W9-BCR-630

MODERN SOCIOLOGICAL THEORY

In Continuity and Change

EDITED BY

Howard Becker
University of Wisconsin

AND

Alvin Boskoff
College of William and Mary

WITH CONTRIBUTIONS BY

FRANZ ADLER
University of Arkansas

HOWARD BECKER
University of Wisconsin

ALVIN BOSKOFF
College of William and Mary

WALTER BUCKLEY
Vassar College

HUGH D. DUNCAN
Homewood, Ill.

ALLAN W. EISTER
Wellesley College

FRANCO FERRAROTTI
University of Milan

LINTON FREEMAN
Syracuse University

C. W. M. HART
University of Wisconsin

GISELA J. HINKLE
Ohio State University

ROSCOE C. HINKLE, JR.
Ohio State University

PAUL HONIGSHEIM
Emeritus, Michigan State University

HOWARD E. JENSEN
Duke University

WILLIAM L. KOLB
Tulane University

JOHN C. McKINNEY
Duke University

DON MARTINDALE
University of Minnesota

W. E. MÜHLMANN
University of Mainz

KUNIO ODAKA
University of Tokyo

RICHARD A. SCHERMERHORN
Western Reserve University

W. J. H. SPROTT
University of Nottingham

JEAN STOETZEL
University of Bordeaux

N. S. TIMASHEFF
Fordham University

ADOLPH S. TOMARS
The City College of New York

BONITA VALIEN
Fisk University

PRESTON VALIEN
Fisk University

KIMBALL YOUNG
Northwestern University

Modern Sociological Theory

IN CONTINUITY AND CHANGE

Holt, Rinehart and Winston

NEW YORK—CHICAGO—SAN FRANCISCO—
TORONTO—LONDON

August, 1966

Library of Congress Catalog Card Number: 57–8839

20864-0117

Printed in the United States of America

PREFACE

"We don't know where we're going, but we're on our way" is a sentiment that, spoken or unspoken, describes many of our day-to-day activities, not only in these United States, but throughout the world. It is by no means a sentiment to be despised; those who gaze fixedly into the crystal ball rarely succeed in doing anything else, and their visions of the future provide no trustworthy guidance. Even when we extrapolate "trends," we may go sadly astray, as witness the American population forecasts made in the early 1940's.

The present book, *Modern Sociological Theory in Continuity and Change,* does not represent an adventure in forecasting. What we mean by "continuity" is "continuity by benefit of hindsight"; our various contributors are looking backward to a period somewhere about World War I, and they are trying to trace developments from that point onward in several sociological fields without assuming that these developments, some of which do seem to follow along fairly definite lines, will continue without interruption, gradual divergence, or even sudden shift. Indeed, a few of the contributors are apparently trying to revitalize certain developments in the sociological enterprise that never really became trends; promising leads either were not followed up or, when they again appeared, did so without evident benefit of the earlier contributions. These breaks in what might have been continuities are encountered with startling frequency from the onset of World War II to the present; all the way from broadly general "systematic sociology" to highly detailed "small-group" analyses, bland disregard or sheer ignorance of vitally important earlier work has become distressingly frequent. The "continuity" of our title page, then, is often in the realm of the "might-have-been," rather than in the actually operative. Perhaps attention to the might-have-been will help to make the actually operative of greater social-scientific worth, but in any case, many of the participants in this symposium give heed to "continuity" in this somewhat Pickwickian sense.

It follows that interest in "change" here goes beyond the happy assumption that since we are demonstrably on our way, we need give no attention to where we seem to be going. Rejecting forecast, we nevertheless feel that close scrutiny of recently evident changes in sociological emphases, in the light of abortive or actual continuity, may help us to steer our course a little less blindly into at least the immediate future. Faddism and opportunism will perhaps always be with us; scientists—yea, even natural scientists—sometimes yield to considerations other than the strictly scientific. Nevertheless, the guild of sober and responsible social-scientific workers may on occasion find it helpful if they are enabled conveniently to recognize ignorance, obscurantism, careless or calculated ignoring of predecessors, careerism, and band-wagon climbing for what they are. Most of the writers in the present symposium have not regarded it as worth while to make painfully clear this particular drift of their presentations, but a little skill at reading between the lines, plus reference to chapter notes and selected readings, will make a few of the things they are driving at reasonably obvious.

Far be it from us, however, to slant this preface in such a way that our symposium would seem to be little more than a random series of commentaries, carrying invidious import, on modern sociology. We have already seen enough and too much, in several widely publicized books, of that sort of thing—often more than a little unfair. Each and every one of our chapters is a thorough survey of its field, in which there has been a sustained effort to present all developments just as fairly as is humanly possible. We think that the coverage has been wide and, limitations of space taken into account, the penetration quite deep. All the contributors were selected with the utmost care, from the standpoints both of their scholarly and scientific competence and of their freedom from warping commitments to this or that "school" of sociology. Once the selections were made, the task of the editors was primarily that of setting up a workable division of labor, grouping the chapters in appropriate sequence, and adjusting space limits to the contributors' interests and the needs of balanced exposition. At no point have we in any way attempted to control the specific content of any of the chapters.

Perhaps it would be suitable to offer here a brief statement as to how the symposium came into being. When Florian Znaniecki was elected, very belatedly, president of the American Sociological Society, he began to plan for the annual meeting of 1954 on a basis somewhat different from that used for several previous meetings of the post-World War II years. Accordingly, in the fall of 1953 he asked a number of persons, including the senior editor of this symposium, to set up a series of section meetings in which the various papers would dovetail fairly closely. The senior editor was assigned the task of securing papers for all five sections dealing with sociology since World War I, and many of the chapters here presented got their start in those sections. Hence, in a very real sense, Znaniecki is among our contributors even though his name heads no chapter. It seemed a pity, given the amount of effort put forth by all concerned, to allow the many excellent papers to lie fallow, or at best to be presented in drastically abridged and scattered form in the professional journals. By special arrangement with The Dryden Press, the publication of the present symposium was assured.

As a consequence, most of the papers presented in the sections mentioned have been brought together here. Several additional contributions (either overlooked in the original program or unfinished by the time of the meeting) have been included. Nearly all the writers involved were given an opportunity to rewrite, expand, or otherwise alter what they had initially offered, and were kept fully advised as to what their co-workers were doing. As is always the case in teamwork, the times when the final versions could be completed differed considerably, but the necessities of the editorial functions and the publisher's plans made it impossible for all chapters to be brought fully up to date in accordance with the final deadline. The approximate dates by which, as far as the direct contributors are concerned, the manuscripts were closed, were as follows: fall 1954: Chapters 13, 14, 20; spring 1955: Chapters 2, 5, 8, 10, 11, 15, 19, 21, 25; summer 1955: Chapter 7; fall 1955: Chapters 1, 3, 4, 12, 18, 23, 24; winter 1955: Chapters 16, 17, 22; spring 1956: Chapter 9; and fall 1956: Chapter 6.

It will be noted, from the table of contents, that the stress of the symposium is strongly on sociological theory in the United States, and that the other countries represented are few in number when compared, for example, with those discussed in the second volume of Becker and Barnes, *Social Thought from Lore to Science,* 2nd ed., 1952 (New York: Dover Publications, reissue, 1956). Because of this stress, inevitable in a volume designed primarily for the use of American students, we decided not to make it still stronger by including a chapter on the United States per se; the greater part of the book can rightly be viewed as fulfilling the function of such a chapter. Where the other countries are concerned, we must in part plead limitations of space and desire to avoid superficiality; given the number of pages possible in a single-volume textbook selling at a reasonable price, it seemed better to deal thoroughly with five countries rather than skimpily with a dozen or more. Even for the five chosen the treatment is not so full as would ideally be desirable. We hope, however, that the selected readings help to remedy this deficiency.

Fortunately, in a way, sociological theory in the United States has been much influenced by leading thinkers and researchers in other countries, as the text and footnotes of the various topical chapters abundantly testify. Hence a certain "at home *and* abroad" *Leitmotif* recurs throughout these chapters. Moreover, although there has been a notable resurgence of interest in sociological theory abroad since World War II, some of it along lines departing considerably from those earlier manifest, a substantial amount of this theory takes account of recent American developments. Consequently, attention to the *Leitmotif* just mentioned will lead to recognition of the fact that even when the explicit references in the topical chapters are primarily to writers publishing in the United States, the contributions of sociologists in other parts of the world, deriving from both past and present, are implicit in much of what is set forth. And those "other parts of the world" are by no means restricted to the five countries for which we have been able to find space. Poland, to choose only one instance, is ably represented by Florian Znaniecki, from whom, as earlier noted, came the program request to the senior editor that resulted in the plans for the present volume.

Thus far, reference has been made only to the various contributors and the senior editor, but the greater part of the actual task of editing the typescripts and putting the book through the press was carried out by the junior editor. Indeed, during the crucial period before publication—from August 1956 until the completion of the index in February 1957—the senior editor was on a research leave financed by the American Philosophical Society and the University of Wisconsin. Part of his time was spent in field work among German peasants, and the remainder in writing up the results. A very heavy load therefore fell on the junior editor. Moreover, during the period when the book was getting under way, several of his suggestions for filling in gaps by securing writers for chapters not initially planned were carefully considered and in one or two cases followed up with success. The relations of junior and senior editors, therefore, are almost literally in terms of age alone; we take equal responsibility—and naturally, equal shares of whatever credit or blame may be assigned—for what we have done.

The chapters by Schermerhorn and Hinkle, in conjunction with which the name of the junior editor appears as co-author, were submitted in substantially their present form by each of the primary authors involved. The junior editor's role was quite minor, particularly in the Schermerhorn chapter, where only parts of the brief introductory section, connecting the chapter with the one immediately preceding, and a few passages in the concluding section, come from his pen. In the chapter by Roscoe C. Hinkle, Jr., the junior editor had a slightly larger but still minor role; he provided about six pages on early European backgrounds (pp. 369-374). In view of the fact that technical difficulties made it impossible to submit proofs to the primary authors, the explicit statement just made should serve fairly to allocate responsibility.

We hope that the symposium will prove to be useful, for although it has many illustrious predecessors, to which reference is made throughout the book whenever relevant, we here offer a selection of fields and a time-span considerably different from any of them. Mere difference is obviously of no merit in itself; hence it must be left to the reader to decide whether our choices have been well advised. If nothing else, we can say that for coverage of modern sociological theory we can date *publication* as of 1957, for all books have time lags.

The contributors, incidentally, must be absolved of any responsibility on the score of length of presentation. Several excellent chapters had to be considerably condensed. We trust that no violence was done to essential meaning at any point, but this is after all only our own opinion. It was not possible, in the greater number of instances, to submit the chapters to the contributors after we had completed this condensation, so that occasional sudden or inadequate transitions, or even culpable omissions, may have been perpetrated. We can only hope that readers will view charitably the inevitable flaws arising when 425,000 words are reduced to about 275,000; but if charity is to be withheld, it should be withheld from the editors only.

Perhaps, however, compression has been advantageous where the classroom utility of the book is concerned. Students do not take kindly to long lists of names, discussions of minute variations having professional significance only, digressions that remain irrelevant even when the presentation has concluded, catalogues of obscure or outdated articles, and bulky footnote asides. We think that our symposium, in its present form, will prove to be quite acceptable and useful in courses at the undergraduate level; students with good basic preparation should be able to read it with interest and understanding.

Moreover, we believe that a carefully organized and comprehensive treatment of modern sociological theory such as that represented here can be read with much profit by all students, including even those well advanced in their graduate work. But in particular, returns should be greatest if the book is used as the mainstay of intermediate courses in sociology in which the instructor wishes to lay stress on the more important theoretical emphases now current. In this way, for example, undergraduate work in "principles of sociology" that has back of it solid elementary instruction can be made more meaningful than is sometimes the case. As Frank H. Hankins once remarked when discussing this point, "Little is to be gained by mere repetition of the same general approach and subject-matter, rendered slightly more difficult through greater abstraction, systematization, and completeness."* The instructor is therefore invited to experiment with this symposium as a textbook for intermediate courses such as those in "principles" already mentioned. Assured of good reading coverage for many key topics, he can devote his lecture time to extensive and penetrating treatment of a few selected aspects; both he and his students may find such procedure enjoyable and rewarding.

From what has just been said, it follows that the editors view this symposium as in large measure substantive; it deals with modern sociological theory *as such,* defining "modern" as "significant today." With few exceptions, the contributors demonstrably share the editorial standpoint; they are not interested merely in the history of sociological theory since World War I. Nevertheless, instructors offering courses in the development of modern sociology may well consider the use of a book such as ours, for most instructors, particularly those of the younger generation, have little antiquarian interest, and their students have less. The history that is meaningful to them, and properly so, must be history that has fairly obvious current relevance. However, it should not be too difficult for the instructor, without in any way disparaging the substantive emphasis, to direct the student reader's attention to this symposium in a way such that the more immediate backgrounds, at least, of sociological theory that is of vital importance today are suitably illuminated. In lecture the instructor can then turn the spotlight, if he wishes, on the remoter settings, or on nearer details that the general illumination may still leave a trifle obscure.

In sum, our book may serve in at least two ways: in courses stressing substantive theory, and in courses giving prominence to the lines along which such theory has developed.

As a finale, we wish to express our heartiest appreciation of Florian Znaniecki's

* H. E. Barnes, Howard Becker, and Frances Bennett Becker (eds.), *Contemporary Social Theory* (New York, 1940), p. xvi.

initiative and encouragement, of the other contributors' team spirit and readiness to give elbow-room to the editors, and of the professional attitude of the director of the publishers. Acknowledgments are also due the following publishers or journals for permission to use a number of quotations: *American Journal of Sociology, American Sociological Review,* Free Press, Harper & Brothers, Harvard University Press, McGraw-Hill Book Company, Philosophical Library, Random House, University of Chicago Press, and University of Georgia Press.

March 1957

HOWARD BECKER
ALVIN BOSKOFF

CONTENTS

PART I

INTRODUCTION

PART II

MAJOR STRANDS IN THEORY AND METHODOLOGY

PART III

SOME SPECIALIZATIONS IN MODERN SOCIOLOGY

PART IV

CONVERGENCES OF BORDERING FIELDS WITH SOCIOLOGY

PART V

SOCIOLOGICAL RESEARCH AND THEORY ABROAD

KEY TO ABBREVIATIONS IN THE NOTES

AA	*American Anthropologist*
ACSR	*American Catholic Sociological Review*
AJES	*American Journal of Economics and Sociology*
AJO	*American Journal of Orthopsychiatry*
AJS	*American Journal of Sociology*
AP	*Archives of Psychology*
APSR	*American Political Science Review*
ARS	*Archiv für Rechts- und Sozialphilosophie*
AS	*Annales Sociologiques*
ASo	*Année Sociologique*
ASR	*American Sociological Review*
ASS	*Archiv für Sozialwissenschaft und Sozialpolitik*
BJS	*British Journal of Sociology*
CIS	*Cahiers Internationaux de Sociologie*
DALV	*Deutsches Archiv für Landes- und Völksforschung*
ESS	*Encyclopedia of the Social Sciences*
FVS	*Forschungen zur Völkerpsychologie und Soziologie*
GSO	*Grundriss der Sozialökonomik*
HR	*Human Relations*
HS	*Handwörterbuch der Soziologie*
HSW	*Handwörterbuch der Sozialwissenschaften*
IJP	*International Journal of Psycho-analysis*
JAP	*Journal of Applied Psychology*
JASP	*Journal of Abnormal and Social Psychology*
JCP	*Journal of Clinical Psychology*
JEP	*Journal of Educational Psychology*
JES	*Journal of Educational Sociology*
JLPS	*Journal of Legal and Political Sociology*
JP	*Journal of Personality*
JPs	*Journal de Psychologie*
JS	*Jahrbuch für Soziologie*
JSI	*Journal of Social Issues*
JSP	*Journal of Social Psychology*
KVS	*Kölner Vierteljahrshefte für Soziologie*
KVSo	*Kölner Vierteljahrshefte für Sozialwissenschaften*
KZS	*Kölner Zeitschrift für Soziologie*
PASS	*Publications of the American Sociological Society*
PB	*Psychological Bulletin*
POQ	*Public Opinion Quarterly*
RP	*Revue de Philosophie*
RS	*Rural Sociology*
SF	*Social Forces*
SJ	*Schmollers Jahrbuch für Gesetzgebung, Verwaltung und Volkswirtschaft*
Soc	*Sociologus*
Socm	*Sociometry*
SR	*Social Research*
SSR	*Sociology and Social Research*
ZS	*Zeitschrift für die gesamte Staatswissenschaft*

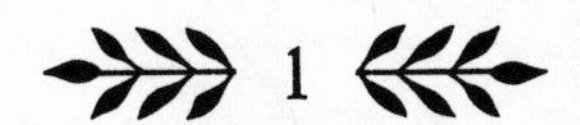

FROM SOCIAL THOUGHT TO SOCIOLOGICAL THEORY

ALVIN BOSKOFF

TO THE VAST PUBLIC THAT HAS HEARD OR READ ABOUT IT OVER THE PAST fifty years, sociology has been a vague, unchanging symbol for the study of social life. When pressed further, most people define sociology in terms of "applied" fields—population, social welfare, crime control, marriage counseling, and others. The result of this tendency has been a failure to appreciate to any extent the basic *distinctiveness* of modern sociology as practiced in many parts of the world and the *developmental* nature of sociology. Implicitly or explicitly, the various chapters of this volume are dedicated to the elaboration of these two features; but since the authors are primarily concerned with specialized aspects of modern sociology, the underlying themes of the entire volume may not always be apparent. Consequently, the purpose of this introductory chapter is to delineate these crucial features by exploring two related questions. In what ways does modern sociology constitute a new or distinctive approach to social life? What is the significance of modern sociology in our efforts to expand our knowledge and understanding of human beings and their problems?

Social Thought and Its Transformation

From the sober, all-encompassing standpoint of the historian, what we now call sociology developed unbelievably late in human affairs—late, in fact, even in the brief, self-conscious interlude of the past 5,000 years that we call "civilization." As far back as archeology will allow us to go in the study of human society, men must have been bothered in some way or another by the problems of living and working together. Culture in general can be interpreted as the more or less conscious solutions of these problems, but certain compartments of culture (notably religion, kinship, and government) probably contain the germ of the increasingly specialized concern for the observation and interpretation of men as associated human beings.

SOCIAL THOUGHT AND SOCIAL PHILOSOPHY

This concern became more explicit as cultures grew more complex, and it was embodied in *social thought* as generalized statements and judgments about a wide range of social phenomena: crime and punishment, war, sex, social responsibilities, relations between groups, etc. Much of this early social thought contained injunctions, evaluations, and ethical objectives that, when codified into laws or the teachings of influential individuals, can be distinguished as *social philosophy*.[1] The essence of this branch of social thought is exhortation, the description of desired states of human experience, and the construction of congenial imperatives for social action—in short, evaluation rather than observation, judgment rather than knowledge.

SOCIAL THEORY

Although it is incorrect to regard the social philosophies of ancient civilizations as purely visionary and unrealistic, it is certainly true that these social philosophies were eventually found to have limitations. The ancients, like modern civilized man and his pre-literate contemporaries, were perfectly capable of analyzing empirical facets of their lives and of adjusting some of their ideals to harsh experience. But rational accomplishment was circumscribed until the relative isolation of societies was shattered by the critical culture contacts of peoples with different experiences and divergent ideals.[2] Consequently, although social philosophy remained the dominant mode of social thought, comparative observation, the conflict of presumable absolutes, and the incursion of doubt and skepticism combined to create the first glimmerings of *social theory*. It is no accident that the Greeks—especially the Ionian Greeks and their intellectual heirs—were the first social theorists, for they lived and thought at the cultural crossroads of antiquity.

Social theory emerges as an auxiliary compartment of social thought when social phenomena are viewed with some measure of objectivity and

[1] See the valuable summaries of social thought by Howard Becker and H. E. Barnes, *Social Thought from Lore to Science* (2nd ed.; New York, 1952), vol. 1, chaps. 1-13; and J. O. Hertzler, *The Social Thought of the Ancient Civilizations* (New York, 1936).

[2] Becker and Barnes, *op. cit., passim,* and especially Chaps. 4, 6, and 11.

when thinkers and philosophers become devoted to generalized descriptions and explanations of social affairs *as they have actually occurred* rather than as they "ought to be." In this sense, social theory professes scientific objectives, whereas social philosophy provides evaluative guides for future social behavior. In practice, however, these tasks are often confused with one another, since each serves a compelling need in man's thinking about his relations with others. If we can accept elements of social philosophy and social theory as persistent strands in the over-all development of social thought, it is important to note the changing relations between these two themes in human history. With the development of Greek thought, social theory effectively enters the arena of social thought, but as a distinctly minor strand. During the next 2,200 years, the dominance of social philosophy is almost unquestioned, although the work of an Ibn Khaldūn or a Machiavelli may be interpreted as premonitory rumblings of new developments in social thought. But in the second third of the nineteenth century, social theory bursts into a feverish, rapid growth, offering for the first time a serious challenge to social philosophy through a temporary alliance with the ascendant physical and biological sciences.

It is clearly beyond the scope of this chapter to present a full history of social theory. The interested reader should consult such valuable reference works as Howard Becker and Harry Elmer Barnes, *Social Thought from Lore to Science;* and Pitirim A. Sorokin, *Contemporary Sociological Theories.* The purpose of this chapter is to sketch the outlines of this intellectual history by analyzing the role of social theory as a *transitional phase* in the transformation of early social thought into the modern sociological theory and research that will be discussed in succeeding chapters.

Types of Social Theory. The development of social theory can be summarized by distinguishing two relatively separate types. From the very inception of this branch of social thought until the present, thinkers have tried to explain observable social phenomena by reference to such factors as geography, climate, physique, physical and chemical relations, and supernatural forces. Sorokin's *Contemporary Sociological Theories* contains an excellent summary and critique of these theories. Considered collectively, many of these *non-social, reductionist* explanations of social phenomena reflected an intense desire for scientific knowledge, but their tenacious dependence on established disciplines invariably blocked the emergence of appropriate categories in the realm of social relations. Although many of these theories had admirable objectives (from a scientific viewpoint) and thus constituted a recognizable advance over the contributions of social philosophy, their conceptual tools were unequal to the task of providing verified generalizations. From our present vantage-point, this type of social theory has served to indicate with the clarity of a well-marked road map some dissappointingly devious roads to be avoided henceforth and forever.

Consequently, we shall take no further note of this species of social theory, although it is certainly true that some of its basic features have continued to appear in more useful theoretical formulations.

Social Theory as Proto-Sociology. The emergence of a second variety of social theory can be located at approximately the middle of the nineteenth century in the work of Auguste Comte. Two characteristics mark this phase of social thought, which can be called "proto-sociology." First, and of extreme importance, is a growing emancipation from most of the concepts and orientations of the physical and biological sciences. This meant a crucial distinction between the spirit and method of science in general and the content of specific sciences. Gradually, social phenomena came to be described in specifically social terms—for example, consensus, society, social group. But this new-found intellectual freedom was quickly followed by attempts to reduce the older social disciples (political economy, history, etc.) to an unwarranted dependance on a fledgling but highly ambitious social science: social physics, or sociology. As developed by the pioneer theorists—Comte, Spencer, Marx, and Ward—this proto-sociology was conceived as an intellectual *synthesis* of the data and generalizations supplied by the specialized social disciplines. The emphasis was so strongly on encyclopedism and intellectual *tours de force* that the new science largely neglected the substantive groundwork required to establish a body of distinctively treated data. As a result, this superimposed discipline and its practitioners became uncertain of its boundaries, antagonized its sister disciplines, and spawned a series of interesting but prematurely developed theories that have, incidentally, provoked continually hostile reactions to more careful attempts at systematic social theory.

THE ROOTS OF MODERN SOCIOLOGY

In the last decade of the nineteenth century, proto-sociology began to be replaced by a more modest, specialized orientation, that is fundamental to the modern practice of sociology as an *analytic* social science. However, the roots of this development are in the work of several proto-sociologists who have, successively and collectively, contributed to contemporary sociological thinking and research. In this chapter, therefore, a selected group of these theorists will be reviewed from the standpoint of their respective contributions to an emerging sociology in the preparatory period 1850 to World War I. In a presentation of the highlights of this development, a number of theorists must be omitted who would certainly deserve inclusion in a more detailed account. Systematic exposition of the life work of any theorist must also be omitted, although it is incontestably true that specific aspects of a theoretical orientation become more meaningful when examined in the context of such an exposition. Our chosen context is a collectively fabricated, emerging system—the outlines of modern sociology. Finally, in order to demonstrate the essential continuity of social theory and sociology, this survey must include the work of proto-sociologists, pioneer modern sociologists, and those who can be classified with some justice in either category, depending on emphasis.

Comte, Marx, and Spencer

COMTE (1798-1851)

The Frenchman Auguste Comte is generally regarded as a synthesizer who sought to construct an intellectually coherent scheme of knowledge about physical, biotic, and social phenomena. But since his ideas about social phenomena were somewhat scattered and were often colored by an insistent search for principles of social reconstruction, Comte's pioneer efforts in proto-sociology were not quite systematic. As a result, he is often remembered for two or three easily cited concepts and theories that fail to indicate his proper place in the development of sociology.

Superficially, Comte supplied sociology with a name and a program, which he preached but did not practice. This program has become so ingrained in our thinking, however, that its earliest formulation often seems tedious and unworthy of close examination. Its major features warrant consideration, regardless of speculative elements that have unfortunately dimmed Comte's reputation in social science.

Though notions of progress and social telesis motivated his entrance into social theory, Comte sharply distinguished social philosophy from a scientific study of social phenomena as an analytically separate realm. To this as yet non-existent discipline he gave the name *social physics* or *sociology,* although it was occasionally referred to as *politics* in a very extended sense. Instead of relying on mere conjecture, he urged the careful use of observation, experimentation, and comparison in establishing social facts and as bases for adequate generalizations. Then Comte proceeded to outline the controversial separation of a projected sociology into social statics and social dynamics. By social statics, Comte meant the investigation of a temporally limited set of social phenomena in terms of the *coexistence* or interrelation of component features—in our present-day terminology, *social structure*. Social dynamics (or, more properly, social kinetics), meant, on the other hand, the analysis of changes or successive states of interrelated social facts. However, social dynamics was largely identified with progress and therefore became the dominant part of his thinking. Despite this uneven emphasis, Comte insisted that statics and dynamics were separable only for analytical purposes and that this distinction should not imply two classes of facts, but rather two aspects of a unified approach to social phenomena.[3] Many contemporary sociologists have not heeded this caution, just as Comte in practice ignored what may soon be regarded as one of his most important principles.

Social Statics. Although Comte's treatment of social dynamics is generally considered to be his major theoretical offering (in spite of the many criticisms directed against it), his scattered analyses of social structure are of great value in preparing a secure foundation for future sociological thought. He approached all social phenomena in the context of the general concept "society," which he saw as representing a *functional system* based on a *division of labor*. One of Comte's fundamental postulates was the *interrelation* of social elements, parts, or divisions. Yet Comte did not hold that the mere fact of interrelationship provided the key to the structure of society. Instead, he foreshadowed the concepts of Tönnies, Durkheim, and others by constructing two basic types of social systems: the *domestic association* and the *political society*. In the former, the continued patterns of association are primarily based on feelings of *solidarity* and *consensus*. As societies come to approximate the latter type, a pronounced division of labor between institutional sectors and a complex organization of economic functions (industrialization in Western societies) are interpreted as threats to stability. The state, a highly developed political form, serves to integrate the specialized functions of component parts, but is supplemented by a system of *social classes* that reflects the dominant institutional sector of society.[4] Thus Comte heralded a genuinely sociological approach to social structure by suggesting three interrelated points. Of primary significance is his insistence on description and analysis of structure in *social* terms—that is, the phenomena of association and its distinctive products. In addition, Comte recognized empirical variety in social systems, which he tried to simplify by devising a pair of structural types—without, however, entangling himself in what were to become the evolutionary dogmas of a Morgan or a Spencer. Finally, Comte sketched the central problems of social institutions, institutional interrelationships, and stratification, although his concern for "dynamics" prevented adequate conceptualization of institutions and social classes.

Social Change. As far as social change is concerned, Comte probably contributed very little to the evolving repertory of sociology. Strangely enough, he was one of the first to separate concepts of progress and per-

[3] Auguste Comte, *The Positive Philosophy*, translated and condensed by Harriet Martineau (London, 1896), vol. II, pp. 216-219, 228; McQuilkin DeGrange, "The Method of Auguste Comte," in S. A. Rice (ed.), *Methods in Social Science* (Chicago, 1931), pp. 23-36.

[4] Comte, *op. cit., passim;* H. E. Barnes, "The Social and Political Philosophy of Auguste Comte," in H. E. Barnes (ed.), *An Introduction to the History of Sociology* (Chicago, 1948), pp. 90-91. [A version edited and augmented by Becker appeared in Becker and Barnes, *op. cit.*, vol. I, pp. 568-593.]

fectability from the neutral concept of *development,* yet his discussions of change were often tinged with moral and political interpretations. The often cited "law of three stages" is basically an analysis of intellectual development (theological, metaphysical, and positivist or scientific stages). But as DeGrange properly indicates, this law was intermittently supplemented by a general theory of social development in which Comte asserted that collective activity passes through successive stages of conquest, defense, and industry.[5] Though Comte never detailed the connection between these two developments, it is perhaps possible to interpret their relation as an embryonic sociology of knowledge; in fact, Scheler has done this. In the important area of social causation and social change, Comte noted the chief factors as race, climate, and political action (by implication, social processes), concentrating his discussion on political action, since that alone seemed to be amenable to human intervention. Without entering into analysis of the dynamic factors or forces in the social process, he did point the direction of Ward's thinking, and perhaps Comte's theoretical omissions can be credited in part with the development of the psychologically oriented sociologists in the latter part of the nineteenth century.

MARX (1818-1883)

Determining the role of Karl Marx in the transition of social theory to sociology is an exceedingly difficult task for at least three reasons. Obviously, his activities as economist, propagandist, and revolutionist blur and confuse the distinctively sociological elements in his writings. Apparently working under the spur of both scientific and political objectives, Marx was in addition often distressingly vague in defining terms; and he could not avoid contradicting himself in the process of recasting his ideas for the political-intellectual controversies that marked his career. Furthermore, the interpretation of his writings by eager disciples has been so incautious that even Marx was compelled to assert "I am not a Marxist." At the same time, just as Comte symbolizes the fruition of a significant development in French social thought, Marx's work may be regarded as a culmination and synthesis of certain branches of Continental thinking which we are accustomed to identify as the *economic interpretation* of history or *historical materialism.* Marx's position in sociological thought has been perhaps less dramatic, although nonetheless quite real and subtly persistent, than the extensive influence of his political and economic doctrines.

The Organization of Society. Marx's conception of society, formulated as early as 1859, is, with some reservations, a distinct improvement upon and further elaboration of the Comtean view. Where Comte tended toward vagueness in analyzing the *composition* of society, Marx defined it as an

[5] DeGrange, *op. cit.,* pp. 23-24. See also the most recent interpretation of Comte's work in McQuilkin DeGrange, *The Nature and Elements of Sociology* (New Haven, 1953).

organic ensemble of social relations among men, meaning by social relations the cooperative associations or bonds between persons. However, whereas Comte found the essence of social phenomena in the family and later in religion, Marx chose to examine the operation of society by focusing on the economic structure. Thus society was further defined as an organized multitude of *productive forces;* unfortunately, the term "productive force" was never clearly defined by Marx, but it is important to note that the interpreted social relations as productive forces, indicating the presence and significance of non-material factors in the economic structure.

With this orientation, Marx proceeded to analyze the economic structure as a *social institution* characterized by: a basic mode of production or productive techniques; a series of cooperative social relations developed in relation to these techniques; and a social division of labor expressed in patterns of ownership of the instruments of production and in a corresponding class structure. According to Marx, this whole structure is a determinate reflection of one component: the mode of production; and the economic structure in turn channels the development and organization of other institutional sectors.[6]

Social Change. If the constitution of society is determined by productive techniques, then social change must be based on developments in those techniques. Yet Marx was forced to approach social change in a much more complex fashion than this logical deduction might imply. One might expect a searching analysis of factors in material and technological innovation, but as a left-wing Hegelian, Marx ignored this problem and leaped to a dilemma-filled exposition of social change as a *dialectical social process.* Marx argued that technological changes come into conflict with established property relations. But is this a conflict on the logical level (one of *consistency*) or on the practical level (relating to the *interests* of implicated groups)? Marx conceded that every social system contains contradictions (lags?) between the economic and other spheres; yet he insisted that these contradictions provoke class struggles and that consequently social change was a function of *social revolution.* Out of respect for facts, Marx was compelled to make a crucial distinction between *objective* changes in productive techniques and the *subjective* reactions of persons in the form of *ideologies.* And although he tried to demonstrate a causal connection between objective conditions and ideologies, he did acknowledge bothersome empirical exceptions—as evidence of "false consciousness."[7] In Marx's *sociological* thinking, then, social change lacks the inevitability usually ascribed to it by Marxists; we might summarize his view of the process as a potential conflict of differen-

[6] Karl Marx, *A Contribution to the Critique of Political Economy,* translated by N. I. Stone (1st ed. 1859; New York, 1904), pp. 11-12.

[7] Karl Marx and Friedrich Engels, *The German Ideology* (1st ed. 1846; New York, 1939), pp. 20, 39.

tially favored groups contingent on the development of appropriate recognition ("consciousness") of the "true" implications of changes in technology.

Marx's Sociological Thought. The essence of Marx's sociological thought, it appears, is not his theories (which are largely unacceptable) but certain *problems* and *concepts* with which sociologists have been continually concerned. In his analysis of economic systems Marx demonstrated the feasibility of an institutional approach and perhaps unwittingly gave prominence to non-economic factors in economic affairs. His efforts to discover the basic position of the economic institution in the total socio-cultural structure led to a classic but erroneous solution of the problem of *institutional interrelations*. As an outgrowth of this institutional approach, Marx, following Comte, strongly indicated the societal significance of stratification and its relation to *focal* social institutions, though he assumed that the economic institution was inevitably central. The Marxian theory of social change, although it is generally fallacious, has emphasized two important features: (1) change is a *processual* phenomenon that can be investigated by analyzing the reactions of implicated groups; and (2) change is often accompanied by strains, maladjustments, and group conflicts on the physical and ideological levels. Finally, Marx noted the phenomena of differential group valuations as important factors in social action, thereby suggesting the importance of the volitional element and by implication a theoretical connection between problems of social change and social causation.

SPENCER (1820-1903)

At the beginning of the twentieth century, no one would have dreamed that Herbert Spencer, prolific English proponent of a new social science, would become an intellectual curiosity, remembered but unread. The evolutionary theory, the organismic analogy, and the vast collections of ethnographic data are still cited out of deference to tradition, yet the old authority of the man and his work as Spencerian is virtually shattered. Like Comte and Marx, Spencer was primarily interested in the broad scope of social change. Today, paradoxically, all that endures of Spencer's work is in the realm of *social structure*.

Basically, Spencer tried to show that human societies constitute a unique form of order or organization (superorganic) in the bio-physical world. The organismic analogy, by which similarities (and differences) between societies and biological entities are noted, was employed as an expository device to convert into more understandable terms the intangible nature of human relations. As part of nature, human societies engage in a struggle for existence with other societies and the non-human environment. In this process societies develop differentiated, specialized "organs" called *institutions*. Spencer distinguished three principal types: *sustaining* institutions (marriage and kinship); *distributing* (or economic) institutions; and *regulating* institutions (religion, political systems).[8] Social structure (society) was therefore conceived as a kind of equilibrium maintained by the interrelated functioning of component institutions. However, although Spencer can largely be credited with stimulating the modern focus on institutions in sociological thought, at no point has he furnished an explicit definition of institutional phenomena.

Gumplowicz, Ratzenhofer, Small, and Sumner

By the 1880's, the general concern with "society" was being subordinated to the analysis of society as an *ongoing process* characterized by relations between constituent parts. The institutional approach of Comte and Spencer had likewise been based on the notion of interrelated parts, but their conceptual focus was primarily on *functions performed* and only secondarily on generalized relations between persons and the dynamics of groups. Although Marx engaged in some exploratory studies of classes, he did not attempt a fundamental inquiry into the nature of groups in general. The threshold of modern sociological thought was probably reached when three problems became the core of sociological research: (1) the nature of social process (or processes); (2) the structure and classification of social groups; and (3) the reciprocal relations among the individual, the group, and social processes.

GUMPLOWICZ (1838-1909)

The pioneering of the Austrian sociologist Ludwig Gumplowicz is sometimes overshadowed by his discredited polygenetic theory of races and by his dogmatic emphasis on *conflict* in social phenomena. Yet Gumplowicz was one of the first to achieve full emancipation for sociology from the nonsocial sciences by insisting that social phenomena are distinctive and can be understood only by reference to social causes. That which is unique about social phenomena, he argued, arises from the observable facts of *human groups in interaction* rather than from the behavior of individuals abstracted from the influence of persistent association and dissociation.

Social Process and Social Groups. Starting from the proposition that the generalizations of sociology are "laws of becoming" and not laws of origins or ultimate patterns, Gumplowicz emphasized the importance of social

[8] Herbert Spencer, *Principles of Sociology* (1st ed. 1876-93; New York, 1923, 3 vols.), vol. I, Parts 1 and 2; vol. II and III, *passim*. See also Becker and Barnes, *op. cit.*, vol. I, pp. 664-667, 680-681. Spencer's classification of institutions is largely followed by Parsons; see Talcott Parsons, *Essays in Sociological Theory: Pure and Applied* (Glencoe, Ill., 1949), pp. 44-51.

process by analyzing the contact and interaction of more or less distinct groups. Because of his interest in the special phenomena of complex societies, Gumplowicz did not furnish a systematic analysis or classification of groups. However, he did distinguish between simple, limited groupings organized on the basis of consanguinity and community of culture, on the one hand, and *compound* groupings, such as the state, formed in the process of amalgamation of originally separate groups, on the other. It is in the second type that social processes of *conflict* (to which he assigned unusual importance), *accommodation, assimilation,* and *internal differentiation* were identified as the dynamics of human association.[9]

Thus Gumplowicz shifted the study of sociology from society in general to relations between specific societies, and thence in part to the interaction of differentiated groups in politically organized societies. In such societies, social process first consists in incorporation of ethnically distinct groups through conquest. When this occurs, external conflicts become internal and social process is manifested in the organization of a new social unit. Two complementary processes arise: the development of *legal norms* to guide the mutual relations between groups, as coercion is gradually replaced by moral obligations; and the differentiation of social classes, first based on ethnic differences and finally on the division of labor.[10]

Although Gumplowicz is often classified as a social Darwinist because of his emphasis on conflict, he was actually one of the first social determinists. In his system, the individual and his motives were useless abstractions, and material needs were a significant influence on conduct. According to Gumplowicz the individual was the product of group experience; his *morals* derived from his relations in the "simple" groups, whereas his notions of *rights* could be traced to the accommodative norms developed by the struggle of interest groups in his society.[11] Gumplowicz therefore anticipated the major theories of Sumner, Baldwin, Cooley, and Mead, although these four thinkers held less deterministic views of the relations of individuals to social groups.

RATZENHOFER AND SMALL

The concept of social process was fully accepted by the turn of the century, but the special interpretations of Gumplowicz were progressively revised. Essentially, Ratzenhofer (1842-1904) and Small (1854-1926), the first Austrian and the second American, can be credited with de-emphasizing (but not disregarding) the role of conflict and conquest in social phenomena and with elaborating in their respective writings the theoretical significance

[9] Ludwig Gumplowicz, *Outlines of Sociology*, translated by F. W. Moore (Philadelphia, 1889), pp. 68, 82-83.

[10] *Ibid.*, pp. 82-87, 146-149.

[11] *Ibid.*, pp. 156-60, 168-169.

of "interests," which Gumplowicz had barely suggested in his discussion of political parties. Ratzenhofer, by his relative emphasis on intra-societal phenomena, gave considerably more attention than did Gumplowicz to the conversion of conflict into the processes of *socialization* (used in a sense different from the contemporary sense), in which selfish interests are subordinated to group welfare (the social interest). Since Ratzenhofer considered society to be an independent structure, except for its interrelations with other societies, he therefore sought to locate the major elements of social process *within* a society. The central significance attached to interests, which were defined in strictly biological terms, served to reduce social phenomena to qualities in individuals. This atomistic conception of the group placed major emphasis upon the role of individuals, in sharp contrast to the views of Gumplowicz. However, Ratzenhofer summarized the operation of social process as progressive differentiation of new sub-groups and harmonization or integration of existing sub-groups, which he explained in terms of inborn interests of the individual and concrete interests of each social structure.[12]

Small further interpreted the social process as indicative of a narrowed scope for dissociative processes. Employing a more socialized conception of interest, he noted a rough progression in the social process in which the interests of individuals become increasingly interwoven. Small regarded both extreme conflict of interests and close conjunction of interests as empirically impossible. Social process instead reflects a general replacement of conflict by consensus; consequently, it involves a "continual formation of [social] groups around interests and a continual exertion of reciprocal influence by means of group action." Interest or purpose, group structure and function, and social process thus were conceptually and realistically intertwined. Later, Small re-interpreted interests as *valuations* guiding conduct; as a result, the social process was significantly redefined as the process of forming valuations, seeking means to realize valuations, modifying valuations in the light of difficulties, and so on.[13] In this revised conception, it should be noted, Small summarized the cardinal sociological problems relating to the *group* in its structural and functional aspects.

Ward, Tarde, Giddings, and Ross

With this dominance of the social-process approach, the former attention to social structure was somewhat reduced, though by no means

[12] This discussion is primarily based on the valuable interpretations of A. W. Small, *General Sociology* (Chicago, 1905), Parts 4 and 5, especially Chaps. 13-17, 25, and 26.

[13] Small, *op. cit.*, pp. 198, 202-204, 209, 240; *The Meaning of Social Science* (Chicago, 1910), pp. 145, 193-195, 203.

eliminated. As a result, a theoretical chasm between *process* and *structure* was implicitly or explicitly recognized by sociologists around 1900; their response was in many cases an attempt to furnish an explanatory bond between social phenomena considered as ongoing networks of interaction (process) and as the abstractable regularities or patterns of association (structure) that are both the effects and the bases of social process. Essentially, this development was manifested in attempts to interpret the social process in psychological terms, or to link the individual to units of social structure through the mediation of such concepts as *motives, desires, wishes, needs,* or *social forces.*

WARD (1841-1913)

Lester F. Ward was probably the first to introduce this orientation effectively into American sociology, and although little remains of his general sociological system today, this specific aspect has endured in the transformations we shall consider below. Defining sociology as the study of human *achievement* (culture)—of functions rather than structure—Ward stressed the importance of feelings, emotions, desires, wants, etc., as motivations in human activities and as causes of human association. These *psychic forces,* which become *social forces* through the interaction of individuals, were classified into essential or physical forces (reproductive and preservative) and spiritual forces (aesthetic, moral, and intellectual)[14]—in modern, albeit question-begging, usage, "basic" and "derived" needs. As interaction proceeds, a typical sequence of social processes develops, out of which social structures, (groups, societies) emerge. Ward called this *social karyokinesis,* a term generally rejected by sociologists as biologistic, and explained the dynamics of the process by the principle of *social synergy,* the successive combination of discrete forces. In this sequence, Ward distinguished stages of collision, conflict, antagonism, opposition, antithesis, competition, interaction, compromise, collaboration, cooperation, and organization.[15] He thus outlined the processual approach later developed by Simmel, Park, and Wiese.

TARDE (1843-1904)

In the meanwhile, a contemporary of Ward, the Frenchman Gabriel Tarde, attacked the same problem with a different psychological emphasis. For Tarde, the basic social process, the character of social facts, and the structure of society were all dependent on the psychological principle of *imitation,* which Tarde defined rather broadly. The socio-cultural structure was therefore explained by an ingeniously simplified process-series: invention, opposition, repetition (imitation), and adaptation.[16] Tarde gave some

[14] F. Ward, *The Psychic Factors of Civilization* (New York, 1892); *Outlines of Sociology* (New York, 1898), pp. 144, 148-149; *Pure Sociology* (New York, 1903), p. 183.

[15] Ward, *Pure Sociology*, pp. 183-184, 205-216.

[16] Gabriel Tarde, *Social Laws* (1st ed. 1899; New York), pp. 38-41, 133-135.

prominence to invention, which he explained largely in terms of mental ability, but it was imitation and its causes and consequences that gave Tarde the opportunity to review fundamental sociological problems.

If imitation is the key to social phenomena, Tarde argued, then the typical social relation is that of "teacher-learner" in a variety of situations. But what determines imitation or its opposite? At this point, Tarde combined the social-forces approach with a quasi-structural analysis, for he takes the causes of imitation to be basically internal, although they are modified or supplemented by the group situation. Thus Tarde discussed *desires,* yet his major emphasis was clearly on social factors: prestige, obedience, and practicality. These desires imply some pre-existing social structure and indicate that imitation is largely a socially conditioned process. Furthermore, imitation is conceived not as an automatic response, but as a process often preceded by *hesitation* (opposition) in adopting or rejecting some model.[17] (Here, incidentally, is perhaps an anticipation of Thomas and Znaniecki's concept of "definition of the situation," MacIver's "dynamic assessment," and the recent "discovery" of "social perception.")

The primary implication of Tarde's analyses for sociological development is an indirect and incomplete recognition of the *socialization process,* of the internalization of norms through social interaction. From our present vantage-point, his apparent emphasis on imitation was essentially a conceptual base from which he was able to explore a crucial sociological problem: the process in which the individual is incorporated into social groups and societies. Like his great rival, Durkheim, he wished to avoid both the atomistic approach and the organismic notions of Comte and Spencer. Thus Tarde explained social structure in terms of individual behavior (imitation) reflecting common models or values, although he failed to stress the latter phenomena as vigorously as some of his contemporaries or successors. He likewise distinguished rough stages (or types) of social structure by reference to differential bases or motivations of imitation. In relatively simple group structures, imitation is predominantly related to *desires* (biological needs), whereas social developments in complexity and differentiation are accompanied by increasing emphasis on *beliefs* (values, organizational principles, and derived needs) that serve as guides for individual behavior.[18] In this manner, Tarde barely defined the important problem of differential relations between the individual and the group which Tönnies, Durkheim, Simmel, and others were exploring in his own lifetime. Yet Tarde may be said to have presaged the direction of thought soon to be taken by Baldwin, Ross, Cooley, Dewey, and the social psychology of modern times.

[17] *Ibid.,* p. 83; Tarde, *The Laws of Imitation,* translated by Elsie C. Parsons (1st ed. 1890; New York, 1903), pp. 78-79, 141, 165.

[18] Tarde, *The Laws of Imitation,* p. 147.

GIDDINGS (1855-1931)

Because of his long career (which encompassed the formative stage of American sociology and the newer emphases of the post-World War I period) and his remarkable synthesis of several sociological currents, Franklin H. Giddings is especially difficult to classify in this review of sociological maturation. He incorporated in his own manner, for example, a psychological approach, an emphasis on social structure and social relations, an extensive consideration of social process and change, a compelling historical analysis, and a vigorous advocacy of both interpretative and quantitative methods. Strangely enough, few sociologists refer to Giddings' writings today and it is probably fair to assume that his books are rarely consulted. Yet he was a transitional figure of major importance and remains the most underrated American sociologist of the past fifty years.

Giddings, like Ward and Tarde, tried to find an elementary principle or method on which a comprehensive sociological scheme could be constructed. The principle he used was his concept of *consciousness of kind,* by which he meant an underlying *feeling of identity* experienced by individuals with respect to their fellows.[19] But consciousness of kind has proved to be of limited value in sociological analysis and may fortunately be detached from Giddings' work without ill effect. In the light of subsequent developments, his greatest achievement was in advancing sociology as a distinctive social science by demonstrating the interrelated nature of four previous emphases: social structure, social process, social forces, and subjective aspects of social phenomena.

Society was defined by Giddings as an interdependent set of differentiated groups and associations in which a constant social process may be observed in the production of social relations and complex organizations. The basic dynamics of human association were expressed in terms of two types of "forces": socializing forces and social forces. Socializing forces include conditions, external or tangential to social structure, which provoke association, develop organization, and promote socialization; soil, climate, and the appetites and passions of individuals are examples. By social forces Giddings meant influences of a group or societal origin that channel behavior toward group ends of any character; public opinion and legislation are examples. As a consequence, Giddings was strongly averse to the Comtean separation of statics and dynamics, which he more appropriately characterized as statics and kinetics. Gidding demonstrated effectively that the problems of sociology are neither static nor kinetic but static-kinetic; thus he anticipated the position of Znaniecki on this point by thirty years.[20]

[19] F. H. Giddings, *The Principles of Sociology* (New York, 1896), pp. v, xi.

[20] *Ibid.*, pp. xv, 3-5, 56-60; Florian Znaniecki, *The Method of Sociology* (New York, 1934), pp. 16-20; see also the comment by Znaniecki in Herbert Blumer, *An Appraisal of Thomas and Znaniecki's* The Polish Peasant in Europe and America (New York, 1939), pp. 95-98.

Accompanying this synthesis of orientations was a crucial distinction between objective and subjective (volitional) aspects of social phenomena. In his earlier formulations, Giddings was concerned with the subjective aspects, principally as a means of elaborating the variable social manifestations of the consciousness of kind. He often referred to the interplay of motives and social forces and even interpreted social process at one point in terms of the interaction of conscious motives (volitional association) and physical forces.[21] Somewhat later, Giddings was to promote the statistical approach to social phenomena,[22] but he must be regarded as one of the first advocates in this country of what we now somewhat loosely call the method of *Verstehen* conceived as the understanding of meaningful aspects of social phenomena.

Social Cohesion and Social Control: Tönnies, Durkheim, Sumner, and Ross

Although the development of sociological theory has not been a smooth progression, it has nevertheless been relatively free from the disturbing discontinuities that reflect intellectual chaos. During the period in which "social forces" and the psychological approach were being explored, a complementary current in sociology, represented principally by the work of four men, came to assume a prominence that has not been equaled by any competitive orientation. Briefly, its significance lies in an implicit redirection of attention toward the *dynamics of social order* through analyses of the causes, variant forms, and consequences of *social cohesion*. The effective source of this development can be traced to a modest work published as early as 1887, just two years after the appearance of Gumplowicz on the sociological scene.

TÖNNIES (1855-1936)

Ferdinand Tönnies, whose justly famous *Gemeinschaft und Gesellschaft* constituted a turning-point in German sociology and likewise heralded a new era in world sociology, contributed what must be regarded as the most fertile and useful set of "master concepts" to general sociological analysis. Before Tönnies, concepts such as society, group, and social relations were not clearly and consistently employed in a distinctively sociological manner; the intrusion of biological, cosmic, economic, or political elements was quite common, as in the work of Comte, Spencer, Marx, Ward, Gumplowicz, and others.

[21] Giddings, *Principles of Sociology*, pp. 13, 75.
[22] F. H. Giddings, *The Scientific Study of Human Society* (Chapel Hill, 1924).

Tönnies was himself not entirely free of such tendencies in his earliest work, but his use of the concepts *Gemeinschaft* and *Gesellschaft* helped to establish a purely sociological approach that might be applied to any and all social phenomena. These concepts became available, therefore, as multipurpose "forms" or "types" by means of which historical and contemporary social data might be classified and interpreted in a fruitful comparative manner. Tönnies has consequently been considered the founder of the "formal" school in sociology,[23] and his work plainly shows that there is no necessary connection between "formal" sociology and stuffiness.

The problems that Tönnies hoped to illuminate by his master concepts were: What is the essential nature of human groups? What process accounts for variation and change in human groups? As interpreted by Tönnies, human association reflects varying manifestations of two analytically distinctive social bonds: those of "community" (*Gemeinschaft*) and those of "society" (*Gesellschaft*). *Gemeinschaft* is based on sentimental attitudes and feelings of intimacy that in turn develop in situations of prolonged social contact or consanguinity. In such relations, which are said to be created and continued by the will of participants, the emphasis is on consensus, on tradition, and on the relationship as an end rather than as an instrument for attaining specific objectives. By contrast, *Gesellschaft* relations grow out of the specific rational objectives of the participants, so that intimacy is replaced by formality, sentiment by calculation and contract, and relative permanence of association by the phenomena of expediency and limited participation.[24]

In the 1920's, Tönnies used these concepts in a careful analysis of three basic types of social entities (social circles, social collectivities, and social corporations), but even his earlier formulation and application of these master concepts contained a number of significant implications for sociology. First, social phenomena were seen to be reflections of determinate *interpersonal bonds;* the nature of groups and structural differences between groups could then be explained by reference to the relative presence of communal and associational relations among persons. Second, changes in group structure could be traced in the process by which new configurations of these types of social relations are established. Third, the dichotomy of individual and group was largely discarded for the concept of a reciprocal relationship in which, on the one hand, persons actively form and re-form groups and, on the other hand, group structures thus established serve to promote the development of characteristic behavior patterns in associated individuals. Personality and social milieu are thus inseparably linked, in anticipation of the famous theories of Cooley, Mead, and others. Fourth, Tönnies, in stressing the unifying function of typical social bonds, also discerned in every

[23] P. A. Sorokin, *Contemporary Sociological Theories* (New York, 1928), p. 491.

[24] Ferdinand Tönnies, *Fundamental Concepts of Sociology*, translated and supplemented by C. P. Loomis from *Gemeinschaft und Gesellschaft* (1st ed., 1887; New York, 1940), Book I.

social bond a *referential system of values* that seems to constitute the basis of group organization. Finally, this line of analysis could be applied to phenomena of cohesion in simple social relationships (e.g., a friendship), social groups (e.g., the family), and organizations of interrelated groups (societies).

DURKHEIM (1858-1917)

Disturbed by the same sociological problem, and even using initially similar concepts, the French sociologist Émile Durkheim developed an approach to social cohesion that complements and in some respects expands the formulation of Tönnies. As his thinking proceeded, Durkheim saw the fundamental interrelations among adequate theory, a methodology appropriate to social phenomena, and the execution of critically selected empirical studies. On this score alone, Durkheim represents a high point in the intellectual drama of sociological exploration and discovery, though it is possible to take exception to some of his theories and interpretations. In his work, for example, we find instructive discussions and illustrations of the following: the functional approach; the nature of social facts; the role of crucial culture case studies in theoretical formulations; the necessity of working from the "exterior" to the "interior" of social facts, from their expression in behavior and artifacts to the *meaning* for actors and observers; and the related problem of analyzing "intangible" social phenomena by the selection of relevant *indices*.

The Essence of Social Cohesion. Durkheim's study of social cohesion began with a preliminary distinction between *societal types*—the simple, encompassing group based on consanguinity; and the secondary, compound group based on specialized functions[25]—comparable in many respects to Tönnies' *Gemeinschaft* and *Gesellschaft,* to Giddings' *social composition* and *social constitution,* and to Simmel's *organic commonness* and *mechanical simultaneousness*. Each type was described primarily in terms of a characteristic *solidarity;* the simple group was said to achieve cohesion through homogeneity (mechanical solidarity), whereas the compound group was shown to function with a more subtle solidarity based on interdependence of specialized functions (organic solidarity). These forms of solidarity were analytically separated, for Durkheim recognized that aspects of each might be found in any specific society. But Durkheim's original contribution to sociology lay in his attempts to (1) connect solidarity and cohesion with orienting rules and norms; and (2) to demonstrate the variable relations between the individual and these norms.

According to Parsons' documentation,[26] Durkheim's work on these related problems was marked by progressive changes in formulation and

[25] Émile Durkheim, *The Division of Labor in Society*, translated by George Simpson (1st ed. 1893; Glencoe, Ill., 1947), Chaps. 2 and 3.

[26] Talcott Parsons, *The Structure of Social Action* (New York, 1936), Chaps. 8 and 10.

interpretation, for Durkheim was apparently not satisfied with the conclusions of his earlier works (*The Division of Labor in Society* and *The Rules of the Sociological Method*). Those interested in the *evolution* of Durkheim's thought can find a convenient starting-point in Parsons' critical review. But in its matured form, the theory of social cohesion incorporated the beliefs that all organized groups and societies operate by means of a "common consciousness" (*conscience collective*), or as sometimes interpreted, a referential value-system; that the various types of organization reflect themselves in different kinds of common consciousness; and that ultimately all social phenomena possess significance for the sociologist through their relation to specific forms of the common consciousness.

Durkheim first noted variations in the common consciousness by distinguishing elements of *repressive law* from *restitutive law,* assuming that law offered an adequate index of solidarity. But it was not until his searching analyses of suicide as a sociological phenomenon that Durkheim was able to discard the formal, legalistic approach to solidarity for a more generalized classification of the phenomena of cohesion. With the help of many simple statistical comparisons of suicide rates, Durkheim demonstrated that suicides could be fruitfully separated into three types in terms of distinctive forms of social groupings and their respective manifestations of social solidarity. *Altruistic suicide* was linked with groups characterized by a value-system that stresses collective ends rather than individual needs, whereas *egoistic suicide* was related to a common consciousness that assigns greater importance to individuality and freedom of choice in periods of personal crisis. In *normless suicide,* however Durkheim was able to demonstrate the existence of groups with weak, undeveloped, or chaotic value systems.[27] Consequently, solidarity was shown to possess a strong *cultural* basis, although Durkheim tried to uncover deeper and more basic conditions of solidarity in *forms of association.* As analyzed in his *Division of Labor*, the primary explanation was bio-social: homogeneity in the mechanical type, concentration of population and resultant intensified social relations (dynamic density) in the organic type. But a more adequate sociological explanation of solidarity and its variations was included under "secondary" factors. Here Durkheim gave belated prominence to the relative development of a social division of labor and degrees of social mobility as sources of variation in the general structure (but not the *content*) of group values. For example, he examined the role of the division of labor in stimulating value-systems marked by a growing abstractness, thus providing greater scope for individual variations, and likewise illuminated the process by which increasing social mobility dilutes the power of traditional values.[28]

[27] Durkheim, *op. cit.,* pp. 71-80, 105-110, 113-120, 129-131; *Suicide,* translated by J. A. Spaulding and George Simpson (1st ed., 1897; Glencoe, Ill., 1951), Book II.

[28] Durkheim, *The Division of Labor*, pp. 256-262, 287-295.

Although Durkheim initially approached social phenomena as they impinge on individuals—through the concepts of exteriority and constraint—he came to recognize the crucial role of the individual's affective reactions. The true basis of solidarity, he concluded, rests neither on enforced acceptance (constraint) nor expedient acceptance (interest), but on an internalized, moral obligation to group norms and on a feeling of "respect" for group dictates. Thus social solidarity emerges from group pressures that create self-discipline, which is manifested in morality and conscience. In this basic attitude of respect, Durkheim discovered a common denominator of society and "religion"; thus the "religious" element (but not necessarily a religious *system*) can be interpreted as the substructure of society, whereas its deterioration produces normlessness.[29] (See Chap. 6, present volume.)

SUMNER (1840-1910)

Folkways and *mores* are terms that have found their way into popular, casual converse, proving that scientific language is useful to laymen. Yet the full significance of these terms is inevitably obscured when they are separated from the work of their originator or from their role in the development of sociology. From our vantage-point, and with the usual benefits of hindsight, these concepts may be interpreted in a manner which would probably be contested by William G. Sumner—that is, the general theory of the folkways and mores may be taken to supplement and expand the major contributions of Tönnies and Durkheim. Sumner, like Ward, was attracted by the functional, processual aspects of society, by what men do, rather than by the entangled social relationships that derive from and condition human behavior. Society for Sumner was in one respect an organization marked by cooperation and specialization, but his "science of society" was largely devoted to detailing the *sequence of values* developed in response to three major interests, which we should now call "institutional areas."[30] In his way, Sumner returned to Spencerian sociology; consequently, the four volumes of the posthumous *Science of Society* (with Keller as alter ego) are today completely overshadowed by the first two chapters of *Folkways,* in which the origin and function of folkways and mores are examined.

In this earlier work, Sumner approached society as a creative process in which control over the environment is achieved by developing, learning, and changing common values. However, environmental control is accompanied by coercive pressures on its members by means of these values. Thus, the individual becomes identified with his group or society not through the

[29] *Ibid.,* pp. 51, 169, 203, 376, 398; Durkheim, *The Elementary Forms of the Religious Life,* translated by J. W. Swain (1st ed., 1912; Glencoe, Illinois, 1947), pp. 36-42, 206-214, 420-424. Our "normlessness" is an Anglicization of *anomie.*

[30] W. G. Sumner, A. G. Keller, and M. R. Davie, *The Science of Society* (New Haven, 1927), 4 vols.

accident of membership but through participation in group activities and acceptance of group norms. Sumner largely ignored the process by which these norms are internalized and instead concerned himself with the resultant cohesion as manifested in conceptions of the "we-group" and the phenomena of *ethnocentrism*.[31] His special contribution, however, was in distinguishing types or degrees of collective pressure. Relatively slight pressures toward conformity are exerted by the folkways, which are based primarily on tradition. (Sumner sometimes employed the term *folkways* vaguely, however.) A second source of pressure to cohesion through value-systems is the mores, which comprise practices endowed with notions of group welfare and survival. The mores contain emotionally charged directives (positive and negative) to individuals; sentiment and strong faith therefore attach to these values, and their violation provokes widespread indignation in the group. From the mores are produced the third and highest form of group pressure—the institutions and laws. Sumner interpreted institutions as matured or formalized mores to which is added some apparatus for *insuring* conformity. But these three social mechanisms do not achieve solidarity by inducing conformity; the basic element in solidarity is instead a by-product of conformity: the common, dominating notions of what is "right", "true", and "good".[32] Consequently, Sumner demonstrated an underlying "division of labor" in the process of maintaining social order, a phenomenon analytically distinct from the interdependence of specialized institutional functions.

ROSS (1866-1951)

The phenomena of group pressures constituted an interest which dominated the early sociological career of Edward A. Ross, but, unlike Sumner, Ross was concerned with the nature of social order and solidarity in relatively complex societies. In fact, Ross regarded division of labor and hierarchical organization, which are characteristic of complex social organizations, as reflecting a "higher" degree of social order than that found in societies marked by mechanical solidarity. As a possible result of this focus, Ross came to emphasize the *problems* involved in maintaining social order rather than the *consequences* of social order. Concepts of solidarity and cohesion were therefore made subsidiary to *social control*, the social processes that coordinate individual and group functions into an organized pattern. Furthermore, this interest in complex societies led Ross to approach the problem of social order not only in terms of the individual *v.s.* the group, but also as a process in which specific component groups confront one another.[33]

[31] W. G. Sumner, *Folkways* (Boston, 1906), pp. 12-15.
[32] *Ibid.*, pp. 2-7, 27-38, 53-60; and Chap. 2.
[33] E. A. Ross, *Social Control* (New York, 1901), pp. 2, 52.

Types of Social Control. Although Ross later gave considerable attention to interests as social forces, his analysis of social control can be regarded as a separable and enduring piece of work It appears that Durkheim, not Tarde, was Ross's guide to this problem, since in general the role of psychological factors was found to be limited and even the principle of imitation offered more problems than solutions in explaining the processes of controls. The key to control, according to Ross, lay in the phenomenon of obedience, which is identical with Durkheim's concept of moral obligation As societies develop, two *contexts of obedience* emerge: the personal-informal and the impersonal-formal In the first of these, order is based on *concord,* a "mechanical solidarity" rooted in homogeneity of blood and values (communal order); in the second, social differentiation weakens concord and thus order is achieved by *control* (societal order). On the other hand, the *mechanisms* of control are distinguished into two types: the *internal* (based on appropriately developed feelings) and the *external* (the use of force and authority). The former is *ethical* control, the latter *political* control; one emphasizes the ends of group life, the other is characterized by an apparatus of *means* (e.g., law, education).[34]

It was Ross's contention that complex society employs and requires both the ethical and the political control mechanisms, although he agreed with Durkheim that the basic and more efficient type of control in modern society is the ethical. Therefore, in anticipation of Cooley's analysis of the primary group, of Linton's theory of social roles, and Kardiner's notions of basic personality structure, Ross regarded the family unit as a moral agent in communication of fundamental ideas and values to an entire generation. Thus the family and other groups were seen as agents of control in their elaboration and inculcation of *patterns* of conduct appropriate to general responsibilities or positions in the wider social configuration. When internalized as *personal ideals,* these values become the bases of the obedience that is the essence of truly efficient social control.[35]

Simmel, Max Weber, and Cooley

The demarcation of distinctively sociological concepts and problems and the progressive identification of the "social" as a scientifically legitimate aspect of experience were considerably advanced by the theorists already discussed in approximately the period 1890 to 1905. In the subsequent decade, sociology emerged as an autonomous and rapidly expanding discipline, with a repertory of problems, concepts, theories, and methods that we can recog-

[34] *Ibid.*, pp. 10-13, 411-12, 432.
[35] *Ibid.*, pp. 181, 218-225, 252.

nize as "modern" despite the added sophistication and specialization of the past thirty years. Sociology was in effect granted a significant degree of coherence by the interaction—cooperative and otherwise—of many sociologists, but it is quite probable that three men can be especially designated as the enduring giants of a particularly fruitful decade: Simmel, Max Weber, and Cooley. Paradoxically, none of these men completed an elaborate theoretical edifice in the manner of a Comte, a Spencer, or a Ward, although Weber might have done so had he not died at a relatively early age. But each man in his own way reworked, illuminated, or extended existing sociological currents, thereby preparing sociology for the voluminous researches of the next generation.

SIMMEL (1858-1918)

In the work of the German sociologist Simmel we find the interesting anomaly of a philosopher who put aside the normative, relatively non-empirical categories of philosophy in favor of more specific concepts dealing with human behavior and interaction. Although he "changed his spots" for only a short period in his intellectual career, Simmel illustrated in numerous capsulated analyses of social phenomena the possibilities of a sociology organized about a series of distinctive concepts. Approaching society as a continuous process of "becoming," manifested in kinetic relations and reciprocal activities among persons, Simmel located the essence of all social phenomena in *sociation* (comprising association and dissociation), the contact and mutual influence of sentient beings. Consequently, he assigned to sociologists the tasks of identifying, classifying, and analyzing the diversity of sociative types or forms that persons employ in building and maintaining society. It is clear that Simmel considered his work an introduction to this kind of analysis; as a result he was not concerned with detailed blueprints but instead contributed brilliantly perceptive essays—brief and often tantalizing in their lack of extensive development—on two major aspects of sociation: social relations and certain aspects of social groups.

The Forms of Sociation. An unusual feature of these essays is their focus on the smaller, semi-institutionalized and somewhat disregarded forms of sociation. In this way, Simmel tried to demonstrate the important function of the more subtle relations in society that were generally ignored in studies of institutions and of the more rigidly classifiable interactions among persons. Although he made perennially useful analyses of such relations as conflict, competition, and superordination-subordination, Simmel's truly original additions to sociological analysis may prove to be his discussions of such minor forms of sociation as *sympathy, gratitude, jealousy, sociability,* and *secrecy.*[36] In

[36] Georg Simmel, *The Sociology of Georg Simmel,* translated and edited by K.H. Wolff (Glencoe, Illinois, 1950), *passim;* N. J. Spykman, *The Social Theory of Georg Simmel* (Chicago, 1925), pp. 27, 31-32, 38-42. The latter work is *important.*

much the same way, Simmel restricted himself to uncovering significant aspects of sociation in relatively small groups. These analytical aspects include: the influence of numbers; differentiation, hierarchy, and the division of labor; centralization; group persistence and cohesion; the degree of reciprocal knowledge between group members; initiation; and the degree of individual de-emphasis.[37]

Whereas Simmel sharply distinguished *forms* of sociation from the *content* of sociation (desires, values, interests), his writings indicate that this was an analytical distinction of complementary aspects. The forms of sociation were abstracted from their respective contents in order to obtain conceptually stable anchorage-points. It was Simmel's intention to spur the creation and use of concepts having wide applicability to social phenomena. Only in this way, he asserted, could sociology attain a scientific identity and in addition overcome the "personal" sociologies of gifted men who were thus unable to establish a genuine discipline in the *mélange* of coteries and schools. Therefore, the forms of sociation cannot be justly characterized as unreal, empty, or non-empirical, for they are derived from analysis of empirical phenomena and their utility can be continually tested in terms of their assistance in clarifying and organizing theoretically relevant aspects of diverse social phenomena.

MAX WEBER (1864-1920)

Max Weber is probably the most discussed sociologist of the past fifty years. Since his premature death in 1920, no less than nine volumes have made his contributions available in more or less adequate English translation from the German, and more are on the way. No other sociologist has struggled with the major problems of sociological analysis more persistently or, on the whole, more successfully. Armed with a remarkable erudition, master of the problems and data of history, economics, and jurisprudence, Weber worked at the very core of modern sociology by serious attention to conceptualization, methodological issues, and research in at least three major institutional areas. In view of this embarrassing richness, nothing approaching full justice to his work can be attempted in this chapter; only the highlights of his thinking as they relate to the emergence of modern sociology will be presented here.

Meaningful Ideal Types. Weber's conceptual scheme continued and in some respects elaborated the "formal" approach of Tönnies and Simmel, for Weber recognized that sociology could not proceed without suitably generalized concepts. But Weber, especially cognizant of the heterogeneous nature of social data, framed his concepts in the form of deliberately accentuated aspects of human behavior: the famous *ideal types*. (These, together with *constructed types*, are analyzed as they appear in contemporary sociology

[37] Simmel, *op. cit.*, pp. 87-117, 181-306, 361-375.

in Chap. 7, pp. 224-228.) However, Weber was guided by his view of sociology as a science concerned with "interpretative understanding" of meaningful human behavior. His ideal types consequently reflected this emphasis on the "subjective" or meaningful as well as the "objective" aspect of social phenomena. Thus, on the basis of the conscious or unconscious meaning involved for an individual (which Weber interpreted as the variable relation between *means* and *ends* in behavior), *social action* was analyzed through four ideal types: traditional, value-rational, purposively rational, and affectual. In a similar manner, Weber developed ideal types of *social relations* (conflict, primary-group, secondary-group, and associational) and of *legitimate orders* (rational, traditional, and charismatic).[38] As a result, sociology was charged with the necessity of uncovering *intentions* of individuals as they confront social situations. This is the famous and controversial operation called *Verstehen* (location of meaning); in modern terms, *Verstehen* is closely allied to analysis of the "definition of the situation."[39] (See Chap. 4, pp. 87-89.)

Institutional Dynamics. These concepts were not employed in piecemeal fashion, for Weber, unlike Simmel, was primarily engaged in analyzing and conceptualizing the *institutional structure* of society as the significant context of sociologically relevant behavior. Institutions were more or less explicitly viewed as complex networks of social relations and interests or functions organized about some structure of obedience, obligation, or to use Weber's term, *legitimacy*. It was this aspect—the nature of legitimate order—that stimulated the major portion of Weber's researches and theoretical formulations; his writings on authority, power, discipline, bureaucracy, the sociology of law, and stratification can be interpreted as attempts to explore the varying facets of legitimate order. Moreover, Weber was one of the first to recognize the crucial role of legitimacy and its variations in a genuinely sociological approach to social change,[40] thereby demonstrating the inadequacy of economic, psychological, and evolutionary theories.

It is in this larger context that we may place Weber's well-known researches in religion and religious kinetics. On the one hand, Weber was engaged in presenting a painstaking analysis of institutional kinetics in terms of the process by which specific legitimate orders are replaced or modified. In religious development, according to Weber, *tradition l* authority is challenged in crisis by the authority of *charisma* through the process of *prophecy*. Prophecy itself was split into two ideal types—emissary prophecy and exemplary prophecy; at the same time, the development of prophetic systems

[38] Max Weber, *The Theory of Social and Economic Organization,* translated by A. M. Henderson and Talcott Parsons (New York, 1947), pp. 88-103, 112-132.

[39] *Ibid.,* pp. 96-100; W. I. Thomas, *The Unadjusted Girl* (London, 1923), pp. 42-43, 81-82.

[40] Weber, *op. cit.,* pp. 324-386; *From Max Weber: Essays in Sociology,* translated by H. H. Gerth and C. Wright Mills (New York, 1946), pp. 196-264.

may emphasize either *ascetic* or *mystic* means of religious organization. The transformation of charismatic authority into more established systems (traditional and/or rational) depends on the social balance of power; in this sense, religious development is basically a struggle for legitimacy.[41]

But Weber was likewise concerned with the interrelation of legitimate orders—with the phenomenon of institutional interdependence. Thus the functional nature of society is stressed in his work. Essentially, he examined the interrelation of three institutional sectors—economic, political, and religious. His general de-emphasis of the kinship and marriage structure is probably related to his focus on complex societies, in which this structure (despite the objections of some observers) plays an important but secondary role. Much of Weber's work in this area served to demonstrate the predominant influence of political institutions in social organization and social change[42] as a corrective of Marxian economic determinism. However, his voluminous but unfinished researches into the relation between religion and economic structure constitute another impressive denial of the universal dominance of any single institutional area in human history. With the aid of detailed comparative culture case studies, Weber was able to expose the causal significance of certain Protestant ethical systems in the emergence of the economic ethics underlying modern capitalism. He did not attempt to "derive" capitalism from Protestantism. Although he recognized the importance of technology and material resources, his historical comparisons seemed to point to the intra-worldly asceticism of some Protestant groups as the *major differentiating factor* in modern capitalism as distinct from other economic systems.[43] The primary implication of these institutional studies therefore corroborates the major thesis of Durkheim: both Weber and Durkheim found the essence of society in the phenomena of moral obligation or legitimacy. But Weber further distinguished social structure as a configuration of *legitimate orders* (institutions) whose mutual interaction constitutes the core problem of sociological analysis.

COOLEY (1864-1929)

Despite the incomparable contributions of such men as Durkheim, Simmel, and Weber, sociology lacked a crucial segment of theory that might establish a reliable connection between institutions, social groups, social pro-

[41] Gerth and Mills, *op. cit.*, Chaps. 11 and 13.

[42] Max Weber, *General Economic History*, translated by Frank Knight (Glencoe, Ill., 1950), pp. 45-46, 316-321, 324-331, 337; *Max Weber on Law in Economy and Society*, translated by Edward Shils and Max Rheinstein (Cambridge, Mass., 1954), Chaps. 4-6.

[43] Max Weber, *The Protestant Ethic and the Spirit of Capitalism*, translated by Talcott Parsons (London, 1930); *The Religion of China*, translated by H. H. Gerth (Glencoe, Ill., 1951); *The Hindu Social System*, translated by H. H. Gerth and Don Martindale (Minneapolis, Minn., 1950), mimeographed; *Ancient Judaism*, translated by H. H. Gerth and Don Martindale (Glencoe, 1953).

cesses, and individuals. The basic need, in short, was a *social psychology* capable of conceptually integrating individuals in groups and institutional orders. Charles H. Cooley provided much of this analysis in three modest works, one primarily social-psychological and the others chiefly sociological, that may well be judged the ablest discussions of sociological problems in America during the first two decades of the twentieth century.

Like Weber, Cooley asserted that social phenomena possess a meaningful aspect that may not be ignored, but Cooley perhaps devoted more attention to the *personal* by concentrating his discussions on small groups in terms of (1) their impact on their members and (2) their relations with more extended groupings. Since he viewed social life as an ongoing organic process in which persons relate to one another by a "tentative method" of trial-and-error adaptation, Cooley could see no alternative to intimate, sympathetic mental participation by the sociologist with the aim of discovering the values and desires of participants and the process by which these values and desires arise and express themselves. This method of *sympathetic introspection*[44] has some apparent similarities to the method of *Verstehen*, although Weber surpassed Cooley in the safeguards imposed.

The Primary Group and Social Organization. In the concept of the *primary group* Cooley sketched the process by which individuals acquire the basic values, ideals, and attitudes underlying social solidarity and the moral obligation to legitimate order. Essentially, then, he regarded social structure as dependent on the *socialization* functions of small, intimate groups, even in societies marked by extensive division of labor.[45] In this manner, Cooley refuted Durkheim's early theory of the cohesive function of interdependence *in itself,* and located the social origins of Durkheim's later and more useful concept of moral obligation.

However, Cooley recognized a certain incompatibility between primary group experiences and the atmosphere of more complex, *voluntary* groupings in the larger social organization. As interpreted by Cooley, this is essentially a contest of value-systems—the primary ideals *vs.* institutional valuations—in the experience of individuals. In place of the informal contacts and controls characteristic of primary groups, impersonal, specialized, and fractional interactions achieve dominance, as manifested in the phenomena of Communication, Public Opinion, Social Class, and Institutions.[46] But the special significance of these developments was for Cooley in the altered nature of social control. Somewhat in the manner of Comte, Cooley viewed institutions as social mechanisms that function through the differentiation of *functionally specialized social classes*, one of which has the primary responsibility for inter-

[44] C. H. Cooley, *Social Organization* (New York, 1909), p. 7; *Social Process* (New York, 1918), pp. 8, 397, 400.

[45] Cooley, *Social Organization*, pp. 23-32.

[46] *Ibid.*, p. 53-57; Cooley, *Social Process*, p. 7.

preting and administering specific institutional values.[47] Thus, by implication, as primary controls are overshadowed by institutional arrangements, the emphasis in interpersonal relations shifts from moral obligation and deep-lying common values to personal and group behavior directed toward *means* of control (power, manipulation, politics)—from *morality* to *expediency*.

Sociology at the Threshold of Expansion

By 1920 the cumulation of many individual contributions had revealed the major outlines of a special social science dedicated to analysis of the fundamental aspects of collective human existence. Unlike the earlier visions of Comte and Spencer, however, this developing discipline was not simply a synthesis of already established social sciences but a new and adventurous field in the scientific division of labor. The intellectual forays constituting this history from Comte to Cooley may be interpreted as a relatively continuous process in which the *social* and *societal* were progressively defined as an analytically separable realm of empirical phenomena. Specifically, this entailed the creation of a special set of concepts suitable to the clear statement and analysis of a wholly distinctive set of problems. What is society and how does it function? What are the essential units of society? How are these combined to satisfy various crucial needs? What processes sustain or threaten stability? How are individuals incorporated into societal structures? What factors differentiate societies, or their component parts, from one another? By 1920, to select only the most general sociological concepts, there was a rather full conceptual kit: society, social group, social institution, social process, social relation, social interaction, social motives, social division of labor, social stratification, social control, and social change.

With these special concepts and problems, sociology attained a semblance of unity, although several nettlesome problems were still apparent at the end of World War I. Of primary importance was the need to refine, modify, and differentiate sociological concepts in the light of numerous and varied empirical researches. Theory and research were largely strangers to one another simply because sociological problems were, in their first stages, understandably vague, and thus truly *sociological* data in the present-day sense were not yet available. A related difficulty was, also understandably, methodological; sociologists were still unable to resolve satisfactorily the apparent dilemma of irrelevant objectivity *vs.* unreliable subjectivity, the respective limitations of physical-science methods and the unevenly brillant but unveri-

[47] Cooley, *Social Process*, pp. 292-302, 336.

fiable insights of personal observation and interpretation. Furthermore, sociology had not yet matched the empirically varied manifestations of social phenomena with an adequate specialization of effort within the discipline of sociology. Finally, in the long quest for identity, sociologists were not devoting much attention to the problems of articulating their studies with other social sciences and thereby exchanging mutually beneficial data, concepts, or generalizations. Interdisciplinary cooperation was not at all in fashion; in fact, sociologists were still suspected of unjustified raids on neighboring specialities.

Despite these difficulties, the emergence of sociology as a *discipline* has, for the first time in human history, provided the distinct possibility of obtaining verifiable, comparative knowledge of an organized nature concerning both the universals and particulars of human behavior. This does not mean that sociology, as "the grammar of social science," can or should supersede the functions of other socially relevant fields such as art, religion, philosophy, and history. Each approach to man as a human being has its proper, specialized objective, which consists of (1) focusing on some aspect or related set of variables of human experience and (2) drawing implications from each line of inquiry for future behavior. But following the revolutionary transformations in social theory, sociology has become a special science that is at the same time a necessary adjunct to any responsible study of man. However, whereas the role of these fields is to understand and prescribe, sociology has increasingly restricted itself to accurate description and verifiable generalization in the quest for knowledge and understanding, largely ignoring the dangerous temptation to convert hard-won theory into hopeful remedies for numerous social difficulties.

This refusal to enter the arena of policy should not be misconstrued as either a lack of interest or an abandonment of social responsibility; it merely signifies that sociology recognizes its limitations as a *direct* participant in policy determination and that it regards genuine understanding as ultimately more "practical" than any hasty program based on partly digested facts and unexamined fancies. Specifically, this indirect approach to problems of social existence has been expressed in a process of *internal specialization,* principally dating from 1920, that has transformed a preliminary, general orientation into a number of sociological compartments bristling with problems of both theoretical and practical interest. Essentially, a specialized sociology has, in its short span, contributed to our understanding by (1) locating and defining relevant problems; (2) gathering and organizing reliable sets of specific facts; (3) indicating the gaps in our knowledge of specific problems; and (4) emphasizing the interrelations between problems ordinarily conceived as discrete and self-contained. The results of these specialized investigations (which are perpetually in need of further correction, since science cannot provide the absolutes of religion or philosophy) often contain implicit or explicit guides to action—for those who appreciate properly qualified cues. But, although there is no lack of socially relevant interpretation, there are no sociological prophets. Indeed, this self-prescribed course has maneuvered sociology into a somewhat delicate position: it disappoints the disturbed multitudes seeking ready answers delivered with certainty; and it enrages a variety of vested interests, who abhor freedom of interpretation and who prefer to let a minimum of handpicked facts "speak for themselves."

SELECTED BIBLIOGRAPHY

Barnes, H. E. (ed.), *An Introduction to the History of Sociology* (Chicago: University of Chicago Press, 1948).

Becker, Howard, *Systematic Sociology on the Basis of the* Beziehungslehre *and* Gebildelehre *of Leopold von Wiese* (New York: John Wiley, 1932; reissued, with a new preface, Gary, Ind.: Norman Paul Press, 1950), Part IV: "Historical Postscript."

Becker, Howard, and H. E. Barnes, *Social Thought from Lore to Science* (2nd ed.; New York: Dover Publications, 1952), 2 vols.

House, F. N., *Development of Sociology* (New York: McGraw-Hill, 1936).

Parsons, Talcott, *The Structure of Social Action* (New York: McGraw-Hill, 1937).

Sorokin, P. A., *Contemporary Sociological Theories* (New York: Harper, 1928).

Timasheff, N. S., *Sociological Theory* (New York: Doubleday, 1955).

II

Major Strands in Theory and Methodology

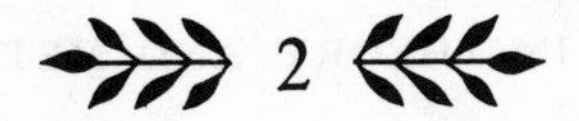

DEVELOPMENTS IN ANALYSIS OF SOCIAL THOUGHT

HOWARD E. JENSEN

STUDENTS OF SOCIAL THEORY HAVE BEEN SINGULARLY TARDY IN APPLYING the techniques of sociological analysis to the development of their discipline, especially in view of Comte's dictum that "a new science must be pursued historically"[1] and of the professional training of many of the founders of American sociology in that field. Even Albion Small himself, a former professor of history and economics, wrote only two years before his death that the earlier neglect by him and his colleagues of what had already been done in their field reflected a "pitiably amateurish attitude." He acknowledged that only in recent years had he come to the conclusion that the historical approach provides "the best way of finding out what sociology is, and what it is worth" but that "until 1917 [he] had not acted on that later belief" in his own graduate teaching.[2]

Small apparently regarded the historical sections of his earlier *General Sociology* (Chicago, 1905) as a contribution to substantive social theory rather than to its history, and his somewhat later book *The Cameralists* as "the study of a single factor of the social process in the German States. . . of importance among the formative forces of the period" but too exclusively concerned with "the central task of furnishing the state with ready means" for the study to comprise a chapter in the history of sociology.[3]

[1] Auguste Comte, *The Positive Philosophy* (London, 1863), vol. 1, p. 22.
[2] A. W. Small, *Origins of Sociology* (Chicago, 1924), pp. 4, 6.
[3] Small, *The Cameralists* (Chicago, 1909), pp. vii-viii.

The General Neglect of Early Social Thought

Nearly a century was to elapse between Comte's first lecture on the subject and Bogardus's pioneer attempt[4] to trace the emergence of man's thought about the more general modes of interpersonal and collective behavior that constitute the immediate background of contemporary sociology. To Bogardus also belongs the credit for placing the history of Occidental social thought in its proper setting in the social lore of primitive peoples and early civilizations. He thus established a tradition followed by Becker and Barnes, and Furfey, but ignored by Seligman, Lichtenberger House, Ellwood, Beach, Barnes, Mihanovich, Kilzer and Ross, and Timasheff.[5]

Sociologists have as yet paid scant attention to the significance of the pre-Comtean period in the study of the origins and development of their science. As early as 1900 Keller had called attention to the great gain which would accrue to sociologists if they "could have at their service separate monographs which would undertake impartially to gather and systematize the sociological material in such documents as the Vedas, the Zend-Avesta, the Eddas, the Hebrew Scriptures the Kalevala, the Nibelungen Lied, the Homeric poems, and the like."[6] For this purpose, Keller considered the Homeric poems superior to all other early literature as the account of sympathetic, first-hand observers of the social conditions and the thoughts, actions, and feeling of men in the age the poems purport to describe. He considered them singularly free from religious or other bias, as well as from extraneous accretions in the processes of transmission, and hence unparalleled in the degree to which they reflect the "quite homogeneous culture stage" that actually existed during the historical epoch of their composition.[7]

[4] E. S. Bogardus, *A History of Social Thought* (Los Angeles, 1922) and its successor, *The Development of Social Thought* (1st ed., 1940; 3rd ed., New York, 1955).

[5] Howard Becker and H. E. Barnes, *Social Thought from Lore to Science* (1st ed., Boston, 1938; 2nd ed., New York, 1952), 2 vols.; P. H. Furfey, *A History of Social Thought* (New York, 1946); E. R. A. Seligman (ed.), *Encyclopedia of the Social Sciences* (New York, 1930), vol. 1: Introduction, and pp. 3-228, 231-249; J. P. Lichtenberger, *Development of Social Theory* (New York, 1923); F. N. House, *The Development of Sociology* (New York, 1936); C. A. Ellwood, *A History of Social Philosophy* (New York, 1938); W. G. Beach, *The Growth of Social Thought* (New York, 1939); H. E. Barnes (ed.), *An Introduction to the History of Sociology* (Chicago, 1948); C. S. Mihanovich (ed.), *Social Theorists* (Milwaukee, 1953); E. F. Kilzer and Eva J. Ross, *Western Social Thought* (Milwaukee, 1954); N. S. Timasheff, *Sociological Theory* (Garden City, 1955).

[6] A. G. Keller, "Sociology and the Epic," *AJS*, 6 (Sept., 1900), p. 267.

[7] Keller, *Homeric Society* (New York, 1902).

Sixteen years later Barnes contended that "from the time of Plato onward, thinkers were approaching, and to a certain extent successfully formulating, the chief problems of sociology," and that there exists therefore "no adequate justification for refusing to go back of Comte for the sources of sociological thought."[8]

But this advice has gone largely unheeded. The general treatises, when they do not ignore or greatly foreshorten the pre-Comtean period, rarely rise above the level of conventional textbook writing in the field of intellectual history. They contain biographical and historical summaries of men and events, but only Barnes and Becker have submitted this material to the penetrating sociological analysis necessary to show the dynamic interrelationships of personality and culture and the emergence of social thought as the joint product of its author and its age. This period still remains a virgin field for sociological research, except for the Becker and Barnes work and except for Keller's early monograph on Homeric society; Becker's culture case studies in his unpublished doctoral dissertation and his projected three-volume work on the social thought of Greece; the monographs of Hertzler on the early civilizations of the Near, Middle and Far East and of Gittler on the Greeks before Plato; Chambliss' textbook summary covering the period from Hammurabi to Comte;[9] and a few articles of varying merit dealing with individual contributors and with problems of limited scope, to be found in the periodical literature and in the introductions to translations of pre-Comtean authors.[10]

SMALL'S ANTI-HISTORICAL POSITION

This neglect is attributable in part to the influence of Small, whose ex officio leadership of the sociological movement Odum has recognized as in several ways greater than that of any of his contemporaries.[11] Small had scant respect for any social thinking prior to the nineteenth century.

[8] H. E. Barnes, "Sociology before Comte: A Summary of Doctrines and an Introduction to the Literature," *AJS,* 23 (Sept., 1917), p. 174.

[9] Becker, "Ionia and Athens: Studies in Secularization" (unpublished Ph. D. thesis, University of Chicago, 1930); ——, *Mind on the Looms of Greece* (manuscript, 3 vols.); vol. 1 made available to the writer through the courtesy of Professor Becker; —— "Church and State in the Cosmos of Crete," International Review of Social History, I, 2 (Fall, 1956), pp. 253-295; J. O. Hertzler, *The Social Thought of the Ancient Civilizations* (New York, 1936); J. B. Gittler, *Social Thought Among the Early Greeks* (Athens, Georgia, 1941). Except for a brief introduction and still briefer descriptions of the three historical periods into which the materials are divided, this volume consists only of classified excerpts from pre-Platonic writings. Rollin Chambliss, *Social Thought from Hammurabi to Comte* (New York, 1954).

[10] Notable among these is M. H. Fisch's "Introduction" to the recent translation of *The Autobiography of Giambattista Vico* (Ithaca, 1940), pp. 1-106.

[11] For a discussion of Small's influence, see H. W. Odum, *American Sociology* (New York, 1950), pp. 94-96.

"There is," he wrote "merely a difference in degree between the man on the street in ancient Rome two thousand years ago, who believed that Atlas carried the world on his shoulders, and the professors who were lecturing on history, and literature, and law, an theology, and politics, and economics in European universities in 1800." He therefore characterized "the body of tradition that has passed as social science up to 1800" as, with conspicuous exceptions, on the whole "unsophisticated, unreliable, [and] irresponsible,"[12] and he concentrated attention upon the early nineteenth-century German critical historians, political scientists, and economists as the most authentic precursors of sociology.

This limitation in range and historical perspective regarding the origins of sociology was taken more seriously by many of Small's contemporaries and successors than he had intended,[13] and his conception of the sharp break in continuity between the social sciences and the inquiries formerly conducted under the name of social philosophy reinforced in the minds of the cruder empiricists the unwarranted belief that a sharp distinction between observing and theorizing distinguishes the sciences from philosophy, an intellectual aberration in which Small himself did not share. Under this influence, it became a current fashion to dismiss the social philosopher contemptuously as an "armchair sociologist who hasn't been working hard recently." The possibility was overlooked that critical reflection is at least as arduous as fact finding, and that sociologists who use their armchairs most fruitfully gather their facts to most purpose.

Small recognized that the intellectual ferment which led to the differentiation of sociology in the first half of the nineteenth century was not "a purely German movement" but part of "an evolution which followed a parallel or converging course throughout the Western World." But he justified the limitation of his study to German sources on the grounds that "the relations of the rapidly developing social sciences to one another are more obvious in German scholarship than elsewhere" and that they are accordingly the most readily available for exposition. He also defended his rejection of a more extended historical perspective by the assertion that the importance of social science is a matter, not of the significance of its problems or its content, but of the reliability of its methods, and that these did not emerge until some time after 1800.

[12] Small, *Origins of Sociology*, pp. 12-13. See also his "Sociology and Plato's Republic," *AJS*, 30, pp. 513-534, 683-702, in which he maintained that "as an example of dialectic, *The Republic* is a foremost example of what sociology is not."

[13] House, a former student of Small, included himself among "the recent writers on the history of social thought" whose historical perspectives have been "unduly influenced by Small's emphasis on the German antecedents of modern social science, or by preoccupation with the great French pioneers, especially Comte and Durkheim." See his review of Gladys Bryson's *Man and Society*, in *ASR*, 11 (1946), p. 373.

But Small did not maintain this view with entire consistency. He introduced occasional qualifications such as the following:

> [If the question] "What have the social sciences done in the nineteenth century toward making out a reliable method of interpreting human experience?" . . . were to be answered in full, it would be necessary to deal with the evolution of philosophy and psychology since Locke in England, since Descartes in France, since Wolff in Germany. Our limitations compel omission of this section of the survey. . . . We shall use as our chief clue to the preparations for sociology some of the significant changes during the evolution of social self-consciousness in Germany. The German factor in the evolution of European self-consciousness is selected, not because the German phase of experience has unique value, but because the links in the chain of experience may be more easily traced in Germany than . . . [in] any other country.[14]

Some Reactions to Small's Position. Small's brilliant analysis of the development of critical history, political science, and economics in Germany and his work in interpreting these contributions to sociological methodology for American readers was of outstanding importance; but neither of his grounds for limiting his study of the origins of sociology to early nineteenth century Germany will bear critical scrutiny. Bryson has shown that the development of the Scottish Common Sense Philosophy of the eighteenth century can be documented with at least equal confidence, and that the social sciences, particularly sociology, have been extensively anticipated and significantly influenced by the philosophers of this school. This was true even on the methodological side, on which Small laid chief stress. In several respects, these philosophers are in the direct line of the intellectual tradition from which modern sociology has emerged: in their conception of man and society as parts of nature which must be investigated as physical systems, in their view of the converging unity of the sciences that forbids that any of them should be developed alone, and in their passion for using mathematical tools in the pursuit of science.

Bryson has demonstrated that among their basic contributions to the development of the modern sociological tradition—contributions which competent research into the origins of sociology can no longer ignore—are their Newtonian convictions that nature must be explained mechanistically and that the correctness of scientific theories must be demonstrated by experiment and not by reason alone; that there is an order and dependability in nature upon which man can count; that the object of science is to discover general principles or laws of nature that have utility for the prediction and control of phenomena; and that in the science of man these principles are to be found not by deductive reasoning from a

[14] Small, *Origins of Sociology,* pp. 15, 29, 31.

priori assumptions but by observing the nature of man and his conduct.[15]

Sorokin has added at least another century to the perspective from which the origins of sociology must be considered. He has shown that the skeptical attitude toward the traditional wiew in the study of social processes and in the adoption of new methods of determining how the observed results are brought about is at least as old as the Social Physicists of the seventeenth century. In their attempts to rule out "subjective" evaluations, to substitute mechanistic for anthropomorphic, teleological, and moralistic conceptions, and to study social phenomena objectively and rationally by the geometrical and quantitative methods that are employed in the study of physical systems, the goals of the Social Physicists were, in plan and aspiration if not also in execution and realization, fundamentally at one with viewpoints and methods regarded by many as peculiarly modern.[16]

Small's exceptions and qualifications noted above do not warrant the conclusion that his view of the origins of sociology differed "only in emphasis" from those of Bryson, Sorokin, and others. The difference in emphasis must be judged in terms of its consequences. Its net effect upon his students and successors has been not that the social scientists of the nineteenth and twentieth centuries differ only in degree from their predecessors in social philosophy but that the latter differ only in degree from the credulous mass mind. Whatever the weight Small may have attached to these exceptions in his own thought, he did not develop them in his writings nor, to my best recollection as his student, in his classes and seminars on the history of sociology, except in his treatment of Adam Smith. Concerning Smith he wrote,

> If one were to come upon *The Wealth of Nations* for the first time, with a knowledge of the general sociological way of looking at society, but with no knowledge of economic literature, there would be not the slightest difficulty nor hesitation about classifying the book as an inquiry in a special field of sociology.[17]

RENEWED EMPHASIS ON THEORY

Another reason for the retarded development of the history of social thought stems from the generally low repute into which theory fell in the period between the world wars. The controversies growing out of the earlier theoretical orientations of positivism, organicism, evolutionism, nominalism, realism, and the various competing economic, racial, geo-

[15] Bryson, *op. cit.*, pp. 16-25, 242-245.

[16] P. A. Sorokin, *Contemporary Sociological Theories* (New York, 1928), pp. 5-13. Sorokin's interest is in a critical evaluation of the contributions to sociological theory over the sixty or seventy years preceding his book rather than in their history. He does, however, give excellent brief summaries of their pre-Comtean predecessors.

[17] Small, *Adam Smith and Modern Sociology* (Chicago, 1907), p. 1.

graphic, technological, and other determinisms had yielded disappointing results in proportion to the time and labor expended and led to a widespread identification of theory as such with apriorism and uncontrolled speculation. The rise and vogue of pragmatism, behaviorism, operationism, and logical positivism, with their emphasis on experimentation and quantification, shifted the interest in research to the accumulation of empirically established facts. But, after the early 1940's, this in turn led to disillusionment and to a clearer understanding that, if the earlier social theory unsupported by verified observations was groundless, the search for facts undirected by theory is aimless, and their accumulation, unintegrated by theory, meaningless.

The result has been a revival of interest in social theory and an increasing emphasis on its significance in contemporary discussions of the problems of education in the social sciences. By all odds the best work of this kind has been done by the economists and is represented especially by the two monographs published as appendices to the *American Economics Review* for December, 1950, and September, 1953. The author of the second of these monographs recommends that, if professional economists are to communicate intelligibly with one another, they must have as a minimum a common core of at least four semesters of systematic training in theory, not merely such economic theory as can be acquired incidentally in the competent treatment of specialized courses throughout the field.

With this recognition of the importance of theory as such, there is growing up a corresponding appreciation of the necessity of the historical approach for a proper understanding of current theoretical problems and issues. The conclusion of the economists' study is that graduate schools should not confine the emphasis on scholarship to the humanities but should make a place for it throughout their programs, and that economists should "require or at least plead with their students, especially those who are destined to be college teachers, to devote to that part of the graduate-school program . . . a modest fraction of their attention." Scholarship, defined as "the pursuit of broad and exact knowledge of the history of the human mind as revealed in written records," should be "one of the ingredients of the education of competent professionals in a field like economics." Graduate professors should "consider it a responsibility to kindle the interest of students in scholarship" in this sense. "This laudable suggestion can be implemented only by introducing students to the history of economic doctrine."[18] What is said here concerning economics is equally pertinent to all the social sciences.

It is not, of course, intended that every social scientist should become his own historian to the extent of being so absorbed in historical researches

[18] H. R. Bowen, "Graduate Education in Economics," *American Economic Review*, 43, pp. 109-110, 115-116.

that he has little time left for empirical research on contemporary problems in his field. But it is important that a few researchers who are familiar with the substantive social theory in each specialty should investigate its history intensively and that their fellow specialists should have a common background of familiarity with the results of these investigations.

THE PROBLEM OF DELIMITING THE FIELD OF SOCIAL THOUGHT

Finally, the history of social thought has been retarded in development because of the difficulty of defining it as a special field of sociological research and of developing a system of concepts and techniques appropriate to the task. Aside from history and political theory, which have venerable ancestries, the social sciences have been recognizable as differentiated fields of critical inquiry only in modern times. Economics as a distinct discipline began to emerge only with the seventeenth century, whereas sociology, anthropology, and social psychology have a history less than half as long. The historians of these disciplines must therefore extract the relevant materials out of their common matrix in folklore, moral and social philosophy, theology, history, economics, and political theory, which constitute the total record of man's increasing awareness of the significance of his life with his fellows. For the political scientist and the economist this is not too difficult a task, for the structures, processes, instrumentalities, and techniques necessary to maintain order within a society and to secure the goods and services which provide the basis for its material existence can be identified with relative ease.

But by what chart and compass shall the historian of social thought find his way through this maze of ideas? By what criteria shall he select out of the common storehouse those materials which are pertinent to his purpose? And how shall he even determine what his purpose is to be? Because of failure to formulate adequate selective criteria, the general treatises on the history of social thought, with few exceptions, are lacking in unity and conceptual clarity. Some writers have defined the field so broadly as to include the entire intellectual history of mankind. Thus Gittler writes that ". . social thought is the reflections about man by men at any given time and place." It does not per se "discriminate between the political, the economic, and the ethical." He adds that "Since the writer is a sociologist by profession, it is evident that his interest is focused on the sociological," but no attempt is made to define that interest more precisely.[19]

Similarly vague is Hertzler's statement that his "concern . . . is specifically with the history of social thought as a background for the sociologist." In his closing summary, however, he provides a list of items of sociological

[19] Gittler, *op. cit.*, pp. 1-4.

interest that his examination of the materials has disclosed. Among these are the following.

> . . . the development of social consciousness; the recognition of the difficulties arising out of personal contacts in group life; a devotion to thought about man's relationship to man in groups; a discussion of human and social values and philosophies of life; much thought about social control, especially the regulative institutions, such as the state, family, and property; some treatment of certain aspects of social organization; some worry about bad social conditions and their effects; the development of massive legal codes governing almost every aspect of group life; much thought about the importance and nature of man's social duties and obligations, with special reference to moral codes and social proprieties; some thought on the preparation for group life, especially education, its theory and technique, but including other means of inculcating institutional lore; the nature of human nature; occasional thought in the form of deft, though partial, social criticism and prophecy; and some treatment of social differentiation, especially the phenomena of class relations and social inequalities.[20]

Lichtenberger describes his work as an attempt "to uncover the foundations upon which the present structure [of sociology] has been erected and to clarify the processes without which, through the achievements of the centuries, it could not have been built at all." Bogardus considers social thought as "abstract. It is complementary to practical thought about social matters, and at times contrasts sharply with popular thinking."[21] Although this definition would exclude the social thought of pre-literate peoples because of its absorption in the practical and the concrete, Bogardus nevertheless devotes a chapter to this type of social thought in his treatise. It would also rule out the overwhelming mass of contemporary social thought as it takes place in drawing-room, luncheon-club, and street-corner discussion, as well as in newspapers and periodicals, radio and television broadcasts, and other media of mass communication, which exercise a most decisive influence upon the course of public policy.

ELLWOOD AND THE SEARCH FOR ANALITIC GUIDEPOSTS

Only Ellwood has delimited his field by adopting at the outset definite criteria for the selection of his materials, and he has consistently applied these criteria in such a way as to enable the reader clearly to relate the contributions of each individual social theorist to what came before and what followed afterwards. After briefly noting the biographical incidents that may have influenced the thought of each author treated, and after summarizing the general social and cultural environment which influenced

[20] Hertzler, *op. cit.*, pp. 1, 340-341.

[21] Lichtenberger, *op. cit.*, p. ix; Bogardus, *The Development of Social Thought* (3rd ed.), p. 4.

his work, Ellwood takes up his methods, or his lack of them, since "thinking is always limited, if not determined, by the method employed." He then outlines "the thinker's doctrine, if he has such," of social origins, of social development, of social organization and functioning, and finally of social order and progress. But he recognizes that "social thinking, with most thinkers, has been so fragmentary that it has rarely covered the whole field of problems outlined"[22] and hence does not employ his plan as a standardized mold into which his materials must be forced.

The treatment throughout reflects Ellwood's general sociological orientation. As a cultural sociologist, he stresses the continuity of tradition and attempts to show how social thought has been conditioned by its own developing tradition. As one of the pioneers of American social psychology, he emphasizes the role of the individual mind within the social process as a center of creativity and true becoming and avoids the pitfalls of both the cultural determinist and the individualistic (or Great Man) theories by his recognition that the mental productions of genius, thought culturally conditioned, are not therefore culturally determined.

CURRENT HISTORIES OF SOCIAL THOUGHT

As a result of the general lack of competent selective criteria, many of the current histories of social thought consist to a large extent of restatements of materials already treated by the historians of philosophy and politics. Others, especially in their treatment of pre-literate peoples and of ancient civilizations where social thought must be deduced from the way men lived and what they did rather than from what they said, have failed to distinguish clearly between *events* and *ideas about events,* and have consequently duplicated much of the contents of social and cultural history and cultural anthropology. What is required to constitute a history of social thought is not a summary of the social structure and institutional practices of pre-literate peoples and early civilizations, together with a classification of their folklore, sacred writings, legal codes, and other documentary remains, but a sociological analysis of such materials to determine the social thought implicit in them.

In the face of the tendency of current empirical research to underestimate the significance of pre-Comtean or even pre-Sumnerian social thought, only a high order of enthusiasm for "what thoughts the wise of old have entertained" can sustain sociological inquiry in this field. From this there has resulted a countertendency to overestimate the social lore of pre-literate peoples and the social wisdom of past civilizations, a difference in evaluation which also is due in part to the tendency of the empirical researchers to employ method and of the historians of social thought to emphasize prob-

[22] Ellwood, *op. cit.,* p. xi.

lems and content as criteria determining the origins of social science.[23] Brilliant intuitions, significant insights, and unsurpassed capacity for sustained reasoning are indeed as universal as mankind and older than history. But they lack the precise formulation which admits of their being brought to the test of empirical fact. They are unsupported by the techniques of documentation, controlled observation, and experimentation that permit the accurate prediction and dependable control of phenomena on which rest both the "truth value" of pure science and the "utility value" of its applications in practice. What is needed is a realistic appreciation of the way in which these generic insights into interpersonal and collective behavior have been winnowed out, extended, and given increasing precision by the work of successive generations who improved upon their predecessors in objective methods of verification so gradually that the most competent of contemporary scholars differ widely in their judgments even as to the century in which social science must be acknowledged to have emerged from the womb of social thought.

Gittler has classified the various conceptions of the origins of sociology into five groups:

> . . . (1) the theory that sociology dates back to ancient times and to the Greeks in particular (this view is upheld by Spann, Bogardus, Lichtenberger, Menzel, Ellwood, and Hankins); (2) the conception of the origin of sociology in the seventeenth and eighteenth centuries (this is supported by such men as Sombart, Brinkmann, and Tönnies); (3) the view that it begins in the romantic period of about 1800 (Small, von Below, and Baxa believed in this conception); (4) the idea that the nineteenth century is the period which gave rise to sociology (this theory has such adherents as Barth, Oppenheimer, M. Weber, Gothein, Freyer, Squillace, Stein, and Mohl); (5) and the theory which places the origins of sociology in the twentieth century (Wiese strongly supports this theory).[24]

THE RATIONALE OF SOCIOLOGICAL ANALYSIS OF SOCIAL THOUGHT

These considerations have led the more positivistically inclined to dismiss the history of social thought as a field of purely antiquarian interest, providing a subject matter for dilettante essays and an opportunity for the prideful display of erudition, but of no value to the scientist in getting on with the job of asking answerable questions about human association. But others, less positivistically inclined, have a profounder appreciation of how many of the basic ideas and value-systems, with their unresolved problems and conflicts, which are today living forces in the

[23] Cf. Small's negative estimate of Plato (note 12 above), with R. M. MacIver's designation of *The Republic* as "the first and greatest of sociological treatises" in his *Community* (London, 1920), p. 54. See also Becker's review of Hertzler, cited in note 28 below.

[24] Gittler, *op. cit.*, pp. 3-4.

world's work, are rooted in man's historic and prehistoric past. They recognize the significance of obtaining as thorough a knowledge of man's total intellectual history as possible for an adequate understanding of contemporary society. They accept the history of social thought as a legitimate field of scholarly research. But they would relinquish it to the historians of philosophy, ethics, and political theory, and restrict themselves to more recent developments.

But ideas about the social process are themselves a part of the social process, and unless these ideas are treated sociologically, an important phase of human culture falls outside the field of sociological analysis Only the sociologist has the broad outlook upon the history of ideas that is so often lacking in contemporary social theory, and only he possesses the tools to make that history yield fruit for further social theory, as a comparison of a Max Weber's excursions into the field with those of a Spengler or a Toynbee will show

If the history of social thought is to justify itself as a sociological discipline, it must yield far richer results for social theory than it has as yet done The problem for sociological research is not primarily to summarize what others have thought For summaries we can turn to the intellectual histories already extant The sociological problem is to find out why they have thought it

Sociology of Knowledge and Social Thought

Our contemporary treatises are, however, largely descriptive and exegetical in character.[25] They record, with varying degrees of success, how our basic ideas about the group factor in human experience have emerged and accumulated and how our methods of dealing with them have been gradually modified and perfected. They are replete with references to the historical conditions under which the individual contributors did their work and to the significant events in their life histories. But they do not pass much beyond placing their materials in a historical continuum. They fail to come to grips with that order and interdependence of phenomena that is to the sociologist the essence of their meaning. They do not organically

[25] This procedure is entirely legitimate if consciously avowed. Thus Sorokin (*op. cit.*, p. xvii) explicitly states his objective as a survey of the principal types of sociological theories over sixty or seventy years preceding 1928 in order "to find out to what extent they are scientifically valid. All other approaches to a study of the theories, such as, for instance, why a certain theory is set forth by a certain author, or why it has become popular, or what is the personality of the author, are intentionally excluded."

relate mental productions to their respective historical epochs by tracing out those interrelations of culture and personality in the processes of becoming that enable us to interpret the thought of any age in terms of its full socio-cultural context. They thus fail to justify their thesis that social thought is the attempt of men to render intelligible the social conditions that environ them.

The demonstration of this thesis requires the use of techniques from the sociology of knowledge in the analysis of social thought. These techniques must be employed to analyze social thought as a body of ideas referring to the social situation not as an externally existing entity but as an integral part of the socio-cultural milieu in which the reflective and creative thinking that produced the ideas took place. Only when the social thought of a writer or of an age has been intensively studied by these methods can the degree of its non-rational and existential determination be appraised and those elements in it which are culturally and historically limited in their application be distinguished from those more rational and universal elements that warrant comparison with the mental productions of other times and cultures.

Sociological theory is not advanced by tracing the equivalents of modern ideas to ancient sources on the basis of superficial and verbal similarities and without regard to fundamental differences in the influence of widely contrasting intellectual milieux upon the problems posed, the postulates assumed, the ends sought, and the socio-cultural meanings of the solutions proposed by the individual theorists. Consider, for example, this gem of historical misinterpretation by Jâszi:

> . . . the ideal state of Plato and that of the Russian communists have many elements in common: both hate commerce and money economy; both regard private property as the sole source of evil; both would eliminate wealth and poverty; both favor a collective education of the children, exempted from parental care; both regard art and literature only as a means of state education; both would control all science and ideology in the interest of the state; both have a rigid central dogma, a kind of state religion to which all individual and social activity must be subordinated.[26]

And this notwithstanding the low repute of Plato with Marx and his modern epigoni! In *Capital,* Marx mentions Plato but once, only to dissent from the "characteristic bourgeois instinct" which he shared with Thucydides and Xenophon.[27]

But the "many elements in common" that Plato is alleged to share with Marx are neither fundamental nor thoroughgoing. They are derived

[26] Oscar Jászi, Introduction to Geza Engelmann, *Political Philosophy from Plato to Jeremy Bentham* (New York, 1927), pp. 4-5. This passage is quoted with approval by Ellwood, *op. cit.*, p. 34.

[27] Karl Marx, *Capital* (New York, 1906), pp. 401-402.

from utterly contradictory postulates to serve completely different ends, each in its unique socio-cultural context. The basic postulates of *The Republic* are not those of dialectical materialism but of the theory of ideas. The end sought is not to bring the class and power structure of society into harmony with its "productive forces" but to realize a concept of justice based upon an assumed analogy between Plato's tripartite individual psychology and the ideal class structure. The communistic solution was proposed not for the instruments of production but for the goods of consumption. It was applicable not to the society as a whole, to secure an equable distribution of necessities, but to the citizen-soldier and guardian classes only, to guarantee their disinterested service to the common good and the permanence of a power structure based on merit and to prevent corruption by the two most subversive influences recognized by Plato, family dynasty and private fortune. Considered in the light of the socio-cultural context, there is nothing in common between the basic theory of the Platonic Utopia and the Marxian dictatorship of the proletariat. Even in the verbal parallels between the particulars cited by Jászi, the differences outweigh the similarities.

Other historians of social thought have, on equally fallacious grounds, identified Plato as the source of the Fascist and "managerial" ideas of our day.[28] It has remained for a Catholic writer, Father Paul H. Furfey, to note that modern sociologists who discuss *The Republic* have been "a bit unimaginative" in becoming "often so fascinated by these subsidiary [communistic] ideas that they miss the principal point of the book." Furfey comments that "Catholic religious secure the same result by holding their property in common while wives and children are eliminated by the vow of chastity."[29]

BECKER AND CONSTRUCTED TYPES IN ANALYSIS OF SOCIAL THOUGHT

Only Becker has attempted to develop the history of social thought as a contribution to sociological theory. In those parts of *Social Thought from Lore to Science* that flowed directly from his pen, and in his editing of the materials contributed by Barnes, he has introduced some semblance of pattern into an otherwise tangled web by employing distinctively sociological concepts and methods of analysis. Through the use of *wissenssoziologische* techniques and the method of constructed types, he has organically related social thought to its proper socio-cultural milieu. He has shown how social ideas emerge and assume their distinctive character in various cultures through the operation of specific factors resulting in the release

[28] Barnes, *An Introduction to the History of Sociology,* p. 7. Similar misinterpretations of Chinese social thought are noted by Becker in his review of Hertzler, *op. cit.,* in *ASR,* 1 (December, 1936), pp. 1020-1022.

[29] Furfey, *op. cit.,* p. 117.

of the critical faculty in the process of societal transition from sacred to secular types of society.

Becker has been criticized for "pointing the thesis toward the justification of a particular conception of sociology and of . . . [constructive typology in] sociological research." But one need not accept Becker's theoretical and methodological standpoint in order to recognize the necessity of introducing *some* sociological concepts and methods into this field if it is to be pursued as a sociological discipline and to appreciate the significance of this pioneer attempt to do so. In the present state of social theory, sociological criticism might profit from Salvemini's remarks on "the constructive use of bias" in contributing to knowledge by determining the value and limitations of conflicting schools through the intensive use of their concepts and techniques in social research.[30]

But even Becker has rigorously employed this method only in the chapters of his *Social Thought* dealing with ancient Greece, which are based on his own intensive culture case studies, and in those concerned with the lore of pre-literate peoples and the social wisdom of the early civilizations of the Near, Middle, and Far East, in which he has subjected to critical reappraisal the results of previous research by Durkheim, Davy, Moret, Max Weber, Myres, Trever, Breasted, J. M. P. Smith, Granet, Creel, and others. Becker has acknowledged this defect, and states that a "more consistent interpretation would have been attempted" had he "become acquainted with the minutiae of *Wissenssoziologie* at an earlier stage in the preparation of the treatise."[31]

But Becker's germinal ideas contain other potentialities for research which he has not himself exploited. In his earlier work the concepts "sacred" and "secular" are used primarily to designate societies. The closed sacred society is one in which "a sort of emotional halo encircles the ways of the fathers and thereby prevents their profanation by change. . . . No comparison, classification, analysis, and abstraction, habitual or otherwise, is practiced; everything is unique, concrete, and personal, for all contacts are primary." There is a maximum of informal and internalized social control through traditional patterns of conduct, and a marked emotional resistance to change in both thought and behavior. The accessible secular society is by contrast one in which social relations have become depersonalized through such social factors as migration, communication, and other modes of cultural contact. Mental mobility, habitual abstraction, rationalism, and individuation constitute the *modus vivendi*. Social control becomes restricted and highly formalized, and new modes of thought and conduct are readily accepted

[30] See C. W. Hart's review of Becker and Barnes, *op. cit.*, in *ASR*, 3 (Aug., 1938), pp. 581-585; Gaetano Salvemini, *Historian and Scientist* (Cambridge, Mass., 1939), pp. 69-84; W. B. Cannon, *The Way of an Investigator* (New York, 1945), pp. 97-107.

[31] Becker and Barnes, *op. cit.*, vol. 1, Preface.

on the basis of "sheer expedient rationality." When this transition occurs, "social thought not only becomes explicit but also tends toward a high degree of generality; when it does not, the implicit or proverbial holds sway."[32]

Sacred and secular societies, as constructed types, represent polar concepts which never precisely describe the empirical realities but to which different aspects of existing societies conform with varying degrees of approximation. As heuristic devices, they are never in precise correspondence with the empirical social reality to which they refer. Nevertheless, criticism of the theory of constructed types on the ground that they are "not sufficiently empirical" is hardly warranted. Scientific concepts and laws do not describe events as they occur in nature but as they are schematized in theory. The absolute vacuums, the perfect elasticities, the frictionless motions of physical science are also heuristic devices. Likewise, the various forms of distribution curves are derived from abstract mathematical equations to which the empirical data conform with more or less "goodness of fit." The chief difference is that in these realms the empirical data are distributed about some specifically defined central tendency in statistically determinable measures of dispersion for each quantitative attribute employed as a criterion of the concept, whereas the constructed types of the social scientist are limiting concepts from which qualitative attributes deviate by observable degrees for which quantitative measures may or may not be ultimately devised.[33]

In his later work, Becker has recognized that this dichotomous classification of societies as sacred and secular is not precise enough to serve as a tool for rigorous analysis in social research. He has accordingly distinguished more carefully the sub-types of sacred and secular societies useful for this purpose. He has also recognized more explicitly that the terms "sacred" and "secular" properly designate the presence or absence in the members of a society of social attitudes of emotional reluctance to change, together with the social phenomena towards which these attitudes are felt.[34] (See Chap. 6 of the present volume.)

Social Thought and the Process of Secularization. The concept of secularization provides alluring possibilities for research that the present writer has for some years been exploring in his seminars on the history of social thought. The transition from the sacred to the secular is a complex and highly heterogeneous process. It takes place in no regular and orderly way. It differs in intensity and tempo within the different complexes of the same culture, and with the classes and other social groupings that constitute

[32] *Ibid.,* vol. 1, pp. 10, 16, 39, and *passim.*

[33] Cf. Anatol Rapoport, *Operational Philosophy* (New York, 1953), pp. 20 *ff.*

[34] Becker, *Through Values to Social Interpretation* (Durham, N. C., 1950), pp. 264-278; Becker and Barnes, *op. cit.* (2nd ed.), vol. 1, Appendix, p. vi.

the social organization. Every society, however sacred, possesses its secular fringe in which problems are faced in a matter-of-fact way. Physical survival requires that certain aspects of nature and of human nature be faced with intense realism. Here detailed and accurate observation serves to direct the trial-and-error processes which lead to the gradual, unmethodical elaboration of vast stores of empirical knowledge, technical skills, and rule-of-thumb procedures through which there is effected that nice adjustment of man to habitat which is the despair of modern men when they are suddenly compelled to face nature in the raw. Likewise, every society, however secular, possesses a sacred core in which the established patterns of life are adhered to with an intensity sometimes approaching martyrdom. On the one hand, most, if not all, societies contain individuals who respect the hallowed ways with a more or less tongue-in-cheek attitude.[35] On the other, all societies, including our own, contain those who regard the overwhelming mass of traditional and customary beliefs and practices as sacrosanct.

The investigation of this sacred core is of vital importance throughout the history of social thought and social science as well, for it is precisely this ubiquitous and hallowed social lore which has hampered the emergence and development of critical reflection about human affairs throughout history. Its upholders still attempt to exclude wide areas of vital social concern from scientific investigation and have succeeded in retarding by decades the application of scientific findings to problems of social policy. It finds expression in our contemporary society in the current spate of restrictive constitutional amendments and in witch hunts into the activities of universities and educational foundations and into the opinions of private citizens whose views on questions of social policy incline slightly to the left of *Homo neanderthalensis*. This circumstance alone should demonstrate the significance for contemporary social research of a sociological analysis of the sacred core.

Equally important is the investigation of the secular fringe, for the tension between it and the sacred core defines the types of problems accessible to critical study and provides the intellectual milieu that determines the nuances of social thought, unique in every age and culture. Only when these nuances are analyzed and intensively explored by the techniques of culture case study can the more subjective and culturally limited "core theorems" of social thought be isolated from the more objective and universal elements "which can with warrant be transferred to the different setting (in some ways *radically* different) in which the contemporary social scientist operates."[36] Only in this way can we justify the spending of time and money on the history of social thought at the graduate level.

[35] Cf. Paul Radin, *Primitive Man as a Philosopher* (New York, 1927), pp. 53-62.

[36] Becker, "Vitalizing Sociological Theory," *ASR*, 19 (August, 1954), pp. 379-380.

SOCIAL THOUGHT AND SOCIO-CULTURAL STRUCTURE

These nuances provide the non-rational and existential determinants of social thought that constitute the legitimate field of the sociology of knowledge.[37] Sociological research into the history of social thought is therefore inextricably intertwined with the investigation of other theoretical problems as well—especially those of the sociology of knowledge and of historical sociology[38]—through their common dependence upon culture case study. From the Greek sophists to the logical positivists, a succession of theorists have challenged the autonomy of the human intellect in the realm of the social and have sought to reduce all of man's conclusions about his life with his fellows to cultural relativity, devoid of objective validity as rational knowledge. An extreme form of this reductionism is found in Oswald Spengler's *Decline of the West* (New York, 1926-28, 2 vols.). Spengler maintains that each culture possesses a style so unique as to be irreducible to the terms of any other—a situation that, as Timasheff[39] points out, would make it impossible for men of different cultures to understand one another, and for Spengler to have written his book.

Another succession of brilliant thinkers, from Plato to Toynbee and Sorokin, have endeavored to deduce from the data of history general laws of social development capable of explaining, or at least describing, the origin, dominance, and decline of societies and cultures. If the conflicts of hypotheses in these fields are ever resolved, it will be through the sort of intensive culture case histories necessary to the development of the history of social thought as a genuinely sociological discipline.

As House has pertinently commented, "the theory of social evolution and the evolution of social theories [are] related by more than a mere punning verbal tie," since they are both embedded in a common matrix of social change.[40] But is their relationship on that account purely causal, as House thinks? If so, the development of social thought is a mere verbal reflex of the evolution of society itself, and its validity becomes wholly a matter of the fidelity with which it reflects the age that produced it. From that point of view, the problems of historical sociology are so intimately related to those of the sociology of knowledge and the history of social thought as cause and effect that the solution of the first set of problems involves the solution of the second and third sets.

But the interrelations of the three fields are not so simple and direct.

[37] See Chap. 13 of this volume.

[38] Unfortunately, some writers have employed the term "historical sociology" as a synonym for the history of sociology. See, for example, Odum, *op. cit.*, p. 95; and Gittler, *op. cit.*, p. 4. This usage should be avoided as confusing.

[39] Timasheff, *op. cit.*, p. 267.

[40] F. N. House, *The Range of Social Theory* (New York, 1929), p. 545.

Their specific problems differ widely in character and complexity. On the one hand, historical sociology, concerned as it is with formulating uniformities or at least comparable aspects of the life courses of societies and cultures, if not also with predictive generalizations concerning their probable future, achieves a higher level of abstraction than the other two. On the other hand, in determining the degree to which the ideas of an individual or an age are conditioned by socio-cultural and hence by non-logical and historically relative factors, an understanding of the sociology of knowledge is essential to a full understanding of the conceptual system of each contributor to the intellectual heritage, hence basic to any discipline that seeks to reconstruct the historical sequence of ideas in any field.

The three disciplines do indeed derive their data from a common historical matrix, but their relationship is not on that account causal, for the main stream of events whose description constitutes the content of history in any age is like the curve of a chart which marks the generalized course of development of social ideas, from which the contributions of individual men of genius diverge in a wide scatter. Individual thinkers are dependent upon the historical process for (1) the problems posed for solution and (2) the basic data which provide the starting point for thought. They are dependent upon the intellectual milieu for (3) the symbolic systems and the initial postulates, categories, and concepts, and (4) the logical and mathematical techniques by means of which the data are described, processed, and generalized. Finally, they are dependent upon (5) the way in which their thought is related to the prevailing theoretical and practical trends of the culture for determining whether their thought is to die a-borning, or to become a part of the developing complex of human thought and action. But the man of genius is also a center of original and creative activity. He may refine the problems posed, invent new symbolic systems, postulates, categories, and concepts, and devise new logical and mathematical techniques by which new data are discovered, described, processed, and generalized, sometimes with new and revolutionary results.

The Limitations of Cultural Determinism. As Goldenweiser has shown, the dictum of the culturologists, *omnis cultura ex cultura,* is sheer dogma. Culture is not the product of external forces operating automatically; it is the contribution of the creative human mind functioning in relation to external forces. Since therefore no point-for-point determinism exists between social thought and the processes of history, the continuity of social thought only approximates the continuity of history. Furthermore, the unity that characterizes these two processes is in each case a unity of a different order of relations. The unity of history is a relation of existential dependence between events; the unity of social thought is a relation of logical, dependence between ideas. The former is "inextricably bound up with the origin of an event or of some qualitative change within an event";[41] the latter is bound up with the identity and non-contradiction of ideas, their coherence, and their meaningful relations. The causal linkage of events is therefore not identical with the logical linkage of ideas. A break in the former constitutes an interruption of the order of nature; in the latter, a violation of logical consistency. The former is a miracle; the latter, an absurdity.

The historian of social thought has therefore something fresh and of extraordinary value to contribute to social theory. The by-product of his work will help to provide the materials for the more precise determination of what pattern or patterns, if any, the course of historical development has followed and the degree to which "man through knowledge can be something more than a loudspeaker for the particular class or the provincial culture in which circumstances happen to place him."[42]

CASE STUDIES OF SOCIAL THOUGHT

Max Weber placed historical sociology on the right track in his extensive use of culture case studies. Durkheim rendered a similar service to the sociology of religion in his use of similar studies of single institutions in their definite socio-cultural contexts, although the materials chosen were unfortunately not precise enough to yield the valid explanatory generalizations he thought he had established. And the work of Simmel on the conflict cycle and of Pareto on the speculator-rentier sequence have demonstrated the effectiveness of the method in establishing beyond question the existence of rhythms, trends, sequence-patterns, cycles, or periodicities in social change. More recently, similar phenomena have been disclosed by Bogardus in his surveys of race relations on the Pacific Coast and by Park and his students in their studies of the development of American communities, strikes, revolutions, and other social movements.

But such studies cover too limited a range of social phenomena and too short a time-span to yield the larger views and more organic conceptions of history required in a genuinely critical sociological treatment of time sequences. Scientific investigation in which phenomena cannot be repeated at will must necessarily turn to the past for the verification of its hypotheses. But the more fundamental the problems and the longer and more complex the cycles of history under consideration, the fewer the instances available for generalization. It then becomes necessary to utilize to the fullest degree and with the most meticulous care the cases that do exist.

In order to utilize existing cases, historical sociology needs what does not yet exist—intensive culture case studies of as many historical epochs

[41] A. E. Goldenweiser, "Psychology and Culture," *PASS,* 19 (1924), pp. 15-23; Maurice Mandelbaum, *The Problem of Historical Knowledge* (New York, 1938), p. 223.

[42] F. S. C. Northrop, Introduction to J. J. Maquet, *The Sociology of Knowledge* (Boston, 1951), p. xix.

as are available for analysis. Generalization of some kind is the objective of sociology. The problems of social dynamics require these date if we are to find meaning and significance in the flow of events and understand the orderly processes or laws of social change. But if explanatory principles applicable to widely varying cultures do not exist, and if the genesis and development of civilizations remain forever outside the realm of scientific sociological treatment, only by such methods as culture case study can we demonstrate the fact.

CASE STUDIES AND CULTURAL RELATIVISM

Finally, the intensive analysis of the mental productions of each thinker in relation to his time, place, and position in the social structure, which is the *sine qua non* of the history of social thought as a sociological discipline, will in turn react upon the development of the sociology of knowledge by providing further data essential to the testing of its present conflicting hypotheses concerning the degree to which social thought is existentially determined. It brings to the test of historic fact such assertions as Mannheim's statement that all social and historical judgments are "perspectivistic"—that is, that they are extrinsically determined by the social and historical conditions under which they were formulated and expressed.[43] For we can verify the hypothesis that the mental productions of any social thinker of the past were existentially determined only if we have independent, non-perspectivistic knowledge of the state of the social system with which his thought purports to deal. In that case, the hypothesis must be qualified to admit the possibility of such factual historical knowledge. It must be revised to recognize in the thinkers of any age a modicum of capacity for social analysis which does not impose itself upon its materials but expresses their order symbolically, and whose validity is a function, not of the thinker's position in the social structure of a specific culture at a specific time, but of the degree of correspondence between the independently existing order of social events and the thinker's symbolization of them, which it is the task of culture case study to disclose. We can know the degree to which social thought reflects the interests of social groups only on the basis of objective knowledge of both the situations symbolized and the interests served. Otherwise, the hypothesis remains an unsupported dogma or bogs down in a morass of cultural relativism which renders futile the quest for an abstract and objectively valid science of society.

Mannheim seeks to evade the charge of relativism by regarding history as a real process that remains unchanged by the perspective from which it is viewed and that therefore contains all the possible perspectives which may emerge from it; it is analogous to a landscape, which contains within

[43] Karl Mannheim, *Essays on the Sociology of Knowledge* (New York, 1952), pp. 84-133.

itself all the perspectives from which it may be viewed or painted.[44] The analogy, of course, breaks down, because the perspective from which the landscape is viewed does not include and condition the viewing subject. But it is precisely upon this conditioning of the subject that Mannheim insists. If, for example, we would understand what Machiavelli said about his times, we must relate his statements to his times. But Mannheim never realized that to do this we must go to some similarly "perspective-bound" observer whose statements about the times of Machiavelli must in turn be related to *his* times, and so on and on in an infinite regression. If, then, the sociology of knowledge is to provide a lever by which to right the world of social and historical knowledge, it must find some Archimedean fulcrum outside itself from which to operate—some degree, however small, of rational autonomy, not existentially determined, by means of which this regression can be transcended.

Furthermore, Mannheim ultimately fails in his attempt to replace the problems of ontology and epistemology with those of the sociology of knowledge by substituting the historical process itself for an atemporal absolute as the ultimate social reality, and by superseding the older "static conception" of truth by a "dynamic" one which includes all the possible perspectives within "the developing totality of [man's] whole psychic and intellectual life." His attempt results only in the reappearance of these problems under new forms. For in this view, history itself becomes the new absolute; and in place of the static view of truth, dismissed because it presumes to view social and historical reality timelessly, as "under the eyes of God," the sociology of knowledge becomes the new "eyes of God," through which we in our day are at last able to view that reality under forms which "the developing totality of the whole psychic life" has lost its power to transcend!

DURKHEIM'S LOGICAL BASIS FOR THE SOCIOLOGY OF KNOWLEDGE

Durkheim was more successful than Mannheim in providing a logical basis for the validity of his sociology of knowledge, but he succeeded only at the expense of accepting in the end an epistemological standpoint with which it was his theoretical objective to dispense. For despite his especial emphasis upon the fact that the "essential ideas which dominate all our intellectual life" are the work of the group, he did not on that account limit their significance to the group alone. He accorded to them an objectivity and autonomy which transcended their social origin. He held that concepts, in contradistinction to percepts, owe their stability and impersonality to their collective origin, but they have "a reason for existence only on condition of being true, that is, objective." Greater than their role in assuring a

[44] *Ibid.*, p. 120.

harmony among minds is "their harmony with the nature of things." The evolution of scientific concepts has been in the direction of symbolizing this correspondence more adequately, so that "the concept which was first held as true because it was collective tends to be no longer collective except on condition of being held as true; we demand its credentials of it before according it our confidence."

It is true, says Durkheim, that the great majority of the concepts we use are not thus methodically constituted; we get them from language —that is, from common experience—without submitting them to any criticism. Nevertheless, between those concepts "which draw all their authority from the fact that they are collective" and "the very slight minority" of concepts which have been "scientifically elaborated and criticised . . . there are only differences of degree." For a collective representation of the former type must also present guarantees of its objectivity. These are found in the very fact of its collectivity; "for it is not without reason that it has been able to generalize and maintain itself with persistence. If it were out of accord with the nature of things, it would never have been able to acquire an extended and prolonged empire over intellect." As a product of the collective life, it "is necessarily submitted to a control that is repeated indefinitely; the men who accept it verify it by their own experience. Therefore, it could not have been wholly inadequate for its subject."[45]

Thus Durkheim, far from finding in the social genesis of logical thought evidence of the ultimately irrational character of conceptual systems, finds in that origin the grounds of their rationality. Ideas impose themselves upon the individual from without and "have within them a sort of force or moral ascendancy. . . . Hence the individual at least obscurely takes account of the fact that above his private ideas, there is a world of absolute ideas according to which he must shape his own; he catches a glimpse of a whole intellectual kingdom in which he participates, but which is greater than he. This is the first intuition of the realm of truth." But as social life expands, the collective horizon enlarges until, with the emergence of international life, the society which was at first conceived as the only whole becomes a part of a vaster social entity with indefinitely expanding frontiers. As the primitive concepts undergo transformation to correspond to the new social reality, they also undergo reorganization according to their own principles. In this process, "logical organization differentiates itself from social organization and becomes autonomous," until rational thought finally becomes "thinking which is imposed on all reasonable beings" and hence is no longer existentially determined by a specific cultural milieu.

Thus the Durkheimian sociology of knowledge, contrary to its original

[45] Émile Durkheim, *The Elementary Forms of the Religious Life* (Glencoe, Ill., 1947), pp. 9, 437-438, 445.

intent, ends in a general epistemology. It accepts a correspondence theory of truth for its collective representations, regardless of their degree of critical elaboration. The validity of their terms depends, not upon their group origin, but upon the adequacy with which they symbolize their referents. The truth of the propositions into which they enter is a function of their capacity to represent or portray the objective order and sequence of events. Collective representations in general differ from those which have undergone scientific elaboration only in the imperfection of the symbols by means of which they express this correspondence, since "scientific symbols themselves are never more than approximative."

SOCIAL THOUGHT AND AN ADEQUATE SOCIOLOGY OF KNOWLEDGE

The legitimate field of the sociology of knowledge is, then, not to furnish a substitute for general epistemology, but to provide a sociological analysis of its history and present status. A sociology of knowledge which does not acknowledge the autonomy of logical principles and the possibility that conceptual systems can transcend cultural relativity, to some degree at least, undermines the basis of its own validity. It must see at the outset of its inquiry what Durkheim acknowledged at the end: "How far it is from being true that a conception lacks objective value merely because it has a social origin." Its proper function is to deal, not with the *evolution* of logical principles, but with the historical processes through which humanity has become aware of them. Its problem is to discover the extent to which the specific content rather than the form of the basic categories of thought are determined by the socio-cultural context of the historical epoch in which they were formulated. It does not seek to reduce them to a function of their culture, but seeks to understand as precisely as possible the functional relationships between them and their culture. Otherwise, the rules of logic lose all autonomy and the reason itself becomes, if not the servant of man's individual passions, at least the handmaiden of group interests in conflict.

A more adequate history of social thought must therefore await the further development of the sociology of knowledge. Admittedly, that development has not proceeded far enough to permit the history of social thought to be fully expressed in its terms. But enough has been accomplished to constitute a sound foundation. It has been made abundantly clear that no phase of intellectual history can be written in isolation from the socio-cultural milieu from which its individual contributions have emerged. Nor can it be wholly reduced to a system of existentially determined propositions. Insofar as the transformation that things and events undergo in the processes of perception, conception, and symbolization is inherent in the relation of being to knowing, it affects research workers in all fields alike. Insofar as things and events relating to society and human behavior are peculiarly liable to such transformation through conditioning by the past and present personal and cultural experiences of the observer, the social scientist must be especially alert to this ever-present possibility. But it may be noted that we become aware of the existence of this transformation only by means of scientific techniques that assume both the autonomy of logical principles and the cognitive validity of the resulting conceptual systems as in approximate correspondence to an objective order of events, subject to change only as further research enables us to formulate closer approximations.

But after our researches have proceeded until they have analyzed the extant data to the remotest detail, many problems in the history of social thought will remain unresolved. There are too many gaps in the historical record, and there are still more in the personal biographies of individual thinkers. As Small has said, "If each writer in the field of social science had also been a Pepys, or if he had been shadowed by a Boswell, the reasons why thinking in social science has meandered in the precise courses which it has followed might be much more evident than they are."[46] But the fact that many of his problems may admit of no definitive solutions is no reason why the historian of social thought should not cultivate his garden.

SELECTED BIBLIOGRAPHY

Barnes, H. E., *An Introduction to the History of Sociology* (Chicago: University of Chicago Press, 1948).

Becker, Howard, and H. E. Barnes, *Social Thought from Lore to Science* (2nd. ed.; New York: Dover Publications, 1952), 2 vols.

Bogardus, Emory S., *The Development of Social Thought*, (3rd. ed.; New York: Longmans, Green, 1955).

Chambliss, Rollin, *Social Thought from Hammurabi to Comte* (New York: Dryden Press, 1954).

Ellwood, C. A., *A History of Social Philosophy* (New York: Prentice-Hall, 1938).

Furfey, P. H., *A History of Social Thought* (New York: Macmillan, 1942).

Hertzler, J. O., *The Social Thought of the Ancient Civilizations* (New York: McGraw-Hill, 1936).

House, F. N., *The Range of Social Theory* (New York: Henry Holt, 1929).

Lowie, R. H., *The History of Ethnological Theory* (New York: Farrar and Rinehart, 1937).

Sorokin, P. A., *Contemporary Sociological Theories* (New York: Harper, 1928).

Timasheff, N. S., *Sociological Theory* (New York: Doubleday, 1955).

[46] Small, "Fifty Years of Sociology in the United States," *AJS*, 21 (May, 1916), p. 722.

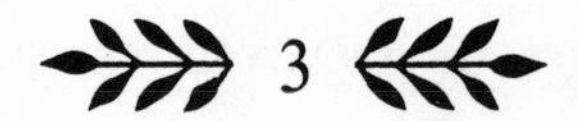

RECENT ANALYSES OF SOCIOLOGICAL THEORY

RICHARD A. SCHERMERHORN
AND ALVIN BOSKOFF

THE HISTORY OF SOCIOLOGY IS DISTINCTLY A SPECIALIZED STUDY IN THE United States. Yet as a required course for undergraduate sociology majors it is too often taught perfunctorily, regarded as a necessary evil by students, and decently forgotten when they fail to see its relevance to the empirical researches of contemporary sociology. At the graduate level, its theoretical implications receive more analysis and it not infrequently serves to suggest topics for thesis research. Nevertheless, the History of Sociology course makes a relatively slight impact on younger sociologists unless it impinges on a specialized interest already awakened elsewhere. It is not infrequent for older sociologists to make the history of sociology an occasion for imposing their memories of days gone by on a captive audience.

But there are notable exceptions to this dismal picture. A number of social scientists have known how to make the history of sociology a gateway to greater scientific awareness for students. The situation is not without its parallels in the natural sciences, where the student arrives quickly at modern theories of atomic energy or genetics without following the long and involved process of the way in which these theories developed. Yet the seminal minds among the pure scientists seem well aware of the methodological and theoretical problems of their predecessors, learn from them, and even introduce advanced students to the works of Singer or Sarton for broadening their intellectual horizons. Instead of concluding that this is fitted for the more enterprising students alone, might we not infer that an earlier acquaintance with the history of a subject like sociology, if properly approached, would make possible the development of specialists who are "broad men sharpened to a point"? The key to the answer lies, of course in the seemingly innocent phrase "if properly approached."

SOCIAL THOUGHT AND SOCIOLOGY

The distinction between "social thought" and "sociology" is an important one. Social thought means any set of ideas about man's relations with his fellows. These ideas, although they are more or less systematic, are for the most part not subjected to rigorous empirical testing by their proponents. Sociology, on the other hand, is a science of human interaction in which the attempt is made to discover systematic evidence for determinate relations between classes of social data in order to develop generalizations that are true under specified conditions. To the extent that these generalizations or hypotheses form a logically interdependent system, sociology is a mature science.[1]

On the way to becoming a science, sociology passed through an initial stage sometimes known as "encyclopedic sociology." For this discussion, encyclopedic sociology represents some of the early attempts to construct a body of comprehensive generalizations about social interaction after the success of the physical and biological science of the seventeenth and eighteenth centuries. It is usually more scientific in aim than in realization, for its general principles are composed of inferences from other bodies of knowledge, uncritical borrowings from the "spirit of the age," personal predilections, and speculation. Beginning with Comte and Spencer, encyclopedic sociology became more and more empirical; sociologists such as Durkheim had a foot in both camps. For purposes of historical analysis, social thought, encyclopedic sociology, and sociology proper may be regarded as constructed types in a continuous series. It then becomes possible to regard the first two as becoming increasingly scientific insofar as they offer increasingly accurate observation, fertile hypotheses for research, and internal consistency. In speaking of the history of sociology, we shall take as our referent the account of theoretical systems since Comte, as well as the reviews of more reliable scientific knowledge that constitute the growing body of our science. Since sociology has not attained the ideal presented in our definition, it is realistic in this discussion to regard it as increasing by approximating that ideal.

Approaches to the Theory of Sociology

A careful review of the literature since 1918 fails to reveal neatly organized periods of special dominance. Many works even fall outside the basic

[1] Cf. Ronald Freedman *et al., Principles of Sociology* (New York, 1952).

trend from generalized historical works to critical and evaluational analyses. An eight-fold typology of the various works, however, may serve as an introduction to the different perspectives that structure the field.

1. *Monographic analyses of the works of leading sociologists or of central concepts such as "progress" and "social forces."* These are chiefly essays in the history of ideas, written with only a secondary interest in what is living and what is dead for the corpus of the science.[2]

2. *Expository textbooks written to give the elementary student a simple, uncluttered summary of leading social thinkers from ancient times to the period of systematic sociology.* Since the aim of these volumes is clarification and simplification, they contain a minimum of critical analysis and a studied effort at popularization with considerable use of biographical detail. The three outstanding works of this type are: James P. Lichtenberger, *Development of Social Theory* (1923) the three editions of a work by Emory S. Bogardus entitled in a recent edition *The Development of Social Thought* (1940); and Charles A. Ellwood, *A History of Social Philosophy* (1938).

3. *Reviews of the social sciences, their methods, and their interdependence, and assessments of the developing specialities within sociology itself.* Although these are not always written from the historical standpoint, they have unusual value for assessing the development of scientific method. Four of these works deserve special attention. The first, edited by H. E. Barnes, *History and Prospects of the Social Sciences* (1925), presents ten essays on different scientific disciplines and their development by ten different authors. Two of these, biology and ethics, would not be included in this form today. But there runs throughout the volume a sense of logical and historical interdependence that would seem modern to our present-day "interdisciplinarians"—a feeling of the unity of social science as a whole.

Daniel Essertier's *Psychologie et sociologie: Essai de bibliographie critique* (Paris, 1927) also deserves attention. Examining the presuppositions of Durkheim, Tarde, and LeBon, Essertier parallels Cooley in his conclusion that the dualism of individual *vs.* collective psychology has been superseded. He foreshadows the culture and personality approach of recent times by insisting that one important way to study social phenomena is through the

[2] Included here, among others, are: Jay Rumney, *Herbert Spencer's Sociology* (London, 1934); Marcel Weinreich, *Max Weber: L'homme et le savant* (Paris, 1938); G. C. Homans and C. P. Curtis, Jr., *An Introduction to Pareto* (New York, 1934); N. J. Spykman, *The Social Theory of Georg Simmel* (Chicago, 1925); H. E. Barnes, "The Doctrines of W. G. Sumner," *AJS,* 25 (July, 1919), pp. 1-23, and "The Doctrines of Lester F. Ward," *ibid.,* pp. 150-170; A. W. Small, "The Category 'Progress' as a Tool of Research in Social Science," *AJS,* 28 (March, 1923), pp. 554-576; F. N. House, "The Concept 'Social Forces' in American Sociology," *AJS,* 31 (Sept., Nov., 1925; Jan., May, 1926), pp. 145-172, 347-365, 507-525, 763-799; A. F. Bentley, "Simmel, Durkheim, and Ratzenhofer," *AJS,* 32 (Sept., 1926), pp. 250-256; G. H. Mead, "Cooley's Contribution to American Social Thought," *AJS,* 35 (March, 1930), pp. 693-717.

study of the formation of personality. Here again is a demand for greater collaboration between sociology and psychology.

In the United States, a symposium edited by George A. Lundberg, Read Bain, and Nels Anderson and entitled *Trends in American Sociology* (New York, 1929) attempted an outline of the domains and methods of sociology. Though the internal divisions of sociology appear to be few and oversimplified to us today (they include social psychology, culture, rural and urban sociology, educational sociology, social work, and the various forms of applied sociology), they were probably representative of the era. Lundberg's statement on the natural-scientific method in sociology is one that might serve as a contemporary basis of *rapprochement:*

> The frontiers of knowledge will always be largely subjective and philosophical. Quantitative and qualitative methods must proceed side by side. They are, after all, only a matter of difference of degree in objectivity. Nor does the quantitative approach mean that all social relationships must or can be described in terms of mathematical symbols now employed in the other sciences. Every science must work out its own concepts, symbols, and details of logic. Only in so far as experience shows the tools of one science to be useful in another are we justified in adopting the same tools and methods. . . . All questions of method are relative to the specific ends sought . . . the broader the purpose the more composite must be the methods employed. . . . In the meantime we are justified in employing all methods which yield some results. Gradually we shall be able to standardize our techniques on the basis of what experience has shown to be the most profitable approaches.[3]

Of even greater historical interest is a work sponsored by the Social Science Research Council under the editorship of Stuart A. Rice.[4] This book marked an enormous step forward in its presentation of diverse methods by actual illustration rather than by description or discussion, and in the sophistication of the categories employed to classify the results. There are few social scientists who could not learn from this case book in their investigations today. At the same time the volume has two major shortcomings: (1) The examples drawn from such diverse fields as economics, political science, social work, psychology, law, sociology, geography, anthropology, history, and philology present a diffuse impression unrelieved by a unified, interpretative summary. (2) For the most part, methods are regarded as techniques constructed *ad hoc,* close to the data and of immediate empirical value, without derivation from any larger body of theory or methodology having greater generality. It is significant that Karl Mannheim expressed admiration for the method of inductive exploration in the field studies

[3] Lundberg *et al., op. cit.,* pp. 404, 415, 416.

[4] S. A. Rice (ed.), *Methods in Social Science* (Chicago, 1931).

but confessed genuine disappointment at the meagerness of results in individual cases.[5]

4. *Critical evaluations of sociological theories and trends, chiefly in the field of systematic sociology*. Perhaps the first in America to go beyond the elementary textbook level in this respect was Floyd N. House. Pursuing the interest of his teacher, Small, he analyzed the contributions of the German sociologists and attempted to interpret their writings in the light of the contemporary social and historical forces of the time.[6] In this he was only partially successful because of the undeveloped nature of his sociology of knowledge. His account of French sociology omits more recent figures like Simiand, Halbwachs, and Mauss.

More comprehensive and critically evaluative was Sorokin's earlier, monumental work dealing with sociological theories of the previous two generations or more.[7] This book probably enlarged the horizons of American sociology more than that of any writer previous to 1928. His erudition and linguistic gifts made it possible for him to survey a vast number of works in the Romance, Germanic, and Slavic languages, hitherto unavailable in English. Because of his philosophical training and acumen, he turned his attention to the broad outlines of contemporary theories and to their presuppositions; his critique of the one-sidedness of certain concepts was positive and trenchant, even when it bordered on the dogmatic. It was a welcome beginning of a trend, not yet fulfilled, of regarding the conceptions and researches of the past as signs and beginnings of a cumulative science still in the process of growth. His classification of theories, however, was highly idiomatic and has had no followers. Although his discussion of theory is comprehensive, Sorokin gives less attention to method (Max Weber's notion of "ideal types" rates only a footnote) not because he is unfamiliar with method, but perhaps because he takes it for granted.

In the same category with House and Sorokin, though much briefer and simpler, is Wiese's account of the development of sociology.[8] His analysis of the beginnings of sociology in Comte and Spencer in keen and judicious,[9] and his analysis of the development of sociology from encyclopedism to the status of an empirical science contains some of the finest passages in

[5] Karl Mannheim, review of Rice, *op. cit.*, in *AJS*, 38 (Sept., 1932), pp. 273-282.

[6] F. N. House, *The Development of Sociology* (New York, 1936). Earlier "social thought" is also included.

[7] P. A. Sorokin, *Contemporary Sociological Theories* (New York, 1928).

[8] Leopold von Wiese, *Soziologie: Geschichte und Hauptprobleme* (1st ed., 1926; 4th ed., Berlin, 1950). Cf. the English adaptation in Howard Becker, *Systematic Sociology on the Basis of the* Beziehungslehre *and* Gebildelehre *of Leopold von Wiese* (New York, 1932), Part 4, "Historical Postscript."

[9] Much of this is a condensation of the earlier *Zur Grundlegung der Gesellschaftslehre: Eine kritische Untersuchung von Herbert Spencers System der synthetischen Philosophie* (Jena, 1906).

the literature. The rest of the work is uneven; French and American sociology receive less space than German, Worms is given as much space as Durkheim, and Wiese is over-sensitive to Max Weber's renown and makes much of the latter's lack of patience for *Kleinarbeit* (monographic detail) and for system. Like many Continental savants, Wiese presents his own work, the *Beziehungslehre* (theory of social relations), as the crown and apex of the sociological movement.

5. *Surveys of the development of sociology in a specific nation.* A few works will serve to represent this type. Bouglé's brief summary of sociology in France[10] is of minor importance; the author professes the positivist tradition, but shows considerable independence, especially in his strong criticism of Lévy-Bruhl. He gives considerable space to the permeation of history with sociological methods and aims, but comparatively little attention to the advancing body of knowledge in sociology proper. Georges Davy's contribution[11] is intensive rather than extensive, consisting of a series of monographs—on the Durkheim-Tarde debate, on Bouglé's sociological analysis of values, on LePlay's theory and method—and a long dissertation on the evolution of the family, taking the researches of Hubert and Mauss as the starting point. The most valuable part of the book is the analysis of family development, which would certainly bear translation. But the volume is not a considered summary of sociological trends in France.[12]

Another type of historical approach to sociology in specific countries is exemplified by Aron's study of German sociology.[13] From the standpoint of a French sociologist not fully committed to any school, Aron reviews the development of German sociology critically and judiciously, showing greater approval of historical writers such as Vierkandt and Alfred Weber than of systematic sociologists. He describes the Germanic abundance of theory as prompted by *l'inquiétude d'autojustification.* In comparing Durkheim's mechanical and organic societies with Tönnies' *Gemeinschaft* and *Gesellschaft,* he remarks that Durkheim preferred a more differentiated society because it liberated the individual, whereas the German preference for *Gemeinschaft* led, by a paradox, to a greater tyranny than the one it sought to destroy—that is, mechanism and brutal economic forces. His review of Max Weber is sober and appreciative, though he notes that Weber presented his main conceptions in opposition to others and that he does not regard psychology as a fundamental science of culture.

Still another review of German sociology written by an outsider is the more restricted work of an American with European roots, Theodore

[10] Celestin Bouglé, *Bilan de la sociologie française contemporaine* (Paris, 1935).

[11] Georges Davy, *Sociologues d'hier et d'aujourd'hui* (2nd ed.; Paris, 1950).

[12] Marcel Mauss, *Sociologie et anthropologie* (Paris, 1950) deserves mention as a significant account of the interdependence of the two disciplines.

[13] Raymond Aron, *La sociologie allemande contemporaine* (1st ed., 1936; Paris, 1950).

Abel.[14] He confines his attention to Simmel, Vierkandt, Wiese, and Max Weber alone. At the time of its publication (1929), this was the most complete and discursive account of these writers in English, affording them a wider influence in American sociology. Although superseded by more definitive studies, it remains one of our most important secondary sources on the development of German sociology. It is unified by the central thesis that sociology is a special and autonomous discipline among the social sciences.

The history of sociology in the United States has been chronicled primarily by Albion Small, the Bernards, and Howard Odum. Small's volume[15] probably did more than any other work to relate American sociology to its European origins, although it is not primarily concerned with American sociology. When combined with his journal articles, however, Small's history comes to a focus in the United States. He describes the initial dissatisfaction of American scholars with the more traditional approaches to the social order—economics and political science—and wryly comments that American sociology was at first primarily an earnest attempt to become something. Initially, this gap was filled by "old-fashioned opinionativeness" parading under the guise of science. Because of his training in Germany, Small credited the historians and economists of the Teutonic world with the greatest share of influence in preparing the way for sociology as a science. Although his style is rambling, discursive, and anecdotal, it reflects a personality that made a powerful impression on his students.

In the forties, the Bernards made a more extensive study of the origins of American sociology in the so-called "social science" movement from which the later associations of the social science specialties split off in the nineteenth century.[16] The authors are more interested in the indigenous features of American sociology than in the European roots and give special attention to sociology as a movement expressed through organization. Interest in theory is therefore secondary.

The most recent study of American sociology,[17] written by Howard Odum, is a work *sui generis* that is probably more intelligible to members of the profession in America than to those abroad. The arbitrary choice of presidents of the American Sociological Society (up to 1950) as the significant figures for biographical and theoretical discussion causes the omission of writers such as Bain, Barnes, Becker, Cavan, Davie, Merton, Sorokin, and a host of others. At the same time, the work includes some lesser figures holding institutional office but without charisma. It is true that many of the great names receive attention in the review of sociological specialities, which

[14] Theodore Abel, *Systematic Sociology in Germany* (New York, 1929).

[15] A. W. Small, *The Origins of Sociology* (Chicago, 1924).

[16] L. L. Bernard and Jessie Bernard, *Origins of American Sociology* (New York, 1943).

[17] H. W. Odum, *American Sociology* (New York, 1951).

is a highly rewarding section of the volume. Perhaps nowhere has the diversity of American sociology been so ably presented; and the summing up is clear and forthright, tinged with genuine American optimism. Evaluation and critical appraisal, however, take a decidedly secondary place; for these the reader must go elsewhere.

6. *Panoramic histories.* Foremost in this category is the monumental Barnes and Becker two-volume work, a landmark in the field now in a second edition, with Becker as senior author and with numerous addenda from his pen.[18] Few books deserve the term indispensable, but this one certainly does. In comprehensiveness, in mastery of the historical materials, and in lucidity, it has set a new standard. Sociology of knowledge has never before been so widely applied as a tool to interpret social thinkers in historical context. The authors themselves would be the first, however, to insist upon some of the inadequacies of such a pioneer venture. Pitched at a high level, it is of more value to the specialist and the advanced student than to the beginner or the layman. Its arrangement has its own intrinsic order which is not easily grasped by the uninitiated. The account of sociological trends in the various countries of the world is more than reasonably complete, although it leaves the reader with a bewilderingly diverse set of impressions. This part of the book is more useful as a reference tool than as a record of the increasingly solid growth of a developing science. Now and then, however, the development of the science is suggested. For example, in the discussion of Halbwachs, the authors clearly show the advances he made over the cruder results of Durkheim in the study of suicide.[19]

We have reached the point today where such analyses have become more and more indispensable—if the study of the history of sociology is not to be irrelevant to the scientific work of the present generation. While Becker and Barnes do not neglect entirely problems of method and research, their attention is focused so completely on the historical task—and on guiding constructed types in particular—that the wide variety of methods and results (frequently obscured by intellectual content) do not appear with clarity. It is, of course, unfair to complain about the omission of aspects of the study that are clearly beyond the authors' aims. One can only suggest that a new form of historical writing may be needed today—a point to which we shall later return.

A second example of the panoramic history is the compendium edited by Barnes in 1948.[20] Of lesser scope than the two-volume work, it begins with a rapid survey of ancient, medieval, and pre-Comtean thought, thereafter devoting separate monographs to leading encyclopedic sociologists of the

[18] Howard Becker and H. E. Barnes, *Social Thought from Lore to Science* (1st ed., 1938; 2nd ed., New York, 1952), 2 vols.

[19] *Ibid.*, vol. 2, p. 844.

[20] H. E. Barnes (ed.), *An Introduction to the History of Sociology* (Chicago, 1948).

nineteenth century, followed by chapters on outstanding Continental, British, and American sociologists. From the standpoint of ready reference, it is an easier book to use than *Social Thought from Lore to Science*. In conception and organization, however, it is less original and more traditional. The use of a large number of authors results in uneven treatment. Post-Durkheim writers in France are given short shrift, and the non-Durkheimians are omitted altogether, as is Vierkandt in Germany. Some of the critical evaluations are quite cogent; special mention should be made, for example, of Mills' chapter on Westermarck, Barnes's analysis of Toynbee, and Speier's interpretative summary of Sorokin.

7. *Monographic studies resulting in refinement of theory and method.* Although only brief mention can be made of them here, these monographs are of great historical and scientific significance. The works of Parsons, Blumer, and, more recently, Volkart furnish examples of this tendency.[21] Parsons' significant contribution was the discovery of certain unified concepts or presuppositions in such disparate sociological systems as those of Marshall, Pareto, Durkheim, and Max Weber. Whether the voluntaristic theory of action, as Parson portrays it, is the only common denominator or whether another theoretician with comparable equipment might have discovered another type of unity is a question that must be raised. (Parsons himself recognized this.) But certainly Parsons, by his historical and logical analysis, raised the essential questions about the way in which historical data can contribute to unification of theory as a guide to our present-day research. And, unlike many others, he has refined and systematized his conception in later works. It is interesting to speculate on the probable outcome if Parsons had turned his attention to a few major American figures, instead of being exclusively concerned with Europeans.

Blumer's analysis of Thomas and Znaniecki is too well-known to need discussion here. But in the historical context adopted here it is important, not only because it led to a much more rigorous pruning of social-psychological concepts and methods, but because it convinced Thomas and Znaniecki themselves of a need for modification and refinement. Volkart's study of Thomas' writings and unpublished papers not only clarified some of the major concepts and showed them in the process of growth, but also placed them in a significant perpective in relation to personality and culture studies of recent anthropology and social psychology. Znaniecki's role, however, seems to have been slighted. This constant

[21] Talcott Parsons, *The Structure of Social Action* (1st ed., 1937; 2nd ed., Glencoe, Ill., 1949); Herbert Blumer, *An Appraisal of Thomas and Znaniecki's* The Polish Peasant in Europe and America (New York, 1939); E. H. Volkart (ed.), *Social Behavior and Personality: Contributions of W. I. Thomas to Theory and Social Research* (New York, 1951). It is significant that the second and third of these books resulted from projects sponsored by the Social Science Research Council.

appraisal of past contributions in the light of contemporary research efforts is of primary importance in making historical studies functional and meaningful.

8. *Critical assessments of theories and methods in specialized fields or broadly related comparative fields.* These assessments include such works as Barnes and the Beckers' (husband and wife) volume on theory, Gurvitch and Moore's symposium, and the recent compendium edited by John Gillin on related social sciences.[22] The compilation by Barnes and the Beckers is not only an appraisal of a variety of specialized contributions but also reviews the influence of sociological theory on other disciplines or fields of applied knowledge, such as economics, political thought, jurisprudence, criminology, social work, education, religion, and ethics. The seventeen authors review theoretical developments of the recent past with reasonable completeness, although rural sociology is too briefly treated and the analysis of social processes and structures is specifically excluded from the plan of the book. For the first time in any comparable volume, Freud receives major attention. Furthermore, social psychology designedly receives more attention here than in *Social Thought from Lore to Science*.

A similar attempt to review the diverse specialties is somewhat less successful in Gurvitch and Moore's volume, where all of human geography is relegated to a few lines in the chapter on ecology, where the advancing tide of statistics receives little attention and the convergences of cultural anthropology with sociology get only passing notice. There are real advances in other respects: Logan Wilson's account of the sociology of groups; MacIver's essay on social causation; Parsons' discussion of systematic theory; and Moore's analysis of the sociology of economic organization are notable contributions. Furthermore, Woodard's synthesis of research results, methodology, and theory in social psychology still deserves separate publication for social psychologists. The concluding section on sociology in European countries and in America is quite uneven. French, German, and American sociology receive the most nearly adequate treatment.

The recent volume edited by Gillin is an attempt to show how the related sciences of anthropology, sociology, and psychology are converging in methods and theory. Each of the seven contributors focuses attention on the conceptualization of two of the three sciences; two of the writers—Becker and Hallowell—give more attention to the historical development of these fields than to theoretical issues. The others—Murdock, Smith, Parsons, Newcomb, and Gillin—subordinate historical to methodological problems.

[22] H. E. Barnes, Howard Becker, and Frances B. Becker (eds.), *Contemporary Social Theory* (New York, 1940) Georges Gurvitch and W. E. Moore (eds.), *Twentieth Century Sociology* (New York, 1945); John Gillin (ed.), *For a Science of Social Man* (New York, 1954). Mention should also be made of L. L. Bernard (ed.), *The Fields and Methods of Sociology* (New York, 1934).

Both Parsons and Newcomb make increasing use of the notion of levels, of the "macroscopic-microscopic range" or "macrostructure and microstructure." Parsons' words on this point bear repeating:

> It is only when sociological and psychological theory—and the various system-reference levels within each—have come to regard themselves and each other as the formulators of very important *special cases* relative to a more general theory, that a higher level of theoretical maturity in our fields will have been reached. The contention that any one of these fields or "levels" provides the "foundations" on which all the others *must* build or be consigned to the hell of perpetual scientific impotence, is only a symptom of the growing pains of a very young family of scientific disciplines.[23]

THE SOCIOLOGICAL PANTHEON

Although these surveys of sociologists and their theories exhibit a certain diversity in intent and emphasis, it is possible to discern an emergent pattern that perhaps reveals as much about contemporary sociology as about its multicolored past. The underlying theme, one that has recently become quite pronounced, is an attitude of critical examination that is reflected in various ways. Increasingly, the basic exposition and summary of theories have been supplemented by attempts at interpretation, at establishing relations with other theoretical works, and at evaluating the potentialities of specific hypotheses (including the related concepts and methodological notions) in the light of subsequent research. There has been a rising tide of concern for the methodological premises—their nature and their feasibility—employed by specific theorists. In fact, the application of a critical attitude has been considerably facilitated by an unplanned specialization in the analysis of sociological theories. As previously indicated, for example, recent surveys have been devoted to individual theorists, to methodological issues, to theoretical trends in given nations, and to the interrelations between sociological theory and neighboring disciplines. The cumulative result of these probings and evaluations is an unofficial sociological pantheon, a provisional Hall of Fame, that functions as a source of inspiration, as a reservoir of concepts and hypotheses, and as a link between the earliest social theorizing and the highly specialized technical developments of modern empirical research.

Some Negative Judgments. Anything resembling unanimity of opinion regarding this group of pre-eminent theorists is, however, clearly absent. Either by neglect or by adverse judgment, several theorists of earlier repute have been partially or wholly relegated to the nebulous realm of faint recognition and fainter influence. But they continue to have their champions, who either trace the basic outlines of modern sociology to their earlier formulations or ascribe to their theories a crucial significance in the development of

[23] Gillin, *op. cit.*, p. 101.

accepted concepts and principles. Thus we have had interesting attempts to demonstrate the importance of Adam Smith and Adam Ferguson.[24] With considerably more persistence, but with no greater success in persuading a generation of sociologists in the United States, DeGrange has tried to revive a serious interest in the sociological system of Auguste Comte. In addition to interpreting the method and conceptual scheme of Comte's *Positive Philosophy,* DeGrange has emphasized what he regards as improvements in the development of theory in the later *Positive Polity,*[25] a work which remains generally repugnant to sociologists because of its abandonment of a scientific approach for a religio-political orientation reminiscent of Plato's philosophical utopias.

Herbert Spencer has fared little better than Comte in the critical surveys of the past thirty years. Reverence for Spencer is still part of the British sociological tradition, though Continental sociologists, from Durkheim to Wiese, have tended to regard his purely sociological work as a series of instructive errors in method and interpretation. Only Znaniecki in recent years has contributed a favorable summary of Spencer's conceptual scheme, in the course of a paper on social organization and institutions.[26] The famous *Principles of Sociology,* distributed in several editions before World War I, has been out of print for over thirty years; just a few years ago it was distinctly a white elephant in many secondhand bookstores in this country. And this in spite of his extended treatment of structure and function!

Sumner, Spencer's intellectual heir, is now more esteemed as a pioneer, particularly for his analyses of folkways, mores, the in-group, and ethnocentrism. Some years after his death, a number of his essays were collected and published by Yale University Press.[27] But some of his basic theories and their implications, as well as his general approach, have been seriously questioned. Cooley, Barnes, and Sorokin represent divergent lines of criticism of Sumner that have not yet been effectively challenged.[28] A decade ago, Myrdal and his associates launched an attack on what they conceived to be conservative connotations in the theory of the mores, particularly as it related

[24] A. W. Small, *Adam Smith and American Sociology* (Chicago, 1907); Albert Salomon, "Adam Smith as a Sociologist," *SR,* 12 (Feb., 1945), pp. 22-42; W. C. Lehmann, *Adam Ferguson and the Beginnings of Modern Sociology* (New York, 1930).

[25] McQuilkin DeGrange, "The Method of Auguste Comte," in Rice, *op. cit.*, pp. 23-87; *The Nature and Elements of Sociology* (New Haven, 1953); *The Curve of Societal Movement* (Hanover, 1930).

[26] Florian Znaniecki, "Social Organization and Institutions," in Gurvitch and Moore, *op. cit.*, pp. 174-178.

[27] *The Challenge of Facts and Other Essays* (New Haven, 1914); *War and other Essays* (New Haven, 1913); *Earth Hunger and Other Essays* (New Haven, 1913); *The Forgotten Man and Other Essays* (New Haven, 1918); also the *Essays of William Graham Sumner* (New Haven, 1934), 2 vols.

[28] C. H. Cooley, *Sociological Theory and Social Research* (New York, 1930), pp. 325-327; H. E. Barnes, "William Graham Sumner: Spencerianism in American Dress," in Barnes, *op. cit.,* Chap. 6; Sorokin, *op. cit.*, pp. 698-700.

to the problem of racial relations in the United States.[29] Currently, the posthumous *Science of Society* is virtually a forgotten work, and the classic *Folkways* probably finds few readers who give serious attention to any but the first two (and most important) chapters.

The rise and decline of Pareto. About twenty years ago, it appeared likely that a major addition to the company of "select" sociologists would be the previously neglected Vilfredo Pareto, who died in 1923. With the exception of a lengthy and generally laudatory summary by Sorokin in 1928[30]—the first to appear in English—Pareto's work did not receive much attention until the mid-thirties, when his *Trattato,* translated as *Mind and Society,* burst like four Roman candles on the American sociological scene. For some reason, Harvard professors found the glow unusually attractive. Henderson, a physiologist, and Homans and Curtis, sociologists, hastened to reduce the enormous bulk of the four volumes to manageable proportions. In particular, they stressed Pareto's analysis of the logico-experimental method, the notion of societal system, the role of the residues and derivations, and the process of change in élites.[31] Meanwhile, Parsons was working on an interpretative study—part of a larger work—in which he sought to establish a basic convergence in the works of Pareto, Durkheim, and Max Weber. Still another Harvard professor, the historian Brinton, tried to apply the concepts of residues and derivations in a comparative analysis of four great revolutions, but not to marked advantage.[32]

The search for examples of derivations became for a time something of an indoor sport. But by 1940 or thereabouts, the bubble had been pricked; critical essays by Ascoli, Becker, Faris, and others[33] helped to locate the latent faults beneath the borrowed charisma of Pareto's posthumous repute. Despite his apparent advocacy of scientific method, according to the consensus of critical accounts, Pareto often abused it in practice, exhibited unadorned political bias and an underlying anti-intellectualism, employed an "instinct psychology" that was thoroughly discredited in the thirties, and, finally, contributed to sociology little that was not already available in the works of

[29] Gunnar Myrdal, *An American Dilemma* (New York, 1944), pp. 1031-1032.

[30] Sorokin, *op. cit.*, pp. 39-62.

[31] L. J. Henderson, *Pareto's General Sociology* (Cambridge, Mass., 1935); Homans and Curtis, *loc. cit....* Franz Borkenau, *Pareto* (New York, 1936); H. E. Moore and Bernice M. Moore, "Folk Implications in Pareto's Sociology," *SF,* 14 (Dec., 1935), pp. 293-300.

[32] Talcott Parsons, *The Structure of Social Action,* Chaps. 5-7; Crane Brinton, *The Anatomy of Revolution* (New York, 1938).

[33] Ellsworth Faris, *The Nature of Human Nature* (New York, 1937), Chap. 16; Max Ascoli, "Society Through Pareto's Mind," *SR,* 1 (Feb., 1936), pp. 78-89; Becker and Barnes, *op. cit.*, vol. 2, pp. 1016-1023; Morris Ginsberg, "Pareto's General Sociology," *Sociological Review* (British), 28 (July, 1936), pp. 221-245; W. Rex Crawford, "Representative Italian Contributions to Sociology," in Barnes, *op. cit.*, pp. 555-568; M. S. Handman, "The Sociological Methods of Vilfredo Pareto," in Rice, *op. cit.*, pp. 139-153.

Freud, Marx, Mosca, and others. At present, Crawford's remark about Pareto probably sums up the future of Paretan thought with succinct precision: "His work is likely to remain a monument rather than a steppingstone."[34]

During the past three decades, the historians of sociology and a sizeable proportion of sociologists devoted principally to more immediate problems have granted particularly high status to a selected number of sociological theorists. This collective judgment is expressed in such evidence of esteem as: frequent inclusion in surveys of contemporary sociological developments; extensive translation of major works, principally but not exclusively into English; and perhaps most significant, the continued application of their concepts and hypotheses in current theoretical formulations and empirical research. But, it should be added, each theorist in this elective élite has likewise been effectively challenged on specific segments of his work, so that we are actually referring to the *net* evaluations of the critics. These theorists do, of course, demonstrably diverge in a number of ways, yet their work contains a basic similarity that might account for their continued eminence, quite apart from the acknowledged value of specific contributions. For each theorist in his own manner and with varying degrees of emphasis devoted serious attention to (1) a suitable conceptual scheme for sociology, rather than to an a priori system; (2) methodological problems peculiar to sociology; (3) the collection and use of historical and contemporary data; and (4) the search for generalizations, uniformities, and verifiable hypotheses.

Simmel. Georg Simmel, who has been widely criticized for what appear to be overly "formalistic" features in his work,[35] has generally been appraised as a pioneer in constructing a distinctive conceptual scheme for a scientific sociology and thus granting it independent status. Park and Burgess included a number of selections from Simmel in their widely used text of the twenties, and in 1925 Spykman presented a full, sympathetic interpretation, soon followed by Abel's very competent analysis of Simmel as a systematic thinker.[36] European reaction was not quite so favorable in the twenties. Sorokin, for example, who had left Russia in 1923, viewed Simmel as a "talented man" in sociology. However, in recent years two substantial English translations from his writings (with interpretative introductions) have appeared,[37] and it is likely that his *Philosophie des Geldes* will also receive a

[34] Crawford, *op. cit.*, p. 568.

[35] Cf. Sorokin, *op. cit.*, pp. 501-502; Hans Freyer, *Soziologie als Wirklichkeitswissenschaft* (Leipzig, 1930), pp. 46-57.

[36] R. E. Park and E. W. Burgess, *Introduction to the Science of Sociology* (Chicago, 1921); N. J. Spykman, *The Social Theory of Georg Simmel* (Chicago, 1925); Abel, *op. cit.*, Chap. 1.

[37] Georg Simmel, *The Sociology of Georg Simmel,* edited and translated by K. H. Wolff (Glencoe, Ill., 1950); *Conflict*, translated by K. H. Wolff and Reinhard Bendix (Glencoe, Ill., 1955). The reader should also consult the lucid translations by Small in the *AJS* from the late 1890's onward.

much deserved translation. The present position of Simmel among sociologists is perhaps reliably illustrated by the fact that, in addition to his prominence among theorists, his writings have been a source of experimental hypotheses for the extremely empirically oriented practitioners of "small-group" research. (See Chap. 9 of this volume.)

Durkheim. Although still the center of considerable controversy, Émile Durkheim occupies a position of special prominence among the critical historians of sociology. He has been repeatedly taken the task for such deficiencies as an immoderate social realism (on occasion almost indistinguishable from the notion of a group mind) and a neglect of the psychological aspects of social phenomena,[38] but it is generally agreed that his analyses of suicide, normlessness (*anomie*), social integration, religious beliefs and practices, and the functional approach contain perennially provoking and useful insights, although some of his formulations remain unacceptable. The most searching and fruitful critiques of his work, by Parsons and Alpert,[39] were published in the thirties; it would therefore be interesting to see how a full-scale contemporary appraisal might affect the essential stature of Durkheim.

Tönnies. It is somewhat paradoxical that the works of Ferdinand Tönnies, who is commonly viewed with great esteem as one of the genuine pioneers in sociology, have not yet been subjected to a full-scale interpretative critique. The famous *Gemeinschaft und Gesellschaft,* first published in 1887, seems to be the primary object of critical concern in the favorable summaries of Becker, Loomis, Parsons, Salomon, and others, and likewise in the variably depreciatory accounts of Aron, Geiger, Sorokin and Wiese.[40] Yet Tönnies lived and worked till 1936, publishing important works during the period 1909-1926 on such topics as social groups, public opinion, and social norms. Only Heberle, Loomis, and Salomon have thus far directed any critical attention to his later theoretical formulations, but these are implicitly viewed as subsidiary rather than central contributions. Since no new or substantial

[38] Sorokin, *op. cit.,* pp. 463-578; Becker and Barnes, *op. cit.,* vol. 2, pp. 829-839; Émile Benoît-Smullyan, "The Sociologism of Émile Durkheim and His School," in Barnes, *op. cit.,* pp. 499-516; Howard Becker, *Systematic Sociology on the Basis of the* Beziehungslehre *and* Gebildelehre *of Leopold von Wiese* (New York, 1932; 2nd ed., with a new preface, Gary, Ind., 1950), pp. 703-704.

[39] Parsons, *op. cit.,* Chaps. 8-11; Harry Alpert, *Émile Durkheim and his Sociology* (New York, 1939). Other helpful reviews include: C. E. Gehlke, *Émile Durkheim's Contribution to Sociological Theory* (New York, 1915); Robert Marjolin, "French Sociology—Comte and Durkheim," *AJS,* 42 (March, 1937), pp. 693-704; Harry Alpert, "Émile Durkheim and Sociologismic Psychology," *AJS,* 45 (July, 1939), pp. 64-70.

[40] Parsons, *op. cit.,*, pp. 686-694; Becker and Barnes, *op. cit.,* vol. 2, pp. 888-889; Albert Salomon, "German Sociology," in Gurvitch and Moore, *op. cit.,* pp. 593-596; Rudolph Heberle, "The Sociological System of Ferdinand Tönnies," in Barnes, *op. cit.,* Chap. 10; C. P. Loomis, "Introduction," in Ferdinand Tönnies, *Fundamental Concepts of Sociology,* translated and supplemented by C. P. Loomis (New York, 1940); Louis Wirth, "The Sociology of Ferdinand Tönnies," *AJS,* 32 (1926).

interpretation of Tönnies has appeared in about fifteen years, we can perhaps look forward to a more definitive account in the near future.

Weber. If we were compelled to select one and only one giant in modern sociological theory, the choice would certainly be Max Weber. With an ever-increasing number of interpretative studies devoted to his writings, Weber has come to be an awesome, almost legendary, figure, remarkable for incomparable erudition, sensitive methodological concern, and seminal theoretical formulations about various aspects of Western social structure. There have, of course, been significant criticisms of methodological and theoretical points,[41] but even these are often tempered by genuine respect for his over-all contributions to sociology. A few decades ago, his theory of the role of Protestantism in modern capitalism was a source of much heated debate, but with the exception of valuable corrections, by Tawney and others, it has become an essentially enduring part of contemporary sociology.[42] More recently, Weber's writings on stratification, bureaucracy, institutional analysis, and religious development have on the whole attracted extremely favorable comment;[43] even more significantly, they have served as conceptual guides in thinking and research. At present, a large portion of Weber's writings are available in English; and as subsequent translations appear, it is safe to assume that the next decade will confirm his reputation with negligible change.

An Agenda for Surveys of Sociological Theory

What can we say of the historian of sociology in the next few decades? He must be thoroughly acquainted with the present state of our science, both empirically and theoretically; preferably he should have made outstand-

[41] Alexander von Schelting, *Max Webers Wissenschaftslehre* (Tubingen, 1934); Talcott Parsons, "Weber's Methodology of Social Science," in Max Weber, *The Theory of Social and Economic Organization,* translated by A. M. Henderson and Talcott Parsons (New York, 1947), pp. 8-29; Reinhold Bendix, "Max Weber's Interpretation of Conduct and History," *AJS,* 51 (May, 1946), pp. 518-526.

[42] See Ephraim Fischoff, "The Protestant Ethic and the Spirit of Capitalism: The History of a Controversy," *SR,* 11 (February, 1944), pp. 53-77; Parsons, "Max Weber's Sociological Analysis of Capitalism and Modern Institutions," in Barnes, *op. cit.,* Chap. 13; Sorokin, *op. cit.,* pp. 673-684; Parsons, *The Structure of Social Action,* Chaps. 14-15. A valuable test of Weber's theory is R. K. Merton, "Science, Technology, and Society in Seventeenth Century England," *Osiris,* 4 (1938), pp. 360-597.

[43] Much of this is available in English in two volumes: *From Max Weber: Essays in Sociology,* translated and edited with an introduction by H. H. Gerth and C. Wright Mills (New York, 1946); and Weber, *The Theory of Social and Economic Organization.* Of genuine value is the diligently collected bibliography on Weber by H. H. Gerth and Hedwig I. Gerth, "Bibliography on Max Weber," *SR,* 16 (March, 1949), pp. 70-89.

ing contributions in both areas. In pursuing his historical task his aim will be to present the findings of Comte, Spencer, Durkheim, Tönnies, Weber, Sumner, Ward, Ross, and all the others to make clear their *present relevance* for sociology. He may prefer to pursue this task by focusing on the history of specialized fields rather than by examining the past from a biographical perspective. Whatever his criteria of selection, his choices must be made in terms of a dominant purpose: to show what the past has to contribute to the advance of science today. He must be relentless in discovering the dead ends, errors, and false starts in previous scientific work, and ingenious enough to show modern parallels of the same deficiencies. He will indicate the high levels of achievement in one or another branch of sociology. He will discover hypotheses still dangling for want of verification that might be of special value for research in his own time. Thus, he must be adept in formulating many issues of the past, in Louis Wirth's words, "in such a fashion that they can be either proved or disproved by means of factual evidence rather than by authoritative pronouncements."

He will be sensitive to indications that certain areas of specialization have peculiar methodological problems; but he must not, in his analysis, allow them the right to declare total independence of the logic of science. He must be non-partisan enough to make it clear that the *logical* character of the natural and social sciences is not different, however varied the applications of method and technique might be. He must expose "planless and pointless empiricism" with the same ruthlessness he would show to systematic theorizing apart from cross-fertilization with empirical exploration. He must lay bare the many series of disconnected investigations with which science is strewn and trace the cycles of interest and apathy in many types of research: in short, he must describe fashions in sociological investigation, together with the incalculable losses that result. He will try to point out "what is fact and what is factitiousness" in our scientific knowledge: more bluntly, what we know and what we don't know. This kind of history might lead to the development of a growing corpus of tested generalizations—something that cannot now be given to students. And it might revive some of the lost interest referred to earlier. It would certainly create more confidence that sociology is a science rather than a series of facts.

SELECTED BIBLIOGRAPHY

Barnes, H. E. (ed.), *An Introduction to the History of Sociology* (Chicago: University of Chicago Press, 1948).

Barnes, H. E., Howard Becker, and Frances B. Becker, *Contemporary Social Theory* (New York: D. Appleton-Century, 1940).

Becker, Howard, *Systematic Sociology on the Basis of the* Beziehungslehre *and* Gebildelehre *of Leopold von Wiese* (New York: John Wiley, 1932; reissued, with a new preface, Gary, Ind.: Norman Paul Press, 1950), Part IV: "Historical Postscript."

Becker, Howard, and H. E. Barnes, *Social Thought from Lore to Science* (2nd ed.; New York: Dover Publications, 1952), 2 vols.

Bernard, L. L. (ed.), *The Fields and Methods of Sociology* (New York: Ray Long and Richard R. Smith, 1934).

Gillin, John (ed.), *For A Science of Social Man* (New York: Macmillan, 1954).

Gurvitch, Georges and W. E. Moore (eds.), *Twentieth Century Sociology* (New York: Philosophical Library, 1945).

Hinkle, R. C., Jr., and G. J. Hinkle, *The Development of Modern Sociology* (New York: Doubleday, 1954).

Odum, H. W., *American Sociology* (New York: Longmans, Green, 1951).

Parsons, Talcott, *The Structure of Social Action* (New York: McGraw-Hill, 1937).

Rice, S. A. (ed.), *Methods in Social Science* (Chicago: University of Chicago Press, 1931).

Sorokin, P. A., *Contemporary Sociological Theories* (New York: Harper, 1928).

Sorokin, P. A., *Society, Culture, and Personality* (New York: Harper, 1947).

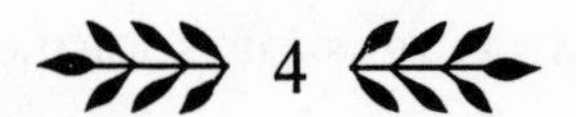

GENERAL SOCIOLOGICAL THEORIES OF CURRENT REFERENCE

PRESTON VALIEN AND BONITA VALIEN

THE TERM "GENERAL SOCIOLOGY" MERITS A BRIEF EXPLANATION. IT STANDS in opposition, naturally, to "special sociology," and the introduction of both terms into sociology is credited to Giddings, who wrote that "sociology may be divided into General, or Fundamental, Sociology and Special Sociology. General Sociology is a study of the universal and fundamental phenomena of societies." The term "special sociology" was applied by Giddings to those inquiries "dealing minutely with some one phase of social organization, social activity, or social development." General sociology deals with efforts to present an all-embracing systematization of sociological theory, with special emphasis upon one or more basic factors or forces in the total social process. It attempts also to develop or present a unified body of principles, a common method of analysis, and broad general concepts. Since it deals with attempts to develop a single integrated system of sociological theory, general sociology is often designated as systematic sociology.

Any attempt to discuss the history of general sociology faces a difficulty inherent in the existence of many and diverse conceptions of "sociological theory." Merton has called attention to "the attractive confusion of sociological theory with the history of sociological thought."[1] In another connection, he assesses the contributions and limitations characteristic of six

[1] R. K. Merton, discussion of Parsons' "The Position of Sociological Theory," *ASR*, 13 (April, 1948), p. 165. For a strong statement of a similar position see Howard Becker, "Vitalizing Sociological Theory," *ASR*, 19 (Aug., 1954), pp. 379-380.

types of activity that are often lumped together as comprising sociological orientation: (1) methodology; (2) general sociological orientations; (3) analysis of sociological concepts; (4) *post factum* sociological interpretations; (5) empirical generalizations in sociology; and (6) sociological theory.[2]

The significance of these six types of sociological activity for general sociology resides in their relation to the problem of system building and the development of fundamental principles in sociology. The earlier leading figures in sociology were large-scale encyclopedists who discussed the origins of human society, the ways of group life, the development and expression of social interests, the modes of social discipline and social control, and the main causes of both cultural lag and social progress. More recently, American sociology has attempted to develop fundamental principles through individual and group research on highly specialized topics, by means of small empirical studies, in the belief that by the accretion of pieces of research, scientific progress can be made.

It was this trend from encyclopedic synthesis to analysis that perhaps motivated Harry Elmer Barnes in 1948 to state in *An Introduction to the History of Sociology* that the "book . . . brings the history of sociological thought down to the era and stage where [encyclopedism] . . . was gradually but rather completely replaced by specialization in some more restricted field of description and analysis." He went on further to predict that "the era of [encyclopedic] . . . sociology has come approximately to an end . . . . Sociological writing from this time onward promises to be mainly specialized forms of social theory."[3]

Trends in American Sociology

Howard Odum, in his *American Sociology* (1951), took note of three trends in the development of social theory in American sociology, one of which was the reawakening of interest in European systematic theory as expressed in Talcott Parsons' revival of the works of Weber, Pareto, and Durkheim; in Howard Becker's systematic theory based upon Wiese and Weber; and in the generally increased emphasis on the works of Tönnies and Durkheim.[4] It should be noted that this reawakening of interest is not expressed merely in appreciative treatments, for Parsons as well as others are critical of, among other things, Durkheim's social psychology and Weber's strictures on the use of psychology in sociology. Dealing with

[2] Merton, *Social Theory and Social Structure* (Glencoe, Ill., 1949), p. 84.

[3] H. E. Barnes (ed.), *An Introduction to the History of Sociology* (Chicago, 1948), p. x.

[4] H. W. Odum, *American Sociology* (New York, 1951), pp. 266-267.

this general point, Becker states, "No useful purpose for sociological theory is served by 'modernizing' the ancients through imputation to them of ideas that, in their day and generation, they simply could not have entertained. The history of social thought can be made vital for substantive sociological theory only by subjecting it to sociology-of-knowledge analysis."[5]

A second trend, according to Odum, has been the tendency of some American sociologists to develop systematized theory in textbooks or in special contributions; and a third trend is reflected in attempts to develop theory by systematizing the results of empirical research. These two trends are illustrated in the work of Howard Becker, George A. Lundberg, Robert M. MacIver, Robert K. Merton, Talcott Parsons, Pitirim A. Sorokin, and Florian Znaniecki. Becker, MacIver, Parsons, and Znaniecki have dealt systematically with social-action theory; their work will be discussed later in this connection. Becker has made important theoretical contributions through the constructed-type methodology and through the application of social-action theory to the study of social change. Parsons' contributions include the structural-functional method of analysis and other important concepts and definitions. MacIver has concerned himself with the problem of social causation through analysis of attitudes, values, and motives. Znaniecki has emphasized what he calls the "humanistic coefficient" in sociology and has stressed the necessity for using personal documents as opposed to quantitative methods in understanding human attitudes, motives, and values. Lundberg, on the other hand, views quantification as the ultimate and indispensable foundation of science. Sorokin's work has been in the tradition of the philosophy of history, and Merton has attempted to link theory with empirical research in what he calls "theories of the middle range." These names do not, of course, exhaust the list of current systematic theorists, but are merely illustrative.

Two events which, perhaps more than any others, laid the foundation for the trend away from individual encyclopedism occurred shortly after World War I. One was the publication of *The Polish Peasant in Europe and America* (1918-1921) by W. I. Thomas and Florian Znaniecki, and the other was the publication in 1921 of the *Introduction to the Science of Sociology* by Robert E. Park and Ernest W. Burgess. *The Polish Peasant* was the first large-scale sociological study in which the entire method and body of data were reported. The work set forth a new method of case studies through personal documents that is still being used and is still the subject of vigorous discussion among sociological methodologists. *The Polish Peasant,* together with the post-World War I expansion in sociological training, research, and publication, directed attention more and more toward extensive

[5] Becker, *op. cit.,* p. 379.

study of a restricted subject. Robert E. L. Faris states that after World War I,

> It was no longer the fashion for each sociologist to . . . become the father of a school of thought. This was the period in which American sociology began to find itself. Its course was no longer governed by the logic of classification of sciences or by any individual's decision but was established by tentative and exploratory efforts in many directions, some of which were rewarded by success. Schools of thought do not survive well in this stage of development, and such schools as were once characteristic of American sociology have been steadily withering away, or perhaps it would be better to say the differences have been dissolving.[6]

Park and Burgess' *Introduction to the Science of Sociology*, which has been called the "most influential textbook in the history of American sociology," was an important agent in the dissolving of sociological differences at this stage. It virtually standardized such concepts as social interaction, communication, social process, competition, conflict, assimilation, accommodation, personality, and collective behavior, and gave great impetus to the trend toward small-scale empirical study. The standardization of these concepts made it much more difficult for sociological schools of thought to develop, because it was now required that sociologists take account of these concepts even where they had theoretical objections to them. In point of fact, this failure to utilize the customary concepts was one of the principal criticisms leveled at Parsons by Ellsworth Faris in his trenchant review of *The Social System*.[7]

EUROPEAN INFLUENCES

Since both the *Polish Peasant* and the *Introduction to the Science of Sociology* were greatly influenced by European social thought, it may be appropriate at this point to indicate some of the major European influences in contemporary American sociological theory.

In recent years, sociological theory in America has shown a revival of the influence of those European thinkers whose theoretical efforts were compatible with the assumptions, problems, and interests of modern American sociologists. Becker estimates that the most lasting European influences in American sociology have been those of Tönnies, Pareto, Durkheim, Max Weber, Znaniecki, and Wiese.[8] To this list should be added the name of Simmel, whose influence was mediated by Park and others of the Chicago

[6] R. E. L. Faris, "American Sociology," in Georges Gurvitch and W. E. Moore (eds.), *Twentieth Century Sociology* (New York, 1945), p. 546.

[7] Ellsworth Faris, review of Parsons' *The Social System*, in *ASR*, 18 (Feb., 1953), pp. 103-106. For an interesting reply by Parsons, describing his personal orientation as a sociologist and the sources of his major theoretical influences, see his "Some Comments on the State of the General Theory of Action," *ARS*, 18 (Dec., 1953), pp. 618-619.

[8] Odum, *op. cit.*, p. 50.

school. We shall consider briefly the contributions of these European scholars that have relevance for contemporary American sociological theory.

Ferdinand Tönnies (1855-1936). Tönnies was the initiator of that type of sociological analysis that we call systematic sociology or analytical sociology. His most important contribution to sociology was his typology categorizing social relations as *Gemeinschaft* and *Gesellschaft*, or "community" and "society." The significance of the work of Tönnies has been twofold. First, he laid the foundation for a typology of social groups that is still influential in American social science in a modified form as "folk society," "urban society," and similar categories. Second, and perhaps more significantly, Tönnies stressed the close association between personality and social structure by distinguishing what he called the two types of human will basic to all social relations: essential will and arbitrary will. He defined essential will as non-rational and sentiment-saturated, and as the unifying bond in community structures dominating the lives of peasants, artisans, and common people. On the other hand, arbitrary will is deliberate, rational, and egocentric and results in the *Gesellschaft* type of society, which is an instrument toward the attainment of some given end. Furthermore, Tönnies, by indicating that *Gesellschaft* must inevitably be preceded by *Gemeinschaft*, anticipated contemporary attempts to place societies in "folk–urban" and similar dichotomies.

Tönnies has been criticized for his identification of essential will with instincts and biotic tendencies and for the oversimplification represented by his dichotomous conception of societies. But critics have elaborated upon rather than discarded the formulations that he based upon this dichotomous conception.[9]

Georg Simmel (1858-1918). Simmel is generally considered to be the founder of sociology as an independent academic discipline in Germany and, in his capacity as teacher, he influenced many of the leading American sociologists of his time. He rejected the position that sociology should be a science of everything human and contended that sociology should concentrate on the *forms* of social interaction. In this context he dealt with forms such as supraordination and subordination, competition, division of labor, and the stranger. Leaving the "content" of interaction to other disciplines, he characterized social psychology as a branch of general psychology and saw no place in sociology for the study of motivation.

Although few would agree today with the limitations that Simmel placed on sociology, his formulations of the forms of social interaction greatly influenced sociological research in his lifetime and continue to influence it through the influence and work of such sociologists as Wiese, Becker, and Park and Burgess.[10]

[9] Cf. pp. 18-20 of this volume.

[10] Cf. pp. 25-26 of this volume.

Vilfredo Pareto (1848-1923). Pareto has the dubious distinction of having the importance of his contribution overestimated by too enthusiastic disciples and underestimated by hypercritical non-disciples. It is generally admitted, however, that Pareto's contributions have been highly influential in American sociology through his conception of society as a system in imperfect equilibrium, his efforts to develop a method of sociological generalization that conformed to the mathematical ideal of modern science, and his attention to the role of non-logical action in social life. His theory of the circulation of the élite probably served more to provoke discussion than to exert influence in American sociology, since it appeared to be based fundamentally on a prejudice against the current conceptions and ideals of democracy.

Pareto's conception of sociology as a "logico-experimental science" attracted much attention. He insisted that sociology must be governed by strictly scientific canons, and he recommended the logico-experimental method as the appropriate investigative procedure to attain this end. Under this method, generalizations and abstractions are arrived at by induction, and observations are formulated so as to involve no evaluative interest and no attempt to prove preconceived propositions. Critics of Pareto have been quick to point out that he failed to follow his own canons, but these canons themselves have nevertheless exerted influence.[11]

Although much of Pareto's work dealt with an analysis of the underlying forces in human conduct that operate in social life, which he designated *residues* and *derivations,* his most influential contributions have been his conception of the social system and his emphasis on the role of non-rationality in human behavior.

Émile Durkheim (1858-1917). Durkheim's influence on American sociology stems in large measure from his emphasis on the necessity for empirical research on specific topics and his analysis of the role of the group in determining human conduct. Durkheim saw sociology as the study of social facts and insisted that social facts be treated as things—that is, as objects in the external world. Social facts, according to Durkheim, are external to the individual and exercise constraint on the individual. Durkheim saw society as a social fact, something real in itself. The Hinkles, in their excellent short study of the development of American sociology, have pointed out that most American sociologists have refused to accept this point of view because of what the Hinkles call the "voluntaristic nominalism" of American sociology.[12] By voluntaristic nominalism they mean "the assumption that the structure of all social groups is the consequence of the aggregate of its separate, component individuals and that

[11] Cf. pp. 72-73 of this volume.

[12] R. C. Hinkle, Jr., and Gisela J. Hinkle, *The Development of Modern Sociology* (New York, 1954).

social phenomena ultimately derive from the motivations of these knowing, feeling, and willing individuals."[13] Stated otherwise, this view holds that society is the sum of individuals in interaction in contradistinction to Durkheim's view that society is a separate and real social fact in itself.[14]

Although Durkheim has been criticized for his acceptance of certain evolutionary doctrines, the chief criticism has come from what appears to be his exaggeration of the role of the group in human life and his minimizing of the social significance of individualism. Timasheff, recognizing the validity of these criticisms of Durkheim, succinctly summarizes Durkheim's important contributions as follows:

> He showed convincingly that social facts are facts *sui generis*. He brought out vividly the social and cultural importance of the division of labor. He analyzed the nature and many of the consequences of social solidarity. He indicated the role of social pressure in areas of human activity where it had previously escaped detection. With Max Weber he brought the attention of sociologists to the significance of values and ideals in social life. And he faced up to complex methodological problems and demonstrated by deed the necessity of empirical research for a science of society.

Max Weber (1864-1920). There can be little doubt that the most influential European scholar for American sociology in recent years has been Max Weber. He viewed sociology as a science of social action—as the study of the behavior of individuals insofar as this behavior is oriented toward the expectations of other individuals. He held that social actions manifest independence and regularity as non-social phenomena do, but social actions are distinct from other phenomena in that social actions are "understandable." Weber maintained that laws of social action could be deduced through the procedure of *Verstehen,* or the interpretation by the observer of the actions of his fellow men.

Weber developed the method of the "ideal" or "pure" type as the most appropriate tool for the study of social actions. In Weber's view, the ideal type had three primary characteristics: (1) it was formulated in terms of subjective categories; (2) it deliberately intensified or overemphasized certain aspects of concrete situations; and (3) it was an instrument and not a goal of social science. He illustrated the application of the ideal type in much of his empirical work.

Weber stressed also the views that science has no normative validity and that scientific work must be free from value-judgments. Science can determine, he stated, the means to be used to produce specific effects, but science cannot state whether or not these effects are desirable. However, Weber clearly did not bar scientific sociology from the study of values as data.

[13] *Ibid.,* p. vii.

[14] Cf. pp. 20-22 of this volume, and index references to "voluntaristic nominalism."

Weber's many influential contributions include (1) the examples he provided of methods for studying specific social situations in order to obtain greater precision in scientific concepts; (2) his insistence on a value-free science that could, however, use values as data; (3) his development of the ideal type as a scientific tool, accompanied by the recognition that the development of types is not the goal of science; and (4) his linking of social causation with meaning in explaining human behavior.[15]

Florian Znaniecki (1882-). Znaniecki has been for many years a leading sociologist in both Europe and the United States, and although he stood for some time in the shadow of W. I. Thomas, his collaborator on *The Polish Peasant,* his mature and penetrating insights have won him independent recognition. In 1953 he was elected president of the American Sociological Society. With the passage of time and with the additional evidence of prior and subsequent work, Znaniecki's role in *The Polish Peasant* has been revealed as increasingly significant.

Znaniecki's recent works have been devoted to the analysis of the structure and process of social action. His *Social Actions* (1936) does not appear to have yet received the attention it deserves. Znaniecki specifies the unit of sociological analysis as "action." Social action is behavior which tends to influence conscious human beings or collectivities. By means of what he calls the "humanistic coefficient" he points up the significance of human consciousness in the lives of both the individual and society. This has led Znaniecki to strong advocacy of the use of personal documents to study human behavior in sociology. His classifications of social actions in the perspective of the actor's appraisal of the social object's attitudes toward the actor's own purposes is an insightful and significant theoretical contribution.[16]

Leopold von Wiese (1876-). Wiese was greatly influenced by Simmel and took over Simmel's objective of making sociology an independent social science. Wiese emphasized the natural-science approach to the study of society and felt that sociology should free itself from reform efforts and from value-judgments. He saw sociology as the study of interhuman relations and devoted the greater part of his work to the analysis of the processes of association and dissociation. His conception of the processes of association (advance, adjustment, accordance, and amalgamation) and of dissociation (competition, contravention, and conflict) focused attention on the need for explicit conceptualization in sociology. This, together with his systematization of plurality patterns (crowds, groups, and abstract collectivities), resulted in valuable insights and furnished the basis for research by Wiese and many of his students. Wiese's influence in American sociology was mediated through Howard Becker, who adapted and augmented his major work

[15] Cf. pp. 120-124, 178-179, and 224-228 of this volume.

[16] Cf. 94-96, and 100-106 of this volume.

in the effort to bring about closer correspondence with American points of view.[17] In the same adaptation, however, Becker introduced a number of points not stressed by Wiese, notably with regard to social action and to constructive typology, thus manifesting Max Weber's influence.

Theory Construction in America

The revival of interest in the theories of European sociologists has greatly stimulated the process of theory construction in American sociology. This process has taken two major directions, one of which is neo-positivism and the other the development of social-action theory.

SOCIOLOGICAL NEO-POSITIVISM

Sociological neo-positivism has its historical roots in three elements: the quantitative approach, behaviorism, and pragmatism.[18] The quantitative approach emphasizes enumeration and measurement as essential factors in scientific investigations in any field. Behaviorism asserts that "consciousness" is not susceptible of "objective" observation and that social science should limit itself to the study of observable behavior.

These elements are represented in the work of George A. Lundberg, who is the most influential exponent of neo-positivism in American sociology. However, his major interest has been in quantification. Although Lundberg has insisted that the role of the scientist acting as a scientist should always be differentiated from that of the scientist acting as a citizen, he regards science as an instrument of human adjustment. He regards the objectives of the adjustment, however, as within the realm of value-judgments and therefore outside the realm of science. Sociology should indicate the consequences of alternative social policies, but it cannot, as a science, specify which consequences are more desirable.

Lundberg's behavioristic approach has been vigorously opposed by the exponents of social-action theory. Lundberg feels that it is "prescientific" and "mystical" for social scientists to deal with motives, values, feelings, and ends, for he believes that the interpretation of these will vary with the prejudices and predilections of the observer. He maintains that introspection cannot be a source of scientific knowledge. He regards as a major objective the bringing of sociology into the domain of the physical and biological sciences; he uses physics as his model, and in this task he has had the enthusiastic assistance of his colleague Stuart C. Dodd.

In keeping with his epistemology, Lundberg insists that concepts be defined in terms of the operations by which data are obtained. "Intelligence

[17] Cf. pp. 180-181 of this volume.
[18] N. S. Timasheff, *Sociological Theory* (New York, 1955), p. 137.

is that which the intelligence test measures." "Space is that which the ruler measures." Lundberg's operationism has drawn heavy fire from his critics, but it has stimulated even them to greater efforts to specify empirical referents for their concepts.

SOCIAL-ACTION THEORY

Social-action theory has been developed by a group of sociologists who have, in large measure, worked independently of one another, but who have been bound together by the common objective of constructing a unified, logically consistent and integrated theory of human behavior with *social action* as the central concept. The Hinkles have designated four sociologists—Florian Znaniecki, Robert M. MacIver, Howard Becker, and Talcott Parsons—as the major figures in the development of social-action theory in America. Although only Becker and Parsons explicitly acknowledge the influence of Max Weber, all four are in fundamental agreement with Weber's conception of social action. All agree that introspection is a proper and indispensable source of scientific data regarding human behavior, and all oppose the application of behaviorist, reductionist psychology to sociology as well as the indiscriminate use of quantitative methods. All four accept means, ends, conditions, and norms as basic components of the social-action system. Since Max Weber furnished the theoretical foundation for social-action theory, we shall deal briefly with Parsons and Becker, who explicitly acknowledge his influence in their work.

Howard Becker (1899-). Becker has made important theoretical and substantive contributions to sociology. As a student of Robert E. Park, he amplified and elaborated the concepts of sacred and secular societies as earlier proposed by Park. Timasheff credits Becker with playing an important role in introducing Simmel's work to American sociologists through his augmented adaptation of Wiese's major treatises.[19] In bringing Simmel to the attention of American sociologists, Becker was again continuing a task begun by Park. He has maintained a consistent interest in the history of social thought and the development of sociological theory, while he has written textbooks on the family and done research on the German youth movement and German peasant villages. He has been particularly concerned to apply social-action theory to the study of social change.

Becker has made an important methodological contribution through his demonstration of the utility of constructive typology in the social sciences. Following Max Weber's position on the ideal type, Becker cautions that the constructed type is merely a tool. He holds that the constructed type gives ample room for relevant quantitative procedure and may have predictive power if the conditions are properly specified.[20]

[19] *Ibid.*, p. 102.

[20] Becker, *Through Values to Social Interpretation* (Durham, N.C., 1950), Chaps. 2 and 4.

Becker's action theory makes use of aspects of the work of Max Weber, G. H. Mead, Znaniecki, and W. I. Thomas. He adapts Weber's means-end typology, Mead's interpretation of the role of the symbol, Znaniecki's analysis of the action situation, and Thomas' four wishes to provide an analysis of social change. In applying social-action theory to social change, Becker makes a significant contribution by relating personality to the social structure. Here he uses the constructed types of sacred and secular societies and describes the polar types of personalities produced by these societies. Becker has avoided the criticism of oversimplification directed at Simmel by dividing sacred and secular societies into subtypes and ranging them on a continuum of sacredness and secularity. Thus, one is enabled to interpret the impact of specific social changes by the increase in sacredness or secularity that they produce. The sybtypes that Becker has elaborated, based upon degrees of readiness and capacity to change, are: (1) proverbial-sacred society, typified by many preliterate societies and some rural Southern communities; (2) prescriptive-sacred society, typified by Nazi Germany or Fascist Italy; (3) principial-secular society, as suggested by middle-class urban American society; and (4) pronormless-secular society, as represented by modern "emancipated" circles of cosmopolitan urban centers. In his recent terminological shift from "normless" to "pronormless," Becker recognizes, even more explicitly than hitherto, that there is a point beyond which even the most extremely secular society cannot go in normlessness and remain a *society*.

Talcott Parsons (1902-). The sociological contributions of Parsons have been both influential and wide-ranging. Boskoff indicated in 1950 several areas in which he felt Parsons had made special contributions: the clarification of the role of theory in research; the structural-functional method of analysis; important concepts and definitions such as the unit act, function, institution, status, and role; the analysis of institutions; the outline of systematic theory in sociology; the voluntaristic theory of action; the analysis of specific structures and roles (kinship, the occupations, and the professions); the analysis of certain modern problems (aggression, fascism, anti-Semitism); and the analyses of the work of Weber, Durkheim, and Pareto.[21]

Parsons has consistently emphasized social action in his work, analyzing social action in terms of: the actor, a situation composed of physical, cultural, and social objects, and the orientation of the actor to the situation. Motivational and value-orientations serve as the basis for Parsons' formulation of the social system, the personality system, and the cultural system. Moreover, Parsons, in viewing behavior as necessarily involving value-orientations, emphasizes the normative aspect of social life.[22]

[21] Alvin Boskoff, "The Systematic Sociology of Talcott Parsons," *SF*, 28 (May, 1950), pp. 393-400.

[22] Cf. the discussions on pp. 110-111, 114-121, and 123-127 of this volume.

Parsons' work has stimulated extensive comment in sociological circles and has been the basis of considerable work by his students. The work of one of his earlier students, Robert K. Merton, has been justly regarded as an independent contribution. Merton maintains the same conception of science and, like Parsons, his theory is based on the means-end schema of social action. But he differs from Parsons as to the level on which he feels profitable theories can be developed. Whereas Parsons' efforts have been directed toward an integrated or master conceptual scheme, Merton is committed to what he calls "theories of the middle range"—theories applicable to limited ranges of data.

Merton has developed a useful analytic paradigm in which he makes explicit, among other things, the distinction between manifest and latent functions. We have already referred to his attempt to assess the contributions and limitations characteristic of six types of activities, each of which is sometimes confused with sociological theory. Merton has been particularly effective in stressing the interplay between research and theory.

Status and Prospects

The status of general sociology can be reviewed briefly as it is exemplified in two of the six types of activity that, as Merton has pointed out, are often regarded as aspects of "sociological theory." The first of these is methodology. Although Merton insists that we should distinguish clearly between sociological theory—which is substantive and has for its subject matter certain aspects of the interaction of men—and methodology, or the logic of scientific procedure, even he acknowledges that the instruments and procedures used in scientific inquiry logically presuppose substantive theories.[23] This can be demonstrated both by the attention that such theorists as Znaniecki, MacIver, Lundberg, Becker, Parsons, and Merton himself have given to methodology, as well as by a mere enumeration of the methodological issues in sociology: reductionism *vs.* *Verstehen;* behavioristic *vs.* meaningful social psychology; the differences of opinion concerning the role of measurement and statistics; and the role of insight *vs.* the analysis of behavior externalities. Certainly, if the history of general sociology has had any continuity since World War I, it has centered around the debates on methodology, many of which are still unresolved.

The analysis of sociological concepts is another sociological activity that has significance for general sociology. In one sense, this is another facet of the disputations regarding methodology. The need for conceptual analysis has its proponents in the holders of such diverse points of view

[23] Merton, *Social Theory and Social Structure,* note 2, chap. 2.

as Blumer and Lundberg. Blumer finds the basic deficiency in social theory to be the ambiguous nature of concepts in sociology, which he defines as "sensitizing concepts" as opposed to "definitive concepts." Blumer makes the following distinction:

> A definitive concept refers precisely to what is common to a class of objects, by the aid of a clear definition in terms of attributes or fixed bench marks. . . . A sensitizing concept lacks such specification of attributes or bench marks and consequently it does not enable the user to move directly to the instance and its relevant content. Instead, it gives the user a general sense of reference and guidance in approaching empirical instances. Whereas definitive concepts provide prescriptions of what to see, sensitizing concepts merely suggest directions along which to look. The hundreds of our concepts—like culture, institutions, social structure, mores, and personality—are not definitive concepts but are sensitizing in nature.[24]

Blumer attributes the existence of sensitizing concepts in sociology neither to immaturity nor to lack of scientific sophistication but to the nature of the empirical world that sociologists are seeking to study and analyze.[25] He suggests that sociologists accept the sensitizing nature of sociological concepts and work for their progressive refinement through adequate study of the empirical instances to which they refer. Like Blumer, Lundberg deplores the ambiguous nature of sociological concepts, but he calls for the operational definition of concepts, that is the acceptance of the definition that develops in the process of research.[26] There are others who hold, of course, that emphasis should be directed not to concepts but to hypotheses and their verification or disproof.

The current trend in general sociology is toward a *rapprochement* between theory and empirical research, toward making sound social theory the essential basis for practical work, and toward developing such theory from the systematization of results of actual research. Howard Becker asserts:

> The vitalizing of sociological theory necessarily includes the require-

[24] Herbert Blumer, "What Is Wrong with Social Theory?" *ASR,* 19 (Feb., 1954), p. 7. See also Merton, *Social Theory and Social Structure,* pp. 85-90.

[25] For another view of the reasons for the present deficiencies in sociological theory see G. P. Murdock, "Sociology and Anthropology," in John Gillin (ed.), *For A Science of Social Man* (New York, 1954), pp. 23-26. He suggests that one reason why cultural anthropology possesses a much more unified body of theory than sociology is that cultural anthropologists in studying non-American culture, have given primary attention to patterned behavior. Sociologists, on the other hand, in studying American culture, assume a knowledge of the major norms of the culture and proceed to a study of unpatterned behavior and deviations from the norms. Murdock cites other reasons for the present defects in sociological theory, one of which is that few sociological propositions have been validated cross-culturally.

[26] For a discussion of operational definitions in an elementary text, see G. A. Lundberg, C. C. Schrag, and O. N. Larsen, *Sociology* (New York, 1954), pp. 32-35.

ment of empirical infusion. . . . Vitalized sociological theory can be provided only by sociological theorists who are also qualified empirical researchers . . .[27]

Becker further makes a case for the coexistence of analytic induction and enumerative induction. And Merton writes as follows:

> The stereotype of the social theorist high in the empyrean of pure ideas uncontaminated by mundane facts is fast becoming no less outmoded than the stereotype of the social researcher equipped with questionnaire and pencil, hot on the chase of the isolated and meaningless statistic. For in building the mansion of sociology during the last decades, theorist and empiricist have learned to work together. What is more, they have learned to talk to one another in the process. At times, this means only that a sociologist has learned to talk to himself, since increasingly the same man has taken up both theory and research. Specialization and integration have developed hand in hand.[28]

Although the platitudinous nature of the foregoing remarks must be recognized, their almost unanimous acceptance by sociologists has significance in itself, for sociologists are equally as susceptible to group pressure to conform to social norms as are the subjects they study. The trend in general sociology can be expected to continue to be away from individual, encyclopedic efforts and great theoretical leaders with loyal disciples, toward the discovery of the regularities in societies through specific pieces of research. According to Durkheim, this period of discovering regularities is a necessary precursor to large-scale theorizing in sociology. If and when this period of theorizing comes, the history of general sociology will have repeated itself with an interesting reverse twist.

SELECTED BIBLIOGRAPHY

Becker, Howard, *Systematic Sociology on the Basis of the* Beziehungslehre *and* Gebildelehre *of Leopold von Wiese* (New York: John Wiley, 1932; reissued, with new preface, Gary, Ind.: Norman Paul Press, 1950).

———, *Through Values to Social Interpretation* (Durham, N. C.: Duke University Press, 1950).

———, *Man in Reciprocity* (New York: Frederick A. Praeger, Inc., 1956).

Durkheim, Émile, *Division of Labor in Society,* translated by George Simpson (Glencoe, Ill.: The Free Press, 1947).

———, *Elementary Forms of the Religious Life,* translated by J. W. Swain (Glencoe, Ill.: The Free Press, 1947).

[27] Becker, "Vitalizing Sociological Theory," p. 381. In this paper, Becker also makes a strong plea for linguistic sophistication on the part of sociologists, a much neglected aspect of the present training of sociologists.

[28] Merton, *Social Theory and Social Structure,* p. 97.

———, *The Rules of Sociological Method,* translated by Sarah A. Solovay and John H. Mueller (Glencoe, Ill.: The Free Press, 1938).

MacIver, R. M., *Society* (New York: Farrar and Rinehart, 1937) [with C. H. Page, in a revised edition (New York: Rinehart, 1949)].

Merton, R. K., *Social Theory and Social Structure* (Glencoe, Ill.: The Free Press, 1949).

Pareto, Vilfredo, *Mind and Society,* translated by A. Bongiorno and Arthur Livingston (New York: Harcourt, Brace, 1935), 4 vols.

Parsons, Talcott, *Essays in Sociological Theory, Pure and Applied* (Glencoe, Ill: The Free Press, 1949).

———, *The Social System* (Glencoe, Ill.: The Free Press, 1951).

———, *The Structure of Social Action* (New York: McGraw-Hill, 1937).

Simmel, Georg, *The Sociology of Georg Simmel,* translated and edited by K. H. Wolff (Glencoe, Ill.: The Free Press, 1951).

Spykman, N. J., *The Social Theory of Georg Simmel* (Chicago: University of Chicago Press, 1925).

Tönnies, Ferdinand, *Fundamental Concepts in Sociology,* translated and supplemented by C. P. Loomis (New York: American Book Company, 1940).

Weber, Max, *From Max Weber: Essays in Sociology,* translated and edited by H. H. Gerth and C. Wright Mills (New York: Oxford University Press, 1946).

———, *The Theory of Social and Economic Organization,* translated by A. M. Henderson and Talcott Parsons (New York: Oxford University Press, 1947).

Znaniecki, Florian, *Cultural Sciences* (Urbana: University of Illinois Press, 1952).

———, *The Method of Sociology* (New York: Farrar and Rinehart, 1934).

———, *Social Actions* (New York: Farrar and Rinehart, 1936).

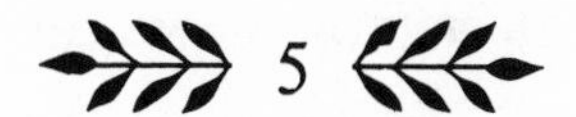

THE CHANGING PROMINENCE OF VALUES IN MODERN SOCIOLOGICAL THEORY

WILLIAM L. KOLB

A HISTORY OF ANY SOCIOLOGICAL CONCEPT RELEVANT FOR CONTEMPORARY systematic theory must be selective. Inevitably, of course, the historian runs the risk of finding order where there is none, or of imposing *his* order on one of a vastly different nature. Yet such risks must be run. Without periodic re-examination of the concepts of a discipline as they have developed through time, the theoretical order that does exist will be dissipated and theorists will continue to make and then to discover the errors that have been made and discovered time and again. But historians of sociological theory must not be antiquarians.

THE FOCUS OF VALUE THEORY: THE NORMATIVE REALM

Fortunately, in considering the recent history of the value concept in American sociological theory, a sharply defined selective standard is available. Almost all writing on values that is of concern to sociologists has to do with the nature and function of normative rules and central normative beliefs in the analysis of social order, social integration, and social change. Realist and nominalist, voluntarist and positivist, historical theorist and functional theorist, all have to deal with norms and values, either as means of explanation or as things to be explained away. This anchoring of the value concept in the realm of the normative has served as a cohesive force holding together an array of conflicting definitions and interpretations of the nature and functions of values. Moreover, it has served as a centripetal force drawing definitions and interpretations constantly closer to the *identification* of values with norms and normative beliefs and gradually creating a consensus on the attribution of functional importance to such normative elements. By concentrating on this central tendency it is possible to discern some order and clarity emerging from conceptual confusion.

Development and Clarification of the Value Concept Since World War I

THE THEORY OF VALUES IN *The Polish Peasant*

In 1918 there was published the first volume of a study that was to stand as a seminal source of theory and method in sociology for a number of years —Thomas and Znaniecki's *The Polish Peasant in Europe and America*.[1] In the "methodological note" of the first volume appears the first systematic discussion of the value concept in American sociological literature. Values are defined by the authors in connection with and in contrast to the psychological concept of *attitude*. For them a value is any *object* having an accessible content and a meaning to the members of a social group. Attitudes are the subjective orientations of the members of the group toward values.[2]

Their definitions of value and attitude, however, were only a starting point for the development of their social theory, for they were interested in a specific phenomenon that had ". . . during the last fifty years . . . constituted the central sphere of interest of the various researches called *sociology*." This focus of attention was the ". . . more or less explicit and formal *rules* of behavior by which the group tends to maintain, to regulate, and to make more general and more frequent the corresponding types of actions among its members." These rules are values, and they are the values with which the sociologist is primarily concerned.

It is apparent that these normative elements of social life are not values for Thomas and Znaniecki because they are normative but because they are data of human experience having an accessible content and meaning for a human group. Nevertheless, for the sociologist such rules are the most important values; and it is on *rules* rather than on values in general that the authors of *The Polish Peasant* build their theory of social organization.[3] From this definition of value as objects meaningful to subjects, combined with the

[1] W. I. Thomas and Florian Znaniecki, *The Polish Peasant in Europe and America* (Boston, 1918-1920), 5 vols. For a discussion of Znaniecki's role in this treatise, see Howard Becker and H. E. Barnes, *Social Thought from Lore to Science* (2nd ed.; New York, 1952), pp. 1075-1077.

[2] *Ibid.*, vol. 1, pp. 21-22. Thomas and Znaniecki recognize the existence of individual values as well as social values, but are primarily concerned with the latter.

[3] *Ibid.*, pp. 32-33.

emphasis on rules as the values important for sociologists, the meaning of the value-concept for sociologists has gradually shifted, so that the element of *normativeness* characteristic of rules has become the determining criterion rather than the element of *objectivity*. In discussing the development of the concept it will be necessary, for the sake of clarity, to use the word "value" to designate this normative element and to abandon the definition of Thomas and Znaniecki. The word "object" will be used to designate meaningful elements of social life toward which members of a social group hold attitudes, since the term implies the existence of an orienting subject or subjects. (For a different treatment of "value," akin to the Thomas and Znaniecki usage, see Chap. 6.).

Values as Elements of Orientation and as Objects of Orientation. Although the definition of value established here departs from that of Thomas and Znaniecki in regarding social rules as values because they are normative rather than because they are objects of concern, it is important to remember that for these men rules were objects, not parts of the orientation of actors. This question as to whether values are *objects* of orientation or *elements* of orientation has plagued the history of the concept from the time of *The Polish Peasant,* for there are weaknesses in the argument by which Thomas and Znaniecki distinguished attitude and object and then use this distinction to establish the objective status of social rules. The difficulty is that the distinction breaks down when applied to the rules.

Superficially, the argument is plausible: Every social group has a system of rules that appear as objects in the experience of the members of the group. These objects evoke attitudes. One rule can evoke many attitudes, and one attitude can be directed toward many rules. Thus a specific norm, such as "Husbands should love their wives and express their love through frequent gestures of affection," can evoke attitude of respect, resentment, conformity, etc.; conversely, the attitude of respect can be taken toward the whole complex of rules of the social group.

Social rules, however, according to Thomas and Znaniecki, not only evoke attitudes; they also express them. They can be treated as indicators showing that the attitude, supposed to exist because it shows itself through the appropriate act, is shared by all the persons who subscribe to the rule. The question that immediately arises in examining any specific rule (such as the one concerning husbands and wives) is that of the nature and content of the attitude so indicated. What shared attitude, to be manifested through the appropriate acts, is indicated by the norm, "All husbands should love their wives and express that love through frequent gestures of affection"? It cannot be the general attitudes of respect, resentment, or conformity, for these are evoked by the rule, and it is obviously impossible for a rule to come into existence as a manifestation of the generalized attitudes it evokes, since its ability to evoke them is dependent on its prior existence.

A second possibility—one toward which Thomas and Znaniecki incline—is that the rule manifests the same central, non-normative attitude that the conforming act apparently manifests (in the present instance, the tendency on the part of husbands to love their wives and to express that love through gestures of affection). This possibility is more complex than the first, and not so easily dismissed. Many husbands who subscribe to and accept the rule of loving and expressing love do actually love their wives and have a non-normative tendency to express that love. This attitude was probably a factor in the creation of the rule and is a basis for its support and a motive for conformity to it. Investigation, however, reveals that not all who subscribe to the rule share this attitude; hence it cannot be the one indicated. There are wives who accept the rule and have the attitude of expecting gestures of affection; unmarried men and women who expect others to act according to the rule; and husbands who do not love their wives but believe they should and try to carry out the appropriate actions, or else feel guilty because they cannot. All these people, together with the husbands who do love their wives, share a common tendency, according to Thomas and Znaniecki; but it cannot be this tendency to love and express love.

There is not, within the framework of theory offered by Thomas and Znaniecki, any further possibility of finding the indicated attitude, because to them the rule is an object and only an object. Once this restriction is abandoned, however, and it is possible to conceive the rule not only as an object but also as an element of normative orientation—a normative attitude—placed within the structure of personality, then new possibilities are opened to investigation. Thus, in the present example, the rule would exist as an element of orientation insofar as it constituted a tendency on the part of the actor to feel and believe that husbands should love their wives and express that love through gestures. This normative attitude taken toward the self can strengthen a non-normative tendency to engage in the action called for, can call into existence a tendency to try to engage in such action, or create a feeling of guilt because of a failure to act in the prescribed manner. Pointed toward others, the actor orienting to it can judge the behavior of others or hold legitimate expectations concerning their actions. Within the framework of this approach, values exist *simultaneously* as objects and attitudes; and in using it to examine a system of social interaction both aspects must be traced, if the place and function of values in the system is to be understood.

VALUES AS ATTITUDES

The period following the publication of *The Polish Peasant* was one of great theoretical development, particularly among the sociologists at the University of Chicago. The formulation of new basic concepts went on apace, as did the examination and reformulation of older concepts. The value concept played an important part in these developments, as attention was constantly paid to the role that systems of normative rules and moral ideals play in social life. The nature of that attention varied, however, according to whether the theorists concerned were interested in the theory of social organization or in the theory of personality and social order. In such areas as human ecology, the theory of urbanism, or the general theory of social organization, the basic objective conception of values as ordering and integrating rules remained unaltered, and the concept was related to new ideas of process, short-run change, disorganization, and urbanization.[4]

To social psychologists, on the other hand, struggling both with the relation of the person to society and with the question of whether human actions are learned or instinctive, the value concept offered a challenge and an opportunity, provided it could be conceptualized as an element of personality. Thomas and Znaniecki had offered a basis for so conceptualizing values in their concept of the social attitude, although they did not use it for that purpose. For the social psychologists of the postwar decade to use the concept, it was first necessary for them to shift emphasis from the social attitudes that objective values evoked to those that they manifested. It was the great contribution of the social psychological theorists of this period that they saw that some of the social attitudes of the person were the subjective aspect of the objective values, and that the internalization of these values was a function of the process of socialization within the human group.

The Contributions of Faris and Mead. Ellsworth Faris and George Herbert Mead were the two most important figures in introducing and developing this new conceptualization of values as elements of personality. It is difficult to overestimate the importance of the essays that Faris wrote during the period under consideration. Two of these are of special significance for our purposes, "Social Attitudes" and "The Concept of Social Attitudes."[5] In them the transition is made from conceiving norms as situational elements for all the actors of a social group to conceiving them as social attitudes.

There are two important theoretical aspects of this transition. The first of these makes it possible to view values as having both an objective dimension, toward which actors singly and collectively can orient their attitudes and actions, and an attitudinal dimension, which constitutes an element of orientation. In other words, social attitudes are, in part, the subjective reflection of the social rules that Thomas and Znaniecki stressed as the central concern of sociology.

If the social psychologists had settled for this, a great many of the difficulties in the path of the value concept would have been avoided. But Faris takes an additional step. Not only are there individual attitudes, but there are

[4] See, for example, R. E. Park, E. W. Burgess, and R. D. McKenzie (eds.), *The City* (Chicago, 1925); and E. W. Burgess (ed.), *The Urban Community* (Chicago, 1926).

[5] Faris' articles were collected in the volume *The Nature of Human Nature* (New York, 1937), pp. 127-131, 132-143.

also group attitudes, and these, too, are social. Group attitudes are "collective phenomena that are not mere summations." The old contrast between values as objects of orientation and as elements of orientation is replaced by the contrast between the collective attitudes as "objective culture" and the somewhat differentiated "subjective" attitudes of the individual corresponding thereto. "The group attitudes are selected in the individual person; public opinion is represented in individual opinion; and personality is the subjective aspect of culture."[6]

If Faris was the outstanding exponent of values conceived as attitudes, Mead was the theorist who formulated the principles according to which normative attitudes come to be a central part of human personality.[7] In the process of building the self, there are, according to Mead, two stages. In the first stage the self ". . . is constituted simply by an organization of the particular attitudes of other individuals toward himself and toward one another in the specific social acts in which he participates with them." In the second stage the self ". . . is constituted not only by an organization of these particular individual attitudes, but also by an organization of the socialized attitudes of the generalized other or the social group as a whole to which he belongs." The social attitudes included in the second stage range from particular normative attitudes relative to particular acts in specific types of situations to a framework of normative attitudes of fundamental orientation that constitute the person's social character. These latter attitudes constitute the person's principles and the acknowledged shared value-orientations of the members of the community toward the world, themselves, and their joint undertaking.[8]

There is nothing in the theoretical system of Mead that prevents the actor from experiencing these normative attitudes as objects of orientation and response. Actually, this status is demanded for them by the dynamics of the system. This is seen most clearly in the conversations an actor may hold with himself in thinking about a possible course of action. If, for example, a man is tempted to steal, he is likely to call out in himself—if he has been successfully socialized—the normative attitude that stealing is wrong. Mead stressed the fact that in a case such as this the person is taking the attitude of the other toward the self, but it is also true that the actor responds to his own normative response and hence is orienting to it as an object.

Difficulties in the Attitudinal Emphasis. It is at this point, however, that the concept of social attitude leads to difficulty in social psychology. Because of the shift in emphasis from the objective aspects of values to the attitudinal aspects, and because of the insistence that values are attitudes without equal stress on the fact that they are *more* than attitudes, the assumption creeps in

[6] *Ibid.*, p. 135.
[7] Mead's lectures were published in *Mind, Self, and Society* (Chicago, 1934).
[8] *Ibid.*, p. 162.

that actors experiencing such attitudes as objects still conceptualize them as their own attitudes or the attitudes of others. The point of view of the actor in this repect is regarded as identical with the point of view of the scientific observer.

This weakness does not become immediately apparent in the writing of Mead himself, but manifests itself in the social-psychological theory of conscience, moral norms, and social rules that developed later. It is true that in *Mind, Self, and Society* there is no thoroughgoing discussion of values in their objective aspects—except as attitudes responded to by the actor—but this is a matter of emphasis and context, not of explicit theoretical rejection of the existence of such aspects. Mead was writing at a time when the concept of the mores was still a focus of attention for those who were writing sociological theory. In that context Mead was offering a social-psychological theory of social attitudes and their internalization, and this theory formed a counterpart to the theory of social organization stressing mores and institutions in their objective aspects. Nevertheless, the definitional stress of Faris and the neglect of the non-attitudinal objective aspects of values by Mead left the road open for a denial of those aspects by later writers. Thus an ever-increasing gap opened up between the sociological theory of the mores and the social-psychological theory of social attitudes.

The trouble probably also grew out of the fact that the sociological theory of the mores was not developing but standing still, whereas social-psychological theory was moving rapidly ahead. As late as 1933, the theory of values as objective mores was essentially the same as it had been at the time of the publication of Sumner's *Folkways* in 1907. It was an evolutionary, behavioral theory that made it possible for theorists to regard the folkways and mores as *irrational* elements of social life, necessary during primitive stages of human development but susceptible of being substituted for by rationally arrived-at and agreed-upon rules in a more scientific age. In this view, folkways are adaptive modes of behavior that change slowly through time as the conditions of a society's life change. Mores develop when the society is faced with a choice and must decide which modes of behavior are necessary for the welfare and survival of the society. Rules of behavior are developed that are supported by sanctions, regarded as real by the actors, and hence evoke attitudes of respect and reverence. Such rules are also supported by religious beliefs, which are essentially irrational in character and will be exploded as man learns more about himself. If, in place of slowly learned folkways, man can substitute scientific knowledge, then mores and religion can be replaced by rationally agreed-upon rules understood to be manifestations of shared attitudes.[9] Thus the theory of the mores offered no really strong opposition to the development that occurred in social psychology.

[9] Cf. Kingsley Davis, *Human Society* (New York, 1949), pp. 510-518, for an account of theories of religion with the rationalistic bias mentioned.

The tendency to believe that human beings viewing values objectively see them as agreed-upon and shared attitudes rather than as realities transcending attitudes can most easily be discerned in the way in which social psychologists have followed their discussions of the rise of the generalized other with a discussion of Piaget's *The Moral Judgment of the Child.* Lindesmith and Strauss, for example, follow their discussion of the generalized other with an account of Piaget's findings. From the evidence that the young Genevan is a "moral realist" up to the age of five, and that following that the child ". . . realizes that moral rules are not objectively real, but reflect group values," they conclude that "Piaget has demonstrated *in general* that the child's conception of moral rules changes from the belief that rules are absolute to the knowledge that they are agreed upon."[10]

The amazing thing about these words is that Lindesmith and Strauss do not, in light of the theory of the mores, see that any problem is posed here. If we know anything from social history, it is that, over most of the span of human existence, human beings have regarded moral values and the mores as real. If what Piaget says about the Genevan children is true, then the source of their conceptions, either as Swiss or as representatives of modern Western culture, constitutes a problem to be solved.

VALUE AS A SUPERFLUOUS CONCEPT

Despite the weaknesses in the way in which social psychologists conceive values, the concept remains for them a central idea crucial to the understanding of human action. For another group of sociologists, the positivists—or, as they sometimes prefer to call themselves, the natural-science sociologists—the concept has little or no significance. Indeed, they view it either as a name for certain established relations among directly observable phenomena that adds nothing to the explanation of such phenomena, or as another of the imaginary entities that have been created by interpretative sociologists out of their abysmal confusion and ignorance of scientific method. The most complete statement of this position is to be found in a recent paper by Adler, although the point of view goes back into the late twenties and thirties.[11]

Adler begins the serious part of his critique with the following charge:

> Interpretative sociologists need the value-concept for a specific purpose. That is, they want to discover entities in the mental behavior of people by which they can "explain and understand" rather than merely "describe" their behavior. . . . This feeling of quasi-aesthetic satisfaction is the final aim of interpretative sociology. In that, it differs from natural-science sociology

[10] A. R. Lindesmith and A. L. Strauss, *Social Psychology* (2nd ed.; New York, 1956), p. 399 [italics mine]. See also Muzafer Sherif, *An Outline of Social Psychology* (New York, 1948), pp. 258-259.

[11] Franz Adler, "The Value-Concept in Sociology" (unpublished paper presented at the annual meeting of the Southwestern Sociological Society, April, 1954).

which sees its primary aim in prediction and does not search for emotional satisfaction for its own sake.[12]

This charge is valid. It can be demonstrated without too much difficulty that most interpretative sociologists really believe people have thoughts, aspirations, and emotions; they tend to consider the total range of man's actions, internal and external, as more important than just the directly observable aspects of action; and they have a genuine desire to understand a wide range of human experience. *However, these proclivities do not necessarily imply soft-headedness*. The interpretative sociologists' primary aim may be explanation and understanding, but he knows, quite as well as the positivist, that one of the major tests of explanation is successful prediction. The difference is one of emphasis, not of the manner in which any scientific concept must finally be tested. This is true of the concept of value. The interpretative sociologist is willing to let the concept stand or fall on the proposition that it does help in explaining and understanding social action, and that proof of this lies in the fact that certain testable predictions concerning action can be made by means of it that cannot be made without it.

According to Adler, this proposition is false. Values are either the summarizing generalizations concerning certain observable actions occurring under certain observable conditions, in which case they do not explain but can be used for purposes of prediction, in that, if one finds the observable conditions in a particular instance, he can predict the course of action; or they are imaginary entities that serve only to confuse the search for the conditions under which social phenomena recur.

The error of the interpretative sociologist lies, according to Adler, in his belief that the generalized principle adds something to the explanation of the relation holding between situation and act in which the principle is exemplified. Actually, he continues, the principle simply summarizes the relation between conditions and action that is present in each instance. But the difficulty with Adler's analysis is that the interpretative sociologist does not use the value-concept in this fashion. If he comes across a series of community studies where the researcher has described the church-going pattern of men, he is likely, because of the inclusion of the value-concept in his theoretical frame of reference, to impute to the members of the communities some such value as "people ought to go to church on Sunday." He is likely to believe that the statements of mothers to their sons that they should go to church manifest this value; that the men experience this value as an object in the statements and actions of the ministers and bankers; and that they themselves share this value as a dynamic attitude, are aware that they hold the value, and attribute to it a transcendental reality as a requirement of God. He believes that he can observe the value directly in the statements and the overt

[12] *Ibid.*, p. 16.

actions of all the people interacting with one another, and that he can impute it as a non-observable element of orientation and object of experience in the internal conversations which each person holds with himself. Thus, whether or not justified in his observations and inferences, he is not simply using the descriptive generalization of the directly observable data as an entity.

REVIVAL OF THE VALUE-CONCEPT: ZNANIECKI

Despite the position taken by the positivists, the value-concept remained in the main stream of American sociological thought. Into the middle thirties, it continued to be bound up, in its objective dimension, with the concept of the mores as formulated by Sumner. In its *subjective* aspects it had become an element of the new social psychology, in which, as we have seen, it tended to become separated from its own objective character as a reality transcending attitudes. Before the close of the decade, however, there was to emerge a new, yet old, conception of value that would once more unite both the objective and the attitudinal aspects of the concept and make it the central concept in sociological theory.

The revival of the value-concept in all its dimensions as a dynamic attitudinal variable and as an object of orientation did not grow out of American social psychology; rather it grew out of the thinking of those theorists who treated values in the first instance as objects experienced by the actor. One of the results of this has been that the sociological theory of values has not yet made full use of the resources of social psychology. Witness the fact that one of the two major contributors to the development of a systematic theory of values, Znaniecki, has denied the relevance for sociology of the theory of personality as an organized system of attitudes and actions; and that the other, Parsons, has integrated the sociological theory of values with a body of psychological theory, but instead of drawing on the symbolic-interactionist tradition of Mead and Faris, has committed himself to the ministrations of Freud.

Turning first to Znaniecki, we find that he starts with the same basic concepts that Faris and Mead had used in laying the foundations of modern social psychology—namely, attitudes and actions.[13] Yet by his use of the cultural-datum concept, which always refers to objects experienced by an agent—objects that must always be taken by the scientific observer as they

[13] See the following works by Znaniecki: *The Method of Sociology* (New York, 1934); *Social Actions* (New York, 1936); and *Cultural Sciences* (Urbana, 1952). The statement of Znaniecki's theory that follows is taken from his most recent book, *Cultural Sciences*, since it presents the most complete statement of his position. It must be remembered that Znaniecki used the word "value" to apply to any meaningful object; hence he presents his theory as a theory of norms and standards, not as a theory of values. For the sake of terminological consistency, the word "object" will be used here for his word "value" and the term "value" will be used to designate the value-concept. But see another usage, closely paralleling Znaniecki's, in Chap. 6.

appear to the actor—he lessens the stress on attitudes as dynamic components of the agent's orientation and places emphasis on the content of the agent's experience. With the lessened stress on attitudes, the personality of the actor as a dynamic motivational system disappears. All that is left on the orientation side of the equation is the conscious agent; everything else is on the object side, including the image of the personality and ideological attitudes organized into systems of rules and norms.

Attitudes as Situational Definitions. Simple attitudes as volitional, affective, and cognitive elements of personality are, Znaniecki believes, of no use in attempting to generalize about human actions. "If the concept of attitude in the sense of 'the attitude of an agent' is to be preserved, it must be used as coextensive with the concept of definition of a situation by the agent." A definition of a situation is a process and a product of reflection on the part of the agent. It is an organization of simple psychological attitudes and hence is a complex psychological phenomenon itself. It is also a cultural phenomenon in that the situation as defined includes common data of human experience and the actor's selection and evaluation of these data may be shared with others.[14]

One type of situational definition is the result of the actor's reflection while in an actual situation and is an integral part of the actor's action in that situation. Znaniecki calls these definitions "realistic attitudes." A second type of definition of the situation is that verbally expressed by actors when they are not acting in the situation to which it refers. The situation is not then actual but is retrospective or prospective, or may even be the situation of another agent, actual or imaginary. The complex attitudes that constitute these definitions are social as well as cultural and psychological because they are expressed in communication, which is a social process. They are also cultural in that the verbal symbols used are cultural products, and the evaluations expressed may be shared by other agents. They have psychological implications in that the expressed definition is evidence of ideas, feelings, and volitions on the part of the agent. They are not, however, the same phenomena as the first type of definitions that have been described: "An attitude manifested by the agent in the course of his action and an attitude manifested by the author in a verbal statement are *entirely distinct* phenomena." The first kind can be studied only in the actions of the agent in the situation, whereas the second can be studied in their verbal form for what they are—namely, attitudes that people express in communicating with one another. The second kind of definitions are called "ideational" attitudes, since they affect directly not the actions to which they refer but thinking about the actions, and since they can be experienced by those who never apply them.[15]

Znaniecki calls the ideational attitudes that include standards and norms

[14] Znaniecki, *Cultural Sciences,* pp. 238-240, 242-248.
[15] *Ibid.,* pp. 248-260.

for judging objects and guiding action "ideological models of attitudes"—that is, these ideational attitudes are examples of right thinking about the situations to which they have reference. They are to be accepted not only by those in the situations to which they refer but by all members of the social group. Acceptance of the validity of such models may be considered more important than actually conforming to them in action; and they may be accepted as valid by people who do not actually conform to them and do not expect to. Nevertheless, many people do make an effort to conform to them in their actions; and actions that do conform constitute "realistic patterns of action." These patterned actions are integrated with other patterned actions through conformity with integrated systems of ideological models of attitudes, so that the actions are rendered mutually helpful and non-conflicting. This principle of organization, which Znaniecki calls "the principle of functional interdependence," makes possible the existence of systems of actions.[16]

A Critique of "The Definition of the Situation." There are several weaknesses in Znaniecki's argument, almost all of them the result of his insistence on minimizing the importance of the psychological dimension of attitudes and on accepting all social and cultural phenomena as the actor experiences them. These weaknesses fall into two groups, the first concerned with definitions of the situation, the second with the problem of conformity.

It will be remembered that Znaniecki defines the "definition-of-a-situation" attitude as a psycho-cultural phenomenon. It is a psychological phenomenon in that it contains elements of affectiveness, volition, and cognition. It is cultural in the sense that the objects of orientation are common data of human experience and that the way in which the actor orders them may be shared with other actors. Now this is certainly a cultural phenomenon in one sense of the term, but not in the sense that it has its primary existence as an object in the experience of the actor. Its primary existence is as an organized orientation of the actor toward the situation, an orientation that need not appear in the consciousness of the actor at all. It is, in other words, primarily a system of volitional, cognitive, affective, and evaluative elements through which the actor orients to the situation. The situation defined is not the definition of the situation. If the actor responds to his definition of the situation as a definition, it then becomes an object of his experience; but not before. Hence it cannot be taken only as the actor experiences it, but must also be taken in its dynamic psychological aspect as the scientific observer is able to observe and impute it.

What is the significance of treating the actor's realistic definition of the situation as an element of attitudinal orientation in the personality structure of the actor rather than as an object of his experience? Essentially it is that the actor may enter the situation with an already formulated definition of the

[16] *Ibid.*, pp. 268-270, 310-311.

situation. Znaniecki has denied this, asserting that the realistic definition of the situation emerges only if the person reflects on the situation, and that it can be investigated only as a part of the action. In order to defend this position he has to admit that people can act *without* defining situations.[17] This may be true in the sense that reflection is sometimes absent; but is it not more reasonable to suppose that the actor enters the situation with a definition already in existence, that he then may act without reflection, or that he may, on the contrary, experience conflicts in his definition, reflect, and formulate a new definition? If he formulates a new definition, the process of redefinition may eliminate some of the existing attitudinal elements, originate new ones, and reorganize the whole; but certainly some of the elements of the initial definition will still be present in the new one. If this is true, then it may be possible to make certain imputations concerning the definition with which the actor enters the situation; then, by observing the situation as it appears to the scientific observer, it may be possible to make some inferences concerning the way in which the actor is *apt* to redefine the situation and, from that, what the probable course of his action will be.

As a final criticism of Znaniecki's treatment of definitions of the situation as organized attitudes, we can say that what is true of ideational attitudes in general must be true of ideological models of attitudes. (The actor has heard these normative attitudes expressed and has expressed them himself.) These models exist as objects of his experience requiring responses of obligation and respect because of their *validity*. This is the important aspect of values that social psychologists tend to ignore. It is also true, however, that these norms are part of the system of ideational attitudes of the actor; and if they are ideational attitudes they can become elements of the realistic complex definition of the situation at the time of action. When the actor enters a situation to which these values are relevant, he starts to define the situation through them. Conflicting definitions already present or introduced by discordant elements in the situation may force reflection in which the situation is redefined.

Limitations in the Theory of Conformity. We now must consider Znaniecki's theory of conformity. Essentially, he explains conformity in terms of normative rules constructed in advance that seek to realize conscious purposes by integrating actions of group members. People must follow these rules because this is the only way particular ends can be achieved. This conclusion on the part of Znaniecki is dictated both by the fact that he treats the system of norms only as *objects* of the actor's experience, at the same time insisting that in sociological theory the reasons for conformity and for requiring conformity must be taken as they appear in the experience of the actor.[18] Even at this level, his explanation of conformity is inadequate, since

[17] *Ibid.,* p. 243.
[18] *Ibid.,* pp. 310-311.

it implies a purely instrumental ground (expediency) for the experienced validity of the norm, whereas in many actual instances, particularly in the case of supreme moral norms, the norm commands obedience, not as a means of realizing a purpose, but for its own sake.

Moreover, the theory is inadequate because it ignores both *attitudinal* and *functional* grounds for conformity. The norm can exercise a powerful influence for conformity to itself through its existence as a dynamic attitude. It may constitute such a dominant element of the definition of the situation that the actor may act according to it without reflection. Conformity may be further reinforced by other unconscious functional needs of the actor that conformity may satisfy. The actor need not be conscious of his desire for the approval of others and for his own self-approval through conscience, but these are nevertheless strong motives for conformity.

Despite these criticisms, Znaniecki's theory of values remains one of the two major systematic contributions to the modern sociological theory of values. His insistence on dealing with norms as objects of experience has its limitations, but it served to keep in the center of attention the fact that values are *objects* as well as attitudes.

REVIVAL OF THE VALUE-CONCEPT: DURKHEIM

The systematic writings of Znaniecki, the continued prominence of the concept of the mores in sociology texts, and the theory of norm internalization of the social psychologists attested to the permanent importance of the value-concept during the thirties. Yet someting more was needed to clarify the attitudinal and situational aspects of values and to place them in their present dominant position in sociological theory. This was a return on the part of American social theorists to the European roots of American theory, a re-appraisal that sought to discover in such theorists as Weber and Durkheim appropriate insights that had somehow been overlooked and that might serve to cast new light on contemporary theoretical problems. The thirties witnessed such a return in connection with a wide range of theoretical and methodological concepts.[19] Our concern, however, is specifically with the value-concept and its dual nature as element and object of orientation. Regarding this problem, our most significant ancestor is apparently Durkheim, and the man who probably recalled attention to him most urgently, Talcott Parsons.[20]

Collective Consciousness and the Division of Labor. According to Parsons, Durkheim had a persistent interest in the normative aspects of social life.[21]

[19] See for example Becker and Barnes, *op. cit.*, vol. 1, pp. 743-790 (primarily by Becker; see Table of Contents).

[20] Talcott Parsons, *The Structure of Social Action* (New York, 1937), pp. 301-470.

[21] For a different view, see Émile Benoît-Smullyan, "The Sociologism of Émile Durkheim and His School," in H.E. Barnes (ed.), *An Introduction to the History of Sociology*

In his concept of the *conscience collective* there is present the idea of shared beliefs and central values, but this concept is used in the description of the undifferentiated society of mechanical solidarity. In a society possessing organic solidarity through the development of a complex division of labor, the source of obligatory rules is to be found in the habitual ways of doing things.[22] Thus, in *The Division of Labor,* Durkheim takes one step beyond the utilitarians in recognizing the necessity for a system of norms in the ordering of a complex division of labor, but he says little or nothing about the nature of these rules in the experience of the actor and is utterly unable to account for their being obligatory.

A further hint is contained in Durkheim's discussion of what he regards as a secondary source of the division of labor. The primary source is to be found in the growth of population accompanied by an increase in the intensity and frequency of contact among the members of the population. Together with this, however, is to be found the "progressive indetermination of the *conscience collective.*" In the society of mechanical solidarity, social action is minutely controlled by shared values and beliefs, but as that society develops, values are detached from particular actions and take the form of general principles. Thus room is left for the development of the division of labor and its accompanying habit-based rules of contractual relationship. There is the suggestion that shared moral values actually play a role in the development of complex societies and hence are more than "mere habit become obligatory," although this description still fits the rules of contract.

Collective Consciousness, Values, and Types of Suicide. In a second empirical study, *Suicide,* the content of the *conscience collective* becomes the focus of Durkheim's attention.[23] In an effort to account for the rates of suicide in various social systems, Durkheim develops a theory based on the nature of shared central values and beliefs and on the breakdown of such systems of belief and their derivative norms.

In a social system where the central value-system stresses the importance of the group and depreciates the individual, one finds *altruistic suicide,* charac-

(Chicago, 1948), pp. 499-537. Benoît-Smullyan's reading of Durkheim places much more stress on Durkheim's social realism than on his account of the normative elements of human action. Becker's comments on Durkheim's strongly partisan role in the French "parochial school" struggle (*cléricalisme-laïcisme*) and his consequent effort to replace God with Society should also be noted. See John Gillin (ed.), *For a Science of Social Man* (New York, 1954), pp. 110-113.

[22] Parsons, *op. cit.*, pp. 318-324. Parsons recognizes that the term *conscience collective* can be translated as "collective consciousness" rather than "collective conscience," but he believes that the first of the two translations is really applicable only when Durkheim shifts his attention away from shared values and stresses the "outsideness" of social facts as a result of his positivistic frame of reference. Cf. however, Howard Becker, "Anthropology and Sociology," in Gillin, *op. cit.,* pp. 111-112.

[23] Parsons, *op. cit.,* pp. 324-338.

terized by sacrifice and the unimportance of the life of the individual. This type of social system has the characteristics of mechanical solidarity, but as a matter of group discipline rather than of lack of group differentiation.

Modern society, however, tends to be characterized by *egoistic suicide,* which is the result of (1) extreme pressure on the person to accept responsibility for himself and (2) of a substantial degree of isolation from other members of the social group. Again, this is brought about by a value-system that forces the individual to be free and that places a high ethical valuation on the individual personality.

A third type, *anomic* (or normless) *suicide,* is found where the normative system breaks down or fails to regulate social actions. In these instances the ends that men seek become boundless and the integration of personality breaks down because of the actor's inability to order his life. In this analysis there is the implication that the *conscience collective* orders and integrates not only social action but the human personality as well.

Social Rules as Constraints and Objects of Respect. In *The Rules of Sociological Method,* first published prior to the publication of *Suicide,* Durkheim is not primarily interested in the functions of rules or values but in defining the nature of "social facts" in the fashion of the positivists of his day. According to Parsons, Durkheim thinks of the actor as pursuing subjective and random ends in a rational manner but being forced to take into account, among other situational objects, certain social phenomena as external and constraining conditions of his action.[24] At this point in Durkheim's thought, the exteriority and constraining power of moral rules is a purely empirical phenomenon observable to both the actor and the scientific observer. Moral rules exist prior to their acceptance by an individual actor and they are forced upon him by the imposition or threat of sanctions.[25]

Parsons finds a very different point of view emerging in *L'Éducation morale.* In this work, Durkheim comes to see that moral norms constrain in the sense that actors feel compelled to obey them because of the attitudes of respect and obligation that they evoke. The element of exteriority remains,

[24] *Ibid.,* pp. 343-375. A careful reading of *The Rules* indicates that Durkheim did not conceive the person as possessing no personal moral values but that he did sharply separate these from values as shared elements of social action and did insist on the exteriority and constraining power of the latter.

[25] Parsons distinguishes two stages in this aspect of Durkheim's thought: The first, which is found in *The Rules,* is a stage in which empirical exteriority and constraint are independent of any human will whatsoever. The second is to be found in *L'Éducation morale* and indicates that the exteriority and constraint of moral rules rest largely in their existing prior to the actor and in their being supported by sanctions. My reading of *The Rules* fails to support this distinction. Exteriority as the existence of rules prior to their acceptance by the individual, and constraint and exteriority as dependent upon the existence of sanctions, are *both* present in the opening statement of the problem in pp. 1-10 of the Free Press edition.

according to Parsons, only in that moral norms constitute ". . . a system of binding norms not private to a given individual, but common to the members of a society." In addition to this redefinition of the nature of exteriority and constraint, Durkheim now holds that a moral rule is not truly moral unless obedience to it is held to be *desirable* as well as a matter of duty—that is, the individual's happiness and self-fulfillment are inextricably intertwined with such obedience.[26]

In Parsons' view, Durkheim has thus moved to a theoretical position in which moral values and norms have become ". . . in the Freudian term, 'introjected' to form a constitutive element of the individual personality itself."[27] In this fashion, Parsons, by his analysis of Durkheim, triumphantly moves to the same point of theoretical development achieved by Faris and Mead a decade earlier. Moral values are central, constitutive parts of human personality and thus are essentially normative attitudes. There is, however, a significant difference in that Parsons has retained the emphasis on the attitudes of respect, obligation, and desire toward moral norms that was characteristic of the earlier approach of Thomas and Znaniecki.

The Religious Aspect of Moral Values. Durkheim never reached a point in his thinking where moral values possess externality only in that they are shared by the members of society. For him, values are exterior to all members of the society and exercise moral constraint to the extent that they are dependent on and part of a reality transcending individuals. This reality is empirically present both for the scientific observer and for the actor; for the actor it is the locus of moral authority that commands the attitudes of respect, obligation, and obedience and that by being present within the actor as well as external to him creates a desire to fulfill one's self by obedience.[28]

The peculiar attitudes that are evoked by this reality cannot be evoked by the self or by others as individuals or as a collection of individuals. The being that can command these attitudes must possess a richer and more complex life than human individuals. Durkheim knows of only two entities that meet this requirement: society considered as a reality transcending its members, and the supernatural. "Between God and society lies the choice."

Although Durkheim recognized that most people at most times and at most places have conceived this reality as divine, he sees in ". . . the Divinity only society transfigured and symbolically expressed."[29] Thus, although the actor may experience the reality in which external values are situated as a

[26] *Ibid.*, pp. 378-390, 407.

[27] *Ibid.*, p. 388. This connection between the thought of Durkheim and of Freud was noted by others at approximately the same time. See Becker and Barnes, *op. cit.*, pp. 930-931.

[28] Émile Durkheim, *Sociology and Philosophy*, translated by D. F. Pocock (Glencoe, Ill., 1953), pp. 44-45, 54-55. The important argument is found in "The Determination of Moral Facts," pp. 35-62.

[29] *Ibid.*, pp. 49-52.

non-empirical supernatural reality, he is actually, according to Durkheim, being constrained and awed by the moral authority of society.

Yet there is in this final formulation of Durkheim's position an insoluble dilemma. Society can command the moral respect of the person only if it is, or appears to the actor as, something more than an organized system of parts struggling simply to maintain itself. For Durkheim it is something more: "In a word, society is nature arrived at a higher point in its development, concentrating all its energies to surpass, as it were, itself." Here is one of Durkheim's most unqualified assertions of social realism. The primary function of society is to be the source and guardian of the highest human values and to be the center of a moral life. If this is true, then society commands respect because and to the extent that it is a moral phenomenon in the eyes of the actor, rather than because it provides a locus for the authority of moral values.[30] In turn, if moral values still require a transcendent reality to give them validity, that reality cannot be society; it can only be superempirical.

Where do we find in Parsons an account of the non-empirical realm to which we have assigned the external location of moral values? It is in his criticism of Durkheim's theory of religion—a criticism that, up to a point, is similar to the one he makes of Durkheim's identification of moral values and society, but that, beyond that point, is extended to include the concept of a non-empirical reality. According to Parsons, Durkheim, in his theory of religion as in his theory of moral values, attempts to assimilate the cognitive orientations of actor and scientist. The result is that in Durkheim's eyes religious ideas are about social reality, and holy objects (empirical and non-empirical) are symbols of society.[31] Holy objects of empirical nature have nothing to identify them as a class of objects except the attitudes of respect, reverence, awe, and obligation that are taken toward them. Thus, for Durkheim, they possess this attribute because they represent some empirical reality that is capable of inspiring these attitudes. Since the attitudes inspired by religious objects are the same as those inspired by moral values, it seems likely that a common reality stands behind both kinds of phenomena. Durkheim's insistence that this reality be empirical leaves society as the only possible entity that can constitute it. Yet if society commands respect only because it

[30] *Ibid.*, pp. 54-55, 80-97; Parsons, *op. cit.*, pp. 390-391. Although Parsons is aware of this fact, he did not use it at this point of his thinking to establish the externality of values in the eyes of the actor.

[31] Parsons, *op. cit.*, pp. 413-414, 417. I have used the word "holy" here rather than Parsons' term "sacred" because of the generally broader meaning given to the latter word, so that it includes all objects treated with extraordinary respect rather than only those that are grounded in the actor's experience of a non-empirical reality. See Howard Becker, "Sacred and Secular Societies," *Through Values to Social Interpretation* (Durham, N. C., 1950), pp. 249-250, footnote 2. See also his essay, "1951 Commentary on Value-System Terminology," in Becker and Barnes, *op. cit.*, vol. 1, pp. i-xxii, and Chap. 6 of the present volume.

is the center of a moral life or is itself composed of moral norms, it cannot be the reality that lends moral authority to norms or to empirical and non-empirical religious objects that symbolize it.[32]

The Place of the Value Concept in Sociological Theory

THE INTEGRATIVE FUNCTION OF VALUES

While sociological research and teaching have been to a large extent concerned with "social problems," social theorists have focused their attention on the more basic problems of social organization, social order, and social change. Although it can be argued that our sociological ancestors from Comte to Park have viewed the emergent urban industrial order as a social problem in itself, and certainly as a source of social problems, it must be recognized that all of them felt the necessity of having a fundamental theoretical conception of the nature of society, its conditions of existence, its structural patterns and dynamic processes, and its modes of change. It is in this context that the value-concept from the very beginning has been treated as a conceptual element in the theory of social order, and more recently in the theory of social integration.

Values as Means of Control. It will be recalled that Thomas and Znaniecki spoke of the values in which sociologists are interested as ". . . more or less explicit *rules* of behavior by which the group tends to maintain, to regulate, and to make more general and more frequent the corresponding types of action among its members."[33] Thus at the beginning of the period with which we have concerned ourselves, we find the major emphasis placed on the *control* function of values in social life. More important, however, is the fact that the passage indicates clearly the sharp limits placed on the use of the value-concept in American social theory prior to the thirties and even later, as was pointed out earlier in this chapter.

In the Thomas and Znaniecki passage, the rules are not seen as an integral element of action creating and directing the very flow of action, but rather as something outside and corresponding to action, serving merely to secure more frequent conformity with an already established pattern of action. The creation of patterns of action, their functional articulation with one another, are, it is implied, problems already solved. There is a separation here between action and symbolic elements of action-orientation that in modern social theory can no longer be supported.

[32] Parsons, *op. cit.*, pp. 414-417.
[33] Thomas and Znaniecki, *op. cit.*, vol. 1, p. 31.

Before examining in detail the use of the value-concept in American theory prior to 1937, it is necessary to return briefly to Durkheim, Spencer, and Sumner, for it is out of the writings of these men that the relatively minor part assigned to values in the twenties and the thirties derives. For Park and other postwar American theorists, perhaps Spencer's greatest contribution was his theory of functional differentiation, organization, and integration. According to Spencer, society is fundamentally an economic system in which men live and work together because they are useful to one another. Out of competition, which is the fundamental societal process, emerges the social order. This order is characterized by an expansion of structure, greater complexity of interrelated functions, and a higher degree of integration as the process of competition occurs among larger and larger numbers of people.[34] Stability of the system is secured because of the interlocking of self-oriented interests and of habits grounded in those interests.

We have already seen that Durkheim attacked this point of view in his *Division of Labor* by arguing that contractual relations presuppose an existing body of laws shading off into moral rules, and in so doing he pointed to his central concern (derived from Comte and from the turmoil of his own times), the problem of moral consensus. But in this early work, it will be recalled, Durkheim derives the division of labor from competition and the dynamic density of population; the rules governing interaction in this system become obligatory in and through habit. Thus, although his focus of interest is different, there is a point of articulation between this stage of Durkheim's thought and the thought of Spencer.

In Sumner, the linkage between the struggle for existence, the emergence of integrated social-habit systems, and finally of folkways and mores is completed. A theoretical synthesis of the Comtean and Spencerian points of view is accomplished in which competition is the process that gives rise to a social order and its integration, the required actions become habitual, the habits become social, and the social habits become obligatory in the face of challenges to the stability of the system. It is essentially this synthesis within which the postwar theorists worked, although it showed constant signs of strain whenever an effort was made to deal with the *dynamics* of moral consensus and its place in the ordering of social life.

Reuter and Hart made the most rigorous effort thoroughly to systematize this point of view in its relation to the value-concept, while others proceeded to stress the area of human ecology, in which they did not feel it necessary to introduce the element of value.[35] The statement of these two

[34] Again because of the focus of our interest on the post-World War I period, the description of Spencer's theory has been taken from his American interpreters. See R. E. Park, "Sociology, Community, and Society," *Human Communities* (Glencoe, Ill., 1952), pp. 178-209, and especially p. 180.

[35] E. B. Reuter and C. W. Hart, *Introduction to Sociology* (New York, 1933), pp. 114-

men constituted the definitive formulation of value-theory in sociology—although not, as we have seen, in social psychology—until late 1937, when the publication of *The Structure of Social Action* provided major stimulus for thoroughgoing revision of the theory.

Values as Products of Interests and Conflicts of Interest. For Reuter and Hart, as for others who worked in the theoretical tradition described above, the initial order arising among an aggregate of human beings is that produced by the process of competition. "The struggle for existence and competition among men inevitably result in some sort of order." This is the order of Spencer, the order of men ". . . who act independently of another, who compete and struggle with one another for mere existence, and treat one another, as far as possible, as utilities."[36] Out of struggle there emerges a division of labor, the complexity of which is dependent on the size of the population and the level of technological development; its functional integration and cohesion, moreover, are dependent on the interlocking of self-interested motives and on adaption to the resources of the natural environment.

Stability of the system developed in the manner outlined above is achieved by the process of habit formation. So long as men can satisfy their needs in the system of interlocking self-interested acts, the required actions will tend to become habitual. The child born into the system finds that his needs are met by developing habits that fit into the habits of others. The uniformities of habit common to the members of the society constitute the folkways or the customs of the group.

Because human beings engage in communication and tend to expect the habitual, some additional motivation to conformity to the folkways is to be found in the effort to avoid being conspicuous or becoming an object of ridicule. Essentially, however, the folkways are simply the shared non-normative patterns of behavior shaped in the struggle for existence and become habitual through success.

The order established initially by competition and supported by custom inevitably possesses a varying degree of instability due to the presence of changing conditions. The major sources of the threat to the social order are first, the introduction of strange people and behavior patterns into the society, and second, the fact that in many instances ". . . customs of long standing become progressively less well adapted to the needs of a changing group."

The result of the strains introduced by these two sets of factors is conflict, and out of conflict there emerges a moral consensus containing norms supported by sanctions and regarded by the members of the society as morally binding on their actions. These norms or values for the most part are simply

172. For the most systematic account of human ecology available, see Amos Hawley, *Human Ecology* (New York, 1950).

[36] Reuter and Hart, *op. cit.*, p. 134; Park, *Human Communities*, p. 180.

the habits and the folkways, or that section of them, become obligatory, now regarded as vital to group welfare.[37]

Critique of the Utilitarian Theory of Values: Parsons and Functional Value-Theory. This implicit theory of values is still to be found in the introductory textbooks, but it has been sharply challenged by several recent writers. The nature of the challenge is perhaps best indicated by Parsons in his statement that "A social order resting on interlocking of interests alone, and thus ultimately on sanctions, is hence hardly empirically possible though perhaps theoretically conceivable, given the order as an initial assumption."[38] Values are thus functionally necessary in the creation and maintenance of social order.

According to the holders of this view, the fundamental deficiency of the Reuter and Hart account of the origin and maintenance of order is their failure to realize that non-normatively oriented interaction among men is not really analogous to or homologous with biotic competition among animals. Animals have limited sets of biological needs, and given an absence of direct contact that results in conflict, an impersonal biotic competition may well be the dominant process of interaction. But man participates in social life as a seeker of culturally defined ends, and such ends, if not normatively limited, tend to be limitless.

The approach to order in social systems, growing out of this critique and manifested in the writings of Parsons, Davis, and others, is not evolutionary or historical in character but focuses on the social system as a going concern.[30] The unit of social systems is the social role, a complex of action-orientation elements and actions, always interrelated with at least one other social role of one other social actor. Thus the prototype of the social system is the interaction of two social actors in the playing of social roles relative to one another, although the only whole social system is a society, a social system that meets all the prerequisites of long-term persistence from within its own resources.

In analyzing the interaction of actors in a social system, the functional value-theorists utilize the *action frame of reference*. The actor is seen as orienting or relating himself to the empirical objects of his situation in ways motivated by the demand for gratification of needs. This process of orienting always contains two fundamental aspects: the first, a cognitive aspect by which the actor discerns and comes to know the qualities and the performance of the

[37] Reuter and Hart, *op. cit.*, 133-136, 144-157.

[38] Parsons, *op. cit.*, p. 404.

[39] The following account of the structural-functional analysis of social systems is drawn from Parsons, *loc. cit.* ... Kingsley Davis, *Human Society* (New York, 1949); Talcott Parsons, *The Social System* (Glencoe, Ill., 1951); Talcott Parsons and E. A. Shils, "Values, Motives, and Systems of Action," in Parsons and Shils (eds.), *Toward a General Theory of Action* (Cambridge, Mass., 1951), pp. 45-275.

object as they relate to his needs and interests; the second, a tendency to respond toward the object as a source of gratification or deprivation, a "cathectic," conative, or desiring tendency. In any situation, however, the objects offer various possibilities of gratification and knowledge, so that orientation always involves an element of selection or "evaluation."[40]

Actions, however, seldom occur singly, but rather in chains or systems developing through time. If these systems or chains of action of a single actor are to be ordered, they must be ordered by evaluative orientation on the part of the actor. If they are ordered in terms of a goal to be achieved at the end of the chain of action—instrumental ordering—the actor utilizes his cognitive ideas and his standards of correct knowledge according to the norm of efficiency. If, on the other hand, within a limited situational context, he is primarily interested in a continuous flow of gratification, he may organize his actions in terms of a scale of preferences using appreciative values as standards for his judgments.[41]

The actor, however, has the additional problem of integrating the total system of orientations and actions that constitutes his personality.[42] Gratifications, either ultimately or immediately available, and instrumentally selected means must be chosen and renounced in relation to their import for the maintenance of the personality as a going concern. Thus action must be oriented to another category of values—namely, moral values, which function in such a manner as to bring about the unity of the personality. These personality-integrative moral values define an ideal mode of personality integration. Conformity to the ideal personality norm itself is defined as a gratifying end and exists coequally with other core ends. These core ends serve to unify (1) the *order* in which subordinate gratifications are sought and (2) the *means* employed to seek them. They require the renunciation both of means and of ends disrupting the integration thus achieved.

To this point we have ignored the social-interactional context of the actor's orientations; social objects are, however, frequently present in the situation. The presence of this class of empirical objects introduces what Parsons calls the elements of double contingency, the fact that the actor's needs are dependent for their satisfaction on the actions of the social objects, and these in turn are to a great degree dependent for their course on the actions of the primary actor. If these actions are to be ordered into a system enduring through time, each actor must be able to predict on the basis of his expectations the actions of the others, particularly in relation to his own available courses of action. But more than predictability is involved, for the ends pursued, the means employed, and the gratifications immediately sought

[40] Parsons, *The Social System,* pp. 6-7. The use of "cathexis" points to Parsons' Freudianism.

[41] *Ibid.,* pp. 48-49.

[42] Davis, *op. cit.,* pp. 238-41.

by each actor must be articulated with and compatible with those of the other members of the system, Here, again, certain ways of orienting to empirical objects in the situation, including the social objects, must be renounced and other ways enjoined. Although certain areas of such a social system can be integrated through orientation to instrumental standards and appreciative standards governing shared orientations toward means and ends on the one hand, and ordered series of shared gratifications on the other, the over-all integration of the system can be obtained only by mutual orientation toward shared moral value-standards. These values perform the function for the social system that personality-integrative values perform for personality. They define a mode of social-system integration both as an ideal, and at the actual organizational level, as a sanctioned achievable end. Further, they define ideal and expected rights and obligations of the actors in their direct relations with one another, and they control and limit the range of private ends and the means used to achieve them insofar as such means and ends impinge on the integration of the social system.[43]

Motivational conformity to moral values at the level of action is secured through the institutionalization of the values. At the deepest level this occurs through the internalization of the values so that the actor develops a motivational need that is satisfied directly through conformity to the value. In addition, the primary actor may find that conformity is directly instrumental to the achievement of other ends, and indirectly instrumental through calling forth interest-furthering actions on the part of the others in the situation. Finally, the actor has certain gratification interests directly related to responses of approval and disapproval on the part of other members of the system.[44]

The Source of Moral Values: Some Unavowed Implications of Functionalism. However, the *source* of moral values remains an unsolved problem with which the functional theorists have shown a peculiar reluctance to grapple. Davis is equally vague on the subject. "They must, therefore, arise as a cultural emergent. They must spring from the dynamics of communicative interaction in a group that maintains itself by cultural adaptation."[45]

These statements are true as far as they go, but they certainly do not go very far. Despite the reluctance of the functional theorists to face up to the problem in specific terms, there are scattered throughout their writings, particularly in *Human Society, The Structure of Social Action,* and *The Social System,* some specific passages and some subtly implicative passages from which a theory of "source" can be tentatively derived. It may be that the functional theorists will be unwilling to agree to the fully developed implications of their theory; but the implications are there, and constitute the

[43] Parsons, *The Social System,* pp. 10-11, 50-52.

[44] Cf. Davis, *op. cit.*, pp. 37-38, 53-54, 144, 526.

[45] Parsons and Shils, *op. cit.,* pp. 171-172; Davis, *op. cit.*, pp. 144, 526.

only adequate answer to the question of source if the older "mores" theory is rejected.

Values and the Non-Empirical Realm. The qualities of moral values, which command the sense of awe, reverence, obligation, and obedience, are closely connected in the minds of the actors with their orientations to non-empirical objects. The values are felt to be valid because of their roots in this realm of the non-empirical. Thus Davis says:

> It seems generally true that religious belief explains and makes real the common-ultimate ends, and that religious ritual strengthens and renews these ends in the minds of the participants. . . . The unseen world is of course fictitious, but it must appear real to the actor if it is to accomplish its function of rationalizing and justifying his ultimate group ends.[46]

But it is necessary to examine the nature of the non-empirical realm. There are, according to Parsons, certain cognitive problems "which are not susceptible to solution by the methods of empirical science." In attempting to find answers to them, therefore, man is forced to develop conceptions of non-empirical entities or of non-empirically determinable qualities of empirical objects.[47] There are also problems of emotional adjustment to the condition of human finitude and helplessness in the face of the cosmos; and, after the institutionalization of a value-system, to the discrepancy between performance and normative expectation.

Levels of Non-Empirical Valuation. Although the problems outlined above can be approached in a cognitive manner, they are of intrinsic cathectic significance to actors, since they are primarily problems of adjustment to the universe and to the vicissitudes of life. When the cathectic dimension is added to the beliefs, they become evaluative or religious in some respects or levels. The first level of evaluation involving the non-empirical is composed of direct *expressive* orientations toward the non-empirical objects and *instrumental* orientations toward achievement of transcendental ends.[48] Since it is a primary characteristic of these non-empirical entities that they command attitudes of respect, obligation, reverence, and awe, both the direct cathectic orientations and the instrumental orientations toward the non-empirical are characterized by these attitudes. It must be remembered that non-empirical entities are not necessarily gods in the popular meaning of that term. They are objects set apart by attitudes of respect, reverence, awe, and obligation. They may be viewed as preternatural rather than supernatural, but the attitudes they evoke are much the same.

There is, however, a second level of evaluative orientation toward the non-empirical. This level is marked by the relationship between the non-empirical and the first level of evaluation on the one hand and by the moral

[46] Davis, *op. cit.*, p. 527.

[47] Parsons, *The Social System*, pp. 329, 360-361.

[48] *Ibid.*, pp. 367-368; Davis, *op. cit.*, pp. 128-129.

norms that serve to integrate the complexes of action in the everyday world of the social system on the other. "Religious beliefs then are those which are concerned with moral problems of human action, and the features of the human situation, and the place of men and society in the cosmos which are most relevant to his moral attitudes, and value-orientation patterns."

Both the cognitive and the cathectic aspects of religious evaluative orientation are of significance for the system of moral norms regulating human behavior. The cognitive aspect justifies and rationalizes the system of moral values by connecting them with the realm of the non-empirical, whether supernatural or preternatural, and with the active orientations that actors take toward the non-empirical. Once this connection is established, the moral norms become suffused with the non-empirical qualities commanding attitudes of respect, reverence, awe, and obligation.[49] In this manner moral norms themselves become anchored in the realm of the non-empirical and derive their own power to command attitudes of respect and obligation from that position.

Moral Norms Based on Imputed Meanings. It is precisely at this point that, in the opinion of the writer, the functional theorists fail to face up to the full implications of their theoretical position. The functional prerequisites of social systems and personalities, and the interests of men in the objects of the empirical world, create the need for integration and impose limits on the variability of the modes of integration possible; but we have seen that they do not and cannot furnish the conditions that produce moral values or their content. On the other hand, if man's cognitive orientation to the non-empirical world results in his imputation to that world of a system of meanings, and if his cathexis of these meanings is determined by his attitudes of reverence and awe toward non-empirical objects, then these meanings can give rise to a system of moral norms and can furnish the basis of their compelling legitimacy.

It is probable that functional theorists have avoided commitment to this explanation of the source of values because of its apparently emanationist nature—that is, it may appear to imply that society is simply a product of religious ideas. Actually, all that its exponents do claim is that the birth and the content of value-systems is rooted in man's orientation to the non-empirical world. It recognizes that worldly interests and the functional prerequisites of personality and society limit the possible modes of integration,

[49] Parsons, *The Social System,* pp. 368-369, seems to derive the holy character of the non-empirical entities from the holy character of the moral norms. This is a reversal of the position he takes in *The Structure of Social Action,* where in his analysis of Weber, for example, the legitimacy of moral norms is seen as "the *institutional* application or embodiment of charisma." And charisma is defined as "the quality which attaches to men and things by virtue of their relations with the 'supernatural,' that is, with the non-empirical aspects of reality insofar as they lend teleological 'meaning' to men's acts and the events of the world" (pp. 668-669).

and that at every point such interests impinge on the process of religious thinking, religious feeling, value-derivation, and value-institutionalization.

VALUES AND SOCIETAL TYPES

If values determine both the fact and the mode of integration in social systems within the limits set by the functional prerequisites of social systems and personality systems, then, in large measure, those values that determine the dominant mode of social integration in a society should be useful for the purpose of classifying societies. These values are describable, according to Parsons and Shils, in terms of a set of five "pattern variables" representing the five choices between pairs of incompatible alternatives (dilemmas of action) that any actor in any situation must make in orienting to any other actor.[50]

Affectivity-Affective Neutrality. The first dilemma the actor faces in orienting to another actor is the question of whether or not he should seek immediate gratification in the situation without regard to any evaluative considerations, instrumental or moral. This pattern variable is called "affectivity–affective neutrality." A value obligating the actor to take evaluative considerations into account is affectively neutral; one requiring the actor to seek immediate gratification is affective.

Self-Orientation–Collectivity-Orientation. The second dilemma involves the conflict between the unshared interests of the actor with either those interests pursued by others in the situation or those shared by the actor and the others. This pattern variable is called "self-orientation–collectivity-orientation." A value requiring or permitting the actor to pursue certain private interests is self-oriented; a value requiring the actor to take the interests of the group or of other members into account is collectivity-oriented.

Universalism-Particularism. The third dilemma is posed by the problem of whether the actor should treat a social object in terms of some particular relationship to him or as a member of some universally defined class of objects. This is obviously a matter of emphasis, since in any interactive situation the fact that the other is related to the actor in some manner is important, and at the same time the other is a member of a class of objects. This pattern variable is called "universalism-particularism."

Ascription-Achievement. The fourth dilemma concerns the question of whether the actor should orient to the object on the basis of the latter's *performance* or on the basis of some *attribute,* such as age, sex, color, or position. The pattern variable is called "ascription–achievement" (more recently, "quality–performance"). A moral value requiring the actor to treat

[50] Parsons and Shils, *op. cit.,* pp. 76-79, 84. Parsons mentions a sixth pattern variable in his article, "Some Comments on the State of the General Theory of Action," *ASR,* 18 (Dec., 1953), pp. 618-631. But to the present time this pattern has not been thoroughly described.

the social object in light of the latter's attributes is ascriptive; a value requiring the actor to orient to the performances of the object is achievement-oriented.

Diffuseness–Specificity. The final dilemma is the question of the degree of involvement of the social actor with the social object. The pattern variable is called "diffuseness–specificity." A moral value requiring or permitting the actor to become involved in a wide range of expectations, rights, and duties with the other is diffuse; a value requiring or permitting an extremely limited range of such interests is specific.

It will certainly be noted that these pattern variables formulate ideas that have been common for a long time in sociological theory. The uniqueness of the pattern variables and their associated values is that *they are assumed to be exhaustive* of the dilemmas of action at the highest level of generality and that hence they can serve as a basis of exhaustive classification and description at that level.

SOCIETAL TYPES IN TERMS OF PATTERN VARIABLES

Parsons reduces the number of major societal types by selecting two of the pattern variables, ascription–achievement and universalism–particularism, as being more directly determinative of the integration of roles between actors. Thus four major types emerge: particularistic-ascriptive, particularistic-achievement, universalistic-achievement, and universalistic-ascriptive.

Instead of attempting to present a detailed description of the characteristics of these societal types, it may be more profitable to indicate their relationship to their source in systems of religious belief. Although this aspect is largely ignored in *The Social System,* the fact that these types are fundamentally drawn from Max Weber's sociology of religion is clearly indicated in *The Structure of Social Action.*[51]

The Particularistic–Ascriptive Type. The particularistic–ascriptive type tends to be organized primarily around kinship and locality structures. The normative patterns of such societies are thoroughly traditionalized and tend to be focused on dangers inherent in unrestricted expressive orientations and on certain situational dangers to the stability of the group. The members of the society tend to be expressively oriented and to adapt passively to the elements of ascription and to any superordinate structures of power and authority.[52]

Parsons cites Spanish-American societies as a good example of this societal type, but it is obvious that most preliterate societies fall into this category and that complex societies of this order must represent processes of immanent development from simpler types organized on the same basis. These simpler types in turn are closely related to Weber's conception of

[51] Parsons, *The Structure of Social Action,* pp. 563-575.

[52] *Ibid.,* pp. 198-199.

"primitive religion." Weber conceived "primitive" religion as a universal starting point for all more highly developed religions, characterized by a relatively undifferentiated complex of religious ideas, interests, value-attitudes, and acts in relation to things and non-empirical entities possessing the quality of charisma.[53]

The relationship between religion and the conformity-inducing qualities of particularistic-ascriptive value systems is clear, but the more central question of the manner in which such values have their source in religion is not. In part this is the result of the fact that Weber used his concept of primitive religion and the kind of traditionalized society to which it gives rise as a point of departure for the analysis of the ways in which more highly rationalized systems of religious belief give rise to other types of societal structure. Parsons' interest likewise is focused on the other three societal types. Yet, in one sense at least, the origin of particularistic-ascriptive value-systems is extremely important in that it poses once again the problem of the possibility of social order prior to the emergence of a value-system, a possibility denied by the modern value-theorists' emphasis on the inordinate goal-seeking of man and the inability of goal-seeking in itself to give rise to an integrated system of order.

As we have seen, particularistic-ascriptive societies are organized around the foci of biological and territorial relatedness. The crucial question, however, centers on the transition of man from a state where, like other animals, his needs are limited to those of biological survival, to the state of true man, where needs become potentially infinite and the realm of means also expands. Thus the need for a moral order emerges simultaneously with the emergence of man as true man, and at the same time the source of a system of values appears with the emergence of the realm of the non-empirical. If we conceive man to be limited at this point to a very low order of conceptual development, the only possibilities of order that would present themselves would be those organized around the already present limited foci of animal order. The emphasis would necessarily fall on the limitation of expressive and instrumental interests manifesting themselves as potential and actual disruptive elements impinging on kinship and locality relations, and on the transformation of the existing elements of animal order into a system of moral order.

The Particularistic-Achievement Type. According to Parsons, Weber was interested in the role of religious ideas as differentiating elements in social development, as factors involved in the challenging or strengthening of tradition in the structure of society. These possibilities emerge when systems of religious ideas move in the direction of rationally systematized attitudes toward significant aspects of life. At some point this development results

[53] *Ibid.*, pp. 564-566, 666-667.

in the challenging of tradition, and the breaker of tradition, speaking in the name of these changed religious conceptions, is a charismatic prophet. The development of religious thought may then take either of two paths, depending on the nature of the prophecy and the nature of the non-empirical realm to which the prophecy is related. There are two major types of prophecy, the *ethical* (or emissary) and the *exemplary,* and these are respectively bound up with transcendent personal conceptions of the non-empirical and immanent pantheistic conceptions. In either case, emphasis may be placed on *asceticism* or on *mysticism* as means of achieving salvation, and these in turn can be *worldly* or *other-worldly* in nature.[54] Out of the combinations of these variables new modes of social integration can therefore arise.

In Weber's view, exemplary prophecy and an immanent conception of the non-empirical are closely bound together. Such an orientation to the realm of the non-empirical cannot result in a set of ethical norms sharply challenging the traditional order, but it can impose upon its adherents certain attitudes toward the traditional order. If the attitudes are rejective of the everyday world, they may take the form of otherworldly asceticism or of otherworldly or worldly mysticism. In this event there may continue to be a passive adaptation to the rules of everyday life or a radical withdrawal from it. If, on the other hand, the attitude is one of worldly asceticism, the ideals set forth at the apex of the traditional order defining the proper relations among men may become the object of achievement-striving.[55] In either case, the points of reference for role-orientation remain particularistic, and certain ascriptive statuses are still of major importance. New achievement roles may emerge, however, and for the worldly type, *performance* in the areas of ascription becomes more important than the *qualities* involved in the ascription. The emergent roles in the case of otherworldly orientations are those of the mystic or the otherworldly ascetic; in the case of the worldly orientation, the role is that of the person who strives to adapt himself and to perfect himself both in relation to his kinship and locality obligations and to larger structures of power and authority, also organized on a particularistic basis.

Although this analysis has been drawn almost exclusively from *The Structure of Social Action,* the description of the patterns involved closely fits that of the particularistic-achievement-oriented society in *The Social System,* especially what might be called the "worldly-oriented particularistic-achievement society." Parsons' example of the particularistic-achievement society is the classical Chinese social structure, which is the society that Weber analyzed as one growing out of an immanent, exemplary-prophet-oriented, worldly system of religious ideas. Although Parsons in *The Social System* does not describe the otherworldly type of the particularistic-achieve-

[54] *Ibid.,* pp. 566-570.
[55] *Ibid.,* pp. 570-574.

ment-oriented society, the description of Weber's treatment of India as an example of this type in *The Structure of Social Action* should be noted.[56]

The Universalistic-Achievement Type. The other major strand of religious development in history is that combining a transcendent conception of the non-empirical and *ethical prophecy*. Non-empirical entities are conceived as standing outside nature, history, and the cosmos; and the ethical prophet proclaims a set of ethical norms challenging the traditional order in the name of the truly supernatural.[57] Such norms are universalistic in that they derive essentially from the relationship of all men or all societal members to the transcendental non-empirical, and they are achievement-oriented in that they define non-empirical and/or empirical goals to be pursued.

If the goals so defined are purely transcendental—for example, the necessity for the individual to strive for salvation in the *next* world—the impact of a transcendental ethical religion on the affairs of the world may be relatively slight. If, on the other hand, the pursuit of, or desire for, non-empirical ends is intimately tied in with strong ethical imperatives for change in the worldly order, universalistic-achievement orientations come to characterize the role-systems of everyday social interaction. The inherent individualism of achievement-orientation then becomes manifest; the person is motivated to pursue private economic goals within a strong framework of universalistic moral norms defining the limits of that pursuit. Large areas of the social structure become organized around instrumental rationality, and institutional restrictions on opportunity and mobility tend to be reduced to the limits set by those functional areas of society, such as kinship, which must remain particularistic and ascriptive. Moreover, the tendency is strong to reduce these areas to the smallest clusters of role-structure possible, so that the small conjugal family tends to replace the larger kinship structures.[58]

The Universalistic-Ascriptive Type. The final societal type delineated by Parsons, the universalistic-ascriptive society, must be approached in a different way from the other three cases. In this instance, the connection between Weber's typology of religion and the value-orientation type is missing, so that description of the type must precede judgment as to whether

[56] *Ibid.*, pp. 542-563, 573-574; Parsons, *The Social System*, pp. 195-198.

[57] Parsons, *The Structure of Social Action*, p. 568.

[58] Parsons, *The Social System*, pp. 178-183. Although the central features of the universalistic-achievement societal types have been derived from Weber's analysis of the rise of capitalism, and from features that other writers have found to be characteristic of urban industrialism in Western nations, these characteristics and their relationship to transcendental ethical religious beliefs have recently found confirmation in Goldschmidt's analysis of the culture of the Yurok, Hupa, and Karok Indians of Northwest California. See Walter Goldschmidt, "Ethics and the Structure of Society: An Ethnological Contribution to the Sociology of Knowledge," *AA*, 53 (Oct.-Dec., 1951) pp. 506-524.

anything can really be said about the nature of its possible religious origins.

The presence of the universalistic element in value-orientations results in the same emphasis on the sphere of instrumental action as in the case of the universalistic-achievement society; but the presence of the element of ascription modifies the nature of the emphasis, which is placed on the *status* of the actor rather than on what he does. His achievements are values almost solely in terms of their relevance to a collective goal, which may be the maintenance of an authoritarian state of affairs or the attainment of an essentially totalitarian state at a future time. The society tends to be highly politicized and aggressive in its relations with other societies. Old Germany is cited as an example of the conservative form of this type, and Nazi Germany and Soviet Russia as examples of the radical form.[59]

What then are the possible religious origins of this type of society? Here the full breadth of the functional definition of religion must be employed. There are, as we have seen, three fundamental aspects of this definition. First, religious beliefs must be concerned with non-empirical entities or non-empirical qualities of empirical objects—that is, the objects or qualities of objects must be ". . . inaccessible to scientific method or the equivalent cognitive value-standards in the culture in question."[60] Second, religious beliefs must answer questions of the meaning of man's existence and relate these answers to man's moral problems. Third, the non-empirical objects, the meanings of man and the cosmos, and the ethical or moral value standards all must have the quality of evoking attitudes of reverence, respect, and obligation—the quality of charisma.[61]

[59] Parsons, *The Social System,* pp. 191-194.

[60] *Ibid.,* p. 359. Becker, it should be noted, in his recent writings rigidly restricts the term "religion" to conduct governed by supernaturalism. In the case of some of the immanent rather than transcendent orientations, of course, the line between the preternatural and the supernatural is hard to draw.

[61] In the first part of this essay we spoke of the quality of holiness; in the present section we have used the term "charisma" more often. It would seem that the second of these terms includes the first, in that holiness appropriately applies only to the transcendent supernatural, whereas charisma is the awe-inspiring quality possessed by the immanent *or* transcendental non-empirical, *or* by the preternatural. The sacred would remain a more inclusive category than the holy or the charismatic, in that there are sources of attitudes of respect and loyalty other than those deriving from the qualities of non-empirical objects or empirical objects believed to possess preternatural attributes. In this manner we can take into account Becker's statement that simple people can make the subtle distinction between the holy and the non-holy, as in the ability of certain German peasants to distinguish between God as transcendent and Hitler as a preternatural charismatic leader, and hence to reject Hitler as a source of religious conduct. In terms of the present analysis this distinction would hold, but the preternatural Hitler would constitute an object tied in with the non-empirical object of the German folk, providing answers to the questions of the meaning of life and imposing those answers and their ethic by means of his preternaturally charismatic quality. In other words, both God and Hitler are foci for systems of sacred belief, but since the Christian God is supernatural

Now the non-empirical objects of universalistic-ascriptive belief-systems are neither transcendent nor immanent in the ways in which we previously have used these terms. There does seem, however, to be a type of historical immanence: empirical objects or processes in history are endowed with preternatural or even non-empirical characteristics that make them objects of respect and obligation. The emergence of these objects and processes may be associated with the decline in the power of transcendent or cosmic-immanent belief-systems and with the resultant need to find new sources of meaning and values. This process may be partly understood by the ease with which non-empirical and empirical beliefs concerning history can become confused, so that preternatural and/or non-empirical qualities may appear to have the status of scientific or at least empirical common-sense knowledge.

More than historically immanent objects and processes, however, are needed to account for universalistic-ascriptive value-systems, for objects and processes of this sort have developed in Western civilization as a support for universalistic-achievement values, as witness such sacred concepts as the doctrine of progress or the nation as a way of life. It is only when these processes or entities become objects of supreme devotion requiring the sacrifice of worldly interests that they can become a source of universalistic-ascriptive values. Thus the nation as a way of life remains traditionally sacred, and as such tends to support values inherited from the past; but "the nation" or "the folk" or "the dialectic of history" become mystical entities hovering above or outside the life of the members of the society through which they can project goals requiring the extreme subordination of all interests to an instrumentally oriented effort directed toward the goal for the sake of the mystical entity. Certainly beliefs of this sort, although they are markedly ideological, have central elements of sacred belief in them that can serve as a source of universalistic-ascriptive values.[62]

and transcendent, God possesses holiness whereas Hitler does not. Cf. Howard Becker, "1951 Commentary on Value-System Terminology," in Becker and Barnes, *Social Thought from Lore to Science,* pp. viii-x. [EDITORS' NOTE: An attempt further to clarify this distinction is made in Chap. 6, "Current Sacred-Secular Theory and Its Development."]

[62] Parsons' only explicit discussion of the development of universalistic-ascriptive values tends to associate them with the functional exigencies faced by a social movement oriented in a worldly direction yet radically rejective of the given institutional order, as that movement gains ascendancy in the larger social system and grapples with the problem of disciplining and integrating the social structure. (*The Social System,* pp. 383, 525-529.)

Yet there are suggestions here and there that those social systems which have tended to remain organized around universalistic-ascriptive values have belief systems in which sacred or even holy elements of the sort described are present. Thus, "There may even, as in Marxist thought, be an attempt to fuse the two, projecting the 'supernatural' into a conception of the 'dialectic' process of history." (*Ibid.,* p. 370.) And "Nazism, on the other hand, projected the ideal state into a political future ideal, conceived to be an emanation of the mystically ideal qualities of the German *Volk.*" (*Ibid.,* p. 193.)

VALUES AND SOCIETAL CHANGE:
BECKER AND THE SACRED-SECULAR TYPOLOGY

One of the major problems of the comparative and historical analysis of large-scale social systems (or societies) has been the question of discernible or theoretically inferable direction in change. Unilinear evolutionary theories of social development, cyclical theories of history, and other patterns have been discerned, only to be criticized and later abandoned. In the functional theory, developed within the action frame of reference, a much more modest concept is present, but it is a concept which nevertheless offers a logical framework for the analysis of large-scale societal change. This is the concept that there is an inherent tendency toward rationalization of the cognitive belief-systems of culture, and probably a corresponding tendency in the patterns of expressive symbolism.[63]

It has, of course, been a common doctrine of culture theory that empirical cognitive belief-systems (science and technology) manifest a cumulative tendency. The functionalists claim, following Max Weber, that a tendency toward *rationalization* is also present in the non-empirical belief-systems (philosophy and religion). Moreover, this tendency toward rationalization and innovation in belief-systems is seen not as a culturally automatic process but as an action process characterized by predominantly cognitive and evaluative orientations. Finally, the tendency is viewed not as empirically dominant in every social system but, like "entropy" in physics, as an inherent trend of change as long as it is not interfered with by a large class of obstacles.[64]

If the central problem today, as in the nineteenth century, is considered to be the development of modern urban industrial society in its universalistic-achievement form, this problem can be seen as one form of the process of rationalization in the spheres of empirical and non-empirical belief. Out of a long irregular development in the systems of empirical belief have emerged the science and technology of the modern world, making possible a complex, instrumentally oriented division of labor. Out of an equally long and tortuous development of religious belief-systems oriented around transcendental non-empirical objects and ethical prophecy, combining the elements of the Greek and Hebrew traditions, have come the modern universalistic-achievement value-orientations integrating the major structural complexes of modern society, including those areas of activity in which scientific and technological knowledge is sought. It was Max Weber's delineation of this process of rationalization in the religious and philosophical sphere, and his demonstration of its importance for the emergence of the

[63] *Ibid.*, pp. 496-503. The analysis of this possibility in patterns of expressive symbolism is still so rudimentary that it will be of little use in the analysis of social change that follows.

[64] *Ibid.*, pp. 336, 499-502.

ethic that makes modern society possible, that constituted his great substantive contribution to the social sciences.

It is not possible to review this contribution here; but it may be instructive to sketch the relationship of Parsons' four societal types to the process of rationalization and other sources of change. To this end, it is helpful to relate the four pattern-variable types of Parsons to the sacred-secular types of Howard Becker as developed from 1928 onwards, for the sacred-secular types are focused specifically on the problem of the relationship of societal types to social change. In so doing, there will be little explicit reference to Becker's repeatedly stated proviso that "the path from one polar societal type to another is not a one-way street," but implicitly it is frequently taken into account.[65]

Proverbial Society and Resistance to Change. The particularistic-ascriptive society is an appropriate starting point because it corresponds to Becker's proverbial type. He defines a sacred society as one that impresses on its members ". . . modes of conduct making for a high degree of resistance to change." The obstacles to the process of rationalization are by definition, therefore, very great. At the heart of the obstacles, of course, is the particularistic-ascriptive value-system itself, with its stress on kinship and locality. The particularism and functional diffuseness of the key roles of the society serve to discourage both instrumental specialization in the tasks of everyday life and the growth of specialized roles in the spheres of cognitive orientation. Additional obstacles to such development are found in the absence of writing and in the vicinal, "social," and mental isolation of the society.[66]

A certain amount of immanent development is possible in a society of this sort. It is probable that a system of differential rewards and privileges —that is, a system of social stratification—and a center of authority will emerge; but these will be based on the same particularistic-ascriptive pattern, and will not in themselves serve as sources of further change. Change, of course, can begin with any element of a system, and the society may be required to adapt to fluctuations in population or in natural situational conditions. But if historical evidence is any indication, such changes cannot break the hold of tradition, but can, if severe, only lead the society in the direction of stagnation and misery. Furthermore, evidence is lacking that changes in these elements will lead to the shattering of the particularistic-ascriptive system.

If the rationalization process theorem is valid, the only way out of the traditionalism of the proverbial society is through the rationalization

[65] For our purposes, the best description of the sacred-secular typology is to be found in Howard Becker, "Values as Tools of Sociological Analysis," *Through Values to Social Interpretation,* pp. 3-92. The passage just quoted occurs on p. 91. [EDITORS' NOTE: Chap. 6 of the present volume supersedes this, terminologically speaking.]

[66] *Ibid.,* pp. 44, 46-49, 52-53.

of the system of religious beliefs, and this in turn must be dependent upon a set of conditions in which the solution of non-empirical cognitive problems becomes very urgent. In Weber's thought, according to Parsons, this was possibly an immanent process, once "primitive religion" reached the level of symbolic formulation. Becker, on the other hand, finds the sources of secularization—in the sense of tendencies toward rationalization of belief systems—in the breakdown of isolation and the development of culture contact. Given this contact, there may be a period of increasing normlessness, but out of it may develop new integrating values, or a revitalization of the old values.

Prescriptive Society and Sanctioned Rationality. The process of rationalization may not proceed far, however, if the non-empirical belief-system moves in the direction either of an otherworldly transcendental religion or in the direction of an otherworldly or this-worldly immanentism. In any of these instances, the new religion becomes essentially a possession of élites. In the case of the otherworldly transcendental religion, a system of universalistic-achievement values in the religious sphere develops, but the mass of the society may be retraditionalized in a particularistic-ascriptive pattern. In the event of a development toward an immanent, pantheistic conception of the supernatural, of either a worldly or an otherworldly variety, a pattern of particularism and achievement is likely to develop to define the roles of élites, and the masses again remain at the level of "primitive religion" and particularism-ascription.

Social change in any of these directions would appear to result in subtypes of Becker's *prescriptive* society. In this type of sacred society there is developed an explicit body of dogma giving rise to sanctioned rationality of action—that is, action in conformity with explicit moral rules enforced by authoritarian or totalitarian sanctions.[68] In the present instances, sanctioned rationality would apply mainly to élite groups, and the masses of society would still be under the domination of traditional rules. Such societies, although perhaps vicinally accessible and to some degree literate, will maintain barriers that insure social and mental isolation. Science and technology may be at a somewhat higher level than in the pure proverbial society, but they are still blocked by traditionalism and religion.

It is a somewhat different matter with the otherworldly, universalistic-achievement type of prescriptive society. This type of society has already partially institutionalized a set of universalistic-achievement values. Its universalism gives it a cognitive emphasis, at least in the realm of the religious and the philosophical, and it is not without interest in cognitive knowledge of the empirical world. Furthermore, as in the case of the

[67] Parsons, *The Social System,* p. 363; Parsons, *The Structure of Social Action,* pp. 566-567; Becker, "Values as Tools of Sociological Analysis," pp. 68-69, 76-79.

[68] Becker, *op. cit.,* p. 57.

Judaic-Christian tradition, there is an element of this-worldly orientation that has emerged as a dynamic factor.

Principial Society and the Shaping of Social Change. Again, it is not vitally important for our purposes to decide whether accessibility and culture contact are necessary conditions for the further rationalization of this system. What is important is that if further rationalization occurs, it moves in the direction of extending universalistic-achievement values to the role systems involved in the everyday life of society. In this event science and technology become positively supported and institutionalized as do the areas of religious and philosophical thought. The institutionalization of universalistic-achievement values permits the emergence of a differentiated system of instrumentally oriented roles tied together in the complex of market relations, so that the division of labor can become increasingly complex. Individuals are permitted to pursue private interests within certain limits, and the political system and the system of social stratification move in the direction of greater democratization. As long as this society remains integrated, it is oriented toward the *acceptance* and *shaping* of social change. Thus the emergent universalistic-achievement society corresponds closely to Becker's principial society, which is vicinally, socially, and mentally accessible and positively oriented toward change.[69] But at its core is a set of values and non-empirical objects, *sacred* in Becker's use of the term, and also *charismatic* in the sense in which the term is here used.

The maintenance of a moving equilibrium in this type of society poses tremendous problems of integration, as the literature of modern social science attests. It is not possible for us to deal with these problems here, nor is there any need to do so, except to note that cumulative failure to solve such problems creates the conditions under which the society may become so relatively normless as to present the opportunity for reintegration on the basis of a different value-system. One aspect of these integrative problems, however, is of direct concern in that it has to do with the continued process of rationalization in the sphere of religious belief.

If a principial society is to remain integrated, one functional prerequisite to be met is that of continuing the sacred and charismatic character of the central value-system. This in turn is related to the consequences of the process of rationalization in both the religious and the empirical spheres. As we have seen above, the origin of the principial society is often to be found in the process of rationalization of religious beliefs focusing on the concepts of a transcendental god, ethical prophecy, and a this-worldly orientation. Thus its source is "holy" in the technical meaning of that term. But two elements in the process of rationalization tend to separate the secular value-system from its source, for as the process of rationalization

[69] Parsons, *The Social System,* pp. 335-348; Becker, *op. cit.,* pp. 74-76.

continues in the religious realm proper, the theologies that develop tend to lose the character of intermediate symbolism which they possessed in the past. Thus there develops a gulf between the religious belief-system of the people and that of sectors of the religious élite. At the same time the belief-systems of both the people and the religious leaders are subject to pressures issuing from the continuing rationalization of the empirical belief-systems. In American Protestantism, at least, the reaction to these pressures has been either the obscurantism of fundamentalism or the adaptation of religious beliefs to thought-systems that deny the existence of a significant non-empirical realm.[70]

It is a characteristic of the process of rationalization that, once the level has dropped, the process is renewed at the lower level. The older religious systems, grounded ostensibly in science and tending to accept the fundamental values of the institutionalized structure—such as the beliefs in evolutionary progress, the nation as a way of life, and man—have in large measure supported universalistic-achievement values and have generated only weak qualities of charisma in their non-empirical objects. Like the "primitive religion" from which they derive and to which they contribute, they serve as a source of mild charisma for the legitimate order.

The Proverbial-Prescriptive Type. But if there are strong trends within the social system toward various types of normless secularization and a series of external crises, there may be a functional demand for the revitalization of the value-system, or a set of conditions requiring some modification in it. Here the only source capable of inspiring the attitudes of respect and obligation is charisma of a powerful order. The "primitive religion" or faith in faith will no longer be sufficient, nor will the mild charisma of the older "naturalistic" empirical religions. The drop in the level of rationalization represented by fundamentalism means that such a faith will have little relevance to the problems of the integration of the universalistic-achievement society, although at a *personal* level there may be some integrative relevance.

Among the naturalistic, historically immanent religions, however, there are some semi-rationalized belief-systems relevant to the problem of integration. These are the systems in which the non-empirical objects, like the nation or history, derive charismatic power by being set over and against the people in their everyday lives. The state, the nation, the folk, and other objects can become objects of devoted worship, respect, and obedience and hence sources of integrative values. But since all these objects are forms of social organization, they inevitably result in the dominance of a mystically conceived social group over its members and an institutionalization of universalistic-ascriptive values. This would seem to be one

[70] Parsons, *The Social System,* pp. 377-378; Reinhold Niebuhr, *The Self and the Drama of History* (New York, 1955), pp. 109-110.

of the major aspects of the transition of a society from any other form to that of universalism-ascription, and particularly an aspect of the transition of the universalistic-achievement type to the universalistic-ascriptive pattern.

This emergent type represents another subtype of Becker's prescriptive society. It differs from the other subtypes that have been discussed by its attempt rigidly to organize the role-structure of the society on an ascriptive basis on the one hand, and, on the other, to maintain an instrumentally oriented dynamism in the scientific and technological spheres. This is true at least of the radical varieties of the universalistic-ascriptive type. The conservative type seeking to stabilize a system in *status quo* may renounce dynamism and change in every area. This type, conservative or radical, seems inherently unstable. If the radical type continues its emphasis on change in science and technology, its universalistic elements may ultimately give rise to tremendous strains that will break down the existing integration. What emerges will depend upon residual elements of other belief-systems and their capacity for rationalization. The conservative type, and the radical type become conservative, may gradually lapse into particularism and ascription through the rationalization and spread of residual elements of aspects of the belief-system supportive of such values; ". . . [prescriptive] societies never remain merely . . . [prescriptive] if they continue as societies for any length of time. What may be termed a . . . [proverbial-prescriptive] type is soon generated."[71]

To return to the universalistic-achievement society under stress for a final word, it may be pointed out that there is one other source of the functionally required charisma that is compatible with the values of that society. This source, in the instance of modern secular society, is the historically rooted belief-system of the Judaic-Christian tradition in its worldly-oriented form. This tradition has continued to be rationalized, but it has not swerved from its basic concepts of a transcendental, non-empirical, ethical prophetism, and worldly responsibility. Its basic values are those of universalism and achievement, although these are seen in the light of a transcendental ethic of love, by which they must be judged.

As sociologists, we cannot pass judgment on the truth or falsity of this faith. But if the functional theory of the relationship between ultimate values and religion is valid, can we, even as scientists, doubt its relevance to the integrative problems of the modern principial society?

[71] Becker, *op. cit.*, pp. 57-63, 66.

SELECTED BIBLIOGRAPHY

Becker, Howard, *Through Values to Social Interpretation* (Durham, N. C.: Duke University Press, 1950).

———, *Man in Reciprocity* (New York: Frederick A. Praeger, Inc., 1956).

——— "A Sacred-Secular Evaluation Continuum of Social Change," *Transactions of the Third World Congress of Sociology* (Amsterdam, 1956), 6, pp.19-41.

Camus, Albert, *The Rebel,* translated by Anthony Bower (New York: Alfred Knopf, 1954).

Mukerjee, Radhakamal, *The Social Structure of Values* (London: Macmillan, 1949).

Parsons, Talcott, "The Place of Ultimate Values in Sociological Theory," *Ethics,* 45 (April, 1935), pp. 282-316.

———, *The Social System* (Glencoe, Ill.: The Free Press, 1951).

———, *The Structure of Social Action* (New York: McGraw-Hill, 1937).

Riesman, David, *The Lonely Crowd* (New Haven: Yale University Press, 1950).

Sumner, W. G., *Folkways* (New York: Ginn, 1906).

Thomas, W. I., and Florian Znaniecki, *The Polish Peasant in Europe and America* (Boston: Richard G. Badger, 1918-1921), 5 vols. [also available in a two-volume edition: Alfred Knopf, 1927].

Weber, Max, *From Max Weber: Essays in Sociology,* translated and edited by H. H. Gerth and C. Wright Mills (New York: Oxford University Press, 1946).

———, *The Theory of Social and Economic Organization,* translated by A. M. Henderson and Talcott Parsons (New York: Oxford University Press, 1947).

Znaniecki, Florian, *Cultural Sciences* (Urbana: University of Illinois, 1952).

———, *Social Actions* (New York: Farrar and Rinehart, 1936).

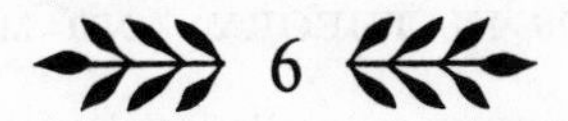

CURRENT SACRED-SECULAR THEORY AND ITS DEVELOPMENT

HOWARD BECKER

THIS CHAPTER PRESENTS SECOND THINGS FIRST; ONLY AFTER CURRENT SACRED-secular theory has been outlined will the background of that theory be dealt with in any detail. A few words may be thereby wasted because of overlap, but the alternative—boring those readers not interested in background—seems worse. The line here chosen enables such readers to stop with the substantive theory.

Terminal facilities like these also seem advisable for related reasons: namely, that the writer will center, even in the substantive portion, on sacred-secular theory as he has himself been concerned with it, and that in the background portion—fortunately quite brief—a kind of intellectual autobiography will intrude itself. Many vexing biases of both omission and commission (in most instances unwitting, let us hope) may therefore become apparent, and the personal note may now and then be found jarring. The reverse order, however, permits avoidance of some of the risk of being vexed or jarred.

One further prefatory comment: Wherever possible, ordinary dictionary English, although perhaps a bit academic in flavor here and there, will be used. In most cases it will do the job, if heed is given to the range of current usage, with—now and again—deliberate concentration on one particular meaning to the exclusion of others. Along with this, there will be an effort to be as direct and intelligible as possible. To be sure, the writer will not always have at his command the skill necessary for the realization of his ideal of simplicity and clarity, more especially as the space that can be granted to illustration is limited, but he can at least try.[1]

Current Sacred-Secular Theory

THE RECIPROCITY OF NEEDS AND VALUES

The terms "sacred" and "secular" are basic to this presentation, but discussion of them is deferred until they can be placed in fuller context. Here it suffices to say that they designate certain kinds of orientation toward any objects of any needs—that is to say, toward values. A value may be tangible or intangible, attractive or repellent, "private" or "public," "real" or "imaginary," vague or definite, and so on; its character as an object is constituted merely by the fact that it is defined as an object by an organism having a need related to it. Swiss cheese, "pie in the sky," well-being, misery, concealed pride, a prestigeful Cadillac, an enemy soldier, Satan, glory, and a ten-dollar debt are all objects of needs of some kind, and in our sense are values.[2]

Needs likewise may be many and various. Needs are always *of* an organism but by no means always *for* an organism in the sense of ministering to survival, much less to "adequate functioning." Putting it differently, there are no needs that are not the needs of living beings, but they may manifest themselves in ways such that the beings possessing them cease to live. A need to devote oneself to Christianity as a value may lead to missionary martyrdom: Father Damien did not survive to the Scriptural three-score and ten; when he went among the lepers on Molokai he knew that the outcome would be an early and loathsome death. Hence it seems that little use can here be made of the current psychological distinction between "primary" and "secondary" needs; what men *learn* to need often has consequences not predictable if "biological needs" are viewed as "primary" by the investigator.

[1] C. R. Mace, a British psychologist, said in his 1951 address to his section of the British Association of Science: "In my studies I have not met a . . . fact or theory that could not be expressed, at the cost of a little reflection, in language which an intelligent schoolboy can readily understand" (as quoted in the London *Daily Telegraph*, July 16, 1951, p. 2). This seems a bit strong, for much depends on the selection of the "intelligent schoolboy"; but if the writer may be permitted to substitute "intelligent college junior," the specification, although still somewhat vague, is nearer to what he here regards as feasible.

[2] This paragraph is based primarily on R. B. Perry, *A General Theory of Value* (New York, 1925); Alexius von Meinong, *Zur Grundlegung der allgemeinen Werttheorie* (posthumous work, ed. by Mally, Gratz, Leuschner, and Lubensky, Vienna, 1923); and Florian Znaniecki, *Cultural Sciences, Their Origin and Development* (Urbana, 1952), pp. 172-174, 183-185, and 238.

Moreover, the reciprocal relation of needs and values, implicit in much of what has just been adduced, presents further obstacles to prediction. To say that there are no values without needs, *and* no needs without values, seems to be hard doctrine. Perhaps it is, but it may be softened somewhat by kneading it slightly in apparently useless ways. To be more definite, the following digressions on the nature of prediction, occurrence, recurrence, "givens," and "takens" may prove helpful even though extremely condensed.

WHAT HAPPENS MAY HAPPEN "AGAIN"

Interest in prediction is of course not necessarily scientific; we all have a bit of "insatiable curiosity" about strange or unusual conduct. Indeed, we often ask the question "What is likely to occur next?" and furnish answers not only when confronted by the unusual, but also where everyday happenings are concerned. Such idle or emotion-laden curiosity is often supplemented or reinforced by more or less clearly realized personal interests of economic, political, and similar character. Again, prediction is obviously of vital importance for general group interests, national and otherwise, and perhaps for mankind as a whole: "Will man be able to use atomic energy without wiping himself out?" seems, to put it mildly, a fairly significant question.

Predictive inquiries about such crucial matters sometimes seem futile in view of the gaps in our knowledge, but in fields where we are better informed, such as those of most technologies and many sciences, a good answer to "What is likely to occur next?" is really the payoff. If we can predict, it is likely that we know enough about the necessary and sufficient conditions of what has been going on to bring about what can be viewed as recurrences of the occurrences in question. In short, when we are reasonably sure about what is likely to happen next, we can ordinarily do something effective toward making it happen again. This is as it should be, for technology and science focus on recurrence, not simply on occurrence. The crucial question with regard to any given occurrence is this: "What is the likelihood of recurrence?" Such a question, in essentials, is basic to pure science in many ways; moreover, applied science aims at preventing or inducing recurrence of this or that kind for the sake of some useful end. "Knowledge for the sake of prediction, prediction for the sake of control" is an old sociological aphorism that, in effect, is often heard today.[3]

ESCAPE FROM THE UNIQUE

Such linking of prediction and control is not accidental, but rather is

[3] For fuller discussion and bibliography, see Howard Becker, *Through Values to Social Interpretation* (Durham, N.C., 1950), Chap. 6. This collection of essays is hereinafter referred to as *TVTSI*. The aphorism is, of course, Auguste Comte's *Savoir pour prévoir, prévoir pour pouvoir*.

inherent in technological and scientific activity.[4] Whether explicit or not, the question basic even to pure science always arises: "Is this *assumed* recurrence controllable, and if so, how?"

But why insert and italicize "assumed"? Certainly it cannot mean that nothing has happened, but it does mean that what has occurred is *assumed* to be "the same" as what has previously come about. To regard one occurrence as identical with another is an assumption undeniably justifiable, but still an assumption. The raw stuff of experience is always and everywhere unique; nothing, literally nothing, is identical with anything else.[5]

The point of view represented by the word *assumed* may be epitomized thus: "*Every* recurrence is an occurrence, but *no* occurrence is ever a recurrence." To speak with Heraclitus, "All things flow," and "We never swim in the same river twice." As I write these lines, I observe an injured spider laboriously crawling across the floor. That spider can be classified by genus, species, variety, and so on and on, but it is still *that* spider and no other, in a situation that will never again be precisely duplicated. If I wished to talk about spiders in such a way that their activities could be predicted and controlled, I should be forced to depart from the utter uniqueness of the immediate observation.[6]

Disregarding here the trains of thought pervading the vast relevant literature of epistemology and philosophy of science, let it be stated that such prediction and control, issuing in "laws of nature," are *without residue* the results of human activity. Man *makes* his "laws of nature"; he does not merely discover the formulas of a Divine Mathematician. This conclusion holds not only for science but also for mathematics itself; however mysterious may seem the correspondence between mathematical symbols and the events they in some way subsume, the mystery resides only in man's inadequate knowledge of his own doings. We *construct* the instruments through which we cope, well or poorly as the case may be, with ourselves and the world around us.[7] Still indulging in phraseology so compressed that, although not so intended, it has a dogmatic ring, let us say that we are finally confronted by "How, using occurrences, are we to *construct* our assumed recurrences?" We may now go over this question in detail while also looking at some of the things we have just said from a slightly different angle (but for more extensive reference, see Chap. 7, by J. C. McKinney, in the present volume).

[4] This use of "prediction and control" as paired terms requires explanation that cannot be offered in present space limits. See *TVTSI* for discussion, especially pp. 285-290. Hypothetical and actual, retrospective and prospective prediction there receive attention.

[5] *Ibid.* pp. 97-101.

[6] *Ibid.* pp. 105-108.

[7] Here see John Doby (ed.), *Introduction to Social Research* (Harrisburg, Pa., 1954), chapter by J. C. McKinney, which has an extensive bibliography on construction.

KNOWLEDGE IS NEVER FINAL

When we refer to "occurrence," we mean that we have experienced some happening or event, vaguely or clearly, in diversity or unity. If asked how we know that we have any experience whatever, the ready reply might be, "Well, we're alive, aren't we?" But the injured spider on the porch floor is alive too; does he "know" anything about the man who is writing about him? Obviously, unless recourse is had to fairy tales, the writer knows about occurrences of which the spider does not and cannot know anything. But does the writer know what the spider knows? No! Its faceted eyes are at a great remove from ours, and we have not the remotest conception as to how the images coming through the hundreds of lenses are fused or coordinated. We can hardly doubt, until evidence to the contrary is produced, that the spider's visual world is strikingly different from our own. Then consider also the demonstrated ability of this creature to sting certain other insects at points precisely right for inducing paralysis; we have only the foggiest notions, if any, as to how this comes about. So one might go on, but the main point is already clear enough: the spider can respond to happenings that our sense end organs do not directly perceive. From what little we can indirectly perceive we draw inferences, and then, if we are experimentally minded entomologists, try to verify them pragmatically. Conceivably we might some day construct instruments, yielding "pointer readings on dials" or whatever, that would eke out our sensory deficiencies; these instruments would cut down the amount of inference necessary, but would never provide for us direct spider experience. We simply do not possess the requisite spider nature.

Leaving this example, and talking now about human deficiencies that limit knowledge, we can assert that nurture is often to blame. Today we perceive happenings completely unknown to our forefathers. Where once the will of God, the Devil, witchcraft, the evil eye, miasma welling up from swamps, night air, and so on were viewed as causing fevers and the like, we now talk about bacteria or even non-filterable viruses. Moreover, the ordinary microscope permits us to see directly anything that falls within the lower limit of the light waves that our eyes can effectively receive, and by means of the proper photographic plates the electron microscope enables us to see indirectly far below the range to which our direct vision is adapted. In other words, our present nurture, including herein acquired ability to use our complex culture, has tremendously increased the world we know as over against that of even as little as a generation ago.

Confronted by this contrast in the nurtures of yesterday and today, and the accompanying contrast in the scope of knowledge, we must take for granted similar contrasts between today and tomorrow. Our world of 1970, barring atomic catastrophe, will certainly be far more and other than our world of 1957.

WE CANNOT TAKE EVERYTHING THAT IS GIVEN

The drift of all this can be summed up as follows: We are today surrounded by "givens" that we are unable, at least as yet, to transform into "takens."[8] Otherwise put, all "takens" are "givens," but not all "givens" are "takens." We do not take everything that is given to us; we cannot capture all that comes our way. Only what we are equipped by nature and nurture to capture enters into the stuff of what we know. Stated still differently, all the things that we experience as knowledge represent "takens," not "givens." A "taken" is a "given" that is actually known in some way by some organism. When organisms differ widely, their experience-worlds are consequently different; the spider's "takens" are not ours and *vice versa.* Arguing in part on the basis of the wide diversity of organisms and the attested growth of human knowledge, it is perhaps permissible to say that out of what may well be an infinite array of "givens"[9] we get only a finite collection of "takens."

Shifting the argument to a closely related topic: All organisms have evolved in a long process of natural selection. The capacities of these organisms to seize upon this or that among the "givens" surrounding them have determined their nature in every fundamental way, *and* the characteristics of the "givens" have determined their capacities. Failure or inadequacy of response to occurrences has meant elimination; every surviving organism "knows" the experience-world that, as a collection of "takens," enables it to survive. What is known is needed; what is needed is known. [10]Although at any given time a particular organism may respond to "takens" that in a sense are matters of indifference to *it,* at some point in the evolutionary development of that general organismic form such "takens" were by no means indifferent, but rather of literally vital concern. Attraction and repulsion, interpreted in organismic terms, are *or have been* inseparably united with

[8] These are Anglicizations of *data* and *capta*—awkward, perhaps, but clear. *Datum* derives from a form meaning "to give, offer, present," and *captum* from "to seize, apprehend, lay hold of, capture." "Concept," "percept," "precept," and so on incorporate this "capture" sense. See *TVTSI*, p. ix, for Howard E. Jensen's suggestions about this terminology.

[9] Such "givens" are of course inferential; we assume that because past "givens" are present "takens" we today are surrounded by "givens" that may eventually become "takens." If anyone wished to say that every "taken" is simply a specially created "given" that had no prior existence, he could of course do so, but the result would be solipsism.

[10] Lest this be thought similar to the assertion that every item in a culture must have a "function" or it would not be "in the culture," note the fact that needs, through continued redefinition *vis-à-vis* changing values, may lose their survival utility—indeed, may militate against survival. Reference may therefore be made to "need" in a *very* broad sense, as long as it is borne in mind that what a given organism that has become human needs, and what a organism *per se* needs, may be in startling contrast.

knowledge itself. Technically put, cognition and conation[11] cannot be separated. What is known is desired, positively or negatively, and what is thus desired is known.

Granted, not all organisms are attracted or repelled by the same things—but this is obvious and repetitive. Further, there is great variation in the vagueness or clarity, diversity or unity, of what is desired; here we need only refer to the wide range of instinctive endowment—from the rigid and definite to the polar opposites of the flexible and amorphous. Man possesses desires of omnivorous, bisexually reproductive, mammalian, non-hibernating, and various other kinds, and in these respects is much like his primitive cousins, but we now know that all these desires are well over toward the flexible and amorphous pole.

Indeed, it may well be that the wide scope of human knowledge has developed in parallel with the loss of rigid and definite instinctive equipment. Further, it is also quite possible that the growth of culture, likewise moving in parallel, has been indirectly responsible for the diminishing of automatically effective instincts. The unlearned but remarkably adroit behavior of the young gibbon in creeping up on and clutching certain food insects may have been similarly exemplified by children a long time ago, but the elaborate baskets, carefully contrived central pit, and coordinated tactics of California Indians staging a grasshopper drive perhaps show that whatever relevant instincts their remote forefathers possessed became progressively unnecessary for survival as the grasshopper-catching culture progressively developed. (Admittedly, such attribution of instinct-lessening power to culture is highly speculative, but there is no reason why the possibility should not be mentioned.) In any case, most contemporary anthropologists and sociologists would agree that man without culture is one of the most poorly equipped of all creatures for making his way in the world.

The implications of the position thus far developed are fairly obvious, but some explicit statement may do no harm. If knowing and desiring are inseparably united, all objects whatsoever are values. The ways in which values are defined vary greatly, of course; a bitter pill spewed out of the mouth of a newborn infant is a value, albeit a negative one, and is such because linked with a vague but nevertheless operative need. Clearly, all organisms, human or infrahuman, are oriented toward values in some way; they are attracted or repelled by them and possess needs that in some fashion correspond to them. The only predictively significant difference between the *human* organism and all other varieties is that both the needs and values of the former are symbolically defined by standard gestures—here including,

[11] This term is used rather than the Freudian "cathexis" because the latter involves commitments to a body of psychoanalytic theory concerning which the writer is quite skeptical. "Desire" as equivalent of conation, positive or negative, is used for the sake of its verbal flexibility—"to conate" and "a conation" seem stiff.

à la G. H. Mead, speech as vocal gesture. Elsewhere the writer has tried to distinguish five levels of needs-values, three of them shared among all organisms, and two regarded as the peculiar province of *Homo sapiens,* who, in interaction with his fellows, has acquired culture and its early-childhood development, self-and-other orientation.[12] No useful purpose would be served here by further elucidation; the literature bearing on these points is abundant and well-known.[13]

THE NATURE OF VALUES AND EVALUATION

The digressions have now served their immediate purpose; let us turn to the values and value-systems to be treated as sacred and secular. The digressions have perhaps called attention to the fact that there is a certain ambiguity in the term "value" as hitherto used.[14] From all that is now known about human beings, it is evident that mere knowing-and-desiring is not characteristically human; the crucial differential is limitation, through culture, of permissibility. Less abstractly stated, all "takens" are subjected to judgments, with awareness or without, of right–wrong, good–bad, proper–improper, convenient–inconvenient, and so on, and these normative judgments involve more than a single actor. In other words, the range of values that may be known-and-desired is far wider than those issuing in actual conduct; perhaps nowhere, to speak popularly, does man do what he *could* wish to do.[15]

In discussing values at the human level, therefore, it would be possible to handle the issues involved in such a way as to require frequent use of the term "norms." Indeed, if it were not so cumbrous a way of putting it, it would be quite proper always to speak of human activity as essentially "knowing-desiring-norming."[16]

Beyond question, the persons engaged in such activity often are not even dimly aware of the fact that their "takens" have been strained through a normative mesh; their choosing has been done for them by predecessors in such ways that no genuine alternatives are perceived. Only the sophisticated observer, presumably holding in view more evidence of the varieties of conduct that could be engaged in than any subject under observation possesses, can state what might or might not be chosen. Again resorting to simpler but not necessarily inaccurate phraseology, it may be a case of "Those fellows

[12] For further discussion, see Howard Becker, *Man in Reciprocity* (New York, 1956, hereinafter referred to as *MIR*), Chaps. 6 and 7.

[13] "Symbolic interactionism" is the key term.

[14] The same is, of course, true of the term "need."

[15] See *TVTSI* p. 21, note 26.

[16] Clearly, it is quite possible to lay stress on any act of "knowing-desiring-norming" in such a way that one aspect is emphasized to the *apparent* exclusion of the others. Thus conduct may be primarily cognitive, conative, or normative. But *pure* knowing, desiring, or norming are nowhere to be found empirically.

just don't know what's good for 'em"—or bad for them, for that matter. Nature and nurture, then, limit the scope of "knowing-desiring-norming" in ways that are at times quite drastic where particular subjects are concerned.

Further, to call an observer "sophisticated" is not to assume that he is omniscient; he too operates within confines, wide though they may be, of permissibility, which is to say that he wittingly or unwittingly imposes normative judgments on what is observed. In the case of the predictively oriented social scientist *qua* scientist, his norms lead to the exclusion of esthetic, playful, religious, and like considerations except as they promise to yield greater predictive power. He consistently makes judgments to the following effect: "All value-judgments other than the supreme value-judgment that prediction is in and of itself worth while are to be set aside by the social scientist in his strictly scientific role." If the predictive statements resulting from the social scientist's activity are verified, he still has no warrant for assuming that he possesses Truth in any final sense; he has merely selected and properly handled those kinds of evidence that have a crucial bearing on the achievement of his supreme value. The difference between the sophisticated social-scientific observer and the persons he observes is in essence the difference between the adherent of a predictive value-system and persons yielding allegiance to other kinds.[17]

Note now that in the previous paragraph the *general* usage has returned to "values." As any object of any need, a value is the outcome of knowing-desiring-norming; what is known is a value, what is desired is a value, what is normed is a value. Similarly, "evaluating" or "evaluation" may and should be used to designate *any* human activity that defines values in terms of needs and *vice versa*.[18] Accordingly, we are back where we began; values and value-systems have once more come into focus.

THE COMPREHENSIVENESS OF SACRED AND SECULAR

Sacred and secular values and value-systems represent a quite abstract level of formulation, although they inductively derive from very substantial bodies of empirical evidence. In the later part of this chapter, dealing with some of the history of sacred-secular constructs, the close interplay of induction-deduction is made reasonably clear; the constructs progressively emerged when certain perplexities arose, and were not set up in advance. But here the writer anticipates unduly; it seems best to continue with substantive presentation.

Reluctance and readiness to accept or initiate social change provide the

[17] See *TVTSI,* Chap. 6.

[18] Implicit throughout this treatment of needs and values is what has come to be known, since the days of Max Weber, as the means-ends schema. See the presentation of this in *MIR*, pp. 111-136, and especially pp. 190-196. It is also dealt with in *TVTSI;* use index for "ends" and "means."

construction lines of what may be called a sacred-secular scale or continuum. Any society or part thereof that imparts to or elicits from its members evaluations that can be altered, if at all, only in the face of definite emotionalized reluctance is a sacred society—a shorthand term for a society bearing a cultural system making for the reluctance indicated. Conversely, any society or part thereof that imparts to or elicits from its members evaluations leading to well-marked readiness to change is a secular society in a similar shorthand sense. Problems relating to social and cultural change (see Chap. 9, by Alvin Boskoff, in the present volume), therefore, are built into the sacred-secular scale, as are also what in some ways are their counterparts, problems of social control.

Given such considerations, and the empirical evidence relating to them, sacred values must be treated as comprising far more than the religious, divine, spiritual, and so on.[19] Any conduct whatsoever may be viewed as hinging on sacred considerations when it is accompanied by characteristic reluctance to change values and/or their related needs. Putting it differently, unwillingness or inability or both—linked with distress or similar signs of tension—to alter any aspect of one's "way of life" is sacred evaluation. The person who makes such evaluation has certain needs so interwoven with certain values that he feels and acts in an "upset" manner when change in those needs and values is even suggested, let alone demanded.

CULTURE IS CRUCIAL

Whether sacred or secular, all values are culturally defined in some manner and degree. What is sacred to any people in eating, mating, fighting, and worshiping is what they have been taught in some fashion or another to hold sacred. In discernibly different but similar ways, the same is true of secular values, for although the secular is not merely the reverse of the sacred, it is still safe to say that readiness for and liking of change must be learned. Ability or willingness to change are, like their opposites, acquired capacities. The learning of secular conduct is clearly, from what has been said above, much more than the acquisition of avowedly or unavowedly non-religious, profane, or skeptical needs and values.[20] These are all secular, of course, but the designation reaches far beyond them. Any sort of conduct may be viewed as centering on values designable in secular terms when well-marked needs to seek those values, whatever the changes entailed, are in some way evident. Persons so evaluating have learned to concentrate on certain ends, tangible or intangible as the case may be, in a manner such that they may even be unable to refrain from pursuing them by any means available

[19] This is discussed at greater length in *TVTSI*, pp. 43-44, 248-250, including notes, and in *MIR*, pp. 137-144.

[20] See references immediately above; also *TVTSI*, pp. 68-69, 277-278 (note 47); and *MIR*, pp. 169-170.

and regardless of the disapproval, however severely expressed, of their fellows.

Here likewise culture is powerfully at work. No innovation ever is entirely without a "cultural base," and from such a standpoint all innovations are culturally conditioned, but over and above this it is obvious that if they are not to disappear when their introducers die, they must be passed on to others who have come to accept or, in some cases, to welcome them. Stated otherwise, changes in culture must be imparted to at least one succeeding generation if they are to become more than merely private variations or deviations; communication over time is indispensable. Cultural changes must be transmitted, learned, and shared quite as definitely as must cultural continuities. Sacred and secular value-systems, then, are both products and producers of culture, particularly when viewed as embodied in evaluative actions leading subsequent actors to evaluate similarly.

FROM RELUCTANCE TO READINESS

The writer earlier remarked that the major theoretical task now under survey is the constructing of a sacred-secular continuum along which evaluations can be ranged. Such a continuum, if it is formalized as a scale, should have specified end-points. The present state of our knowledge makes specification of this kind rather venturesome or even somewhat arbitrary, but it cannot be avoided. Therefore, let us array several types of evaluation along a line leading from estimated maximum reluctance to change old values to estimated maximum readiness to seek new values. (Incidentally, "old" and "new" must be assigned the definitions offered, in whatever ways, by the *subjects* concerned; it makes no difference for present purposes whether the values involved are "really" old or new.) As long as unduly precise connotations are not thereby introduced, the scale in question may be constructed algebraically—that is, from maximum plus to maximum minus, with a zero or transitional point somewhere about the middle.[21]

WHAT IS HOLY MUST BE KEPT HOLY

Starting with maximum plus as the strongest empirically manifested reluctance to change, we may give appropriate attention to the frequent embracing of martyrdom for oneself or the inflicting of it on others that men have time out of mind practiced for the sake of preserving religious needs and values. Their orientation toward what they have regarded as supernatural forces or beings has frequently been so compulsive that they have sacrificed

[21] This is not the proper context for discussion of the properties that a suitable scale should possess, but certainly the mere specification of end-points is not sufficient. The writer does not here wish to take a position regarding unidimensionality, cumulativeness, etc., especially as a forthcoming paper by a colleague, Robert B. McGinnis, raises a number of issues casting doubt on some of the accepted conceptions.

themselves or their fellows rather than permit changes in the evaluation of those orientations, or supernatural agencies, or both. Now and then, it may be admitted, there prevails a conception that impious innovators are supernaturally punished, and that hence the pious need not themselves take action. "Vengeance is mine; I will repay, saith the Lord." When this is the case, the heretical deviant merely becomes an outcast or, less frequently, may be allowed to remain a member of the society, albeit at the lower levels. But in spite of this and other exceptions noted later, holy evaluation in one or another form bringing sacrificial extinction with it has so often been evident that there seems considerable warrant for placing it at the maximum-plus pole of the sacred-secular scale.

Indulging in terminological comment: "Holy" is expressly limited, following established precedent, to evaluations bound up with supernaturalism, which is to say with religion as here viewed. Much confusion has resulted, and will probably continue to result, from the loose use of "religion" to designate non-supernaturalistic evaluations of compelling kind—for example "Communism as a religion." Similar confusion comes about when the sacred and the religious are treated as coterminous; religion *per se* is but one aspect of the sacred. A very large amount of sacred conduct has little or nothing to do with the supernaturalistically oriented—which is to say, with the religious. The holy, on the other hand, has long been properly restricted in English to religious manifestations in the narrow and only suitable sense: holy water, holy days, holy wedlock, holy communion, holy orders, the Holy Land, His Holiness the Pope, the Holy Bible, and so on.[22] Attention to the holy as a kind of evaluation inseparably linked with supernaturalism was taken as a matter of course by anthropologists and sociologists until well beyond Tylor's time—in fact, until Durkheim and Sumner (to name only the more prominent) befogged significant distinctions by using all-inclusive and vague categories. Only in the second quarter of the present century, with Otto and other students of comparative religion, was the importance of the holy again recognized. Even now only a few sociological investigators such as Goode seem to have kept abreast of the newer evidence and emphasis;[23] for the most part, anthropologists as well as sociologists seem confused and out of date. Unless religion, which is to say holy evaluation, which is to say conduct oriented toward objects regarded as supernatural, is analytically distinguished from other varieties of the sacred, little predictive worth attaches to it as a category.

[22] See especially *The New Century Dictionary* (New York, 1940), section on "Synonyms, Antonyms, and Discriminations," p. 2319. Cf. also Howard Becker and H. E. Barnes, *Social Thought from Lore to Science* (2nd ed., New York, 1952, or reissue), hereinafter referred to as *STFLTS* (1952), "1951 Appendix on Value-System Terminology," pp. iii-x.

[23] W. J. Goode, *Religion Among the Primitives* (Glencoe, 1951), *passim*.

NOBODY LOVES A TRAITOR

Having at least provisionally placed the holy at the plus extreme of the evaluation scale, it must nevertheless be noted that the basic criterion, action involving martyrdom or its equivalents, is also present in several other kinds of sacredness. The loyalistic, for example, comprising clan allegiance, patriotism, identification with one or another race, class, faction, party, or what not, calls forth everything from "altruistic suicide" to murder—or shall we say "liquidation"? It is easy to bring to mind instance after instance of the terrific power of loyalism; multitudes of men have perished because of their own or their opponents' devotion to groups of one or another kind. So numerous are the instances, in fact, that loyalistic sacredness seems closely to rival and now and again to surpass the holy variety as a contender for the maximum-plus position on the scale.[24]

The historical record is by no means clear, and it may well be that supernaturalism is not the most important source, numerically speaking, of "supreme sacrifice." The obscurity enshrouding much of the past is increased by the fact that the holy and the loyalistic are often difficult if not virtually impossible to separate, not only empirically but also analytically. Just where the line can be appropriately drawn between Hindu religious belief, practice, and feeling as such, on the one hand, and the intermeshing evaluative conduct constituting the structure of Hindu castes, guilds, village councils, and similar loyalty-eliciting groups on the other, baffles the most thoroughly informed students of such matters.

Moreover, there is a substantial amount of evidence showing that it may occasionally be far safer openly to denounce a god than to assert independence of a group, much less to become traitor to it. A researcher, in his work among the Winnebago, found that one skeptic boldly expressed contempt for the holiest of the tribal deities and that, when the deity in question appeared in order to inflict lethal disease as punishment, his impious critic remained immune. The consequence was that the deity, hoping to escape ridicule, begged the man to succumb, but in vain. The same researcher also found that non-observance or defiance of established social relations carried far more serious consequences than did religious dissent; those unable or unwilling to conform socially faced banishment or death. In short, religious heretics sometimes held their own, but social mavericks never did.[25]

In spite of this and like evidence, however, the writer feels that although the loyalistically sacred, together with several other varieties to be mentioned later, may come very close indeed to the holy in life-or-death power, the

[24] Here in particular see Howard Becker, *Systematic Sociology on the Basis of the* Beziehungslehre *and* Gebildelehre *of Leopold von Wiese,* hereinafter *WBSS* (New York, 1932, and Gary, Ind., 1950 ed. with new preface). For discussion of abstract collectivities, use index, but especially pp. 556-642. See also *MIR,* pp. 434-435.

[25] Paul Radin, *The Method and Theory of Ethnology* (New York, 1933), pp. 42-43, 50-51.

holy has probably been stronger in a somewhat greater number of cases. This feeling arises from a considerable amount of reading in the relevant sources, but proof or disproof would require elaborate and costly research.

THE BONDS OF INTIMACY

Thus far we have dealt only with the holy and the loyalistic, but several other kinds of sacredness must be discussed, among them that connected with what have long been called primary groups. Intimate sacredness, represented by ties with playfellows, friends, comrades, mates, and partners, is encountered on every hand. Intimacy, once well and favorably established, is usually regarded as not lightly to be terminated or even altered in slight degree.

Manifestly, the grounds of intimacy, as of all other aspects of the sacred and the secular, differ strikingly from one society to another, but the world over we encounter evidence of the supreme devotion that it calls forth; it also often rivals the holy in the sacrificial zeal it evokes. Cooley's praise of democracy had little realistic reference to the mass political phenomena apparent to other than Pollyanna observers even in his day, but what he had to say about kindly give-and-take, shared responsibility, good faith, willingness to cooperate, and neighborliness was warranted for what he saw among face-to-face and relatively small groupings practicing—however short of perfection—a kind of rural and small-town American version of nineteenth-century Protestant Christianity. The core of his sociology was a cheerful exaggeration of the scope and power of the intimately sacred, but he did validly point to its importance.[26]

THE MORALISTIC AND ITS QUALIFICATIONS

Proceeding further along the scale, it seems that moralistic sacredness may be assigned the next section of the continuum. This variety has a range more limited than that of the familiar mores, for the latter has been so loosely used, from the very beginning, that it takes in everything from the holy to the fitting and has been applied to some aspects of secular conduct as well. What is here meant by the moralistic covers evaluations referring directly to enjoined or forbidden types of conduct specifically distinguishable from the total personalities of those engaged therein. Concretely, a man may be viewed as having bad morals but not as being a hopelessly bad man; further, his morals can be improved piecemeal, as it were. In contrast, grave breaches of the holy, loyalistic, and intimate put the offender beyond the pale in many societies; condemnation is complete.

In the case of the moralistic, to be sure, the "manners and customs" concerned are often so entrenched that marked indignation is the immediate

[26] C. H. Cooley, *Human Nature and the Social Order* (New York, 1902); *Social Organization* (New York, 1909); and *Social Process* (New York, 1918).

consequence of even the mere suggestion that they should be changed. Nevertheless, the potential or actual violator is not exterminated, cast out, or wholly ostracized; there is some possiblity of making amends. This may be illustrated by the fact that in American society, particularly of almost bygone rural type, violations of sexual morals among the unmarried could be remedied by the "shotgun wedding." With moralistic requirements thus satisfied, the ensuing conduct of the once outraged guardian of the moral code was ordinarily the reverse of violent; the son-in-law acquired by threat was frequently treated as though no major deviation had occurred. Obviously, this example also serves to indicate that on occasion the moralistically sacred carries with it the ultimate sanction of death—but usually as alternative, not as inevitability.

Placing the moralistic at a considerable remove from the maximum-plus end of the scale therefore seems warranted. Again, however, there must be inserted the proviso that the wide variations between one culture and another may bring about *notable shifts* in scale position, not only of the moralistic, but also of other types of sacredness.

Still another qualification must be imposed with regard to the ethical, viewed as the moralistic at a more general level. Ethical sacredness, as is well known, often engenders exalted and passionate devotion. That is to say, abstract ethical precepts may approximate the holy in the zeal they call forth. Further, in form they are often highly rational (in the formal, discursive sense), although in content they are usually, at least with regard to origin, quite as nonrational as the moralistic. Moreover, ethical precepts may be held with such intensity as to lead to rejection of ritual; take the example of the Hebrew prophets who declared that Yahveh desired justice rather than burnt offerings. Ethical demands, in other words, may be closely linked with the transcendent claims of the holy. Consequently, the treatment of the ethical as merely the moralistic at a more abstract level may beg some questions in favor of the present scaling procedure. Let it be understood, then, that there is nothing sacred about this procedure. If it proves predictively useful, well and good; if not, alterations are certainly advisable.

"IT JEST AIN'T FITTIN'!"

Next along the scale comes a kind of evaluation of distinctly lower intensity than any of those thus far considered. This may be called the fittingly sacred; it occupies the hazy band between the moralistic and the merely appropriate. Designations for conduct falling in this band are many; a short list includes proper–improper, "done"–"not done," "good form"–"bad form," mannerly–unmannerly, decent–vulgar, and the like. This list draws on the vast fund of what is viewed as etiquette in the formal sense, but there are equivalents, likewise representing a low intensity of the sacred, for all other forms of the fitting. Few persons would regard the custom, observed in some circles, of not immediately picking up one's change on the bar when a drink has been served as in the realm of etiquette, for example; but it may nevertheless be viewed as eminently fitting even by those not conversant with Emily Post.

One of the most convenient ways of distinguishing the fittingly sacred from closely related varieties is to take account of the conduct attending its violation. Moralistic offenses evoke indignation, whereas failure to observe the fitting elicits little if anything more than contempt. The almost imperceptible shrug of the shoulders, the raised eyebrow or the curled lip, the sudden and noticeably continued silence when the obtrusive newcomer enters the clubroom frequented only by the long-established members, are all unspoken but nevertheless definite judgments that the fitting is being disregarded in a culpable way.[27]

Reference has been made to the low intensity of the fitting, yet there may be a high degree of reluctance to change even in what those of us inclined toward informality call "mere manners." Men seldom die for the sake of the fitting, but they may undergo extreme discomfort and sometimes danger. Those of us who have watched Britishers quietly finish their tea-drinking before proceeding to air-raid shelters, even though the noise of bursting bombs was to be heard all through teatime, have gained some notion of the fact that though the fitting is not oriented toward holiness, it represents a reluctance to change that can hardly be viewed as other than sacred.

"DINNER JACKETS WOULD BE APPROPRIATE"

The sacred on the fringe of fadeout has sometimes been placed in the realm of the folkways; but like the mores, the folkways take in too much of both sacred and secular. It here seems best to make use of a more limited term such as the appropriate. There is a minimum of any controls savoring of indignation or contempt, but resort to ridicule is still possible. "Suitable," "customary," "regular," "expected," "normal," "usual," and similar more or less interchangeable words often have a sacred tinge; they indicate that "right" and "wrong" ways of doing things are not matters of indifference, and that there is some reluctance to relinquish, or to see others relinquish, the appropriate ways.

At the same time, those who wittingly or unwittingly perpetrate the inappropriate are not viewed as unworthy, but rather as uninstructed. Their remediable ignorance, indifference, or impatience may be viewed with nothing more than mild and courteously concealed amusement. The man

[27] Violation of the fitting, as noted, elicits negative sanction primarily as contempt, etc. Whether or not the baring of the teeth, or tendencies thereto, in the sneer represents an attenuated inclination to use physical violence in defense of the fitting, is debatable, beyond question, but the possibility should be mentioned. If the mere suggestion seems to involve too much biological preoccupation, the writer asks, "Is man a disembodied spirit?"

who wears yellow-tan shoes and bright blue socks with a green suit and a pictorial necktie at a garden party will, it is assumed, learn better after a while. In the interval, the temptation to smile in his presence remains only a temptation. Defense of the appropriate, which is to say of the sacred almost at the vanishing point, here amounts to no more than an inadvertent twitch at the corners of the mouth;[28] the shift to the secular is close at hand.

THE PERVASIVENESS OF CEREMONIAL

Discussion of this shift must be delayed, however, until some reference is made to an aspect of sacred conduct evident in all its varieties, from the holy to the merely appropriate, that may be labeled the ceremonially sacred. Its importance is readily perceived when we focus on the holy, for ritual, in the sense of religious ceremonial *per se,* is often the most obvious mark of supernaturalistic orientation. In fact, Jane Harrison and others have pointed out that *dromena*—"things done" rather than "things believed"—may be overwhelmingly more evident in some kinds of religion than are doctrines and creeds. Ritual in the strict sense, as set forms of worship, may be performed when the worshipers have only the vaguest of notions as to what the supernaturalistic forces or beings worshiped may be like. The misty outlines of the supernaturalistic object may fluctuate tremendously, as it were, in accordance with the hazily defined and therefore fluctuating needs of the worshiper, while the ritual varies little if at all. Stock ejaculations in ancient tongues, dimly comprehended but rote-learned formulas, elaborate genuflections, and intricate processions may be accurately repeated again and again by men who have achieved no *explicit* orientation toward a *definite* supernaturalistic object.

Ceremonial as bound up with the holy, which is to say as ritual in the strict sense, is clearly of great importance, but there are many other significant kinds of ceremonial. This fact is usually overlooked, and confusion between ritual and other ceremonial is induced and increased,[29] because we lack terms for distinguishing these other varieties, except for a few such as "commencement" for graduation ceremonial, "commemoration" for anniversary or otherwise time-defined ceremonial, and the like.[30]

[28] Note 27 is also relevant here, There are many theories of laughter and its derivatives, but among them are several stressing the quasi-sadistic enjoyment of discomfiture. See Max Eastman, *The Enjoyment of Laughter* (New York, 1936), especially the notes. In view of such theories, we can at least suggest that our basic criterion is not irrelevant.

[29] This distinction is not observed, unfortunately, in the otherwise excellent book by J. H. S. Bossard and Elinor H. Boll, *Ritual in Family Living* (Philadelphia, 1950). However, as recently as 1955 the present writer failed to make the distinction; see Howard Becker and Reuben Hill, *Family, Marriage, and Parenthood* (2nd ed., Boston, 1955), p. 20.

[30] See the classic treatment, Herbert Spencer, *Principles of Sociology,* II, 1 (2nd ed. reprinted, New York, 1897), chapter on "Ceremonial Institutions."

COMMEMORATIVE CEREMONIAL

As long as those varieties of ceremonial for which we lack specific terms are not overshadowed by commemoration, some discussion of the latter is relevant in the present context. Such relevance does not arise merely because of the existence of the term, but primarily because of the very large amount of commemoration plainly evident as such in all known societies. Disregarding, in view of our sociological slant, commemoration of "natural" happenings such as the seasonal cycle in and of itself, we still encounter multifarious ceremonials that, although time-defined, are not necessarily bound to the more obvious seasonal, annual, or similar divisions of the prevailing calendar system. The ancient Hebrews, for example, observed every forty-ninth year as a sort of moratorium commemorating an earlier tribal communalism; debts were wiped out and slaves liberated in a general jubilee. Similar "occasions," as Granet calls them,[31] owing little if anything to "naturally" recurring intervals except as these are needed for fixing the culturally defined events, are to be found among many other peoples. Much more frequent, of course, is the close conjunction of the natural and the cultural; the natural, however, is not dealt with as such, but is defined in cultural terms. Ramadan, Yom Kippur, the Sabbath, Easter, Christmas, Independence Day, Columbus Day, wedding anniversaries from paper to diamond, and centennials, sesquicentennials, and so on of many descriptions provide ample evidence.

Holy, loyalistic, and intimate kinds of sacredness are powerfully reinforced by commemoration, for simple sacred continuity is thereby endowed with coherent structure. Evaluative activities can be reckoned with in advance and their significances interrelated; a sequence sacred not only in its distinguishable parts but also as sequence is thereby established.

A related aspect of commemoration is its effect on socialization. Using Myres' definition of culture as "what remains of men's past, working on their present, to shape their future,"[32] there is involved the problem of how much of the past remains and how it works on the present. If departed ancestors, as far back as memory can reach, are commemorated and their virtues systematically extolled, a very great deal of the past may remain to work on the present. Not only parents and other living relatives and custodians directly influencing offspring as they are reared, but also a host of departed worthies, "actively" participate in socialization.

American society grants some importance to bereavement ceremonial, but except for sporadic cemetery visitation, there is little commemoration. Socializing influences are therefore temporally shallow; intimate sacredness, for instance, must rely for its social-control effect, in most cases, only on living representatives.[33] Holy and loyalistic sacredness are better supported,

[31] Marcel Granet, *La Pensée chinoise* (Paris, 1934), pp. 119, 127, 151-160, 173-208.

[32] J. O. Myres, *The Political Ideas of the Greeks* (Cincinnati, 1927), p. 16.

[33] Evidence bearing on this point has been assembled in Howard Becker, "Social

for prophets, saviors, saints, revolutionary heroes, and great presidents and lawgivers need not be intimates in order to be invoked as socializing examples. Relatively little attention has been given by American social scientists to commemoration, except for occasional reference to matters such as Chinese "ancestor-worship," which is the more surprising in view of the widespread interest in culture and the means of its transmission.

CEREMONIAL REINFORCEMENT OVER THE LOYALISTIC-APPROPRIATE RANGE

Turning now to ceremonial of less general reference, let us note the fact that it abounds in the realm of the loyalistically sacred. Choosing only one example, men may mutually pledge, as did the Founding Fathers, "our lives, our fortunes, and our sacred honour." The intimately sacred also has its ceremonies, comprising everything from vows of blood-brotherhood to marriage. So too with the moralistically sacred; the acceptance of contractual obligations may be ceremonialized by a simple handclasp or, where the state exercises influence, by signature, notarization, and so on for many other major and minor routines with moralistic overtones. Further, where these overtones are faint and at most contempt is expressed toward the deviant, as in the fittingly sacred, ceremonials such as granting precedence to "the weaker sex," elders, or those of higher rank, the loser's jumping over the tennis net to congratulate the winner, and other formalizations of sportsmanship, politeness, refinement, and respectability are abundant. Even where the social controls are only more or less mildly manifest as good-humored ridicule, that is, where the appropriately sacred holds sway, there is much ceremonial that, in our society, takes forms such as "small talk," avoidance of "talking shop," and accepted ways of "breaking the ice," greeting, "dating," and leave-taking—in fact, the full array of what is viewed by the various social strata concerned as ordinary tact and discretion. There is seldom vigorous resistance to variations in such conduct, but those who are naive, negligent, or brusque may slowly come to the realization that their conduct is a source of hidden mirth.

We have again reached what was earlier called "the sacred on the fringe of fadeout," again shifted our gaze from maximum to minimum resistance to change. The somewhat arbitrarily designated steps along the reluctance part of our scale may now be listed: holy, loyalistic, intimate, moralistic, fitting, and appropriate, and pervading all of these in greater or lesser degree, ceremonial.[34] Considerable attention has been given to commemorative

Psychology of Bereavement," hereinafter *SPOB*, unpublished M.A. thesis, Northwestern University, 1926, Appendix 2. This thesis also includes a lengthy bibliography.

[34] Whether to treat ceremonial as a special category in the continuum, or to view it as a subcategory of several of the others, or to regard it as pervading all of the sacred and some of the secular (principial, comfortable, and thrilling) has been a difficult problem.

ceremonial, for it plays a significant part in the perpetuation of many of the evaluations we have surveyed. It must again be stressed, however, that it is by no means the only major aspect of ceremonial, even though at the empirical level it is sometimes mingled in prominent and almost inseparable fashion with other aspects.

HOW THE SACRED MAY BE SYMBOLIZED

Before proceeding further along the scale, it seems advisable to mention some of the ways in which the symbolizing of sacred reluctances takes place. Such symbolization may be implicit or explicit, adequate or inadequate, in large measure because of the fact that many reluctances can be put into words or other explicit symbols only with considerable difficulty, if at all. The outlines of the values involved are often hazy: the force or spirit, kinship group, friend or other intimate, moralistic requirement, propriety, or normatively tinged procedure endowed with this or that amount of sacredness may be defined in important respects by chills of fright, throbs of joy, qualms of nausea, and thrills of ecstasy, as well as by furrowed brows, quickened pulses, contorted mouths, beaming eyes, and rapturous chest-heavings. Manifestations such as these enter into the definitions of sacred values and their reciprocal needs in many essential ways; they represent, however, only a small quota of the obscure actions, potentially or actually symbolic, that not only reinforce those having more clarity but also, in numerous instances, furnish key parts of the value-definition. In short, not all effective symbols are verbal or visual in a directly intelligible sense; postures, gestures, fleeting facial expressions, and a host of similar bits of conduct, down even to the level of faint kinesthetic tensions, often play crucial symbolic roles.

PROVERBIAL RELUCTANCES ARE NOT MERELY VERBAL

With these qualifications before us, perhaps little harm will be done at this point and in our later presentation of what we shall call proverbial societies and their characteristically sacred systems by referring to the value-defining conduct involved as though it were chiefly a matter of "putting things into words." In using "proverbial"[35] we expressly include what might be called, were we coining words, "propostural," "progestural," "proexpressive," "protensional," and so on indefinitely. The same holds, with differences in degree, for those prescriptive, principial, and pronormless societies also to be discussed in more detail later.

The compressed bits of verbalized experience called proverbs in the narrower and usual sense often contain much more meaning than is imme-

The third possibility seems to be the only one suitable; but in earlier formulations by the present writer, the first was erroneously chosen.

[35] If it were not for the many liabilities of "folk" (briefly mentioned later, note 83), we could speak of "folkish" evaluation.

diately apparent. Usually only long-continued saturation in the society concerned will reveal to the investigator what a given proverb actually conveys to the "natives." That is to say, proverbs are full of *implicit* symbolism; their explicit significance may be of lesser importance. However, comparison of proverbs will show that they are often contradictory in content even when full account is taken of both explicit and implicit aspects.[36] The users of proverbs glibly repeat first one and then another, without seeming at all disturbed by what to outsiders are obvious discrepancies which would be viewed as such by insiders too if they had ever taken the trouble to codify their proverbs. They feel no need to do so; the needs of the immediate situation are met well enough, and reflection is after all a habit slowly and painfully acquired.

This is tantamount to saying that the implicitness of at least part of the proverb, concretely considered, is accompanied by the related implicitness of its systematic linkage with other proverbs, when that linkage has been established at all. Proverbs are seldom if ever arranged in such a way as to constitute a creed or a coherent ideology. Granted, the jumbled masses of proverbs encountered in many relatively simple societies, although uncodified, are frequently interwined, grown together, or merged; using technical language, they are accrete in the same way as are the outer floral leaves, initially separate, of wintergreen when they finally fuse into an inseparable whole.[37] In sum, value-systems composed chiefly of proverbs are likely to be largely implicit in content and connection, primarily uncodified, and almost always accrete.

These systems manifest the traits just mentioned because they are chiefly of traditional and nonrational character. The imparting of culture in proverbial societies is a process overwhelmingly informal in the sense that it comes about through communication among intimates rather than through being entrusted to specialized instructors functioning in formal organizations such as schools. What remains of man's past in the society in question is informally embodied and implanted by the intimates, and this tradition—for that is what "what remains of man's past" here amounts to—is accepted merely because it *is* tradition. Traditionalism and nonrationality go hand in hand.[38]

[36] Here see S. G. Champion, *Racial Proverbs* (New York, 1938), for many interesting and amusing examples. See also *STFLTS* (1952), pp. 15-17, and notes, vol. I, pp. xxxv-xxxvi.

[37] "Accrete" is a botanical term meaning "at first distinguishable but later so fused as to provide little evidence of earlier separateness." It is here borrowed for sociological purposes. The wintergreen reference is only one of the hundreds possible. "Accrete" seems a better term, for present purposes, than "integrated," for the latter implies functional unity, and we do not wish to beg the "functionalism" question.

[38] This is discussed at some length in *TVTSI*, pp. 26-29, and in *MIR*, pp. 118, 120, 162-166.

THE GREATER DEFINITENESS OF PRESCRIPTION

The effect of tradition is not, of course, limited to proverbial societies, but in other types it operates differently. Take, for example, sets of prescriptive evaluation such as the Eightfold Path, the Torah, the Code of Justinian, the Apostles' Creed, catechisms of every variety, knightly injunctions, "rules of the game," and countless other explicitly stated and codified values and their correlatively sanctioned needs; these are traditionally derived, but explicitly and in codified arrangement. The various prescriptions are formulated as pointedly as is possible at the time in the given cultural context, but beyond this they are stacked, so to speak, in piles more or less orderly as contrasted with higgledy-piggledy heaps of proverbs. Such orderliness lends itself to at least the semblance of deductive systematization, although much more often than not it is merely semblance. The system amounts only to a crude catalog sequence, determined by historical happenings, convenience of memorization, or peculiarities of the method, if any, of making some sort of record. Then, to resume the metaphor, in many cases the stack is solidified by troweling deductive mortar between the joints, and a great deal of ingenuity may be lavished on this task. The separate prescriptions remain distinguishable, however, and each one is as sacred as any other; even apparently insignificant fragments are held inviolate. Nevertheless, the resulting value-system is explicit and codified, and in addition is accrete.[39] In spite of differences in other respects, both proverbial and prescriptive societies have value-systems that are viewed as unalterable both as wholes and in their minutest parts.

Still, in spite of such accreteness and the oftentimes "afterthought" nature of their deductive solidification, prescriptive value-systems are formally rational. That is to say, "good reasons" can usually be given by their adherents for the existence and perpetuation of every one of the parts and the totality. As we know, the offering of "good reasons" usually amounts to nothing more than what has come to be called rationalization or *ex post facto* justification, but the justification may be very consistently carried out. Indeed, it may be a task specifically assigned to highly trained scribes, priests, "doomsmen," and the like.[40] Their explicit articulations (in both senses of this term) stand in strong contrast to the traditional nonrationality of a proverbial system where "It's always been done that way, and that's the way it's got to be" closes all issues—in fact, often prevents issues as such from arising.

Concisely, proverbial formulations are implicit, uncodified, unintentionally accrete, and traditionally nonrational; prescriptive formulations are explicit, codified, in some degree intentionally accrete, and at least formally rational or even apparently deductive.

[39] See *MIR*, pp. 166-168.

[40] *Ibid.*

LOOKING FOR A CENTER OF INDIFFERENCE

Now that this sketchy outline of the sacred parts of our scale, together with their characteristic modes of symbolization, is before us, a rough draft of the secular sections must be provided. In dealing with readiness to change, we shall proceed from minimum to maximum, but the criterion for estimating the degree of this readiness—namely, extinction of oneself or others—is much more difficult to apply consistently than is the case with reluctance. It will nevertheless be used here and there, although relatively little direct reference will be made to it.

Following the algebraic procedure, account must now be taken of our zero point. This is represented by those seldom-encountered kinds of conduct evidencing almost complete indifference to change or the lack thereof. Sparsely spread throughout some societies there may occasionally be encountered a few persons who seem not to care much one way or the other about the change-involved conduct of their associates, but on investigation such unconcern is usually found to be no more than verbal. When it comes down to a situation that can be defined as "either-or" in ways meaningful in a given context, what at first seemed to be indifference takes on positively or negatively evaluative characteristics. By far the greater number of the members of any society possessing even a slight amount of organization do have active concern about conduct that on the surface looks insignificant. In other words, a true zero point may be hard to discover when the empirical evidence is examined, although we may grant that from the analytic angle such a point must be postulated.

THE EMERGENCE OF PRINCIPLES

However this may be, when transition through the zero point occurs, the secular portion of the scale begins, which is to say that readiness to change, no matter what the reason, supplants reluctance. The two may be almost in balance, of course—almost, but not quite. There is acquiescence in change, active assent to it, or even search for it; nevertheless, certain restrictions stemming from the sacred are placed on its nature, speed, or range. As has been noted, sacred reluctances frequently are not well symbolized where proverbs and their nonverbal or subverbal equivalents are concerned; at the prescriptive level, clearly, symbolization is much more adequate. Both proverbs and prescriptions lose power as the intensity of the sacred diminishes; indeed, this is in some ways a tautologous statement. At the same time, it should be noted that on occasion a good deal of their remaining efficacy may be transferred to somewhat more abstract formulations functioning as ethical, governmental, professional, and similar principles.

Just as the differences between proverbs and prescriptions are matters of degree in some respects, so too are the differences between them and principles. No hard and fast line can be drawn, but broadly speaking, principles are much more abstract and hence are considerably more flexible, admitting of many changes in application without rendering them worthless.[41] By contrast, proverbs and prescriptions are so concrete that they are tightly bound to their immediate manifestations in conduct; extensive variation in the way they are applied therefore destroys their effectiveness. If their content is to be salvaged at all, it must be separated from the specific actions enjoined or prohibited and given general bearing. Essentially, this is what abstraction means here, and when it is successfully carried out the result is emergence of principles in the secular realm. Such abstract principles are still viewed as sacred, for they are regarded as basically unalterable, but the scope of the circumstances to which they have become applicable is so great that striking changes may come about under their auspices—changes that their formulators rarely if ever concretely envisage, but that may be foreseen as the vague "shape of things to come." Presumably inviolate and inviolable, abstract principles nevertheless lend themselves to changes that as time goes on may be very far-reaching indeed. Implementing amendments and other adaptations progressively modify the principles to which they are pursuant—that is, from which they follow or derive.

PURSUANT SECULARITY AS PRINCIPIAL EVALUATION

Pursuant evaluation is secular, for change is viewed as both possible and desirable as long as basic principles are kept in force. Instance the fact that the principles of "unalienable rights" such as those to "life, liberty, and the pursuit of happiness" were built into the fundamental documents of our republic, but at the same time procedures were provided for specifying those principles to be viewed in practice as suitable for amendment. The extent to which the Supreme Court would lay claim to its broadly comprehensive prerogative of interpretation apparently was not fully foreseen, but the prerogative, although repeatedly challenged, has come to be regarded as warranted in the light of the basic principles.

Readiness to concede such interpretative powers is in part the outcome of the deductively rational form in which interpretation is delivered. Taking the principle as end, the means chosen, however new in actuality, must still be regarded as pursuant to it, and in this sense as deducible from it *before* a specific occasion for implementation arises. Obviously, this is seldom possible. What really happens is that advocates of change say, in effect, "The measures we propose are essential for the well-being of us all, and fortunately they fully accord with the principles to which we all adhere." In other words, pursuant rationality may differ from prescriptive rationality in little more

[41] See *TVTSI*, pp. 74-76; p. 279, note 49. Karl Popper's able polemic, *The Open Society and Its Enemies* (Princeton, 1952), is in essence a defense of principial or "open" societies as against prescriptive or "closed" societies.

than level of abstraction; justificatory argument rather than genuine deduction may appear in both. The difference in level may be so great, however, that the principle proves adaptable to a vastly wider scope of change. It may become so abstract, indeed, that the interpretations connecting it with the concrete enactments it ostensibly sanctions must be highly sophisticated and hence beyond the grasp of most laymen. When this occurs, it is sometimes difficult to persuade such laymen that the principle is still being preserved; their identification with the value-system therefore diminishes to an extent endangering the continuance of the system.[42] Principial rationality, then, as a kind of rationality presumably representing "first principles" in operation, may by abstraction be so far removed from those principles that there comes about either reversion to more concrete prescriptions or abandonment of such abstract secular guides based, all too remotely, on sacred considerations.

THE CONSEQUENT KIND OF EXPEDIENCY

When such abandonment occurs, it means that the limitation of expedient changes to those that can somehow be brought into accord with the principles is no longer thought imperative. Expedient rationality begins to take over. Note, however, that in one quite valid sense "expediency" means only acting in such ways as to free, release, or extricate—to remove hampering restrictions. Of course, in general and popular usage, "expediency" frequently has the connotation of being always directly opposed to "principle." For our purposes here this connotation should be excluded; expedient changes may be consistent with recognized principles or they may not.[43] *There is no inherent contradiction.* Nevertheless, it is clear that changes regarded as expedient, as the most convenient ways, from both short-run and long-run standpoints, to alter what must be altered anyway, are seldom easy to harmonize with pursuant rationality—indeed, the contrary is ordinarily the case. Furthermore, emergencies of one kind or another, as well as ultra-rapid changes that foreseeably will give rise to emergencies, may so limit the time available for adaptation on the part of those who wish to hold expediency within the confines of principle that their efforts necessarily come to nothing.

[42] See *MIR*, pp. 184-188, especially the sections entitled "Abstraction Is Necessary for Principle, But Harmful to Principle," and "What We Don't Know About the Fifth Amendment."

[43] Etymologically, *expedire* means simply "to free the feet, to release, to extricate." This meaning is free from moralistic bias; so also the close parallel that follows:

"The Eskimo culture is the growth of centuries. . . . Survival has been the criterion. The succession of variations, followed by the elimination of the inexpedient, and the selection and retention of the expedient, has perfected . . . [a great deal].

". . . Expediency or inexpediency in most culture traits is not a matter of immediate life or death. Yet selection continually goes on." Edward M. Weyer, Jr., *The Eskimos: Their Environment and Folkways* (New Haven, 1932), pp. 65-66.

The upshot is that along with expedient tactics, as it were, that can sooner or later be brought into conformity with some strategy of pursuant rationality, others are introduced that may eventually burst all controlling bonds and disrupt the society that initially granted leeway to them. Examples are provided by totalitarian regimes of many kinds, which have often got their start out of concessions to crisis reluctantly vouchsafed by principial regimes unable otherwise to adapt to such crisis quickly enough. Concretely, the use of Article 48 of the Weimar Constitution in the last three years of its operation was essentially both a concession to demands for dictatorship and an admission of the inelasticity of parliamentary government in Germany, and the precedent thereby afforded was directly referred to when Hitler seized power. Communist Russia, Integralist Portugal, and Falangist Spain, along with several other instances that might be mentioned, provide additional examples. Such totalitarian systems should be discussed further, but space is lacking; about all that can be said here is that they unite, in seemingly incongruous but none the less effective ways, both rigid prescription and far-reaching expediency.

Relatively "unlimited" or "consequent" efforts to achieve ends by any means whatever, so long as these means are not regarded by their users as self-defeating, represent the essence of consequently expedient evaluation. Let it be noted, however, that a "so long as" qualification has been imposed; this means that unlimited expediency is unlimited only where the *range* of possible means is concerned, even though no limits are placed on the choice of means as such and therefore anything from gas-chamber extermination to brain-washing may be used. It is also true, of course, that ruthless planners may eschew certain means on the ground that they are likely to be worthless for the ends in view or in opposition to more effective means. This amounts to saying that "unlimited" secularity may actually undergo rational restriction; only that which seems likely to work is put into operation. Consequent secularity, then, is a type that is unlimited only in one sense—namely, that any workable means may be adopted. Restricted only by rational judgments of instrumental efficiency, it stands in striking contrast with pursuant secularity which, although likewise rationally limited in the means used, is further limited in the ends toward which they may be directed; consistency with presumably unalterable principles is demanded.

Values of consequently expedient type usually command the efforts of persons not constrained by the sacred as proverb or prescription, caring little about the direction change may take, or oriented toward the sacred only as an aspect of abstract principle lending itself to secularization. Discussion of pursuant secularity thus far has dealt primarily with those totalitarian manifestations repugnant to many of us. Therefore, it must also be pointed out that much of what is ordinarily called progress is directly attributable to consequent secularity. Science, in all its pure and many of its applied forms, is consequently secular; only those evaluations yielding prediction and control, regardless of other ends, are scientifically relevant. *The fact that even the most devoted scientists permit humanitarian norms to limit the scope of experimentation—for example, vivisection of human beings is seldom so much as contemplated—should not lead us to confuse the issue.* Science as such may be either angelic or devilish.

Although consequently expedient evaluation in the scientific and other realms produces what we may call the profits of progress, many of the costs of progress are simultaneously incurred. Social disorganization disastrous to many peoples contentedly abiding by proverb, prescription, or principle has often been introduced by zealously consequent modernizers from outside the society who promptly decamp when the effects of their efforts become embarrassing. Total warfare, utilizing the services of scientists for the wiping out of old men, women, and babes in arms, in strictly consequent fashion, is an even more disturbing manifestation, particularly when carried out in the service of irrational ends. We have recently witnessed scientifically conducted total warfare involving fantastic dreams of superior and inferior races, of a revival of Cæsarism, of an emperor as descendant of the Sun Goddess, and of a "proletariat" with the dialectically guaranteed destiny of world domination. The consequently rational use of means may combine with the pursuit of ends that social scientists, at least, would call nonsensical.[44]

NONRATIONAL SECULARITY AS COMFORTABLE AND THRILLING

Such combinations certainly are not the only possibilities in secular conduct. For example, both means and ends may be nonrational—indeed, they may both be so remote from even formal rationality that the distinction between them is virtually impossible to make. They are so heavily charged with emotion, so to speak, that they frequently are strikingly irrational, which is to say *counter*-rational, rather than merely nonrational.

Sweepingly secular evaluation of this kind can be split into at least two types, the comfortable and the thrilling. Readiness to seek any value that yields comfort, as long as the search itself is comfortable, and regardless of entailed breach of proverbial, prescriptive, or principial restrictions on change, is characteristic of the first variety. If such evaluation were put into words, they might run thus: "I like it because I like it, and what's to stop me?" There is no sharp break in the transition from this to the second variety, thrilling secularity, even though if charted the increase in degree might look like a steeply ascending exponential curve. The Roman slogan "Bread and the Circus" shows both the connection and the contrast of the two types. Gratifications linked with the attainment of thrillingly secular values form an array comprising anything from rabid spectatoritis as a

[44] This is a highly condensed restatement of the writer's earlier formulations, and as such may be hard to follow. See *TVTSI*, pp. 23-24; 32-42, 281-305.

wrestling fan to sadistic murder committed "for the hell of it." These are of course extreme instances; many less intensely thrilling evaluations, not far removed from the merely comfortable, are evident on every hand.

Wide prevalence of the various manifestations of comfortable and thrilling secularity brings about interpenetration of means and ends to an extent that in many cases amounts to virtual fusion;[45] distinction between them is difficult if not impossible. Furthermore, persons flinging themselves into the nonrational pursuit of the new as new overstep most if not all proverbial, prescriptive, and principial limits; indeed, even the rational requirements of consequently secular conduct exercise little or no control. This amounts to saying that a high proportion of the previously functioning norms, whether merely "external" or "internalized" in considerable measure, are evaded, disregarded, altered, or flouted as whim decrees.

NORMLESSNESS HAS LIMITS

This relative normlessness reaches beyond the form and content of the norms themselves in that the connections, whether nonrational or rational, linking the norms into some ascertainable kind of system, weaken rapidly, fluctuate, or almost vanish. Otherwise stated, the accrete character of proverbial and prescriptive value-systems, the at least ostensibly deductive and end-limited character of principial value-systems, and even the rationally means-restricted character of consequent value-systems are so fundamentally changed by the hither-and-yon search for transitory and disconnected ends by any and every means as hardly to warrant use of the term "system."

Note, however, that qualifications have been placed on the span and amount of normlessness by use of "relative" and similar words; no society that continues to operate for any length of time is ever entirely without "public" norms of some kind, however much it may favor normlessness. Short of complete societal dissolution, which rarely if ever occurs, needs and their correlative values are never utterly discrete, never wholly "private," never completely at random, never without functioning system. Moreover, when dissolution threatens, any society that manages to survive does so because of a "normative reaction to normlessness" that at the very least salvages fragments of its value-system around which stabilizing crystallization, so to speak, can proceed. Occasionally, it must be granted, conquest exterminating nearly all of the key value-carriers may wipe out a society, but this occurs very rarely. Even a few surviving women and children can preserve or reconstitute, perhaps as the hidden lore and practice of outwardly assimilated slaves, important segments of the subjugated society.

These qualifications begin to carry us beyond present relevance. Later in this chapter, some mention will be made of "pronormless" societies; as embodiments of value-systems, they *favor* a normless state of affairs, but

[45] *Ibid.*, pp. 29-32.

are not actually without guiding norms. Here, however, it should still be clear that although the normlessness manifested in thrilling and comfortable secularity is seldom if ever complete, it may go a very long way,[46] and that the pronormless societies in which it is continually and pervasively present are likely to be highly unstable.[47]

The end of the secular part of the scale has now been reached; we have surveyed the range from the minimum of willingness and/or ability to change, from change permissible only in the service of principle,to change for the sake of change. Otherwise put, we have seen how expedient rationality may veer toward either its pursuant or consequent varieties, and how the emotion-laden, nonrational search for the new is characterized by both comfortable and thrilling manifestations.

THE SCALING CRITERION FOR SECULAR EVALUATION

Brief reference to the criterion for estimating the degree of readiness to change—extinction of oneself or others—should perhaps be made here. It has already been noted that the criterion is hard to apply consistently even where reluctance to change is concerned; difficulties are even greater in the secular part of the scale.

However, it is probably true that principles, lacking identification with the concrete as they ordinarily do, can undergo amendments, interpretations, and other alterations so far-reaching that the principles themselves are slowly altered without the necessity of any sacrificial zeal for change. Pursuant rationality, as the kind of mentality involved, may be extremely flexible in judging what is actually pursuant, and such flexibility is hardly congruous with enthusiasm for change leading its advocates to suffer or inflict death.

Shifting to consequent secularity, it occasionally happens that scientists, for example, conduct experiments that may have lethal effects on themselves or others for the sake of changes increasing prediction and control, but such occurrences are not frequent. Further, when they do appear it is likely, to say the least, that evaluations of other than consequently secular type play prominent parts. Using our earlier example, humanitarian considerations, representing intimate, moralistic, and other sacredness in combination, may intrude. Certainly other aspects of consequent rationality, such as attention to economic efficiency and the like, do not engender indifference to survival in and of themselves. Again, consequent rationality as it enters into total warfare obviously is not operating autonomously; supreme loyalty to nation, class, or race enlists consequent rationality under its banner, and that is all.

[46] Those who have experienced a Rhineland carnival, for example, can testify to the astonishing lengths to which ordinarily staid and sober persons will go during this period, and how much this is taken for granted by all concerned. American "office parties" provide a parallel.

[47] See *MIR*, pp. 173-180.

Here too, the criterion seems usable; "extinction" for the sake of consequent secularity *per se* may tend to be infrequent if not minimal.[48]

Where nonrational secularity confronts us, there seems to be a definite increase, particularly at the thrilling end of the scale, in the correlation between readiness to change and readiness to risk death in pursuing it. In fact, even craving for the comfortable, when it brings about acquiescence in shortened life-prospects, may properly be viewed as having results adverse to personal and perhaps group survival and therefore as conforming to the criterion. The thrilling, obviously, often induces extreme risk of death, and sometimes its open acceptance. Many examples, ranging from "flame-divers" and "hell-drivers" to drug addicts, might be listed.

These, it may be granted, sometimes represent norms that are not of merely "private" or egocentric bearing; many societies make a definite place for thrill-seeking and expressly set leisure time aside for it. Moreover, those whose risking of death elicits thrills in others as well as themselves may be yielded much deference—the bullfighter, confronting "death in the afternoon," is but one of numerous instances. At the same time, however, it is hard to imagine a society in which everyone regularly takes crucial risks on every possible occasion; most death-defying thrills are vicarious.

Thrill-seeking *via* risks taken by others may nevertheless be destructive of many parts of the value-system important for general stability; avid delight in gladiatorial spectacles together with craving for increase in their cruelty, for example, are not usually regarded as having fostered the coherence of Roman society.

But in any case, it seems reasonably clear that the "extinction" criterion is applicable, with suitable provisos, not only to the sacred part of the scale but also to the secular. Other criteria may be found that are equally usable, if not more so, and some of them, given the empirical derivation of the clusters along the scale on which the analysis has concentrated, may well be implicit in what has thus far been set forth.

For example, ceremonialism undoubtedly has played a part. It appears, however, in pursuant secularity in relation to the preservation of principle,

[48] But see *TVTSI*, pp. 293-305. The "extinction" criterion becomes difficult to apply in the case of scientific value-monotheists. Here the pursuit of prediction and control becomes the chief or sole end of life, perhaps to be identified with other efforts at attaining new experience as in and of itself worth while, and as such non-scientific. That is to say, emotional neutrality in the selection of means is displaced by intense emotionality in the search for the thrill of new experience, which search is furthered by the latitude in the means available that science affords. Some scientists, in other words, pursue science not for the sake of science but for the sake of the thrilling experience that science provides. Although life may be sacrificed for the sake of such experience, it can still be said that science *per se* is not necessarily involved. Hence strictly scientific activity, as consequent secularity, may still conform to our scaling criterion; "extinction" may not be much beyond the minimal.

and also in some aspects of the comfortable and the thrilling. In other words, the *anti*-ceremonialism that should appear in the negative part of the scale, if it were to serve as a useful criterion, is only partially in evidence. At the same time, the "ceremonial" that may accompany a strip-teaser's conduct, for instance, is not ceremonial *per se,* for it may be freely changed "to give the bald-headed row a bigger bang." So likewise with ceremonial in some "luxury" restaurants; the waiters may be garbed as Arabs during one season and as Robin Hood yeomen the next. Hence, "ceremonial" may be essentially anti-ceremonial if it has no proverbial, prescriptive, or principial halo.

Once more, there is clearly a shift from the concrete to the abstract throughout the range from the proverbial to the thrilling, except that in the case of the latter, abstractions have become so attenuated that they have virtually disappeared. The concrete again is dominant—*but* as non-traditional or even anti-traditional.

Speculation about the scaling criteria might also center about the familiar "pattern variables" or their equivalents.[49] Given the present expository task, however, more pressing matters demand attention, and to them we now turn.

THE USES AND ABUSES OF LANDMARKS

Although we have been dealing primarily with types of reluctance and readiness to change rather than with the societies that embody them, a good deal has necessarily been said about such societies, and in fact some of the same designations can be applied to them: proverbial, prescriptive, principial, and pronormless. Further, a warning much the same as that bearing on the scale presentation must be issued; namely, that as empirically manifested the societal types in question are certain to be found only in mixture with one another.

This holds even for proverbial societies. The empirical instances approximate the type construct quite closely in many cases, but it is virtually impossible to find proverbial societies without prescriptive traits, and evidence of normlessness, albeit in minor respects, is seldom altogether lacking. Concretely, then, it is the *proportion* of proverbial and other discernible characteristics that must guide the researcher in detailed investigation; his types are only general landmarks.[50]

But landmarks serve useful purposes, and in addition to those listed above, two others must be set up if the predictive orientation of the theory being presented is to be not only maintained but also made more definitely

[49] The writer has paid some attention to this in *MIR*, pp. 191-196, there quoting and commenting on a 1930 presentation. See also Chap. 5, by W.L. Kolb, in the present book, esp. pp. 120-131.

[50] This has often been stressed, but see *TVTSI*, pp. 106-107, and Chapter 7, by J. C. McKinney, in the present book.

applicable in empirical investigation. The additional landmarks have long been known as isolation and accessibility; they refer to the general situations in which societies of certain types are ordinarily found.

ISOLATION AND ACCESSIBILITY AS SITUATIONS

Both isolation and accessibility have at least three distinguishable aspects: vicinal, social, and mental.

The physical absence of or separation from other societies in the vicinity constitutes the vicinal isolation of any society so situated. Every society has both geographical location and vicinal position, and the former has nothing to do with the presence or absence of other societies in the vicinity—latitude, longitude, altitude, and so on, suffice for its specification. In contrast, vicinal position cannot be specified unless reference is made to the possibility of relations with other societies. Such reference immediately brings into consideration the level of the culture or cultures involved. The inhabitants of desert Nevada at a time when not even the horse was available for transportation were in a vicinal position very different from that of those living in the same region today, for the railroad, automobile, and airplane have brought about a drastic change in what may be called "effort distance."[51] In the first case, the missions of the California coast might as well have been at the South Pole as far as the possibility of reaching or being reached by them was concerned; in the second, a Piute chief can make his appearance on a Hollywood movie lot within three hours or less.

Culture is responsible for such shifts from isolation to accessibility. The geographical location of the society remains precisely the same after the advent of the airplane, but its vicinal isolation is transformed into vicinal accessibility. Nature presents man with his geographical location; culture provides his vicinal position.[52]

The possibility of coming into contact with other societies in the vicinity, however, remains only a possibility where vicinal accessibility as such is concerned. The fact that other societies can easily be reached does not mean that there will be an effort to reach them. Differences in color and language, to choose obvious instances, may block associative relations or even bring about dissociation so extreme that one society exterminates another without ever having defined its members as human beings. Here there has been vicinal accessibility, but "social" isolation.

Clearly enough, culture plays a key part in social isolation too—for example, there is ample evidence showing that when marked dislike of this or that skin color is evident, such dislike is learned. The same holds for language. Having acquired one symbolic system that in many ways is funda-

[51] Called "time-cost" distance by some ecologists.

[52] The term stems from E. C. Semple, who Anglicized Ratzel's *Lage*. See *TVTSI*, p. 47 including note 53, and p. 68; also *STFLTS*, *passim* (use index).

mental to the knowing-desiring-norming processes that we have lumped together as evaluation in general, children, and adults as well, are necessarily disquieted when confronted by another system. They literally undergo, in some cases, the shock of incipient disorientation; their bewilderment is more than momentary and superficial. The consequence is unwillingness or inability to associate in mildly congenial or even neutral ways with beings who in the nature of the case "don't seem human." Association thus blocked, the continued physical presence of persons whose strangeness is repeatedly evident intensifies the tendency to social isolation; the process is circular. Less extreme instances of course abound, but at bottom social isolation roots in failure, for whatever reason, of effective communication.[53]

Mental isolation is closely linked with social; nevertheless, it is sufficiently distinct to require special consideration. The overcoming of vicinal isolation may make it possible for peoples to come into physical contact. Social isolation may yield, in considerable measure, to painfully acquired ability to communicate which, although sometimes partially at nonverbal and hence inadequate levels, still permits association of rudimentary type. Bridging these gaps, however, is not enough; isolation may be kept intense if not intact by more or less clearly outlined ideas. Culture is at work here too.

Take, for example, the mental isolation of the Gypsy from the various host peoples among whom he has moved. There soon was no vicinal isolation of any consequence, and social isolation rapidly diminished to the point where the Gypsy became an extensively patronized specialist in coppersmithing, horse-trading, fortunetelling, and so on. Some social isolation remained, for communication was partial; the Gypsy still resorted to his own language when necessary for secrecy, but partial communication there nevertheless was, quite sufficient to produce romantic infatuation of the kind described in the old ballad, "She sleeps with a blackjack Gypsy, O." Mental isolation, however, continued to be strikingly apparent in most cases. The host peoples defined the Gypsies as pariahs, thieves, tricksters, and kidnappers, and the Gypsy in turn often derided and despised his hosts, viewing them as fair game. The resulting mental isolation has only today begun to disappear because the Gypsy as Gypsy is disappearing.

Isolation of this kind is particularly interesting because it was based, generally speaking, on proverbial value-definitions; there were no such elaborate ideologies involved as those linked, for instance, with anti-Semitism, which tend to be prescriptive. Such prescriptive evaluation, because of its explicitness, codification, and formal rationality, engenders mental isolation of quite intense kinds, but on the other hand, the implicit and uncoordinated character of proverbial isolation makes it more difficult to attack by

[53] In terms of effective self-and-other definition. See *TVTSI*, p. 43, and *MIR*, p. 108.

means of a counter-ideology. Passive resistance, coupled with occasional resort to guerilla tactics, so to speak, may sometimes be harder to overcome than rigidly disciplined, planfully organized defensive warfare.

HOW PROVERBIAL SOCIETIES ARE SITUATED

However this may be, proverbial societies often evidence all three kinds of isolation in marked degree, and are notoriously hard to change. Societies most closely conforming to the proverbial type are usually remote from those routes of travel facilitated by the prevailing level of culture; they are difficult both to get away from and to reach.

Granted, some proverbial societies have not been marked by extreme vicinal isolation, but in such instances, social and mental isolation have amply compensated for the lack of vicinal. The customary modes of interaction and organization usually contrast so strongly with those of the strangers who, singly or in groups, find their way among the natives, that the strangers are *ipso facto* offenders against sacred patterns almost every time they turn around.[54] Social isolation is thereby not only left as impermeable as before, but is frequently walled still higher. Even trade may be almost impossible to carry on without perpetual danger of assault, and the more intimate relations are simply out of the question.

With such interaction at a minimum, there is every opportunity for mental isolation to maintain and intensify itself. Notions of the unclean, immoral, hostile, and heathenish conduct of the outsiders readily arise, quickly spread, and sooner or later find standard proverbial expression.

PRESCRIPTIVE SOCIETIES AND THEIR SITUATIONAL COMBINATIONS

As repeatedly noted, the empirical boundaries between our main societal types can seldom if ever be definite. Prescriptive societies, although ordinarily larger and culturally more developed than proverbial, often preserve many of the components of the latter; they are simply made slightly more explicit, given a semblance of codification, and subjected to a degree of formal rationality while still remaining accrete. In spite of this, however, fairly close approximations of prescriptive societies can be found. Witness the fact that at certain periods in the development of ancient Greece, and particularly of Athens, much proverbial lore was superseded by prescriptive law—indeed, prescription at times became abstract enough to show many principial features. The same was true of several phases of Roman development and, now and again, of a number of large states in the Near East and in the Orient proper.

In most of these cases, the advance of prescription was enormously facilitated by the advent of writing; many prescriptive societies were literally so in the etymological sense. Script took the place of mere words and their

[54] But see *TVTSI*, p. 47, note 54.

partially symbolic equivalents. But let it be hastily noted that not all proverbial societies are or have been nonliterate, nor all prescriptive societies literate.[55] *A limited kind of literacy may readily coexist with proverbial dominance,* and well-worked-out techniques of memorization and repetition may render a society essentially prescriptive at a time when the art of writing is unknown. There is a *tendency* for nonliteracy to go hand in hand with the proverbial and literacy with the prescriptive, and that is all.

Prescriptive societies, their value-systems crystallized by elaborate codification and the like, may survive for a long time in situations of considerable vicinal accessibility. Several of the totalitarian regimes of yesterday and today evidence many cultural facilities transcending vicinal isolation. Nevertheless, Iron, Bamboo, and similar "curtains" may counteract man's devices of transportation and communication. Refusal to grant exit or entry permits may mean that societies so restricted are quite as effectively removed from one another's vicinity as they would be if all cars, trains, ships, and planes were suddenly to undergo atomic disintegration. Culture, in other words, may counteract culture; what makes for vicinal accessibility may be put out of operation by social obstacles and mental barriers. Ideological conflict, in particular, may vicinally isolate a prescriptive society.

Except for such "cold-war" manifestations, however, the kinds of isolation appearing most often in prescriptive societies are (1) the vicinal varieties stemming from paucity of culture rather than the thwarting of one of its aspects by another, (2) social isolation deriving, for example, from absence of so much as Pidgin English or from offensively contrasting food habits, and (3) mental isolation stretching all the way from Zionist conviction of being God's chosen occupants of Palestine to the Franco Spaniards' belief that Baptists are emissaries of the Evil One.

Significant proportions of the social isolation helping prescribed societies to keep in balance are produced or strengthened, as several of the foregoing illustrations indicate, by governmental, ecclesiastical, and similar social organizations authoritarian enough to induce or enforce submission. Oftentimes governmental and ecclesiastical systems are so interlinked that the cleric can rely on the policeman or the soldier whenever necessary, and like the soldier can issue edicts in a prescriptive chain of command that reaches down to the parish layman as a kind of religious G. I. (see Chap. 15, by Paul Honigsheim, in the present volume, for discussion of the "ecclesia").

State and church are by no means the only institutions that in prescribed societies promulgate authoritative edicts, even though it may be granted that they are the ones most often able to back up such edicts with spiritual or physical coercion. Educational institutions inculcate many prescriptions; so likewise do economic.

[55] The writer earlier used "preliterate" as an equivalent of "proverbial," but has since abandoned the former as erroneous. See *STFLTS* (1952), Chap. 1.

Occasionally, to be sure, the prescriptions promulgated or inculcated may be at variance with one another. In contemporary France, for example, what ecclesiastical authorities decree is not infrequently gainsaid by governmental officials. Moreover, there are other institutional conflicts; the French schoolteacher is quite likely to be a left-wing Socialist or even a Communist, poles removed from everything represented by the local factory owner, who is nevertheless equally fervent *and* dogmatic. This points to the fact that in a principial society—and contemporary France can hardly be placed in any other category—many prescriptive systems may be in full swing, and the function of the principial regime then consists primarily in maintaining a somewhat uneasy balance of power among them.

Still, we are chiefly concerned at this point with societies that are primarily prescriptive in their dominant value-systems. Totalitarian regimes, covering the span from the Egypt of the Pharaoh's taskmasters to the East Germany of a Communist "people's democracy," provide the most relevant illustrations.

Extreme social isolation frequently appears under totalitarianism. Not only are foreigners distrusted and in many cases excluded, but in addition many groups within the society are held to be subversive, at the very least, and are therefore expelled, imprisoned, or liquidated. But if mental isolation yields in some measure, for whatever reason, to mental accessibility, social isolation, and vicinal as well, may likewise yield. Isolation is by no means irreversible.

For the present analysis, one conclusion to be drawn from such examples is already familiar: it is very hard to distinguish sharply between social and mental isolation. Another instance to the same effect is the prohibition of mixed marriage that has so long prevailed among Orthodox Jews, Roman Catholics, Boer Calvinists, and others. Such prohibition socially isolates one group from another, with increase in mental isolation as the inevitable consequence, but the social isolation, if we look at the historical record, seems to have been largely the outcome of the mental. Regardless of which came first, however, one reacts on the other; the process is circular, and disentanglement, concretely speaking, is to say the least bafflingly difficult.

VICINAL AND SOCIAL ACCESSIBILITY AID PRINCIPIAL TRANSITION

Shifting attention to isolation and accessibility among principial societies, where the transition from sacred to secular becomes reasonably well marked, it seems safe to say that except when warfare, "cold" or "hot," is going on—and when it is, principles are likely to turn into prescriptions anyway—there is much vicinal accessibility. It goes almost without saying that virtually any society that has become principial has been exposed to frequent visits by strangers; the barriers of nature have been penetrated, in this way or that, by the devices of culture and their carriers.

Further, outsiders not only reach the society easily, but can also go to and fro in it without being everywhere rebuffed; hence the erstwhile outsider often attains the rank of insider, and sometimes speedily. In contemporary terms, he gains admission to private homes and clubs as well as to offices and hotels, and although a few restrictions ostensibly remain, they are not taken very seriously by anybody. On occasion it even happens that visitors encounter fewer social barriers than do underlings, whether or not so labeled, who are presumably fully-accredited members of the society concerned; "the charm of the exotic" is by no means uncommon as a rapid solvent of social isolation.

MENTAL ACCESSIBILITY AND PRINCIPIAL ADAPTATION IN BRITAIN

It was earlier pointed out that prescriptive values are frequently codified, but that such codification usually amounts to little more than "cataloging."[56] In spite of the formal rationality used, the deductive interconnections are only putative; the prescriptive values are really accrete—inseparably merged.

When prescriptive evaluation gives ground to the principial variety, expedient rationality has begun to operate. However, it has only begun, for it is still limited by persisting reluctance to change the core of the abstract principle or principles. This core ultimately derives, in virtually all instances, from historically traceable concrete prescriptions. That is to say, pursuant rationality, as a limited kind of expedient rationality, makes its appearance in principially secular societies.

In such societies, there must always be something to which rationality can be pursuant. There are many examples other than the American "natural rights" principle to which reference was previously made, and among them British developments may be conveniently singled out. Starting with the divine right of the ruler, eventually established after long dynastic struggles and exclusion of papal jurisdiction, numerous adaptations to changing circumstances brought about a limited constitutional monarchy in which the sovereign is not much more than "a human flag." Important policy declarations read to "subjects" by the supposed ruler are actually formulated by ministers coming to power in ways owing little or nothing to the sovereign's sanction.

A large part of the ceremonial inseparable from coronation and similar supreme symbolizations is still ritual in its proper meaning, for it is directed toward the deity who is believed to vouchsafe and protect divine right. Nevertheless, many other aspects of the ceremonial are imbued with little if anything more than loyalistic and commemorative sacredness, and a number, significantly enough, are pursuantly secular.

[56] For an apt discussion of "catalog" codification, see Marcel Granet, *op. cit.*, especially Chap. 3, "Les Nombres."

The secularity is recognizable not only in the tacit acceptance by the sovereign of restrictions such as the Royal Marriage Act, but also in the open avowal, through oath, of firm intention to abide by the law of the realm. "Pursuant to the British Constitution" (which although only partially codified is viewed as a coherent whole), changes that have led to restrictions on previously untrammeled divine right are expressly accepted. "The sovereign reigns, but does not govern."

How effectively principle had become dominant over prescription was shown by the abdication of Edward VIII, forced by a mere commoner, Stanley Baldwin. Protests there were, issuing from adherents of both proverbial and prescriptive conceptions, plus other protests deriving from a good deal of comfortable and even thrilling nonrationality, but the pursuantly secular won out.

In spite of this, however, any observer thinking that the sacred core of the monarchical principle had been eliminated would be in serious error. It triumphantly survived the abdication of the sovereign who has now become the feckless Duke of Windsor, to find a focus in devotion to a legitimate and earnest successor, George VI, and at his death there resounded the shout, "The King is dead—long live the Queen!" A limited constitutional monarchy such as today's Britain upholds still stems, then, from a sacred first principle, but the abstractness of the principle makes pursuant rationality widely applicable. Contemporary Britain is best characterized as a principial secular society.

This is as much as to say that a society that once had a closed sacred system, partially based on the proverbial but to an even larger extent on the prescriptive, opened at least as early as the sixteenth century to principles previously unknown. Some of these, at least, are traceable to prescriptions or principles earlier evident in countries with contrasting ideologies. Only yesterday, the principial secular society of Britain found it possible to espouse for a time the pursuant rationality of a monarchical State Socialism denounced by some Britons keenly aware of historical antecedents as fundamentally foreign.[57] They were right, where the State Socialism was concerned, but they overlooked the fact that in the minds of ordinary citizens the principle of monarchical reign had become so remote from ordinary governmental exigencies that it survived, and continues to survive, one supposedly revolutionary change after another. In short, fears of destructive contradictions have proved unfounded; normlessness does not necessarily follow drastic innovations if the principial society within which they occur is possessed of principles abstractly sacred manifested in changes concretely secular.

[57] Herbert Spencer correctly termed the State Socialism he knew "Bismarckian." Let it be noted, however, that in the stress on "culture contact" here and elsewhere, there is *no* intent to restrict the sources of social change to such contact alone. Strains arising from *within* a society may induce change, as the writer has stressed in TVTSI, pp.264-278, dealing with *indigenous* and *exogenous* change.

NORMLESSNESS IN FRONTIER AND RURAL SOCIETIES

Passing reference was earlier made to pronormless societies—that is, to societies having value systems *favoring* an extremely free-and-easy state of affairs, and that are therefore *pro*normless in this sense. Nevertheless, although such societies are unstable, they often have enough continuity flowing from established proverbial, prescriptive, and principial value-systems to maintain a measure of functional effectiveness over fairly long periods. It would therefore be quite unrealistic to call them normless without qualification, and continually to insert "relatively" is cumbrous. By building the prefix "pro" into the designation of the society itself, stress is simultaneously laid on the wide spread of normlessness and on the fact that any society surviving *qua* society, whatever its instability, is never wholly without some normative structure. Indeed, only when expedient rationality is largely unlimited—which is to say, when the consequent is virtually unchecked by the pursuant—do confortable and thrilling nonrationality, always and everywhere present in some degree,[58] begin to play so overwhelmingly prominent a part in evaluation that serious threat to the survival of a pronormless society arises.

In most empirical instances, obviously, the vicinal accessibility of pronormless societies is extremely high. Ready at hand, therefore, is the assumption that *all* such societies are predominantly urban, since urban centers stand at the crossroads, as it were, of traffic and communication. Such an assumption must be rejected.

Take, for example, the many frontier societies dotting the record of man's to-and-fro expansion over the face of the earth. Most of these have been marked by normlessness in startling measure, but only by very strained interpretation could they be called urban. The mutually destructive clash of value-systems need not run its course in anything remotely approximating a city.

Further, the slow deliquescence of restrictions on change ultimately bringing about a pronormless state of affairs may go on in vicinally isolated rural societies where "cultural loss through lapse" culminates in many equivalents of Tobacco Road. Under some circumstances the transmitting, learning, and sharing of sacred reluctances cannot be carried out effectively; each succeeding generation possesses fewer of the technical, expressive, and control facilities[59] of the ancestral culture than did its predecessors, and the outcome is a sprawling, formless collection of creatures whose conduct is almost unpredictable, even to themselves, except in the most vaguely general terms. They will eat, drink, sleep, and copulate, but what? when?

[58] This is an important point; see *MIR*, pp. 174, 188.

[59] J. W. Woodard, "A New Classification of Culture and a Restatement of the Culture-Lag Theory," *ASR*, 1 (Feb., 1936), pp. 89-102.

where? and how? may be questions almost unanswerable. Normlessness, in short, is sometimes rural in setting.[60]

THE FICKLENESS OF URBANITY

These provisos inserted, it may then be freely granted that many striking examples of normlessness have urban locales. Further, "urbanism as a way of life" is often so powerfully exemplary that it is practiced in at least some respects throughout most of the hinterland. Frequent trips to Athens made even the Attic shepherd, for many purposes, a representative of urban standards of political conduct, if nothing else, and "Sears and Sawbuck" and "Monkey Ward" notably assist the denizens of the American countryside in imitating, although a trifle belatedly, the styles of Hollywood and "Gay Paree." In urban centers *per se,* strangers usually are physically present in large numbers and are often accepted with little question. Those native to the society either travel freely themselves, or through the mass communications that an advanced culture affords, vicariously participate in travel and thus become fairly well aware of cultural contrasts of all kinds, with attendant growth of relativism. Otherwise put, there is much actual or vicarious vicinal mobility.

Added to this, social accessibility is high; strangers are welcomed as sources of novel thrills as well as for the cash they contribute. Intermingling of every variety goes on; secular societies yielding to normlessness frequently resemble, in some sections, conglomerations such as slum Liverpool, Saloniki, Algiers, Chicago's Near North Side, and Hamburg's Reeperbahn. Social accessibility prevails between classes, castes, and like groupings that in societies not in rapid flux tend to remain separate. Social stratification is certainly not absent in pronormless societies, but the various layers rapidly shift up and down in ways blurring their distinguishing traits. Briefly, social mobility is marked. City spot-maps centering on social phenomena show this clearly; quarters once impenetrable by *hoi polloi* become free-and-easy. Equalitarianism prevails in practice, not so much through adherence to "natural rights" conceptions as through the near-impossibility of discriminating among anonymous fragments of an almost formless aggregate.

Easygoing "open-mindedness," representing mental accessibility leading toward normlessness, is widely prevalent, and usually is nonrational, in contradistinction to the willingness rationally to debate the advisability of various pursuant methods of adaptation characteristic of principial societies.

[60] Such considerations, and many others, have led to the writer's rejection of the folk-urban dichotomy. See *TVTSI*, pp. 256, including notes 19, 20, and 21; and *MIR*, 154, 168, 176-177, 196, and 349-350.

Interesting sidelights on this topic are afforded by some of the writings of Hemingway and, of course, much of Faulkner—indeed, the whole "decay under the magnolias" school.

Pronormless societies, in other words, grant great leeway to facile tolerance reflecting, at bottom, indifference to principle. This tolerance may reach the point where criminal conduct proves attractive as affording the kind of thrill that imaginary participation in such conduct yields.

To be sure, many sacred formulas are in circulation, but they are treated as magical expedients in "playing the numbers" or whatever. They do not act as checks on comfortable and thrilling deviations.

The society is also fully open to scientific developments, even though these may clearly be detrimental to the remaining vestiges of once operative value-systems. Using our familiar example once more, total warfare casting aside all humanely proverbial, prescriptive, and principial restraints is heartily advocated if victory can thereby be assured—"Use the atom bomb before they use it on us." At less drastic levels also science is judged praiseworthy, but not for its own sake or for its real or supposed pursuit of exalted principial goals such as "the welfare of mankind." On the contrary, it is supported because when applied as a sort of wand-waving magic it brings improved health, better food, more leisure, and greater thrills. Futurism, of which fantasies of space travel provide a current example, is freely indulged in, and in this and other respects mental mobility takes extreme form.

In sum, the epitome of consequent rationality, science, is held to be worth while primarily because it promises easy attainment of nonrational or even irrational ends.[61]

THE NORMATIVE REACTION TO NORMLESSNESS

Most of the illustrations just used bear chiefly on contemporary normlessness, but a few of them have pointed toward earlier manifestations. This was done by design, for it is often erroneously believed that extreme secularization is an affair of modern times. Numerous cases, many of them analyzed in detail rather than used merely for illustrative purposes, have been presented by others, and the writer has dealt with several himself.[62]

Moreover, secularization in well-marked form is not only evident in the remoter record but, in addition, has been repeatedly followed by its reverse, sacralization. At many times and places we encounter a "normative reaction to normlessness"[63] that not only puts a stop to ultrarapid secular-

[61] All ultimate ends are viewed by the writer as nonrational, but most persons in the contemporary world hold some, at least, to be rational in the meaning they attach to the latter term.

[62] Here see *STFLTS* (1952), using index for "secularization." See also F. J. Teggart, *Theory and Processes of History* (Berkeley, 1941), *passim.*, on topics such as "breakup of idea-systems," "release," etc. A. J. Toynbee's *A Study of History* (Oxford, 1934-1952) is in several respects a study of secularization-sacralization in many societies.

[63] Briefly discussed in *STFLTS* (1952), pp, 834-836; *TVTSI*, pp. 76-78, 270; *MIR*, pp. 182-184, 189.

ization but also introduces and/or reinstates reluctances to change that soon take on, or attempt to take on, the features of stabilizing value-systems. The Protestant Reformation, the Catholic Counter-Reformation, the Fascist and Nazi seizures of power, the founding and revival at various times of the Ku Klux Klan, and the establishing of Methodism all provide partial illustration.

One of the reasons for this is that societies are rarely of one piece.[64] Normlessness may be gratifyingly comfortable and thrilling to some members and perhaps to a majority, but for others it is uncomfortable and even frightening. For these the slackening or breaking of normative ties presages disaster; the reckless pursuit of irrational ends at the risk or because of threat to survival spurs those not cherishing those ends to oftentimes frantic endeavor to avert what they regard as the foreseeable consequences of their fellows' contumacy.

Indeed, the consequences may be viewed as not merely foreseeable but as actually present; stark ruin confronts not only the wicked but also the righteous. Such major disaster need not be clearly demonstrable; all that is necessary is that a sufficient number of the populace believe it already to have occurred, to be occurring, or about to occur.

Given firm conviction, the next phase is search for a saving solution. If memories of proverbial, prescriptive, or principial formulas are still strong, demand for return to the good old days is almost automatic. Archaism in one or another form is held to be the way out.

What the good old days really were is always a matter of interpretation, however, and whose interpretation is to be accepted? The same question arises if the solution is found in a social order never yet concretely exemplified *in toto:* futurism, in other words, must also find an authoritative interpreter. In either case, the problem of leadership comes to the fore.

THE TIME, THE PLACE, AND THE MAN

Inasmuch as pronormless societies are *ipso facto* chaotic or at the very least syncretic—that is, characterized by intermixture of oftentimes irreconcilable value-systems—short-lived gospels of political, economic, moral, religious, and other import flourish luxuriantly. Such gospels spring from soil and seed, true enough, but their successful cultivation is usually the accomplishment of some extraordinary person surpassing others who, although also extraordinary, are not favored by time, place, circumstance, and skill.

Sociologists will at once recognize that the charismatic leader is here being alluded to, not as the possessor of the charisma of office but rather of the person. The man, his mission, and his extraordinary gifts are all bound together, and out of the welter of contending solutions this particular

[64] It would be difficult to overstress this point. See *MIR*, p. 190, and the article by C. W. M. Hart, "The Sons of Turimpi," *AA*, 56, (April, 1954), pp. 242-261.

trinity-in-unity emerges triumphant. Followers flock to him, a cult of regeneration takes shape, and with good fortune, a center of successful sacralization is firmly established.

WHO CARRIES ON FOR THE LEADER?

Note the qualification "with good fortune." In order solidly to found any sacralizing system, continuity beyond the life span of the initiating leader must somehow be insured. The vexed question of succession arises, which is to say that the problem of effective transmission of the follower-facilitating extraordinariness must be confronted.

In earlier periods, reliance was often placed on the familiar "Blood will tell"; biological heredity, however reckoned, was held to be assurance of legitimate charisma. Other methods were: the direct designation of the successor, regardless of kinship, by the aging or ailing leader; selection jealously controlled by a small group of adherents thought to be able to speak in his behalf after his dotage or death; more formal and neutral choice by a wider circle, and so on. Whatever method was followed, preternatural qualities—which is to say, those assumed to represent the natural in altogether unusual degree of force or concentration—were, at the very least, held to be indispensable. In many cases, of course, supernatural traits in the strict sense were the only valid grounds for recognition.

THE RETURN OF THE SACRED

In this modern day, the preternatural seems almost wholly to have crowded out the supernatural, but it is amazing to observe how often the distinction between the two is blurred during the lifetime of the leader. The net effects of such blurring, in the short run, are almost indistinguishable from the open attribution of supernatural powers.

In any event, it can be said with some confidence that far-reaching secularization not infrequently engenders intensified sacralization; extremes meet. The new or revised sacred system may not be holy in its orientation, but the loyalistic and similar sacredness that it calls forth and intensifies is often so powerful that the unwary are persuaded to speak of racism as a religion, class-consciousness as a religion, nationalism as a religion, democracy as a religion. Disregarding such errors, it must still be said that although value-systems go, value-systems come.

A SUBSTANTIVE SUMMARY

The rough survey of sacred-secular theory as interpreted by the writer has now been completed. A sketch of the basic epistemology issued in the conclusion that all knowing-desiring-norming, characteristically human because occurring in such combination only in cultural contexts, represents actions reciprocally linking needs and values, which actions may therefore be viewed as evaluations. A scale of evaluations was constructed along a continuum leading from maximum reluctance to maximum readiness to change. It used as criterion the sacrifice of life in behalf of both extremes ("extinction" for the sake of preventing change *vs.* "extinction" in pursuit of change). In conjunction with the scale of evaluations, and using in addition the situational criteria of isolation and accessibility in their vicinal, social, and mental aspects, four constructed types of societies—proverbial, prescriptive, principial, and pronormless—were set up and analyzed. Repeated reference was made to the empirical intermixture of any and all societies approximating these types. Along with this, stress was laid on the fact that no society whatever is concretely "all of one piece"; when any society is treated as a whole, this is necessarily by definition, witting or unwitting. Shifts from one societal type to another were also discussed, but not in order to demonstrate evolutionary or even developmental sequence; skipping and reversal is not only possible but also frequently evident. Finally, some attention was paid to the fact that extreme secularization has sometimes been transmuted into its direct opposite, extreme sacralization, and that in this process the combination of felt crisis and charismatic leadership plays an essential part. The result is that the societal phoenix springs from its own ashes; the chaos of today becomes the cosmos of tomorrow.

The Background of Sacred-Secular Theory

WE ALL OWE DEBTS TO OUR FORERUNNERS

In the first main portion, now concluded, of the present chapter, little reference was made to the manifold sources of the ideas presented. This second portion, although much less lengthy, attempts to list and comment on as many of these sources as can be dealt with in appropriate space limits. At the beginning of the attempt it is perhaps permissible to belabor, by echoing the farmer's plaintive remark, what to most readers is already obvious: "I milked fifty cows for the little butter I got."[65]

Moreover, the various concepts that have coalesced in the foregoing sacred-secular theory did not precipitate in relation to that theory alone. On the contrary, awareness of their apparent worth arose in conjunction with social-scientific problems of several kinds. Naturally, any researcher finds that most of his efforts somehow interact, but rarely if ever does he foresee what the results of such interaction will be. Using Kantian language loosely, percepts call forth concepts and concepts call forth percepts in a reciprocal process having no ascertainable beginning or end. For the most part, refer-

[65] "Fifty" is a distinct understatement; see *STFLTS* (1952).

ence hereinafter is to the concepts, but that argues nothing about actual priority in time, as the earlier discussion of "givens" and "takens" may have helped to show.

Further, the fact that it is often hard for us to remember when we first heard the word that eventually acquires content and systematic significance, thereby becoming a genuine concept, often leads us to think that we can date accurately the emergence of such a concept in our own experience. Few would wish to deny that appropriate terms may bring flashes of insight; a mere jumble of evidence may kaleidoscopically fall into pattern at the touch of a word—but the jumble must somehow have preoccupied us, and there must somehow have been something to be jumbled. How are we to assign dates to what in such cases are culminations of experience?

Enough. The concepts used in the first portion of the chapter have many parallels and progenitors, but they took on meaning for the writer only in close conjunction with various perplexities and tentative solutions thereof. Concepts and perplexities will consequently be discussed together without, it is hoped, in any way minimizing indebtedness to the concepts and their originators.

MOURNING IS NOT A SIMPLE MATTER

Among the first of the baffling problems were those resulting from an over-ambitious study of bereavement.[66] No accepted terminology enabling easy distinction between rites of tendance or commemoration, on the one hand, and evil-averting (apotropaic) or placatory conduct, on the other, could then be found in the literature. Malinowski's revealing analysis was discovered only after the study had been completed.[67] Reverence, piety, hope for continued fellowship, and simple affection were obscured by unduly comprehensive terms such as blessed, cursed, tabooed, and what not. Commemoration of holy bearing as contrasted with that having only intimate reference, and consequent aversion of magical type, plus many other kinds of bereavement conduct, were all mixed together. No way out of the *impasse* could then be found, and the study remained analytically incomplete. Nevertheless, the relevance of Malinowski's distinctions eventually dawned on the writer, as did also that of Rudolf Otto's "idea of the holy."[68] Further,

[66] *SPOB.* By "over-ambitious" is meant "requiring conceptual equipment and facilities for research far exceeding what was then available."

[67] Bronislaw Malinowski, "Magic, Science, and Religion," in Joseph Needham (ed.), *Science, Religion, and Reality* (London, 1925). Much later (1948, in fact), the writer became familiar with the revealing "Baloma: The Spirits of the Dead in the Trobriand Islands" (1916), reprinted in Malinowski's *Magic, Science, and Religion and Other Essays*, edited by Robert Redfield (Glencoe, 1948).

[68] Rudolf Otto, *The Idea of the Holy: An Inquiry into the Non-Rational Factor in the Idea of the Divine and Its Relation to the Rational*, trans. by J. W. Harvey (2nd ed., London, 1950). The writer referred to an early edition of the original in *STFLTS* (1st ed., 1938),

Simmel's small-group and Cooley's primary-group analyses belatedly assumed significance for intimate sacredness. In short, the search for adequate concepts had begun, and with the lapse of time brought what still seem to be usable results.

THE YOUTH MOVEMENT PUZZLE

At about the same time as the bereavement study was undertaken—indeed, in some respects a trifle earlier—a study of the German youth movement was launched. At that time, the writer possessed virtually no sociological equipment, but even when, after several years, there was again opportunity for first-hand research, very few suitable concepts could be used; the necessary conceptual sophistication had not yet been acquired. The existing literature incorporated several highly relevant concepts, as rereading has shown, but most of them failed to register at that time. Certain "givens" did not become "takens."

Moreover, even limited participation in the movement on the part of the writer led to identification with some parts of its value-system to the point where the detachment necessary even for good observation was hard to maintain. Needless to say, the vocabularies of the more ardent devotees were full of "highly diagnostic" words and phrases, and many of them were set down in the records the writer kept; nevertheless, there was no realization at the time that they were, so to speak, symptomatic. It therefore proved impossible readily to label, much less systematically to connect, devotion to the self-appointed *but* chosen leader, loss of self-identity in merging with a group, acceptance of situations as defined by prescribed ideologies, and a maze of similar phenomena.[69] Appropriate terminology for those already characterized as well as for the value-systems likely to have been involved will already have occurred to the informed reader, but for a considerable time the writer possessed no clues of any consequence.

When these emerged, the contributions of Max Weber on charismatic leadership, Troeltsch's distinctions between the various kinds of social structure, small and large, carrying supreme value-systems (see Chap. 15, by Paul Honigsheim, in the present volume), and Scheler's attention to unipathy as one of the many ways in which identification with others may take place proved most helpful. Traces of all of these are to be found in sacred-secular theory as heretofore presented, particularly where reference is made to loyalistic and intimate sacredness, to prescriptive societies, and to the normative reaction to normlessness.

Vol. I, p. xxiv of notes. See also Robert F. Davidson, *Rudolf Otto's Interpretation of Religion* (Princeton, 1947).

[69] Here see the bibliography in Howard Becker, *German Youth: Bond or Free*, hereinafter *GYBOF* (London, 1946; or reissue, New York, Humanities Press). The book itself may also be of use with reference to the points noted.

STUBBORNESS MAY BE MISUNDERSTOOD

Shortly after the youth movement project had come to a halt, not to be resumed for a dozen years or more, joint field research—supervised by Leopold von Wiese—in which the writer participated led to concentration on rural German Lutheranism. Particularly prominent among the kinds of evidence collected were interviews disclosing a kind of "emotional halo" surrounding traditional practices, many of them having no apparent supernaturalistic implications—at least not for the subjects concerned. It therefore became apparent that traditionalism had to be handled very carefully—more specifically, with due regard to the way in which the situations into which it enters are defined by naive participants, as over against definitions offered by outside observers unfamiliar with the cultural context. Glimmerings of the difference between implicit and uncodified evaluations, in contrast to explicit and codified, slowly emerged but were too faint to be properly followed up at the time. Consequently, too much was then attributed to specific historical occurrences and definite religious doctrine; [70] the nature of traditionally grounded reluctance to change was misinterpreted, leaving a feeling of dissatisfaction that could not be dispelled until much later.

PHENOMENOLOGICAL FLASHES

At about the same time that rural Lutheranism was being studied, phenomenology and sociology of knowledge were first encountered in the lectures and seminars of Max Scheler. Much was learned from his social psychology, offered in phenomenological guise, describing and analyzing personality types. Leadership was illuminated from several unfamiliar angles and the part played by felt crisis in the rise of leaders was clearly indicated. Other results were fuller comprehension of the difference between the holy and the less intense or divergent aspects of the sacred, as well as better appreciation of the corresponding difference between the profane and the secular.[71]

The terms just mentioned, however, had not yet come to the writer's attention in any problematic sense, hence there was nothing around which the confused array of equivalents and near-equivalents could crystallize. A further handicap was linguistic; although words could be translated, their connotations remained vague, in part because of the several radically divergent points of view from which words and connotations had to be extracted and then, if possible, reconciled.

[70] Howard Becker, "Sargasso Iceberg: A Study in Cultural Lag and Institutional Disintegration" (study of German peasant village, Hunsrück in the Palatinate), *AJS*, 34, 3 (Nov., 1928), pp. 492-506.

[71] *STFLTS* (1952), pp. 906-912; and *WBSS*, pp. 186-188.

THE COMING OF DAYBREAK

Work with Robert E. Park soon added a fresh set of perplexities, but also brought indications of ways to resolve some of the old along with the new. He had used sacred and secular as terms for designating societies in their value-system aspects for a considerable time, as his publications from the early 1920's onward show.[72] Under his discerning and kindly guidance it became possible to see how these concepts could be handled in ways making them of great utility. All the possibilities were of course not fully foreseen, but many of Park's hints, viewed in retrospect, now seem to show that he envisaged some of the possibilities. Moreover, he had already suggested the use of sacred and secular to Everett C. Hughes, who is the first of those working with Park, so far as the writer knows, to have utilized the concepts in dealing with an empirical problem.[73] In addition, Robert Redfield had profited from Park's advice and had begun to develop the well-known folk-urban dichotomy.[74] Given these examples of applicability, the results of work with Park that were most significant for sacred-secular theory as presented in this chapter were the following: (1) the catalytic effect of the concepts mentioned; (2) the impact of fresh evidence, gathered at his suggestion, pointing toward the connections of various forms of isolation and accessibility with mental mobility and immobility, and these in turn with sacred and secular evaluations; (3) growing awareness of the need for sharper distinction between the many aspects of the sacred and the secular; and (4) startlingly sudden realization of the importance, for the relevant problems, of concepts and evidence offered by a long array of authors (referred to in the notes) with whom the writer had been previously familiar but who had nevertheless not become fully meaningful.[75] The debt to Park on all four points, as well as many others not mentioned, can hardly be overestimated; his mind threw off stimulating ideas like sparks from a grinding wheel.

[72] R. E. Park and E. W. Burgess, *Introduction to the Science of Sociology* (2nd ed., Chicago, 1924), pp. 260-263. This same passage appeared in the first edition. The most extended reference is in Park's *Race and Culture* (Glencoe, Ill., 1950), pp. 10-14, dating from about 1933.

[73] E. C. Hughes, "Personality Types and the Division of Labor," *AJS*, 33 (March, 1928), pp. 754-768.

[74] Robert Redfield, *Tepotzlan, A Mexican Village* (Chicago, 1930), and his many subsequent writings.

[75] A full list would be much too lengthy here; see the names prominently mentioned in *TVTSI*, Chap. 3, adding Fustel de Coulanges, and in John Gillin, (ed.), *For a Science of Social Man* (New York, 1954), pp. 115-128, *passim*. By 1938 there was an overwhelming array; see *STFLTS* (1952), but especially Chap. 20. P. A. Sorokin, in particular, exerted influence, partly because his polemic against "sensate" societies forced the writer to reflect on the relations of principial and pronormless societies.

APPRECIATION IN RETROSPECT

Some little time after frequent conferences with Park were no longer possible (because of residence elsewhere), cumulative effects of earlier work with Leopold von Wiese began to appear. The task of adapting and expanding his major treatises for American readers proved engrossing. It led to much more precise knowledge not only of Wiese's contributions but also those of many other sociologists, primarily German and French, who hitherto had not been much more than names. Simmel, Tarde, and Durkheim loomed larger and larger, and so also did Tönnies and Max Weber. Along with heightened appreciation of their conceptual skill and vast erudition, however, came some reservations, but these have heretofore been taken account of, implicitly or explicitly, and need not now detain us.

In spite of qualifications, what was derived from Weber, to single out only one of those mentioned, was a great deal. In particular, there came realization of the need for monographs placing social actions in the context of value-systems, and these in turn in larger cultural contexts setting the possible range of such systems—i.e., for culture case studies. Beyond this, interest in problems of self-and-other orientation, interpretation, type construction, epistemology, and a host of other matters was effectively aroused. (See Chap. 7.)

Further, Wiese's own masterly analyses of structure and function,[76] concrete social actions and their classification, association-dissociation, small groups, and so on,[77] contributed essential foundations on which to build sacred-secular theory.

SUGGESTIONS FROM FRANCE

Although Durkheim's ideas about the crucial importance of value-systems, as incorporated in his discussions of *conscience collective,* had already been encountered, close contact with Halbwachs, Blondel, Berr, and Granet during a stay abroad intensified belief in his importance. These men, who were in varying ways both Durkheim's devoted disciples and his searching critics, were indispensable in arriving at an adequate interpretation of his treatment of the "sacred" and the "profane." They made it possible to apply sociology of knowledge to Durkheim's concepts, and thereby to see how his peculiar elevation of society to the rank of "an entity *sui generis*" had come about.

[76] For his treatment of structure and function, independent of Durkheim, Radcliffe-Brown, and their imitators, dating from as early as 1924, see *WBSS*, pp. ix, 6-7, 11-113, 119, 215, 252-257 and many scattered references thereafter, 364, 401-412, 430, 443, 476, 487, 493-495, 500-501, 502-505, 526-527, 540-541, 578-582, 594, 599-600, 602, 606, 618-619, 649, 650-651, 656, 698-699.

[77] *WBSS*, use subject index. References to Wiese have been sedulously omitted by several American sociologists who owe him a debt embarrassingly large. See Howard Becker, "*Systematic Sociology* and Leopold von Wiese," *Sociometry and the Science of Man,* 18, 4 (Dec., 1955), pp. 262-268.

His effort to provide supreme values devoid of supernatural content was bound up with the struggle against the parochial school. Unless a sociological substitute for God could be offered, he felt, the Roman Catholic clerics to whom he was opposed would be victorious. Consequently, he provided the substitute, and in so doing expunged "holy" (*sainte*) from the French sociological vocabulary in favor of "sacred" (*sacré*). A similar procedure was followed with reference to profane (*profane*), secular (*seculier*), and lay (*laïque*); "profane" was given meaning that permitted full scope to Durkheim's polemic skill.[78]

It should not be thought, however, that increased familiarity with Durkheim brought negative results only, for along with several other positive influences, his stress on culture in all its forms, his attention to symbolic systems, and his distinctions between social controls that are effectively internalized as contrasted with those that remain largely external made a deep impression. The writer's treatment of proverbial and prescriptive societies owes much to him. Further, his studies of law in its major forms, the division of labor, and the prerequisites of social solidarity are all reflected, in one way or another, in the description and analysis of principial societies.

THE WAY TO LEARN A SUBJECT IS TO TEACH IT

The many stimulating and suggestive ideas gleaned in the ways indicated began to be deposited by the writer in his publications, but more important was systematization enforced by the demands of graduate instruction. Several students, by their criticisms and their own writings, contributed notably in this direction.[79] As a result, the conception of the cultural context of social actions, described in a culture case study structured with reference to a specific social-scientific problem and laying emphasis on the discernible value-system or systems as the sociologically significant aspect of that context, was further developed. In the process, it became apparent that societies as carriers of value-systems could not be analyzed in useful ways unless divided into more than the two broadly general types of sacred and secular. Accordingly, an effort was made to distinguish types that were somewhat less general, beginning with four,[80] exuberantly expanding to twenty-two,[81] and soberly coming back to four[82] as sufficient for most research purposes—at least for initial sketches of research designs. Terminology for the four

[78] *STFLTS*, pp. 750-751, 829-839; Gillin (ed.), *op. cit.* pp. 109-114.

[79] A list is given in *TVTSI*, p. 14. To this should be added: Andrew Breines, Walter Buckley, Robert Doel, John Flint, Vytautas Kavolis, Jack Lucas, Thomas Mathiesen, Vatro Murvar, Robert Notestein, Juris Veidemanis, Howard Polsky, and several others.

[80] In Howard Becker and Reuben Hill, *Family, Marriage, and Parenthood* (Boston, 1948 ed.), Chap. 1.

[81] In the 1950 article presented in unabridged form in *TVTSI*, Chap. 5.

[82] In the lectures included in *MIR*, Chaps. 10-13.

types was altered in several ways from time to time, primarily in order to avoid confusion arising from implied value-judgments and certain ambiguities evident in general usage.[83] Much more might be said on this score, but the first portion of the chapter implicitly raises many of the points that might be considered here, and for explicit mention the notes will suffice.

VIVAT POLONIA!

The influence of Park has long persisted, and so likewise has that of the hitherto unmentioned Znaniecki, albeit in less specific ways. Most important has been his treatment of values as objects, and the pragmatic epistemology therewith associated. What has heretofore been said about "givens" and "takens," evaluation, and so on owes much to him, especially where the insights and formulations provided in his work on the cultural sciences are concerned.[84] These, to be sure, are scattered throughout many of his earlier writings, but it was not until he organized them into a close-knit whole that they made maximum impact. In addition, his long insistence on defining situations as the subjects involved define them, and his skilful use of life-histories as a means of ascertaining the nature of such definitions, has entered basically into the writer's treatment of knowing-desiring-norming.

Clearly, however, the immediate stimulus toward dividing evaluation into three analytically distinguishable but empirically inseparable aspects came from Parsons, who starts from epistemological premises considerably differ-

[83] What is here termed "proverbial" has been at various times termed "preliterate," "folk," "folk-sacred," and "preceptive". This last term was used in *Societies Around the World*, shorter edition in one volume, with Irwin Sanders *et al.* (New York, 1956), section entitled "Looking at Values and Value-Systems." "Precept," however, is too often opposed to "practice" in current usage to be suitable.

"Prescriptive" has been "prescribed" and "prescribed-sacred." The flexible form seems best.

"Principial" has been "principled" and "principled-secular." Again the flexible form seems more usable, primarily because "principled" almost always evokes its antithesis, "unprincipled," and thus calls forth value-judgments. "Principial" is unfamiliar but the meaning, "deriving from first principles," is exactly what is required.

Further comment on "folk" seems advisable. In *MIR*, p. 162, an effort was made to apply the term to *any* society bearing a value-system that is in very high degree traditional, implicit, uncodified, and accrete. Such wide meaning, however, stretches unduly terms such as folksong, folklore, folktale, etc. Moreover, it is almost inevitably taken as committing the user to the popular but untrustworthy folk-urban dichotomy. Hence the writer will henceforth use it, if at all, only in contexts where precision is not required, or when referring primarily to peasants and similar "retarded" or "underdeveloped" contingents of industrial civilizations.

"Expedient" has value-judgment liabilities, but is retained for lack of a good substitute. See note 43. Pursuant secularity represents expediency limited by principle; consequent secularity points to expediency that is unlimited except by rational considerations as to choice of means.

[84] Florian Znaniecki, *Cultural Sciences: Their Origin and Development* (Urbana, 1952).

ent from Znaniecki's.[85] Nevertheless the tripartite division has proved useful in making the concept of evaluation (the term as used by Parsons is less inclusive) a good deal more clear than it might otherwise have been. Fundamentally, however, Znaniecki's discussion of values as objects was and is fundamental.

"THE EVIDENCE, GENTLEMEN, THE EVIDENCE!"

Throughout all the foregoing part of this section, attention has centered on the conceptual contributions to sacred-secular theory of a number of sociologists whose accumulated knowledge is available in any good library. In closing this survey, however, reference must be made to the impressions coming from field work.

Experience with "black propaganda" operations brought no new concepts, true enough, but it vastly intensified appreciation of those the writer already possessed.[86] At the same time, it brought keener awareness of the need for saturation in the evidence bearing on any theoretical problem; conceptual jugglery is not enough. If sacred-secular theory can be fruitfully applied in empirical research, fine; if it cannot be so applied, it represents sadly wasted effort. Reversing the Kantian order, and inserting one emphatic word, "Percepts without concepts are blind, [but] concepts without percepts are empty."

This conviction has been reinforced by recent field work in Germany and Britain.[87] To the writer, it becomes more and more plainly apparent that without culture case study, both of documentary and field-work character, there is danger of treating sociological theory as an end in itself rather than as an indispensable tool in the scientific enterprise. That enterprise hinges on the attainment of sound predictive knowledge, capable of systematic transmission and expansion. Here, for the sociologist, is the one thing needful.

[85] Talcott Parsons, *The Social System* (Glencoe, 1951), Chap. 1. Parsons is a critical realist, although his commitment to Freudianism seemingly introduces some discrepancies.

[86] Here see the following by Howard Becker: "Peoples of Germany," Chap. 15 in symposium ed. by T. C. McCormick, *Problems of the Postwar World* (New York, 1945), pp. 342-390; "The Nature and Consequences of Black Propaganda," *ASR*, 14, 2 (April, 1949), pp. 221-235: "The Regimented Man: Interviews with German Officials under the Nazis," *SF*, 28,1 (Oct., 1949), pp. 19-24; "Intellectuals, Concentration Camps, and Black Propaganda," *American Journal of Economics and Sociology*, 10, 2 (Jan., 1951), pp. 139-144; "Propaganda and the Impotent German Intellectual," *SF*, 29,3 (March, 1951), pp. 273-276; "Max Weber, Assassination, and German Guilt," *American Journal of Economics and Sociology*; 10, 4 (July, 1951), pp. 401-406; and the Epilogue of *GYBOF*.

[87] Some preliminary results, quite sketchily treated, are to be found in Howard Becker, "Field Work among Scottish Shepherds and German Peasants: 'Wholes' and Their Handicaps," *SF*, 35, 1 (Oct., 1956), pp. 10-15.

SELECTED BIBLIOGRAPHY

Arensberg, Conrad M., *The Irish Countryman* (New York: Macmillan, 1937).

Becker, Howard, "Processes of Secularisation" *Sociological Review* (British), 24 (April-July, and Oct., 1932), pp. 138-154; 266-286.

Boskoff, Alvin, "Structure, Function, and Folk Society," *ASR,* 14, 6 (Dec., 1949), pp. 749-758.

———, "Postponement of Social Decision in Transitional Society," *SF,* 31, 3 (March, 1953), pp. 229-234.

Bourne, George, *Change in the Village* (London: Duckworth, 1912).

Carpenter, Niles, *The Sociology of City Life* (New York: Longmans, Green, 1931), Chaps. 6-10, 13, 14.

Cohn, Werner, "Jehovah's Witnesses as a Proletarian Movement," *American Scholar,* 24, 3 (Summer, 1955), pp. 281-298.

Davis, Kingsley, "The Origin and Growth of Urbanization in the World," *AJS,* 60, 5 (March, 1955), pp. 429-437.

Gadourek, I., *A Dutch Community* (Leiden: Stenfert Kroese, 1956).

Keur, John Y. and Dorothy L., *The Deeply Rooted* (Assen, Holland: Van Gorcum, 1955).

LeTourneau, Roger, "Social Change in the Muslim Cities of North Africa," *AJS,* 60, 6 (May, 1955), pp. 527-535.

Loomis, C. P., and J. C. McKinney, "Systemic Differences Between Latin-American Communities of Family Farms and Large Estates," *AJS,* 61, 5 (March, 1956), pp. 404-412.

Martindale, Don, and E. D. Monachesi, *Elements of Sociology* (New York: Harper, 1951:, Chaps. 7, 13, 14, 21, 22.

Munch, Peter, "Cultural Contacts in an Isolated Community: Tristan da Cunha," *AJS,* 53, 1 (July, 1947), pp. 1-8.

Parsons, Talcott, *The Social System* (Glencoe, Ill.: The Free Press, 1951), Chap. 5.

Redfield Robert, *The Little Community: Viewpoints for the Study of a Human Whole* (Chicago: University of Chicago Press, 1955).

Rose, Arnold, *Sociology: The Study of Human Relations* (New York: Alfred A. Knopf, 1956), Chap. 14.

Sanders, Irwin T., *A Balkan Village* (Lexington, K.: University of Kentucky Press, 1949).

——— *et al.*-Becker, Howard, *Societies around the World,* one-volume ed. (New York: Dryden Press, 1956).

Sklare, Marshall (ed.), *The Sociology of the Jews in America* (Glencoe, Ill.: The Free Press, 1957) selection by Howard Polsky on context and construction of a scale designed for the measurement of secularization among Orthodox Jews in Milwaukee.

Sorokin, P. A., *Social Mobility* (New York: Harper, 1927), especially Chaps. 21 and 22.

———, C. C. Zimmerman, and C. J. Galpin (eds.), *A Systematic Source Book in Rural Sociology,* 3 vols. (Minneapolis: University of Minnesota Press, 1930), Vol. I, Readings 11-13, 18, 25, 35, 38, 39, 41-51, 68; Vol. II, Readings 83, 86, 91, 113, 117, 119, 122.

West, James, *Plainville, USA* (New York: Columbia University Press, 1946).

Williams, W. M., *The Sociology of an English Village: Gosforth* (London: Routledge Kegan Paul, 1956).

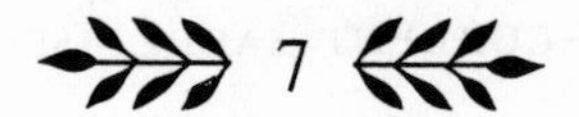

METHODOLOGY, PROCEDURES, AND TECHNIQUES IN SOCIOLOGY

JOHN C. McKINNEY

ONE OF THE SIGNIFICANT DEVELOPMENTS IN SOCIOLOGY IN THE DECADES since World War I is the increase of sophistication with respect to methodology, procedure, and technique. It is necessary to define these three terms clearly at the outset, for "methodology" or "method" is sometimes used to cover all of them.

THE DISTINCTIVE NATURE OF METHODOLOGY

Methodology can be defined as the principles of organized investigation—the "norms" by means of which procedures and techniques are selected and articulated. Methodology must be distinguished from *sociological theory*, which has as its subject matter certain aspects of the interaction of people and hence is *substantive* in character. Although methodological and substantive theory are closely associated, they are not identical. In most of its aspects methodology is not bound up with sociological problems per se; therefore it transcends any body of substantive theory. Most of its problems are common to a number of disciplines, those of a more general character being common to all scientific procedure. Sociologists must be methodologically competent in that they must understand the design of investigation, the norms of procedure, the nature of inference, and the appropriate use of theoretic systems; but methodological competence does not determine the *content* of any theory or study. In short, methodology essentially answers the question of "how"; substantive theory answers the question of "what."

Methodology must also be distinguished from philosophy, epistemology, and logic, although there are obvious areas of overlap. Although methodology is in one sense a "normative" discipline, it does not in any practical scientific sense belong to any of these three fields. The problems dealt with in the field of philosophy tend to become so general and abstract that they have little bearing on those of the working scientist. This is best illustrated by the fact that philosophic discourse is customarily geared not to the *procedural question of how* but to questions of ontology and metaphysics.

One would expect that the research sociologist would receive a great deal of help from the logician, but unfortunately this has not been true. The abstract and technical problems of the logician have little applicability in the sociological realm of theorizing and fact-gathering. The esoteric symbols, syllogisms, forms of proof, and paradoxes of implication of the logician have contributed little to the methodology of the sociologist. Similarly, the problems of the epistemologist have in large part been irrelevant to the work of the methodologist. The epistemologist (of any school or brand) starts with the immediate experience of the individual and attempts by way of this cognitive reference to reach a realm outside the individual. The methodologist, on the other hand, starts with a problem that lies within an unquestioned world of objects and relations between objects that is subject to observation and experiential control. The methodologist makes certain necessary assumptions about the world and then *proceeds to structure the inquiry concerning it*. On the other hand, the philosopher, the logician, and the epistemologist focus upon and wrestle with the assumptions themselves. The methodologist (with respect to any substantive field) is more pragmatically inclined; since his object is to investigate the world, he continues to use his assumptions as long as they work.

For the reasons mentioned above, then, the sociologist has had to be his own methodologist to a great extent. This is not to say that methodology, epistemology, logic, and that branch of philosophy concerned with science will not *eventually* converge; it is to assert merely that the substantive disciplines (particularly the biologic and social sciences) have had to develop their methodology largely through their own efforts.

THE RELATION OF PROCEDURES AND TECHNIQUES IN SOCIOLOGY

The growth of substantive disciplines has always been closely related to the refinement of *procedure* and the development of *techniques*. A plenitude of techniques does not in itself guarantee substantive expansion, but it does represent an indispensable prerequisite of that expansion. The increased emphasis on procedure and technique in sociology in the past few decades is an unmistakable sign of maturation.

Procedure can be defined as a general form or system of operating in investigation. *Technique* is differentiated from procedure as a specific fact-finding or manipulating operation adapted from the basic (generic) procedure. By adhering to this distinction it is possible to isolate five generic procedures that are a part of the methodology of any science. These are the statistical, experimental, typological, historical, and case procedures. On the other hand, there are innumerable techniques derived from these procedures, directly or in combination, which vary in the specificity or generality of their application. Some techniques are resticted to one discipline or to a group of closely related disciplines. Examples of what are here considered to be techniques are the Guttman scale, participant observation, the non-directive interview, and the questionnaire.

The *process* of developing techniques, rather than the specific techniques themselves, is the significant feature of contemporary sociological growth from the standpoint of methodology. For instance, many substantive "types" have been developed and forgotten, but the process of refining the procedure of constructive typology has continued. Similarly, innumerable "scales" have come into existence and been discarded in the past thirty years, but the process of scale construction has advanced enormously. Technical proficiency cannot be dismissed as "mere gadgetry," because ultimately it has methodological ramifications.

In the epoch since World War I, empirical and quantitative research in sociology has experienced promising growth.

Under the pressure of instituting and conducting such research, sociologists tended to become preoccupied with techniques. Consequently, this period was not characterized by a great deal of methodological order and systematic development of substantive theory. American sociologists were so absorbed in making their discipline an empirical science that there seemed to be no time to plan thoroughly and handle basic methodological concerns. Bushnell, writing in 1919, made the following comment on the state of sociology:

> . . . the working equipment of sociology up to date often looks more like a museum full of curios than a workshop full of tools; and such is necessarily largely the fact: for as a new science, sociology has been engaged extensively in raking together things that might prove useful in constructing a better social order, rather than accurately adapting the materials assembled.[1]

To the casual observer, this might appear to be the case today, but the professional sociologist knows that his discipline has come a long way in this period. Not only has the sociologist a workshop full of tools with which he can perform tasks impossible in 1919, but also there is emerging an organizational pattern (methodology) that is definitely less fragmentary than earlier patterns.

One of the most significant symptoms of movement into the epoch of

[1] C. J. Bushnell, "Scientific Method in Sociology," *AJS,* 25 (July, 1919), pp. 45-46.

unparalleled growth in sociology was the publication of *The Polish Peasant*.[2] This work certainly cannot be held to be the single cause of later developments in sociology; nevertheless, it represents in significant fashion the break with the speculative sociology of the classical encyclopedists and the entry into the period of empirical development with all its methodical and technical accoutrements. Indeed, Thomas and Znaniecki made the following comment:

> Our work does not pretend to give any definite and universally valid sociological truths, nor to constitute a permanent model of sociological research; it merely claims to be a monograph, as nearly complete as possible under the circumstances, of a limited social group at a certain period of its evolution, which may suggest studies of other groups, more detailed and more perfect methodically, thus helping the investigation of modern living societies to rise above its present stage of journalistic impression and preparing the ground for the determination of really exact general laws of human behavior.[3]

Methodology

Methodology has not developed uniformly; on the contrary, broad frontal movements in the field have diverged radically. Several distinct trends are discernible, but their theoretical "opposites" are also usually apparent. Consequently, all the trends dealt with here will be understood as constructed types. Instead of treating these trends as unitary and mutually exclusive categories into which men and approaches can be sorted, the major trends will be conceptualized as "polarities" on continua. Thus, although empiricism has been a dominant trend, its logical opposite, rationalism, is set up as a "type" at the opposite pole of the continuum. No man or approach need be viewed either as "purely" empirical or as rationalistic in all respects, but all will fall somewhere short of either absolute pole. In this way important developments in "rationalistic" methodology as well as those of the more prevalent empiricism are brought into focus. This device is used in order to emphasize the fact that developments have come from very different positions and that methodology has many ambivalent characteristics.

The continua representing the major methodological trends are: empiricism–rationalism; neo-positivism–anti-positivism; induction–deduction; quantitative–qualitative; and nomothetic–idiographic. On analysis, it would appear that the strong tendency toward the empirical-positivistic-inductive-

[2] W. I. Thomas and Florian Znaniecki, *The Polish Peasant in Europe and America* (2nd ed.; New York, 1927).

[3] *Ibid.*, pp. 1822-23.

quantitative-idiographic poles has produced a complex responsible for the emergence of several minor trends that are treated here as unitary sub-types of that complex. They are: behaviorism, operationism, and pragmatism.

THE INCREASING DOMINANCE OF EMPIRICISM OVER RATIONALISM

Some of the methodological issues that have troubled sociology have become obsolete, but others have persisted. One of the persistent "polarities" is evident in the relative roles of empiricism and rationalism as approaches to sociological knowledge. Empiricism became dominant soon after World War I, and during the twenties and thirties rationalism almost completely capitulated. The mid-forties, however, witnessed a rationalistic revival that at the present time can be interpreted as a distinct modification of radical empiricism.

Empiricism is a way of thinking and working with data. It indicates an attitude-complex characterized by the utmost faith in the senses, firm belief in the power of observation, willingness to be ruled by observable evidence, and belief that scientific conclusions should never get beyond the realm of extrapolation and that the rational universe of science is nothing more than the habitual association of certain ideas in the mind of the perceiver.

In rationalistic method, by contrast, the criterion of truth is not sensory but intellectual and deductive. Rationalism assumes the universality of natural laws; hence it appeals to sense-perception only in its search for particulars. It is preoccupied with conceptual schemes, constructions, and logical manipulations. *The supreme embodiment of rationalism is in pure mathematics.*

Rationalism, as exemplified in crude non-mathematical form by the "classical" sociologists, was dominant prior to World War I. At present, although rationalism has recouped considerably in recent years, there is no more honorific word in all of American sociology than the adjective "empirical." Evidence of this appears in the work of the modern representatives of sociological rationalism; the constructors of mathematical models and formal deductive systems, for example, consistently lay claim to be doing empirical work.[4]

The Mixed Fruits of Empiricism. The spread of empiricism in American sociology has been responsible for several important emphases. There has been a sincere striving for objectivity and a direct concern with modesty of conclusion. The aim has been precision in statement with respect to the evidence that has been collected by the most trustworthy of instruments. Quantitative methods and standardized modes of inquiry have been em-

[4] See Robert Bierstedt, "A Critique of Empiricism in Sociology," *ASR,* 14 (Oct. 1949), pp. 584-92.

phasized because of their promise of objectivity and precision. "Brute fact" has been king at the expense of *explicit* theory.

These emphases have had a variety of consequences for methodology. First, the refreshing contrast of empirical research with the apriorism of the classical writers discredited the completely speculative approach. Second, empiricism established the necessity of controlled observation and research design as components of scientific investigation. Third, the necessity of keeping theory in touch with evidence and relating it to the bedrock of accumulative fact is basically an empirical contribution. Fourth, empiricism made an outstanding contribution to the procedural rules of research. It is the empirically oriented who to a great extent have codified the research rules and practices. Fifth, the empiricists have accomplished an enormous amount of investigation, much of it trivial but most of it arduous.

On the other side of the ledger, empiricism has had several limiting consequences for methodology.[5] First, it has contributed to a specific form of methodological naiveté. Although empiricism has eliminated some surface forms of subjectivity, it certainly has not eliminated certain more subtle and tenacious forms. Focusing attention almost exclusively on areas of obvious objectivity has lessened awareness of the dangers of (a) subjectivity on the higher levels by use of implicit rather than explicit theory, (b) loose delineation of research problems, (c) careless articulation of techniques, and (d) faulty interpretation of results. Failure to give due attention to the assumptions and limitations of their own theory seriously limits the validity and utility of much of the work of the empiricists.

Second, a great many recent sociological investigations have closely resembled mere collections of facts and hence have not even approximated the scientific model ostensibly subscribed to by the empiricists.

Third, the roles of theory and research have been reversed in empirical method as compared to standard scientific practice. Instead of evaluating research in terms of its contribution to theory, empiricists tend to evaluate theory solely in terms of its current utility in research. Stated simply, scientists have never been interested in particulars for their own sake but rather for their potential relation to uniformities. This implies that research begins and ends with substantive theory and is conducted in terms of methodological principles. The tendency to reverse the traditional roles of theory and research has not only been obvious in the work of the avowed empiricists but also is explicit in the statements of such carriers of the rational tradition as Merton. His "serendipity" is close to "trust to luck."

Fourth, radical empiricism has led to random, helter-skelter, petty, uncodified research. Moreover, its adherents have emphasized immediate rather than long-range accomplishments because they distrust theory as a

[5] *Loc. cit.*, for a penetrating critique of empiricism in sociology.

guideline. This concern for immediacy seems inevitably to produce the "practical" and undoubtedly leads away from basic research.

Fifth, the deëmphasizing of systematic theory for the sake of empirical "free enterprise" has increased the difficulty of extracting sociological principles and generalizations from the mass of idiographic facts. It is a generally accepted view that the ideal of science is to achieve a systematic network of statements that account for the facts in the area of abstraction in which the science is working. Neither isolated propositions nor aggregates of facts constitute a science. The tendency of American sociology to proceed along empirical lines almost exclusively has not hastened its arrival as an accepted science in this respect.

The foregoing statements apply to the period of rampant empiricism of the twenties and thirties and to a lesser extent to the modified empiricism of the present. Rationalism, however, was never entirely discarded as an avenue to knowledge, and since World War II several developments have strengthened the rational tradition. Although the vast majority of sociologists were in the empirical camp during the twenties and thirties, nevertheless a few outstanding carriers kept the rational tradition alive and vital. Men of such diverse interests and accomplishments as Znaniecki, Wirth, Blumer, MacIver, Hiller, Sorokin, Becker, Hughes, Parsons, Merton, Bierstedt, Lazarsfeld, Loomis, Furfey, Guttman, and Dodd, among others, fought against radical empiricism by one means or another.

The Recent Tempering of Empiricism. Resistance to radical empiricism has developed along several different lines, but in general they can be reduced to three. First, an emphasis on *system* was perpetuated in the work of several of the men mentioned above. Those who espoused the doctrine of "system" during the twenties, thirties, and forties were fighting the battle of "explanation" as opposed to "description." The delineation of systems of behavior by Znaniecki in the late twenties, subsequently accepted by Sorokin and then Parsons; the transformation of "formal" sociology into the structural-functional approach of Wiese-Becker in the early thirties, which emphasized structural aspects (currently developed with somewhat more emphasis on functionalism by Parsons); and the recent concern with social systems, largely through the impetus of Parsons, are a few examples of this trend. In each instance, these sociologists were striving for explanation in the sense of providing a conceptual context within which individual elements could be meaningfully interpreted.

Second, there was a continued emphasis on conceptual apparatus, primarily in the form of constructed types, empirical and mathematical models, and conceptual schemes. A few persistent sociologists have felt compelled to emphasize the fact that there can be no body of scientific fact without conceptualization and no system of science without theory. The symbolic element in all fact, the conceptual element in all percept, and the organizational role of theory in all inquiry have been stressed by the sociological rationalists. Such diverse examples as Becker's work on the logic of constructed types, Guttman and Lazarsfeld's work on scalogram and latent-structure analysis respectively, and Parsons' delineation of the function of the conceptual scheme are representative.

Third, emphasis was placed on research design within the *logic* of the experimental method. Here one may add to the list of contributors such persons as Chapin and Stouffer, who normally are classed as empiricists but in this respect are located near the rational pole. The experimental method is usually regarded as an aspect of empirical science. This ascription is legitimate, but on closer observation one cannot overlook the tremendous role of reason in experimental design. Questions of what to study, what hypotheses to examine, what operations to perform, what data to collect, and where to apply the experimental design—all these are questions of primary importance in the conduct of research. The vastly improved design of research undertaken in recent years attests to the rational modification of extreme empiricism.

The Convergence of Theory and Research. Although there has been some tendency recently for sociologists to avoid the extreme poles of either empiricism or rationalism, and although the two methodologies have showed a significant tendency to converge, it would be entirely misleading to leave the impression that either the "collectionalists" or the "closed-system logicians" are extinct. Both, however, are subject to tremendous pressure to enter the crucial area of convergence. For instance, Parsons and his associates obviously feel under strong compulsion to demonstrate the "utility" of their theory. Conversely, more sociologists today than earlier tend to ask "So what?" of a purely descriptive study.

The speciousness of trying to separate theory and research is gradually being recognized. In many respects theory was earlier monopolized by verbal specialists who demonstrated little interest in formulating verifiable propositions. On the other hand, research in sociology was under the control of those who were technically equipped but who through sheer theoretical incompetence were blinded by naked fact. There was a recognition that some bridges had to be built before the scientific situation improved. This meant that some intermediary theory had to be devised—e.g., that of Merton. It also meant that some empirical investigations involving working theory had to be undertaken—for example, the studies of military personnel by Stouffer and others.[6] Moreover, it meant that theory had to be adapted to some operational procedures; witness the convergence in the work of Riley *et al.*[7] of the methodological line of Lazarsfeld, Guttman,

[6] See S. A. Stouffer *et al., Studies in Social Psychology in World War II* (Princeton, 1949), 4 vols.

[7] See Matilda W. Riley *et al., Sociological Studies in Scale Analysis* (New Brunswick, 1954).

and Stouffer with the theoretical work of Parsons, Merton, Mead, Cottrell, and Moreno. In addition, recognition of the need for bridges meant the adaptation of grand-scale theory to empirical problems through extraction and reduction of models; witness the use of "the social system" by Loomis *et al.*, with respect to the problem of instigated change in *Turrialba.* These events seem to indicate that American sociology has learned the lesson of "fact" and "research" that empiricism had to teach but now feels the need of improved conceptual equipment from the rational tradition in order to comprehend its facts and intelligently conduct its research.

NEO-POSITIVISM AND ITS OPPONENTS

Positivism in modern trappings has had a distinct vogue in American sociology. Although evidence of it has been discernible for many years, the classic statement of neo-positivism was not made until Lundberg published his *Foundations of Sociology* in 1939.

The neo-positivist approach is double-barreled in nature. First, it is methodologically oriented to the position of physical science, striving for a unified view of the world of phenomena through an adaptation of the viewpoint of physical science to all phenomena. In this respect it develops an ascetic methodology based on the following premises; (1) societal phenomena are subject to natural laws; (2) there is no distinction between sciences that deal with human beings and those that deal with other phenomena; and (3) the subjective aspects of societal phenomena can be studied scientifically only on the basis of their objective, overt manifestation.[8] This methodology, although it has been widely criticized,[9] is at least clear-cut.

One of the focal points of attack by the neo-positivists has been the concept of causation. Neurath criticizes the causal frame of reference and states the basis for avoiding it.[10] Lundberg refers to causation as an "animistic, theological" viewpoint. Dodd makes the radical proposal that correlation be substituted for causation. Frank contends that no real progress in the social sciences can be made until the idea of causality is dropped.[11] The

[8] See G. A. Lundberg, "Contemporary Positivism in Sociology," *ASR,* 4 (Feb., 1939), pp. 42-55.

[9] The critics of neo-positivism have not been silent. See Sorokin's review of Lundberg's *Foundations of Sociology,* in *AJS,* 45 (March, 1940), pp. 795-98; Ethel Shanas, "A Critique of Dodd's Dimensions of Society," *ibid.,* 48 (Sept., 1942), pp. 214-30; Florian Znaniecki, "The Proximate Future of Sociology: Controversies in Doctrine and Method," *ibid.,* 50 (May, 1945), pp. 514-21; Talcott Parsons, *The Structure of Social Action* (2nd ed.; Glencoe, 1949), *passim.*

[10] Otto Neurath, *Foundations of the Social Sciences* (Chicago, 1944), vol. 2, pp. 20-22, 51.

[11] Lundberg, *Foundations of Sociology,* p. 260; S. C. Dodd, *Dimensions of Society* (New York, 1942), pp. 822-23; L. K. Frank, "Causation: An Episode in the History of Thought," *Journal of Philosophy,* 31 (1934), pp. 421-28.

opposition to this vigorous point of view is best expressed by MacIver, who states in great detail the case for causation.[12]

The outcome of this controversy has been the virtual elimination of the "cause as a force" notion and the substitution of a very broadly expanded version of causality. Sociologists now generally prefer to put their statements of uniformity in terms of relating an event to the conditions under which it occurs. Since these uniformities are empirical, they can be stated only in terms of probability. Consequently, the statement of probability in the form of empirical generalization about relations has tended to replace causation in the traditional sense. This methodological modification is largely the product of neo-positivist pressure.

The second of the factors that give neo-positivism its double-barreled structure is the typical pattern of "moral" and "practical" considerations featured by positivists in their desire for a scientifically articulated world. Lundberg makes this comment: "Positivists do not admit the assumed dichotomy between the pursuit of science on the one hand and social action on the other. We contend, on the contrary, that the pursuit of science is the most fundamental of all social action."[13] The fusion of science and action does not, however, make it any easier to attain the ideal of a natural science of society. On the contrary, this fusion might act as a positive hindrance as a result of the fact that the methodological rigor of the physical sciences aspired to by the neo-positivists becomes subjugated to the problems of society rather than to problems that have theoretic significance in the discipline. The results are an emphasis on "practical" and "immediate" research useful in societal action and, indirectly, deëmphasis of the role of systematic theory.

Critics of Neo-positivism. Although the opposition to neo-positivism in American sociology has been powerful and effective, it has been so diversified that it is difficult to label. Unquestionably, however, the strongest single source of opposition lies in the tradition of *verstehende* (interpretative) sociology. An open revolt against Comtean positivism, growing out of the German concept of *Geisteswissenschaften,* was led by Dilthey, Rickert, and Windelband, who attempted to develop a methodology based upon an understanding (*Verstehen*) of history and society. In anti-positivistic fashion, they distinguished between the nomothetic or generalizing character of the physico-mathematical sciences, and the idiographic or individualizing character of the historico-cultural sciences. Moreover, they emphasized the difference between the knowledge of being (*Sein*) and the awareness of and relation to norms (*Sollen*). Against this background, Max Weber brought the movement to its culmination with the substitution of "ideal types" for mechanical laws

[12] R. M. MacIver, *Social Causation* (New York, 1942).

[13] Lundberg, "Contemporary Positivism in Sociology," p. 54.

and of probability for invariance, thereby bolstering the conception of sociology as a nomothetic science. The emphasis was on *understanding* social behavior, which meant that mere statistical regularities had to be supplemented by knowledge of the subjective motivation before causality could be imputed *on the level of meaning*. The essential difference between *verstehende* theory and neo-positivism is that in the former emphasis is placed upon the subjective categories of action—that is, action as it is viewed from the perspective of the actor—and hence is oriented toward the "meaning" of behavior as it is being conducted rather than to the mere uniformities of behavior.

This *verstehende* line of thought has assumed an increasingly important role in American sociology in the past two decades. It has infiltrated in and become a working part of American methodology in several ways. Initially, it was brought in largely by American scholars of German training or background who managed to disseminate the orientation in several of the leading graduate schools. In the late twenties, this group began to produce a series of translations and interpretations of the important works in German sociology. Then, the rise of Hitler meant that the United States was fortunate enough to receive a number of refugee German scholars, who have exerted significant influence upon American graduate students since World War II.

The foremost proponents of the various forms of *verstehende* sociology include such persons as Blumer, Hughes, Loomis, MacIver, Merton, Parsons, Redfield, Sorokin, Becker and Znaniecki.[14] This methodological position has resulted in an emphasis on: (1) the value of theory in research; (2) the significance of the concept of system; (3) the potential of the "structural-functional" approach; (4) the need of motivational theory and the instruments by means of which it can be tested; and (5) the necessity of giving attention to the qualitative aspects of research.

At the present writing, the conflict has died down considerably. No "victory" has been registered by either side, but methodology has benefited from the fact that proponents of the different positions have had to give intensive consideration to the problems involved. The metaphysical assumptions remain, for neo-positivism as well as for its opponents, but on the procedural level the extreme positions have been distinctly modified.

[14] Howard Becker, *Through Values to Social Interpretation* (Durham, N.C., 1950); Talcott Parsons, *The Social System* (Glencoe, 1951); Florian Znaniecki, *The Method of Sociology* (New York, 1934); R. K. Merton, *Social Theory and Social Structure* (Glencoe, 1949); C. P. Loomis and J. A. Beegle, *Rural Social Systems* (New York, 1950); P. A. Sorokin, *Social and Cultural Dynamics* (New York, 1937-41), 4 vols.; Herbert Blumer, "Science Without Concepts," *AJS*, 36 (Jan., 1931), pp. 515-33; MacIver, *loc. cit.;* E. C. Hughes, "Institutional Office and the Person," *AJS*, 43 (Nov., 1937), pp. 404-13; Robert Redfield, "The Art of Social Science," *ibid.* (Nov., 1948), pp. 181-90.

THE SUPREMACY OF INDUCTION

One of the basic methodological polarities develops between inductive and deductive procedures. In the most general sense, induction may be defined as the process of inferring a general assertion from the observation of a number of particular facts. Conversely, deduction is the process of analytical reasoning from general to particular or less general. This involves logical inference of a conclusion from one or more given premises. These two procedures are not mutually exclusive; indeed, it is possible to interpret either one as a special case of the other in given situations. The interplay between deduction and induction is an observable feature in the conduct of any research project, and to conceive of either one as being "purely" adhered to is unrealistic. Nevertheless, it is possible to conclude that sociology has become increasingly inductive since the days of its break with classical encyclopedism.

There are still sociologists who tend to start with purely abstract rules, premises, or systems, develop them rationally, and correct them in various ways so that the results fit the actual occurrences. Proportionately, however, there are now fewer of these sociologists. On the other hand, there is a preponderance of sociologists who begin with ordinary and restricted notions, who try to refine them more and more by making them more definite, removing contradictions, and delimiting their area of applicability. This kind of investigator is content if he can make a modest generalization that applies to a limited universe of particulars. Thus, most modern sociologists employ inductive method in one of its two major forms: analytic and enumerative induction.

Enumerative induction is by far the most commonly used method in sociology. It takes the form of a statistical generalization based on the examination of cases within a defined universe. If *all* the individual instances that come under the generalization are examined, the method is called *complete* induction. Since most subject matter does not lend itself readily to complete induction, *incomplete* induction, based on a sample of the universe, is the most commonly used form. It is in the use of this method that statistical procedures become a substitute for induction in the classical analytic sense.

A special complex of problems is involved in the utilization of statistical procedures for establishing causal relations (that is, of constant uniformities). It has become increasingly clear that in sociology the statistical method comes into use wherever—that is, almost everywhere—classic induction, the direct inference from one instance to other instances, fails. The most notable characteristic of the statistical search for causal relations is that the method relates cause-and-effect universes wherein, in addition to the cause-and-effect elements, other components are included that have no bearing on the causal relationship. Moreover, the statistical method ignores the individual units in the universe and concentrates on their common or average manifestations. The homogeneity of the universe is a working assumption but is not necessarily an actuality. In summary, this means that statistical inferences about causal relations always belong to the realm of probability and lack the incisiveness of analytic induction. Probability is not based solely on the fact that the universe is only *sampled* and not completely enumerated, but also on the fact that the elements being related contain additional conceptual components that are not a necessary part of the relationship.

This complex of problems has been regarded by some sociologists—Znaniecki, for example—as the weakness of enumerative induction. On the other hand, it can also be viewed as the strength of that method. The statistical method allows us to *proceed* and establish uniformities which, although sometimes crude and often highly variable, nevertheless represent an advance of knowledge. The applicability of a method is as much a measure of its strength as is its degree of logical perfection.

Znaniecki contrasts enumerative induction with what he calls the true scientific method, *analytic induction*.[15] Since Znaniecki's classic discussion of analytic induction in 1934, this approach has received several research adaptations[16] and has been a controversial issue in methodology.[17] Znaniecki maintains that analytic induction supplies universal statements instead of mere probability statements based on correlations (to which there are always exceptions). In contrast to enumerative induction, which abstracts by generalizing, analytic induction generalizes by abstracting. Enumerative induction examines many cases for characteristics that are similar and abstracts them because of their generality. Analytic induction proceeds from the opposite position by abstracting from the concrete case the characteristics essential to it and then generalizing these characteristics on the basis of their assumed essential nature. According to Znaniecki, a well-conducted analytic induction leaves no real problems for enumerative induction. He asserts that analytic induction leads to genuinely causal laws and exhaustive knowledge of whatever cases are studied.

Procedurally, analytic induction begins with an explanatory hypothesis and a provisional definition of something to be explained. The hypothesis is subjected to verification by examination of the data involved, and then two modifications are made. The hypothesis is modified so that *all* the facts fall under it, and the phenomena under examination are redefined to exclude

[15] Znaniecki, *op. cit.*, pp. 235-331.

[16] See R. C. Angell, *The Family Encounters the Depression* (New York, 1936); E. H. Sutherland, *Principles of Criminology* (3rd ed.; New York, 1939); A. R. Lindesmith, *Opiate Addiction* (Bloomington, 1947); D. R. Cressy, *Other People's Money* (Glencoe, Illinois, 1953).

[17] See W. S. Robinson, "The Logical Structure of Analytic Induction," *ASR*, 16 (Dec., 1951), pp. 812-18; R. J. Turner, "The Quest for Universals," *ibid.*, 18 (Dec., 1953), pp. 604-11; and the interesting comments of Angell and Turner in "Communications and Opinions," *ibid.*, 19 (Aug. 1954), pp. 476-78.

any cases that are not explained by the hypothesis. The range of applicability of the hypothesis and the area of the universe then stand in a one-to-one logical relationship. The hypothesis is limited to explanation of the facts that fall in that universe; and the universe is inclusive only of the facts explained by the hypothesis. Other facts turned up in the investigation are held to be elements of other universes susceptible to other hypotheses.

Robinson has recently pointed out that the differences between analytic and enumerative induction are differences of degrees and not of kind.[18] The extent to which a statistician limits a hypothesis to observably uniform cases, and the extent to which he limits the universe to meet the range of applicability of the explanatory hypothesis, are measures of the extent to which he has made an analytic induction. Conversely, the failure of the researcher practicing analytic induction to achieve perfection in the statement of relationship indicates an incomplete induction based on the use of a statistical universe.

The question of the superiority of either of the two inductive forms is irrelevant. The two simply serve different purposes with respect to different research problems and situations. Wherever analytic induction is inapplicable, either because of our lack of conceptual equipment or because of the nature of the subject matter, then, obviously, enumerative induction should be applied. Wherever the statistician exposes relations that he subjects to continuing refinement by progressive elimination of the irrelevant, he is moving toward analytic induction. It should be evident that enumerative induction will continue to be, at least in this epoch, the primary approach. The chief significance of analytic induction, for the present at least, is that it may make statistical practitioners dissatisfied with crude correlations and low probabilities and thus force them to refine their hypotheses and limit their universes wherever practicable. Analytic induction denies the statisticians the right to ignore exceptional instances, for they obviously require explanation in terms of other hypotheses and universes.

Deduction as a Major Tool. Although induction reigns in American sociology, deduction still plays an important role and probably will play a more important role in the future. The inductive myth that the true scientist starts by observing the facts without any conceptual anticipations has been responsible for the unnecessary discrediting of deduction. This myth, sometimes called the *tabula rasa* fallacy, has gained a firm foothold in American sociology; it is unusual to find other scientists who feel that they can or should approach their subject matter with a blank mind. On the other hand, the traditional "methods books" in sociology have frequently encouraged sociologists to approach their material without any "preconceptions," "theories," "concepts," or "evaluative judgments." It is important to realize

[18] Robinson, *op. cit.,* p. 816.

that this is logically impossible and contrary to the actual history of science. Without anticipatory ideas and conceptual directions, one cannot know what facts to look for and cannot recognize what is relevant to the inquiry. It would be difficult to start by observing the facts, for to determine which facts are relevant is a primary object of scientific inquiry. Deduction is thus a necessary part or instrument of research.

Deduction has been best exemplified in American methodology by conceptual schemes in the form of systematic theory, by constructed types (to be considered below), and by mathematical and empirical models. Conceptual frameworks such as that of Parsons[19] can perform at least two scientific functions. First, they can help in the codification of our constantly accumulating concrete knowledge. This means that discrete hypotheses and observations can be unified under general categories and tentatively "placed" in a larger context; consequently their "meaning" can be assessed in the light of more general implications. In a sense the distinction between description and explanation is that between fragmentary knowledge and systematic knowledge. Second, conceptual frameworks can serve as a guide to research. They enable us to locate and define the areas of our knowledge and ignorance by pointing up problematic areas. In the light of system one can "see" problems of interest and significance relative to hypothetical "interconnections" or relationships.

Typology as a Deductive System. Constructed types represent a bridge between systematic theory and empirical observation and hence have some of the same functions as systematic theory. Actually constructed types are "systems" on a small scale and are usually susceptible of empirical treatment. A constructed type is a purposive, planned selection, abstraction, combination, and accentuation of a set of criteria *that have empirical referents* and that serve as a basis for comparison of empirical cases. It has the function of a model remaining in close touch with the "takens" from which it derives. (See Chap. 6, esp. pp. 135-140, 182-183.)

Although models have actually been used by sociologists for years (types and systems, for example, are models), interest in the explicit construction and interpretation of models has increased recently.[20] Models may be in prose or mathematical notation; they can be long or short, simple or complex, but their heuristic value has been indisputably demonstrated. In general terms, analysis by means of a model involves a definition of the

[19] Parsons, *The Social System, passim.*

[20] See Paul Lazarsfeld (ed.), *Mathematical Thinking in the Social Sciences* (Glencoe, Illinois, 1954) for the most complete treatment extant of use of models in the social sciences. Also K. J. Arrow, "Mathematical Models in the Social Sciences," in Daniel Lerner and H. D. Lasswell (eds.), *The Policy Sciences* (Stanford, 1951); and M. A. Girscick and Daniel Lerner, "Model Construction in the Social Sciences," *POQ,* 14 (1950-51), pp. 710-28.

model and a test to determine how well a sample of data approximates the model. The model as a deductive device is given an empirical interpretation by means of comparison with data. If the discrepancy between the model and the sample data can be reasonably ascribed to chance rather than to factors not contained in the model, then it can be assumed that the data have a structure akin to the model. A pre-eminently "inductive" statistical sociologist is really following this procedure when he fits a frequency distribution to a "normal curve" and then tests the goodness of fit by chi-square. All "analytic" statistical devices involve this element of deduction.

Lately, several mathematical models have been developed in sociology that are indicative of a trend. The area of attitude study has been particularly productive in this respect, especially in view of the fact that the models apparently are applicable to many elements of behavior besides attitudes. Among these models are the Guttman scale and the "latent-structure" model of Lazarsfeld.[21] The sociologist's concern with models has increased since World War II, a trend which is indicative not only of the strength and persistence of deduction as a component of methodology but also of the increased quantitative sophistication of the American sociologist.

THE RISE OF QUANTIFICATION

There has been a great deal of controversy about the role and value of quantitative techniques in sociology. Extreme positions with respect to quantification were common during the twenties and thirties. But recently the polemic fervor has died down considerably. The tendency now is to look upon quantitative techniques as essential parts of the conceptual equipment of the sociologist rather than as an end in itself.

Conspicuous in the methodological thought of the twenties and thirties was the belief that sociology could become a natural science through statistical procedure. The neo-positivist orientation at the basis of this belief is apparent. The reasoning went as follows: The success of natural science may be attributed to the objective character of its data and the quantitative treatment of its results. Hence, if sociology is to emulate that success, it must change its ways of getting and handling data. This means that sociology must develop techniques that secure objective social data suitable for quantitative treatment by statistical means. There were numerous proponents of this thesis, but it was perhaps first clearly stated by Lundberg in 1928.[22]

The opposition to this view was stated in its most extreme form by those who were certain that human behavior was "different" enough from other phenomena to make it incapable of being treated statistically. It was

[21] See Stouffer *et al., op. cit.*, and Riley *et al., op. cit.*, for excellent treatments of these techniques.

[22] Lundberg, *Social Research* (New York, 1928).

asserted that the portion of sociological data that could be expressed in quantitative form was by its nature the least important of behavioral data, and moreover, so insignificant as to be barely worth the effort of getting it. This view was characteristic of many of the "outgoing" generation of sociologists. More important, it was advocated capably by such champions of "qualitative" research as Sorokin, MacIver, Waller, and Znaniecki.

Growing Recognition of the False Dichotomy. Although the sides were clear-cut, a number of leading sociologists were made very uncomfortable by what they considered to be a false dichotomy. As competent researchers they had technical leanings toward the quantitative or qualitative poles but nevertheless could not sympathize with the oversimplified "either-or" formulation of the argument. Such enthusiastic and yet conservative proponens of quantification as Ogburn, Dorothy Thomas, Thurstone, and Stouffer could not sympathize very strongly with optimists such as Lundberg, Dodd, and Bain, who wanted to start measuring social phenomena immediately with all the precision of the physical sciences. Conversely, there were those skilled specialists in qualitative research—such as Becker, Blumer, Hughes, Parsons, and Wirth, to mention only a few—who could not sympathize with those "intuitionists" who denied that men's behavior could ever be quantified in any important respect and that quantification could help in the understanding of society.

This "middle-range" group of sociologists recognized, and pointed out with increasing clarity, that both extreme positions rested on an assumption that was demonstrably false. This assumption was that sociological study could be carried on only in terms of one *particular* approach. It was increasingly recognized that a quantitative scale was no more *the* answer to sociology's problems than analytic induction, logico-experimentation, the case history, or any other device in the hands of the sociologist. Granted that some devices might have greater *instrumental* value than others, it remained true that there was no master key or royal road to scientific knowledge. There were many ways of conducting systematic study in sociology, and their value did not lie in the potential elevation of any one of them to supremacy, but rather in their articulation in a complementary and integrated set of tools. These "middle-range" sociologists explicitly recognized that enumerative and measuring devices were useful, but at the same time recognized that there were many other valuable components of the research endeavor.

The rise to pre-eminence of such "middle-range" scholars as Angell, Becker, Guttman, Lazarsfeld, Loomis, Merton, Stouffer, and Suchman has demonstrated that there is a *direct line of logical continuity* from systematic qualitative research to rigorous forms of measurement. A whole battery of intermediate devices fill the gap between the quantitative and qualitative poles and thus create a research *continuum* rather than a dichotomy. The sociologists in this group, through their leadership in the work with systematic ratings, classifications, ranking scales, constructed types, simple quantitative indices, codification, research design, logic of proof or demonstration, and "continuities in research," have made an immense contribution to the rejection in modern research of the logical separation of qualitative and quantitative endeavor.

This rejection has emphasized the fact that the application of mathematics to sociology does not insure validity of results any more than the use of "insight" or "intuition" guarantees the significance of the results. This point may be illustrated by the failure of Dodd's *Dimensions of Society* to have any appreciable effect on American methodology. A radical formalistic attempt to develop sociological theory in mathematical guise, it can be adjudged a magnificent failure, although it was a laudable attempt, involving a great deal of effort, to create a mathematical model. Nevertheless, it was scathingly dismissed by a mathematician (E. T. Bell) and a theoretician (Talcott Parsons) in a dual review.[23] Bell found that, except for a chapter on correlation theory, there was no mathematics in the book. A translation to an esoteric set of symbols had been accomplished, but no solvable equation had been constructed. On the other hand, Parsons concluded that "general adoption of S-theory would positively impede the achievement of the highest levels of generalized analysis attainable in the present state of the subject." The lesson learned from Dodd is that mathematicization independent of working theory and research procedures of demonstrable reliability amounts to mere symbolic gymnastics.

To illustrate the opposite aspect of the point, one may cite the work of Sorokin. Without questioning the importance of Sorokin's substantive contribution to the field, one can truthfully assert that his twenty or more books will have less methodological impact than such formulations as Guttman's scale analysis, Lazarsfeld's latent-structure analysis, Parsons' version of structural-functional theory, and Becker's logic of test of the constructed type—all of which can be presented in a few chapters. To know something (and Sorokin's works give evidence of a great deal of knowledge) is not enough for science; the procedures by which one knows are an essential part of the scientific process.

The rejection of extreme positions in the field with respect to quantification has had several consequences. For one thing, it has now become a commonplace that, no matter how precise measurement may be, what is measured remains a *quality*. Quantification is a tremendous asset insofar as it achieves greater reliability and precision in measuring the *qualities that are theoretically significant*. The indispensable working partner of quantifying procedures is obviously the theory that determines what is to be measured.

[23] E. T. Bell and Talcott Parsons, review of *Dimensions of Society,* in *ASR,* 7 (1942), pp. 707-14.

Second, it is also a commonplace that the most completely qualitative type of research employs measurement in limited fashion. The use of such terms as "growing," "increasing," "rising," "more," and "less" are indicative of *latent* quantification. In the broadest sense of the terms, social phenomena are being "measured" and "enumerated" constantly by both theoreticians and applied social researchers. Third, it seems to be generally agreed that it is desirable to treat quantitatively those data that can be theoretically formulated in units. Fourth, the measurement of subjective phenomena is *legitimate* as long as it is accompanied by recognition of the fact that it is accomplished indirectly through objective indices. Fifth, it is generally agreed that statistics afford verification or disqualification of hypotheses but only *suggest* explanation. In sum, quantification is now accepted as a normal and indispensable aspect of sociological endeavor. The controversies that surround it no longer refer to whether it is or is not possible in the behavioral sciences; they now are technical controversies concerning the applicability of given techniques, under stated circumstances, to particular kinds of phenomena.

NOMOTHETIC AND IDIOGRAPHIC TRENDS

In principle, American sociologists are almost universally committed to a nomothetic ideal for their science—an ideal which stems from a modified version of the original Windelband formulation of the nomothetic-idiographic dichotomy. Windelband distinguished two classes of sciences: those studying the general, and enunciating natural laws (nomothetic); and those studying particulars in their historically determined configurations (idiographic). The problem of whether sociology enunciates natural laws is not a current issue. It is agreed that sociology studies the *general, regular* and *recurrent* aspects of phenomena and hence can *generalize* and *predict* within the limits of its substantiated theory. This makes it a nomothetic discipline despite the substitution of empirical generalizations for natural laws.[24]

Like all other sciences, sociology has a necessary idiographic aspect. It contains numerous particular statements as well as generalizations. The problem centers around the extent to which the search for these particulars dominates the attempt to generalize, insofar as the attainment of general knowledge is the admitted aim of the discipline. Sociology has amassed a tremendous amount of descriptive data about specific people, places, and events. There are case studies of specific delinquents, surveys of specific communities, ecological descriptions of specific cities, observations of specific strikes, etc. The value of these descriptive treatments goes unquestioned insofar as they serve as the center from which empirical generalizations evolve. Their value is questioned, however, when they remain in the form of particulars and are not brought into the framework of substantive theory.

[24] A notable adherent of the concept of natural law is Znaniecki.

A promising, if modest, body of empirical generalizations has been built up in the past few decades, and it is legitimate to assume that this process will continue in the future. Nevertheless, most theoretically oriented sociologists are seriously concerned with the paucity of generalization as compared with the mass of particulars. Stated briefly, their concern has its basis in the fact that most sociologists affirm the desirability and necessity of formulating the general and recurrent and then in actual practice settle for the gathering of data and the amassing of descriptive particulars.[25]

Major Sources of Idiographic Emphasis. There is actually a very strong idiographic trend in sociology, then, despite the aims explicitly agreed upon by most sociologists. There seem to be several sources of this trend. One of the sources is interdisciplinary contact, wherein some representatives of closely related fields place strong emphasis on idiography. Among these, cultural anthropologists such as Boas, Herskovits, Lowie, Willey, and Wissler; social psychologists such as Kantor; institutional economists such as Mitchell; and almost all American historians emphasize the uniqueness, and hence concreteness, of every social situation. Sociologists who come under the influence of these representatives and their procedures tend to become idiographic observers and recorders.

A second source of the idiographic trend is the growth of the "community study" movement in recent years. Under the powerful stimulus of the Lynds' *Middletown*, a remarkable number of community studies have been conducted, none of which has attained the stature of *Middletown* and most of which have been almost entirely idiographic. The point of diminishing returns from such studies probably set in a long time ago; the need for more Middletowns, Plainvilles, Yankee Cities, and Jonesvilles is at least questionable. From the standpoint of sociology as science, what is needed is the examination of *general forms* of behavior in communities. This means that communities should not be studied as specific communities, but should be approached with some general considerations in mind. The growth of sociography rather than of sociology is the alternative.

Another primary source of idiographic emphasis is in the use of the statistical method. This is not to be taken as an assertion that the statistical method is exclusively idiographic in character. Indeed, its nomothetic aspects have been consistently gaining ground and at the present the value put upon statistical correlation, variance, and probability statements is probably greater than that put upon statistical description. The statistical method involves an essential nomothetic element because statistical enumeration is seldom exhaustive. The rapid growth of sampling theory is evidence of this. Nevertheless, the early statistics were primarily descriptive, and this is true also of much current statistical work. There are still many sociologists who enjoy

[25] An able defense of idiography is given by N. S. Timasheff, "On Methods in the Social Sciences," *ACSR,* 6 (1945), pp. 169-76.

assembling arrays of statistical data presumably independent of hypotheses and general categories.

Finally, and most important of all methodologically, a source of the idiographic trend—or, more specifically, of idiographic-nomothetic confusion—centers around the problem of abstraction. If considered on a low enough level of abstraction, all phenomena are unique. It has always been the task of science to conceptualize these phenomena in abstract terms in order to comprehend their general character. The fact that World War II was a unique war is no more a deterrent to the sociological study of wars than the fact that any given earthworm is unique is a deterrent to the study of the general structure of earthworms. Abstraction is a general scientific problem. It is true, however, that the problem persists in sociology because the sociologist is often interested in unique events or occurrences in a small number of cases. The interest is stimulated by the very fact that the cases are exceptional and hence "curious." The answers here seemingly lie in the adaptation of Znaniecki's analytic induction; or, in the situation involving few cases, the adaptation of a developing small-sample theory.

BEHAVIORISM AND ITS MODIFICATION

Immediately after World War I, behaviorism emerged as a movement of considerable proportions. Although relatively few sociologists accepted the extremism of Watson,[26] the movement nevertheless had a significant influence on sociological thinking, particulary in that fringe area of sociology known as social psychology. Behaviorism was a neo-positivist attempt to assimilate the study of human behavior to the natural sciences. As a discipline, it rejected the concepts of consciousness, sensation, perception, will, image, mental experience, and the significance of motives in determining behavior. Those concepts which it did retain from the older psychology (as for example, thinking and emotion) it redefined as forms of observable or directly inferred activities. The emphasis was on the stimulus-response bond, and it was overt behavior that was of central importance.

This approach was in keeping with the growing empirical and pragmatic tendencies of the twenties; it seemed to satisfy the demand for objectivity and mechanical certainty in the conduct of research. Because of its emphasis on the mechanical character of the stimulus-response relation, it seemed particularly amenable to quantification; hence it gave promise of freeing sociology from its subjectivism and thus converting it into an "exact" science. A comment by Bain, written in 1928, is an example of this line of thinking: "The development of sociology as a natural science has been hindered by: (1) emphasis on its normative rather than upon its de-

[26] For an early statement see J. B. Watson, *Psychology from the Standpoint of a Behaviorist* (Philadelphia, 1919); for a later work, see his *Behaviorism* (rev. ed.; New York, 1930). One of the few Watsonians of today, among sociologists, is Franz Adler, a recent convert.

scriptive aspects; (2) too much attention to subjective factors, such as ideas, ideals, motives, sentiments, wishes, and attitudes, and too little attention to objective, overt behavior. . ."[27]

Unfortunately, the promise of radical behaviorism did not "pay off" in research. Scarcely any contributions really based on the principle emerged, possibly because the very things it sought to explain did not easily (if at all) reduce to the mechanical circulation of stimulus-response. Nothing approaching scientific knowledge in the radical-behavioristic sense has accumulated regarding such phenomena as fashions, fads, crazes, conventions, rumors, public opinion, attitudes, customs, institutions, and social systems. As a consequence, in the thirties a much more modest type of behaviorism quickly supplanted the older variety and is still current—the "symbolic-interactionist" version, championed especially by Mead.[28] The positive significance of modified behaviorism lies primarily in its partial closing of the gap, which appeared larger than it was, between objectivism and subjectivism; its emphasis on symbolic interaction, which has led to the development of a sociology of communication; the reorientation of attitude study so that attitudes are no longer studied in a "vacuum" but are related to the social structure; and the promise that the Meadian approach holds for the growth of a peculiarly American sociology of knowledge in the future.

THE CONTROVERSY OVER OPERATIONISM

The doctrine of operationism established in physics by Bridgman in 1927 was transported into sociology in the thirties by several of the more pragmatically inclined sociologists. It was the subject of considerable controversy during the thirties and forties, but the issue died down somewhat by mid-century.[29] The central notion is expressed by Bridgman as follows: "In general, we mean by any concept nothing more than a set of operations; the concept is synonymous with the corresponding set of operations. . . . The meaning of a proposition is its verifiability."[30] Lundberg in particular took this as a cue to recast the conceptual framework of sociology. He asserted that the continued use of current sociological symbols would doom the discipline to "subjectivity." He pointed out the lack of agreement as to the

[27] Read Bain, "An Attitude on Attitude Research," *AJS,* 33 (May, 1928), p. 940.

[28] G. H. Mead, *Mind, Self and Society* (Chicago, 1934).

[29] See Lundberg, *Foundations of Sociology,* pp. 58-61; also his "Operational Definitions in the Social Sciences," *AJS,* 47 (March, 1942), pp. 727-43, with a "rejoinder" by Herbert Blumer, *ibid.,* pp. 743-45; S. C. Dodd, "Operational Definitions Operationally Defined," *ibid.,* 48 (Jan., 1943), pp. 482-89, with comment by Ethel Shanas, *ibid.,* pp. 489-91; Franz Adler, "Operational Definitions in Sociology," *ibid.* 52 (March, 1947), pp. 438-444; Harry Alpert, "Operational Definitions in Sociology," *ASR,* 3 (Dec., 1939), pp. 855-61; and Hornell Hart, "Toward an Operational Definition of the Term 'Operation,'" *ibid.,* 18 (Dec., 1953), pp. 612-17.

[30] P. W. Bridgman, *The Logic of Modern Physics* (New York, 1927), p. 5.

"meaning" of even common concepts, the typical use of them in a variety of senses, the fact that they mean many things to many people, and even different things to the same people on different occasions. This he considered fatal to the scientific approach, and consequently he also asserted that the ". . . only way of defining anything objectively is in terms of the operations involved."[31]

The objections to operational sociology tended to center around the limitations this approach placed on the role of concepts and of systematic theory. If Bridgman's original statement is taken literally—and it was by some sociologists—then it entails a severe limitation on concepts. For example, the traditional meaning of "magnitude" as a concept cannot be made synonymous with the "physical operations" involved in measuring magnitude. The physical operation of measuring magnitude never determines more than the magnitude of some specific object. The meaning traditionally ascribed to magnitude as a concept, however, determined the operation of measuring; for without knowing that meaning the physicist would have been incapable of selecting a relevant measuring device appropriate to the object. To measure a plowed field with a thermometer and call it "size" would be no more incongruous, however, than to measure intelligence with an achievement test and call it "intelligence." The operationists ignored the fact that concepts are always "general" and that an operation is always "specific" and hence subject to determination by the general. Radical operationism of the Lundberg type discounted the role of synthesizing rational thought in concept construction and consequently became a form of raw empiricism.

Operationism vs. *Systematic Theory.* The second ramification of radical operationism was the reduction of the role of systematic theory. Such typical operational statements as "intelligence is what intelligence tests test" implies that there can be as many "intelligences" as there are "tests." If so, extreme eclecticism results and it becomes impossible to establish a system of interrelated concepts of general empirical reference.

Although operationism has not experienced success in attaining incorporation into any of the important research developments in sociology, it nevertheless has left its imprint. First, a considerable amount of operationism is evident in much empirical research, particularly that reported in theses and dissertations. Second, and more important methodologically, operationism has assisted in bringing about the development and general acceptance of a more moderate approach known as *instrumentalism.* Originally formulated by Dewey, it is now a prevailing orientation of both the theoretically and the empirically inclined. Instrumentalism (often still traveling under the label of operationism) simply maintained that concepts should be made subject to inquiry and susceptible to hypothetical statement

[31] Lundberg, *Foundations of Sociology,* p. 69.

for purposes of examination. Moreover, instrumentalism asserts that theories, discrete or systematic, must be evaluated in terms of their research adaptability, verifiability, and fruitfulness. This orientation is implicit in the work of Stouffer and his associates and of Merton and Lazarsfeld, and even in the comprehensive systematic theory of Parsons.[32]

THE PRAGMATIC DEVELOPMENT

Pragmatism, although it is a philosophic label, stands for an attitude of mind rather than for a system of ideas; hence it appears in many diverse approaches and systems. Pragmatism is represented in the habit of interpreting ideas or events in terms of their consequences. As a result, it is closely allied with the logic of experiment, which is the basis of modern research science. In general, then, pragmatism does not seem to imply any final philosophic conclusions but merely manifests a tendency to accept anything that works in the conduct of research. It is thus an amplified empiricism that has become aware of the relation of conceptualization and theory to research.

The practice of research science has been continually to approach new problems and with these new problems to formulate new hypotheses. The test of these hypotheses lay in the experience of man as researcher, with whatever instruments he had at hand. The test, then, was found in the actual process of cognition. From this standpoint, then, mathematics, substantive theory, instruments, observational techniques, etc., simply represented the apparatus for working out hypotheses with respect to experience. Pragmatism as a doctrine is nothing more than an expression of scientific method as it has worked in the past.

It is still too early to ascertain the influence of pragmatism on sociology. Unquestionably, pragmatism has gained considerable headway in recent decades, and aspects of its orientation may be detected in many of the methodological positions dealt with here. It shows itself in several different ways. It is manifest in the decline of sociological dogmatism and the growing tendency to refuse to accept as final or definitive any single approach, theory, or instrument. The pragmatic attitude in sociology identified itself closely with the use of scientific method as that method entails the continuing analysis of problematic situations, the development and consideration of alternative hypotheses relative to the problems, and the verification of the alternatives by some test of experience.

The Implicit Role of Pragmatism in American Sociology. The pragmatic attitude permeates American methodology and characterizes not only the work of avowed empiricists but also that of our outstanding theorists. For

[32] Stouffer *et al., loc. cit.;* R. K. Merton and Paul Lazarsfeld (eds.), *Continuities in Social Research: Studies in Scope and Method of the American Soldier* (Glencoe, 1950); Parsons, *The Social System.*

example, Talcott Parsons has constructed the most "rationalistic" and "deductive" system in modern sociology; nevertheless, it has powerful pragmatic overtones. In espousing the "structural-functional" approach as essential to the development of sociology, Parsons indicates that he conceives of it as the most "fruitful" or "useful." In line with his contention that every empirical investigation is carried out in terms of a conceptual scheme that is either implicit or explicit, Parsons states that the "sole sanction of such a conceptual scheme is its utility, the degree to which it works in facilitating the attainment of the goals of scientific investigation."[33] His final test and justification is therefore a pragmatic one.

This American tendency to view and evaluate any heuristic device from the standpoint of its instrumental value in continuing an experiential (research) process gives considerable flexibility and adaptability to methodology; nevertheless, there are certain dangers involved in it. The dangers are similar to those of empiricism and can be briefly summed up as involving opportunism, lack of direction and continuity, vacillation between conflicting approaches, concern with immediacy of problems, and hence a lack of "long-run" vision. The primary contributions of the pragmatic point of view to methodology seem to be its emphasis on instrumentalism, experimental design (controlled experience), and modest working theory. Insofar as it has benefited from these contributions of pragmatism, American methodology has attained "hard-headedness" rather than succumbed to "headlessness."

Major Procedures and Techniques

American sociology has placed a concentrated emphasis on procedures and techniques since World War I. Each of the generic procedures—statistical, experimental, typological, historical, and case-study procedures—has been considerably used and developed. Unquestionably, however, the statistical procedure, with its varied enumerating and measuring techniques, has been developed and adapted more than any other. In addition, a consistent preoccupation with techniques as adapted to specific fact-finding or manipulating has brought about an enormous development of both qualitative and quantitative techniques. This emphasis on procedure and technique has resulted in the emergence of a generation of technically skilled sociologists and remains the outstanding characteristic of the rapidly developing American sociology of this period.

[33] Parsons, *Essays in Sociological Theory Pure and Applied* (Glencoe, Illinois, 1949), p. 66.

TEXTBOOKS ON RESEARCH

One of the quickest ways to grasp the growth of American sociology is to look at the various "methods" handbooks. The rapidity with which these books have become obsolescent is a gratifying thing. The best of the methods books of the twenties, for example, look very unsophisticated in comparison with the current crop. In 1920 Chapin published a work on methods, *Field Work and Social Research,* that represented the first real attempt to codify sociological research procedure. The first "manual" that surpassed it was Bogardus's *The New Social Research*, published in 1926. Its brief heyday was cut short by the appearance of Palmer's *Field Studies in Sociology* in 1928, representative of research developments at the University of Chicago in that period. Then, in 1929, sociology experienced a banner year. Odum and Jocher published *An Introduction to Social Research* and Lundberg his *Social Research*. Although they differed in emphasis, both these books excelled anything previously published in comprehensiveness and sophistication. The next year witnessed the appearance of a book of wider scope than those previously published: Spahr and Swenson, *Methods and Status of Scientific Research with Particular Application to the Social Sciences.*

In 1931 a major sociological milestone was reached. Until that time, all the methods books could be classed as "manuals." In 1931, however, the Social Science Research Council brought out *Methods in Social Science: A Casebook*, edited by Rice. This was not a "how-to-do-it" book; it consisted of fifty-two methodological analyses of contributions to the social sciences. For the first time, methodology entered the picture in a significant sense. Very different from the Rice book, but nevertheless representative of the same concern, was Znaniecki's *The Method of Sociology*, published in 1934. This can be labeled America's first great work in methodology. (Znaniecki is appropriated here for the United States even though Poland has a prior claim.) These two works were forerunners of the major developments that were to take place in the next twenty years.

To return to the "how-to-do-it" books: Bogardus brought out *Introduction to Social Research* in 1936; Pauline Young published the excellent *Scientific Social Surveys and Research* in 1939. The same year also brought Elmer's *Social Research*. In 1941 the two best statistical books oriented toward sociology came out: Hagood's *Statistics for Sociologists* and McCormick's *Elementary Social Statistics*. The second edition of Lundberg's work appeared in 1942, and in 1949 a revision of Young's earlier work appeared. In 1950 Gee's *Social Science Research Methods* was introduced.

Then came the present array of books concerned with research—books that have a "new look" compared to those previously published. In general, the older books, with the exception of those of Rice and Znaniecki, concentrated on the practical procedures of empirical research and had relatively little to say about the justification and articulation of techniques in the light of the logic of science. The current works represent a considerable shift in emphasis toward techniques, although they retain the earlier emphasis. *Research Methods in Social Relations* by Jahoda, Deutsch, and Cook; *Methods in Social Research* by Goode and Hatt; *Research Methods in the Behavioral Sciences* by Festinger and Katz; *Introduction to Social Research* by Doby *et al.; The Scope and Method of Sociology* by Furfey; *The Design of Social Research* by Ackoff; and *The Language of Social Research* by Lazarsfeld and Rosenberg all represent the remarkable present-day technical enrichment of sociology in comparison to former decades, the product of many significant developments in procedure and technique since World War I.

THE STATISTICAL PROCEDURE

The statistical procedure comprises a body of theory and techniques dealing with data secured through enumeration and measurement. Hence the problems of statistical analysis generally center around the valid enumeration and measurement of units of the phenomena under consideration. Initially, statistical techniques were applied to behavior in which interaction or communication was of little or no importance—in demography, for example. Increasingly, however, sociologists have been concerned with the application of statistical techniques to areas of behavior where the "units" are not self-evident or obvious. Despite the continued controversies over the "proper" quantification of some aspects of behavior and the persistent problem as to whether a great deal of that behavior can be enumerated and measured at all, sociologists have experienced a gradually increasing success in applying statistical techniques to their body of substantive material.

Sociologists have made little contribution to the rapidly developing body of statistical theory. The major contributions in this field have been made by mathematicians, geneticists, psychologists, educators, economists, and agricultural biologists. Sociologists have been kept busy trying to apply the body of techniques developed in and made available to them from other disciplines. Consequently, although one cannot cite basic contributions of sociologists to statistical procedure, one can cite significant contributions in the application of statistical techniques to sociological behavior for the first time.

The Descriptive Function of Statistics. The whole body of statistical techniques can be divided into two parts: the *descriptive* and the *generalizing*. The descriptive techniques are those that condense and summarize data on enumerable or measurable characteristics of a series of units and thereby describe selected aspects of those units. The measures most commonly used in descriptive statistics are ratios, rates, percentages, frequency distributions, measures of central tendency and of dispersion. These summarizing measures condense masses of data into a form that makes them more comprehensible and communicable.

Use of statistics in sociology at the time of World War I was almost wholly restricted to this descriptive function. Even at the present time, *most* sociological application of statistical techniques is at this descriptive level. This use of statistics goes largely unquestioned in the field today, except for the fact that many theoretical sociologists question the significance of much of the data amassed in this fashion. This area is representative of one of the strongest idiographic trends in the discipline.

During the twenties and thirties it became increasingly common to extend the descriptive techniques in two ways. One extension involved the time series in the description of characteristics of the same unit at different periods.[34] The other extension involved the construction of compound, indirect measures in the form of index numbers or scale scores.[35] These techniques still represented the descriptive function, but it is important to note that they quantitatively described sociological subject matter that had previously been dealt with only in strictly qualitative terms.

Analytic and Generalizing Functions of Statistics. The *generalizing* statistical techniques are those that the sociologist was inevitably forced to use because of the requirements of certain types of inquiry. Many inquiries are necessarily restricted to the study of only a portion of the units involved in the problem. This restriction necessitates the use of a limited number of units as a *sample* of the entire series conceived of as a *universe*. Theoretically, the sample must be representative of the universe with respect to the characteristics being investigated. The data gathered from the sample are handled by descriptive techniques, which afford a summary description of the sample itself. In addition, however, there is a more elaborate body of techniques that permits the sociologist to make certain estimates about the larger group from which the sample was drawn. The techniques used in this function may be called generalizing statistical techniques. These techniques make it possible to compute for the whole series of phenomena (the universe) estimates of the same summarizing measures (ratios, rates, measures of central tendency and dispersion, etc.) that the descriptive techniques furnish for the sample.

The ability to generalize about data in this fashion is related to two factors not involved in mere description: probability logic and sampling theory. Both are necessary in view of the sociologist's inability to examine *all* the cases involved in his inquiry. The frequency theory of probability enables the sociologist to extrapolate from his findings within certain confidence limits. Sampling theory, as a specific form of probability logic, enables the sociologist to study significant problems that would otherwise

[34] See Dorothy S. Thomas, *Social Aspects of the Business Cycle* (London, 1925).

[35] For illustration, see Margaret J. Hagood, "Construction of County Indexes for Measuring Change in Level of Living in Farm Operator Families, 1940-45," *RS*, 12 (June, 1947), pp. 139-50; A. L. Porterfield, "Rank of the States in Professional Leadership and Social Well-Being," *SF*, 25 (March, 1947), pp. 303-9.

be beyond his reach if he had to study all the units involved. It gives him greater theoretical justification for asserting the representativeness of his observations. Unquestionably, the development of sampling theory (entirely outside the field of sociology) has played a major role in liberating the sociologist from sheer description. Moreover, there is great promise that the sociologist will experience increasing success in validly sampling whatever groups he is interested in and hence increasing the accuracy of sociological knowledge. The rapidly increasing literature on aspects of sampling appearing in the professional journals and research handbooks, particularly in the past fifteen years, is an indication of the sociologist's intense awareness of the pertinence of sampling theory and procedure to his inquiry.[36]

Importance of Sampling Design. Sampling design is increasingly becoming a part of research projects undertaken by sociologists. There are many different kinds of design, but several are very common. Most of the early sampling, and even much of that being done today, is *accidental* sampling. This is a form that is not subject to codification but can only be described after the fact. Certain cases are used as the basis for generalization because of their ready accessibility. It would be impossible to estimate the effect that this type of sampling had had on the accumulation of sociological knowledge, but it obviously has been the source of considerable bias. Examples of its use are the selection of "volunteer" cases or the use of one's students or friends as the basis of generalization. Sociologists have been prone to take the data that they have ready access to and to ignore the more inaccessible. However, this habit is less prevalent today than earlier. Perhaps the greatest single force counteracting this tendency was the type of research fostered at the University of Chicago in the twenties, where, under the vigorous leadership of Park, students were encouraged to do research in problematic areas that were certainly not readily accessible.

In the twenties, most sampling was rather hit-or-miss, but there was a growing awareness that work had to be done on the development of techniques for selecting "fractions" of the phenomena of interest that *represented* larger universes of that phenomena. The field studies conducted by rural sociologists, often reflecting the stimulus of Galpin, were a part of this movement. One of the early studies of this kind was the one reported in 1922 by Zimmerman and Taylor in *Rural Organization, A Study of Primary Groups in Wake County, N.C.* The Missouri Crime Survey, reported in 1926,

[36] See, for example, F. F. Stephan, "Practical Problems of Sampling Procedure," *ASR,* 1 (August, 1936), pp. 569-80; T. C. McCormick, "On the Amount of Error in Sociological Data," *ibid.,* 3 (June, 1938), pp. 328-32; P. H. Furfey, "The Sampling Problem," *ACSR,* 8 (1947), pp. 258-65; F. F. Stephan, "Sampling," *AJS,* 55 (January, 1950), pp. 371-75; and the treatments accorded the subject in recent research handbooks.

represented a large-scale attempt to survey the administration of criminal justice by means of careful sampling.[37]

In the thirties, largely as a result of the depression, the federal government served as a powerful stimulus to the further application of sampling. A great number of sample surveys, undertaken directly or indirectly under federal auspices, set the pace for changes in sampling technique during this period. The general direction of these surveys was away from subjective and accidental selection toward *systematic* and *random* selection. Also, toward the end of the decade, developments occurred in various types of *stratified* sampling, as well as in *area* and other *mixed types* of sampling.

The rising popularity of public opinion polls and market research gave considerable emphasis to *quota* sampling during the thirties and forties, although the technique has numerous limitations for other types of research. Quota sampling is stratified non-random sampling and represents the only common technique in which randomness is not essential. Simple random sampling itself is not applicable to most sociological problems, but the principle of randomness is involved in all the techniques that are applicable.

Stratified sampling and *proportional stratified* sampling have both come into considerable use lately. Their major impetus has come from the Departments of Agriculture, Labor, and Commerce; the Bureau of the Census; the field of attitude study; and the study of rural and urban community structure. Area sampling got its true start at Iowa State College in the late thirties, was used by the Bureau of the Census in its sample surveys of congested areas in 1943 and 1944, and came of age in the 1945 Census of Agriculture.[38]

The events of the past two decades have indicated that sampling techniques are powerful tools for studying universes too large to be studied in their entirety. Most of the technical development has taken place in the extensive "large-scale" studies devoted to the analysis of specified characteristics. There is still a need for more successful adaptation of "small-sampling" theory to units that are more amenable to "structural-functional" or "process" analysis. The fact that sampling is necessarily subject to error because of its probability character is not its major drawback. The major obstacle to the application of sampling techniques, as in all other statistical manipulation, is the fact that there are vexing and persistent *problems of enumeration and measurement of units* of sociological data involved.

Statistics and the Search for Relationships. In addition to a descriptive-generalizing classification of statistical techniques, another twofold division

[37] C. C. Zimmerman and C. C. Taylor, *Rural Organization, A Study of Primary Groups in Wake County, N.C.* (Raleigh, 1922); *The Missouri Crime Survey* (New York, 1926).

[38] See R. J. Jesson, *Statistical Investigation of a Sample Survey for Obtaining Farm Facts* (Ames, Iowa, 1942); and A. J. King and R. J. Jesson, "The Master Sample of Agriculture," *Journal of the American Statistical Association,* 40 (March, 1945), pp. 38-56.

is based upon complexity of application[39]: first, the *simple* techniques that either through description or generalization treat single distributions of characteristics; and, second, the *complex* techniques that deal with distributions of two or more characteristics simultaneously, either descriptively or by generalization. The techniques in the second group are designed to reveal association or relationship between characteristics and may be called the statistics of relationship.

Although the description of the incidence or distribution of a characteristic is in itself important, and although much sociological research renders this sort of report, it nevertheless remains true that such description is not sufficient for the inquiry into sociological *problems*. Such problems are always problems of *relationship,* hence a statistics of relationship is essential to the purposes of sociological inquiry. Increasingly, sociological research has attempted to ascertain and precisely describe the existence, direction, degree, and character of the association between two or more factors. When the conclusions of the investigation are limited to the units studied, *descriptive statistics of relationship* have been employed. In attempts to generalize about the universe from which the sample is drawn, *generalizing statistics of relationship* have been employed. The first of the two is far more characteristic of current sociology than the second; explicit generalization tends to be very scanty at the present time.

Especially since the twenties, sociologists have become very familiar with certain summarizing measures of association. They have used coefficients of contingency to relate two or more non-quantitative characteristics; coefficients of correlation (total, partial, and multiple); linear and curvilinear correlations to relate two or more quantitative characteristics. Factor analysis is entering the picture here as a potential tool, but its practical adaptability to sociological problems has not yet been demonstrated.

The invention of analysis of *variance* and *covariance* by R. A. Fisher in the forties introduced two more tools of powerful potential for the sociologist. It is still too early to evaluate their utility for sociology, but unquestionably a serious attempt will be made in the future to integrate these techniques into the sociological battery.[40] Analysis of variance is designed to relate one quantitative characteristic and one or more non-quantitative characteristics. It seems best suited to experimental studies where approximately equal groups are assigned to known values of the experimental variable. Analysis of covariance is designed to relate two or more quantitative characteristics and one or more non-quantitative characteristics. The utility of covariance lies in the fact that it can be substituted for rigorous

[39] Hagood's classification is followed here for convenience. See Margaret J. Hagood and D. O. Price, *Statistics for Sociologists* (2nd ed.; New York, 1954), pp. 4-5.

[40] See the recent treatment by R. L. Ackoff, *Design of Social Research* (Chicago, 1954), pp. 229-55.

matching techniques in research.[41] Successfully adapted to sociological material, covariance might give the sociologist an approximation to experimental control over data without the use of artificially "contrived" situations.

Problems of Measurement and Scaling Techniques. The attempt by sociologists to adapt statistics of relationship to their discipline is a laudable one, although its history is dotted with excess and error. Headway has been made, however, and much of it is due to the increased ability to enumerate and measure units. *Measurement* presupposes the assumption of a continuum, and it has been increasingly profitable for sociologists to conceive of their subject matter as distributed along continua. When a continuum is assumed, the task becomes one of scaling it so that distinctions can be made between the phenomena distributed along it. The problem to which scaling techniques are applied is that of ordering a series of items along a continuum in order to convert a series of qualitative attributes into a quantitative series of some sort. Sociologists have wrestled with this problem since the twenties, with rather promising results. They have encountered and attacked the problem in such diverse areas as the study of attitudes, institutional practices, housing adequacy, social status, occupational prestige, neighborhoods, concept formation, personal relations, and social systems. Many different scales have been devised in the past thirty years, but most of them fall into five general types: social-distance scales (including sociometric); rating scales; ranking scales; internal-consistency scales; and latent-structure scales.[42] This, incidentally, represents their chronological order of development.

The question as to whether sociological scales employing cardinal numbers can ever be developed is a persistent one. Such a scale would have to have two attributes: its point of origin would have to be at the value zero; and each component element of the scale would have to add an equal increment. In the view of some sociologists, only a scale of this sort would render "true" measurement. Whether this is true or not is a moot question; no sociological scales in current use possess these attributes, all of them being *ordinal* scales. Sociological measurement to date is merely ordinal measurement.

The first scales to be widely used were social-distance scales, often called *Bogardus scales* in recognition of Bogardus' pioneering work in this area. The concept itself was used early in the century by Park and had reference to the grades and degrees of understanding and intimacy which characterized pre-social and social relations. Bogardus took this concept in the early twenties and developed a crude measure for it—crude because it involved the assumption of equidistance between scale points and the

[41] See M. J. Taves, "The Application of Analysis of Covariance in Social Science Research," *ASR*, 15 (June, 1950), pp. 373-81.

[42] See W. J. Goode and P. K. Hatt, *Methods in Social Research* (New York, 1953), p. 243.

premise that each point on the scale was beyond the preceding one. In addition, its reliability could only be tested by the frequently impractical test-retest technique. Nevertheless, the contribution was a basic one and the technique received wide application in the study of various types of groups (especially minority and occupational groups), and in the study of values.

In the mid-thirties, Moreno and Jennings developed a new technique called *sociometry,* which may be classed under the social-distance rubric, although it differs radically from the Bogardus approach.[43] Sociometry has been an extremely useful sociological technique because it is concerned with group structure in terms of the attractions and repulsions between the individuals composing the group. The technique has been applied in such diverse areas as informal groups, institutionalized groups, school classes, prisons, and military establishments and has been used to investigate problems such as morale, compatibility, integration, leadership, and isolation. The technique has been used competently by a number of people, but Zeleny's use in his studies of morale and of compatibility of flying partners probably represents the most refined use of the technique as it was originally developed.[44] The only instance of extension of the technique beyond its original scope may be attributed to Loomis. The early sociometrists restricted themselves to choices and rejections of people built around the notion of "preferred associations." Loomis and others have shifted the technique to include actual associations (as in visiting patterns, for example) in specific activities rather than mere preferences.[45] This emphasis on actual structure has enhanced the sociological utility of the technique in contradistinction to the earlier "therapeutic" emphasis.

Rating scales represent another common approach to sociological measurement. Innumerable scales of this type have appeared since the twenties and have added considerably to sociological knowledge. The rating technique is based on a working definition of three elements: the judges who make the ratings; the subject or subjects that are rated; and the continuum along which they are rated. However, the validity of the technique is based on the adequacy of selecting and relating the three. Rating scales have appeared in a great many different forms, the most common being point scales, graphic scales, compound rating scales, the "guess-who" test, the check list, and forced-choice scales. They have been applied as rating devices

[43] J. L. Moreno, *Who Shall Survive?* (Washington, D.C., 1934); and Helen H. Jennings, "Structure of Leadership-Development and Sphere of Influence," *Socm,* 1 (July-Oct., 1937), pp. 93-143.

[44] L. D. Zeleny, "Sociometry of Morale," *ASR,* 4 (Dec., 1939), pp. 799-806; and his "Selection of Compatible Flying Partners," *AJS,* 52 (March, 1947), pp. 424-31.

[45] For illustration, see C. P. Loomis, *Studies of Rural Social Organization in the United States, Latin America and Germany* (East Lansing, 1945); and his *Studies in Applied and Theoretical Social Science* (East Lansing, 1950).

to such diverse phenomena as personnel evaluation, home and social environment, occupations, teaching proficiency, and social systems. The technique remains a valuable tool in the hands of careful investigators who control the instrument as they use it. Its great advantage is its extreme flexibility and its adaptability to situations in which it is the first step toward quantification.

Ranking scales are very similar to rating scales, with the exception of one factor. The judgments of the subject are not made on a preconceived continuum used as an absolute scale; they are made on the basis of comparisons of the units themselves. These comparisons "produce" the scale. The ranking technique represents the main line of scale development and leads directly to current developments. Thurstone, adapting ideas from psychological testing, was the prime mover in developing scale technique during the twenties and thirties.[46] His earlier techniques of "paired comparisons" and "just discernible differences" culminated in the technique of "equal-appearing intervals" that is normally referred to as the Thurstone technique.

The Thurstone technique of equal-appearing intervals became the dominant type of ranking scale during the thirties. Although the technique provided an instrument that produced admirable results under certain circumstances and was simple in administration and scoring, it nevertheless had certain drawbacks. First, its basic dependence on judges constituted a limitation; second, the amount of labor involved in construction limited its applicability. Thurstone was aware of the difficulties involved in his technique, and his own suggestions for improvement led to the development of the internal-consistency scales widely used by sociologists. Thurstone's criticism of the use of judges and his development of the notion of an objective criterion of irrelevance were crucial factors in the emergence of internal-consistency scales. The fundamental difference between this and the earlier ranking techniques is that the subjects take the place of the judges and produce the scale in terms of their own responses. There were many contributors to this development in the late thirties; notable among them were Murphy, Likert, Rundquist, and Sletto.[47]

Although attitude study represented the dominant application of this mode of scaling, sociologists found ample opportunity to apply it to other phenomena. One extension involved the scaling of a variety of social values. Chapin's scaling of social status and community participation; Sewell's scaling of rural social status; and Leahy's scaling of the adequacy of home

[46] L. L. Thurstone, "Attitudes Can Be Measured," *AJS,* 33 (January, 1928), pp. 529-54.

[47] Gardner Murphy and Rensis Likert, *Public Opinion and the Individual* (New York, 1938); E. A. Rundquist and Raymond Sletto, *Personality in the Depression* (Minneapolis, 1936).

environment[48] were representative of this line of development. The area of "prediction" studies is also based on the idea of internal consistency. The general form of these studies consists of selection of criterion groups, determination of differences among them, and combination of the differences into a scale to predict the behavior of other groups. Prediction scaling has been applied to such problems as likelihood of delinquency, parole success, probation, success, happiness in marriage, and occupational adjustment.[49] The technique of internal consistency has been basically integrated into the sociological approach.

The Guttman Scale and Related Developments. The next major development in measurement came with the appearance of "scalogram analysis" in the forties. Guttman was the theoretician of this development, and the scales growing out of it bear his name. One of the basic criticisms of the technique of internal consistency contained the charge that scales constructed by it were multidimensional and hence gave only a crude measure of the factors they were presumed to measure. As a consequence Guttman provided a technique whereby the "unidimensionality," hence "scalability," of a set of items could be assessed. The notion of a "scalable unidimensional universe" has added considerable precision to the measurement of manifest behavior.[50] The Guttman assumptions are formal and take account of both the strong and the weak points of the earlier Thurstone scales. The technique makes no attempt to adjudge items as constituting a scale on the basis of content; on the contrary, the scale is a function of its "reproducibility." An attitude questionnaire, for example, is a scale if the items arrange a group of people so that their responses can be reconstructed from their ranks. This means that there is a unique combination of responses for each rank; hence a person's response pattern is determined by his rank. In other words, persons with the same scale score produce the same pattern of responses to all the items in the scale. If a set of items does not have high reproducibility of this sort, the items are judged to be multidimensional and hence not scalable by the Guttman technique.

The Guttman technique received extensive application in the area of

[48] Chapin, "A Quantitative Scale for Rating the Home and Social Environment of Middle Class Families in an Urban Environment," *JEP,* 19 (February, 1928), pp. 99-111; William Sewell, *The Construction and Standardization of a Scale for the Measurement of the Socio-economic Status of Oklahoma Farm Families* (Stillwater, 1940); Alice M. Leahy, *The Measurement of Home Environment* (Minneapolis, 1936).

[49] H. A. Weeks and M. G. Smith, "Juvenile Delinquency and Broken Homes in Spokane, Washington," *SF,* 18 (October, 1939), pp. 48-55; G. B. Vold, *Prediction Methods and Parole* (Hanover, N.H., 1931); E. D. Monachesi, *Prediction Factors in Probation* (Hanover, N.H,, 1932); E. W. Burgess and L. S. Cottrell, *Predicting Success or Failure in Marriage* (New York, 1939); E. L. Thorndike *et al., Prediction of Vocational Success* (New York, 1934).

[50] For a detailed treatment see Stouffer *et al., op. cit.,* especially Chaps. 2-11 by Louis Guttman and E. A. Suchman.

attitude study during and following World War II, and it is gradually being adapted to more general sociological problems. For instance, Wallin used a Guttman scale to measure women's neighborliness, Schmid used it to establish ecological pattern types, and Schuessler and Strauss used it to analyze the development of concepts by children. Moreover, Riley and his associates have recently described the ways in which the Guttman scale can be adapted to a wide range of theoretical problems—for example, to such familiar sociological concepts as status, consensus, and interpersonal communication.[51] Furthermore, these authors attempt to handle collective data involving patterns of acts and social structures. They regard as their central contribution the demonstration that scale analysis can be used to order either groups or the objects of group action along a unidimensional continuum. It is now rather obvious that the Guttman scaling technique is destined to be a major research tool in sociology.

Another development of the forties was Lazarsfeld's generalized latent-structure theory, which derives Guttman's scale as a special case.[52] Although it is too new and untried to be evaluated as a research tool, it is quite likely to elicit testing and application for years to come. It not only represents a challenge to conventional procedures in attitude scaling, but it has a potential for a much wider empirical application. Unlike the Guttman scale, it does not depart from factor analysis; rather, it appears as a technique for factoring qualitative data. It is based on the notion of a latent-attitude structure that can under certain conditions be derived from manifest data. The technique does not appear to oppose either the Thurstone or Guttman approaches; it is a complementary analytic tool.

THE EXPERIMENTAL PROCEDURE

The experimental procedure is commonly looked upon as crucial to the inductive base of science. The notion of experimental procedure, however, has been very loosely used in sociology. Optimistic expressions regarding the application of the procedure to social data were made quite frequently during the twenties and thirties. References to the "sociological laboratory" were commonplace. Even today, the term is frequently applied to empirical studies in which it is an obvious misnomer with reference to actual procedure. Increasingly, however, sociologists have faced up to the fact that much of human behavior is not susceptible of the sort of control that is the distinctive characteristic of the experimental procedure. This is

[51] Paul Wallin, "A Guttman Scale for Measuring Women's Neighborliness," *AJS,* 59 (Nov., 1953), pp. 243-46; C. B. Schmid, "Generalizations Concerning the Ecology of the American City," *ASR,* 15 (April, 1950), pp. 264-81; Karl Schuessler and Anselm Strauss, "A Study of Concept Learning by Scale Analysis," *ASR,* 15 (Dec., 1950), pp. 752-62; Riley *et al., loc. cit.*

[52] See Stouffer *et al., op. cit.,* Vol. 4.

not to say that sociologists have lost faith in the *logic* of the experiment; on the contrary, they maintain that it is equally as important in the social as in the natural sciences. Sociologists have simply recognized that the *direct* manipulatory control which accompanies that logic to a high degree in the natural sciences is largely lacking in sociology. The modern tendency is to accept the experiment as a *model* for research design; the basic problem has become one of articulating the observational and collectional procedures to the experimental *design*.

Briefly, the methodological core of the experiment is represented in the ability to isolate a set of factors or immunize them to external influence. These factors are the potential variables within the defined "boundaries" of the experiment. Then a single determinate change is effected with reference to one variable while all other potential variables are held simultaneously constant. Determinate differences in the end result are then noted. Scientific custom decrees that the variation in results was produced by the change induced in the variable. Direct *manipulatory* control is evident throughout in this method, which is the prototype of the experimental method.

With respect to this prototype, two courses have been open to the sociologist. One involves the attempt to use the method in "contrived" situations; the other involves settling for the logic of experiment as the pattern of research design and depending on observational and statistical control in place of direct manipulation. Both courses have been taken, although the second appears to be of much greater long-run significance.

A wide variety of studies labeled "experimental" have been conducted since World War I; they reflect varied levels of competence, rigor, ingenuity, fruitfulness, and control.[53] The following are examples of the better known of these studies. In 1920 F. H. Allport studied the influence of the group on various mental activities. In 1927 Gosnell investigated the causes of non-voting; in the same year Gillis studied the outcome of two different teaching approaches to health practices. In 1933 Mayo issued a preliminary report of an investigation into the influence of a variety of techniques of remuneration and of physical and social factors on the productivity of workers in the Hawthorne Western Electric plant. Dodd conducted an experiment contrasting hygienic practices in Arab villages in 1934. Newstetter studied the nature of group adjustment by adolescent boys in a boys' camp in 1937. In 1938 Menefee tested the effect upon students of typical propaganda appeals for and against a strike. The "experimentation" of the Group Dynamics organization under the leadership of Lewin and Lippitt also started in the thirties at Iowa, moved to M.I.T., and is currently being

[53] For summary treatment of some of this work, see Chapin, *Experimental Designs in Sociological Research* (New York, 1947); and Ernest Greenwood, *Experimental Sociology* (New York, 1945).

conducted at Michigan. Probably their most famous study is the one concerned with the effects on behavior of "autocratic" and "democratic" atmospheres. One of Chapin's more representative studies was reported in 1940; it concerned the hypothesis that the rehousing of slum families in a public housing project would result in improving their social life.[54]

These few examples of the work carried on since World War I indicate that sociologists have been deeply concerned with the experimental concept. However, the "experimental" does not bring the great bulk of the work done in the past into any favorable comparison with much routine work in other sciences. This is not to disparage the work being done at the "laboratories" at Harvard and Michigan, for example; it is merely to point out that despite the extravagant claims of some experimental enthusiasts, experimentation has certain severe limitations in sociology. Obviously most important social situations cannot be "contrived" and structured at the will of the sociologist; hence this endeavor must necessarily remain as a subsidiary approach in sociology.

The Logic of Experiment. On the other hand, there is nothing to prevent the sociologist from borrowing the logic of experiment and adapting it to any problem he may be studying. In recent years, sociologists have begun to understand the logic of experimentation *as it can be applied sociologically* rather than in its merely formal character. A review of the situation with respect to experimentation as it existed in 1929 was given by Odum and Jocher; and Brearly surveyed the situation in 1931.[55] Their reviews indicate the diversity of view and the confusion about experimentation that prevailed in the field at that time. Since that time, however, the logic of experiment has been brought down to earth and thus made more meaningful procedurally. Several factors have apparently played a role in this development: (1) the empirical work that has been done where an approximation to the experimental model is sought (as in the case of the examples previously cited); (2) the continual analysis of these attempts, with resulting gain in

[54] F. H. Allport, "The Influence of the Group upon Association and Thought," *Journal of Experimental Psychology,* 3 (June, 1920), pp. 159-82; Harold Gosnell, *Getting Out the Vote* (Chicago, 1927); Gillis, "An Experimental Study of the Development and Measurement of Health Practices of Elementary School Children," *JES,* 1 (November, 1927), pp. 164-65; Elton Mayo, *The Human Problems of an Industrial Civilization* (New York, 1933); S. A. Dodd, *A Controlled Experiment on Rural Hygiene in Syria* (New York, 1934); W. I. Newstetter, "An Experiment in the Defining and Measuring of Group Adjustment," *ASR,* 2 (April, 1937), pp. 230-36; Selden Menefee, "An Experimental Study of Strike Propaganda," *SF,* 16 (May, 1938), pp. 754-82; Ronald Lippitt, "Field Theory and Experiment in Social Psychology: Autocratic and Democratic Group Atmospheres," *AJS,* 45 (July, 1939), pp. 26-49; F. S. Chapin, "An Experiment on the Social Effects of Good Housing," *ASR,* 5 (Dec., 1940), pp. 868-79.

[55] H. W. Odum and Katharine Jocher, *Introduction to Social Research* (New York, 1929), pp. 260-83; H. C. Brearly, "Experimental Sociology in the United States," *SF,* 10 (Dec, 1931), pp. 196-99.

experience (Chapin has unquestionably been the leader in this aspect of the development over the years, although he received an important assist from Greenwood in 1945);[56] (3) the importation of European methodology (particularly German) with its emphasis on conceptual apparatus, which enriched the American sociologist's methodology; (4) the development of statistical theory and technique with the increased promise of control over data; and (5) the increased concern with study *design* and the inevitable recognition that the *logic* of experiment is pervasive throughout scientific endeavor and hence is implicit in the most fruitful use of all of the procedures of the sociologist.[57]

The convergence of the above factors has gradually brought about the realization that the logic of experimental procedure is as important to the sociologist as it is to those scientists fortunate enough to possess direct manipulatory control over their data. The logic of experimental procedure is the logic of the *explanatory* use of the statistical, typological, case, and historical procedures. The use of any of these procedures as predictive devices demands that they be testable under empirical conditions. This means making comparisons in the sense of experimental logic. The fact that most of these comparisons must be made with reference to "naturally" occurring data and cannot be "willfully" produced is a handicap to the sociologist, but it does not deny him explanation in the scientific sense.

As Stouffer remarked in 1950:

> . . . the heart of our problem lies in study design *in advance,* such that the evidence is not capable of a dozen alternative interpretations. . . . Basically, I think it is essential that we always keep in mind the model of a controlled experiment, even if in practice we may have to deviate from the ideal model.[58]

THE TYPOLOGICAL PROCEDURE

The constructive typological procedure has played an important role in all the sciences although it has not in all cases been explicitly recognized, rigorously used, or carefully interpreted. The "formal" clarification of the procedure of constructive typology must be credited to the discipline of sociology, more specifically to a number of leading German sociologists of the late nineteenth and early twentieth centuries, despite the fact that the procedure itself is as old as science.

In the United States the procedure was established, under German influence, primarily at the University of Chicago under the leadership of Park. In the late twenties and early thirties several excellent typological

[56] Chapin, *Experimental Designs in Sociological Research;* Greenwood, *loc. cit.*

[57] For a brief, concise, and yet convincing exposition of this emerging point of view see R. G. Francis, "Principles of Experimentation" in J. T. Doby (ed.), *An Introduction to Social Research* (Harrisburg, 1954), pp. 101-22.

[58] Stouffer, "Some Observations on Study Design," *AJS,* 55 (Jan., 1950), pp. 355-61.

dissertations were produced there. Hughes and Redfield have carried on the tradition at Chicago, although the continuity has been maintained primarily at the University of Wisconsin under the influence of Becker. The typological procedure, in its explicit formulation, is now more generally used than it formerly was and a larger number of competent typological studies are being produced.

Constructive typology may be identified with methodology in that it is a way of handling and ordering the data of any substantive field. On the basis of the more fruitful instances of typological procedure in research, it would seem that a constructed type is a purposive, planned selection, abstraction, combination, and accentuation of a set of criteria that have empirical referents and that serve as a basis for comparison of empirical cases.[59]

The definition above indicates that the constructed type is a concept that is determined to a great degree by the selective and creative activity of the scientist. The primary distinction between it and other concepts, however, is that its value as a component of knowledge is not to be measured by the accuracy of its correspondence to perceptual reality but in *terms of its capacity to explain.* The constructed type has the scientific function of "ordering" the concrete data so that the experience obtained from one case, despite its uniqueness, *may be made to reveal with some degree of* probability *what may be expected in others.*[60]

The constructed type is therefore a heuristic device. It is an abstraction designed to eliminate the research minutiae and to achieve a structured order of observations that more readily lend themselves to statement and verification. The type is thus a means of reducing the diversities and complexities of phenomena to a coherently general level. It does not describe a concrete structure or course of action. The abstraction deviates from perceptual reality in that it frequently accentuates to a logical extreme some attribute or group of attributes that are relevant to a problem or system of analysis.

The constructed type is a devised *system* of attributes (characteristics, criteria, traits, elements, aspects, etc.) that is *useful* as a *basis* for understanding empirical objects and events. It is a construct made up of abstracted elements and formed into a unified conceptual pattern in which there may be an intensification of one or more aspects of concrete reality. The elements of the type have discoverable empirical referents or at least can be legitimately inferred from existent evidence. As a logical expedient, the type does not purport to be empirically valid in the sense of retaining the unique aspects of the empirical world. The constructed type as a conceptual device represents an attempt to advance concept formation in sociology from the

[59] For the development of this see J. C. McKinney, "Constructive Typology and Social Research," in Doby, *op. cit.*

[60] See Becker, *op. cit.*, pp. 97, 261-62, for the "logic" of probability as it is used here.

state of description and strictly "empirical generalization" to the construction of theoretical systems.

The Constructed Type and Sociological Theory. The constructed type is a special kind of concept—special in the sense that it deliberately emphasizes and states the *limits* of the case. Moreover, it is special in the sense that it consists of a set of attributes in which the *relations between the attributes are held constant* for heuristic purposes. Hence, the constructed type is a system in itself; it has the character of a *theoretical model*. As such, the type functions as an *explanatory schema* and as an implicit theory. The drawing out of this theory results in the explicit statement of hypotheses about the type. What these hypotheses will be, however, is regulated by the structure of the type, for the type is really a hypothetical model course of action, of process, structure, entity, etc. What one is saying when one uses a constructed type is that this is the *expected* behavior of the "sect," the "clan," the "union man," the "scientists," the "falling body," or whatever is being studied. But something different has actually happened. What factors have interfered with the expectancy? That is the question that must be answered before empirical explanation can be said to exist.

The answer to this question entails the examination of empirical cases and their comparison with the type as model. Although examination of empirical cases never reveals anything more than "approximations" or "deviations" from the constructed type, it is essential that the type be formulated on the basis of empirical evidence. The attributes are purposively selected on the basis of empirical evidence and put into a pattern that the researcher hopes will serve as a *significant base of comparison*. When formulated in this fashion the type implies an explanatory predictive schema. For example, the concept of "rational man" implies the adaptation of means to ends. Granted certain ends and norms as "given," then the test of rationality is the adequacy of selection of available means and their adaptation to the attainment of ends. Obviously no "actual" man is rational in all aspects of his behavior, and yet his behavior can be comprehended in terms of the rational mode. There is an *expectancy* of man when he is viewed as "rational man" that is only partially met by any given man. A comparison of the extent to which actual men meet the expectancy nevertheless serves as the basis for explaining "differences" in their behavior.

To illustrate further, any type, such as the "feudal system," "proverbial society," or "academic man," on the basis of its criteria will imply a predictive schema. Feudal behavior will vary from one concrete situation to another, and yet despite these variations there is a "feudal expectancy" different from any other expectancy that enables one to comprehend the variations within the pattern. Likewise, expectancies of the course of action and character of relations within a "proverbial society" are different from those of any other type of society. "Academic man" is not found on university campuses; nevertheless, it is the predictive schema of the academic man that makes empirical approximations (actual professors) comprehensible. In summary, the constructed type is a *model,* and as such it throws actual structures or courses of action into a comparative light. The type focuses on *uniformity,* and it is only through the notion of uniformity that we comprehend variations or deviations. Obviously, any variation or deviation must be a variation or deviation *from something.* To identify that something is necessarily to determine a uniformity represented by the type.

The foregoing treatment of typology represents the method in its present logical status in the field. It has attained that clarified status through the persistent empirical and theoretical labors of a small but active group of sociologists. All these workers are of course tremendously indebted to Max Weber, who performed the major task of delineating the procedure in Germany prior to World War I. In the United States, Becker has unquestionably played the major role in developing the logical character of the type as well as in demonstrating its empirical utility. Tracing his writings, beginning in 1932 with those parts of *Systematic Sociology* which came directly from his pen, gives one the best single insight to the development of the procedure.[61] The theoretical work of Abel, Goode, Kolb, Lazarsfeld, Loomis, McKinney, Parsons, Redfield, Rose, Sorokin, and Winch[62] must also be cited with reference to the development of typology in the past twenty-five years.

There has also been a gradual increase in competent empirical adaptation of typology. Hughes studied the relation of personality types to the sacred and secular aspects of the division of labor; Hiller examined the "strike cycle" as it appeared in "patterns"; Redfield introduced the folk-urban continuum as a basis for examining empirical cultures; Schmid intensively examined the German youth movement; Becker analyzed this movement and traced its ultimate perversion to Hitlerism; Foreman reported on the Negro lifeways in the South; Yinger analyzed the sociological significance

[61] *Ibid.* See bibliography, pp. 308-332, present volume, for key Becker references.

[62] Theodore Abel, *Systematic Sociology in Germany* (New York, 1929); W. J. Goode, "A Note on the Ideal Type," *ASR,* 12 (Aug., 1947), pp. 473-74; W. L. Kolb, "The Peasant in Revolution: A Study in Constructive Typology" (unpublished Ph.D. dissertation, University of Wisconsin, 1943); C. P. Loomis, "The Nature of Rural Social Systems: A Typological Analysis," *RS,* 15 (June, 1950), pp. 156-74; Paul Lazarsfeld, "Some Remarks on the Typological Procedures in Social Research," *Zeitschrift für Sozialforschung,* 6 (1937), pp. 119-39; Parsons, *The Structure of Social Action,* especially Chaps. 14-17; Sorokin, *Social and Cultural Dynamics;* Arnold Rose, "A Deductive Ideal-Type Method," *AJS,* 56 (July, 1950), pp. 35-42; R. F. Winch, "Heuristic and Empirical Typologies," *ASR,* 12 (Feb., 1947), pp. 68-75; Robert Redfield, *The Folk Culture of Yucatan* (Chicago, 1941); McKinney, "The Role of Constructive Typology in Scientific Sociological Analysis," *SF,* 28 (March, 1950), pp. 235-40; and his "Constructive Typology and Social Research" in Doby *et al., op. cit.*

of religion in the struggle for power; Pauline Young studied the secularization accompanying acculturation of a Russian peasant group in Los Angeles; Kolb examined the role of the peasant in revolution; Murvar studied pastoral nomads who became traders and politicians; Eister investigated the factors inducing and supporting the movement for Moral Rearmament; and Loomis began the work of typing and comparing "social systems" and contributed to the quantification of typology.[63]

THE HISTORICAL PROCEDURE

American sociology has been generally *ahistorical* in its approach to the study of society. It has instead concerned itself with the realm of "contemporary" events. This fact is one of the best single indications of the "culture-bound" state of any research discipline. American society itself is largely ahistorical in outlook and consequently indifferent to the "dead past." The rapid transitions to life in American society, plus the sharp cleavages between it and "the old country," have produced a cultural unconcern or even an unconscious disavowal of historical continuities. Doubtless, many other factors are involved in the situation; it nevertheless remains true that most American sociologists are ahistorical and have shown little interest in historical perspective. The sociologists of the early part of this century scarcely touched upon historical factors in their "grand-scale" sweeping classifications. The sociologists of the post-World War I era, subjected to the pressing influence of developments in ecology, demography, attitude study, public opinion polling, statistical method, case study, sociography, and applied sociology, have scarcely had the time, much less the inclination, to deal with historical continuities. The methods *primarily* adhered to by them have been those best adapted to the survey of contemporary conditions.

It is obvious that the research tasks of sociology and history are different as *disciplines,* for their procedures answer to their respective research purposes. Nevertheless, since all data are historical in one sense, the data of history and sociology are the same. The logical difference between the

[63] E. C. Hughes, "Personality Types and the Division of Labor," *AJS,* 33 (March, 1928), pp. 754-68; E. T. Hiller, *The Strike Cycle* (Chicago, 1928); Robert Redfield, *Tepoztlan: A Mexican Village* (Chicago, 1930); and his *The Folk Culture of Yucatan* (Chicago, 1941); Robert Schmid, "German Youth Movements: A Typological Study" (unpublished Ph.D. dissertation, University of Wisconsin, 1941); Howard Becker, *German Youth: Bond or Free* (New York, 1946); P. B. Foreman, "Negro Lifeways in the Rural South: A Typological Approach to Social Differentiation," *ASR,* 13 (Aug., 1948), pp. 409-18; J. Milton Yinger, *Religion in the Struggle for Power* (Durham, N.C., 1946); Pauline V. Young, *Pilgrims of Russian Town* (Chicago, 1932); Kolb, "The Peasant in Revolution," *loc. cit.;* Vatro Murvar, *The Balkan Vlachs: a Typological Study* (unpublished Ph. D. dissertation, University of Wisconsin, 1956); A. W. Eister, *Drawing-Room Conversion: A Sociological Account of the Oxford Group Movement* (Durham, N.C., 1950); Loomis and Beegle, *Rural Social Systems.*

disciplines lies in what they do with the data. The research task of the sociologist is to generalize; that of the historian, to individualize. Both are legitimate enterprises and are complementary rather than conflicting.

It is acceptable to maintain that all objects or events are unique in time and space. No sociologist has any quarrel with this position. This thesis need not involve the argument that objects or events are *merely* temporal and that they can be known *only* in their uniqueness, with their time and space markings clearly evident. On the contrary, it is possible through the use of concepts to conceive of the "identical," the "recurrent," and the "typical." History is event-structured even to the idiographic historian, and events not only can be viewed chronologically and individually, but also can be viewed as relationship-series involving necessary and sufficient antecedents of consequents. Such conditions and consequents can be categorized, and types and the relations involved can be abstractly stated as general relations. It is thus the *perspectives* of the historian and sociologist that differ.

Historical Perspective and Techniques. The historian is concerned with processes and structures that are singular in their space-time occurrence; hence he does not conceive of them as being repeatable, whereas the sociologist adopts the opposite view. The sociologist is concerned with the repetitive and constant factors, or tendencies to regularity, of human society. For example, the sociologist's purpose may be to describe the recurrent aspects involved in the process of "urbanization"; the historian's purpose, on the other hand, will be to state the specific course that "urbanization" has taken in a given place at a given time. This is another way of saying that the sociologist attempts to extract whatever is "general" from the phenomenon, whereas the historian attempts to expose the relevant "particulars" of one case of the phenomena. The difference between the disciplines does not lie in the data but in the relevant *perspectives, problems,* and *techniques*. Granted this, then it is entirely justifiable and indeed necessary that the sociologist concern himself with data that are unquestionably historical. History is not merely the business of the historian; it is also of crucial concern to the sociologist, for it offers him a wealth of material that must be accounted for in his "general" formulations.

It is not logically defensible for the sociologist to refuse to consult data merely because it is considered to be "historical." If his formulations are truly general they must stand the test of time, and their "generality" resides in the bracketing not only of "spatial" but also of "temporal" markings. To arrive at processes and structures that are not merely "unique," it is necessary to examine them in the light of the data of history. The idiographic data of the historian and the data of the descriptive (idiographic) statistician have the *same function* for the sociologist. They are *materials* that he can place in *scientific* perspective.

What, then, is the relation of the historical procedure to sociology? The answer lies in what are considered to be the processes of historical method. Gottschalk reports that there is striking unanimity among writers on historical method with respect to these processes. He points out that historical procedure is generally considered to consist of ". . . (1) the collection of probable sources of information; (2) the examination of those sources for genuineness (either as a whole or in part); and (3) the analysis of the sources or parts of sources proved genuine for their credible particulars."[64] Any synthesis or articulation of the particulars thus derived is *historiography,* and there is considerable lack of agreement about historiography. This is irrelevant to the sociologist, however, for it is not the historiography that he is interested in; it is the procedure. Historiography reflects the perspective, problems, and research purposes of the historian, whereas the procedure defined above is generic and can be of aid to any scientific discipline.

The materials turned up by this procedure have elicited little attention from the majority of sociologists, but a significant few have concerned themselves with them. The materials consist of chronicles, annals, biographies, memoirs, diaries, genealogies, inscriptions, official documents, dispatches, letters, public reports, business papers, newspapers, travelers' tales, folktales, anecdotes, ballads, paintings, sculpture, architecture, language, artifacts, implements, and literature. There is a widespread American belief that such materials are somehow "less valid" than those collected by a doorbell-ringing interviewer with a schedule in his hand; by a mechanical "interaction recorder"; or even by a "participant observer" who can get quite close to his data. Over the years a few persistent sociologists have steadily rejected this belief. It is primarily these few who have kept the historical procedure productive in sociology, although it must be noted that *many* studies bring in history incidentally or use it as an implicit part of their design.

Illustrative Applications of Historical Materials by Sociologists. Among American sociologists who have concerned themselves with the methodological implications of the historical procedure, it is Becker who has contributed most consistently. His contributions may be found scattered among his various writings of the past twenty-five years and the essentials may be found in his *Through Values to Social Interpretation,* published in 1950. Eliot, writing in 1922, made several concrete suggestions with regard to sociological use of historical materials and offered pertinent criticism with respect to sociological practice. Hertzler offered suggestions with respect to sociological uses of history in 1925.[65] F. S. Teggart, in his *Processes of*

[64] Louis Gottschalk, Clyde Kluckhohn, and R. C. Angell, *The Use of Personal Documents in History, Anthropology, and Sociology* (New York, 1945), p. 10.

[65] T. D. Eliot, "The Use of History for Research in Theoretical Sociology," *AJS,*

History (1918) and *Theory of History* (1925), made a major contribution to methodology which has been largely ignored by sociologists. His *Rome and China* (1939) is an interesting attempt to study correlations in historical events. Several of the books on social research (see, for example those by Odum and Jocher, Elmer, Pauline Young, and Gee) contained chapters on historical method—albeit scarcely adequate chapters.

With respect to substantive contributions through the use of the historical method, it is possible roughly to distinguish two levels: those on the "grand scale" and those restricted to more specific phenomena. Of the former, Sorokin unquestionably is the leading American representative.[66] He has handled a truly stupendous amount of data in producing his cycles, periodicities, and types. Barnes's various works can be thought of as being on the grand scale also.[67] MacLeod did an extensive job of tracing the main forms of political society from primitive tribalism in his *Origin and History of Politics*. Chapin's *Cultural Change* and Ellwood's *Cultural Evolution* represent attempts to trace the development of certain phases of culture and leading social institutions. Somewhat more restricted in scope are Wright's *Study of War*, Zimmerman's treatment of the family in *Family and Civilization*, and Gerth and Mills' social psychology as found in their *Character and Social Structure*.

Other sociologists have used historical materials in a much more restricted way. The following are representative examples. Young's study of the acculturation of an immigrant group in *Pilgrims of Russian Town* is almost in the classical "before-and-after" experimental design. Becker's study of the German youth movement in *German Youth: Bond or Free* is a demonstration of the ability to articulate a "small-group" movement into the larger pattern of events. Yinger's *Religion in the Struggle for Power* is also in this tradition. Elliott, in studying frontier history, established the historical antecedents of our cultural disrespect for formal legislative controls. Slotkin studied the development of jazz as a special case of acculturation. Cressey conducted a study of Chinese traits in European culture as an example of diffusion. Moore and Williams examined stratification in the Old South and thereby contributed to comparative analysis. Frazier used the records of the past extensively in order to throw light on the contemporary status of the Negro.[68]

27 (March, 1922), pp. 628-36; J. O. Hertzler, "The Sociological Uses of History," *ibid.*, 31 (Sept., 1925), pp. 173-98.

[66] Still outstanding among his numerous works is *Social and Cultural Dynamics*.

[67] Barnes has been a prolific writer. Probably his outstanding work is in collaboration with Becker, *Social Thought from Lore to Science,* (1st ed.; 1938; 2nd ed.; with numerous additions by Becker, New York, reissue, 1952).

[68] Mabel A. Elliott, "Crime and the Frontier Mores," *ASR,* 9 (April, 1944), pp. 185-92; J. S. Slotkin, "Jazz and Its Forerunners as an Example of Acculturation," *ibid.*, 8 (Oct., 1943), pp. 570-75; Paul Cressey, "Chinese Traits in European Civilization:

These few examples should indicate that despite its secondary role in the American sociological past, the historical procedure has been retained in sociology for its utility. Retrospective or *ex post facto* explanation *may be* subject to more hazards than prospective explanation; nevertheless, it remains an important part of the sociologist's approach.

THE CASE PROCEDURE

The proponents of the "case study" and those of the "statistical method" engaged in extensive controversy during the twenties. Today the controversy has largely died out, and both procedures remain in use. This may be taken as evidence that both have been adjudged "useful" by the research sociologist and have been incorporated with some degree of success into the total sociological approach.

The case study is a way of ordering social data with a view to preserving the unitary character of whatever is being studied. It merely selects and treats a socially defined object or act as a *whole*. This whole constitutes the case unit, and the case unit may involve any level or base of abstraction. The case may be a person, an episode in a person's life, a group, a set of concrete relationships, a specific process, a society-culture—in short, any aspect of empirical reality defined as a unit. The function of the case study is to describe the unit or case in terms of the observable particulars. This means the intensive examination of the specific factors implicated in the case.

The wholeness or unitary character ascribed to the case is a *construct*. Objects and acts have no concrete limits; the limits imposed reflect the perspective and the theoretical interest of the observer. For example, the limits defining an individual may be "dissolved" when one is observing from the perspective of the group. In turn, the limits defining the group may be dissolved when one is conceptualizing in terms of a larger structure. All units are thus constructs delimited for pragmatic purposes. Any unit that has been abstracted out may be examined and described in its uniqueness.

Any unit that has been abstracted out is temporally and spatially bounded. It has its own historical development and is a unique configuration; it may be described as a case by an indefinite number of facts obtained from documents, from life-histories, from the individual, from members of a group, from participant observation, from the use of various techniques available to the sociologist. However, the imputation of these facts to the case merely *describes;* facts do not have *explanatory* value in the scientific sense. Something further must be done with them.

Conflicting Uses of Case Studies. There is considerable disagreement among sociologists about the logical role and research value of the case

A Study in Diffusion," *ibid.,* 10 (Oct., 1945), pp. 594-604; W. E. Moore and R. M. Williams, "Stratification in the Ante-Bellum South," *ibid.,* 7 (June, 1942), pp. 343-51; E. Franklin Frazier, *The Negro in the United States* (New York, 1949).

procedure. The adherents of analytic induction, following Znaniecki, have maintained that the intensive study of cases, with appropriate modification of the hypothesis and limiting of the universe, produces valid scientific generalizations. Among the studies designed with this orientation are Angell's study of the family in the depression, Sutherland's study of crime causation, Lindesmith's study of opiate addiction, and Cressey's analysis of embezzlement.[69]

The proponents of constructive typology, under the leadership of Becker, have maintained that the intensive study of cases is an essential preliminary to the inductive establishment of types having general applicability and susceptible of theoretical prediction. The most complete theoretical statement of this position is found in Becker's *Through Values to Social Interpretation*. Studies that fall into this category include Loomis' studies of comparative social systems, Becker's study of the German youth movement and his analysis of the impotent German intellectual, Edwards' analysis of revolutions, Redfield's study of folk society, Kolb's study of the peasant in revolution, Murvar's work on Balkan nomads, and the study by Mintz of the rural proletarian community in Latin America.[70]

Those sociologists who have identified themselves with the idiographic tradition maintain that the comprehensive description of any case is valuable knowledge in itself and does not require any nomothetic justification. Many of the Chicago studies of the twenties and most community studies, particularly those conducted by the rural sociologists, belong to this tradition. Representative examples of idiographic case studies include Healy's study of pathological stealing by children, Anderson's study of the hobo, Shaw's examination of the jack-roller, and West's study of the community of Plainville.[71]

Quantitatively oriented sociologists have maintained that the main function of the case study is to furnish insights, hunches, and clues. These adherents of enumerative induction maintain that cases cannot yield valid generalizations until they have been subjected to a defensible sampling procedure defining the universe that they represent. Lundberg's position here is representative.[72]

A number of sociologists have concerned themselves with the logical

[69] See footnote 16 for references.

[70] Loomis and Beegle, *Rural Social Systems;* Becker, *German Youth; Bond or Free;* and his "Propaganda and the Impotent German Intellectual," *SF*, 29 (March, 1951), pp. 273-76; L. P. Edwards, *Natural History of Revolution* (Chicago, 1927); Redfield, *The Folk Culture of Yucatan;* Kolb, *op. cit.;* Murvar, *op.cit.;* Stanley Mintz, "The Folk-Urban Continuum and the Rural Proletarian Community," *AJS,* 59 (Sept., 1953), pp. 136-43.

[71] William Healy, *Mental Conflicts and Misconduct* (Boston, 1917); Nels Anderson, *The Hobo* (Chicago, 1923); C. R. Shaw, *The Jack-Roller* (Chicago, 1930); James West (pseud.), *Plainville, U.S.A.* (New York, 1945).

[72] Lundberg, *Social Research* (rev. ed., 1942), pp. 115, 385-87.

limits and application of the case procedure, as well as with the relation of the case study to other methods. Particularly notable contributions have been made by Angell, Becker, Burgess, Dollard, Stouffer and Lazarsfeld, and Thomas and Znaniecki.[73]

The continuing logical clarification of the case study, accompanied by the continuing use of the procedure in the diverse ways mentioned above, indicates that it is a useful tool. There appears to be general agreement to the effect that the case procedure has one important theoretical advantage: it preserves the structural unity of what is being conceptualized. This would seem to be a necessary research function in view of the fact that statistical analysis is essentially "trait" or "attribute" analysis. Moreover, even the most quantitatively minded make use of cases as sources of insight, understanding, and hypothesis.[74]

Some of the methodological issues that have troubled sociology have indeed become obsolete, but several underlying controversies have been remarkably persistent. This very persistence has played a role in enriching the methodology of the sociologist, for it has constantly emphasized the point that there are many ways of knowing and many perspectives from which social phenomena can be viewed. The continuing examination of the assumptions, characteristics, limitations, and possibilities involved in divergent methodological positions has contributed considerably to the sociologist's understanding of his ways of work and their relation to his ultimate objective.

[73] Thomas and Znaniecki, *op. cit.;* E. W. Burgess, "Statistics and Case-Studies as Methods of Social Research," *SSR,* 12 (Nov.-Dec., 1927), pp. 103-20; Becker, "Culture Case-Study and Ideal-Typical Method: With Special Reference to Max Weber," *SF,* 12 (March, 1934), pp. 399-405; John Dollard, *Criteria for the Life History* (New Haven, 1935); R. C. Angell, "A Critical Review of the Development of the Personal Document Method in Sociology 1920-1940," in Gottschalk *et al., op. cit.,* pp. 175-232; "Note on the Statistical Treatment of Life-History Material," *SF,* 9 (Dec., 1930), pp. 200-203. In collaboration with P. M. Hauser and S. A. Stouffer: "Note on the Logic of Generalization in Family Case Studies," in their *Research Memorandum on the Family in the Depression* (New York, 1937), pp. 187-201.

[74] Stouffer, "Experimental Comparison of Statistical and Case History Methods in Attitude Research" (unpublished Ph.D. dissertation, University of Chicago, 1930).

SELECTED BIBLIOGRAPHY

Becker, Howard, *Through Values to Social Interpretation* (Durham, N.C.: Duke University Press, 1950).

Chapin, F. Stuart, *Experimental Designs in Sociological Research* (New York: Harper, 1947).

Doby, J. T. (ed.), *An Introduction to Social Research* (Harrisburg: Stackpole, 1954).

Jahoda, Marie, Morton Deutsch, and Stuart Cook, *Research Methods in Social Relations* (New York: Dryden Press, 1951), 2 vols.

Lazarsfeld, Paul, and Morris Rosenberg (eds.), *The Language of Social Research* (Glencoe, Ill.: The Free Press, 1955).

Lundberg, G. A., *Foundations of Sociology* (New York: Macmillan, 1939).

MacIver, R. M., *Social Causation* (New York: Ginn, 1942).

Merton, R. K., *Social Theory and Social Structure* (Glencoe, Ill.: The Free Press, 1949).

Merton, R. K., and Paul Lazarsfeld (eds.), *Continuities in Social Research: Studies in the Scope and Method of The American Soldier* (Glencoe, Ill.: The Free Press, 1950).

Parsons, Talcott, *The Structure of Social Action* (New York: McGrawHill, 1937).

Riley, M. W., *et al., Sociological Studies in Scale Analysis* (New Brunswick: Rutgers University Press, 1954).

Sorokin, P. A., *Sociocultural Causality, Space, Time* (Durham, N.C.: Duke University Press, 1943).

Stouffer, S. A., *et al., Studies in Social Psychology in World War II* (Princeton: Princeton University Press, 1949), 4 vols.

Thomas, W. I., and Florian Znaniecki, *The Polish Peasant in Europe and America* (Boston: Richard G. Badger, 1918-1921), 5 vols.

Znaniecki, Florian, *The Method of Sociology* (New York: Farrar and Rinehart, 1934).

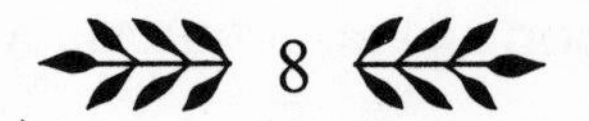

STRUCTURAL-FUNCTIONAL ANALYSIS IN MODERN SOCIOLOGY

WALTER BUCKLEY

IMPORTANT IDEAS INVARIABLY HAVE THEIR ROOTS IN THE CROSS CURRENTS OF earlier speculation; therefore naming single authors or dates as points of origin is an arbitrary matter. So it is with "functionalism," which will here be arbitrarily confined to the American scene since World War I. But in order to construct this narrower context, a brief excursion must be made back to Herbert Spencer as an important instigator of a line of thought in social science that contributed to the development of functional analysis.[1]

Background of Functionalism

Precursors: Spencer and Schäffle. Spencer's sociology is replete with the terminology of modern functionalism but was built on a basically different methodology. His wide use of the biologic analogy and biological theory suggested a view of society as an organism in a very nearly literal sense. This view was picked up and developed to its logical extremes by the "organismic school" of social theorists, which included among its members the German sociologist Albert Schäffle. Unlike most of his colleagues, Schäffle came to hold a tempered organismic position, recognizing the analogy for what it

[1] See the discussion of Comte, pp. 7-19 of this volume.

was and strongly qualifying its application to society.[2] His interpretation influenced at least two of America's important pioneers in sociology. The first is A. W. Small, who introduced Schäffle's structural-functional analysis to American audiences in the first American textbook of sociology and in the first issue of the *American Journal of Sociology*.[3] The second is C. H. Cooley, who tells us that he spent more time and energy perusing the work of Schäffle than he spent on that of any other single author.[4] Cooley did not immediately and directly utilize a functional framework, but the germ of such a framework is present in his "organic" interpretation of society and especially in his later treatment of the "tentative social process" as "that which works or functions."[5]

Sumner and Keller: A Functional Theory of Culture. Another important line of development may be traced directly from Spencer to the implicit functional view of W. G. Sumner, whose work has been characterized as "Spencerianism in American dress." Sumner's theory of folkways as group patterns that, through trial and error, prove to work or function successfully in the struggle for survival was more fully developed by his disciple, A. G. Keller, whose elaboration, completed in 1928, antedates Malinowski in proposing a theory of culture as adaptive or functional in subserving the basic needs of its carriers and evolving by a sort of mass trial-and-error process.[6]

Durkheim and the Distinction between Functional and Causal Approaches. Finally, we must include Durkheim, who was influenced primarily in a negative way by Spencer's psychologistic appeal to the "need for greater happiness" and the corresponding utility of social structures as an explanation and justification for their existence. Durkheim insisted on the separation of the two methods of explanation—the functional and the causal—but maintained that both were necessary. "When, then, the explanation of a social phenomenon is undertaken, we must seek separately the efficient cause which produces it and the function it fulfills." A social fact, he held, could not generally maintain itself if it were not useful, and social life would be impossible if the majority of social phenomena were not useful. Thus, to gain a satisfactory understanding of social life, "it is necessary to show how the phenomena comprising it combine in such a way as to put society in harmony with itself and with the environment external to it." But the term "function" is used in preference to "end" or "purpose"

[2] Cf. Howard Becker and H. E. Barnes, *Social Thought from Lore to Science* (2nd ed.; New York, reissue, 1952), pp. 684-686.

[3] A. W. Small and G. E. Vincent, *Introduction to the Study of Society* (New York, 1894); *AJS,* 1 (July, 1895), pp. 110-112.

[4] C. H. Cooley, *Sociological Theory and Social Research* (New York, 1930), p. 6.

[5] C. H. Cooley, *Social Process* (New York, 1918), p. 8.

[6] A. G. Keller, *Societal Evolution* (New York, 1915).

... precisely because social phenomena do not generally exist for the useful results they produce. We must determine whether there is a correspondence between the fact under consideration and the general needs of the social organism, and in what this correspondence consists, without occupying ourselves with whether it has been intentional or not.[7]

Thus he devoted Book I of his *Division of Labor in Society* to "the function of the division of labor" and Book II to "causes and conditions." The division of labor thus functioned as the basis of the "organic" solidarity of advanced, complex, and highly differentiated societies. The underlying causes and conditions included increasing spatial and social "density," increasing individual differentiation arising from disintegration of the "common consciousness" and different hereditary predispositions.

Functionalism in Germany and Britain. By the time of World War I, then, functionalism was no stranger to the American scene, either figuratively or literally. But despite Small's efforts before the turn of the century to publicize the idea in this country, it remained dormant,[8] coming to full fruition only after some three decades under the stimulus of new injections from outside. Schäffle's compatriot, Leopold von Wiese, is our only other widely known German source of explicit functionalism. His treatment of the subject, first appearing in essays published in 1918 and 1924 in Germany, was presented to readers of English in 1932 by Howard Becker in the Wiese-Becker volume, *Systematic Sociology.*[9] In England in the early post-World-War I period, under the influence largely of Durkheim's views, Malinowski and Radcliffe-Brown were laying the research foundations for the radically new functional interpretation in cultural anthropology. Important publications by these two Englishmen,[10] appearing in the twenties and thirties, proved a decisive impetus behind the reappearance in the United States of serious thinking along structural-functional lines.

Implicit Functionalism in Pareto's Thought. We may recognize a further external stimulus to functionalism, though less influential in this respect, in the work of the Italian Vilfredo Pareto. His *Treatise on General Sociology,* appearing in 1916, was digested and made more accessible to American readers in a concise and stimulating form by L. J. Henderson in 1935. As

[7] Émile Durkheim, *The Rules of Sociological Method* (Chicago, 1938), pp. 95, 97.

[8] Functionalism provides the central orientation of Small's first text of 1894. In his *General Sociology* of 1905, a few pages are devoted to Schäffle's functionalism. But in his *Origins of Sociology* of 1924, functionalism is scarcely referred to.

[9] Howard Becker, *Systematic Sociology on the Basis of the* Beziehungslehre *and* Gebildelehre *of Leopold von Wiese* (New York, 1932; 2nd ed., with a new preface, Gary, Indiana, 1950). See page 181, note 76, in the present volume.

[10] A. R. Radcliffe-Brown, *The Andaman Islanders* (Cambridge, 1922); "On the Concept of Function in Social Science," *AA,* (New Series) 37 (1935), pp. 394-402; Bronislaw Malinowski, "Anthropology," *Encyclopedia Britannica,* First Supplementary Volume (London, 1926); "Culture," *ESS,* (New York, 1936), vol. 4, pp. 621-645.

Henderson was especially concerned to demonstrate, Pareto's "logico-experimental" method was modeled primarily after classical mechanics—treating of systems of mutually dependent variables—and it is for this strictly logical method of attack that Pareto's work is best known. However, he did make some use of what we have come to call the functional method, especially in treating the problem of the social utility of religion. Henderson explains this as follows:

> For this purpose he adopts a norm of utility that is nearly equivalent to *survival value* in biology, and unfortunately, though fairly serviceable, equally vague. He notes that the greater part of the residues that exist in a given society . . . can hardly be incompatible with the survival of the society. . . . He next states that this conclusion is confirmed by the facts and that the survival value of the greater part of the residues of a society may be clearly observed . . . thus morals and religions may be seen to be essential to the survival of the society. In general it is observed that the weakening of these forces is accompanied by the decline of the society.[11]

The Biological Bias of Earlier Functionalism. Before proceeding to outline the interpretations of Wiese-Becker and of the British functionalists, it is important to inquire more deeply into the general character of functional methodology and its significance for the development of sociological theory. A beginning may be made by considering the difference between the Spencerian "organismic" view of society and the "organic" view stressed especially by Durkheim and Cooley. Both views derived, for the most part, from principles of biological functionalism, according to which an organism is an integrated whole made up of certain differentiated organs or structures through which certain functional requirements for the survival or effective operation of the organism are typically met.[12] The "organismic" school, as pointed out above, accepted the biologic analogy literally and viewed society as a true organism, going so far as to equate social structures or institutions with such animal organs as the brain, the heart, the circulatory system, etc.[13] In a word, they borrowed the content as well as the general method of biology and, emphasizing the former, concerned themselves mainly with a static description, classification, and analysis of social structures. The "organic" view, on the other hand, rejected the content of biological theory and any literal application. Society was seen as "organic" in the sense that it is composed of differentiated, interrelated structures reacting

[11] L. J. Henderson, *Pareto's General Sociology* (Cambridge, 1935), pp. 53-55. Note the close correspondence to Durkheim.

[12] W. B. Cannon, *The Wisdom of the Body* (New York, 1932) is a favorite source for a model of biological functionalism. For a more detailed treatment, cf. R. K. Merton, *Social Theory and Social Structure* (Glencoe, Ill., 1949), pp. 47-49.

[13] For the more detailed original organismic-organic distinction, see Becker and Barnes, *op. cit.,* vol. 1, pp. 677-692.

on one another and constituting an integral whole on a *psycho-social,* rather than a biological, level. The emphasis was on interrelation or organization rather than on structure per se.

It was this emphasis on interrelation that was seized upon by the functionalists, who proceeded to build a dynamic theory of society and culture on the *logic* or methodology of biology. Thus, reacting against the static structural sociology of Spencer and his followers we find Small, Cooley, and Wiese emphasizing *function* or *process*. Reacting against an anthropological historicism of static description, and a view of culture as consisting of independent "shreds and patches," we find Malinowski and Radcliffe-Brown emphasizing the "functional integration" of culture.

Modern Functionalism

The Search for Connections in the Socio-Cultural System. The significance, then, of this newer orientation consisted essentially in a shift from "structure" to "function" as the principal tool of scientific explanation and interpretation of society, with function now tending to be regarded as the independent variable, structure being demoted to a derivative and a consequence of the play and sequence of functions.[14]

Thus Radcliffe-Brown, in the introduction to his latest collection of essays,[15] asserts that his point of departure is an aspect of the social theory of Montesquieu, which constituted what Comte later called the first law of social statics. According to this law, in a specific form of social life there are among the various features relations of interconnection and interdependence that unite them into a coherent whole and account for the persistence of that form of social life. This law defined for Radcliffe-Brown the problem of social statics, which was to investigate the nature of the coherence. His investigation was made in terms of the concepts of structure and function, two abstractions made from the total social process. "Structure" referred to some sort of ordered arrangement of components or traits of culture; "function" referred to the interconnection between the social structure and the process of social life, the part the structure played in accounting for the coherence and persistence of the social whole. Thus, a culture trait or structure was "explained" in terms of its functional relation to other traits and its contribution to the maintenance of structural continuity.

In like manner, Malinowski subscribed to a scheme of functional inte-

[14] Cf. H. M. Kallen, "Functionalism," *ESS*, vol. 6 (1931), pp. 523-525.

[15] A. R. Radcliffe-Brown, *Structure and Function in Primitive Society* (London, 1952).

gration but went further in tracing the function of culture components to the part they played in satisfying individual needs. For him, culture appeared as a vast instrumental reality that existed and functioned in response to basic or derived human needs. These needs defined the function of unit structures, rather than the persistence of the whole, as Radcliffe-Brown maintained.

A more methodology-conscious British anthropologist, tracing his views not only to Malinowski and Radcliffe-Brown but also to Ruth Benedict and Margaret Mead, is Gregory Bateson. Recognizing the divergent emphases of the first two anthropologists and—in his turn—the ambiguity of the term function as including both the sense of causal interdependence and adaptive or teleological relation, Bateson attempts to bring more system into the method. Unlike most of his functionalist colleagues, he is particularly sensitive to the dangers of teleology and tries to counteract the extremists. Thus he defines "adaptive function" as follows:

> When we say of some part of a functional system that it behaves in such and such a way in order to produce such and such a desirable effect in the system as a whole, we are attributing adaptive function; and we are verging upon teleological fallacy. But it is a cold plunge from this to realizing that no cell or organ cares two hoots about our survival. We can avoid some of the dangers of teleology by acknowledging that undesirable effects occur not infrequently.[16]

What is of particular interest to us here is that, because of these misgivings, Bateson is almost unique in choosing to use the term function "to cover the whole play of synchronic cause and effect within the culture, irrespective of any consideration of purpose or adaptation." As a result, his analysis of "Naven" cannot be accurately described as pure functionalism. Subdividing Benedict's concept of culture "configuration" into "ethos" and "eidos"—respectively, standardized *affective* and *cognitive* characteristics—he analyzes the interrelation between the ethos of a culture and individual affective behavior, and between culture eidos and cognitive behavior. His concern is with the double hypothesis, derived from Benedict, that "the pervading characteristics of the culture not only express, but also promote the standardization of the individuals." In other words, his study belongs primarily to social psychology, since it is concerned with the reciprocal cause-and-effect relations between culture and personality; it approaches what we think of specifically as functional analysis only in his selection of a separate category, which he calls "social function," in which to deal with the effects of elements of culture in satisfying the needs of groups.

Of further interest is Bateson's fairly well developed anticipations of some important aspects of modern functional (and also non-functional) sociological theory. These include not only the analytic separation of cogni-

[16] Gregory Bateson, *Naven* (Cambridge, 1936), pp. 26, 29, 34, 281.

tive and affective aspects of behavior, but also his interesting use of the notion of dynamic equilibrium as characterizing the *status quo*. He defines dynamic equilibrium as "a state of affairs in a functional system, such that although no change is apparent, we are compelled to believe that small changes are continually occurring and counteracting each other."[17] Such a view, following from his recognition of dysfunctional as well as functional effects of culture elements, led him to an analysis of disruptive processes (schismogenesis) that, if heeded, might have gone a long way to modify the one-sided emphases of Malinowski and Radcliffe-Brown.

Wiese-Becker: Social Process and Structure as Functional Systems. In 1932 appeared the first important American publication since that of Small to give functionalism an explicit, systematic methodological role in the development of social theory: Wiese-Becker's *Systematic Sociology*. Here the unit of analysis is the "socius," an abstraction from the individual virtually identical with the concept of "actor." These units are oriented to one another in terms of the basic processes of "sociation," which characterize different patterns of interhuman relations and serve as analytical tools in the analysis and classification of social structures. But the study of such social processes merely as existent processes, it is urged, is very restricted and only preliminary; we must also determine the *function* of the process under investigation, asking what functional value a process or relation has in the maintenance of a structure.

The ambiguous meaning of the term function is recognized (once again) as referring to the notion of task or achievement on the one hand, or designating the mathematical relation of dependence of correlated variables on the other. The first sense, that of task, is used here, but cleared of its wider teleological implications by the understanding that function or end is not the same as purpose in the proximate sense. On this basis, the Wiese-Becker scheme seeks to determine the functional interconnection of the separate processes or relations with the total sociative process (social system) in either its constructive (eufunctional) or destructive (dysfunctional) aspects.[18]

Social structures are seen at bottom as networks of social processes functioning to help men in mastering the obstacles of the external world and thus to perpetuate the results of certain types of human endeavor. Thus an institution is defined—in modification of Sumner's famous definition—as consisting of a structure and a function (as seen by the investigator) preserving or otherwise serving the larger "plurality pattern" within which it operates. And the type of plurality pattern called the "abstract collectivity" represents organized attempts of men to achieve mastery over extrahuman obstacles and to attain primary gratification. But a methodological distinction—closely recalling that of Durkheim—is insisted upon: although such analyses may

[17] *Ibid.*, pp. 175, 282.

[18] Becker, *op. cit.*, pp. 111 *ff.*

concentrate upon the functional aspects of social structures, "it must not be forgotten that they are also phenomena of interhuman life which become effective under certain conditions as a result of definite causes, and that they must consequently be explained without primary reference to the purposes they serve."[19]

The subsequent rapidly increasing interest in the functional view is indicated by the appearance of several other American works in the 1930's in which it played a more or less important part. Some of these used it as a general orientation for substantive analysis and interpretation of social phenomena, tacitly accepting its efficacy as a theoretical base; such for example were E. T. Hiller's *Principles of Sociology* and F. S. Chapin's *Contemporary American Institutions*. Others concerned themselves directly with its methodology. In his *Study of Man,* the anthropologist Ralph Linton acknowledged a general functional principle but with strong reservations and no lack of criticism of important details. Shortly thereafter, Sorokin published his *Social and Cultural Dynamics,* in which the problem of the integration of cultures and their functioning is central. And, like Linton, Sorokin accepted the functional principle only with important qualifications and much negative comment.

Critiques of Functionalism

The Bias of Functional-Integration Theory. As functionalism matured into a major theoretical orientation, criticism rapidly mounted. Along with explicit and extensive caveats issued by a few of its exponents, especially Wiese-Becker, have come attacks on every important facet of the theory. The central concepts involved in the earlier formulations, as we have seen, were "integration of culture," "function" as explaining the existence and persistence of structures, and "survival" or "continuity" as an ultimate criterion. Critiques of these, along with general questionings of the theory's empirical fruitfulness, teleological weakness, and ideological bias will be briefly surveyed.

Linton and Sorokin accused the functionalists of failure to analyze and define clearly what they meant by "integration of culture." Linton held that, to the functionalist, integration is primarily a matter of the mutual adaptation and interdependence of behavior patterns, and as such the concept is rather superficial. The resulting picture of culture is that of a mass of gears all turning and grinding each other, but with no focal point for all the activity. Even the mutual adaptation of behavior patterns can be accounted for without

[19] *Ibid.,* p. 582.

an appeal to anything more significant than the process of trial and error. On this view, a culture system appears mechanical and two-dimensional. Linton suggested that we might find the focal point of culture integration in Abram Kardiner's concept of "basic personality structure."[20]

Sorokin makes a similar point but in a different way. For him, cultures are "integrated" in four basic types: (1) spatial or mechanical adjacency; (2) association due to an external factor; (3) causal or functional integration; and (4) logico-meaningful unity. Each represents a higher or more comprehensible level than the preceding type. "Functional" is here used in its mathematical sense, synonymous with "causal" and referring to "direct interdependence (mutual or one-sided) of the variables or parts upon one another and upon the whole system." But, although "causal-functional" unity represents a higher degree of integration than the first two types, it is not essential and its importance has been grossly overrated. The "supreme form" of integration is the "logico-meaningful" type. Here the ordering principle is not the uniformity of relationship between fragmentary variables, but

> . . . identity of meaning or logical coalescence. Hidden behind the empirically different, seemingly unrelated fragments of the culture complex lies an identity of meaning, which brings them together into consistent styles, typical forms, and significant patterns.[21]

It is this level of integration that gives any culture its "individuality," its "physiognomy and personality."

Such attempts as these to characterize cultures as wholes or realities *sui generis* play no great role in subsequent functional theory, but the deeper probing into the notion of functional integration was of great significance in modifying the common assumption of complete unity of culture. As stated by Wiese-Becker and by Robert Merton, such an assumption is not only often contrary to fact but of doubtful heuristic value, since it diverts attention from dysfunctional or disintegrative consequences of structures. (See Wiese-Becker on "society and plurality patterns" and "destructive processes.")

This one-sided emphasis on unity is seen as a reflection of the sweeping and ambiguous application of the concept of function to culture elements. Speaking from the anthropological point of view, Alexander Goldenweiser complained that Malinowski read too much meaning and unequivocal determination into every bit of culture, thus refusing to admit diffusion of single traits, or the existence of "necrotic survivals" and fortuitous trait complexes.[22]

Merton's Analysis of the Postulates of Functionalism. In a thorough cri-

[20] Abram Kardiner, *The Individual and His Society* (New York, 1939), pp. viii-ix.

[21] P. A. Sorokin, *Social and Cultural Dynamics* (New York, 1937-1941), vol. 1, pp. 15, 23.

[22] H. E. Barnes, Howard Becker, and Frances B. Becker (eds.), *Contemporary Social Theory* (New York, 1940), pp. 470 *ff*. Cf. also the fuller discussion in Howard Becker, *Through Values to Social Interpretation* (Durham, N.C., 1950), pp. 137-140.

tique, Robert Merton has analyzed in some detail the various meanings of the term "function." This analysis culminates in his well-known statement that exposes the fallacies in the three postulates most commonly adopted by functionalists. These postulates hold that *all* standardized social items fulfill positive functions in a social system, that such items are functional for the *entire* system, and that they are thus *indispensable*.[23] Merton argued that, on the contrary, there may be some items that are partially dysfunctional or non-functional; some that are, on balance, dysfunctional; and thus some that are quite dispensable. Thus one must be on guard against inferring that, because some culture item or recurring activity is organically integrated with the other activities of a society, it *therefore* makes a contribution to the continuity or survival of the society. This is a hypothesis to be investigated, not an a priori assumption that may be freely made.

Likewise, attention has been focused on the lack of clarity in the meaning of the term "survival" or "continuity" of society. Homans, for one, pointed out that history has shown that few societies have actually failed to survive, and since a society may decline considerably before it dies, the notion of survival of a society as a whole is too indefinite to be useful. We might distinguish between a society characterized by a specific type of social organization and a society as a general grouping characterized mainly in terms of territorial, biological, and some minimal degree of cultural continuity. Perhaps it is the survival of a society in this second general sense that should be the ultimate criterion and not the survival of a more limited, specific social system. The social system of France, for example, changed radically between 1780 and 1850; but the French nation, or society, as a distinct general grouping, survived and was continuous—territorially, biologically, and in many respects culturally.

Functional Theory and the Problem of Empirical Change. Seen from another angle, the question becomes: how can functionalism account for the fact that specific social systems do not survive—that change seems as basic as stability?[24] To answer that disruption occurs because certain functions cease to be fulfilled would indeed be begging the question. Such social systems must at some time have functioned adequately, and an explanation of the intervening internal factors that resulted in the disintegration of the system requires an analysis of the mechanisms, forces, and interrelations that underlie the bare fact that a structure ceased to function.

This brings us to criticisms questioning the significance of functional theory for empirical research—criticisms that were made early in its history. Parsons reports that Max Weber, for example, was suspicious of an approach that took as its point of departure the social "whole" rather than detailed

[23] Merton, *op. cit.*, pp. 27-38.

[24] Cf. Sorokin's rather extreme view in his *Society, Culture, and Personality* (New York, 1947), pp. 696-699.

analysis of individual motivation.[25] The implication seems to be that it is too easy to impute a function to an item merely by definition; or that, though the theory tells us to look for the function of a culture item and to assess it against the survival of the society, it tells us nothing of how to go about doing these things. It gives us no directions or operational procedures for connecting the concepts to empirical data and for validating functional hypotheses. Further, certain functional relations "seen" by one observer may not be at all evident to others.

The Strategy of Functional Methodology and Research. In greater detail, Merton has listed some of the "basic queries" that must be answered in facing the problem of empirical validation of functional theory. Some of these queries are: (1) What must enter into the protocol of observation if it is to be amenable to systematic functional analysis? (2) What is involved in the problem of evolving canons for assessing the net balance of the aggregate of functional and dysfunctional consequences in a social system? (3) What is required to establish the validity of such an intervening variable as "functional requirement" where rigorous experimentation is impracticable? (4) What is the presently available inventory of social mechanisms through which social functions are fulfilled? (5) What available procedures will permit the sociologist most adequately to gauge the accumulation of stresses and strains in a given social system?[26]

The Teleological Bias in Functionalism. All of these criticisms may be summarized in terms of the well-worn argument revolving around teleological *vs.* mechanistic explanation. Explicitly or implicitly, this question is posed time and again. We have already seen the distinction between the causal relation and the teleological relation made by Durkheim, Pareto, Henderson, Wiese-Becker, and Bateson. We also have Sorokin's unequivocal charge that the functionalists substitute teleological speculation for causal dependence and tend to solve a problem by inventing some utilitarian explanation of a relationship according to the schema of means and ends. Or, as the British anthropologist S.F. Nadel put it, ". . . to pronounce at once upon the ultimate functions subserved by social facts, is to short-circuit explanation and reduce it to generalities which, so prematurely stated, have little significance."[27]

Nevertheless, a certain degree of teleology is seen to be implied in functionalism in its appeal, not to purpose, but to an end effect or "final cause." In a recent essay[28] concerning the methodological implications of

[25] Talcott Parsons, *Essays in Sociological Theory Pure and Applied* (Glencoe, Ill., 1949), p. 83.

[26] Merton, *op. cit.,* pp. 50-54.

[27] Sorokin, *Society, Culture, and Personality,* p. 15; S. F. Nadel, *Foundations of Social Anthropology* (Glencoe, Ill., 1951), p. 375.

[28] Ernest Nagel, "Teleological Explanation and Teleological Systems," in Herbert Feigl and May Brodbeck (eds.), *Readings in the Philosophy of Science* (New York, 1953), pp. 537-558.

teleology or functionalism in biology, Ernest Nagel has attacked the problem of whether the nature of an organic system is such as to require for its study a peculiar, autonomous methodological procedure such as functionalism rather than the "mechanistic" or causal type of analysis of the physical sciences. Although biologically oriented, most of his arguments are of great relevance here. His main thesis is that teleological or functional explanations, as utilized in science today, are equivalent to non-teleological ones, so that the former can be replaced by the latter without loss of asserted content. For example, "The function of religion is to relieve anxiety in a group." This asserts nothing not asserted by "Anxiety in a group is relieved if (or perhaps, only if) it practices religion," or by "A (sufficient, necessary, or sufficient and necessary) condition for relief of anxiety in a group is the practice of religion." These latter statements are clearly non-functional. If this example is taken as a paradigm, it seems to Nagel that when a function is ascribed to a constituent of some organic whole, the content of the teleological statement is fully conveyed by another statement that simply asserts a condition for a certain trait or activity of that whole. On this assumption, therefore, a teleological explanation states the *consequences* for a given system of one of the latter's constituent parts or processes; the equivalent non-teleogical explanation states some of the *antecedent conditions* under which the system persists in its characteristic organization and activities. The difference between the two types of explanation is thus comparable to the difference between saying that *B* is an effect of *A*, and saying that *A* is a cause or condition of *B*. In brief, the difference is one of emphasis or selective attention rather than of asserted content.

Although there may be sufficient reason on the methodological level for the functionalist's selective attention to consequences, ends, and wholes, there is another motivating force of some importance not considered in Nagel's discussion. This is man's normative concern with the problem of order and disorder in society—a concern manifested in a reformist orientation in social science prevalent from the beginnings of systematic sociology. Such an orientation appears clearly, for example, in the functionalism of Radcliffe-Brown. We may recall that the functional view implied for him that a social system has a "functional unity," which he defined as "a condition in which all parts of the social system work together with a sufficient degree of harmony or internal consistency, i.e., without producing persistent conflicts which can neither be resolved nor regulated." He discusses the problem of characterizing this condition of unity, harmony, or social order, considering for this purpose the possibilities of the organismic analogy. In an organism we distinguish between "health" and "disease." Durkheim, he points out, sought to lay the basis for a scientific social pathology based on a morphology and a physiology. He sought objective criteria for judging whether a society at a given time is normal or pathological (normless or anomic). One such proposed criterion was the suicide rate.

Such a view, Radcliffe-Brown recognized, may be criticized by realizing the imperfections of the organismic analogy. In relation to organisms, we can find strictly objective criteria for distinguishing disease from health, the pathological from the normal, for disease leads to death or disruption of activities characteristic of the type. But since societies do not die in the sense that animals die, we cannot define disorder or functional disunity as that which leads, if unchecked, to the death of a society or to a disturbance of the usual activities of a social type, as Durkheim tried to do. However, Radcliffe-Brown himself maintains the hope that, although we may not be able to find strictly objective criteria for distinguishing social disease from social health, we may be able to distinguish between different *degrees* of health, or functional unity.[29]

The Ideological Bias in Functionalism. We may note a further closely related criticism leveled against earlier functionalism. Since emphasis was placed on functional consequences as bringing about social unity, full integration, stability, and continuity, many felt that an ideal state of society was too easily implied—despite the opposite implications of the above discussion early made by Radcliffe-Brown. From many statements made by functionalists, it seemed possible to conclude that since a social system persisting a long time is functionally integrated, or has reached a state of "equilibrium," it must have attained an ideal state of adjustment, whether in terms of individual happiness or common welfare. Such a situation, therefore, is evaluated as "good," and must not be changed: what is, is best, and any change is for the worse.[30] Merton deals with this criticism at some length, suggesting that ideological bias is not at all *inherent* in structure-function analysis but derives mainly from adherence to the false postulates mentioned above. He strengthens his argument by pointing to the fact that functionalists have been accused not only of conservative bias but of radical bias as well. Thus, it is not the *method* of analysis itself but the analyst who may inject implicit valuations.

Recent Structural-Functional Analysis

Notwithstanding an increasing volume of criticism, structural-functional analysis continued to develop and, to a great extent because of the criticism, it has become quite highly refined. Since World War II, it has had a large number of adherents and has served as a principal, if not *the* principal,

[29] Radcliffe-Brown, "On the Concept of Function in Social Science," *loc. cit.*, pp. 397-398.

[30] Cf. Gunnar Myrdal *et al.*, *An American Dilemma* (New York, 1944), p. 1055.

basis of sociological thinking. But there seems to be some confusion as to what is and what is not functionalism, and who is and who is not a functionalist. If the label means only that social systems are seen as integrated to some extent and can be analyzed into certain elements that may be related to certain other elements and to the operation of the system as a whole—then, as someone has suggested, we are all functionalists. But according to the view we are specifically labeling as structural-functional—a view which derives its main inspiration from biological methodology—integrated social wholes are analyzed into structures and functions; the term "function" is used primarily in its non-mathematical sense; and the focus is primarily on the *consequences* of the operation of structures for the "survival" or "maintenance" of some specified or unspecified state of the whole.

Parsons and Generalized Functional Analysis of Social Systems. Most of the development of structural-functional analysis has issued from a few major sources. Sacrificing breadth for depth, we shall concern ourselves here only with the more highly systematized refinements of Talcott Parsons and his close follower, Marion Levy,[31] and the highly constructive critique of Robert Merton, to which this account is already heavily indebted.

Parsons believes he first approached the formulation of the theory of social systems in structural-functional terms in 1941. Furthermore, he has come to believe that the most fruitful systematic theory must conform to this type, which is similar to the type effectively utilized in physiology, except that an actor-situation frame of reference is substituted for an organism-environment reference. The reasoning behind this is as follows. Adequate dynamic analysis of a social system, with its complex of numerous interrelated variables, requires the continuous and systematic reference of every problem to the state of the system as a whole. In the history of science we find only two types of conceptual scheme logically capable of performing this task. The most efficient is an analytical system of dynamically interrelated variables, modeled after classical mechanics and expressed in terms of a set of simultaneous equations that make possible the direct solution of dynamic problems. But sociology in its present state of development is hardly ready to adopt such a system. The other alternative, very inferior but better than nothing, is a "generalized structural-functional system." In essence, this system simplifies the problem of dealing with a complex of interrelated variables by removing groups of them—treated as generalized categories—and viewing them as constants within the system. In this way, dynamic problems become manageable without refined mathematical analysis.

Considered more fully, this type of analysis requires a complete system of structural categories that can provide a determinate description of the

[31] Talcott Parsons and E. A. Shils (eds.), *Toward a General Theory of Action* (Cambridge, Mass., 1951); Parsons, *The Social System* (Glencoe, Ill., 1951); M. J. Levy, *The Structure of Society* (Princeton, 1952).

empirical social system. However, these more static "structural categories" must be linked to the dynamically variable elements of the system. This linkage is provided by the central concept of function, whose role is "to provide criteria of the *importance* of dynamic factors and processes within the system." Thus, an additional requirement is a set of "dynamic functional categories" that describe the important processes by which particular structures are maintained or upset and the relations of the total system to its environment. In Parsons' words:

> Functional significance in this context is inherently teleological. A process or set of conditions either "contributes" to the maintenance (or development) of the system or it is "dysfunctional" in that it detracts from the integration, effectiveness, etc., of the system. It is thus the functional reference of all particular conditions and processes *to the state of the total system as a going concern* which provides the logical equivalent of simultaneous equations in a fully developed system of analytical theory.[32]

Necessary Modifications in Parsons' Functionalism: Merton's Contribution. Before going on to the later development of this schema, we shall consider some of the more constructive aspects of Merton's critique, written partly in close reference to it. We have already noted several of Merton's cogent criticisms of different aspects of functional theory, and shall briefly outline some of his suggestions for alleviating the difficulties. (1) To combat the tendency to confine sociological observation to the positive contributions of social items to the social system, he offers the concepts of "dysfunction," "functional alternatives," and "multiple consequences." To avoid confusing the subjective category of purpose or motive with the objective category of consequences or function, he suggests the concepts of "manifest function" (objective consequences intended and recognized by participants of the system), and "latent functions" (those neither intended nor recognized). (2) To remove one-sided emphasis on positive consequences and bias connected with the notion of functional unity or integration, he suggests the concept of "a net balance of an aggregate of consequences." (3) Noting the very cloudy and empirically debatable concept of "functional requirements" or "prerequisites" that inheres in functional analysis, he suggests that clarification must involve the difficult problem of (a) establishing types of functional requirements—distinguishing requirements holding on a universal level and those holding for a highly specific level of analysis; (b) establishing procedures for validating the assumptions of these requirements; and (c) providing for a concrete and detailed account of the mechanisms that operate to perform a given function.[33]

[32] Parsons, *Essays in Sociological Theory,* p. 22.
[33] Merton, *op. cit.,* pp. 49-55.

In elaborating his theoretical frame of reference, Parsons acknowledged and profited by Merton's critique. The Parsonian schema, however, is much more than simply a structural-functional method of analysis. It is an "action" frame of reference built on a structural-functional base. Practically speaking, this seems to mean that the latest knowledge of motivational processes is combined with modern sociological and anthropological thinking, the whole articulated and given significance on the theoretical and empirical levels in terms of the structural-functional relation. The structure of a social system is formally categorized, and the categories provide the "morphological" setting within which a "physiology" of the social system may be developed. The "dynamic motivational processes" of goal-oriented, role-playing actors interacting in culturally patterned situations—which constitute the independent variables of the system—are located in the structural setting, and the test of their significance is their functional relevance for the maintenance or change of the system.[34]

Consequent Refinements: Functional Requisites and Equilibrium. Without attempting to delve into the intricacies of this schema, we shall try to extricate in general terms those aspects of particular relevance. It may be instructive to correlate these aspects with the proposals of Merton outlined above, with the aim of ascertaining how some of the earlier critical difficulties are met.

First, it is quite clear that the concept of function is now used in the more general and neutral sense of "consequences," which may or may not be intended or recognized, and which may or may not contribute positively to the social system. This is made most explicit by Levy, who defines function as a condition or state of affairs resulting from the operation of a structure through time. "Eufunction" and "dysfunction" are its subtypes; the first of these terms refers to consequences favorable to maintenance, continuity, or survival, and the second to consequences leading to disintegration or structural change.

A further refinement includes recognition of the relative degrees of relevance of structures and functions for the social system. Some functions may represent conditions of little or no relevance for maintenance, some may represent sufficient conditions, and others necessary conditions. Strictly speaking, then, the link between the structural categories and maintenance of the system is provided by the more restricted concept of functional requisites, prerequisites, or "imperatives": those conditions which *must* be provided for if the system is to be maintained. It is further acknowledged that different structures may serve the same requisite, and different requisites may be fulfilled by the same structure.

Second, as it was most recently presented, the Parsonian schema incor-

[34] Parsons, *The Social System,* pp. 19-22.

porates the concept of "equilibrium"[35] as of central importance. This concept tends to replace a more normatively evaluated state of the total system as a fixed point of reference for analysis—although there is still *much* ambiguity here. This mechanistic concept is analogous to the principle of homeostasis in biology, performing a similar function for sociology. Just as it had been postulated earlier that a social system tends to maintain a state of internal unity or harmony, it is now postulated that equilibrium—which we may recognize as a more neutral term implying a "net balance of an aggregate of consequences"—tends to be maintained.

Third, the important role of the concept of functional requisites now leads to closer consideration of its implications, especially for empirical research. Following the explicit formulation of Levy, it is first required that a unit social system be defined in terms of the interrelatedness of its elements and its distinctiveness *vis-à-vis* its non-social setting or environment. The question is then asked, "What conditions must be met if such a system is to exist or be maintained in such a setting?" The answer establishes the functional requisites, which may be determined for different levels of generality. We may thus seek the necessary conditions for *any* system, or for a *particular* system empirically defined. For Parsons the "functional imperatives" of *any* system include adaptation to the external situation, instrumental goal-attainment, integration among the units of the system, and latent pattern-maintenance and tension-management.[36] On the *particular* level, dominant structures of an empirical system force "structural imperatives" upon the rest of the system: given certain central patterns, the variability of the others is sharply limited.

The Application of Functional Requisites in Research. It is claimed, then, that despite many logical and empirical difficulties, the concept of functional requisites is analytically useful in directing attention to crucial problems for social structure and hence furnishes a starting point in the search for and analysis of social structures. Once a list of requisites has been worked out, there exists a systematic way of ascertaining whether or not in a given problem all of the minimally required structures have been studied. Thus, in analyzing our own society, Parsons views the dominant economic structure in terms of the functional imperatives of allocation and integration, showing the limits set by these patterns on other patterns, such as those of kinship, courtship, and religion. From this he traces the strains or inconsistencies that occur as the integrative or equilibrium limits of the different sets of patterns are

[35] For an exposition of Pareto's use of the equilibrium concept, see L. J. Henderson, *op. cit.;* G. C. Homans and C. P. Curtis, Jr., *An Introduction to Pareto* (New York, 1934); and the *Revue internationale de sociologie,* 44 (Sept.-Oct., 1936), entirely devoted to "Les Équilibres sociaux."

[36] Talcott Parsons, "Some Comments on the State of the General Theory of Action," *ASR,* 18 (Dec., 1953), pp. 624-625.

approached, and from them derives special structures that act as "mechanisms of social control" and maintain the system in a relatively balanced state. To the degree that these mechanisms fail, the social system disintegrates or changes its structural type.

The Persistence of Teleology in Functionalism. The discussion of recent functionalism may suffice to suggest that, although many of the difficulties of earlier functionalism have been cleared up, not all of them have been resolved. A case may perhaps be made for the thesis that the resolution of earlier difficulties has resulted, in effect, in a transition from a more teleological type of interpretation modeled after biological method, toward a more "mechanistic" or causal type of analysis following the lead of physical-science methodology. (Nagel's contention as to the basic equivalence of the two types would seem to be exemplified here in practice. On this view, the problems that remain in modern functionalism may be seen as due in part to the intermingling and confusion of the two types of method.) Such a thesis seems especially plausible in view of the tendency toward interchangeability of important concepts derived from the two realms. First, as has been noted by N.S. Timasheff,[37] the terms "function" and "mechanism" are given almost identical definitions by Parsons, the latter term taking on a more and more important role. Second, the earlier normative notions of "integration," "harmony," etc., of the whole tend to give way now to the notion of "equilibrium" correlated with concept of "order" in its logical sense as the opposite of randomness. However, as will be seen below, this is only a tendency, inconsistently adhered to, with "order" sometimes reverting to the normative sense. Third, a similar trend may be seen in the transition of the notion of social "needs" to "requirements" or "prerequisites" to "necessary and/or sufficient conditions"—the second being a logical notion quite clearly separated connotatively from the first.

Let us consider in a little more detail the usage of "equilibrium" and "order." We have noted that in the functional methodology of biology the fixed point of reference against which structures and functions are given significance, and criteria of health and disease are determined, is the normal state of the total organism as a structurally fixed, surviving whole. In earlier sociological functionalism, the analogous fixed point of reference was a more or less unspecified state of the total social system as a surviving whole. We have also noted the attempt of Radcliffe-Brown, following Durkheim, to specify more carefully this fixed point of reference, despite his recognition that the biologic analogy breaks down at this point. It is here that modern functionalism has picked up the trail. In answer to the demand that the idea of "survival of society" be more carefully specified, one response was made in terms of the specification of the level of generality of the social system

[37] N. S. Timasheff, "The Basic Concepts of Sociology," *AJS,* 58 (Sept., 1952), pp. 176-186.

under consideration. But our problem has not been completely solved.

An answer seems to be provided by the concept of equilibrium. A social system, if it is truly an on-going system, represents a state of equilibrium that tends to be maintained. But confusion easily results from the ambiguous meaning of the concept. Thus, in one place Parsons states:

> The most general and fundamental property of a system is the interdependence of parts or variables. Interdependence consists in the existence of determinate relationships among the parts or variables as contrasted with randomness of variability. In other words, interdependence is *order* in the relationship among the components which enter into a system. This order must have a tendency to self-maintenance, which is very generally expressed in the concept of equilibrium.[38]

It must be kept clear that, in this sense, equilibrium—or, more strictly, order in the component relationships—represents an evaluatively neutral condition—that is, a condition implying nothing about "order" in the Hobbesian sense, concerning the degree of conflict, inconsistency, frustration, or tension existing in the system. All that is said is that a persisting system represents a net balance of an aggregate of interdependent variables.

Because he feels that we are unable at present to define and relate the variables with any precision, Parsons appeals to the functional principle, introducing the concept of functional prerequisites as a device for locating the more significant variables in the social system. But at another point, Parsons tends to revert to an earlier position, characterizing the total system in terms of an ideally evaluated condition, stating that "Order—peaceful coexistence under conditions of scarcity—is one of the very first of the functional imperatives of social systems."[39]

This raises important problems. If "order"—and therefore "equilibrium"—is defined in the first sense of logical interdependence of the variables of a system, then we have no real fixed point of reference corresponding to the "normal" in biology and applicable for any social system. Some degree of order in this sense will exist and some level of equilibrium will persist as long as we have a *system* to talk about. In Bateson's terms, any *status quo* represents a condition of dynamic equilibrium. By way of concrete example we might cite Benedict's analysis of the Zuñi and Dobu cultures: each represents a social system; each is in equilibrium; but these equilibria exist on very different levels measured in terms of conflict, frustration, tension, or peaceful coexistence.

The Neglect of Deviation by Functional Theory. On the other hand, if equilibrium, or persistent order, is to be defined in terms of "peaceful coexistence," then criticisms discussed earlier are applicable. Statements

[38] Parsons and Shils, *op. cit.*, p. 107.

[39] *Ibid.*, p. 180; Parsons, *The Social System*, pp. 26-27.

holding that *any* society tends to maintain such a state are doubtful as to factual correctness and ideological neutrality. Such considerations lead to the crucial point, suggested in one way or another by Merton, Homans, and Sheldon, that an adequate theory must allow for the social structuring of "deviance" on a par with that of "conformity." These two categories are indistinguishable as far as the logical meaning of "order" is concerned. A great deal of clarification, then, is needed if we are to attempt to reconcile a mechanistic concept such as equilibrium, which implies a "Gibbs system," with a functional orientation, which implies a normative system.

Circular Reasoning Implied in Functionalism. It may be that the two definitions of "order" were intended to be distinct and independent, the second —order as peaceful coexistence—being a functional prerequisite postulated or derived from the theoretical system. This raises the question of the logical and empirical significance of the concept of functional prerequisites. Merton is only one of many to object to its tendency to produce mere truisms, tautologies, or *ex post facto* statements. Such statements do not tell us anything new about society or a specific social system; rather they *are* what we mean by society or by a specific system. On the general level our statements are broad and far removed from concrete structures. On the lower level, if we define a system in terms of specific structures, it becomes too easy to pick out these same structures as fulfilling requisite functions. Such a process would appear to be circular and lead nowhere.

Let us consider, for example, the general requisites of any society suggested by Aberle and others.[40] Society is defined as "a group of human beings sharing a self-sufficient system of action which is capable of existing longer than the life-span of an individual, the group being recruited at least in part by the sexual reproduction of the members." The prerequisites for the persistence of such a society are given as: provision for adequate relationship to the environment and for sexual recruitment, role differentiation and role assignment, communication, shared cognitive orientations, a shared, articulated set of goals, normative regulation of means, regulation of affective expression, socialization, and the effective control of disruptive forms of behavior. Levy insists that these prerequisites are not derived merely by definition but are the minimal implications of the existence of a society in its setting: they are not empty deductions but empirical relationships to be independently discovered.[41]

Some clarification of what is involved here may result from a consideration of Ernest Nagel's contention that functional statements are equivalent to non-functional statements of the type commonly used in physical science. It may be asked how the concept of functional requisites, defined as the

[40] D. F. Aberle *et al.*, "The Functional Prerequisites of a Society," *Ethics*, 60 (Jan., 1950), pp. 100-111.

[41] Levy, *op. cit.*, pp. 40 *ff.*

necessary conditions of a system, might be interpreted in the light of physical-science systems. As discussed earlier, a model theoretical system in physical science includes a set of equations that state the relationships between the several variables and define the state of the total system for given values of the variables. The theoretical system represents a logical structure or deductive system from which certain implications necessarily follow and which are subject to empirical test. Given, for example, such a theoretical structure as that of celestial mechanics, what would it mean to state that if the solar system is to persist, certain necessary conditions must be met? Such a statement could have no independent significance, if it has determinate meaning at all. The "conditions" are already defined or described by the structure of the theoretical system in terms of its set of equations. On the general level the conditions are given by equations relating variables; on a particular empirical level they are given by the equations with numerical values substituted.

Similarly in the case of a sociological system. If we start with a social-system theory, defining and relating all the necessary concepts involved, such as society, situation, actor, interaction, etc., then the functional requisites, or conditions necessary for the persistence of such a system are, ideally, implied by the system as delineated. Such implications are not to be disparaged as "mere deductions." Empirical research then enters as a test of validity of these implications and thus of the theoretical system. Thus, viewed from the theoretical system, functional prerequisites are implications or deductions; viewed from the process of verification, they are empirical relations to be discovered.

However, as Parsons argues, sociologists are not ready yet for a precise theoretical formulation of social systems. But this is as much as to admit that they cannot trace the logical implications of the existence of a social system: from such theory as exists, the necessary conditions (functional prerequisites) of social systems on the general, or particular, level cannot be determined. In other words, just how does the concept of function serve as a criterion of importance or relevance for social structures? It is supposed to do so by relating them to the functional prerequisites or necessary conditions of existence of the social system. But these are, logically, end-points of a theory; they are verifiable derivations from the theory and can only be a subject of loose speculation until the theory is fairly well on the way to construction. An appeal, then, to the notion of functional prerequisites would seem to be gratuitous. The concept plays no formalized part in the theory, and it is at best an open question whether its use can add anything more than the illusion of scientific procedure to what must admittedly remain at present a confession of inadequacy and guesswork.

On the other hand, construction of any theory necessarily involves a large initial amount of guesswork; if such a concept as "functional prerequisites" proves to have important heuristic value, there can be no objection to its use as long as its highly tentative character is clearly acknowledged. Thus, S. F. Nadel, himself critical of the concept, nevertheless hastens to suggest that its use may not be entirely sterile, leading only to truisms and tautologies.

Attempts to Validate the Theory of Functional Requisites. Let us consider the test of Aberle *et al.*, for establishing the validity of the above-listed functional requisites on the most general level for any society. A given function is a requisite of any society if in its absence the relationship between the society and its setting can be shown to be such that one (or some combination) of the following four conditions for the termination of the society would result. The four conditions are: (1) the biological extinction or dispersion of the members; (2) the apathy of the members (lack of adequate motivation); (3) the war of all against all; and (4) the absorption of the society into another society. It is claimed that this can be demonstrated clearly in some cases, convincingly in others. But the authors do not, however, "demonstrate" anything, but rather appeal to prevailing knowledge of society and its implications on the primarily intuitive level. A rigid logic of validation, of course, would require experimental setups and techniques either not feasible or not yet developed.

However, one may ask if validation is really demanded of such general requisites as those proposed. For the most part, they would seem to be quite "self-evident"—that is, clearly implied in the definition of "society" and the terms included in it, such as "sharing," "self-sufficient system," and "action." It is on the lower empirical levels that difficulty is likely to be encountered. It is here that most of the interesting problems for the sociologist are encountered. And it is here that the question of validation becomes most crucial.

General Deficiencies in the Theory of Functionalism

Criticism has laid a heavy burden of proof on functionalism. Whether it is to play some kind of important role in the construction of sociological theory will only be shown conclusively in its future fruits. The fact that it is now given a *central* position is causing much uneasiness among fellow theorists. Speaking for those who feel dissatisfaction with the functional approach, Richard Sheldon—himself a collaborator in the Parsonian theory of action—traces the underlying difficulties to a lack of realization of the facts of theory construction, and in doing so, cuts across and thus sums up many of the critical points we have previously considered. He points out that there are three basic ingredients in any scientific theoretical structure. The first is a set of concepts and postulates, categories, and axioms, which are "free creations of the human intellect" in that they are not given in nature but represent principles created by abstraction and convention. Since they have no necessary or direct relation to observational data, they are by nature untestable. The second is a set of operations by which the principles or categories are attached to sense data. By means of this independently defined set, propositions of the first set are empirically testable. The third is a logical system or structure whereby conclusions may be derived and stated in terms of relationships other than those originally given in the first set of principles.

Functionalism as exemplified in the Parsonian system abounds in principles and categories of the first set, but is quite deficient in the other two. "Function" operates as a principle of the first type, relating categories also of the first type. There are no independent operations or logical structures attaching these to sense data and providing for empirical tests and new derivations.[42] Rather, relationships seem to be made more or less intuitively by the structure of the observer's language, or are assumed to be in nature. In a word, ". . . the theory has content but not structure. All one can do with such a theory is to fill in the content, and the end result can be statements such as, 'suicide is functional because it promotes peace of mind.' "[43]

SELECTED BIBLIOGRAPHY

Bateson, Gregory, *Naven* (Cambridge: Cambridge University Press, 1936).
Becker, Howard, *Systematic Sociology on the Basis of the* Beziehungslehre *and* Gebildelehre *of Leopold von Wiese* (New York: John Wiley, 1932; reissued with a new preface, Gary, Ind.: Norman Paul Press, 1950).
Bennett, J. W., and M. M. Tumin, *Social Life* (New York: Alfred Knopf, 1948).
Durkheim, Émile, *The Rules of Sociological Method,* translated by S. A. Solovay and J. H. Mueller (Glencoe, Ill.: The Free Press, 1938).
Fortes, Meyer (ed.), *Social Structure: Studies Presented to A.* R. *Radcliffe-Brown* (Oxford: at the Clarendon Press, 1949).
Goldenweiser, A. E., *History, Psychology, and Culture* (New York: Alfred Knopf, 1933).
Goode, W. J., *Religion Among the Primitives* (Glencoe, Ill.: The Free Press, 1951).
Levy, M. J., *The Structure of Society* (Princeton: Princeton University Press, 1952).
Malinowski, Bronislaw, *Argonauts of the Western Pacific* (London: Routledge, 1922).
———, *Coral Gardens and Their Magic* (New York: American Book Company, 1935), 2 vols.

[42] However, more recent close collaboration with colleagues working directly on the empirical level (interaction-process analysis) gives promise of meeting these deficiencies. Cf. Talcott Parsons, R. F. Bales, and E. A. Shils, *Working Papers in the Theory of Action* (Glencoe, Ill., 1953).

[43] Parsons and Shils, *op. cit.,* p. 35.

———, *Magic, Science, and Religion and Other Essays* (Glencoe, Ill.: The Free Press, 1948).
———, *A Scientific Theory of Culture and Other Essays* (Chapel Hill: University of North Carolina Press, 1944).
Merton, R. K., "Intermarriage and the Social Structure: Fact and Theory," *Psychiatry* (August, 1941), pp. 361-374.
———, *Social Theory and Social Structure* (Glencoe, Ill,: The Free Press, 1949).
Parsons, Talcott, *Essays in Sociological Theory Pure and Applied* (Glencoe, Ill.: The Free Press, 1949).
———, *The Social System* (Glencoe, Ill.: The Free Press, 1951).
Parsons, Talcott, R. F. Bales, and E. A. Shils, *Working Papers in the Theory of Action* (Glencoe, Ill.: The Free Press, 1953).
Radcliffe-Brown, A. R., *The Andaman Islanders* (Glencoe, Ill.: The Free Press, 1948).
———, *Structure and Function in Primitive Society* (Glencoe, Ill.: The Free Press, 1952).
Thompson, Laura, *Culture in Crisis* (New York: Harper, 1950).
Warner, W. Lloyd, *A Black Civilization* (New York: Harper, 1937).

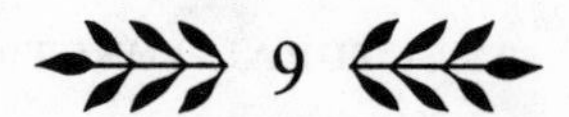

SOCIAL CHANGE: MAJOR PROBLEMS IN THE EMERGENCE OF THEORETICAL AND RESEARCH FOCI

ALVIN BOSKOFF

FEW IF ANY PROBLEMS IN SOCIOLOGY HAVE BEEN MORE FASCINATING, MORE tantalizing, or more elusive than social change. Ever since Heraclitus, and problably well before his era, change has been a theme that called forth sweeping statements and vague speculation. But until recently, change was approached with an assertiveness and intellectual confidence that guaranteed a basic simplicity. The modern attitude among sociologists, however, is marked by a series of instructive paradoxes that provide the key to our present difficulties and achievements in this significant area.

Social Change: Central Problem or Afterthought. Although social change was, in one form or another, an immensely popular topic in the half-century before World War I, it has received remarkably little serious attention from either the present or the preceding generation of sociologists. Indeed, despite widespread use of the term, sociologists tend to be more concerned with *structure, organization,* and *configuration.* Textbooks in sociology, an excellent index of what most sociologists are thinking and teaching, often relegate discussions of social change to a final chapter, or sometimes to a small section located well to the rear of numerous chapters on culture, socialization, social groups, and the community.[1] Unfortunately, the usual textbook approach is superficial and unenlightening and often appears to be a belated but extended footnote to the volume.

[1] The major exceptions to this trend seem to be: R. M. MacIver, *Society* (New York, 1937) [a revised edition of this work, with Charles H. Page as coauthor, appeared in 1949]; and Arnold Green, *Sociology* (New York, 1953).

At present, as a consequence of this decline of interest, we have no text or special volume that analyzes social change as a distinct area of sociological concern, with the exception of N. L. Sims' *The Problem of Social Change* (New York, 1939). This is in sharp contrast to the mushrooming output of texts on marriage and the family, criminology, social problems and disorganization, race relations, and the urban community. Furthermore, it is difficult to label specific sociologists as "experts" on social change in the same sense in which we might refer to criminologists or industrial sociologists as experts. In other words, the study of social change has become something of a part-time concern in recent years, although men like Weber, MacIver, Sorokin, Becker, and Znaniecki have written perceptively on one or more aspects of the problem. The essential anomaly is that the study of social change has become a specialty without specialists.

The Disorganized State of Social-Change Studies. As a consequence of this diminished interest, social change tends to remain in practice a fragmented, embryonic specialty rather than a concise, distinctive area of mutually relevant research and thinking. In part, this condition derives from the tacit assumption that sociologists lack the requisite knowledge to organize and appraise an adequate body of concepts and theories. However, as we shall see later, a considerable and growing amount of data and theoretical probing is readily available in such relevant fields as social movements, social mobility, urbanization, specific institutional changes, acculturation, broad historical interpretations, and the nascent specialty of social planning.[2] In fact, there is already some evidence that serious attention to the implications of these studies can result in fruitful organization of research in social change, particularly necessary in an era bristling with change and its attendant problems. A tentative schema, drawn from analyses of some of these related problems and designed to furnish a key to scattered works on social change, is presented in the final section of this chapter; basically it explores one manner of systematizing the problems and the data of social change and thereby seeks to establish genuine unity in an amorphous compartment of modern sociology.

Structure vs. *Change: The Diversion of a False Problem.* Perhaps the most fundamental enigma lies in the search for the true relation between problems of structure and problems of change. Essentially, this requires development and explicit use of two complementary assumptions. The first involves the degree of analytical distinction between social structure and social change; the second is concerned with the relative priority of these problems in conceptualization and research.

Until about the time of World War I, sociologists tended to place questions of change, "dynamics," and "progress" in the forefront of their thinking and writing; in a sense, they accepted Comte's separation of social

[2] See below, pp. 270-287.

statics and social dynamics, but their concern for the stream of human history and contemporary social problems often led them to construct "dynamic sociologies" in which structure was somewhat subservient to change. This approach is evident, for example, in the later works of Comte and in those of Spencer, Ward, Durkheim, Marx, Ross, Gumplowicz, Hobhouse, and others.[3] In reaction to the sweeping generalizations of these men, modern sociologists have re-emphasized the distinction between structure and "dynamics." Furthermore, although consideration of problems of change is conceded to be basic to any respectable sociology, the assumption seems to be quite general that analysis of structure necessarily precedes proper understanding of change. Consequently, change is treated both as a *synthetic* problem, dependent on "primitive" delineations of structure, and as a fundamental and semi-autonomous sociological realm.[4] The result is a methodological dilemma of great magnitude, from which escape has sometimes seemed hopeless.

Undoubtedly, the clearest voice in this theoretical wilderness has been that of Florian Znaniecki, whose association with W. I. Thomas was one of the fortunate accidents of contemporary sociology. Criticizing the traditional antithesis of social statics and social dynamics, Znaniecki has suggested that the false problem of "order *vs.* change" can be obviated by approaching sociological data in terms of *dynamic systems*. The only form of stability (i.e., of structure) in the social world is *relative* organization, which reveals elements of and tendencies toward difference, dis-order, and change. Thus structure and change become *intersecting* and overlapping problems. It therefore follows, according to Znaniecki, that social change must not be relegated to a balmier future, since, if properly studied, it can contribute to our understanding of structure—in the same way that analysis of structural problems yields insight into the nature of change.[5] At present, Znaniecki is developing

[3] Auguste Comte, *The Positive Philosophy,* translated and condensed by Harriet Martineau (London, 1896), vol. 2, Book 6; Herbert Spencer, *Principles of Sociology* (3rd ed.; New York, 1905), vol. 1; L. F. Ward, *Pure Sociology* (New York, 1903); and *Dynamic Sociology* (New York, 1883), 2 vols.; Émile Durkheim, *The Division of Labor in Society,* translated by George Simpson (Glencoe, Ill., 1947); Karl Marx, *A Contribution to the Critique of Political Economy,* translated by N. I. Stone (New York, 1904), pp. 11-12; E. A. Ross, *Social Control* (New York, 1901) and *Foundations of Sociology* (New York, 1915); Ludwig Gumplowicz, *Outlines of Sociology,* translated by F. W. Moore (Philadelphia, 1899); L. T. Hobhouse, *Social Development* (New York, 1924); A. G. Keller, *Societal Evolution* (New York, 1916); F. H. Giddings, *Studies in the Theory of Human Society* (New York, 1922).

[4] See Talcott Parsons, *The Social System* (Glencoe, Ill., 1951), pp. 486-494, and Florian Znaniecki, *Cultural Sciences* (Urbana, 1952), pp. 281, 392, for contrasting positions on this problem.

[5] Znaniecki, *op. cit.* pp. 281, 372. See also Znaniecki's "Comment" in Herbert Blumer, *An Appraisal of Thomas and Znaniecki's* The Polish Peasant in Europe and America (New York, 1939), pp. 95-98.

this orientation in a "principles" text in which social change is not only introduced in the opening chapter but is also discussed in most of the succeeding chapters.

The Proper Balance of Theory and Research. A final paradox is a resultant of those already noted. Simply stated, although heretofore the study of social change was marked by an abundance of theory and little research, we are now faced with an amazing mass of undigested but variably relevant research and surprisingly little organized theory. Thus far, few sociologists have been able or willing to pause in their occupational flight for reflection or possible redirection.

Social Change as a Distinctive Area of Investigation

Since the study of social change has been somewhat marked by paradox and doubt, one might expect that adequate definition and conceptualization would be difficult to achieve. Unfortunately, this expectation coincides uncomfortably well with reality. But is this not the situation in other problem areas of sociology? For example, it is still a fact that any careful observer can distinguish a variety of nuances of meaning in the use of such basic terms as society, social group, institution, and social class. Yet it is believed that a provisionally acceptable definition of social change can be formulated—one which reflects the best thinking of our predecessors, current attempts to resolve the paradoxes discussed above, and the contributions of pertinent research.

A Definition. Social change refers to the intelligible process in which we can discover significant alterations in the structure and functioning of determinate social systems. The implications of this definition can be explored by focusing attention on the key terms: social system, structure, function, and significant alteration.

The Social and the Cultural. The crucial aspect of this definition is an analytic separation of the "social" and the "cultural" and of social and cultural systems. This is a relatively new distinction—less than fifty years old —and some sociologists find it difficult to accept, principally because the social and cultural aspects are so obviously interrelated. But close relationship should not blind one to the distinct identity of each of the related parts. A father and his son, for example, are related physically and socially, yet it would be an error to confuse one with the other. This principle applies to the whole realm of human behavior. The basic facts are observable interactions among persons; from these facts we can distinguish: (1) patterns of association and relations through which persons influence or motivate one another; and (2) certain products of these regularities in the form of communicable values, norms, and standards. The former we designate as the "social" aspect, the latter as the "cultural," recognizing that these are not antithetical but merely reflect differing though complementary facets of human experience.[6]

This abstraction of a distinctively social dimension can be traced to Simmel, who argued that sociology as a special science was primarily concerned with the *forms* of reciprocal relations among persons rather than with the *content* (the interests, goals, or values underlying specific associations); and to Tönnies, who classified what we now call social systems into social relations, social circles, social collectives, and social corporations.[7] In their own way, both Durkheim and Weber pursued the same line of development; whereas Durkheim focused on the serial classification of organized groups, Weber concentrated his analysis on specific aspects of the "social" and social structure (*e.g.*, order and authority, hierarchy, bureaucracy, legitimacy, and stratification).[8] In 1921, Alfred Weber explicitly separated *social* processes from their products, subdividing these products into *cultural* processes and *civilizational* processes. By the thirties, most of the leading sociologists recognized a fundamental distinction between society and culture, although in practice they were not always faithful to this distinction. Finally, in 1934 and again in a recent paper, Znaniecki outlined the proper subject matter of sociology in four types of *social systems:* social relations, social roles, social groups, and societies.[9]

The Nature of Social Structure. Each social system, from the simplest to the most complex, exhibits certain *regularities* in the relations of its members with one another. Taken together, these uniformities constitute the *structure* of a social relation, a social role, social group, or society. It should be remembered that structures in the social realm are only relatively stable, that

[6] Znaniecki, *Cultural Sciences,* pp. 336 (footnote), 396-398; P. A. Sorokin, *Society, Culture, and Personality* (New York, 1947), Chap. 3; Fred Eggan, *Social Organization of the Western Pueblos* (Chicago, 1951), p. 6; MacIver, *op. cit.,* p. 395; J. H. Steward, *Area Research: Theory and Practice* (New York, 1950), pp. 98-101; A. L. Kroeber, *The Nature of Culture* (Chicago, 1952), pp. 157, 165.

[7] Georg Simmel, *The Sociology of Georg Simmel,* edited and translated by K. H. Wolff (Glencoe, Ill., 1950), pp. 21-23, 40-57; Ferdinand Tönnies, *Fundamental Concepts of Sociology,* translated and supplemented by C. P. Loomis (New York, 1940), Introduction; Ferdinand Tönnies, *Soziologische Studien und Kritiken* (Jena, 1925-1929), 3 vols.

[8] Max Weber, *The Theory of Social and Economic Organization*, translated by A. M. Henderson and Talcott Parsons (New York, 1947), Parts 3 and 4; and *From Max Weber: Essays in Sociology,* translated by H. H. Gerth and C. Wright Mills (New York, 1946), Chaps. 6-10.

[9] Alfred Weber, *Fundamentals of Culture Sociology,* translated by G. H. Weltner and C. F. Hirshman (New York, 1939); Florian Znaniecki, "Basic Problems of Contemporary Sociology," *ASR,* 19 (October, 1954), pp. 521-523, and *The Method of Sociology* (New York, 1934), pp. 107-121.

social systems operate in time and space, and that therefore any careful statement about structure involves an attempt to reduce empirical variations to a minimum. The sociologist has discovered, however, that structure is best analyzed by locating and appraising (both qualitatively and quantitatively) certain *dimensions* or aspects of social systems. In most general usage are analyses of the following: characteristic types of interaction (cooperation, competition, accommodation, etc.); differential frequency of interaction between implicated actors; the induction of new members and withdrawal of existing members (turnover of personnel); distribution of rights and privileges, duties and responsibilities; the division of labor; the form of status differentiation (stratification); the system of integration through structures of power and authority; the social needs of members met by the normal operation of the social system; and the consequences of relative autonomy or interdependence with other social systems.

Function. The function of a social system refers to the contributions of that system to (1) the basic and acquired needs of its members and (2) larger social systems in which it may be realistically included as a subsystem. Since, as has been noted, social systems exhibit constellations of interrelated features, the function of any single element of structure can be analyzed. It is now common practice to distinguish readily accessible (or *manifest*) functions from those which are unintended or unsuspected by participant actors (*latent* functions).[10] Unfortunately, functional analysis, and particularly analysis of latent functions, has not yet achieved sufficient precision, but it is plainly a method which possesses immense potentialities for a meaningful sociology. (See Chap. 8.)

Significant Alterations. Since social reality is marked by flux, dynamism, variation, and an acknowledged absence of exact repetition in any area of human experience, social change would become equivalent to social reality; and the student of social change would, through this theoretical imperialism, find himself overwhelmed by raw, insistent facts. Consequently, it is indisputably necessary—for the dignity of sociology and the sanity of sociologists—to devise some consistent standard of selection. Hence the key term in our definition: *significant alteration.* This criterion is *implied* in most of the careful studies of social change, but it should be explicitly stated for critical appraisal. Essentially, this standard of "significance" initially concentrates the attention of sociologists on variations that generate *objectively different consequences for the social system being studied.* Then, as analysis proceeds, the process by which these significant alterations emerge can be explored by reference to earlier, less developed bodies of pertinent data. The advantage of this orientation is that the sociologist can thereby move from the descriptive to the analytical level, from the "what" and "where" to the "how" and "why" of social

[10] R. K. Merton, *Social Theory and Social Structure* (Glencoe, Ill., 1949), pp. 50-53, 60-61.

change. Lundberg's definition of change, in his *Foundations of Sociology,* as "successive positions of societal phenomena in time" clings to the descriptive level cherished by behaviorists. Perhaps this explains the limited contribution of this able sociologist to our understanding of social change.[11]

Social Change and Related Terms. Discussion of the problem of social change has been accompanied by such a profusion of terms that the result has often bordered on confusion; we have, for example, such variously related terms as social interaction, social process, social development, social evolution, social progress, and social dynamics. All these terms have value if we recognize that each is a different label for a different order of fact or interpretation. *Social interaction* is the stuff of social change, as previously defined, but it is not change. Interaction refers to all the basic facts of human association, whereas social change comprehends *certain variations from accustomed interaction patterns*. Put another way, social interaction may exhibit little or no significant change, whereas social change always derives from the process of social interaction.

Social process is another general term which, as used over the past thirty or forty years, seems to comprehend social interaction and the accumulated socio-cultural products of interaction. For this reason, social change can be included as a part of social process (cf. Wiese's concept of "process-series").

Social development, social evolution, and *social progress* are terms that involve special interpretation or evaluation of extended processes of social change. All three have reference to the *direction* of successive changes and all seem to imply some judgment about the desirability or inevitability of an imputed direction in change. The most neutral concept in this group is social development, although, as used by Hobhouse and others, it definitely comprehends some over-all movement toward greater efficiency and complexity—but with the recognition of concomitant problems. Social evolution, on the other hand, classifies long-term social changes into a series of graded stages or phases, each of which is assumed to possess greater complexity, greater social opportunities, and greater ethical qualities than its predecessor. With the concept of social progress, however, neutrality disappears, and in place of more or less constructed stages, there appears the notion of a continuous development toward some supposedly realizable objective such as happiness, brotherhood, or rationality—an inevitable accumulation of wished-for social changes.

Social dynamics or *kinetics,* like social change, is a culturally neutral concept. Of course, Comte identified social dynamics with social progress, but in the last few decades social dynamics has come to signify an enduring quality of social phenomena: namely, the inherent possibility of alteration in social affairs. Social change rests on the potentialities supplied by social

[11] G. A. Lundberg, *Foundations of Sociology* (New York, 1939), pp. 504-511.

dynamics as these are acted upon by discernible causes or agencies of change. In reality, we infer social dynamics from comparative studies of specific social changes.

The Interaction of Social and Cultural Change. Although the distinct conceptual status of social change has been emphasized, it is quite obvious that cultural change is often correlated with social change.[12] Each order of change provides valuable data for the fuller comprehension of the other. But it is also important to recognize that, for any given socio-cultural system functioning within a determinate time period, there is no necessary correspondence between developments in the social and cultural spheres. Whatever the fundamental causes, the social and cultural aspects each evidence a measure of independence, as well as interdependence. We can ignore this semi-autonomous condition only at the price of diminished understanding of complex social phenomena. Indeed, a basic reason for the peculiar impotence of many social reform movements and the persistence of social problems is the hopeful but erroneous assumption that desired adjustments in one realm will produce corresponding adaptation in the other. The persistent difficulties of international organization, for example, can be diagnosed sociologically as a situation in which momentous social changes have not yet been matched by appropriate cultural changes (toward a global morality). On the other hand, such problems as delinquency, criminality, divorce, corrupt government, minority-group relations, and mental health seem to resist satisfactory treatment because of undue reliance on attempted cultural changes (e.g., legislation) without proper regard for the alterations in social organization that might sustain new systems of valuation.[13]

Major Trends in the Study of Social Change

The conception of social change presented in the preceding section indicates a general development in this problem area that roughly corresponds to the recent development of sociology itself. Neither sociology nor the study of social change has clearly divested itself of earlier confusions and

[12] For general discussion, see MacIver, *op. cit.*, pp. 443, 462, 466; Znaniecki, *Cultural Sciences*, p. 396; P. H. Landis, *Three Iron-Mining Towns* (Ann Arbor, 1938); W. F. Ogburn, *Social Change* (New York, 1923), pp. 58-60; Sorokin, *Social and Cultural Dynamics* (New York, 1941), vol. 4, pp. 127, 377. For some empirical illustrations, see: Esther Goldfrank, *Changing Configurations in the Social Organization of a Blackfoot Tribe During the Reserve Period* (New York, 1945); Laura Thompson, *Culture in Crisis* (New York, 1950); J. W. Bennett, "Culture-Change and Personality in a Rural Society," *SF*, 23 (Dec., 1944), pp. 123-132.

[13] Znaniecki, *Cultural Sciences*, pp. 396-398.

adolescent immodesties, but a number of promising trends can be discerned in the recent history of social-change analysis which also reflect variously evolved tendencies in modern sociology. These include:

1. A crucial analytical distinction between social and cultural change, corresponding to the development of sociology as a *special* social science. This has been discussed at length in the previous section.

2. The nascent recognition of social-change analysis as a complement to studies of social structure, replacing the view that knowledge of change depends upon and follows analysis of structure. This likewise was sketched in the previous section.

3. An important theoretical and methodological connection between social change and *social causation.*

4. Increased emphasis on a factual, objective study of change, as contrasted with the speculative debates and grandiose theorizing of the nineteenth century.

5. The expanding study of specific societies or constituent communities, as case studies of change, rather than the traditional attempt to treat "all mankind" through a biased comparative approach.

6. A marked concentration on social, cultural, and psychological factors in social change rather than on the well-worn biological, physical, and climatic factors.

7. The emergent conception of social change as a complex *process* involving analysis of abstracted or typical stages or phases.

8. A continuing concern for the operation of values, meaning, and "subjective" aspects in general in the whole process of social change.

9. A concomitant, though rather recent, emphasis on the human agents in the social-change process—their essential characteristics, motivations, needs, etc.

10. The recognition of difficulties, problems, and maladjustments in social change, with a consequent de-emphasizing of progress.

The last seven items in this summary seem to constitute the essential pattern in contemporary analysis of social change. The remainder of our discussion is devoted to an extended description of these features, and to an investigation of the significance of item 3, which is often overlooked in any extensive survey of relevant research, theory, and methodology.

SOCIAL CHANGE AND SOCIAL CAUSATION

In the period of the great theorists, between Comte and World War I, sweeping theories of change and implicit notions of causation were intimately connected in the thinking of such men as Spencer, Marx, Ward, Ratzenhofer, and Ross.[14] As sociologists began to strive for methodological sophistication and purity, this coalescence of problems became suspect. On the one hand, the general problem of social change came to be redefined as a series of special research problems with increasing emphasis on accurate *description.* At the same time, in headlong imitation of the new physics, the concept of "cause" was largely replaced by the concepts of "relation" between "variable" and "function." These refinements were generally justifiable, but they had the unhappy consequence of diluting both the meaning and the dynamic qualities of the whole problem of social change. Even today, we receive remarkably little illumination on social change from the positivists and neobehaviorists among sociologists.

Despite a generation of empiricism and inhibited theorizing, however, the quest for intelligible and meaningful research is still alive, although this kind of research is represented only by a thin but continuing thread. The major inspiration has undoubtedly been Max Weber, whose methodological reflections and research served to reunite for modern sociology the critical problems of causation and change. In the thirties, moreover, Znaniecki detailed the connection by distinguishing "closed" or "limited" social systems whose development could be traced either *genetically* or *causally.* In the first instance, social systems are conceived to exhibit a process of modification explainable solely in terms of potentialities inherent in the component parts of the system. A good example, from the field of biology, is the "normal" maturation process for any species. These modifications are "expected," internal to the system, and therefore, according to Znaniecki, present no causal problem. Genetic sequences are consequently one type of variation. The principle of causation is appropriate only in situations of "change"—that is, situations in which a social system presents evidence of variation traceable to external influences.[15]

Thus analyzed, both change and causation are concepts applicable to situations in which an established line of development is interrupted. Causation is therefore the creation of *deviations,* whereas change encompasses the accumulated products of a specific process of causation. MacIver has further elaborated Znaniecki's formulation by locating the basic element in social causation and social change in a process of *dynamic assessment* (cf. "definition of the situation"), in which individuals and groups *interpret* social situations in a manner which gives rise to variant social actions. Moreover, MacIver distinguishes three typical forms of social causation and change. The first is

[14] Spencer, *loc. cit.;* Karl Marx and Friedrich Engels, *The Communist Manifesto* (many editions); L. F. Ward, *Psychic Factors in Civilization* (Boston, 1906); *Pure Sociology;* and *Dynamic Sociology;* Gustav Ratzenhofer, *Soziologische Erkenntnis* (Leipzig, 1898); Ross, *Social Control,* pp. 17-19, 85, 136, 252-255, 395.

[15] Znaniecki, *The Method of Sociology,* pp. 19, 293-297, and *Cultural Sciences,* pp. 164, 229-231; R. M. MacIver, *Social Causation* (Boston, 1942), pp. 63-65, 176.

distributive phenomena, resulting from independent but converging assessments, such as crime rates, changes in mores, trends of opinion. The second is like or converging assessments which lead to concerted social action, as in the case of social movements, legal enactments, and organizational policies. This is the important category of *collective phenomena*. And finally, there are the dissimilar assessments and activities of interdependent persons and groups that create unpremeditated social resultants—what MacIver calls *conjunctural phenomena*. Here can be included such phenomena as the social division of labor, the business cycle, the various patterns of social disorganization and social problems, and even the complex development of the basic institutions in any society (cf. Sumner's analysis).[16]

Admittedly, few sociologists trained outside the European tradition have been explicitly aware of this connection. Yet, if we may borrow one of MacIver's terms, there is some evidence that modern sociologists, in their daily thinking and research, have been producing a conjunctural phenomenon which, in implication at least, approximates the general viewpoint of Znaniecki and MacIver. Indeed, the last section of this chapter seems to provide considerable support for this judgment.

Major Types of Social-Change Studies

With few exceptions, the study of social change has come to be weighted toward an empirical study of specific aspects of change; and the consequence is a strategy of *indirect* analysis of the larger problem. Although this is a fundamentally desirable trend, the resulting specialization in research has not been followed by a proper synthesis and appraisal of a staggering quantity of variably pertinent investigations. Aside from the fact that the intellectual labor involved is admittedly gargantuan, a possible reason why this work has not been done is a peculiar reluctance to profit from neighboring specialties unless some academic fashion lends it glamour and sophistication. (See Tomars' trenchant discussion in Chap. 17 of this volume.) In the absence of such a fashion, we can only indicate these more or less relevant fields of special research and thinking and perhaps attempt to give a preliminary, tentative summary of the implications of each specialty for the more general problems of social change.

STUDIES IN DEMOGRAPHIC AND ECOLOGICAL CHANGE

These studies have largely emphasized a descriptive, quantitative orientation, with occasional concern for the related problems of social mobility and social movements. A significant contribution of this sort of research is

[16] MacIver, *Social Causation,* pp. 298, 333, 372-388.

the necessary recognition that social processes are affected by the composition of a population and its distribution through culturally appraised physical environments.[17] Durkheim employed this approach, with unsatisfactory results, in tracing the development of a social division of labor to an increase in *dynamic density*. More recently, Park and his followers have tended to consider demographic and ecological changes as important indices (and even as factors) in social change.[18] However, the study of internal migration promises to supply the most fruitful insights into social change by inquiring into the (1) changing social characteristics of migrants; (2) changing trends in the location of migrants; (3) changing problems of social adjustment faced by migrants; and (4) the social consequences of migration for communities of origin.

URBANIZATION STUDIES

The processes of urbanization embody a second locus of related data, particularly since much of contemporary social change is associated with the dominance of urban social structures. Urban research is devoted to numerous types of development, but a few are of immense importance to the student of social change. One of the older problems, the causal factors in the emergence of cities and their particular geographic locations, has been resolved by distinguishing functional types of cities and by reference to a series of cultural and physiographic prerequisites. A second problem, the search for and understanding of growth patterns in cities, has been a source of much controversy during the past quarter-century; the purely competitive, economic explanation has been supplemented by concern for broader cultural factors and the effect of political factors, with increasing attention to urban developments outside the U. S.[19]

Studies of the processes of urban specialization represent several pertinent kinds of research. First, there is the problem of change or lack of change in the segregation of groups and functions within the city. Most studies point to definite territorial specialization, with a consequent limitation of social interaction between social strata and other groups (particularly ethnic groups).[20] Second, we have the phenomena of *suburbanization* and the

[17] For interpretative summaries and numerous references, see: Amos Hawley, *Human Ecology* (New York, 1950), Parts 2-4; and J. A. Quinn, *Human Ecology* (New York, 1950), Parts 2-3.

[18] Durkheim, *op. cit.*, pp. 256-262; R. E. Park, "Succession: An Ecological Concept," *ASR*, 1 (April, 1936), pp. 171-179.

[19] R. E. Park, E. W. Burgess, R.D. McKenzie (eds.), *The City* (Chicago, 1925); Walter Firey, *Land Use in Central Boston* (Cambridge, 1947); Kingsley Davis and Hilda Hertz, *The Pattern of World Urbanization* (New York, 1954); P. K. Hatt and A. J. Reiss (eds.), *Reader in Urban Sociology* (Glencoe, Ill., 1951), Parts 3 and 4.

[20] Consult Quinn, *op. cit.*, Chaps. 7, 15-16 for references and summaries of research investigations.

growth of an urban fringe. Although the data in these studies are not yet adequate, there is some prospect of discovering the emergence of a social system (particularly in the area of family organization) unlike that found in farm areas or in the city proper.[21] Whether or not a unique social structure is developing in suburbs and fringe areas, there is considerable evidence that rural-farm and rural–non-farm areas are undergoing social changes which are erasing the solidary, folk-like communities of the past. This is, for example, reflected in such trends as lower birth rates and higher crime and suicide rates. And finally, the rapid growth of internally differentiated metropolitan communities, in which a dominant central city integrates the specialized functions of numerous smaller communities within its hinterland, is being charted. Studies by McKenzie, Bogue, and others have documented the increasing specialization in population characteristics and economic services which accompanies this trend; and we are just beginning to investigate the sociological changes in types of component communities prompted by this division of labor.[22]

Some Implications. In general, the study of urbanization seems to furnish four important clues for the comprehension of social change. Most obvious is the conclusion that urban changes have occurred without plan or calculation (cf. MacIver's conjunctural phenomena). Equally important, but not often recognized, is that the phenomena of urbanization seem to result from the innovative actions of economic and political élites and the subsequent adjustments of both urban masses and initially non-urban groups. Furthermore, the process of urbanization proceeds without the imposition of force or coercion, but through subtle, indirect, economically tinged pressures. Finally, the social changes implicit in urbanization seem to have been possible in social systems that have embraced two cultural premises: the desirability of material progress; and a genuine rejection of established patterns based solely on the authority of tradition.

SOCIAL MOBILITY, CHANGES IN STRATIFICATION, AND DYNAMICS OF ÉLITES

The Great Depression stimulated enormous interest in problems of stratification in the U.S., although European sociologists had been seriously working on this difficult question since Comte. In the U.S., much of strati-

[21] E. Gartly Jaco and Ivan Belknap, "Is a New Family Form Emerging in the Urban Fringe?" *ASR,* 18 (Oct., 1953), pp. 551-557; W. T. Martin, *The Rural-Urban Fringe* (Eugene, Ore., 1953); "Some Socio-Psychological Aspects of Adjustment to Residence Location in the Urban Fringe," *ASR,* 18 (June, 1953), pp. 248-253; and "A Consideration of Differences in the Extent and Location of the Formal Associational Activities of Rural-Urban Fringe Residents," *ASR,* 17 (Dec., 1952), pp. 685-694.

[22] R. D. McKenzie, *The Metropolitan Community* (New York, 1933); D. J. Bogue, *The Structure of the Metropolitan Community* (Ann Arbor, 1949); W. H. Whyte, Jr., "The Transients," in *Prize Articles of 1954* (New York, 1955), pp. 39-112 [originally in *Fortune,* 1954].

fication research was designed to confront the myth of social equality with undeniable facts, and it was not until the early thirties that the problem of vertical mobility achieved some prominence. Sorokin furnished an excellent summary and interpretation of research in his classic *Social Mobility* and, in addition to analyzing the social channels of vertical mobility—military, religious, economic, political, familial, professional—probed for the causes of mobility in such factors as population differentials between social strata, and specific cultural and social changes which require new qualities in certain strata. Since the thirties, research in vertical mobility has concentrated on the extent of *occupational mobility* for specific professions and communities. In general, students of occupational mobility are quite cautious about assigning causes, though a recent report discovered changes somewhat correlated with economic periods.[23]

Changes in systems of stratification had not been given much attention until very recently. Indeed, Marxian theories of a succession of internally hostile class structures probably hindered, by their extremeness, the undertaking of more judicious and empirical studies of class dynamics. However, Landtman ably analyzed the general process of class formation and progressive differentiation, basing his study on ethnographic materials.[24] During the thirties, and again within the past few years, the major changes in class structure noted by sociologists were either the tightening or the loosening of class lines, as indicated in the studies of the Lynds, Riemer, Sorokin, Hollingshead, Sjoberg, and Goldschmidt.[25] In a somewhat different vein, Boskoff tried to correlate specific developments in American Negro class structure with rough historical periods and, more significantly, with the movement of Negroes to more complex communities.[26] But, as Hinkle and Boskoff have shown in Chap. 12 of this volume, the vagueness of concepts in stratification research has severely limited our knowledge of changes in this important dimension of social structure.

[23] P. A. Sorokin, *Social Mobility* (New York, 1927); F. W. Taussig and C. S. Joslyn, *American Business Leaders* (New York, 1932); W. Lloyd Warner and J. C. Abegglin, *Big Business Leaders in America* (New York, 1955); Natalie Rogoff, "Recent Trends in Urban Occupational Mobility," in Hatt and Reiss, *op. cit.*, pp. 406-420; Stuart Adams, "Trends in Occupational Origins of Business Leaders," *ASR*, 19 (Oct., 1954), pp. 541-548.

[24] Gunnar Landtman, *The Origin of the Inequality of the Social Classes* (Chicago, 1938).

[25] R. S. Lynd and Helen M. Lynd, *Middletown in Transition* (New York, 1939); Svend Riemer, *Upward Mobility and Social Stratification;* A. B. Hollingshead, "Trends in Social Stratification: A Case Study," *ASR*, 17 (Dec., 1952), pp. 679-686; Gideon Sjoberg, "Are Social Classes in America Becoming More Rigid?" *ASR*, 16 (Dec., 1951), pp. 775-783; W. R. Goldschmidt, "America's Social Class—Is Equality a Myth?" *Commentary*, 10 (Aug., 1950), pp. 175-181; P. K. Hatt and Virginia Ktsanes, "Patterns of American Stratification as Reflected in Selected Social Science Literature," *ASR*, 17 (Dec., 1952), pp. 670-679.

[26] Alvin Boskoff, "Negro Class Structure and the Technicways," *SF*, 29 (Dec., 1950), pp. 124-131.

A related line of analysis during the past thirty-five years is embodied in the focus on élite groups and their alteration through time. This is, incidentally, one of the major contributions of three very different kinds of sociological explorers: Pareto (drawing on Mosca), Mannheim, and Toynbee. Following a partially developed germ of theory by Gaetano Mosca, Pareto summarized historical development as a "circulation of élites" in which the foxes (experts in the use of deceit and "speculative" measures) alternately replace and are replaced by the lions (who emphasize the use of force and extreme conservatism in ideas and techniques). According to Pareto, this incessant cycle of leadership qualities results from the fact that each type possesses *immediate* advantages that fail to satisfy the enduring problems of leadership; the maintenance of social equilibrium therefore "requires" a continuous process of replacement as recurrent social situations confront the élites.[27] For Mannheim, the dynamics of élites lay in certain formal aspects which have been observed to vary in recent Western history. Principally, he found evidence of (1) an increasing number of élites, with a consequent cancellation of a clear leadership function; (2) a decrease in the creativity of élites traceable to a declining insulation of élites from their followers; (3) increasing selection of élites on the basis of descent and tradition; and (4) a growing emphasis on localism and parochialism in the background and thinking of contemporary élites. More recently, Toynbee, in a manner reminiscent of Pareto but with extremely different objectives, portrays societal leadership as the alternation of creative minorities and dominant minorities, the former meeting societal challenges through proper contemplation and reason, whereas the latter, eschewing "withdrawal and return," maintains its ascendancy through force.[28]

Some Implications. For the student of social change, this vast field of research, barely sketched above, constitutes one of the key contributions to our growing understanding of social kinetics. The most immediate of these is, of course, the heightened awareness of social change as fundamentally a problem of redistribution of power and authority—a theoretical point broached by Marx and more carefully examined by Max Weber.[29] But these studies have implicitly pointed to the importance of searching for the differential opportunities and frustrations created by specific social changes; it is therefore extremely necessary to consider specific groups in terms of the differential impact of change and their respective responses to situations of

[27] Vilfredo Pareto, *Mind and Society,* translated by A. Bongiorno and Arthur Livingston (New York, 1935), vol. 4.

[28] Karl Mannheim, *Man and Society in an Age of Reconstruction* (New York, 1940), pp. 81-96; A. J. Toynbee, *A Study of History,* abridged by D. C. Somervell (New York, 1947), pp. 50, 67-77, 217-246.

[29] Marx, *op. cit.,* pp. 11-12; Max Weber, *Essays in Sociology,* Chap. 9; Max Weber, *Theory of Social and Economic Organization,* part 3.

change. However, the most far-reaching implication, one which is yet to be pursued with vigor in the U.S., is the notion that social change is a function of the peculiar hierarchical structure of given societies and that the nature and direction of change can be substantially clarified by knowledge of the characteristics, problems, and relations of social strata. This, it seems, is the significance of research on political, economic, and esthetic élites and their social circles.

STUDIES OF INSTITUTIONAL AND COMMUNITY CHANGE

Since sociology is to a large extent concerned with the analysis of the institutional level of human phenomena, the relation of institutional change and social change in general requires little explanation. But what precisely is the "institutional" level? Although it is by no means uniformly defined by sociologists, we can agree that institutions have two related aspects: the social and the cultural. The cultural aspect of institutions consists of the shared, learned values bearing on the satisfaction of some generally recognized need—for example, sex, hunger, care of the young, defense against other groups. This aspect is not be to underestimated or ignored, but the sociologist finds it insufficient *by itself;* he is concerned with the differentiated patterns of behavior required of specific categories of persons, and their functional interrelation, directed toward given needs. Thus the *social* institution comprehends a constellation of interdependent social roles relative to some biological and/or social function. And institutional change signifies any important alteration in the interrelations of interdependent social roles.

So much attention has been lavished on institutional change, in one form or another, that we cannot even attempt a substantive résumé of this embarrassing richness. In general, however, institutional change is principally represented by studies of familial, economic, political, and religious institutions, with important secondary attention to scientific, educational, and artistic institutions. Familial change has become a highly specialized field, with research emphasis on: changing roles and functions of family members; changes in the process of mate selection; changes in relation between family of orientation and family of procreation; changes in continuity of family life, as in studies of divorce and of reactions to such crisis situations as depression and wartime separation. A particularly noteworthy emphasis is the rather recent concern with class differences in familial changes.[30] Sociological analysis has not been extensively applied to *economic* change, although

[30] Texts concerned with these aspects include: E. W. Burgess and H. J. Locke, *The Family* (New York, 1945); W. W. Waller, *The Family,* revised by Reuben Hill (New York, 1951); Ruth S. Cavan, *The American Family* (New York, 1953); Howard Becker and Reuben Hill (eds.), *Family, Marriage, and Parenthood* (Boston, 1948). See also Reuben Hill, *Families Under Stress* (New York, 1949); and Mirra Komarovsky, *The Unemployed Man in the Depression* (New York, 1939).

the new speciality, industrial sociology, or perhaps the sociology of economic organization, can conceivably remedy this partial neglect of an immensely important institution. However, in addition to scattered social analyses by cultural anthropologists, there is a considerable literature on the development of capitalism as a social institution, the most representative being the work of Max Weber, Sombart, Merton, Veblen, Berle and Gardner, and Drucker.[31] As far as the developmental pattern of religious institutions is concerned, little of scientific importance was accomplished until Troeltsch, stimulated by Max Weber, supplied his famous conceptual scheme of religious types, although, again, cultural anthropologists and classical scholars have been furnishing descriptive accounts of developments in magic and ritual. Since Weber's death in 1920, we have had a number of studies constructed on the basis of his orientation; among these we might mention the work of Troeltsch, Wach, Honigsheim, Niebuhr, Becker, Francis, and Yinger.[32] (For a fuller account of this literature, consult Chap. 15 of this volume.)

In the field of political change, sociologists have focused attention on five tasks. Most often, it seems, they have analyzed revolutionary phenomena; this will be discussed in connection with the study of social movements. Earlier in this century, as a consequence of the "evolutionary" emphasis, the origins of the state were a source of fascination, as in the work of Oppenheimer, Hobhouse, MacIver, and Lowie.[33] A third focus has been the consideration of one facet of political development, for example, the development of military organization and warfare, or the development of political parties. More recently, political dynamics has been approached through certain characteristics of political personnel—for example, psychological features, occupational origins, and class position—as in the studies

[31] Max Weber, *General Economic History,* translated by F. A. Knight (Glencoe, Ill., 1950); Werner Sombart, *The Quintessence of Capitalism,* translated by M. Epstein (London, 1915); R. K. Merton, "Science, Technology, and Society in Seventeenth Century England," *Osiris,* 4 (1938), pp. 360-597; Thorstein Veblen, *The Theory of Business Enterprise* (New York, 1904); A. A. Berle, Jr., and G. C. Means, *The Modern Corporation and Private Property* (New York, 1935); Peter Drucker, *The End of Economic Man* (New York, 1939); and *The Future of Industrial Man* (New York, 1942).

[32] Max Weber, *Gesammelte Aufsätze zur Religionssoziologie* (Tübingen, 1920-1921), 3 vols. [a partial translation appears in *Essays in Sociology*. Part 3]; Ernst Troeltsch, *The Social Teaching of the Christian Churches* (New York, 1931); Joachim Wach, *The Sociology of Religion* (Chicago, 1944); H. Richard Niebuhr, *The Social Sources of Denominationalism* (New York, 1929); Howard Becker, *Systematic Sociology on the Basis of the* Beziehungslehre *and* Gebildelehre *of Leopold von Wiese* (New York, 1932; reissued, with new preface, Gary, Ind., 1950), Chap. 44; E. K. Francis, "The Russian Mennonites: From Religious to Ethnic Group," *AJS,* 53 (Sept., 1948), pp. 101-107, and "The Adjustment of a Peasant Group to a Capitalistic Economy," *RS,* 17 (Sept., 1952), pp. 218-228; J. Milton Yinger, *Religion in the Struggle for Power* (Durham, N.C., 1948).

[33] Franz Oppenheimer, *The State* (Indianapolis, 1913); R. M. MacIver, *The Modern State* (London, 1926); R. H. Lowie, *The Origin of the State* (New York, 1927).

of Lasswell, Mannheim, Gerth, and Abel.[34] Finally, there have been attempts at broad interpretations of political development in the Western world; outstanding in this respect are such writers as MacIver, Toynbee, Merriam, Holcombe, Barnes, and Nisbet.[35]

From Institutional to Community Change. Institutional change may of course be studied at the societal or community level, but the tendency has been to shift analytical focus from the former to the latter. Since the community is, from the sociologist's standpoint, a constellation of institutions, one complexity is thereby replaced by another; if specific institutional change on the societal level requires generalization of numerous communities or community types, the study of institutional change on the community level involves the task of coordinating and assessing varying degrees of change in several interdependent institutional areas. This task is not so easy or routine as it might seem; consequently, we have many community studies and community surveys but relatively few attempts to describe and interpret community change as we have defined it. The pioneer studies, principally in Britain and the U.S., were of rural communities and small towns. In the twenties and thirties somewhat larger units were included, as in the famous Middletown and Yankee City series. In the same period the Rural Life Studies of the Department of Agriculture provided several fine descriptive accounts of the commercialization and urbanization of farm communities.[36] Finally, there have been a few studies of rapid wartime changes in new or revivified communities.[37] Yet, despite the variety of locations and populations, an essential uniformity of results has emerged; basically, economic innovations and expansion of communication networks have intensified social differentiation, secularization, and urbanization, with resultant problems of social adjustment familiar to any alert newspaper reader.

Some Implications. The study of institutional change during the past

[34] H. D. Lasswell, *Psychopathology and Politics* (Chicago, 1930), and *Power and Personality,* New York, 1948); Karl Mannheim, *Ideology and Utopia,* translated by Louis Wirth and E. A. Shils (New York, 1936), part 3, section 2; Hans Gerth, "The Nazi Party: Its Leadership and Composition," *AJS,* 45 (Jan., 1940), pp. 517-541; Theodore Abel, *Why Hitler Came into Power* (New York, 1938).

[35] MacIver, *Society,* pp. 482-498; Toynbee, *op. cit.,* pp. 367-370; C. E. Merriam, *Political Power* (New York, 1934); H. E. Barnes, *Sociology and Political Theory* (New York, 1924); R. A. Nisbet, *The Quest for Community* (New York, 1953).

[36] Lynd and Lynd, *loc. cit.;* W. Lloyd Warner and P. S. Lunt, *The Social Life of a Modern Community* (New Haven, 1941), and *The Status System of a Modern Community* (New Haven, 1942). The most relevant studies made by the Department of Agriculture are: E. H. Bell, *Culture of a Contemporary Rural Community: Sublette, Kansas* (Washington, 1942); and E. O. Moe and C. C. Taylor, *Culture of a Contemporary Rural Community: Irwin, Iowa* (Washington, 1942).

[37] L. J. Carr and J. E. Stermer, *Willow Run* (New York, 1952); E. C. Banfield, *Government Project* (Glencoe, Ill., 1951); R. J. Havighurst and H. B. Morgan, *The Social History of a War-Boom Community* (New York, 1951).

four decades has thus far been apparently distinct from the question of social change in general. In the previous half-century, institutional change was studied as inseparable from social change, although this theoretical insight was marred by the bias of evolutionism. If more recent studies do not allow us to view social change as a series of inevitable stages, what *can* we extract from them of theoretical importance? First, these studies indicate that each institutional sector undergoes the same general *process* of change in all societies, regardless of varying tempi in change or of differing products of change. (This point will be elaborated in the last section of this chapter.) Second, a comparison of studies of developments in different institutional sectors reveals the importance of all institutional areas as foci of change, at one time or another. Consequently, any attempt to discover a *single* lever of change in the economic, religious, political, scientific, or familial institutions constitutes a dangerous oversimplification. Third, these studies offer evidence of an often neglected connection between institutional change and the development of stratification systems, a contribution of such different theorists as Marx and Cooley.[38] Fourth, we are given a mass of evidence that strongly confirms social and cultural explanations of change and virtually extinguishes, for all but the most recalcitrant minds, the theoretical validity of physical, biological, or geographic factors. Finally, although any theory of substantive stages in social change must remain suspect, these studies do suggest a *basic direction* (but not a final destination) *for limited periods of time* toward increasing social complexity, secondary social relationships, and urbanization. They do not indicate *inherent* limits in trends of change, as Sorokin insists; indeed, no form of inevitability can be deduced without some violence to the facts.

SOCIAL MOVEMENTS

One of the richest sources of data for the student of social change is the realm of social movements, the organized attempts to effect one or more basic institutional changes. Until very recently, most studies of social movements were careful descriptive accounts by social historians, rather than sociologists, but what was lacking in conceptualization and generalization was often compensated for by fullness of detail and an implicit concern for what some sociologists now call *group dynamics*. At present, there is an impressive literature dealing with political, economic, religious, and other types of social movements. In the field of religion, for example, we have several analyses of cultish and sectarian development, such as Father Divine and the Oxford Group Movement, and in the economic sector, mention should be made of various studies of European and American labor move-

[38] Marx, *op. cit.*, pp. 11-12; Karl Marx and Friedrich Engels, *The German Ideology* (New York, 1939), pp. 7-13; C. H. Cooley, *Social Organization* (New York, 1909), p. 140, and *Social Process* (New York, 1918), pp. 292, 302, 336.

ments, the social security campaign, and the development of business organization and integration.[39] However, political movements have so captured the imagination and attention of both historians and sociologists that social movements seem to many people to be largely political phenomena. We can distinguish two types of political movements: the peaceful, constitutional variety; and the revolutionary or violent type. The first is best illustrated by studies of agrarian movements in the U.S., the CCF in Canada, the Progressive movement, and prohibition.[40] Communism, fascism, and nazism are excellent examples of revolutionary social movements. Revolutionary movements have somehow stimulated more analytic explorations than constitutional movements and a number of attempts have been made to discover a generalized pattern or sequence in revolutions—attempts which seem to involve virtually all the theoretical problems of social change in general.[41]

SOCIAL PLANNING

Although social planning is at present in a theoretical jungle, its relevance to the study of social change may be provisionally clarified by viewing planning as a special case of the phenomena that make up "social movements." For if social movements include *all* organized attempts to produce institutional change, social planning largely encompasses those *rationally organized* activities which derive from attempts to anticipate, produce, and control social changes on the institutional and societal levels. Social planning may then be viewed as the crystallization of precedent politico-economic movements, a special but infrequent product of successful movements whose leaders genuinely seek social change, and not merely a replacement of élites. In the past few decades, there have been more controversies about planning than actual planning itself, and relatively few sociological studies of planning have appeared. The British experience in town-and-country planning, Scan-

[39] See, for example, A. W. Eister, *Drawing-Room Conversion* (Durham, N.C., 1950); R. A. Brady, *Business as a System of Power* (New York, 1943); P. S. Foner, *History of the Labor Movement in the United States* (New York, 1947); C. Wright Mills, *The New Men of Power* (New York, 1948); Adolph Sturmthal, *The Tragedy of European Labor* (New York, 1944); Hadley Cantril, *The Psychology of Social Movements* (New York, 1941), Chap. 7.

[40] S. P. Buck, *The Agrarian Crusade* (New Haven, 1920); J. D. Hicks, *The Populist Revolt* (Minneapolis, 1931); Theodore Saloutos and J. D. Hicks, *Agricultural Discontent in the Middle West, 1900-1939* (Madison, 1951); Alvin Boskoff, "The Farm Bloc and Agrarian Ideology" (unpublished Master's thesis, Columbia University, 1948); C. A. Chambers, *California Farm Organizations* (Berkeley, 1952); S. M. Lipset, *Agrarian Socialism* (Berkeley, 1950); K. C. MacKay, *The Progressive Movement of 1924* (New York, 1947); P. H. Odegard, *Pressure Politics* (New York, 1928); A. M. Lee, "Techniques of Social Reform: An Analysis of the New Prohibition Drive," *ASR*, 9 (Feb., 1944), pp. 65-77.

[41] L. P. Edwards, *The Natural History of Revolutions* (Chicago, 1927); Crane Brinton, *The Anatomy of Revolution* (New York, 1938); P. A. Sorokin, *The Sociology of Revolution* (Philadelphia, 1925); R. D. Hopper, "The Revolutionary Process: A Frame of Reference for the Study of Revolutionary Movements," *SF*, 28 (March, 1950), pp. 270-279.

dinavian family and population control, French *planification,* Soviet Russia's vast experiments in socio-economic transformation, and the varied efforts in city and regional planning in the U.S., plus the instructive essays in planning under the New Deal—all have been well documented, although generalized analyzes of wider relevance have been made only in the case of the TVA, the New Deal, and Soviet planning.[42]

Some Implications. In general, studies of social movements and social planning have emphasized four aspects of social change that underlie the modern approach to change. First, they inevitably focus on conditions of strain and maladjustment. Second, there is often an attempt to determine the social characteristics of leaders and active participants. Third, the crucial question of power and force is explicitly confronted as a reality (good or bad) in matters of social change. Fourth, the widespread concern for understanding the success or failure of specific movements has produced many hypotheses basic to the comprehension of change.

ACCULTURATION STUDIES

When anthropologists study acculturation, or culture change, as a process of contact between different peoples, they almost invariably furnish excellent evidence of social change; in fact, the recent anthropological emphasis on acculturation has all but shattered any theoretical barriers between anthropologists and sociologists (see Chap. 18, pp. 528-549). It is quite common, for example, to find creditable observations on such basic sociological phenomena as developments in intragroup processes, emergence of new groupings, social distance, power relations, stratification, and leadership, and, in view of the anthropologists' partiality toward kinship, family structure. And now that studies of acculturation give us a broad coverage of that phenomenon—among American Indians, in Central and South America, the South and Central Pacific, and various regions of Africa—there is developing a generalized picture of acculturation based on appropriately comparative situations. Moreover, this fund of acculturation research probably constitutes one of the more significant sources of data and ideas relevant to the study of social change. No other body of data, for example, so clearly substantiates and illustrates the *processual* nature of social change. Furthermore, we can extract from this type of research several important theoretical leads. Two such clues also derive from studies of social movements: the role of coercion and the characteristics of key personnel in social change. But acculturation studies often furnish, in addition, comprehensive accounts of social and

[42] Alva Myrdal, *Nation and Family* (New York, 1941); R. A. Brady, *Crisis in Britain* (Berkeley, 1952); Gregory Bienstock *et al., Management in Russian Industry and Agriculture* (New York, 1944); David Lilienthal, *TVA: Democracy on the March* (New York, 1944); Philip Selznick, *TVA at the Grass Roots* (Berkeley, 1949); Alvin Boskoff, *Social Planning in Modern Society* (unpublished manuscript), Chaps. 1-2.

psychological tensions and appraisals of specific innovations, of transitional social structures, and of reaction patterns of defense against innovation. We shall return to some of these aspects in the last section.

SYNTHESES OF HISTORICAL CHANGE

Finally, there have been classic and near-classic attempts to survey and interpret the essential pattern of change in recorded human experience. These broad theoretical excursions into the materials of history invariably mix sociology and philosophy (and even theology), but, although they are open to detailed criticism on questions of fact, methodology, and interpretation, they contain enough valuable insights to justify continual reference and study. Four of these panoramic theories of social change will serve as examples.

Brooks Adams. Brooks Adams, tracing change from the Greeks to modern times, published his famous analysis, *The Law of Civilization and Decay,* in 1896; but his thesis was quite popular in the twenties and a handsome edition, with a preface by Charles A. Beard, appeared as late as 1943. According to Adams, social change is cyclical and reveals itself in four concomitant processes. The most fundamental of these is the change from physical dispersal to population concentration, which is correlated with a movement from "barbarism" to "civilization" on the socio-cultural level. But societies also exhibit change in the manifestation of human energy, from an emphasis on fear to the sinister motivations of greed. As these processes develop, the dominant social institution shifts from the religious to the military and then to the economic sectors; contrapuntally, social dominance of the priesthood passes to a warrior class and thence to a commercial class symbolized by the usurer. The development of "ripe" civilization—characterized by greed, urbanization, economic dominance, and a commercial élite—inevitably brings decay, since both moral integration and military ability diminish to the point at which fear and its associated factors resume central significance.

Spengler. In 1918, a previously unknown German secondary-school instructor, Oswald Spengler, seasoned this world view with generous dashes of symbolism and fatalism in his *Decline of the West.* Approaching the major societies as organismic entities, Spengler diagnosed their life-histories as the emergence of an adolescent, early "culture" stage, inevitably followed by a matured "late culture," and finally yielding to a decadent civilization phase comparable to senility. At the "culture" stage, society is marked by rural, dispersed organization and the dominance of priesthood and nobility (a warrior class). As cultures reach maturity, well-articulated estate groups give way to an increasingly urbanized class structure (at the town level), after which intensified urbanization produces new classes (the *third estate* and the *mass*) and the eventual destruction of the traditions and social organization of earlier phases. Civilization represents, paradoxically, both the height of development and the incubus of social degeneration. And history is the record of successive cycles of socio-cultural development in which *cause* is replaced by Destiny and social mechanisms are but manifestations of race, blood, the cosmic, and sex. "History is heavy with fate but free of laws." Social change is therefore a process edged in black.

Toynbee. Spengler's fatalism was fashionable in the twenties and even later, but the passion for objectivity, or at least for some semblance of objectivity, produced two other intellectual exercises in social-change analysis that contain interesting variations in method and interpretation. In the late thirties, a scholarly English historian, Arnold J. Toynbee, began publication of his massive *A Study of History,* which now consists of ten volumes. If we can disregard his oddly assorted objectives (theological-philosophical and sociological), there is much food for thought in his analysis of the rise, growth, and decline of recorded societies and their affiliates. Toynbee views these societies comparatively and collectively as the data of a comprehensive global process of social change in which the "grand serial order" flows from primitive societies (the relatively stationary structures) to the primary civilizations, to the later affiliated secondary civilizations, and finally, to their specialized offspring, the so-called higher (worldwide) religions. In contrast to Spengler's trendless cycle, Toynbee posits a teleological cumulation of human efforts that creates an incompletely realized but novel social unit—which we might call the *developed religious community.*

Toynbee's abstraction of a basic social mechanics is far from Spengler's biological symbolism. Essentially, primitive societies reach the level of civilization by developing *creative minorities,* who devise adequate *responses* to the successive *challenges* of their total environment. An adequate response appears to emerge from the "withdrawal-and-return" of creative persons, but the reader is not enlightened as to *how* this temporary isolation produces "correct" responses. As challenges appear and are satisfactorily removed, societies become progressively differentiated and complex, until inevitably, the creative minority degenerates into a *dominant minority* relying on force rather than invention to maintain its position. This occurs, Toynbee asserts, because the successful creator finds his success a handicap in newer, stranger, more difficult challenges: the so-called *nemesis of creativity;* a required change in élites is not easily obtained since previous success is no spur to abdication. This is the Time of Troubles, prelude to disintegration, in which the dominant minority eventually responds by creating a *universal state* to check social breakdown, and the internal proletariat (primarily urban masses) in turn produces a socio-cultural schism by elaborating a higher religious system as the basis of a *universal church.* To complicate matters, the external proletariat (the less-developed peoples on the periphery of the universal state) aggravates the process of disintegration by becoming a military menace precisely when the civilization is at its weakest.

Sorokin. In his full-scale survey of social change, Pitirim Sorokin, a leading sociologist, also draws on the major historical societies. Sorokin has reduced the bewildering complexity of world social change to a basic cycle of *cultural change*. Instead of discovering any recognizable trend in *social* dynamics, he marshals an impressive but unconvincing battery of frequency distributions to support his contention that social processes are "varyingly recurrent." However, there are certain limited regularities in social change that accompany an underlying process of cultural replacement. The character of social relations, systems of authority and stratification, war and revolution, etc., are all responsive to the development of three relatively integrated systems of *cultural premises* about the nature of reality: the *ideational, sensate,* and *idealistic* "supersystems." These alternative premises—that reality is supersensory, sensory, or mixed—constitute the three possible ways of apprehending reality; but Sorokin fails to tell us why any one becomes predominant in any given era. He tells us instead that the sensate and ideational supersystems are each partial and inadequate representations of genuine reality and that therefore each, when overdeveloped, leads to its own eventual displacement.[43]

Although Sorokin freely criticizes all theories of social change, and particularly those that emphasize sequence or stages of development, his approach does not completely repudiate the notion of some abstract regularity. His principle of immanent change, although modified by his recognition of the secondary role of external factors and "the principle of limits," implicitly involves a relatively definite developmental pattern. Furthermore, he posits an inner dialectic in socio-cultural processes: overabundance of some emphasis in social systems leads to the dominance of its opposite, etc. But Sorokin in addition points to an independent convergence in theory among Spengler, Toynbee, and himself. His ideational supersystem corresponds to Toynbee's growth phase of civilization, while his idealistic and sensate supersystems respectively coincide with the breakdown and disintegration stages in Toynbee's analysis.[44] Thus, although Sorokin pays more attention to unanticipated variation and indeterminancy, his central analysis does not radically deviate from the apocalyptic conception of social change developed by Adams, Spengler, and Toynbee.

Some Implications. Despite the high level of generality at which they are pitched, these four systems of interpreting social change give dramatic focus to several specific problems crucial to the study of social change. Adams and Sorokin strongly emphasize the importance of value-systems and changes in what Herskovits has recently called "cultural focus." All four, in

[43] Sorokin, *Social and Cultural Dynamics,* vol. 4.

[44] Sorokin, *Society, Culture, and Personality,* pp. 643-644.

varying degrees, recognize the necessity of viewing social change through the phenomena of stratification, power, and coercion; and all four likewise repeately demonstrate that social change involves tensions, maladjustments, and often regressions—although their interpretations tend to be pessimistic. Furthermore, although each theorist develops the basic insight in different ways, each identifies social change as a more or less *intelligible process* that can be investigated in terms of successive problem-phases. Toynbee, in addition, has given some prominence to the nature of the innovative phase in his discussion of creative minorities and challenge-and-response.

Understanding Social Change

METHODS OF STUDY

After laboring to redress the balance between empirical research and theory, modern students of social change do not seem to have discarded the ultimate objective of their several efforts: the comprehension and understanding of change, its causes, conditions, and its general direction. But with the evolutionary approach in deserved disrepute, there has been a continuous search for alternative methods of organizing the accumulated data, concepts, and hypotheses bearing on this difficult sociological problem. In general, the statistical method has been of limited utility—principally in studies of special aspects of social change, such as social mobility, and in organizing the materials of *cultural* change, as in studies of inventions and their cumulation through time.[45] What is emerging instead, despite the enveloping fervor of quantitative enthusiasts, is a reliance on two or three complementary qualitative orientations designed to capture the maximum of meaning and order from the myriad manifestations of social change.

Constructed Types. A device favored in the past twenty-five years is the use of *constructed types* of social and cultural systems in analyzing the data of social change. There is, in fact, clear evidence of the use of this approach in the work of Tönnies (1887) and perhaps Durkheim (1893), but whereas this method was then used incidentally in connection with other problems, it has now become a key tool in the study of social change. Essentially, the use of constructed types involves the conceptualization of opposed (or more recently, graded) sets of socio-cultural systems, purposely accentuated and simplified in order to provide unambiguous reference points when analyzing specific cases. Whereas Tönnies viewed change as the displacement of *Gemeinschaft* by *Gesellschaft,* modern sociologists have developed more ela-

[45] An interesting application of the statistical method in this area is Alice Davis, "Technicways in American Civilization," *SF,* 18 (March, 1940), pp. 317-330.

borate analyses in terms of *sacred* and *secular* types (Park, Hughes, Becker); *folk* and *urban* types (Redfield, Linton, Miner, Kroeber); *folk society* and *state civilization* (Giddings, Odum); *repetitive* and *changing* types (Ogburn, Gluckman); *ideational, sensate,* and *idealistic* types (Sorokin); and *chance-discovery, invention,* and *planning* types (Mannheim). Redfield's comparative account of four Yucatan communities and Becker's study of change in Ionia and Athens are perhaps the best examples of this approach.[46] But as experience has widened, sociologists, particularly Becker, have seen fit to construct a number of intermediate, transitional, or subtypes to facilitate analysis of social change processes previously lumped together by the use of paired, dichotomous types.[47] This increasing sophistication in the construction and application of referential social types promises gratifying results, if the potentialities and limitations of the types are continually appraised throughout the next decade or so.

Personality and Change. With the recent cross-fertilization of disciplines devoted to the "study of man," there has begun to develop an interesting approach to social change that combines the typological emphasis and the orientations of the psychologist and the cultural anthropologist. This approach is the attempt to grasp the pattern of change as it reveals itself in the behavior of typically implicated persons whose personality structure indirectly "records" the new potentialities, problems, and valuations accompanying some identifiable series of social changes. In practice, this involves the construction of empirically based personality types whose manifestation and predominance are correlated with specific eras of socio-cultural variation. In effect, this method provides an additional index of social change and enables the investigator to check his research on the critical institutional level with properly analysed findings on the behavioral level. Hughes and Becker first demonstrated the possibilities of such an appraisal by distinguishing several

[46] R. E. Park, *Race and Culture* (Glencoe, Ill., 1951), pp. 12-16; Howard Becker, *Through Values to Social Interpretation* (Durham, N.C., 1950), Chap. 1; Robert Redfield, *The Folk Culture of Yucatan* (Chicago, 1941); Ralph Linton, *The Study of Man* (New York, 1936), Chap. 16; Horace Miner, "The Folk-Urban Continuum," *ASR,* 17 (Oct., 1952), pp. 529-537; A. L. Kroeber, *Anthropology* (2nd ed.; New York, 1948), pp. 280-286; F. H. Giddings, *Civilization and Society* (New York, 1931); H. W. Odum, *Understanding Society* (New York, 1947), Chaps. 12-14, 20; W. F. Ogburn, "Stationary and Changing Societies," *AJS,* 42 (July, 1936), pp. 16-32; Max Gluckman, "Some Processes of Social Change Illustrated from Zululand," *African Studies,* 1 (1942), pp. 243-260; Sorokin, *Social and Cultural Dynamics,* vols. 1, 4; Mannheim, *Man and Society,* pp. 50-54, 369-381; Howard Becker, "Ionia and Athens: Studies in Secularization" (unpublished Ph.D. thesis, University of Chicago, 1930).

[47] See especially the following works by Howard Becker: "Current Sacred-Secular Theory and Its Development," (Chap. 6 of the present volume); *Man in Reciprocity* (New York, 1956), Chaps. 10-13; and "Looking at Values and Value-Systems," in I. T. Sanders, J. R. Schwendeman, R. B. Woodbury, and Howard Becker, *Societies Around the World* (one-volume abridgment; New York, 1956), pp. 318-398.

personality types in the transition from sacred to secular social systems. In a bold combination of anthropological, sociological, and psychiatric insights, Kardiner and Linton traced with much care and analytical skill certain changes in the "basic personality type" of simpler peoples which were presumed to be correlated with antecedent social and cultural innovations.[48] In the meanwhile, with the aid of Rorschach tests and TAT's, anthropologists were unwittingly experimenting with the same approach by gathering impressive data on personality changes associated with the process of acculturation—as in the work of Hallowell, Esther Goldfrank, and Laura Thompson. And most recently, David Riesman and his associates have examined the consequences of the change from tradition-directed to inner-directed to outer-directed character types as these have emerged in consecutive phases of American social and demographic structures.[49]

The Functional-Process Approach. The third modern approach to social change studies is, paradoxically, the most significant, yet the most difficult to portray in brief compass. Students of social change have implicitly used it in a more or less fragmentary fashion for decades; it has apparently emerged unplanned and largely unnoted, an excellent example of *conjunctural phenomena* (MacIver's phrase). It may be provisionally labeled the functional-process approach. It is not a product of a single thinker or even a sociological *coterie* but rather a crescive configuration of numerous insights that seem to constitute a distinctive pattern of investigation.

Following a basic tradition established principally by Cooley, Park, Simmel, Wiese, and MacIver, the functional-process approach serves to reduce the multiform phenomena of social change to a manageable complexity by conceptualizing the approach to any social change (regardless of content, location, or direction) as an *analytic process* composed of separable but consecutive research problems or phases. Unlike the evolutionary approach, this method does not involve the search for inevitable substantive "stages" but merely conceives social change as generically consisting of a sequence of problems (not solutions) for implicated actors. These problems of specific persons become, on proper conceptualization, the key scientific problems for the student of social change. In this way, the broad and often speculative problems of social change are converted into definite research questions on which truly comparative data can be gathered. As a matter of fact, this also

[48] Becker, *Through Values to Social Interpretation,* pp. 78-90; E. C. Hughes, "Personality Types and the Division of Labor," *AJS,* 33 (March, 1928), pp. 754-768; Abram Kardiner, *Psychological Frontiers of Society* (New York, 1945).

[49] A. I. Hallowell, "Aggression in Salteaux Society," *Psychiatry,* 3 (1940), pp. 395-407, and "The Rorschach Technique in the Study of Personality and Culture," *AA,* 47, (1945), pp. 195-210; Esther Goldfrank, "Historic Change and Social Character," *ibid.,* 45 (Jan.-March, 1943), pp. 67-83; Laura Thompson and Alice Joseph, "White Pressures on Indian Personality and Culture," *AJS,* (July, 1947), pp. 17-22; David Riesman, *The Lonely Crowd* (New Haven, 1950).

provides a logical and practical basis for specialization in research on social change.

Moreover, each analytical phase is regarded both as a limited field of investigation, complete in itself, and as the product of antecedent phases, so that process and continuity are not sacrificed on the altar of analysis. In practice, each phase of the social-change process is treated as a system of functionally interrelated parts (e.g., social groups, social roles, institutions) whose relative equilibrium is disturbed by the deviant operation of one or more component structures. This is of course a form of the structural-functional approach, which, despite the otherwise deserved strictures of its critics, seems to be useful in the study of change as well as of order. Essentially, then, the functional-process approach offers an integrated *schema* for further research and a guide for collating and appraising a formidable mass of variably relevant investigations over the past forty years.

SOME CONCLUSIONS BASED ON THESE METHODS

The fruits of these methods constitute an immensely variegated yield and at first glance appear to be sadly indigestible. However, sociological interest in social change has expressed itself on two distinct levels. First, there is an abiding concern for broad generalizations applicable to all or most of recorded history—the *macroscopic* view. At the same time, research has been partly deflected to limited ranges of social change discernible in brief time periods of particular societies or communities— the *microscopic* view. Since the available data and the problems posed are clearly different on each level, the results are not directly comparable. Perhaps this difference is best described as one of *intent:* whereas the macroscopic view searches for the basic causes and direction in social change, the microscopic view regards these as ultimate problems, to be deferred until empirical generalizations can be made about specific phases of the change process.

Causes of Social Change. With negligible exceptions during the past forty years, macroscopic theorists of social change have demonstrated a remarkable tendency to converge in their explanations of social change. In no real sense can we now distinguish contending "schools" among sociologists, as Sorokin did twenty-five years ago in his account of not-so-contemporary sociological theories. Instead we find a widespread emphasis on socio-cultural factors in change, although this is expressed in at least three forms. The primacy of *economic* and *technological* factors has been a basic theme in the work of such writers as Veblen, Keller, Ogburn, Chapin, Odum, Barnes, Murdock, and Leslie White.[50] Under the influence of cultural anthropologists (parti-

[50] Thorstein Veblen, *The Theory of the Leisure Class* (New York, 1934); Keller, *Societal Evolution,* pp. 143-149, 261; Ogburn, *Social Change,* pp. 200-211; F. S. Chapin, *Cultural Change* (New York, 1928); Odum, *op. cit.,* Chap. 15, 19-20; H. E. Barnes, *Historical Sociology* (New York, 1948), p. 158; G. P. Murdock, *Social Structure* (New York, 1949),

cularly Kroeber, Goldenweiser, Lowie, and Herskovits), there has also been a pervasive tendency to explain social change as a product of *general cultural processes* of variation, diffusion, and acculturation, as in the relevant theories of Vierkandt, Alfred Weber, Sorokin, MacIver, Hobhouse, Ginsberg, and Parsons.[51] Finally, and by no means in opposition to tempered versions of the preceding explanatory models, there are specifically *social* theories of social change, which ascribe a critical role to the operation of normally dynamic aspects of social structure—such as systems of stratification, the power structure, institutional role-configurations. No systematic exposition of this theoretical position has been formulated, but some indications of the potential value of this explanatory tool can be found in the work of Max Weber, Teggart, MacIver, Mannheim, Sorokin, Redfield, Becker, Pareto, Gluckman, Merton, Toynbee, and Bateson.[52]

The Direction of Social Change. It has been extremely difficult for theorists of social change to resist supplementing causal inquiries with generous conclusions about major trends in social change. The search for dominant *patterns* of change, for an over-all *direction* in change, possesses a perennial fascination, despite the enormous complexity of social changes and the patent failure of the evolutionary doctrines so popular before World War I. Faced with these difficulties and yet attracted by the seductive nature of the basic problem, sociologists in recent years have come to exercise a commendable caution that has channeled discussion along two notable lines. One respectable solution summarizes historical trends in an objective but highly generalized fashion that bars the door to inevitability and teleology. A good illustration is MacIver's "schema of social evolution," in which the level of *communal customs* (a primitive *fusion* of political, economic, familial, and religious practices) is superseded by *differentiated communal institutions* (distinctive forms of political, economic, and other procedures), and finally by *differentiated associations* (specialized groups, such as the state, the corporation and the church performing particularized cultural functions). This analysis of trends holds substantially for specific peoples and, with modifications, for the length and breadth of human social organization.[53] Incidentally, Mac-

p. 137; L. A. White, "Energy and the Evolution of Culture," *AA,* (July-Sept., 1943), pp. 335-356.

[51] Alfred Vierkandt, *Die Stetigkeit im Kulturwandel* (Leipzig, 1908); Alfred Weber, *loc. cit.;* Sorokin, *Society, Culture, and Personality,* Chaps. 39, 43, 46; MacIver, *Society,* pp. 443, 462-466; L. T. Hobhouse, *Social Development;* Morris Ginsberg, *Sociology* (London, 1934); Talcott Parsons, *The Social System* (Glencoe, Ill., 1951), p. 487.

[52] See especially Max Weber, *Theory of Social and Economic Organization,* Part 3; F. J. Teggart, *Theory and Processes of History* (Berkeley, 1941), pp. 196-197, 278-279; Mannheim, *Man and Society,* Parts 1, 2, 5, and *Freedom, Power, and Democratic Planning* (New York, 1950), pp. 46-56; Becker, *op. cit.,* Chaps. 2, 3; and Gregory Bateson, *Naven* (Cambridge, 1936), pp. 176-194.

[53] MacIver, *Society,* pp. 497-498.

Iver's schema is somewhat like Toynbee's "grand serial order" of social change, although Toynbee explicitly posits a spiritual ultimacy that is unacceptable to most sociologists.

Another approach to the trend of social change is characterized by concentration on the nature of change in a limited segment of human history, principally Western civilization and its component societies in the last millennium. With this specialized focus, sociologists have generally interpreted major trends through the use of somewhat similar sets of constructed types and as a consequence a gratifying unanimity has been reached with respect to the basic development of the Western world. This collective appraisal summarizes the pattern of modern change as one of steadily increasing secularization and reliance on formalized organizations, with the result that the potentiality of further change has approached maximization. This is the position, for example, of Tönnies, Max Weber, MacIver, Znaniecki, Park, Odum, Redfield, Becker, Mannheim, Ginsberg, Sorokin, Toynbee, and Parsons.[54] However, there is a persistently "cautious" group—principally among American cultural anthropologists—that is quite skeptical about reducing the phenomena of change to any particular pattern. Alfred Weber is probably the leading exponent of this view, ably seconded by Kroeber, Lowie, and Herskovits.[55]

The Process of Social Change

There is little doubt that these general theories of social change have been provocative and valuable exercises in synthesis and interpretation; but they provide rather diffuse explanations that have extremely limited applicability to concrete, ongoing changes. Fortunately, the current emphasis on *processual* analysis of change promises to augment our understanding by furnishing data and a set of more modest generalizations for specified phases of the over-all process. Although this approach is still somewhat embryonic, it is possible to summarize pertinent investigations in the form of a provisional *schema of social change* consisting of five crucial problem-areas.

1. SOURCES OF SOCIAL DEVIATION

Practically speaking, social change presents itself to the sociologist as *collective deviations from established patterns*. Consequently, attention is often

[54] Consult the previously cited works of these authors.

[55] A. Weber, *op. cit.*, pp. 31, 47, 57-60; A. L. Kroeber, *Configurations of Culture Growth* (Berkeley, 1944), and *The Nature of Culture*, pp. 157-165; R. H. Lowie, *Culture and Ethnology* (New York, 1929); M. J. Herskovits, *Man and his Works* (New York, 1947), Chaps. 34, 36.

given to a structural description of antecedent social systems as a basis for fruitful comparison. But the major objective of analysis at this point is to uncover *proximate* sources of deviation, in contrast to the nineteenth-century quest for ultimate origins clothed in speculation and immune to verification. Thanks to anthropological studies of diffusion, acculturation, and culture contacts, an obvious but important factor in deviation has been well documented; and it is particularly noteworthy that many of these studies provide evidence not only of culture change (in acculturation) but also of *social* accommodations (to coin a term: *associalization*). Out of these studies has arisen a body of theory, constructed by Teggart, Park, Redfield, Becker, and others, which explains fundamental deviations by reference to migrations, intrusions, social collisions, and the development of prolonged accessibility to alien influences.[56]

As our focus has shifted to complex societies, external sources of deviation have been found to offer limited clues. With the modern emphasis on societies as functioning systems, deviation has proved to be a relatively "normal" aspect of concrete societies and thus much research and thinking is devoted to revealing "internal" situations which produce deviation and change. Essentially, this quest has involved analysis of two types of conditions: sources of strains, tensions, and practical contradictions; and permissive but somewhat unconscious variations. Thomas, Ellwood, Gillin, and Hallowell have noted the continued variable effects of the socialization process as an underlying source of unspectacular deviation. Parsons reminds us that approved behavior usually falls within a certain *range of acceptability,* even on the important institutional level.[57] Similarly, as Merton and Mandelbaum have shown, societies normally operate with at least three sorts of directives to actors: the *prescriptive* or *invariant,* which embody unequivocal definitions of one acceptable form of behavior; the *preferred,* in which moral weight is attached to one of several permissible alternatives; and areas of *free choice* or *neutral variation,* where all possible responses are regarded as acceptable within the scope of some over-all guiding pattern or theme.[58]

[56] Teggart, *op. cit.,* pp. 151, 195-197, 272; Becker, *op. cit.,* Chaps. 1-3, and "Forms of Population Movement," *SF,* 9 (Dec., 1930; Mar., 1931), pp. 147-160, 351-361; Park, *Race and Culture,* pp. 10-13, 350-355; Redfield, *op. cit.,* Chap. 12.

[57] W. I. Thomas, *Primitive Behavior* (New York, 1937), pp. 7, 612; John Gillin, "Parallel Cultures and the Inhibition to Acculturation in a Guatemalan Community," *SF* (October, 1945), pp. 1-14; C. A. Ellwood, *The Psychology of Human Society* (New York, 1925), pp. 214-215; A. Irving Hallowell, "Sociopsychological Aspects of Acculturation," in Ralph Linton (ed.), *The Science of Man in the World Crisis* (New York, 1945), pp. 182-183; Talcott Parsons, *Essays in Sociological Theory Pure and Applied* (Glencoe, Ill., 1949), p. 278.

[58] R. K. Merton, "Intermarriage and the Social Structure: Fact and Theory," *Psychiatry* (Aug., 1941), pp. 366-368; David Mandelbaum, "Form, Variation, and Meaning of a Ceremony," in R. F. Spencer (ed.), *Method and Perspective in Anthropology* (Minneapolis, 1954), pp. 74-79; Linton, *The Study of Man,* Chap. 16.

In a sense, these universal structural features comprise a substratum of deviation that may be tentatively characterized as potentially significant, given sufficient time and the aggravation of more dramatic conditions. During the past few decades, increasing concern for both the obvious and the more subtle *dysfunctioning* of societies has opened new possibilities by providing careful analyses of strains, tensions, dissatisfactions, and discrepancies traceable to specific parts of concrete societies or communities. According to this functional approach, deviation is a variably conscious response to personal and group difficulties experienced in the process of enacting accepted social roles and occupying assigned status positions. This functional source of deviation has been phrased in four related ways that have become conceptual mooring-points in contemporary sociology.

Role Conflicts. The first approach traces deviation to unanticipated role conflicts generated by a presumably "normal" ongoing social system. Parsons and Merton have elaborated the basic theory of this process with particular incisiveness, and Merton has clarified the major type of discrepancy between culturally defined goals and institutionalized means in his oft-quoted analyses of innovation, ritualism, and retreatism. Cultural anthropologists seem to point to a similar condition (drawn from acculturation research) when they refer to *dominant cleavages* (Gluckman), *radical oppositions* (Godfrey and Monica Wilson), and the process of *schismogenesis* (Bateson).[59] Strangely enough, schismogenesis has been largely neglected by sociologists, although the concept provides the most general theoretical explanation of internalized deviation. As conceptualized by Bateson, who has contributed comparative analyses of the process among the Iatmul and the Balinese, schismogenesis refers to differentiation of norms and roles resulting from cumulative interaction among persons of the same society or of acculturating societies. Role differentiation develops as a by-product of the search for maximization of such universal values as prestige, esteem, and security. Unless the process is checked by specific socio-cultural controls (e.g., government intervention), conflicts may arise between opposite roles (complementary schismogenesis). or between similar but competing roles (symmetrical schismogenesis). In either case, the give-and-take of acceptable interaction produces patterned deviations which both originate and express strains and incompatibilities.

Blockage of Need Patterns. A related search for deviation emphasizes the instrumental character of social systems and hence traces deviant behavior to inadequate satisfaction of biological and socially acquired needs. This is of course the basic position of psychoanalytic theory in its variant forms, but

[59] R. K. Merton, "Social Structure and Anomie," *ASR,* 3 (Oct., 1938), pp. 672-682; Gluckman, *op. cit.,* pp. 249-250; Godfrey Wilson and Monica Wilson, *The Analysis of Social Change* (Cambridge, 1945), pp. 125-134; Bateson, *Naven,* pp. 184-193, and "Bali: The Value-System of a Steady State," in M. Fortes (ed.), *Social Structure* (Cambridge, 1949).

the major exponents of a comprehensive functional analysis are probably Radcliffe-Brown and Malinowski. The former, for example, explains all deviation and change as adaptations to significant need-frustrations. Malinowski, who became interested in culture contact late in his career, allows even wider scope for deviation by regarding the creation of new needs (whatever their source) as an important source of deviation.[60] In recent years, this general position has been incorporated into sociology by Parsons and his disciples, who have abstracted a set of "functional prerequisites," the relative satisfaction of which serves to explain degrees of conformity and deviation. An interesting development in this area is the attempt by John Gillin to apply the principles of learning theory to the process in which need-frustration results in deviation.[61]

Crisis. Crisis and its variant conceptualizations have been perennial analytical tools in the quest for internalized sources of deviation. The classic formulation by W. I. Thomas in 1909 interpreted social order as the routine satisfaction of biological needs and, by implication, social needs. Smooth functioning of a social system involves adequate *control,* or need-satisfaction. However, when habitual activity fails to obtain such control, the resultant di urbance of routine creates a *crisis* which in turn awakens *attention,* the attitude which seeks to manipulate things in order to obtain control. Thus, attention, reborn in crisis, expresses itself in new or deviant behavior designed to restore control. Thomas did not clarify the factors in crisis, but he did try to relate the character of deviation to such factors as mental ability, the level of cultural complexity, and socially structured attitudes toward change. Max Weber employed essentially the same scheme in his sociology of religion, particularly in his analysis of the origins of prophecy, conceptualized as deviant religious ideas. More recently, the concept of crisis has been successfully applied to deviant behavior connected with revolutions and acculturation.[62]

Cultural Integration. Sorokin has developed a fourth functional approach to deviation. Distinguishing between logico-meaningfully integrated

[60] A. R. Radcliffe-Brown, "On the Concept of Function in Social Science," *AA,* 37 (July-Sept., 1935), pp. 394-402, and "Kinship Terminologies in California," *ibid.* (1935), p. 531; Bronislaw Malinowski, *A Scientific Theory of Culture and Other Essays* (Chapel Hill, N.C., 1944), p. 41, and *The Dynamics of Culture Change* (New Haven, 1945), pp. 27, 54, 71.

[61] Parsons, *Essays,* pp. 6, 33-36; M. J. Levy, *The Structure of Society* (Princeton, 1952), pp. 43-45, 62-72, 151; John Gillin, "Acquired Drives in Culture Contact," *AA,* 44 (Oct.-Dec., 1942), pp. 545-554, and *The Ways of Men* (New York, 1948), Chaps. 11, 25.

[62] Weber, *Essays in Sociology,* Part 3; W. I. Thomas, *Source Book for Social Origins* (Boston, 1909), pp. 16-21; Paul Meadows, "Behavioral Bases of Social Movements," *SSR,* 28 (Nov.-Dec., 1943), pp. 112-117; Laura Thompson, *Culture in Crisis* (New York, 1953); E. N. Anderson, *Process Versus Power* (Lincoln, 1952), pp. 20-25; Ralph Linton (ed.), *Acculturation in Seven American Indian Tribes* (New York, 1940).

social systems (those organized in terms of guiding sets of logically consistent values) and "congeries" (accidental or temporary juxtaposition of socio-cultural systems), Sorokin relates the possibility and significance of deviation to the character of these two referential types of social system. Congeries, representing a minimum of meaningful integration, consequently manifests the maximum vulnerability to external influence; deviation, therefore, is unavoidable and incessant. Since no genuine order exists in congeries, deviation is a type of "order" rather than divergence from order. On the other hand, integrated socio-cultural systems, which are said to be relatively immune from external influences, develop changes (Sorokin does not call them "deviations") which are inherent in the normal, interrelated functioning of their component parts. The source of change, according to this approach, is not in difficulties of adjustment or need-frustration, but in an unexplained "unfolding of . . . inherent potentialities."[63] Consequently, the concept of deviation is inapplicable, since all or most changes in such systems express an "expected" line of development.

These four attempts to locate sources of deviation, collectively considered, have incidentally clarified two important issues often confronted in general discussions of social change. For one thing, they tend to indicate the equivocal nature of social-control mechanisms; although we have been accustomed to view social control as a process that *inhibits* deviation, at least two of these approaches compel us to regard social control as sometimes unwittingly inspiring deviation. Secondly, the old controversy about diffusion *vs.* independent variation as factors in social change is rather deftly consigned to the realm of fruitless forensics by all four analyses. Essentially, the functional analysis of deviation recognizes both internal and external potentials for deviation, but neither source attains significance until members of a given social system are thereby confronted with difficulties, strains, undesirable discrepancies—which are taken to be the motive power for deviation. Thus, external pressures become critical only when they are "internalized" within a social system and are experienced derivatively as strains and tensions. What this accomplishes especially is a recognition of the fundamental theoretical similarity—as far as process is concerned—between immanent change and the phenomena of conquest and acculturation.

2. INNOVATION

Whatever its source, deviation manifests itself in a process of innovation, either in some independent creation or in creative application of some alien pattern. Innovation is of course extraordinarily widespread, although most innovations probably remain unrecognized or fail to achieve social acceptance. Nevertheless, sociologists have only recently begun to given careful

[63] Sorokin, *Society, Culture, and Personality,* pp. 332-335 and Chap. 46.

attention to innovation as a stage in the over-all process of social change. At present, we are not very clear about the connection between innovation and the presumed sources of deviation; and it is no longer possible to intone "necessity is the mother of invention" with unassailable assurance. Instead, two exploratory approaches to innovation are emerging, each with the apparent aim of understanding this phase in itself before tackling its relation to other analytic stages in the social-change process.

The *structural-institutional* orientation, primarily employed by sociologists, emphasizes the socio-cultural matrix of innovation and tries to determine the major institutional areas and component social systems from which innovations are principally derived for given societies. One of Max Weber's most important contributions is his recognition of the key innovative role of the military and religious institutions, in addition to the economic, in the development of classical and modern societies. Parsons has pointed also to philosophy, theology, the law, and perhaps the social sciences as important foci of innovation in contemporary society.[64] And the physical sciences and technology should be added to the list. Within these areas, as Mannheim has suggested, significant innovation (technical or social) seems to be primarily derived from small groups (presumably of intellectuals) which remain on the periphery of the established social structure. Perhaps this general approach is best summarized by Herskovits' concept of *cultural focus,* which might be profitably renamed as *socio-cultural* or *institutional focus*. According to Herskovits, every society develops a limited area of particular interest to which much attention and many resources are devoted—the cultural or institutional focus. Unlike other areas, this is neither taken for granted nor accorded a sacred, inflexible status. Though significant innovation (i.e., radical changes) is not intended, intensive interest leads to experimental "improvements" (not interpreted as "change" by participants) which normally eventuate in cumulative innovations. As Herskovits and Gillin have carefully noted, socio-cultural focus may and does shift from one institutional sector to another (e.g., the shift from the religious to the economic in the development of the United States); their reference to historical accident and cultural drift, however, does not seem to be satisfactory.[65] Nonetheless, this structural approach clearly reveals the presence of built-in and sanctioned processes of innovation that achieve a certain autonomy from the presumed sources of deviation (strains, etc.). And it strongly suggests what has long been suspected, that innovation is itself a source of strain rather than a mere response to anticipated difficulties. It is now distinctly possible that the relation between strain and innovation differs in simple and in complex social structures (as analyzed in the various constructed types now in use), although this problem has not yet been seriously investigated.

[64] Parsons, *Essays,* pp. 296-297.

[65] Herskovits, *op. cit.,* Chaps. 32, 34; Gillin, *The Ways of Men,* p. 552.

Generally speaking, anthropologists have pioneered in the *personal* approach to innovation, which focuses on the differential characteristics of innovators and the manner in which such persons recombine or reinterpret the socio-cultural materials. This is still a virgin area subject to continuing controversy, principally because no adequate classification or typology of innovators has been devised. For example, are there significant differences between successful and unsuccessful innovators, between social and technological innovators, or between occasional and professional innovators? One important clue to innovators is embodied in Toynbee's concept of *withdrawal-and-return,* but this has not been tested. Max Weber stressed the importance of *charismatic* qualities in religious and political innovators, although charisma may only serve to differentiate between successful and unsuccessful innovators. Recently, Homer Barnett seriously examined the whole process of cultural innovation from the standpoint of the persons involved rather than of the innovations themselves. Although he does not furnish a description of the typical innovator, he presents an illustrative catalogue of personal incentives toward innovation, without, however, assigning weights to each item. In addition, Barnett identifies the major mental processes employed by innovators (discrimination, assimilation, configuration, substitution, projection, identification, and recombination), which, together with knowledge of the socio-cultural sources available to innovators, help somewhat in understanding the empirical variety of innovations. Perhaps the greatest contribution of Barnett's analyses, and of others employing the personal approach, is the de-emphasizing of the innovator and in part of the innovation itself and a recognition of the critical role of the acceptance-rejection process in socio-cultural change.[66]

3. APPRAISAL OF INNOVATIONS

Not many decades ago, it was steadfastly assumed that "needed" inventions would be readily accepted, since the march of "progress" was virtually preordained. However, with growing doubt about the meaning of progress and the recognition that the criteria of necessity were disturbingly inconsistent, sociologists and anthropologists began to study the reaction of persons to innovations and new experiences as a critical phase in social and cultural change. A.G. Keller was one of the first after the turn of the century to suggest this approach, but Thomas and Znaniecki gave it classic formulation in their concept, the *definition of the situation.* In recent years, MacIver has restated this position by viewing change as a resultant of *dynamic assessment* or evaluation of new situations by specific groups of persons who subsequently adjust their behavior in terms of their assessments.[67] With this

[66] Toynbee, *op. cit.,* pp. 217-240; H. G. Barnett, *Innovation* (New York, 1953), Chaps. 4-7, 10-14.

[67] Keller, *op. cit.,* pp. 51, 54; W. I. Thomas and Florian Znaniecki, *The Polish Peasant*

theoretical modification, students of social change have increasingly sought the crux of social change by analyzing the factors in the appraisal process.

Basically, four foci of research and thinking can be distinguished in this quest for significant factors and fertile generalizations: the *innovation*, the *innovator*, the *agents of diffusion*, and the *appraisers*. In the twenties and early thirties, much attention was given to the innovation itself, based on a theoretically crucial distinction between material and non-material innovations. For a time, sociologists and anthropologists such as Ogburn, Chapin, Barnes, Barnett, Linton, and Leslie White seemed to be secure in their judgment that material items are more readily accepted than new ideational patterns. Others, including Max Weber, MacIver, Sorokin, Dixon, and Kroeber, have pointed to contrary evidence.[68] At present, this is a moot question, but Sorokin and others have correctly indicated that any innovation possesses both material and ideational aspects which can be analytically but not practically separated. It seems likely that we have reached a theoretical *cul de sac* from which a hasty exit is more than desirable.

A second focus of analysis, primarily derived from acculturation studies of the thirties, has sought understanding of the appraisal process in certain characteristics of the innovator. Before World War I, it should be recalled, Max Weber demonstrated the importance of personal charisma, particularly in successful religious innovators. Ralph Linton has extended this explanation by pointing to the *prestige* of innovators (particularly those from other societies) in terms of superior might, economic position, social class, etc.[69] Unfortunately, this hypothesis has not been adequately tested. There is some tendency to shift from the innovators themselves to a third focus, the agents of diffusion, but amazingly little work has been done on this problem. However, Linton, again drawing from acculturation materials, regards the prestige of these intermediate groups as a key factor in appraisal. Perhaps this question could be profitably explored by appropriate analysis of such notable agents of diffusions as publicists, advertising men, and lobbyists in our society.

Since the forties, however, the dominant theme in studying the appraisal process has been the nature of the appraiser and its relation to acceptance-rejection of proffered innovations. Most investigators have implicitly or explicitly adopted the concepts of dynamic assessment and definition of

in Europe and America (Boston, 1918-1921), vol. 3, pp. 21-27, 48-49; W. I. Thomas, *The Unadjusted Girl* (London, 1923), pp. 42-43, 81-82; Znaniecki, *Cultural Sciences*, pp. 242-265; MacIver, *Social Causation*, pp. 298-301.

[68] Ogburn, *Social Change*, pp. 140, 200-211; Linton, *op. cit.*, p. 485; Max Weber, *The Protestant Ethic and the Spirit of Capitalism*, translated by Talcott Parsons (London, 1930); MacIver, *Society*, pp. 466, 474-478; Sorokin, *Social and Cultural Dynamics*, vol. 4, p. 377; R. B. Dixon, *The Building of Cultures* (New York, 1928), p. 147; A. L. Kroeber, "Stimulus Diffusion," *AA*, 42 (Jan.-March, 1940), pp. 1-20, and *Anthropology*, Chap. 10.

[69] Linton, *op. cit.*, p. 473.

the situation by giving prominence to the role of *socially conditioned and personally interpteted need-patterns* of individuals confronted by innovation. Gillin, for example, approaches appraisal as a learning process in which the appraiser experimentally estimates the comparative rewards and punishments of the old and the new. In this scheme, reduction of anxiety and maximization of security seem to be cardinal motivations. But Gillin also indicates that changes in the physical and social environment may induce new needs which affect the individual's reception of specific innovations. Now this basic theory has been phrased or elaborated in several complementary ways. According to Barnett, acceptors of innovation are characterized by personal conflicts, dissatisfaction, and marginal status; however, a study of Peruvian change by Richard N. Adams suggests that dissatisfaction and acceptance are correlated only in disintegrating societies and that innovations in more stable societies are evaluated in terms of the reflected prestige of the innovator or agent of diffusion.[70] With more emphasis on the social characteristics of appraisers, Ogburn, Parsons, and Bernhard Stern (following Marx) have underscored the role of "vested interests" and class position in the differential evaluation of inventions. Surprisingly little work has been done to substantiate this important hypothesis, though Gross and Ryan have accomplished some excellent spadework in their studies of the diffusion of agricultural innovations. Carl Zimmerman insists that dynamic assessment operates under the key conditioning influence of *family experience*, a position apparently based on Cooley and Freud. Finally, we have the recent blend of psychological and sociological factors in Kardiner and Linton's concept of *basic personality structure*, which, based on early social conditioning, constitutes a typical need-structure that largely determines the reaction to given innovations.[71]

4. THE TRANSITIONAL PHASE

Social appraisal of innovation is a constant feature of change but may be analytically divided into *experimental* and *decision-making* phases. Initial

[70] Gillin, "Parallel Cultures," *loc. cit.*, and "Acquired Drives in Culture Contact," *loc. cit.;* H. G. Barnett, "Culture Processes," *AA,* 42 (Jan.-March, 1940), p. 29, and "Personal Conflicts and Cultural Change," *SF,* 20 (Dec., 1941), pp. 160-171; R. N. Adams, "Personnel in Culture Change: A Test of a Hypothesis," *SF,* 30 (Dec., 1951), pp. 185-190.

[71] Parsons, *Essays,* pp. 313-317; Ogburn, *Social Change,* pp. 167-169; B. J. Stern, "Restraints on the Utilization of Inventions," *Annals* (Nov., 1938), pp. 13-31, and "The Frustration of Technology," *Science and Society,* 1 (Winter, 1937), pp. 3-28, and *Society and Medical Progress* (Princeton, 1941); Bryce Ryan and N. C. Gross, "The Diffusion of Hybrid Seed Corn in Two Iowa Communities," *RS,* 8 (March, 1943), pp. 15-24; Neal C. Gross, "The Differential Characteristics of Acceptors and Non-Acceptors of an Approved Agricultural Technological Practice," *RS,* 14 (Jan., 1949), pp. 148-158; C. C. Zimmerman, "The Family and Social Change," *Annals,* 272 (November, 1950), pp. 22-28; Kardiner, *op. cit.*, pp. xviii, 34-35, 414, 433, 448-449.

acceptance of innovations corresponds to a trial period, which imperceptibly gives way to a period of social decision when sufficient numbers have become acquainted, through practice and discussion, with the potentialities of some innovation. Three empirical possibilities in decision can be distinguished: (1) the rejection of a provisionally acceptable innovation, as in the case of the Zafimaniry clan among the Tanala, which discarded wet rice cultivation because of the injurious social consequences; (2) full acceptance of new patterns with corresponding displacement of established practices and relationships; and (3) a precarious attachment to both the established and the innovative, with a resultant chaos of contradictory alternatives that soon leads to new tensions and recurrent social cleavages (between generations, classes, etc.). From all accounts of identifiable change, and particularly in acculturation studies, the last situation is quite common and constitutes a *period of transition* in which neither the traditional nor its substitute (and their respective practitioners) is secure.

The phenomena of transition in social change have been recognized for many years, but they have not been systematically analyzed. Teggart, Ellwood, and Lowie sketched the first fruitful definition of the problem of transition, but not until the late thirties did the transitional phase in change receive needed structural analysis. Linton, classifying degrees of participation in culture, pointed to the importance of competing Alternatives in the change process and even suggested the problems that derive from the prominence of Alternative patterns.[72] In much the same way, Odum conceptualized transition as a period in which the folkways and mores are rivaled by the technicways (behavior adapted to newly accepted innovations). Mannheim, in characterizing transitional phases in modern society, noted as its distinguishing feature a conflict between the principles of competition and planning, thereby interpreting the transitional phase as a conflict of *social techniques* (practices and relationships designed to shape human behavior). His analysis has been basically accepted by the anthropologist Lowie in his approach to "transition" in acculturating pre-literate societies; by Godfrey and Monica Wilson, also anthropologists, in their concept of *radical oppositions* (situations in which people come to to support contradictory concepts and conventions); and by the historian Eugene Anderson, who, in his concept of *cultural crisis*, emphasizes conflicts between groups supporting contradictory ideas and techniques, as well as a significant aspect of transition—the stimulation of norm violation and extreme tendencies toward behavior scorning regulation or moderation.[73] As a result of these conditions,

[72] Teggart, *op. cit.*, pp. 278-290; Ellwood, *op. cit.*, pp. 242-243; Lowie, *Culture and Ethnology*, pp. 80-81; Linton, *The Study of Man*, pp. 279-283.

[73] R. H. Lowie, "The Transition of Civilizations in Primitive Society," *AJS*, 47 (Jan., 1942), pp. 527-543; Odum, *op. cit.*, Chap. 20; Mannheim, *Man and Society*, Introduction and pp. 252-259; Anderson, *op. cit.*, pp. 20-25; Wilson and Wilson, *loc. cit.*

the transitional phase is one of apparent disorder and numerous tensions presenting problems that match or exceed those experienced in the first phase of the social-change process.

5. INSTITUTIONAL AND INTEGRATIVE PROBLEMS

If the major problem of the transitional phase is unequivocal selection among alternatives, the predominant feature of this final phase of the social-change process consists of a compelling concern with two related tasks: the *legitimation* of new patterns; and the integration of these patterns with strategic areas of the existing socio-cultural pattern. From all the available evidence on change "in process," both of these problems are normally complicated by the development of *secondary* or *derivative* patterns, which seem to represent experimental attempts either to (1) maximize the benefits of an accepted innovation or (2) aid in adjusting to unforeseen difficulties or strains generated by newly approved patterns. In either case, innovations (original or derivative) require legitimation or institutionalization to insure continued and predictable acceptance. Essentially, this process involves some reorganization of social controls and in particular a discernible transformation of authority and power systems. Given sufficient time, institutionalization of change alters the importance of different social categories and groups and thereby affects stratification systems, since, as Cooley and MacIver have so well analyzed the relationship, (1) class-and-caste systems are pre-eminent expressions of particular institutional structures in all complex societies, and (2) class and institution are but related aspects of the phenomena of social control. The empirical evidence of this connection, both in acculturation studies and in analysis of change in Western societies, is so consistent and clear that we might now venture to assert that a change in stratification systems is *one* of the invariable hallmarks and indices of genuine socio-cultural change.

However, institutionalization does not represent a completed process of change, although it certainly is an advanced point in that process. Although societies and their cultures are never perfectly integrated, societal continuity demands a minimum articulation and compatibility among component parts—a strain toward consistency that, incidentally, usually involves more strain than consistency. Consequently, the supreme problem of social change lies in accommodating various institutional sectors to recently institutionalized or partly institutionalized innovations. This functional problem of social change—institutional malintegration—has been almost uniformly phrased in terms of "lags" or discrepancies in the development of related socio-cultural parts. Vierkandt, Lippert, Müller-Lyer, and Keller may be considered the precursors of our modern conception of "cultural lag" and its terminological variations, but Alfred Weber probably contributed the concepts and theory basic to our current usage in his separation of *cultural*, *civilizational*, and *societal* processes.[74]

As interpreted by Ogburn, Weber's three processes reduce to two in the problem of socio-cultural integration. Ogburn combines the social and cultural processes under the concept "adaptive culture," whereas his term "material culture" corresponds to the civilizational process. Cultural lag derives from the presumed inability of the adaptive culture to keep pace with developments in material culture, particularly in modern societies. As applied by Ogburn, Chapin, Barnes, Barnett, and Leslie White, this theory describes the fundamental problem of malintegration as one of overdevelopment of the economic institution (and its subsidiary sectors, science and technology) as compared to political, religious, familial, educational and other institutions.[75] However, other sociologists do not regard cultural lag as the *universal* form of institutional imbalance. Odum, for example, restricts the applicability of cultural lag to folk societies in process of rapid change. In societies that approach state civilization, on the other hand, he notes (with Sorokin) that material culture fails to develop quickly enough to meet the demands of relatively new scientific, ethical, and political systems.[76]

The concept of lag has dramatized the problem of integrating innovations but, as currently used, does not quite adequately explain the conditions that underlie the *persistence* of malintegration. Ogburn points to the presence of social heterogeneity—to the differential effect of lag on various social groupings. Barnes believes that a sacred aura, now stripped from our material culture, still clings to other institutional areas, implying that reluctance to secularize adaptive culture prolongs and extends institutional imbalance in societies experiencing rapid change. Recently, Carr developed the concept of *social lag* to designate a continued failure of specific individuals and groups to remove or mitigate cultural lag.[77]

The importance of these explanatory attempts is that they tend to shift discussion from supposedly inherent qualities in different cultural areas (e.g., differential rates of development, differential diffusibility) to the larger societal context within which some degree of integration is ultimately achiev-

[74] Vierkandt, *loc. cit.;* Julius Lippert, *The Evolution of Culture,* translated by G. P. Murdock (New York, 1931); Franz Müller-Lyer, *The History of Social Development,* translated by Elizabeth C. Lake and H. Lake (London, 1923); Keller, *op. cit.,* p. 149; A. Weber, *op. cit.,* pp. 8-10, 25-36, 57-60.

[75] Ogburn, *Social Change,* pp. 200-211. There is, however, little or no evidence that Ogburn knew anything of Alfred Weber's work at the time the "cultural lag" theory was formulated.

[76] H. W. Odum, "Notes on the Changing Structure of Contemporary Society" (unpublished memorandum, Nov. 12, 1948), p. 3; Sorokin, *Society, Culture, and Personality,* pp. 659-662.

[77] Ogburn, *Social Change,* pp. 257-263; Barnes, *Historical Sociology,* p. 158; Carr and Stermer, *op. cit.,* pp. 17-18, 206-207, 321-322.

ed. The search has been begun, therefore, for specifically social factors in problems of integration. One theoretical focus, prominent in the work of Mosca, Pareto, Mannheim, and Toynbee, relates institutional malintegration to delays in recruiting élites that possess social characteristics appropriate to the challenge of current, rather than outmoded, problems. Still another approach in this vein tries to discover patterns of imbalance typical of certain kinds of societal systems—for example, Odum's distinction between cultural lag and achievement lag. In much the same way, Boskoff has described presumably typical problems of integration as basic to the experience of *transitional society* (a constructed type). By definition, transitional society is marked by numerous innovations and contradictory valuations that seem to underlie the phenomena of *social indecision*—those responses in behavior and ideology which reveal (1) delay in acknowledging problems of integration and (2) attempts to apply unrealistic solutions, which often produce intensification of social crises.[78]

SOCIAL PROBLEMS AS PROBLEMS OF INTEGRATION

Very often, for reasons that sociologists do not fully understand, there emerges in the process of social change a period of deferred integration. This is the period in which *social problems* abound and social crisis succeeds social crisis. Students of social problems generally approach their phenomena as derived from dramatic social changes, although scarcely three decades ago heredity, poverty, sin, defective intelligence, and climate were favorite "causes of social problems." Social problems seem to be relatively late products of the social-change process; yet because of their impelling quality, and because they are readily accessible and have immediate significance, social problems have probably received more attention from sociologists than has been granted to the preparatory phases of social change. For this reason, it is not necessary to dwell on the nature of social problems; instead it should be noted that unsuccessful integration of innovations and resultant social problems give rise to various types of social movements (discussed on pp. 278-279 above) whose role in the process of social change may be interpreted as last-ditch attempts to achieve proper incorporation of past changes, rather than as bold initiators of change. Since social movements are in reality only partly successful in attaining this gener-

[78] Gaetano Mosca, *The Ruling Class,* translated by Hannah D. Kahn (New York, 1939), pp. 65-66, 415, 460; Pareto, *op. cit.,* vol. 4, § 2485-2487; Mannheim, *Man and Society,* pp. 81-96; Toynbee, *op. cit.,* pp. 246, 309.

For analyses of "transitional society," see J. W. Bennett, "Culture Change and Personality in a Rural Society," *SF,* 23 (Dec., 1944), pp. 123-132, and "Some Problems of Status and Solidarity in a Rural Society," *RS,* 8 (Dec., 1943), pp. 396-408; Alvin Boskoff, "Postponement of Social Decision in Transitional Society," *SF,* 31 (March, 1953), pp. 230-231, and "Social Indecision in Two Classical Societies," *Midwest Sociologist,* 15 (Spring, 1953), pp. 10-17.

alized objective, the persistence of tensions is expressed in recurrent deviation and thus the *process* of social change resumes the generalized course outlined in these pages.

SELECTED BIBLIOGRAPHY

Barnett, H. G., *Innovation* (New York: McGraw-Hill, 1953).

Becker, Howard, *Through Values to Social Interpretation* (Durham, N.C.: Duke University Press, 1950), Chap. 3 "Prospects of Social Change as Viewed by Historian and Sociologist," and bibliography.

MacIver, R. M., *Social Causation* (Boston: Ginn, 1942).

———, *Society* (New York: Farrar and Rinehart, 1937).

Mannheim, Karl, *Man and Society in an Age of Reconstruction* (New York: Harcourt, Brace, 1940).

Ogburn, William F., *Social Change* (New York: B. W. Huebsch, 1923).

Sims, Newell L., *The Problem of Social Change* (New York: T. Y. Crowell, 1939).

Sorokin, Pitirim A., *Social and Cultural Dynamics* (New York: American Book Company, 1937-1941), 4 vols.

———, *Social Mobility* (New York: Harper, 1927).

Teggart, F. J., *Theory and Processes of History* (Berkeley: University of California Press, 1941).

Toynbee, A. J., *A Study of History,* abridged by D. C. Somervell (New York: Oxford University Press, 1947).

Wilson, Godfrey, and Monica Wilson, *The Analysis of Social Change* (Cambridge: Cambridge University Press, 1945).

Znaniecki, Florian, *Cultural Sciences* (Urbana: University of Illinois Press, 1952).

———, *The Method of Sociology* (New York: Farrar and Rinehart, 1934).

III

Some Specializations in Modern Sociology

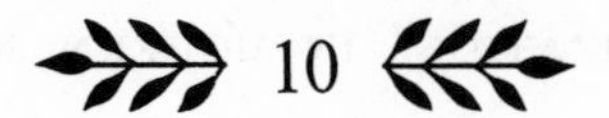

10

BASIC CONTINUITIES IN THE STUDY OF SMALL GROUPS

ALLAN W. EISTER

The Development of Research Interest in Small Groups

WHAT IS CURRENTLY CALLED SMALL-GROUP ANALYSIS IS AN INTEREST THAT has antecedents running back for some decades in a variety of fields as diverse as sociology and professional education, social group work and industrial management, social psychology, group psychotherapy, and applied anthropology. Until recently, at least, much of the work that has been done appears to have been done with a minimum of cross-disciplinary communication and with neither common theoretical orientation nor concepts.

Varied Origins of Interest in Small Groups. Not only have there been a number of specialties expressing interest of some sort in small groups, but the nature of the interests has varied considerably within fields and from field to field. Whereas for some the emphasis has been upon research for practical application—for example, the improvement of morale in military units—for others the emphasis has been upon theoretical problems and basic research. In some cases—the Mayo studies of factory production, for example—the interest emerged unexpectedly and was incidental to research on quite different problems. In others it has grown directly out of the development of more sophisticated theoretic insights rooted in one or more of the academic disciplines or borrowed from related fields such as psychiatry.

A result of this is that research problems, concepts, and experimental and other findings in this area bear only slight evidence of explicit mutual relevance. Hence the job of tracing out the development of interests in small groups and of surveying research accomplishments is not a case of simple exposition and chronology. In sociology alone, for example, only the first steps have been taken in the direction of collating and articulating research problems and findings.

Sociologists and social scientists generally, however, are well aware of a recent surge of interest in small groups, particularly during and directly after World War II. Moreover, within sociology small-group analysis has now achieved the status of a "specialty." This fact, along with the increased volume of research on small groups, suggests the need for review of some of the sources of interest in small groups and for recurrent scouting of the directions in which these interests appear to be moving.

Ambiguity in the Concept of Small Groups. Certain difficulties are encountered in any attempt to determine the scope and direction of the small-group research movement, and it may be well to consider at least two of these at the outset. Perhaps the most serious of the difficulties is the vagueness surrounding the concept of the small group itself. In the nature of the case, some agreement on what a small group is would seem to be essential. However, on such questions as how large a group may be and still be considered a *small* group, or how clearly structured relations among actors in a social situation must be in order for a group to exist, many sociologists and social psychologists have tended to be somewhat evasive—this in spite of their central and direct theoretic involvement in the movement. Some, apparently, have proceeded on the assumption that the upper limits of the small group can or will be established empirically; others have adopted arbitrary limits or simply have not regarded the problem as an issue for immediate consideration.

Approaching the problem of the size of the small group inductively, James and his associates, for example, observed some 9,129 groups classified as "informal, simulated informal, and work groups." They found these ranging in size from two to seven, with a modal number of two (71 percent of the cases) and a sharp decline to 21 percent of the cases with three members, 6 percent with four, 1½ percent with five, and less than 1 percent with six or seven.[1] Simmel and Wiese-Becker[2] in their theoretical descrip-

[1] John James, "A Preliminary Study of the Size Determinant in Small Group Interaction," *ASR,* 16 (Aug., 1951), pp. 474-477.

[2] See *The Sociology of Georg Simmel,* translated by K. H. Wolff (Glencoe, Ill., 1950), pp. 87-177; Howard Becker, *Systematic Sociology on the Basis of the* Beziehungslehre *and* Gebildelehre *of Leopold von Wiese* (New York, 1932; 2nd ed., with a new preface, Gary, Ind., 1950), pp. 488-530; ———, "*Systematic Sociology* and Leopold von Wiese," *Sociometry and the Science of Man,* Sociometry, 18, 4 (Dec., 1955), pp. 262-268.

tions of small groups focused their discussion chiefly on dyads and triads, suggesting that the addition of a third person was more significant in its consequences for interaction, and so on, in the group itself than the addition of the 4th, 5th, or *n*th person. (Note however the Wiese-Becker treatment of *b*- and *B*-groups.)

On the other hand, there appear to be sound reasons (and well-established precedent) for including groups with somewhat larger numbers of members as small groups. Bales, for example, following in part Cooley's conception of the primary group, defines the small group as

> . . . any number of persons engaged in interaction with one another in a single face-to-face meeting or a series of meetings, in which each member receives some impression or perception of each other member distinct enough so that he can, either at the time or in later questioning, give some reaction to each of the others as individual persons, even thought it be only to recall that the other was present.[3]

Although this is an operational definition, it leaves us with an open-ended conception of the small group, since it is an open question how many other persons in a given situation or group an individual can perceive in relation to himself and also retain images of when all the actors are not together.

This conception of the small group is similar to that used by Jennings when she speaks of "sociogroups" and of "psychegroups," or by Krech and Crutchfield when they speak of "psychological groups" (as distinguished from what they call "social organizations," i.e., formally structured associations).[4] It is also a conception that appears to be implicit in the sociometric technique for defining cliques or other small groups, as well as in the field-theory approach of Lewin and the group dynamists.

Cooley's conception of the primary group as a face-to-face group was not necessarily of a small group in the sense of limitation to a very few members. He and others used it to refer not only to the nuclear family and to congeniality or play groups but also to neighborhoods and even to whole communities in rural settings. Villages of several hundred persons could, under certain circumstances, function as primary groups, though not as small groups. The difficulty seems to lie, in part at least, in the variable capacities of human beings to interact (and to perceive and recall their relations) in various types of social situations; and it suggests rather clearly, perhaps, the futility of attempting any definitive specification of the maximum size of the small group, if the basis is to be the psychological grounds of perception and recall. Still, these factors are necessarily operative in any

[3] R. F. Bales, "A Theoretical Framework for Interaction Process Analysis," in Dorwin Cartwright and Alvin Zander (eds.), *Group Dynamics: Theory and Research* (Evanston, Ill., 1953), p. 30.

[4] Helen H. Jennings, *Leadership and Isolation* (New York, 1943); David Krech and R. S. Crutchfield, *Theory and Problems of Social Psychology* (New York, 1948), pp. 366 ff.

small group (as indeed in every social situation); and relations that are personal and "particularistic," or non-categoric, do stand out as distinctive. Hence attempts to include reference to such aspects as face-to-face interaction in the concept of the small group are readily understandable.

Conceptual Variations in Small-Group Structure. Another aspect of the vagueness that exists in the concept of the small group in the body of research concerning it appears in the varied requirements in the kind and amount of structuring of the relations among the actors. Social psychologists, for example, have sometimes conducted, in the name of small-group research, experiments in which they used as groups subjects selected more or less at random and set to competitive or other tasks with comparatively little attention given to the roles or role-relations involved or to the feelings and attitudes that the subjects might have toward each other, including awareness of themselves as a group In many cases, subjects have been total strangers to each other prior to the single experimental session in which they are brought together, and no data are gathered about any structuring that may occur in the course of the experiment. (Here see Chap. 7, pp. 221-224.)

Although similar procedures have been followed by some sociologists in laboratory experiments, attention has invariably been focused on the structuring that develops and on the processes by which it occurs. *Role* and *status* as well as other structural concepts have figured prominently in sociological thinking about the small group, whereas in other disciplines structure and structural factors have tended to be less emphasized. More will later be said about this.

Although groups in small-group research have included spontaneous, free-forming groups in which roles are only informally defined and in which there is a minimum of cultural patterning, many small-group research studies have clearly included groups that are highly structured by external agents. Work groups established by employers, fighting units established by military authority, and even some kinds of experimental groups set up by laboratory investigators are examples of these.[5] The monogamous family, patterned by custom and law, is an additional example. These variations in the structuring of groups identified as small by one or another investigator make it difficult to speak of the small group in any generic sense

The Dominance of Disparate Frames of Reference. Reference has already been made to a second major difficulty in surveying small-group research. It stems from the fact that much of the work done so far appears to have

[5] Muzafer Sherif's recent work argues for the possibility of combining the advantages of natural groups with experimental control in a field setting. See his "A Preliminary Experimental Study of Intergroup Relations," in J. H. Rohrer and Muzafer Sherif (eds.), *Social Psychology at the Crossroads* (New York, 1951), pp. 388-424; "Integrating Field Work and Laboratory in Small-Group Research," *ASR*, 19 (Dec. 1954), pp. 759-771.

been done by investigators or by groups of investigators working without close and continuous contact with research being done by others. In consequence, there has been a proliferation of different words for essentially the same or similar phenomena and a growing variety of disparate and unrelated theoretic orientations. Borrowings of concepts and procedures have occurred and are hard to trace, particularly where ideas and techniques borrowed from one source are recast in different phrases and set in quite different theoretical contexts. Within a given discipline, moreover, whole areas of research have frequently not been seen as related by a common frame of reference. In sociology, for example, it is probably safe to say that comparatively little of the large volume of research on interpersonal relations in courtship, marriage, and the family has been dealt with explicitly in small-group terms.

Sociological Interest in Small Groups. Sociologists working on small-group research have tended in the recent literature to restrict their use of the concept *small-group research* to experimental or descriptive studies of very small numbers of persons (two to six or eight, occasionally as many as twelve), among or between whom various details of interpersonal communication can be observed and recorded or obtained in other ways. Most often, the groups studied have been informal groups—cliques, gangs, and other natural small groups, or else contrived groups brought together in an experimental situation by the investigator himself. Where family and subfamily groups or other culturally prescribed and highly structured plurels have been used, it has been under conditions where details of this sort can be obtained. The emphasis, too, has tended to be on the dynamic and the functional as well as on the processual and structural aspects of the groups involved.

Limitations in usage of the small-group label, however, if applied too rigorously, could lead us to overlook relevant work or prove too restrictive to permit for even a brief review of the interest displayed by sociologists in small groups. Hence, despite valid arguments to the contrary, the frame of reference will be broadened here to include some of the other approaches sociologists have made to the subject. Reference here is to studies of primary groups as well as to the formal descriptive and even taxonomic treatments of small groups. Useful summary surveys of work done in this broader context have been made by Wilson, Shils, and Faris; and an extensive bibliography, compiled by Strodtbeck and Hare[6] and including other than sociological studies, is available.

[6] Logan Wilson, "Sociography of Groups," in Georges Gurvitch and W. E. Moore (eds.), *Twentieth Century Sociology* (New York, 1945), pp. 139-171; E. A. Shils, *The Present State of American Sociology* (Glencoe, Ill., 1948), pp. 40-52; also "The Study of the Primary Group," in Daniel Lerner and H. D. Lasswell (eds.), *The Policy Sciences* (Stanford, 1951), pp. 44-69; R. E. L. Faris, "Development of the Small-Group Research Movement,"

TYPES OF SMALL-GROUP RESEARCH

Small Groups and Social Process: Simmel. Promising—even impressive—beginnings were made in the direction of small-group analysis early in the history of sociology. In general, however, as Shils has pointed out, sociologists in the late nineteenth century and the early decades of the twentieth century were more interested in processes and characteristics of total societies than they were in small groups as such. As a consequence, suggestive leads in the work of LePlay and Durkheim, for example, were not followed up. Of the sociological writings before World War I, only those of Simmel and Cooley are cited with any degree of frequency today for contributions to small-group analysis.

Simmel's interest in small groups was directed primarily to the formal properties of dyads and triads and to the kinds (and consequences) of relationships that might logically be expected to occur in them. One of his observations, utilized recently, for example, by Mills and also by Strodtbeck, was that a majority becomes possible in a triad but is non-existent in a dyad and that this has important consequences for the functioning of the group. Another, selected at random, is that

> . . . the larger the group is, the more easily does it form an objective unit up and above its members . . . [participants] in a given [pair] relationship see only one another, and do not see, at the same time, an objective, super-individual structure which they feel exists and operates on its own.[7]

Although he wrote in a period and in part as representative of a tradition that has been described as "historicist," Simmel's propositions were formulated at a level sufficiently abstract for sociologists to be able to make use of them in a variety of contexts. Those with strong interests in the dynamics of interaction—in the motivations of actors and the functions of acts—may experience some difficulty in fitting their thinking to the more severely abstract categories which Simmel in part utilized. Despite this, however, there has been periodic revival of interest in Simmel's thought.

Small Groups and Personality: Cooley. In connection with small groups, Cooley is best known for his concept of the primary group—although the two types of groups are not precise equivalents, as we have seen. Cooley's interest was not so much in small groups per se, however, as it was in the significance that small groups of the primary type were thought to have

in Muzafer Sherif and M. O. Wilson (eds.), *Group Relations at the Crossroads* (New York, 1953), pp. 155-184; F. L. Strodtbeck and A. P. Hare, "Bibliography of Small-Group Research," *Sociometry,* 17 (May, 1954), pp. 107-178.

[7] T. M. Mills, "Power Relations in Three-Person Groups," *ASR,* 18 (Aug., 1953), pp. 351-357; F. L. Strodtbeck, "The Family as a Three-Person Group," *ibid.,* 19 (Feb., 1954), pp. 23-29; Simmel, *op. cit.,* pp. 127-28, 136.

in the formation of personality and of specific attitudes and responses, on one hand, and in the functioning of large social organizations or societies, on the other. With respect to the first area, his orientation was as much social-psychological as it was sociological.

Although a great many other sociologists, both European and American, writing before World War I, gave explicit attention to the concept of the group (including, of course, small groups), it was Cooley's primary group that came to be accepted most widely in the United States as the classic theoretic frame within which to handle small groups. Until quite recently, American sociologists, by and large, appeared content to accept at face value and to repeat, without closer scrutiny of the processes involved, the propositions advanced by Cooley. As a result, those standard textbooks in the field which have dealt with small groups have seldom gone beyond general, and often speculative, statements about socializing functions of the family, the play group, the neighborhood, and so on.

Large numbers of descriptive studies, however, were beginning to be made following World War I, and the primary-group concept was employed in investigations as wide-ranging as those by Thomas and Znaniecki of Polish peasants in Europe and America and by Thrasher in his study of gangs.

The Small Group in Its Social and Ecological Setting. The emphasis of Thrasher's work was somewhat different, however, from that of Cooley and others. Here, as in other studies influenced by Park and Burgess, the interest centered on the processes of social interaction—conflict, competition, cooperation, and so on—through which groups were formed, and on such phenomena as group morale or *esprit de corps.* Thrasher's study not only focused attention on these processes but also, in line with the particular ecological orientation of the Chicago school in the late twenties, sought to relate ganging to "interstitial areas" and to social conditions characterizing specific zones of the city. Whyte's later work on gangs in *Street-Corner Society,* as the subtitle and later chapters of the book indicate, also pointed to the broad problem of social organization in a slum area of a large city and to the relation of small groups to larger social structures—in this case, that of an urban area.[8]

The Search for Analytic Properties of Small Groups. Still another emphasis is present in the discussion of small groups in the Wiese-Becker *Systematic Sociology* and in studies made by Kuhn, Ruth Useem, and others. Drawing in part on Simmel, this approach called for scrutiny and comparison of various types of pair and three-person relations and other small-group patterns and led to a number of studies of this sort at the University of Wisconsin and elsewhere. Meanwhile, several attempts

[8] F. M. Thrasher, *The Gang* (Chicago, 1927); W. F. Whyte, *Street-Corner Society* (Chicago, 1943).

either at identifying logically the characteristics of groups of different types (including small groups) or at describing and analyzing groups empirically had been made or were being made. In a series of articles in the *American Journal of Sociology,* Bodenhafer, for example, compared the use made of the group concept in Ward's *Dynamic Sociology* and in later sociological work. Brown, Coyle, and others before 1930 called further attention to concepts then available for studying groups. L. J. Carr, in his analysis of the interaction occurring in committee work, pioneered in the direction of detailed observation of small-group processes.[9] They were joined by a number of others (e.g., Palmer, Young, Eubank, Bogardus, Sanderson, Menger, and Lundberg),[10] who promoted the search for additional analytic concepts or for methods of gathering data about groups in the thirties.

Beginning in the mid thirties, however, several changes in the research and theoretical treatment accorded small groups appeared in sociological writing. These came about partly as a result of further insights and skills developed within the discipline itself and partly through the impact of psychoanalytic and other psychiatric thinking, partly from the introduction of sociometric and other techniques for handling data about small group structure and process, and partly from the diffusion of concepts such as *role* and *status*.

Research in Small Groups: Sociometry. Sociometric concepts and techniques, introduced by Moreno in 1934, appear to have been especially influential, among developments outside sociology itself, in giving direction to research. The technique, originally intended for use in identifying friendship circles in a girls' training school, was quickly adapted to a variety of uses and applied, for example, by Lundberg, Zeleny, Chapin, and others.

[9] Manford Kuhn, "The Engagement," in Howard Becker and Reuben Hill (eds.), *Marriage and the Family* (Boston, 1942), esp. pp. 216-218; ———, "American Families Today: Development and Differentiation of Types," in Howard Becker and Reuben Hill (eds.), *Family, Marriage, and Parenthood* (Boston, 1948), especially pp. 134-144 (see also pp. 246-275); Becker and Ruth H. Useem, "Sociological Analysis of the Dyad," *ASR,* 7, 1 (Feb., 1942), pp. 13-26; W. B. Bodenhafer, "The Comparative Role of the Group Concept in Ward's *Dynamic Sociology* and Contemporary American Sociology," *AJS,* 26 (1920-1921), pp. 273-314, 425-474, 588-600, 716-743; B. W. Brown, *Social Groups* (Chicago, 1926); Grace Coyle, *Social Process in Organized Groups* (New York, 1930); L. J. Carr, "Experimental Sociology: A Preliminary Note on Theory and Method," *SF,* 8 (Sept., 1929), pp. 63-74.

[10] Vivien M. Palmer, *Field Studies in Sociology* (Chicago, 1928), pp. 102-128; Pauline V. Young, *Scientific Surveys and Social Research* (New York, 1939); E. E. Eubank, *The Concepts of Sociology* (Boston, 1932), especially pp. 116-168; E. S. Bogardus, *An Introduction to Social Research* (Los Angeles, 1936); Dwight Sanderson, "Group Description," *SF,* 16 (March, 1938), pp. 309-319, and "A Preliminary Structural Classification of Groups," *ibid.,* 17 (Dec., 1938), pp. 196-201; Karl Menger, "An Exact Theory of Social Groups and Relations," *AJS,* 43 (March, 1938), pp. 790-798; G. A. Lundberg, "Some Problems of Group Classification and Measurement," *ASR,* 5 (June, 1940), pp. 351-360.

Among other things, Moreno's technique for sociogramming group structure may have given added impetus also to the several studies of leadership that were reported in this period.[11]

Functional Concepts in Small-Group Research. Role and status concepts, rediscovered in the work of Mead and also borrowed from Linton, fitted easily into interest in group structure that had been evolved in general sociology. Psychiatric concepts (introduced to sociologists through the writings of Sullivan, Horney, Fromm, and others), "configurational" and "situational" concepts, emphasis on operational definitions of terms, as well as developments in the application of mathematical concepts to social phenomena—all appear to have contributed to small-group research. In addition to these, several techniques for observing and recording interpersonal interaction used by social group workers and by some social psychologists and others[12] were being found useful for sociological purposes.

Meanwhile, there were other "outside" developments that appeared to have contributed in one way or another to the change in the character of sociological interest in small groups. These include the studies by Mayo and his associates of informal group behavior in factory settings, by Warner and others of cliques and clique behavior in communities and in formal organizations,[13] as well as the theoretic writings and experimental studies by Lewin and his associates at the University of Iowa and later at M.I.T., the University of Michigan, and elsewhere. The latter group of investigators were chiefly responsible for the development of the specialty known as "group dynamics" and have contributed heavily to the literature on small groups, as we shall see later.

Family Studies as Implicit Small-Group Research. Within the field of sociology itself, by the early forties, several additional ideas for interpreting, observing, or describing groups—in some cases small groups specifically—

[11] J. L. Moreno, *Who Shall Survive?* (Washington, D.C., 1934); G. A. Lundberg and M. Lawsing, "The Sociography of Some Community Relations," *ASR,* 2 (June, 1937); Lundberg and M. Steele, "Social Attraction Patterns in a Village," *Socm.,* 1 (Jan., 1938), pp. 375-419; L. D. Zeleny, "Sociometry of Morale," *ASR,* 4 (Dec., 1939), pp. 799-808, and "Sociometry in the College Classroom," *Socm.,* 3 (Jan., 1940), pp. 102-104; F. Stuart Chapin, "Trends in Sociometrics and Critique," *ibid.,* 3 (July, 1940), pp. 245-262, and "Sociometric Stars as Isolates," *AJS,* 56 (Nov., 1950), pp. 263-267; C. P. Loomis, "Informal Grouping in a Spanish-American Village," *Socm.,* 4 (Feb., 1941), pp. 36-51.

[12] See W. I. Newstetter, *Wawokiye Camp: A Research Project in Group Work* (Cleveland, 1930); Dorothy S. Thomas, "Some New Techniques for Studying Social Behavior," *Child Development Monograph,* 1, 1929; and Thomas *et al. Observational Studies of Social Behavior,* vol. 1: *Social Behavior Patterns* (New Haven, 1933).

[13] See especially Elton Mayo, *The Human Problems of an Industrial Civilization* (New York, 1933); and F. J. Roethlisberger and W. J. Dickson, *Management and the Worker* (Cambridge, Mass., 1939); W. Lloyd Warner and P. S. Lunt, *The Social Life of a Modern Community* (New Haven, 1941), pp. 301-355.

were being proposed,[14] along with numerous empirical studies. Specifically, a change had occurred in the analysis of small groups in that closer attention was being given to details of status structuring and of in-group processes observed in action, as well as in dynamic processes operating within the personalities of the group members in relation to each other and to rules and norms, especially those developed within the group itself. Interest in the dynamics of interpersonal behavior in courtship, marriage, and the family, for example, was evident in the late thirties and early forties in the work of Waller, Burgess and Cottrell, Becker and Hill,[15] and others. Earlier studies had directed attention to residential propinquity, ethnic differences, and other ecological and social-distance factors in relation to mate-selection, or had concentrated on changes in the functions of the family as an institution and the like; later studies placed heavier emphasis on the study of interpersonal feelings and attitudes, roles and role-taking in the family, and similar subjects. Much of the research on the family and of other primary groups, however, was done independently of other sociological interest in small groups and hence, with some exceptions, has tended to remain largely outside of the context of systematic small-group analysis as this has developed in the postwar decade.

Extra-Theoretical Factors in Small-Group Research. During World War II, sociologists, along with other social scientists, were drawn into research in the structure and functioning of both military and civilian organizations and on problems germane to their effective operation. Perhaps the most ambitious of these projects involving sociologists were those undertaken by Stouffer and his associates on the American army. Other studies on a much more limited scale, or dealing with smaller organizations, were also being made.[16] In general, these served again to underscore the importance of informal small groups in the operation and maintenance of larger formal organizations and of society itself.

Sociologists, however, were not drawn into research done under contract with the military services to the extent that psychologists were—with a result that in the postwar flood of publications of research on leadership in small groups and other aspects of small groups, sociological studies have tended to be eclipsed by the sheer volume of work reported by psychologists.

[14] Including: Florian Znaniecki, "Social Groups as Products of Participating Individuals," *AJS,* 44 (May, 1939), pp. 799-811; L. D. Zeleny, "Measurement of Sociation," *ASR,* 6 (April, 1941), pp. 173-188; Becker and Useem, *op. cit.*

[15] W. W. Waller, *The Family* (New York, 1938); E. W. Burgess and L. S. Cottrell, *Predicting Success or Failure in Marriage* (New York, 1939); Becker and Hill, *op. cit.*

[16] S. A. Stouffer *et al., The American Soldier* (Princeton, 1949), 4 vols.; G. C. Homans, "The Small Warship," *ASR,* 11 (June, 1946), pp. 294-300; L. D. Zeleny, "Selection of Compatible Flying Partners," *AJS,* 52 (March, 1947), pp. 424-431; E. A. Shils and Morris Janowitz, "Cohesion and Disintegration of the Wehrmacht in World War II," *POQ,* 12 (June, 1948), pp. 280-315.

For a time, differences and similarities in the focuses of sociology and of social psychology on small groups have been hard to discern. This has been a problem, particularly in the relationships existing between group dynamics and some other social-psychological orientations and the sociological approaches. These have become increasingly clear, however, in the light of cross-disciplinary theoretical orientations in social science that have begun to develop recently. (For a discussion of such matters, see Chap. 17, "Sociology and Interdisciplinary Developments," by Adolph S. Tomars; and also Chap. 19, "Social Psychology and Sociology," by Kimball Young and Linton Freeman, esp. pp. 550 and 552-556.)

The Growing Convergence of Theoretical and Experimental Studies. Especially prominent among sociological contribution to the analysis of small groups since 1945 have been the investigations and theory of Bales and of Homans, and, more recently, of Strodtbeck, Mills, and others associated in one way or another with the Harvard Social Relations Department or Laboratory.[17] Contributions to the growing body of substantive research findings as well as to research methodology have been made by James, Whyte, Stephan, Adams, Riley *et al.*, and others.[18] In general this research interest in small groups has been largely experimental (see Chap. 7, pp. 221-224) and much of it has been done against the background of a still evolving general theory of action developed cooperatively by Parsons, Shils, Bales, and others, to which further reference will be made in the final section of this chapter.

[17] Bales, *op. cit.*, and "A Set of Categories for the Analysis of Small-Group Interaction," *ASR*, 15 (April, 1950), pp. 257-263; (with F. L. Strodtbeck, T. M. Mills, and M. E. Roseborough), "Channels of Communication in Small Groups," *ibid.*, 16 (Aug., 1951), pp. 461-468; (with Strodtbeck), "Phases in Group Problem-Solving," *JASP*, 46 (Oct., 1951), pp. 485-495; and "The Equilibrium Problem in Small Groups," in Talcott Parsons *et al.*, *Working Papers in the Theory of Action* (Glencoe, Ill., 1953), pp. 111-161; G. C. Homans, "A Conceptual Scheme for the Study of Social Organization," *ASR*, 12 (Feb., 1947), pp. 13-26, and *The Human Group* (New York, 1950); F. L. Strodtbeck, "Husband-Wife Interaction over Revealed Differences," *ASR*, 16 (Aug., 1951), pp. 468-473; Mills, *op. cit.*

[18] James, *op. cit.*, also "Clique Organization in a Small Industrial Plant," in *Research Studies of the State College of Washington*, 19 (1952), 125-130; W. F. Whyte, "Small Groups and Large Organizations," in Rohrer and Sherif, *op. cit.*, pp. 297-312; F. F. Stephan, "The Relative Rate of Communication Between Members of Small Groups," *ASR*, 17 (Aug., 1952), pp. 482-486; (with E. G. Mishler), "The Distribution of Participation in Small Groups: An Exponential Approximation," *ibid.*, pp. 598-608; Stuart Adams, "Status Congruency as a Variable in Small-Group Performance," *SF*, 32 (Oct., 1953), pp. 16-22; "Social Climate and Productivity in Small Military Groups," *ASR*, 19 (Aug., 1954), pp. 421-425; Matilda W. Riley *et al.*, *Sociological Studies in Scale Analysis* (New Brunswick, 1954), especially pp. 150-267, and "Interpersonal Orientations in Small Groups: A Consideration of the Questionnaire Approach," *ASR*, 19 (Dec., 1954), pp. 715-724.

Applications of Small-Group Research

Small Groups and Applied Fields: Social Work and Welfare. In point of time, the next field after sociology to define an interest in small groups was a somewhat heterogeneous group of specialties concerned with discovering what could be learned about small groups that would be useful for improving the "democratic" process, for re-training delinquents, and for other essentially therapeutic or explicitly value-laden purposes. These include professional social work and a variety of other fields directly concerned with practical application of their findings. They were joined by students of child development and child welfare and later by professional educators, industrial-management specialists, and others. Many of these groups were avowedly concerned with improving morale, bettering human relations, increasing production, and so on. These aims were somewhat different from the objectives of some of the earlier specialists studying small groups to gain insights in helping individuals toward "better personal and social adjustment."

At least as early as the turn of the present century, workers in correctional and other institutional organizations were beginning to study and utilize small groups for something like therapeutic purposes. In the broader interests of improving the "democratic" process in society, Follett, Lindeman, and some other social philosophers, for example, were recognizing in the twenties the potentialities of small groups for implementing democratic behavior and other ethically defined objectives. Some of this interest was focused fairly sharply on improving the quality of "group thinking" in the small group, with some attention given to the functions of "the group leader" in this process. Several social psychologists and some professional educators joined in the search for experimental answers to such questions as "Do groups think more effectively than individuals?"[19]

Social-work contributions toward small-group study soon began to come from a number of directions. Following somewhat closely along lines suggested by Park and Burgess for studying groups, Coyle sketched out a schematic account of "the social process in organized groups" and undertook to trace out interaction processes in informal settlement house and playground groups. Simultaneously, before 1930, Newstetter was developing

[19] Mary P. Follett, *The New State* (New York, 1918); E. C. Lindeman, *Social Discovery* (New York, 1924); Ada D. Sheffield, *Creative Discussion* (New York, 1927); H. S. Elliott, *The Process of Group Thinking* (New York, 1928); Ordway Tead, *The Art of Leadership* (New York, 1935); Goodwin Watson, "Do Groups Think More Effectively than Individuals?" *JASP,* 23 (Oct., 1928), pp. 328-336.

a program of observational studies of groups in a boys' camp that called for running accounts of interaction in group situations and included suggestions for ways to record these. Following formal recognition around 1935 of group work as a social-work specialty requiring distinctive skills and techniques, social workers gave increasing attention to what was termed *the group process*. The concept embraced not only sequences in activities and interaction in a given group, but also steps toward organizational structure, as well as movement toward more "mature" attitudes and overt behavior believed to be related to these.[20] This particular concept has not been widely adopted outside of group-work circles, however, in part, perhaps, because of its spongy, all-inclusive character.

The Small Group and Problems of Motivation: Psychiatry and Psychoanalysis. An important contribution of social group work to subsequent small-group analysis, however, was the emphasis on the dynamic or motivational and other emotional factors in the personalities of group members and in their interaction with each other. Although professional social work has been only one of the channels through which psychiatric concepts and interpretations were introduced into small-group analysis, social workers have been generally alert, particularly since World War I, to the use of psychiatric principles in relation to group behavior. Actually, psychiatric patterns of thinking were applied almost exclusively to social case work at first, and some time elapsed before they were more widely extended to the small-group context in social group work. Although Freud's *Group Psychology and the Analysis of the Ego,* for example, was available in English translation as early as 1922, it was generally not until the later thirties and early forties, following the work of Slavson and of Moreno especially,[21] that group psychotherapy, sociatry, and other psychiatrically oriented approaches to group work came into vogue.

Emphasis in the Freudian approach was almost exclusively on the emotional, and primarily the unconscious, elements in the interaction process and on influences emanating from family experiences of individuals since these were believed to carry over into subsequent small-group relations. In this view, all groups—and especially small groups—tended to be thought of as "symbolizing" relations found in the family with the leader presumably representing the powerful parental figure and the other members siblings. Recent proponents of this general approach include Redl, Bion, Scheidlinger,[22] and others.

[20] Grace Coyle (ed.), *Studies in Group Behavior* (New York, 1937); Newstetter, *op. cit.;* H. B. Trecker, *Social Group Work: Principles and Practice* (New York, 1948); and G. Wilson and G. Ryland, *Social Group Work Practice* (Boston, 1949).

[21] S. R. Slavson, *An Introduction to Group Therapy* (New York, 1943); Moreno, *op. cit.*

[22] F. Redl, "Group Emotion and Leadership," *Psychiatry,* 5 (Nov., 1942), pp. 573-596; "Group Psychological Elements in Discipline Problems," *AJO,* 13 (Jan., 1943),

Group work in various types of groups—in some cases with and in other cases without psychiatric or even psychoanalytic orientation—has been carried on rather widely since the beginning of World War II. Examples of research in these terms have been reported by Rosenthal, Shulman, Powdermaker and Frank, and others.[23] Some sociologists have maintained interests in group work and participated in group work, or similarly oriented research.

By 1950, associates of Moreno at the Sociometric Institute in New York were seeking to clarify and sustain a sharp distinction between group therapy and group psychotherapy, the latter being proposed to designate any intended "improvement" in attitudes, "social adjustment," interpersonal relations, and so on, which takes place as a consequence of deliberate professional guidance of the group process in groups where "the therapeutic welfare of the group is the immediate and sole objective and these ends are attained by scientific means, including analysis, prognosis, and prediction." According to this distinction, the term "group therapy" applied to cases where the desired changes occurred incidental to play and other activities without the particular kind of planning and direction provided by psychiatrists.[24]

Industrial Research and Small Groups: Mayo and His Disciples. In the meantime, interest in small groups and additional techniques for examining them in their natural settings were arising in another quarter. Without originally intending to study cliques or other small groups as such, Mayo and his associates (studying factors related to productivity, morale, and so on, in two industrial plants—a textile factory in Philadelphia and an electrical equipment factory in Hawthorne, Illinois) were virtually driven to recognize the existence and importance of informal groups or cliques and their norms of work performance in the factory setting when other factors failed to account for observed variations in rates of production. Apparently, it was the insights that Mayo, Roethlisberger, Dickson, and others developed on

pp. 77-81; W. R. Bion and J. Rickman, "Intra-Group Tensions in Therapy: Their Study as the Task of the Group," *Lancet,* 245 (1943), pp. 678-681, and "Group Dynamics: A Review," *IJP,* 33 (1952), pp. 235-247; Saul Scheidlinger, *Psychoanalysis and Group Behavior* (New York, 1952); "Freudian Concepts of Group Relations," in Cartwright and Zander, *op. cit.,* pp. 52-61.

[23] P. Rosenthal, "Group Studies of Pre-Adolescent Boys," *AJO,* 12 (January, 1942), pp. 115-126; H. M. Shulman, "Delinquency Treatment in the Controlled Activity Group," *ASR,* 10 (June, 1945), pp. 405-414; J. Abrahams and L. W. McCorkle, "Group Psychotherapy of Military Offenders," *AJS,* 51 (March, 1946), pp. 455-464; W. W. Wattenberg and J. J. Balistieri, "Gang Membership and Juvenile Misconduct," *ASR,* 15 (Dec., 1950), pp. 744-752; F. B. Powdermaker and J. D. Frank, *Group Psychotherapy* (Cambridge, Mass., 1953); B. Kotkov, "A Bibliography for the Student of Group Therapy," *JCP,* 6 (Jan., 1950), pp. 77-91.

[24] "Open Letter to Research Workers and Friends of Group Psychotherapy," in *Group Psychotherapy: Journal of Sociopsychopathology and Sociatry* (April, 1950).

the spot, rather than familiarity with theoretical work or research done in other fields, that led industrial management and management-engineering groups to this interest in small informal cliques among factory workers and other small groups in formal organizations. These phenomena, studied through observational techniques similar to those developed by Mayo and his associates, and through additional techniques such as those worked out by Chapple, were examined subsequently by applied anthropologists,[25] industrial sociologists, and others, with the result that a fairly extensive literature on work groups and informal groups in formal organizations is now available. In contrast with some of the other approaches to the study of small groups, this one has tended to "see" the small groups in the contexts of larger organizations and, in some cases, has led to attempts to trace the connections between relations existing outside of the factory (or other organization) and those existing within it.

Education, Manipulation, and the Study of Small Groups. Both sociometric techniques and psychiatric concepts, as well as several other concepts and observational techniques developed in these various fields, attracted considerable attention in education and drew professional educators into the widening circle of investigators concerned with small groups.[26] Like professional social group workers, they have been interested chiefly in the possibilities of developing more effective techniques for handling individuals in groups. the chief difference being in the degree of formality of the groups and in the avowed purposes of investigators in the two fields.

Similarly, hospital, military, certain governmental administrators, and other executives became exposed to small-group concepts and research findings. This development has occurred chiefly during and since World War II, and in all of these cases the interest has been frankly in the usefulness of knowledge about small-group processes, particularly where "better human relations" and the like were among avowed objectives.

Social-Psychological Interest in Small Groups. Interest in small groups (or more precisely in the interactions of persons in small-group situations) is a comparatively recent development in experimental social psychology, brought to focus most recently on such problems as leadership and the exercise of power, communication, group cohesiveness, group productivity, morale, and the exercise of group pressures and interpersonal influence.

[25] Mayo, *op. cit.*; Roethlisberger and Dickson, *op. cit.*; see also T. N. Whitehead, *The Industrial Worker* (Cambridge, Mass., 1938); F. J. Roethlisberger, *Managament and Morale* (Cambridge, Mass., 1941); E. D. Chapple, "Measuring Human Relations: An Introduction to the Study of Interaction of Individuals," *Genet. Psych. Monogr.*, 22 (Feb., 1940), pp. 9-147, and "The Measurement of Interpersonal Behavior," *Trans. N.Y. Acad. Sci.*, 4 (1942), pp. 222-223.

[26] See, for example, K. D. Benne and Paul Sheats, "Functional Roles of Group Members," *JSI*, 4 (Spring, 1948), pp. 41-49; K. D. Benne and B. Muntyan, *Human Relations in Curriculum Change* (New York, 1951).

Although much of the experimental work that has given both content and direction to small-group analysis along these lines originated in the investigations and theory of Kurt Lewin and others associated with him in group dynamics, other social psychologists, outside this particular orientation, have contributed heavily to the literature on small groups—and there are important sources of social-psychological interest in small groups other than group dynamics that need to be taken into account in any attempt to survey what has been done or to characterize this interest.

Small groups in the sense of pairs or other sets of experimental subjects have commonly been used in research studies in social psychology. In many of the earlier studies on group and social factors in relation to performance of various tasks, for example, such groups were used. Current research interests and conceptions of the small group, however, appear to owe less to these studies than to the large number of observational studies of child behavior in the twenties and thirties, where attention was drawn specifically to the interactions among the subjects and, in some cases, to their feelings and attitudes toward each other. Both in these respects and in the attention that was given to the status behavior of members and to certain structural characteristics of groups, these earlier studies foreshadowed several of the later developments. In some of these studies, techniques were developed for observing and recording interaction, for identifying and describing status positions and other group characteristics.[27] Several of the concepts relating to roles and role-performances as well as to dynamic processes and elements in interpersonal relations were also introduced into social psychological thinking about small groups in these kinds of studies.

Many of the pioneering studies that began to draw together these and other concepts and techniques for social psychology began to appear in the thirties. The problems on which work was done, however, were not necessarily small-group problems—and in many cases the groups that were used were groups in the most minimal sense, sometimes demanding or permitting very little structuring or even interaction among subjects except that response presumably being "tested for" in the experimental situation. Even in these cases, comparatively little attention was given to the details of content, direction, etc., of the interaction process.

The Dynamics of Interpersonal Relations. When small groups have been used in later studies—whether they were simply sets of experimental subjects or groups in which some structure was recognized as existing—the emphasis has rather clearly been upon the communication process itself and on other aspects of interpersonal relations in the situation, especially as these

[27] See, for example, *The Psychology of Social Norms* (New York, 1936). For compact surveys of these and later developments, see R. W. Heyns and Ronald Lippitt, "Systematic Observational Techniques" and G. Lindzey and E. F. Borgatta, "Sociometric Measurement," both in Lindzey, *op. cit.*, pp. 370-448.

relate to needs, satisfactions, motivations, etc., in the subjects. These emphases, together with some use of *role, status, group membership,* and other concepts of abstract relationship, parallel rather clearly some of the developments in sociological and other social-science thinking in the period, and they stand in fairly sharp contrast to conceptions of the group accepted and utilized in many earlier experimental studies.

In general, it has been the dynamic rather than the structural and developmental aspects of social interaction that have interested social psychologists; hence the problem of defining the small group structurally—for example, in terms of functionally interdependent roles, formal or informal roles, "symbols of the group," or other concepts of patterned relationship—has tended to remain secondary in their orientation.

The Experimental Emphasis. It may be suggested in addition that small groups may have entered into social-psychological (including group dynamics) research largely because of the greater ease with which they can be handled in experimental laboratory situations or because possibilities for observing and recording communication as well as for obtaining interpersonal status ratings and the like are greater in small groups than in larger ones. Comparatively less concern, in any case, seems to have been expressed in social-psychological research over the matter of size and structuring in the small group itself than in sociological thinking and research, although, as a matter of course, the number of subjects was invariably reported in each study.

Similarly, except in some of the studies of leadership done by Shartle or of interpersonal perception in groups begun by Tagiuri,[28] there has been somewhat less regard for inquiry in any detail into the functions that cultural prescriptions of group roles, formal role-expectations, and role-awareness have in small groups.

Nevertheless, social psychologists have contributed extensively and importantly to the research literature on small groups and, in fact, seem to have done considerably more experimental work on them than have sociologists to date. Outstanding in this respect have been the research and theoretic formulations of Lewin and his associates in group dynamics, although, as has been mentioned earlier, the work of others not closely identified with group dynamics such as Sherif, Stogdill, Shartle, and Cattell, must also be included.[29] Since these social-psychological studies have contri-

[28] C. L. Shartle, "Studies in Naval Leadership, Part I," in H. Guetzkow (ed.), *Groups, Leadership, and Men* (Pittsburgh, 1951), pp. 119-133; R. Tagiuri, "Relational Analysis: An Extension of Sociometric Method with Emphasis upon Social Perception," *Socm.*, 15 (February, 1952), pp. 91-104.

[29] See, for example, Kurt Lewin and Ronald Lippitt, "An Experimental Approach to the Study of Autocracy and Democracy: A Preliminary Note," *Socm.,* 1 (Jan., 1938), pp. 292-300; Lewin, *Field Theory in Social Science* (New York, 1951), and "Frontiers in Group Dynamics," *HR,* 1 (June and Nov., 1947); R. B. Cattell, "Determining Syntality

buted substantially to current experimental knowledge about small groups, more than passing reference to them must be made in the following section of this chapter.

Representative Research on Small Groups

Major Problems in Small-Group Research. Preliminary sampling of the literature reporting research on small groups shows that investigators in this field have been working on such problems as (1) how and under what conditions small groups are formed; (2) what factors account for the size and structure of small groups; (3) what determines the patterning and direction of interaction within the group or to individuals and groups outside; (4) how small groups influence their members and in what directions; (5) what determines the strength of the influence; (6) how group goals and group norms are formed; and (7) what factors affect the level of morale, productivity, and so on in groups. The sheer volume of output, particularly since World War II (largely because of armed forces contracts), makes it possible to cite here only a few of the studies that may be taken as representative of what is being done, chiefly experimentally, in the area of small-group research.

Research on the Formation and Maintenance of Small Groups. In general, sociologists have been more concerned than other investigators with the question of how groups come into existence. Earlier sociological thinking on the subject was replete with speculations concerning "consciousness of kind," instincts of gregariousness, and the like. This was followed by a period of empirical studies of social contact aimed at discovering the significance of such factors as residential propinquity, ethnic affiliation, race, age, sex, and other attributes or variables in relation to contact and choice of mates, friends, or other associates.

Present-day sociologists have not given up the problem, but have taken a more sophisticated view of it. On the assumption, for example, that general needs to interact with others are firmly embedded in the habit patterns of individuals long before they are aware of them, later investigations have turned the inquiry toward such items as the cultural imperatives and prescriptions (e.g., formal social roles) that enter into the process, or have attempted to observe interaction and specify the conditions under which people associate together in small groups. Of special interest to some is the process (or processes) through which roles (in this case usually *informal* roles) come

Dimensions as a Basis for Morale and Leadership Measurement," in Guetzkow, *op. cit.*, pp. 16-27, and "The Sociometry of Working Relationships in Formal Organizations," *Socm.*, 12 (Aug., 1949), pp. 276-286; Muzafer Sherif, "A Preliminary Experimental Study of Inter-Group Relations," in Rohrer and Sherif, *op. cit.*, pp. 388-424.

to be defined and simultaneously linked up in functional interdependencies with each other.

Some studies in the methodological tradition of earlier field studies have taken a fairly simple inductive approach to the problem and have used on-the-spot observations, aided by sociometric testing and so on, to determine conditions under which small informal groups take shape. Various factors, such as physical proximity, homogeneity in respect to one or more traits, and so on, have been reported. James, to cite only one sociological study in this connection, reported a strong tendency toward homogeneity in the 187 cliques he found among 478 employees of a small woolen mill.[30]

Several studies of children's groups have pointed to specific variables that appear to be associated with the formation of small groups. F. B. Moreno noted, for example, that pre-school children formed into small groups with a certain amount of stability, that members developed status in their groups, and that the groups showed a tendency to be homogeneous with respect to prestige, intelligence, and family income of members.[31]

Emphasis on Needs in Group Operation. Social psychologists—and particularly group dynamists—have generally considered the question of how groups are formed and maintained as a question of what sorts of needs impel social behavior or must be satisfied in order to attract and hold persons as active participants in a group or in a simple social situation. The research in these cases has tended to deal only with informal (and *ad hoc*) groups, and comparatively little attention has been given, as we have suggested above, to role-prescriptions and other cultural components in the situation, including symbols that subjects may be using for identifying themselves and others as members of a group. In group dynamics, phrases such as "group attraction" and group cohesion (a term, incidentally, used by Simmel) are commonly used to refer simultaneously—and rather ambiguously—to dynamic processes operative both in the origin of groups and in their development and maintenance. Hence it is sometimes difficult to determine which of these two processes is being discussed. Actually, the emphasis has tended to be more on the problem of what holds people together in groups rather than on what specifically brings them to initial contact and to the interaction that creates a group. To the extent that the same needs and need-satisfactions (or at least certain ones among them) that draw persons together in the first instance are assumed (or found) to continue in force into subsequent gatherings of the same persons, the distinction becomes relatively unimportant, and, for some research purposes, the first meeting of the group or its twentieth may serve equally well.

Relative Neglect of Origins of Small Groups. Perhaps in consequence of

[30] James, "Clique Organization in a Small Industrial Plant," *loc. cit.*

[31] F. B. Moreno, "Sociometric Status of Children in a Nursery-School Group," *Socm.*, 5 (Nov., 1942), pp. 395-411.

this or similar reasoning, the question of how groups actually originate is often not even raised in some research orientations—or if it is, the answer is likely to be essentially in common-sense terms, that is, that the group was simply "set up" by an investigator who managed to offer sufficiently attractive incentives and rewards to get subjects to come together in a laboratory to follow his instructions.

There are some exceptions to this, however. For example, research in the Westgate Housing Project, conducted by Festinger and others, gave some attention to how cliques developed. It was found, in this case, that although proximity of residence within the project and such factors as the arrangements of sidewalks, mailboxes, and stairways were important in determining the persons with whom one made friends, the attractiveness of whatever groups were formed depended on how well these groups met the needs of their participants. In another instance, basing his report on research among participants in the National Training Laboratory for Group Development at Bethel, Maine, French found that friendship choices were made "mostly on the basis of similarity of occupation, personality characteristics, and the extent of actual and expected reciprocation of the choice." He noted also that such choices were being made shortly after the entire population assembled.[32]

Psychological Variables in Small Groups. Regarding those needs and need satisfactions that draw and hold individuals together in small groups, a number of experimental findings have been reported. Research along these lines by Bovard, Deutsch, French, Lewin, Thibaut, and others, indicates the general kinds of need satisfactions on which "group attraction" depends and at least some of the conditions under which these appear to be maximized. Position in the group, acceptance by others, type of leadership in the situation, clarity of objectives, opportunity for participation, and several other factors have been cited as relevant once the group has been set in motion.[33]

Bion and others with strong psychoanalytic orientation emphasize emotional needs deriving from the nature of earlier intrafamily relationships and reason that individuals are satisfied with groups in proportion as their needs—for direction (from a father figure), for modified erotic pleasure,

[32] Leon Festinger, S. Schachter, and Kurt Back, *Social Pressures in Informal Groups* (New York, 1950); J. R. P. French, Jr., "Group Productivity," in Guetzkow, *op. cit.*, pp. 44-54. For a critique of some aspects of small-group research see Howard Becker, "Vitalizing Sociological Theory," *ASR*, 19,4 (Aug., 1954), esp. pp. 383-385.

[33] See, for example, Lippitt, "Group Dynamics and Personality Dynamics," *AJO*, 21 (Jan. 1951), pp. 18-31; Lewin, "The Dynamics of Group Action," *Educ. Leadership*, 1 (Jan., 1944), pp. 195-200; French, "The Disruption and Cohesion of Groups," *loc. cit.*; Morton Deutsch, "A Theory of Cooperation and Competition," *HR*, 2 (April, 1949), pp. 129-152; E. W. Bovard, Jr., "Group Structure and Perception," *JASP*, 46 (July, 1951), pp. 398-405; J. W. Thibaut, "An Experimental Study of the Cohesiveness of Underprivileged Groups," *HR*, 3 (Feb., 1950), pp. 251-278.

etc.—are gratified. Operational definitions of group cohesion in this case are not offered. Although he did not attempt to develop his case experimentally, Bion has shown that, among other things, systematic and persistent refusal on the part of the nominal leader to give expected authoritarian direction arouses hostility and insecurity among those who expect strong direction and presumably spells intense dissatisfaction with the group experience until the member has been brought around to insight into his own need structure (as interpreted in psychoanalytic terms).

Structure and Interaction Channels in Small Groups. Closely related to the problem of identifying factors in the formation and maintenance of small groups is the general problem of locating the factors that help to determine such structural features of small groups as size, hierarchy of positions, complexity of the relations, and so on, as well as those which appear to govern the direction, amount, and kinds of interaction that go on within a given situation.

Explorations into the Size of Groups. Size of the group (including the questions of modal, and possibly of optimum, size) has been treated in some contexts as a consequence of the given purposes of the group and of other more or less determinable factors; in other contexts it has been treated as a datum to be specified on the basis of observation. An instance of the second of these approaches is the study by James and others, previously cited, in which a modal size of two was found. It was concluded from these observations that groups characterzed by face-to-face and spontaneous interaction tend to gravitate to the smallest size—*i.e.*, two—or, stated otherwise, to the point of the least number of relations. Hollingshead, incidentally to his study of class factors in clique formation and interpersonal interaction among high-school students in Elmtown, found a size of four or five members prevailing for cliques of town dwellers and three for rural youth attending high school in the town.[34]

One factor in determining the size of many groups, especially those existing within formal organizations (as well as experimental laboratory groups) is, of course, the action of power figures, who, by administrative fiat or other manipulative action, set up the groups and often order some of the relations that are to exist among members within the group. Another, of course, is the character of the cultural prescriptions (including formal rules, such as laws specifying monogamous marriage) prevailing in the society. Other factors, both within the personalities and external to the intentions and wishes of the participants, might also be cited. Chevaleva-Janovskaja, Moreno, Jennings,[35] and others have suggested that age of members

[34] James, "A Preliminary Study of the Size Determinant in Small Group Interaction," *loc. cit.;* A. B. Hollingshead, *Elmtown's Youth* (New York, 1949); see also Faris, *op. cit.*

[35] E. Chevaleva-Janovskaja, "Les Groupements spontanés d'enfants à l'âge préscolaire," *AP,* 20 (Feb., 1927), pp. 219-233; J. L. Moreno, "Evolution of Group

and/or their level of psycho-sexual development and other variables determine not only the size of informal groups but also their level of complexity.

Studies of Structural Variables: Prestige, Communication, Power. A rather large number of experimental research findings are available on the subject of factors related to structural and interactional patterns in small groups. Again only a few of these can be cited here to suggest the directions in which investigations into this aspect of small groups are moving. Structural variables are here taken to include not only the number of statuses or positions in the group and the relationships in which these stand to each other, but also the degrees of formality and rigidity that characterize these relationships apart from idiosyncracies in the behavior of persons who "act out" the roles.

Strictly speaking, there is not one structure but several structures for every group—among these a prestige structure, a friendship or choice structure, and a power structure. Studies by Bales and others, Festinger and Thibaut, French, Kelley, Schachter, and Strodtbeck[36] indicate a close and, in general, reciprocal relation between the flow of communication and specified structures in small groups. It has been observed that direction and flow of communication within the group in some instances make it likely that certain people (especially those centrally located in the physical arrangement of the situation in this case) will assume responsibility for certain functions and acquire, or be accorded, high status; and *vice versa*, that persons in prestige-bearing positions themselves control in some measure at least the channels and the patterning of communication. Means and media of communication, spatial location, and arrangements of actors within the situation (presumably whether planned or not) have also been found significant. Experimenting with circular, linear, and inverted-**Y** patterns of physical placement of subjects in five-member "groups" and permitting subjects to communicate in writing only—and only in specified directions—Bavelas and associates found that in both the linear and inverted-**Y** arrangements the person in the central position invariably became the leader, that is, the most influential in guiding the decisions of the group.[37]

Organization" in Eugene Hartley *et al.* (eds.), *Outside Readings in Psychology* (New York, 1950), pp. 639-648; Helen H. Jennings, "A Sociometric Study of Emotional and Social Expansiveness," in R. G. Barker *et al.*, *Child Behavior and Development* (New York, 1943), pp. 527-543.

[36] Festinger and Thibaut, "Interpersonal Communication in Small Groups," *loc. cit.;* H. H. Kelley, "Communication in Experimentally Created Hierarchies," *HR,* 4 (Feb., 1951), pp. 39-56; French, "Group Productivity," *loc. cit.;* Schachter, *op. cit.,* See Bales' works, especially "Channels of Communication in Small Groups," *loc. cit.,* and Strodtbeck, "Husband-Wife Interaction Over Revealed Differences," *loc. cit.*

[37] Alex Bavelas, "Communication Patterns in Task-Oriented Groups," in Cartwright and Zander, *op. cit.,* pp. 493-506.

T. M. Mills, in his study of power relationships in three-person laboratory discussion groups, found that when what he called the strong members of a trio formed a mutually supportive pair, the third person was firmly excluded and a stable social structure occurred; but when the strong members were in conflict, no stable structure developed and the two competed for the favor of the third member.[38]

Stratification in Small Groups. Differentiations of status positions—especially those identified as leadership positions—and development of hierarchies of status in small groups have occupied the research attention of a large number of social scientists. Both total hierarchies of status (sometimes seen as systems of linked roles) and assignments of positions to individuals have been studied as possible functions of such items as the nature of the task, the kind of observed interaction in the situation, and the inferred needs of various participants. In some cases, the problem has been phrased to point up the effects on size, role-differentiation, degree of stratification and other structuring, complexity and persistence of in-group relations, etc., of the activities being engaged in, the type of interaction, and the nature of the task presented; in other cases, such factors as type of interaction and channeling of communication are examined as consequences of size of the group, type of structuring, style of leadership, prestige of the group among other groups, and the like. Again, positions assigned to specific individuals, including "the leaders," have been looked at in terms of the amount of their participation, the nature of their contributions to the group, etc., as well as in terms of dominance-submission "needs" in the actors in the situation. Size of the group in relation to number and complexity of intragroup relations, amount of fracturing into subgroups, and so forth, have also been examined.[39]

In broad theoretical contexts, these items are seen increasingly to be mutually related (as much earlier sociological thinking had anticipated they would be), but experimental research has had to proceed in more pedestrian or fragmentary fashion, testing for relations first in one direction and then in another.

[38] T. M. Mills, "The Coalition Pattern in Three-Person Groups," *ASR*, 19 (Dec., 1954), pp. 657-667.

[39] E. P. Torrance, "The Behavior of Small Groups Under the Stress Conditions of Survival," *ASR*, 19 (Dec., 1954), pp. 751-755; Lewin *et al.*, "Patterns of Aggressive Behavior in Experimentally Created 'Social Climates,'" *JSP*, 10 (May, 1939), pp. 271-299; J. I. Hurwitz *et al.*, "Some Effects of Power on the Relations of Group Members," in Cartwright and Zander, *op. cit.*, pp. 483-492; Lippitt, "Field Theory and Experiment in Social Psychology: Autocratic and Democratic Group Atmospheres," *AJS*, 45 (July, 1939), pp. 26-49; L. Carter *et al.*, "The Behavior of Leaders and Other Group Members," *JASP*, 46 (Oct., 1951), pp. 589-595; O. J. Harvey, "An Experimental Approach to the Study of Status-Relations in Informal Groups," *ASR*, 18 (Aug., 1953), pp. 357-367; Hare, "Study of Interaction and Consensus in Different-Sized Groups," *op. cit.*

Group Pressures and Interpersonal Influence in Small Groups. The significance of small primary groups in relation to personality development and the formation of attitudes has long been recognized in social science, and various hypotheses as to how this aspect of socialization occurs were advanced by Cooley, Mead, Freud, and others before World War I. More recently, however, experimental inquiry into exactly how group pressures and interpersonal influence are attempted—in what directions and on what specific sorts of issues—and under what conditions they are successful or effective has tended to supplement or replace the less expressly empirical approaches. In this respect—as in others we have considered thus far—close observation and experimentation have been employed more and more throughout the social sciences generally. Again, however, important leads in the experimental design of research on the general problem have come from social psychologists, some of whom no doubt would also identify themselves as sociologists.

One general point should be made clear at the outset. This is that it is not so much the smallness of the group as it is the intimacy—the emotionally charged, personal interaction and relations that smallness makes possible—that appears to be the basic desideratum in the process. Even without the presence of intimately personal relations, however, as group dynamists have shown, it is possible to observe and trace patterns and consequences of intragroup pressures exerted among members and to hypothesize about them.

For the latter, Festinger, Schachter, and Back formulate the general position succinctly with the proposition that:

> the strength of the influence which the group could effectively exert [in the direction of gaining acceptance of group norms and securing homogeneous, conforming responses, etc.] . . . depended partly upon the attractiveness of the group for the member and partly on the degree to which the member was in communication with others in the group.

Back found subsequently that in "high-cohesive groups" (i.e., those most attractive to their members in an experimental series) not only did the subjects try harder to influence their partners, but partners were more willing to accept each other's opinions. This appeared to be true regardless of the source of the attractiveness that the high-cohesive groups had for their members. It was also proposed that pressures (toward uniformity at least) are exerted differentially in groups, tending to be stronger in high-cohesive groups and in groups which are already homogeneous in other respects or which have clearly defined and widely accepted goals and norms—and with varied consequences.[40] Deviates, up to a certain point, are targets for greater amounts

[40] Festinger, "Informal Communication in Small Groups," *loc. cit.;* Back, "Influence Through Social Communication," *op. cit.*

both of communication and of pressure than conforming members, but pressures, if "stronger" than the "positive valences" that hold the person to the group, can drive members out of the group entirely. In general, individual persons in high status positions in small groups have been found to be subjected to less pressure of certain kinds than other members. Whyte has suggested, however, that a leader, in order to remain a leader, must conform more closely to the group's norms than other members, and in this sense he is less "free" than the others.[41]

Leadership and Influence in Small Groups. Lippitt, Polansky, and others, to cite another example, found that power figures among children in a summer camp, as a consequence of being imitated voluntarily by other children, influenced others even when they did not want to do so or were not aware of doing so. In cases of deliberate attempts by leaders to "influence" others in the group, Preston and Heintz found a "participatory" style of leadership more effective than a "supervisory" style in creating changes in attitudes. In similar studies, reminiscent of some of Lewin's earlier experiments, Bovard and Levine and Butler[42] found that individuals were more apt to change their attitudes and overt behavior (and more apt to change in the direction of a common norm) when they have participated in group discussion and other interaction in reaching a decision than when they have been told what to do either by command or by formal lecture by a leader-instructor.

Schachter and others found that cohesiveness serves to heighten susceptibility of group members to influence from other members. Liking of one individual for another increases the probability of one's being influenced by the other. Similarity of position, occupation, and certain other attributes appear also to be significant in determining whether (and how much) interpersonal influence will be exerted. This has been pointed out in studies by Lazarsfeld concerned with voting behavior, and similar effects have been observed in informal work groups and in other contexts by Hughes, Van Zelst, Riley and Flowerman,[43] and many others.

[41] See R. M. Emerson, "Deviation and Rejection: An Experimental Replication," *ASR,* 19 (Dec., 1954), pp. 688-693; W. F. Whyte, "Corner Boys: A Study of Clique Behavior," *AJS,* 46 (March, 1941), pp. 647-664; J. G. March, "Group Norms and the Active Minority," *ASR,* 19 (Dec., 1954), pp. 733-741.

[42] Lippitt *et al.,* "The Dynamics of Power," *HR,* 5 (Feb., 1952), pp. 37-64; Preston and Heintz, *op. cit.;* Bovard, *op. cit.;* J. Levine and J. Butler, "Lecture *vs.* Group Discussion in Changing Behavior," *JAP,* 36 (Feb., 1952), pp. 29-33.

[43] S. Schachter *et al.,* "An Experimental Study of Cohesiveness and Productivity," *HR,* 4 (Aug., 1951), pp. 229-238; Paul Lazarsfeld *et al., The People's Choice* (New York, 1944); E. C. Hughes, "The Knitting of Racial Groups in Industry," *ASR,* 11 (Oct., 1946), pp. 512-519; R. H. Van Zelst, "Validation of a Sociometric Regrouping Procedure," *JASP,* 7 (April, 1952), pp. 299-301; Matilda W. Riley and Samuel Flowerman, "Group Relations as a Variable in Communication Research," *ASR,* 16 (April, 1951), pp. 174-180.

Butler, Sacks, and others suggest that there are some special cases where influence is facilitated by inequality of status and by absence of homogeneity (although not necessarily of *rapport*)—one of these being in the therapeutic relationship existing between client and therapist[44] and another in the educational process involving student and teacher. Discrepancies in findings among several studies make it clear that the nature of the content to be communicated or the kind of influence that is attempted, or what within the behavior system of the person is being "influenced," must be discriminated. In addition to these, there are personality variables in the actors themselves, as well as variables in the situations, that have been found to affect the kind and amount of influence possible. Asch, for example, in a study of some affects of group process on the modification and distortion of judgments, found that persons with a strong degree of "confidence" in their own perceptions resisted making changes in their expressed judgments in the face of group pressure designed to get them to relinquish these in favor of "inaccurate perceptions" deliberately reported by others acting as experimental stooges in the group.[45] He found also that the "support" of one other person in a group often sufficed to give the subject enough resistance to pressure to retain his original judgment. Findings from some studies support the common-sense observation that where subjects expect to find (or do find) that their opinions are sufficiently different from those prevailing in the group to invite criticism or pressure, they will suppress rather than change these opinions. Gorden, for example, found that a large proportion of the members of a group of twenty-four persons held private opinions that were different from those they publicly stated in the group.[46]

Group Norms and Personal Influence in Small Groups. Sociologists, as we have suggested, have tended to investigate this problem in somewhat different perspective from that of social psychologists. Strodtbeck, for example, in his study of husband-wife interaction in three different cultures, concluded that cultural norms and role-expectations partly determine how much and what kind of influence is attempted and how successful it will be. He reported the attempts to be "most successful" in the case of Mormon spouses (with husbands attempting to influence more frequently and insistently than wives in this particular instance), "less successful" in the case of Texans, and least so in the case of Navajos, who, incidentally, attempted more frequently

[44] J. M. Butler, "The Interaction of Client and Therapist," *JASP,* 47 (April, 1952), pp. 366-378; E. L. Sacks, "Intelligence Scores as a Function of Experimentally Established Social Relationships Between Child and Examiner," *ibid.,* pp. 354-358.

[45] S. E. Asch, "Effects of Group Pressure upon the Modification and Distortion of Judgments," in Guetzkow, *op. cit.,* pp. 177-190; see also G. M. Hochbaum, "The Relation between Group Members' Self-Confidence and Their Reactions to Group Pressures to Uniformity," *ASR,* 19 (Dec., 1954), pp. 678-687.

[46] R. L. Gorden, "Interaction Between Attitude and Definition of the Situation in the Expression of Opinion," *ASR,* 17 (Feb., 1952), pp. 50-58.

than couples in the other categories to win by imploring concurrence from the spouse rather than by argumentation and persuasion.[47]

Approaching the phenomenon of influence of the small group on behavior from a different direction, Stouffer *et al.* and Shils and Janowitz have shown that the motivation to fight among soldiers both in the American Army and in the German *Wehrmacht* derived not from individuals' acceptance of large strategic or political goals, but rather from their experiences with, and feelings of loyalty toward, others in their military primary groups. These findings parallel those of Mayo, Roethlisberger, and others in industrial work groups, where what fellow workers thought about their performance was observed to be, in general, more effective in influencing how workers worked than the persons or groups external to the immediate work situation. Several refinements or extensions of these hypotheses have been made. Babchuck and Goode report, for example, that something other than simple rejection of management's demands can be involved.[48] The mere fact of being singled out for observation in one case, however, according to one report from the Mayo group, was sufficient to affect the work performance, at least temporarily—the "influence" in this case emanating from outside the immediate work group.

Development of Group Goals and Norms in Small Groups. Comparatively less work appears to have been done on tracing in detail the processes by which group goals are formulated and norms of performance are evolved within small groups than other problems outlined here—partly, perhaps, because of the difficulties involved in specifying what is denoted by the concept of "group goal" in the first instance. Norms generally are recognized as culture patterns, and the processes by which these are created in small groups have been given somewhat more attention. Sherif's classic study of the formation of norms, previously cited, is particularly germane although the norms in this case were norms of perception rather than of performance. Differences, again, appear between social psychologists and group dynamists on one hand and sociologists and anthropologists on the other, with the former confining their analyses largely to processes operating within single sessions of interacting subjects—or to short-term groups lifted out of their full social contexts for reasons that have already been suggested.

Homans and other sociologists have given explicit attention to the problem of describing the formation and the functions of norms in small groups. One hypothesis, advanced by Homans, is that an increase in the frequency of interaction among members of a group and in the number of

[47] Strodtbeck, "Husband-Wife Interaction over Revealed Differences," *loc. cit.* Strodtbeck also found that, in general, the spouse who talked most won the decision most frequently.

[48] Stouffer *et al., op. cit.*; Shils and Janowitz, *op. cit.*; N. Babchuch and W. J. Goode, "Work Incentives in a Self-Determined Group," *ASR* 16 (Oct., 1951), pp. 679-687.

activities they participate in together leads to an increase in the extent to which norms are common and clear. Others are that the members of the group are often more nearly alike in the norms they hold than in their overt behavior; or that norms, once established, tend to change more slowly than actual social behavior.[49] Progress made thus far toward tracing the processes by which norms are created in small groups has depended heavily upon theory about the nature of language and of symbolic communication generally.

Productivity, Morale, Consensus, and Related Variables in Small Groups. Research on the problems of locating variables associated with productivity, consensus, morale, and what Cattell has called *syntality* factors in small groups has been done recently in a wide variety of contexts. As a result of the wide interest in "applied knowledge," the research literature in this particular area is voluminous. Again, only a sampling of studies can be made.

As might be anticipated, discrepancies in interpretations of findings occur. For example, Bavelas and others suggest that, in small groups of workers meeting together with skilled discussion leaders to discuss work problems, to decide whether they were to set a group production goal, and to determine the content and level of that goal, productivity underwent a very marked increase that was sustained over a period of time. Babchuck and Goode challenge this with evidence that decisions of the "self-determined" work group do not lead necessarily either to high morale or to high productivity.[50] Similarly, whereas some studies have reported both productivity and morale to be higher in groups that have been formed on the basis of sociometric preference or in groups that are highly cohesive, others have denied or sharply qualified this conclusion. Schachter, for example, suggests that cohesiveness as such does not necessarily make for increase in productivity; rather it serves to heighten susceptibility to influence, which can then be turned toward either higher *or* lower productivity.[51] Other conditions, such as prestige of the group as a whole, aspirations of participants, actual power of the group to make decisions, and cooperative working conditions, have been reported in other studies to lead to higher productivity.

Many investigations have been directed toward aspects of group performance other than productivity. Thus, for example, speed and accuracy in problem-solving (a research problem frequently studied in social psychology) were reported by Bavelas to be functions of the kind of communi-

[49] Homans, *The Human Group* pp. 12, 126, 362.

[50] Alex Bavelas, unpublished study cited in Lewin's "Frontiers in Group Dynamics," *op. cit.*, pp. 25-26. See also R. L. Kahn and Daniel Katz, "Leadership Practices in Relation to Productivity and Morale," in Cartwright and Zander, *op. cit.*, pp. 612-628; Babchuch and Goode, *op. cit.*

[51] See, for example, Van Zelst, *op. cit.*; B. Norfleet, "Interpersonal Relations and Group Productivity," *JSI*, 4 (Spring 1948), pp. 66-69; Schachter, "An Experimental Study of Cohesiveness and Productivity," *loc. cit.*

cation structure existing in the group. Again, significantly fewer incorrect solutions to complex problems have been found in situations where group members who differ in expertness were willing to accept expert knowledge, as compared with groups where experts were ignored.[52]

Bovard found more noticeable shifts toward common norms and greater intermember friendliness in "group-centered" groups than in "leader-centered" groups—a finding similar to those of Preston and Heintz, Kahn and Katz, and others. Lewin, Lippitt, and White, in their earlier studies of behavior under "authoritarian" and "democratic" conditions, had previously reported higher morale, more "we-feeling," stronger group unity, more effective attack on group tasks, etc., in the "democratic" social climate. Maier and Solem report that groups with "trained leaders" are superior in the quality of their performance to leaderless groups or to groups with "untrained" leaders, because the trained leader helps the group make effective use of minority opinions.[53]

Experimental studies on consensus and on *esprit de corps* are also found in the research literature on small groups. Hare, for example, reports that groups of five were more successful in achieving consensus, or achieved it more rapidly, than groups of twelve members. Sharper specialization of role-functions and fewer positions in the smaller groups, he suggests, might tend to facilitate achievement of consensus as well as to reduce an apparent tendency for groups of twelve to split into factions. Testing for the significance of other factors, French, for example, found that "organized" groups not only had more "we-feeling" and showed more interdependence under conditions of fear and frustration than "unorganized" groups, but also remained more cohesive in spite of the more frequent quarrels that developed over goals and methods of achieving them (presumably because of greater ego-involvement in the group, etc.).[54]

Relation of Small Groups to Larger Social Systems. Investigation of the interrelations among small groups and larger social systems has been the concern, apparently, of a larger number of sociologists and more recently of anthropologists than of other groups of specialists who have given attention to this general problem—Stogdill,[55] for example.

[52] Alex Bavelas, "Communication Patterns in Task-Oriented Groups," in Lerner and Lasswell, *The Policy Sciences,* pp. 193-202; French, "Group Productivity," *op. cit.*

[53] Bovard, *op. cit.;* Preston and Heintz, *op. cit.;* Kahn and Katz, *op. cit.;* N. R. F. Maier and A. R. Solem, "The Contribution of a Discussion Leader to the Quality of Group Thinking: The Effective Use of Minority Opinions," *HR,* 5 (Aug., 1952), pp. 277-288.

[54] Hare, *op. cit.;* French, "Organized and Unorganized Groups Under Fear and Frustration," *loc. cit.*

[55] Stogdill, "Leadership, Membership, and Organization," *loc. cit.,* and "The Sociometry of Working Relationships in Formal Organizations," *Socm.,* 12 (August, 1949), pp. 276-286.

As was pointed out earlier, problems of this nature were among the first raised by sociologists using the primary-group concept. The problem was usually considered in terms of functions of primary groups in relation to larger social systems as a result of either preparing or failing to prepare their members for participation in the larger systems. If the question of what constituted satisfactory participation in the larger system was raised, it was generally answered in the light of prevailing values of the organization or the community—or, in some cases, of the investigators themselves. Both sociological and social-work studies of boys' gangs, for example, were frequently done in this perspective, social workers being concerned primarily with formulating principles that might guide group workers and others active in social-service agencies.

In sociological literature, functions of the family and of gangs, cliques, and other small groups have commonly been viewed in relation to the organization and social processes operative in the local community or in the society—for example in relation to the ecological patterning of the community, the class system, the political structure, and so on. In family studies, processes bridging the relationship have been examined frequently in terms of personality structure of individuals as they carry habits and attitudes, for example, from the smaller group to the larger, and *vice versa*. In broad perspective, the family has been seen not only as a socializing agent but also as a necessary refuge to which individuals can periodically turn from the impersonal, secondary, and categoric types of relations prevailing in larger communities of certain types. According to this view stresses emanating from the larger society, as these are carried back to the family through the attitudes of individuals or in other ways, have been interpreted as one of the major sources of difficulty in maintaining the small family group intact.

Examples of experimental studies designed to test the significance of primary-group participation for subsequent personal "adjustment" of individuals, especially in large social contexts, are those by Mandel, Hill, Shulman, and others cited by Chapin in *Experimental Designs for Sociological Research.*

The Community Context of Small Groups. In another direction, Whyte's study of *Street-Corner Society*, for example, aimed to show among other things some of the consequences for the social organization of a slum area of the existence of street-corner gangs and other small groups that grew up alongside—or inside—the formal political organization of the community. Still other studies, such as Hollingshead's report on high-school cliques in a small city in Illinois, have showed how small groups both reflect and help to perpetuate the social class structure of the community.[56] Other studies of the organization and functioning of small groups in school and college com-

[56] Whyte, *Street-Corner Society;* Hollingshead, *Elmtown's Youth.*

munities, and in such specialized kinds of communities as prisons and military camps, have also been reported.

The Institutional Context of Small Groups. Small groups in relation to social movements—that is, religious, political, revolutionary, reform, and youth movements, and so on—have been recognized as having important functions. Sociologists of religion, for example, have been keenly aware—at least since Weber—of the importance of the charimatic leader and his band of apostles in the development of religious organizations; and small circles of "like-minded" worshippers have frequently existed in religion. Similarly, the phenomenon of the *cell* in revolutionary movements, the troop, the patrol, and other small groups in scouting and other youth movements has been noted,[57] though not frequently studied in full empirical detail.

Recently, more and more sociological studies of small groups—usually identified as informal groups—have been made in the context of formal, bureaucratic organizations such as industrial plants, commercial organizations, and the military services. In some cases, fleeting dyadic relationships (e.g., between customer and waitress in the restaurant) have been included; in others, attention has been focused on groups that are more highly structured, although still largely informal. Studies of the functions of small groups within larger organizations—particularly of cliques among factory workers—have not yet produced consistent findings, however, any more than have studies of other small-group phenomena. Gross, for example, complains of "an unfortunate tendency in the literature on the sociology of work to regard cliques as innocuous play groups or else as being antithetical to the purposes of the organization as exemplified in the restriction of output." Although this is the case in some situations, he argues, there is evidence at hand to suggest that "primary controls on behavior are far from being inconsistent with institutional controls."[58]

Small Group Analysis and General Sociology

Mutual Relevance of Social Theory and Small Group Research. It is difficult to insolate and identify what might be called *small-group theory* in sociology. General schemes of analysis and interpretation of social phenomena, such as those of Park and Burgess, Znaniecki, Wiese-Becker, Lundberg and Dodd,

[57] See, for example, A. W. Eister, *Drawing-Room Conversion: A Sociological Account of the Oxford Group Movement* (Durham, N.C., 1950), pp. 101 ff.; Howard Becker, *German Youth: Bond or Free* (New York, 1946).

[58] W. F. Whyte, "The Social Structure of the Restaurant," *AJS,* 54 (Jan., 1949), pp. 302-310; Edward Gross, "Some Functional Consequences of Primary Controls in Formal Work Organizations," *ASR,* 18 (Aug., 1953), pp. 368-373.

Sorokin,[59] and others, have made explicit, and occasionally detailed, reference to small groups; but what is appropriate theory for small-group analysis is not often clearly distinguished from what applies also—perhaps more appropriately—to larger social systems. Except when the specific size of the group—as two-member, three-member, or other—has been made a starting point for theoretic analysis (as in portions of Simmel's *Sociology* or in the Wiese-Becker *Systematic Sociology*), small groups have tended to be bracketed with primary groups and analyzed in primary-group terms or else treated as abstract categories in classificatory series without further efforts to hypothesize about processes and the functions that are peculiar to them.

In general, although some structural-functional types of theories appear to have avoided any tendency toward purely taxonomic treatment of groups, the focus of attention has tended not to be on the small group as such, but rather on the functional interrelations among roles and other general aspects of social systems. Although some of the findings in the empirical studies by Bales and his associates have served to underscore empirically the probable significance of the number of actors in the situation as an important variable, this has not been a focal point around which research and theory have been organized. Rather it has simply been a condition to vary or hold constant from one observation or experiment to another. Emphasis has been on examining such phenomena as the processes in which functionally interlocking roles and integrated role-systems come into being in problem-solving groups, etc. The larger, more comprehensive theory against which these findings are being viewed, however, purports to describe processes in social systems generally, not in small groups only. The small group is, in a sense, only a kind of social system that permits handling in a laboratory setting—one that allows some control of various factors in the situation and also reasonably detailed observational recording and analysis of the details of interpersonal interaction and relationship as these develop. Given the need for inclusive frames of reference in social science, these broader theoretic settings should eventually make it possible to fit research findings together more satisfactorily and to trace out more readily the lines of possible or probable relevance among various studies.

Several theoretic schemes in sociology, nevertheless, are useful in connection with small group-analysis and research—among them the proposals for analysis of small groups found in the Wiese-Becker *Systematic Sociology*, concepts and hypotheses found in Homans' *The Human Group*, and proposi-

[59] R. E. Park and E. W. Burgess, *Introduction to the Science of Sociology* (Chicago, 1921); Florian Znaniecki, *The Method of Sociology* (New York, 1934); Becker, *Systematic Sociology;* G. A. Lundberg, *Foundations of Sociology* (New York, 1939); S. C. Dodd, *Dimensions of Society* (New York, 1942), pp. 389-435; P. A. Sorokin, *Society, Culture, and Personality* (New York, 1947).

tions about small groups as social systems found in Bales and Parsons' papers in *Working Papers in the Theory of Action*, and elsewhere. These three by no means exhaust the possibilities, but they may serve to point up some available theoretical resources.

An Early Functional Approach to Small Groups. Earliest (1932) of the three formulations listed above is that of Wiese-Becker. This approach is notable for its clear statement of the close correspondence that exists at the empirical level between interaction and structure—or as Becker called them, between *action patterns* and *plurality patterns*. It is simply a matter of arbitrary choice, guided by research interests of the investigator, in other words, whether he focuses attention on "live" social *action* and on-going *processes*, or upon the *relationships* that have grown out of (and that, in some measure, in turn channel) any subsequent interaction. In short, these are two sides of the same coin. Similar distinctions are sometimes drawn between "dynamic" and "static" or between "horizontal" or "cross-sectional" and "genetic" or "longitudinal" analysis—although these dichotomies generally fall short of differentiating out from *process* those phenomena that, in current psychological usage, are identified as "dynamic." This distinction is suggested but not developed at length in Wiese-Becker.

An important contribution to the clarification of the concept of the *group* made in the Wiese-Becker treatise was its listing of the characteristic criteria of "genuine" groups. These were intended to distinguish groups in a specifically sociological sense from other kinds of plurels and especially from loose aggregates, statistical categories or classes, etc. Genuine groups must, for example, have formal or informal "organization . . . based on a division of function among its members."[60] This is a conception not far removed from that which sees groups as systems of functionally interrelated or interlocked role-statuses, especially when note is taken of the Wiese-Becker distinction between *processes* and *relationships*.

The Small Group and Its Systems: Homans and Parsons. In Homans' treatment of groups, including small groups but again not confined to them, the emphasis was placed on tracing interrelations among "activities, interactions, and sentiments." all of which were regarded as phenomena that could be observed and analyzed at a comparatively low level of abstraction. These phenomena were held to be found in all groups—and interrelations among them to be operative and analyzable *within* the group (considered more or less in isolation as an "internal system") and within the group *in relation to* factors of various kinds seen as impinging upon it from without ("external system"). Field observations and various kinds of data, including on-the-spot recording of interaction, interview, and questionnaire responses and reports of these were expected to provide the basic case material out of

[60] Becker, *op. cit.*, pp. 490 ff.

which certain hypotheses might be derived inductively and in which other hypotheses similarly derived in other cases might be "tested" for goodness-of-fit. An example of hypotheses put forward by Homans, to cite only one, is "An increase in the size of the group and in the specialization of activity will tend to increase the number of positions in the chain of interaction between the top leader and the ordinary members."[61]

Probably the most ambitious and comprehensive theoretical framework within which small-group research is presently being conducted is the general theory of action, in process of being worked out by Parsons, Bales, Shils, and others.[62] Here the effort—as far as small groups are concerned—is to examine small-group phenomena in the light of hypotheses derived from systematic theory and in such a way that explicit reference can be made to systems of social action on other levels. It is argued that what makes this kind of reference possible is a theory that utilizes as its central concept the idea of *system* and that "sees" social action as organized, or as occurring, within systems at different levels of analysis. The system concept, which is a familiar one in the physical and biological sciences, simply holds that phenomena can be thought of as coming in constellations of interrelated units affected by variables that emanate from within the system itself or from outside in such a way that a change or alteration in one is felt by, or influences, in some degree, all other units. In this pattern of contemporary social-science thinking, not only groups but also personalities and cultures can be investigated in system terms, with various kinds of units used according to the level on which the analysis is to proceed. In this scheme, systems are conceived to exist *within* systems or to interpenetrate with one another. A limited number of "system problems" and a few general structural features are thought of as running like a series of threads through all these types or levels of systems—or at least through those which are identified as *action* systems.

Small-group research in this setting is expected to yield information about role-formation, interaction sequences, role-relations, and regular or recurrent shifts in the patterning of these, etc.—knowledge that is expected to have relevance beyond the confines of the specific group studied and beyond the level of the small group. Although it is not expected to generalize loosely across system levels—from microcosm to macrocosm or vice versa—without recognition of different orders of variables, it is anticipated, apparently, that more detailed knowledge about role-formation and other pro-

[61] Homans, *The Human Group,* p. 406.

[62] Talcott Parsons *et al., Toward a General Theory of Action* (Cambridge, Mass., 1951). See also R. F. Bales, "The Equilibrium Problem in Small Groups," and Parsons *et al.,* "Phase Movement in Relation to Motivation, Symbol Formation, and Role Structure," both in Parsons *et al., Working Papers in the Theory of Action* (Glencoe, Ill,, 1954), pp. 111-161, 162-269.

cesses will be possible in the framework of analysis of social action systems. More effective integration of research, not only among sociological specialties but also among social-science disciplines, is also anticipated. If, in the context of small-group observation and analysis, the processes by which roles come to be created and functional interdependencies among them established can be traced, such information can be "placed" in a wider context with consequent gains in its relevance and usefulness for social-science theory on a larger and broader scale.

THE FUTURE OF SMALL-GROUP RESEARCH

It is difficult at this point to estimate the place that small-group research and analysis may occupy in general sociology. But what has already been said suggests that such research may be expected to have implications extending beyond small-group phenomena as such, that it may serve to advance social-science theory and sociological theory in ways that might not have been anticipated as recently as three decades ago. Whether this current surge of interest in small groups will last, or whether it will fulfill some of the expectations held for it, whether conceptual difficulties can be resolved and discontinuities bridged—these and other questions remain to be answered in some future survey of small-group research and analysis.

SELECTED BIBLIOGRAPHY

American Sociological Review, "Special Issue on Small-Group Research" [with the aid of F. L. Strodtbeck], 19 (December, 1954).

Cartwright, Dorwin and A. F. Zander, *Group Dynamics* (Evanston: Row, Peterson, 1953).

Faris, R. E. L., "Development of the Small-Group Research Movement," in Muzafer Sherif and M. O. Wilson (eds.), *Group Relations at the Crossroads* (New York: Harper, 1953).

Lewin, Kurt, *Field Theory in Social Science* (New York: Harper, 1951).

Moreno, J. L., *Who Shall Survive?* (Washington: Nervous and Mental Disease Publishing Company, 1934).

Parsons, Talcott, R. F. Bales, and E. A. Shils, *Working Papers in the Theory of Action* (Glencoe, Ill.: The Free Press, 1953).

Shils, E. A., "The Study of the Primary Group," in Daniel Lerner and H. D. Lasswell (eds.), *The Policy Sciences* (Stanford: Stanford University Press, 1951).

Simmel, Georg, *The Sociology of Georg Simmel,* translated and edited by K. H. Wolff (Glencoe, Ill.: The Free Press, 1951).

Strodtbeck, F. L., and A. P. Hare, "Bibliography of Small-Group Research," *Sociometry,* 17 (May, 1954), pp. 107-178.

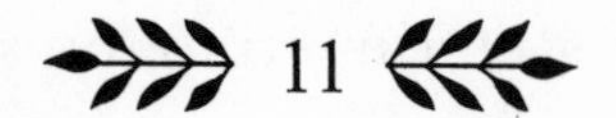

SOCIAL DISORGANIZATION: THE CONFLICT OF NORMATIVE AND EMPIRICAL APPROACHES

DON MARTINDALE

THE THEORIES THAT HAVE SO FAR BEEN ADVANCED IN THE AREA OF SOCIAL problems have for thousands of years been judgmentally normative (hereinafter referred to simply as "normative"). Indeed, the great confusion in this area has resulted from the tendency to disguise normative social theories as empirical types. It is important to distinguish between normative and empirical theory, since the only type appropriate to the study of social problems is normative social theory.

In science, a developed theory consists of a logically interrelated body of laws. Although such laws are crucial to scientific explanations, they are not the sole requirement for making scientific predictions; a knowledge of particular properties and circumstances is also required. Description consists in establishing the "facts" of the event or events under study. Two vital phases of description are: (1) the identification of properties of the events and (2) the establishment of relevant quantitative aspects of these properties. *Explanation,* so far as it is distinguishable from description, consists in discovering relations between the various properties described. There are two important types of explanation: (1) those that seek to *generalize* the relations between the facts—that is, to establish the existence of laws; and (2) those that apply established laws to sets of observed facts—in the process of prediction. Both forms of explanation are frequently present in a given scientific study.

In a recent study, these distinctions have been clarified by Feigl, who has treated explanation as essentially an inferential procedure. One may distinguish, according to Feigl, among various levels of explanation in terms of their generality. Reading from the bottom up they are:

Theories, 2nd order	Still more penetrating interpretation (still higher constructs).
Theories, 1st order	Sets of assumptions using higher-order constructs (results of abstraction and inference). (Deeper interpretation of the facts as rendered on the Empirical-Law Level.)
Empirical Laws	Functional relationships between relatively directly observable (or measurable) magnitudes.
Description	Simple account of individual facts or events (data) as more or less immediately observable.[1]

In Feigl's presentation a "law" is a relatively low-order explanation. It simply states a regularity in a number of specific facts. The number of deductions that can be made from it is relatively limited. A theory is a higher-order explanation that states regularities abstracted from a number of laws; the total base of descriptive material which it encompasses is thus tremendously greater. By the same reasoning, the higher the order of theory, the greater its eventual empirical power.

The Essentials of Empirical Theory. The results of this process of exposing degrees of regularity in facts may be called empirical theory. It has no object other than explanation, and in the pursuit of this object the only ultimate criteria of acceptability are (1) the highest possible generality that gives (2) the maximum explanatory power. Typically, such theory develops in complete disregard of what *ought to be*. It is not anti-ethical but non-ethical.[2]

The Nature of Normative Theory. If theory making is broadly considered as the construction of concepts into systems from which deductions can be logically made, only one kind of theory making serves scientific explanation. Scientific explanation is concerned with facts and relations, and theory construction has also been addressed to objectives and aids in reaching them. There is no reason why the conceptualization of such action desirabilities should not be given theoretical form. When it is, the result may be called *normative theory* in contrast to empirical theory.

The contrasts between empirical and normative theory are important. The ultimate materials of empirical theory are facts; the ultimate materials

[1] Herbert Feigl, "Some Remarks on the Meaning of Scientific Explanation," in Herbert Feigl and Wilfrid Sellars (eds.), *Readings in Philosophical Analysis* (New York, 1949), p. 512.

[2] See Howard Becker, *Through Values to Social Interpretation* (Durham, N.C., 1950), pp. 281-305.

of normative theory are value-*imperatives*. As noted above, empirical theory is formed out of a system of laws. Normative theory converts facts and laws into requisite means and conditions and is unique in being addressed to a system of objectives desired by the formulator or by those in whose service he stands.

Social Change as a Major Approach to Social Problems

Normative (dogmatic) and empirical theory are never parallel. The values to be *achieved* determine the content of a normative theory, and anything that clarifies the conditions affecting the values becomes relevant. It is not inconceivable that the findings of a half-dozen empirical disciplines can be drawn upon. However, some branches of empirical theory will normally be closer than others to any given normative position. In terms of our analysis, the closest empirical counterpart to the theory of social problems is the theory of social change.

The theory of social change attempts to explain such things as the formation and dissolution of institutions, social orders, societies, social strata, social roles, etc. It is occupied with those structures and situations in which human social values are anchored. No other field continuously raises so many questions relevant for a normative theory of social problems. However, these theories should be kept distinct: an empirical theory of social change does not prescribe goals; nor does a normative theory of social action ever make complete or exclusive use of the theory of social change. This, of course, is not to say that in the literature these two kinds of theory are always kept distinct.

Theories of Social Evolution: Comte and Spencer. The works of Auguste Comte and Herbert Spencer were to sociologists the most important sources of theories of social problems prior to World War I. These works may also serve to illustrate the relation between normative and empirical theories.

Despite considerable differences in the manner in which they worked it out, Comte and Spencer held the same general theory of social change—a conception of large-scale societal evolution. To be sure, Comte was idealistic, Spencer materialistic. Comte developed only broad outlines; Spencer conceived a theory of evolution of single institutions as well. But in spite of numerous differences, some essential similarities remain: evolution is a transformation of the forms of life of all mankind; century-long changes form the only proper unit for comparison; all societies develop from simple to complex forms; the general form of change is from military to industrial types;

and, finally, development can occur only through a specific series of basic steps.[3]

Social Evolution and the Emergence of Social Problems. The question of how social problems arise is interesting for a social evolutionist. Since the development of society is envisaged as a natural process with certain fixed stages, problems must in some sense also be natural. The stages of development for Comte were three: from a Military-Theological form, society developed through a Critical-Metaphysical, to an Industrial-Scientific stage. Each stage was necessary and although each was the most perfect form possible, each had typical limitations. Indeed, the limitations of any given stage of social evolution are its social problems.

But what are the limitations of any given stage of social evolution? One can scarcely read a line of Comte without sensing the presence of basic valuations. The values dearest to Comte were order, stability—and, above all, peace of mind. Human progress was viewed as the increasing control of the intelligence over feeling. Problems are failures of control. The first great advance of the human mind was found in the control of the physical environment. The task for the future is securing control over human nature. (Even war had its value insofar as it established order; industry, through its discipline in abject obedience, had even more. The family is essential as a source of stability in private affairs; only religion can provide ultimate stability in public affairs.) Comte's thought tended in later years to be addressed to the designing of a "scientific community" in which everyone was to have his proper place. Women's place was in the home, where they should rule supreme over domestic morality. Society was to be under the tutelage of sociologist-priests of the religion of Humanity—Humanity being conceived as the Great Being, predecessor of Durkheim's "Society *sui generis*." They were to function as educators, conciliators, arbiters of disputes, as the conscience of the people, recommending to them their stations and classes, the formulators of public opinion and the censors of thought and action.

Herbert Spencer gave the doctrines of social evolution a more materialistic twist. Society still moves from Military-Theological to Industrial-Peaceable types. The notable contrasts between Spencer and Comte appear, however, (1) at the level of their values and (2) in their programs to implement these values. Comte desired order, stability, and peace of mind, but he feared to leave the pursuit of these values to individuals. Spencer, by

[3] In the discussions of Comte and Spencer, the arguments are not developed in detail but are only outlined, for they are intended primarily to illustrate the early form of the theory of social problems in sociology. See Auguste Comte, *The Positive Philosophy*, translated by Harriet Martineau (3rd ed.; London, 1893), 2 vols, and *Système de politique positive:* (Paris, 1851-1854), 4 vols. Also see Henri Gouhier, *La vie d'Auguste Comte* (Paris, 1931); Herbert Spencer, *The Principles of Sociology* (New York, 1896), 3 vols., *The Study of Sociology* (New York, 1897), and *Man* vs. *the State* (New York, 1908).

contrast, wanted to be let alone and given freedom to act; he therefore became a passionate opponent of reform and state activity.

The important point to note is that the same general theory of social change (evolutionism) was for both Comte and Spencer the anchorage point of the sanctions of desirable goals and a concept of social reform. Thus, it is not the theory of social change that makes the programs of Comte and Spencer different; it is the set of values each brings to bear on the concept of change. The very thing Comte held most dear—the fixation of individuals in a caste-like order—was conceived by Spencer as the bitterest of all fates.

Evolutionism in American Sociology: Ward, Sumner, and Giddings. Prior to World War I, the positions of Comte and Spencer represented the most important alternative points of view offered by sociology regarding social problems. However, the only major follower of Comte in America was Lester Ward.[4] In a sense, Ward was far more orthodox than either Comte or Spencer. To the extent to which he accepted Spencer's goals and Comte's program, he re-aligned a radicalism of method with a liberalism of values. But sociology has never been noted as a hive of radicalism, and Ward was without heirs. Spencer fared better; such major academic and intellectual figures as William Graham Sumner and Franklin H. Giddings manned the battalions against the reformers in the name of the forgotten man[5] and vigorously ferreted out evidences of suspected tendencies toward socialism.

The "Conflict School" of Social Problems. A possible rival to evolutionism in interpretation of social problems during these years was Social Darwinism, as represented by Bagehot and Gumplowicz[6] in Europe and Small[7] in America. The novelty of the approach was the conception of conflict as a fundamental social process. Gumplowicz, for example, saw society as a product of conquest of groups and its more developed structural forms as the product of military subordination. However, the conflict point of view did not appear favorable to the conceptualization of ideal social states, perhaps because moral formulas approached from this perspective often appeared to be the will of the conqueror or the uneasy compromise formulas accepted to preserve peace. In any case, something in the approach was sobering, tending to suppress the elaboration of normative theories. Spencer's formula, moreover, was too attractive to be denied—it permitted one to be a thoroughgoing conservative in every act and thereby to achieve the liberal goals. Who could ask for more?

[4] See L. F. Ward, *Applied Sociology* (New York, 1911).

[5] W. G. Sumner, *The Forgotten Man and Other Essays,* edited by A. G. Keller (New Haven, 1919). Sumner complained bitterly of the sad lot of the middle class, which was most heavily taxed and benefited least by legislative aids.

[6] Ludwig Gumplowicz, *Der Rassenkampf* (Innsbruck, 1909), and *Sociologische Essays* (Innsbruck, 1899).

[7] A. W. Small, *General Sociology* (Chicago, 1905) was influenced not only by Gumplowicz but by Ratzenhofer, among others.

Rise of the Concept of Social Disorganization

Urbanization and the Decline of Optimism. A number of things combined to bring the easy optimism of the past century to an end. The most significant general process of the period was the rise of urbanism. In the period after the Civil War the prevailing atmosphere had been characterized by the excitement of the boom town. Everything tended, to be sure, to be slipshod and jerry-built. But everyone knew this to be temporary. Almost every major city of the period saw a crowding of people it was not prepared to receive. Service lanes were converted into shantytowns; streets too narrow and crooked and inefficient for new volumes of traffic disintegrated completely; methods of garbage and waste disposal were so badly understood that streams and waterways were polluted; a series of dramatic fires revealed the general failure to think in terms of a new level of risks. Even in a physical sense, the new urban complex was beginning to force thinking people to take stock. If industrialism and urbanism are the highest product of social evolutionism, change is not an unmixed blessing.[8]

The event most significant in helping transform the easy optimism of sociologists into a more sober type of reflection was World War I. Spencer, among others, had assumed that society had grown so complex and interdependent in its industrial stage that as a natural result of the evolutionary process war had become virtually impossible. If evolution was to be retained as a basis for a conception of social problems, a radical change of emphasis from the Spencerian point of view was therefore indicated. However, the theory of evolution was itself being brought under critical review. In time social problems came to be conceptualized on a new base which was found, not in a theory of social change, but in a theory of social structure. Social problems were increasingly viewed as the negative or contradictory aspects of social organization. Subsequently, new approaches to social problems have been organized around the concept of *social disorganization.*

Durkheim's Theory of Disorganization and Anomie. Although he accepted the evolutionary framework that prevailed in his time, Durkheim was primarily interested in it as a base for understanding social facts and societies.[9] Social facts are collective representations (including such things as ideas,

[8] See Howard Becker and H. E. Barnes, *Social Thought from Lore to Science*, 2nd ed. (New-York, 1952), vol. 1.

[9] See Émile Durkheim, *The Division of Labor in Society*, translated by George Simpson (Glencoe, Ill., 1947), and *The Rules of Sociological Method,* translated by Sarah Solovay and J. H. Mueller (Chicago, 1938).

sentiments, habits, norms, etc.), identifiable by their general acceptance and by the constraint exercised in their name over the actions of individuals. Societies are not mere aggregates of people; they are shared ways of life characterized by social solidarity. Whereas the social solidarity of mankind in the past was merely *mechanical* (based on such things as kinship, friendship, etc.), in the modern world social solidarity is increasingly *organic* (based on a division of labor).

Yet the division of labor sometimes creates the very negation of solidarity. Division of labor makes criminal organizations more elaborate and effective. Moreover, the various social and industrial crises, such as class disturbances, labor struggles, etc., indicate how things may go awry. But Durkheim tended to locate the source of all such difficulties in the collective sentiments—the rules, regulations, and norms—which were the essence of society and social solidarity.

> If the division of labor does not produce solidarity . . . it is because the relations of the organism are not regulated, because they are in a state of *anomie*. . . . Since a body of rules is the definite form which spontaneously established relations between social functions have taken in the course of time, we can say, a priori, that the state of *anomie* is impossible wherever solidary organs are in contact or sufficiently prolonged.[10]

One of the most interesting things about Durkheim's development is the tendency for his formulations to grow less optimistic. The concept of *anomie* ("normlessness") is expanded in the course of his studies and given ever broader formulation.[11]

Cooley and the Dissipation of Primary Groups. A second form of social-disorganization theory appears in the writings of Charles Horton Cooley, who attacked the central issues of sociology from the standpoint of the relation of the individual to the group. In general, Cooley's ideas bear a close resemblance to Durkheim's concepts of collective representations, social solidarity, and the central importance of regulating norms. The novelty of his work lies mainly in the location of the source of norms in primary groups, which are characterized by close association and cooperation, play a primary role in the formation of the social nature (the ideas) of the individual, and are typified by the family, the play group, the neighborhood community, and the community of elders. They are the source of primary ideals.

Larger society is, at least in its more acceptable phases, a construction out of primary ideals. Democracy and Christianity are, for Cooley, simple primary ideals writ large on the scale of world history. However, the presentation of the primary-group ideals at the level of society at large leads

[10] Durkheim, *Division of Labor,* p. 368.
[11] See Durkheim, *Le Suicide* (Paris, 1897).

to mechanization, formalism, and the draining away of the energies of human nature. Religion becomes intolerant, deadening routine appears in the schools, the universities become filled with cant, the cheap press and habits of hasty reading are fostered. In his later work the view is further extended as Cooley calls attention to the conflict of group standards within the larger society.[12]

Personal and Social Disorganization: The Theories of Thomas and Znaniecki. Thomas and Znaniecki were led to their concept of social disorganization from a starting point quite different from that of either Durkheim or Cooley. For some years Thomas had been interested in a phenomenon particularly characteristic of American cities after the Civil War and through the first decade of the twentieth century: the pool of cheap labor. Pursuing this interest, Thomas had begun assembling masses of facts on the Polish immigrant in America and in the course of his work came in touch with the brilliant young Polish philosopher-sociologist, Florian Znaniecki.

The process Thomas and Znaniecki were trying to understand was the reception of the immigrant Polish peasant into the American community. In the course of their study, they were led to introduce: (1) a typology of motivational categories; (2) the concepts of life-organization and social organization; (3) a typology of individual life-organizations; and (4) special concepts of personal and social disorganization. Only the last two of these contributions are directly relevant to our purposes.

The typology of individual life-organization introduced by the authors represented a characterization of formal differences in the adjustment of life to social organization. The *Bohemian* is the person who finds no point of stability in himself, but flows into the social mold of the moment. He is all things to all people because he is nothing to himself. He pursues no consistent career because he cannot. He drifts and eventually tends to fill the ranks of the hobo. The *Philistine* represents an inelastic adjustment to the social order. He, too, finds no point of order in himself; he can only cling fanatically to *tradition*. The *Creative Man* finds a stable basis for development within himself and is capable of a dynamic adjustment of personality.

Anyone of average intelligence reading Thomas and Znaniecki's work would hardly regard either Bohemianism or Philistinism as particularly desirable. Bohemianism is, in a sense, the epitome of individual disorganization. The difficulty with Philistinism is that the individual who finds no stability in himself can hardly rebel without falling into Bohemianism.

Applying these distinctions, Thomas and Znaniecki defined social disorganization as the decrease in the influence of social rules over the behavior

[12] C. H. Cooley, *Human Nature and the Social Order* (New York, 1902), *Social Organization* (New York, 1909), pp. 5, 7, 9-10, 23-24, 35, 342, 347, and *Social Process* (New York, 1919), p. 106.

of group members. They understood this decrease in influence as existing in varying degrees, from the breaking of a particular rule by a particular individual to a general decay of institutions. They recognized the fact that an individual may break rules because he is losing the capacity for life-organization required by his society, or because he rejects rules as hindrances to his attainment of a more inclusive life-organization. But the assumption that individual and social organization are directly related is not necessarily warranted; individual demoralization is not equivalent to social disorganization. Social disorganization is thought of as a universal process. During eras of social stability, *incipient* disorganization is neutralized by actions that re-enforce the social rules and norms. It is only during periods of change that it tends to become important.[13]

Criticism of Disorganization Theories. The entire theory of social disorganization was brought under vigorous attack by Mills,[14] who found it to be a facile display of "a paste-pot eclectic psychology" demonstrating an "occupationally trained incapacity to rise above a series of 'cases.'" If social-disorganization theorists were really capable of examining the norms, Mills suggests, they would perhaps have been led to see the "total structure of norms" and to "relate these to distributions of power."

Unfortunately, dispassionate analysis of social disorganization *has* generally been lacking. Wirth quite rightly pointed out that there are elements of evaluation in the conceptualization of both social organization and social disorganization.[15] And Lemert made a responsible and suggestive analysis of some aspects of both.[16] But these analyses leave many significant problems untouched.

The one thing that all the critics—from Mills to Lemert, and many others in addition—are agreed upon is the presence of valuations in the theory of social disorganization. There is no question whatsoever about the fact that they are correct. The criticism is frequently marred, however, by the fact that the critic objects to *particular* evaluations rather than to the confusion of values with facts.

The type of analysis suggested by the critics of social-disorganization theory is a comparative analysis of the different value-presuppositions of its advocates. It is quite correctly pointed out that Cooley's values seem to be those of the small town—friendly feeling, neighborliness, etc. There seems, however, to be a strong unwillingness to admit that social-disorgan-

[13] W. I. Thomas and Florian Znaniecki, *The Polish Peasant in Europe and America* (Boston, 1919), vol. 2, p. 74.

[14] C. Wright Mills, "The Professional Ideology of Social Pathologists," *AJS,* 49 (Sept. 1943), pp. 165-180.

[15] Louis Wirth, "Ideological Aspects of Social Disorganization," *ASR,* 5 (Aug., 1940), pp. 472-482.

[16] E. M. Lemert, *Social Pathology* (New York, 1951), Chap. 1.

ization theorists ever preferred anything else. But Thomas and Znaniecki seem not to have grieved at the decline of the small town. Their highest value clearly appears embodied in their Creative man. Throughout their work, the assumption is that the natural environment of the Creative Man is the larger urban center. Moreover, Thomas and Znaniecki are no more remote from the criticism of provincialism than is Durkheim, although Durkheim does not commit himself to a "creative man" as an ideal. Durkheim everywhere prefers what he called "organic" to "mechanical" solidarity, indicating a preference for an urban, industrial, and scientifically minded social order.

These examples certainly demonstrate that the distinction between normative and empirical social theory still remains when the concept of social problems is generalized into a concept of social disorganization. However, in part because this distinction was not drawn, the evaluative aspects of the issue were not sharply separated from the empirical. It is evident, moreover, that the highest values of the chief authors of the concept of social disorganization were not identical.

Rise of the Concept of Cultural Lag

Although the concept of cultural lag is frequently treated as a form of the concept of social disorganization, in the present discussion it is examined separately. Social disorganization is here taken to refer to those approaches to social problems that involve a concept of social *organization* as an empirical base. Cultural lag, on the other hand, entails an analysis of social problems projected on the foundation of a conception of social *change*.

In the new edition of *Social Change,* with the wisdom of an old man looking back on his life work, Ogburn observes that at the time of the first edition, social evolution had been a lode temporarily worked out. On reflection, nearly thirty years later, it seemed to him that social evolution —modified, to be sure, and identified with cultural evolution—provided the best account of social change after all. Four fundamental processes are seen to compose social evolution: (1) *invention,* including both material and social innovations, as the product of mental ability working on a material base addressed to wants; (2) *accumulation,* which generally adds more to culture at any given time than is lost—a process that tends to accelerate; (3) *diffusion,* the spread of inventions and the process by which people profit from innovations they have not made themselves; and (4) *adjustment* of one part of society to another, such as the economy to the family, the family to education, and so on.[17]

[17] W. F. Ogburn, *Social Change* (2nd ed.; New York, 1950), pp. 369 *ff*.

The Theory of Cultural Lag. Ogburn observed that cultural elements persist for at least two reasons: they may have a practical utility; or they may satisfy a psychological need. These two kinds of things can, of course, coincide; but if they were not distinguishable, it would be difficult to account for "survivals" having no apparent utility. Magical practices of all types are an excellent example; they satisfy psychological needs and at the same time tend to suppress the development of genuine utilities. Similarly, change occurs in response to material and psychological needs through the processes of innovation and diffusion.

Yet a number of conditions may obstruct change. It may be resisted by vested interests, which tend to preserve the *status quo* at all costs. Resistance to change may also be due to traditional hostility to the new, to habit, to pressure toward conformity, the tendency to forget the unpleasant, and fear. Curiosity, restlessness, pain, and ambition are among the psychological forces making for change.[18]

It is in these terms that Ogburn laid the basis for his theories of social problems. The position taken here is that Ogburn presented not one but two theories of social problems. The first of these may be considered under its usual designation, "cultural lag." Ogburn argued that the accumulation of culture is occurring at an ever-accelerating rate.

> The thesis is that the various parts of modern culture are not changing at the same rate, some parts are changing much more rapidly than others; and that since there is a correlation and interdependence of parts, a rapid change in one part of our culture requires readjustments through other changes in the various correlated parts of culture.[19]

The general argument is that material culture tends to develop relatively rapidly, "adaptive" culture much more slowly. The lag between the two, then, is the source of tensions. This is illustrated by forestry and conservation. In the early history of our culture there were vast forests, a tremendous need for wood for fuel and building, and men with an eye to the main chance. The forests were slashed in the quickest but most wasteful manner possible. This, together with the growth of population and industry, led to the approaching exhaustion of the forests. Consequently, the new "adaptive" culture of the "conservation" movement arose to meet changed material conditions.

Among the reasons for cultural lag are: (1) the scarcity of invention in the adaptive culture;[20] (2) mechanical obstacles to adaptive changes—for instance, legislatures meet at infrequent intervals and for too short times, whereas needs continue without intermissions or holidays; (3) closeness of

[18] *Ibid.*, pp. 170, 176, 180, 186, 190-191.
[19] *Ibid.*, pp. 200-201.
[20] *Ibid.*, p. 257.

contact with material culture—sometimes the relation between adaptive and material culture is indirect and hence takes much longer to be brought into correspondence; (4) the connection of adaptive culture with other parts of culture—for instance, the mores of exploitation serve to increase resistance to forest conservation; and finally, (5) group evaluations, the emotionalism of groups, love of the past, etc., may lead to resistance to adaptation.

The Implicit Theory of Biological Lag. The theory of cultural lag seems to have been viewed by Ogburn as capable of accounting for only a limited range of social problems, for after advancing it, he went on to introduce another theory that, for want of a better name, may be called a theory of *biological lag*. Indeed, he wrote:

> It was shown that a number of social problems arise because the different parts of culture change at unequal rates. In the present chapter we wish to consider some of the problems that arise, not from the lack of adjustment of the various parts of culture, but from the lack of adjustment between human nature and culture.[21]

Summing up the facts known about the physical evolution of man, Ogburn observed that man has been on earth for several hundred thousand years or so, and that skeletal remains indicate that his evolution has been slow. Generally, there is agreement that there has been no significant evolution, biologically, in man since the last glacial age. Man's psychological nature is quite similar to that of the anthropoids. Man's nature would thus seem to be "much more like that of the cave men than the appearance of cultural differences would lead one to think."

Ogburn thus suggests that, although man is the same biologically as in the ice age, his culture has profoundly changed. He further suggests that we may be like a group of Cro-Magnon children in a modern city. And he considers the hypothetical possibility that modern man suffers from indigestion because he does not eat the food of cave men and does not experience primitive hunger. He also suggests that adjustment to marriage and to rigid sex codes may be difficult for the same reason.

> It is claimed that a great many social problems such as war, crime, sexual phenomena and disease arise because of the inability or difficulty of the original nature of man to adapt itself to modern conditions and cultural standards. So also it is claimed that much of our unhappiness, nervousness and insanity is traceable to the same general causes.[22]

Our biological nature, Ogburn argues, has not been adapted to civilization because of the short time available for such adjustment. We cannot be absolutely sure where the greatest discrepancies lie. However, at the

[21] *Ibid.*, p. 283.
[22] *Ibid.*, p. 287.

present time there is probably far more demand for intellectual concentration, sustained thought, and attention than ever in the past. There is at present probably far less opportunity for an equivalent range of emotional experience. Modern man undoubtedly has the same instinctive equipment as his ancestors, just as he has the same musculature. He must therefore suffer at least as severely for lack of proper exercise of his instinctive nature as he does from the failure to act physically according to the needs of his apelike body.

To the tensions born of discrepancies between modern civilization and the nature of the old ape—to biological lag—Ogburn attributes much nervousness and insanity. He observes that some nervous troubles are due to accidents, injuries, or hereditary defects; but over and beyond these are such things as hysteria, morbid compulsions, anxiety-neuroses, paranoia, melancholia, and manic-depression, in which the difficulty lies in the *functioning* of structure and which are hence occasioned or modified by the cultural environment rather than by physical or organic factors.

Further examples of problems due to discrepancies between human nature and culture are found in crime. "In periods of economic depression there is more temptation to violate laws regarding property. The amount of crime fluctuates with economic conditions." Thus "crime is clearly evidence of lack of adjustment between human nature and culture." In the field of sex, such things as adultery, prostitution, and illicit sexual intercourse are seen as social problems. These, together with divorce and family breakdown, indicate that the "conflict of sex codes and human nature" is a frequent "cause of unhappiness." Moreover, human nature seems to be basically self-seeking. Given half a chance, it creates an "inequality in the distribution of wealth." This, in turn, is a factor in "poverty, disease, taxation, labor, government, war, and many other problems."[23]

Cultural Lag vs. *Biological Lag*. Not the least interesting feature of Ogburn's two theories of social problems is the fact that they are in some measure contradictory. Cultural lag attributes problems to tensions between material and non-material culture. Biological lag attributes problems to tensions between man's original nature and his acquired nature (culture). It could perhaps be argued—and it is rather surprising that no one ever confronted Ogburn on this point—that these are complementary approaches applying to different spheres. But if this is the case, it is not immediately evident. The lag between the exploitation of the forests and conservation was utilized to illustrate the first kind of theory. However, orgies of unrestrained selfishness were also thought to be characteristic of the second type of problem explanation. Forest exploitation could as easily be fitted into the second as into the first scheme. This is true for almost every illustration of either type of problem; with slight changes of emphasis each one can be fitted into either mold.

[23] *Ibid.*, pp. 33, 290, 293, 312, 332-334.

It is impossible to escape the conclusion that the same old valuative points of view are present. The most striking feature of Ogburn's discussion is that he presents both in turn. If one accepts the culture-lag theory, the solution to problems seems to be an extension of scientific intelligence. If one accepts the biological-lag theory, presumably one must either adjust human nature to culture or culture to human nature. In the first approach, problems appear because man is rather stupid; following the second approach, man is still a savage and civilization a thin veneer. The cultural-lag theory inclines toward liberal perspectives, the biological-lag theory toward conservative orientations.

Critique of "Lag" Theories. Moreover, important theoretical and methodological problems are raised by both theories. Cultural-lag analysis, for example, presupposes a distinction between material and adaptive culture, but neither of these has been adequately defined conceptually or specified operationally. The examples were developed so vaguely that the ideas are unclear. Presumably, for example, there is a lag between forest exploitation and forest conservation. But why is forest exploitation any more "material culture" than forest conservation? Ideas seem to be non-material whereas things are material. But science is thought of as material culture; yet it is not a thing. It hardly makes sense to think of science as a set of material facts without ideas, intentions, enterprise. In none of the examples is the distinction between material and non-material culture made clear and unambiguous. Why should a general property tax be material, whereas some other type of tax is not? Is an instrument material? The least interesting properties of an instrument are its purely material properties; it is significant for the ideas and activities for which it is designed. But these latter seem more properly to belong to non-material culture.

The Evaluative Basis of "Lag" Theories. The failure to draw the distinction between normative and empirical theory adds to the confusion. The very notion of "lag" seems to imply that something is "ahead." The only way to answer the question of what is lagging is to state the aims, goals, and values—the basis of judgment. The old saw holds in this area as well as in others: what is one man's meat is another's poison. What is viewed as a lag or even a positive regression by one person may represent an advance or gain to another.

Clarity in cultural-lag theory depends upon a formulation of culture goals. And these are only implied in the theory. It is clear that Ogburn was "for" the following: conservation, the more adequate compensation of victims of industrial accidents, a revision of the tax laws, and organizations to promote international peace. Stated in this way the theory of cultural lag takes on some of the properties of the program of a political party—which, at bottom, it is.

The theory of biological lag also presents problems. The most important theoretical and methodological problems consist in the necessity of adequately conceptualizing and empirically verifying "original human nature." An interesting but risky series of assumptions appears to be made in the concept of biological lag. The two most important are: (1) that there is an original human nature, and (2) that there is a culture appropriate to it. But what is the solution to a set of simultaneous equations made up completely of unknowns?

The kinds of goals presupposed by this second approach seem to be the direct opposite of those suggested by the first. The cultural-lag approach seems to suggest that the general body of social life be brought into accordance as fast as possible with the latest gadget or combination tool. The biological-lag theory, however, seems to suggest either that human nature be adjusted to culture or that culture be adjusted to human nature. The ideal here seems to be stability and peace of mind and thereby the elimination of most psychoneurosis, crime, and suicide.

From Conflict to Ecology

It has been observed that the analysis of social life from the point of view in which conflict is accepted as the basic process had its most important American representative in Albion Small, who, at the University of Chicago, became the primary representative of this view in America. As he developed the theory, interests conceived as unsatisfied capacities corresponding to unrealized conditions were held to be the simplest modes of motion in human beings. The basic interests were health, wealth, sociability, knowledge, beauty, and rightness. All action occurring in society consisted of movements of persons compelled by various interests. Society was the resultant at any given moment of all the efforts of particular persons to achieve particular satisfaction. *"All social problems are problems of the relations of personal units that have in themselves distinct initiative and choice and force. This personal equation must be assigned its real value, in order to reach a true formula of the social reaction."*[24]

The Role of Interests in Social Problems. The incidents in the life of a person are contacts with the physical world or with other individuals. In the process of making social contacts, a constant differentiation of interests occurs from which follow differentiation of structure and function. Numbers of people whose relation to each other is sufficiently important to require attention constitute a group. People are continuously in associative combinations, and human social life is primarily group life. The social process

[24] Small, *General Sociology,* pp. 426, 433, 481.

is thus a perpetual action and reaction of interests lodged in individuals who are in contact. In spite of disguised or open struggle, people fuse into groups. Conflict then goes on at the new level, between group and group. Although conflict (following Ratzenhofer) is primary and universal, it tends to resolve itself into cooperation. In brief, socialization is the transforming of conflict into cooperation.[25]

At first glance, this conception of conflict would seem to recommend itself as the most direct of all possible positions for analyzing social problems. It is difficult to conceive of a simpler model of trouble: two hungry dogs, one bone. The more nearly equal in size, strength, and ability the dogs are, the more interesting the events.

Yet the character of the ordinary type of analysis of social problems is nowhere more completely shown than in the reluctance of some thinkers to approach social problems from the standpoint of conflict. Such a standpoint makes assignment of praise and blame strangely inappropriate. This is not to say that conflict itself is viewed as desirable—reluctance to rush into the middle of human affairs with a mouthful of moral condemnations is not equivalent to making perverted value-judgments. However, when people are seen as acting on a plurality of interests that lead them in pursuit of limited values and into encounters in which both cannot win; when cooperation is seen, as it so often is, as a combination to achieve more effective group conflict; when a peaceable social state is seen as a slow compromise of diverse interests—such perceptions tend to dampen an overenthusiastic reforming zeal. This is particularly true when reforming zeal is observed to be often itself an instrument in conflict. For these reasons, it is interesting to trace those shifts of emphasis that lead from an empirical examination of conflict processes back to a normative consideration of social problems.

The Ecological Approach to Social Problems. The concept *social process* (with conflict at its core), which was being moved into central position by Small, was adopted by Park and Burgess.[26] When it was brought under closer analysis, social process was subdivided into four major types of interaction: competition, conflict, accommodation, and assimilation. Competition was thought of as the human form of that struggle to survive which is characteristic of all life. It was not social; it was *sub*-social. It was constant, largely unconscious and impersonal. In the economic order, it was ecological in nature. It was the force that creates the territorial and vocational distribution of the population basic to the division of labor and organized economic interdependence.

Conflict, on the other hand, was thought to be more social in nature, as competition become conscious, with other persons taken into account.

[25] *Ibid.*, pp. 49-491, 495, 499.
[26] R. E. Park and E. W. Burgess, *Introduction to the Science of Sociology* (Chicago, 1921).

The political process shows *par excellence* how competition may become conscious and take the form of conflict.

Accommodation is the attempt by individuals and groups to make the internal adjustments to the situations created by competition and conflict. When they are made, conflict subsides. Assimilation completes the process with a thoroughgoing transformation of personality under the influence of intimate social contacts.

But it was the concept of *competition* as the human form of the universal struggle to survive that served as the bridge from a theory of social process in which conflict was central, to the conceptualization of the city. The modern city was thought of as a system of interactive life produced in the course of modern man's commercial activity. Economic activity is the primary field of competition; economic competition tends to produce the kind of order known as *ecological*. Just as in the plant world the biological competition of diverse forms tends to produce an order in which various habitats are natural to a given plant form, in which one form may invade the area of another, and in which the plant "community" is seen as an integrated balance of vegetative types, so the human city, constructed out of competition, has its natural habitats for social groups, its potentials for invasion of areas by different groups, and typical successions of groups through an area.[27]

The Urban Matrix of Social Problems. Burgess centered attention on the order that was, theoretically, produced by the operation of the urban ecological processes and presented an idealized picture of the characteristic zones produced. Zone I was the central business district; in Chicago it was the Loop.

> Encircling the downtown area there is normally an area in transition, which is being invaded by business and light manufacture (II). A third area (III) is inhabited by the workers in industries who have escaped from the area of deterioration (II) but who desire to live within easy access of their work. Beyond this zone is the "residential area" (IV) of high-class apartment buildings or of exclusive "restricted" districts of single family dwellings. Still further, out beyond the city limits, is the commuter's zone—suburban areas, or satellite cities—within a thirty-to-sixty-minute ride of the central business district.[28]

[27] R. E. Park, E. W. Burgess, and R. D. McKenzie (eds.), *The City* (Chicago, 1925). See Park's suggestions, pp. 1-46. The stimulus for this approach is often traced to C. J. Galpin, *The Social Anatomy of an Agricultural Community* (1915). Between 1918 and 1920 Park was promoting the study at the University of Chicago and utilizing the concepts developed by the plant ecologists. See his "The City: Suggestions for the Investigation of Human Behavior in the City Environment," *AJS*, 20 (March, 1915), pp. 577-611; and R. D. McKenzie, "The Neighborhood," *AJS*, 27 (Sept. and Nov., 1921; Jan., March, and May, 1922).

[28] Park, Burgess, and McKenzie, *op. cit.*, p. 50.

This conception of the competitive processes of the city producing a characteristic ecological order made possible a unique investigation of social problems. One was able to examine them, not from the standpoint of the basic character of human social conflict, but from the standpoint of their physical location in the physical structure of the city. At the time Park and Burgess were developing these formulations, Burgess reported the following projects under his direction. "Nels Anderson, *The Slum, An Area of Deterioration in the Growth of the City;* Ernest R. Mowrer, *Family Disorganization in Chicago;* Walter C. Reckless, *The Natural History of Vice Areas in Chicago;* E. H. Shideler, *The Retail Business Organization as an Index of Business Organization;* F. M. Thrasher, *One Thousand Boys' Gangs in Chicago: A Study of Their Organization and Habitat;* H. W. Zorbaugh, *The Lower North Side; A Study in Community Organization.*"[29] Almost all the studies in progress at that time resulted in familiar publications. They were the first of a flood of similar studies: of the physical location of areas of high incidence of crime, juvenile delinquency, suicide, disease, etc.; of variations and differences in incidence of almost everything in one area after another of the city.

The Conversion to Environmentalism. As studies of the location by areas of various types of ills and socially disapproved behavior become more frequent, the theoretical origins of the research—conflict theory—are eclipsed. Appeal to this theoretical core disappears. With increasing frequency the observation is made that a specific area of a city tends to show a uniform problem-incidence regardless of who occupies it. More implicitly than explicitly, the idea that human problems are a function of environmental location rises to the surface. The formula, thus, tends to be reversed. The properties of a neighborhood, rather than conflicting interests, become important.

The inevitable result was a new program of reform, and this was not long in coming. By 1930 the conception had already developed that a program of neighborhood reform was the proper way of meeting these issues. In one of the more recent reports on developments in one of the projects, it is observed:

> Since its inception in 1930, the Chicago Area Project, with a small staff of competent, zealous workers had introduced its distinctive philosophy and program of neighborhood betterment into thirteen different areas in the metropolitan district, areas of varied racial and national strains, but all of them definitely underprivileged and with comparatively high rates of juvenile delinquency.[30]

[29] *Ibid.*, p. 62.

[30] C. R. Shaw, "The History and Basic Principles of the Chicago Area Project," (mimeographed report, Chicago, 1942), and Celia Stendler (Burns), *Bright Shadows in Bronzetown* (Chicago, 1949), p. 10.

Thus, the conflict point of view was gradually transformed into an environmental account of social problems, making a place after all, for the reformer.

In a fairly short period, during and immediately after World War I, an array of new ideas was addressed to social problems. With some simplification they have been reduced to three groups: (a) social disorganization concepts, (b) concepts of cultural and biological lag, and (*c*) neighborhood-situational explanations of social problems. By 1925 the main outlines of these approaches was complete.

Social Problems on the Textbook Front, 1925-1945. It would be quite inappropriate to single out any particular work for either theoretical blessing or blame during the next fairly long period. The typical social-pathology or social-problems text tended to have generally the following format: There was either a chapter or a series of chapters on "social problems," "social disorganization," "social change," or "social pathology." This was normally followed by a series of chapters on particular social problems ranging from homosexuality and suicide to war and revolution. And there was usually a concluding chapter expressing hope for a better future.

The so-called theoretical phase of the ordinary study usually—and in most cases fortunately—has been confined to the opening sections of the book as a kind of ceremony that must be observed before settling down to business. Some preferences are shown for given theories or approaches: one prefers the social-disorganization terminology, another cultural-lag theory, a third a situational approach. Not infrequently, all three types of approach are confused. The divergent implications of locating problems in the framework of social structure rather than of change, or by means of the situational approach, are ignored. But these approaches, although stirred together vigorously, cannot be made to mix.

The social situation in which these works were written was one of world-wide depression and war. What was needed at the time was the application of any available body of thought to social issues. When any given work made a serious contribution to the field, it was usually in the form of an addition to the knowledge of concrete issues or an organization of empirical data rather than an addition to theory. One must in fairness conclude that these are works by men of good will trying to measure up to their social responsibilities.

The Dominance of Social Disorganization and the Normative Approach. Quite apart from the fact that ideas with different derivations were usually stirred together in one pot, the concept of social disorganization tended to be central. There was even some tendency to simplify and codify it. Organization was increasingly thought of as a system of actions in a state of equilibrium, disorganization as a system in a state of disequilibrium. But when this is utilized as a criterion for analyzing particular problems, it quickly proves to be inadequate. Crime rings, for example, are treated as examples of disorganization. Yet they are often more "organized" than the society in which they appear and in which they are assumed to represent "disorganization." Clearly, normative judgments, in these instances, are being disguised as factual judgments. Crime rings are not objected to because they are examples of disequilibrium but because they are normatively objectionable.

Perhaps the most misleading aspect of the whole field is the reluctance to examine just what is and what is not in equilibrium. At times a given author appears to assume that society as a whole is one great system. Its equilibrium states are good; its disequilibrium states are bad. But this would assume (1) the existence of social wholes of enormous size and (2) the uncritical identification of the *status quo* as good. Yet almost all the writers on social problems would reject the first idea on theoretical grounds and the second on value grounds.

Recent Developments

Old Wine in New Bottles. Since World War II, there has been a renewed interest in social disorganization with the reissue of old books in revised form and the appearance of many new studies. A brief review of a few of these books may indicate some of the trends. In the foreword to Brown's *Social Pathology*,[31] Mowrer, who had himself contributed much to the study of personal and family problems, observes that the study of social disorganization has gone through two stages and is entering a third. In the first stage, the student of society, confronted with social problems, was motivated by reform. In the second, a scientific spirit was introduced and social maladjustments were treated as pathologies. In the third, the need to harmonize scientific knowledge about both individuals and societies is being recognized and approached.

Brown himself treats social organization as the result of social processes. Social process is in itself neither normal nor abnormal. Social disorganization is in principle not different from social organization; it is, in fact, that kind of social organization that is not culturally approved.[32] With these basic statements there can hardly be any quarrel. The key question is: what is culturally approved? Presumably in answer to this, Brown develops his notion of the place of ideologies in social disorganization. Ideologies rise in human nature and social order, and any ideology may be manifested in war, religion, or education, even in vice and crime. The operation of

[31] L. G. Brown, *Social Pathology* (New York, 1946), p. vii.
[32] *Ibid.*, pp. 358-359, 365.

social forces produces many diffuse elements, each with its own ideology.[33] Apparently one's conception of social problems depends on which ideology one holds. Since Brown designated some things as problems, he presumably made a choice among ideologies. Unfortunately, however, he did not specify which "ideology" underlay his treatment.

Robert E. L. Faris' study is somewhat closer to the strict social-disorganization schema. A successful society is conceived as one that achieves a fairly stable system adapted to its surroundings and permitting its members to carry on their generally accepted tasks. Social disorganization is thought of as the disruption of the functional relations to the point that the performance of accepted group tasks is made difficult. There are then many symptoms of disorganization. Among the more important are: formalism, decline of the sacred, individualism, hedonism, mutual distrust, etc.[34]

It may be noted that in the studies of Brown and Faris society is implicitly thought of as a kind of organic whole. Value-judgments are not clearly specified but are buried under such notions as "accepted" group behavior.

Back to Cultural Lag. A. P. Herman makes a serious attempt in his *Approach to Social Problems* to review alternate approaches to social problems and to isolate his own. He wishes to relocate social problems against the concept of social change. "Social problems arise, and existing problems are aggravated, when a society creates or accepts instruments of change, yet fails to understand, anticipate or deal with the consequences of such action." Among the kinds of issues which either create new issues or aggravate old ones are: mechanical inventions (radio, industrial machines, drug therapy, x-ray, soil analysis, etc.); population movements (decline in rate of growth, migrations, age trends); changes in natural resources (changes in the supply of raw materials that can be exploited); natural occurrences (floods, tornadoes, earthquakes, insect pests); physiological changes (disease and the other organic pathologies).[35] Herman's work is an attempt to revise and bring up-to-date an approach similar to that of Ogburn.

The Value-Conflict Approach. In 1950 two books on social problems were reissued: the third edition of Elliott and Merrill's *Social Disorganization* and the second edition of Barnes and Ruedi's *The American Way of Life*.[36] The point of view of Elliott and Merrill was roughly that of the earlier social-disorganization theorists, a view whish has been sufficiently commented on above. Barnes and Ruedi dealt with social problems wholly

[33] *Ibid.*, pp. 378 *ff*.

[34] R. E. L. Faris, *Social Disorganization* (New York, 1948), pp. 4, 19.

[35] A. P. Herman, *An Approach to Social Problems* (New York, 1949), Chap. 1 and pp. 51, 57.

[36] Mabel Elliott and Francis Merrill, *Social Disorganization* (New York, 1950); H. E. Barnes and I. O. Reudi, *The American Way of Life* (New York, 1950).

in terms of cultural lag: "In the case of nearly every problem, we shall find the underlying cause to be culture lag—the failure to adapt our institutions to new material conditions of life."[37]

In Weaver's *Social Problems,* which appeared in 1951, social problems are treated as conditions that involve strain, tension, conflict, frustrations, and interference with the fulfillment of a need. The theory is, and was apparently intended to be, rather cursory. Cultural lag and social disorganization are treated as identical or at least complementary.[38]

Of the major volumes appearing in 1952, Phelps and Henderson avoided as far as possible any theoretical commitments. Reinhardt *et al.* developed a form of disorganization approach under the new terminology of disadjustments, and Herbert Bloch reintroduced a new version of the fused cultural-lag and social-disorganization approaches, performing, by all odds, the most serious theoretical job of the year.[39]

Like Herman's study, Jessie Bernard's *American Community Behavior* appeared in 1949. Bernard sees the basic problem of American society as the result of "the gap between our professed, official, documented ideals —sometimes called overt ideals—and our unprofessed, unofficial, even repudiated, but nevertheless actually sought goals . . ." But more than this, she goes on to state that there is no genuine consensus and we want a multiplicity of conflicting things.

A genuine conflict approach is thus presented; in fact, even reform is treated as a special case of conflict. "Because the goals sought by reform are usually controversial, reform activity is simply a special case of conflict in general." The parties to the conflict are those who try to correct the evils and those who profit from the evils. The conflict nature of planning is recognized in the formula of "freedom under planning," which represents either a much higher degree of consensus than was present earlier or an ironing out of some of the basic differences of interests. Social engineering is conceived as the highest level of planning implemented by science. "Science . . . can be a powerful weapon for the control of community welfare. But it is not omnipotent. It can give us data on which to make decisions, but it cannot make our choices for us."[40]

Cuber, working from the general description of a social problem as an undesirable social condition, indicates that this assumption presupposes the existence of value-premises, which may be the value-judgments either

[37] Barnes and Reudi, *op. cit.*, p. 13.

[38] W. Wallace Weaver, *Social Problems* (New York, 1951), pp. 3, 40 *ff*.

[39] H. A. Phelps and David Henderson, *Contemporary Social Problems* (New York, 1952); J. M. Reinhardt, Paul Meadows, and J. M. Gillette, *Social Problems and Social Policy* (New York, 1952), pp. 2 *ff;* H. A. Bloch, *Disorganization: Personal and Social* (New York, 1952), pp. 1-130.

[40] Jessie Bernard, *American Community Behavior* (New York, 1949), pp. 67, 609, 631.

of an expert or of the public. However, since a man is an expert only if the public so recognizes him, all value-judgments are ultimately made by the public. Value-conflicts are treated as the *source* of social problems and the disorganization point of view is rejected.[41]

An Empirical Approach to Social Disorganization. Lemert's discussion contains one of the better analyses of current theories of social disorganization, though it differs in a number of respects from the present one. Lemert proposes positive criteria for a systematic theory of social problems. This, he believes, should include clear delimitation of the field and its conceptualization in terms of a limited number of postulates that are both logically interrelated and empirically adequate to the facts to which they are addressed. Moreover, the hypotheses should follow as logical consequences from this conceptual structure.[42]

Lemert's proposal has particular interest, since for the theory of social problems he advances criteria of *empirical* theory. His specific proposals for such a theory include the following ideas: (1) that behavior varies; (2) that deviant behavior arises from culture conflict; (3) that social reactions to deviant behavior vary; (4) that sociopathic behavior is effectively disavowed; (5) that a deviant person is one who has been basically influenced by deviant behavior and its consequences; (6) that the restrictions on deviant behavior are more completely social than biological; and (7) that deviates differ with respect to their susceptibility to influence by the social reaction.[43]

This general formulation is in all key essentials so close to that of Thomas and Znaniecki that it may be best viewed as a modern version of the same general view. The most important—and most hazardous—idea is that contained in point (4), that sociopathic behavior is behavior that is effectively disavowed. The danger is that in practice this tends to mean that behavior is a problem only when it is no longer a problem, or that the *status quo* exhausts what is legitimately to be considered good.

Homans and the Group Variables of Social Disorganization. Not all of the interesting recent developments in the study of social problems are to be found in textbooks. One important step was taken by Homans. In his study, *The Human Group,* Homans proposed to analyze the group in terms of such variables or clusters of variables as sentiment, activity, norm, and value. The group was conceived essentially as a system of action in equilibrium. Actually, it was thought of as composed of two systems: (1) the *external* system, consisting in part of its formal structure, in part of its relations to the external environment; and (2) the *internal* system, or the system of activities of members toward each other. In Homans' framework,

[41] J. F. Cuber and R. A. Harper, *Problems of American Society* (New York, 1951), pp. 25, 27, 446.

[42] Lemert, *op. cit.,* pp. 3-27.

[43] *Ibid.,* pp. 22-23.

changes taking place in one system tend to work themselves out in the companion system as well.

After completing an analysis of a number of groups in terms of this schema, Homans raised the problem of social disorganization, giving a new accent to its conceptualization. Taking the case of Hilltown, a New England town that underwent serious decline toward the end of the nineteenth century and into the present, Homans introduced a special version of disorganization theory. Following Durkheim, Homans describes a situation in which the group is losing control over its members as an example of "normlessness" or *anomie,* in which the organization is going to pieces and which should not be confused with conflict, where there is no difficulty in the control of the group over its members.[44] This distinction is proposed as clearing up one primary confusion in social-disorganization theory.

Homans' analysis of the steps in the social disintegration of Hilltown takes the following form. The difficulty started in the external system: (1) the sentiments that led group members to collaborate declined in number and power; (2) the number of activities the members carried on together declined; (3) the frequency of interaction between members decreased. These changes in the external system reacted on the internal system; (4) as interaction in the external system decreased, so it declined in the internal system; (5) decrease in the frequency of interaction brought a decrease in interpersonal sentiments; (6) decrease in interpersonal sentiments led to a decline of the norms; (7) leadership became less firm; and (8) social control thereby weakened.[45]

The extent to which Homans' analysis can be generalized to social problems is a question. It depends, among other things, on the adequacy of this analysis of the forms and variables of the group and the extent to which all social life has essentially this form. There are reasons, which cannot be examined here, for seriously questioning both. It cannot be denied, however, that Homans took a step long needed in the area. Social disorganization has suffered from the failure to be spelled out in terms of particular variables and brought down to concrete cases. Homans therefore took an important forward step.

Social Problems and Structural Sources of Deviation. Robert Merton's increasing interest in social problems is shown in his analysis of "social structure and *anomie*." The general problem he wishes to examine is the manner in which social structure itself may be a source of deviant behavior. Normally, Merton argues, social structures tend to do two fundamental things: (1) to define goals and (2) to enforce ways of achieving them. However, in a society where there is tremendous emphasis on the goals without emphasis on institutional procedures, Durkheim's state of *anomie* is produced.

[44] G. C. Homans, *The Human Group* (New York, 1950), pp. 336-337.
[45] *Ibid.*, pp. 359-360, 362, 366.

Contemporary American culture is in Merton's mind a peculiar type tending to emphasize success-goals without emphasizing institutional means.

> The culture enjoins the acceptance of three cultural axioms: First, all should strive for the same lofty goals since these are open to all; second, present seeming failure is but a halfway station to ultimate success; and third, genuine failure consists only in the lessening or withdrawal of ambition.[46]

The effect of this is to deflect criticism of the social structure onto the persons in society who do not have full access to opportunities. It forces persons to judge themselves not by their peers but in terms of those they hope to join and threatens those who do not accept such ambitions.

The result of this, as Merton sees it, is the emergence of a variety of typical individual adaptations: (1) the *conformist* accepts both the cultural goals and the institutional means; (2) the *innovator* accepts the cultural goals but not the institutional means; (3) the *ritualist* accepts the means but not the goals; (4) the *isolate* withdraws from both the goals and means; and (5) the *rebel* cannot make up his mind on either.

Like Homans, Merton has presented a challenging new approach to social problems based on Durkheim's *anomie*. The rather startling novelty of Merton's approach is the notion of laying the responsibility for *anomie* on the very doorstep of social structure itself!

A second innovation in Merton's approach to social problems appears in his proposed development of functionalist theory. Functionalism is that modern version of sociological organicism assuming that cultural items can be properly analyzed only if conceived as parts of organic or even organismic wholes. Merton proposes to change the fundamental postulates he ascribes to the prevailing type of functionalism. These postulates are (1) that social activities are functional for the entire social system; (2) that all such activities fulfill sociological functions and are indispensable. Merton, by contrast, seems to be convinced that functionalism must operate with functional wholes smaller than the entire social system and hence with limited numbers of items. Thus he distinguishes between functional prerequisites and functionally necessary items and advances a concept of functional alternatives.

But the point in Merton's analysis that is of interest to us is his introduction of the distinction between manifest and latent functions, and hence his transition to the theory of social disorganization.

> Numerous . . . sociological observers have . . . from time to time distinguished between categories of subjective disposition ("needs, interests, purposes") and categories of generally unrecognized but objective functional consequences ("unique advantages," "never conscious" consequences, "unin-

[46] R. K. Merton, *Social Theory and Social Structure* (Glencoe, Ill., 1949), pp. 125, 128, 132-133.

> tended service to society," "function not limited to conscious and explicit purpose").

Merton urges that functional deficiencies in the official structure tend to generate unofficial structures to fulfill the needs. These fulfill functions for groups not otherwise provided for and demonstrate that eliminating an existing structure without providing for the requirements abolished makes failure certain. Hence, "To seek social change, without due recognition of the manifest and latent functions performed by the social organization undergoing change, is to indulge in social ritual rather than social engineering."[47]

In the course of his analysis, Merton not only introduced the concept of manifest and latent function as providing the basis for a conception of conflict and reinforcement between different aspects of a given system but insisted as well that a conception of dysfunctions was also required.

> A theory of functional analysis must call for specification of social units subserved by given social functions and . . . items of culture must be recognized to have multiple consequences, some of them functional and others, perhaps, dysfunctional.[48]

As far as one can tell, the concept of dysfunction has a role in Merton's theory comparable to that of the concept of disorganization in a theory of social problems. *It, too, raises issues that can only be settled on normative grounds.*

The Attack Against "Scientism." A general spirit of good will pervades almost all the thinking about social problems. However, it should be no surprise, perhaps, that ill-will and misrepresentation do appear in this area. A. H. Hobbs has recently launched a slashing attack on all persons who have suggested that science may be of some help in the solution of social problems. If Hobbs had held to his own definition of what he calls scientism ("a belief that science can furnish answers to all human problems," a view which he says "makes science a substitute for philosophy, religion, manners, and morals"), he would have had fewer people to attack. For example, Hobbs has accused Professor Monachesi and me of "scientism" on the basis of the following quotation:

> In spite of the many obstacles that curb social planning in the various spheres of social behavior, planning has come to be regarded as the most effective way to anticipate and to solve social-problem situations. This view is unavoidable, since planning is an efficient way of creating a solution to an anticipated problem before the problem actually occurs.[49]

[47] *Ibid.*, pp. 27, 35, 63, 73, 79-80.
[48] *Ibid.*, pp. 37, 41, 51, 139.
[49] A. H. Hobbs, *Social Problems and Scientism* (Harrisburg, 1953), pp. 17, 45.

From the suggestion that science might help people solve their problems, Hobbs reasons: "Since scientism attempts to regulate the lives of people, it must begin by making puppets of them." He argues further that there are many professors and Ph. D.'s among the scientists who, technically not Socialists or Communists, are joiners of front organizations. Hence, they are not Communists only in the sense that they are not members of the Communist Party.

> Failure of scientistic liberals to accept the communism or socialism implied in the extension of their principles may be due, not to convictions about the evils of such regimentation, but because . . . [they] lack the character for communist faith because they lack the character for any faith.[50]

Perspectives

At the beginning of this chapter two sets of distinctions were introduced. The first contrasted general value-perspectives. An interplay can be discerned between different approaches to social problems at any one time and between the elements constituting a given position over a period of time. The two perspectives were groupings of values into liberal and conservative types respectively. Perhaps the most novel approaches were those of Comte and Spencer: Comte presented a radicalism of method in the interest of conservative values; Spencer presented a conservatism of method in the interest of liberal values. In disorganization theory, Durkheim advocated a conservative type, Thomas and Znaniecki a liberal type; Cooley presented an old-fashioned (Jeffersonian) liberal form. In his field analyses, Ogburn advanced first a semi-liberal and later a semi-conservative approach to social problems. In general the uniformity of value-judgments so often imputed to the social-problem thinkers is a myth, although by and large the so-called liberal type of orientation tends to prevail.

The second set of distinctions introduced in the early pages of this chapter was the contrast between a normative and an empirical theory. Empirical social theory was defined as a system of hypotheses developed in the interest of explanation. Normative social theory was defined as the systematic exploration by means of empirical theory of the procedures for achieving a given program of action. The general theses of this study were: (1) only normative social theory is appropriate to social problems, and (2) whenever a set of normative formulations is disguised as empirical, only confusion results. This study has repeatedly verified both these theses. Time after time, in one form or other, value-premises have been discovered

[50] *Ibid.*, pp. 22, 38, 124, 170.

in the positions reviewed. The presence of these value-premises is not in itself bad; it was to be expected. What is bad is to have value-judgments disguised as judgments of fact.

If these theses are accepted, and if they are felt to be at least in some measure verified, then the most important question of all may be posed. What is the student of social problems to do?

Fundamentally, he appears to be in a dilemma. The theory of social problems cannot assume efficient form unless it is recognized for what it is—a judgmentally normative social theory. Moreover, so long as we admit the legitimacy of alternative value structures, we must recognize that there is no *single* theory of social problems, but many *theories* of social problems. Meanwhile, insofar as the theories of social problems are of a normative rather than an empirical type, they are outside the province of the scientist as scientist. As a scientist, one can apply one's knowledge to any given set of goals, demonstrating (1) whether they are attainable; (2) if so, how they can be most efficiently attained; and (3) what the consequences of attaining them may be. However, as a scientist one cannot prescribe goals.

Thus the peculiar adolescence of this particular field, its tendency to blow hot and cold by turns, its sudden embarrassments and hollow pretensions—these, it is maintained, are due to the attempt to cast contradictory role requirements in a single mold. It has been the peculiar destiny of thinkers in this field to search for a single solution to social problems—as if there were only one—and to seek scientific objectivity under conditions where it was in principle impossible.

SELECTED BIBLIOGRAPHY

Bain, Read, "Our Schizoid Culture," *SSR,* 19 (1934-1935), pp. 266-276.

Bloch, H. A., *Disorganization: Personal and Social* (New York: Alfred Knopf, 1952).

Faris, R. E. L., *Social Disorganization* (New York: Ronald Press, 1948).

Frank, L. K., *Society as the Patient* (New Brunswick: Rutgers University Press, 1949).

Herman, A. P., *An Approach to Social Problems* (Boston: Ginn, 1949).

Merton, R. K., *Social Theory and Social Structure* (Glencoe, Ill.: The Free Press, 1949).

Mills, C. Wright, "The Professional Ideology of Social Pathologists," *ASR,* 3 (October, 1943), pp. 165-180.

Odum, H. W., *Understanding Society* (New York: Macmillan, 1947), Parts IV and VI.

Ogburn, W. F., *Social Change* (New York: B. W. Huebsch, 1922).

Thomas, W. I., and Florian Znaniecki, *The Polish Peasant in Europe and America* (Boston: Richard G. Badger, 1918-1921), 5 vols.

SOCIAL STRATIFICATION IN PERSPECTIVE

ROSCOE C. HINKLE, JR.,
AND ALVIN BOSKOFF

CURRENT STRESS ON STRATIFICATION PROBLEMS IN AMERICAN SOCIOLOGY is so pronounced that two simple yet significant facts are often overlooked. First, American sociologists have only lately developed a serious interest in stratification. Second, this interest has been greatly facilitated by prior developments in European stratification theory. Later in this chapter, the emergence of stratification research as a sociological specialty in the United States will be examined. This development is, however, intimately related to a cardinal contribution of European sociology—the conceptual distinction between stratification in general and the phenomena of social class, estate, and caste.

Stratification of all types involves the differential evaluation and ranking of persons and groups according to some scale of values. In many instances, stratification reflects the development of a single criterion of ranking—for example, age, sex, physical prowess, wealth, family status. But these "unibonded" types of stratification have most significance in relatively simple social structures. As sociologists came to devote their attention to more complex societies, stratification systems were found to derive from a variable set of complementary ("multibonded")[1] criteria that segregated communities and societies into broad socio-cultural groupings. These divisions have been analogically conceptualized as *social strata,* various forms of which have been labeled "social classes," "estates," and "castes."

In general, the analyses of social strata by European theorists reveal

[1] See P. A. Sorokin, *Society, Culture, and Personality* (New York, 1947), pp. 236-55.

a more or less consistent focus on specific *institutional sectors* as contexts of the structure and dynamics of stratification. Indeed, this orientation has engendered a spurious controversy about the relative importance of the *economic* and *political* institutions, but the results of this long debate have in recent years clarified the conceptions of class and caste to the point where polemic and ideological assumptions are clearly distinguishable from conceptual analyses of a verifiable character.

Early European Backgrounds

The Economic Approach to Social Stratification. Although economic conceptions of class can be shown to be quite ancient—going back at least as far as Plato—it was Karl Marx who constructed and dramatized a comprehensive view of the economic foundations of class and related phenomena. If Marx neglected to supply a textbook definition of "class," he has nevertheless become the classical locus of economic interpretations, to be criticized assuredly, but not to be disregarded. Basically, social strata represented for Marx the products of a division of social labor in which the ownership and control of productive facilities and access to the market constitute the fundamental criteria of differential position. Unfortunately, Marx did not distinguish among "class," "caste," and "estate," or among their interconnections in the *process* of stratification. However, he asserted that systems of social strata inevitably, but not immediately or automatically, respond to changes in productive techniques through the latter's effect on property relations. Anticipating the theory of cultural lag, Marx emphasized the logical and sociological discrepancies between technical developments and established systems of stratification; and thus interclass antagonism and struggle were derived as meaningful expressions of "social" lags.[2] Yet members of social strata are conscious in varying degrees of their identity and of the potential contradictions between technical change and existing patterns of social stratification. Marx therefore resorted to a non-economic, residual category, the *ideological,* which he tried unsuccessfully to link with an economically oriented position. "False consciousness," the economically inexplicable ideas of economically differentiated groups, remains the Achilles heel of the Marxist approach, along with the dubious assumptions that stratification systems are inherently unstable and consequently menace both social order and "progress."[3]

[2] Karl Marx, *A Contribution to the Critique of Political Economy,* translated by N. I. Stone (New York, 1904), pp. 11-12; Karl Marx and Friedrich Engels, *The German Ideology* (New York, 1939), pp. 7-9, 18-20.

[3] Marx and Engels, *op. cit.,* pp. 20, 39, and *The Communist Manifesto* (various editions).

The Marxist conception of class has been variously interpreted and extended by presumed or self-styled disciples, among others, but relatively few theorists have seriously retained the purely economic approach. Tönnies and Durkheim, for example, gave some attention to economic strata in their respective analyses of *Gesellschaft* and organic solidarity, although they did not accept the Marxist explanation of class development and class struggle.[4] Similarly, Franz Oppenheimer could not accept the technological determinism of Marx. However, Oppenheimer contributed a detailed study of major forms of the state in terms of distinctive class structures based on distribution of property and access to the market. He therefore envisaged the form of the state as a reflection of the social organization of property.[5]

In recent years such men as Sombart, Mannheim, Lederer, and Landtman have tended to retain an emphasis on the economic component of social class. Mannheim, however, has come to regard the system of stratification as, in addition, a function of non-economic factors or "social techniques" (i.e., ways of organizing human interaction, such as persuasion, manipulation, etc.). Even the problems of ideology and class antagonism were finally interpreted by Mannheim as "marginal situations." In the first case, Mannheim recognized that economic position was only one significant determinant in the creation and acceptance of ideologies; similarly, class struggle was conceived as an *alternative* consequence, not as an inevitable expression, of separable, antagonistic economic interests.[6] Lederer, who is often classified as a Marxian, nevertheless viewed the class structure—based on an economic division of labor—as a necessary and normal component of complex societies. Indeed, like Mannheim, he interpreted contemporary social difficulties as deriving from *destratification,* in which the "masses" are expanded and institutionalized, and not as class struggle.[7]

An interesting but somewhat neglected discussion of social strata has been furnished by the Swedish ethnologist Gunnar Landtman.[8] Based on comparative analyses of contemporary preliterates, this approach defines classes initially as "homogeneous divisions separated from each other by precedence and privileges." Landtman concludes that in preliterate societies

[4] Ferdinand Tönnies, *Fundamental Concepts of Sociology,* translated and edited by C. P. Loomis (New York, 1940); Émile Durkheim, *The Division of Labor in Society,* translated by George Simpson (Glencoe, Ill., 1947), pp. 182, 374, 384.

[5] Franz Oppenheimer, *The State* (Indianapolis, 1914). Cf. Howard Becker, "Pastoral Nomadism and Social Change, *SSR,* 15, 5 (May-June, 1931), pp. 417-427; "Conquest by Pastoral Nomads," *SSR* (July-August, 1931), pp. 511-526; and *Man in Reciprocity* (New York, 1956), pp. 265-299.

[6] Karl Mannheim, *Man and Society in an Age of Reconstruction* (New York, 1940), pp. 101-104, 242-252, 308, 342.

[7] Emil Lederer, *The State of the Masses* (New York, 1940), pp. 29, 45-50, 142.

[8] Gunnar Landtman, *The Origin of the Inequality of Social Classes* (Chicago, 1938), pp. 36, 68, 78-81.

such divisions represent different employments or vocations, a view that is essentially but independently Marxist. More significantly, Landtman found that class differentiation emerged whenever and wherever accumulation of individual fortune was made possible, a condition presumably attributable to a developing division of labor. The consequent inequality in property, sustained by inheritance rules, appeared to promote and deepen social inequalities. But Landtman did not clearly distinguish the respective roles of wealth and vocation in systems of social strata. In general, however, he was inclined to accept a functional explanation of stratification based on specialization of vocation or trade and differential evaluation or preference given to various "callings." Since the scale of preference is itself implicit in the general mores of a society, purely economic explanations become inadequate; Landtman thus shifted stratification to the *borders* of economics.

Power, Politics, and Stratification. The major rival of an economic conception of stratification was for a long time the political explanation, first brought to the attention of modern sociologists in the works of Gumplowicz and Ratzenhofer. According to the earliest expression of this approach, stratification was assumed to derive initially from military conquest of ethnically divergent groups. Gradually, as Gumplowicz asserted, the relations between "classes" lost their pristine coercive nature with the development of legal norms and moral obligations between differentiated groups. However, this process, the *legitimation* of class differences, is a reflection of power differences that likewise determine subsequent division of labor and the allotment of social responsibilities and skills.[9] Although Ratzenhofer also located the origins of social differentiation in conquest, he devoted considerably more attention to the progressive development of subgroups (classes) organized around the biological interests of individuals and the "concrete interests of each social structure." Thus the relations between groups are mediated by similarity and difference in interests (values, objectives, ideologies). Ratzenhofer seems to conclude, in contrast to Gumplowicz, that eventually power differentials become consequences of the organization of competing interests, rather than that antecedent power differentials determine subsequent development of specialized interests.[10]

Eschewing questions of ultimate origins, Mosca and his followers have approached contemporary stratification as a simple distinction between politically dominant groups and the masses—the ruling minority and a politically dependent majority. Such a division is regarded as a universal, normal condition of societies with developed political systems. Mosca even goes so far at one point as to state that the character of the ruling class determines

[9] Ludwig Gumplowicz, *Outlines of Sociology,* translated by F. W. Moore (Philadelphia, 1898), pp. 68, 82-87, 146-149.

[10] A good discussion and interpretation may be found in A. W. Small, *General Sociology* (Chicago, 1905), Parts 4 and 5.

the political structure and the level of civilization in a given society.[11] But the major theoretical contributions of such men as Mosca, Michels, and Pareto consist of their attempts to discern (1) the significant characteristics of dominant groups and (2) the process by which changes in class structure occur.

Mosca was perhaps the first to emphasize the necessity of analyzing the growth, composition, and organization of ruling classes. As a result of comparative studies, he concluded that the ruling minority is selected in varying ways, but always in terms of certain desired qualities or resources. Indeed, Mosca believed that the power of a ruling élite (the legal or moral principle or the "political formula") was ultimately based on the extent to which the qualities of the élite correspond to the peculiar needs of a given era. These needs in turn reflect characteristic changes in religion, political thought, scientific, technological, and economic developments, and new sources of wealth. Consequently, differentials in power and political authority appear to rest on a wide range of socio-cultural conditions ("social forces").[12] According to Mosca, changes in class structure can be summarized by noting changes in the composition of the ruling minority, which in turn is a measure of vertical social mobility.

Both Michels and Pareto closely followed Mosca's analysis of stratification, although each stressed a different aspect of his general position. Michels seemed to underscore the *functional necessity* of power distinctions (the so-called "iron law of oligarchy") in all complex societies and organizations, including those of a democratic, socialistic, or communistic nature.[13] Pareto, on the other hand, was convinced that the stratification system is primarily based on the structure and dynamics of the dominant class.

Starting from the premise that stratification is ultimately dependent on biological and social heterogeneity, Pareto analyzed political and economic élites—with a certain emphasis on the former—in terms of their significant characteristics and corresponding methods of maintaining social ascendancy. Every élite manifests the relative dominance of two major "residues" or motivations: the "instinct for combinations" or manipulative tendencies (the *speculator*-fox type); and the "instinct for group persistences" or a dogged conservatism (the *rentier*-lion type). Consequently, every élite —and pre-eminently the governing élite—remains in power by some combination of force and manipulation, coercion and consent. Unfortunately, Pareto failed to define the conditions that promote changing proportions of these motivations. Instead he noted that manipulative tendencies appear stronger in periods of economic prosperity, but refused to regard

[11] Gaetano Mosca, *The Ruling Class,* translated by Hannah D. Kahn (New York, 1939), pp. 50-51.

[12] *Ibid.,* pp. 65-70, 244, 415, 438.

[13] Roberto Michels, *Political Parties* (New York, 1915).

this as a relation of cause and effect. Yet Pareto seemed to locate the cardinal problem of stratification in the phenomena of renewal and "succession"—the "circulation of the élite." Since the élite is numerically small and quite mortal, its members must often be replaced from the non-governing class. This process serves to reapportion the major residues between the two classes, and its effects are quickly evident in a small group.[14] In summary, then, Pareto emphasized the *processual* aspect of stratification, the mechanisms of control by the élite, and the personal characteristics of élites appropriate to these control mechanisms.

Both economic position and political power have proved to be oversimplified dimensions in stratification analysis. Essentially, each approach constitutes a reversion to "unibonded" analysis of what is fundamentally "multibonded." Consequently, the last few decades of this period (until the interlude between the two World-Wars, let us say) in stratification theory can be interpreted as a continuing analysis, critique, and accommodation of economic and political theories. The fruits of this reappraisal, bolstered by empirical, comparative investigations by such men as Max Weber and Sorokin, constitute an impressive heritage that modern sociologists have not yet fully explored.

Weber and the Three Orders. To Weber the crucial feature of stratification lies in the necessity of distinguishing three analytically separable aspects or orders: the social, the economic, and the legal. Each order contains a peculiar system of ranked groupings that is analytically distinct from those of the other orders. The social order is composed of *status groups* based on differential *honor,* which is in turn a consequence of divergent styles of life, education, occupation, and family reputation. Caste systems are conceptualized by Weber as a special type of status-group organization, based on presumed ethnic differences, political position, or economic situation. Following Marx and others, Weber locates "classes" in the economic order; here differential rank and "life chances" derive from differential access to property and income and from distinctive roles in the market. Finally, he associates the legal order with power-seeking groups (parties) whose relation to one another is determined by the interests of their respective status and class groups.[15]

With these distinctions, Weber was able to furnish a more generally applicable analysis of stratification, suitable to (1) the exploration of interdependent criteria of stratification and (2) the potential or actual conflicts

[14] Vilfredo Pareto, *Mind and Society,* translated by A. Bongiorno and Arthur Livingston (New York, 1935), vol. 4, § 2236, 2244, 2254, 2311, 2413, 2487.

[15] Max Weber, *From Max Weber: Essays in Sociology,* translated and edited by H. H. Gerth and C. Wright Mills (New York, 1946), Chap. 7; Max Weber, *The Theory of Social and Economic Organization,* translated and edited by A. M. Henderson and Talcott Parsons (New York, 1947), pp. 424-429.

between stratified groups. In the first case, Weber seemed to make an implicit distinction between some *original* standards of differential position and the *current* bases. Status groups, for example, can be ultimately traced to some process of usurpation and property acquisition that prevailed earlier; similarly, class groups and their respective market situations reflect the dominance of a specifically congenial legal order.[16] Nevertheless, a system of stratification is notable for the unique configuration of honorific, legal, and economic criteria in a *contemporary* setting. Of most general significance is Weber's conclusion that the dominance of any order (and its special criteria of ranking) varies considerably in terms of the total socio-cultural system, thereby demolishing the persuasive half-truths of any monistic explanation of stratification.

This conceptual scheme likewise acknowledges a critical distinction between objective characteristics and interests (stratum situation) and conscious awareness and organization (stratum action). As a result, differential ranking cannot be conceived as automatically promoting interstratum conflicts. Furthermore, as Weber was one of the first to demonstrate, "class struggle" may not only be limited to contending groups in the economic order but often involves a competition for position between class groups and status groups, between the principles of *acquisition* and *consumption*. Generally speaking, however, economic stability favors status groups, whereas technological change normally brings class groups into prominence.[17]

Sorokin's conception of multibonded social classes—as semiorganized collections of persons with similar occupational, economic, and political statuses—is substantially Weberian, although Sorokin declares Weber's analyses to be "very vague" and even classifies Weber with the Marxians.[18] But Sorokin appended to the conceptions of Weber the dynamic problems of Mosca and Pareto. The result is the classic *Social Mobility,* which is particularly notable for its theoretical distinction between horizontal and vertical mobility and a thorough discussion of the principal means or channels by which individuals achieve vertical mobility.[19]

To explain the emergence of the modern American approach to social stratification, it is necessary not only to summarize its current characteristics but to review the related concern with rank in the two periods prior to the present.[20] The contemporary interest, discussed here in the section "The

[16] Gerth and Mills, *op. cit.*, pp. 185-190. Cf. Howard Becker, "In Defense of Morgan's 'Grecian Gens': Ancient Kinship and Stratification," *Southwestern Journal of Anthropology,* 6, 3 (Autumn, 1950), pp. 309-339.

[17] *Ibid.*, pp. 184-185, 192-194.

[18] Sorokin, *op. cit.*, pp. 271-275.

[19] P. A. Sorokin, *Social Mobility* (New York, 1927), Chaps. 7-9.

[20] The periods in social-stratification theory follow the periods of the history of American sociology generally as presented in R. C. Hinkle, Jr., and Gisela J. Hinkle, *The Development of Modern Sociology* (Garden City, N.Y., 1954).

Field of Social Stratification (1936-1954)," owes its inception most directly to modifications in the basic assumptions making social inequality problematic in the period discussed here as "Indirect Interest in Social Stratification (1918-1935)". However, the nature of these presuppositions during the twenties cannot be understood without a summary of the characteristics of the earliest approach to social stratification, which centered on "Rank, Individual Talent, and Progress" throughout the formative years of sociology (1906-1917).

Rank, Individual Talent, and Progress (1906-1917)

Emerging during the formative era when sociology was unspecialized, undifferentiated into subject fields, and unprofessionalized, and when its representatives were personally acquainted with one another, the interest in social stratification was directly derived from the general intellectual characteristics of the discipline. Consequently, the concern with matters of status and rank was inextricably interrelated with the preoccupation of sociologists with the conditions of their own society and the intellectual commitments that prompted this direction of attention.

Like many other intellectuals of the period, sociologists observed the phenomena of centralization of control, concentration of population, and the impersonalization of relations that accompanied the post-Civil War trend toward urbanization and industrialization. What they saw were the major social problems: poverty, unemployment, dependency, relief, child labor, women wage earners, crime, delinquency, family instability, mobility, immigration, race and ethnic conflict, and disputes between management and labor.

Sociologists were then commited to progress, melioirstic interventionism, and science. They believed that the direction of social change, which was construed as social evolution, was toward a more acceptable society. Such upward development could be accelerated by direct human intervention enlightened by knowledge of sociological laws for planning, education, and legislation. These scientific laws—to the search for which sociology was dedicated—resembled invariant natural laws governing physical and organic phenomena.

These dominant commitments of the discipline as a whole are the source from which were largely derived the following basic characteristics of the concern with status and rank:[21]

[21] These characteristics are drawn from an independent investigation of the nature and context of references made to social stratification phenomena in the *Publications*

1. Interest in social stratification did not take the form of direct, explicit, and detailed analysis, except in textbooks. Only two of the 125 papers presented at the annual meetings of the American Sociological Society before 1917 treated subjects having to do predominantly and obviously with some aspect of rank. Nevertheless, the papers contained frequent references to various facets of the social hierarchy. This seeming paradox may be explained by American sociologists' preoccupation with the specific social problems of their society. The references to rank in the literature involve its more concrete manifestations, and appear to be incidental to and to deal with rank as subordinate to social problems.

2. Since most sociologists assumed that the laws of sociology and of social change in particular are evolutionary, they interpreted the condition of social stratification of their era within the schema of social and cultural evolution. This formulation ordinarily invoked, at some point, the conflict principle of struggle for existence, although most American sociologists rejected extreme Social Darwinism. Perhaps Gumplowicz and Ratzenhofer provided the most commonly used evolutionary formula of social stratification. According to this formula, present-day classes are ultimately the outcome of a sequence of processes: conquest, caste, mitigated inequality, law, and the state.

3. For the most part, these early American sociologists took class to mean an aggregate of persons with similar economic characteristics. Despite the primary importance attached to economic criteria in class demarcation, no economist stands out as exerting a dominant influence on the class conceptions of American sociologists. With perhaps few exceptions, American sociologists were acquainted with and employed Thorstein Veblen's analyses. But almost none of them was prepared to accept his views as a whole. Nor did the common recognition of class control by the state incline them favorably to Marxist notions. The more common criteria of class included: relation to a system of production, occupation, wealth, amount of income, property, possessions, power, and privilege. Type of income, degree of skill, and standard of living were utilized less frequently. Education was the most conspicuous of the non-economic characteristics (although it was often viewed as an effect of occupation or income). Variations in taste, moral standards, goals, values, or culture generally were seldom mentioned. This emphasis on economic criteria relegated questions of group organization, solidarity, and consciousness to a position of secondary importance.

4. All the arguments involving consideration of rank seemed ultimately to focus on the question of whether or not the existing social hierarchy afforded full expression of individual differences in mental capacity for

of the American Sociological Society, I-XII (1907-1918), as well as from C. H. Page, *Class and American Sociology* (New York, 1940).

contributing to maximum acceleration of progress. But there were two divergent positions concerning the effect of the class hierarchy on individual differences. One, represented especially by Sumner and Giddings, construed the social-class hierarchy as the outcome of natural social-evolutionary processes, with the members of the various strata arranged in accordance with their individually unequal physical, moral, and intellectual endowments for progress. Social superiority and contribution to progress were identical. Individuals who achieved superior status—Sumner's "classes" and Giddings' "natural aristocracy" or "pre-eminent class"—were the favorable biological variant who contributed innovations, made progress possible, and comprised the instrumentalities through whom society makes its adaptations. However, Giddings, who was an adherent neither of *laissez faire* nor of unqualified evolutionism, was disturbed by the possibility that social selection might oppose, if not counteract, natural selection. Hence he urged state intervention to secure adoption of eugenic measures by which the ratio of gifted to the inadequate or deficient might be increased.

The other position, represented by Ward, Ross, and Cooley, regarded the class hierarchy as an arbitrary and artificial arrangement having no correlation with individual capacities and thus requiring equalization of opportunities to provide for the necessary ascendance of talent for creative innovation. Sociologists who subscribed to this viewpoint accepted Cooley's interpretation, embodied in his study of "Genius, Fame, and Comparison of Races," that unusual ability is no monopoly of any social class but that the disadvantages of inferior class position constitute an obstacle to the attainment of fame. Low-class position was not an index of low innate potentiality for contributing to progress. Although many of these sociologists doubted that society could dispense with its class divisions, they enthusiastically endorsed a democratic extension of education as a major means of maintaining open classes, enlargement of opportunity, and the ascendance of the exceptional individual.

Indirect Interest in Social Stratification (1918-1935)

Throughout the second era of American sociology—the dominant feature of which was the quest to make the discipline scientific—the concern with social stratification phenomena continued as an interest subordinate and secondary to other intellectual problems. In the developing professional division of labor, the differentiation of specialized fields, and the preoccupation with scientific method, social stratification did not become a separate and independent field. Rather, the chief channels for the indirect expression of concern with matters of rank were the areas of rural sociology, labor unrest and radicalism, social biology (especially) and its later bifurcation into ethnic and race relations and population, and statistical research techniques.[22]

The failure of social stratification to emerge as a separate field in the twenties was a consequence of the effects of changes in the social context and in the discipline as a whole upon the pre-World War I concern with social inequality. First, sociology's orientation to the events in the larger society and its earlier conception of class and ethnic–race problems allowed the implications of differential individual mental capacities—which developed from the accumulation of data on the I.Q.'s of Army inductees—to be interpreted primarily in terms of race- and ethnic-group differences and only secondarily as a matter of social stratification. Second, the increased academic stature of sociology was acknowledged during this period in the establishment of independent departments of sociology in colleges and universities. This independence was often the consequence of a withdrawal from a joint department with economics. The almost complete disappearance of sociologists' concern with the field of labor unrest and radicalism—a concern they had shared with economists—by the mid-twenties may perhaps be explained by the intellectual independence accompanying this academic separation. At this time sociologists were energetically endeavoring to make their discipline a separate, recognized social science. This trend may have had a significant influence in deterring direct sociological analysis of class, for classes, were still conceived primarily in economic terms. Third, the occurrence of World War I, the subsequent attempt to make sociology scientific, and the cross-disciplinary contacts with cultural anthropology resulted in the jettisoning of "progress," meliorism, and social evolutionism which had been the rationale for interest in the interrelations of individual differences, the class hierarchy, and innovation. When sociologists reflected on the implications of World War I in the immediately subsequent years, many of them became pessimistic about the rationality of man and the possibility of progress. Direct contact with cultural anthropologists at the annual meetings of the American Sociological Society in the mid-twenties and publication of anthropological papers in sociological journals communicated the facts of cultural relativism and accentuated the demand for objectivity.

Social stratification probably found its most definite, recognized expression in the area of labor unrest and radicalism. Sensitive as sociologists were to the concrete conditions of their society by virtue of their commitment to progress and meliorism, their interest in this area was intensified

[22] A more detailed treatment of this subject is to be found in Roscoe C. Hinkle, Jr., "Theories of Social Stratification in Recent American Sociology" (unpublished Ph. D. dissertation, University of Wisconsin, 1952), Chaps. 3-4.

by the widespread labor-management conflict and the growth of the I.W.W. movement prior to World War. I. The research of Carleton H. Parker, the labor economist, was especially important in focusing sociologists' attention on these events. Yet this area never became a special field of sociological endeavor, for interest seems to have waned almost completely by the mid-twenties, when demarcation of fields was clearly appearing.

The area of labor unrest is unique in that for the first time it involved the analysis of social stratification with Freudian principles. Ernest W. Burgess' comments at the 1920 annual meetings of the American Sociological Society were significant in their anticipation of the subsequent prevalent use of the concepts of "balked instincts" and "repression."[23] Of the many sociologists who employed psychoanalytic notions to explain labor unrest —and they included Jerome Dowd, Seba Eldridge, and Stuart Rice—none made more extensive contributions to Freudian interpretation in this area than F. Stuart Chapin and Herbert Adolphus Miller.[24]

Rural sociology became one of the major fields for the expression of interest in social stratification because sociologists observed that urbanization, mechanization, tenure differences, and urbanward migration had hierarchical implications for rural society. Carl Taylor connected "The Rise of the Rural Problem" and the emergence of agrarian-interest organizations with the economic and social inequalities between the rural and urban populations.[25] Dwight Sanderson saw rural society being stratified and segregated as the result of swift and easy transportation, family intervisitation delimited by common specialization of tastes and interests, and church affiliation restricted by status. And throughout the twenties and early thirties, the volume of state agricultural-experiment-station bulletins and occasional publications of the United States Department of Agriculture bore witness to the conception of farm tenancy as a facet of rural stratification.[26]

However, rural–urban migration was probably the chief problem through which the more general study of stratification was approached.

[23] E. W. Burgess, "Discussion," *PASS,* 14 (1920), p. 240.

[24] J. H. Bond, "Discussion," *PASS,* 14 (1920), pp. 78-82; Seba Eldridge, "Discussion," *PASS,* 15 (1921), pp. 170-173; Jerome Dowd, "Industrial Democracy," *AJS,* 26 (March, 1920), pp. 581-587; S. A. Rice, "Motives in Radicalism and Social Reform," *AJS,* 28 (March, 1923), pp. 577-585; F. S. Chapin, "Democracy and Class Relations," *PASS,* 14 (1920) pp. 100-110; H. A. Miller, *Races, Nations and Classes* (Philadelphia, 1924).

[25] Carl Taylor, "The Rise of the Rural Problem," *SF,* 2 (1923-24), p. 33; "Organizing Farmers for Economic and Political Action," *PASS,* 17 (1923), pp. 194-199; and "Farmers Movements as Psychosocial Phenomena," *PASS,* 23 (1929), pp. 153-162.

[26] Dwight Sanderson, "The Relation of the Farmer to Rural and Urban Groups," *PASS,* 22 (1928), pp. 104-106. See the partial bibliography in E. A. Schuler, "The Present Social Status of American Farm Tenants," *RS,* 3 (1938), pp. 22-24, footnote 10.

Just as the eugenist social biologists used Social Darwinist assumptions to infer population selectivity in the birth and death rates of the several social classes, so students of rural sociology interpreted the urbanward migration as a selective process negatively affecting population quality in the status hierarchy of rural society. In 1921, for example, John M. Gillette was convinced that the flow of migrants from country to town was accompanied by a stream of talent in the same direction.[27] Assuming achieved social status as an index of innate capacity, Gillette was led to argue that cityward migration of persons who became leaders in industry, commerce, finance, engineering, journalism, and the ministry depleted the rural districts of extraordinary individuals.

But the most common medium for the expression of interest in social stratification was the field of social biology, which was devoted to an examination of the biological quality of the various segments of the population. This field owes its chief importance as a channel for consideration of status and rank to three circumstances. First, the historical sequence of waves of culturally distinct immigrants in this country resulted in the objectification of the status hierarchy in terms of visible ethnic and, sometimes, physical differences. Second, the experience of World War I led many intellectuals, including a number of sociologists, to conclude that the existence of lower strata of partially assimilated European ethnic groups and presumably unassimilable Oriental and Negro racial groups impeded the maximum integration and coordination of national skills and talents. Third, the dissemination of the army I.Q. data, arranged by racial and nationality groups, reinforced the tendency to interpret status subordination as racial and ethnic inferiority. This mass of information, which J. P. Lichtenberger first brought to the attention of sociologists in his paper on the "Significance of Mental Levels" at the 1920 annual meetings of the American Sociological Society, was rapidly incorporated into the Social Darwinist interpretation of the role of hereditary individual inequalities in the formation of the social hierarchy, in status placement, in vertical mobility, and in the creation of innovations for progress.

Probably the most important consequences for the biological assumptions that conferred theoretical significance on social stratification in the field of social biology resulted from the intrusion of cultural–anthropological arguments, with which sociologists became increasingly conversant during the mid-twenties. Some sociologists came in contact with cultural anthropology during their graduate training (e.g., Ogburn), but probably more often they became acquainted with the field through the direct participation of Alexander Goldenweiser, Melville Herskovits, Margaret Mead,

[27] J. M. Gillette, "Points of Contact between City and County," *PASS,* 16 (1922), p. 219. However, see Gillette's article "Urban Influence and Selection," *PASS,* 23 (1929), pp. 1-14 for a change in his interpretation.

and Ralph Linton in the annual meetings of the American Sociological Society and through articles published in the sociological journals. Cultural anthropologists drew on their accumulating information from cross-cultural studies of race and ethnic groups and especially on Alfred Kroeber's distinction between biological (organic) and cultural (superorganic) phenomena to contribute to the attack on the premise of differential racial intellectual capacities, by which eugenists accounted for the inferior status of the unassimilated race and ethnic groups.[28]

The field of race and ethnic relations—the first of the two divisions derived from social biology—is especially identified with Robert E. Park and his students. In this as in other areas, Park used and recommended the application of the case-study technique and the natural-history approach. The voluminous research into race and ethnic problems, which he and his students conducted by means of this investigative procedure, is replete with references to social stratification, although only a few of his immediate students made rank a direct object of systematic study.[29]

All the stratification-related concepts employed in this field and in others disclose the persistent individualism of American sociology in their focusing on interpersonal relations and the personality. Status, Park's basic concept, is the personal position of an individual in relation to others in a group. One position or status is ultimately separated from another by social distance—the degree of intimacy and understanding with which individuals feel their life-experiences can be shared. As a kind of consciousness of difference that provokes categorical rather than personal definitions of the people involved, race-consciousness prevents intimacies and understandings, sustains distances, and determines social status accordingly.[30] Studies by Park and his students emphasized personality characteristics—restlessness, aggressiveness, ambitiousness, sensitivity, self-consciousness, egocentricity—of marginal individuals. Yet E. B. Reuter, Everett Stonequist, Paul Cressey, and especially William O. Brown did investigate the

[28] See Margaret Mead, "The Methodology of Racial Testing: Its Significance for Sociology," *AJS,* 31 (1925-26), pp. 657-667; M. J. Herskovits, "Social Pattern: A Methodological Study," *SF,* 4 (1925-26), pp. 57-69.

[29] Although H. W. Zorbaugh's *The Gold Coast and the Slum* (Chicago, 1929) is generally predicated on Park's ecological frame of reference, it does contain an entire chapter on the rank consciousness, style of life, social ritual, formal and informal structures, prestige competition and social climbing of Gold Coast "society." Also relevant are E. C. Hughes, "Institutional Office and the Person," *AJS,* 43 (Nov., 1937), pp. 404-413; "Position and Status in a Quebec Industrial Town," *ASR,* 3 (Oct., 1938), pp. 709-717; and "Dilemmas and Contradictions of Status," *AJS,* 50 (1944-45), pp. 353-359.

[30] R. E. Park, "Sociology and the Social Sciences," *AJS,* 27 (Sept., 1921), p. 181; "Sociology," in Wilson Gee (ed.), *Research in the Social Sciences* (New York, 1929), p. 31; and "The Concept of Position in Sociology," *PASS,* 20 (1926), p. 14. See also Park, *Race and Culture* (Glencoe, Ill., 1950).

struggle for status of the marginal personality.[31] But generally, whatever facets of stratification were examined were interpreted in terms of the personality or personal relations. Even Park's conspicuous lack of interest in social class relations seems to derive from his individualistic conception of American society, in which "distinctions and distances must be of a purely individual and personal nature" and in which "there are no class distinctions" so that "changes in status are correspondingly rapid."[32]

However, the field of population—the second of the two areas into which social biology divided—showed a much more direct and obvious interest in social stratification. Probably the attention frequently and explicitly given to the vital statistics of social-class divisions was the result of the persistence of the earlier presuppositions of eugenist biology in this field. As late as 1933, students of population attempted to relate the cultural and intellectual development of the nation to the major occupational categories (regarded as social classes) and their differential fertility. Thus the doctrine of progress, which had become suspect in sociology in the mid-twenties, continued implicitly as the justification for research in population.

The field of methods was the last area in which interest in social stratification appeared in the second era of American sociology. Chapin's social-status scale is especially important because it reveals how the controversy over the scientific method (especially statistics *vs.* case study and objectivism *vs.* subjectivism), the legacy of progress and meliorism, and individualism all converge in the construction of a measuring device. Like Ogburn, Chapin was influenced by Giddings' instruction to employ and promote statistical procedures as the means for making sociology scientific. Chapin's status scale is a practical application of this conception of science. And just as science was justified earlier as the most efficient technique to accelerate progress by amelioration, so Chaplin's scale has the melioristic objective of providing social workers "with an objective measure of the home environment for prospective foster homes."[33] But the instrument is even more important for the conception of social status on which it is alleged to be predicated. Chapin insisted, in the course of an objectivist-subjectivist methodological argument with Floyd House, that the living-room scale involves a notion of socio-economic status that is founded on a psychological

[31] E. V. Stonequist, "The Problem of the Marginal Man," *AJS,* 41 (July, 1935), pp. 1-12; P. F. Cressey, "The Anglo-Indian: A Disorganized Marginal Group," *SF,* 14 (Dec., 1935), pp. 263-268; W. O. Brown, "Culture Contact and Race Conflict," in E. B. Reuter (ed.), *Race and Culture Contacts* (New York, 1934), pp. 44-45.

[32] Park, *Race and Culture,* pp. 233, 258.

[33] F. S. Chapin, "A Quantitative Scale for Rating the Home and Social Environment of Middle Class Families in an Urban Community: A First Approximation to the Measurement of Socio-Economic Status," *JEP,* 19 (1928), p. 99, and "A Home Rating Scale to Check Social Workers' Opinions," *SSR,* 14 (Sept.-Oct., 1929), pp. 10-11.

or attitudinal factor.[34] Income and material possession, cultural acquisitions, and social participations of individuals in community affairs are compositely the economic and social evidence of position to which the "attitudes of subordination or domination (and their variations) are conditioned."

The Field of Social Stratification (1936-1954)

After 1936 the study of social stratification came to be consolidated and unified as a separate field. Its designation as a field is confirmed by common consent and practice, by acknowledged professional specialization, and by the accumulation of a body of theory, concepts, methodology, techniques, and empirical findings. A widespread commitment to functionalist theory and a preoccupation with the nature of, and appropriate techniques for studying, social-class stratification in American communities are the dominant features of the recent sociological inquiry into social stratification. Despite its rapid emergence after 1936, the field of social stratification continued to reflect its association with certain earlier interests as well as with the changes transpiring in sociology generally.

Only as the inquiry into rank was modified to meet the changing demands of the discipline itself did the remarkable efflorescence of research occur in this field during the past two decades. Two major modifications appear to have been required for the present proliferation of stratification research: (1) the explicit emergence of a newer and more utilitarian rationale to make rank directly problematic, and (2) the construction of appropriate empirical research techniques by which data on social inequality could be reliably studied.

Both these intellectual requirements were satisfied by the two lines of endeavor out of which present-day empirical studies of social class have arisen—the rural-sociological and the modern anthropological approaches to the study of American communities. Since the older doctrines of progress, meliorism, and evolutionism had become generally suspect, they could no longer afford justification for the study of social inequality as they had in the early and middle twenties. Rural sociology became concerned with social stratification in American rural communities largely as a consequence of the increase in farm tenancy and the devitalization of the smaller rural centers, which had been occasioned by the impact of the rural depression beginning in the twenties, urban influences, and the increased capitalization demanded by agricultural mechanization. Many rural sociologists were con-

[34] F.N. House, "Measurement in Sociology," *AJS*, 40 (1934-35), p. 8; F.S. Chapin. "Measurement in Sociology," *ibid.*, pp. 476-477.

vinced that leadership in the rehabilitation of rural life was affected by class stratification, both directly and indirectly (through urbanward migration of population). The series on contemporary rural life, published by the Bureau of Agricultural Economics, and the research of Gee, Schuler, and others, suggest the emergence of this utilitarian rationale.[35] The study of social stratification in a prairie town by John and Ruth Useem and Pierre Tangent also documents the continued and independent interest of rural sociologists in this field in the late thirties and early forties.[36] Rural sociological research is equally significant for its early experimentation with the prestige-rating technique for distinguishing classes and for allocating the community's residents to the strata discovered.

The rural sociologists seem to have played an important, although largely unrecognized, role in providing a new justification and new technique for studying social inequality. Their work, the effect of the general depression of the early thirties, and the re-examination of the analyses of European social theorists appear to have established a favorable intellectual climate for consideration of the Warner research, which has now become the basis for much of the controversy in the field and which will be discussed below in some detail. Although Warner contributed several papers prior to the publication of his or his students' monographs on the South and Yankee City, sociologists generally do not seem to have been clearly aware of the rationale or the research procedures of his studies until *Deep South* and *The Social Life of a Modern Community* appeared in 1941. The Yankee City investigations, which were undertaken to enlarge the understanding of the factors in the inefficient productivity of the industrial worker in the modern factory, have a relatively explicit utilitarian justification. Preceded by sociologists' positive interest in the study of social rank supported by direct, observational data, Warner's findings and his methods provoked immediate and continuing reaction from researchers in sociology.

However, much of the social-stratification inquiry from 1936-1942 centered on problems that were identified with the older areas of social biology, race and ethnic relations, population, community, rural sociology, and methods. Studies of the differential intellectual talents of occupational

[35] Bureau of Agricultural Economics, Rural Life Studies, 1-6, published from Nov., 1941 to Jan., 1943, as *Culture of a Contemporary Rural Community* (El Cerrito, New Mexico; Sublette, Kansas; Landaff, New Hampshire; the Old Order Amish of Lancaster County, Pennsylvania; Irwin, Iowa; and Harmony, Georgia). Note also Wilson Gee, "A Qualitative Study of Rural Depopulation in a Single Township, 1900-1930," *AJS,* 39 (Sept., 1933), pp. 210-221; Wilson Gee and Dewees Runk, "Qualitative Selection in Cityward Migration," *AJS,* 37 (Sept., 1931), pp. 254-265; E. A. Schuler, "The Present Social Status of American Farm Tenants," *RS,* 3 (1938), pp. 20-33, and "Social and Economic Status in a Louisiana Hills Community," *RS,* 5 (1940), pp. 69-83.

[36] John Useem, Pierre Tangent, and Ruth Useem, "Stratification in a Prairie Town," *ARS,* 7 (June, 1942), pp. 331-343.

strata (using the I.Q.'s of college students and their fathers' occupations, or the I.Q.'s and scholastic records of public school students and the vocations they subsequently entered), of the bio-social characteristics of inventors, of the occupational mobility of notable persons, and of the role of class origins and historical circumstances in the achievement of fame—all these studies issue from assumptions or interests characteristic of the older social biology. The investigations of the effect of American life on the social-class status of the immigrants, the impact of industrialization on position in an ethnic hierarchy, the role of status in assimilation of a racial group, the development of an intermediate position for Orientals in a Negro-white area, the social status of migrant Negroes, ritual and stratification in Negro churches, and the relationship of race and class and caste and class stem from the earlier race and ethnic preoccupations. Research into selective migration, differential fertility of different occupational categories, and the demographic clues of stratification is linked with the field of population. The first studies of social stratification in small towns or cities were classified as community studies. Rural sociology is represented by the inquiries into rank in American rural life, which were especially important in pointing both to the earlier concern with the quality of the residual population after urbanward migration and to the newer development of prestige rating by judges as a technique for determining community strata. Finally, specialists in statistical techniques, many of whom were also proponents of operationism, elaborated and extended the construction of social-status scales.

Although antecedent expressions of interest were important in the emergence of social stratification as a specialty, changes occurring in the discipline at large were no less influential. The shifts included particularly the utilitarian justification of research, use of teams to conduct large-scale investigations, more fundamental interdisciplinary stimulation, and the widespread acceptance of the view that advancement of science and the extension of theory are interdependent. The studies of Warner and his associates exemplify all of these trends current in the discipline as a whole. The original Yankee City research, which was conducted by a team of investigators, was one of several efforts—arising from the investigations of the Western Electric Company's Hawthorne plant by the Committee of Industrial Physiology at Harvard University—to contribute to the solution of the problem of worker inefficiency in the modern factory. In the more recent *Social Class in America* (1949), the utilitarianism of knowledge about social classes is more explicit, for Warner and his colleagues specifically set forth the advantages of such information for teachers and school administrators, personnel directors, market analysts, and advertising experts.

Other inquiries into social stratification also reveal certain of these general trends. The utilitarian implications of financial sponsorship by the

Air Force of Stuart Adams' and Raymond Mack's projects are unavoidable.[37] The interdisciplinary influences in and the theoretical focus of the studies of Talcott Parsons and his associates are readily recognizable. Parsons has acknowledged indebtedness to Malinowski's functionalist anthropology, Max Weber's postulates of social action, Vilfredo Pareto's concept of the system, and Sigmund Freud's personality theory. Thus Parsons' work discloses another general feature of contemporary American sociology—the selective incorporation of the viewpoints of recent European social theorists.

Like the discipline as a whole, the field of social stratification is generally committed to the investigation of social rank by means of a theoretical schema. Although its basic postulates have never been systematically subjected to cross-cultural study, *functionalism* has become the prevalent framework for empirical inquiry and theoretical elaboration. Thus social inequality is interpreted as in some way functionally indispensable to the maintenance of a society, the parts of which are conceived to be integrated and mutually interrelated as a system in equilibrium. This conception of society is the accepted point of departure for the social stratification theories both of W. Lloyd Warner and Talcott Parsons.[38]

Adhering to this interpretation, Warner contends that a certain minimum structural differentiation within the society is prescribed by the adaptations required for its continued existence. Three types of adjustive structures must be developed. The physical survival of the group in a natural environment demands the skills and tools of a *technology*. The necessity for a degree of orderliness in the interactions of individuals makes *rules of social organization* imperative. Finally, the existence of those unknown or other forces which technology and social organization cannot control sufficiently to give man the safety he feels he needs necessitates *religion* or a sacred symbol system.

However, additional adaptations may be required as social complexity increases, as internal groups and social relations are augmented, as social differentiation within the total number of relations comprising the society expands. *Rank stratification* is just this kind of requisite functional adjustment in a complex society, "with a large number of individuals pursuing diverse and complex activities and functioning in a multiplicity of ways," because differentiation of power and prestige must accompany the coordination of the efforts of all a society's members into a common enterprise which is necessary for the preservation of the group. Warner notes that

> . . . as division of labor increases and the social units become more numerous

[37] Stuart Adams, "Social Climate and Productivity in Small Military Groups," *ASR*, 19 (Aug., 1954), pp. 421-425; R. W. Mack, "The Prestige System of an Air Base: Squadron Rankings and Morale," *ASR*, 19 (June, 1954), pp. 281-287.

[38] See C. Arnold Anderson, "The Need for a Functional Theory of Social Classes," *RS*, 19 (1954), pp. 152-160; M. M. Tumin, *Caste in a Peasant Society* (Princeton, 1952); and J. W. Bennett and M. M. Tumin, *Social Life* (New York, 1948).

and diverse, the need for coordination and integration also increases and, when satisfied, enables the larger groups to survive and develop.

Those who occupy coordinating positions acquire power and prestige. They do so because their actions partly control the behavior of the individuals who look to them for direction. Within this simple control there is power. Those who exercise such power either acquire prestige directly from it or have gained prestige from other sources sufficiently to be raised to a coordinating position.[39]

What this argument suggests is that the type of status order which a society manifests is functionally dependent on the degree of social complexity and social differentiation. Now a status—the position, place, or location of the individual or his behavior in the social structure—may or may not be ranked as superior or inferior. Non-ranked statuses are characteristic of simple and relatively undifferentiated societies. These statuses imply the least social inequality and signify that all the social positions of a society are available to all members of the same sex at some time in their life spans. Rank statuses are found in more complex, differentiated societies and involve a social hierarchy allocating individual or groups of individuals in superior and superordinate places and other individuals in inferior and subordinate positions because the members of the society evaluate certain social positions and the behavior found there as superior and inferior.[40]

Just as there is the functional implication that each status-system represents a functional response to a particular—though unspecified—degree of social complexity and social differentiation, so there is the functional postulate that the statuses in any type of society are mutually interrelated and interdependent. Warner's construction of a generalized typology of 89 positions in the Yankee City class system is an effort to demonstrate the validity of this postulate. Through the analysis of the kinds of interconnections between these positions viewed as contact-situations in which status relations may be super-, sub-, or co-ordinate, the role of each position may be described in terms of the function it plays in the entire positional system. In their totality, these 89 positions represent an interrelated, interconnected, and interdependent system in equilibrium.

Unlike Warner, Parsons derives social stratification as a dimension of any social system by use of the action frame of reference in conjunction with a set of functional prerequisites specifying the necessary conditions to be met if the particular system is to persist as a system. Stratification is, consequently, implicated in a system of social relations by virtue, on

[39] W. Lloyd Warner, Marchia Meeker, K. W. Eells, *Social Class in America* (Chicago, 1949), p. 8.

[40] W. Lloyd Warner and Allison Davis, "A Comparative Study of American Caste," in E. T. Thompson (ed.), *Race Relations and the Race Problem* (Durham, N.C., 1939), p. 220.

the one hand, of the actor-situation orientations and, on the other, of the scarcity of desired objects, the nature of the human organism, and the realities of coexistence. By slightly modifying the Kantian conception of human nature, Parsons interprets all role-playing between and among persons as motivationally oriented toward the situation by combinations of cognition, cathexis, and evaluation.[41]

Parsons proposes that social stratification ultimately arises from the evaluation inherent in actor (inter-)action. In Parsons' frame of reference all action necessarily entails choice, selection, or preference. What persons do or how they do it cannot be a matter of indifference. "Exactly equal valuation of two or more entities may of course occur, but it is a special case of evaluative judgment, not a demonstration of its irrelevance." The probability is that evaluation "will serve to differentiate entities in a rank order of some kind."[42] Thus, such preferential appraisal implies a ranking of the system's units in terms of the common value-orientations of the social system.

There must be such standards for evaluation, for the inherent scarcity of desired objects in a situation will provoke conflict so that orderly coexistence becomes impossible. By definition, actors are motivated toward one another in a situation for direct or indirect gratification of their needs-dispositions. The desired objects in the situation may be physical, cultural, or social (e.g., actions or attitudes of another actor or actors). But whether these objects operate as *facilities* (which are desired for the instrumental uses to which they can be put) or as *rewards* (which are desired for direct cathexis) in the actor's motivational system, they are inherently scarce. Hence, claims to their use, control, or disposal as possessions must be institutionally regulated. The facts of scarcity also require that inequality be institutionalized.

Just as power is a consequence of the distribution of scarce facilities, so prestige is a consequence of the distribution of scarce rewards. And of all the types of rewards, esteem is the most important for the emergence of a generalized system of rank or prestige. Esteem, as Parsons uses the concept, is a composite gratificational response allocated to the entire person. Since it is awarded to the person as a generalized entity, it is diffuse and cannot be segregated to a particular context or contexts (as can approval, the other type of affectively neutral reward). Its diffuse generalized character implies a degree of prestige in a general prestige hierarchy because the

[41] An analysis of Parsons' assumptions concerning science, methodology, epistemology, the action frame of reference, and the social system as a theoretical system (and their intellectual antecedents) may be found in Hinkle, *op. cit.*, Chap. 7.

[42] Talcott Parsons, "A Revised Analytical Approach to a Theory of Social Stratification," in Reinhard Bendix and Seymour Lipset (eds.), *Class, Status, and Power* (Glencoe, Ill., 1953), p. 93.

functional prerequisite that the social system must be integrated demands an institutionalized, generalized, and common evaluative scale cutting across different classes of rewards as a condition of social stability. Therefore, the person actually has esteem relative to a graded hierarchy; his relative esteem in an ordered total system of differentiated evaluation is prestige, which signifies comparative evaluation. In turn, differential prestige is the basis of stratification.

In addition to derivation by evaluation and by the inherent scarcity of desirable facilities and rewards, stratification can be functionally deduced from the prerequisite of adequacy of motivation. Kingsley Davis and Wilbert Moore have employed this argument.[43] They contend that certain positions in a social system are functionally more important than others and require special skills for their performance. However, the number of individuals who have these talents and who are willing to undergo the sacrifice demanded for training is limited. Hence, inducements in the form of differential access to the scarce and desired rewards of the society must be attached to these positions in order to motivate the talented persons to subject themselves to the sacrifices and acquire the training. These differential rewards lead to a differentiation of prestige of strata and, consequently, to social stratification, which is, in turn, functionally contributory to the maintenance of the social system. Viewed in the historical perspective of social-stratification study in American sociology, Davis and Moore's argument is noteworthy because it reiterates the persistent voluntaristic theme, so prevalent among the earlier students of social inequality, that differential rewards (or social and economic conditions) are a motivational requisite to the maintenance of the society.

When the actual character of the empirical investigation of stratification is examined, it appears to be confined predominantly to the study of classes in the local community. American sociologists, who are the legatees of an older "social-problems" tradition, of the social survey, and of the instrumentalism *implicit* in the doctrine of progress and meliorism, have concentrated on class (or caste-class) as the most appropriate designation for the hierarchical arrangement of American society.[44] Despite the evident localistic delimitation of their research projects, they have seemingly been relatively unaware that they have been studying only an American variety

[43] Kingsley Davis, "A Conceptual Analysis of Stratification," *ASR,* 7 (June, 1942), pp. 309-321; Kingsley Davis and Wilbert Moore, "Some Principles of Stratification," *ASR,* 10 (April, 1945), pp. 242-249. See also Melvin Tumin, "Some Principles of Stratification: A Critical Analysis," *ASR,* 18 (Aug., 1953), pp. 387-394, and the rejoinders by Davis and Moore, pp. 394-397.

[44] Stone and Form have warned against a conception of social stratification that is exclusively hierarchical: G. P. Stone and W. H. Form, "Instabilities in Status: The Problem of Hierarchy in the Community Study of Status Arrangements," *ASR,* 18 (April, 1953), pp. 149-162.

(or varieties) of classes in towns or smaller urban communities. However, Artis, Duncan, Gross, Hatt, Kaufman, and Sewell have all insisted that class structure is a function of the values of the mass society as well as those of the local community.[45]

For the most part, the earlier local community studies (such as those by Warner, Hollingshead, Kaufman, and Wheeler) resulted in operational definitions of social class. In the case of the Warner studies, participant observation and/or interviews with samples of long-time residents purportedly elicited the community class designations. If judges of prestige were used (e.g., Hollingshead and Kaufman), a consensus of their ratings established the classes. Frequently, these earlier researches also adhered to a conception of class that was based on prestige rather than power and regarded the strata as discrete groupings segregated by participation and culture, as real rather than heuristic entities.

These community investigations of social class in rural centers, towns, and small cities proposed varying numbers of classes. According to Warner, Jonesville and Yankee City had five and six social classes respectively. Hollingshead, who used a rating method, corroborated the five classes of Jonesville (or Elmtown). Allison Davis, Burleigh B. and Mary R. Gardner, Mozell C. Hill and Bevode C. McCall, Harold F. Kaufman, and Morton Rubin noted five classes in the communities they respectively studied. Evan Z. Vogt and James West located three and four strata respectively, whereas Wayne Wheeler and William H. Form found seven strata in Plains and in planned communities.

As the number of community investigations has increased, the opportunities for critical analysis have grown. Sociologists have begun to re-examine the theory, concepts, and techniques by which stratification is being studied. Pfautz, for instance, notes that it is crucial that "distinctions be made between the task of delineating the class structure of a community and that of placing individuals within it; between the correlates and the determinants of class status; and, finally, between class structures and assignments which are a function of the individual's self-conception, the researcher's analytic device, and the community's judgment."[46]

Since the research of Warner and his colleagues has bulked so large

[45] O. D. Duncan and J. W. Artis, *Social Stratification in a Pennsylvania Rural Community* (State College, Pa., 1951), Bulletin No. 543; H. W. Pfautz and O. D. Duncan, "A Critical Evaluation of Warner's Work in Community Stratification," *ASR,* 15 (April, 1950), pp. 205-215; H. F. Kaufman, O. D. Duncan, Neal Gross, W. H. Sewell, "Problems of Theory and Method in the Study of Social Stratification in Rural Society," *RS,* 18 (March, 1953), pp. 12-24; H. F. Kaufman, "An Approach to the Study of Urban Stratification," *ASR,* 17 (Aug., 1952), pp. 430-437; P. K. Hatt, "Stratification in the Mass Society," *ASR,* 15 (April, 1950), pp. 216-227.

[46] See Pfautz's summary: "The Current Literature on Social Stratification: Critique and Bibliography," *AJS,* 58 (1952-53), pp. 391-418. The citation is from p. 394.

in the field, much of the criticism has been directed at Warner.[47] Immediately after the publication of the first volume of the Yankee City series and long before Warner had formalized his techniques as "Evaluative Participation" and the "Index of Status Characteristics," the work was attacked by C. Wright Mills because it employs a conception of class that indiscriminately absorbed three analytically separate dimensions of stratification, although it actually emphasized but one. Most sociologists seem to concur with Mills that stratification embodies the three separate types of variables distinguished by Max Weber, the legal (political coercion), the economic (access to goods and services), and the social (prestige status). Despite their rejection of exclusive preoccupation with prestige and their acceptance of a multidimensional view of social stratification, they have scarcely begun to probe the relationships among the three types of variables. Perhaps the pervasive voluntaristic convictions of American sociology have discouraged inquiry into power and political coercion.[48] Within the past several years, sociologists have started empirical study of the occupational component of the economic variable in stratification.[49]

More recently, sociologists have come to question the validity of construing American classes as discrete, segregated categories.[50] Lenski, Cuber, and Kenkel advance a continuum conception of strata, insisting that there "are several privilege, power, and status ranges, more or less continuous from top to bottom, with no clear lines of demarcation." They claim that the following arguments reveal that Warner's position is untenable: (1) the number of classes seem to vary with the number of observers; (2) significant numbers of persons cannot be categorized on the basis of any criterion; (3) the bases of ranking are subject to continuous change; (4) whenever variables of differential status are measured, a continuous

[47] For a summary of the criticisms of Warner's position, see Ruth R. Kornhauser "The Warner Approach to Social Stratification," in Bendix and Lipset, *op. cit.*, pp. 243-255. Cf. C. Wright Mills, review of *The Social Life of a Modern Community,* in *ASR,* 7 (June, 1942), pp. 263-271.

[48] Hence there are few articles on this subject: C. C. North, "Class Structure, Class Consciousness, and Party Alignment," *ASR,* 2 (June, 1937), pp. 365-371; Herbert Goldhamer and E. A. Shils, "Types of Power and Status," *AJS,* 45 (Sept., 1939), pp. 171-172; Robert Bierstedt, "An Analysis of Social Power," *ASR,* 15 (Dec., 1950), pp. 730-738; Reinhard Bendix, "Social Stratification and Political Power," *APSR,* 46 (June, 1952), pp. 357-375; T. M. Mills, "Power Relations in Three-Person Groups," *ASR,* 18 (Aug., 1953), pp. 351-367.

[49] See Pfautz, *op. cit.*, pp. 398-399.

[50] J. F. Cuber and W. F. Kenkel, *Social Stratification in the United States* (New York, 1954); G. E. Lenski, "American Social Classes: Statistical Strata or Social Groups?" *AJS,* 58 (1952-53), pp. 139-144; S. A. Hetzler, "An Investigation of the Distinctiveness of Social Classes," *ASR,* 18 (1953), pp. 493-497; A. M. Rose, "The Popular Meaning of Class Designation," *SSR,* 38 (Sept.-Oct., 1953), pp. 14-21.

series of data emerges; (5) criteria of rank do not show significant correlations with one another; (6) the procedures of the proponents of the categorical conception of classes "fall short of statistical research methods which have come to be accepted as essential if reliability and validity are to be claimed"; (7) investigations (such as those by Kenkel and Lenski) that have employed methods comparable to those used by Warner and his colleagues and, in addition, have adhered to acceptable statistical procedures, have not revealed that society "divides itself" into class categories, but rather that a continuum of strata result; (8) the data from socio-economic-scale and discrete class studies are actually consistent with the continuum theory, for they also tend to assume the form of continua.[51]

Nevertheless, it may be ill-advised, if not inaccurate, at this juncture to contend categorically that all class strata in the United States are *either* continuous *or* discrete rather than more or less continuous *and* more or less segregable. There is evidence that greater breaks may exist between some strata than between others in the same community. (Moreover, Warner has not argued that classes are segregated to the absolute maximum of isolation.) In comparing and in generalizing from the stratification arrangements of different communities, much more rigorous consideration needs to be devoted to precisely how similar or dissimilar the communities are—for instance, in age, regional location, stability of local population (immigration and emigration), ethnic, racial, and possibly religious diversity, the rapidity and continuity of economic development, the nature and diversification of local industry, the extent of mechanization and standardization of work operations, the bureaucratization of worker relationships, and the ultimate source of decision in local industrial, commercial, and financial spheres.

Interestingly, vertical mobility, which is probably the most crucial feature of class stratification, was not consistently studied by American sociologists before 1949. Much of this recent research has been directed to compiling relevant factual information within single communities, to comparing regional variations, to establishing the role of migration in, and to ascertaining the social-psychological correlates of, upward and downward mobility.[52] Sociologists tend to agree that such inquiries must differentiate the various dimensions of vertical mobility: that within the individual's life-career, that between generations in the same or different communities; and that for groups as a whole. Since class analysis is still so new and marked by controversy, most investigators (except for two of Warner's students) have used *occupation* rather than class as the hierarchy of ascent and descent. Ruth Albrecht, who examined status changes in life-careers of older persons, noted in her summary that upward "mobility in a lifetime characterized

[51] Cuber and Kenkel, *op. cit.*, pp, 25-26, 303-307.

[52] See H. W. Pfautz, "The Current Literature on Social Stratification: Critique and Bibliography," *AJS*, 57 (Jan., 1953), pp. 391-418.

the upper and both middle classes, while downward mobility centered in the two lower classes." Carson McGuire commented that his conclusion that 25 percent of a generation must be upwardly mobile to maintain the status system of Jonesville is applicable also to the American stratification system. In their analysis of the labor market of Oakland, California, Reinhard Bendix and Seymour Lipset found that most of the life-career status shifts transpire within manual and non-manual occupations rather than between them. Using information drawn from the marriage-license applications of two samples of 10,000 males in 1910 and 1940 in Marion County, Indiana, Natalie Rogoff has probably contributed the most extensive and substantial findings on vertical mobility. Her calculations are based on a ratio of actual to expected recruitment proportions by which variations in the social origins of occupational strata can be measured through time. Stuart Adams studied variations in the occupational origins of attorneys, physicians, and businessmen. Ronald Freedman and Amos Hawley concluded that there was a marked association between migration and occupational mobility within Michigan during the Depression. Richard Scudder and C. Arnold Anderson reported that their recent study supports the hypothesis that "sons who migrate out of small or moderate-size communities are more likely to rise above their parents' occupational status than sons who remain in the home town."

As sociologists have studied vertical mobility, they have been compelled to examine the historical dimensions of the hierarchical arrangements through which the rates of ascent and descent increase or decrease. They have come to recognize—perhaps belatedly—that their investigations of upward movement assume a temporal relationship to a system the characteristics of which cannot be accepted as constant. Nelson Foote's "destratification" and "restratification" concepts symbolize this recently acquired interest in process and change in the national, regional, and local status systems.[53] Both Hertzler and Sjoberg have approached the problem of change in the social hierarchy from the perspective of vertical mobility. Hertzler believes that restraint, rigidity, and even reversal of vertical mobility have already set in, whereas Sjoberg claims that "the class system is less well defined [now] than it was a half-century ago, particularly in the urban community. . . ." C. Arnold Anderson and Mary Jean Bowman have used

[53] Nelson Foote, "Destratification and Restratification: An Editorial Foreword," *AJS*, 58 (1953), pp. 325-326; J. O. Hertzler, "Tendencies Toward a Closed Class System in the United States," *SF*, 30 (1952), pp. 313-323; Gideon Sjoberg, "Are Social Classes in America Becoming More Rigid?" *ASR*, 16 (1951), pp. 775-783; C. Arnold Anderson and Mary J. Bowman, "The Vanishing Servant and the Contemporary Status System of the American South," *AJS*, 69 (1953), pp. 215-230; A. B. Hollingshead, "Trends in Social Stratification: A Case Study," *ASR*, 17 (1952), pp. 679-686. See also C. Wright Mills' analysis of the emergence of the new middle classes in his *White Collar* (New York, 1951).

the decline of servants as an index of modification of the South's status system. From his study of New Haven, Hollingshead infers that the development of highly stratified, parallel social structures has resulted in a compartmentalization of the social life of the inhabitants, which is likely to become more rigid with the passage of time.

In addition to the specialized study of the characteristics of classes, vertical mobility, and changing rank-arrangements in American communities, differentiation of the field of social stratification has involved the application of status analysis to many of the phenomena of the older social-problems fields and to segmental, institutional structures. Sociologists have investigated in particular the rural community, ethnic and race relations, family and marriage, and personality organization and disorganization from a stratification perspective. Similarly, they have studied the status relations in voluntary organizations, in the professions and occupational-industrial systems, in the public schools, colleges, churches, and the military hierarchies.

The last major feature of the field of social stratification is the emergence of interest in rank systems in other societies. Before World War II, a few relevant papers on French Canada, Haiti, Hawaii, and South Africa had been contributed. The war appears to have facilitated research on the nature and arrangements of strata in Latin-American countries, such as Argentina, Brazil, Colombia, Bolivia, Costa Rica, El Salvador, and Cuba. Frequently, these studies were the work of rural sociologists who participated in missions sponsored by the American Departments of State and/or Agriculture. During and after the war, German, Yugoslavian, and Chinese stratification systems were analyzed. Since the war, inquiries on Micronesia, Japan, India, Ceylon, Israel, Norway, England, and especially Russia have been made available. In the study of foreign social stratification the utilitarian rationale, which typifies American sociology generally, is most conspicuous in the research on Latin-America and Russia. It is also noteworthy that only Barrington Moore, Joel B. Montague, and Natalie Rogoff have attempted comparative studies of social-ranking systems.

The sociological study of social stratification appears to have undergone its most extensive changes during the recent period of American sociology. Indeed, by the mid-thirties a definite field of social stratification had begun to emerge, with its own theory, concepts, methodology, research techniques, and empirical studies. In less than twenty years, the field has rapidly achieved specialized status and internal differentiation. However, there remains much to be done in the comparative study of status structures and the analysis of processes of change in stratification systems.

SELECTED BIBLIOGRAPHY

Bailey, W. C., *et al., Bibliography on Status and Stratification* (New York: Social Science Research Council, 1952) [mimeographed].

Bendix, Reinhard, and S. M. Lipset (eds.), *Class, Status, and Power* (Glencoe, Ill.: The Free Press, 1953).

Centers, Richard, *The Psychology of Social Classes* (Princeton: Princeton University Press, 1949).

Cox, O. C., *Caste, Class, and Race* (New York: Doubleday, 1948).

Cuber, J. F., and W. F. Kenkel, *Social Stratification in the United States* (New York: Appleton-Century-Crofts, 1954).

Hiller, E. T., *Social Relations and Structures* (New York: Harper, 1947).

Pfautz, H. W., "The Current Literature on Social Stratification: Critique and Bibliography," *AJS,* 57 (January, 1953), pp. 391-418.

Sorokin, P. A., *Social Mobility* (New York: Harper, 1927).

Warner, W. Lloyd, Marchia Meeker, and Kenneth Eells, *Social Class in America* (Chicago: Science Research Associates, 1949).

Warner, W. Lloyd, and J. O. Low, *The Social System of the Factory* (New Haven: Yale University Press, 1947).

Warner, W. Lloyd, and P. S. Lunt, *The Social Life of a Modern Community* (New Haven: Yale University Press, 1941).

———, *The Status System of a Modern Community* (New Haven: Yale University Press, 1942).

Weber, Max, *From Max Weber: Essays in Sociology,* translated and edited by H. H. Gerth and C. Wright Mills (New York: Oxford University Press, 1946).

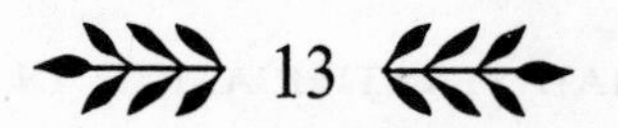

THE RANGE OF SOCIOLOGY OF KNOWLEDGE

FRANZ ADLER

THERE IS UNFORTUNATELY NO GENERALLY ACCEPTED DELIMITATION OF THE field of "sociology of knowledge." However, the term "sociology" is quite generally understood as referring to the science of social actions. "Science" primarily involves the methods of observation, generalization, systematization, and verification—a meaning given to the term by most American sociologists. By "social actions" we mean any behavior oriented toward the behavior of others or from which the behavior of others can be predicted. The primary aim of sociology, therefore, is to arrive at generalizations that permit the prediction of the behavior of some individuals from the behavior of others—in other words, the discovery of the *social* nature of human behavior.

The sociology of knowledge, then, is a branch of science. It deals with the socio-cultural factors associated with thought and its various forms of expression. The sociology of knowledge consequently overlaps with the sociologies of religion, of art, of literature, of law, of politics. Discussions of relations between knowledge and religion and discussions of esthetic and political valuations are not presented in this chapter, since they are treated elsewhere in this volume. Another systematic omission concerns the relation of linguistic behavior to cognitive behavior.

Ethnological Contributions: The Durkheim School

One of the major roots of present-day sociology of knowledge lies in the French developments of the Durkheim school. Following the master's lead, there is in present-day sociology of knowledge an ethnological emphasis and socio-psychological emphasis. Both trends are based on the notion of collective representations—group determination of concepts, thoughtways, and even categories of perception in the individual.

Thus, Marcel Granet derives Chinese conceptions of time and space from early village life and its cycle of events.[1] In his study of gift-giving, Marcel Mauss emphasizes the irrational, non-utilitarian thinking that accompanies preliterate gift-giving. This emphasis on the non-rationality of preliterate thinking also marks the writing of Lévy-Bruhl. Preliterate thinking is said to be based on the *law of participation*, which points to the fusion of logically distinct aspects of reality into mystical wholes. In other words, the preliterate is a "wholist" or Gestaltist. In his conception of causation, the original cause and the final consequence are seen in immediate conjunction. Intervening stages are consequently ignored. Thinking in general is prelogical; that is, the principle of contradiction is disregarded.[2] However, the exact nature of the relationship between being primitive and being prelogical is not stated in these works.

Present-day anthropologists, at least in this country, reject the concept of a primitive mentality that is basically different from a civilized mentality. They point to the fact that the kind of thinking which Lévy-Bruhl considers typically primitive occurs in modern society, not only among the uneducated, but even among the intellectual élites, particularly philosophers. Aside from the dubious pleasure of name calling, nothing can be gained by accusing a neo-Thomist or a phenomenologist of being a primitive merely bebause he starts from philosophical premises of which Lévy-Bruhl disapproves. But this is, after all, the only objection that can be raised against this description of the logic of preliterates, as Malinowski, for example, has convincingly demonstrated.[3]

The Durkheimian line of inquiry is also followed by Hans Kelsen in his study of the concept of causation. The eminent jurist tries to show the

[1] Marcel Granet, *La Pensée chinoise* (Paris, 1925); Marcel Mauss, "Essai sur le don: forme et raison de l'échange dans les sociétés archaiques," *ASo,* new series (1925), pp. 30-186.

[2] Lucien Lévy-Bruhl, *How Natives Think,* translated by Lilian A. Claire (London, 1926), and *Primitive Mentality,* translated by Lilian A. Claire (London, 1923).

[3] Bronislaw Malinowski, *Magic, Science, and Religion and Other Essays* (Garden City, 1954), pp. 25-36. See also M. J. Herskovits, *Man and His Works* (New York, 1948), p. 74.

development of the idea of cause from the idea of guilt in the course of a transition from mystical to rational thinking. This development he regards as paralleling general cultural developments. It is completed when social monism, which sees society and nature as one, is overcome and society and nature become effectively separated in the minds of men.[4]

Kardiner and Linton: The Fusion of Ethnology and Psychodynamics. An anthropological contribution to the sociology of knowledge comes from a confluence of anthropology with Freudian psychology. Kardiner and Linton studied personality and culture in the totality of their manifestation, including those that might be considered as "knowledge," as the results of primary institutional experiences, for example, toilet-training and weaning practices current in given cultures.[5] Related to their efforts is a line of investigation that may be designated by the general term "culture and personality" and that over varied paths tends to merge into a general social psychology with some emphasis on exotic illustrations.[6] The sociology of knowledge aspects of these writings tend to be implicit rather than explicit. In this context, it is well to remember Sewell's empirical test of some of the Kardiner-Linton pronouncements, since his findings did not support their hypotheses.[7]

Social-Psychological Contributions of the Durkheim School. The other line of thinking in the sociology of knowledge deriving from Durkheim employs a psychological approach. Bouglé considers logical outlines as derived from social outlines; logical thought deals with concepts that are social products. Logic and concepts embodied in language thus determine the ways of thinking.[8] Maurice Halbwachs considers *memory* as the key to an understanding of mental processes. The isolated individual has practically no memory; only in a group with which he feels solidarity does memory develop. The individual and the collective memory interact, the content of the collective memory being not history but tradition. Ideas of time and space are products of social groups, acquired by the individual by way of memory of experiences. The individual participates in many groups and thus forms many kinds of time and space ideas.[9]

[4] Hans Kelsen, *Society and Nature* (Chicago, 1943); cf. Howard Becker's treatment of social monism in Becker and Barnes, *Social Thought from Lore to Science,* 2nd ed. (New York, 1952), pp. 46-55, 57, 60, 99-100, *et passim.*

[5] Abram Kardiner, *The Individual and His Society* (New York, 1939); Abram Kardiner [with the collaboration of Ralph Linton, Cora DuBois, and James West], *The Psychological Frontiers of Society* (New York, 1945).

[6] Exemples of this are: Ralph Linton, *The Cultural Background of Personality* (New York, 1945); S. S. Sargent and Marian W. Smith (eds.), *Culture and Personality* (New York, 1949); J. S. Slotkin, *Personality Development* (New York, 1952).

[7] W. H. Sewell, "Infant Training and the Personality of the Child," *AJS,* 8 (Sept., 1952), pp. 150-159.

[8] Celestin Bouglé, *The Evolution of Values,* translated by Helen S. Sellars (New York, 1926).

[9] Maurice Halbwachs, *Les Cadres sociaux de la mémoire* (Paris, 1925); "La mémoire

American Social Psychology. The approach of the Durkheim school was primarily speculative. American social psychology, by contrast, has introduced experimental techniques into the study of the influence of group situations upon the thinking of the individual. It is impossible to list here all the studies that indicate the actual influence of group situations upon perception and judgment. It is similarly impossible to go into a complete review of the whole field of communications, propaganda, and public opinion—a field which Merton and Lazarsfeld were perhaps among the first to recognize as of essential relevance to the sociology of knowledge.[10]

Marxist Philosophy and Sociology of Knowledge

German contributions to the sociology of knowledge are the best known in this country and have left their distinctive mark on the whole field. Three lines may be clearly distinguished in the German development: the Marxian, the anti-Marxian, and the synthesizers who tried to reconcile the opposing views.

The Marxist Theme and Variations. Our discussion of Marxist sociology will be based mainly upon the study by Ernst Grünwald,[11] who had many materials at his disposal that are unavailable to the present writer and who summarized and analyzed these materials with great acuity. Grünwald distinguishes two lines of Marxist thinkers: "positivists" and "anti-positivist." The former, more correctly referred to as "nominalists," derive from the later Marx and Engels, whereas the latter take the earlier Marxist works for guidance. Although the patriarchs of Marxism were influenced strongly by Hegel in their youth, they increasingly embraced empiricist attitudes in their older age. The term "positivism," although inaccurate, is preferable to the value term "vulgar Marxism" often used by Hegelian Marxists and other anti-empiricists.

The Positivists. Paul Szende believed that sense experience proper is reliable, but that its *interpretation* is open to social influence. These interpretations form an ideology that veils reality in the interest of the ruling class. If the suppressed class acquires knowledge of this reality, it not only destroys

collective chez les musiciens," *Revue Philosophique de la France et de l'Étranger,* 64 (1939), pp. 136-165; and *La Mémoire collective* (Paris, 1950). See also Leopold von Wiese, "Einsamkeit und Geselligkeit als Bedingungen der Mehrung des Wissens," in Max Scheler (ed.), *Versuche zu einer Soziologie des Wissens* (Berlin and Leipzig, 1924), pp. 218-229; and Wilhelm Jerusalem, "Die soziologische Bedingtheit des Denkens und der Denkformen," *ibid.,* pp. 182-207.

[10] R. K. Merton and Paul Lazarsfeld, "Studies in Radio and Film Propaganda," in R. K. Merton, *Social Theory and Social Structure* (Glencoe, Ill., 1949), pp. 265-285.

[11] Ernst Grünwald, *Das Problem der Soziologie des Wissens* (Vienna, 1934).

the ideology imposed by the ruling class, but it also proceeds to overthrow this ruling class.[12] (This view presupposes, as Grünwald states, that reality is really bad.)

Bogdanow, leaning on Ernst Mach's positivist-pragmatist philosophy, considers consciousness as a means of adaptation in the struggle for survival. Thus each person's consciousness is a concrete copy of his social existence. The history of mankind consists of four epochs, in each of which a specific economic development (which in turn is technologically determined) brings forth a certain way of thinking; each epoch has its own conception of causality. The second epoch, for example, models its concept on the patriarchal social organization with its direct command-obedience pattern.[13]

Otto Bauer, the foremost theoretician of Austro-Marxism, distinguishes between the immanent and the transcendent interpretation of mental products. The immanent interpretation refers to their social roots, but it is needed only if the work to be interpreted comes from a very rapidly changing period of history. In such periods, the immanent development is interrupted by outside interferences. In applying his views to the history of ideas, Bauer finds that he has to apply the transcendent interpretation continuously; that is, the imagined quiet flow of undisturbed immanent developments either never takes place or, if it does, fails to produce anything worth talking about. The individual's way of life is the source of his views on nature and the world. The member of the leisure class who plans work but does not carry it out himself feels the overwhelming importance of the plan and construes his world view accordingly in terms of idealism. The manual worker, on the other hand, develops a materialist view of a universe consisting of force and matter, an extrapolation of his working experiences. This theory, whether true or false, can be checked against the evidence.[14]

Fogarasi defended the nominalist Marxists against Karl Mannheim, who pointed out that not only the thought of the bourgeoisie is situationally determined but also the thought of the proletariat, and that if the one is *ipso facto* false, the other must also be false (see the discussion of Mannheim on pp. 409-411). Fogarasi admits that the proletariat as well as the bourgeoisie has a class-conditioned outlook; whether it is true or false depends on the historical situation.[15]

The Anti-Positivists. Georg Lukács is safe from suspicion of any pos-

[12] *Ibid.* pp. 118-120; Paul Szende, "Das System der Wissenschaften und die Gesellschaftsordnung," *KVSo,* 2 (1922), pp. 12 *ff;* see also Arthur Child, "The Theoretical Possibility of the Sociology of Knowledge," *Ethics,* 51 (July, 1941), pp. 392-418.

[13] A. Bogdanow, *Die Entwicklungsformen der Gesellschaft und die Wissenschaft* (1st ed.; 1913; Berlin, 1924); Grünwald, *op. cit.*, pp. 120-121.

[14] Otto Bauer, "Das Weltbild des Kapitalismus," in *Der Lebendige Marxismus: Kautzky Festschrift* (1924); Grünwald, *op. cit.,* pp. 122-124.

[15] A. Fogarasi, "Die Soziologie der Intelligenz und die Intelligenz der Soziologie," *Unter dem Banner des Marxismus,* 4 (1930), p, 366; Grünwald, *op. cit.,* pp. 125-127.

itivist taint. His story of the sociology of knowledge is a poetic sort of imaginative wish-fulfillment for frustrated Marxians. His key concept is "class consciousness." This state of mind does not occur in individuals, nor does it, for the time being, occur anywhere else. It is an ideal to be realized in the course of history. In other words, it is a Platonic ideal or an Aristotelian form. The realization of the proletarian class consciousness will coincide with the moment of world revolution. The only class that can perceive all economics adequately with regard both to objective fact and to its own class position is the proletariat. The bourgeoisie necessarily sees the economic system in a manner that is both factually and situationally inadequate. This is the result of the dialectics of the historical process in which the bourgeoisie fights a desperate battle, trying to close its eyes to the truth presented by the proletariat. A class consciousness that includes Marxism is then "imputed" to the proletariat as its adequate reaction to its situation. It is apparently a normative decision of the theorist, who decrees that a class ought to hold a certain set of convictions. Why a situationally inadequate class consciousness should be imputed to the bourgeoisie, except for the purpose of prophesying its impending doom, can hardly be explained.[16]

Max Adler distinguishes two branches in the sociology of knowledge: an epistemological one and a substantive one, the second depending on the first. He decides that Kant's a priori elements of perception—space, time, causality, etc.—are incomplete. The "social" is also an a priori element of perception. (Kant indicates his awareness of this necessity implicitly, and Marx agrees with his view.) All knowing is thus socially conditioned, and this insight forms the metaphysical basis for all substantive inquiry. Mental phenomena can be understood only in terms of the stimuli that concrete conditions of life have given to or withheld from particular thinkers. Ideologies, derived from the connection between mental activity and the systems of production and distribution, are powerful social forces. Consequently there are two distinct sciences—a bourgeois science and a proletarian—but there is only one truth. The two classes, however, accept different propositions as true. This duplicity of science is particularly marked in the social sciences. The proletariat is more likely to develop true science because the developmental interests of the proletariat correspond to the true findings of true social science. Denial or doubt of this tendency is proof of bourgeois mentality and as such is invalid. Proof of the truth of proletarian science is found in the logic of dialectics.[17]

[16] Georg Lukács, *Geschichte und Klassenbewusstsein: Studien über Marxistische Dialektik* (Berlin, 1923); Grünwald, *op. cit.*, pp. 128-137; Raymond Aron, *La sociologie allemande contemporaine* (Paris, 1935), pp. 78-80; Arthur Child, "The Existential Determination of Thought," *Ethics*, 52 (Jan., 1942), pp. 153-185.

[17] Max Adler, "Marxismus und kantischer Kritizismus," *Archiv für die Geschichte des Sozialismus und der Arbeiterbewegung*, 11 (1925), p. 345; "Wissenschaft und soziale

This position contains little of interest to non-Hegelians or non-Marxists, except for one rather important insight: that acceptance or rejection of an ideology at large is the object-matter of the sociology of knowledge. The rise of an idea in the individual may be due to unique past experiences, but the *acceptance* of an idea by large sections of the population or even by a small professional public points to experiences shared among those who accept it.[18]

Lederer considers himself a cultural sociologist. Although the "spirit" of an era arises from the relations of production, it is, however, not possible to deduce cultural phenomena (including thought) from the relations of production. All that can be deduced is what *cannot* possibly occur. What does occur has to be explained by creative achievement arising out of personal spontaneity. Lederer's philosophy, too, is akin to Scheler's (see pp. 406 ff.). On the other hand, he resembles Bauer in stressing that ideas show an immanent development, only disrupted by social elements at the breaking-points of social and economic developments.[19]

Lerner and the Power of Class Ideas. Turning to the United States, Max Lerner's sociology of knowledge shows similarities to nominalist Marxism. He believes that the discovery of the power of irrational elements in the motivation of human actions is the great achievement of the twentieth century. This discovery makes it necessary to interpret history as the expression of broad social-class forces. In interpreting thought in terms of class interests one must avoid overemphasis on rational self-interest. The increased influence of the propagandizer, the popularizer, and the public often overshadows the influence of the thinker. To understand an idea, it is not sufficient to take it at its face value. "For in the history of ideas even their distortions are part of their meaning—the unfolding of a line of direction inherent in the idea itself."

The full meaning of an idea is found in four components: (1) the thinker and his biography; (2) the intellectual tradition in which he functioned; (3) the social context in which he made his ideas public; (4) the historical consequences of his ideas and the successive audiences he found. Ideas not only arise under specific conditions, but are also *used* under specific conditions, not necessarily the same. In every culture they are used as weapons, either instrumentally or manipulatively. In the former there is regard for (1) the validity of the idea used; (2) the social cohesion that will result; and (3)

Structur," *Verhandlungen des Vierten Deutschen Soziologentages* (Tübingen, 1925); *Lehrbuch der materialistischen Geschichtsauffassung* (1930); *Kant und der Marxismus, Gesammelte Aufsätze zur Erkenntniskritik und Theorie des Sozialen* (Berlin, 1925).

[18] Ernst Lewalter, "Wissenssoziologie und Marxismus," *ASS,* 64 (April, 1930), pp. 63-121; Grünwald, *op. cit.,* pp. 152-155.

[19] Emil Lederer, "Aufgaben einer Kultursoziologie," in Melchior Palyi (ed.), *Hauptprobleme der Soziologie, Erinnerungegabe für Max Weber,* vol. 2 (1923); Grünwald, *op. cit.,* pp. 156-158.

the minds of those who are being influenced. In the latter case only the end in view is considered; the truth or falsity of the idea is irrelevant, and the minds of those who are to be influenced are held in contempt.[20]

Some Empirical Studies of Marxian Clues: Centers and Eysenck. Centers, in his study of the psychology of social classes, found that conservative views were more frequently found among business people than among workers and most frequently found in those strata that have most to gain from the preservation of the *status quo*. The radicalism–conservatism cleavage is increasing between the classes.[21]

Centers' quantitative method in the study of class attitudes was expanded and improved upon by Eysenck in England. He envisions two continua instead of one; to Centers' variable "radicalism–conservatism" he adds another, "toughness–softness." Thus, holding party preferences constant, he is able to locate his individuals and groups in a field determined by two coordinates instead of merely along one line. Some of his findings are: all working-class groups are more tough-minded than the corresponding middle-class groups; liberal working-class groups are more conservative than conservative middle-class groups; socialist working-class groups and liberal middle-class groups show about the same score in radicalism; middle-class Communists are more radical than working-class Communists. He found substantial agreement among members of the working class, regardless of party membership, on certain issues and on certain statements of fact.[22]

Occupation, Education, and Ideology. Williams and Mosteller studied the relationship of certain opinions to education and economic status. They distinguished five educational levels and five levels of wealth or poverty and analyzed the following aspects of opinion: (1) information, estimates, awareness; (2) social stereotypes; (3) opinions on peace; (4) intervention in the war; (5) economic problems; (6) political approval.

> Education is found more important where factual knowledge gives an insight . . . also . . . in creating, through more consistent indoctrination, greater allegiance to certain general social stereotypes as, for example, those toward law and the reward that comes from individual ability. Economic status . . . determines opinion more than education on all issues . . . [dealing] with financial return. . . . The opinions of the poor can be generally described as a desire for growth through change in the social structure; the opinion of the upper group as a desire for growth without change in the social structure.[23]

[20] Max Lerner, *Ideas Are Weapons* (New York, 1939), pp. 3-12. The quoted portion is from p. 6.

[21] Richard Centers, *The Psychology of Social Classes* (Princeton, 1949), pp. 55-74; see also H. J. Eysenck, "Social Attitude and Social Class," *BJS*, 1 (1950), pp. 56-60.

[22] H. J. Eysenck, "Primary Social Attitudes as Related to Social Class and Political Party," *BJS*, 2 (1951), pp. 198-209.

[23] Frederick Williams and Frederick Mosteller, "Education and Economic Status

Gwynne Nettler used questionnaire and polling methods to find differences in the manner in which members of ten occupational groups predicted certain major events then in the making. The 1,500 individuals were selected from various directories. The occupations chosen were: business executives, journalists, politicians, natural scientists, political scientists, historians, philosophers, psychologists, sociologists, and economists. All of these, except the first three groups, may be considered as belonging to the intelligentsia in Mannheim's sense of the term (see pp. 410-411). No significant differences between groups appeared in the responses, except with regard to one question, predicting who would be the next president. Nettler concludes that occupational differences of this kind do not influence all knowledge. He is led to assume that no simple social position conditions all knowledge. The following factors, however, condition the relationship between social position and knowledge: (1) the criterion of social position used by the researcher; (2) the type of knowledge measured; and (3) the time at which the relationship is measured.[24] Studies of this nature show clearly that it is quite possible in this area of thought to submit one's ideas, Marxist or otherwise, to empirical tests.

Stratification Studies in the U.S. Studies of social classes in America are often carried on as part of community studies. This tradition began with the Middletown investigations of the Lynds, in which characteristics of class members in action and ideology form important parts of the information sought and reported. Perusal of these works, and of others in the same tradition, with the problems of the sociology of knowledge in mind—problems which were not of great interest to those who did the studies—yields some empirical data and suggests methods of obtaining relevant facts.[25]

Mills studied ideologies of small businessmen and white-collar workers in middle-sized cities. The views held by them are seen to be often not in keeping with what appears to be their class interests. Similarly, Andrzejewski shows that individuals often accept what is personally disadvantageous to them and that institutions generate ideologies which are avowedly antagonistic to them.[26]

as Determinants of Opinion," in Hadley Cantril *et al., Gauging Public Opinion* (Princeton, 1944), pp. 195-208. The quotation is from pp. 207-208.

[24] Gwynne Nettler, "A Test for the Sociology of Knowledge," *ASR,* 10 (June, 1945), pp. 393-399.

[25] R. S. Lynd and Helen M. Lynd, *Middletown* (New York, 1929), and *Middletown in Transition* (New York, 1937); Allison Davis, B. B. Gardner, and Mary R. Gardner, *Deep South* (Chicago, 1941); James West (pseud.), *Plainville, USA* (New York, 1945); W. Lloyd Warner *et al., Democracy in Jonesville* (New York, 1949); W. Lloyd Warner and P. S. Lunt, *The Social Life of a Modern Community* (New Haven, Conn., 1941); W. Lloyd Warner and J. O. Low, *The Social System of the Modern Factory* (New Haven, Conn., 1947).

[26] C. Wright Mills, "The Middle Classes in Middle-Sized Cities: The Stratification

Schütz distinguishes three types of persons according to what information they consider relevant and what they take for granted: the expert, the man on the street, and the well-informed citizen. Experts and well-informed citizens are what they are by the force of social approval, which gives weight to what they know. Hendrik de Man, on the other hand, deplores the virtual disappearance of the well-informed citizen. The speed of modern means of communication and the spread of mass media provide the individual with more information than he can possibly absorb. Consequently, he notices only the sensational and loses sight of the important. For business reasons, the mass media aim at the sensational, which is wanted, rather than at the important, which is needed. To be saleable, everything has to be extremely simplified.[27]

Park did not share this interest in the class character of information that is implied in Schütz's and de Man's essays, but used a broader approach. His findings, however, support theirs.

> The extent to which news circulates determines the extent to which the members of a society participate in its political action. News . . . is characteristically limited to events that bring about sudden and decisive changes. Exclusive attention to some things inhibits responses to others, resulting in a limitation of the range and character of the news to which a society will respond collectively or individually. The function of news is to orient man and society in an actual world.[28]

Socialization as an Ideological Mechanism. The sociologies of child development and education show the concrete mechanisms by which social and economic factors of class and status are translated by child-rearing practices and educational procedures into differential attitudes, kinds and degrees of knowledge, and general outlook on life. Again, the specific questions of the sociology of knowledge have been pursued in this field, but much of the material needed for answering them and the methods for further investgation are available.[29]

and Political Position of Small Business and White-Collar Strata," *ASR,* 11 (Oct., 1946), pp. 520-529; Stanislaw Andrzejewski, "Are Ideas Social Forces?" *ibid.,* 14 (Dec., 1949), pp. 758-764.

[27] Alfred Schütz, "The Well-Informed Citizen: An Essay on the Social Distribution of Knowledge," *SR,* 13 (Dec., 1946), pp. 463-478; Hendrik de Man, *Vermassung und Kulturverfall* (2nd ed.; Munich, 1952), pp. 87-108.

[28] R. E. Park, "News as a Form of Knowledge: A Chapter in the Sociology of Knowledge," *AJS,* 45 (March, 1940), pp. 669-686.

[29] J. H. Bossard, *The Sociology of Child Development* (New York, 1948), pp. 283-328; W. Lloyd Warner *et al., Who Shall Be Educated?* (New York, 1944); A. B. Hollingshead, *Elmtown's Youth* (New York, 1949); Allison Davis and R. J. Havighurst, *Father of the Man* (Boston, 1947); Allison Davis, *Social Class Influences upon Learning* (Cambridge, Mass., 1948).

The Anti-Marxians

Explorations in Non-Economic Determinism. The term "anti-Marxist sociology of knowledge" might in a sense be considered a contradiction in itself. As long as "existential determination" is thought of exclusively as economic determination, the rejection of economic determination will be considered by some to imply the rejection of all sociology of knowledge. But it is possible to consider other aspects of life as equally or more important than the economic aspects; or the relation between the mental and existential elements of a culture may be seen in a relation other than one-way determinism.

Scheler: the Relation Between Real and Ideal Factors. Both views of the sociology of knowledge appear in the writings of Max Scheler, who approached the sociology of knowledge with the definite intention of "overcoming" Marxism as well as positivism. He derives certainty from phenomenological and organismic assumptions. Society is the true and original reality; it is the individual's most immediate experience, which he knows, not by partial information and observation, but by immediate total intuition. He also knows the other members, because of their organic relationship to him, by direct insight. Any further knowledge is acquired in social terms. However, the social conditions or *real factors* do not determine knowledge or thought. They merely make it possible; only those potential thoughts actually occur that are permitted by the factors. The origin of thought is to be found in the *ideal factors*—a realm of eternal truths, ideas, and values that subsist in an eternally valid hierarchy of their own. The real factors open and close the sluice gates for thought to pass from possibility to actuality. The sociology of knowledge must therefore discover the "law of succession" according to which real and ideal factors interact in history.

According to Scheler, the structure of human drives determines the real factors prevalent in a given society. There is a definite sequence of types of integration; domination of blood and kinship ties characterizes the first stage; emphasis on political power and power over nature characterizes the second; the third and current stage is characterized by an increasing importance of economic motivations. This sequence in the drives of man derives from a kind of "aging" of human societies and corresponds to the changes related to aging in the individual human being. The similarity of these stage to those of Comte is fairly obvious.[30]

[30] Max Scheler, "Vorrede" and "Einleitung," in his *Versuche zu einer Soziologie des Wissens,* and *Die Wissensformen und die Gesellschaft* (Leipzig, 1926); Hans-Joachim Lieber, *Wissen und Gesellschaft, Die Probleme der Wissenssoziologie* (Tübingen, 1952);

Honigsheim and the Significance of Non-Rational Elements. Honigsheim has written important essays dealing with the unity of style in economic and spiritual culture, the relationship between the youth movement and knowledge, scholasticism, realism and nominalism, and mysticism. A unity of style between mental and economic life is found in three stages of an evolutionary sequence, viewed typologically. In the first stage, magic and economy are one in the undifferentiated society of the non-reflective horde. Later both mental and economic life are part of a universal *theocracy*, as in medieval scholasticism. In the Renaissance, science and economy find unity of style and a free connection with each other in the rise of *individualism*. Absolutism establishes state domination over both science and economy. Liberalism sees state, economy, and science in free coexistence. In our age, mental life is under economic domination and appears as an expression of the mechanization of the world. Thus Marxism is true for its own time.[31]

Honigsheim stresses irrational striving and the submission to charismatic leadership as characteristic of the German youth movement. He sees a diminished ability to observe concrete things, an inability to approach anything scientifically, a belief that only experiences born from love can give knowledge. He explains the rise of the movement by pointing to certain social and economic conditions, but can show only one reason why the same conditions did not bring forth similar movements in other countries. This singular element is the German philosophic attitude, which is reinforced and exaggerated in the youth movement.[32]

Mysticism flourishes primarily in times of prelogical thinking. In times of states and written religions, it flourishes whenever the state supports the mystic in his opposition to highly organized religion. Most helpful to the mystic is a religiously oriented, unified culture with an all-encompassing value-hierarchy structured in a pyramid of universal theocracy. Mysticism can be connected with science whenever science is a kind of scholasticism. The mystic claims to have direct insight into essences and essential connections; thus the phenomenologist is in a sense a mystic.[33]

Howard Becker and H. O. Dahlke, "Max Scheler's Sociology of Knowledge," *Philosophy and Phenomenological Research,* 2 (March, 1942), pp. 309-322; H. O. Dahlke, "The Sociology of Knowledge," in H. E. Barnes, Howard Becker, Frances B. Becker (eds.), *Contemporary Social Theory* (New York, 1940), pp. 64-87; Arthur Child, "The Existential Determination of Thought," *loc. cit.,* pp. 153-185; R. K. Merton, "The Sociology of Knowledge," *Isis,* 27 (Nov., 1937), pp. 493-503; R. K. Merton, *Social Theory and Social Structure,* pp. 217-245; Maurice Mandelbaum, *The Problem of Historical Knowledge* (New York, 1938), pp. 147 *ff.* Grünwald, *op. cit.,* pp. 158-171; G. L. DeGré, *Society and Ideology* (New York, 1943), pp. 10-22.

[31] Paul Honigsheim, "Stileinheit zwischen Wirtschaft und Geisteskultur," in Max Scheler (ed.), *Versuche zu einer Soziologie des Wissens,* pp. 256-262.

[32] Paul Honigsheim, "Jugendbewegung und Erkenntnis," *ibid.,* pp. 389-406. Cf. Howard Becker, *German Youth: Bond or Free* (New York, 1946).

[33] Paul Honigsheim, "Soziologie der Mystik," in Scheler, *op. cit.,* pp. 323-346.

The Cultural–Mental Determinism of Sorokin. The most monumental study in the sociology of knowledge, Pitirim A. Sorokin's inquiry into social and cultural dynamics,[34] deals with the criteria of truth. Sorokin affirms that the prevailing culture conditions what a society considers as true or false, scientific or unscientific, right or wrong, lawful or unlawful, beautiful or ugly. The "nature of the culture" is determined by the "major premises of the culture"—assumptions concerning "the nature of reality, the nature of the needs and ends to be satisfied and the method of satisfaction."

In terms of these premises, Sorokin distinguished three main forms of culture. In the *ideational* culture, reality is seen as non-material and ever-lasting Being; needs and ends are spiritual; the extent of their satisfaction is the largest and the level the highest; and the method of fulfillment is asceticism. The *sensate* mentality views reality as that which is presented to the sense organs; it is thought of as changing or becoming; needs are physical and their maximum satisfaction is sought; they are realized by modification and exploitation of the external world. Although mixtures of these two types occur, only one of these mixtures is logically integrated, the *idealistic* mentality. Here, reality has aspects of everlasting Being as well as of Becoming and includes aspects of the spiritual as well as of the material. Needs and ends are both spiritual and material, but in their satisfaction the material is subordinated to the spiritual. The method of realization of needs involves modification of self and of the external world.

To each of these types of culture-mentality there corresponds a predominant system of truth. Revealed truth—truth of faith—corresponds to the pure ideational mentality. A "scientific" empirico-sensate system of truth corresponds to the sensate mentality. With a mixed idealistic mentality there develops rationalism, or an inconsistent mixture of the truths of faith, of reason, and of the senses. Skepticism, a belief in the impossibility of obtaining valid truth, prevails in the passive-sensate and cynical mentality. Fideism, a desperate will to believe by those who are disbelievers, occurs in the ideational-desperate mentality. Thus by definition the criteria of truth are part of the given mentalities or cultures.

Sorokin used a quantitative method to measure what most people before him considered unmeasurable: fluctuations of systems of truth and fluctuations of first principles—that is, criteria of truth. Taking twenty-year intervals as his units of time, he listed all the well-known thinkers who lived in each time unit and assessed their importance on the basis of twelve criteria that, unfortunately, are not sufficiently clearly defined to permit repetition of his weighting procedure. Then he classified them as to their use of one or the other systems of truth and first principles. Thus each twenty-year

[34] P. A. Sorokin, *Social and Cultural Dynamics* (New York, 1937-1941), 4 vols. Vol. 1 contains the general approach, Vol. 2 Sorokin's "Sociology of Knowledge," and Vol. 4 discussion of basic principles and methods.

period was assigned a numerical value that indicates the number and importance of thinkers active in this period and representing one of the various lines of thought. These numbers were then ranged in time series for each kind of first principle and for each kind of system of truth. In correlating the appropriate time series, very high coefficients of correlation were obtained. This is not surprising if it is considered that the related time series contain largely the same thinkers, classified from different viewpoints, but weighed by the same weight. Thus, the coefficients measure logical consistency of the thinkers more than they measure sociological factors.

Sorokin does not relate the criteria of truth, the first principles, to art, warfare, or any of the other variables discussed in his work. With regard to these he uses a "culture-mentality" variable, which, however, contains a strong epistemological component. He makes it quite clear that he feels supported by his data in considering the mentality, including the ideas on the nature of reality, as the determining factor and the non-mental elements as dependent variables. Unfortunately, his statistics are purely descriptive and no correlation coefficients or other measures showing relationships are presented.

Two features give Sorokin's work importance: one, it approaches a sociology of knowledge that attempts to show that mental factors determine existential factors, rather than vice versa; second, quantitative techniques were applied to long-range historical data for the purpose of achieving statements of general relationships. Yet Sorokin himself would tend to depreciate the second point, for he uses statistics largely to show that he could have done just as well without them by using logic and intuition.

Synthesizers and Eclectics

Karl Mannheim and Constructed Types. Several authors tried to unite the conflicting ideas of Marxist and anti-Marxist sociologists of knowledge. The outstanding figure here is Karl Mannheim, with whose name the sociology of knowledge has been most firmly linked in the minds of Americans inside and outside the ranks of sociology. His outstanding position in the field may be partially due to the fact that Mannheim's *Ideology and Utopia* was the first publication in the English language to employ the term "sociology of knowledge" in its subtitle; that Wirth, in his preface to the book, promised that the book would make important contributions to theory, research, and the solution of many of the practical ills of our time;[35] and that certain American

[35] Louis Wirth, "Preface" to Karl Mannheim, *Ideology and Utopia: An Introduction to the Sociology of Knowledge*, translated by Louis Wirth and E. A. Shils (New York, 1936), pp. xxix-xxx.

sociologists hoped that all these blessings would accrue by the use of the procedures they had long been championing without being able to show the desired results. Because of his outstanding position, Mannheim has been the object of many attacks and criticisms. And he has not found many defenders. In addition to Wirth, Paul Kecskemeti, in the course of a broadly favorable discussion, defends Mannheim against only two charges out of the many leveled against him. And Wagner points out that the charge of inconsistency and confusion collapses if it is understood that Mannheim's writings are not related to empirical inquiry, "not even the kind envisaged by Max Weber or Dewey."[36]

Mannheim basically accepts the Marxist idea of ideological thinking. The *particular* conception of ideology arises when an adversary's opinion is considered to be distorted by the unconscious and unintended effect of his life situation. The *total* conception of ideology, on the other hand, implies that the opponent's total system of thought is inevitably ideological. The first is based on the psychological imputation of motives to individuals, the second on the establishment of a correspondence between the system of thought and the conditions under which it is said to occur. Although Marxism is considered by its adherents to be true on Hegelian historicist grounds, Mannheim considers Marxism to be as "ideological" as the views it attacks.

Yet political ideologies are the only kind of knowledge Mannheim analyzes in his substantive work. In his theoretical writings, the concept of "knowledge," though undefined, appears to be extended to include any kind of knowledge, belief, or thought. He rejects the separation of value from fact as essentially different and treats the "knowledge" of both as one and indivisible. He maintains, however, that formal knowledge and exact sciences, but not social sciences, are unaffected by social or historical situations. The relation between the conditions that "determine" and the thought that is "determined" is not full causal determination, but some other undefined form of connection, occassionally called "correspondence." This unknown connection refers to systems of thought and to various intellectuals representing social classes. However, classes are conceived in ideal fashion rather than as factual aggregates of persons. In his substantive work, he seems to imply that acceptance of the class ideology constitutes class membership. The *Weltanschauung* of the class or group is again construed ideally, for no one in the class holds or even knows the complete view. The observer shapes it as a logical unity from separate manifestations of thought; it is the view the people *ought* to hold, finding themselves in a given position. Later observation will reveal the extent to which the *Weltanschauung* has been realized.

[36] Paul Kecskemeti, "Introduction," in Karl Mannheim, *Essays on the Sociology of Knowledge,* translated by Paul Kecskemeti (London, 1952), pp. 1-32; H. R. Wagner, "Mannheim's Historicism," *SR,* 9 (Sept., 1952), pp. 300-321.

"Existentially determined" thought —for example, class-oriented thought —is not in and of itself invalid. But the thought system of a group smaller than the whole of society will probably not contain the whole truth. A number of ideologies with differing perspectives coexist, each claiming to represent the whole truth but actually containing only a part of it. The real and full truth can be found by the unattached intellectuals, who are not tied to any existential position, but are free to put themselves, actually or imaginatively, into any position. Thus they gain understanding of all ideologies from all viewpoints and can discover full and real truth. Truth in this absolute sense is judged in terms of adequacy to the historical stage. Views that help man to adjust in the present are true; adjustment, however, remains undefined. Views are true if, put into action, they will shatter the existing order and bring about a new one. The intellectual who is to judge a view for its truth content must, then, have a clear knowledge of the future course of the historical process. Mannheim does not explain how this knowledge of the future is to be acquired.[37]

Only a few of the points that have been raised against Mannheim by his critics will be mentioned. Aron speaks of "*un Marxisme caricatural*" in which reality is based, as in Marxism, on a kind of "religious" faith; so likewise does H. Otto Dahlke. Wagner lists a number of important questions Mannheim neglected to answer and accuses him of not having adhered strictly enough to historicism. Merton finds, among other things, that by leaving the relationship of existential factors and thought undefined, Mannheim has "virtually precluded the possibility of formulating problems for empirical investigation." Mandelbaum feels that in spite of his efforts, Mannheim was unable to escape relativism. Becker makes the same charge, and several others equally damaging.[38]

Child takes issue with Mannheim's procedure of imputation. He shows that Mannheim designates the totality of the thought of a group or class as an ideal type, but also as a reconstruction of reality. But where is this reality to exist, if it does not exist in the individual group or class members? Mannheim makes it quite clear that it is not even to be considered as the sum or integration of the thoughts of the group members. But the individual participates in this totality. How, asks Child quite correctly, can the group member participate in and be influenced by a thought system built in the mind of the observer?[39]

[37] See the already cited writings of Mannheim and his *Essays in Sociology and Socia Psychology*, edited by Paul Kecskemeti (New York, 1953).

[38] Aron, *op. cit.*, pp. 85, 93; Wagner, *op. cit.*, p. 303; R. K. Merton, *Social Theory and Social Structure*, pp. 247-264; Mandelbaum, *op. cit.*, p. 82; Becker and Barnes, *op. cit.*, pp. 921-927—the passages in question also appeared in the 1st ed. (1938).

[39] Arthur Child, "The Problem of Imputation in the Sociology of Knowledge," *Ethics*, 51 (Jan., 1941), pp. 200-219.

Schelting and the Sociological Implications of Types of Knowledge. Schelting's sociology of knowledge is an attempt at a synthesis of the conflicting theories in terms of Max Weber's approaches to sociology. Alfred Weber's distinction of the "cultural" and the "civilizational" is basic in his thinking, which developed partly out of his criticism of Mannheim.[40] Positive or objective knowledge—that is, civilizational knowledge—develops according to its immanent structure. Only the *selection* of problems is socially determined, not the solution. Knowledge of the cultural sort, on the other hand, flows from the existence of man as a thinking, willing, and affectual being. This gives rise to ideas, which are essentially different from factual knowledge. In the history of science and ideas, knowledge and ideas generally appear in different mixtures. These mixtures are to be separated by the application of the unchangeable canons of logic. The sociology of knowledge must be applied quite differently to four different types of mental phenomena: (1) those that have no validity as knowledge whatsoever; (2) knowledge at a lower stage of development, incomplete and imperfect; (3) knowledge considered now as fully valid; and (4) knowledge that would be considered valid by anyone putting himself in the situation of the creator of that knowledge. In these types, the sociology of knowledge must focus upon the social constellations and extra-scientific attitudes that generally, or in a particular historical situation, favor or inhibit the rise of scientific thought.[41]

Grünwald and a Return to Relativism. Grünwald, however, criticizes Schelting severely for employing Weber's distinction between civilizational and cultural knowledge. He points out that in actual fact a separation of this nature is impossible. Nevertheless, he distinguishes sharply between a sociology of society and a sociology of culture and places the sociology of knowledge in the latter. It is a social science; its proper method is "understanding." It asserts that mental life ("culture") is determined by the social; thus it stands on the same level as other determinisms—racial, characterological, geographic, glandular, etc. None of these propositions is unconditionally valid for everyone. Each of these theories, including the sociology of knowledge, merely represents one possible interpretation. If it is chosen as an avenue of interpretation, then thought is seen as manifesting existence. What social conditions produce here are not judgments, but the "material of judgment." This entity Grünwald declares to be undefinable

[40] Critical accounts include: Grünwald, *op. cit.*, pp. 186-217; Becker and Barnes, *loc.cit.*, pp. 921-927; Dahlke, *op. cit.*, pp. 64-89, particularly pp. 82-85; R. K. Merton, "The Sociology of Knowledge," in *Social Theory and Social Structure.* One attempt to test Mannheim's theory is Alvin Boskoff, "The Farm Bloc and Agrarian Ideology" (unpublished master's thesis, Columbia University, 1948).

[41] Schelting, *op. cit.*, pp. 65-177, and "Zum Streit um die Wissenssoziologie," *ASS*, 62 (1929), pp. 1-66.

in words. In the material of judgment exists meaning as a potentiality; in the actual judgments resides the immanent meaning.[42]

The Conversion of Reality by Thought: Lieber. Lieber, by studying the history of the sociology of knowledge, arrives at certain conclusions about an adequate sociology of knowledge. His history of the field is truly remarkable in that it does not refer to any French studies at all and does not contain any data from the English-speaking world after Sir Francis Bacon. Lieber decides that all sociologies of knowledge must ask two questions: (1) Is there a kind of knowledge that can be considered as tied to existence? (2) What is the nature of these ties? Lieber finds unanimity among sociologists of knowledge in stating that only knowledge in the social sciences is tied to existence. As to the second question, either a moderate or a radical stand can be taken. The moderate one considers real factors, in the manner of Scheler, the only elements for the realization of mind, or spirit, but not as having any influence on its content. The radical answers see mind as a function of the dynamism of reality. Thus mind itself becomes historical, instead of remaining above history or guiding it. The relation between reality and mind may be one of *causation* or one of *expression*. Acceptance of the radical answer excludes any possibility of belief in an absolutely valid science. The sociology of knowledge merely provides an added tool for understanding in the social sciences, which must be considered as coordinated on the same level with other such tools. Man can always overcome his ties to reality by his thinking. Relativism cannot be based on the findings of the sociology of knowledge: scientific thinking, even in the social sciences, is governed by an ethos that guarantees objectivity, excludes the effect of ties to real factors, and is itself unconditioned by such ties.[43]

The European Impact on American Eclectics: DeGré. Related to the German synthesizers are some American thinkers who also try to combine the thinking of various and often opposing sources. Their approach is, however, generally not based upon the dialectic idea of synthesis. They choose from various sources leading ideas that are used independently, are unrelated to any wider system of thought, or are combined into a more or less well-knit pattern. It is characteristic of the eclectic thinkers that European thought is favored; American contributions are largely disregarded.

DeGré well represents this eclectic school of thought. His mosaic of thoughts gleaned from various opposing views is enriched by references to Nietzsche, Sorel, Pareto, Znaniecki, and others. In his approach, the substructure of human actions is provided by objective situations. The attitudinal structure of the human agent interprets the substructure and brings forth concrete social actions that in their totality form the superstructure. But social actions involving the communication of "truth" from one indi-

[42] Grünwald, *op. cit.*, pp. 52-106, 182-183, 228-234.
[43] Lieber, *op. cit.*, pp, 139-146.

vidual to others are of primary interest to the sociology of knowledge. It studies the sociology of the gnostician (the utterer of "truth") and of the "truths" he communicates. Basically, the relation of ideas to the attitudinal structure of the proponent of the idea must be discovered. This presupposes that constructed types of attitudinal complexes are already available. The subjectively meaningful elements or complexes are then to be related to the external socio-historical situation in which they occur. In effect, then, the method of the sociology of knowledge is to be the same as that of sociology in general.[44]

The Distinction Between Ideological Creation and Acceptance: Speier. Speier wishes to avoid the pitfalls of sociological determinism. Needs and satisfactions may or may not be relevant to the accomplishment of a thought process. However, where research is motivated by the desire to know, practical needs are irrelevant. Technical and promotive reasoning, on the other hand, are clearly related to the needs of the situation and should be studied in this context. The nature of the relationship is not to be stated a priori, but must be empirically discovered. The quest for a public by a promoter is to be studied sociologically by analyzing the public in terms of its social composition and ethos. On this basis, the specific type of the promoter and his emergence are to be explained. Finally, the means of communication are to be investigated. In studying philosophers, the problem is complicated by the fact that the philosopher's environment, unlike the promoter's, stretches through all the ages. The sociologist of knowledge will have to find out to what extent the philosopher was a promoter in his own time and to what extent he transcended the needs of his own time and became a lasting influence upon the ethos of later generations. He also studies to what extent freedom or restraint of the search for truth have facilitated, stifled, or directed this search. The mere fact that ideas are being used to answer needs does not prove that they arose from those needs. The intelligentsia that produces theoretical and ideological thoughts is not socially detached, as Mannheim asserted, but is a leisure class with definite social and economic dependences and ties.[45]

The Social Psychology of Ideological Production: Child. Child, a philosopher, does not move along strictly sociological lines. After discussing with outstanding clarity many of the sociologists of knowledge, he advances his own views, which turn out to be psychological in nature. He constructs a psychology of his own, introducing sets of "categories," entities that formalize intentions, and predispositions, which in turn are shaped by attitudes. The attitudes are socially acquired in terms of Meadian social interactions, but the components of the "social" are neither enumerated nor defined. In the

[44] DeGré, *op. cit.*, pp. 94-111.

[45] Hans Speier, "The Social Determination of Ideas," *SR*, 5 (May, 1938), pp. 182-205.

last analysis, Child is talking about events and relations within the thinker rather than relations between acts of thought or knowing on the one hand and other persons' acts of a different nature on the other.[46]

Major Issues in the Sociology of Knowledge

A Paradigm for the Sociology of Knowledge. Merton arrived inductively at a set of questions, the answers to which will provide a complete theory of the sociology of knowledge. The first question concerns the existential basis of mental production. He sees two classes of possible answers: either social bases, such as class, generation, occupation, etc., or cultural bases, such as values, ethos, folk spirit, etc. He omits the possibility that mental productions may be seen as the basis of existential developments or that the relation may be considered a reciprocal one. On the other hand, he does not restrict the existential basis to non-mental phenomena. Thus a sociology of knowledge in his definition could be a study of psychology or of logic.

The next question to be asked is what mental productions are to be analyzed. This question implies two others: What spheres—such as ideologies, ethics, science, categories of thought, etc.—are to be studied? And which of their aspects—as foci of attention, level of abstraction, models of verification, etc.—are to be analyzed? Third, how are mental productions related to their existential bases? The answer may stress causal and functional relations; it may stress symbolic, organismic, meaningful relations; or the matter may remain vague or ambiguous.

The fourth question deals with manifest and latent functions imputed to the mental productions; such functions include maintenance of power, orientation, exploitation, etc. The final question is directed at the time in which the relationships obtain. The answer may be either in historicist terms (confined to particular societies or cultures), or in terms of a general analytical theory.[47]

Problems of Empirical Research and Imputation: DeGré and Wolff. DeGré asks primarily for monographic studies of divergent social groups and of attitudinal complexes through which experience is interpreted. The roles played in different societies by highly charged complexes like communism, fascism, freedom, etc., ought to be studied. Finally, the sociology of knowledge should discover "the reciprocal influence" of socio-historical conditions and

[46] See the following works of Arthur Child: "The Theoretical Possibility of the Sociology of Knowledge," *Ethics*, 51 (July, 1941), pp. 392-418; "The Existential Determination of Thought," *loc. cit.;* "The Problem of Imputation in the Sociology of Knowledge," *loc. cit.;* "The Problem of Imputation Resolved," *Ethics*, 54 (January, 1944), pp. 96-109.

[47] Merton, *Social Theory and Social Structure,* pp. 221-222.

the most general structure of knowledge on the formal level. Wolff agrees with DeGré that there is need for more substantive research in the sociology of knowledge. Is there, for example, such a thing as a "central attitude," a total context in which one element renders all others understandable? Are there typical central attitudes? Is there a justification for speaking of magical, religious, artistic, philosophical, scientific, etc., attitudes? Can terms such as "distance" (the intensity of participation of an author of a mental event in certain elements of the event), "area of the taken-for-granted," "residual area," be empirically founded? Wolff lists research topics that show the wide range of his interests. They are not restricted to *ex post facto* studies of historical events, but also contain problems aimed at the establishment of general relationships.[48]

An Agenda for Research: Wagner. Wagner feels that Mannheim and others have not dealt sufficiently with certain crucial problems: the social preconditions of human knowledge; the origin and distribution of knowledge on the common-sense level; the formation of social and political ideologies; the influence of social factors on the formulation of social theories and on the steering of scientific interests; the selection of particular items of research for popularization; the transformation of specialized into general knowledge on the scientific level; the eventual limitations imposed on cognitive processes by the particularities of cultural situations and social structures; the subtle influences that "feeling tone," "climate of opinion," and the "relative natural aspects of the world" exert in different social units on the general ideas and orientations of thinkers and researchers, on their operational frame of reference, and on both the direction of their inquiries and the interpretation of their findings.[49]

Some Tangential Studies

The Sociology of the University and of the Learned Man. Veblen's *Theory of the Leisure Class* could have become the starting point of an American sociology of knowledge but was not followed by concrete investigations or even further expansions in speculative thought. His *The Higher Learning in America*, however, irritating an apparently permanent sore spot of American scholars, opened a line of investigation that is an important native contribution to an American sociology of knowledge.[50]

[48] DeGré, *op. cit.,* pp. 105-107; K. H. Wolff, "The Sociology of Knowledge: Emphasis on an Empirical Attitude," *Philosophy of Science,* 10 (April, 1943), pp. 104-123.

[49] Wagner, *loc. cit.*

[50] Note the recent reissue of *The Higher Learning in America* with an introduction by David Riesman (Stanford, Cal., 1954).

Wilson's study of the "academic man," his recruitment and status; Sibley's report on the recruitment, selection, and training of social scientists; Beck's study of the social and economic composition of boards of trustees of universities; parts of Jordan's spirited outcry, *Business Be Damned;* and parts of Barber's more inclusive investigation of the relations between science and the social order—all are stepping stones on this path. Also related is a study by Kent that deals with the vicissitudes befalling refugee intellectuals in America.[51] Wilson, Jordan, and Barber are particularly concerned with the effect of the conditions of academic life, as they describe them, upon the scholar. Kent's study is so strongly focused on "Americanization" and "adjustment" that any answer to the question of what influences the American academic environment exercises upon the output of the European scholar can only be gleaned from accidental implications.

Related to this trend, the study of the "academic man," is Znaniecki's study of types of men of knowledge. He does not inquire into the specific position of contemporary American scholars within their academic communities, but asks the broader question: What social function does the man of knowledge perform in all cultures and at all times? By use of constructed types—that is, by planned selection and manipulation of culture-historical materials—Znaniecki arrives at four types of men of knowledge who function in certain types of cultural conditions. Technologists, sages, schoolmen, and explorer-creators each serve their times with a specific kind of knowledge. As it stands, Znaniecki's work will lend itself better to the *ex post facto* "understanding" of past periods than to prediction. With the development of measurements of correspondence to types, it may be possible to transform his qualitative statements into quantitative predictive formulas.[52]

Typologies of Intellectuals and Their Functions. As early as 1926, Paul Honigsheim, discerning a crisis in German higher learning, arrived at a typology of individuals engaged in producing or acquiring the contents of higher learning. The types of professors—the savant, the aristocratic state employee, the industrial capitalist, the *literatus* or journalist, the prophet, and the organizer—are discursively related to characteristic backgrounds and groups of followers. The same is done for the students: fraternity members, blossoming businessmen, philologists, government officials studying part-time, and adherents of youth movements are distinguished. These and other

[51] Logan Wilson, *The Academic Man* (New York, 1942); Elbridge Sibley, *The Recruitment, Selection and Training of Social Scientists* (New York, undated); H. P. Beck, *Men Who Control Universities* (New York, 1947); Elijah Jordan, *Business Be Damned* (New York, 1952); Bernard Barber, *Science and the Social Order* (Glencoe, Ill., 1952); D. P. Kent, *The Refugee Intellectual* (New York, 1953).

[52] Florian Znaniecki, *The Social Role of the Man of Knowledge* (New York, 1940); Israel Gerver and Joseph Bensman, "Toward a Sociology of Expertness," *SF*, 32 (March, 1954), pp. 226-235. Cf. James K. Feibleman, "On Quality," *Journal of Philosophy*, 53, 21 (Oct., 1956), pp. 625-634.

influences—economic, political, and religious in nature—are blamed for the disappearance of *Gemeinschaft* and its replacement by an undesirable *Gesellschaft*. Writing in the same symposium as Honigsheim, Helmut Plessner discovered similarities in the activities of expert impersonal business management and expert impersonal research in science. At the university, principles of research become the rules of social interaction among the academicians. Thus university organization, although inhuman, furthers research.[35]

Theodor Geiger of Denmark rejected these problems in much the same way as did the writers of this country. His starting point, however, is a rejection of Karl Mannheim's conception of the synthesizing function of the intellectuals with regard to knowledge. Geiger believes that the intelligentsia has a social mandate. They are expected to create new cultural values, just as entrepreneurs are expected to create new economic values. As carriers of these expectations, intellectuals and entrepreneurs form the two élites of modern society. The intellectuals, furthermore, are expected to rationalize life, to make it efficient. Finally, they are supposed to criticize existing institutions and thereby to achieve moderation in the exercise of established powers. It is their function to produce many conflicting ideologies. Ideologies arise from overgeneralization or from treating the metaphysical as existential. For their existence, intellectuals depend on the availability of economic surpluses and on cultural willingness to spend them for intellectual endeavors. To function adequately in a society, they depend upon two conditions. First, their efforts must be received and responded to by the society; second, there must be freedom of production. Geiger sets up several types of intellectuals according to the form of economic support they receive, types of their way of life, and the relations of various types of cultures to different preferred types of knowledge. The book is based on quantitative work in the study of élites, which is, unfortunately, not included.[54]

The Sociology of Science. During the depression years, when the contribution of science was brought into dispute, natural scientists in Great Britain tried on the one hand to persuade the public at large of the advantages to be derived from the continued application of the scientific method to ever enlarging fields; on the other hand, they began to worry about the very basis of their existence in society. Thus, a sociology of science came into being. After the dropping of atomic bombs on Hiroshima and Nagasaki,

[53] Paul Honigsheim, "Die Gegenwartskrise der Kulturinstitute in ihrer soziologischen Bedingtheit," in Scheler (ed.), *Versuche zu einer Soziologie des Wissens,* pp. 426-250; Helmut Plessner, "Zur Soziologie der modernen Forschung und ihrer Organisation in der deutschen Universität," in Scheler, *op. cit.,* pp. 407-425.

[54] Theodor Geiger, *Aufgaben und Stellung der Intelligenz in der Gesellschaft* (Stuttgart, 1949). See also Theodor Geiger, *Den Danshe Intelligens fra Reformationen till Nutiden: En Studie i Emperisk Kultursoziologi* (Aarhus, 1949); Claire Leplae, *Recrutement et mobilité sociale des universitaires* (Louvain, 1946); Roberto Agramonte y Pichardo, *Sociologia de la Universidad* (Universidad Nacional, Mexico, 1948).

and the ensuing bad publicity science received in the United States, American natural scientists first, and American social scientists later, became aware of the existence of a problem. Enforced secrecy and Congressional committee hearings sharpened their awareness.[55]

Extrascientific Factors in Research. The topic of planned research has been investigated by Gerard Piel. Great experimental designs, financed with large amounts of public or private money, demand large research teams. In recruiting these, good research men are diverted from the research that they would choose on their own initiative either to direct research technicians or to devote themselves to research topics not of their own choosing. It is the design of the project that counts, rather than who carries out the work. Preoccupation with little problems prevails and controversy is soft-pedaled. Academic and personal freedom are eroded.

> Freedom of conscience, speech, publication, and assembly are required alike by the advancement of science and the self-government of a democracy. . . . No scientist can surrender his freedom as a citizen without resigning his independence as a scientist.[56]

Hart likewise discusses extrascientific factors affecting ongoing research. He points to time, capital, qualified personnel, whims of administrators, *modus operandi* of controlling agencies, the mores, and the availability of respondents. For reasons of his own, he also considers a nominalist bias—namely, the assumption that science is a body of techniques rather than a body of laws and principles, and the assumption that research projects aim at the establishment of generalizations—as extrascientific.[57]

The Social Origins of Science. An older approach to the sociology of science is the quest for its origins. In a nomothetic discipline like sociology, the study of a unique event (the rise of modern science) has no place. Only if the unique event is considered as one case of many possible similar and comparable cases does its study fit into sociology. Merton is fully aware of this in his study of origins. His question is not: How did science arise? It is: How did it arise here and here, but not here? He derives hypotheses from the rise of science in England and applies them to the rise of science in France

[55] The British journal, *Science*, contains numerous articles by British natural scientists and others on the relation of science and society. *Nature,* another British magazine for natural-science interests, also shows this trend. The *Bulletin of the Atomic Scientists,* since its inception in 1945, has been continually occupied with questions of the relationship between science and government, science and public opinion, science and peace or war, etc.

[56] Gerard Piel, "Scientists and Other Citizens," *Scientific Monthly,* 78 (March, 1954), pp. 129-133. See also M. S. Stahl, "Splits and Schisms: Nuclear and Social" (unpublished Ph. D. dissertation, University of Wisconsin, 1947).

[57] Clyde W. Hart, "Some Factors Affecting the Organization and Prosecution of Given Research Projects," *ASR,* 12 (Oct., 1947), pp. 514-519. See also R. A. Bauer, *The New Man in Soviet Psychology* (Cambridge, Mass., 1952).

and Germany. The trouble with this procedure is that the rise of science in any one of these countries may not have been isolated from its rise in the others; their cultures were not really isolated from one another—at least not as far as those layers of society were concerned in which science arose. The rise of science in these three countries may be but one and the same phenomenon, so that no generalization can be derived from it alone.[58]

Social Factors in Specific Disciplines. In addition to the sociology of science in general, there are, of course, the sociologies of the special disciplines. Hashagen found that historians were rarely historians only but also had other occupations. These occupations, as well as their class positions, color their findings and presentation. Honigsheim, in discussing the sociology of jurisprudence, seems to have mistaken the content of the law for the content of jurisprudence, thus offering a sociology of the former rather than of the latter.[59] A sociology of economics was attempted by Gunnar Myrdal in Sweden. He found economic theory influenced by political theory on the one hand and by the use of traditional language and traditional concepts on the other. Political discussion implies beliefs concerning economic facts and the relations between them. These beliefs tend to be erroneous. Early economic thought was based on a natural law philosophy that colored its language. The sentiments implied in this philosophy still cling to the concepts used by today's economists.[60]

The Search for Implicit Ideologies in Sociology. A sociology of sociology, strictly speaking, is non-existent. But distant approximations to it may be seen in some attacks upon and defenses of sociology, which in this context is often tied to positivism because of the identity of the inventor of the names for both lines of thought.

A spirited attack on positivism is offered by Frank Hartung. He accuses the positivists of being instruments of reaction. Thus sociology, too, is basically reactionary and counterrevolutionary. Practical positivism excludes democracy and implies by logical necessity a fascist system. Hartung advocates an interpretative approach related to that of the German schools.[61]

Hartung's views find support in an essay by Kurt Wolff, who discovers in sociology a general orientation characterized by conservatism, reflected

[58] R. K. Merton, "Science, Technology, and Society in Seventeenth-Century England," *Osiris* (Bruges, 1938); also *Social Theory and Social Structure,* pp. 329-346 and 347-363; Paul Meadows, "Science as Experience: A Genetic and Comparative Review," *ASR,* 14 (Oct., 1949), pp. 592-599.

[59] Justus Hashagen, "Ausserwissenschaftliche Einflüsse auf die neuere Geschichtswissenschaft," in Scheler, *op. cit.,* pp. 233-255; Paul Honigsheim, "Soziologie der Jurisprudenz," *ibid.,* pp. 263-272.

[60] Gunnar Myrdal, *The Political Element in Economic Theory,* translated by Paul Streeters (Cambridge, Mass., 1954). The original Swedish edition dates back to about 1929.

[61] F. E. Hartung, "The Sociology of Positivism," *Science and Society,* 8 (Fall., 1944), pp. 328-341.

in the use of the "caste" concept and the concepts of folkways and mores; the absence of studies of man's greatness, meanness, and suffering; and the consequent absence of a search for improvement. These attitudes are to be explained by a socio-cultural interpretation that takes in account social backgrounds of individuals, power distribution, classes, attitudes, beliefs, values, etc.[62] Wolff seems to conclude that a non-evaluative, fact-finding approach necessarily implies approval of the facts found.

Nisbet explains Comte's sociology as a return to medievalism. In the enlightenment, state and individuals combined forces to destroy the established groups, family, church, guilds, etc. This process culminated in the French Revolution, to which Comte reacted by again calling attention to the group. F. A. Hayek likewise inveighs against positivism and positivist sociology.His trump in the argument is that positivism, sociology, and socialism come from the same source, namely the *École Polytechnique* of Paris.[63] It would be interesting to test Hayek's assertion by investigating whether or not today's schools of engineering, particularly institutes of technology, encourage similar differences in the ways of thinking of their teachers and students from those existing at other schools of higher learning. Only if this is generally the case could Hayek's explanation be considered as valid.

The rare phenomenon of a real Marxian in American literature was provided by Behice Boran:

> Nineteenth-century European sociology, with dual roots in Marxism and the bourgeois ideology of Comte, had a class character. American sociology was, from the beginning, animated by an unrealistic, optimistic bourgeois spirit. In the early twentieth century, American sociology discarded the philosophy of history and was reduced to the study of practical social problems. Since the twenties, in spite of revolutionary world-wide changes in society, sociologists have been preoccupied with questions of method. Lundberg speaks now of faith in science as a cure-all for social ills; but while scientists dally, the ills grow apace. Lynd more realistically points out that the central problem of the social sciences is the premises of culture, which, themselves, condition science.[64]

Lundberg replied to Boran by restating his faith in the irrelevance of political situations to science, a faith that unfortunately will not bear the burden of proof. He emphasizes that only that is science which has general validity—a statement valid only if differences among the cultural criteria of truth are disregarded. He states that science is itself a major part of

[62] K. H. Wolff, "Notes Toward a Sociocultural Interpretation of American Sociology," *ASR,* 11 (Oct., 1946), pp. 545-553.

[63] R. A. Nisbet, "The French Revolution and the Rise of Sociology in France," *AJS,* 49 (September, 1943), pp. 156-164; F. A. Hayek, *The Counterrevolution of Science* (Glencoe, Ill., 1952).

[64] Behice Boran, "Sociology in Retrospect," *AJS,* 52 (January, 1947), p. 312.

history and therefore cannot be conditioned by history. True enough; it cannot be conditioned by total history. But being one part of history, it may very well be conditioned by other parts of history. Science, the normative desideratum defined by Lundberg and others, as well as the actual phenomenon at various times and places designated by that term, has been very variable, probably in relation to other variables. The arguments that more specifically answer and destroy Boran's attacks do not refer to the sociology of knowledge and are therefore not relevant here.[65]

House and Bowman brought some calmer thinking to this controversy. As early as 1928, House showed that social change brings about changes in social thinking. In a time of change, the leisurely study of unique events of the past for the sake of understanding them is less important than the finding of generalizations that hold true timelessly in spite of change. The latter is the aim of sociology. Bowman points out that all kinds of sharp cleavages in a society, political, national, religious, and others, make it difficult to develop an objective social science. He sees, however, a useful function in ideologies, in that they may serve as material for scientific hypotheses.[66]

Ideological Bias in Subfields of Sociology. For smaller units within sociology, the question of a progressive *vs.* a conservative character has been discussed by Bowman for family sociology and by Mills for the study of social problems. Bowman finds that sociology has replaced theology in his field. Textbooks emphasize a positive attitude toward sex, the development of the child at the expense of parental comfort, contraception and family planning, feminism and equalitarianism. On the other hand, little research is being done on the *sociology* of sex. The traditional beliefs concerning mariage, love, and sex are upheld in the teachings and writings on family sociology.[67]

Mills, in discussing the "Professional Ideology of the Social Pathologist," finds that these scholars are born in small towns or on farms; they have participated in reform groups of the professional or business class; they associate in homogeneous groups; they have Ph.D. degrees and are college professors, etc. This similarity in their backgrounds may explain their unanimity in interpreting facts. Pathologies are defined as deviations from invariable norms taken to be the standards of society. Pathologists' organismic view of society makes it hard for them to see the possibility of change. They use the term "social" as equivalent to "good," "individual-

[65] G. A. Lundberg, "Sociology *versus* Dialectical Immaterialism," *AJS,* 53 (Sept., 1947), pp. 85-95.

[66] F. N. House, "Social Change and Social Science," *SF,* 7 (Sept., 1928), pp. 11-17; C. C. Bowman, "Polarities and the Impairment of Science," *ASR,* 15 (Aug., 1950), pp. 480-489.

[67] C. C. Bowman, "Hidden Valuations in the Interpretation of Sexual and Family Relationship," *ASR,* 11 (Oct., 1946), pp. 536-544, and "Cultural Ideology and Heterosexual Reality: A Preface to Sociological Research," *ASR,* 14 (Oct., 1949), pp. 624-633.

istic" to "bad." Their ideal society is Cooley's primary group. Their aim is to preserve rurally oriented values and stability. The term "adjustment" is used to advocate conformity. The ideal member of society is seen as an independent middle-class person, verbally living out Protestant ideals in the small towns of America. Consequently, sociology is reactionary, because, after all, most sociologists are at least part-time social pathologists.[68]

Recapitulation. It appears that in its history the sociology of knowledge has changed from an instrument of political discussion to an esoteric philosophy of the history of thought. Now it seems to be moving from the second phase toward becoming an empirical branch of scientific sociology. Substantive studies of specific problems hold much promise, and represent a desirable line of development. It is, of course, quite possible that sociology of knowledge will be deflected from this path before reaching the goal, but knowledge of past errors may prevent further wavering.

SELECTED BIBLIOGRAPHY

Cowell, F. R., *History, Civilization, and Culture: An Introduction to the Historical and Social Philosophy of Pitirim A. Sorokin* (Boston: Beacon Press, 1952).

Dahlke, H. Otto, "The Sociology of Knowledge," in H. E. Barnes, Howard Becker, and Frances B. Becker (eds.), *Contemporary Social Theory* (New York: D. Appleton-Century, 1940), Chap. 4.

DeGré, G. L., *Society and Ideology* (New York: Columbia University Press, 1943).

Grünwald, Ernst, *Das Problem einer Soziologie des Wissens* (Vienna: Wilhelm Braumüller Universitäts Verlag, 1934).

Mannheim, Karl, *Essays in the Sociology of Knowledge* (New York: Oxford University Press, 1952).

———, *Ideology and Utopia,* translated by Louis Wirth and E. A. Shils (New York: Harcourt, Brace, 1936).

Maquet, J. J., *Sociologie de la connaissance* (Louvain; Institut de Recherches Économiques et Sociales, 1949).

Merton, R. K., *Social Theory and Social Structure* (Glencoe, Ill.: The Free Press, 1949).

Scheler, Max (ed.), *Versuche zu einer Soziologie des Wissens* (Munich: Duncker and Humblot, 1924).

Sorokin, Pitirim A., *Social and Cultural Dynamics* (New York: American Book Co., 1937-1941), 4 vols.

Znaniecki, Florian, *The Social Role of the Man of Knowledge* (New York: Columbia University Press, 1940).

[68] C. Wright Mills, "The Professional Ideology of Social Pathologists," *AJS,* 49 (Sept., 1943), pp. 165-180.

GROWTH AND SCOPE OF SOCIOLOGY OF LAW

N. S. TIMASHEFF

THE HISTORY OF SOCIOLOGY OF LAW SINCE WORLD WAR I IS CHARACTERIZED by numerous but rather unrelated efforts to build up a new discipline the need for which is recognized by many, but relative to the scope, structure and methods of which there is little agreement[1]. The number of volumes explicitly devoted to the sociology of law has been small; but there have been many more volumes and articles devoted to its individual problems. Moreover, the idea that law could and should be treated sociologically has conquered the minds of several legal philosophers or scholars specializing in the "general theory of law" (approximately "jurisprudence" in the American meaning). On the other hand, law has gained some recognition in sociology and cultural anthropology where, until recently, it was commonly mentioned as something located on the periphery of folkways and mores, which have been topics of genuine sociological and anthropological interest. But interaction between general sociology and the sociology of law has been superficial and probably will remain so until the sociology of law develops something tangible and sufficiently verified to offer for incorporation into the central core of sociological theory.

Let us therefore survey a number of studies that focus on the following problem: How can the law, which for millennia was treated as a system of norms or ideas, be actually integrated with society and culture viewed as parts of biopsychic reality? But, of course, when contributions to the soci-

[1] See N. S. Timasheff, *An Introduction to the Sociology of Law* (Cambridge, Mass., 1939), pp. 44-63; and Georges Gurvitch, *Sociology of Law* (New York, 1942), pp. 68-197.

ology of law have gone beyond this central problem, the relevant efforts will also be considered. The individual efforts may be grouped into six major classes, the first of which includes the contributions of the American neo-realists in jurisprudence.

American Neo-Realism

The American neo-realists do not claim to have founded sociology of law; many among them have probably never heard that such a discipline was in the making. But the school has boldly proclaimed the goal of rendering the science of law a true science, approaching law as a category of time and space subject to human devising and direction. The school opposed this science to "fundamentalism," which regarded law as a realization of an absolute verity, beyond change, time, and space.[2]

The earlier works of the neo-realists stated the thesis rather sharply. Among them, none is more representative than Jerome Frank's *Law and the Modern Mind* (1931). The main objective of the work is to expose the "basic legal myth" that ascribes to the law "unrealistic certainty." Men adhere to the myth because they have not yet relinquished the childish need for an authoritative father and try to find in the law a father-substitute—obviously a psychoanalytically inspired statement.

Moreover, legal certainty is a myth because, through judge-made law, the rights and obligations of the parties may be decided retroactively. For any particular person, the law with respect to any particular set of facts is a decision of a court. Until a court has passed on these facts, no law on the subject is yet in existence.

How are judical decisions arrived at? Judging begins with a conclusion, more or less vaguely formed. Only afterwards does the judge try to find premises that will substantiate them. In doing so, the judge is influenced by political, economic, and moral prejudices; since these vary from person to person, judges differ in an amazing degree in their treatment of similar classes of cases. It is clear, therefore, that Frank's approach to the proximate causes of a judicial decision strikingly resembles that of Pareto.

At about the same time, another member of the school, Karl Llewellyn, published an article[3] in which he well summarized its creed. To Frank's thesis he added these: Law is always in flux and is a means to social ends. But society is also always in flux, although at a greater tempo than law. Hence there is necessarily discrepancy between the law as an instrument of

[2] H. E. Yntema, "Law and Learning Theory Through the Looking Glass of Legal Theory," *Yale Law Journal,* 53 (1943-44), pp. 338-339.

[3] Karl Llewellyn, "Some Realism about Realism," *Harvard Law Review,* 44 (1930-1).

social engineering and the social facts, a discrepancy that must be, and partly is, overcome by judge-made law that is unpredictable from the point of view of historically established rules.

Retreat from Neo-Realism: Some Evidence. It is noteworthy that, in the next decade, both Frank and Llewellyn retreated toward much more moderate positions. In a volume entitled *Courts on Trial* (1949), Frank no longer asserts that the system of legal rules is too vague to allow any prediction as to the outcome of a trial. On the contrary, he concedes that a good lawyer is commonly able to advise his client correctly on the chance of winning a judicial contest. But he attacks another "myth," the commonly held belief that a judicial decision is the result of the application of pre-established rules to the relevant facts. He gives a lengthy and challenging survey of the obstacles met by the most sincere efforts to establish the real facts; among these obstacles, he mentions the very organization of the trial, which, in his opinion, is a survival of judicial combat. In consequence, legal uncertainty is emphasized almost as strongly as it was in the earlier volume; but now the cause seems to be different, and the emphasis is not primarily on change in the methods of realistically studying the law, but on judicial reform, a problem outside the scope of this paper.

Why has there been such a retreat? Probably because the views of the neo-realists, in their original form, proved to be sterile. No one among them has ever undertaken or even suggested a method for the systematic study of the actual behavior of the judges. Moreover, it is common knowledge that the vast majority of judicial cases are routine cases decided almost automatically on the basis of precedent; in actuality, the main challenge against any known judicial system is lack of individualization and not at all unpredictability. Therefore, the earlier works of the neo-realists seem to have posed a kind of pseudo-problem.

But the problem could be, and actually has been, restated to cover a much wider field of facts. Law, concurrently with other factors, is supposed to condition human behavior. Could we not, then, carry out well-controlled observation of change in human conduct under the impact of change in law? The most painstaking study of this kind has been undertaken by Moore and Callahan.[4] It concerns itself mainly with the impact on actual parking behavior of a regulation limiting the duration of parking in New Haven. Observations were made before and after the introduction of the new regulation. As might be expected, a significant difference was established, as well as considerable regularity in parking behavior. Similar observations were made by Frederickson and associates[5] on the reactions of motorists to a

[4] Moore and Callahan, "Law and Learning Theory," *Yale Law Journal,* 53 (1943-44), pp. 1-143.

[5] N. Frederickson *et al.,* "A Study of Conformity to a Traffic Regulation," *JASP,* 34 (1939), pp. 118-123.

traffic regulation requiring them to keep in line, and by Britt on pedestrian conformity to a traffic regulation enforced in Washington, D. C.[6] Britt's study is interesting because it distinguishes between absolute conformity, two degrees of partial conformity, and absolute non-conformity. It was discovered that conformity was greater downtown than in residential areas and more marked in the first days after the change in regulations than later.

With respect to the Moore-Callahan investigation, Yntema, another authoritative representative of neo-realism, published an article[7] in which he stated that, during the past fifteen years, there had been a relaxation of the effort to expand the scope and depth of the pragmatic scientific knowledge of legal phenomena. Moreover, Yntema raised this question: What should be mainly studied, the area of non-litigious behavior or behavior connected with actual or possible litigation? In the latter case, should one start from the client, the advocate, the expert witness, the judge, or the bystander? Thus, a very interesting and promising research program has been formulated, but little progress along these lines has taken place.

However, pertinent remarks, but no developed theory, can be found in Max Radin's *Law as Logic and Experience* (1940). Radin concentrates his attention initially on the legal experience of non-lawyers, who are commonly unaware of having this experience since, most of human experience is habitual and unconscious and consequently rarely determined by conscious application of norms, least of all legal norms. That experience becomes truly legal when lawyers start talking about it. This does not happen in common and usual situations, but rather in *marginal* and *exceptional* situations with which the law deals. In the hands of lawyers, law becomes part of logic, since the lawyers who are very realistic in what they do are conceptualists in what they say. Lawyers study what was said about old legal quarrels and what was said about these statements; this is law in books. To that material they add real experience of their own, dependent on records and memory. To arrange that vast amount of material, they actually need logic and a system of notations—that is, the technical terms that earn them the animosity of laymen. The whole discourse of the lawyer is, however, oriented to the statement he imagines the judge might make. But who are the judges? Not only persons so-called officially, but also "judicasters" or persons issuing statements involving "oughts" insofar as these statements are treated as binding on them by those who are in actuality judges.

After all, writes Radin, law is merely a small part of the mechanism of social management, closely connected with the mechanisms of political administration. Not justice or a good society, but convenience of commercial practice, appeasement of individual quarrels, and increase of good will among

[6] S. H. Britt, "Pedestrian Conformity to a Traffic Regulation," *JASP*, 35 (1940), pp. 114-119.

[7] Yntema, *op. cit.*, pp. 340-341.

competitors are the purposes of law, if we examine its actual operation.

An Assessment of Neo-Realism. Summing up, one may say that the American neo-realists have brought forward a number of valuable ideas about studying the law as a particular kind of human behavior in society. But no tangible body of knowledge has emerged from their efforts, and no convenient method of gaining such knowledge has been offered. The quantitative methods of Moore and his followers seem to be applicable only to the simplest situations and these "sophisticated" methods merely confirm and perhaps refine what is common knowledge.

Max Weber and Analysis of Legitimate Order

Another effort to build up the sociology of law, contemporaneous with the early writings of the American neo-realists, has been that of Max Weber in *Wirtschaft und Gesellschaft* (1922).[8] This effort, largely developed in painstaking and illuminating studies of concrete developments in the field (for instance, the formation of contesting schools of jurists) has been influential in a particular regard. To define the law and related phenomena, Weber has used in place of necessity, commonly applied by those who want to make their study rigorously "scientific," the concept of probability.

Weber's approach to law begins, significantly, with the concept of order. Order is present, says Weber, if actions are oriented toward more or less definite maxims of conduct (norms). But an order is valid if there is the *probability* that an action will be at least partly determined by the actor's idea that the order is valid. Two main types of order are distinguished: *convention* (in the sense of mores) and *law*. Convention is an order the validity of which is externally guaranteed by the *probability* that deviation will result in a relatively general and practically significant reaction of disapproval. Law is an order the validity of which is guaranteed by the *probability* that deviation will be met by physical or psychic sanction by a "staff" especially empowered to carry out this function. This staff, obviously, must have power, and power is defined by Weber as the *probability* that an actor can impose, within a social group, his will even against resistance. Thus Weber relates a probabilistic definition of law to a probabilistic definition of power.

Weber has also applied the concept of probability to the problem of legal change. In his opinion, the probability that a definite legal institution will be invented in the context of a given legal order is mainly determined by

[8] The sections on the sociology of law are now available in an excellent English translation by E. A. Shils and Max Rheinstein, under the title *Max Weber on Law in Economy and Society* (Cambridge, Mass., 1954).

the prevailing thought techniques. Economic conditions do not automatically engender new legal forms, but only increase the probability that an invention in the field of legal technique, if and when it is made, will be accepted.

Weber's Typology of Legal Activity and Structure. Moreover, Weber's work is important as a counterpart to the court-centered views of the American neo-realists (and of Anglo-Saxon lawyers and jurists in general). Weber asserts that court-centered law is a peculiarity of Western civilization and therefore cannot be the starting-point for generalizations of universal validity. He makes an attempt to formulate a more general theory of the two basic types of legal activity: creating the law and finding the law. These activities may be distinguished ideal-typically as *rational* or *irrational,* and in each case with respect to either *formal* or *substantive* criteria. The activity of judges in Western civilization corresponds to the class of activities that are both rational (that is, guided by general rules) and formal—more explicitly, logically formal. This is in fact true because this activity is characterized by the use of abstract concepts and conceived as constituting a complete system. A contrast appears in the so-called *cadi justice* of the Moslems, which is irrational (that is, not guided by abstract rules), and substantive or concerned with the individual case. In Weber's work, these points appear in a rather obscure form; but they have been brilliantly elucidated by Max Rheinstein, in his introduction to the English translation of that part of Weber's monumental work which is devoted to the law.

Not all the definitions and theorems of Max Weber, however, are acceptable. Especially dubious is his attempt to consider as "legal" those activities unrelated to pre-established maxims of conduct (to use Weber's terminology). But his use of the concept of probability relative to the law as a social fact has directly affected the further development of the sociology of law, whereas his views on the "ideal types" of actions oriented to law making or law finding (adjudication) deserve more attention than they have yet received.

Distinction Between the Legal and Moral Orders

A third group of efforts consists of the works of scholars who studied in Russia shortly before the revolution of 1917 and who continued their work in various countries of the West. None of this group has fully adopted the ideas of the great Russo-Polish master Petrazhitsky, whose major works, *An Introduction to the Study of Law and Morals* (1905) and *The Theory of Law and the State* (1907), are now be available in an abridged English translation.[9]

[9] Petrazhitsky, *Law and Morality* (Cambridge, Mass., 1955).

Petrazhitsky's main thesis is a denial of the reality of what forms the central core of jurisprudence, namely of legal norms, rights and duties. Reality is ascribed only to the experiences of individuals who assume rights and obligations and who, to explain and vindicate these experiences, construct norms. This seems to atomize the legal world into individual experiences; but there are forces that tend to unify these experiences and render them meaningful wholes. Legal experience is contrasted by Petrazhitsky with moral experience. The latter is unilateral, purely imperative, imposing obligations to which no rights correspond; the former is bilateral, attributive-imperative, imposing obligations and granting rights. The two classes of experiences may be united into a higher class, that of ethical experience, which differs from all other kinds of motivating experiences in that it evaluates past or future actions in themselves with no regard to pleasure, pain, utility, or beauty. It must also be noted that, according to Petrazhitsky, all attributive-imperative experiences are legal; coercion or possibility of coercion is not required. Obviously, this is a view which expands the scope of law much further than the conceptions prevailing in jurisprudence.

Sorokin: Law and the Major Cultural Supersystems. Of this group, Pitirim A. Sorokin has probably remained closest to the ideas of the master. He does not, however, share Petrazhitsky's skepticism about the reality of law—more exactly, of law norms. Law, in the form of norms, is part of culture; the position of law in culture is defined in close approximation to the ideas of the master. According to Sorokin, the supersystem of culture consists of five major systems, one of which is ethics, containing two subsystems, law and morals. Sorokin has also preserved the idea that every attributive-imperative norm is legal. This proposition plays an important part in his treatment of organized groups, which he identifies as groups in which the reciprocal relations of the members are determined by law norms, in the meaning he ascribes to this term. It is obvious that legal order becomes almost identical with social order in its totality. But Sorokin differs from Petrazhitsky in that, for him, law norms imply sanctions.[10]

On the other hand, Sorokin has made an important contribution to the very "stuff" of the sociology of law. In his *Social and Cultural Dynamics* (1937) (Vol. II, Chap. 15), he has established certain tendencies in the expansion or contraction of actions considered criminal by various societies as well as fluctuations in the development of punishment. The correlations that he draws between these movements and the basic movement of culture (from ideational through idealistic to sensate, and vice versa) may be not quite convincing. But the findings refute the idea that law depends on the whim of the legislator and is therefore scientifically inscrutable. Research along the lines of the chapter just mentioned could bear abundant fruit.

Gurvitch: Law and the Forms of Sociality. Another member of this group

[10] P. A. Sorokin, *Society, Culture, and Personality* (New York, 1947), pp. 70-85.

is Georges Gurvitch, who is a legal philosopher rather than a legal sociologist; nevertheless, he is one of the rare men to publish a book entitled *The Sociology of Law* (in French, 1940; in English, 1942). He firmly believes that the definition of law must be contributed to legal science (on its various levels) by philosophy; and since as a philosopher he belongs to the phenomenological school, his definition must be molded according to the teaching of that school. In practice, this does not mean very much; as is the case with all the phenomenologists in the field of sociology, the method actually followed is based on participant-observation and empiricism than rather on informal inference. Very definitely, Petrazhitsky's ideas have played a large part, for Gurvitch defines law as an attempt to realize in a given social environment the idea of justice through multilateral attributive-imperative regulation deriving its validity from normative facts that give it social guaranty and may (but *must* not) be conducive to precise and external constraint.

Three ideas appearing in this complex definition have been taken over from Petrazhitsky: (1) the attributive-imperative character of legal norms; (2) the reference to normative facts that, in Petrazhitsky's system, are authoritative facts referred to by persons ascribing rights or obligations to everyone; and (3) the idea that external constraint is not a necessary trait of law. This is at variance with Sorokin and, in later parts of Gurvitch's work, proves to be disastrous, since it expands beyond any reasonable limit the scope of the investigation. The body of the sociology of law, according to Gurvitch, should consist of (1) a systematic part studying the manifestations of law as a function of the forms of "sociality"; (2) a differential part studying the manifestations of law as a function of real collective units; and (3) a genetic part studying the regularities in the change, development, and decay of law within particular types of society.

In the first or systematic part, Gurvitch distinguishes between social law (to which he has devoted a long monograph in French) and interindividual law. Social law is subdivided into the law of the masses, of the communities, and the communions; interindividual law into the law of separation, of approaching, and mixed law. Additional classifications are then introduced, all independent of each other. The result is about 162 types of law; but, relative to the vast majority of these types, Gurvitch has nothing to add beyond the matter of definitions—a symptom of scientific sterility.

In the second or differential part, Gurvitch asserts that each active group affirms itself as a normative fact engendering its own jural regulation. Here, as in Sorokin's discussion of organized groups, legal stands for social. There follows a short abstract survey of legal orders found in various types of groups; among others, there appear political, economic, and mystic-ecstatic law. In several places, statements representative of old-fashioned natural-law theory appear; for example, the author asserts that the international legal order prevails over the national ones, a statement at variance with observable facts. The third or genetic part is treated so briefly that there is as yet little basis for discussion of it.

Timasheff: Law, Power, and the Learning Process. A third member of the group is the present writer. His membership in the group is, however, limited to (1) strict adherence to the proposition that an empitical study of law must be a study of facts, not of ideas; (2) the proposition that the reality of law must be ascertained in terms of man's biopsychic experiences; and (3) that law and morals form together the higher class of ethics.

Man's biopsychic experience related to law is, however, of a collective kind; therefore, it can and must be treated sociologically. Two social facts have been considered as basic for the scientific understanding of the reality of law: first, the existence in every durable group of an order that may be articulated in norms and that, through complex mechanisms, is imposed on group members; and second, the existence of social power. These two phenomena may be analyzed into complex systems of learned behavior tendencies. They may exist independently of one another; but they may merge, and their merger is law.

Such are the fundamental ideas of the *Introduction to the Sociology of Law,* which appeared in 1939. The book has been the object of much criticism, positive and negative. One of the sharpest attacks came from Karl Olivecrona, a member of the Upsala school (see pp. 434-436), who seems not to have recognized a great affinity between that work and the teaching of the school to which he belongs.[11] More especially, Olivecrona has tried to prove that in Timasheff's book there remains an objective and therefore nonempirical "ought."

In an article entitled "The Social Reality of Ideal Patterns,"[12] Timasheff made two additions to the view expressed in his book. First, he called attention to the striking parallelism between the structure of a legal norm and of a learned behavior tendency. To the hypothesis of the norm there corresponds the stimulus situation; to the disposition, the response; and to the copula (ought to be), the biopsychic mechanism calling forth the response. This parallelism may explain the somewhat mysterious force of the sense of duty; it may also be a contribution to the theory of the internalization of culture, especially of its normative elements. Another idea was that of the functional interchangeability of ideal and real patterns; whereas originally norms (ideal patterns) appear as abstractions from actual conduct sanctioned by group conviction, later on the technique of legislation (in a broad sense of the term) is discovered (independently in many places and at various times)—that is, of the planned imposition of new norms to be converted into actual behavior.

[11] Timasheff, "Is Sociological Explanation of Law Possible?" *Theoria,* 14 (1948), pp. 181 ff.

[12] Timasheff, "The Social Reality of Ideal Patterns," *JLPS* (Autumn, 1944).

The Upsala School

A fourth group of efforts to construct a sociology of law may be seen in the work of the so-called Upsala school. The members of the school share the idea that a really scientific theory of law demands the elimination of the dualism of law as a fact (expressed in observable human behavior) and law as a system of normative ideas said to be valid. In the development of this school, two periods can be distinguished. During the earlier period, the purpose of the school was rather negative—to unveil as unrealistic such basic concepts of jurisprudence as right, obligation, and norm. The members of the school concentrated on the task without knowing that, many years earlier, a similar work of demolition had been performed, with much more vigor, by Leo Petrazhitsky.

The recognized head of the Upsala school is A. Hägerström, until his recent death Professor of Legal History and Legal Philosophy at the University of Upsala. He started writing on the subject of the sociology of law as early as 1915-1916. In 1953, a most useful compilation of his theoretical writings appeared in English under the title *Inquiries into the Nature of Law and Morals,* edited by one of his followers, Karl Olivecrona.

Hägerström and the Non-empirical Basis of Legal Rights. Hägerström's reasoning begins with a blunt denial of the reality of rights and duties. "Rights and duties," he says, "are metaphysical sham-concepts; it is impossible to identify that which we call a right or a duty with any fact. The notions must be discarded *en bloc.*" But these terms are used by legislators, private individuals, and judges. What do they mean when employing them? Being aware of his considerable authority, the legislator describes certain types of anticipated situations, gives advantage to some persons involved in them, and imposes corresponding disadvantages on others. He knows that in the majority of cases the former (called the possessor of a right) will receive the advantage as against the person who is under obligation.

A private person, informed of these anticipatory statements of the legislator, makes certain "declarations of intention" (to use Hägerström's term), believing that they will have the described effect through the mechanism of law. Of course, he cannot be sure that his case will not be one of those exceptional cases in which recourse to courts is necessary. After all, he means that either the right (the advantage secured by the legislator) will in fact obtain from the party under obligation, or that he will acquire a power (to coerce that party) through a process of law.

In its turn, a court understands, under right and duty, situations corresponding to the anticipatory statements of the legislator. The judge conceives right as a certain state of affairs to which there corresponds an alternative of power, backed by compulsion. What the judge does is merely this: he proclaims that the plaintiff "ought" (or eventually ought not) to have the anticipated advantage.

The complex network of beliefs and actions described above can function only insofar as there exists, objectively, an organized system of coercion. Unlike most legal philosophers and sociologists of law, Hägerström believes that *illegality* rather than law is the basic concept to be analyzed first. Illegality, in his words, is the behavior which calls forth certain coercive reactions in accordance with rules that are in general applied and are irresistibly carried out in a human community. Legal behavior is behavior with the opposite character. Let us notice that, at this point, realistic purism is abandoned by the Swedish scholar: like rights and duties, norms cannot be observed; they can be only inferred.

Sources of Legal Behavior. What is behind the functioning of irresistible coercion? The real cause of the maintenance of legal order is concurrence of *imponderabilia.* The individual refrains from illegality because of (1) a "social instinct" that involves an inclination to follow, without reflection, certain general rules of action; (2) a positive moral disposition that Hägerström, at one point, calls "feeling of duty," thus ascribing to duty psychological reality; (3) fear of external coercion; and (4) reference to divine power. The third of these points is amplified in the following way: There are authorities charged with the enforcement of law. If they do not act according to the rules, other authorities interfere in their turn; the question of an eventual *regressus ad infinitum,* posed at this point by Petrazhitsky,[13] does not occur in Hägerström's system. Finally, the existence of legal order is characterized by the fact that fixed rules for the exercise of coercion are maintained and that the arbitrariness associated with terrorism is excluded.

Legal Rules as Ideals of Conduct: Olivecrona. Here again the problem of the reality of rules or norms emerges. The problem is all the more important since another representative of the school, Karl Olivecrona, in his *Law as a Fact* (1939), attacks the conception of law as a body of rules binding on the members of a community. The binding force of a legal rule (conceived to precede, logically, the sanction that is supposed to be inflicted because a binding rule has been violated) is not a fact; it has no real place in the real world of time and space.

The only way to create a realistic theory of law is to take up such facts as are covered by the expression "rules of law." The function of these rules is to influence people's actions in specified situations. The content of the rules of law may be defined as ideas of imaginary[14] actions by people (among them,

[13] Petrazhitsky's reasoning is presented in Timasheff, *An Introduction to the Sociology of Law,* p. 364. (The corresponding passage does not appear in the translation cited in footnote 9.)

[14] In this context, of course, "imaginary" means not fantastic but anticipatory.

judges) in imaginary situations. The application consists in taking the imaginary actions as *models* for actual conduct when the corresponding situations arise in real life. This view agrees with that of Hägerström, with a shift of emphasis from rights and duties to rules.

Legal Rules and the Phenomena of Respect and Obligation. How does this conversion of models into real actions take place? After refuting current theories of law, Olivecrona bluntly asserts that the rules of law (as well as the rules of morality) are "independent imperatives." Here, the Swedish realist seems to come very close to the position of Kelsen and of a whole line of his German predecessors, who asserted that legal rules, once promulgated, were detached from the will of the legislator and became valid per se.

Why do these independent imperatives work and influence human conduct? The explanation is a modified idea of Kelsen's. The basic fact is the *respect* in which the constitution is held. Of course, Olivecrona has in mind not only formal constitutions, but also informal ones ascribing supreme power to some individual or groups of individuals. This respect for the constitution is transferred into ordinary legislation and causes people positively to accept duly promulgated laws as binding. At this point, Olivecrona contradicts himself, having denied earlier in his treatise that one could identify the binding force of rules with the feeling of being bound.

Now arises the crucial question: How can reverence for the constitution be explained? In Olivecrona's opinion, time and again there arises a temporary assemblage of forces strong enough to effect that change in the attitudes of the citizens which is implied in the acceptance of a new constitution as binding; here again, Olivecrona refers to the feeling of being bound. He adds, however, in agreement with Hägerström, that the principal source of the strength of a constitution is in the social habits and instincts of the people. Also in the style of Hägerström are Olivecrona's interpretations of rights and duties. Right is considered to be a fictitious or imaginary power; it is used by the law as a means of directing people's action. Duties are also based on imagination, being completely determined by the rules of law. The generic technique of law consists of interpolating imaginary rights and duties between the relevant facts. There follows an idea often recurring among sociologists of the Durkheim school: All these techniques based on imagination are closely related to magic. "We have retained the outer structure of magic in legal matters while the specific belief in supernatural forces has faded out."[15]

Law as a Reflection of Social Power. Having explained the working of legal rules by respect for the constitution as reflecting a past configuration of social forces, Olivecrona says: "If the law is not binding in the traditional sense, then law must be essentially organized power. This is in fact so."[16] Law consists chiefly of rules about force; the citizens have to make their

[15] *Law as a Fact*, p. 115.
[16] *Ibid.*, p. 123.

behavior conform to them. The immediate effects of individual sanctions are relatively unimportant in comparison with the pressure exerted on the minds of the citizens by the existence of organized force. In order to avoid the burden of fear, one must exclude even the thought of an unlawful action. This is, however, possible only if there are some generally accepted reasons why sanctions are applicable to specified actions; otherwise the system is terroristic rather than legal. In other words, power must be limited. But it is not a question of limiting a power which is unlimited per se; on the contrary, the problem consists in building up a concentration of force of limited scope and subjecting it to limited ends.

Law as Normative Interpretation of Reality. During the more recent period of the existence of the Upsala school, its younger members have made a number of positive contributions to the solution of the main problems of the sociology of law. One of them is Alf Ross who, in 1929, in a German work entitled *Theorie der Rechtsquellen,* clearly formulated the most difficult of these problems. Since law cannot be considered as a mere fact or as mere "ought," the task is to resolve the opposition between the two and show that the "ought" is not anything independent and absolutely opposed to the "is." In that work, however, Ross did not make any significant advance toward the goal itself.

He has been much more successful in another work, which appeared in 1946 in English and is entitled *Toward a Realistic Jurisprudence.* Following Hägerström (to whom he acknowledges his indebtedness) and Olivecrona, he bluntly states that law is a fact, not an ideal, or a logical system. The legal propositions are not *real* propositions; they have no meaning in themselves but are statements about special phenomena—expressions of attitudes that function as parts in a comprehensive social reality.

Nevertheless, law is expressed in the form of normative propositions to which validity is ascribed; in Ross's system, validity is almost identical with Olivecrona's binding force. This dualism of fact and validity must be overcome, but this cannot be done by ignoring validity, as the older members of the school have done. Validity is a term implying rationalization of subjective experiences; when the process of rationalization is reduced and expressions of validity are taken according to their symbolic value, the alleged dualism between fact and validity can be seen to reflect the interaction between actual elements of legal reality, whereas the traditional concept of law (emphasizing validity) is of a magical nature.

The Fusion of Coercion and Obligation: Socio-Legal Order. The reduction of the opposition between law as a fact and law as a system of valid norms is performed by Ross through contemplation of two "pure" systems—one dominated by compulsion (which, after all, appears to be the central core of law as a fact), the other based on the acceptance by group members of norms issued by an authority recognized by them. Both systems tend to evolve and to meet one another. In the former system, there emerge collective customs caused by interest in avoiding compulsion when compulsion becomes rarer; the collective custom tends to produce spontaneous, disinterested impulses having the stamp of validity. In the latter system, the authority resorts to compulsion only in exceptional cases, when authority as such does not suffice: after a while, compulsion establishes itself as the real state of things. In reality, development does not start from any one of these extremes, but there is a genuine interaction and fusion between the two factors. The phenomenon thus created is a particular social order. (The statement by Ross is probably a *lapsus calami;* what is emerging is *legal* order.) The discussion of the fusion of two primarily independent phenomena strikingly resembles Timasheff's views on the merger of ethical group conviction and power into law.

The social (or legal) order, continues Ross, must have an organized procedure for the (valid) exertion of physical coercion (valid stands here, of course, for the experience of validity). Moreover, it must contain an element of authority for the establishment of (generally compulsive) rules for what is valid (to be experienced as valid). In other words, the law is a social system that implies judicial and legislative power.

Although, in Ross's schematic presentation of the emergence of law, compulsion plays a large part (one of the two systems involved is entirely based on it, and the other uses it in exceptional cases), he denies the possibility of reducing the reality of law to manifest or latent coercion. Some rules, he says, derive their power from their own authority—from the belief in their validity. What he probably has is mind is the fact that these rules are issued by authorities whose rules are commonly endowed with sanctions. It is impossible, he continues, to separate these non-sanctioned rules from other rules because, all together, they constitute a coherent whole. But, somewhat inconsistently, Ross is inclined to classify international law as part of conventional morality (which he opposes to personal morality) with some characteristics derived from the law.

Geiger: Law as a Distinctive Sector of the Social Order. Of equal importance is a work written by a German scholar, Theodor Geiger. His *Vorstudien zu einer Soziologie des Rechts* (1947) is characterized by ample use of symbolic notation. In his opinion, the sociology of law must study actual relations. This is the position of the Upsala school, of which he declares himself to be a member; but the sociological shortcomings of the school must be overcome. Especially, the denial of the norm must be replaced by its reduction to reality—that is, discovery of the actuality behind the norm. These statements are directed against the theories of the older members of the school; Alf Ross's work, which appeared one year before Geiger's, was probably unknown to him.

In a very abridged form, Geiger's ideas may be summarized as follows: Social order is coordination of the behavior of group members. Law is a specific structure of order within a social aggregate. Its nature may therefore be best discovered by studying social order in general. Within the social aggregate there exists a definite relationship between situations and behavior; for the observer, this relationship is reflected in social expectations. Legal order is then an observable regularity in group life; from this regularity, we may infer rules that are distinct from verbal norms. These real rules may be habitual, but they may also be intentionally issued. A norm exists (is real) if the relationship $s–g$ is endowed with binding force (v). Put another way, a norm is real if there exists an exterior power that in situation s pushes A towards g. The reality of a norm is, consequently, the probability of its effectiveness, a statement traceable to Max Weber.

The exterior pressure may be exerted by all group members collectively, by specified segments of the group, by the victim of misbehavior, or by a special agency endowed with the function to react in the name of the whole group. Despite all these pressures, instead of g, behavior $\bar{g}$, or its opposite, is possible; then, pressure becomes reaction, r. In the final account, the reality of v is neither obedience nor reaction, but exactly intermediate to these two. The cause of this phenomenon (binding force) is social interdependence; this probably means that v (in the meaning described) is necessary for group survival.

Law is, therefore, only part of the social order. The social order becomes "legal" if the social aggregate, in the midst of which it develops, is a state. The state is a supreme power structure. Law is possible only in a differentiated *milieu* where an overwhelming central power has arisen—a view which is in accordance with the views of the majority of German as well as of American jurists. Law is, however, never the *only* social order; but we do not know either why some of the patterns emerging in a certain society are endowed with v or what is the principle of selection that separates legal from non-legal rules. In these remarks, Geiger seems to display an ignorance of sociology similar to that he ascribes to the Upsala school. Since Tarde, a rather complete theory of social change has developed that may be well used in answering the questions posed by Geiger. Moreover, in *Society, Culture, and Personality,* Sorokin has shown at least preliminary insight into the problem of the selection of norms to be endowed with sactions enforced by the state.

The Conversion of Power into Law. Contrary to Olivecrona, Geiger asserts that, functionally, power precedes law. This is obvious because, to achieve dominant power—that is integral power in equilibrium—one must first use natural power. Geiger has many things to say about the consequences of the emergence of law and of the endowment of norms with power. The effects of the first fact are these: (1) reaction, instead of being spontaneous, becomes organized; (2) norms appear concerning reaction to g; (3) special agencies are formed to carry out these reactions; (4) the activities of these agencies are regulated; (5) a monopoly of reaction is created in their favor.

Effects of the second fact are these: (1) the probability of voluntary obedience is increased; (2) the issuing of legislative norms by agencies receives a high probability of molding the conduct of the citizen; (3) the sanctions imposed by the competent agencies are regularly carried out. These statements are similar to those contained in Timasheff's *Introduction to the Sociology of Law*. This is an obvious case of "parallel invention," since Timasheff's book was unknown to Geiger.

Other Representatives of the Upsala Orientation. The Upsala school comprises many other sociologists, but only two can be mentioned here: A Finnish scholar, O. Brusiin, the author of *Ueber die Objektivität der Rechtssprechung* (1949) and *Ueber das juristische Denken* (1951), concentrates on finding "sociological constants" in the law and the courts. Among these, he emphasizes the very existence of the courts and the tendency of the judicial practice toward objectivity—that is, the elimination, in decisions, of all elements extraneous to the case. To substantiate his statements, the author studies a number of mechanisms: the structure of the courts; the regulation of procedure; control of public opinion (which, he acknowledges, may work against objectivity); the obligation imposed on the judges to justify their decisions; the reliance on precedents; the supervision by ministries of justice; sanctions against eventual lawbreakers among the judges; and the structure of legal education. Taken together, these mechanisms create a remarkable unity in judicial practice, contrary to the alarmist statements of the early American neo-realists. But, the author concedes, his material is largely normative and his constants obtain only in advanced Western civilization.

Like Brusiin, Lahtinen (*Zum Aufbau der rechtlichen Grundlagen,* 1951) is inclined to regard science, including the science of law, as the search for constants. His main effort is directed towards the exploration of the main legal constant covered by the elusive term "ought." He begins by defining demand *(Forderung)*. This term denotes a situation in which *A*, by definite means, tries to cause *B* to behave in a definite way. Looking at the situation from the point of view of *B* reveals something quite different: what is connoted by the term "ought"—a very dubious statement indeed. Neither is Lahtinen's attempt realistically to identify the law very fruitful. He seems to move along a dangerous path in separating norms into conscious and emotional types, which, he believes, are identical with "legal standards" of American jurisprudence.

The development of the Upsala school can be summarized as follows. From the rather negative and sometimes eclectic positions of Hägerström and Olivecrona it has made a tremendous advance best presented in the works of Ross and Geiger. These works seem to show at least one possible way toward the solution of the major problem of the sociology of law: the realistic explanation of normative elements inherent in it. Many of their statements could and should inspire research projects to be executed in the manner customary in American sociology—by concrete case studies and investigations of the statistical type.

Contributions of Legal Philosophers

A fifth group of efforts to integrate law with society and culture is represented by the contributions of legal philosophers more or less affected by the emergence of the sociology of law. Of course, very few contributions can be surveyed here. One of the most significant developments is this area has been the conversion of Hans Kelsen. In the beginning of his brilliant career, Kelsen wrote that a sociological concept of law was just as impossible as a mathematical concept of a biological phenomenon or an ethical concept of a physical phenomenon;[17] a few years later he devoted a book to the refutation of the very *possibility* of a sociology of law.[18] But during the thirties he began to acknowledge that a sociological study of law was possible provided it did not interfere with the pure, exclusively normative theory of law. In a more recent book, he has declared that, since the laws of natural science are now formulated as assertions of statistical probability instead of absolute certainty, there exists no essential difference between natural and social laws.[19]

Kelsen never could avoid reference to law as fact. According to his view, all legal norms are valid because they have been created in accordance with a "basic norm" that cannot be derived from any superior norm. This basic norm is commonly a *constitution:* "Ultimately," he writes, "we reach some constitution that is the first historically and that was laid down by an individual usurper or by some kind of assembly."[20] There may be a sequence of constitutions, and there are also revolutions; in the latter case, the order in force is overthrown and replaced by a new order in a way which the former had not anticipated. This means that the validity of legal rules ultimately depends on a social fact—the existence of a political power that is able and willing to sustain the legal system. We have already met similar ideas when discussing Olivecrona; but, of course, uncontested priority belongs to Kelsen.

Horvath and the Interrelation Between Law and Power. Among the contributions of European legal philosophers, that of Barna Horvath should be mentioned first. In 1934 he published a book in German, entitled *Rechts-*

[17] Hans Kelsen, "Eine Grundlegung der Rechtssoziologie," *ASS* (1915).

[18] Kelsen, *Der juristische und der soziologische Staatsbegriff* (Tübingen, 1922).

[19] Kelsen, *Society and Nature* (Chicago, 1943), p. 266.

[20] Kelsen, *General Theory of Law* (Cambridge, Mass., 1945), p. 115.

soziologie, that is very definitely of philosophical inspiration. After a thorough discussion of the relation of the sociology of law to other sciences, expecially jurisprudence, he concentrates his attention on the correlation of law on the one hand, and economics, combat, power, knowledge, and procedure, on the other. The purpose is praiseworthy, because very few studies of correlation exist. But, unfortunately, the author's philosophical position forces him to treat every problem from the points of view of historical evolution, social correlation, juridico-logical fluctuation, and axiological limitation.

Of these correlation studies, that of power seems to be most constructive. From the very beginning, says Horvath, objective power depends as much on the law as the law depends on power. Power is instrumental for the law. If one identifies law with the regularities obtaining in a society and achieved through a complicated procedural apparatus, then law, as structure, is also the prerequisite of social power. It is, however, wrong to assume that power presupposes law. This is true only of supreme social power. Power is the probability that a certain human action becomes the condition of another human action, a statement obviously inspired by Weber. In small groups, this can be achieved by person-to-person contact. But in "a large human society, personal charm cannot work directly; so here, without law, only unstable power relations may obtain."

But the multiplicity of the points of view forces the author to make statements inconsistent with those just reported. All things considered, he says, law is not grounded in power; to be valid and efficient, it requires not so much power as *freedom.* Power is necessary when resistance is met. But no power can exist in opposition to a well-developed procedural apparatus; under such conditions, power must either become law or cease to exist—a statement which can be easily refuted by pointing to such organizations as the Mafia and Camorra in Italy and the revolutionary organizations in Ireland and Russia that survived decades of struggle against a well-developed apparatus of state coercion.

Schindler: Law as a Social Constant. At approximately the same time as Horvath, the Swiss jurist D. Schindler published a book entitled *Verfassungsrecht und soziale Struktur;* in 1944 a second edition appeared, and the author was preparing a third when death interrupted his labor. His disciples published a posthumous volume entitled *Recht, Staat, Volksgemeinschaft* (1948) that incorporates several articles and unpublished manuscripts. The starting point of Schindler's analysis is the proposition that the nature of law is to transfer that which *ought to be* into that which *is.* Law is not only norm, but also fact. This is the ineluctable dualism that has become the main problem of the Upsala school. Schindler, interested in the same problem, offers a quite different solution.

Existence of an approximately universal human nature, he says, breaks through conflicting ideologies and imposes itself in approximately identical regulations of specified fields because they correspond with the nature of things and human nature. In spite of all variations, social life is grounded in *constants* that appear as structures and functions. Their study is among the major tasks of the social sciences.

One of these structures is the law. The kind of reality that distinguishes the legal norm from other norms is the state, for the relationship of law to the state is essential. That which makes a norm legal is its incorporation into a state organization. Even norms of international law are related to the state. Contrary to common opinion, Schindler holds that power behind the legal norms must not be overwhelming; it suffices that power *could* be applied. But this is only one dimension of law. The law is also oriented to *ethics*. Positive law needs, as foundation, something transcending it; this is the idea of law. At this point Schindler, like many legal philosophers, appears to believe that one can create a kind of yardstick that, applied to norms, can determine whether or not they are legal. But this formidable problem arises: The state, endowed with power, may impose a coercive order that does not correspond to the idea of law. This is unjust law—a law that "ought not to be." The solution offered by Schindler is this: *theoretically,* the decisive factor is the legal idea; but, *in practice,* the final decision belongs to the state.

Haesaert: An Instrumental Philosophy of Law. Recently, Jean Haesaert, a Belgian jurist, legal philosopher, and sociologist, has published a series of works[21] from which can be derived the fundamentals of a sociological theory of law. The jurists, he says, agree that there is "legal reality." What is it? The social order consists of functional relations of varied human activities; they converge and form complex wholes that can be reduced to a limited number of broad categories. Of these potential activities, the systems retain only those required to constitute such systems and, depending on conditions, grant them the freedom to go ahead or to subside. In legal terms, these activities become rights and obligations. This is very close to the derivation, in American sociology, of statuses and roles.

The legal sphere of life, so constituted, is a particular manner of realizing social ends by means of human activities considered instrumental by those who apply them. This way of achieving social ends is based on the fact that those engaged in the corresponding activities consider themselves bound in such a way that there is no possibility of acting otherwise. (At another point, the author formulates this proposition somewhat differently, declaring that the persons involved consider the corresponding norms "unconditionally obligatory," a statement in the style of Stammler's legal philosophy.) Nevertheless, the underlying imperatives are considered to be categorical, although the system is willed and artificial and not based on natural necessity. In accordance with these imperatives, the parties interpret and carry out their

[21] Jean Haesaert, *Essai de sociologie* (Brussels, 1946); *Théorie générale du droit* (Brussels, 1948); *Préalables du droit international public* (Brussels, 1950).

relations; they consider the situations and the relations to be as necessary as physical causality. This, then, is the criterion of a legal rule.

The legal phenomenon is therefore a *technique* that must meet the approval of the community. It is produced by correlated mental attitudes of *coercion* and *obedience*. The former is spontaneous; the latter is originally tied to immediate violence, but is also partly based on religion and on the emergence of individuals to whom the competence of making law is ascribed (an idea akin to that of Alf Ross). In advanced society, immediate coercion is replaced by conditioned reflexes.

Haesaert is a recognized expert in international law. Therefore, he must relate his general theory to international law, and he does so in the following manner: When the states desire to bind themselves unconditionally, nothing prevents their doing so. But once they have chosen to submit their relations to law, they are bound as unconditionally as if they were bound by natural causality. Here the Belgian scholar abandons the standpoint of realism (which is that of the sociology of law) and seeks refuge in the natural-law proposition *pacta sunt servanda*.

Coing and a Formalistic Philosophy of Law. Much less sociologically relevant is the work of the most representative of German postwar legal philosophers, V. Coing, whose work is entitled *Grundzüge der Rechtsphilosophie* (1950). Law is a binding order of human relations within a human group, but it is only one of the forms under which people live together. The legal order must not be confused with human representations about the law, because it is there even if at a given time nobody thinks of it. The law is an order that is (1) durable; (2) abstract (typological); (3) anticipatory (forming part of the conscious molding of life); (4) based on human decisions (in which instincts participate); and (5) imperative. It is finally grounded on conformity with moral norms, which, of course, is an unrealistic proposition.

Pound: The Incomplete Search for a Functional Philosophy of Law. When one turns to the contributions of American jurisprudence and legal philosophy (outside the neo-realistic school already discussed), one cannot but begin by pointing to Roscoe Pound's work, which started before World War I and has continued until the present day. It must, however, be acknowledged that his work has remained on the periphery of the sociology of law, since it has been devoted to sociological jurisprudence.[22] In that direction, Pound has mainly followed the lead of the German *Interessenjurisprudenz* initiated by R. Jhering and best represented by Philipp Heck.[23] From the very start, Pound has emphasized that jurisprudence has to look more to the working of law than to its abstract content and lay more stress on the social purposes it subserves than upon sanctions. In later works, he has distinguished between "law in books" and "law in life" and attempted to distin-

[22] *Cf.* Timasheff, *An Introduction to the Sociology of Law,* pp. 25-29.

[23] M. Magdalena Schoch (ed.), *The Jurisprudence of Interests* (Cambridge, Mass., 1948).

guish three different things in law: the legal order; the authoritative methods in which to find the ground of judicial and administrative determination; and the judicial process. But, remaining on the level of sociological jurisprudence, he has never tried to formulate theoretical propositions about the relationship between law in books and in life, or between the three components just mentioned. In the forties, he contributed a chapter on the sociology of law to Gurvitch and Moore's *Twentieth Century Sociology*. There, as in innumerable articles, he has displayed his incomparable ability for systematically surveying and critically analyzing the theories on the subject. But one can hardly find there any statement that could be reported as Pound's sociology of law.

Cairns: Law as a System of Invariant Factors. Closer to the common preoccupations of the sociologist of law stands Huntington Cairns' *Theory of Legal Science* (1941). Like Hägerström (with whose work Cairns is probably not familiar), Cairns sees the starting point for study not in order, but in human behavior as a function of *disorder*. Yet this does not mean very much, since it is immediately recognized that order is a necessary element in all societal achievements and is the primary objective of social control (to which law obviously belongs). The ideal of a theoretical science of law is the formulation of statements asserting invariant or almost invariant relations in the field and the organization of such principles into a coherent system. More exactly, the theoretical science of law (Cairns does not use the term "sociology of law") should have as object not law itself, but human behavior influenced by or in relation to it.

Nevertheless, Cairns must define the law, and he does it according to the common opinion of the jurists: law is identified with the order of politically organized society. This does not preclude the fact that legal rules are often obeyed entirely apart from any thought of the judicial process or compulsion; but they are distinguished from customary rules in that behind them lies a specific agency of political society for their enforcement.

According to Cairns' view of the science of law, one of the main objectives is the isolation of invariants or constants. In his opinion, in all areas in which relatively homogeneous systems of law prevail, these six constants are observable: (1) regulation of behavior with regard to persons; (2) associations; (3) the structure of the community; (4) property; (5) promises (in the sense of acts preparatory to contracts, etc.); and (6) administration, including the political system. Relative to these constants, he seeks to establish uniformities of change, not in the sense of *evolutionary* stages, but of universally recurring mechanisms. In each change he sees the appearance of new relations and tries to enumerate their physical and psychic elements. The physical elements are time, space, and interaction; the psychic factors are communication, isolation, association, and social distance. He hopes that, on the basis of this list of elements, a comparative study of the six constants could yield material for a quantitative study of change. No specimen of such a study is, however, offered. One cannot but feel skeptical about the outcome of such an enterprise. As Horvath correctly observes,[24] the constants chosen by Cairns are much too complicated to serve as elements for a historico-comparative analysis aiming at theoretically fruitful results.

Law as the Coalescence of Formal, Valuational, and Factual Aspects. Another work in the field, Jerome Hall's *Living Law of Democratic Society* (1949), is somewhat disappointing for a legal sociologist just because, in another work, to be discussed below, Hall has displayed an exceptional ability to think along sociological lines. In *Living Law,* Hall comes to rather unrealistic conclusions. The main purpose of the book is to answer the question: What is positive law—a question that cannot but preoccupy the legal sociologist. The inquiry is conducted in three stages. First, the legal method is investigated and the conclusion is that positive law consists of propositions having the form of hypothetical imperative judgments and that the formal source and the enforcer of these rules is the maximum power center of society. The second step of the inquiry shows that an element of *valuation* is inherent in law; in other words, the rules of law are coalescences of ideas with values. This can hardly be denied; more dubious, however, is the proposition that there exists intuitive knowledge of answers to moral problems, so that the better ones are defensible. The third step consists in the study of law as a cultural fact, which gives Hall's work socio-legal relevance. The findings are quite meager. Legal rules, says the outhor, contain generalizations about facts, but what he probably intends to say is that, in drawing these rules, men rely on recurring observations of facts.

These three steps are then integrated in the statement that law is a distinctive coalescence of *form, value,* and *fact.* The value element as understood by Hall compels him, however, to distinguish among state norms (a term appearing in the later parts of the book), legal norms, and other types of norms that he calls power norms, technical state rules, and so on. It is, however, obvious that the courts apply all these types of norms indifferently, that the professors at the law schools teach all of them, and that functionally (*i.e.*, in their action in society) they form one class. This shows that Hall's attempt to limit law to what conforms to our impeccable moral judgment does not stand the test of adequacy.

The acceptance of the very idea of a sociology of law by legal philosophers has remained incomplete. In any case, in one of the recent and most comprehensive books on the subject, Julius Stone's *The Province and Function of Law,* one finds the idea rejected because, in the author's opinion, the very distinction between nomothetic and idiographic sciences has become obsolete.[25]

[24] Barna Horvath, "Neuere Richtungen in der Rechtsphilosophie in den Vereinigten Staaten and Skandinavien," *Oesterreichsche Zeitschrift für offentliches Recht,* 6 (1953), p. 70.

[25] Julius Stone, *The Province and Function of Law* (2nd ed.; Sydney, 1950), p. 394.

Cultural Anthropology: Malinowski

The sixth and last group of efforts to be considered involves the work of some outstanding cultural anthropologists. During the period under review, the prevailing tendency has been to assert the existence of law in very early stages of social and cultural development, which requires dropping the attribute of organized coercion from the concept of law. This tendency has a conspicuous parallel, as we have seen, in the works of Petrazhitsky and some of his followers.

Most representative has been Malinowski:

> There must be in all societies a class of rules too practical to be backed by religious sanctions, too burdensome to be left to mere goodwill, too personally vital to individuals to be enforced by any abstract agency. This is the domain of legal rules. The positive law governing all phases of tribal life consists of a body of binding obligations, regarded as right by one party and acknowledged as a duty by the other and kept in force by a specific mechanism of reciprocity and publicity inherent in the structure of their society. . . .
>
> . . .Such rules are sanctioned not by a mere psychological motive, but by a definite social machinery of binding force based upon mutual dependence.[26]

This position is, however, untenable because the distinction between legal and non-legal rules is in fact projected by the proponents of the theory into primitive society on the basis of their knowledge of the scope of law in advanced society. In a later work, *A Scientific Theory of Culture* (1942), Malinowski has expressed in a rather vague form the view that, for the understanding of culture, especially of its normative elements, one must resort to the learning theory of modern physiology and psychology.

Statuses as Foci of Rights and Duties: Linton. Ralph Linton has made contributions of quite a different kind. In his *Study of Man* (1936), he has offered a functional and realistic theory of "ideal patterns," a term he prefers to the term "norms." Society must develop more or less conscious patterns of expected behavior for individuals in certain positions. These ideal patterns are, however, quite different from actual behavior. As systems of ideas, they become part of the culture of the group and are transmitted from generation to generation. The patterns rarely if ever achieve a complete expression in behavior. But behavior is strongly influenced by them, since they are constantly demonstrated to individuals as models. The fact that they are shared by many members of the society gives them a super-individual character.

[26] Bronislaw Malinowski, *Crime and Custom in Savage Society* (London, 1926), pp. 55, 67-68.

They possess a substantial degree of organization and are susceptible to objective study.

In connection with ideal patterns, or norms, Linton has suggested the introduction into sociology of the concepts of status and role, and, as is well known, his suggestion has received wide acceptance. Ideal patterns, says Linton, determine reciprocal behavior between individuals and groups. The polar positions in such patterns are *statuses*. A status is a position in a particular pattern; it is simply a collection of rights and duties. The *role* represents the dynamic aspect of a status; when the individual puts the rights and duties that constitute the status into effect, he performs a role.

It is noteworthy that, as shown in previous sections, about the time when Linton suggested the incorporation of the legal concepts of rights and duties into general sociology, doubts arose in the sociology of law as to their reality. Therefore, one of the basic topics of the sociology of law (much discussed by the Petrazhitsky group and the Upsala school) coincides with one of the basic problems of general sociology. It must be acknowledged that the sociologists of law have not yet succeeded in conveying to sociologists at large the idea that, when accepting the concepts of status and role, they face new and difficult problems.

The Search for "Legal Constants": Conflict and Sanctions. Largely of anthropological inspiration is a remarkable book written by Karl Llewellyn, an outstanding member of the neo-realist school, in collaboration with the ethnologist, E. A. Hoebel. In this volume, entitled *The Cheyenne Way* (1941), the authors, following the view of many cultural anthropologists, make an attempt to discover law in simple, undifferentiated societies lacking any machinery for enforcement; and then, by comparison with contemporary American law and, incidentally, with Roman law, try to find "legal constants." The findings are approximately these:

The "law-stuff" is furnished by the integration of persons in groups and the correlative patterning of their behavior with the rise of divergent urges and claims among group members. Thus the "law stuff" is intimately related to *conflict* situations. But law is not the totality of group order. That part of the social order is legal that is endowed with sanctions, that prevails in conflicts with other parts of the order (a very dubious proposition indeed), and that has an aspect of officialdom.

However, one is not obliged to accept the authors' theorem that an order complying with the above criteria is *legal;* on the contrary, one may with good reason consider it *pre-legal,* and use the findings of the coauthors (as well as those of Malinowski) in constructing a sociological theory of the emergence of law.

Social Change and the Law: A Case Study. Somewhat outside all the groups of efforts directed towards the construction of a sociology of law, there stands a unique work, Jerome Hall's *Theft, Law, and Society* (1935;

especially 2nd ed., 1952). The book is primarily a study in legal history, but it is a study undertaken with the understanding of "the need for scientific knowledge of interpersonal conduct in relation to law."[27] More specifically, the author wanted to find out whether there is a one-way process, or something more complex in operation between economic institutions and law. He chose eighteenth-century England as a laboratory because the social and legal problems of that period were obviously related to major social changes.

On the basis of his concrete studies, the author has formulated these generalizations: (1) The functioning of courts is significantly related to concomitant cultural needs. (2) The chronological order of the principal phases of legal change is *(a)* lag between substantive law and social needs; *(b)* spontaneous efforts of judges, other officials, and laymen to make successful adaptation; and *(c)* legislation. (3) The law-process represented in the norm-oriented and directed conduct of large sections of the population provides the conceptual framework of legal sociology.

Of course, these generalizations are not spectacularly new; but one may believe that, if several studies of a similar type—that is, studies of legal history with an eye to the problems of the sociology of law—are carried out with the insight and penetration of a Jerome Hall, the sociology of law will be provided with valuable building-stones.

Conclusion

This survey of the development of the sociology of law since World War I seems to demonstrate that advance has not been spectacular. Two factors have obviously inhibited progress: first, the disruption of communication among scholars of various nationalities, especially during World War II and the years immediately following it; second, the scarcity of scholars trained both in sociology and jurisprudence. Although the first of these unfavorable factors is passing, the second is here to stay—especially in America, where the lawyers and sociologists are trained in separate schools.

There are also favorable factors, however. They lie in the recent advances in the general theory of society and culture and in the theory of the interaction between culture and personality, especially of the internalization of cultural items. These new advances seem to pave the way for the solution of the difficult problem of how to "reduce" norms or ideas to social reality consisting of human behavior and attitudes. As a by-product, Max Weber's probabilistic approach may receive a solid foundation.

[27] Jerome Hall, *Theft, Law, and Society* (2nd ed.; Boston, 1952), p. v.

Furthermore, modern views on the social system may offer an adequate conceptual scheme for the analysis, first, of the relatively narrow social system centered around the court (here questions posed by Yntema should be explored) and, second, of the total system insofar as it is influenced by law as an instrument of peace essential for the survival and development of society.

SELECTED BIBLIOGRAPHY

Ehrlich, Eugen, *Fundamental Principles of the Sociology of Law,* translated by Walter L. Moll (Cambridge: Harvard University Press, 1936).

Gurvitch, Georges, *Sociology of Law* (New York: Philosophical Library, 1942).

Hoebel, E. Adamson, *The Law of Primitive Man* (Cambridge: Harvard University Press, 1955).

Petrazhitsky, Leo, *Law and Morality* (Cambridge: Harvard University Press, 1954).

Seagle, William, "Sociological Trends in Modern Jurisprudence," in H. E. Barnes, Howard Becker, and Frances B. Becker, *Contemporary Social Theory* (New York: D. Appleton-Century, 1940). See also bibliographical appendix, pp. 898-900.

Simpson, S. P., and Julius Stone, with the collaboration of M. Magdalena Schoch, *Cases and Readings on Law and Society* (St. Paul, Minn.: West Publishing Co., 1948-49).

Timasheff, N.S., *An Introduction to the Sociology of Law* (Cambridge, Mass.: Harvard University Press, 1939).

Weber, Max, *Max Weber on Law in Economy and Society,* translated by E. A. Shils and Max Rheinstein (Cambridge, Mass.: Harvard University Press, 1954).

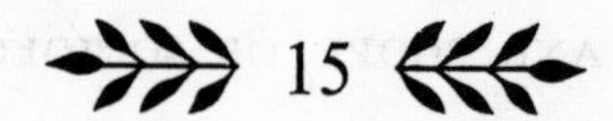

15

SOCIOLOGY OF RELIGION: COMPLEMENTARY ANALYSES OF RELIGIOUS INSTITUTIONS

PAUL HONIGSHEIM

SINCE WORLD WAR I, THE ROLE OF RELIGION HAS BEEN OF INCREASED importance, at least in some countries and among some social groups, and interest in the sociology of religion has also increased. Historically, Thomas Aquinas, Franciscan Nominalists, Jesuit missionaries, British and French exponents of the Enlightenment, and German Romanticists had shown interest in the relationship between religion and social structure. Their work, however, cannot be said to constitute a sociology of religion, if we define this discipline as a special science that tries to build up a system of statements concerning relations between religion and group life. In this sense, the sociology of religion actually originated and developed in the nineteenth century. But among the groups in the nineteenth century that showed interest in religion and accordingly could be supposed to have been productive within the field of sociology of religion, we can once and for all omit the American pragmatists, as well as some American philosophers of other schools, such as Royce, Santayana, and Whitehead, from whom a contribution in this field might be expected, but whose contribution is actually not very substantial.

Seven groups made widely noticed and influential contributions prior to World War I. These groups remained in existence after the war, and some of their members continued to pursue studies that are of importance to the sociology of religion. The seven groups[1] are as follows: (1) pre-

[1] Surveys of the schools that played roles of relative importance before World War II may be found in Paul Honigsheim, "Romantik und neuromantische Bewegungen,"

Marxian socialists and Marxians of more or less orthodox attitude; (2) Darwinian evolutionists; (3) positivists such as Auguste Comte, Émile Durkheim, and their schools; (4) Catholics, who first perpetuated romanticism with Platonic-Augustinian elements, as represented by Frohschammer, Günther, Knoodt, Vogelsang, and others, and then increasingly reactivated scholasticism, especially Neo-Thomism; (5) psychoanalysts, at that time still mainly interested in traits supposedly common to all men (such as the Oedipus situation) as well as in religious behavior, which they presumed to be connected with such attitudes; (6) anthropologists (who partly overlapped with the aforementioned groups), who considered religious groups, originally and mainly in Europe and the United States, to be independent parallel developments; then, in contrast to this and primarily in the German and Austrian schools of Graebner and Wilhelm Schmidt and their Latin-American followers, from the viewpoint of diffusion of cultural goods, of forms of life and kinds of religious groups; (7) German neo-Kantians, such as Georg Jellinek, Ernst Troeltsch, and Max Weber. Weber, especially, in part following Heinrich Rickert, elaborated an epistemological system on which he based his religio-sociological system, most of which was published posthumously and which gained a number of adherents.

Weber, prior to World War I, made the following important assertions.[2] The religio-ethico-political sphere and the sphere of special sciences are distinguished from one another; sociology, among other disciplines, is classed with the latter. Within sociology, judgments of value must be excluded. States, churches, and other sociological phenomena must be, in the mind of the investigator, nothing but terms used in a strictly nominalistic sense, to denote patterns of ongoing collective activities. These patterns can be classified by the use of so-called "ideal types," and it is feasible to

HSW (Stuttgart, 1953), and "Neukantianismus," *ibid.* (forthcoming); Howard Becker and H. E. Barnes, *Social Thought from Lore to Science* 2nd ed. (New York, 1952), vol. 1, Chaps. 17-20, and vol. 2, Chap. 22; Howard Becker, *Through Values to Social Interpretation* (Durham, N.C., 1950), Chap. 3; H. E. Barnes (ed.), *An Introduction to the History of Sociology* (Chicago, 1948), Parts 3 and 4.

[2] The main writings of Max Weber dealing with epistemology and methodology are collected in Max Weber, *Gesammelte Aufsätze zur Wissenschaftslehre* (Tübingen, 1951), especially pp. 146-565. Some of his writings are also collected in Max Weber, *Schriften zur theoretischen Soziologie; zur Soziologie der Politik und Verfassung* (Frankfurt/Main, 1947). Translations of *some* of this material appear in *Max Weber on the Methodology of the Social Sciences,* translated and edited by E. A. Shils and H. A. Finch (Glencoe, Ill., 1949).

For description of the personality of the man and the framework into which Weber's epistemology and sociology of religion are incorporated, see the following writings of Paul Honigsheim: "Max Weber als Soziologe," *KVS,* 1 (1921); "Max Webers geistesgeschichtliche Stellung," *Die Volkswirte,* 5 (1930); "Max Weber as Historian of Agriculture," *Agricultural History,* 23 (1943); "Max Weber: His Religious and Ethical Background and Development," *Church History,* 19 (1950); "Weber, Max," *HSW* (forthcoming); "Neukantianismus," *ibid.* (with detailed bibliography).

make statements concerning the possibility of regularity of sequence of such types.

CRITERIA FOR ANALYZING PERTINENT STUDIES

Such, in brief, was the situation of the sociology of religion at the beginning of World War I. In dealing with the sociology of religion since that time, several practices will be observed. The term *religion* will be used to denote every attitude based on, and connected with, the convictions that supernatural forces exist and that relations with them are possible and significant. Publications dealing exclusively or primarily with religiously based social-reform programs will not be considered in this study, and value-judgments on social or religious phenomena will be avoided, as well as judgments concerning correctness and suitability of methods used and statements made (except in our concluding section). In the three sections that follow, pertinent material will be analyzed according to: (1) the epistemological and methodological conceptions used regarding sociology of religion; (2) the contributions to the sociological aspect of *special* religio-cultural items; and (3) contributions to *general* concepts of religio-sociological character. The concluding section will contain evaluation of the suitability of the methods and contributions described in the three sections that precede it.

The Range of Methodological Premises in Sociology of Religion

Certain groups of sociologists will be excluded from this survey of methodology because they did not contribute to the epistemological background of sociology of religion. These include the disciples of prewar socialists, Darwinists, and positivists, as well as the postwar Existentialist philosophers and the somewhat existentialistically minded theologians—much discussed at the present time—Karl Barth, Reinhold Niebuhr, and Albert Schweitzer. Six groups remain, then, as representatives of the various types of methodology in sociology of religion.

Catholics.[3] After romantic Catholicism had lost much of its influence as a result of the ascendency of neo-scholasticism, there developed within

[3] Gustav Gundlach, *Zur Soziologie der katholischen Ideenwelt und des Jesuitenordens* (Freiburg, 1927), p. 20; Alois Dempf, "Kulturphilosophie," *Handbuch der Philosophie* (Munich, 1932), pp. 109 *ff.;* "Die Hauptform mittelalterlicher Weltanschauung," *ibid.* (1925), p. 67. As to the history of these controversies, see E. K. Winter, *Die Sozialmetaphysik der Scholastik* (Leipzig, 1929).

the latter group an antagonism between, on the one hand, an older, mainly Dominican concept according to which economic and social sciences, including sociology, were a branch of theology, and, on the other hand, a concept according to which the social sciences were relatively independent of theology. The second of these concepts was represented mainly by Jesuit fathers such as Pesch, Nell-Breuning, and Gundlach who individually made further differentiations in the concept. Gundlach in particular aimed at a formal, *verstehende* sociology of a special cultural item—the Catholic religion. Largely independent of all of them is Aloys Dempf, who considers the sociology of religion (as well as the sociology of knowledge and other fields) as a special branch of cultural sociology. He makes use of Max Weber and developed, among other things, the new category *geschichtstheologische Kulturanschauungen* —concepts about culture that are themselves based on a theological concept of history.

The Modern Psychoanalysts. Fromm and his followers are the foremost members of this group.[4] The psychoanalysts have emphasized, among other things, problems concerning special kinds of relations of individuals to groups, among them religious groups, including those of "primitive" peoples.

Anthropologists. Whereas in Europe and Latin America the main antagonism in the field of anthropology was between evolutionary-minded parallelists on the one hand and diffusionists on the other, in the United States the older evolutionism, as represented by Morgan, was superseded by the newer historical school of Boas.[5] This school opposed, first, the evolutionists by refusing to accept their supposedly undemonstrable schemas of regularly occurring sequences and second, the European diffusionists, whom they accused of making allegedly unwarranted one-sided statements. There were some attempts, however, to build a synthesis of European diffusionism and American historicism. Goldenweiser, for example, considered "diffusion, adaptation and invention as omnipresent," and Kroeber asserted that every group, including such uncomplicated groups as the Tasmanian, has its history. Within such groups there may be diffusion, but often it represents an innovation suggested by the observation of a foreign pattern.

This American historical school was then criticized for being unduly satisfied with the historical analysis of special cultures in their uniqueness.

[4] Erich Fromm, *Escape from Freedom* (New York, 1941), pp. 10-14, 23, 248, 280, 290-293, and *Psychoanalysis and Religion* (4th ed.; New Haven, 1952), pp. 10-12, 85, 99-113; Geza Roheim, *Psychoanalysis and Anthropology* (New York, 1950).

[5] Alexander Goldenweiser, "The Diffusion Controversy," in Elliot Smith *et al.*, (eds.), *Culture: The Diffusion Controversy* (New York, 1927); A. L. Kroeber, *The Nature of Culture* (Chicago, 1952), pp. 5, 61-64, 79-84; Bronislaw Malinowski, *Magic, Science and Religion* (Garden City, N.Y., 1952), pp. 23, 145; *The Dynamics of Cultural Change* (New Haven, Conn., 1945), pp. 29, 34; "The Life of Culture," in Smith, *op. cit.*, pp. 40-42.

This criticism was especially directed toward them by the Functionalists, whose best-known representatives, Malinowski and Radcliffe-Brown, expressed, more or less independently, their interest in a culture, not as it had occurred in its historical uniqueness, but rather as an "organic whole." They contended that a culture must be considered "organically" if one is to understand the meaning and significance of any single item of the culture being studied. Separate items can then be understood as they function within the whole. Although the aforementioned antagonisms remained in existence, attempts were made to build a synthesis from these heterogeneous concepts, and Malinowski himself later considered history as an indispensable complement of functionalism.

German Neo-Kantianism After World War I. Troeltsch,[6] in his post-war book, *Der Historismus und seine Probleme,* asserted that the historian must approach religious phenomena primarily from the viewpoint of their uniqueness and their inexplicability by purely rationalistic methods, recognizing both the rare appearance of truly new ones and the importance of new phenomena in the development of Occidental Christian culture. In spite of this limitation, a sociology of religion is possible because history builds these unique phenomena out of substantial elements that are basic to many phenomena and that only at first glance are completely different from one another.

Methodologists Influenced by Neo-Kantian problems. The chief representatives of this group are Wach and Becker. Other studies partially influenced by Neo-Kantian problems—Van der Leeuwe's *Phänomenlogie der Religion,*[7] and Karl Mannheim's sociology of knowledge,[8] are for us of only indirect and specialized importance. Joachim Wach,[9] whose background is German, has written and taught in the United States since the beginning of the Hitler regime. He rejects the neo-Kantian concept of group as a sum of individuals or as collective activity, as well as the elimination of value-judgment. Howard Becker, a native American who received American, German, and French training, initially defines the historian as one who deals with the unique. In order to do so, however, according to Becker, the historian must not only have in mind the traits common to the phenom-

[6] Ernst Troeltsch, *Gesammelte Schriften* (Tübingen, 1912-1925), vol. 3, pp. 1-11, 22-122, 164, 173, 656, 706-720, and vol. 4, pp. 7, 11-13, 25, 118-120. See also J. Milton Yinger, "The Sociology of Religion of Ernst Troeltsch," in Barnes, *op. cit.*, pp. 309-315; Paul Honigsheim, "Troeltsch, Ernst," *HSW* (forthcoming).

[7] Gerardus van der Leeuwe, *Phänomenologie der Religion* (Tübingen, 1933), pp. 223-247, 613-652.

[8] Karl Mannheim, *Ideology and Utopia* (New York, 1936), and *Essays on Sociology and Social Psychology* (New York, 1953).

[9] Joachim Wach, *Sociology of Religion* (2nd ed.; Chicago, 1949), and *Types of Religious Experiences, Christian and Non-Christian* (Chicago, 1951), pp. 3-5, 18; Becker, *Through Values to Social Interpretation* (consult index).

enon to be described in its uniqueness but also those common to comparable phenomena. This is true in the opposite sense for the systematizer, who must base his work upon a knowledge of the particulars of historical phenomena in order to be able to elaborate "constructed types" of general significance. These types, which are different from Max Weber's ideal type, are characterized by the following traits: they must be able to provide the *probability* as well as the possibility of meaningful applicability to the phenomena that are to be classified; moreover, they are neither of a statistico-quantitative nor a wholly qualitative nature; and by virtue of their existence as concepts in the mind of the classifier, exceptions from them within historical reality will necessarily occur.

Intuitionists, Neo-Romanticists, and Anti-Optimists. The following seven men are the main representatives of this group: (1) Oswald Spengler[10] conceives the history of every cultural unit, including its religious life, as a sequence of stages, such as early development, climax, and inescapable decline, following one another automatically. (2) Arnold Toynbee[11] resembles Spengler in his concept of stages through which every culture, including its religion, must pass, but differs by setting aside "abortive" and "arrested" cultures and by being less pessimistic as to the future of Christianity. (3) Othmar Spann[12] and his collaborators, Baxa, Sauter, and Manfred Schroeter, deny the necessity and possibility of eliminating value-judgments, as well as the possibility of obtaining knowledge "individualistically" by the analytical method of special sciences; they insist rather on the perceptibility of entities and apply this concept also to the cognition of religion. (4) Ludwig Klages[13] contrasted intellect, which is supposed to be the "adversary of life," to the emotive psyche or *Seele,* with its intuitive capacity to perceive the essential, and asserted that the latter kind of cognition had been dominant in the matrilinear society with its corresponding religion. (5) Henri Bergson,[14] although he did not deny the need for quantitative analytical investigation, emphasized intuition and *élan vital*, and with this approach attained considerable influence for some time over some French Catholics as well as anarcho-syndicalists. (6) Max Scheler[15] passed

[10] Oswald Spengler, *The Decline of the West,* authorized translation with notes by Charles Francis Atkinson (New York, 1926-1928), 2 vols.

[11] A. J. Toynbee, *A Study of History* (London, 1935-1954), vols. 1 and 6. See also *A Study of History* [abridgment of vols. 1-6] (New York, 1947), pp. 153-55, 168-174, 307-338.

[12] Othmar Spann, *Der wahre Staat* (2nd ed.; Leipzig, 1923).

[13] Ludwig Klages, *Der Geist als Widersacher der Seele* (Leipzig, 1929-1932), 3 vols.

[14] Henri Bergson, *L'Évolution créatrice* (Paris, many editions); and *Les deux sources de la morale et de la religion* (Paris, many editions).

[15] Max Scheler, *Vom Umsturz der Werte* (Leipzig, 1923), 2 vols.; and *Vom Ewigen im Menschen* (Leipzig, 1923). See also Paul Honigsheim, "Max Scheler als Sozialphilosoph," *KVS,* 8 (1929); Helmuth Plessner, "Scheler, Max," *HSW,* pp. 115 ff.

through non-scholastic Catholicism, panentheism, and other stages and considered the emphasis given to reason by Thomism, Neo-Thomism, Kantianism, and Neo-Kantianism as proof of psychical impoverishment; he claimed a *Wesenschau* or "envisagement of essences" as defined by Husserl (i.e., a conception of the essence of an entity in the form of a synopsis combining intuition and reason), and as a form of such a synopsis, also the perception of a religious group as an unitary entity, composed of individuals as well as institutions. (7) Pitirim Sorokin[16] rejects the belief in automatic progress, believes in ever-new recurrence of the same pattern, and classifies cultures according to three types: ideational, idealistic, and sensate. The latter is conceived of as being a primarily rationalist and analytically minded culture; the former, on the contrary, is the culture to which belong the beginnings of every complex religio-ethical system and its founders.

Sociologically Relevant Analyses of Specific Relgiious Systems

From the viewpoint of sociological relevance, we shall examine the contributions to the study of a number of religions systems made by the following groups: the methodologists already mentioned; sociologists and specialists in other fields who have made relevant contributions, such as anthropologists belonging to the various schools mentioned above or following the tradition of Durkheim, as well as Oriental, classical, and other philologists; and Catholic, Protestant, and Jewish theologians of orthodox or Biblio-critical background, including missionaries as well as natives of Oriental countries who may be more or less assimilated into the Occidental culture. In this discussion, no account will be taken of statements about problems that appear in every culture (e.g., Wach's religio-sociological classification of religious groups according to the degree of pessimism toward the world—a topic to be dealt with later) or of problems in which the investigations under consideration—although important from other viewpoints—are religio-sociologically irrelevant.

Preliterate Cultures. The study of preliterate cultures includes four topics principally. First is the causal role of the collective consciousness of the primitive group, as asserted by the Durkheim school but rejected as of metaphysical character by Gurvitch[17] and the functionalist Mali-

[16] P. A. Sorokin, *Social Mobility* (New York, 1927); *Social and Cultural Dynamics* (New York, 1937-1941), 4 vols.; *The Crisis of Our Age* (New York, 1941); *Man and Society in Calamity* (New York, 1942); *Society, Culture, and Personality* (New York, 1947).

[17] Georges Gurvitch, *Essais de sociologie* (Paris, 1938), *passim.*

nowski.[18] Second is the religio-sociological importance of the matrilinear society. This type of society was supposed by Engels and some other Marxians to be connected with collective property. It was conceived by the romanticist Johann Jakob Bachofen,[19] and more recently by Klages and Schroeter and others who were to some extent related to Othmar Spann, as connected with a special kind of mystical insight. The matrilinear society became, then, an object of interest in the diffusionist system of Father Schmidt and in the sociological system of Franz Oppenheimer. Both considered the matrilinear structure as a characteristic element of a cultural cycle that had spread through diffusion. The sociological importance of the matrilinear society has also been emphasized by some psychoanalysts, such as Georg Groddeck, and by the functionalist Malinowski.

The third of these topics is totemism.[20] Its importance as a widely dispersed and very old form of sociologically conditioned religious attitude was asserted by men of such heterogeneous basic attitudes as the French positivists (especially Durkheim), by their antagonist Bergson, and also by psychoanalysts such as Fromm-Reichmann, Rank, Reik, and Zullinger. The psychoanalysts used Freud's attempt to correlate the Oedipus situation and totemism and to interpret religious phenomena that appear in more complex cultures.

The fourth topic included in the study of preliterate cultures is the religio-sociological position and function of the magician.[21] Robertson

[18] Malinowski, *Magic, Science, and Religion,* pp. 19, 25, 34-63, 75-77, 87-88, 124, 140; *Dynamics of Cultural Charge,* p. 49; *Crime and Custom in Savage Society* (New York, 1951), pp. 55, 92-94.

[19] J. J. Bachofen, *Gesammelte Werke* (Basel, 1943-1945). The best selection is *Der Mythos von Orient und Occident aus den Werken von J. J. Bachofen* (Munich, 1926). The most useful survey of the corresponding theories of William Schmidt may be found in S. A. Sieber and F. H. Mueller, *The Social Life of Primitive Man* (St. Louis, 1941), Chaps. 17-23. Cf. also the review of this book by Paul Honigsheim in *ASR,* 6 (1941), pp. 898-902; Franz Oppenheimer, *System der Soziologie* (Jena, 1922-1924), vol. 2, pp. 187-199, and vol. 4, pp. 7-8; Georg Groddeck, "Der Symbolisierungszwang," *Imago,* 13 (1928), p. 219.

As to the history of the whole problem see the following writings of Paul Honigsheim: "Die geistesgeschichtliche Stellung der Anthropologie, Ethnologie, Urgeschichte und ihrer Hauptrichtungen," *Festschrift, Publication d'hommage offerte au P. W. Schmidt* (Vienna, 1928); "Adolf Bastian und die Entwickelung der ethnologischen Sociologie," *KVS,* 6 (1927); "Soziologische Fragestellungen in der gegenwärtigen praehistorischen und ethnologischen Literatur," *ibid.,* 7 (1928).

[20] Émile Durkheim, *Elementary Forms of the Religious Life* (Glencoe, Ill., 1950); Malinowski, *Magic, Science, and Religion,* pp. 44-47; Siegmund Freud, *Totem und Tabu* (Leipzig, 1913); Otto Rank, *Psychoanalytische Beiträge zur Mythenforschung* (Leipzig, 1924); Theodor Reik, *Das Ritual* (2nd ed.; Leipzig, 1924), pp. 88-101, 282-304, and "Psychoanalytische Studien zur Bibelexegese," *Imago,* 5 (1917), p. 381.

[21] Lucien Lévy-Bruhl, *La Mentalité primitive* (Paris, 1922), and *La Mythologie primitive* (Paris, 1935), pp. 45-47, 90, 214-215; Gurvitch, *loc. cit.;* Malinowski, *op. cit.,* pp. 19,

Smith, and more recently Lucien Lévy-Bruhl, considered magic as the beginning of or as a special kind of early religious and prelogical feeling. In contrast, Gurvitch, as well as Malinowski and Ruth Benedict, asserted that the magical attitude is one that is sociologically distinct from religion, is connected with individualism and selfishness, and is involved in a practice undertaken by special persons who are different from priests and who are often disdained, but who, on the other hand, according to Malinowski, are also among the exponents of consequent secularity who prepared the way for science.

Pre-Columbian American Cultures. Various investigators, such as Baudin, Bennett-Bird, Cunow, Emmart, Morley, Thompson, and others,[22] have pointed out certain facts with respect to Indian religions. Among Aztecs and Incas the gods of subjected peoples have been accepted by the conquerors; indeed, priests made a living because the church owned land and magicians functioned among lower classes.

China. Max Weber in his posthumously edited studies described the social position and way of life of the leading group of "gentlemen-intellectuals" of China. Marcel Granet, a French adherent of Durkheim, went into further detail and described the shift from small feudal courts with "wise men" like Confucius as councilors to large, subjugated empires with advisors who knew the techniques of governing. The Chinese Fung-Yu-Lan went even further and insisted on the existence of an interrelation between special kinds of social life and special schools of philosophy, including Taoism. The latter had been described by Max Weber as having originated out of magical techniques with the purpose of vouchsafing a long life, and as having developed into a multitude of sects for people of lower socio-economic status. No essential additions have been made to this analysis up to the present.[23]

Religions of the Hindus. In his posthumously published work, Weber asserted that Hindu philosophers were primarily interested in salvation by means of contemplation and asceticism and that they actually left various

34, 75-88, and *Coral Gardens and Their Magic* (New York, 1935), 2 vols.; Ruth Benedict, *Patterns of Culture* (New York, 1953), pp. 131-132.

[22] Louis Baudin, *L'Empire socialiste des Inkas* (Paris, 1928); Wendell Bennett and J. B. Bird, *Andean Culture History* (New York, 1949), pp. 234-237; Heinrich Cunow, *Geschichte und Kultur des Inkareiches* (Amsterdam, 1937), p. 21; Emily W. Emmart, *The Badianus Manuscript* (Baltimore, 1940), p. 47; S. G. Morley, *The Ancient Maya* (Stanford, 1946), p. 50; Eric Thompson, *Mexico Before Cortez* (New York, 1933), p. 226.

[23] Max Weber, *The Religion of China: Confucianism and Taoism*, translated and edited by H. H. Gerth (Glencoe, Ill., 1951); Marcel Granet, *La Pensée chinoise* (Paris, 1934), pp. 420-427, 554-557; *Chinese Civilization*, translated by Kathleen E. Innes and R. Brailsford (New York, 1951); *La Religion des Chinois* (2nd ed.; Paris, 1951); and *Catégories matrimoniales et relations de proximité dans la Chine ancienne* (Paris, 1939); Fung-Yu-Lan, *A Short History of Chinese Philosophy* (New York, 1948), pp. 18, 37.

spheres of life free of religio-ethical constraint, as for example the politico-economic sphere. To this observation Becker and Wach each independently added that the distinction between more or less perfect men actually led to the toleration of and even stimulated the building up of big states, even under the control of adherents of Buddhism. The case of King Asoka is one in point. Various newer Hindu sects, as well as Buddhism in its changed form outside India, were looked upon by natives such as Chang Lee, Masaharu, Satoni, Zuzuki, and others from the viewpoint of assimilability.[24]

Sikhism. Similar to Buddhism in its rejection of the caste system but rather exceptional because of its incorporation of some Mohammedan elements, this religion has been the object of very little investigation; Weber, for example did not examine it in his unfinished comparative study. It has recently been described, however, by Archer with respect to its shift from a non-aggressive to an activistic peasant (and especially warrior) religion.[25]

Zoroastrianism and Its Continuance in India; Parsism. Although already in the eighteenth century, especially through the work of Anquetill Duperron, Zarathustrianism and Parsism had become an object of interest for adherents of the Enlightenment, they were studied much less than Hinduism by the Romanticists and philologists of the nineteenth century. The books of Ernst Herzfeld and of Dhalla, the latter himself a Parsee high priest, also contain only a few useful remarks on Zoroastrian priests and Parsee assimilation.[26]

Ancient Egypt. According to investigations undertaken by Cerny, Frankfort, Mercer, Wilson, and others, the reputation of gods, temples, and priests depended increasingly on the amount of land owned. The land was accumulated through gifts by the state as a result of its conquests.[27]

Greek Antiquity. The Frenchmen Gernet and Boulanger, who were somewhat guided by Durkheim, have insisted that one of the essential

[24] Max Weber, *The Hindu Social System*, translated and edited by H. H. Gerth and Don Martindale (Minneapolis, 1950); Becker and Barnes, *op. cit.*, vol. 1, pp. 74-81; Joachim Wach, *Sociology of Religion*, pp. 74-81; Shao Chang Lee, *Popular Buddhism in China* (Hawaii, 1939); Anesaki Masaharu, *History of Japanese Religions* (London, 1930), pp. 145, 260-262; Kishis Satoni, *Japanese Civilization* (New York, 1924), pp. 211, 229-231; Daisetz Teitaro Zuzuki, *An Introduction to Zen Buddhism* (New York, 1948), pp. 118-127.

[25] J. C. Archer, *The Sikhs* (Princeton, N.J., 1946), pp. 140-141, 169-170, 196, 233-235.

[26] Karl Geldner, "Die altpersische Literatur," in Paul Hinneberg (ed.), *Die Kultur der Gegenwart* (Berlin, 1906), vol. 1, pp. 233-234; Ernst Herzfeld, *Zoroaster and His World* (Princeton, N.J., 1947), p. 124; M. N. Dhalla, *History of Zoroastrianism* (New York, 1938), pp. 474-488.

[27] Jaroslav Cerny, *Ancient Egyptian Religion* (London, 1952), Chaps. 3 and 4; Henri Frankfort, *Ancient Egyptian Religion* (New York, 1948), Chap. 2; S. A. Mercer, *Horus, Royal God of Egypt* (Grafton, 1942), pp. 94-95.

facts was the early shift from village to city life, with each city having its own officially worshipped gods. But it is the unofficial mystery cults connected with Demeter, Dionysos, Eleusis, and the Orphics that have become objects of greater interest, first to the romanticists—Friedrich Creuzer, Otfried Mueller, and Bachofen, the aforementioned emphasizer of the matrilinear society—then later to Alfred Baeumler and Manfred Schroeter, as well as to Guthrie, Nilsson, and the positivists Gernet and Boulanger. Almost all of these sociologists stressed the fact that such cults diverted men from their city-state religion and from the ethnocentrism of their own social groups.[28]

Celtic Religion. Celtic-speaking peoples, although they live near the centers of Occidental culture, appeared on the horizon of scientists relatively late, and consequently not much is known of them even now. Therefore a brief recapitulation of the development of interest in Celtic peoples is appropriate.

Macpherson's translation of the lays of Ossian appeared at the end of the eighteenth century and was considered by Johnson and others to be a forgery. Many romanticists, however, considered it to be an original folk product (the view of Goethe and of Herder, a forerunner of the romanticists), or a free adaptation by Macpherson but by no means a forgery —a view shared by some more recent investigators.

The edition of old Bretonic literature, published in 1839 by Hersart de la Villemarque, was followed by a similar controversy. A general reawakening of interest in their own past took place among Irish, Manx, Welsh, Cornish, and Scottish-Gaelic peoples; and teaching of Celtic philology began in Bonn, Berlin, Heidelberg, Leipzig, Paris, Cambridge, and Madison. For a long time, however, interest centered in grammar and in the history of Irish monasticism, Welsh heroic literature, and their influence on the Continent, which included influence upon Wagner's *Lohengrin* and *Tristan.* The Englishman Spence and the Frenchman Bayet were concerned with the Celtic tree-cult rather than with priests and their functions, which were dealt with to some extent by German Celtologists such as Heinrich Zimmer, Kuno Meyer, and Ludwig Christian Stern, and more recently by the Frenchman, Henri Hubert, who is methodologically akin to the Durkheim school. His theory is that, at the time of Caesar as well as later, there existed a pan-Celtic religious organization with a center in Britain, with Druids,

[28] Louis Gernet and André Boulanger, *Le Génie grec dans la religion* (Paris, 1932), pp. 34, 116, 131-142, 153, 318, 350; W. K. Guthrie, *Orpheus and Greek Religion* (2nd ed.; London, 1952), pp. 205, 238, 256, and *The Greeks and Their Gods* (Boston, 1955), Chaps 6, 9, 11; Martin P. Nilsson, *Greek Piety,* translated by Herbert Jenning Rose (Oxford, 1948), pp. 46-49. As to the history of these, see Alfred Baeumler, "Einleitung," *Der Mythus von Orient und Occident, loc. cit.;* Paul Honigsheim, "Schelling als Sozialphilosoph," *KZS,* 6 (1953-1954), pp. 613 ff. (with detailed literature).

often of royal descent, as diviners and educators and with bards and soothsayers as less powerful seers for the lower classes.[29]

Judaism. As far as the epoch before Christ is concerned,[30] there is at present agreement among authors of divergent background with respect to nine subjects: (1) The unacceptability of the older pan-Babylonian theory, as put forward by Hugo Winckler and Eduard Hahn, who derived almost all important socio-cultural attitudes of the Near East from Babylon. (2) Predominance of the patriarchal family structure in the epoch of nomadism. (3) The slow decline of patriarchy. (4) Superiority of the agriculture of the natives of Canaan to that of the Hebrews. (5) Forbearance of the Canaanites after the conquest. (6) The role of judges as charismatic leaders. (7) Increasing dependence of the rural population upon cities, kings, and their residences. (8) Prophets as representatives of old nomadic-rural life in contrast to urban and foreign influences. (9) Sects, after the Babylonian exile and at the epoch of Jesus, as differentiated by their social affiliation and their attitude toward Greek thinking and the Roman Empire. To these generally accepted items, Leonard Wooley has added the remark that in the patriarchal epoch a powerful family, which had its own god, could occasionally impress adherence to it on others.

Five aspects of the epoch after Jesus have been intensively dealt with. (1) The Jews in Mohammedan Spain, wealthy and in high position,[31] have attracted much attention. (2) Chassidism,[32] a popular Jewish movement

[29] Lewis Spence, *The History and Origin of Druidism* (New York, 1949), pp. 128 *ff.*, 141, 178 (very disputable); Albert Bayet, *La Morale des Gaulois* (Paris, 1930), pp. 17-48, 221-225; Heinrich Zimmer, "Sprache und Literatur der Kelten im Allgemeinen," *Die Kultur der Gegenwart* (Berlin, 1909); Kuno Meyer, "Die irisch-gaelische Literatur," *ibid.;* Ludwig Christian Stern, "Die schottisch-gaelische und die Manx-Literatur"; and "Die kornische und die bretonische Literatur," *ibid.;* Henri Hubert, *The Greatness and The Decline of the Celts,* translated by M. R. Dobie (London, 1934), pp. 227-247.

[30] Max Weber, *Gesammelte Aufsätze zur Religionssoziologie* (Tübingen, 1921), vol. 3; Paul Honigsheim, "Edward Hahn und seine Stellung in der Geschichte der Ethnologie und Soziologie," *Anthropos,* 24 (1929); Leo Baeck, *The Pharisees and Other Essays* (New York, 1947), pp. 47; S. W. Baron, *A Social and Religious History of the Jews* (New York, 1952), vol. 1, pp. 26-35, 56, 61-75, 83, 89, 152; Louis Finkelstein, *The Jews; Their History, Culture, and Religion* (New York, 1949), pp. 29, 49, 97, 115-117; T. Croutter Gordon, *The Rebel Prophet: Studies in the Person of Jeremiah* (New York, 1932), pp. 73-75, 103-105; William Graham, *The Prophets and Israel's Culture* (Chicago, 1934), pp. 69-71, 98; C. A. Guignebert, *The Jewish World in the Time of Jesus,* translated by H. S. Hooke (London, 1939), pp. 94-99, 180-201, 210, 231; Elmer Leslie, *Old Testament Religion* (New York, 1936), p. 265; Sir Leonard Wooley, *Abraham: Recent Discoveries and Hebrew Origins* (New York, 1936), pp. 170-177, 197, 234-249; Becker and Barnes, *op. cit.*, vol. 1, pp. 115-130.

[31] Valeriu Marcu, *The Expulsion of the Jews from Spain,* translated by Moray Firth (New York, 1935), pp. 41-43, 57.

[32] Martin Buber, *Tales of the Hasidim,* translated by Olga Marx (New York, 1947-48), 2 vols. See also Paul Honigsheim, "Martin Buber 70 Jahre," *Die Friedens-Warte,* 48

which arose in the eighteenth century in Poland, centered around a charismatic leader, Rabbi Baal Schem, and emphasized emotion and face-to-face relations in contrast to Talmudism and institutionalization. Although it later became an object of derision or was forgotten, it was rediscovered by Martin Buber, who considered it an especially characteristic expression of Jewish mentality. (3) The ghetto and assimilation[33] have been studied by Louis Wirth, who analyzed the life in American ghettos, especially that of newcomers who settled in the neighborhood of their coreligionists because they were not familiar with the language and labor conditions. They later tried to leave the ghetto to settle elsewhere and to assimilate into the new surroundings; by so doing they often lost contact with their former neighbors and looked at non-assimilated newcomers with condescension and compassion. (4) Judaism, capitalism, and anti-Semitism constituted a complex which has attracted a great deal of attention.[34] German romanticists, their followers the Russian Slavophiles (including Dostoevski), and the earlier German non-racial anti-Semites (such as Constantin Frantz, Otto Roeckel, and others) in their struggle for return to a pre-capitalistic society and against an ascendant capitalism, put the blame for the evils of capitalism on the Jews. Indeed, Max Weber insisted on the existence of an interrelation between some kinds of religion and capitalism (to be dealt with later), but at the same time he rejected the notion that the Jews more than others had contributed to its development. Werner Sombart, however, who at least for some time was connected with the Weber-Troeltsch epistemology, methods, and problem area, although he accepted Weber's insistence on the possibility of religious influence on economy, nevertheless, in contrast to Weber, asserted that capitalism was in the last instance of Jewish origin. Writers of Jewish as well as non-Jewish descent have combated this theory, among them, Jacobs, Sachs, Sorokin, Waetgen, Wirth, and others. Although contemporary anti-Semitism is less a religious than an economic or ethnic phenomenon, the literature that deals with its socio-psychological background deserves attention; for example, Robert Byrnes, who analyzes the French movement, and the *Studies in Prejudice,* edited by Horkheimer and Flowerman, dealing among other things with the newest movements, in-

(Zurich, 1948); and Jack Lucas, "Leadership in the Religious Movement: the Hasidim of the Eighteenth Century" (unpublished master's thesis, University of Wisconsin, 1954).

[33] Louis Wirth, *The Ghetto* (Chicago, 1928), Chaps. 4, 6-7, 9-12.

[34] Werner Sombart, *The Jews and Modern Capitalism,* translated by M. Epstein, with an introduction by Bert F. Hoselitz (Glencoe, Ill., 1951); Joseph Jacobs, *Jewish Contribution to Civilization* (Philadelphia, 1919); A. S. Sachs, *World That Passed* (Philadelphia, 1928), pp. 70-75; H. J E. Waetgen, *Das Judentum und die Anfänge der modernen Kolonisation* (Berlin, 1914); Wirth, *op. cit.,* Chap. 4; R. F. Byrnes, *Anti-Semitism in Modern France* (New Brunswick, 1950); Max Horkheimer and S. H. Flowerman (eds.), *Studies in Prejudice* (New York, 1951).

cluding those in the United States. (5) Zionism[35] is primarily a reaction against anti-Semitism, as well as against assimilation and the fear of losing attitudes that are supposed to be of a special Jewish character (and for this reason, worthy of maintenance). Almost all existent Occidental politico-socio-economic concepts reappear here: for example, economic liberalism and socialism; the program of Franz Oppenheimer for developing rural collectivities and that of Martin Buber for creating a state that should be basically Jewish with respect to the form of face-to-face relations, and in that respect different from Occidental states. Thus several problems concerning the interrelation between Jewish religiosity and social structure reappear in the literature published by and about various Zionistic movements.

Islam. The Islamic religion was at one and the same time neighbor, enemy, and stimulus to the Christian world. Thorough knowledge of Islam was never lost; it was strongly developed by a division of German romanticism, especially represented by Friedrich Rueckert, and then implemented by Russian, Austrian, French, and English expansion, as well as by the various forms of reaction to expansion among natives themselves. The men who are of primary importance for us are: Hitti, a Lebanon-born Christian who is now teaching in the United States; various Americans, Britishers, and Frenchmen, such as Arnauld, Gibb, Guillaume, Landon, and Massé; the missionaries Watson and Mott; and above all, Gustave Edmund von Gruenebaum. They have examined three areas of special interest. (1) *Official Islam* accepted the forms of life of subjected peoples; immanent urbanization and rationalization; the threefold social position of every Moslem as sinner or saint, as descendant from Arabs or converts, and as a member of a special social group within the social hierarchy. (2) *Sectarian movements* manifested such typical traits as the illiteracy and low socio-economic status of charismatic leaders and emotionalism of the adherents. (3) *Assimilation* is evidenced in a tendency to interpret the Koran in a modern manner and to imitate Occidental forms of nationalism.[36]

[35] Franz Oppenheimer, *Die Siedlungsgenossenschaft* (3rd ed.; Jena, 1922), and *Wege zur Gemeinschaft* (Munich, 1924). As to rural collectivities established by Zionistic Jews in Palestine, see Paul Honigsheim, "Rural Collectivities," in C. P. Loomis and J. Allan Beegle, *Rural Social Systems* (New York, 1950), pp. 846 *ff.* Also Martin Buber, *Kampf um Israel* (Berlin, 1933); Honigsheim, "Martin Buber 70 Jahre," *loc. cit.;* Josef Patai, *Star Over Jordan* (New York, 1946); Solomon Liptzin, *Germany's Stepchildren* (Philadelphia, 1944), pp. 113-124, 255-270.

[36] P. K. Hitti, *The Arabs* (Princeton, 1943); Sir Thomas Arnold and Alfred Guillaume, *The Legacy of Islam* (London, 1952), pp 298-301; H. A. R. Gibb, *Mohammedanism; An Historical Survey* (London, 1949), pp. 13-15, 45-113, 151-162; K. P. Landon, *Southeast Asia: Crossroad of Religion* (Chicago, 1947), pp. 47 ff.; Henri Massé, *Islam,* translated by Halid Edib (New York, 1938), pp. 79-89, 259; C. R. Watson, *What is the Moslem World?* (New York, 1933), pp. 97-118; J. R. Mott, *The Moslem World of*

Christianity. Only three groups of problems can be dealt with here: Greek Orthodoxy, neo-Kantian theories, and Christianity in the United States.

Since the split between Eastern and Western Christianity, Greek Orthodoxy has been at times a preoccupation of Western scholars because of the following factors: the flight of Byzantine scholars, such as Bessarion, to Italy after the conquest of Constantinople by the Turks; the interest of Westerners in an ecumenical Union of Christian Churches[37] as stressed by Schelling, Baader, and other German Romanticists, by members of the Anglican and the German Old Catholic Church (both emphasizing the common episcopal element), and by ecumenically minded theologians of recent times, such as Friedrich Heiler, Hans Ehrenberg, Ernst Benz, and others; the interest of anti-rationalistically minded philosophers, such as Max Scheler[38] in Greek Orthodox intuitionism, especially in Dostoevski; the emigration of Greek Orthodox theologians, philosophers, and sociologists,[39] such as Nicolai Berdiaev, Sergius Bulgakov, Pitirim Sorokin, and Fedor Stepun, to Western Europe and the United States after the Soviets came into power; the interest of independent scholars[40] in the history of Byzantine and Russian economy, religion, and literature, from Bessarion to the foundation of special professorships for Byzantine or Slavic philology.

These factors center about two phenomena in particular. First, the mystical rather than juridical interpenetration of state and church in Czarist Russia, and earlier in Byzantium, made possible the continuance of non-institutionalized religious attitudes, such as that of Stylites and Hesychiasts.

Today (New York, 1926), pp. 311-313; G. E. von Gruenebaum, *Medieval Islam* (Chicago, 1946), pp. 173-185, 188, 204. American Anthropological Association, *Islam: Essays in the Nature and Growth of a Cultural Tradition,* vol. 57 (April, 1955), Chaps. 11, 12.

[37] As to the history of the interest in Greek Orthodoxy, see Ernst Benz, *Die Östkirche im Lichte der protestantischen Geschichtsforschung von der Reformation bis zur Gegenwart* (Freiburg, 1952); Paul Honigsheim, "Schelling und seine Stellung in der Geschichte der Voelkerannaeherung," *Die Friedens-Warte* (Basel, 1954), pp. 249-251; Friedrich Heiler, *Evangelische Katholizität* (Munich, 1926), vol. 1, pp. 304-325; Serge Bolschakoff, *The Doctrine of the Unity of the Church in the Works of Khomyakow and Moehler* (London, 1946), pp. 59-61, 77, 108.

[38] Max Scheler, *Der Genius des Krieges und der Deutsche Krieg* (Leipzig, 1915), pp. 95, 269, 305, and *Schriften zur Soziologie und Weltanschauungslehre,* (Leipzig, 1923), vol. 1, pp. 117, 127, 136, 169; vol. 2, pp. 95, 269, 305.

[39] Nicolai Berdiaev, *The Russian Idea* (New York, 1948), pp. 87-123, and *The Origin of Russian Communism* (London, n.d.), pp. 1-37.

[40] W. F. Adeney, *The Greek and Eastern Church* (New York, 1928), p. 442; N. H. Baynes, *The Byzantine Empire* (New York, 1926), pp. 112; Charles Diehl, *History of the Byzantine Empire,* translated by G. B. Ives (Princeton, N.J., 1925), p. 102; Steven Runciman, *Byzantine Civilization* (New York, 1933), pp. 111-113; Matthew Spinka, *A History of Christianity in the Balkans* (Chicago, 1933); Alexander Vasiliev, *History of the Byzantine Empire* (Madison, 1929), vol. 1, pp. 372, 407; Georgii Vernadsky, *Kievan Russia* (New Haven, 1948), p. 348.

Second, the sects' problems of leadership, as well as of relation to the state and other institutions, were in some cases similar to those of Western sects.

Neo-Kantian theories concerning Protestantism and the modern world were formulated principally by Jellinek, Weber, and Troeltsch. The main theories had already been elaborated prior to the beginning of World War I, but significant discussion occurred after the war and still continues today. In order to understand the discussion, a short survey of the main theories themselves is essential. Georg Jellinek, the first of the theorists, tried to trace the declaration of the rights of man made by the French Revolution back to the constitutions of some North American States. These in turn he traced to the declarations signed by early Protestant settlers in New England, and finally to British Calvinism.[41] Weber then elaborated the most discussed portion of this group of theories.[42] Among ascetic Protestants, such as Calvinists, Anabaptists, Quakers, and Methodists, Weber argued, the systematic performance of economic work and the receipt of money was considered an indication of being chosen by God, a view which did not prevail among Catholics and Lutherans. The impossibility of using this money for secular pleasures and the felt need to demonstrate salvation to others and oneself, supplied a new impulse to reinvest it. Thus the religious attitude of these groups led to the capitalistic mentality and became one of the factors in the development of capitalism.

Troeltsch elaborated a more general theory concerning the history of Christian social ethics.[43] He asserted that Jesus considered economic problems as belonging to this world; further, that Paul in his propaganda felt the necessity of taking the state and other institutions into consideration but remained naive, conservative, anti-revolutionary. The church fathers, according to Troeltsch, went a step further in eliminating indifference toward this world. Augustine still considered the Roman Empire and culture as being outside Christian ethics, and he was still far away from the concept of the Christian, church-subjected Empire of the Middle Ages. The Middle Ages, especially as represented by the Thomistic social ethics (which was different from that of the Church Fathers), penetrated all spheres of life through a church-mentality, and at the same time abandoned an otherwordly radicalism. In contrast, later medieval sects represented attempts

[41] Georg Jellinek, *The Declaration of the Rights of Man and of Citizens,* authorized translation by Max Farrand (New York, 1901). See also Paul Honigsheim, "Georg Jellinek," *KZS,* 3 (1950-1951).

[42] Max Weber, *The Protestant Ethic and the Spirit of Capitalism,* translated by Talcott Parsons (London, 1930).

[43] Ernst Troeltsch, *The Social Teaching of the Christian Churches,* translated by Olive Wyon (London, 1950); *Protestantism and Progress,* translated by W. Montgomery (London, 1912); "Protestantisches Christentum und Kirche in der Neuzeit," in Hinneberg, *op. cit.,* vol. 1, pp. 431-755; *Augustin, die christliche Antike und das Mittelalter* (Munich, 1915).

to realize a radical but non-assimilating Christian law. Luther and Lutheranism represented renewed approaches to a medieval, church-directed society and culture. Anabaptist groups, in contrast to Lutheranism and Calvinism, represented a new attempt to realize life according to unrestricted Christian natural law. The British non-conformists who emigrated to colonial America represented Anabaptist elements rather than Calvinism, as Jellinek believed.

Some of the foregoing statements were supported or enlarged upon on the basis of new materials and considerations; several examples must suffice for illustrative purposes. The later appearance and lesser importance of the capitalistic mentality in Catholic countries, especially certain Germanic principalities, was shown by the Catholic Wilhelm Schwer.[44] The attitude of British non-conformists toward natural science, commerce, and slavery was emphasized by Herbert Schoeffler and his school in Cologne.[45] Moreover, the development of Methodism in England[46] as an ambivalent and intermediary phenomenon demanded loyalty toward the capitalistic employer on the one hand, and, at the same time, produced leaders of cooperatives and strikes in the nineteenth century (pointed out especially by Becker, Edwards, and Wearmouth).

In reply to Jellinek, French scholars insisted that the French revolutionary declarations were independent of the American declarations, which in the final analysis means Calvinistic ideas.[47] This controversy, however, has almost died out. With respect to the famous Weber controversy, the following arguments have appeared. The Catholic mind, contrasted here with Calvinism, is theocentrically structured and cannot for this reason be understood by Weber's way of thinking (according to the Jesuit father Gundlach);[48] Calvinistic mentality was already in existence prior to and outside Calvinism according to Sombart (who in other respects paralleled Weber), Sorokin, Tawney, and Yinger; Calvin himself and original Calvinism

[44] Wilhelm Schwer, "Der Kapitalismus und das wirtschaftliche Schicksal der deutschen Katholiken," in Wilhelm Schwer and Franz Mueller, *Der deutsche Katholizismus in Zeitalter des Kapitalismus* (Augsburg, 1932).

[45] Herbert Schoeffler, *Protestantismus und Literatur* (Leipzig, 1922); *Die Anfänge des Puritanismus* (Leipzig, 1933), pp. 54, 175-177; E. F. Hoevel, *Die soziale Herkunft der neuzeitlichen Dialekt-literatur Englands* (Leipzig, 1929); Adolf Lotz, *Sklaverei, Staatskirche und Freikirche* (Leipzig, 1929), pp. 3 *ff.*, 31-34, 48, 86; Albert Rosin, *Lebensversicherung und ihre geistesgeschichtlichen Grundlagen* (Leipzig, 1932), pp. 67, 77-80, 102; cf. Paul Honigsheim, "Zur Religionssoziologie des englischen Protestantismus," *KVS,* 11, pp. 402-411.

[46] Howard Becker, *Systematic Sociology on the Basis of the* Beziehungslehre *and* Gebildelehre *of Leopoid von Wiese* (New York, 1932; 2nd ed. with a new preface, Gary, 1950), [hereinafter Wiese-Becker] pp. 639-642; Maldwyn Edwards, *After Wesley* (London, 1945), pp. 21, 37, 41, 47, 57, 91, 154; R. F. Wearmouth, *Methodism and the Working Class Movement of England, 1800-1850* (London, 1847), pp. 41-43, 143, 173, 186, 205, 222.

[47] E. G. Boutmy, *Études politiques: La souveraineté de peuple: La déclaration de droit de l'homme et Mr. Jellinek* (Paris, 1907).

[48] Gustav Gundlach, *Zur Soziologie der katholischen Ideenwelt,* p. 20.

retained a medieval mentality in their economic ideas (Hyma, Tawney, Yinger); belief in predestination was not a common trait of the various sects and other groupings referred to by Weber (Becker, Hall, Marshall, Knappen, Sorokin); the "calling" was of less importance than Weber supposed (Robertson, Yinger); the non-conformists in Britain merely adapted themselves to an already changed situation in eliminating their economic restrictions (Robertson, Tawney, Richard Schlatter); the Pilgrim fathers did not come to the New England colonies primarily for religious freedom, but rather for economic opportunities (Yinger).[49]

Troeltsch was attacked[50] in connection with his beliefs about Jesus, Paul, and the Church Fathers mainly by Catholics, such as Franz Xavier Kiefl, who nevertheless agreed with him in some respects, whereas Otto Schilling insisted on the more positive attitude of the Church Fathers toward the "world" and accordingly in the relatively smaller difference between them and Thomas Aquinas. With regard to Luther, Troeltsch had been mainly attacked by German Protestant church historians, such as Boehmer, Brieger, Kattenbusch, and Loofs; as to Reformation sectarians, especially in regard to Thomas Muenzer, he was mainly criticized by Hugo Ball and Ernst Bloch. Both went further than Troeltsch and considered Muenzer as the true climax of the Reformation.

Work on Christianity in the United States in recent times has been done mainly by Americans themselves and has centered largely upon the following seven topics. (1) *The American denomination.*[51] Basing his analysis

[49] Becker and Barnes, *op. cit.*, vol. 1, pp. 324-328; Wiese-Becker, *op. cit.*, pp. 632-634; T. C. Hall, *The Religious Background of American Culture* (Boston, 1930), pp. 210, 233; Albert Hyma, *Christianism, Capitalism, and Communism* (Ann Arbor, 1937); Marshall Knappen, *Tudor Puritanism: A Chapter in the History of Idealism* (Chicago, 1939), vol. 1, pp. 422-424; Talcott Parsons, "H. M. Robertson on Max Weber and His School," *Journal of Political Economy*, 43 (1935); H. M. Robertson, *Aspects of the Rise of Economic Individualism: A Criticism of Max Weber and His School* (Cambridge, 1933); R. B. Schlatter, *The Social Ideas of Religious Leaders 1660-1688* (Oxford, 1940), Appendix 3; Werner Sombart, *The Quintessence of Capitalism*, translated and edited by M. Epstein (London, 1915); Sorokin, *Social and Cultural Dynamics*, vol. 1, p. 500, vol. 3, p. 224, and vol. 4, pp. 123 [footnote 25], 175, 312, 362 [footnote 14]; Sorokin, *Society, Culture and Personality*, pp. 591 [footnote 4], 657, 672 [footnote 30]; W. W. Sweet, *Religion in Colonial America* (New York, 1942), pp. 100-101; R. H. Tawney, *Religion and the Rise of Capitalism* (New York, 1922), pp. 78, 84, 113, 119, 226, 233; J. Milton Yinger, *Religion in the Struggle for Power* (Durham, N.C., 1946), pp. 37, 90, 111.

[50] Otto Schilling, *Die Christlichen Soziallehren* (Munich, 1926). As to the attacks made by German Protestant Church historians against Troeltsch, cf. *Theologischer Jahresbericht* (1906), and Troeltsch's answers in his "Protestantisches Christentum und Kirche in der Neuzeit," in Hinnebert, *op. cit.*, vol. 1, pp. 745-747; Hugo Ball, *Die Flucht aus der Zeit* (Munich, 1927); Ernst Bloch, *Thomas Muenzer als Theologe der Revolution* (Munich, 1921); Heinrich Boehmer, *Gesammelte Aufsätze* (Gotha, 1927), pp. 35-37, 61-65, 187-190.

[51] H. Richard Niebuhr, *The Social Sources of Denominationalism* (New York, 1940); Wiese-Becker, *op. cit.*, pp. 629-630.

in part on Richard Niebuhr (a brother of Reinhold Niebuhr), Howard Becker has pictured the denomination as a characteristic American sect in an advanced stage characterized by concessions. For example, the denomination no longer admits only those adults who have already given proof of being children of God.

(2) *Newer sects.*[52] Elmer Clark has described among others the following types: charismatic Pentecostal groups, whose members attend their meetings in anticipation of being blessed; Perfectionist sects, whose members feel that they are basically involved in sin and expect to be definitely delivered from it; world-escaping groups, to which the great number of rural collectivities based on special religious beliefs also belong; spiritualistic groups, primarily interested in the certitude of the continuance of life after death through communion with departed spirits.

(3) *Jehovah's Witnesses.* This group has increased in Germany as well as in the United States. Herbert Stroup[53] asserts that in the United States Jehovah's Witnesses attract largely those who feel insecure, such as small businessmen and immigrants who have economic or adaptation difficulties. Further, that the attitude toward marriage, state, elections, etc., is ambivalent, dependent upon the nearness of the millenium.

(4) *Negro religious life.*[54] Two problems persist: The possibility and desirability of the gathering of whites and Negroes in the same church, especially in the South, has been dealt with historically, for example, by Dwight Culver. The factors that may explain the singular nature of Negro religious attitudes are traced by the followers of Herskovits in part to African heritage; by others, especially by Fauset, such attitudes were attributed to the fact that Negro religious groupings are often in the stage of transformation from an almost exclusively religious institution to an institution acquiring new social functions under changing politico-economical circumstances.

(5) *Rural churches.*[55] Because of the great role that rural sociology plays in the United States, the membership, economic background, relation to

[52] E. T. Clark, *The Small Sects in America* (New York, 1949); C. S. Braden, *These Also Believe* (New York, 1949); W. L. Sperry, *Religion in America* (New York, 1946).

[53] H. H. Stroup, *The Jehovah Witnesses* (New York, 1945); see also Royston Pike, *Jehovah's Witnesses* (New York, 1954).

[54] D. W. Culver, *Negro Segregation in the Methodist Church* (New Haven, Conn., 1953); A. H. Fauset, *Black Gods of the Metropolis: Negro Religious Cults in the Urban North* (Philadelphia, 1944).

[55] C. L. Fry, *The New and Old Immigrant on the Land: A Study of Americanization and the Rural Church* (New York, 1922); Loomis and Beegle, *op. cit.*, Part 4; E. de S. Brunner, *Church Life in the Rural South* (New York, 1923); *Churches of Distinction in Town and County* (New York, 1923); *Surveying Your Community: a Handbook of Method for the Rural Church* (New York, 1925); *Tested Methods in Town and Country Churches* (New York, 1930); and *Industrial Village Church* (New York, 1930).

immigrant origin, training of rural ministers, and similar problems have become objects of investigations by Beegle, Brunner, Fry, Loomis, and others.

(6) *Catholicism in the United States.*[56] The attitude of Catholicism toward society and its different institutions, as it appears in the writings of Grace, Lecler, Snell, and others, for example, does not differ essentially from the general Catholic (and especially the Neo-Thomistic) attitude. Thus a special survey of this literature is omitted.

(7) *Mormons*. Having played a special role in the history of the settlement of the West, the Mormons are playing an increasingly important role in American life and are the object of a voluminous literature which deserves intensive study. The *Book of Mormon* is considered by adherents to be the text written on golden plates that was translated by Joseph Smith, and to contain the history of ancient Hebrews who immigrated to America (some of whom became Indians). With respect to this text, critics contested primarily four things. First, critics have questioned its truth, which on the other hand was recently reasserted by the Mormon writers Hunter and Ferguson in their reference to archeological material and the post-Columbian writings of Ixtrilxochitl and others. Second, it is suspected to be plagiarized from an earlier book written by Spaulding. This was originally asserted by the Catholic church historian Hergenroether, among others, but is now largely abandoned, even by Catholic writers such as Algermissen. Third, the supposedly "Reformed Egyptian" characters allegedly written on the golden plates and copied by Joseph Smith, are disputed by the contemporary philologist Anton and the majority of later critics. Fourth, the creditability of assertions by witnesses claiming in the *Book of Mormon* and in *The Doctrine and Covenants* to have seen the plates was recently re-emphasized by the Mormon writer Evans but again denied by Beardsley. The "charismatic" leadership of Smith has been conceived by Max Weber as perhaps that of a conscious swindler and by Beardsley, Howard Becker, and others as that exercised by a psychopathic personality.

The "second one," Brigham Young, has been the subject of studies because of his willingness to subordinate himself with his practical-mindedness to Smith, the possessor of a completely different mental structure, in a relationship compared by Howard Becker to that of Paul to Jesus, Abu Bekr to Mohammed, and similar pairs. The group-life in isolation, with the development of an in-group feeling, has been dealt with by Eduard Meyer, a German historian of Oriental and Greek antiquity, and recently by Anderson and Kimball Young. The process of assimilation is especially

[56] Frank Grace, *The Concept of Property in Modern Christian Thought* (Urbana, 1953); Joseph Lecler, *The Two Sovereignties: A Study of the Relationship between Church and State* (New York, 1952); Roberta Snell, *The Nature of Man in St. Thomas Aquinas Compared with the Nature of Man in American Sociology* (Washington, 1942).

exemplified by the abandoning of "plural marriage" (i.e., polygyny, as recently described by Kimball Young) despite the fact that it had originally been introduced on the basis of a purported revelation. The religiously based cooperatives and the rural collectivity, the "United Order" planned by Smith and later realized by Brigham Young, have been described especially by Allen, Anderson, Evans, Gardner, Hunter, and the German sociologist, Franz Oppenheimer.

Major Concepts and Theories in the Sociological Approach to Religion

The Typological Approach: Weber-Troeltsch.[57] In the types developed by Weber and Troeltsch, the most essential feature is the distinction between church and sect. The former is a group strongly inclined toward universality and institutionalization; the latter a group that accepts the fact that it is small and tends toward primary contacts and face-to-face relations. Sects themselves were divided into three subtypes: The *aggressive sect* appears mainly in times of unrest. The members are convinced not only that they are the chosen ones who know the right way but also that they are entitled, and even obliged, to use the sword. If the aggressive sect is not successful, it may shift to the second subtype, the *assimilating sect,* and by doing so, it approaches *the church type.* The third possibility is the refusal either to make concessions or to use the sword. In this case, the members are satisfied with realizing the kingdom of God in a small group where they are not persecuted. That is, the group becomes the *tolerated sect.*

Howard Becker introduced two new elements in this typology.[58] First, he classified societies themselves into two types, namely, sacred and secular —carefully pointing out, however, that sacredness includes far more than the specifically religious (i.e., the "holy"), and that secularity may embody principles, such as "natural rights," of powerfully binding character. Moreover, Becker added two constructed types: the *denomination* and the *cult.* The denomination he viewed as a sect in an advanced stage that has made compromises, for example, as to the admission of new members. Moving in the opposite direction from the sect type is the cult, normally an ephemeral

[57] Max Weber has elaborated his concept of religious groups, leaders, attitudes toward the world, etc., systematically in his posthumously published work, *Wirtschaft und Gesellschaft* (Tübingen, 1922).

[58] Wiese-Becker, *op cit.,* pp. 613-642; Becker, *Through Values to Social Interpretation,* pp. 114-117, 248-280; Joachim Wach, *Sociology of Religion,* pp. 47, 55-88, 114-147, and *Types of Religious Experiences,* pp. 195-201.

group clustered around a *religiously* charismatic leader, such as the various Catholic or Protestant mystical cults. Similarly, Wach distinguishes churches, denominations, sects, and smaller groups that cannot be considered as belonging to one of the three former types. Finally, Leopold von Wiese uses the term "church" in a somewhat more universal sense and points to the dilemma that rests in the fact that the church must combine two kinds of activities basically different from one another—namely, the collective gratification of religious needs, and organization, which usually includes the use of coercion.

The older evolutionary notion of the existence and perceptibility of an automatic and deterministic sequence no longer finds support. On the other hand, in contrast to many German church historians who denied the possibility of establishing a sequence, Max Weber in his later years increasingly insisted upon the possibility of making statements about the regularity of sequence in his ideal types. Howard Becker did something similar in noting the possibility of making statements as to the sequence of his constructed types—cult→sect→denomination, or cult→sect→ecclesia→denomination, etc.[59]

The Function of the Individual Within the Religious World. The older conviction, especially of German historians, had been that history to a large extent is made by "great men." Partly in contrast to this belief, Marxians and the Durkheim school particularly emphasized group structure and group consciousness as one of the central factors in historical occurrence. Both concepts have receded in influence and increasingly a more moderate viewpoint has been accepted, especially by those who follow Weber and Troeltsch.[60] According to this concept, the religious individual is indeed indispensable, but nonetheless he is only one of the various factors causing change.

Types of Religious Leadership. Weber[61] has classified leaders generally (though not exclusively with regard to religion), as well as the corresponding forms of obedience, into three types. The *charismatic leader* in epochs of unrest stands at the beginning of revolutionary, religio-emotional, and sectarian-schismatic movements. He finds adherents because he is believed to be the one who knows what is needed. The *traditional* leader appears in a situation in which authority derives from immemorial custom, connected with certain family lines or the ownership of a special feudal estate. The *bureaucrat* exists in situations where persons are obeyed by others, not because of personal merits or because of tradition, but rather because those

[59] Max Weber, *The Theory of Social and Economic Organization,* translated by A. M. Henderson and Talcott Parsons (New York, 1947), pp. 109-110; Becker, *Through Values to Social Interpretation,* pp. 107-108, 121-124, 207, 215-219, 287-289.

[60] Troeltsch, *Gesammelte Schriften,* vol. 3, pp. 101, 720.

[61] Weber, *The Theory of Social and Economic Organization,* pp. 324-363.

who obey know that the bureaucrat has received his position in a legally instituted, or "legitimate," way.

The charismatic leader has often appeared in our epoch of unrest and accordingly has received much attention in the literature.[62] Wach as well as Dempf have described the function of the charismatic leader as seer and prophet; likewise Sorokin has pointed out the function of the charismatic leader in founding new religious movements. Moreover, the charismatic leader has been shown to function in the following special cultures: preliterates (Bergson, Boulanger, Gernet, Gurvitch, Malinowski); China (Granet); Judaism (Buber, Gordon, Scholem); Islam (Gibb, Hitti, Landon); Greek Orthodoxy (Berdiaev, Beynes, Bulgakov, Runciman, Vasiliev); modern America (Braden, Beardsley, Fauset).

Weber demonstrated how charisma may become hereditary, how a form of traditionalism consequently originates, and how a group of followers becomes so large and yet is so geographically dispersed that bureaucratization occurs.[63] Archer, Arnauld, Gruenebaum, and Guillaume have further illustrated these situations by examples taken from the history of the Sikhs and Mohammedans.

Studies of the social organization of religious leaders are exemplified by the sociological description of Catholic monastic orders as elaborated by Gundlach and Calmes.[64] Priestly organizations among Chinese, Persians, and Celts have been described by Granet, Herzfeld, and Hubert, respectively.

Religious Attitudes of Special Social Strata: Weber's Classification. Weber was the first to survey the religious attitudes of social strata.[65] His conclusions are as follows: Peasants are very close to nature and therefore likely to be involved in magic. Except for such involvement, peasants are almost never crucial to the origin, maintenance, and development of a special kind of religion. Rather, they are dependent upon the will and interest of other groups, such as the nobility.

The feudal nobility abhor humility and similar attitudes required by religions claiming redeeming qualities, but accept such religions when their rituals can be incorporated into the characteristic structure of fashionable feudal life. Moreover, the feudal noble is usually not greatly bothered by considerations concerning life after death, and even less so when he not only owns land but also ships. In this way, an intermediary phenomenon appears between piracy and the early tradesman culture, as exemplified by

[62] Wach, *Sociology of Religion,* pp. 347-354; Aloys Dempf, *Kulturphilosophie,* pp. 109-111; Sorokin, *Social and Cultural Dynamics,* vol. 1, pp. 277-285, and *The Crisis of Our Age,* pp. 111, 134-136.

[63] Weber, *The Theory of Social and Economic Organization,* pp. 363-392.

[64] Gustav Gundlach, *Zur Soziologie der katholischen Ideenwelt;* Michael Calmes, *Zur Soziologie des katholischen Ordensstandes* (Munich, n.d.).

[65] Weber, *Wirtschaft und Gesellschaft,* pp. 267-296.

Homer. Professional officers, although they may have originated from the nobility, actually become specialists when regular armies develop; to a larger or smaller extent, this professional group is rationalistically minded and hostile to emotional religion, which they approve only as a means of subjugating the masses.

Bureaucrats are even more hostile to emotional religion. Accordingly, in China and in modern Occidental states, the bureaucrats have persecuted many emotional, revivalistic, and mystical movements. Capitalists, certainly one of the most rationalistically minded groups, belong either to non-emotional or to non-magical religions, show no interest in religion, or use it as a means of dominating the masses. Middle-class artisans belong either to very rationalistic or, in contrast, to emotional and eschatological movements, as for example in the later Middle Ages and the Renaissance period, but mainly when they fear loss of status.

Slaves are never carriers of special religions of their own, but either espouse the religion of their masters, as in stratified societies, or adhere to those sectarian groups open to heterogeneous strata, as may occur in epochs of unrest. The proletariat complements the high-capitalists, with whom they share a basically non-religious rationalism. Slum dwellers, called *Lumpenproletariat* in German (literally, "rags-proletariat") are former members of the lowest middle class, include those who have declined in status, emigrants who failed in their attempts to assimilate, and intellectual bohemians. These groups are not rationalistically minded; and insofar as they have any hope, they expect change resulting from crisis and may therefore accept a radical ideology—either a secular anarchism or a religious apocalyptic belief.

Pariah-groups, which for ethnic, national, or religious reasons are considered by the surrounding world as inferior, feel underprivileged. On the other hand, such groups may consider their suffering as a proof of their own superiority and expect a future retaliation or "justification," either in this world (as in orthodox Judaism) or in a future world (as do some Greek Orthodox believers under non-Christian rule). Intellectuals since the development of writing have often formed literary guilds, and when the religion under consideration becomes a mass religion, the guild distinguishes itself from the masses as an organized priesthood. The intellectuals may also develop a rationalized religion and to a large extent shift away from religion; or, finally, they may, when sinking socially, in part accept mystical and emotional religions as, for instance, the Russian *Narodniki*.

Further Studies of Stratification and Religious Participation. The religion of nomads was dealt with by Weber in his book on ancient Hebrews but was not incorporated systematically into this scheme. More recently, Wooley and others have emphasized the importance of the family god of the nomads. When certain tribes became powerful, they often imposed their god on other tribes. The shift from rural to urban life and its importance to changes in religious life have been emphasized with regard to the Greeks and the Moslems by Gernet and Gruenebaum, respectively.

The religion of subject peoples occupies an unimportant place in Weber's survey, but three types of pertinent observations have been made in recent years: First, reference is made to the maintenance of religious independence of the conquered people by Gruenebaum, Hitti, and Massé, with special regard to Christians in the Islamic empires. Second, observations have been made by Oppenheimer concerning the decline of the gods of the conquered to the role of demons. And third, some evidence points to the incorporation of elements of the religion of the conquered into the religious system of the Incas by Baudin, Bennett, and others.

The religion of lower social strata, especially their tendency to espouse charismatic prophets and to expect retaliation, has been studied by Dempf. Finally, the shift to magical, mystical, and emotional attitudes on the part of lower social strata has been illustrated through studies concerning primitive groups (Gurvitch), the Chinese (Granet), Mohammedans (Gibb, Hitti, Landon), and recent North Americans (Stroup).

The Relationship Between Religion and the Non-Religious World. According to Weber,[66] three problems have to be taken into consideration. The first problem is the two ways to salvation with regard to their influence on life. One of these ways is one's own work, which may assume three different forms, each modifying life in a special way: (1) magical means; (2) work of a social character—that is, an occasional and unorganized form of almsgiving or a systematized form of welfare work; and (3) self-sanctification through mysticism or asceticism or through a combination of both. Both mysticism and asceticism are either otherworldly or worldly; indeed, this difference decisively modifies their attitude toward the world.

The second means to salvation is supplied by the work of others, and is accompanied by various types of saviors as well as by a process of institutionalization. Institutionalization arises from the fact that, from the work supposed to have been done by the savior, an institutionalized church originates that is supposed to be a "vessel of grace."

The second problem concerning the interrelation of religion and the non-religious world is what Weber calls the *theodicy-problem,* by which he meant analysis of the attempts made to explain (perhaps to justify by religio-theological means) the existence in the world of phenomena supposed to be evil. Here Weber sees two essential types constantly recurring. First is the messianic eschatology, which asserts that the great change will come in the form of retaliation here on earth and will give high status and power

[66] *Ibid.*, secs. 8-12, pp. 296-363; in part also translated into English in *From Max Weber: Essays in Sociology,* translated and edited by H. H. Gerth and C. Wright Mills (New York, 1946), pp. 323-359.

to those of low status and power. The best example is furnished by the ancient Hebrews. Second is retaliation in another world, which is promised by faith in God's goodness and by the dogmas of predestination, reincarnation, or metaphysical dualism. Connected with this metaphysical dualism is the belief that ultimately the good, or God and his adherents, will dominate, as emphasized most strongly in Zoroastrianism.

The third problem, according to Weber, is the position taken by religious groups toward primarily non-religious spheres. Compared to the two previously presented areas, the numerous problems in this area have been treated to a lesser degree by Weber in his posthumously published work. Rather, these problems have been approached in a series of concrete examples, as in the discussion of religion and interest on capital, as well as in the description of the attitude of various types of religion toward different kinds of states. In contrast, Weber deals more intensively with alms and the use of violence. In many societies, alms are highly prized and their desirability is often used to justify the existence of the poor as a stratum within the state. Only religions of an extremely economico-rationalistic character (such as Calvinism, which considers unemployment as attributable to one's own guilt) reject general almsgiving. As to the use of violence, Weber advanced the formula of an inverse ratio between optimism (in the sense of a belief in ameliorating conditions of *this* world) and belief in the possibility of eliminating the use of violence and war. A religion confident that the world can be improved and saved will emphasize the right and even the obligation to use the sword to save the world, as did Zoroastrianism, Islam, and Christianity. In opposition to this is the belief in the basic incorrigibility of the world, as viewed by the pacifistic "true" Buddhist.

Interest in the forms of salvation as related to social structure has decreased somewhat. As to the theodicy-problem, Wach,[67] although he did not usually use that term, has supplied the following continuum of choices: the world can be considered basically good (as exemplified by the early Hinduistic Vedas and Homer), to be sanctifiable (as in the Zoroastrian, Mohammedan, and Christian faiths), or to be rigorously rejected (as by Buddha himself). Moreover, Becker and Scheler have respectively cited examples taken from Hinduism and Greek Orthodoxy.

With regard to the attitudes of religion toward primarily non-religious spheres of life, many studies have been made. The interrelationship between religion and economic life has been the subject of a twofold interest. On the one hand, the economic background of leading groups within some religious groups (for example, the life of priests in Peru, Mexico, China, and Egypt as dependent on landownership and land rent or on tribute)

[67] Wach, *Sociology of Religion,* pp. 299-313.

has been investigated by Baudin, Bennett, Cunow, Frankfort, Granet, and others. The other approach, of course, concerns the reverse relation: the influence of some religious attitudes on economic life. Here it may suffice to recall the two major controversies centering around the Sombart-problem, concerning Jews and capitalism, and around the Weber-controversy, concerning the relation between certain types of protestantism and capitalism, including the Schoeffler school and the writings of Edwards, Wearmouth, and others on Methodism. The extensive new Catholic literature on religion and economy, as represented by the publications of Gundlach, Franz Mueller, Nell-Breuning, Peter Tischleder, and others, deals not with actual phenomena but rather with the ideals that should be realized.

Religion and the Political Order. As to the interrelations between religion and the state, Wach[68] has presented still another continuum ranging from *complete identification,* through *juxtaposition* (exemplified by Zoroastrianism and the Sunnistic form of Islam), to the *complete separation* of both. Related to this and his classification of the degrees of belief in the salvation of the world is Wach's complementary classification of the possibility, capability, and willingness of constructing a state philosophy—proceeding from complete non-existence of such a philosophy (as in original Buddhism), through the use of a theory of the existence of cosmic laws justifying the existence of secular rule (as in Hinduism), to a complete social philosophy (as elaborated by those religious concepts, which, according to another of Wach's classifications, consider the world as savable—for instance, Zoroastrianism, Islam, and Christianity). Additions to this have been made by Benoy Kumar Sarkar as to the state philosophy of the Hindus (which was developed only within limits) and by Berdiaev, Bulgakov, Diehl, Fedotov, Spinka, Vasiliew, Venansky, and Zernow concerning various epochs in the history of the Greek Orthodox Church. The corresponding Catholic literature, by Joseph Biederlack and some other writers mentioned above, is outside the scope of this article.

Finally, Weber's theory of the inverse relationship between optimism and the permissibility (and even the obligation) of using violence has also been generally amplified by Wach, as well as by specific examples with respect to Sikhism, Greek Orthodoxy, and modern American sects by Archer, Scheler, and Stroup respectively. The interrelationship between religion, on one hand, and nations, political parties, and labor unions on the other played a minor role in Weber's work, but more recently some additions have been made. Matthew Spinka stressed the predominance of national feeling over, or its absorption into, the Greek Orthodox feeling in many Balkan situations. Edwards and Wearmouth emphasized the Methodist antagonism to the Tory position and their gradual shift from conservat-

[68] *Ibid.*, p. 323.

ive anti-Chartism to leadership positions in cooperatives and strikes. All this is closely connected with the general problem of the assimilation of religion into the environing social world, as shown in a previous section.

Concluding Remarks and Evaluations

Hitherto we have restricted ourselves to statements of facts, of causal interrelationship, and of novelty of ideas. We have refrained from making value-judgments concerning either religion in general or particular religions, as well as from making value-judgments with respect to social structure. Although we shall continue to abstain from value-judgments about the two items mentioned above, we shall try to evaluate the accuracy of the statements and theories with which we have dealt. This evaluation, made on the basis of historical fact and the rules of logic, may occasionally go further and indicate which theories have high probability of being productive with respect to new knowledge. In this section, we shall proceed according to the sequence of the chapter; when all assertions made in the section under consideration are in correspondence with the facts, we shall simply use the phrase "all statements mentioned" in order to avoid repetition. When only some of the assertions are correct, we shall list them individually.

METHODOLOGICAL PREMISES IN SOCIOLOGY OF RELIGION

Psychoanalysis, as developed under the influence of Fromm, promises to become an important contributor if it can free itself from the one-sidedness of early Freudianism. As to the investigation of simple cultures, the unrestricted use of the diffusionist, functionalist, and parallelist-evolutionary perspectives can only be considered working hypotheses, whereas the complementary use of all these approaches may produce new results. Neo-Kantianism, by limiting the sociology of religion to the position of a special science, without value-judgment and distinguished from philosophy, theology, and history (although based on the latter in the most general sense), has actually developed an increasingly complete sociological method with an epistemological base. The transformation of the "ideal type" into the "constructed type," as accomplished by Howard Becker, is also important. By contrast, Wach's two criticisms (against the elimination of value-judgments and against the use of the concept of group as a term that denotes merely ongoing collective activities) must be considered a return to metaphysics, with a consequent imposition of a genuine handicap on the development of the Occidental special sciences.

This is true to an even greater degree with regard to some of the authors mentioned at the end of the first section. Spengler, for example, is basically wrong in assuming that succeeding cultures do not accept anything from their predecessors. On the other hand, his theoretical conclusions about decline as a general law of ontological character are logically correct, given his premises. Contrariwise, Toynbee sees the possibility of an exception from the general law of decline; and this one exception actually makes *his* theory (supposedly of an ontological character) a non-ontological law. Othmar Spann is purely metaphysical—except for the work done by his school in the history of ideas—and that is also true, with the exception of a few statements concerning the matrilinear society, with regard to Klages. Bergson, Scheler, and Sorokin, even in the eyes of those who do not accept their general philosophical position, must be considered as stimulating theorists who offered some useful viewpoints.

SOCIOLOGICALLY RELEVANT ANALYSES OF SPECIFIC RELIGIOUS SYSTEMS

Preliterary Cultures: Gurvitch's and Malinowski's refutation of the group-consciousness concept, as conceived by the Durkheim school; the insistence on the role of the matrilinear and totemistic groups with their corresponding religion by functionalists, psychoanalysts, and diffusionists —all are acceptable, as are all statements relating to pre-Columbian America.

China: Fung-Yu-Lan's, and even more so, Granet's sociological classification of intellectuals, represented a step beyond Weber.

Hindus: Wach's and Becker's extrication of the causes of the attitudes of religion toward secular power likewise meant a step beyond Weber.

Sikhism, Zoroastrianism, Egypt, and Greek Antiquity: All statements mentioned are in correspondence with the facts.

Celtic Religion: Hubert's classification of religious leaders corresponds to fact.

Judaism in the Epoch Before Jesus: Details confirming Max Weber's main concept as well as additions made by Wooley and others concerning family gods of powerful families are valuable. In the epoch after Christ, the following are acceptable: adaptation in Spain; Chassidistic sectarianism (Buber); ghetto-life, ghetto-escape, and assimilation (Wirth); refutation by Weber, Wirth, and many others, of the untenable assertion made by Sombart about the primarily Jewish character of modern capitalism; the socio-psychological background of anti-Semitism, as elaborated by Horkheimer and his collaborators; the interrelationship of and antagonism between religion and the economic viewpoint in modern Zionism.

Islam and Greek Orthodoxy: All statements mentioned, especially those put forward by Gruenebaum, are acceptable.

Christianity and the Jellinek-Weber-Troeltsch Problem Area: Jellinek's theory, with the modifications offered by Troeltsch, is generally accepted and is now no longer discussed. The following critics of Weber have made exaggerated cases: Gundlach as to the impossibility of comparing Catholic with Calvinistic mentality by Weber's method; Sombart, Sorokin, Tawney, and Yinger as to the capitalistic mentality of the Middle Ages; Yinger in his underestimation of the importance of the "calling" and of the religious impulses of the non-conformists who came to colonial America. Although Robertson was at obvious cross-purposes with Weber, it is still true that Becker, Hall, Knappen, and Sorokin were correct in pointing to the fact that predestination is not a trait common to all the groups used as examples by Weber.

Thus the common denominator lies primarily in the common ascetic character and the common belief that economic success is a proof of having lived a life that pleased God. The central theory stands, nevertheless, and there is substance to the assertion that ascetic Protestantism was one of the essential promoters of capitalistic mentality and, as a consequence, of capitalism as an economic system. As far as Troeltsch's theories are concerned, some legitimate modifications were made by Catholics in his picture of the Church Fathers. Some modifications of his concept of the medieval character of Luther are likewise pertinent. Nevertheless, his main theories on the position of protestantism in the history of Occidental culture remain intact and have been illuminated by the additions offered by Edwards, Schlatter, Schwer, Wearmouth, and the whole Schoeffler school.

Christianity in the United States in Recent Times: Except for some exaggeration as to the African heritage in the religion of the American Negro, the statements mentioned can be considered to be fruitful.

MAJOR CONCEPTS AND THEORIES IN THE SOCIOLOGICAL APPROACH TO RELIGION

Types of Religious Groups: There are four extensions of the somewhat crude Weber-Troeltsch classification that are worthy of commendation. They are as follows: (1) Becker's general distinction between "secular" and "sacred" societies (with the important qualifications noted on p. 470), as well as the addition of the two types, denomination and cult; (2) Wach's classification according to the degree of pessimism; (3) Wiese's characterization of the "church"; (4) Niebuhr's, Becker's, Clark's, and Fauset's characterization of the "denomination."

Regularities as to the Sequence of Religio-Sociological Phenomena: Weber's theories, as corrected by various critics, are acceptable.

The Function of the Individual: The concepts of Weber-Troeltsch and their followers correspond to the facts.

Types of Religious Leadership: All the statements mentioned are acceptable.

Transformation from One Type of Leadership to Another: All the statements mentioned are acceptable.

Organization of Religious Leaders: All the statements mentioned are acceptable.

Religious Attitudes of Special Social Strata: Four gaps in Weber's incomplete scheme have been filled in by the investigations mentioned.

Relationship Between Religion and the Non-Religious World: Weber's stimulating but incomplete remarks on "theodicy" found a more fruitful continuance in the corresponding typologies elaborated by Wach.

SOCIOLOGY OF RELIGION: RETROSPECT AND PROSPECT

In conclusion, it would seem justifiable to assert that the most weighty contributions in the field of sociology of religion—as to epistemological foundation, special investigations, typology, and description of special types—were supplied by the Neo-Kantian school and its adherents in the United States. The primary representative of this school (with pragmatic overtones) is Howard Becker. His main epistemological contribution lies in his work on the "constructed type," whereas his major substantive contribution centers around his sacred-secular typology and the addition of the cult-denomination types to the Weber-Troeltsch formulation. Although epistemologically unrelated to all the above, Wach must be mentioned here because of his interest in similar problems. In particular, his typology and his definition and description of special types are of importance.

Wach and Becker and his students must accordingly be considered with regard to the aforementioned spheres as among the most productive and fruitful writers since Max Weber. Since that time, there has not been much influential work carried on by the neo-Kantians and their followers with regard to the less complex religions. Indispensable special contributions, however, on methods of investigating the latter and on knowledge of particular religions have been elaborated by such diverse thinkers as the functionalists, the French positivists, the Catholic diffusionists, and the anti-diffusionist but nevertheless historically minded American anthropologists.

As to specific countries, French positivism generally, and the Durkheim school especially, is not exerting epistemological and methodological leadership. On the other hand, France is represented by works in at least three areas that deal with a religio-sociological complex in a sociologically relevant way: Gernet and Boulanger on Greece; Granet on China; and Hubert in connection with the Celts. All of them stand in a more or less loose relation to the Durkheim viewpoint.

In the United States, native Americans as well as Russian, German, Hungarian, and other refugees, in addition to natives of Oriental countries such as Chinese, Moslems, and others, have made contributions of four different kinds. These have reference to: (1) ancient and contemporary Oriental peoples (for example, the contributions of Chang Lee, Fung-Yu-Lan, Gruenebaum and others); (2) the past and present of Greek Orthodoxy; (3) the Weber-Troeltsch-problem; (4) American religious life as manifested in the many churches, denominations, sects, and cults.

Many religious groups in the world, nevertheless, have not been adequately investigated from the religio-sociological point of view: for example, to mention only a few, Shintoism, Central Asiatic Buddhism, Manichaeism; and (among Christian groups) Armenian, Coptic, and Ethiopian Monophysitic churches; as well as American variants of Episcopalianism and Lutheranism. A great deal remains to be done before it will be possible to construct an even relatively complete sociology of religion.

SELECTED BIBLIOGRAPHY

American Journal of Sociology, Sixtieth Anniversary Issue, on Religion, 60 (May, 1955), Part II.

Becker, Howard, *Systematic Sociology on the Basis of the* Beziehungslehre *and* Gebildelehre *of Leopold von Wiese* (New York: John Wiley, 1932; reissued, with a new preface, Gary, Indiana: Norman Paul Press, 1950), pp. 613-642.

Becker, Howard, and H. E. Barnes, *Social Thought from Lore to Science,* 2nd. ed. (New York: Dover Publications, 1952), 2 vols.

Durkheim, Émile, *Elementary Forms of the Religious Life,* translated by J. W. Swain (Glencoe, Ill.: The Free Press, 1947).

Malinowski, Bronislaw, *Magic, Science, and Religion and Other Essays* (Glencoe, Ill.: The Free Press, 1948).

Sorokin, P. A., *Contemporary Sociological Theories* (New York: Harper, 1928), Chap. 12.

Tawney, R. H., *Religion and the Rise of Capitalism* (New York: Penguin Books, 1947).

Troeltsch, Ernst, *The Social Teaching of the Christian Churches,* translated by Olive Wyon (London: Allen and Unwin, 1950), 2 vols.

———, *Gesammelte Schriften* (Tübingen: J. C. B. Mohr, 1922-1925), vols. 1-4.

———, *Christian Thought: Its History and Application* (London: University of London Press, 1923).

Wach, Joachim, *Sociology of Religion* (Chicago: University of Chicago Press, 1949).

———, *Types of Religious Experience: Christian and Non-Christian* (Chicago: University of Chicago Press, 1951).

Weber, Max, *From Max Weber: Essays in Sociology,* translated and edited by H. H. Gerth and C. Wright Mills (New York: Oxford University Press, 1946).

———, *Gesammelte Aufsätze zur Religionssoziologie* (Tübingen: J. C. B. Mohr, 1920-1921), 3 vols.

———, *The Protestant Ethic and the Spirit of Capitalism,* translated by Talcott Parsons (London: Allen and Unwin, 1930).

SOCIOLOGY OF ART, LITERATURE AND MUSIC: SOCIAL CONTEXTS OF SYMBOLIC EXPERIENCE

HUGH D. DUNCAN

BY 1914 SOCIOLOGISTS INTERESTED IN ART WERE ABLE FOR THE FIRST TIME to make use of philosophic, sociological, and psychological views that offered possibilities of creating an ordered body of knowledge about the function and structure of art in society. Dilthey provided the sociologist with much-needed philosophical underpinnings for theory. Marx and Engels related art to forms of ownership and production. Frazer indicated how art organized primitive life. Durkheim and Max Weber, although they dealt primarily with religious experience, created theoretical and methodological tools for the analysis of *all* symbolic material. Some of Simmel's forms of sociation were developed out of analysis of art and play. By the end of the twenties, hermeneutics, the study of symbolic interpretation, was a well-defined field in the writings of Wach and Cassirer. Marx and Weber taught us, further, that men use art in the struggle for power among classes. Malinowski summed up anthropological views in his description of myth as a kind of social charter. Durkheim and Lévy-Bruhl showed how magical art was used to create and sustain collective sentiments and thought. Collingwood stressed the use of art to inspire us to undertake tasks necessary to group survival. From Freud, finally, we learned how art dissipated tensions through make-believe, which, like dreams, lets us imagine what we cannot have.

Art as Communication. But Freud's emphasis on subconscious elements in art, and Malinowski's stress on the function of art (as myth) in the creation of social charters, provided sociologists of art with no way to think about art as *communication.* Until social theory could supply a view of sociation based on role enactment through symbolic interaction (as communication), the sociologist of art was bound to European views of art that explained much about art but little about the specific use of art forms in the communicative aspect of role-taking. In America, Peirce's triadic analysis of sign situations, his insistence on the public nature of truth, offered American social scientists a way of thinking about the social function and structure of meaning, as meaning arises in action, long before the appearance of Malinowski's and Richards' widely accepted discussions of the triadic elements in "the meaning of meaning" in the early thirties.

George H. Mead and John Dewey understood the significance of Peirce's stress on the public nature of truth for the development of social theory. Mead's view of the social genesis of the self through the reflexive gesture, the role-taking of the "I" and "We" within the group (the "They"), although it stresses the biological level of symbolic interaction, offered for the first time a promise of a theory of personality that would simultaneously free sociological theory from the restriction of Marxian materialism, the excesses of Darwinian naturalism, the new Hegelian "spirit" of Durkheim in his *conscience collective,* and Freud's genetic theories of psychic causation in an archaic heritage. For Mead, the social was a category in its own right, to be explained by the social aspects of role-taking in communication, rather than by analogy to physical nature, biological environment, or the substantiation of Spirit, God, or Society.

Cooley's stress on dramatic rehearsal in the imagination as the means by which we understand, and thus communicate, was very fruitful for the development of a sociology of art, and in turn, for the creation of a sociological theory of communication. But the prestige of early biological psychology and the wonderful discoveries of the physicists soon overwhelmed American sociologists. That great figures of Darwin, Freud, Frazer, and Einstein overshadowed the American pragmatists, Peirce, Mead, and Dewey, who were seeking to develop a theory of sociation based on communication. The next generation of American sociologists, who believed that Mead's theories of sociation arising in communication were the base from which sound sociological theory could be developed, failed to turn to art experience—the specifically *symbolic* experience. It was not until the appearance of the work of Kenneth Burke (not a sociologist) that the indigenous tradition of Peirce, Mead, and Dewey was carried forward in a series of theoretical and methodological propositions on the function of art as communication in society.

Art and Society: The European View. In Europe, orthodox Marxist analyses of art by Plekhánov, the brilliant early work of Lukács on drama and the novel, Antal's work on Florentine painting, and Caudwell's study of the sources of poetry, were soon accompanied by studies that, although they did not accept Marx's transcendent proletarian, still adopted Marxist theories of social class in their analyses of art. Huizinga's *The Waning of the Middle Ages,* like Burckhardt's great work on the Renaissance, used art works and art theory for interpretation of society.[1] Max Weber's essay on the rational and sociological basis of music, as well as his essay on the function of the Chinese *literati,* indicated that insofar as German sociology was concerned, the problem was no longer one of how to think about art and society, but what elements in society and art should be related.[2] In the thirties a number of sound studies by Martin and Balet on art; Schücking, Ehrenberg, Bab, Kohn-Bramstedt, and Misch in literature; the articles on art in the *Handwörterbuch der Soziologie,* edited by Vierkandt in 1931, fulfilled the early hopes of Dilthey (subsequently echoed in philosophy by Cassirer and Collingwood) that the study of art would be considered a study of human understanding.[3] The persecution and slaughter of German scholars under Hitler's terror retarded but did not destroy the important work whose power is again becoming manifest in such recent works as Hauser's *The Social History of Art,* Blaukopf's *Musiksoziologie,* and Honigsheim's studies in the sociology of music.[4]

Lalo, Baldensperger, and Souriaux in France continued the tradition of Taine and Guyau. In common with Dilthy, Bergson, Maritain, and more recently Malraux, they concerned themselves with the meaning of art in society.[5] In French minds, however, "meaning" was not limited to the problem of art as a form of knowledge (as in Dilthey and Cassirer) or as a problem in interpretation (as in Wach and Cassirer); it also included art as a moral problem.

[1] Georg Lukács, *Die Theorie des Romans* (Berlin, 1920), and "Zur Soziologie des modernen Dramas," *ASS,* 38 (1914), pp. 303-345, 662-706. Now available in English is Georg Lukács, *Studies in European Realism* (London, 1950). Frederick Antal, *Florentine Painting and its Social Background* (London, 1947); Christopher Caudwell, *Illusion and Reality* (London, 1937).

[2] Max Weber, "Die rationalen und soziologischen Grundlagen der Musik," *Wirtschaft und Gesellschaft* (2nd. ed.; Tübingen, 1925), and *From Max Weber: Essays in Sociology,* translated and edited by H. H. Gerth and C. Wright Mills (New York, 1946), Chap. 17.

[3] Alfred von Martin, *Sociology of the Renaissance* (New York, 1944); Leo Balet, *Die Verbürgerlichung der deutschen Kunst, Literatur, und Musik in 18. Jahrhundert* (Leipzig, 1936); L. L. Schücking, *The Sociology of Literary Taste* (London, 1944); Victor Ehrenberg, *The People of Aristophanes: A Sociology of Old Attic Comedy* (Oxford, 1943); Julius Bab, *Das Theater im Lichte der Soziologie* (Leipzig, 1931); Ernst Kohn-Bramstedt, *Aristocracy and the Middle Classes in Germany* (London, 1937), especially the introduction, "The Sociological Approach to Literature"; Georg Misch, *A History of Autobiography in Antiquity* (London, 1950), 2 vols.

[4] Arnold Hauser, *The Social History of Art* (London, 1951), 3 vols.; Kurt Blaukopf, *Musiksoziologie* (Berlin, n.d.) (contains bibliography).

[5] Charles Lalo, *Notions d'esthétique* (3rd. ed.; Paris, 1948); Ferdinand Baldensperger, *La Litterature: creation, succes, durée* (Paris, 1913); E. Souriau, *L'Avenir de l'esthétique* (Paris, 1929), and *Les Correspondances des arts* (Paris, 1947); Jacques Maritain, *Creative Intuition in Art and Poetry* (New York, 1953); André Malraux, *The Voices of Silence* (New York, 1953).

Although there arose in France no separate field of the sociology of art comparable to the work in religion of Durkheim, Hubert, Mauss, and Bouglé, this was not because there was no sociological thinking about literature. As in the United States, sociological thought on art was developing within the profession of art itself. Durkheim's sociological views soon influenced French study of art, however. The work of Saussure and Meillet in linguistics; of Granet, Schuhl, and Luquet in the history of ideas; of Lalo in the function of art in social life; of Lévy-Bruhl in primitive use of symbols; the recent work of Beljame, Cohen, and Mongredien on the literary life of the seventeenth and eighteenth centuries; and the work of DeRougement, Benda, Briffault, as well as the many discussions among French men of letters over the function of art (the exchange of letters between Gide and Claudel on the nature of art and religion is but one example) indicate French concern with the social function of art.[6] Malraux's recent work on art, although written from the viewpoint of the artist—not the critic or the public—shows clearly that French thought on art has strong sociological orientations.

In Britain, Jane Harrison's *Themis* offered a statement of myth and ritual, based on thorough documentation taken from Greek tragedy. Her *Ancient Art and Ritual* showed how Greek graphic and plastic arts were affected by magic and ritual. Cornford's *The Origin of Attic Comedy* described ritual origins for comedy similar to those Harrison had discovered for tragedy. Weston's treatment of the Grail romance, Murray's studies of witches, Cook's work on Zeus myths, Hocart's study of kingship, Hooke's symposium on Hebraic-Christian myth in ritual, Welsford's treatment of the fool, and finally Raglan's *Jocasta's Crime,* investigating the incest taboo in myth and ritual, and his summary of the ritual approach in *The Hero*—as well as the later work of Thomson, Carpenter, Spence, and Williamson—indicate the value of ritual concepts.[7] Once Raglan pointed out the common features of all hero myths and stressed the origin of myth in ritual, myth was related to

[6] Ferdinand de Saussure, *Cours de linguistique générale* (Paris, 1916); Antoine Meillet, *Linguistique historique et linguistique générale* (Paris, 1921-1936), 2 vols.; Marcel Granet, *Fêtes et chansons anciennes de la Chine* (Paris, 1919); *Danses et légendes de la Chine ancienne* (Paris, 1926); *La civilisation chinoise* (Paris, 1929); and *La pensée chinoise* (Paris, 1934); M. Schuhl, *Essai sur la formation de la pensée grecque* (Paris, 1934); G. H. Luquet, *L'art primitif* (Paris, 1930); Alexandre Beljame, *Men of Letters and the English Public in the Eighteenth Century* (1st ed., 1881; London, 1948); Gustav Cohen, *La vie littéraire en France au moyen-âge* (Paris, 1949); Georges Mongredien, *La vie littéraire au xvii*^e^ *siècle* (Paris, 1947); Denis DeRougement, *Passion and Society* (London, 1940); Julien Benda, *Du style d'idées* (Paris, 1948); Robert Briffault, *Les troubadours et le sentiment romanesque* (Paris, 1954).

[7] Jessie L. Weston, *From Ritual to Romance* (New York and London, 1920); Margaret A. Murray, *The Witch Cult in Western Europe* (London, 1921); A. B. Cook, *Zeus* (Cambridge, 1925); A. M. Hocart, *Kingship* (Oxford, 1927); S. H. Hooke (ed.), *Myth and Ritual* (Oxford, 1933); Enid Welsford, *The Fool* (London, 1935); Lord Raglan, *The Hero: A Study in Tradition, Myth, and Drama* (New York, 1937); George Thomson, *Aeschylus and Athens* (London, 1941); Rhys Carpenter, *Folk Tale, Fiction, and Saga in*

social process and could be defined in terms of how it functions. Radcliffe-Brown, Malinowski, and others extended these ideas to primitive societies through their analyses of how social cohesion was maintained through dance, song, magic spells, legends, tales, and myth proper.[8]

The use of art as an index to cultural change by Spengler and others is summed up in the massive work of Sorokin, who proposed to abstract laws of culture change from developmental processes in the reciprocal relations between art and society.[9] Tomars used MacIver's theories of community for his *Introduction to the Sociology of Art,* while Mukerjee, in his *The Social Function of Art,* compares European, Asiatic, and Indian art as means of creating "social" feelings and understanding.

Freudian Theories of Art. Freud opened up several avenues for the sociologist of art. His Oedipus theory, for example, shows how art works can be used to create hypotheses for empirical study. In *Wit and The Unconscious* he stressed the need for analyzing reciprocal relations between author and public in terms of status as well as of sexual concepts. In the specific application of his theory of the structure and function of the id, ego, and superego systems to actual cases, he showed how rhetorical and dramatic forms offered clues to the structure of the psyche. Rank, Jung, Reik, and Jones made it possible for other workers—such as Baudouin, Kris, Sachs, and Wolfenstein—to begin concrete analyses of how art and the sexual wish are related.[10] Thus by 1930 students interested in the sociology of art no longer found it necessary to discuss whether art and society were related, but could analyze the connection and, above all, begin to show it in terms of the form and content of the art work itself. It was obvious that any theory of motivation could be substantiated from some kind of art. But once students of art who were interested not only in using art to explain or illustrate other social phenomena tried to use the ideas of Freud, Marx, Weber, and Simmel[11] for concrete sociological analysis of art works, all sorts of difficulties arose. Freud, Weber, and Marx *ascribe* sexual or class characteristics to art and then "derive" these from art. Even if sexual, status, and class determinants

the Homeric Epics (London, 1946); Lewis Spence, *Myth and Ritual in Dance, Game and Rhyme* (London, 1947); H. R. Williamson, *The Arrow and the Sword* (London, 1947).

[8] A. R. Radcliffe-Brown, *The Andaman Islanders* (Cambridge, 1922); Bronislaw Malinowski, *Magic, Science, and Religion and Other Essays* (Garden City, N.Y., 1954).

[9] Oswald Spengler, *The Decline of the West* (New York, 1926-1928), 2 vols.; P. A. Sorokin, *Social and Cultural Dynamics* (New York, 1937-1941), 4 vols.

[10] Otto Rank, *Art and Artist* (New York, 1932); Ernst Kris, *Psychoanalytic Explorations in Art* (London, 1953) [excellent bibliography]; C. G. Jung, *Psychology of the Unconscious* (London, 1921); Theodore Reik, *The Secret Self* (New York, 1953), and *The Haunting Melody* (New York, 1953); Ernest Jones, *Hamlet and Oedipus* (London, 1949); C. Baudouin, *Psychoanalyse de l'art* (Paris, 1929); Edmund Bergler, *The Writer and Psychoanalysis* (New York, 1950); Hans Sachs, *The Creative Unconscious* (Cambridge, 1942); Martha Wolfenstein, *Movies: A Psychological Study* (Glencoe, Ill., 1950).

[11] Georg Simmel, *Philosophische Kultur* (Leipzig, 1911).

are accepted, it is these relations as *symbolically* constituted that concern the sociologist of art. Social class in Marx is not the same as in Henry James. One is an economic, the other an artistic depiction.

A Sociological Schema for the Interpretation of Art. The task of analyzing art sociologically was undertaken in America outside the profession of sociology. Thomas and Znaniecki had made use of symbolic material, but as Blumer's critique showed, there was really no way to evaluate such work because there was no sociological theory of communication. Park and Burgess had discoursed at some length on interaction under such categories as competition, conflict, accommodation, and assimilation in what Simmel termed forms of sociation.[12] *How* social interaction took place was never made clear. The small amount of progress made by some academic sociologists in creating any kind of theory of communication is likewise evident in Parsons' and Shils' uncritical use of the Freudian concept of cathexis.[13]

Mead, although not (according to his students) specifically interested in art, concentrated on how the psyche arises in *function* (i.e. communication) rather than on the structure of the psyche alone. *How* the "I" and the "We" communicate must be known, according to Mead, if we are to know anything about the forms of sociation. For as Dewey held, along with Mead and Cooley, sociation exists in and through communication; hence communication must be a basic, not a residual, category in theory.[14]

Burke's Conceptual Scheme. Although Burke was in no sense a student of Mead, and certainly not a professional sociologist, he too held that only as we understand symbolic phases of interaction can we understand society. He proposed that we think of art as symbolic action, a phase of the act in which attitudes are formed as incipient *acts,* not only as wishes. Unlike Thomas, he did not categorize wishes and then "apply" these to symbolic material but emphasized the need for developing sociological concepts of the function of art. His first statement of this in terms of art as dream, prayer, and chant—like Collingwood's categories of make-believe, magic, and art proper[15]—attempted to synthesize many approaches. By 1945 Burke was able to expand his earlier synthesis of Marx, Frazer, and Freud into a fully developed theory.

[12] Herbert Blumer, *An Appraisal of Thomas and Znaniecki's* The Polish Peasant in Europe and America (New York, 1939); R. E. Park and E. W. Burgess, *Introduction to the Science of Sociology* (Chicago, 1921).

[13] Talcott Parsons and E. A. Shils (eds.), *Toward a General Theory of Action* (Cambridge, Mass., 1952); Talcott Parsons, *The Social System* (Glencoe, Ill., 1951), Chap. 9. Max Scheler, on the other hand, confronted the problem of communication directly; see Howard Becker, "Empathy, Sympathy, and Scheler," *International Journal of Sociometry,* 1, 1 (Sept., 1956), pp. 15-22.

[14] G. H. Mead, *The Philosophy of the Act* (Chicago, 1938), Chap. 23; John Dewey, *Art as Experience* (New York, 1934); C. H. Cooley, "The Roots of Social Knowledge," in his *Sociological Theory and Social Research* (New York, 1930).

[15] R. G. Collingwood, *The Principles of Art* (Oxford, 1945).

> In a rounded statement about motives, you must have some word that names the *act* (names what took place in thought or deed), and another that names the *scene* (the background of the act, the situation in which it occurred); also, you must indicate what person or kind of person *(agent)* performed the *act,* what means or instruments he used *(agency),* and the *purpose.*[16]

Burke thus supplies us with a specifically sociological theory, precise enough in formulation to allow us to develop analytic tools for the investigation of concrete works of art. The specific societal function of art, in his view, is to create and sustain social hierarchies through legitimation of various powers. Burke's view seems very close to Weber's, but Burke shows *how* legitimation occurs in symbolic action. This is done by glamourizing symbols that transcend conflict by appeals to "higher" powers; that is, to symbols that the artist and his society charge with that highly sacred aura, the power of the group itself. Art works must be analyzed in terms of what dramatic struggle goes on, under what conditions, by what means, between what kinds of actors, in what kinds of actions, and for what purpose. This is done by showing how, in the form and content of the art work itself, values held inimical to the survival of the society are destroyed, as in the symbolic killing of the villain; how values held necessary to the survival of the group are preserved or brought into being, as in the symbolic birth, rebirth, or victory of the hero. Symbols of passage from birth to rebirth, from defeat to victory, from the old to the new self make social change possible. The artist keeps paths to change open through the creation of ambiguous, playful, or comic symbols that enable us to experiment in symbolic action with attitudes before we must realize them in the irrevocable moments of completed acts.

Art as a Social Institution

Analyzing the structure of art as a social institution, in terms of the function of art itself, is a task that those trained in the sociological traditions of Cooley, Simmel, and Weber can now undertake. Once Dilthey, Cassirer, Mead, Collingwood, and Burke gave us a theoretical, methodological, and technical base for the analysis of the function of art in society, it became possible to think about the *structure* of art life.[17] The institutional structure of art

[16] Kenneth Burke, *A Grammar of Motives* (New York, 1945), p. xv.

[17] Good introductions to Dilthey's work may be found in H. A. Hodges, *The Philosophy of Wilhelm Dilthey* (London, 1952), and *Wilhelm Dilthey: An Introduction* (New York, 1944); Ernst Cassirer, *An Essay on Man* (1st. ed., 1944; Garden City, N.Y., 1953), and *The Philosophy of Symbolic Forms* (New Haven, Conn., 1953); Susanne K. Langer, *Philosophy in a New Key* (1st. ed., 1942; New York, 1948), and *Feeling and Form* (New York, 1953).

in society must be approached in terms of the interactive forms taken in the relationships between artist, critic, and public.[18] The role of the critic is decisive for sociological analysis of the structure of art life, for he mediates between the artist and his public in terms of what he considers to be values necessary for the survival of the group. Who may select, criticize, judge, or distribute what kind of art, through what media, on what occasions, in what way, and for what purposes, are questions the answers to which describe the structure of art as a social institution. Focus of attention on criticism in complex societies avoids the overly simplistic type of tribal art experience that characterizes ritual approaches. In our society art is used to stress, and yet at the same time transcend, differences.

From a sociological viewpoint, the uses publics make of art, and the reciprocal relationships between these publics and their artists, as expressed through the critic who must act as intermediary, are of crucial importance. But what is said about structure must be said in terms of the institutional function for which the structural theory is designed. And unless we can apply our sociological concepts to art as experienced in symbolic interaction, we cannot be sure we are talking about art at all. Art must be recognized as a *category* of experience. Artists create and maintain the symbols by which we communicate; hence the study of art becomes the study of society, and no science of society will reach fully rounded theoretical expression until we develop a science of communication.

Typology of Social Structures of Art. In fully developed art institutions several elements can be clearly distinguished. These are: the kinds of expression considered to be art by artists and their publics; the times and places in which art is used; the kinds of writers, painters, musicians, etc., who are considered to be artistic (as well as those who are not); the means used to produce and distribute art works; and the values, purposes, or goals of art. This kind of analysis assumes that the practice of art in modern society involves four separable yet interdependent functions. These are: (1) a concern with specific social problems; (2) the creation of symbolic forms that will order social experience in certain ways for those who can make use of these forms (the public as well as the artist); (3) the creation of publics who use art productions for various kinds of satisfactions; and (4) the development of critics who make judgments for their various publics.

The sociologist may single out any element for analysis, but the most important element in structural analysis of art as a social institution will be *criticism*. For it is the emergence of the critic as we know him in our society—that is, as one who passes judgment on the function of art for the group he represents—that probably constitutes the best single clue to the structural analysis of art institutions. The critic must think in terms of what the artist is

[18] H.D. Duncan, *Language and Literature in Society* (Chicago, 1953) [contains extensive bibliographies].

trying to do, and at the same time pass judgments on the use of the artist's work by various publics.

When the evidence from historical and primitive societies is considered, it is doubtful whether there is any situation in which the audience is not differentiated in terms of power to judge art. Once we know the basis for such hierarchies in criticism, we can understand the forms taken in the judgment of art. Judgment of some kind is always being made, and this judgment in its final effect does much to determine art, since it sets standards for the production, distribution, and consumption of art. In this kind of analysis it is important to know who is assigned the right to criticize; what institutions assume the guardianship of criticism; how these institutions defend their roles in competition with other institutions; how those who are to criticize are selected, trained, and supported; to whom criticism may be communicated; and on what occasions criticism is required.

From a sociological viewpoint, critics who base their judgments on esthetic canons are only one type among many. Church, state, business, school—each institution criticizes art in terms of its own needs. The church wants its dogma upheld; the state wants patriotic citizens who will join its armies; business wants profit; the school wants useable material for purposes of instruction. Whether it is called criticism, censorship, market analysis, or revision for learning, such judgments have a profound affect on what kind of art will be produced.

For purposes of analyzing the structural aspects of arts as a social institution, three component elements have been distinguished; namely, artist, public, and critic.[19] It will be assumed that each acts in terms of the other, but that varying degrees of strength in the relationship between any two may be discerned. Such distinctions will be made in terms of what tasks are assigned to those responsible for artistic activity in their society and of what means are allotted to the production of art. Finally, it will be assumed that art institutions, like other institutions, are struggling to achieve a degree of autonomy that will make it possible for artists to communicate their view of the world as they see fit.

A typology of the forms of interaction of artist, critic, and public may be conceived on a continuum beginning with the most direct kind of relationship between artist and public—in which there is very little differentiation in the various undertakings concerned with the production and communication of art works—to a final construct in which artists, publics, and critics may be actually unknown to one another as persons and communicate only in the most indirect manner, yet in which each assumes a responsibility for upholding a standard of art and all are agreed that art should be a power in society on the same level as religion, science, education, politics, etc.

[19] This typology is more fully analyzed in Duncan, *op. cit.,* Chap. 4.

1. Wherever art is produced in small, intimate groups, the purposes for which art is being used are understood by everyone present. Speaker and hearer in the drama know each other's reactions almost immediately through reciprocal responses that are clearly understood by everyone because they are using symbols learned in common and upon which they place a common value. The speaker considers himself to be speaking for the group as a whole. Whatever directly expressed criticism there may be is not thought of as a specialized statement derived from a specific standard, but simply as a statement about the right words that anyone in the group might be capable of making. Older people, or those more widely experienced, may be listened to with more deference than others and thus exercise a kind of criticism. But in general only the speaker and his audience can be clearly distinguished. The accompanying diagram illustrates this type of relation between artist, public, and critic. The heavy line indicates a strong reciprocal relation between artist and a public; the dotted ones indicate the relatively weaker relations between public and critic and between artist and critic.

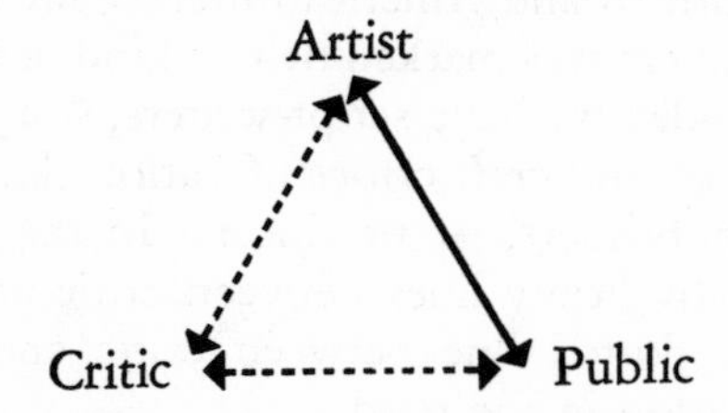

2. Whenever the production of art is monopolized by a class, an order, an institution, or a craft group; whenever those creating art think of themselves as writing not for a general public, but for those in power, the artist reaches what we think of as a public only indirectly—through censors, judges, or critics. The clerics of the Middle Ages, the Chinese *literati,* and the court writers of Europe were of this type. In the diagram, the heavy lines indicate a strong reciprocal relation between artist and critic; the dotted ones the weaker relations between critic and public and between artist and public.

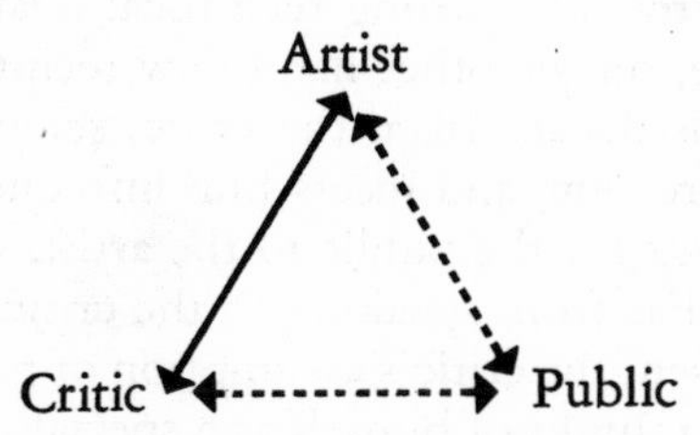

3. In a third type of relation, the artist considers himself strongly related to critics and to his public, but there is no strong reciprocal relation between

critic and public. Critics conceive of their role as guardians of a craft skill or tradition; as advocates of specific social institutions, such as the gentry, the connoisseur, the salon, the publisher; or—a final, highly specialized variant of this type—as a play "doctor" for producers. In all these variants the public is "known" to exist (as far as the critic is concerned), but the critic conceives of his public from the standpoint of the connoisseur or the man of taste. The general public is "vulgar," and it is considered demeaning to criticize for them. The public may be manipulated, its tastes formed, or it may even be permitted to overhear what the critic is saying, but there is no feeling of direct relation to a general public.

The artist, on the other hand, conceives of himself as speaking to and for a general public. He welcomes the enlargement of this public and assumes a responsible role in guiding its taste. He strives to communicate on the widest possible base to the largest number of people, and in every sence treats his public seriously. In a final variant of this type of relation, the artist may consider himself to be speaking to the people as a prophet, a literary priest, or a leader. British and American literary life from the days of Pope through the Victorian era was marked by this kind of relation between artist, public, and critic. Today we have script-writers, story conferences, authors' agents, play "doctors," and craft critics of various kinds who are supported directly by artists, publishers, or producers. In the diagram, this type of relation is indicated by heavy lines between critic and artist, and artist and public, whereas the dotted line between critic and public indicates the weakness of this relation in the triad.

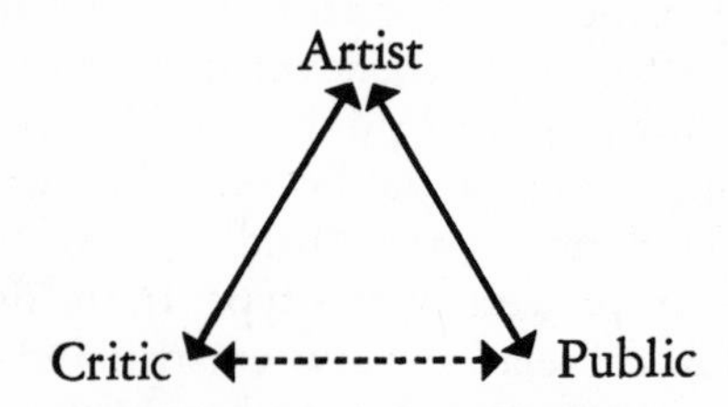

4. In the fourth constructed type of relation, both artist and critic consider their roles in terms of a strong reciprocal relation to a general public. Artist and critic have, on the other hand, few reciprocal relations with each other. The artist feels distant from the critic, seldom submits his work to him for preliminary review, and meets him infrequently and informally—if at all. The critic speaks for the public to the artist, whereas the artist speaks only for the people. Far from speaking to the critic, he may even be hostile to him and deeply resent the critic's assumption of power over their common public. The critic also thinks of himself as a specialist in public taste. He may even be "neutral" in his judgment of the value of this taste. Pollsters of all kinds are a good example of this type of critic. They pretend to no judgment

but simply report what the people want. Whether people should want it, how the people could be made to want something better, in what way the writer could communicate better with his publics—the kind of concern that the critic manifests in every other type of relationship between artist, public, and critic—these elements are lacking.

Newspaper and periodical criticism, in which critics of drama, music, literature, art, and the movies speak as delegates of publics whose taste is accepted as a standard, are the most familiar examples of this type of relation. The "neutrality" of the pollsters is cast aside, and the taste of the public is defended. Artists are even taken to task for not creating in terms of this taste, whereas the critic makes little attempt to evaluate, since his function is to "reflect" taste as he finds it. The purest form of this critic is the one who holds that in art, as in politics, the voice of the people is the voice of God. The following diagram indicates the strong reciprocal relation between artist and public and public and critic (the solid lines) and the weaker relation between artist and critic (the dotted line).

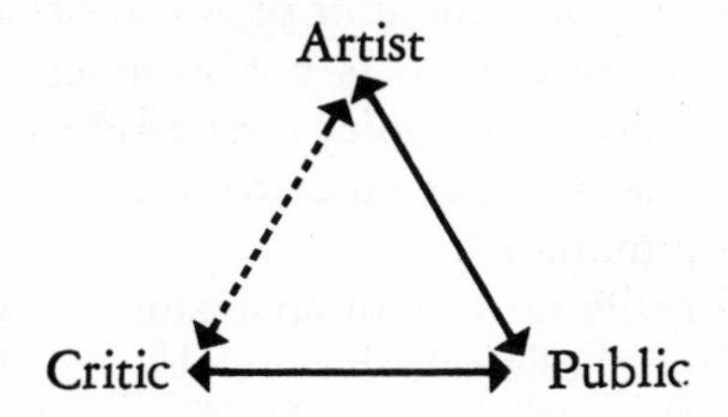

5. In a fifth type of relation, artist, critic, and public assume a mutual responsibility to one another in the belief that art should have an autonomous function in society. The artist, like the priest, the stateman, the soldier, the philosopher, is considered in terms of his social office. He is no longer simply a clown, a magician, a dreamer, a "lucid neurotic," or an "irresponsible," but becomes a creator of forms whose function is to help us explore consciously—through imagination in the service of reason—what certain actions can mean. Here art emerges as an institution in its own right and seeks power on the same level as business, the church, or the school. Artists may seek this power as allies of other institutions, when they are in complete agreement with the ends of those institutions; but when this is so, artists and critics feel that they must be included on policy levels of discussion.

Another example of art taking the form of an independent institution can be seen in the rise of artists to corporate status, where they organize themselves to control the production, distribution, and consumption of art works, as in the Book-of-the-Month Club, which has incorporated and issued stock. This assumption of corporate form by groups of modern *literati* is, however, a somewhat different expression of autonomy from that of the "studio life" of nineteenth-century Europe. American *literati* seem to be abandoning the inverted aristocracy of Bohemia for a professionalization that reflects the organizational structure of American corporations.

The following diagram indicates the strong and reciprocal relations between each pair of elements in the triad by heavy lines.

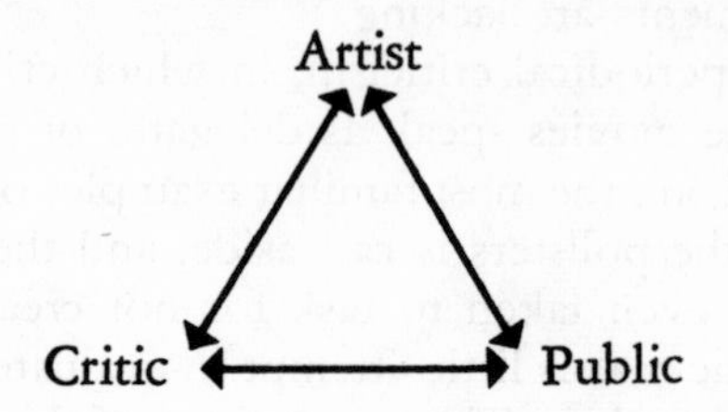

Some such schema as this may therefore help us to rely less on "thought styles," "existential bases," "cultural bases," "organismic relations," and other highly general concepts used in the literature gathering about the sociology of knowledge. For purposes of concrete study of art works, we need structural conceptions of some unit of social organization that is sufficiently clear as a functioning unit. It is not so much a matter of making a case study of small institutions (as Cooley advised)[20] as of creating some kind of institutional concept that will permit us to deal with art in terms of structure and function as communication.

Although there is really no way of analyzing an art work without considering it as a unified symbolic act, the sociologist, like the psychoanalyst, must select certain key ideas and images. He cannot do so until he is able to state clearly what sociological perspective he is taking. In a future highly developed state of sociological analysis of symbolic works, more specialized views will be applied. At present, it seems best to stress a sociological principle general enough to offer possibilities for many types of sociological analysis: the principle of social hierarchy.

SYMBOLS AND HIERARCHY

Essentially, the final power of a symbol is not attained until it is detached from a specific context and becomes powerful in itself. The achievement of this task is, in fact, one of the prime functions of art. For the artist is not content with symbols either as signs (as in scientific discourse) or as ideological weapons (as in political discourse), but seeks to endow them with an "ultimate" radiance that will be a "final" ground for the creation of attitudes necessary to community survival in whatever kind of action he believes necessary. In a scientific context, the power of the symbol arises in demonstration; in politics, through persuasion; but in art, symbols move us because of the process of identification and, from the sociological view, identification

[20] Cooley, *Sociological Theory and Social Research* (New York, 1930), pp. 313-322.

with the *group* as we enact our roles in specific positions of a social hierarchy. Identification arises in forms similar to those evoked by the politician when he begins telling us that he too once lived in our fair city, worked as a humble laborer, etc. There is also an unconscious factor in identification. Then too, symbolic identification can become a highly individual end, as when we earnestly yearn to identify ourselves with some specific group. Here we are not necessarily being acted upon by a conscious external agent, but may act upon ourselves to achieve this end.

The function of art, from the sociological view taken here, is to celestialize hierarchy.[21] Those in power expect their artists to dignify, ennoble, and spiritualize their symbols of power with such radiance that institutional, party, status order, or national demands become individual duty. In view of this, sociological analysis of art works may proceed by distinguishing hierarchic terms as follows: First, there are terms assigned to the celestial order alone. Sacred symbols of images and ideas are always ultimate terms; the form and content of such terms indicate the deepest beliefs of the society. Second, there are terms used only in the depiction of the social order. They are predominantly secular terms. Third, there are terms that bridge sacred and secular realms; these are terms of passage. Fourth, there are terms explicitly celestial but implicitly social. Fifth, there are terms explicitly social but implicitly celestial. Sixth, there are terms speciously social but actually celestial. Seventh, there are terms speciously celestial but actually social. Terms of the third through the seventh type function as terms of passage from one social condition to another and thus offer clues to how the principle of identification with authority functions in communication, considered as a public phenomenon.

Hierarchic Ladders. Social needs for authoritative ladders are satisfied in art (as well as in science and religion) by ideas of steps or stages. Action must go forward in proper order, processes must be carried out in the "right" way or their efficacy will be damaged. The university president approaches the platform in a certain way, as do kings their thrones or presidents the speaker's platform in Congress. Status processes are not only regular but *ordinal,* with canons of first, second, third, etc., order—canons ranging from absolutes in presidents, kings, etc., down to whatever rank is necessary to carry out action on a local level. The magician performing his rites, the king's processional toward his throne, the army parade—these take a form in which progress from one stage to another is regulated by considerations of propriety—that is, by relationships between each step in a developmental sequence. Certain words must be uttered before others, the university marshal must proceed the president, scientific experiments must be done in a certain sequence. The power of such orderly process in art, the working out

[21] See Kenneth Burke, *Rhetoric of Motives* (New York, 1950) for an exposition of this theme in greater detail.

of various forms, thus has its counterpart in society; and art in turn enhances the power of these social forms. How we go from one position to another is thus as important as our points of departure and arrival.

Social courtship, the communication between differentiated classes of persons, however these persons are symbolized, is a basic sociological phenomenon in art. In its purely social manifestations, an art work expresses differences in social conditions, but at the same time, transcends differences through *symbols of community integration.* Differences may be of age, as in *Alice in Wonderland;* of sex, as in *Lady Chatterley's Lover;* of race, as in *Native Son;* but the resolution of these differences takes place through symbols of social hierarchy. Even a "sexual" drama such as *Lady Chatterley's Lover* cannot be understood without reference to status. Sexual impotency occurs not as the result of biological or psychological facts alone, but of social causes as well.

In comic and tragic art we have formal dramatic expression of the problem of hierarchy. Superiors must create and sustain symbols that enhance belief in their power; inferiors must create and sustain symbols that offer relief from the burdens of power. Superiors must be majestic, inferiors loyal. Both, however, feel the burden of power. The superior must be great, sublime; his sin is pride, and unless it is checked it must have greater and greater scope for expression. The inferior must be humble and attentive; his sin is churlishness, a refusal to give full and complete loyalty. Yet the inferior, unless he really believes that his superior exercises power through a principle binding on both, must resent what he cannot think just. With the best of intentions, despite the most carefully forged symbols, there will still be areas where majesty and duty do not jibe. In such failure, the scapegoat or the fool must be invoked. Majesty must purify itself through transferring evil to a scapegoat. The death of the scapegoat, the villain's corpse on the stage, relieves our society of its evil, and we are ready to follow our leaders once more. But the birth of the fool relieves us, too, for now we know that things can at last be said (in laughter) that we ourselves long to say but dare not, for fear of displeasing those we must love, or those whose displeasure may cause us pain.

Our leaders, too, can say things through the fool that could not be said seriously without damage to their majesty. A proud leader commands; he does not request. A successful leader cannot admit failure openly. In laughter both leader and led put aside their solemn masks of devotion and belief to take up the comic mask of doubt and question. Comedy uncovers the mysteries lurking in symbols of social cohesion; tragedy enshrouds them. In great comic art, the fool is the voice of the community. He transcends both the superior and the inferior because he can take the point of view of one toward the other without becoming weak or evil. The tragic hero, on the other hand, must treat difference as heresy and destroy it. The comic hero kills off evil, too, not through the horrors of victimization, but by submitting the differences to community reason through laughter. As we laugh together, we cannot hate, for now we feel a deep sense of brotherhood in our common plight. As we laugh, for example, at the haughty gentleman who slips into the swimming pool as he backs away from the lady to whom he is bowing, we feel superior because his status trappings of formal dress become ridiculous in a swimming pool, and the elaborate status pantomine of bowing to a lady has ended incongruously. We laugh because status tension suddenly dissipates. If, in helping the drenched plutocrat out of the pool, we too tumble in, laughter mounts in a complete disregard for the expense, and hence the sacredness, of our plutocratic status trappings. In doing so, we reaffirm once again our common humanity.

As sociologists, we should keep in mind that for thousands of years art has been offering mankind ways of reducing status tensions to manageable proportions. It would be simple enough for us to recognize this and begin with the assumption that all forms of victimization (tragic and comic alike) are but attempts to regain, sustain, or create conditions where divisiveness may be overcome through transcendent symbols of cohesion. Study of *how* great artists do this might do as much for sociologists as Freud's use of art did for psychoanalysis.

SELECTED BIBLIOGRAPHY

Burke, Kenneth, *The Grammar of Motives* (New York: Prentice-Hall, 1945).

Daiches, David, *The Novel in the Modern World* (Chicago: University of Chicago Press, 1939).

Dewey, John, *Art as Experience* (New York: Minton, Balch, 1934).

Duncan, H. D., *Language and Literature in Society* (Chicago: University of Chicago Press, 1953).

Hauser, Arnold, *The Social History of Art,* translated by S. Godman, (London: Routledge and Kegan Paul, 1951), 3 vols.

Johns-Heine, Patricke, and H. H. Gerth, "Values in Mass Periodical Fiction, 1921-1940," *POQ,* 13 (Spring, 1949), pp. 105-116.

Kohn-Bramstedt, Ernst, *Aristocracy and the Middle Classes in Germany* (London: P. S. King, 1937).

Schücking, L. L., *The Sociology of Literary Taste* (London: Kegan, Paul, Trench, and Trubner, 1944).

Smith, H. L., *The Economic Laws of Art Production* (Oxford: Oxford University Press, 1924).

Sorokin, P.A., *Social and Cultural Dynamics* (New York: American Book Co., 1937), vol. 1.

Tomars, A. S., *Introduction to the Sociology of Art* (Mexico City, Mexico: no publisher given, 1940).

Wolfenstein, Martha, and Nathan Leites, *Movies: A Psychological Study* (Glencoe, Ill.: The Free Press, 1950).

IV

Convergences of Bordering Fields with Sociology

SOCIOLOGY AND INTERDISCIPLINARY DEVELOPMENTS

ADOLPH S. TOMARS

IN THIS CHAPTER THERE IS IN NO SENSE ANY ATTEMPT AT A FORMAL HISTORY of interdisciplinary movements involving the participation of sociology. What is undertaken here is a consideration of some of the implications of interdisciplinary developments in the light of the history of sociology.

At one time sociologists devoted an inordinate amount of energy to discussion of the nature and purposes of sociology, how it differed from other disciplines, whether it was a general or a special science, etc. The reaction, especially in America, has been to develop the science of sociology rather than to discuss what sociology should be—a perhaps not uncharacteristic American tendency to prefer research to theory and action to reflection. Although there is much to be said for this proclivity, it has undeniable drawbacks. It must be admitted that our subject has made a much more impressive record in the amassing of empirical data than in the meaningful ordering of its material into a coherent structure of knowledge—that is, a discipline.

Interdisciplinary Collaboration in the Light of the History of Sociology

Whatever one's preferences, there is a periodic need to ask basic questions about the direction a science is taking in relation to its avowed nature and purposes and to assess current work in the light of the historic aims of the discipline. No amount of stress upon activism can long avoid it.

This assessment becomes peculiarly necessary when the sociologist engages in interdisciplinary activity conjointly with other social scientists. Such collaboration inescapably calls into question the relation of sociology to other subjects and the nature and purposes of its own discipline.

These questions pose themselves insistently: What is the distinctive contribution of sociology? In what capacity does the sociologist collaborate and upon what terms? Are the purposes of the collaboration consistent with the purposes of sociology?

The questions become the more urgent because, for better or for worse, the idea of interdisciplinary collaboration is in the ascendant, and interdisciplinary developments are increasing in number and prestige on a variety of levels.

Academic Collaboration: The Integrated Course and the Combined Department. Attention has been focused largely upon interdisciplinary research in which sociologists join other social scientists in a concerted investigation of a problem or problem area. On another level, recent years have seen the development of the interdisciplinary course, combining several social disciplines in the "integrated" course in social science. In some cases, valiant attempts are made to interrelate the materials in some way, with debatable degrees of success. Many such courses are interdisciplinary only in the nominal sense that several disciplines are taught in one course, possibly on the theory that if four instructors, each teaching a discipline in which he is competent, cannot provide integration, it may somehow be achieved by one instructor teaching four disciplines in three of which he is incompetent.

For these courses interdisciplinary texts are provided. But the interdisciplinary text has long been with us in sociology itself. Many sociology texts contain huge slices of material lifted bodily from anthropology, social psychology, geography, economics, political science, etc. Contentwise, sociology frequently finds itself occuying a minority position in its own textbooks. Years ago Howard Becker referred to this propensity as "academic kleptomania," but that was before the term "interdisciplinary" became fashionable.

There is also the interdisciplinary university division in which sociology is one of several disciplines comprising a separate educational unit devoted to criminology, or social welfare, or area studies. Finally, there is the interdisciplinary department. Academically, sociology usually began as a division within an older department, in a junior partnership with economics or government. For some years the tendency was for sociology to split off into a separate department; more recently, the trend has been again toward combination, most often with anthropology. In most cases, however, the connection appears to be purely administrative, each subject going its own way.

The Rationale of the Interdisciplinary Movement. There are a number of recognizable reasons for the ascendancy of the interdisciplinary idea. The issues most frequently verbalized center about conceptions of integration as opposed to specialization (the latter usually preceded by the adjective "narrow"), or part *vs.* whole. Among the social disciplines, the exclusiveness of specialization must be countered by integration of disciplines. Knowledge of the separate parts of human society is not enough; we must see the unity of social life and view human conduct in all its aspects as a total configuration.

Behind these explicit reasons lie implicit conceptions derived indirectly from various specific sources or from general values in our climate of opinion. For instance, from progressive education comes the idea that it is desirable to break down the barriers between departments with the ultimate goal of abolishing pedagogical subjects as units of instruction. Another source, coupled with this, stems from a tendency of educational administrators, especially on the college and university level, to see departments as entrenched vested interests, severally jealous of each other's expansion, prone to jurisdictional disputes, and jointly resistant to administrative encroachment, thus presenting so many stumbling-blocks to educational innovation as embodied in the proposals espoused by administrators.

In the lexicon of many administrators, "departmental" has come to be a bad word, "interdepartmental" to have a virtuous sound. Such an attitude readily passes from departments to the disciplines they administer, and imperceptibly "disciplinary" and "interdisciplinary" come to acquire a similar polarity of wickedness and virtue. Not infrequently the scholar devoted to the integrity and advancement of his discipline finds himself regarded by a reproving administrative eye as but the crassest departmental chauvinist.

From the general ethos of our society comes the notion that cooperation is always superior to isolation and teamwork to solitary work, a notion easily extended from persons to entire disciplines. Teamwork carries connotations of democratic *camaraderie*. Individual work bears the odium of snobbish, aristocratic exclusiveness. The present tendency toward the exaltation of the cooperative research team over individual research almost causes one to wonder if ultimately the practice of individual investigation by the single scholar working alone may not come to be looked upon with suspicion as a kind of solitary vice if not evidence of subversion.

The superior virtues of cooperative effort are, however, predicated as much upon the ground of efficiency as democracy. Do not the egalitarian mores tell us that, on any problem, two heads are better than one, so that, by analogy, in scholarly investigations, two sciences are better than one? These are some of the implicit influences making for the current vogue of the interdisciplinary idea, and the sociologist, sensitive to the cultural climate, cannot fail to discern them.

A Critique of Current Arguments for Integration. Although some of these implicit ideas have considerable validity, there are large areas of dubiety, as in the highly questionable procedure of reasoning by analogies from persons to disciplines. And with respect to the aim of abolishing pedagogical subjects, whatever its merits for elementary education, its extension to higher education could threaten the integrity of the social sciences as organized disciplines.

"General education" has become a catchword among college educators. A healthy reaction to the undeniable dangers of overspecialization is understandable. But a swing of the pendulum from "learning more and more about less and less" to "learning less and less about more and more" may be a doubtful corrective that creates dangers of no less gravity. This is by no means a purely pedagogical matter of no concern to social scientists. The future practitioners of sociology are now being trained in the colleges. In a science as young and amorphous as sociology it may well be that what is needed is the strengthening of its autonomous organization rather than the weakening of it.

Whatever the numerous overtones, the core of the issue does lie in the explicit "specialization *vs.* integration," or part–whole, dichotomy in its specific application to the role of sociology in interdisciplinary collaboration. It is here that we must ask the basic questions about the nature and purposes of sociology as a discipline *vis-à-vis* other disciplines when they collaborate in pursuit of the goal of social integration and unity.

This goal of complete coverage of the societal whole is frequently expressed in such familiar phrases as "political, religious, economic, and social" to indicate the broad range of human behavior. In this phrase it is the significance of the words "and social" that goes to the heart of the questions we must ask with respect to interdisciplinary collaboration.

THE DEVELOPMENT OF SOCIOLOGY AND THE SIGNIFICANCE OF INTEGRATION

Questions involving the purposes of sociology cannot be answered a priori, but only in the light of the historic development of the discipline as it has formulated its aims. The suggestion is here put forward that sociology has developed in two distinct ways, one of which may be termed purposive, the other accidental, and that in the light of each of these ways interdisciplinary collaboration has a different significance and presents different problems.

The Purposive Development of Sociology. The purposive developmental history of sociology is found essentially in the development of social theory as the orderly and systematic formulation of the discipline. This history is familiar enough to permit statement in highly compressed form with deliberate oversimplification of its phases.

Sociology began with the recognition that it was as necessary to undertake objective study of the social realm as of the natural. This was the Comtean call for a social physics. Sociology was to be the science of social life, the study of everything that happens in society. With respect to the social sciences already existing (economics, political science, linguistics, comparative religion), the attitude developed that these were specialized studies, dealing with parts of the social order. If every conceivable part were studied by a separate science, the collective totality of special sciences would not constitute a science of society. The integration of the parts into an organic social order would still be lacking. Sociology was to provide the integrated whole. On the Spencerian model, sociology was to be thought of as a synthetic science of society whose purpose was to integrate the entire corpus of social sciences into one general, encyclopedic social science.

A further phase brought rejection of this purpose as untenable. A synthetic general science would not be a genuine science, but an impossible superscience requiring superscientists. Diverse frames of reference of the special social sciences could not be integrated within a single encyclopedic unit—at least the goal was highly premature.

The goal was reformulated. Sociology was still conceived as the science of society, but society and the social were redefined as a structure of social relations and groups. Sociology was not to concern itself with the entire cultural realm of all happenings in social life, but with the nature, forms, and processes of interhuman behavior—with institutions and groups as such. Sociology became a special science within its own specific framework and yet remained a general integrative science in the sense that the social structure it studies is basic to and underlies the subject matter of all the other social sciences. Not economics *qua* economics or religion *qua* religion but economic and religious institutions and groups as types of social structures is the focus. One thinks of Simmel as a key figure in this reformulation.

The other social sciences do not thereby become branches of sociology, but the material they study may. Thus Max Weber foresaw that besides general sociology there would develop various special sociologies of economics or religion or art in which these areas would be studied within the broad conceptual framework of sociological theory, thereby relating them to the total social structure and to each other. This has been the great tradition of systematic social theory in which stand such present-day theorists as MacIver, Znaniecki, Wiese, Becker, Parsons, and others.

In the light of this purposive developmental history, interdisciplinary collaboration between sociology and other social disciplines raises some vexatious questions. The sociologist collaborates with other disciplines in seeking the goal of integration, the very goal which is the avowed purpose of his own discipline! He is placed in a curious dilemma; acceptance of collaboration on equal terms seems to be a negation of his role as practitioner of a discipline purporting to be the science of society. In the phrase "political, religious, economic, and social," the sociologist represents the caudal appendage "and social." Yet in his own discipline the "social" is defined as something broader and deeper than all the others and as essentially encompassing them. What does the "social" represent in the collaboration? Can the incompatibility be reconciled?

Three possibilities appear. Perhaps sociology has repudiated its avowed purpose and no longer regards itself as engaged in the creation of a science of society. Yet there are no overt signs that sociologists have abandoned their claim to deal with basic social structures and processes involved in all social behavior. The textbooks continue to define sociology as the science of society, however phrased. For instance, a recent text terms sociology as the science of human groups, emphasizing that although other sciences study particular types of groups, sociology alone studies human groups as such.[1]

Another possibility is that in agreeing to the need for interdisciplinary collaboration in achieving an integrated view, sociologists thereby concede the complete failure of sociology to realize its own stated purpose. Sociologists may have been humble about their achievement, but again there is no evidence of any general feeling that we have made no progress in clarifying the nature of society.

A third possibility remains. Perhaps sociology has only failed to convince others of the validity of its aims and its progress toward realizing them—a failure in public relations. Having hid his light under a bushel, the sociologist faces a dilemma when called upon to join in interdisciplinary work. To refuse collaboration on the ground that he is already committed to the same purpose within his own discipline stamps him as a scientific snob. To make conditions by insisting that he has the broad conceptual frame within which the others should work makes him appear to seek a scientific hegemony, refusing to play unless captain of the team, a churlish fellow unworthy of the democratic fraternity of scientists. So he keeps silent and meekly accepts the ambiguous role of representative of the "and social."

However this may be, it seems that in the light of the purposive developmental history of sociology, interdisciplinary collaboration presents the sociologist with an embarrassing situation.

The Accidental Development of Sociology. What of the situation in the light of the other way in which sociology has developed, the one here termed its accidental development? This historical process can be summarized very briefly.

Sociology came upon the academic scene as an upstart among older and well-entrenched social disciplines, and soon developed a tendency to appropriate and cultivate those problem areas and social fields either not claimed or else permitted to lie fallow by other sciences. This tendency ex-

[1] Ronald Freedman *et al., Principles of Sociology* (New York, 1952), pp. 2, 4.

pressed itself in empirical research and curricular specialization. The development is accidental in that the criterion of selection appears to lie almost exclusively in the fact that a given area was not already studied by another discipline.

In this way, sociology took over large areas of demographic inquiry and of social statistics, the study of immigration and assimilation, broadening into race relations and minority groups, criminology, urbanization, human ecology, marriage and family relations. The last-named area had been untouched in the colleges, presumably because, involving sex, it was considered dangerous. Sociologists rushed in where others feared to tread and, when shortly the climate of opinion changed, found in their hands not a dangerous subject, but the most popular subject on the campus.

THE NEED FOR INTERNAL INTEGRATION

By this historical development, sociology has become a congeries of social specialties, loosely joined without theoretical integration into an over-all discipline, and consequently possessing little systematic internal organization. The bulk of sociological growth has proceeded in this fashion.

Most of these specialties are potentially among the special sociologies that Weber envisaged. Yet despite a few valiant attempts, it can scarcely be said, in all candor, that any one of them illuminates its materials in the light of a specifically sociological focus of conceptual formulations so that it bears the distinctive aspect of a branch of sociology. We are familiar with marriage and family books and courses that contain a minimum of sociology with large segments of pure psychiatry, law, demography, psychoanalysis, anthropology, and home economics, and that could as legitimately come under rubrics other than sociology. In what sense is this a legitimate specialization within a sociological discipline? We may be glad that sociology has cultivated this important field, but it is difficult to take pride in the fact that it is a sociological field only because the sociologist got there "fustest" with the "mostest" courses.

In the light of this accidental historical development of sociology, interdisciplinary collaboration presents a different aspect, free from the difficulties suggested above, yet not without its embarrassing features. The sociologist is called in to collaborate as a technical expert in a specific set of problems, not as the representative of a discipline. His expertness has no necessary relation to his being a sociologist. He merely possesses information that no one else has acquired.

When the phrase "political, religious, economic, and social" expresses that whole which is the aim of interdisciplinary collaboration, it is clear what "and social" means under these circumstances, since the phrase can only mean political, religious, economic, and whatever is left over. Such collaboration can scarcely be considered interdisciplinary in any meaningful sense.

Perhaps integration, like charity, should begin at home. It might be suggested that for the sociologist, interdisciplinary collaboration in search of integration may be somewhat premature before sociology has achieved integration among its own sprawling and as yet undigested specialties. Unless this is achieved, we may well find interdisciplinary developments taking over some of our own fields of specialization. One need not be a cynic to recognize, as a practical reality, the desire of other disciplines to cut in on some of the more popular sociological specialties as at least one motivation behind some interdisciplinary movements—witness the considerable pressure in some universities to have marriage and family relations become an interdisciplinary area of specialization removed from purely sociological auspices. The moral and the warning is unmistakable. He who possesses a field by squatter's rights without ever acquiring legitimate title may some day come to find himself dispossessed.

Sociology in the Grand Design of Unified Knowledge

Current advocacy of interdisciplinary activity goes far beyond mere collaboration on specific problems or even whole problem areas. The goal envisaged by many is nothing less than a grand design into which all the sciences concerned with the study of man and his works are combined into one unified social science of man.

The increasing enthusiasm for the realization of this grandiose objective as the next task for the joint efforts of the social sciences makes it all the more necessary that the premises, assumptions, and implications of such a project be examined with the greatest care. The prerequisite for such a long leap, proposed with so much enthusiasm, should be an equally long look and much calm reflection.

What is purposed here is a brief examination of a few of the underlying questions and implications involved in the leap towards a synthesis of the social sciences. These will be, for the most part, general considerations, not more pertinent to sociology than to other disciplines, but the discussion will attempt to keep matters of special sociological relevance in view wherever possible.

THE RATIONALE OF AN OVER-ALL SOCIAL SCIENCE

The current interdisciplinary agitation has been brought to a focus in the recent volume edited by John Gillin under the title, *For a Science of*

Social Man.[2] If this title expresses the editor's envisaged goal of a cross-disciplinary integrated science, the work of the book's six contributors is better described by the subtitle, *Convergences in Anthropology, Psychology, and Sociology.*

Two distinguished authorities from each of the three disciplines assess, respectively, the impact of one of the other two disciplines upon their own, emphasizing conceptual interpenetrations and possibilities for further synthesis. Thus Howard Becker and Talcott Parsons consider, respectively, the interrelations of anthropology and psychology with sociology. Such surveys of interdisciplinary cross-fertilization are highly valuable and serve to point up the fact that without any conscious plan or design the "compartmentalization" of the several disciplines has never prevented their constant interpenetration, whether such influences have proved helpful or hindering. Becker, for instance, makes this very clear when he skillfully condenses the complicated history of the cross-fertilization between anthropology and sociology and also traces its differential pathways in four different countries.[3]

In the editor's scheme, these historical surveys are preparatory to the noble goal of the unified science of man for which he pleads. Not all of the contributors to the survey are as sanguine as the editor about the readiness of the sciences for integration, and although all envisage unification as an ultimate goal, some clearly regard its realization as in the nature of some far-off divine event. Gillin, however, sees unification as the imperative next step for which the ground must be prepared without delay, a view shared by some of his collaborators. His concern is to "bring to light certain agreements and convergences, especially in theory, among these sister disciplines and to point to promising possibilities that will. . . contribute to the further development of a science of social man." Because Gillin's book so well sums up an intellectual trend now gathering momentum, it can well serve as a point of departure for inquiry into some of the premises upon which this trend in based.

It may be noted that the "core disciplines" whose integration is to create the grand synthesis are, here, sociology, anthropology, and psychology. Since this premise is not discussed it is presumably regarded as self-evident. Conspicuously absent are economics and political science, disciplines sometimes thought to play a not inconsiderable part in the study of man.

It is possible to discern an implied train of reasoning here. The economic and the political long since became differentiated from each other, and the political in turn was distinguished from the social. Consequently, these two disciplines have become modest in their assertions, claiming no more

[2] John Gillin (ed.), *For a Science of Social Man: Convergences in Anthropology, Psychology and Sociology* (New York, 1954).

[3] Howard Becker, "Anthropology and Sociology," in Gillin, *op. cit.,* Chap. 5.

than certain areas of social life and restricting their concern to specific problems of man.

Sociology, anthropology, and psychology make more inclusive assertions, each in turn claiming or having claimed to be the science of man. As noted before, sociology made earlier claim to taking in economics, political science, and other specialized social disciplines, and still regards itself as basically underlying them. Anthropology includes all the cultural sciences, regarding the economic, political, etc., as areas of culture; and psychology has long looked upon itself as the proper subject devoted to the proper study of mankind. The reasoning then appears to be that if these three disciplines have severally claimed to be the science of man, then a general science of man must surely exist somewhere between them jointly if only they can be put together. An additional element here may represent the influence of anthropology, which, dealing so much with primitives, who for the most part lack complex political elaboration and possess economies that can be examined largely in terms of their technologies, has tended to look at economics and political science as parochial "culture-bound" disciplines (i.e., restricted to our culture), therefore not on a par with disciplines with a comparative perspective worthy of inclusion among the sciences of man as such. This notion is not likely to commend itself to social theorists concerned with economic and political sociology and mindful that the interest in economic and legal science of Durkheim, Weber, and MacIver, to mention only a few names, was sufficiently comparative to take in all the great civilizations of the world.

Another conspicuous absentee among the sister disciplines who are to join hands in collaborative unity is history. Since the mother of all the social sciences can scarcely be excluded on the grounds of narrowness of specialization, one seeks other possible grounds. Is it, perhaps, because history is an idiographic discipline rather than a true nomothetic science? This is, however, belied by the stress laid upon ethnography in assessing the significance of the contribution of anthropology. To this issue we must return again later. Here it suffices to note that the premises of inclusion and exclusion are not discussed.

It might be reasonable to suppose that in any proposals for interdisciplinary integration, the first step would be to determine what disciplines are to be integrated and why; how and what each would contribute to the grand design. If the work under examination is typical of the interdisciplinary trend, as it appears to be, it can hardly be said that this preliminary problem has received adequate attention.

SOME OBJECTIONS TO AN INTEGRATED SOCIAL SCIENCE

What are the basic premises of the argument for a concerted push to create a comprehensive social science? Taking the Gillin book as representative, two arguments against a science of man are recognized: the objection that human behavior is not amenable to scientific explanation, and the objection that a coordinated social science, although desirable, is premature.

The first argument seems irrelevant to the issue, being an objection to the feasibility of any social science, separate or integrated. The second argument however, goes to the heart of the matter. There is generally universal agreement upon the desirability of the eventual consolidation of all the social sciences into a unified body of knowledge of man and, eventually, ultimate unification of all knowledge in existence. The issue is one of readiness, and the objection warns that premature attempts at unification, as far as the social disciplines are concerned, would have stultifying rather than liberating effects.

Refutations. In refutation of this central objection on the grounds of prematurity, Gillin presents several arguments: the extent of existing convergence is indication of readiness; interdisciplinary collaboration is necessary because the social sciences have much to learn from each other; and, finally, the need for integration into a unified science is socially urgent and imperative.

The first two of these arguments are not elaborated and are somewhat inconclusive. The surveys made by Gillin's six contributors, although they point up some impressive convergences, are heavily weighted in this direction, since the objection was to draw out the convergences, not to emphasize the differences. When the focus is shifted to the intradisciplinary level, the notable lack of integration between the schools and factions within the several disciplines themselves makes the case for interdisciplinary integration considerably less impressive. It might indeed suggest that the next step could well be a determined effort to achieve a greater measure of self-integration before reaching out to comprehensive integration on a still wider and more ambitious level. This problem requires further discussion and we will return to it later.

The second argument, stressing the value of cross-fertilization, is undeniable but not altogether pertinent. The social disciplines have learned much from each other and have much more to learn. The argument, however, does not clearly distinguish between collaboration for the purpose of mutual learning and fruitful collaboration for the building of a comprehensive science. For the latter, it does not suffice for sciences to learn to take from each other such material as they can use for their own ends; it requires first learning each other's language, then forging a common language before beginning the erection of a common scientific structure. Otherwise the structure becomes a Tower of Babel. Gillin is fully aware of this problem and is sharply critical of much current interdisciplinary collaboration that involves no genuine meeting of minds and produces no real integration. Yet he seems to feel that if enough interdisciplinary channels of communication are kept open for the reciprocal flow of knowledge, a general integration will eventuate.

It is the third argument, in terms of practical urgency, upon which the case for a unified social science is mainly grounded. Although Gillin's immediate goal is a unified body of theory, his main concern is that such a science of social man would yield a valid body of knowledge for the solution of man's pressing social problems. The need is too urgent for delay; man's very survival is at stake. The social sciences must attain coherent unification comparable to that of the physical sciences, and there is no time to lose. The situation is too desperate for petty quibbling over disciplinary boundaries while a world demands usable knowledge. That this view has become a platitude repeated daily by social scientists, educators, and publicists does not lessen its significance. Long ago H. G. Wells called it the race between education and catastrophe. Currently, it is more likely to be phrased as social science catching up with physical science.

It cannot be denied that these considerations are among the most powerful motivating forces behind the present enthusiasm for interdisciplinary integration. Nor can it be denied that they are noble in purpose and praiseworthy in motivation. Indeed, social scientists would be unworthy citizens if they did not feel impelled to make greater contributions to human welfare in these troubled times. But there remain underlying assumptions that require more careful examination and whose validity must be brought into question, however laudable the aspirations based upon them may be.

The basic assumption here is that our troubles are due to a lack of coherent and dependable scientific knowledge of man and that when such knowledge is achieved it will be put to good use for the welfare of man. Although Gillin is too sophisticated not to be aware of the pitfalls of "scientifetishism" and specifically disclaims such addiction, it is clear, nevertheless, that he looks to social science for man's salvation. There is in this view an obvious and important truth. Comprehensive and valid knowledge of man cannot be put to social use except insofar as it becomes available. This is a partial truth, however, in that availability of knowledge carries no guarantee that it will be used. The point could well be made that if only a fraction of the knowledge already gained by the social sciences, separately or collectively, were put to intelligent use, the world might not be in quite so parlous a state. In fact, Gillin himself makes this point elsewhere but does not draw its full implications.

The implied picture of a world of men desperately looking to social scientists as the last best hope of staving off disaster, and of social scientists stung by a sense of guilt into the creation of a full-fledged science of man with which to leap into the breach—this is a picture containing strong elements of both naive optimism and unconscious arrogance. It is, of course, the old Platonic dream of the intellectuals, the utopia in which philosophers are kings and kings philosophers (for philosophers here read "social scientists," for kings, makers of public policy). And despite all experience, the conviction never dies that if only the philosophers can perfect their philosophy they will surely be kings, or at least the counselors of kings.

The Uses of Scientific Knowledge. There is an even more basic and more disturbing consideration that should be squarely faced. The real issue is not society's use or non-use of social science, but the *kind* of use. And consideration of the purposes for which science is used, their wisdom or folly, takes us straight into issues of morality and ethics, realms wholly beyond the competence and authority of the scientist.

The lesson for social scientists is plain, if not pleasant, and surely preferable to comforting illusions. If nuclear physicists are not today the happiest of men, it is not because society has failed to utilize their knowledge. Let us suppose that the unified social science so devoutly wished for is possible within the near future and that a reliable body of knowledge of man yielding a high degree of prediction and control could be attained by, let us say, 1984. How certain can social scientists be that they would thereby have cause to rejoice? Social scientists should be capable of realistically facing up to this possibility.

If the view of social science as salvation is compounded of arrogance as well as optimism, it must be admitted that the counter-view here put forward can involve elements of cowardice as well as of compassion and can easily lead to conclusions equally arrogant and misleading. It is not here proposed that social scientists should arrogate to themselves the decision to make available or to withhold knowledge according to their predictions of the probable uses to which it might be put and their own judgment upon such uses. What is suggested is that if a comprehensive science of man is not a present or imminent reality, the social scientist should be able to view that situation with patience and equanimity, perhaps not unmixed with some feelings of relief. Physical science has flourished greatly and the world has had unloosed upon it the threat of the atom bomb. We may wish for social science to flourish even as mightily, but it must be in full and unblinking awareness that there could be horrors worse than atom bombs.

The scientist *qua* scientist is concerned with the search for and extension of knowledge and with the maintainance of conditions permitting and facilitating such endeavor. This is *his* responsibility. What use society will make of his knowledge is something he can neither control nor foresee and about which he is no wiser than other citizens. Here he has neither responsibility nor competence. In this he must take his chances along with the rest on the wisdom or folly of men.

These considerations have been stressed here because the conception of a brave new total science of man as the urgent need for the solution of man's ills is, implicitly and explicitly, the chief motivation behind so much of the mounting enthusiasm for interdisciplinary integration. If this view is to be held, it is vital that its full implications be examined and that those who hold it are free of illusions about it.

A DISSENTING OPINION ON INTEGRATION

Apart from practical motivations, there are important questions relating to the theoretical possibility of interdisciplinary integration. These questions center about the key issue of the readiness of the social sciences for conceptual unity; and they do not seem to be receiving adequate study.

One cause of this situation may well be that the enthusiastic advocates of integration have succeeded in identifying their view as "advanced," "progressive," and "broad-gauged," whereby the dissenters become "narrow specialists," "stand-patters," or "reactionaries." This has tended to inhibit voicing of skepticism, which expresses itself most often in silence, cautious acceptance, or minimal enthusiasm. It is, then, all the more noteworthy to find a distinguished scientist raising his voice in vigorous dissent against the currently fashionable trend, as the anthropologist, A. L. Kroeber, does in a recent paper.[4] He does not hesitate to point out the fetishistic value acquired by the word "integration" and to remind us that, although it is a fundamental goal to recognize integration where it exists, there is an equal responsibility to recognize its absence where it is not present or has not been found.[5]

In the compulsive drive for integration as a current shibboleth, Kroeber discerns an extrascientific and emotional element, an infantile monism yearning for the simplicity of unity in the face of the complex pluralism of reality—a kind of pantheistic belief in oneness that is religious rather than scientific.

As an anthropologist, Kroeber is concerned with that distinctive aspect of man called culture, which he sees as resting upon society and personality. He has no objection to making a beginning upon the ultimate task of relating culture, society, and personality, provided this will not deflect or inhibit the development of the study of culture. But since he regards the social sciences as only in the early stages of understanding their own distinctive fields, he clearly fears that such deflection will occur, that the emotional drive of social scientists apparently hell-bent for integration will

[4] A. L. Kroeber, "The Knowledge of Man," (paper prepared for Columbia University Bicentennial Conference V, "The Unity of Knowledge," October 27-30, 1954). Since conference rules do not permit quotation from unpublished papers, it is necessary to paraphrase.

[5] One wonders how much encouragement would be given a book serving as a counterpart to Gillin's, surveying the disagreements, divergences, and incompatibilities among the social disciplines. Though negative in emphasis, such a work would be especially valuable for those interested in integration. It is still a basic tenet that in testing hypotheses negative results are as important as positive results.

not advance their disciplines toward genuine conceptual union, but will rather have a regressive and stultifying effect upon all of them. And he cautions again that analysis is as important as synthesis and is what makes real synthesis possible and meaningful.

It is characteristic of disciplines in the early stages of development that they attempt a general total-front attack upon their phenomena, an attack usually ineffectual because of its diffuse character. Separate approaches are then developed for separate aspects of the phenomena; and it is by this isolation that the chaotic unity of the crude phenomena of experience is broken down into differentiated bodies of validated knowledge. These are then gradually linked and integrated with each other under successively broader principles of organization.

Kroeber traces this process in the development of biological and chemical science and regards the present condition of the social sciences as comparable to the state of biology and chemistry about the year 1700—that is, still in their relatively undifferentiated condition, attempting simultaneous total-front attacks upon their subject matter, and lacking even the foundation of an adequate taxonomic organization of their data. Thus the very fact of the agitation over integration into a total science of man becomes itself evidence of the immaturity of the social disciplines.

Kroeber speaks primarily as an anthropologist, and it is likely that his estimate of scientific immaturity is less true for sociology than for anthropology. For anthropology has been especially characterized by a total-front, holistic approach to the study of man. The field it has claimed for its own would cover all the social sciences and all the humanities, all seen as specialized subfields of culture (the special field called "social organization" being relegated to sociology), together with large portions of the biological and geographical sciences as applied to man and his environment as well as to prehuman forms. Kroeber himself has consistently de-emphasized the biological and natural-science aspect in order to restrict anthropology to the study of culture; however, to the observer, this restriction seems somewhat as though he were limiting himself by hitching his wagon not to the farthest star but only to the nearest. Sociology, beginning with almost as grandiose claims, has gradually redefined itself within a more restricted and more sharply focused theoretical field.

It may be noted that this over-inclusiveness did not produce serious difficulties as long as anthropology concentrated its attention upon primitive cultures. Not only were these small enough as units to permit a holistic, configurational approach, but they had been ignored by the other social scientists, who were scarcely aware of their existence. Anthropologists had no choice but to be their own historians, economists, political scientists, sociologists, religionists, linguists, ecologists, anatomists, and anthropometrists.

It is likely, also, that Kroeber's strictures on the lack of an adequate system of classification are less applicable to sociology than to anthropology. Sociological theory has made some progress here, especially in the development of categories of social groups and in distinguishing the basic social features of such polarities of social structures as those involved in simple and complex societies (*Gemeinschaft–Gesellschaft,* folk–urban, sacred–secular, communal–associational, etc.).

It would appear, indeed, that the influence of anthropology upon sociology has been an inhibiting one here, for the failure of anthropology to develop a sound classification of cultures is apparently rooted in the fact that such classifications were originally associated with stages of evolution. In throwing out the early sociological–anthropological theories of *unilineal* evolution, anthropologists seem to have thrown out everything with the bath—baby, tub, soap, and towel—for example, "evolution" as organizing concept and systematic attempt at culture classification. Insofar as this attitude also permeated sociology, as it clearly did, it serves as an example of interdisciplinary influence of at least questionable, if not detrimental, effect.[6]

Whatever the relative immaturity of the various disciplines, the basic fact remains that the search for wholeness as implied in much of the yearning for integration, the very notion of a whole truth, at once sociological, psychological, economic, cultural, etc., represents an attitude that is quasi-religious, extra-scientific, and even anti-scientific. The whole truth is something expected from theologians in the churches and witnesses in the courts, but not in science, all of whose truths are partial, circumscribed, relative to defined frames of reference, achieved by the creation of closed systems through which what is included becomes meaningful precisely because of what is excluded. Answers are possible only because of the refusal to ask all questions simultaneously.

MATURITY AS A PREREQUISITE OF INTEGRATION

Only as systems are developed can they be brought into wider articulation with each other in broader systems within which the constituent systems fall into place as special cases. There are no short cuts. The problem is to distinguish between early and mature phases of the process. The appearance of integration or wholeness shown in the early phases is due to the fact that differentiation has not yet occurred. The genuine integration of the

[6] A number of Kroeber's observations imply anthropological views of sociology not acceptable to sociologists. In a paper prepared for the Columbia Conference mentioned above, under the title, "Comments on Professor Kroeber's Paper," Talcott Parsons takes issue with some of these. Thus he shows that Kroeber's implication that both sociology and psychology deal with underlying subcultural interaction grounded in a subhuman level would make culture the only distinctively human field and would neatly leave anthropology as the only science of man as man.

mature phase is the result of differentiation, making possible organic interrelationships within larger structures, as when astronomy and mechanics are integrated into a Newtonian synthesis and brought within the reference system of general laws of motion. The passage to successively wider spheres of interrelationship is marked by the creative formulations of great synthesizing minds such as those of a Newton, a Darwin, an Einstein.

There is little disagreement that, compared with the natural sciences, the social sciences represent an early phase of scientific development, in terms of systematic organization and integration, far behind the mature theoretical development of physical science. Nor have the social disciplines anything to be ashamed of in this. Developing as disciplines largely during the past sixty years or so, as opposed to several times that span for the physical sciences, and working with peculiarly complex and intractable materials, they have made notable progress in bringing some order out of the welter of human phenomena.

It is curious to note that some of the people most decrying the "primitive" and "backward" state of the social sciences *vis-à-vis* physical science are the very persons who want the social disciplines to undertake an over-all unification that would imply a maturity of development equal to that of the physical sciences. By some short-cut called interdisciplinary collaboration, the social sciences are somehow to raise themselves by their bootstraps and enter a stage of over-all integration only recently achieved by physical science and far from completed there. Presumably, by some magic inherent in interdisciplinary teamwork, the social sciences would be expected to produce Einsteins even before they have found their Newtons. The danger in such short-cuts is not merely that they are illusory, but that attempts to force integration upon disciplines not ready for it might well introduce confusion and interfere with their chances of orderly internal development.

The present situation in sociology is especially pertinent here. Many contemporary sociologists, reacting against earlier premature attempts at developing sociological theory on a broad scale and without adequate factual base, have turned their backs on any generalized social theory. Deliberately restricting themselves to "theories of the middle range" of a relatively low order of abstraction and remaining close to empirical data, they hope that by some gradual process of accretion such theories arising from concrete research will assemble themselves into a body of sociological theory of society.

Opposed to these "empiricists" are the "theorists" who stress the importance of broader systematic theory as a necessary framework for the guidance and integration of empirical research that will prevent the fragmentation of sociology into disjointed segments and the dissipation of research into relatively trivial problems by providing key hypotheses and directing research to the crucial experiments. At present, this cleavage is the major issue among sociologists and there are signs that a *rapprochement* is coming about, with "empiricists" increasingly aware of the need for broader theory and "theorists" increasingly focusing upon possibilities of empirical validation. It would be unfortunate if, just as this situation is beginning to come into balance in a new attempt to create a systematic sociology, it were to be upset by any large-scale redirection of effort to the forcing of a still broader all-out integration of sociological theory with the entire gamut of social disciplines. It seems unlikely that sociologists would want to divert their attention to massive collaboration with other disciplines in creating a science of man at a time when they are beginning to learn how to collaborate fruitfully with each other to create a sounder discipline of sociology.

The Absence of Internal Integration in Specific Social Sciences. The decisive proof, if proof is required, that the social sciences are not ready for integration and unification lies in their own lack of internal integration into systematized disciplines. Until such self-integration has advanced a good deal further, until each discipline has defined its own boundaries more clearly, questions of further interdisciplinary integration seem highly premature. The common enterprise of unified knowledge can hardly be fruitful until each contributor has been able to determine the precise nature of his distinctive contribution to it.

From the standpoint of internal organization, all the social sciences are beset by unsolved difficulties. Despite very serious problems of this kind, sociology seems almost unified when compared to a subject in such a schizoid condition as psychology, which has yet to determine if it is a biological or social science or whether it deals with a separate psychic order apart from both.

It can be assumed that the solution of these internal problems is likely to occupy the attention of all the social sciences for some time until *intra-disciplinary* integration is sufficiently advanced to justify interdisciplinary integration. Those who assume the present readiness of the social sciences and the imminence of their unification are men strong in faith, even as the early Christians were confident in the imminence of the Second Coming. Now, as at that time, the devout need not abandon their faith; they need only adjust their timetable.

A cynic might begin to suspect that some of the enthusiasm for a general interdisciplinary science springs from a confession of failure and a desire to evade these problems of internal organization—as if, conceding failure to determine clear boundaries for the several disciplines, it were then proposed to ignore all boundaries and let everyone range everywhere in a grand "free-for-all" over the entire field of the study of man. It is quite possible that there may be some unconscious motivation here to thus escape the pressing need for the social disciplines to clarify their own focus and their relationship to each other.

Intradisciplinary Integration: The Relation Between Descriptive and Generalizing Concepts. One matter that surely requires clarification is the relation within each discipline of the descriptive and generalizing aspects. Put another way, this can be stated as the relationship of all the social sciences to history. Here is one interdisciplinary collaboration that the idiographic–nomothetic relationship makes mandatory for all the disciplines. They must all use for raw material the description of events, past and present, that constitutes human history and that provides the data from which to abstract and by which to validate generalizing propositions. All the more curious, then, is the fact, noted earlier, that most proposals for interdisciplinary unification leave out the discipline of history and that interdisciplinary collaboration almost never includes formal collaboration with historians, where collaboration would appear to be most fruitful.

This omission is evidently the result of the influence of anthropology, in which ethnography plays such a prominent part and which consequently envisages itself in the role of supplier of descriptive data for the social sciences. Thus Murdock asserts that, in the riches of ethnography, anthropology has "evidence concerning an immensely wider range of variation in human behavior than has any other discipline. It has access to thousands of nature-made experiments . . . of social and cultural life . . . impossible to reproduce artificially. They provide the ideal ultimate testing ground for theories of human behavior . . ." Murdock consequently claims that anthropology is destined "to become the final proving ground of behavior theory in the future . . . the final arbiter of the universality of social-science propositions."[7]

These are claims sociologists will find it difficult to accept. The descriptive riches gathered by anthropology have been of great value for many comparative purposes. But from the point of view of sociology they have only limited utility by virtue of the fact that these materials are themselves limited in that they are, for the most part, restricted to (1) primitive cultures and (2) contemporary cultures. The propositions sociology is most concerned with apply primarily to complex societies and require the time dimension of history (and only complex societies have a recorded history) in order to suggest and test theories of causation and change.

The quantitative richness of primitive societies does not make the anthropological material less limited. The smaller number of complex historic societies provide more significant answers to the questions asked by sociol-

[7] G. P. Murdock, "Sociology and Anthropology," Gillin, *op. cit.*, pp. 29-30. For discussions of the issues involved in the suitability of anthropological methods for the study of non-primitive society and the adequacy of ethnographic as compared with historical data see: Howard Becker, *Through Values to Social Interpretation* (Durham, N.C., 1950), pp. 106-110, 141-147; Robert Bierstedt, "The Limitations of Anthropological Methods in Sociology," *AJS*, 54 (July, 1948), pp. 22-30; A. S. Tomars, "Some Problems in the Sociologists' Use of Anthropology," *ASR*, 8 (Dec., 1943), pp. 625-634.

ogy than any number of non-literate societies. For these sociological questions, history is indispensable, as it is for most of the social disciplines. Wheter each social discipline can best provide its own descriptive materials (its "-ography" to accompany its "-ology"), or whether all can draw upon a common pool provided by the discipline of history as such, is a questton that will have to be threshed out before any adequate clarification of the interrelations of the social sciences is possible.

Informal Cross-Fertilization and its Benefits. The history of the social sciences amply belies the notion that their compartmentalization has isolated them from each other behind iron curtains of specialization. Interdisciplinary cross-fertilizing influence has taken place all along, and is likely to accelerate without the necessity of any hothouse forcing by enthusiasts for a science of man that is as pretentious as it is premature.

Whether one regards a unified science as in the offing or only a very remote possibility, normal interdisciplinary intercourse and collaboration will proceed with all its obvious benefits and carry with it some definite dangers to be guarded against. It has not been an unmixed blessing in the past; like other things conferring great benefit, interdisciplinary interpenetration must be used with reasonable care and caution. It may be worth while to conclude here by noting a few of the benefits and some of the cautions to be observed and the way in which advantages and dangers are inextricably intertwined.

An obvious benefit accruing from interdisciplinary fraternization is the avoidance of unnecessary duplication and rediscovery, as when workers in one discipline "discover" conceptual formulations and arrive at conclusions already known for years to their colleagues in another discipline. Although no science has had a monopoly of prior discovery, sociologists can point with pardonable pride to an excellent record in this respect. Thus the anthropologist Murdock writes:

> . . . most of what modern anthropology has absorbed from the functionalists it could have learned decades earlier from American sociology had it chosen to listen . . . the lesson from functionalism has been that cultures and subcultures are organically related to the structured groups and subgroups that carry them, which has been axiomatic in sociology at least since . . . Summer.[8]

According to Murdock, not until Linton's *Study of Man* in 1936 did any American anthropological work recognize this fact. In similar vein, the psychologist Smith, discussing recent developments in psychology, states:

> One of the most hopeful features in the current situation . . . is the emergence . . . of incipient consensus on a [conceptual] model that rejects the sterile dichotomy of isolated individual *vs.* disembodied group. The model is by no means new; Cooley and G. H. Mead had the essential insights early in

[8] Murdock, *op. cit.*, pp. 19-20.

the century. But the tradition springing from Mead and Cooley tended to remain the private property of sociologists . . . today . . . the insights are being rediscovered on all sides . . .[9]

And, writing as a social psychologist, Newcomb, discussing the impact upon current psychology of various sociologists and their concepts of individual–group relations, social self, attitudes-values, status, role, etc., notes:

> [C. H. Cooley's]. . . calm and non-defensive insistence on the indivisibility of "Human Life" was belatedly discovered by many a psychologist. . . . At their own level . . . with remarkably little help from psychology, micro-sociologists of the 1920's . . . had developed a framework for handling many of the observed facts, conditions and consequences of interaction among persons. [Until] the late 1940's psychologists made little use of the potential contribution.[10]

Newcomb even goes so far as to say:

> If it had proved possible for an earlier generation of sociologists to develop a body of theory . . . both reasonably complete and internally self-consistent, sociology itself would have been on the highroad to a unified science of man.[11]

Theoretical Blind Alleys. Whereas it is true that greater cross-disciplinary communication between the social sciences might profitably reduce much needless rediscovery of each other's achievements, it is also true that we cannot be sure this rediscovery is always needless. What appears as a defect of wasted effort can have virtue and value of its own. Two kinds of value can be discerned, which we may here designate by the terms *dialectic value* and *convergence value.*

By dialectic value is meant the thinking through of an issue in the dialectic of development within a discipline to the point where a specific concept or formulation becomes meaningful *in terms of that discipline*, even though another discipline had evolved it earlier in its own terms. This is another way of saying that a science is unable profitably to appropriate conceptions from another science until it is ready to assimilate them. In the logic of development of a particular discipline, such separate rediscovery cannot be dismissed as so much wasted effort. For psychologists of the twenties, extricating themselves from the morass of instinctivism only to stumble into the pit of behaviorism, the ideas of a Cooley could scarcely have held much meaning. It would seem that disciplines, like individuals, can learn only through their own experience and from their own errors.

[9] M. B. Smith in Gillin, *op. cit.,* p. 64.

[10] T. M. Newcomb, in Gillin, *op. cit.,* pp. 233, 236.

[11] *Ibid.,* p. 230.

The alternative, when concepts are taken over from another discipline before such a dialectic process has been gone through, has generally led to an appalling superficiality. One has only to think of the ill-digested and shallow use of psychiatric and psychoanalytic concepts by sociologists and anthropologists, in particular some of the latter, who have applied methods of tribal investigation to contemporary large-scale civilizations and blithely generalized national character from a few details of infant care, such as swaddling, weaning, toilet training, etc.—"diaper determinism," to use Becker's phrase.

If taking over concepts from another discipline before being ready to assimilate them has the effect of negating dialectic value through superficiality, it also negates convergence value through uniformity. That is to say, premature conceptual borrowing invites the danger of becoming sheer imitation. Such imitative uniformity defeats the cross-fertilizing convergence that is the desired outcome of interdisciplinary influences. Convergence is significant precisely because, and only to the extent that, it is an arrival at a similar destination by different routes. Convergence reinforces validity and can lead to significant integration; uniformity only holds up the mirror to itself and may create the illusion of integration.

There are strong pressures that sometimes lead to the imitative borrowing of concepts and methods not compatible with the logical development of the discipline adopting them. The greater prestige of longer established disciplines may often cause such pressure, as in the well-known inferiority feelings of social scientists with respect to the achievements of their own younger disciplines *vis-à-vis* the natural sciences, and the equally well known history of attempts to imitate from the natural sciences concepts and methods of doubtful applicability. The danger here has been the wasteful deflection of effort and attention from legitimate concerns indicated by the logic of the social sciences and a consequent inhibitory effect upon their development. It may be that young sciences, like infant industries, require some sort of protective tariff against the pressure of ideas from outside.

Although it is true that sociologists may feel proud that other disciplines are only now discovering seminal sociological ideas such as the insights of a Cooley, it is also true that such pride will not be unmixed with some feelings of guilt. For it cannot be said that sociologists ever gave those seminal ideas any great attention and development; they were largely permitted to lie fallow. Indeed, it is possible that through the medium of other disciplines, such as psychology, sociology may rediscover the significance of its own pioneers. If so, this too would have to be included among the positive values of interdisciplinary influence.

Extra-Scientific Factors in Previous Borrowings. Factors of prestige and inferiority have undoubtedly been at work also in the many instances where the social sciences have been deflected from their own proper concerns by excessive preoccupation with each other's concepts and methods. In their collective feeling of inferiority in relation to physical science, the social sciences have tended to watch each other narrowly, each with some anxiety that perhaps the other has struck a rich vein of scientific gold. Undoubtedly this has been a factor in spurring interdisciplinary curiosity. Certainly many sociologists have exhibited a tendency to undervalue their own achievements, to take over and be unduly impressed with psychological or anthropological concepts and methods as somehow possessing greater validity. This suspicion, which makes other fields look greener and richer, is perhaps a manifestation of insecurity that can be outgrown with increased maturity and cross-disciplinary communication. At least one value of accelerated interdisciplinary collaboration might be to allay such anxieties by reassuring all the collaborators of their mutual impoverishment and making it clear that, scientifically speaking, no one of them has yet "struck it rich."

In this all-too-human anxiety of scientists, there is an inevitable time-lag in the appropriation of material from other disciplines, with the result that by the time the ideas are appropriated they are already becoming outmoded in the disciplines from which they are taken. Thus at the time behaviorism was already going out of fashion in psychology, some sociologists were becoming greatly excited over the possibility of a behavioristic sociology. The cynic might scornfully describe this process as disciplines taking up each other's discards.

Yet this phenomenon, too, is not to be derided, for it is never possible to predict in which discipline a concept will become most fruitful. Ideas and methods not found rewarding in one field may turn out to have great significance in another. Perhaps a classic example is the recapitulation concept, an idea at least as old as Vico. Despite persistent effort, it was never possible to validate it as a principle for social or individual development in the fields of social theory, culture history, or educational psychology; yet it turned out to have application in biology in the field of embryology.

The Importance of Diversity. So inextricably interwoven are the benefits and disadvantages of interdisciplinary collaboration that it becomes a delicate matter to decide when it makes for creatively stimulating cross-fertilization and when it has inhibiting, deflecting, and other detrimental effects upon the disciplines involved. Yet if anyone can clarify this question it should be the social scientist. For years sociologists and anthropologists have been studying such processes as invention *vs.* imitation, invention and diffusion, parallelism, convergence, acculturation, assimilation, etc. All of these apply to interdisciplinary influences, and specialists in these processes should be able to throw much light here.

One principle underlying all creative change and innovation seems almost self-evident, namely, that change comes about by the interaction of differences. Two conditions, therefore, must be met: (1) enough communication to insure the maintenance of interaction; (2) enough isolation to insure the maintenance of differences. Without a proper balance between the factors of communication and isolation, cross-fertilization cannot occur. Increased communication requires more, not less, emphasis upon the preservation of differences.

Nowhere does this apply with greater force than to the cross-fertilization between disciplines where the maintenance of the distinctiveness of each of the disciplines is the *sine qua non* of the fertility of their contacts. The prospective acceleration of influences crossing scientific boundaries makes it all the more imperative that the boundaries themselves be clearly defined; and the increase of interdisciplinary communication can itself aid the process whereby the disciplines clarify their relationship to each other (i.e., the ways in which they differ from each other).

The Necessity of Clearer Definition. The suggestion put forward here, therefore, is that the most valuable use of interdisciplinary collaboration would be, not the elimination or blurring of disciplinary boundaries, but the redefining, relocating, and tightening of those boundaries along more logical and meaningful lines, focusing more sharply upon the genuine differences that legitimately separate the social sciences.

This suggestion will not be popular with enthusiasts for an immediate drive toward integration and unification, but what basically stands in the way of interdisciplinary integration is obvious lack of self-integration—the need for increased self-discipline before the sprawling agglomerations called the social sciences can be true disciplines and hence ready for further unification. If the social sciences have any clear and present duty, it is not at this time to begin building the grand mansion of unified science, but first for each to put its own house in order. By all appearances, this is not likely to prove an easy task, yet it must be attacked with determination if the sciences of man are ever to reach that level of maturity on which they can properly consider a science of man.

One important result of such intradisciplinary tidying up would be the recognition that much that is presently thought of as integration is spurious. It is not infrequently found that there are greater theoretical differences between practitioners of the same discipline than between representatives of different disciplines. This is sometimes hailed as a sign of cross-disciplinary integration; it is much more likely to be evidence of the disorganized state of the disciplines.

When the sociologist finds himself coming closer to the psychologist, before this convergence is hailed as *rapprochement*, integration, or unification, it might be well to ascertain if it does not mean merely that the sociologist has been asking psychological questions of his material rather than sociological ones. No one need condemn this as high treason, but it is important to recognize it. It is possible to become so "enthused" over crossing boundaries as to forget that unless we can determine where the boundaries lie we can no longer know when we are crossing them.

A case in point is the present status of social psychology, a field cultivated within both sociology and psychology, although increasingly gravitating to the latter. There are now two kinds of social psychology, a sociological social psychology (microsociology, in Newcomb's terminology) and a psychological social psychology. If the former came under sociology and the latter under psychology, the distinction would be troublesome, but at least it would have a logic to justify it. The point is that at present both can be found within each discipline.[12] Unless this sort of thing is checked by an orderly re-examination and relocation of boundaries, there is a distinct possibility that undisciplined social-science growth will lead, not in the direction of integration, but toward chaos. (See Chap. 19, "Social Psychology and Sociology.")

It can be expected that increasing interdisciplinary collaboration will make it possible to determine more easily to which disciplines specific problem areas are to be most effectively allocated, how existing boundary lines can be re-aligned so as to be more meaningful, and what territory is to be included within the boundaries consolidated.

Integration. The actual carrying out of such a re-focusing of disciplines into more systematically and coherently organized bodies of knowledge will undoubtedly encounter great difficulties in the face of vested interests and entrenched traditions; and no discipline will escape the necessity for some agonizing reappraisals. The integration of any one of the major social sciences bristles with difficulties so formidable as to make the task seem almost as visionary as the project of a unified science.

For psychology, one major problem of integration will involve the reconciliation of psychology as biological science and as social science; another, the reconciliation of psychology as theory and as technology; and both of these the problem of different schools' and factions on each level. For instance, many psychologists have considered social psychology as an applied field on a par with educational or industrial psychology, whereas others regard it as a special body of theory, and some as providing the basic theoretical framework for most of general psychology.

Anthropology seems relatively free of problems involving confusion of theory and technology. Here the problem will lie in the possibility of finding some integrating focus, some distinctive approach in a field now

[12] At one college known to the author, social psychology is taught under psychology. For some years it was given both semesters but by two different instructors, one oriented sociologically and the other from individual psychology. Their courses had almost nothing in common, and students were left with radically different conceptions of the subject according to whether they had taken it in the fall or spring semester.

totalitarian in its all-out claims, embracing all the social sciences and humanities and reaching into the biological level. Even if physical anthropology is cut loose, the problem of finding a distinctive theoretical focus on the inclusive level of the cultural will still raise great difficulties.

In contrast, sociological theory appears in a better position, having already passed through its stage of all-inclusive claims and having, gradually, in its central tradition, concentrated upon a more specifically focused and manageable area.

Specific Problems. But if sociology is in a more definable state than anthropology, this is so only with respect to formal theory. On the practical level of research and teaching activity the situation is reversed. Despite its omnivorous inclusiveness, anthropology, in practice, has restricted itself to a distinctive area by its concentration on primitives—units small enough to be amenable to a total approach and with which no other disciplines had concerned themselves. Anthropologists had not succeeded in validating a science of man, nor had they conclusively established a valid science of culture. But beyond question they had created a distinctive science of primitive culture. Only as anthropologists have been reaching the end of the road with primitives and have begun to turn to the study of large-scale contemporary civilizations, where they find themselves preceded by other disciplines, have they begun to face the problem of finding a distinctive place for themselves on the practical level.

Sociology, as indicated above, despite increasing theoretical concentration, has become increasingly dispersed on the practical level, expanding haphazardly within the interstices of the other disciplines until sociologists today are literally "all over the place" and the proportion of their research and teaching that is specifically *sociological* has become surprisingly small. The problem of integration will involve reappraising the many sprawling specialties now included within the field by asking to what extent they can be given a sociological orientation and legitimately incorporated, and to what extent it may be necessary to relinquish them. This will be further complicated by the fact that some of these specialties are considered theoretical, others technological, and, as in psychology, there is frequently lack of agreement over which is which.

This task of re-evaluation, reappraisal, and redefinition of the spheres of the social sciences into more unified, integrated, and distinctive areas is certain to prove Herculean, but it is difficult to see how it can be evaded much longer. By entering a stage of systematization and consolidation, the social disciplines would be signalizing their coming of age as genuine disciplines. Not until the achievement of such maturity would it be possible to look forward to the further step of interdisciplinary consolidation. It may be that eventually the various social sciences acting in concert will comprise a harmonious orchestra, each player contributing his part to the grand symphonic synthesis of the science of man. But before that, it will be necessary to make certain that each player has mastered his instrument through knowledge of its nature, its possibilities, and its limitations.

SELECTED BIBLIOGRAPHY

Cairns, Huntington, "Sociology and the Social Sciences," in Georges Gurvitch and W. E. Moore (eds.), *Twentieth Century Sociology* (New York: Philosophical Library, 1945), Chap. 1.

Gillin, John (ed.), *For a Science of Social Man* (New York: Macmillan, 1954).

Laski, H. J., *The Danger of Obedience and Other Essays* (New York: Harper, 1930), Chap. 6.

Ogburn, W. F., and Goldenweiser, A. E. (eds.), *The Social Sciences and Their Interrelations* (Boston: Houghton, Mifflin, 1927).

Parsons, Talcott *et al.* (eds.), *Toward a General Theory of Action* (Cambridge: Harvard University Press, 1951).

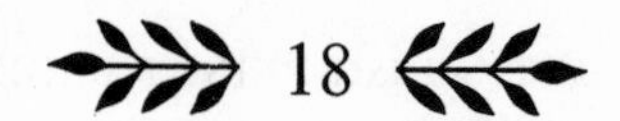

CULTURAL ANTHROPOLOGY AND SOCIOLOGY

C. W. M. HART

SINCE WORLD WAR I, ANTHROPOLOGY MUST BE HELD TO HAVE PROGRESSED and flourished greatly, if we judge it by the usual standards of number of practitioners, place in universities, size and number of professional societies, and professional journals. Less formal criteria point in the same direction. An anthropologist has been a leading character in a Broadway play, and another, in a Hollywood movie, has been cuckolded by Clark Gable. Perhaps the final proof that anthropology has really arrived has been its selection by the Ford Foundation as one of the chosen behavioral sciences. If however, we begin to select from the enormous body of anthropological literature since World War I that portion of it that has sociological relevance, we find that much of it must immediately be excluded. Without question physical anthropology and archeological advances have to be excluded, and there is little doubt that a great part of anthropological progress in the past thirty-five years has been in those fields. In fact, if we accept Kroeber's *Anthropology* of 1948 as an adequate summary of contemporary knowledge, a comparison of that book with the same writer's *Anthropology* of 1923 shows that practically all the advance between the two dates has been in physical anthropology or in archeology, or in obtaining better and more certain answers to the questions which those subfields are in the habit of asking.

When we categorically decide, as we do, that progress in physical anthropology and in archeology is not of sociological relevance, then we are left with cultural or social anthropology. (It is a nuisance to have to write "cultural [or social]" whenever reference is made to the third segment of the subject, but there is good historical reason for it, as will become clear later in this paper.) Even in this third segment we are tempted to exclude a good deal. During the past year, the three most impressive books in general anthropology (excluding college texts) that have appeared in the United States are Linton's *Tree of Culture,* Coon's *Story of Man,* and Howells' *Back of History.* Are such books as these of sociological relevance? They are all very similar in outline and are all firmly grounded in the tradition of world culture history, the area of knowledge that Ronald B. Dixon, Kroeber, and most German ethnologists were cultivating long before World War I, and an area of knowledge to which American sociology has paid little or no attention, either before World War I or since. Comparison of these three books with Dixon's *Building of Cultures* (1928) shows no change in theory, no change in problem, no change in handling of data, no change in focus of interest or attitude of mind. The interest is a straightforward desire to know what happened in the past, especially in the ages before writing and in the areas without writing. The problem remains the simple task of reconstructing, from any and all available sorts of evidence, the history of the cultures without history, and the only things needed for improvement in this area of knowledge are more facts and more certain facts. Because they possess more facts than their predecessors, Linton and Coon and Howells are able to improve upon Dixon or the Kroeber of 1923 or Bastian or Graebner. This type of book is culture history, and culture historians, like orthodox historians, are simply fact collectors, whose constant question—"What happened?"—gets answered better as more facts accumulate with the passage of time and the increase of coworkers.[1]

The vigor and growth of culture history over the past thirty years, as evidenced by the improvement shown from Dixon to Coon or Linton, should cause some soul-searching among cultural (or social) anthropologists. Perhaps it is *only as culture history* that cultural anthropology can advance. Certainly the numerous critics of culture history within anthropology would be hard-pressed to show any correspondingly impressive advance in the areas of knowledge or in the frames of reference that they urge as alternatives to culture history. This growth of culture history in range and certainty demonstrates most of all the dominating position that Kroeber has come to occupy during the period. For Kroeber has always maintained that cultural anthropology can never be more than culture history. "Anthropology is history or it is nothing" was his position at the time of World War I, and from that position he has never been shaken. During the thirties, when many of

[1] A. L. Kroeber, *Anthropology* (New York, 1923, and New York, 1948); R. B. Dixon, *The Building of Cultures* (New York, 1928); C. S. Coon, *The Story of Man* (New York, 1954); W. W. Howells, *Back of History* (New York, 1954); Ralph Linton, *The Tree of Culture* (New York, 1955). For a detailed comparison of Kroeber's 1923 and 1948 editions, see C. W. M. Hart, review of Kroeber's *Anthropology,* in *AJS,* 54 (1949), pp. 572-574.

his colleagues began doing things that seemed not to resemble history in the slightest, Kroeber attempted to legitimize their peculiar activities by a remarkable article[2] in which he produced such an all-embracing definition of history that he was able to bring even Margaret Mead's study of Samoan adolescence within it. To Kroeber, since all anthropology is history, then everything anthropologists do must be history, no matter how the meaning of history has to be strained to get it all in.

Since Kroeber is the ablest and most influential living exponent of culture history, we tend to identify culture history with him. Since he has always maintained that culture history is not science, not even social science, but merely better world history than produced by the professional historians, then we are left with the conclusion that the Kroeber type of cultural anthropology, which is the type to which Coon's, Howells' and Linton's recent books belong, is part of humanistic history and as such, lacking any social-science claim, it has no more sociological relevance than any other sort of history has. We could therefore dispense with any further reference to culture history in this essay were it not for the fact that the other types of cultural and social anthropology that have made some headway since World War I are best seen as explicit reactions against culture history and against Kroeber's ultimately anti-social-science position. Most of the new trends in cultural anthropology during the past thirty years represent attempts to prove that Kroeber's "history or nothing" dictum is false.

This becomes clear from a brief summary consideration of what has happened in American anthropology since World War I and particularly in the very significant decade between 1926 and 1936. It is the familiar story of an established church beginning to develop discontents within its bosom, the discontented groups not being at all sure or clear as to what they are for, but being perfectly sure what they are against.

By the middle of the twenties, the established church in American anthropology was the school of Boas. There is no need here to enter into the thorny question of what Boas' position really was; the disciples of the founder are still quarreling about that. To any reasonable outsider it is perfectly obvious that Boas at different times preached the desirability of different things, including the desirability of culture history. We have his own word for it (in 1935) that as early as 1910 he was bored with culture history and was advocating other lines of development in its stead, but justice compels us to add that there is no indication in his 1910 writing that he was moving away from culture history as early as that. If he was tired of culture history by 1910, he apparently kept quiet about it and let the Frankenstein monster of his own creation roll along. And roll it did, in the hands especially of Wissler and of Kroeber, the former confining himself to the culture history

[2] Kroeber, "History and Science in Anthropology," *AA*, 37 (1935), pp. 539-569.

of the American Indian, the latter showing a more universalistic interest. By the middle twenties, whatever Boas may have thought or wished, it was the work of Wissler, Kroeber and their associates that dominated American cultural anthropology—that, in fact, *was* American cultural anthropology. Other interests were present—Boas' abiding concern with linguistics, Lowie's with kinship, Kroeber's "psychological" period—but these were ancillary to the main task, which Boas had laid down as the "providing of a chronology for the American Indian." Even the superintellectual Sapir was engulfed in the prevailing orthodoxy and produced the most sophisticated statement of the methodology of the culture history movement.[3]

The true church was one and indivisible, Boas was its Pope, and Wissler's work and Kroeber's were the models for all younger men to follow. The murmurs of heresy and the rumblings of discontent become audible as the twenties move into the thirties. Leslie Spier, one of the inner circle, repudiated the culture-history methodology in 1929.[4] Sapir, another of the inner circle, insulted the sacred cow of culture by calling it a "statistical fiction" in a series of psychologically oriented articles that begin in 1928.[5] Herskovits and Margaret Mead went on field trips to non-Boasian parts of the world in 1927-1928, Herskovits to Africa and Mead to Samoa; and Mead, at least, explicitly chose Samoa not to study its "culture," but as a setting in which to seek an answer to a social-psychological question, that of adolescent stress and strain. And 1928 was the date of the first of a series of articles by Ruth Benedict that attracted little attention at the time but were soon (1934) to culminate in *Patterns of Culture*.[6] Of course, not all of these are to be interpreted as symptoms of formal revolt, but they all represent at least gropings for some basis around which to orient anthropology, and they all come from scholars closely indentified with Boas. Out on the periphery there were appearing other heretics—less spectacular because less closely associated with the sacred stream—such as Redfield, with his Tepoztlan study (1930), and

[3] Edward Sapir, *Time Perspective in Aboriginal American Culture: A Study in Method* (Ottawa, 1916).

[4] Leslie Spier, "Problems Arising from the Cultural Position of the Havusupai," *AA*, 31 (1929), pp. 222-232.

[5] See the following works of Sapir: "The Unconscious Patterning of Behavior in Society," in C. M. Childs *et al.* (eds.), *The Unconscious* (New York, 1928); "Cultural Anthropology and Psychiatry," *JASP*, 27 (1932), pp. 229-242; "The Emergence of the Concept of Personality in a Study of Cultures," *JSP*, 5 (1934), pp. 408-415; "The Contribution of Psychiatry to an Understanding of Behavior in Society," *AJS*, 42 (1937), pp. 862-870; "Why Cultural Anthropology Needs the Psychiatrist," *Psychiatry*, 1 (1938), pp. 7-13.

[6] Ruth Benedict, "Psychological Types in the Cultures of the Southwest," *International Congress of Americanists*, 23 (1928), pp. 572-581; "Configurations of Culture in North America," *AA*, 34 (1932), pp. 1-27; *Patterns of Culture* (Boston, 1934); "Continuities and Discontinuities in Cultural Conditioning," *Psychiatry*, 1 (1938), pp. 161-167.

Hallowell, who in the early thirties began his long-continued attack on the problem of personality among the Chippewa Indians.[7]

These sporadic outbursts of new sorts of anthropological activity are alike only in their indication that the time was ripe for a change. Mead and Redfield were at least the younger generation, even if Spier and Sapir were not; and the younger generation was clearly dissatisfied with traditional culture history. But what was to be substituted for it? That was not so clear. One of the few attempts to meet the issue squarely came in a paper by Alexander Lesser, which, although it did not appear until 1939 and apparently had little overt effect when it was published, best sums up the main problem of the early thirties. What Lesser challenges and criticizes is not so much culture history as antiquarianism. He is critical of the tradition that selects tribes entirely because nobody has studied them before or to fill in gaps on a distribution map, and he advocates instead that fieldworkers select their tribes because of particular problems that they expect those tribes to answer. That is, Lesser is urging anthropology to become problem-oriented instead of tribe- or trait-oriented, but he was much too tactful to add that the chief responsibility for making anthropology tribe-oriented lay with Boas, or to point out that by doing so Boas had left anthropology without any problem at all until Kroeber and Wissler had provided one by attempting to integrate the mass of tribal information into the age-area framework.

Lesser's solution to the problem of prevailing historicism and antiquarianism was the proposal to substitute problems for collecting tribal facts, which is precisely what Margaret Mead had done in her selection of Samoa as a place to study female adolescence on her first field-work trip and in her later selection of Manus and the Upper Sepik for the study of other problems. Somewhat earlier, Mead herself had argued the same case as Lesser, although in a slightly different way. Her formulation of what anthropology needed was that field workers should pay more attention to the "informal aspects" of culture, of which child training was emphasized as an outstanding example. At first sight, neither Lesser not Mead appeared to be attacking culture history as such, but by implication both were, since the inference clearly was that the older tribe-centered anthropology (in Lesser's terms) or the older preoccupation with the "formal" aspects of culture (in Mead's terms) were not concerned with "problems" at all, inasmuch as the older anthropology of Kroeber and Wissler had been very much concerned with the growth of cultures through time, especially by such mechanisms as cultural diffusion, and inasmuch as questions of growth through time cannot be "problems" at all in Lesser's and Mead's opinion. In advocating the study

[7] Hallowell's earliest article in the personality and culture area was in 1934. Most of his writings on the subject (but not his article of 1934) have been collected in his *Culture and Experience* (Philadelphia, 1955).

of "problems" as something new, both imply that the problems have to be other than historical or culture-growth problems to make them worth studying. Mead's examples of what might be done with the results of field work oriented along the lines she advocates suggest that the most fruitful problems are social-psychological or comparative psychological ones. Lesser is not so explicit in stating what sort of problems he would direct the field workers' attention towards answering, but apparently he saw the Meadian social-psychological interest as only one of several possibilities.[8]

For brevity's sake the label "non-historical" may be used for all the various attacks upon, movements away from, and suggested alternatives to culture history of the Kroeber-Wissler type. This oversimplifies the general situation *circa* 1930, but it enables us to say that all the assorted heretics and dissenters of the period were agreed that cultural anthropology had to become something other than culture history, but were at variance as to what to substitute. Mead's social-psychological alternative was one possibility, but for the time being at least it commanded little general acceptance. The true church of anthropology was reasonably tolerant of eccentricity; as long as young people did "good field work" they were encouraged to experiment with new forms of expression and presentation of results. Kroeber in his usual benign way gave Mead and Benedict's early work his apostolic blessing; Boas introduced Mead's Samoan book with at least superficial approval, and it was only the more doctrinaire Lowie who asked nasty questions about how it was possible to learn a native language in three months.[9] But even there Lowie was not challenging Mead's right to investigate the sort of problems she had chosen to investigate; he was questioning whether her field work was "good." The ordeal by field work was fundamental for acceptance into anthropology; if that were passed successfully, then nobody in authority was likely to challenge whatever the young fieldworker chose to do with his results. On the other hand, the innovator was not likely to be widely imitated either, and for much of her early career at least Margaret Mead had few imitators or followers. Whereas her influence on the general public has been enormous and she has alone done more than all other anthropologists combined to make cultural anthropology a household word in the United States, her influence within the profession has been only as part, although a very

[8] Alexander Lesser, "Problems *versus* Subject Matter as Directives of Research," *AA,* 41 (1939), pp. 574-582; Margaret Mead, *Coming of Age in Samoa* (New York, 1928); *Growing Up in New Guinea* (New York, 1930); and "More Comprehensive Field Methods," *AA,* 35 (1933), pp. 1-15.

[9] R. H. Lowie, "Queries," *AA,* 35 (1933), pp. 288-293. Mead attempted to answer Lowie's question in her "Native Languages as Fieldwork Tools," *AA,* 41 (1939), pp. 189-199, in which she appeared to claim that no fieldworker had used the native language before Malinowski and herself. This absurd claim was demolished by Lowie in one of his most ruthless efforts: "Native Languages as Ethnographic Tools," *AA,* 42 (1940), pp. 81-87.

dynamic part, of the wider, more diffused, anti-historical movement that we are here discussing.[10]

During the thirties, the strongest influence within the anti-historical movement was exerted by the Englishman Radcliffe-Brown, and for some time it appeared that the various currents of discontent would crystallize around his teachings. Sapir and Redfield were instrumental in bringing Radcliffe-Brown to the University of Chicago in 1931, apparently as a tentative answer to their search for an alternative to culture-history. Radcliffe-Brown, in two papers, one in his Capetown period, the other as President of Section H of the British Association for the Advancement of Science in 1931, had vigorously attacked culture history in general and American culture history in particular, as being, if not useless, at least beneath the dignity of social scientists, and advocated as a clear-cut substitute his own version of what has since come to be called the structural-functional position.[11]

In his British Association paper, seeking for a way of differentiating his type of anthropology from culture history, Radcliffe-Brown suggested the use of ethnology for the latter and comparative sociology for the former, and this apparent sociological affiliation was of course in line with the strong Comtean and Durkheimian influences in his system. But since he had doubly passed the ordeal by field work, and in two very primitive areas (Andaman Islands and Australia), he could not be dismissed as "just another sociologist," even though he wanted to call himself by that (to American anthropologists) obnoxious name. His criticism of American cultural anthropology was the criticism of a brother anthropologist (even though an Englishman), and he was perfectly acceptable as a professor of anthropology at Chicago, where he quickly learned to drop "comparative sociology" as a designation for his type of anthropology and to substitute the "social anthropology" label that still continues to be used interchangeably with cultural anthropology in present-day writing.[12]

[10] In a recent paper covering much of the same ground as is being covered here, Eggan has omitted Mead entirely from mention in his treatment of the rise of the non-historical tradition in the early thirties: "Social Anthropology and the Method of Controlled Comparison," *AA,* 56 (1954), pp. 743-763. This is a remarkable instance of Chicago chauvinism in an otherwise judicious treatment. Neither anti-historicism in theory nor modernity in field research were immaculately conceived within the University of Chicago.

[11] A. R. Radcliffe-Brown, "The Methods of Ethnology and Social Anthropology," *South African Journal of Science,* 20 (1923), pp. 124-147; and "The Present Position of Anthropological Studies," *Proceedings, British Association for the Advancement of Science,* Section H (1931).

[12] When it became known in 1930 that Radcliffe-Brown (then in Australia) was willing to accept an American appointment, both Harvard and Chicago were interested. But "Harvard wrote, Chicago cabled." It is interesting to speculate what might have been the consequences for American anthropology had Harvard been better acquainted with the advantages of modern technology.

During his sojourn at Chicago (1931-1937), Radcliffe-Brown supplied a rallying point and a source of intellectual leadership for some of the anti-historical trends in American anthropology. He consistently adopted an all-or-none position with regard to history, and for a time the line was tightly drawn. At one meeting of the American Anthropological Association during this period, separate sessions on "Social Anthropology" and "Cultural Anthropology" were listed on the program, and when one prominent anthropologist inquired what was the difference between the two sessions, he was pointedly told by the chairman of the Social Anthropology session (Dr. Redfield) that "those who wished to discuss history should go to the session on cultural anthropology, those who wished to discuss social science should stay here." But for a number of reasons Radcliffe-Brown failed to unify the widespread opposition to culture history. Undoubtedly his British nationality was a factor; it was quite all right for Spier and Sapir, or even Mead and Redfield, to criticize American cultural anthropology; it was quite a different thing when it was done by an Englishman with a monocle. Moreover his indictment of history tended (publicly at least) to be too sweeping and all-condemnatory; those who had to judge his system by his public pronouncements failed in many cases to realize that not only was there room in it for genuine historical interests and problems, but that in his own research work he was constantly striving to integrate the synchronic and diachronic approaches. Too often he appeared to be condemning *all* history, *all* interest in the past, *all* problems where time-sequence is involved, and this was going much further than many of those dissatisfied with culture history were prepared to go.

Ultimately, however, the failure of Radcliffe-Brown to found a new type of American anthropology must be attributed not to the man but to the time. Not only was his system rigid and (on the surface at least) bigotedly anti-historical, it was likewise rigidly sociological and hence anti-psychological. And any system that found no place for "psychology" was bound to have little appeal in the United States in the early thirties. Redfield and the younger Chicago men became Radcliffe-Brown "functionalists" in varying degree; but, outside Chicago, whatever acceptance the functional system has had has been covert rather than overt and diffuse rather than specific. Even Sapir, although he had been instrumental in bringing Radcliffe-Brown to Chicago, seems to have found little in the teachings of the Englishman to meet his intellectual difficulties, whereas Linton, after a brief honeymoon of intense enthusiasm, became a bitterly hostile critic.

Probably the main factor in reorienting American anthropology during the thirties was the relatively sudden emergence in American social science generally, and indeed in the wider area of American culture, of that intense and all-consuming interest in "personality" and "the individual" that shows itself between World War I and World War II. Nobody seems to have explained satisfactorily the factors and trends in American culture which caused America and American social science to become so "psychology-conscious" during that period, and this is no place to attempt an explanation, except to remark that the increasing knowledge of psychoanalysis in the United States and the rising tide of Freudianism seem to have been effects rather than causes of a wider intellectual current. In the light of developments in American social science since 1930, and particularly the vogue of that strange American monster, social psychology, it seems reasonable to attribute Radcliffe-Brown's failure to gain wider acceptance in the United States for his sociologically oriented anthropology to the absence in his system of any place for or indeed of any interest in problems of "personality" and the "role of the individual."[13] His system was too sociological or not psychological enough; the two criticisms mean the same thing. A system that was thoroughly nineteenth-century in its treatment of the "individual" and derived ultimately from Comte's positivism and proximately from Durkheim's "society as a reality *sui generis*" position could not compete in the new psychologizing climate. Not nineteenth-century Paris but late nineteenth-century Vienna was the Mecca towards which American social science was looking for a new revelation. So that, outside Chicago, Radcliffe-Brownian functionalism, as an acceptable alternative to culture history, had but little acceptance.

Hence the sudden vogue of Ruth Benedict and her configurational approach as a more acceptable and fashionable alternative. In the role of a new Messiah to lead anthropology out of the wilderness of culture history, Benedict had the serious disadvantages of being a woman and a poetess, but she had the inestimable advantage of being Boas' chosen successor at Columbia. Her early articles, therefore, although to many they appeared to be more literary than scientific, commanded some attention. Basically, what Benedict was doing was reviving the old antiquated issue of racial or national psychology, which in the hands of Houston Stewart Chamberlain, Gobineau, and their various disciples had flourished in the 1870's and 1880's. But Benedict revived the issue (in the beginning of her work anyway) not in relation to the dynamite-laden question of European national psychologies, but in relation to American Indians, the private property of American anthropologists, those people about whom anthropologists claimed exclusive expertism. The surface excitability of the Northwest Coast Indians as contrasted to the

[13] Actually, there is a place in Radcliffe-Brown's system for "psychology," but since exploring its possibilities in *The Andaman Islanders,* he has neglected it in favor of problems of comparative social structure. An excellent demonstration of how to give a psychological dimension to structural analysis is to be found in E. E. Evans-Pritchard's treatment of time and space concepts among the Nuer: *The Nuer* (Oxford, 1940). Explicit recognition of this dimension in the formulations of Radcliffe-Brown has recently been made by G. C. Homans in his review of Radcliffe-Brown's *Structure and Function in Primitive Society,* in *AA,* 56 (1954), pp. 118-120.

withdrawn, introverted surface appearance of the Pueblos must have been noticed by many observers through the years, but such were the conventions of the classic Boas school that it was not considered to be a valid anthropological observation until Benedict brought it up as a problem. And having raised the problem, she then had to demonstrate that it was a valid problem for anthropological treatment by somehow bringing it into a cultural frame of reference. Granting the observation to be a true one, it was still, *prima facie,* an observation of a contrast between Northwest Coast mentality and Pueblo mentality—that is, a matter of tribal psychology. But what "causes" tribal psychology? Obviously culture does; it molds the psychology or personality of those born into it into a typical and standardized local form like the Dionysian Kwakiutl or the Apollonian Pueblos. In this plausible but logically loose series of assertions, an essential relationship of psychology to anthropology is postulated, "psychological" questions are brought within the orbit of cultural anthropology, and the new field of "personality and culture" is on its way.

Patterns of Culture, first published in 1934, is the fruition of these ideas of Benedict, and through its many editions has become one of the widely read books in social science of the past twenty-five years. Whether it is an anthropologically sound book is, however, a question that many anthropologists prefer to dodge, if possible. No other front-rank anthropologist has attempted to imitate Benedict's type of operation, and *Patterns of Culture* remains a sort of comet on the anthropological horizon, without ancestors and without direct successors. It lines up better with Spengler, Toynbee, and Northrup than it does with the corpus of anthropological literature. Kroeber compared it with Burckhardt's *Renaissance,* a comparison that would have occurred to few readers except Kroeber. Benedict's importance in the anthropological trends of the middle thirties stems not from her book but from her legitimization of psychological interests, which was achieved more by her professional prestige than by her specific formulations. Mead's work on Samoa and on Manus was also psychological in a slightly dissimilar but allied sense, and the two of them combined to produce the same general statement of the relation of culture to personality: the "gamut" theory.

Edward Sapir also, especially after his move from Chicago to Yale to be one of the stars in the Institute of Human Relations project, produced a series of papers that encouraged his students to explore some aspects of personality without feeling they were thereby forfeiting their anthropological union cards.[14] Sapir's position may have been very far indeed from that of Benedict, but in the story of anthropological development the vitally important point is that Benedict, Mead, and Sapir were all in their diverse ways performing the wonder of psychologically orienting anthropology and of making

[14] See the works cited in footnote 5.

"psychologizing" an anthropologically respectable occupation—a feat which enabled them to find ways of cooperating in research and of speaking a common language with psychologists, psychiatrists, and social pyschologists, these being disciplines with which the culture historians had traditionally had no communication. Indeed, it is probably true that Benedict, Mead, and Sapir, by making psychology and psychiatry conscious of culture, had a greater impact during the thirties upon those fields than they had upon their own field. They certainly contributed more to those disciplines than cultural anthropology has received in exchange from them.

This brief and oversimplified résumé of trends in American anthropology between 1926 and 1936 (the crucial period) enables us to locate three foci of interest: the traditional culture-history of the Boas-Wissler-Kroeber tradition, the sociological position of Radcliffe-Brown (so-called British functionalism with its well-established Chicago branch), and the personality and culture movement. It is in relation to these three foci that trends in American anthropology since the middle thirties should be viewed. They are called foci rather than schools or sects because the basic unity of cultural anthropology was preserved and the adherents of the different viewpoints were still held together by the two features that give anthropology its distinctive position among the social sciences—namely, the fieldwork requirement and the natural-history tradition. Whatever focus his teachers may adhere to, the novice must still "go to the field," and his main task there is to "describe the culture."

Nothing better demonstrates the natural-history birthright of cultural anthropology than the fact that sheer description of a natural phenomenon, or of human behavior treated as a natural phenomenon, is still regarded as both a primary duty and a problem in itself (a fact that has also prevented cultural anthropology from being much affected by the craze for statistics that is engulfing other social sciences in a morass of technological futility). Provided the field-work requirement has been met, then the frame of reference of the field work itself, the description of the culture, and most of all the topics the field worker selects about which to write anthropological articles and books in his later career—all these may be very variable indeed, although they can usually be placed in relation to the three foci, as predominantly culture-historical or sociological-functional or psychological.

Various compromises and intermediate positions are of course possible and even usual: Eggan, for example, has combined the historical with the sociological in his *Social Organization of the Western Pueblos;* Margaret Mead is unrivalled in her ability to distill psychological findings out of functional analysis; Linton in the course of his career traveled between all three foci, ending as he began, in culture history; and Murdock's *Social Structure* cannot be clearly related to any one of the three markers although it has faint overtones of all of them, dimly heard through the heavier strains of nineteenth-century social evolutionism. Indeed, it is one of the great strengths of contemporary anthropology that few, at least of the younger generation, adopt an all-or-none position with regard to any of the three emphases. Addiction to personality and culture, to structural-functional analysis, or to culture history are distinct enough as addictions to be recognizable in any given piece of research. Selecting examples only from studies published in the past few years and by younger scholars, it is possible to apply the psychological label to Spindler's work on the Menomini, to call Goodenough's work on Truk sociological-functional, and to cite Eleanor Leacock's study of Montagnais-Naskapi as culture-historical.[15] Yet such labeling gives a very partial and distorted picture. All three are important contributions to anthropology, and any one of the three could be used to illustrate the theorem that whatever its addiction, good field work is readily identifiable as good anthropology, at least by other anthropologists. And this identification by the test of good field work quite overshadows the minor differences introduced by Spindler's addiction to projective tests, Goodenough's addiction to genealogies, and Mrs. Leacock's extensive use of documentary material.

The ferments and the arguments of the restless thirties were still unsettled when World War II arrived and the non-Western cultures were suddenly of concern to many other people besides anthropologists. The result was a quick and dramatic expansion of anthropological opportunities to get to strange parts of the world, either in uniform or out of it; and of course such opportunities multiplied even more *after* the war. It is difficult, however, to see that this increased activity by anthropologists had very much effect upon anthropological theory. Anthropologists did queer things during the war and immediate postwar years (not the least queer being Ruth Benedict's *The Chrysanthemum and the Sword*); but then so did everyone else; and whereas there was good propaganda to be made from the fact that armies and navies needed anthropological help in dealing with Asiatic and Oceanic peoples, one has only to read *The Teahouse of the August Moon* to realize how little use was made of anthropological knowledge by the armed services in places where it might have helped them. In the postwar period and particularly after the launching of the Point Four program and its alphabetic successors and offspring, the expansion of anthropological jobs has continued, and many strange operations are currently being carried on in strange parts by anthropologists under U.S. governmental, United Nations, or (more recently) Ford Foundation auspices.

But the assessment of anthropological achievement by the Wenner-Gren Foundation in 1952 revealed an over-all record, at least in cultural

[15] G. D. Spindler, *Sociocultural and Psychological Processes in Menomini Acculturation* (Berkeley. Cal., 1955); W. H. Goodenough, *Property, Kin, and Community on Truk* (New Haven, Conn., 1951); Eleanor Leacock, *The Montagnais "Hunting Territory" and the Fur Trade* (Menasha, Wis., 1954).

anthropology, that would have been much the same if the assessment had been made ten years earlier. Had there been a Wenner-Gren Foundation to undertake the task in 1940, substantially the same people would have written the same articles making the same points and using the same arguments to substantiate the same theses. By 1952 the main difference was that the bibliographies were longer and the illustrative material more diversified. The more anthropologists who go to more places to do more and more different sorts of field work, the more the body of anthropology remains the same; that is the main impression conveyed by the cultural sections of *Anthropology Today.*[16]

Among the wartime and postwar pressures on anthropology was the feeling in many quarters that anthropology should have some practical application somewhere, and indeed such an aim had brought into existence the Society for Applied Anthropology (S.A.A.) even before Pearl Harbor. This society has grown and continued to flourish, but if there is any generally accepted agreement within the profession as to what constitutes "applied anthropology," or to what sort of problems anthropology can be "applied," it is very hard to find. The main figures in the society pursue very diverse research interests, united only by the very practical thread that in all of them the purpose of the research is laid down by some employing or financing agency. The value of the S. A. A. has been to act as a ginger group of young Turks (most of them by now not so young) demanding that anthropology be made more "practical" or more "useful for achieving something." Since any reasonably competent anthropologist, whatever his addiction, is capable of performing an applied operation within the existing limits of his normal frame of reference if called upon to do so, little marked change in anthropological theory has been noticeable in response to the nagging of the S. A. A.

The one marked emphasis in the theoretical position of the leaders of the S. A. A. has been a good deal of criticism of the prevailing anthropological concept of culture. Dealing as they do with living people, since all the diverse "applied" problems at least have that feature in common, the concept of culture as developed by Kroeber, Boas, Linton, *et al.* seems to them too mechanical and depersonalized a concept to be useful. Positively stated, this dissatisfaction with "culture" has grown out of their strong feeling that human behavior can be best structured in interactional terms—as occurring *between* people rather than within individuals or between cultural items. Since this involves them in a situational point of view rather than a psychological one, the result is to move them, somewhat paradoxically when we remember the number of psychiatric articles in their journal, towards the sociological position of Radcliffe-Brown and the British functionalists. The underlying nature of this convergence, if indeed it is convergence, has been

[16] A. L. Kroeber *et al., Anthropology Today: An Encyclopedic Inventory* (Chicago, 1953).

well brought out by Homans in his treatment of Firth's data on Tikopia, Whyte's *Street Corner Society* study, and the material from the Bank Wiring Room at Hawthorne as being essentially similar data existing at the same level of abstraction.[17] If Homans is correct, then obviously any attempt to treat Firth's data as "cultural" and the other two studies as "social" becomes meaningless.

The applied anthropologists are not alone, however, in their dissatisfaction with the current theory of culture. Other anthropologists, not usually grouped with the S. A. A., are demanding that representatives of their subject stop talking about culture and begin talking about people, especially and specifically people-in-interaction. Radcliffe-Brown has pointed out that such a change would involve substituting the study of "societies" for the study of "cultures" as the basic operation of anthropology, and that this substitution has long since been accepted in England. Such a shift would of course be much more difficult to achieve in the United States, where comparative peace between anthropology and sociology is maintained largely by giving the anthropologists a bone marked "culture" to chew on while the sociologists chew on a bone marked "society." And in American anthropology it may not be necessary to approach the problem quite in this semantic way. There are signs that the concept of culture and the theory of culture are likely to change, not as the result of the attacks of explicit critics, but by some sort of inner evolution. If such an inner evolution of cultural theory is about to take place, or is already taking place, it can be attributed to "the demands of the external system"—that is, to the new conditions of fieldwork created by the postwar world.

In these new conditions of fieldwork we can only single out two considerations that are already having and will continue to have increasing effects on anthropological theory. The first is the weakening of the traditional tendency for anthropologists to concentrate upon the most primitive peoples available for study, the tendency to make the Eskimo, the Australians, the Navaho, and the Hottentots the spoiled darlings of anthropology. In deciding on locations for fieldwork, contemporary anthropologists have to take cognizance of the current American preoccupation with the "underdeveloped areas," which contain rather more advanced and sophisticated cultures than those just mentioned. The first American anthropologist to have an opportunity for field work in India characteristically chose to do it with the Todas and Khotas of the Nilghiri hills, but that was in 1938. Today there are swarms of American anthropologists in India, but the terms of their grants are such that they avoid the Todas and the Bhils and the Gonds like the plague and concentrate instead on standard Hindu villages. A similar moving away from exotic or exceptionally backward cultures towards what Redfield

[17] G. C. Homans, *The Human Group* (New York, 1950).

has called cultures "with a great tradition" is also marked in such areas as Japan, Siam, the Islamic world, and Latin America. In theoretical terms, this means that the unit of anthropological fieldwork is no longer the "tribe," since, whatever we are to call the new peoples being studied, we can hardly call them tribal. Certain enthusiasts are suggesting that the new unit is the nation, but that is largely window-dressing and part of academic imperialism. In the meantime, although it is not yet clear what the new unit of anthropological study ought to be, the workers in the new areas have obviously found it expedient to study villages. Anthropologists will scarcely rest content to have their subject defined as "the study of villages"; such a definition is infinitely worse than the old label of "people who study tribes." The folk–urban continuum theory of Redfield has been sucked nearly dry of whatever theoretical content it may have had, and attempts by Oscar Lewis and others to substitute "peasant cultures" for "primitive tribes" do not look very promising. The problem of what anthropology becomes when it moves away from concern with "primitive peoples" to concern with "underdeveloped areas" is wide open, but it seems certain that concern with Hindu or Siamese or Lebanese villages instead of Eskimo or Arunta or Navaho customs must radically alter thinking about the whole area of social and cultural structure, since if it ever was valid to treat the very backward cultures as well-integrated, homogeneous, and autonomous systems, it is certainly incorrect and indeed absurd to treat the societies of the underdeveloped areas similarly.

The new fieldwork opportunities in the underdeveloped areas have had a second consequence that must in time affect anthropological theory. By forcing anthropologists to move away from the very primitive and backward peoples and work instead with folk or peasant or underdeveloped peoples, the postwar trend has destroyed the anthropologists' monopoly. Time was when the Eskimo, the Arunta, the Toda, and the rest were the exclusive and private property of the anthropologists. But the underdeveloped areas are nobody's exclusive subject matter. In endeavoring to do research in such areas, the anthropologist has to compete with economists, political scientists, sociologists, and the members of various assorted "missions," all of whom, in self-defense, tend to question, if not dispute, the applicability of anthropology to the basic problems of political, economic, and social development with which most of them are concerned. Thus put on the spot, the anthropologist finds it necessary to soft-pedal his static theory of culture and come up instead with some useful remarks about social and cultural change, a topic concerning which anthropological literature is well-supplied with detailed case-studies but deplorably deficient in generalizations of the middle range.

It is widely believed in anthropological circles that this new concern with change in place of the older concentration on social statics will have an invigorating effect upon anthropological thinking. But this does not necessarily follow. Merely to recognize change as an important problem is not enough; Wissler at least, if not also Kroeber, studied little else but change all their working lives, as did all the people who worked within the age-area framework. A satisfactory theoretical framework to handle social and/or cultural change seems desperately difficult for social scientists to formulate, although case studies of particular changing situations are relatively easy to make. And anthropologists have always been good at case studies, largely because, as was pointed out above, they regard sheer description as a problem calling for hard work and not soluble by IBM machines. Therefore, by leaving the economists and the political scientists and the other "missions" to carry on their activities in the national capitals of the underdeveloped areas, and sticking closely themselves to the villages, those anthropologists who are working in the underdeveloped regions are in an excellent position to sidestep the urgent necessity for some new theoretical ideas by concentrating instead on producing endless studies of particular Asiatic villages, focused either on the details of the local culture or on the details of change at the local level.[18]

If this should be the line followed by the new fieldworkers (and the completely planless and random research operations of the Ford Foundation in India and the Near East seem a direct encouragement for it to happen), the result will be a continuation and proliferation, for the underdeveloped areas, of the same old line of unending, particularistic monographs and articles and papers that the Boas school produced for the American Indians. The Boas school was always saved from the necessity of theorizing about anything (including change) by the long line of tribes and tribelets still awaiting fieldwork. Hence the uncongenial and difficult job of evaluating and assessing the facts could be constantly relegated to "the anthropologists of the future," in favor of collecting more facts from more tribes before "the native cultures all die out." The substitution of the Asiatic village for the American Indian tribe can obviously prolong this process indefinitely; the supply of villages in India alone is inexhaustible, and although the likelihood of the Asiatic peoples dying out is minimal, the urgency of the fieldwork operations can be justified by substituting the equally grim threat of speedy Westernization.

The chief result, then, of the postwar demands for anthropological services has been to add a fourth focus of interest—that of "change at the local level"—to the three foci that became apparent in the thirties. This new focus is not in serious conflict with the other three, since it is suitable for all manner of combinations with each and all of them. Projective tests can be used as indicators of cultural change, for instance, as by Hallowell and by Spindler,

[18] Cf. C. W. Stillman, "Academic Imperialism and Its Resolutions: The Case of Economics and Anthropology," *American Scientist*, 43 (1955), pp. 77-88.

thus combining the psychological with the change interest; or rural reorganization in India can be related through village factionalism to the kinship system, thus linking the change focus to the structural focus. Indeed, it would almost appear that to highlight change as the core of all current research projects may be the answer to all anthropological difficulties. To do so provides innumerable advantages; it commends the projects to the foundations; it enables anthropologists to go on making more field trips to underdeveloped areas and to achieve some acceptance by their colleagues from other disciplines who are working in the same regions; it shields them from charges of antiquarianism and of being committed to a static view of culture; it provides a lot of "busy work" for them without necessitating any drastic change in current theoretical habits of thought; and an interest in change can easily be combined with any other interests or addictions that a particular anthropologist may have. Lastly, it can be used to give a "problem-emphasis" to later restudies of a culture studied several years before either by the same anthropologist (as in Mead's studies of Manus in 1930 and in 1953), or by a different fieldworker (as in the two studies of Tepoztlan by Redfield and by Lewis).[19]

This quick survey of what has happened since World War I seems to suggest that the true church of American cultural (or social) anthropology has survived the past thirty-five years remarkably well and with remarkably little change in its basic ideology. The doubtings and potential schisms of the thirties, the disruption of the World War II period, and the anthropological prosperity of the postwar period have had numerous effects and repercussions, but these must be judged to be superstructural rather than fundamental. The basic configurational shape of cultural anthropology continues to be what it has been since the days of Bastian and Tylor—essentially a natural-history approach to human diversity. When the natural-history museums of the nineteenth century became departmentalized and the zoologists appropriated the stuffed birds and the beetles and the geologists took over the rocks and the meteorites, anthropology organized itself around the residue, which consisted of human bones, human tools, and "uncivilized" human customs. And it has remained fascinated by these ever since. What has held this apparently diverse subject matter together for nearly a century has been an attitude of mind—the attitude of mind of the nineteenth-century natural historian. (On what other basis can we explain the extraordinary fact that the social and cultural anthropologists have put up with the archeologists as fellow-anthropologists for so long—and vice versa?) Kroeber's *Anthropology* of 1948, or Linton's *Tree of Culture,* or the Wenner-Gren proceedings embodied in *Anthropology Today* disclose the same attitude of mind as that of Tylor or Bastian. The diversity of human custom is part of the wonderful

[19] Robert Redfield, *Tepoztlan* (Chicago, 1930); Oscar Lewis, *Life in a Mexican Village: Tepoztlan Restudied* (Urbana, Ill., 1951).

diversity and complexity of nature; and the typical cultural anthropologist, either of Tylor's time or of now, is excited by a new custom or a new twist to an old custom in exactly the same way as the entomologist is excited by a new butterfly or the birdwatcher by a new warbler.

Bennett[20] has recently questionnaired a sampling of sociologists as to their picture of anthropology and anthropologists. One respondent cited by him replied tersely "Nature-lovers." This was no doubt meant to be derisive, and Bennett at least seems unhappy about it. But it is a judgment showing great insight into anthropology and the best demonstration of its essential correctness is to be found in the history of anthropology, including its recent history. The culture-history movement was a direct development out of the natural-history movement of the nineteenth century. And the culture-history movement *was* American anthropology until *circa* 1930. Since 1930 culture history has been vigorously attacked by the spokesmen for all the new fashions—by those who, like Radcliffe-Brown, advocated systematic social science; by those who, like Malinowski, called it antiquarianism; by those who, like the applied anthropologists, wanted it to be more useful for something; by those numerous sectarians who wanted to make it an adjunct of psychology and psychiatry; and finally, since World War II, by those who think it should have greater relevance to the problem of industrializing the non-industrial areas of the contemporary world. But despite all these attacks, and despite the various new fashions in fieldwork and in research-project writing, the essentially natural-history approach of anthropology to its problems remains unchanged.

Kroeber and Kluckhohn unearth and publish 257 different definitions of culture (the core concept of anthropology), all of them different and most of them contradictory, and nobody in anthropology is particularly worried, or even particularly interested. What culture "really" is interests cultural anthropologists as little as what "species" really is interests the field naturalists. Cultures are things you find in the field, not in definitions.

The American Anthropological Association, at its 1954 annual meeting in Detroit, scheduled twenty-two different sessions in a three-day meeting, but only one session bore the title "Theory," and that contained such a rag-bag group of miscellaneous papers that it is obvious that the program committee used the "Theory" session as a residual depository. The other twenty-one sessions were all devoted in one way or another to empirical data or questions arising from and grounded in empirical data. Ninety percent of the papers were case studies—of structure or change or functional integration or contact or comparison, or even explanation, but all case studies, firmly located in time and place, of whatever the problem was. As

[20] J. W. Bennett and K. H. Wolff, "Towards Communication Between Sociology and Anthropology," *Yearbook of Anthropology*, 1 (1955), pp. 329-351.

case studies the papers at the 1954 annual meeting were vastly superior to the papers that were being given at annual meetings twenty years ago, but their rigid, down-to-earth empiricism had not changed in the slightest. "This is what happens in Bingo-Bingo-land (or in one Indian village or one Siamese district) and these are the factors that I, the fieldworker, judge to be operative in causing it to happen in that way." Anthropological papers at meetings have not changed; they are merely better at saying the things they have always said. Kroeber's description of the early American archeologists can actually be applied to all anthropologists, of any period, including the present: "They liked going places; they liked finding [out] things; . . . and the longer it lasted the better pleased they were." Bennett's respondent might have come even closer if he had said "beach-combers"—the beaches that anthropologists like to comb being the societies and cultures of the non-Western world.

That this attitude of mind is not just an American legacy from Boas but is characteristic of all cultural or social anthropology is demonstrated by a quick comparison with contemporary British activities. At first sight the impressive achievements of the British functionalists since World War I seem to indicate a different intellectual climate, but on closer study the difference is largely in the type of fieldwork monographs that they produce rather than in anything deep in basic attitude. Like their American colleagues, they show little interest in their own society or culture, despite the great advantage they have over these colleagues in their freedom from sociological competiton. They infinitely prefer Africa or Asia or the Pacific as the locus of field research. Like their American colleagues, they prefer the piling up of particularistic monographs to grappling with "theories" at a general level, Nadel being the one exception that proves the rule.[21] Despite his advocacy of systematic law-seeking, Radcliffe-Brown ranks with Linton or Kroeber in his encyclopedic knowledge of ethnographic data, and in practice he has never shown anything like the same constant enthusiasm for working out his systematic laws that he has shown for collecting and analyzing the kinship systems of the world. Evans-Pritchard has explicitly rejected any belief that anthropology can be made into a social science and is content to have anthropologists recognized merely as "regional specialists." (Again the natural-history parallel is apparent; just as naturalists break up readily into bird-specialists, bug-specialists, etc., so anthropologists are really Africanists, Indianists, and so on.) And Leach, one of the younger rising stars of British anthropology, suggests that to get an adequate framework for studying social change we should go back to fundamentals and analyze all over again what precisely is comprised in the thing we call a social system. And how is that to be done? Not at all in the speculative manner of a Talcott Parsons,

[21] S. F. Nadel, *The Foundations of Social Anthropology* (Glencoe, Ill., 1951).

but by the careful, meticulous analysis of the endless details of the doings that go on among the Kachin tribes of the Burma Hills.[22]

The British, largely by separating social structure from the rest of culture and giving it primacy in descriptive integration, have patented a type of monograph that has greater unity, greater integration of its detail, and hence greater depth of social understanding, than most American monographs achieve; but like their American colleagues the British still remain essentially monograph-writers concerned with describing particular societies as they are, without attempting to prove anything much except how this particular example of human diversity works.[23] The British counterpart of Boas was A. C. Haddon, and Haddon and Boas were both nineteenth-century field naturalists, with striking parallels in their respective formulations of what anthropologists should do and what anthropology should be.[24] And today the common naturalist tradition is still there. While the grandchildren of Haddon "beachcomb" African tribes instead of Melanesian islands, the grandchildren of Boas "beachcomb" East Indian villages instead of the Eskimo, the Kwakiutl, and the Blackfoot. "And the longer it lasts the better pleased they are."

So at last we return to the basic question of this essay: What, among all these trends in anthropology since World War I, has sociological relevance? And we are immediately reminded that Tylor was confronted with that same question nearly a hundred years ago. After the first publication of *Primitive Culture* in 1871, the question arose as to what the relevance of that work was to the work of Mr. Spencer, the great sociologist of the day. Apparently it was raised so insistently that Tylor had to acknowledge the existence of the question. And acknowledge the question he did, in the preface to the second edition. But he could not answer it. His reply seems a weak one, and yet it is devastating. "The absence of particular reference [to Spencer] is accounted for by the present work, arranged on its own lines, coming scarcely into contact of detail with the work . . . of the eminent philosopher."[25]

[22] E. R. Leach, *Political Systems of Highland Burma*.(London, 1954). For an extended discussion of the approach of Parsons, compared with the normal anthropological approach to theory, see C. W. M. Hart, review of Talcott Parsons' *The Social System*, in *AA*, 56 (1954), pp. 118-120.

[23] The technical excellence of the British monographs has so dazzled Murdock that he can only account for them by denying them to be anthropology at all and by calling them "sociological"—apparently now a dirty word in the university of William Graham Sumner. See G. P. Murdock, "British Social Anthropology," *AA*, 53 (1951), pp. 465-473. Kroeber, on the other hand, uses the British monographs as a standard of excellence against which to measure American monographic achievement. See his comments on Mandelbaum's paper: "Critical Summary and Commentary, 2" in R. F. Spencer (ed.), *Method and Perspective in Anthropology* (Minneapolis, 1954), p. 291.

[24] Cf. A. H. Quiggan, *Haddon, The Head-Hunter* (Cambridge, 1942); and Franz Boas, *Race, Language and Culture* (New York, 1948).

[25] E. B. Tylor, *Primitive Culture* (1st ed., 1871; 2nd ed., London: 1873), preface.

"The present work, *arranged on its own lines*"—this is the basis upon which Tylor laid the integrity and the autonomy of anthropology, and it is the basis upon which the relevance of anthropology to sociology must still be discussed. Anthropology in the 1950's, as in Tylor's time, is nobody's handmaiden and nobody's adjunct. It is a discipline arranged on its own lines. Tylor's apparently weak formula becomes better the more we mull it over. And the most constant thread in those lines is the unceasing exploration of social and cultural diversity. Sociologists will doubtless complain that cultural diversity and cultural relativism need no further proof, since they are already proved up to the hilt and every introductory text in sociology devotes an early chapter or two to cultural variability. But the anthropologist, being nothing but a human naturalist, is not concerned with proving anything. He is satisfied just to know more about the endless variations that man has achieved in his efforts to solve the universal problems of living in groups. Such a modest aim leaves cultural and social anthropology with only two problems (apart from the problem of sheer description), and it is with these that all the new trends and developments since World War I have been concerned. One is the question of how to improve field observations, and the other is the problem of making some sort of better sense of field observations so as to answer the question, "Why do these people do the things I observe them to be doing?"

This gives us at least a bare minimum statement of what anthropology has been doing since World War I. If sociologists consider anthropology as thus described to be of value to their field, then it follows that all the cultural- and social-anthropological literature of the past thirty-five years must be sociologically relevant.* Conversely, if the multifarious ways in which groups of men throughout the world have adapted themselves to nature and to each other are not of interest to sociologists, then none of the anthropology since World War I can be sociologically relevant. But if the latter alternative is correct, then most anthropologists are at a loss to know what they can do to give their work sociological relevance, short of changing their habits of work and their attitudes of mind so drastically that the results would no longer be recognizable as anthropology at all.

* The editors *do* regard anthropology as of sociological value. They are impressed, however, by the *very* limited range of reference to cultural and social anthropology found in sociological textbooks—and even in works presumably transcending the textbook level. The names of at most a dozen American, two or three British, and a scant sprinkling of French and German anthropologists exhaust the list. Has anthropology been unduly particularistic, narrowly technical, or smugly esoteric? Or has sociology been impatient, easily swayed by *Ladies' Home Journal* anthropology, or afraid of the unfamiliar? At any rate, the lines of communication have not been working well.

SELECTED BIBLIOGRAPHY

Barnett, H. G., *Innovation* (New York: McGraw-Hill, 1953).

Becker, Howard, "Field Work among Scottish Shepherds and German Peasants: 'Wholes' and Their Handicaps," *Social Forces,* 35, 1 (Oct., 1956), pp. 10-15.

Bierstedt, Robert, "The Limitations of Anthropological Methods in Sociology," *AJS,* 54 (July, 1948), pp. 22-30.

Hallowell, A. Irving, *Culture and Experience* (Philadelphia: Anthropological Society Publications, 1955).

Kardiner, Abram, *The Individual and His Society* (New York: Columbia University Press, 1939).

———, *Psychological Frontiers of Society* (New York: Columbia University Press, 1945).

Kroeber, A. L., *The Nature of Culture* (Chicago: University of Chicago Press, 1952).

Linton, Ralph, *The Study of Man* (New York: D. Appleton-Century, 1936).

Lowie, R. H., *The History of Ethnological Theory* (New York: Farrar and Rinehart, 1937).

Malinowski, Bronislaw, *A Scientific Theory of Culture and Other Essays* (Chapel Hill: University of North Carolina Press, 1944).

Radcliffe-Brown, A. R., "On the Concept of Function in Social Science," *AA,* 37 (July-September, 1935), pp. 394-402.

Redfield, Robert, *The Folk Culture of Yucatan* (Chicago: University of Chicago Press, 1941).

———, *The Primitive World and Its Transformation* (Ithaca: Cornell University Press, 1953).

Tomars, A. S., "Some Problems in the Sociologists' Use of Anthropology," *ASR,* 8 (December, 1943), pp. 625-634.

SOCIAL PSYCHOLOGY AND SOCIOLOGY*

KIMBALL YOUNG AND LINTON FREEMAN

THE CONCEPT OF INTERACTION HAS ALWAYS BEEN REGARDED AS CENTRAL TO social psychology as well as to sociology. From birth on, the survival of the human being depends on the intercession of another individual, normally his mother or mother-surrogate. As he grows up, he lives in social interaction with other members of his family and later with individuals in other primary associations; finally, he moves into the world of specialized secondary and segmentalized groupings. Thus from birth on he is part and parcel of a series of interconnected, interactional units, the model of which is the dyadic parent-child, child-child, or adult relationship.

TYPES OF INTERACTION

Earlier sociologists and social psychologists dealt with various forms of interaction. This is amply clear in the writings of Ward, Small, and Giddings,

* Social psychology, as interpreted in this chapter, seems to the editors to embrace a realm of subject matter that has in great part been traditionally studied by other disciplines. The wide range of topics treated here—for example, the group, social processes (cooperation, etc.)—points to an interpretation of social psychology as a kind of imperialistic social science, a tendency working against a fruitful division of labor among the *several* social sciences. However, it must be granted that this encyclopedic view has many adherents among contemporary social psychologists; it should therefore be carefully considered. For a more restricted delimitation of the field of social psychology, the reader is urged to compare this chapter with another in which the same senior author participated: Kimball Young and Douglas W. Oberdorfer, "Psychological Studies of Social Processes," in H. E. Barnes, Howard Becker, and Frances B. Becker (eds.), *Contemporary Social Theory* (New York, 1940), Chap. 12.

to mention only three earlier American writers. Yet it remained for Park and Burgess in their *Introduction to the Science of Sociology* (1921) to give us a more systematic statement of social processes. Drawing heavily upon the German philosopher and sociologist Simmel, they extended the analysis and stimulated various studies which used such concepts.[1]

Competition and Cooperation as Forms of Interaction. A more organized attack on the concepts of opposition and cooperation was stimulated in the twenties by certain committees of the Social Science Research Council that were interested in the emerging field of personality and culture. Margaret Mead compiled and edited a book entitled *Cooperation and Competition among Primitive People* (1937), which consisted of chapters on selected non-literate peoples illustrating model patterns of cooperation, competition, and individualistic enterprise. A second publication was a brochure by May and Doob in which they reviewed concepts and contributions centering around competition and cooperation.[2]

Language as Interaction. Language, which is a system of phonetic symbols, is the chief agent of communication, and is hence of central concern to social psychology. Much of the early work on language, however, had an ethnocentric bias. This is clearly seen in the old argument that there was a basic language or *Ursprache*, an idea linked with certain racialist dogmas in Germany and elsewhere. Similarly, bias is evident in generalizations concerning the growth of vocabulary formed on the basis of studies the overwhelming bulk of which took their data from middle class, and usually professional, families. Yet with the extension of interest to non-European societies and their cultures, much of this earlier limitation has disappeared. Not only has the former ethnocentrism been dissipated, but earlier discussions about the origin of speech, such as the interjectional and onomatopoetic theories, as well as attempts at rigid classification of languages in terms of form, no longer greatly interest students of language.[3]

Language plays a large part in socialization. The acquisition of speech itself is necessary to most later learning. Furthermore, along with the use of tools, language is the *sine qua non* of culture. It is the basic carrier of culture, and the growth of one's vocabulary is a measure on one's encultura-

[1] See N. J. Spykman, *The Social Theory of Georg Simmel* (Chicago, 1925); *The Sociology of Georg Simmel,* translated by K. H. Wolff (Glencoe, Ill., 1950). As one example of the Chicago studies, see F. M. Thrasher, *The Gang* (Chicago, 1927).

[2] M. A. May and L. W. Doob, *Competition and Cooperation* (New York, 1937). See Gardner Murphy *et al., Experimental Social Psychology* (2nd ed.; New York, 1937) for reviews of such research.

[3] The following will provide an introduction to the large literature in linguistics: Edward Sapir, *Language* (New York, 1921); Otto Jesperson, *Language* (New York, 1922); Leonard Bloomfield, *Language* (New York, 1933); B. Bloch and G. Trager, *Outline of Linguistic Analysis* (Baltimore, 1942); and Z. S. Harris, *Methods in Structural Linguistics* (Chicago, 1951).

tion. Psychologists have worked out the stages of linguistic development for children in our Western society, but whether like stages are to be found in all societies is not known. In any case, it is clear that in learning any given language, the individual uses only a fraction of the potential phonetic elements possible in human speech. Although many psychologists would not agree with Watson that thinking is essentially subvocal talking, no one doubts that language and thought are closely linked. Furthermore, language is essential to the development of the social self, as George H. Mead so definitely indicated.[4] In this connection, speech plays a central part in the moral training of the child and thus becomes an important feature of social control. Finally, speech and non-linguistic vocalisms provide a means of expressing individuality. All societies and their cultures permit a certain range of idiosyncratic verbal habits that serve to reveal individual variation.[5]

Status and Role in Processes of Interaction. The interpersonal relations of individuals who make up a group have, with increasing astuteness, been analyzed in terms of roles and statuses. Some important theoretical consideration of these matters, moreover, came from cultural anthropology rather than from psychology or sociology. Linton's discussion of status and role has become something of a landmark in the literature.[6] There have been several cross-cultural studies of personality that have made use of the role-status formulation. (See pp. 564-567.) In this connection, Linton developed his concept of *status personality*. Essentially, he attempted to show that the "basic personality" is largely unconscious. Other aspects of personality, however, at a more conscious level, revolve around taking on, and functioning with respect to, certain known status positions and their associated roles. Of these, he notes, occupation is one of the most important.[7]

INTERACTION AND GROUP DYNAMICS

Viewed in a larger perspective, so-called "role theory" has taken on a great deal of importance in social psychology.[8] This is partially the result of the fact that it has become enmeshed in another new area known as "group

[4] G. H. Mead, *Mind, Self, and Society* (Chicago, 1934). See also J. F. Markey, *The Symbolic Process* (New York, 1928); and Kimball Young, *Personality and Problems of Adjustment* (2nd ed.; New York, 1952), both of which borrow heavily from Mead. Joseph Bram's *Language and Society* (New York, 1955) is a concise and well-written discussion of the interrelations of society, culture, and language.

[5] Sapir, "Speech as a Personality Trait," *AJS*, 27 (1927), pp. 892-905.

[6] Linton's first discussion of role and status appears in his *Study of Man* (New York, 1936). A later and somewhat expanded treatment is found in his *The Cultural Background of Personality* (New York, 1945). See also W. F. Ogburn, *Social Change* (New York, 1922).

[7] See Linton, "Problems of Status Personality," in S. S. Sargent and M. W. Smith (eds.), *Culture and Personality* (New York, 1949).

[8] See, for example, T. R. Sarbin, "Role Theory," in Gardner Lindzey (ed.), *Handbook of Social Psychology* (Cambridge, Mass., 1954), vol. 1.

dynamics." As a theory as well as a methodology, group dynamics owes its origin to Lewin. At the outset of his professional career Lewin had more or less followed the Gestalt school of psychology; but later he developed his own "field theory." Unhappily, communication of the new theory to those working in social psychology at the time was made difficult because Lewin had invented a number of new terms for what were old and well-recognized dimensions of group behavior.

Not content to stop with theoretical formulation, Lewin and his students set up an experiment to test his thesis. The chief experiment aimed to study variations in productivity and interactional patterns among groups of subjects—junior-high-school pupils—working at given tasks under three distinctive conditions: (1) an "authoritarian" type of control wherein directions and advice were handed down from a predesignated director; (2) a "democratic" type in which the participating subjects discussed the project in advance, agreed on a certain division of labor, and sought advice from the director on a permissive level; and (3) a working condition called "laissez faire" in which there were only general directions and little or no planning or supervision.[9]

This study showed clearly that groups may be investigated under reasonably well-controlled conditions. Unfortunately, many long-range and unwarranted generalizations have been made from this research with respect to the advantages of "democracy" over "totalitarianism." Such an extension does raise the broader problem of the applicability of the findings of studies on small groups to wider and more highly institutionalized ones. Then, too, critics have pointed out that the subjects in the Iowa investigation came from middle-class families with their heavy emphasis on competitive attitudes and habits. Children from a cultural setting that stressed strong authoritarian controls might have performed quite differently.

The expansion of this type of research was rapid. In 1945 the Massachusetts Institute of Technology established The Research Center for Group Dynamics. In 1948, after the death of Lewin, the center was moved to the University of Michigan. As was the case with sociometry, a certain cult developed in connection with this whole program, but fortunately some of the cultish attitudes have been dissipated.[10]

[9] See Kurt Lewin, Ronald Lippitt, and R. K. White, "Patterns of Aggressive Behavior in Experimentally Created 'Social Climates,'" *JSP,* 10 (1939), pp. 271-299; Ronald Lippitt, "An Experimental Study of Authoritarian and Democratic Group Atmospheres," *University of Iowa Studies,* 16 (1940), pp. 43-198. For a full review and bibliography, see Morton Deutsch, "Field Theory in Social Psychology," in Lindzey, *op. cit.,* vol. 1.

[10] Note should be made of the fact that a good deal of the research done under the aegis of the Tavistock Institute in London, England, follows the Lewin tradition. The Center at Michigan and the Tavistock Institute publish jointly a periodical, *Human Relations,* which devotes much of its space to publications in this area.

It would take us too far afield to attempt to list, let alone to summarize, the varied aspects of social behavior that have been investigated under the rubric of group dynamics. But some of the more important and suggestive topics may be mentioned. Lewin was much concerned with the topic of intergroup conflict, especially as it was related to prejudice. One study dealt with the relative effectiveness in problem-solving of group-members working under conditions of cooperation or competition. Others dealt with group decision making, with the conditions making for group cohesiveness or division, with the emergence and role of leaders, and with the place of the isolate or peripheral member.[11]

The Group. The term *group* has been used to conceptualize the fundamental interactional process—that is, the dyadic A ⟷ B unit of interstimulation and response. In this generic sense as a substantive, it is synonymous with the concept of *society*. To speak or write of "group effects" is the same as to make statements about "social effects." Of course, the terms "society" and "group" also refer to specific ordering and functioning of individuals with respect to some particular goal and the interactional patterning related thereto. However, in this context it is usual to think of society as a larger and more complex aggregate of individuals, and the group as a sub-element of the larger society.

The Primary Group and Its Significance. Two early studies of patterned group behavior stand out: those of Sumner and Cooley. In *Folkways* (1901) Sumner gave us the basic functional distinction between the in-group or we-group and the out-group. Cooley's theory of the primary, face-to-face group was made explicit in his *Social Organization, A Study of the Larger Mind* (1909), although it had been foreshadowed in his earlier *Human Nature and the Social Order* (1902), in which he treated the development of the self within the matrix of the family. The family, in one form or another, is the universal primary group and is found in all societies. Play groups of children and the small village are other examples of universal or near-universal primary association. Surely the family is the first human collectivity with which the infant and child comes into contact and from which he learns the fundamental attitudes, values, and habits of his society.[12]

In contrast to the primary group is the secondary or specialized group. Although Cooley did not develop the significance of the secondary group in any great detail, or even refer to it as such, his discussion of the extension

[11] Some of these researches are reported in Dorwin Cartwright and Alvin Zander (eds.), *Group Dynamics: Research and Theory* (Evanston, Ill., 1953); see also F. L. Strodtbeck (ed.), "Special issue on small group research," *ASR,* 19 (Dec., 1954).

[12] For reviews and comments on an extensive literature, see Harold Orlansky, "Infant Care and Personality," *PB,* 46 (1949), pp. 1-48; and Clyde Kluckholn, "Culture and Behavior," in Lindzey, *op. cit.* On problems of methodology in this field, see also J. W. M. Whiting, "The Cross-Cultural Method," *ibid.*

of the social order covered many of its important features. The secondary group is characterized by its limited-interest motivation, that is, by the fact that it concerns only a specialized sector of social behavior.

Farewell to the Group-Mind Approach. Although the group-mind theory is no longer seriously discussed, no serious history of social psychology can completely ignore it. The older notion of group-mind has a way of reappearing under different guises. As G. W. Allport has pointed out, the basic problem of some unit larger or over and above the individual has sorely tried philosophers and psychologists for ages. He notes an ancient analogy between human society and a combination of individual men operating as a supermind and superman.[13] This was essentially the idea of Thomas Hobbes in his *Leviathan* (1651). Then there was the idea of some *collective unconscious* larger than the conscious or unconscious parts of the individual mind. Jung's "racial unconscious" is a modern instance of this.[14]

G. W. Allport has tried to meet the recurrent problem of the individual as related to the group in what he calls a theory of "common and reciprocal segments of behavior." For him, groups, institutions, culture patterns, etc., are high-level abstractions, or perhaps projections "of certain attitudes and beliefs from the personal mental life of individuals." Individuals share with others "common segments," that is, they have attitudes and habits similar to those of their fellows with respect to given institutions and groups. Individuals are, in addition, in certain "reciprocal relations" to each other. That is to say, within the framework of interaction there are certain reciprocal roles in operation.[15]

The Social Group and Social Control. Another perennial topic concerns the function of the group as the carrier and enforcer of the social norms. The earlier treatment of norms and their influence on personal conduct tended to be couched in terms of social control, a topic of continuing interest to sociologists. A classic in this area was Ross' *Social Control* (1901), which for nearly a quarter of a century was regarded as the standard work in this subject. Seen against the background of psychology and sociology of that day, it was an important contribution to an understanding of the way in which the norms—both formal and informal—impinged on individuals and groups to keep them in line with the fundamental values of a given society. An important and incisive cross-cultural note in the study of social control was introduced in Thomas and Znaniecki's *The Polish Peasant in Europe and America* (1918-1920). Prior to this, Thomas had developed his theory of the "four wishes" and later linked them to social control through his concept

[13] G. W. Allport, "The Historical Background of Modern Social Psychology," in Lindzey, *op. cit.*

[14] C. G. Jung, *Collected Papers on Analytical Psychology* (2nd ed.; London, 1922).

[15] Allport, *ibid.*, pp. 39-40.

of "the definition of the situation."[16] In this study of the problems of adjustment of the old-world peasant to urban, industrialized America, the authors showed clearly the difficulties involved in dropping one set of norms in order to take up a new one. Whatever criticism of this study has been made subsequently,[17] it remains a landmark in the study of the decay of old norms and the acceptance of new ones.

The Emergence of Group Norms. The discussion of norms through the twenties continued largely in the sociological tradition in social psychology. But in the mid-thirties serious research on small groups was begun, and among the early (and still classic) studies was that of Sherif on the process by which group norms arise and function. From the standpoint of the individual, the norm represents a certain prescription of role, a special case of expectation, that tends to be enforced by the carriers of power and authority within a given group or community. Later Sherif went on to make applications of his findings by reviewing material on stereotypes, fashions, and other social phenomena, showing how norms serve as frames of reference in perceiving, interpreting, and controlling social events.[18] There have also been a number of empirical studies on the manner in which the norms, already at hand through the culture or established through the experimental situation, operate with regard to individuals.[19]

Collective Behavior: Crowds. The concept *collective behavior* has usually been employed in social psychology and sociology to refer to the relatively unstructured activities of aggregations such as crowds, mobs, audiences, followers of fashions and fads, and various publics.

Taking his clue from psychoanalysis, Martin has pointed out the repressed and unconscious formulations behind crowd thinking and acting. He contends that the crowd is essentially filled with that egotism, hatred, and the sense of absolute rightness that characterizes the paranoiac. Although his treatment of the crowd is enlightening, it does not recognize the relation of culture to those attitudes and, moreover, it neglects the interactional factors.[20]

[16] W. I. Thomas, *The Unadjusted Girl* (Boston, 1923).

[17] Herbert Blumer, *An Appraisal of Thomas and Znaniecki's* The Polish Peasant in Europe and America (New York, 1939).

[18] Muzafér Sherif, "A Study of Some Social Factors in Perception," *AP,* No. 187 (1935), and *The Psychology of Social Norms* (New York, 1936).

[19] See H. H. Kelley, "Attitudes and Judgments as Influenced by Reference Groups," in G. E. Swanson, T. M. Newcomb, and E. L. Hartley (eds.), *Readings in Social Psychology* (rev. ed.; New York, 1952); P. F. Lazarsfeld and R. K. Merton, "Mass Communication, Popular Taste, and Organized Social Action," in Wilbur Schramm (ed.), *Mass Communications; A Book of Readings* (Urbana, Ill., 1949), pp. 459-480; Morton Deutsch and M. E. Collins, *Interracial Housing; A Psychological Evaluation of a Social Experiment* (Minneapolis, 1951). For a review of the research in this field, see J. Harding, B. Kutner, H. Proshansky, and I. Chein, "Prejudice and Ethnic Relations," in Lindzey, *op. cit.,* vol. 2.

[20] E. D. Martin, *The Behavior of Crowds* (New York, 1920).

The ideas of Freud on group and collective behavior became widely available to the English-speaking world with the publication in 1921 of his *Group Psychology and the Analysis of the Ego*. Although he dealt with institutionalized groups, his thesis is that such mechanisms as identification, projection, and rationalization may be used in analyzing crowd behavior. For Freud, the leader, either of a formal group or of a crowd, is a father-figure of some sort.

With but slight elaboration and modification, the basic ideas of Freud, Martin, and F. H. Allport regarding crowd conduct were accepted throughout the twenties and thirties. In 1941 Miller and Dollard, writing largely from the behavioristic standpoint of Hull, recast certain earlier formulations of imitation to make it the crucial form of social learning.[21] On the basis of their interpretation, they made an analysis of the behavior of a lynching mob and of other forms of collective behavior. This marked a definite step away from an eclecticism of the earlier two decades that had somehow tried to keep house with both behaviorism and Freudian psychology.

From time to time efforts have been made to uncover the causal factors in more violent behavior, such as that found in the Negro-white conflicts in this country. In general, the attempted explanations range from contentions that the fundamental factor is economic—either low standards of living and unemployment or intense competition between whites and Negroes—to contentions of a social-psychological nature. A number of studies have reported on the economic backgrounds,[22] and there have been some perceptive analyses of social-psychological and cultural factors that enter into such violence.[23] Although it might seem almost impossible to set up satisfactory experiments to study mob behavior, a few such efforts have been reported. Panic, likewise, has to be studied *ex post facto*.[24]

Fashion Distinguished from Crowd Behavior. Fashion is a phase of collect-

[21] N. E. Miller and John Dollard, *Social Learning and Imitation* (New Haven, Conn., 1941).

[22] For a summary review of the more important discussion of these studies, see R. W. Brown, "Mass Phenomena," in Lindzey, *op. cit.*, vol. 2.

[23] See, for instance, K. B. Clark, "Group Violence: A Preliminary Study of the Attitudinal Pattern of Its Acceptance and Rejection: A Study of the 1943 Harlem Riot," *JASP*, 40 (1944), pp. 143-148; H. O. Dahlke, "Race and Minority Riots: A Study in the Typology of Violence," *SF*, 30 (1952), pp. 419-425; Durward Pruden, "A Sociological Study of a Texas Lynching," *Southern Methodist University Studies in Sociology*, 1 (1936), pp. 3-9.

[24] N. C. Meier *et al.*, "An Experimental Approach to the Study of Mob Behavior," *JASP*, 36 (1941), pp. 506-524; D. Grosser *et al.*, "A Laboratory Study of Behavioral Contagion," *HR*, 4 (1951), pp. 115-142; R. T. LaPiere, *Collective Behavior* (New York, 1938); I. L. Janis, *Air War and Emotional Stress* (New York, 1951); Hadley Cantril, *The Invasion from Mars* (Princeton, N. J., 1940); S. H. Britt, *Selected Readings in Social Psychology* (New York, 1950); A. Mintz, "Non-Adaptive Group Behavior," *JASP*, 46 (1951), pp. 150-159.

ive action that has much in common with crowd behavior. It rests in large part on physical contiguity, but today is dependent for its spread and persistence on rapid communication and transportation. It is, therefore, related to the behavior of the public as well as to that of the crowd. Fashions are not in the mores; they are a phase of the non-moral folkways. In modern Western society, with its swift changes and heightened animation of life, its mobility and rapid communication, fashions shift rapidly, and such changes are really a part of social ceremonial. Moreover, fashions move in cycles, and certain fashions run to extremes. Fads, crazes, rages, and "mental epidemics" likewise reveal varying features of emotionalized crowd behavior.[25]

The Audience and the Public. Although *audiences* vary in degree of structuring and cultural definition, for the most part both situation and convention tend to control them. Historically there has been rather limited research on audience behavior. In 1916 Bentley discussed needed research in a number of topics in social psychology, including the audience. His student, Woolbert, followed this up with a theoretical analysis of the audience with some concrete examples. Bentley and Woolbert studied more formal audiences which Brown terms intentional rather than casual. Formal or intentional audiences have been subdivided into information-seeking and recreational groups.[26]

A *public* is a loosely conjoined secondary grouping, not necessarily dependent on any physical contiguity of participants. It does depend on common interest of members but is often quite transient and only slightly structured. There is not only one public but rather, in our complex world at least, a variety of publics. These revolve around interests or needs such as political, economic, educational, religious, civic, recreational, and esthetic needs, which are some of the more important sources of publics.

The term *opinion* refers to a belief or conviction or notion regarding some situation, event, or issue. Consequently, the term *public opinion* refers to belief about some problem or topic that is regarded as of widespread public interest. When a belief or conviction is relatively stable, we may say that public opinion supports this view or that. When the beliefs vary among

[25] On cycles of fashion change, see J. Richardson and A. L. Kroeber, "Three Centuries of Women's Dress Fashions: A Quantitative Analysis," *Anthropological Record,* 5 (1940), pp. 112-150. For a psychoanalytic interpretation of clothes and fashion, see J. C. Flugel, *The Psychology of Clothes* (New York, 1930). See also Kimball Young, *Social Psychology* (3rd ed.; New York, 1955); Hadley Cantril, *The Psychology of Social Movements* (New York, 1941). Also Brown, in Lindzey, *op. cit.,* for discussion and bibliography.

[26] See M. Bentley, "A Preface to Social Psychology," in Bentley (ed.), "Studies in Social and General Psychology from the University of Illinois," *Psychological Monographs,* 21 (1916), pp. 1-25; C. H. Woolbert, "The Audience," *ibid.,* pp. 37-54. For a review of many of the earlier studies, see H. L. Hollingsworth, *Psychology of the Audience* (New York, 1928); Young, *Social Psychology* (2nd ed.; New York, 1944). See also La-Piere, *loc. cit.*

people, as they may over public problems, then we say that public opinion is in flux or in the process of formation. Earlier students of public opinion formation accepted an older theory of rational discussion concerning well-recognized issues or differences. Although discussion remains the essential mechanism, we now know that irrational and emotional elements, as well as rational ones, enter into much public debate.

Some important landmarks in the shift from the older rationalist views to more modern views are Wallas' *Human Nature and Politics* (1908), which drew heavily on McDougall's theory of instinct, and his *The Great Society* (1914), which showed clearly how Western peoples had shifted from a localism to a concern with world-wide problems. Then came the brilliant and telling book by Lippmann, *Public Opinion* (1922), in which, through his concept *stereotype* and by his use of historical examples of the rise of humor and the play of myth and legend, it became clear that emotional and irrational factors entered deeply into opinion formation. In another book, *The Phantom Public* (1928), Lippmann shows the limitations of public discussion of issues in the face of these forces which have grown up in our complicated industrial world.[27]

PUBLIC OPINION AND THE APPARATUS OF PERSUASION

The importance of recently developed mass media—motion pictures, radio, television, and comic books—in providing the building blocks of man's belief system has only recently begun to be understood. Very little is known about the possible effects of mass suggestion and mass imitation. We have just begun to glimpse the psychological needs and gratifications of individuals who become emotionally "possessed" by attending motion pictures, from listening to "soap operas," by watching and listening to television, or by becoming absorbed in comic books.[28]

Propaganda. As a device to alter people's views, propaganda is as old as written history. In its present-day meaning, the term first came into wide use during World War I. George Creel's *How We Advertised America* (1920) was an unofficial account of the propaganda operations of the Committee

[27] For materials on, and interpretation of, public opinion for the years between World War I and 1930, see Young, *Source Book for Social Psychology* (New York, 1927) and *Social Psychology* (New York, 1930). For a complete overview and summary of research and discussion down to 1939, see J. W. Albig, *Public Opinion* (New York, 1939).

[28] Hilda Herzog, "What Do We Really Know About Daytime-Serial Listeners?" in P. F Lazarsfeld and F. N. Stanton (eds.), *Radio Research*, 1942-1943 (New York, 1944). See also Rudolph Arnheim, "The World of the Daytime Serial," *ibid.* For some earlier studies on the possible influence of the motion pictures on ideas and conduct, see Herbert Blumer, *Movies and Conduct* (New York, 1933). On the influence of comic books on children, see K. M. Wolf and M. Fiske, "The Children Talk About Comics," in P. K. Lazarsfeld and F. N. Stanton (eds.), *Communications Research*, 1948-1949 (New York, 1949).

on Public Information, 1917-1919.[29] Not long after the close of hostilities, articles and books dealing with wartime propaganda began to appear. The most complete account of that period is H. D. Lasswell's *Propaganda Technique in the World War* (1927).

Another aftermath of World War I was the effort in some quarters to reassess its causes and to attempt to fix the blame elsewhere than on Germany. And in connection with this there was an effort to "debunk" the propaganda associated with the war.[30]

The earlier studies were chiefly historical and analytical. But beginning in the thirties there appeared reports on experimental research designed to discover more precisely how propaganda influences individual views and attitudes.[31] About the time World War II broke out the word *propaganda* began to be replaced by the concept *psychological warfare*. Yet the techniques were largely the same. There is a vast literature on Nazi-Fascist propaganda, and we can but cite the most readily available bibliographies.[32]

The rapid growth of interest in propaganda and in its relation to public opinion is also evidenced in the establishment in 1937 of the Institute for Propaganda Analysis and the inception of its publication, *Propaganda Analysis: A Monthly Letter to Help the Intelligent Citizen Detect and Analyze Propaganda.* This periodical, which gave its chief attention to Nazi propaganda and little, if any, to Communist efforts in this field, voluntarily dissolved in December, 1941. Another indication of the expansion of concern with communication, including propaganda, was the founding in January, 1937, of *The Public Opinion Quarterly*, under the aegis of the School of Public Affairs, Princeton University. The propaganda of World War II was both extensive and elaborate. One of the most striking differences in the content of propaganda in the two World Wars is brought out by Kris and Leites, who point out that in the World War I much of the propaganda was highly emotional

[29] See J. R. Mock and C. Larson, *Words That Won the War: The Story of the Committee on Public Information,* 1917-1919 (Princeton, N.J., 1939).

[30] See H. E. Barnes, *The Genesis of the World War* (3rd ed.; New York, 1926); A. W. H. Ponsonby, *Falsehood in Wartime, Containing an Assortment of Lies Circulated Throughout the Nations During the Great War* (New York, 1928).

[31] A. D. Annis and N. C. Meier, "Induction of Opinion Through Suggestion by Means of Planted Content," *JSP*, 5 (1934), pp. 68-81; W. H. Wilke, "An Experimental Comparison of the Speech, the Radio, and the Printed Page as Propaganda Devices," *AP* (1934), No. 169; and S. P. Rosenthal, "Change of Socio-Economic Attitudes under Radical Motion Picture Propaganda," *ibid.*, (1934), No. 166. See also Cantril and Allport, *loc. cit.*

[32] The Committee for National Morale published two books under the editorship of L. Farago: *German Psychological Warfare: A Critical, Annotated and Comprehensive Survey and Bibliography* (New York, 1941), and *The Axis Grand Strategy: Blueprints for Total War* (New York, 1942). For extensive listings of both domestic and wartime propaganda, see H. D. Lasswell, R. D. Casey, and B. L. Smith (eds.), *Propaganda, Communication, and Public Opinion* (Princeton, N.J., 1946). The student of propaganda should not overlook Hitler's *Mein Kampf* (Boston, 1943).

(as witness the atrocity stories), moralistic, and often given to outright falsification. Although the Germans and the Russians, each on their own side, indulged in some atrocity stories in World War II, for the most part propaganda from both sides tended to be more factual, sober, and non-moralistic.[33]

Since the close of World War II, there have been a number of descriptive works on the use of propaganda in wartime. But perhaps more significant has been the continuation of experimental research in this field, which has been concerned with media, content, and forms of presentation.[34]

LEADERSHIP

Systematic observation of the rise and functioning of leadership among children began with modern child psychology, but more carefully controlled studies were first made in this country after World War I when a number of institutes were set up to facilitate research in child behavior.[35] Although patterns of dominance and submission appear in novel and unstructured groups, culture soon sets the stage for appropriate roles. Moreover, at the adult level, students of social behavior usually distinguish *voluntary leadership*, as in election to a position of high status by the other members of a group, and *headship*, which is a matter of office derived from an institutional ascription of role.

There have been a number of psychological approaches to leadership. Some have stressed a unit trait or some constellation of traits as the determinant of dominance. Others have emphasized some form of typology such as the old distinction between leadership in action and leadership in thought.[36] Still others have regarded the interactional factors as basic. This latter position is clearly evident in the followers of Lewin and his field theory.[37] The

[33] Ernst Kris and Nathan Leites, "Trends in Twentieth-Century Propaganda," *Psychoanalysis and the Social Sciences,* 1 (1947), pp. 393-409; P.M.A. Linebarger, *Psychological Warfare* (Washington, 1948); Howard Becker, "The Nature and Consequences of Black Propaganda," *ASR,* 14, 2 (Apr., 1949), pp. 221-235.

[34] Among others see R. E. Summers (ed.), "America's Weapons of Psychological Warfare," *The Reference Shelf,* 23 (1951); C. I. Hovland, I. L. Janis, and H. H. Kelley, *Communication and Persuasion* (New Haven, 1953); P. F. Lazarsfeld and F. N. Stanton (eds.), *Communication Research,* 1948-1949 (New York, 1949). For recent surveys of much pertinent literature, see C. I. Hovland, "Effects of the Mass Media of Communication," in Lindzey, *op. cit.;* and L. Lowenthal (ed.), "Special Issue on International Communications Research," *POQ,* 16 (1952-53), pp. 481-708.

[35] The most important of the earlier researches on leadership in children's groups are summarized in W. I. Thomas and Dorothy S. Thomas, *The Child in America* (New York, 1928).

[36] For a handy review of the earlier literature on traits in leaders, see S. H. Britt, *Social Psychology of Modern Life* (rev. ed.; New York, 1949); C. A. Gibb, "Leadership," in Lindzey, *op. cit.;* O. L. Schwarz, *General Types of Superior Men* (Boston, 1916); E. B. Gowin, *The Executive and His Control of Men* (New York, 1915).

[37] The Lewinian standpoint is illustrated in the following books: David Krech and

studies in groups and leadership by Moreno, although they represent a less extreme view, would also, in general, tend to fall into this third category. Investigations of leaderless groups, stimulated largely by Lewin and Moreno, have thrown much light on the manner in which dominance emerges in a newly formed group.[38] The device of observing behavior under such conditions was used, among others, in the selection of field operatives for the Office of Strategic Services (OSS) during World War II.[39]

A review of the extensive literature on so-called traits of leadership shows that, whereas group members often perceive particular combinations of traits as adhering to a person whom they regard as a leader, there is no general consensus as to which constellation, if any, always goes with leadership. On the other hand, it hardly seems adequate to attempt to deal with the phenomena of dominance without paying some attention to personality factors.[40] Some suggestive work on personality and leadership, approached essentially through typology, is that of Adorno and his collaborators in their comparisons of the so-called "authoritarian" and "democratic" personalities. Sanford, following up on this work, and using a scale of authoritarian-equalitarian attitudes, has reported that "authoritarians" and "equalitarians" differ in the type of dominance they prefer and in their reactions to leadership.[41]

DIVERGENT APPROACHES TO PERSONALITY

At the beginning of the present century most social psychologists were concerned with matters of collective behavior. Inspired in large part by the French school of group psychology, American scholars such as Ellwood

R. S. Crutchfield, *Theory and Problems of Social Psychology* (New York, 1948); S. E. Asch, *Social Psychology* (New York, 1952) [no separate chapter on leadership]; and in many papers in Cartwright and Zander, *loc. cit.*

[38] J. L. Moreno, *Who Shall Survive?* (Washington, 1934); Gibb, *ibid.;* and Cartwright and Zander, *op. cit.* The two last-cited sources contain ample lists of publications in this area.

[39] OSS assessment staff, *Assessment of Men* (New York, 1948).

[40] For strong support of this position, see R. B. Cattell, "Concepts and Methods in the Measurement of Group Syntality," *Psychological Review,* 55 (1948), pp. 48-63; and L. Carter, "Leadership and Small-Group Behavior," in Muzafer Sherif and M. O. Wilson (eds.), *Group Relations at the Crossroads* (New York, 1953).

[41] F. H. Sanford, "Research on Military Leadership," in J. C. Flanagan (ed.), *Current Trends—Psychology in the World Emergency* (Pittsburgh, 1952). See also T. W. Adorno *et al., The Authoritarian Personality* (New York, 1950); also R. Christie and Marie Jahoda (eds.), *Studies in the Scope and Method of The Authoritarian Personality* (Glencoe, Ill., 1954); S. A. Stouffer *et al., Studies in Social Psychology in World War II* (Princeton, N.J., 1949), vol. 1; C. L. Shartle and R. M. Stogdill, *Studies in Naval Leadership* (Ohio State Research Foundation, 1952); J. K. Hemphill, *Situational Factors in Leadership* (Ohio State University Personnel Research Board, 1949); Melvin Seeman and R. T. Morris, *A Status-Factor Approach to Leadership* (Ohio State University Research Foundation, 1950). Gibb, *loc. cit.,* has a good review of the Ohio studies.

and Ross investigated the mental structure of the crowd, but it was not until the publication of McDougall's *An Introduction to Social Psychology* in 1908 that the attention of American social psychology was shifted to the systematic study of personality.

The central feature of McDougall's system, as originally expounded, is a systematic and definite linkage of instincts and emotions. He listed seven paired instincts and emotions and added some "less well defined" impulses and emotions, such as instinct of reproduction (with sexual jealousy and female coyness associated therewith), the gregarious instinct, and instincts of acquisition and construction. Through experience, the various emotions combine into more complicated forms. When the complex emotions have a relatively stable object about which they are organized, we have the birth of the sentiment, and on the basis of complex emotions and sentiments the self arises. The particular form it takes will be greatly affected by social background. Character of a consistent sort grows up by relating the instincts, and the emotions and habits developed from them, to a goal or ideal.

Behaviorism derived largely from the work of the Russian physiologist Pavlov, whose method was introduced into this country by Watson. Their heavy stress on environmental, as against innate, elements in determining behavior, led to a wholesale attack on the instinct theory of McDougall and his followers. The main point of criticism seemed to be that the instinct hypothesis is a naive and particularistic explanation for the complexities of human behavior. The whole argument is well summarized in Bernard's *Instinct: A Study in Social Psychology* (1924).

A systematic approach to the subject matter of social psychology based upon the *reflex hypothesis* of the behaviorists is F. H. Allport's *Social Psychology* (1924), which soon gained wide acceptance. Its basic assumption is that "the human being has inherited a number of prepotent reflexes which are fundamental not only in their original potency, but in the control which they exert over habit formation throughout life. Ultimately, as well as genetically, they are prepotent." Allport recognizes six important classes of human prepotent reflexes: starting and withdrawing, rejecting, struggling, hunger reactions, sensitive zone reactions, and sex reactions. Upon these foundations all social behavior is built.

To these reflex theorists the human group is merely an aggregation of individuals. Although some habits may be common to all or to some of the group members, each individual has his own habits and characteristic ways of acting. The mechanism of conditioned response is used to explain how the individual develops his behavior in association with other people. Through such associations the child learns a language and acquires the habits and characteristic modes of behavior of his group. This behavior is a response to sensory stimulation; it is learned through the process of reinforcement in which acceptable acts are rewarded and unacceptable ones punished. In this manner the individual develops his personality.

Although regularly attacked by the sociologically oriented social psychologists,[42] this reflex or reinforcement scheme gradually gained currency until it reached its peak just prior to World War II in the writings of Hull. Hull developed reinforcement theory into an hypothetico-deductive general theory of behavior. Using survival as a key concept, he viewed the organism as adaptive in terms of need reduction. A large-scale and somewhat controversial application of Hull's theory to social psychology was made by Miller and Dollard and published in their book, *Social Learning and Imitation* (1941). This work was followed by a series of empirical studies, [43] and these in turn were followed by a stream of criticism.

Contributions of Cooley and Mead. In contrast to this approach to the study of personality development is that of the symbolic-interactionist school. The chief aim of this group has been to describe and interpret the manner in which the self or personality arises and functions in social interaction. The groundwork of symbolic interactionism was laid by James, Baldwin, Dewey, and Cooley. Cooley's major contributions to the theory of personality and its relation to society appear in his three books: *Human Nature and the Social Order* (1902); *Social Organization, A Study of the Larger Mind* (1909); and *Social Process* (1918). His chief thesis is the inseparable connection between the person and society. The child's idea of himself is the reflection of others about him.

Following the basic premises of Baldwin and Cooley, and strongly influenced by functional and behavioristic tendencies in psychology, Mead has presented a naturalistic and more or less objective description and analysis of the processes involved in the rise of the self. Mead published only an occasional paper, but his lecture notes and other unpublished writings have been edited posthumously; his theory of the self is elaborated in *Mind, Self, and Society* (1934). According to Mead, "The self arises in conduct, when the individual becomes a social object in experience to himself. . . . The child gradually becomes a social being in his own experience, and he acts toward himself in a manner analogous to that in which he acts towards others."

Role Theory and Personality. Of all the concepts suggested by the symbolic interactionists, the term *role* has perhaps got most attention. It has been used both by sociologists, including Cottrell, Merton, Hughes, Kuhn, Waller, Parsans, and Kimball Young, and by psychologists such as Cameron,

[42] See Herbert Blumer, "Social Psychology," in E. P. Schmidt (ed.), *Man and Society* (New York, 1937).

[43] C. L. Hull, *Principles of Behavior* (New York, 1943); W. W. Lambert, "Stimulus-Response Contiguity and Reinforcement Theory in Social Psychology," in Lindzey, *op. cit.;* Dorrian Apple, "Learning Theory and Socialization," *ASR,* 16 (1951), pp. 23-27; A. R. Lindesmith and A. L. Strauss, "Comparative Psychology and Social Psychology," *AJS,* 58 (1952), pp. 272-279.

Newcomb, Sarbin, and Sargent.[44] Whereas earlier work was largely qualitative and anecdotal, recent literature includes a growing body of empirical investigations of social roles and the development of the self. The trend is toward explication and empirical establishment of these concepts; it is probable that they will continue to gain adherents in the future.

Personality as Viewed by Freud and the Revisionists. Another important and influential theory of human personality is that developed by Freud, the founder of psychoanalysis. The subject matter of psychoanalysis "is human behavior viewed as conflict."[45] The individual is regarded as in a more or less constant state of striving or struggling for satisfactions which a hostile environment, especially the social world, tends to redirect, restrict, and often completely deny him. Freud's theory is essentially the developmental story of this conflict. (See Chap. 20, "Sociology and Psychoanalysis," by Gisela J. Hinkle.)

As the practice of psychoanalysis spread from its original center in Vienna, deviations from Freud's own views were bound to arise. Two of the earlier defections centered around Jung, who stressed the archaic ego and developed a theory of interactive personality types, and around Adler, who viewed life as characterized by a fundamental, inherent, purposive striving toward some anticipated goal of perfect achievement. Of the various deviations from Freud that do not completely reject his work, those of Horney, Fromm, and Sullivan have had considerable vogue, especially among certain social scientists in the United States. Horney's basic contention is that Freud overemphasizes the importance of instincts and of organic development by inevitable stages from birth to maturity. Fromm approaches the topic of personality as a lay analyst and social psychologist with a strong interest in history and cultural anthropology. He, like Horney, holds that the satisfaction of instinct is not the central task of the individual; rather, it is adjustment or learning in line with the social-cultural demands of time and place. Sullivan, a psychiatrist, was what might be called a quasi-Freudian. Out of his clinical observations he fashioned a "theory of interpersonal relations" or "theory of the self-system."[46]

Social Perception and Personality. Perception is a basic process in the relating of the individual to his environment, physical and social. Historically, the experimental psychologist dealt chiefly in simpler perceptual judg-

[44] See T. R. Sarbin, "Role Theory," in Lindzey, *op. cit.*, vol. 1.

[45] For discussions of Freud's theory of personality see Kimball Young, *Personality and Problems of Adjustment* (2nd ed.; New York, 1952); and C. S. Hall and G. Lindzey, "Psychoanalytic Theory and Its Applications in the Social Sciences," in Lindzey, *op. cit.*, vol. 1.

[46] C. C. Jung, *Psychological Types* (New York, 1922); Alfred Adler, *The Neurotic Constitution* (New York, 1916); Karen Horney, *The Neurotic Personality of Our Time* (New York, 1937); Erich Fromm, *Escape from Freedom* (New York, 1941); H. S. Sullivan, *Conceptions of Modern Psychiatry* (Washington, 1947).

ments, such as are found in the Weber-Fechner phenomena. A consideration of possible social–cultural influences on perception did not interest him. So, too, for a long time the social psychologist took perception for granted and gave his attention to motivation, emotion, and social interaction. Recently, however, under the rubric "social perception," there has appeared a growing interest in studying social–cultural factors in this important adaptive process.[47] In view of the intimate relationship between perception and needs, perceptual processes become the critical intervening variables for this personality theory, and, conversely, personality processes are crucial in determining perceptions.

Culture and Personality. Gradually, social psychologists began to take cognizance of the findings of cultural anthropology. What men perceive is influenced, on the learning side, by the content of what is acquired, and most of this will have direct or indirect roots in the culture of a given time and place. Klineberg contributed to the growing appreciation of such factors in his account of the Chinese interpretation of gestures. Adams showed the place of cultural stylization in his comparison of emotional expressiveness of the rural Japanese with that of the Japanese-Americans in Hawaii. LaBarre brought together a wide range of examples to demonstrate deviations in emotional expression. And Efron's study of the gestures of East European immigrants, recently arrived in the United States, with those of second and later generations of these same groups has given us detailed documentation on this general topic.[48]

Historically, the "culture and personality" approach had its chief source in Freud's attempts to explain cultural and social phenomena in terms of his psychoanalytic theory. Freud was largely biologically oriented and tended to regard the individual as a product of growth and maturation along biological lines, modified or redirected by the impact of social or cultural forces. The neo-Freudians place less stress on biological factors and more stress on cultural factors in their interpretation of the dynamics of personality development and function.

From this source, cultural anthropologists, social psychologists, and others have attempted to study the effects of culture upon personality development. In many cases the materials have been largely of a descriptive and historical sort familiar to cultural anthropology. The early study by Benedict and the more recent work of Margaret Mead, Gorer, and others exemplify

[47] See J. S. Bruner and Leo Postman, "Personality Dynamics and the Process of Perceiving," in R. R. Blake and G. V. Ramsey (eds.), *Perception: An Approach to Personality* (New York, 1951).

[48] See Otto Klineberg, *Social Psychology* (2nd ed.; New York, 1954); Romanzo Adams, *Interracial Marriage in Hawaii: A Study of the Mutually Conditioned Processes of Acculturation and Amalgamation* (New York, 1937); Weston LaBarre, "The Cultural Basis of Emotions and Gestures," *JP,* 16 (1947), pp. 49-68.

this approach.[49] But others, notably Kardiner and Linton, Hallowell, and DuBois have attempted to present a dynamic picture of cultural learning.[50]

METHODOLOGY IN SOCIAL PSYCHOLOGY

Of the phenomenal developments in social psychology since World War I, the most important have been those in methodology.* Whereas early social psychologists built their theoretical systems on the basis of meager evidence collected informally, recent research tends to produce limited generalizations on the basis of systematic, controlled study. Whereas older reports involve qualitative anecdote and later more extensive and formal case study, in contemporary research stress is placed upon the collection, processing, and interpretation of mass data. Statistical procedures have been improved and their applications extended. Observational techniques have become more rigorous, interviews more sophisticated, and experiments better controlled. Furthermore, a number of special research techniques have been devised that have enriched the repertory of the social psychologists.

Within the field of social psychology there has been a perennial debate centered around the relative importance of theory and data. In order to understand this conflict, we must look to its origins.

In the beginning, embryonic social psychology emerged from an antecedent tradition of social philosophy. Its initial break took the form of an increased attention to empirical data. Yet the early social psychologists attempted to construct universal encyclopedic schemes that had much in common with the social philosophy of the time. Spencer, Tylor, Durkheim, and LeBon are examples of these encyclopedic theorists.[51] Although the contribution of these men in laying the groundwork for scientific social psychology is undeniable, many of their theories have not stood the test of time.

Behaviorism. After World War I behaviorism became increasingly dominant in psychology, and it soon attracted such adherents as F. H. Allport and Kimball Young in social psychology.[52] As a sort of reaction-formation to

[49] Ruth Benedict, *Patterns of Culture* (Boston, 1934); Margaret Mead, *Soviet Attitudes toward Authority* (New York, 1951); Geoffrey Gorer, *The American People* (New York, 1948).

[50] These approaches are summarized in Alex Inkeles and D. J. Levinson, "National Character: The Study of Modal Personality and Socio-Cultural Systems," Lindzey, *op. cit.* The interest in interdisciplinary treatment of social psychology is evident in J. E. Hulett, Jr., and Ross Stagner (eds.), *Problems in Social Psychology: An Interdisciplinary Inquiry* (Urbana, Ill., 1952).

* The editors have not tried to make the terminology of this "methodology" section uniform with Chap. 7, which provides a more extended treatment.

[51] For a discussion of the contributions of these men, see Howard Becker and H. E. Barnes, *Social Thought from Lore to Science*, 2nd ed.; (New York, 1952), vol. 1.

[52] F. H. Allport, *Social Psychology* (Boston, 1924); and Young, *Social Psychology* (1st ed.; New York, 1930).

the grandiose generalizations of their predecessors, these behaviorists initiated a rigid empiricism. They avoided theory and saw science chiefly as a process of data collection. During this era, the individual who openly admitted an interest in theory invited inquiry into his personal competence, his professional ethics, or both.

However, theory was implicit in the work of even the most rigid of these empirically minded scholars. Today, therefore, most social psychologists demand an integration of theory and data, but many questions are still undecided and controversies continue to arise. Currently, attempts to erect a bridge between theory and data are bogged down because of the question concerning the level upon which theory should be pitched. Should theory be of a broad or narrow nature? Although there is a place for both broad and narrow theory, the latter is certainly more common today and is likely to dominate the field for some time to come.

Along with the shift in the relative emphasis on theory and data there is a second trend. Social psychologists have moved from the descriptive presentation of data toward the analytic or explanatory. Descriptive science is preoccupied with classifying data. Its generalizations are enumerative, resulting in aggregates of facts rather than in systems of knowledge. Explanatory science, on the other hand, stresses the search for systematic interconnections of experiences. It produces generalizations of covariance and cause.

Case Study and Statistics: The Passing of a Controversy. After World War I, most social psychologists could agree that the aim of their research was scientific—to predict and control social interaction. Agreement was lacking, however, on the best *means* for achieving such prediction. A controversy over the relative merits of case study *vs.* the statistical method loomed large, and adherents of each position made exaggerated claims.

Formal case-study procedures utilizing the life history and other personal documents were introduced into social psychology by Thomas and Znaniecki in their monumental work, *The Polish Peasant in Europe and America* (1918-1920). In it the authors attempted to demonstrate the utility of case study in producing scientific generalizations. Their method quickly gained popularity and a number of such studies resulted.[53] More recently, this method has been employed in modified form by Angell in studying the reactions of families to the depression, by Lindesmith in investigating opiate addiction, and by Cressey in his studies of violation of financial trust.[54]

[53] See William Healy and Augusta Bronner, *New Light on Delinquency and Its Treatment* (New Haven, 1936); Thrasher, *op. cit.;* Shaw, *op. cit.;* H. W. Zorbaugh, *The Gold Coast and the Slum* (Chicago, 1929); H. D. Lasswell, *Psychopathology and Politics* (Chicago, 1930); Nels Anderson, *The Hobo* (Chicago, 1931).

[54] R. C. Angell, *The Family Encounters the Depression* (New York, 1936); A. R. Lindesmith, *Opiate Addiction* (Bloomington, Ind., 1947); and D. R. Cressey, *Other People's Money* (Glencoe, Ill., 1953).

The fruitfulness of the case study method has been a topic of long debate and today we must recognize that it no longer holds the central position in social psychology it once did. However, the comment of Burgess is pertinent: "Almost all sociologists agree upon the usefulness of the case study for the exploration of the problem, for disclosing leads, for deriving hunches, and for raising questions and hypotheses."[55]

The Quantitative Emphasis: Tests, Scales, and Factor Aanalysis. The current trend is toward statistical manipulation of mass data in testing hypotheses. Among the first American social scientists to utilize these new statistical procedures were the educational psychologists. Here, the names of Cattell, Thorndike, Terman, and Thurstone are outstanding.[56] These investigators devised tests and measurements of a large number of human attributes, but their primary interest was in statistical application to intelligence testing. The first mass psychological testing in any country was the application of the Army intelligence test during World War I. Following the success of the intelligence testers in the schools and in the Army, social psychologists were quick to pick up statistical techniques. Since opinions and attitudes constitute one of the central substantive elements in the field, the construction of instruments for their measurement became of vital importance. The most striking development was in the use of scales and of factor analysis. The origins of scales in social psychology derive from the application of rating schemes devised by Thorndike for measuring the speed of reading and the like. Then, too, in the mid-twenties Bogardus invented his social-distance test.[57] An early attempt to get at the problem of measurement in a more exact fashion came when Thurstone, applying the techniques of just-perceptible differences, developed a scale that had eleven equidistant units. This means was used for making scales to measure a wide range of social-psychological phenomena: conservatism–radicalism, prejudice–tolerance, and so on. During World War II, Guttman began analyzing the responses to questionnaires collected by the Research Branch of the Information and Education Division of the Army Service Forces, with a view to developing a set of scales of unidimensionality.[58]

Factor analysis had its origin in Spearman's theory of a general and specific factor as an explanation of the nature and functioning of intelligence. With the aid of matrix algebra, Thurstone began developing techniques to

[55] E. W. Burgess, "Research Methods in Sociology," in Georges Gurvitch and W. E. Moore (eds.), *Twentieth Century Sociology* (New York, 1945).

[56] See R. S. Woodworth *et al.*, "The Psychological Researches of James McKeen Cattell," *AP* (1914), No. 30; E. L. Thorndike, *Educational Psychology* (New York, 1913), 3 vols.; L. M. Terman, *The Measurement of Intelligence* (Boston, 1916); L. L. Thurstone, "Attitudes Can be Measured," *AJS*, 33 (1928), pp. 529-554.

[57] E. S. Bogardus, "Measuring Social Distances," *JAP*, 9 (1925), pp. 299-308.

[58] See S. A. Stouffer *et al.*, *Studies in Social Psychology in World War II* (Princeton, N.J., 1950), vol. 4.

handle the results of a wide variety of tests in such a way as to show that the test responses might be interpreted as dependent upon single or multiple factors. More recently Eysenck, Stephenson, and R. B. Cattell have worked out rather elaborate techniques accompanied by theoretical formulations to enable them to deal with a wide range of phenomena, from personality traits to the content of widely diverse culture systems.[59]

Students of social psychology have long wished for some method of handling qualitative data in more objective, preferably statistical, terms. The recent development of the "latent-structure approach" through the use of factor analysis at the hands of Lazarsfeld and Stouffer and others may provide a beginning in this direction.[60]

Sampling Problems. Sampling has always been a difficult problem in social psychology. This is particularly true in public opinion polling where the collection of mass data is fundamental. Early public opinion polling gave little attention to sampling. It grew out of the attempts of "inquiring reporters" to take "straw votes" prior to elections. These attempts aroused public interest, and in 1916 the *Literary Digest* began regular forecasts of national elections. The *Literary Digest* was dominant in the field until, in 1936, it made a gross error in predicting the results of the presidential election because of a biased sample. This led the opinion pollsters to re-evaluate their sampling attempts.

Soon the Gallup Poll, Roper's *Fortune* survey, and the Crosley Poll were gaining stature, and their areal sampling procedures were apparently successful. However, in 1948 the polls again failed in their predictions. A serious error was evident in almost all pre-election polls, and again stock-taking resulted. A controversy immediately arose over the relative effectiveness of quota or cluster *vs.* probability sampling.[61]

Participant-Observation and the Interview. Observational techniques constitute a basic tool of social psychology. Present techniques have grown out of the unsystematized observations of the early social psychologists discussed above. Some refinements and attempts at control were made during the first quarter of the present century by Park and his students. They form-

[59] C. E. Spearman, "General Intelligence Objectively Determined and Measured," *American Journal of Psychology,* 15 (1904), pp. 201-293; L. L. Thurstone, *Multiple Factor Analysis* (Chicago, 1947); H. J. Eysenck, *Dimensions of Personality* (London, 1947); W. Stephenson, *The Study of Behavior* (Chicago, 1953); R. B. Cattell, *Factor Analysis* (New York, 1952).

[60] S. A. Stouffer, "Scaling Concepts and Scaling Theory," in Marie Jahoda *et al.* (eds.), *Research Methods in Social Relations* (New York, 1951), vol. 2; and Stouffer *et al., op. cit.,* vol. 4.

[61] Frederick Mosteller *et al., The Pre-Election Polls of 1948* (New York, 1949); F. F. Stephan, "Sampling in Studies of Opinions, Attitudes, and Consumer Wants," *Proceedings of the American Philosophical Society,* 92 (1948), pp. 387-398; Harry Alpert "Some Observations on the Sociology of Sampling," *SF,* 31 (1952), pp. 30-33.

alized their procedure into the technique of participant-observation, but they never developed any systematic means to eliminate bias and insure reliability of their data. The first attempts at systematic treatment of these problems were made by Bühler and Thomas.[62] Observational techniques have been receiving increased attention in recent years. The movement has been away from recording the totality of interaction and toward noting only specifically predetermined aspects of behavior. Category sets and rating scales have been developed to specify the phenomena to be observed. In addition to specification of observations, controls have been introduced in recent observational work through application of various mechanical recording devices.[63]

Interviews, in one form or another, are one of the most fundamental tools of social psychology. They range from the deep, intensely personal, free association of psychoanalysis to the brief check-list questionnaires sent through the mail by commercial pollsters. The informal deep-level interview has been employed chiefly in various techniques of psychotherapy. It was outlined first by Freud and his followers, and has recently been adapted by Rogers and his client-centered therapists.[64]

The Experimental Approach. According to Murphy, Murphy, and Newcomb, the systematic study of suggestion by Braid between 1841 and 1860 represents the inception of experimentation in social psychology. From that time forward psychological literature was sprinkled with reports of experimental studies in this field. After World War I, Moede and F. H. Allport outlined their demands that social psychology be placed on an experimental basis.[65] Since that time, experimentation has increased at a rapid rate until, currently, it is one of our major methods. Although, as the discussion above indicates, increased use of experimental research designs has been a major trend in social psychology, modifications in the experimental model itself have also taken place. Most of these have aimed at improving control and eliminating bias. One school of thought has moved toward greater complications in design—resulting from the addition of more experimental and control groups—culminating finally in Solomon's four-group design. Another tradition, stemming from the statistician-biologist, Fisher, has minimized exper-

[62] W. F. Whyte, "Observational Fieldwork Methods," in Jahoda *et al., op. cit.*, vol. 2; Charlotte Bühler and H. Hetzer, *Testing Children's Developments from Birth to School Age* (New York, 1935); Dorothy S. Thomas *et al., Observational Studies of Social Behavior* (New Haven, Conn., 1933), vol. 1.

[63] For discussions of these developments, see R. W. Heyns and A. F. Zander, "Observation of Group Behavior," in Festinger and Katz, *op. cit.;* and R. W. Heyns and Ronald Lippitt, "Systematic Observational Techniques," in Lindzey, *op. cit.*, vol. 1.

[64] C. R. Rogers, *Counseling and Psychotherapy* (Boston, 1941).

[65] Gardner Murphy, Lois B. Murphy, and T. M. Newcomb, *Experimental Social Psychology* (2nd ed.; New York, 1937); W. Moede, *Experimentelle Massenpsychologie* (Leipzig, 1920); F. H. Allport, *Social Psychology* (Boston, 1924).

imental controls, utilizing statistical controls instead.[66] Here the emphasis is on random sampling and on the more elegant statistical devices, such as analysis of variance. (See Chap. 7.)

In concluding this discussion of methods some mention should be made of a few of the various special research techniques that have been employed in the field.

Projective Techniques. The use of projective techniques has assumed increasing importance. They represent a combination of some quantification with a good deal of qualitative analysis. Projective tests are believed capable of getting at deeper levels of personality than are the devices developed by Thurstone, Likert, Guttman, and others. The interpretation is based on the meaningful content, on the emotional expression accompanying the replies, on gestures, hesitations, and other expressive movements thought indicative of unconscious features of the personality. The projective tests rest on the assumption that the free-flowing associations aroused derive from the unconscious and dynamic underpinning of the personality.[67]

Sociometric Techniques. Sociometry may be designated as the study of interpersonal relations, with special reference to determining attractions and repulsions within the group structure. Its chief sponsor, Moreno, has written a natural history of group formation using both statistical and geometric modes of presentation to indicate the dynamics of interindividual relations. Currently, sociometric measures are receiving widespread attention and are being modified through the development of more sophisticated statistical techniques.[68]

Content-analysis arose as a device to identify specific or general themes in various form of verbal material: novels, essays, public speeches, news stories, editorials, and the like. The detection, tabulation, and analysis of such themes provide a means of describing changes through time in political propaganda, in party policies, and in international relations—to note only a few applications. Berelson believes that an examination of content changes over time may give us a way of predicting future trends.[69]

The Cross-Cultural Approach. Strictly speaking, cross-cultural study is not a research technique but a means of gathering data. However, its use represents a substantial advance for social psychologists in that it allows them to build generalizations that are not restricted to a single culture. Early studies were performed by Tylor and by Hobhouse, Wheeler, and Ginsberg using cross-cultural comparisons to test evolutionary hypotheses. But it was

[66] R. L. Solomon, "An Extension of Control-Group Design," *PB,* 46 (1949), pp. 137-150; R. A. Fisher, *The Design of Experiments* (Edinburgh, 1935).

[67] See J. E. Bell, *Projective Techniques* (New York, 1948).

[68] Moreno, *op. cit.;* Gardner Linzey and E. F. Borgatta, "Sociometric Measurement," in Lindzey, *op. cit.,* vol. 1.

[69] Bernard Berelson, *Content-Analysis in Communication Research* (Glencoe, Ill., 1952).

not until the past decade that the cross-cultural method was used to test social-psychological hypotheses.[70]

SELECTED BIBLIOGRAPHY

Cartwright, Dorwin, and A. F. Zander, *Group Dynamics* (Evanston, Ill.: Row, Peterson, 1953).

Dennis, Wayne (ed.), *Current Trends in Social Psychology* (Pittsburgh: University of Pittsburg Press, 1948).

Hulett, J. E., Jr., and Ross Stagner (eds.), *Problems in Social Psychology* (Urbana, Ill.: University of Illinois Press, 1952).

Karpf, F. B., *American Social Psychology* (New York: McGraw-Hill, 1932).

Kluckhohn, Clyde, and H. A. Murray (eds.), *Personality in Nature, Society, and Culture* (New York: Alfred Knopf, rev. ed., 1953).

Lindzey, Gardner (ed.), *Handbook of Social Psychology* (Cambridge, Mass.: Addison-Wesley, 1954), 2 vols.

Murchison, Carl (ed.), *A Handbook of Social Psychology* (Worcester, Mass.: Clark University Press, 1935).

Swanson, G. E., T. M. Newcomb, and E. L. Hartley (eds.), *Readings in Social Psychology* (rev. ed.; New York: Henry Holt, 1952).

Young, Kimball, and D. W. Oberdorfer, "Psychological Studies of Social Processes," in H. E. Barnes, Howard Becker, and Frances B. Becker (eds.), *Contemporary Social Theory* (New York: D. Appleton-Century, 1940), Chap. 12.

Woodard, J. W., "Social Psychology," in Georges Gurvitch and Wilbert E. Moore, *Twentieth Century Sociology* (New York: Philosophical Library, 1945), Chap. 19.

[70] E. B. Tylor, "On the Method of Investigating the Development of Institutions, Applied to the Laws of Marriage and Descent," *J. Royal Anthropological Institute,* 18 (1889), pp. 245-269; L. T. Hobhouse, G. C. Wheeler, and Morris Ginsberg, *The Material Culture and Institutions of the Simpler Peoples* (London, 1915); J. W. M. Whiting and I. L. Child, *Child Training and Personality* (New Haven, Conn., 1953); J. W. M. Whiting, "The Cross Cultural Method," in Lindzey, *op cit.,* vol. 1.

20

SOCIOLOGY AND PSYCHOANALYSIS

GISELA J. HINKLE

THE THEORIES OF SIGMUND FREUD HAVE BECOME PERVASIVE IN AMERICAN thought-ways of the mid-twentieth century and in contemporary American sociology. Many sociologists are using adaptations of psychoanalytic method, segments of its theories, and such selected and varied concepts as latent qualities, manifest qualities, repression, rationalization, projection, sublimation, identification, frustration, aggression, parental surrogate, superego, guilt feeling, withdrawal, displacement, security, and insecurity. Freudian and neo-Freudian notions have also diffused into many specialized areas of sociology where they are employed both with and without awareness of their intellectual origins. They have been, in a sense, "diluted" to fit into a sociological framework in social psychology; collective behavior, public opinion and communication, sociology of the family, race and ethnic relations, social stratification, bureaucracy, social disorganization, social psychiatry, and sociological theory.[1] "Freudianism" in American sociology may thus be said to involve conscious and unconscious, pure and diluted, and correct and incorrect usage of psychoanalytic ideas.

Ambivalent Attitudes Toward Psychoanalytic Theory. Nevertheless, sociologists have severely and fundamentally criticized psychoanalysis. Occasionally, rejection of Freudianism is categorically based on its excessive emphasis on sex, its use of the recapitulation theory, its theory of totem and

[1] Franz Alexander interprets the "dilution" of psychoanalysis in American social science as evidence of its acceptance. See Franz Alexander and Helen Ross (eds.), *Twenty Years of Psychoanalysis* (New York, 1953), p. 18.

taboo, and its use of biological, instinctive determinants of behavior. Most sociological appraisals are fundamentally strictures on procedure and technique. Sociologists criticize psychoanalysts' frequently insufficient, inadequately selected, and irrelevant data; their overgeneralizations based on such evidence; their tautologically defined, imprecise concepts; their tendency to label rather than explain behavior; and their disregard of the facts of cultural relativity in propounding a universal theory of motivation and personality development.[2]

This paradoxical acceptance and rejection of psychoanalysis justifies a detailed investigation to determine how extensive use of these ideas by sociologists has come about. Such a history of psychoanalysis in American sociology is best summarized in terms of three major eras of American sociology.[3]

The First Period, 1905-1918

Initial Hesitation in Accepting Freudian Theory. The impact of psychoanalysis on American social thought dates from the year 1909, when Freud presented five lectures on the origin and development of his theories at the twentieth anniversary celebration of Clark University.[4] He outlined the principle of psychic determinism and, utilizing the case of the young girl studied by him and Breuer, specified how hysteria results from actively conflicting mental forces rather than from congenital degeneracy. He also explained the concept of "resistance," the nature of the "wish" and its manifestation in dreams and wit, infantile sexuality, the Oedipus complex, and the function of sublimation in the development of modern civilization. Through the many American and foreign scholars who attended these meetings, Freud's theories became widely known. Indeed, G. Stanley Hall, then president of Clark University, argued that these meetings provided the initial momentum for the spread of Freudianism throughout the United States.[5]

[2] See A. R. Lindesmith and A. L. Strauss, "A Critique of Culture-Personality Writings," *ASR,* 15 (Oct., 1950), pp. 587-600.

[3] The history of American sociology can be conveniently described in terms of three periods: 1905-1918, 1918-1935, and 1935-1955; see R. C. Hinkle, Jr., and Gisela J. Hinkle, *The Development of Modern Sociology,* (Garden City, N.Y., 1954). The history of psychoanalysis approximates these same three periods. However, 1920 is a better terminal date for the first period in the history of psychoanalytic influence on sociology since the first formal recognition of psychoanalysis by sociologists occurred during that year.

[4] Sigmund Freud, "The Origin and Development of Psychoanalysis," *Lectures and Addresses Delivered Before the Departments of Psychology and Pedagogy in Celebration of the Twentieth Anniversary of the Opening of Clark University,* Part I, Lectures before the Department of Psychology (Worcester, Mass., 1910), pp. 1-30.

[5] G. Stanley Hall, *Life and Confessions of a Psychologist* (New York, 1923), p. 332.

Hall's interpretation applies more directly to American literature, philosophy, education, and psychology than to sociology.[6] Since sociologists were recruited predominantly from Protestant social backgrounds characterized by strict morality, they avoided extensive discussion of psychoanalysis. They regarded Freudianism as synonymous with sex, and the general problem of sex as outside their realm of inquiry. Prior to World War I, sociologists were acquainted only with W. I. Thomas' *Sex and Society* (1907) and Havelock Ellis' *Studies in the Psychology of Sex* (1898). Although they were hesitant or unwilling to investigate and evaluate Freud's theories publicly, early sociologists' citations and reviews of psychoanalysis suggest substantial familiarity with these ideas. Nevertheless, the reticence to discuss Freudianism justifies characterizing the earliest phase of psychoanalysis in American sociology, 1909 to 1920, as one of "cautious hesitancy."

Some Parallels Between American Sociology and Freudian Theory. The first phase of psychoanalysis coincided with the formative era of American sociology, when sociologists sought to discover the natural laws of social life in order to ameliorate social problems associated with industrialization and urbanization. The basic interests and assumptions of early sociology were thus congenial to the acceptance of Freudian psychology. Seeking to explain problems of pauperism, crime, insanity, suicide, and illegitimacy, sociologists adhered to four basic assumptions that are consistent with those held by psychoanalysts: (1) sociologists accepted the task of searching for universal scientific laws of human behavior that resemble invariant natural laws governing physical and organic phenomena; (2) they identified social change as social evolution and interpreted it as progress toward a better society; (3) they regarded such upward human development as subject to acceleration by direct human melioristic intervention, using knowledge of sociological laws; and (4) they conceived of social behavior and society as constituted by individual behavior, and particularly emphasized the motivation of individuals in association.

Conducive to a positive interpretation of Freudianism is the adherence to an individualistic conception of society, which has persisted throughout the last fifty years of the discipline, and which can be succinctly described as *voluntaristic nominalism*.[7] Expressing the points of agreement among early

[6] Gisela J. Hinkle, "The Role of Freudianism in American Sociology" (unpublished Ph. D. dissertation, University of Wisconsin, 1951); E. W. Burgess, "The Influence of Sigmund Freud upon Sociology in the United States," *AJS*, 45 (Nov. ,1939), pp. 356-374; C. S. Hall and Gardner Lindzey, "Psychoanalytic Theory and Its Application in the Social Sciences," in Gardner Lindzey (ed.), *Handbook of Social Psychology* (Cambridge, Mass., 1954), vol. 1, pp. 143-180.

[7] Hinkle and Hinkle, *op cit.*, p. vii: "This term describes the assumption that the structure of all social groups is the consequence of the aggregate of its separate, component individuals and that social phenomena ultimately derive from the motivations of these knowing, feeling, and willing individuals."

sociologists, Albion W. Small wrote in 1906 that "nothing is social which is not psychical" and that sociologists' "distinctive center of attention and . . . principle of synthesis is the personality."[8] Although their primary study is individuals in association, sociologists should be especially concerned with the elements of attention, valuation, and volition operative in the dynamics of social action.

The stress placed on the psychic nature of man as the basic source of social phenomena is evidenced in the theories of social forces found in the writings of all the earlier major sociologists. Lester F. Ward set forth a theory of social forces that emphasized emotions. William G. Sumner believed man to be motivated by the instincts of hunger, sex love, vanity, and ghost fear. Albion W. Small thought that the six interests of health, wealth, sociability, knowledge, beauty, and rightness prompt man to action. And Edward A. Ross, who wrote the first American text in social psychology, conjoined Ward's theory of social forces with Small's theory of interests.

Given the assumption of *voluntaristic nominalism,* sociologists generally viewed social problems as results of maladjustment of individuals to the complexities of modern civilization. This individual maladaptation was considered the direct product of man's psychological and mental make-up. Within this general orientation toward social problems, sociologists began to employ selected Freudian notions, as, for instance, the concepts of "wish," "repression," and "sublimation." How these and other Freudian ideas became incorporated into sociological research dealing with crime, social change, and labor unrest will now be examined.

Disseminators of Freudian Theory: Hall and Groves. G. Stanley Hall was the first to describe the potentialities of Freudian discoveries for sociology.[9] Addressing himself to the problem of crime, he indicated that the mental process associated with criminality involves revolt by individuals against those social institutions that compel conformity, inhibit self-realization, and restrict the expression of the feeling of justice. Criminals rebel against social pressures because they possess certain elementary qualities to an excessive degree.

No references to psychoanalysis can be found in the official records of the American Sociological Society for the five years succeeding Hall's paper. Beginning in 1917, however, several articles, book reviews, and abstracts pertaining to Freudianism were published. Ernest R. Groves wrote the first full-length book review in 1918. Robert Gault published a lecture that he had presented in March, 1917, at Northwestern University.[10] Reinterpreting

[8] A. W. Small, "Points of Agreement Among Sociologists," *PASS,* 1 (1907), p. 67.

[9] G. Stanley Hall, "Social Phases of Psychology," *PASS,* 7 (1913), pp. 38-46.

[10] E. R. Groves, review of W. A. White's *Principles of Mental Hygiene,* in *AJS,* 23 (May, 1918), p. 841; Robert Gault, "Psychology in Social Relations," *ibid.,* 22 (May, 1917), pp. 734-748.

Freud's theory of the unconscious, Gault maintained that there is both an instinctual and an acquired unconscious, and that knowledge about and control of the latter could be used to create greater national unity.

Incidental references to psychoanalysis appeared in several articles. Robert E. Park suggested in 1919 the hypothesis that the conduct of Negroes can be viewed as an expression of their racial character just as dreams are manifestations of deep-seated wishes. Ulysses G. Weatherly proposed that makers of social policy become familiar with scientific psychology and the role of unconscious and repressed wishes in human behavior, because "the conscious wish is often not the real wish at all." F. Stuart Chapin viewed the prevailing social-class upheavals, industrial unrest, and radicalism as resultants of repression of basic impulses, especially the powerful urge toward self-realization and the operation of displacement, projection, symbolism, compensation, and rationalization.[11]

One of the most consistent interpreters of psychoanalysis during this early period was E. R. Groves. Not only did he write several of the earliest articles on psychoanalysis, but he was the most frequent reviewer of psychoanalytic books.[12] In summarizing the major contributions of Freud, Adler, and Jung, he cited the following three psychoanalytic discoveries as significant for sociology.[13] By demonstrating that the mental attributes of the insane are intensified versions of the attributes found in normal persons, Freud had, first, discovered a theory of mental life that is universal and subject to quantification. Secondly, he had extended the boundaries of psychology beyond physiology to the study of the psychic processes of mental activity. And, finally, he had discovered the "wish" as the key to the human mind. Groves was the first sociologist to recognize a similarity between the Freudian theory of the sublimation of the "wish" and the sociological theory of the psychic causation of human behavior. Anticipating subsequent theoretical formulations of personality, Groves wrote:

> Human society is made possible by this sublimation, and each person who becomes a member of the social group has to pass through the experiences

[11] R. E. Park, "Education in Its Relation to the Conflict and Fusion of Cultures: With Special Reference to the Problems of the Immigrant, the Negro, and Missions," *PASS,* 13 (1919), pp. 38-63; U. G. Weatherly, "Democracy and Our Political System," *ibid.,* 14 (1920), pp. 23-35; F. S. Chapin, "Democracy and Class Relations," *ibid.,* 14 (1920), pp. 101-110.

[12] E. R. Groves, review of W. A. White's *Principles of Mental Hygiene,* in *AJS,* 23 (May, 1918), p. 841; review of S. E. Jeliffe's *The Technique of Psychoanalysis, AJS,* 25 (July, 1919), pp. 100-101; review of W. Lay's *The Child's Unconscious Mind, ibid.* (Nov., 1919), pp. 367-368; review of W. A. White's *Thoughts of a Psychiatrist on the War and After, AJS,* 26 (Sept., 1920), p. 239; and review of W. S. Swischer's *Religion and the New Psychology, ibid.* (Nov., 1920), p. 376.

[13] E. R. Groves, "Sociology and Psycho-Analytic Psychology: An Interpretation of the Freudian Hypothesis," *AJS,* 23 (July, 1917), pp. 107-116.

of conflict between inner instinctive impulses clamoring for gratification and the pressure from the outward social environment which demands from the individual what seems best for the group as a whole.[14]

In December, 1920, as co-chairman of a round table discussion of the "Social Significance of Psychoanalytic Psychology," Groves summarized the several papers and re-affirmed his earlier observations.[15] Solving the problems of crime and labor unrest requires better knowledge of "instinct controls." Since human cravings for sex, self-assertion, hunger, fear, and gregariousness are universal, sociologists must study the socially acceptable forms in which they are expressed in different cultures. And before instituting changes in the expression of these instincts in American society, sociologists must study and understand how social pressures mold the personality during the early years of childhood.

Healy's "Mental Analysis" of Social Deviation. Another significant contribution to the diffusion of Freudianism was made by the criminologist William Healy, who incorporated selected psychoanalytic tenets into his research and writing. Conversant with both German and English psychoanalytic literature by 1915,[16] Healy regarded misconduct as a form of behavior intermediate to socially acceptable conduct and neurosis. Similarities to psychoanalysis exist especially in his method of "mental analysis" and his theory of the development of behavior.[17]

Healy's technique of inquiry, "mental analysis," is like psychoanalysis in that its ultimate aim "is synthesis [and] its immediate method is the digging up of links of mental knowledge of causal relationship." When dealing with juvenile misconduct, mental analysis differs from psychoanalysis because it involves relatively short, direct interviews instead of intensive, time-consuming free association. The origins of mental conflicts in children are still relatively uncomplicated, near the surface of mental life, and easily discoverable even though they exist in the unconscious. Healy's theory of personality formation posits that social and anti-social behavior proceeds from the unconscious operation of basic, irrational mental elements called motives, impulses, drives, or inner urges. Through various mental mechanisms, some of which are borrowed from psychoanalysis—e.g., repression, dissociation, and substitution—the adult personality evolves. Conversely, every thought and action is linked to a past idea through association and is thus, fundamentally, based upon an inner drive, motive, or impulse.

[14] *Ibid.*

[15] *PASS,* 15 (1921), pp. 203-216. Participants included: E. R. Spaulding, W. A. White, F. Blanchard, C. C. Robinson, and I. L. Peters.

[16] William Healy, *The Individual Delinquent* (Boston, 1915), p. 116, footnote 1.

[17] William Healy, *Mental Conflicts and Misconduct* (Boston, 1917), especially chapters 1-4.

Particularly significant for misconduct are "complexes." Following psychoanalytic theory, Healy regarded them as constellations of mental elements or associations of ideas characterized by a vigorous emotional tone. When complexes fail to harmonize with one another, they produce mental conflicts that lead, through dissociation and repression, to various forms of misconduct including theft, truancy, pyromania, etc. In his clinical treatment, Healy sought to discover complexes in order that the child could acquire an understanding of the causal nexus between his own mental conflict and misconduct. Finally, to prevent the recurrence of delinquent action, substitute behavior was provided as an outlet for the repressed energy associated with the complex. Thus, Healy's mental analysis, his stress on unconscious, irrational motives in behavior, and his analysis of mental conflict and misconduct are similar to Freudian theories. However, he is not Freudian in his rejection of the psychoanalysts' intensive free-association technique, the theory of symbolism, and analysis of dreams.

Thomas and Psychoanalytic Aspects of the Four Wishes. Another significant relationship between psychoanalysis and sociology is present in the writings of W. I. Thomas, whose career spanned two eras in American sociology. Like his colleagues of the formative period, he was originally interested in developing rational, scientific means for aiding and controlling social progress.[18] This concern about social change provided the meaningful context for his empirical investigation of the assimilation of ethnic groups (the Polish peasant), delinquency, prostitution, and maladjustment among children. He explained these various forms of behavior by an internal, dialectic theory of personality development that contains the concept of "wishes."

Although some of Thomas' personal acquaintances argue that he repeatedly denied any direct influence of psychoanalysis on his own work, a definite relationship between the "four wishes" and the psychoanalytic concept of "wish" can be demonstrated to exist. This connection, moreover, suggests the basis for more recent utilization of psychoanalytic tenets by adherents of Thomas' theory of social behavior.

The concept of the four wishes first appeared in *The Polish Peasant in Europe and America* (1918-1919). Previously Thomas had used "instincts" and subsequently he employed a multiplicity of terms: attitudes, attitudes and values, fields of values, and impulses. Significantly, the study of the Polish peasant was published only four years after E. B. Holt's popular *The Freudian Wish and Its Place in Ethics* (1915). This coincidence is not accidental, for Thomas had read Holt's book and been deeply impressed by it. Florian Znaniecki, co-author of the study of the Polish peasant, has indicated that:

Soon after we had formulated (I believe mostly on his [Thomas'] initiative)

[18] Gisela J. Hinkle, "The 'Four Wishes' in Thomas' Theory of Social Change," *SR*, 19 (Dec., 1952), pp. 464-484.

the theory of the four main desires which motivate individual participation in primary groups, he suddenly became interested in "the Freudian wish" as it was called at that time by some American followers of Freud. He did not accept the *libido,* but changed our term *desire* to *wish* and applied "the four wishes" in the analysis of unadjusted personalities in a way somewhat analogous to the Freudian analysis.[19]

This indirect relationship bespeaks a similarity in theoretical formulation. Analysis reveals that both Thomas and Freud adhered to an internal, dialectic theory of change, positing the dynamics and direction of human behavior within man himself. In spite of his shift in terminology, Thomas always maintained that man strives to seek satisfactions and that these strivings—or wishes—are in constant dialectic conflict with one another and with the external environment. Wishes, insisted Thomas, are universal. Some wishes (like the wishes for security and new experience) belong to the *individual* side of personal evolution; and others (like the wishes for response and recognition) to the *social* side of personal evolution. The individual and social forces of the personality compete for dominance within the personality at the same time that they struggle to obtain satisfaction from the external world. An equilibrium among these forces is eventually established in every individual, although sudden alterations of the social situation require new adjustments and a new equilibrium. More recently, in his *Primitive Behavior* (1937) Thomas indicated that such adjustive behavior always contains an emotional element. Thus Thomas' notion of the wishes resembles the Freudian one, since (1) wishes are universal human tendencies to seek goals; (2) wishes are continuously in conflict among themselves and with the external world; (3) adjustive behavior involves an emotional factor; and (4) the constant struggle is the source of personal evolution and social change.

These similarities account in part for the coexistence of references to Thomas' theory of behavior and Freudianism in sociological literature. In discussing the role of social forces in behavior, Robert E. Park and E. W. Burgess, in their *Introduction to the Science of Sociology* (1921), integrated Thomas' four wishes into a theory of personality development similar to Freud's notion of the evolution of the libido. Indeed, they referred directly to the use of the "wish" by psychoanalysis. Thomas himself explained delinquency among girls by conjoining Healy's theory of mental conflict with the notion of blocked wish-fulfillment. Although he rejected the emphasis on sex, he expressed agreement with the Freudian stress on wishes and concluded that non-satisfaction of the wish for recognition elicits the same mental states that Freud had attributed to frustration of sexual drives.[20] This similar usage of two otherwise separate concepts can be attributed to their common intellectual antecedent, Nietzsche's "will to power."

[19] Personal letter to the author, April 3, 1950.

[20] W. I. Thomas, *The Unadjusted Girl* (Boston, 1923), p. 32.

Ogburn and Parker: The Psychoanalytic Approach to History, Economic Affairs, and Social Problems. In a variety of ways, William F. Ogburn has played an important role in the history of Freudianism in early American sociology. His explanations of many sociological problems invoke psychoanalysis; his knowledge of Freud's discoveries is directly traceable to the lectures at Clark University; and his writings influenced other social scientists to explore the potentialities of psychoanalysis.

While a student at Columbia University in 1910, Ogburn was introduced to Freud's theories during a seminar address by Franz Boas, who had attended the Clark University lectures. At this time he was also attending discussions at the home of Alexander Goldenweiser, where, upon one occasion, Louis Lorwin reviewed Freud's *Three Contributions to the Theory of Sex*. Pursuing his own interest in the relationship between mental phenomena and bodily states, Ogburn subsequently read Bernard Hart's *Psychology of Insanity,* H. W. Frink's *Morbid Fears and Compulsion,* Edward J. Kempf's *Psychopathology,* and Sigmund Freud's *The Interpretation of Dreams, Psychopathology of Everyday Life,* and *A General Introduction to Psychoanalysis.*[21] Finally, in 1918, Ogburn underwent a didactic psychoanalysis, which was performed by Trigant Burrow.

While actively pursuing his interest in psychoanalysis from 1910 to 1918, Ogburn became a close friend of the labor economist, Carleton H. Parker. He influenced the latter, who was particularly interested in labor unrest on the West Coast, to read psychoanalytic literature. Parker had always regarded strikes to be inimical to social progress and had criticized classical economists for their failure to anticipate or deal with labor problems. Parker had become aware of the irrational forces operative in labor unrest through his early descriptions of riots and strikes and had, consequently, emphatically denied the economists' assumption of the rational man. In 1915, at Berkeley, Ogburn introduced Parker to the writings of Freud. Henceforth Parker's writings, including a paper read before the American Sociological Society in December, 1917, employed Freudian assumptions about the operation of human nature for the interpretation of strikes, riots, and labor unrest.[22] Striking workers, argued Parker, are being denied satisfactions for basic dispositions, needs, and instincts that man has inherited without change from his cave-man ancestors. Social circumstances, especially those of modern civilization, which prevent or repress the satisfaction of certain instincts, produce "psychic revolt." This state of mind leads to revolutionary behavior among both lowly migratory workers and the upper classes of society. Among the striking workers is a form of neurosis, a kind of industrial psychosis, comparable to

[21] Personal letter by W. F. Ogburn to the author, May 5, 1950.

[22] C. H. Parker, "California Casual and His Revolt," *Quarterly Journal of Economics,* 30 (Nov., 1915), pp. 110-126; "I. W. W.," *Atlantic Monthly,* 120 (Nov., 1917), pp. 651-662; and "Motives and Economic Life," *PASS,* 12 (1918), pp, 131-151.

the neuroticism described by Freud, since the sex instinct as well as needs for food and shelter remain unsatisfied. Sociologists were familiar with this explanation of unrest, as the literature after 1917 indicates.

Convinced of the significance of this explanation of labor unrest as a form of industrial psychosis, Parker undertook a nation-wide tour to discuss his empirical findings and theoretical conclusions with prominent scholars in psychology, psychiatry, sociology, economics, law, political science, philosophy, and public administration. This trip, concluded just before his untimely death in 1918, introduced many leading American social scientists to the teachings of Freud and their applicability to American social conditions.[23]

Ogburn himself applied psychoanalysis to various topics, including the writing of history, selected social problems, and conservatism and radicalism. At the American Economic Association meeting in December, 1918, he outlined an essentially psychoanalytic psychology of knowledge.[24] The writing of history in terms of dominant themes of ethics, great men, religion, or politics disregards the real force of historical change—the economic one. This distortion of history, argued Ogburn, results from the operation of the same mechanisms that Freud had discovered in the behavior of individuals. Just as neurotics repress sexual motives and ideas into the unconscious, so in the memories of the group, about which history is written, selfish economic motives are forgotten. Thus, the economic forces in history manifest themselves only in disguised form as rationalizations, since this is the only way in which they can slip by the watchful eye of the censor—that is, the social controls.

Like his fellow sociologists, Ogburn sought to explain the increase in neurosis and in the social problems of industry, labor, family life, immigration, and crime. Accepting both Freud's universal theory of neurosis and Parker's theory of industrial psychosis, Ogburn argued that undesirable social conditions result from the nature of modern culture. Human nature, which includes the motives of fear, sex, curiosity, new experience, adventure, pugnacity, anger, flight, gregariousness, sociability, and altruism, has changed little since prehistoric times. Civilization has changed, and modern urban life represses some, and provides insufficient satisfaction for other, basic human desires and motives. Thus a readjustment between human nature and society is necessary.[25]

Reformers who endeavor to correct this disharmony between man and his culture are frustrated in their attempts by both radicals and conservatives. Conservatives attempt to re-establish past social conditions because they forget the unpleasant aspects of the past and are hesitant about trying the new,

[23] Cornelia S. Parker, *An American Idyll* (Boston, 1919).

[24] W. F. Ogburn, "The Psychological Basis for the Economic Interpretation of History," *American Economic Review* (supplement), 9 (March, 1919), pp. 291-308.

[25] W. F. Ogburn, *Social Change* (New York, 1922).

unknown and untested ways of the future. On the other hand, radicals, as Parker discovered, are persons who have nothing to lose but their chains, and, who as a result of non-fulfillment of wishes or of mental conflicts, sublimate thair energies through radical forms of behavior.

In spite of their hesitancy, sociologists thus became familiar with psychoanalysis, particularly during the later years of the formative period. The small group exploring the applicability of Freudian psychology to social problems was notably composed of young sociologists just beginning their scientific careers. Unlike the founding fathers of American sociology, these men did not concentrate on the formulation of theories of social evolution. They explained social problems not as corollaries of social progress, but as behavioral difficulties involving the motivation, instincts, social forces, or wishes of individuals. Consequently, they were favorably inclined towards Freud's theories of the wish, wish-fulfillment, repression, sublimation, and the unconscious.

The Second Period, 1920-1935

The United States as a Fertile Field for Freudian Theories. Both changes in American intellectual and popular thought after World War I and the expansion of sociology as a scientific discipline affected the history of psychoanalysis in the second era of American sociology, 1920 to 1935. Through the medium of inexpensive periodicals, a new interest in private love and sex affairs developed. Apparently, magazine editors hired special personnel to give "advice to the lovelorn" and to rewrite or edit personal confessions submitted by the public during widely advertised contests. The MacFadden Company took the lead in printing this confessional literature separately as *The True Story Magazine*. Other companies followed with *True Confession, Dreamworld, Cupid's Diary, Love Story, I Confess, True Romance,* and *My Story.*[26] As the repetition of this theme of love and sex weakened public morality, scientific discussions of sex increased. Sensing, encouraging, and profiting from this new interest in private problems, American publishers reversed their earlier refusal to print English versions of Freud's major books and made nine translations publicly available during the brief period 1917 to 1923.[27]

[26] E. T. Kreuger, "Autobiographical Documents and Personality" (unpublished Ph. D. dissertation, University of Chicago, 1925).

[27] *The History of the Psychoanalytic Movement* (1917); *Wit and Its Relations to the Unconscious* (1917); *Totem and Taboo* (1919); *Thoughts for the Times on War and Death* (1918); *Selected Papers on Hysteria and Other Psychoneuroses* (1920); *Dream Psychology: Psychoanalysis for Beginners* (1921); *Beyond the Pleasure Principle* (1922); *Group Psychology and the Analysis of the Ego* (1922); and *Introductory Lectures on Psychoanalysis* (1923).

At the same time, public interest in mental health increased. The mental hygiene movement, formally recognized in 1910 by the formation of the National Committee for Mental Hygiene, received further impetus through the psychiatric activities of World War I. Having attained acceptance by the medical profession,[28] psychiatry itself began to recognize psychoanalysis. This movement culminated in 1926 in the joint meeting of the American Psychiatric Association and the American Psychoanalytic Association, at which William A. White, a proponent of psychoanalysis, was elected to the presidency.

As popular interest in sex and mental health increased, sociologists slowly altered their former reluctance to discuss Freudian ideas. During the early twenties, for instance, the *American Journal of Sociology* was still reviewing primarily secondary psychoanalytic works. Robert E. Park reflected sociologists' skepticism when he reviewed Freud's book on group psychology: "Sigmund Freud's comment on any aspect of human life and conduct is always interesting, even if not always convincing. That must one say even of his essay into the field of group psychology."[29] The actual usage of psychoanalysis by sociologists must be understood within the context of sociology's expansion, its specialization, its cooperation with other social sciences and social technologies, and its increasing emphasis on scientific method.

Factors in the Growing Acceptability of Freudian Theory. Sociology probably changed more rapidly and more extensively during the twenties than at any prior or subsequent time. This was largely the result of the general numerical increase in college students, graduate students, and recipients of Ph. D. degrees, and a similar growth in the membership of the American Sociological Society. More significant than the numerical increase of sociologists, however, was the displacement of the pre-World War I generation by younger men. Since the leadership within sociology was increasingly assumed by representatives of Middle Western educational institutions, a younger group of Middle Western sociologists was particularly important in determining the role of Freudianism during the second era of American sociology. Other changes in sociology included the differentiation of fields, based primarily on the social problems studied during the formative era. Among the principal problem fields and fields of theoretical, methodological, or technical import, Freudianism was particularly associated with the life history method, social psychology, urban–rural conditions, criminology, and family relations.

Sociologists' use of psychoanalysis, which itself represents a kind of cross-disciplinary activity, was affected by a general increase in interdisci-

[28] American Psychiatric Association (ed.), *One Hundred Years of American Psychiatry* (New York, 1944).

[29] R. E. Park, review of Sigmund Freud's *Group Psychology and the Analysis of the Ego*, *AJS*, 30 (Jan., 1925), pp. 485-486.

plinary cooperation with respect to formally organized discussions, publications, research, and academic interdepartmental organizations. One of the earliest interdepartmental ventures was the Yale Institute of Human Relations, organized effectively in 1929 to conjoin the biological sciences, social sciences, and law in the study of man. Its first research project was a study of the family and delinquency by William Healy and Augusta F. Bronner, *New Light on Delinquency* (1936), and subsequently it sponsored research in culture and personality by Edward Sapir, John Dollard, and others.

Finally, sociologists changed their outlook on progress, rationalism, and science, and reformulated the basic *rationale* of their discipline. World War I made them pessimistic about the inevitability of progress, which had previously been regarded as the product of man's increasing rationality. Many sociologists concurred in the interpretation of other intellectuals that the war had demonstrated the essential irrationality of human nature. Indeed, sociologists considered modern man to be as primitively emotional as he had been in prehistoric times. Consequently, the advance of sociology and the solution of social problems necessitated the discovery of the laws governing human irrationality. Thus, a favorable setting for the incorporation of theories about the operation of human emotions and the development of the personality existed within sociology itself.

Sociological Critiques of Freudianism: Overemphasis on the Sexual Instinct. Nevertheless, sociologists did not accept Freud's theories without qualification. Since sociologists were striving to make their discipline scientific, they evaluated theories about human irrationality and personality formation in terms of the criteria of science. Having rejected philosophies of history as impressionistic, as armchair speculation, sociologists placed particular emphasis on induction and empiricism as hallmarks of science.

They rejected certain basic Freudian theories. One of the first concepts to be criticized was the instinct of sex. Although Freud interpreted the meaning of sex broadly, including many of the specific instincts usually cited by other social scientists, he posited the source of all human behavior in an innate tendency to strive for the satisfaction of sexual energy. During the postwar years, sociologists, psychologists, and philosophers re-examined the entire instinct doctrine. Ellsworth Faris attributed the misuse of the instinct concept to the "mistake of thinking that hypotheses are data" and to a disregard for the description of behavior among non-civilized peoples.[30] L. L. Bernard wrote in his *Instinct: A Study in Social Psychology* (1924) that he had discovered references to 15,789 different instincts in the literature, and that personal whim had seemingly governed their formulation. Even when grouped into 6,131 types, usage of instincts was still too inaccurate, inconsist-

[30] Ellsworth Faris, "Are Instincts Data or Hypotheses?" *AJS,* 27 (Sept., 1921), pp. 184-196; and "Ethnological Lights on Psychological Problems," *PASS,* 16 (1922), pp. 113-120.

ent, and uncritical to be scientifically acceptable and useful. Moreover, Bernard demonstrated that most of the instincts result from environmental conditioning. Since the "psychoanalysts share in the popular fallacies regarding the instinctive control of human action,"[31] they are subject to the same criticisms: adherence to biological determinism, lack of precision, and treatment of instincts as if they were real data. This hypothetical nature of the sex instinct contributed to a second stricture on psychoanalysis, since Freud had assumed the reality of instincts in his explanation of the origin of the Oedipus complex and totemism. Sociologists accepted Kroeber's criticism that a scientific explanation of totemism, the custom of not killing one's totem animal or having sexual relations with members of one's own totemic group, could not be based on hypothetical instincts and on an event that had never occurred. "The old man story," which Freud had used to explain the origin of totemism, was simply an imagined situation.[32] Bronislaw Malinowski's *Sex and Repression in Savage Society* (1927) was often cited by sociologists as further empirical evidence disproving the universality of the Oedipus complex.

Secondly, sociologists attacked Freud's theories as scientifically unsound because they were particularistic and violated the assumption of the multiple causation of social behavior. That social phenomena and human behavior result from the operation of many factors and conditions was regarded as an obvious fact of experience by sociologists. Accordingly, explanations relying solely on one cause, such as sex, were prejudged as scientifically inadequate.

The Problem of Verification in Freudian Theory. A third criticism of psychoanalysis derived from sociologists' emulation of the quantitative procedures of the natural sciences. From this perspective, behavioristically and quantitatively inclined sociologists classified psychoanalysis as a form of the life-history method and as subject to the same criticisms of subjectivism and non-measurability. Freudian procedures cannot lead to verifiable conclusions because they rely on the patient's reconstruction of his experiences and the subjective interpretation of the analyst. Thus psychoanalysis was often regarded as art rather than science.

Ironically, psychoanalysis itself was suggested as a means for obtaining greater objectivity in social-scientific research.[33] In a paper read at the annual sociological meeting in 1922, William F. Ogburn proposed that bias in scientific research is a form of prejudice, an attitude characterized by emotion

[31] L. L. Bernard, "Instincts and the Psychoanalysts," *JASP* (Jan.-March, 1923), p. 350.

[32] A. L. Kroeber, "Totem and Taboo: An Ethnologic Psychoanalysis," *AA*, (new series), 22 (Jan.-March, 1920), pp. 48-55. See also Howard Becker and D. K. Bruner, "Some Aspects of Taboo and Totemism," *Journal of Social Psychology*, 3, 3 (Aug., 1932), pp. 337-353.

[33] W. F. Ogburn, "Bias, Psycho-Analysis, and the Subjective in Relation to the Social Sciences," *PASS*, 18 (1923), pp. 62-74.

and ignorance of the facts. The emotional factor is the most significant, since it "tends to keep us ignorant and to prevent us from getting the facts." Emotion in the form of desire leads men to see what they want to see or to distort the facts in conformity with their wishes. Ogburn insisted that bias, which is common in the study of such emotionally charged topics as the family, sex, religion, income, industrial relations, and politics, must be avoided or minimized if sociological activities are to be scientific. Sociologists must acquire an understanding of the relationship between desire and thought as outlined by the psychoanalysts, who have demonstrated that the emotion experienced at the time of the act determines how men recall ideas from memory and how they conceive of the world of reality. Since ideas that transcend time and space are especially prone to emotional association, sociologists should reinvestigate their use of logical and reflective thought as commonly employed in sociological theory. Social theorizing has largely been a form of daydreaming, and as Freud has shown, dreams are caused by unconscious, emotional forces that achieve expression during times of relaxation. Ogburn concluded that these hazards in scientific activity could be avoided if sociologists employed psychoanalysis and learned to understand their own wishes and biases, and if they quantified, whenever possible, their observations and interpretations.

The Life-History Method in Sociological Research. Utilization of psychoanalysis as a form of the life-history method was, however, more common. As early as 1921, sociologists had linked "life-history and psychoanalysis" as a separate topical subfield of sociology.[34] Among early expositors of the life-history method was William Healy. At the annual meeting of sociologists in 1923, he described its advantages for sociological research. The life-history method is the best means whereby sociologists can correct the outstanding deficiencies in their knowledge of man's behavior, mental life, and the circumstances that condition them: inheritance, physical upbringing, early mental experiences, education, family life, modes of living, and social contacts. Besides knowledge of external conditions, the mechanisms whereby behavior in turn affects the actor must be discovered.

The general acceptance of life histories for sociological research is attested to by the special round-table discussion at the annual sociological meetings in 1927. Under the chairmanship of Stuart A. Queen, the discussants considered the nature, usages, results, and reliability of the case-study method in sociological research. The following year, Ruth Shonle Cavan exhaustively reviewed the literature, surveying books and articles in seven journals (primarily in sociology and social work) from 1920 to 1929.[35] On the

[34] "A Tentative Scheme for the Classification of the Literature of Sociology and the Social Sciences," *AJS*, 27 (July, 1921), pp. 128-129.

[35] Ruth S. Cavan, "Topical Summaries of Current Literature: Interviewing for Life-History Material," *AJS*, 25 (July, 1929), pp. 100-115.

basis of seventy-five bibliographical citations, she defined the life-history as "an account of the life of a person presented in such a manner that the development of habits and attitudes can be traced. The term implies a complete account of all phases of life." Each profession tends to have its own particular emphasis: sociologists stress cultural conflict; social psychologists study the integration of attitudes and habits; social workers emphasize the flexibility of human nature; and psychoanalysts and psychiatrists center their attention on the causes of neurosis and psychopathy. Since the method is common to many disciplines, it provides the basis for fruitful interdisciplinary cooperation in the study, analysis, and treatment of social and personal problems.

The actual usage of life histories dates back to the formative era of sociology. Healy used personally reported data as the basis for his mental analysis of juvenile misconduct. Thomas and Znaniecki employed the technique in their Polish peasant study, especially in Volume 3, "Life History of the Immigrant." Several years later Thomas related the importance of life histories to the determination of individuality, which derives not so much from social institutions as from the meaning of crucial events and critical experiences for the individual. Experiences, as studies of psychoneurotics firmly established, may have totally different meanings for different persons. Moreover, these meanings largely determine the structure of institutions and the customs of society. Consequently, if sociologists hope to explain these societal phenomena, they must view them from the perspective of man's desires and the development of personality as revealed in personal documents and life histories.[36]

During the twenties, E. T. Kreuger investigated the force of the autobiographical motive for the reorganization of disorganized personalities. Having collected personal documents and classified them as egoistic, naive, scientific, or confessional, he concluded that the most complete life records are obtained when the confessional type of method is used. Underlying the confessional document is the mechanism of catharsis or release from tensions created by mental conflicts. Worry, fear, dread, restlessness, depression, moodiness, loss of self-confidence, and feelings of inferiority are all symptoms of the existence of such conflicts. Assuming Thomas' theory of the four wishes, Kreuger argued that such conflicts result from defeat or failure in the realization of wishes, mental accumulation of forbidden experiences, or disturbance by new social conditions of deep-seated habits and sentiments. Writing a confessional document releases unconscious, repressed, or suppressed ideas and satisfies the wish for recognition, since readers of the document are regarded as a sympathetic audience. Like the psychoanalytic interview, therefore, the confessional document provides a means for untangling experiences and events in mental disturbances. Kreuger's cases

[36] W. I. Thomas, "The Problem of Personality in the Urban Environment," *PASS*, 20 (1926), pp. 30-39.

confirmed the Freudian contention that the experiences originating the conflict are frequently found in long-forgotten events of childhood. Thus, although Kreuger accepted the social interactionists' assumptions of personality formation, his research disclosed similarities between the nature and conclusions of the psychoanalytic interview and the writing of confessional life histories.[37]

This similarity of psychoanalytic and life-history methods was again noted in 1939 by Harold D. Lasswell.[38] Indeed, Lasswell employed the two concepts interchangeably and noted that some of the most fruitful research in sociology resulted from the use of the life-history method by students of Park, Burgess, and Faris. The frequent association of the life-history method and psychoanalysis by sociologists at the University of Chicago who adhered to a social interactionist social psychology suggests a more basic similarity.

Freud and Cooley: Basic Similarities. The early proponents of social interactionist social psychology included Charles Horton Cooley, who emphasized primary groups and the development of the self; George Herbert Mead, who formulated the distinction between the "I" and "me" and emphasized the importance of language in personality development; and W. I. Thomas, who contributed the concepts of the four wishes or attitudes and values. Among other adherents of this orientation were Faris, Park, Burgess, Blumer, and their various students. Although these men examined different aspects of man's mental life, they shared the following theory of personality development.

> The child is born neither human nor social; at birth he is simply an animal organism belonging to a particular biological species. Ordinarily he is born into a small, face-to-face social group—the family—where he experiences social interaction with parents, siblings, and others, and acquires language, behavior patterns, and familiarity with and acceptance of the values and goals of his society. Along with this indoctrination into the culture of his group, he develops a notion of himself as a self, or ego, which makes him all the more human and social because he now responds directly to the expectations of others and to the internalized moral codes of the group. The child thus becomes self-conscious and plays social roles in accordance with the expectations of others in order to attain their respect and acceptance. As the individual matures he modifies and adjusts his personality developed in childhood by extending the attitudes and values acquired in primary groups to other social situations.[39]

In spite of obvious differences, intensive analysis of the writings of most proponents of the interactionist theory reveals similarities to Freud's explana-

[37] Kreuger, *op. cit.* See also E. T. Kreuger, "Technique of Securing Life History Documents," *Journal of Applied Sociology*, 9 (March-April, 1925), pp. 290-298.

[38] H. D. Lasswell, "The Contribution of Freud's Insight Interview to the Social Sciences," *AJS*, 45 (Nov., 1939), pp. 375-390.

[39] Hinkle and Hinkle, *op. cit.*, p. 30.

tion of personality formation. Sociologists differ insofar as they emphasize the role of language, reject the Freudian stress on sex, or do not precisely detail the relations among family members—for example, mother-son relations.

Similarities can well be indicated by analyzing Cooley's writings, developed independently of Freud. Rejecting the Cartesian dualism of mind and matter, or self and society, Cooley focused upon the interaction of man and environment in the development of personality. The formation of personality begins with the inherited instincts of anger, fear, love, and self-assertion. "These instinctive emotions predetermine, not specific actions, but in a measure, the energy that flows into actions having a certain function with reference to our environment." During the first five years of life, through the "instinct of self-feeling,"[40] the self develops in primary groups, such as the family, and assumes the task of mediating the demands of the biological and moral forces playing upon the person in everyday life. Interaction with other persons in primary groups teaches children to control and subordinate their passions of lust, greed, revenge, pride, power, etc., (which are survivals of their animal nature) to the demands of society as expressed in primary ideals. Although the kinds of primary ideals vary from one society to another —in American society they include love, freedom, justice, and morality— they exist in some form everywhere and are always internalized forces in mature personalities.

Freud's concept of the id differs little from Cooley's instinctive emotions, for the id "contains everything that is inherited . . . [and] is fixed in the constitution—above all, therefore, the instincts which originate in the somatic organization and which find their first mental expression in the id in forms unknown to us." "Under the influence of the real external world," the ego evolves from the id and assumes the function of umpire between the demands of the id and the external world. Paralleling Cooley's concept of primary ideals, Freud posited the internalization of parental dicta or other moral prescriptions of the society by the superego. In its judical function, man knows the superego as his conscience.[41]

Although Freud and Cooley differed in their emphasis on sex and the detail with which they elaborated various aspects of their theories, they both posited a biological inheritance that relates man through evolution to lower animal forms. This biological force interacts with the environment and produces the ego or self. Finally, the moral tenets of society are internalized through participation in the family and come to govern individual behavior through the superego or internalized primary ideals. These three forces, the biological, the individual, and the societal, are in constant conflict and create a "dynamic equilibrium" that is essentially the personality. The ego or self

[40] C. H. Cooley, *Human Nature and the Social Order* (New York, 1902), pp. 26, 168-210.

[41] Sigmund Freud, *An Outline of Psychoanalysis* (New York, 1949), pp. 14-15, 43, 121.

is the crucial arbiter in all disputes and the organizing power in each person.

Accordingly, Freud's and Cooley's theories of *personality maladjustment* and *social maladjustment* are also similar. Social disorganization is the result of personal disorganization, and the latter derives from a disquilibrium between the organic forces, the ego, and the internalized social forces. Maladjustment exists when the normal sequence of personality development is interrupted, arrested, or inverted through an external force or through the weakening of the ego and its resultant capitulation either to the id or the biological cravings, or to the superego or the moral standards. Social reconstruction thus ultimately involves readjustment of individual personalities by re-establishing their mental equilibrium.

The Application of Freudian Concepts in Research on Social Types. Through the use of life histories by adherents of social interactionist social psychology, selected concepts or tenets of Freudianism were integrated into social research pertaining to personality types. Park expressed considerable interest in the formulation of personality types. Some of his students combined the life-history method with Freudian and social interactionist theories in order to determine typical personalities for natural areas in the urban community. The criteria for these types usually involved the assumption that a normal personality is one that evolves from birth to death in such a way that the four wishes, set forth by Thomas, are constantly satisfied in a balanced fashion. These investigations generally pertained to maladjusted personalities—for instance, the dwellers in rooming houses, residents of hotels, and criminals and delinquents.

Harvey Zorbaugh employed the life-history method to sudy the adaptation of single men and women to life in the transient rooming-house area of Chicago.[42] He found that people conform to certain social types that are characterized by constellations of attitudes related to the social situation in which they live. Social types result from the changeable factors—the individuals' attitudes and their social situation—and one non-changeable force, the individuals' wishes. Residents of furnished rooms are socially isolated, restless, lonely, in a world which thwarts their wishes for security, response, and recognition. The resultant mental tension is expressed by withdrawal in the form of suicide, by repression of reality and living in a dream world, by substitution, or finally, by action governed by impulses rather than cultural convention.

In a similar manner Norman Hayner studied hotel life and discovered four personality types.[43] Some persons characterized by restlessness, loneliness, and an unhappy state of mind, find adjustment difficult and satisfaction of wishes impossible in this anonymous, impersonal atmosphere. Others give

[42] H. W. Zorbaugh, "The Dwellers in Furnished Rooms: An Urban Type," *PASS,* 20 (1926), pp. 83-89.

[43] N. S. Heyner, "Hotel Life and Personality," *AJS,* 33 (March, 1928), pp. 784-795.

free play to their impulses and become individuated when the customary social restraints are removed. A third group reflects overstimulated wishes and engages in *blasé* behavior. Finally, some persons are accustomed to hotel life and experience hotels as their "real home."

By analyzing life histories of delinquents and criminals, Clifford Shaw demonstrated how institutions and customs in certain natural areas are related to the inner, personal world of "the subject, his attitudes and wishes, his interpretation of the situation and his conception of himself."[44] In contrast to Shaw, Hayner, Zorbaugh, and others who studied personal and social maladjustment, Harold D. Lasswell applied the life-history method to *normal* persons. As early as 1927, he attempted to develop political types by arranging personality traits on a continuum ranging from neuroticism to normalcy.[45] Accepting Park's natural history method, Lasswell analyzed the political act into four phases: unrest, public opinion, enactment, and enforcement. Although variations on this theme are possible, he concluded that three types of personalities are always involved: the agitators, the bosses, and the responsible leaders. In his *Psychopathology and Politics* (1930), Lasswell used psychoanalysis more extensively to discover the significant events and crises in the typical processes of personality formation associated with political agitators and political administrators. Lasswell hoped that knowledge of these causal processes could be applied so that politicians' personal biases and mental conflicts would no longer affect major policy decisions.

Psychoanalytic Theory and the Sociology of the Family. Finally, through interdisciplinary ventures, psychoanalysis came to the attention of students of the family. Beginning with the annual convention of the American Sociological Society in December, 1925, problems of family living became regular topics for round-table discussions among psychoanalytically oriented social workers, psychiatrists, and sociologists—e.g., E. W. Burgess, E. R. Mowrer, Harriet Mowrer, Kimball Young, Groves, L. Guy Brown, Thomas D. Eliot, F. D. Frazier, and Meyer Nimkoff. Burgess' writings are of special interest because some of his students have recently made extensive use of psychoanalysis.

According to Burgess, the family, as a "unity of interacting personalities," is the social situation within which individuals acquire their personality; it also reflects the relative state of social organization and social disorganization of the larger society. Since personality development of well-adjusted persons requires wholesome expression and satisfaction of the wishes, the nature of the social limitations of wish-fulfillment in the family and elsewhere is important. During periods of rapid social change and social upheaval, the direct or substitute avenues for wish-fulfillment become ineffective and behavior becomes disorganized. Thus modern urban society

[44] C. R. Shaw, *Delinquency Areas* (Chicago, 1929), p. 8.

[45] H. D. Lasswell, "Types of Political Personalities," *PASS,* 22 (1928), pp. 159-168.

produces excessive adolescent unrest, juvenile delinquency, cynicism, pessimism, and *tedium vitae*. More specifically, Burgess attributed this personal disorganization to inadequate parent-child relations.[46] During the socialization process in the family, children acquire "social images" that are often not realized in later life because the family itself is in disequilibrium. Mental conflict ensues and produces problem behavior. When American society has completed its present period of social change, the internal and external functions of the family will once more be stabilized and inconsistencies between the acquisition and realization of social images will disappear. In the meantime, social disorganization can be alleviated by using life histories to determine the causal processes involved in personal disorganization and readjusting individual personalities.

Some Psychoanalytic Preconceptions in Social Psychiatry. Psychoanalysis has seemingly exercised more significant impact on sociology through these investigations of concrete problems than through the specially designated area of "social psychiatry." Students of this subfield, popular during the thirties, assumed the existence of a direct relationship between personal and social disorganization. Ultimately, they derived social disorganization from neurotic tendencies within individuals. They usually viewed social disorganization as an extension of personal disorganization, which they interpreted psychoanalytically; or they reasoned analogically that the same mental mechanisms are operative in both neurotics and disorganized societies. Although numerous sociologists wrote social–psychiatric articles—for example, Bain, Burgess, Dollard, Eliot, Groves, Young, Park, Dunham, Sapir (an anthropologist), and others—pyschiatrists are more specifically associated with this field. Outstanding among the latter are Franz Alexander, Trigant Burrow, Lawrence K. Frank, Ben Karpman, Harry Stack Sullivan, William A. White, and James Plant.

One of the earliest and most frequently cited social–psychiatric articles was Bain's "Our Schizoid Culture."[47] Having briefly examined fundamental conflicts in major American social institutions, Bain concluded that cultural contradictions, unreason, and irrationality are normal aspects of American society and essential for dynamic social change. Cultural integration, a temporary (and perhaps undesirable) phenomenon, signifies the absence of culture-creating individuals and presages cultural decline. In a speculative vein, he warned that removal of cultural contradictions by a natural science of sociology might destroy our culture.

Other adherents of social psychiatry were often similarly philosophical.

[46] E. W. Burgess, "The Family as a Unity of Interacting Personalities," *The Family*, 7 (March, 1926), pp. 3-9; "The Trend of Sociological Research," *JAP*, 8 (Jan.-Feb., 1924), p. 137; and "The Sources and Methods of Family Study," in L. L. Bernard (ed.) *The Fields and Methods of Sociology* (New York, 1934), pp. 447-448.

[47] Read Bain, "Our Schizoid Culture," *SSR*, 19 (Jan.-Feb., 1935), pp. 266-276.

As part of a symposium in the *American Journal of Sociology* in 1937, Blumer summarized the points of agreement among social psychiatrists. They usually regard social disorganization as a projection of individual disorganization; they view social interaction in disorganized social systems as governed by autistic or illusory images that camouflage repressed, unconscious motives; they posit the genesis of personal disorganization in childhood experiences within the family; and, finally, they advocate improvement in child training and education as the best means for social reconstruction.[48]

In 1948 H. Warren Dunham examined the significance of social psychiatry for American sociology and concluded that "the question as to whether a field of social psychiatry has been developed is certainly a moot one."[49] This interpretation is essentially correct. On the one hand, sociologists are skeptical of social–psychiatric conclusions, since excellent personal organization is known to exist in some socially disorganized areas. And on the other hand, the abstract and speculative tenor of many articles in this field limits their application to concrete research problems. Nevertheless, social–psychiatric influences are evident in current formulations of social-disorganization theories.

The Essential Integration of Psychoanalytic and Sociological Orientations. The influence of psychoanalysis on American sociology of the second era is thus persistent though unspectacular. Aided in part by the weakening of the sex taboo throughout American society, by sociologists' quest for scientific goals, and their shift to an interest in human irrationality, the integration of Freudian ideas proceeded slowly. Since they emphasized scientific procedure in their own research, sociologists criticized psychoanalysis for its biologism, particularism, and subjectivism. Yet they agreed with the assumption of psychic determinism, the stress on childhood experiences, and the theory of wish-fulfillment in human behavior. Indeed, the Freudian theory of personality formation is congenial to the social interactionist one that was widely used in empirical investigations of personality development and adjustment. Consequently, selected psychoanalytic mechanisms were frequently employed to explain personality maladjustment. The prevalence of the life-history technique also contributed to sociologists' selective adaptation of Freudianism, which was a convenient frame of reference for interpreting the data of personal documents. Finally, interdisciplinary cooperation between sociology and psychiatry increased and culminated in the recognition of social psychiatry as a special subfield of sociology.

[48] Recently David Riesman has expressed many of these same ideas in his studies on the changing American character, *The Lonely Crowd* (New Haven, 1950).

[49] H. Warren Dunham, "Social Psychiatry," *ASR,* 13 (April, 1948), pp. 183-197.

The Third Period, 1935-1955

Factors in the Renewed Appreciation of Psychoanalysis. Psychoanalytic developments in American sociology since the mid-1930's reflect and have been in part a response to new emphases in sociology, trends in other behavioral sciences, and major social and political events related to World War II. By emphasizing prediction and control and studying phenomena related to the welfare of the nation, sociologists both implicitly and explicitly endorsed utilitarianism. In seeking to make their knowledge useful, sociologists have recognized the need for theoretical formulations and theoretical integration. Psychoanalysis is congenial on both counts, for it has amply demonstrated its therapeutic possibilities and it has been presented as an integrated frame of reference.

Throughout the social sciences, moreover, interdisciplinary activity has increased in the form of large-scale research, academic integration, and joint literary production. Some major research projects that have employed psychoanalytic theory have been undertaken by men trained in several disciplines. Although they cannot be associated solely with sociology, the studies of Dollard, Allison Davis, Lasswell, Havighurst, and others are regarded as significant contributions to American sociology. As cooperation among sociologists, anthropologists, social workers, and psychoanalytically oriented psychiatrists has increased, Freudian tenets have continued to spread into sociology.

Developments in other disciplines have, accordingly, contributed to the diffusion of psychoanalytic ideas. American anthropologists are no longer primarily preoccupied with exhaustive descriptions of preliterate cultures but have increasingly investigated personality development, personality types, and personality deviation. Psychoanalysis has achieved the status of a separate, mature discipline with a great number of trained professionals, many of whom emigrated from Europe during the political and social upheavals of the thirties and subsequently contributed to the American psychoanalytic movement. As psychoanalysis developed, specialization and modification of views proceeded rapidly and the genesis of man as a social being became an important problem. Neo-Freudian literature dealing with the social nature of man was favorably received in sociological circles, notably the writings of Karen Horney and Erich Fromm.

While participating in governmental projects during World War II, many sociologists became familiar with other behavior sciences. They engaged in interdisciplinary research of such war-related problems as army life, German national character, leadership, war, morale, propaganda, and communication. Not uncommonly, psychoanalytic concepts and theories were introduced into the description and interpretation of these topics.

Since the mid-1930's the importance of psychoanalysis for sociology has been repeatedly acknowledged. Most new publications by orthodox or neo-Freudian writers are regularly reviewed in sociological periodicals. In November, 1939, the *American Journal of Sociology* contained a special issue on Freud's contribution to the social sciences. Articles outlining the relation of psychoanalysis and sociology have been written by Bain, Burgess, Dunham, Young, and Green. Goldenweiser, Shils, Parsons, Simpson, and the Hinkles[50] have included special discussions of Freudian psychology as part of general surveys of trends in American sociology. These articles tend to agree that the acceptance and adaptation of concepts has been the chief influence of psychoanalysis on sociology. Secondary emphasis is usually placed on the Freudian deterministic theory of personality as a means for integrating sociology and psychology.

Psychoanalytic Currents in Sociological Specialisms. Psychoanalytic elements can be demonstrated to exist in three groups of subfields of contemporary sociology. There are specialties that have accepted and utilized psychoanalysis continuously since the twenties: family sociology, social and personal disorganization, and other social problem fields. Areas that began to be influenced by psychoanalysis during the middle period but are primarily associated with the recent era of American sociology include: culture and personality, political sociology, public opinion, and race relations. Finally, there are relatively new or renewed sociological interests and social problems, such as the sociology of war, social stratification, bureaucracy, and systematic sociological theory, that have lately borrowed Freudian ideas. Usage of psychoanalysis is especially prominent in the six areas of: social disorganization, culture and personality, political sociology, race relations, family sociology, and sociological theory.

Social Problems and Social Disorganization. Social disorganization is today ordinarily regarded as the theoretical basis of the great variety of social problems that sociologists have investigated for nearly five decades. Although sociologists do not accept one integrated theoretical framework, and although their theoretical formulations are often insufficiently related to actual

[50] Read Bain, "Sociology and Psychoanalysis," *ASR,* 1 (April, 1936), pp. 203-220; Dunham, *op. cit.;* Kimball Young, "The Impact of Freudian Psychology on Sociology," *American Journal of Orthopsychiatry,* 10 (Oct., 1940), pp. 869-876; A. W. Green, "Sociological Analysis of Horney and Fromm," *AJS,* 51 (May, 1946), pp. 533-540; Alexander Goldenweiser, "Some Contributions of Psychoanalysis to the Interpretation of Social Facts," in H. E. Barnes, Howard Becker, and Frances B. Becker (eds.), *Contemporary Social Theory* (New York, 1940), pp. 391-430; Edward Shils, *The Present State of American Sociology* (Glencoe, Ill., 1948); Talcott Parsons and Bernard Barber, "Sociology, 1941-1946," *AJS,* 52 (Jan., 1948), pp. 245-257; George Simpson, *Man in Society* (Garden City, N.Y., 1954), pp. 39-45; Hinkle and Hinkle, *op. cit.,* p. 52.

discussions of social problems—as recent textbooks amply demonstrate—they usually agree on certain assumptions about the nature and causes of social disorganization. In part, these presuppositions have been inherited from the social psychiatry movement of the thirties.

Personal and social disorganization are presented as interdependent, since the former is the individual, behavioral manifestation of conflicts within the culture. The discordant elements in society are generally regarded as corollaries of social change and cultural lag. Current world crises, contradictions in institutional structures and behavior, and especially conflicts in values and ideas are said to make modern man fearful, tense, frustrated, insecure, and anxiety-ridden. The modern child, growing up in a schizoid culture, is thus unlikely to develop a stable, integrated personality. Since poorly organized personalities find adjustment to the complexities of modern life difficult, they often engage in crime, alcoholism, sex offenses, and other undesirable behavior. In extreme cases they become neurotic or psychopathic.

The existence of a high rate of neurosis, which sociologists are including among the major social problems, is ultimately attributed to conflicting cultural conditions. Sociologists cite the writings of Karen Horney and Erich Fromm in confirmation. Fromm is credited with presenting the historical antecedents of the strains in American culture; and Horney is accepted as having explained how the American emphasis on individualism, competition, and success produces anxiety, envy, and hostility, which lead to compulsive behavior and neuroticism.

Not only has Freudian literature confirmed the general presupposition about social disorganization, but it has also been the source of hypotheses about the relations between social conditions and neurosis. Sociologists are increasingly investigating the relationship between neurosis or severe personal maladjustment and specific social conditions such as age, sex, rural–urban residence, college life, social class, ethnic background, and military life. Arnold Green, for instance, has described how certain middle-class social conditions enter into the socialization process and predispose the child to neurosis.[51] Faris and Dunham have studied, though without recourse to psychoanalysis, the ecological distribution of neurosis, implying that the social conditions in different areas of the city evoke differential rates of mental deviance. Henry Elkin has studied aggressive behavior in military life,[52] and Dollard, Allison Davis, Warner, and others have studied the effect of "caste" status on the mental adjustment of American Negroes.

[51] A. W. Green, "The Middle-Class Male Child and Neurosis," *ASR*, 11 (1946), pp. 31-41.

[52] R. E. L. Faris and H. Warren Dunham, *Mental Disorders in Urban Areas* (Chicago, 1939); Henry Elkin, "Aggressive and Erotic Tendencies in Army Life," *AJS*, 51 (March, 1946), pp. 408-413.

A singular and elaborate integration of psychoanalytic theory and social disorganization has recently been published by Herbert A. Bloch, *Disorganization: Personal and Social* (1952). Relying on basic psychoanalytic theories, he assumes that all individuals must make adjustments to their social conditions during early childhood in order to satisfy basic needs. Having achieved adjustments, individuals are reluctant to change their basic habits and attitudes even though social conditions have changed. These behavior patterns, which become ineffective in meeting prevailing social realities, Bloch calls "latencies." When latencies exist in a plurality of individuals, social disorganization exists.

Related to the field of social and personal disorganization is psychotherapy, which is still retained in some quarters as a legitimate interest of sociology. A discussion of the extensive influence of psychoanalysis on therapeutic practices, however, rightfully belongs to the history of American social work.

Culture and Personality: Psychoanalysis and Socialization. The culture-personality field is primarily the product of anthropological research, although it apparently had its inception in sociology.[53] With the publication of the works of Kardiner, Linton, Mead, Benedict, Kluckhohn, Leighton, Hallowell, and others during the later thirties and early forties, the field became basically psychoanalytic in orientation. It uses Freudian psychology as its frame of reference for determining basic personality structures of total societies, and for studying personality development and personality deviance in different cultures. Its empirical studies have been consistently reviewed in sociological periodicals. Information concerning feeding habits, mother-child relations, weaning, toilet training, life crises, masturbation, and strict, permissive, or ambivalent discipline has been widely accepted as part of the sociological literature on socialization. As an approach, or frame of reference, for the study of personality formation, sociologists have utilized "culture-personality" to study personality development in American subcultures.[54]

Psychoanalytic Concepts in Public Opinion Research. Analyses in the fields of communication and public opinion also manifest considerable psychoanalytic influences. The research and writings of Lasswell, who was influenced by psychoanalysis in his early studies of personality among politicians, have been particularly responsible for this trend. Lasswell and his associates have used psychoanalytic interviews to develop a classificatory schema that was subsequently applied as "content analysis" to analyze the ideas presented

[53] Among the earliest usages of the phrase "personality and culture" is that made by Blumer in 1930, when he used it synonymously with the phrase "privacy and social order." See his review of Wilson Gee's *Research in the Social Sciences,* in *AJS,* 35 (May, 1930), pp. 1101-1111. Ellsworth Faris subsequently described the "Culture and Personality of the Forest Bantu," *PASS,* 28 (May, 1934), pp. 3-11.

[54] Rural sociologists have recently used this approach. See W. H. Sewell, "Infant Training and the Personality of the Child," *AJS,* 58 (Sept., 1952), pp. 150-159.

in media of mass communication and propaganda. Other sociologists have also used psychoanalytic notions in studying public opinion. Goldhamer, for instance, investigated the applicability of the concepts of withdrawal and displacement to the formation of public opinion.[55] He concluded that the relevance of withdrawal for determining interest in public affairs has not been demonstrated, but that the concept of displacement has potential value. Research is needed, however, on the nature of public questions and the processes whereby they become objects of displacement.

Race Relations and Psychoanalytic Theories of Prejudice. The field of race and ethnic relations is a third area in which interdisciplinary activities and psychoanalytic influences have more recently converged. Inaugurated by the American Council on Education studies of Negro youth, the tendency to employ Freudian theories in the investigation of race prejudice and personality development of members of racial and ethnic groups has become well established. Prejudice is commonly regarded as a function of fear, guilt feelings, and hostility acquired during socialization. Most widely known is the frustration–aggression theory associated with Dollard, Davis, and others, who have repeatedly acknowledged their indebtedness to psychoanalysis. They represent the American Negro as a person whose goals and aspirations, although derived from American culture, are constantly restricted, blocked, and frustrated by his "caste" status. Consequently, mental conflict characterizes the Negro personality, and whether Negroes acquiesce or rebel, their behavior is interpreted as aggression. Although many students of race relations do not accept the universal, one-to-one relationship between frustration and aggression, most writers give general credence to this theory. Other psychoanalytic concepts current in the literature on the psychology of prejudice include displacement, projection, rationalization, and anxiety. Indeed, Arnold and Caroline Rose maintain that of all contemporary schools of psychology "only psychoanalysis has proved to be of any assistance"[56] in the analysis of prejudice.

Family Sociology: Emotional Interaction and Institutional Structure. Throughout all three eras of American sociology, students of family sociology have been interested in and influenced by psychoanalysis. With the efflorescence of literature on the sociology of the family after World War II and with the growing interest in small-group analysis, this trend has become even more pronounced. Some of the most extensive theoretical integration of psychoanalytic psychiatry has occurred in family sociology as this field itself has accepted the crucial importance of happy childhood experiences and of the acquisition of the conceptions of family roles during childhood in effecting happy marriages.

[55] Herbert Goldhamer, "Public Opinion and Personality," *AJS,* 55 (Jan., 1950), pp. 346-354.

[56] Arnold Rose and Caroline Rose, *America Divided* (New York, 1950), p. 305.

Although Groves was the first of many family sociologists to favor psychoanalysis, recent developments have been particularly associated with Burgess and his students. In his most recent text, *The Family* (1953), Burgess, in collaboration with Harvey J. Locke, allows over one hundred pages for a discussion of personality formation within the family. Borrowing extensively from the psychoanalytic theories of Freud, Adler, Jung, and Rank, Burgess regards all individuals as motivated internally by impulses. He interprets the functional significance of these impulses from a sociological perspective by translating them into Thomas' schema of the four wishes for security, new experience, response, and recognition. Wish-fulfillment and the importance of wishes in actual behavior are then explained by using the Freudian mechanisms of sublimation, dominance, and frustration. These and other "psychogenic processes"—identification, differentiation, overprotection, projection, self-expression, restrictiveness, and compensation—are employed to describe the emotional interaction within the family—that is, the family "psychodrama."

Winch has presented an even more encompassing theoretical formulation of psychoanalysis and family living. In *The Modern Family* (1952), Winch seeks to present an integrated social psychology of personality based on Mead's social behaviorism, the neo-social behaviorism of Dollard, Miller, O. H. Mowrer, and Sears, and both orthodox and neo-Freudiansim. According to Winch, the family is the basic social institution because the emotional patterns of the personality, which are significant in producing a happy marriage, are first and fundamentally established in it. In explaining both the experiences of infancy and childhood, which he considers as crucial, Winch draws heavily on psychoanalysis. During infancy, activity is primarily on a bio-physical level of tension-release through gratification, which leads to infantile love for the mother, and involves the child in frustration, anxiety, and repression, whereas the parents experience ambivalence. Through subsequent learning, the child acquires social needs and internalizes values, norms, and goals prevalent in the group. Thus, theoretically, the family becomes the pivotal social situation meshing the private, individualistic aspects of the personality with the cultural patterns of the society.

Functionalism, Psychoanalytic Theory, and the Family. Recently this same pivotal nature of the family has been recognized by Talcott Parsons and has led him to borrow many psychoanalytic concepts for his systematic sociological theory. Parsons contends that the social-action frame of reference permits viewing the family as a social system in which the new organism attains a relationship with the environment.

This relationship is said to develop though the operation of mechanisms of socialization and motivation.[57] Although the laws of motivation are

[57] Talcott Parsons, *The Social System* (Glencoe, Ill., 1951), especially Chap. 6.

universal, the mechanisms of motivation are relative and must be interpreted in terms of personality as a system and the mechanisms of personality. There are three major mechanisms of personality that account for its growth and development. First and basic is the mechanism of learning new cognitive, valuative, and expressive elements of action-orientation through interaction with other persons. Learning entails further mechanisms of socialization. Second is the mechanism of defense, which adjudicates conflicting needs and is closely related to the third mechanism, that of adjustment, which sublimates conflicts in relation to external objects. Such adjustment involves internalization of social controls and is comparable to the superego.

Socialization occurs through cathectic-evaluative, cognitive, and value-acquisition mechanisms. The cathectic-evaluative mechanism includes reinforcement-extinction, which is based upon the pleasure-pain principle of reward and punishment; inhibition, which is comparable to Freud's concept of repression; and substitution, which is bifurcated into transference and displacement. The two cognitive mechanisms are imitation and identification, which are based on feelings of esteem or love. Identification, which requires attitudes by the alter towards the ego, develops attachments for other persons so that these alters' value-orientations can be internalized. To use Freudian terminology, the individual internalizes parental dicta and acquires a superego.

As a system, the personality is constantly changing through the mechanism of learning. Yet it remains in equilibrium through the mechanisms of adjustment and defense, which control those factors both within and outside the individual tending toward disequilibrium. This view of a personality evolving through interaction with the environment and controlled by psychic mechanisms is similar to the psychoanalytic conception of dialectic personality formation.

Other instances of Parsons' use of Freudian ideas for his theory of personality can be found throughout his major recent books and articles. For example, he accepts weaning as frustrating because the child is forced to relinquish old, familiar need-disposition objects for new, unfamiliar ones; he views erotic gratification during infancy as crucial in personality development; he traces interpersonal attachments to an early affective relation between mother and child; he requires normal personality development to be continuous and not "frozen" at any point—that is, not characterized by fixation or regression; and he accepts the existence of egocentric sex attachments in the family and relates them to the incest taboo.

In one of his most recent publications, Parsons relates the social system and the personality system by emphasizing the role of the symbolic process.[58] He regards it as comparable to the development of the superego and insists

[58] Talcott Parsons, "Psychoanalysis and Social Science," in Alexander and Ross, *op. cit.*, pp. 186-215.

that through it the personality system acquires and internalizes moral values, defines goals, makes choices, and thus organizes its motivations into meaningful systems. The establishment of the Oedipal relationship between parents and children requires the operation of this same symbolic process. The Oedipal relation itself is the means whereby the child attains differentiated role conceptions. Whereas the infant's motivations are guided by anxieties about security—being loved—Parsons maintains that the child, upon reaching the Oedipus-complex stage, becomes motivated by anxieties about performance—reciprocating the love of the parent by giving love. Thereby the child acquires differentiated role conceptions that are elements in the social system. The sociological significance of this role-differentiating process present in the family derives from its being generic and present in other social systems, as Parsons demonstrates by analysis of the relationship between client and therapist.

Psychoanalytic Concepts and General Sociological Theory. Although other sociological theorists have explored the potentialities of psychoanalytic concepts and ideas—for example, Robert Merton's use of latent and manifest functions and Louis Schneider's comparative analysis of Veblen and Freud—Talcott Parsons' writings have been conspicuous in this respect. Of special significance is his attempt to use the Oedipus complex to interrelate personality and the social system, which are analytically separate and distinct. Since the organismic and cultural forces are not necessarily complementary, Parsons posits that the individual ultimately *wishes to accept* the cultural patterns that will restrict and limit his behavior. Thus Parsons articulates the persistent voluntaristic theme of American sociology.

SELECTED BIBLIOGRAPHY

Alexander, Franz, and Helen Ross (eds.), *Twenty Years of Psychoanalysis* (New York: W. W. Norton, 1953).

Dunham, H. Warren, "Social Psychiatry," *ASR,* 13 (April, 1948), pp. 183-197.

Goldenweiser, A. E., *History, Psychology, Culture* (New York: Alfred Knopf, 1933).

———, "Some Contributions of Psychoanalysis to the Interpretation of Social Facts," in H. E. Barnes, Howard Becker, and Frances B. Becker (eds.), *Contemporary Social Theory* (New York: D. Appleton-Century, 1940), pp. 391-430.

Hall, C. S., and Gardner Lindzey, "Psychoanalytic Theory and Its Application in the Social Sciences," in Gardner Lindzey (ed.), *Handbook of Social Psychology* (Cambridge, Mass.: Addison-Wesley, 1954), vol. 1, pp. 143-180.

Kardiner, Abram, *The Individual and His Society* (New York: Columbia University Press, 1939).

———, *Psychological Frontiers of Society* (New York: Columbia University Press, 1945).

Parsons, Talcott, *The Social System* (Glencoe, Ill.: The Free Press, 1951).

V

Sociological Research and Theory Abroad

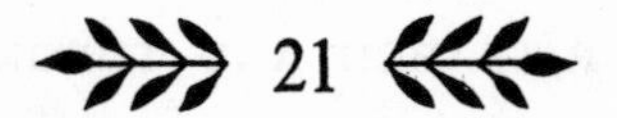

SOCIOLOGY IN BRITAIN: PREOCCUPATIONS

W. J. H. SPROTT

THIS IS NO PLACE TO DISCUSS THE DEFINITION OF SOCIOLOGY, BUT PERHAPS it is convenient to distinguish between sociologists interested in the general problems of social phenomena (such as the nature of society, the implications of social action, social control, and the relation between social structure and belief) and those who certainly call themselves "sociologists" but who are mainly concerned with the study of specific social problems (such as, for example, town planning) from a sociological point of view. The distinction is not clear-cut—few distinctions of this kind ever are—and there may be works that would be difficult to place; but I think that so far as British sociology is concerned, the distinction of emphasis is worth making. By way of providing labels, let me call the first group "theoretical sociologists" and the second "applied sociologists." The second label is not very satisfactory because the group has but little "sociology" to "apply." However, the labels can stand as indicating the distinction I have in mind.

THEORETICAL AND APPLIED SOCIOLOGY IN BRITAIN

Now social research of any kind is itself part of the social process, and one branch of the sociology of knowledge will, no doubt, contain a chapter on the sociology of sociology. In France, for example, the sociological inquirers influenced by *L'Ecole Polytechnique* were out to "put paid" to the revolutionary clash of opinion by applying scientific principles to the social machine.[1] In England, things were different. Spencer, it is true, thought

[1] Cf. F. A. Hayek, *The Counter-Revolution of Science* (Glencoe, Ill., 1952).

that societies could be understood like any other organism, but as to interfering with the beneficial evolutionary process of Nature, that was out of the question. Of planners he wrote: "A fly seated on the surface of the body has about as good a conception of its internal structure as one of these schemers has of the social organization in which he is embedded."

Mill thought that a science of society would be possible when we knew enough psychology to relate the total psychological complex of an age with the social results to which it could give rise. It was understanding rather than inquiring that he sought. In any case, neither of these eminent Victorians was an academic man. Worse still, they were not "sound" when it came to religion. It would be ridiculous to suggest that Spencer and Mill had no effect upon English social thought in general, but they certainly did not found schools of sociology; they did not even make it a "subject."

There was, however, considerable social unrest in early Victorian England, and the noses of the comfortably off became sensitive to the stink of poverty. We need not refer to Engels' celebrated book on *The Condition of the Working Class in England;* perhaps we might mention the Chadwick reports of 1833 and 1844. But noses were not the only organ to be stimulated. Hearts were touched, and philanthropic ladies and gentlemen hastened to supply blankets. "But," said the Charitable Organization Society, "we must not pamper the poor. We must help the deserving to help themselves." And then Charles Booth, the ship-owner, asked: Who are the poor? And how poor are they? Receiving no satisfactory answer, he took a step: he actually went to find out for himself. The result was his *Life and Labors of the People of London* (1891-1903), a work which was reviewed by the London School of Economics under the title of *The New Survey of London Life and Labor* in the 1930's, which is not only a milestone in the history of social surveys in England (I suppose we ought to count Stowe's *Survey of London* as a predecessor), but is also symbolic of the turn taken by social research in this country. The mood it engendered was: Let us not rely on superficial appearances, let us find out the facts. This is the mood of British sociology: fact finding.[2]

The Revolt Against Empiricism: Hobhouse and Ginsberg. Two figures, and, I think, only two, stand for something different. They are L. T. Hobhouse and Morris Ginsberg, both holders of the only chair of Sociology in Great Britain, the Martin White Chair of Sociology at the London School of Economics. Hobhouse was a man of wide interests, considerable learning, and profound intellectual ability. He was interested in comparative psychology and comparative anthropology, and he knew a great deal about the history of civilization. Surveying the scene, he saw an evolutionary pattern. There was, he thought, a tendency toward the harmonizing of desires and

[2] The significance of fact-finding is ably insisted on by Barbara Wootten, *Testament for Social Science* (London, 1950).

needs in the individual, and a tendency toward the harmonizing of the claims of all individuals in the societies that they comprise. He sought for evidence by a comparative study of institutions and moral systems. He accepted no facile answer, and, as one travels in the vehicle of his well-upholstered prose, one feels oneself in the presence of a noble and far-seeing mind. And yet it all seems somewhat old-fashioned. That this should be the case is undoubtedly to be deplored, but we are all too busy with practical problems to pay the attention we should to wide-sweeping and all-encompassing visions.

His successor, Morris Ginsberg, has inherited Hobhouse's philosophical interest and balanced approach. He has not produced a *magnum opus*, but his essays, collected in *Studies in Sociology* (1932) and in *Reason and Unreason in Society* (1947), are masterpieces of their kind. In the latter volume the studies "National Character" and "The Cause of War and Moral Progress" are outstanding; so, too is his analysis of the concept of the group mind in his *Psychology of Society* (1938). He has kept alive the "Hobhouse tradition," which combines a balanced analysis of social phenomena with a philosophical wariness against both egregious error and glib superficiality.

Ginsberg is to be followed by T. H. Marshall, a most elegant thinker. Marshall has likewise not written much, but whenever he puts pen to paper the result is a piece of subtle analysis expressed in perfect language. His *Citizenship and Social Class* (1950), to which reference will be made below, contains one of the best introductions to the problem of class in the language. The essays of Ginsberg are all short, and his recently published *Ideas of Progress: A Revaluation*, is but an expanded lecture. Marshall's output is similarly in essay form. The only two introductions to sociology, one written by Ginsberg and the other by me,[3] are both small volumes. We do not go in for large theoretical works or large, comprehensive textbooks; for these we rely on the United States. Theory and encyclopedism are for the moment unfashionable. Perhaps an exception should be made of Arnold J. Toynbee. Few would deny the adjectives "theoretical" and "encyclopedic" to his great *A Study of History*. Its reception among sociologists can scarcely be regarded as enthusiastic. This is no doubt partly due to what is felt to be a central defect: the choice of a pattern of development—creative minority, solidification into a world state, growth of the external and internal proletariat, collapse—that fits the Roman Empire and by making artificial historical dimensions is proved to apply everywhere else. It may well be due also to our hesitation in accepting the promise of redemption from the cycles of history if we adopt Christianity. It is not the "Hobhouse tradition" that we follow, it is rather the fact-finding tradition of Booth. Research is in the hands of the applied sociologists, not in those of the theorists.

The Present Neglect of Theory. As for such theorists as we have pro-

[3] Morris Ginsberg, *Sociology* (London, 1934); W. J. H. Sprott, *Sociology* (London, n.d.).

duced—we tend to ignore them; their names are known and mentioned, but their thought does not form the basis for research. In the case of applied sociologists of the past, we tend to forget them altogether. This has been the fate of two sociologists, Patrick Geddes and Victor Branford. Geddes was a biologist by profession and brought the sociological concept of biology to bear upon society. His survey of Edinburgh (1911) was one of the earliest of the social surveys, and to it he added surveys of cities in India, where he was appointed Professor of Civics and Sociology in 1920. His emphasis on empirical research is, to be sure, remembered, but he was also a systematizer, a maker of diagrams, and this tends, alas, to be lethal to any reputation. Vast stacks of unpublished notes still collect the Edinburgh dust. He is very probably cast for the role of a topic for Ph. D. research in the 1980's.

Branford, a financier, was a pupil of Geddes. He is remembered, if at all, as prime mover in the founding of the Sociological Society in 1903 and its journal, the *Sociological Review*, now published from the University College of North Staffordshire. He and Geddes were, in a sense, disciples of LePlay, and the headquarters of the Society was known as LePlay House. Several social surveys were conducted from this center, but it must be confessed that they have not joined the corpus of knowledge placed at the disposal of the modern student.

RESEARCH AND PRACTICAL PROBLEMS

The fact is that the research that is done, and there is a considerable amount of it, is directed to the solution of social problems—directed, one might say, to reform. The topics are dictated by our preoccupations. In what follows I propose to indicate what these preoccupations are, and to mention some of the research to which they have given rise. The account does not pretend to be exhaustive, and for the most part books alone will be referred to.

Population Problem: Age Distribution and Family Stability. We were disturbed by our declining population, or some of us were, for J. C. Flugel[4] told us that our alarm was simply due to our fear of impotence, whereas the late C. M. Joad took the line that in this island the fewer the roomier. Our fears have been somewhat allayed by the preliminary reports of the 1951 census. A Royal Commission on Population was set up, and it reported in 1949. Of particular interest are the Memoranda submitted to the Commission, especially Volume V, which contains a section on the *Relation Between Intelligence and Fertility* to which the psychologists Sir Godfrey Thomson and Sir Cyril Burt contributed, and Volume I on *Family Limitation.*

Volume V is concerned with the issue of the *quality* rather than the

[4] J. C. Flugel, *Population, Psychology and Peace* (London, 1947).

quantity of the population. We were warned that the level of national intelligence was declining because the inept poor were breeding more rapidly than the clever rich. This led to a variety of investigations—for example, Gray's *The Nation's Intelligence* (1936)—and a conflict between the environmentalists, represented among others by Julian Blackburn,[5] and the innateists, represented by Sir Cyril Burt. This is mainly a matter of investigation for educational psycholologists, but another aspect of the incidence of intelligence was soon pointed out: the negative correlation between family size and intellectual ability. There was some evidence that this was the case irrespective of social class, but Blackburn[6] again championed the environmental factor. In any case, if the negative correlation were to be what it seemed to be, surely it ought to have shown itself to the unsophisticated eyes of school teachers by now. But in the great replication of the 1932 intelligence survey of Scottish children carried out in 1947, no significant decline was shown. We breathe again, but a little uneasily. In any case, we feel that the best use must be made of the brains we have. This topic will be resumed later.

The second volume of papers submitted to the Royal Commission confirms the results of an investigation carried out by the Council of the Royal College of Obstetricians and Gynecologists into the general problem of the influence of family limitation during the past fifty years.

The decline in the birth rate began, of course, in the nineteenth century, and J. A. Banks[7] has investigated the conditions of life among the Victorian middle classes. He has collected evidence from books on household management, written for the instruction of the *nouveaux riches*, catalogues of furniture, and other sources to show exactly how the rising aspirations of the middle classes put a serious pressure on their income and restricted the number of children they were prepared to have.

The population problem is not only concerned with numbers; it is also concerned with age-distribution. In the not far distant future there will be too many old people and too few young ones to look after them. Old age is forced upon us, not only because we are all bound in that direction, not only on humanitarian grounds, but also because it is providing so many exhibits. We want therefore to keep them at work as long as possible, and investigations are afoot to see what kind of jobs they can do. The Nuffield Foundation has initiated research into this,[8] and also into the special needs and housing requirements of the aged.[9]

Closely associated with the problem of population is the problem of

[5] Julian Blackburn, *Framework of Human Behavior* (London, 1947).
[6] Julian Blackburn, in *Population Studies,* 1 (1947), p. 165.
[7] J. A. Banks, *Prosperity and Parenthood* (London, 1954).
[8] B. Seebohm Rowntree, *Old People* (Oxford, 1947).
[9] A. T. Welford *et al., Skill and Age* (Oxford, 1951).

family life. The alleged break-up of family life is a familiar topic for publicists and the Cassandras of journalism. A serious study was, however, made by Eliot Slater and Moya Woodside.[10] They compared the marital experience of two groups: a group of 100 service men admitted to a hospital because they were suffering from a neurosis, and a similar group admitted to medical and surgical wards. From the evidence they collected they show the features of unhappy married life that are associated with the presence of neurotic symptoms. This book is mainly concerned with the relations between man and wife. John Bowlby, who had detected the significance of separation from the mother at a very early age as a factor conducive to the development of an "affectionless" delinquent character,[11] has made a survey of the literature in *Maternal Care and Mental Health* (1951) for the World Health Organization. We here find ourselves well over the invisible barrier which separates sociology from psychology.

Town and Country Planning: Economic and Psychological Aspects. The population is, of course, unevenly distributed over the country. Towns sprawl, and agricultural land is absorbed. Towns are also frequently hideous and inconvenient. This preoccupation has given rise to a large number of social surveys, to which a useful short introduction, now a little out of date, has been written by F. A. Wells,[12] and a general history of the troubled history of town planning has recently appeared, written by William Ashwith.[13] Among the more important surveys are the following: *Midland City* (Wolverhampton) by Tom Brennan (1948); *Survey of Merseyside* by Caradog Jones (1934); *Work and Wealth in a Modern Port* (Southampton) by P. Ford (1934); *Conurbation* (Birmingham and the Black Country) by the West Midland Group (1948); and *English County* (Hereford) by the same group (1946).

These and certain other surveys are mainly aimed at fact finding and contain information about the location of industries, residential areas, and public services. Somewhat more concerned with the life of the citizens is Ruth Glass (ed.), *The Social Background of a Plan* (1948). This deals, among other matters, with the rational siting of utilities. Another factor that is significant in town planning is the distance people have to go to work. This topic is the subject matter of Kate Liepmann's *Journey to Work* (1945). Of recent years a new note has been struck. Towns must have streets, houses, schools, shops, and so on. The first question is: Where should these be located for the convenience of their users? The view, however, has been frequently expressed that urban life is somehow unsatisfactory. We are, they say, lonely. Paul Halmos in his *Solitude and Privacy* tells us that the cult of privacy is now out of date, only cultivated by the neurotically withdrawn.

[10] Eliot Slater and Moya Woodside, *Pattern of Marriage* (London, 1951).
[11] John Bowlby, *Forty-four Juvenile Thieves* (London, 1946).
[12] F. A. Wells, *The Local Social Survey in Great Britain* (London, 1935).
[13] William Ashwith, *Genesis of Modern British Town Planning* (London, 1954).

Neighborhood units are consequently recommended. In the unpublished Pilot Survey of Oxford, J. Mogey compares the neighborly intercourse of people living in one of the poorer districts of Oxford with that in a new housing estate. The same interest in neighborliness in a new housing estate was a central theme in Mrs. Durant's study of *Watling* (1939). In Coventry the matter was explored by Leo Kuper.[14] He found that it makes a difference, with regard to the amount of social intercourse into which you are drawn, whether you live at the corner of a *cul-de-sac* or on one of its sides. He also made the not unexpected discovery that some folks do not care for their neighbors anyway. The neighborhood-unit controversy is characteristic of the British sociological scene. We have a theory that people ought to be more friendly with their neighbors, we devise plans on paper to ensure it, we then get round to finding out what actually happens. A preoccupation—the loneliness of people in cities—starts the ball rolling. Assumptions are made, action is taken, and then the investigator steps in.

Surveys of Poverty and Social Services. Besides general descriptions of towns, there are also studies of their inhabitants from a different point view. Tom Brennan made a survey of Swansea (unpublished) in which he describes the changes that have taken place in the importance of the Chapel and its ministers. Rowntree has made a series of investigations of poverty in York, showing the changing conditions of the working classes.[15]

We have long been conscious of the poor. The surveys of Booth and Rowntree and the fixing of a "poverty line" fastened attention on poverty. As time went on we became increasingly "class-conscious" in the sense that we became preoccupied with the whole question of class. Citizenship, as T. H. Marshall has put it in his *Citizenship and Social Class*, of which mention has already been made, has three elements: freedom of speech and freedom from arbitrary arrest; the right to have some say in the making of the laws the citizens have to obey; and the right to such opportunities of living and developing as will ensure that no one shall be impeded by the sheer chance of birth. The first set of rights were won in the seventeenth and eighteenth centuries, the second in the nineteenth century, whereas the third is in progress of some sort of achievement in the century in which we now live.

The Social Services are yet another preoccupation. They are described by Penelope Hall in her *Social Services in Modern England* (1952). An account of the psychiatric social services has been compiled by Margaret Ashdown and S. Clement Brown in their *Social Service and Mental Health* (1953). The operation of social services during the crisis of World War II has been related by R. M. Titmus in his *Problems of Social Policy* (1950). The general

[14] Leo Kuper (ed.), *Living in Towns* (London, 1953).

[15] B. Seebohm Rowntree, *Poverty: A Study of Town Life* (London, 1902), and *Progress and Poverty* (London, 1941).

scheme for a co-ordination of relief was expounded by Lord Beveridge in the celebrated Beveridge Report, followed by his book on the implications of full employment.[16] This book, as the title implies, deals with full employment as a condition of effective welfare provision. Welfare has its costs, and this subject is the concern of Gertrude Williams in her *Price of Social Security* (1944). But statutory services are not enough; there is a need for voluntary services to cope with the cases that are not handled by the bureaucracy. A series of studies discuss this problem: Lord Beveridge (ed.), *Voluntary Actions* (London, 1943) and his *Evidence for Voluntary Actions* (London, 1949); Constance Braithwaite, *The Voluntary Citizen;* and Mess *et al.*, *Voluntary Social Services Since 1918* (London, 1947).

The social services aim at improving the standard of life of the lower-income groups, and studies have been made of the kind of life they live. Two lively sketches of their general way of life have been provided by F. Zweig,[17] who has also written a study of miners.[18] These books are of the order of reportage, but they are vivid and informative. The same may be said of Mark Benney's *Charity Main*, a study of a mining village. Mention should also be made of the Pilgrim Trust report on *Men Without Work* (1938), a comparative study of unemployment in different cultural backgrounds—Deptford, Leicester, Liverpool, Blackburn, Crook (County Durham), and the Rhondda (S. Wales).

Three more studies may be mentioned in this connection. The first is B. M. Spinley's *Deprived and Privileged* (1953), a comparison of methods of child rearing in a slum district with those experienced by groups of middle-class boys, in the hope of throwing light on the cultural differences between the two classes. The second is the soon-to-be-published study by Robb, in his *Anti-Semitism in an English Town*, of life in Bethnal Green. The point here is that anti-Semitism is a function of personality unbalance; this, in turn, is a function of the cultural pressures to which the personalities have been subjected. As a preliminary to his research Robb had, therefore, to get the key to Bethnal Green life, where children are lavishly treated when they are small to keep them quiet so that the "old man" can sleep, but are thrown out to play in the streets when they are older because bribery at that age is too costly. The third is a piece of research in progress at Nottingham University on the variety of cultural standards to be found in the working-class districts of a neighboring town.

The Status of the Middle Classes. The poor are, on the whole, accessible and ready to talk. The middle-classes are not so available for research in this country. The standard work on the professions is still the book by A. M.

[16] William Beveridge, *Full Employment in a Free Society* (London, 1944).

[17] F. Zweig, *The British Worker* (London, 1952), and *Labour, Life, and Poverty* (London, 1949).

[18] F. Zweig, *Men in the Pits* (London, 1948).

Carr-Saunders and P. Wilson,[19] but T. H. Marshall discusses the spread of "professionalism" in new occupational spheres in his *Citizenship and Social Class*. Studies of the Civil Service have been made by H. E. Dale and H. R. G. Greaves,[20] and a somewhat petulant account of their social handicaps in a changing world has been provided by R. Lewis and A. Maude,[21] whose description of the plight of the middle classes[22] is almost equally gloomy. The results of an inquiry into the recruitment of the Civil Service by H. K. Kelsall is on the way to publication.

Channels of Vertical Social Mobility. People do not, however, remain in the social class in which they were born; they are, to a limited extent, mobile. A pioneer study of vertical social mobility was made by Morris Ginsberg in 1927.[23] His sample was heavily weighted with students and teachers and his results were but tentative. However, it did appear that there was a limited amount of mobility from the manual working-class into the upper regions, and that this had increased in the generation with which he was concerned, as compared with the previous one. Lately a much more extensive inquiry, covering England, Wales, and Scotland, has been organized at the London School of Economics, under the direction of D. V. Glass, our most distinguished demographer. The sample is much more satisfactory, both geographically and occupationally. The results are estimated both in the crude terms of the percentage of sons who remain at the same occupational level as their fathers, rise above it, or fall below it, and also by the use of the concept of "perfect mobility." Using the second method of calculation, it appears that the "index of association," i.e., the extent to which children remain in the same class as their parents, is very much higher in the upper classes than in the lower regions except for the lowest occupational level of all. This study of social mobility was recently published by Kegan Paul in the International Library of Sociology and Social Reconstruction.

Among the pieces of research connected with the social-mobility project are studies of the educational opportunity afforded to different classes of the community. The "1944 Act," which aims at providing a wider range of educational opportunity to all children than they have had in the past, is the culminating event of years of preoccupation with the general problem of education. It is impossible to summarize the recent history of British education, the reports on the secondary schools, the "public" schools, and so on. Only a few books of recent date will be mentioned. The researches referred to above, which are collected in the volume edited by D. V. Glass,

[19] A. M. Carr-Saunders and P. Wilson, *The Professions* (Oxford, 1933).

[20] H. E. Dale, *The Higher Civil Service of Great Britain* (London, 1941); H. R. G. Greaves, *The Civil Service in the Changing State* (London, 1947).

[21] R. Lewis and A. Maude, *Professional People* (London, 1952).

[22] R. Lewis and A. Maude, *The English Middle Classes* (London, 1949).

[23] Morris Ginsberg, *Studies in Sociology* (London, 1932), Chap. 9.

Social Mobility in Britain (Glencoe, 1954), show how narrow the educational ladder was before the Act of 1944. The significance of secondary education is discussed by H. C. Dent in his *Secondary Education for All* (1949). Since then he has described the transition that is taking place in his *Education in Transition* (1952), which is an account of the impact of war on English education, and its sequel, *Growth in English Education* (1954), which brings the story up to 1952. A more general work on the sociology of education has recently appeared.[24]

Problems of Formal Education. An obvious topic of controversy is the persistence of independent "public" schools, the curious contribution of which is described by J. P. Wolfenden in his *Public Schools Today* (1948). But secondary education is not our sole matter of concern in the provision of educational opportunities: there are the universities. The provincial universities are discussed in brief critical terms by a writer whose identity has been kept a close secret, masquerading under the pseudonym of Bruce Truscot.[25] These books, alarmingly well-informed, describe life and labor in universities other than Oxford and Cambridge. And now another preoccupation is making itself felt. Granted we have adequate "grammar school" accommodations, with the possibility of transferring to such schools boys and girls whose intellectual abilities have developed later, do we then select the right ones for university education? Apparently, according to R. R. Dale, we do not.[26]

Educational opportunity is, naturally, only one of the anxieties that trouble us in communities with young people. There is also the entry into industry of those who do not go on to higher forms of education. In this field an interesting piece of research has been carried out in Glasgow.[27]

Studies of Delinquency. But youths do not, as we all know, merely enter quietly into industry or higher academic institutions. They sometimes enter Approved Schools, Borstals, and, when they are old enough, prisons. Here, again, the compilation of a bibliography of British books on deliquency is out of the question, but a few books might be selected of a more obviously sociological rather than psychological character. The outstanding figure in the field of delinquency studies in this country is Hermann Mannheim. The title of his major work indicates clearly enough the nature of our problems. In 1940, just after the beginning of World War II, he published *Social Aspects of Crime in England Between the Wars*. In the following year came *War and Crime*. The London School of Economics was evacuated to Cambridge and a study, *Young Offenders* (1942), was made by Mannheim, Carr-Saunders,

[24] A. K. C. Ottaway, *Education and Society* (London, 1953).

[25] Bruce Truscot (pseud.), *Redbrick University* (Harmondsworth, 1943), and *Redbrick Revisited* (Harmondsworth, 1951).

[26] R. R. Dale, *From School to University* (London, 1954).

[27] T. Ferguson and J. Connison, *The Young Wage Earner* (Oxford, 1951).

and E. C. Rhodes, which was followed by a more general survey of crime in Cambridge under the somewhat misleading title of *Juvenile Delinquency in an English Middletown*.[28] This had been preceded by a more general work on *Criminal Justice and Social Reconstruction*, published in 1946. At present Mannheim teaches and directs research at the London School of Economics. Liverpool University has also produced research in this field, such as J. H. Bagot's book on *Juvenile Delinquency* (1941) and the same author's *Punitive Detention* (1944). Bristol University is at present mounting a long-term research project under the direction of John Spencer, whose *Crime and the Services* (1954), contains a valuable investigation into the influence of armed forces experience on delinquency, and vice versa. To these may be added *Society and Its Criminals* (1949), a collection of essays by Norwood East, sometime head of the Prison Medical Service.

As to the treatment of delinquents, the Chairman of the Prison Commission has brought up to date his account of the Borstal and prison system,[29] which gives an exhaustive description of the prison system, with its new classification of open prisons and prisons for persistent offenders. The more experimental types of treatment are dealt with by other writers. Joseph Trenamen, for example, describes an experiment in reconditioning unsatisfactory soldiers by methods more likely to get a response than those normally associated with the "Glass House." David Wills, following in the footsteps of the Viennese Aichorn, experimented with the "discipline" of freedom, allowing his charges to do exactly what they liked, short of murder and suicide, until they got sick of it. He has given an account of these in his *Hawkspur Experiment* (1941) and *Borns Experiment* (1945). Very little is known about the influence of subcultural background on delinquency, although we notice that delinquency produced by a "good home"—that is to say, a "respectable" upwardly mobile home—would have a different causality from that produced by (as most of it seems to be) a less "respectable" home, where a more generous attitude is taken toward the property of others. It is hoped that the researches at Bristol and Nottingham will throw light on this aspect of criminology.

Race Relations. The next preoccupation is one with which the United States of America is only too familiar, but one which has only comparatively recently given rise to anxiety: the color problem. We have always had communities of colored men in our parts, but we have never taken any "scientific" interest in their relations with the white population. Our interest has been aroused partly because of an increased number of colored immigrants and partly because we have become increasingly ashamed at the "incidents" that occur from time to time, showing the existence of a color-bar in some circles. The first serious study was carried out by K. L. Little, the anthro-

[28] Hermann Mannheim, *Juvenile Delinquency in an English Middletown* (London, 1948).
[29] Lionel Fox, *The English Prison and Borstal System* (London, 1952).

pologist, who made a survey of Tiger Bay, a Negro settlement in Cardiff.[30] More recent is A. H. Richmond's *Color Prejudice in Britain*, a study of Negro technicians in Liverpool. There also exist many unpublished theses on the subject, such as M. P. Barton's study of Negroes in Stepney; a study of Negroes in Manchester by Ego Barsey Ndem, a native of Nigeria; and another on Moslem and Negro groupings in Tyneside by S. F. Collins.

Industrial Relations. Industry presents its social-psychological problems. The general structure of industrial relations has been given textbook form recently by J. Henry Richardson,[31] who describes the devices for negotiation at shop-floor level, by joint consultation, by trade-union argument, and by arbitration. The structure and problems of the nationalized industries have been investigated by the Acton Society Trust, whereas the complex structure of trade unionism has been analyzed by the members of an invaluable organization called Political and Economic Planning (P.E.P.),[32] who also publish bulletins on social issues from time to time. To this latter topic a contribution has been made by J. Goldstein in a book called *The Government of British Trade Unions* (1952). The variety of traditions which are incorporated into the general body of trade unions is so complicated that a guide is essential. The works cited above are mainly descriptive. Another approach to industrial relations is exemplified by the work of the Tavistock Institute of Social Relations. In their consultative work and in their research they aim at analyzing the unconscious tensions that disturb good relations. In *The Changing Culture of a Factory* (1951), Elliot Jacques describes the hidden motives that impeded the transformation of a factory with a more or less conventional structure into a more integrated organization in which the workers played a more responsible part in the making of decisons. Unconscious irritations, fear of responsibility, and unspoken feelings of neglect constantly seemed to divert attention from painful issues onto innocuous topics. Joint consultation, with its two opponent sides, was revealed as a vested interest for both parties because of its scapegoat function. Other work of a similar nature is reported in various volumes of *Human Relations*, a journal published by the Tavistock Institute and the Research Center for Group Dynamics at Ann Arbor, Michigan.

Leisure. As one might suppose, other people's leisure-time activities are a perennial worry. In 1950 the staff and students of Westhill Training College in Birmingham published an account of *80,000 Adolescents* and how some of them spent their leisure time. In the same year we had *Patterns of British Life* from the Hulton Press, and in 1951 there appeared *English Life and Leisure* by B. Seebohm Rowntree and J. Laver, based on a sample that even an unsympathetic reader may be excused for thinking a little odd, to

[30] K. L. Little, *Negroes in Britain* (London, 1948).
[31] J. Henry Richardson, *Introduction to the Study of Industrial Relations* (London, 1954).
[32] P. E. P., *British Trade Unionism* (1947) and *Trade Unionism in Britain* (1950).

say the least. On the whole, of course, the impression is given that other people waste their time more than is the case with the authors. Perhaps, indeed, they do.

A Broad Approach to Legal Problems. Finally, I should mention a topic that is not a preoccupation as the others are, but rather a matter that I believe to be of interest. Roscoe Pound contributed a chapter on the Sociology of Law to Gurvitch and Moore's *Twentieth Century Sociology* (1945). It would, I believe, be unthinkable for a distinguished English lawyer to contribute an article under that title to an English compilation of such a kind—if one could imagine such a thing, anyway. Sociological considerations have, however, penetrated the Royal Courts of Justice. As a matter of insignificant reminiscence, I might say that it was the present Master of the Rolls who forced me to read Cardozo's *Nature of the Judicial Process.* The position is that the law, sustained in judgments and legislation, does not keep pace with rapid social changes, and the interpretation of the letter is frequently in conflict with the spirit. There are, of course, those who insist on the letter, awaiting legislation to change it, but there are also those who, like Cardozo, recognize the significance of interpretation. It is impertinent for one who is not a lawyer—especially in this country—to venture an opinion, but from his judgments, one cannot help recognizing that Lord Justice Denning is of the latter party, and his *Changing Law* (1953) bears this out. The influence of changing public opinion and changing social situations on legal thought and utterance is the subject matter of W. Friedmann's *Law and Social Change in Contemporary Britain* (1951). The general influence of economic development and law form the material of A. S. Diamond's *Evolution of Law and Order* (1951).

SUBSIDIZATION OF RESEARCH

Research into social problems in Great Britain is financed by a variety of agencies. The Government, through its own social research unit, the Social Survey, through the Department of Scientific and Industrial Research, which is now turning its attention to the "human factors" in industry, and through its various departments of state pays for a certain amount of it. The great foundations in this country and America, such as the Rockefeller Foundation, the Nuffield Foundation, the Pilgrim Trust, the Carnegie Trust, and so on, provide funds. Furthermore, special grants were made to Universities between 1948 and 1952 for the development of "social-science" departments. This last provision is parochially known as "Clapham money" because it was the implementation of the advice given by a Committe on the Provision for Social and Economic Research (1946), which met under the chairmanship of Sir John Clapham.

Now it is agreed that social research in this country should be done mainly through the universities and university colleges, and mention of

Clapham money is not amiss. In the first place the earmarked grant, given annually in increasing amounts reaching £400,000 in 1951-52, was recommended at a time when the social services were expanding, so that the intention was to provide an improved basis for planning. In the second place it will be noted that economics was included as a social science, as was politics. Now, of course, when there is money to be had, hands will be stretched out to take it, and the decision as to who should have it will be partly determined by existing departments in universities and by the presence in them of distinguished and forceful men.

In reviewing the ditribution, P.E.P.[33] noted that the bulk of the new appointments since the grant was given were in the "departments of economics, politics and allied subjects, leaving the rest to be shared by demography and all the subjects included under the general head of 'sociology'. And a good deal of this latter amount went in to providing for the teaching of social workers. The trouble was—if "trouble" it be—that there were no departments of sociology outside the London School of Economics. Something, however, was certainly done. In Liverpool, the Department of Social Science was expanded, as was the Faculty of Commerce and Social Science in Birmingham. In Edinburgh and Glasgow, social research was established, but mainly to deal with local and Scottish problems. A considerable amount of the grant went to the London School of Economics, which has an extremely active Department of Sociological and Demographic Research. All this government aid was further supplemented by grants from research foundations, particularly in the London School of Economics and in Oxford, where Nuffield College was founded to encourage research in the social sciences. The result of it all is that such of the earmarked grant (which has now been merged into the total grants to universities) as remained after the economists and political scientists had had their whack, has been applied to the teaching of social workers and the financing of research, with the aid of the foundations, and into social problems of a local or urgent national character. Sociology as a *theoretical* science has scarcely benefited.

The over-all picture is provided in a UNESCO pamphlet on the *Teaching of the Social Sciences in the United Kingdom* (1953). In Cambridge there is a chair in social anthropology, and the university went so far as to break with their old habits and invite an American professor of sociology, Talcott Parsons, to give courses of lectures in 1953-54. In Oxford, sociology is taught to graduates and social trainees. Howard Becker lectured throughout the spring term at Birmingham in 1951, and the university has a regular professor of social science; so have Liverpool and Nottingham. Lecturers in sociology are to be found in Exeter, Hull, Leicester, Oxford, and

[33] P.E.P., *Government Aid for the Social Sciences* (1950), Planning Vol. 17, No. 321.

Southampton. Only in two universities, London and Nottingham, can honors degrees in sociology be taken, and there is still only one chair of sociology, so-called—the Martin White Chair, to which reference has already been made.

Variety of Research in British Universities. Let it not be thought that, with this meager supply of funds and personnel, no research is done. The *Register of Research in the Social Sciences*, published annually by the Cambridge University Press, tells a very different story. The London School of Economics is active with its demographic and criminal research, as is the Department of Criminal Science at Cambridge. Birmingham, Bristol, Durham, Edinburgh, Glasgow, Oxford, and London are all surveying the regions about them. There us an active Social Research Centre in Edinburgh and others in Sheffield and Bristol, the Bristol center being attached to the Institute of Education. In Liverpool the Merseyside provides a field of inquiry, and research proceeds with dock-workers and in hospitals. It would be too tedious to repeat the list provided by the Register; I have obly extracted a handful of items, which may, indeed, look rather puny compared to the formidable activities in the United States. To us, too, it is puny enough, but we try to find comfort-though certainly not complacency—in the reflection that to us it is all so new. When one thinks back to the twenties and thirties, there was, no doubt, social research of some kind going on, but if one was not in it one heard nothing about it. Nowadays it is the concern of every university and university college in the country, although in some places, no doubt, it is looked upon askance. In all universities except Cambridge it is taken as a matter of course that "social science" or sociology should be part of their establishment.

PROSPECTS FOR SOCIOLOGY IN BRITAIN

The future is not easy to predict. The holders of the Martin White Chair and its future holder have made contributions to sociological theory. In addition to these we have had Westermarck and Karl Mannheim, both of whom have thrown considerable light upon general sociological problems, and both of whom, be it noted, came to us from the Continent. Nowadays, if we except Leo Silberman's *Analysis of Society* (1951) and my own *Science and Social Action* (1954), very few, if any, books seem to be published that are concerned with the general field of sociology as a science. As I have said, social science here is applied science, tied to current events. It is impossible to say whether this will always be so. At a conference held in London in 1953, under the auspices of the British Sociological Association, an address was given by Gunnar Myrdal, who made a plea for abstention from direct participation in practical tasks on the part of at least some sociologists. In a report on the conference, T. H. Marshall wonders whether we ought not to do more than "shovel up the facts needed by the politicians and administrators."[34] I think myself that a study of sociological theory is important and that it is neglected in this country. For its development we require senior posts to be created in universities for sociologists who aim at making their research serve their theories, rather than hanging around making themselves useful. I must hasten to add that this is a minority opinion. Reform and Service fire the hearts of my colleagues; to most of them my interest in sociological theory is as wicked as Nero's interest in music.

Sociology, at any rate in its applied form, is on the map. *The British Journal of Sociology* was started in 1950; *The Sociological Review*, which almost died—although in its sickness it still contained interesting material—has recovered, and is published at the University College of North Staffordshire. The British Sociological Association was founded in 1951. An enormous amount of research is being done, much of which, alas, is buried in thesis form in the libraries of universities. My own hope is that among the increasing number of students who study the subject some may come forward, endowed with scientific imagination, who will refrain from knocking at doors and presenting questionnaires until they have formulated some theoretically significant hypothesis for verification.

SELECTED BIBLIOGRAPHY

Becker, Howard, and H. E. Barnes, *Social Thought from Lore to Science*, 2nd ed. (New York: Dover Publications, 1952), vol. 2, Chap. 21.
Ginsberg, Morris, *Sociology* (London: Thornton, Butterworth, 1934).
———, *Studies in Sociology* (London: Methuen, 1932).
Glass, D. V. (ed.), *Social Mobility in Britain* (Glencoe, Ill.: The Free Press, 1954).
Marshall, T. H., *Citizenship and Social Class* (Cambridge: Cambridge University Press, 1950).
Rumney, Jay, "British Sociology," in Georges Gurvitch and W. E. Moore (eds.), *Twentieth Century Sociology* (New York: Philosophical Library, 1945), pp. 562-585.

[34] T. H. Marshall, in *BJS*, 4 (1953), p. 206.

SOCIOLOGY IN FRANCE: AN EMPIRICIST VIEW*

JEAN STOETZEL

FRENCH SOCIOLOGY HAS UNDERGONE SOME VERY IMPORTANT MODIFICATIONS during the past thirty-five or forty years. Several previous surveys present the situation in various eras, notably those by Davy, Essertier, Bouglé, Aron *et al.*, Lévi-Strauss, and Girard.[1] Reference to these works is indispensable for understanding modern French sociology. The passage of years, nevertheless, makes new scrutiny necessary, not only because of significant additions, but because our perspective changes with time.

The General Character of French Sociology: 1918-1954

A very general examination of work done during the whole period, divided into five-year intervals (except for the first, 1919-1924: six years),

* Translated by Alvin Boskoff.

[1] Georges Davy, "La Sociologie française de 1918 à 1925," in his *Sociologues d'hier et d'aujourd'hui* (Paris, 1931), pp. 1-23 [first published in the *Monist* in 1926]; Daniel Essertier, *La Sociologie* (Paris, 1930); Celestin Bouglé, *Bilan de la sociologie française contemporaine* (Paris, 1935); Raymond Aron *et al., Les Sciences sociales en France: enseignement et recherche* (Paris, 1937); Claude Lévi-Strauss, "French Sociology," in Georges Gurvitch and W. E. Moore (eds.), *Twentieth Century Sociology* (New York, 1945); Alain Girard, "Travaux récents de sociologie en France," *Population,* 7 (1952), pp. 109-126.

enables us to assemble a group of rather sharply defined characteristics that help in distinguishing several periods.[2]

1. Except for the war and occupation period, production has continued to increase at an accelerated pace. Figured on a base of 100 for the initial period, the index of production reached almost 300 on the eve of World War II, and approaches 900 for the most recent five-year period (See Table 1).

TABLE 1

INDICES OF SOCIOLOGICAL PRODUCTIVITY IN FRANCE
By Five-Year Periods
(Base Period — 100)

Five-Year Periods	1919-1924	1925-1929	1930-1934	1935-1939	1940-1944	1945-1949	1950-1954
Index	100	102	150	285	99	700	860

2. The attitude and method of sociological work have been profoundly modified. Although the philosophical or reflective method, and the scholarly approach, characterized three fourths of the work done during the first interval, they now account for only one quarter. This change has been relatively gradual; however, it has become quite apparent chiefly since 1930. These changes, it should be noted, must be understood in a purely relative sense. Along with the considerable increase in production during this period, the absolute number of philosophically oriented sociological works more than quadrupled between the 1919-1924 period and the 1950-1954 period. We must therefore not think that the philosophical tendency in modern French sociology has totally disappeared; if it has diminished, it has done so only relatively.

This relative diminution has been accompanied by an increase—both relative and absolute—in works based on facts. In this regard, we should distinguish between works that depend on data that are already available, whether quantitative or qualitative, and those that are based on individual investigations of the author. Research, in a relative sense, reached its full height in the period of 1930-1934, as a result especially of the contributions of ethnography. Subsequently, research developed considerably, in an absolute sense, in other sociological specialisms, and notably in political sociology

[2] This survey is based on about 800 titles of works and articles considered to be sociological; generally, the choice of these articles was based on reviews in one of the leading French sociological journals. We have added works, notably articles, that were not reviewed but that clearly belonged to the sociological realm. Inevitably this involved some arbitrary elements, since a given work often belongs to several disciplines. Messieurs Bourricaud, Mendras, Pauvert, and Romefort were of great aid in the survey.

and demography. Works with a documentary and statistical base, on the other hand, became more prominent a bit later—especially after 1944.

The remainder of sociological production is featured by description and critical analysis of authors and theories, by surveys and methodological discussions, by works aimed at popularization, or by other methods (e.g., theoretical calculations of school needs). These kinds of work have tended toward stability, relatively for the first two intervals, absolutely for the last two. Changes in attitude and method are summarized in Table 2.

TABLE 2

CHANGES IN ORIENTATION AND METHOD OF SOCIOLOGICAL WORK IN FRANCE

Five-Year Periods	1919-1924	1925-1929	1930-1934	1935-1939	1940-1944	1945-1949	1950-1954
Philosophy	41	29	20	22	12	21	20
Scholarship	33	37	14	12	6	9	2
Research	0	11	32	28	32	21	30
Documentation	7	3	18	16	21	21	23
Statistical	0	0	4	6	6	16	9
Critical	7	6	6	2	6	5	5
Methodological	0	3	2	2	3	4	7
Popularization	7	11	4	7	6	2	2
Other	5	0	0	5	6	1	2
Totals	100	100	100	100	100	100	100

The changes in approach and method between 1918 and 1954 are essentially characterized by a weakening, clearly recognizable since 1930, of the philosophical and scholarly viewpoint—in other words, by a rationalistic, humanistic approach; and by a strong emphasis on research and empirical investigation (whether quantitative or qualitative) dating from the same period, augmented since 1940 and especially since 1945, for production was particularly weak between 1940 and 1945.

3. Changes is the *content* of sociological work during the whole period likewise show well-defined features. What is initially striking is the decrease in the relative importance of works in general sociology and moral sociology, which flourished during the first interval. The decrease in the first category is only relative, the number of works and articles in general sociology being four times more numerous in 1950-1954 than in 1919-1924. But works in moral sociology have completely disappeared since 1940. By contrast, at the end of this period we can see a considerable development of works in political sociology and demography.

In the intermediate period, between 1930 and 1945, the sociology of law, economic sociology, ethnography, and human geography occupied important positions. We shall later comment in detail on this invasion of sociology by sociologically relevant disciplines, which, however, probably deserve a place at its periphery—in its orbit, if you will—rather than at its center, properly speaking.

Social psychology, collective psychology, and the sociology of religion —scanning the indices for each division of sociology—appear to have been on the downgrade. In reality, a dual phenomenon is involved: psychosociology and religious sociology in the first intervals relied almost exclusively on the humanistic approach; and in this category these two disciplines have tended to disappear. At the same time, they reappear in an empiricist form, without having reached the full development to which they seemed destined in France.

It is to be noted also that the category "others" tends to increase noticeably. The table shows the appearance or the development of such disciplines as the sociology of migration, of acculturation, of classes, and of age groups, which were virtually non-existent till 1930. At the same time, such disciplines as the sociology of art and the sociology of language are seen to have regres-

TABLE 3

CHANGES IN THE DISTRIBUTION OF VARIOUS SPECIALISMS IN FRENCH SOCIOLOGICAL WORK
(By Percent of Total Output)

Five-Year Periods	1919-1924	1925-1929	1930-1934	1935-1939	1940-1944	1945-1949	1950-1954
General Sociology	11	17	8	7	3	5	6
Moral Sociology	13	3	2	3	0	0	0
Sociology of Law	8	3	12	11	6	4	1
Political Sociology	8	6	2	6	6	5	20
Sociology of Religion	13	17	6	11	6	5	4
Sociology of the Family	5	9	0	2	0	4	5
Economic Sociology	2	13	16	0	12	13	7
Industrial Sociology	0	0	0	1	3	8	3
Urban Sociology	0	3	2	3	6	4	5
Rural Sociology	0	0	6	9	0	6	3
Human Geography	0	0	0	5	12	7	2
Ethnography	2	11	16	16	22	6	4
Demography	0	0	2	6	3	12	13
Social and Collective Psychology	23	9	0	4	15	5	6
Expository works	5	3	8	3	0	2	2
Others	10	6	20	13	6	14	19
Total	100	100	100	100	100	100	100

sed, which is to say that specialties linked with the humanistic approach so characteristic of the first interval shared its decline.

Table 3 supplies statistical evidence that supports the preceding remarks. We must repeat that this inevitably involves some doubtful and arbitrary elements in classification and that, on the other hand, it disregards overlapping categories. It should therefore be consulted with extreme care.

In short, it is probably not too arbitrary to distinguish three periods in French sociology between 1918 and 1954. From 1919 to 1924, the dominant character of work is one of philosophical reflection and scholarship; general sociology and moral sociology are in full bloom and the sociology of religion and psychosociology are also very important, approached in the same humanistic spirit. Between 1930 and 1944, these features give way and studies of this type show a marked decline. The sociology of law, economic sociology, human geography, and ethnography attain the first rank. The dominant temper is empirical; individual research expands, but the central disciplines of sociology are somewhat neglected. Since 1945 the empirical note has continued to increase, reaching those branches of sociology that had hitherto been approached in a rather reflective manner—such as the sociology of religion, political sociology, and social psychology—and giving birth to new disciplines.

The Humanistic Period: 1918-1929

It is doubtless unnecessary to recall that French sociology in 1918, at the end of World War I, emerged from a double ordeal. On the one hand, it experienced grave losses from the war itself. Among the sociologists killed on the battlefields, one at least had already to his credit some promising works: Robert Hertz (1882-1915). Others had begun to follow in the footsteps of their teachers: Maxime David, Antoine Bianconi, Jean Reynier, R. Gelly, André Durkheim (see *L'Année Sociologique,* new series, 1925, pp. 19-29). On the other hand, the leader of the most illustrious school of French sociology, Émile Durkheim, had just passed away at fifty-nine (November, 1917). The most important periodical of French sociology, *L'Année Sociologique,* whose twelfth volume appeared in 1913, ceased from that date. In the eleven-year period separating the war's end from the thirties, sociologists were greatly to feel the effects of this situation.

The period is marked, first—among sociologists connected with the *L'Année Sociologique*—by an effort to re-form their group, in order to revive its spirit and thereby to restore the productive impetus checked by the war. This effort is primarily reflected, thanks to the loyal concern of Durkheim's disciples, in a series of publications of the master's manuscripts: in 1920, the

Revue Philosophique welcomed an "Introduction à la morale"; in the following year there appeared (in the form of two articles entitled "The Conjugal Family") the conclusion of Durkheim's favorite lectures on the family, of which the *Annales de la faculté des lettres de Bordeaux* had published the introduction in 1888 ("Introduction à la sociologie de la famille"). In 1922 Alcan published a little volume, *Education et philosophie,* followed in 1924 by *Sociologie et philosophie,* a collection of previously published articles. Finally, in 1925, there appeared *L'Éducation morale* and in 1928 *Le Socialisme.* At the close of this first period, the harvest of scattered or unpublished works by Durkheim was almost at an end. Not until 1937, in *La Revue de métaphysique et de morale,* did the three lectures on "professional morality" given in 1898-1900 appear, and much later, in 1950, through the efforts of the Turkish sociologist H. Nail Kubali, *Les Leçons de sociologie: Physique des mœurs et du droit* (with a preface by G. Davy).[3]

The connection with the preceding period was the more easily established, on the other hand, as many investigations, completely halted in 1914, could not appear because of the war; and even those well advanced toward completion had to await the end of hostilities to achieve full maturity. This was true of the thesis by Paul Fauconnet, *La Responsabilité,* which expands on the ideas of four lectures by Durkheim in his course on the theory of sanctions, given at Bordeaux in 1894. This work, finished in 1914, finally appeared in print in 1920. The same was true of the works of Georges Davy, whose *La Foi jurée* and *Le Droit, l'idéalisme et l'experience* both appeared in 1922. Similarly, the important sociological chapters contained in the *Traité de psychologie* (edited by Theodor Ribot)—"La Sociologie," by Davy; "Les Volitions" and "La Personnalité," by Charles Blondel—appeared in 1924. The subsequent publication of a major share of the work of Marcel Granet during this period is explainable in the same manner. Granet, who had scarcely published anything before 1914, and who would publish little after 1930, was nevertheless ready. He produced a considerable number of works at once very sophisticated sociologically and very much inspired by Durkheim's ideas, to which he reverted without any conscious intention of doing so.[4]

The desire to continue the great Durkheim tradition manifested itself

[3] The same devoted efforts brought about the publication of a collection of works by Robert Hertz, killed in 1915: *Mélanges de sociologie religieuse et de folklore* (Paris, 1928).

[4] "Quelques particularités de la langue de la pensée chinoise," *Revue Philosophique* (1920); "La vie et la mort: Croyances et doctrines de l'antiquité chinoise," *Annales de l'École des hautes études* (1920-21); "Le dépôt de l'enfant sur le sol: Rites anciens et ordalies mythiques," *Rev. Archeol.* (1922); "Le langage de la douleur d'après le rituel funéraire de la Chine classique," *JPs* (1922); *La Religion des Chinois* (Paris, 1922); "L'esprit de la religion chinoise," *Scientia* (1929); "Remarques sur le Taoisme ancien," *Asia Major* (1925); *Danses et legendes de la Chine ancienne* (Paris, 1926) 2 vols.; *La Civilisation chinoise* (Paris, 1929); *La Pensée chinoise* (Paris, 1934).

in the revived publication of the annual *L'Année Sociologique* (1924) and in the creation in 1925 of the French Institute of Sociology, under the presidency of Durkheim's nephew, Marcel Mauss. It appears, however, that this group entertained some rather optimistic illusions about its possibilities; although the French Institute of Sociology succeeded in surviving, the journal, which was one of its major objectives, was forced to suspend publication after the second volume (1926).[5]

We shall later have the opportunity, in outlining the characteristics of the next period, of examining the underlying reasons for these difficulties. It is likely that they were not only of a financial nature. In any case, it is certain that the group formed around *L'Année Sociologique* is not the only one in this period to participate actively in sociology. Various dissident viewpoints soon came to be heard. In 1920, in a "Introduction à la sociologie" *(Revue de métaphysique et de morale)*; Joseph Wilbois stressed the notion of the *totality* of society, a leading idea of the École de la science sociale, a bitter rival of *L'Année Sociologique* in Durkheim's time. But above all, Paul Bureau, who had published his *L'Indiscipline des mœurs* in the same year, did not hesitate in his work, *La Science des mœurs: Introduction à la methode sociologique* (1923), to take advantage of the absence of his illustrious adversary: "Furthermore," he writes in his preface, "the time seems favorable; the recent demise of the undisputed leader of the French school of sociology has left this group in some disorder . . . [This] was inevitable, the day when the fascinating ability and prophetic influence of the incomparable dialectician, Émile Durkheim, would no longer be available to conceal the overweening certitude of his conclusions, which are deduced from an a priori philosophical system rather than from a methodical analysis of facts." Bureau then seeks an understanding "doubtless polite, but clear and frank" with his Durkheimian colleagues. He criticizes their "sociological materialism" and comprehensively contrasts it with the monographic method of LePlay, aided as it is by statistics and history, and its characteristic conception of social facts: the basic trinity—Place, Work, and Folk.

La Science des mœurs was the last book by Bureau; he died the same year in which it was published (1923). Despite this manifesto, the École de la science sociale was to produce few important fruits in its short span (although we might cite the work of M. Descamps, *La Sociologie experimentale,* 1934, even though it belongs to the next period). But the work of Bureau proves that opposition to *L'Année Sociologique* was not extinguished; in fact,

[5] It is interesting to list the succession of presidents of the French Institute of Sociology: Marcel Mauss, 1924-1927; Lucien Lévy-Bruhl, 1927-1930; François Simiand, 1930-1933; Marcel Granet, 1933-1934; Paul Fauconnet, 1934-1939; Maurice Halbwachs, 1939-1944; Georges Bourgin, 1945-1946; Henri Lévy-Bruhl, 1947-1948; Georges Davy, 1948-1950; Louis Gernet, 1950-1952; Maurice Leenhardt, 1952-1953; Georges Gurvitch, 1953—.

many other critics belonged to this opposition: René Worms, founder of the International Institute of Sociology, of the *Revue internationale de sociologie,* who also published *La Sociologie: Sa nature, son contenu, ses attaches* (Paris, 1921); Gaston Richard, successor to Worms (who died in 1926) in the International Institute of Sociology—*L'Evolution des mœurs* (1924); Raoul Allier, who aimed his barbs especially at Lévy-Bruhl—*La Psychologie de la conversion chez les peuples non-civilisés,* 2 vols. (Paris, 1925), and *Le non-civilisé et nous* (Paris, 1928); Daniel Essertier, *Les Formes inférieures de l'explication* (Paris, 1927) and *Psychologie et sociologie* (Paris, 1927).

On the other hand, we shall later see to what extent the methodological inspiration of LePlay, mediated by such writers as Bureau and Descamps, remains tenacious and fertile. True, it eventually loses its strength as a doctrine. And to the degree that it is no longer a question of discovering the essence of social facts and of contrasting idealism and materialism, sociological and psychological viewpoints, totality and specificity; to the degree, on the contrary, that it is concerned solely with description of social facts and on occasion with enumeration, in the sincere belief that the facts are not known, and likewise seeks to explain them because of conviction that they require explanation—to this degree are writers employing the monographic method in accord with those who continue to represent the tradition of *L'Année Sociologique.*

However, we must admit that between 1919 and 1930 the most significant works came from the group identified with *L'Année Sociologique.* Many of these works still are classics of French sociology. We can even say that, apart from Durkheim's works, this period may truly be termed the most fruitful one for *L'Année Sociologique* adherents, and also that great individuality emerged in this period among members of that "team."

In 1919, Georges Davy, currently dean of the Sorbonne, and a leader of French sociology, had as yet published only one volume of selected fragments from Durkheim (preceded, it is true, by a carefully planned introduction): *Durkheim, Choix de textes* (Paris, 1911). But he was on the way: in 1919-1920 he contributed two important articles to the *Revue de métaphysique et de morale:* "Emile Durkheim, l'homme et l'œuvre"; and his thesis *La Foi jurée,* appeared in 1922, plus a profoundly critical work on the principal conceptions of the contemporary legal thinkers, Duquit and Hauriou: *Le Droit, l'idéalisme et l'experience.* The following year (1923), with Alexandre Moret, he published *Des Clans aux empires: L'Organisation sociale chez les primitifs et dans l'Orient ancien* (in the series *L'Evolution de l'humanité*), in which he sketched a synthesis of ethnographic facts of the earliest historic period. His chapter on "La Sociologie," in the *Traité de psychologie,* was published in 1924. In the same year his *Eléments de sociologie appliquée à la morale et à l'éducation* also appeared. We should also remember that almost all the chapters of his *Sociologues d'hier et d'aujourd'hui* (1931) were separately published during this period.[6] The rigorous precision of his thought and writing, in which some remark a "determination somewhat impatient with doctrine" (Essertier, p. 179), combined with an impeccable fund of accurate information, mark Davy as an outstanding, possibly the most representative, member of the Durkheimian group.

Yet another writer of the first rank in this period is Marcel Mauss (1872-1950). Twelve years older than Davy, and like him possessor of a degree in philosophy, Mauss is in many respects quite different from Davy.[7] A nephew of Durkheim, he worked on *L'Année Sociologique* from 1899 onward as well as on various other learned journals. He had already written an imposing list of articles and treatises. In 1909 he collected in one volume three studies done in collaboration with Henri Hubert, called *Mélange d'histoire des religions*. For nineteen years he was director of studies on the history of religion among preliterates at the École des hautes études. Then he resumed his lectures and publications, which were both learned and inspiring; and, until 1930, scarcely a year passed in which he did not publish a work or even two; they were usually short but always creative or penetrating.[8] Furthermore, after 1923 he inspired and managed the renewed publication of *L'Année Sociologique*, and he was the first president of the French Institute of Sociology.

However, Mauss did not succeed Durkheim in his teaching position. It was rather the coauthor of the article-manifesto contributed to the *Encyclopedia,* Paul Fauconnet, who would later inscribe the name of Mauss with gratitude in the preferace to his thesis. Professor at Toulouse since 1907, Fauconnet in 1921 was called to the Sorbonne in the chair of "the science of education and sociology." Fauconnet had written very little, and his thesis on *Responsabilité* was ready in 1914. However, he has a central place in the period under review, not so much because *Responsabilité* appeared in 1920, but because in the university position occupied by Fauconnet since 1921, this work and its underlying spirit exercised a very great influence on students of philosophy. As Bouglé aptly remarks in his *Bilan de la sociologie française contemporaine* (1935), this "much debated notion of responsability," thanks to

[6] "L'œuvre d'Espinas," *Revue Philosophique* (1923); "La psychologie sociale de McDougall et la sociologie durkheimienne," *JPs* (1923); "La famille et la parenté d'après Durkheim, "*Revue Philosophique* (1925); "La sociologie française de 1918 à 1925," *Monist* (1926). Only the last chapter, "La psychologie des primitifs d'après Lévy-Bruhl," comes as late as 1930, in *JPs*.

[7] See Essertier, *op. cit.,* pp. 116-122; Claude Lévi-Strauss, "Introduction à l'œuvre de Marcel Mauss," in Marcel Mauss, *Sociologie et anthropologie* (1950; posthumous), pp. ix-lii; Henri Lévy-Bruhl, "In Memoriam Marcel Mauss," *ASo* (1951), pp. 1-4.

[8] Besides his social-psychological and ethnographic interests, the most significant works by Mauss are: "Essai sur le don: Forme archaïque de l'échange," *ASo* (1925) [English translation published by the Free Press, Glencoe, 1954]; "Divisions et proportions des divisions de la sociologie," *ibid.,* 2 (1927).

Fauconnet, finally appeared as a relevant concept thenceforth, not only in philosophical analysis, but also in the examination of facts in ethnographic and historical investigations.

Still another central figure is Celestin Bouglé, who in 1922 published his *Leçons de sociologie sur l'évolution des valeurs*. From 1907 Bouglé occupied a chair at the Sorbonne (history of social economy). He was to become associate director of the École normale supérieure in 1927. A large part of his work had already appeared. Under his influence and that of the book on the evolution of values, Davy in 1926 began his review of the accomplishments of the Durkheimian school. This "little, clear-sighted, and brilliant book," writes Davy *(Sociologues d'hier et d'aujourd'hui,* p. 12), "furnishes a balance-sheet of contemporary sociology." In his address, "Jugements de valeur et jugements de réalité," presented to the International Congress of Philosophy at Bologna in 1911,[9] Durkheim had maintained that values are creations of the social consciousness and that their objectivity rests on this social character. The realm of the ideal is not transcendent, "it is in and of nature."

Bouglé took up these ideas and applied them to various orders of values, notably to the economic, which had always had for Durkheim a repugnant flavor. Economic values are matters of attitude, but these attitudes are imposed, as reflections of values, "in accordance with the structure of society." Values thus understood, he adds, "are the essential object of sociology." Bouglé's book, of course, is only an essay and is not amenable to empirical verification. But it is an impelling and rich essay, which has turned French attention toward the problem of values.[10] However, it is chiefly in the next period that Bouglé's influence was to be felt.

We have already pointed out the breadth of Granet's work between 1919 and 1934. This work, highly esteemed by Sinologists, now enjoys renewed interest among sociologists; this explains the recent reprinting of Granet's articles and reports in the volume *Études sociologiques sur la Chine* (Paris, 1953).

A work that also deserves renewed attention is Albert Bayet's *Le Suicide et la morale* (1923). The author, Professor of Letters (more recently Professor of Sociology) at the Sorbonne, by a careful analysis of classical literature, demonstrates that a society, apart from the simple morality that applies to the broad masses, maintains a divergent morality congenial to the élite. This contribution to the science of morality, which Bayet developed in his *Histoire de la morale en France* (Paris, 1930-1931, 2 vols.), is at the same time a methodological contribution whose larger significance was apparent two years later in *La Science des faits moraux* (1925).

[9] Bouglé himself wrote the preface to the reprinting of this essay, in 1924, in the volume titled *Sociologie et philosophie.*

[10] M. Deat also prepared a thesis on the sociology of values. *La Compréhension des valeurs* (Paris, 1945), by R. Polin, is dedicated to Bouglé's memory.

Maurice Halbwachs produced three works in the period 1919-1930: *Les Origines du sentiment religieux d'après Durkheim* (1924); *Les Cadres sociaux de la mémoire* (1925); *La Population et le tracé des voies à Paris depuis 100 ans* (1928); —not to speak of the *Calcul des probabilités à la portée de tous* (1923) with the mathematician Fréchet. These are quite divergent works, differing from his thesis of 1913, differing in content, method, and basic attitude. They suggest the varied interest and manifold talents and techniques of Halbwachs. This will be even more evident in the following period, for which we shall reserve an overview of his work. At this point his *Les Cadres sociaux de la mémoire* will receive our attention.

The psychological emphasis was new with Halbwachs, but it will be a persistent one, since he often spoke of it to his friends and since his posthumously published papers (he died in a German concentration camp in 1945) contained a manuscript on "Mémoire collective" (published in *L'Année Sociologique,* 50, 1949, pp. 11-177). Halbwachs' intention was to demonstrate that memory, which is taken as a psycho-physiological function, is in reality a psychosocial function. Men do not recollect in their dreams, in the full sense of the term; memory relates only to social life, which supplies the benchmarks and the categories in which memories reside. Consequently, the form and even the contents of an individual's memory are dependent, at least in part, on the social group to which he belongs, and notably to his social class.

This theory was extremely new at that time, dependent, it is true, on current orientations, on individual psychological analysis, or, at most, on literary considerations, rather than on laboratory research or field investigations. It has attracted a good deal of criticism, but it is intimately related to the psychosocial trend—a very strong and varied one—that was popular among partisans of *L'Année Psychologique*. Durkheim, in various places in his works, has discarded the foundations of a social psychology, not only as a theory, but even as a method of analysis and as an ultimate goal for sociology. But one wonders whether a modern analysis of his work, basically so weak in the analysis of social structure, would not judge it as being essentially psychosocial. On such principles the contributions of Davy and Blondel in the *Traité de psychologie,* discussed above, seem to be constructed. Furthermore, the frequent attendance of Granet and Mauss at the meetings of the Psychological Society is especially significant; not only do sociological philosophers maintain that psychological functioning reveals itself in social situations and is deeply affected by those situations; indeed, they recognize the elements of such situations even in the products of individual psychological phenomena, and likewise in the mechanisms of such phenomena. Moreover, Mauss and Granet, an ethnologist and Sinologist respectively, provided concrete and variegated detail for such general theories. Although they were unwilling to use the term *ethnographic psychology,* this concept well expresses their thinking. We can extend this formulation to psychological phenomena in general, without risk of distortion.[11]

Social psychology, or rather ethnographic psychology, as pursued by the *L'Année Sociologique* school, plainly culminates in the work of Lucien Lévy-Bruhl.[12] His basic thesis was that preliterates possess a mental structure different from our own; the former is prelogical and mystical, characterized by indifference to the principles of identity and causality and by devotion to the law of participation and mystical experience. The informational base and problems are the same in both cases; the only difference is in point of view.

Lévy-Bruhl, in the introduction to his last book, states: "In this work, a natural continuation of preceding works, I cannot deviate from the manner of formulating questions or from the general method that I have employed till now." We should perhaps appreciate the fact that, if the first and second volumes were concerned with the general functioning of primitive mentality, as was expressly stated by the author—the first volume from the standpoint of the principle of identity, the second from that of causality—after 1927 he studied this functioning in its application to more specific realms: the soul, the supernatural and nature, myths, mystical and symbolic experiences. We should also note, perhaps, that his terms become blurred, that he writes more and more of "functions" and less of "structures," and that the "laws of thought" give way progressively to "mental habits." But it is questionable how much there is that is new in the essential ideas of this well-written, clearly thought-out work.

This impression is not entirely justifiable, however, for his thinking was developing. Progressively, Lévy Bruhl's thought evolved, and as he himself wrote with brutal honesty in his *Carnets:*

> I had begun by postulating a primitive mentality different from ours . . . and I found myself hard put to it to explain the similarities between this mentality and ours. . . . I had after all only discovered parallels. . . . This was a position I had never been able to defend, one that was untenable in

[11] The principal social-psychological contributions of the two writers are as follows: Mauss: "L'expression obligatoire des sentiments," *JPs* (1921), pp. 425-434; "Salutations par le rire et les larmes," *ibid.* (1922); "Rapports réels et pratiques de la psychologie et de la sociologie," *ibid.* (1924); "Effet physique chez l'individu de l'idée de mort suggérée par la collectivité," *ibid.* (1926); "Les techniques du corps," *ibid.* (1936); "Une catégorie de l'esprit humain: la notion de personne, celle de 'moi,'" *Journal of the Royal Anthropological Institute* (1938). Granet: "Le langage de la douleur d'après le rituel funéraire de la Chine classique," *JPs* (1922); *La Pensée chinoise* (Paris, 1934).

[12] His most important works include: *La Morale et la science des mœurs* (1893); *Les Fonctions mentales dans les sociétés inférieures* (1910); *La Mentalité primitive* (1922); *L'Âme primitive* (1927); *Le Surnaturel et la nature dans la mentalité primitive* (1931); *La Mythologie primitive* (1935); *L'Expérience mystique et les symboles chez les primitifs* (1938). In 1949, ten years after his death, his private diary of scientific reflections, *Carnets,* was published, edited by Maurice Leenhardt, in *CIS,* 6 (1949).

> the long run. In restricting myself to discussing mental habits, I took refuge in a circular position. But the thesis thus embroidered is no longer defensible (p. 131).

In reality, he had not thought clearly; he had missed a portion of the truth:

> I have always felt that there was something inadequately distinct in the manner in which I described the world of myth (p. 80). . . . What I had never seen at all when I spoke of participation in mental functions was that it is tightly linked with the representation of the world of myth (p. 157). . . . From a strictly logical viewpoint, no essential difference is established between primitive mentality and ours (p. 70).

Indeed, it is Leenhardt who notes the passage in which (according to Lévy-Bruhl) the entire problem should be reversed: the inquiry should be not how participation is explained, but, on the contrary, how the mind has freed itself from judging everything from the standpoint of participation. The most trenchant criticism of Lévy-Bruhl thus came from his own pen.

But what is quite apparent today was not so between 1919 and 1930. By 1930 Essertier could write: "The importance of a theory depends on the current of ideas that it provokes and the works it inspires. In this regard, Lévy-Bruhl's theories occupy the first rank in contemporary thought" (p. 60). These lines are incontestably apt, Lévy-Bruhl, more than any other writer, impressed upon philosophers, psychologists, and the entire educated public a doubt as to the universality of human intelligence, thus initiating the problems of a social psychology.

The preceding survey was limited to the leaders; however, it is quite in accord with the results of our initial quantitative analysis. This first period is not only marked by humanistic features (i.e., philosophical or scholarly); it is further distinguished by the fact that the great majority of its publications are precisely those of the leaders. Following World War I, French sociology re-formed its ranks of survivors. But it recruited few new investigators. We can indeed assert that there is almost no other name to be cited that had not already appeared in previous bibliographic listings. Undoubtedly, despite the losses due to the war, the period was a prosperous one for sociology. But sociology had not sufficiently prepared for the future From 1930 on, we sense the absence of a breeding-ground for sociologists. The features of the next period, which we can fairly call transitional, will be largely understood by reference to this situation.

The Transitional Period: 1930-1944

The second period of French sociology did not begin under the best of auspices. Difficulties were great in 1918: many men had died, institutions were either disorganized or destroyed. At least the survivors returned; they resumed their work, finished incomplete jobs, and prepared their overdue publications. Even the dead left their heritage; that of Durkheim was considerable, for it richly contributed to the work of the following decade.

In 1930 the situation was even more serious. *L'Année Sociologique* had disappeared for the second time. Many of the leaders who epitomized the preceding period slackened or halted their production. Davy, for example, branched out toward administration of secondary instruction in philosophy—as inspector general. Fauconnet prepared for retirement without publishing anything further. Mauss and Granet reduced their rate of publication to a third of what it had been in the preceding period. If we except the cases of Bouglé and Halbwachs, which had different features to which we shall return, we find that scarcely anyone except Lévy-Bruhl maintained his level of activity. He continued, and even tended to accelerate, the progressive publication of his monumental work. But the strength of this work was inwardly sapped by the anxieties revealed in his *Carnets*. To anyone who examined the profession around 1930, French sociology (and here we refer to personal recollections) gave the impression—by contrast with the enthusiasm that animated young sociologists around 1900 or the atmosphere of abundance that could be sensed around 1920—of labored breathing, if not of exhaustion.

What is still more serious, we can reproach these leaders, whose first generation of students had been decimated by the war, for not having sought to replace it—or, in any event, for not having succeeded, if they did try—and for being more concerned with producing works than with recruiting workers. Advanced instruction in sociology itself remained very limited. Doubtless on the primary level, or rather in the training of its teachers, Durkheim and his associates had executed an important institutional reform, thereby establishing basic instruction in sociology. Between 1920 and 1930 there was a veritable efflorescence of handbooks, which Davy cites, not without pride, in his article in *The Monist* (cf. *Sociologues d'hier et d aujourd'hui*, p. 23) and likewise Bouglé in *Les Sciences sociales en France: Enseignement et recherche* (1937), p. 19, foot-note 2.[13] But secondary-school instruction gave

[13] The opponents of Durkheim, and particularly the Catholics, read political motives into this reform. Bouglé cites the opinion of one of these: "The obligation of teaching M. Durkheim's sociology in two hundred normal schools of France constitutes the gravest national danger our nation has encountered in a long time."

sociology a farcical position as an optional subject to which were devoted no more than six lectures during the last year of study. On the university level, the teaching of sociology had attained only an extremely circumscribed place in the curriculum of philosophy students; it was dubiously linked with ethics, and in the pursuit of a certificate of higher studies was valid only for the general degree. Moreover, this latter diploma was only offered in a very small number of universities.[14] As for organization of research, it was simply non-existent. The French Institute of Sociology was only a sort of academy; nowhere was there a research laboratory.[15]

Consequently, at the beginning of and during a good part of the transitional period 1930-1944, no one in France, literally no one, replaced the leaders of the preceding era. The only newcomer was a foreign philosopher who arrived with a collection of already significant works on ethical, juridical, and political theories—Georges Gurvitch. His writings in French[16] were cautiously received by the legal theorists connected with *L'Année Sociologique*. This group, relatively closed to outsiders, evidently placed obstacles in the path of any revival. Gurvitch nonetheless was placed in charge of the sociology program at the Faculté des Lettres at Strasbourg and published several important works before World War II.[17]

We may well wonder how the French school of sociology was able to survive this period. The answer is in great measure external conditions and the emerging role of related disciplines. The latter for the most part enabled a faltering sociology to weather this transitional period.

We should emphasize that collaboration between the sciences of man, which became obvious after 1930, was not new. It was in fact characteristic of the social sciences in France. Durkheim and his group had, in effect, always believed that sociology was not a separate science; the social sciences constitute a family whose various members mutually complement one another. These ideas pervaded the article "Sociologie et sciences sociales," which he wrote with Fauconnet for the *Revue Philosophique* in 1904. They

[14] Aron, in his chapter on "Sociology" in *Les Sciences sociales en France* (pp. 27-28), emphasizes the inadequacy of this instruction as well.

[15] Consequently, research is rare among students. In 1937, Aron could find only two cases in which advanced diplomas were awarded for empirical inquiries: Polin, *Les Coopératives en Tchécoslovaquie* (Paris, 1934) and Stoetzel, *La Publicité* (unpublished). See Aron, *op. cit.*, p. 29 and footnote 1.

[16] See his *L'Idée du droit social: Notion et système du droit social, histoire doctrinale du 17e jusqu'à la fin du 19e siècle* (Paris, 1931); *Le Temps présent et l'idée du droit social* (Paris, 1931); *Droit naturel ou droit positif intuitif* (Paris, 1933); *L'Expérience juridique et la philosophie pluraliste du droit* (Paris, 1935). For criticism of some of this work, see René Maunier, review of *L'Idée du droit social*, *AS* (1935), pp. 102-105; and J. Ray, review of *L'Expérience juridique, ibid.* (1937), p. 67.

[17] These include *Morale théorique et science des mœurs* (Paris, 1937); "Essai d'une classification pluraliste des formes de sociabilité," *AS* (1938), pp. 1-48; *Essais de sociologie* (Paris, 1938); *Éléments de philosophie juridique* (Paris, 1940).

are found in the treatise by Mauss, "Division et proportions des divisions de la sociologie," which appeared in *L'Année Sociologique* (1927). In 1930 Essertier, describing French sociology, devoted one fourth of his book to the "mental sciences." He reviewed the contributions to sociology of the linguists, geographers, historians, legal thinkers, and economists, pleading lack of space for omitting the ethnographers, historians of religion, literature, and the arts, technologists, folklorists, etc. In the same spirit, in his *Bilan* (1937) and also in the two symposia that he edited in the same year, Bouglé closely linked with sociology the various disciplines that have traditionally comprised the family of mental sciences in France.

A good example of this contribution is the work of François Simiand, who reached his height of productive power during the period under study with the monumental work *Le Salaire: L'Evolution sociale et la monnaie* (1932, 3 vols.). Simiand (1873-1935), an assistant professor of philosophy but quite early oriented toward economics, was an early collaborator on *L'Année Sociologique* and more than once broke lances for his sociological friends, notably against the historicist historians.[18] His earliest works, "Études sur le prix du charbon en France au XIXe siècle," *L'Année Sociologique,* 5 (1902) and *Le Salaire des ouvriers dans les mines de charbon en France* (1907) were models of empirical analysis, entirely based on statistical material that unrelentingly discriminated, among the ingenious a priori hypotheses of previous economists, those that were verified from those that were only probable.

The same exacting method produced, after almost thirty years of research, the work *Le Salaire: L'Evolution sociale et la monnaie*. We are reminded of the general implication of this investigation, expressed in a provocative fashion in an oft-cited passage at the beginning of the work:

> What is in the nineteenth and twentieth centuries the cause of the rise in wages and, more broadly, of a generally favorable orientation toward economic development entirely, is not the structure of the economic system, not economic freedom, not technological change, not capitalism or socialism; it is the discovery and exploitation of the gold mines of California, the Transvaal, and the Klondike. And furthermore, at the beginning of the nineteenth century, as in the second and third decades of the twentieth, it is what we commonly designate as monetary inflation.

The attacks launched by Simiand against the a priori economists and against the normative interpretations (liberal or socialistic) of economic evolution did not displease the sociologists. They likewise appreciated writers whose theory of sociological relativism was opposed to a rationalistic absolutism—for example, Simiand's demonstration that the law of supply

[18] Cf. his "Méthode historique et science sociale," *Revue de synthèse historique* (1903); "La causalite en histoire," *Bulletin de la société française de philosophie* (1907).

and demand produced its effects only under socially determined conditions and under a well-defined legal structure. Finally, they recognized a genuine member of their group in the writer of the treatise "La Monnaie: Réalité sociale" (*L'Année Sociologique* [1934], pp. 1-86), in which this medium of exchange is viewed as much superior to a simple conventional standard of values, as the expression of the "faith" of a group, of an expectation, a hope, a shared trust, which is by no means a result of explicit agreement or the doings of any specific individual.[19]

The same attitude of sociological relativism, the same concern for placing phenomena in their sociological context, is encountered in this period among a certain number of legal theorists.[20]

In a summary that aimed at complete coverage of related but not purely sociological works accepted by French sociologists between 1930 and 1940, a significant place should be reserved for ethnography and human geography. We would certainly include such works as those by Robert Montagne, Labouret, and others.[21] On many points, in fact, it is clear that ethnologists and geographers were a stabilizing force in the critical period of an exhausted sociology. They touched on religious sociology, political sociology, the sociology of the family, urban and rural sociology, and demography. They produced field investigations that sociologists in the strict sense of the term still hesitated to undertake. Their example and their interest in sociology eventually turned that discipline toward direct field research. It is highly significant that in 1936, the armchair ethnologist Lévy-Bruhl, aged seventy-eight, visited Maurice Leenhardt one morning and expressed a desire to board ship for Oceania.

But other symptoms of a renovation of method (and even in interests) among French sociologists were thenceforth visible. In 1934 a new journal appeared, the *Annales Sociologiques* (which was to run to sixteen volumes before publication ceased in 1942), in which one group of articles and the main share of bibliographic reviews were to emphasize more than ever the unity of the social sciences. In 1931 Gabriel LeBras published in the *Revue d'histoire de l'église de France* a note on statistics and religious history containing

[19] Cf. the interpretations of Bouglé: *Bilan de la sociologie française contemporaine*, pp. 127-133, 141-150; and the articles in *AS* (1934), pp. 83-89; (1936), pp. 5-28.

[20] Emmanual Lévy, *Le Fondement du droit* (1935); "Notes rétrospectives," *AS* (1937), pp. 1-5; Jean Ray, *Essai sur la structure logique du code civil* (1926); "La communauté internationale d'après les traités du 16e siècle à nos jours," *AS* (1938), pp. 14-49; Henri Lévy-Bruhl, *Quelques problèmes du très ancien droit romain* (Paris, 1934); *Aspects sociologiques du droit* (Paris, 1955); René Maunier, *Loi française et coutume indigène en Algerie* (Paris, 1932); *Essai sur les groupements sociaux* (Paris, 1929).

[21] Robert Montagne, *Les Berbères et le Maghzen dans le sud du Maroc* (Paris, 1930); Henri Labouret, *Paysans d'Afrique occidentale* (Paris, 1941); Maurice Leenhardt, *Gens de la Grande Terre* (Paris, 1937); *Do Komo: La personne et le mythe dans le monde mélanésien* (Paris, 1947); Pierre Gourou, *Les Paysans du delta tonkinois* (Paris, 1936); and many others.

a questionnaire that he requested priests to fill out for their parishes. At first little heard of, LeBras later stimulated a considerable sociological research movement, at least in religious sociography.

On the other hand, Bouglé, who came to the École normale supérieure as associate director in 1927, had rapidly formed a Centre de documentation sociale. This Center had many functions; for the first time a substantial library of books and sociological journals (French and foreign) was assembled. Conferences initiated by sociologists attracted students of the most varied specialties each semester. Publications were undertaken: a series on "social reformers," a series on the conferences of 1935, 1936, and 1938 (under the title of "Evaluations"), and various other works. Bouglé especially encouraged active research, in France and outside. A small amount of research funds made possible the support of several researchers. Future sociologists consequently had the opportunity of traveling during their enrollment at the school. Thus, as bibliographers or as assistants at the Centre de documentation sociale, Georges Friedmann, Raymond Aron, Robert Marjolin, Raymond Polin, Jean Stoetzel, and others, temporarily released from teaching duties, had the leisure to pursue individual research. Aron went to Germany, Polin to Czechoslovakia, Charron to Roumania, Marjolin and Stoetzel to the United States, Soustell to Mexico, Le Cœur to Morocco.

A whole group of studies and finished works, mainly encouraged and directed by Bouglé himself, was the product of this experimental program operating at the Ecole normale supérieure, or with the group of Bouglé's students at the Sorbonne.[22]

During the same period, 1930-1940, several theses in sociology were prepared under Bouglé's direction.[23] An analysis of these works, several of which are of outstanding merit, would show how French sociology, at the eve of World War II, was already being revivified. The young authors cited in footnote 22 had perhaps forgotten a good deal of Durkheim's contributions. Their major preoccupations, the problems they posed, the methods they employed, even the style—the phraseology, if you will—in which they expressed themselves, indicated a sharp discontinuity with the period 1919-1929, which carried on with great fidelity the successes of the period of the first *L'Année Sociologique*.

What is perhaps most striking is that, being members of the same generation, and almost all of them schoolmates in a very selective school

[22] For example, René Mauduit, *La Réclame* (Paris, 1933); J. Charron, *La coopérative agricole en Roumanie* (Paris, 1934); Raymond Aron, *La Sociologie allemande contemporaine* (Paris, 1935); Robert Marjolin, *L'Évolution du syndicalisme aux États-Unis* (Paris, 1936); Jacques Le Cœur, *Le Rite et l'outil* (Paris, 1939); Jean Stoetzel, "La psychologie sociale et la théorie des attitudes," *AS* (1941) [the latter was delayed by the war].

[23] Raymond Polin, "Les classes moyennes en Belgique," *Inventaires*, 3 (1939), pp. 159-189; Henri Mougin, "Un projet d'enquête sur les classes moyennes en France," *ibid.* (1939), pp. 287-342; and many others.

that could only be entered after several years of a strict, basic, humanistic regimen, the sociologists of the new generation between 1930 and 1940 constituted nothing less than an united group, a coterie, quite opposed to the characteristic features, so often stressed by themselves and their opponents, of the writers on *L'Année Sociologique*. These of the new generation agreed to select, each for himself, his own tasks and not to be burdened with any doctrine or tradition. Thus the masters of the preceding period disappeared from the scene, or greatly diminished their activity; many sympathizers, though drawn from different disciplines, assumed the task of continuing the movement led by Durkheim, notably in the *Annales Sociologiques*. The young ones have shied away from an inspiration that seemed threadbare.

However, the school survived in one author, Maurice Halbwachs, and we can say that his personality dominated the period. Professor at the University of Strasbourg for eleven years and invited to the University of Chicago, Halbwachs had in 1930 important accomplishments to his credit.[24] From the standpoint of method, Halbwachs had always followed two tendencies, if not two temptations. From his contact with Bergson, who was his teacher at the Henry IV secondary school and whom he never ceased to admire, he retained the flavor and the manner of reflective analysis—sometimes introspective, sometimes based on objective fact, but always of a qualitative character.[25]

But still another methodological tendency recurs in Halbwachs' work: the quantitative empirical method, based on numerical items recorded in statistics which must be carefully analyzed. For Halbwachs, a friend of long standing of Simiand, symbolically inherited Simiand's calculating machine. He was likewise a comrade of normal-school days—and a colleague at Strasbourg and Paris—of the mathematician and statistician Maurice Fréchet, with whom he published in 1924 a *Calcul des probabilités à la portée de tous*. This method was already dominant in his law thesis of 1909 on the price of land in Paris. It was the basis of a critical, historical analysis on another thesis: *La Théorie de l'homme moyen: Essai sur Quetelet et la statistique morale*. And it supplied the basic results of his major work on *La Classe ouvrière et les niveaux de vie,* expanded in 1933 in his *L'Évolution des besoins dans les classes ouvrières*. The statistical method inspired Halbwachs, struck by the inadequate

[24] *Les Expropriations et le prix des terrains à Paris, de 1860 à 1900* (Paris, 1909); *La Classe ouvrière et les niveaux de vie* (Paris, 1913); *Les Cadres sociaux de la mémoire* (1925); *Les Causes du suicide* (Paris, 1930). For accounts of Halbwachs' work, see Essertier, *La Sociologie,* pp. 159-162; Jeanne Alexandre, "Maurice Halbwachs," *ASo* (1949), pp. 3-10; and the preface by Georges Friedmann to Halbwachs, *Esquisse d'une psychologie des classes sociales* (Paris, 1955), pp. 9-23. The latter work contains a reasonably complete bibliography on pp. 25-28.

[25] Cf. his *Les Cadres sociaux de la mémoire;* "La psychologie collective du raisonnement," *Zeitschrift für Sozialforschung* (1938), pp. 357-375; and "Mémoire et société," in the posthumously published *La Mémoire collective* (Paris, 1950).

means available to Durkheim in 1897 when he studied suicide, to re-examine the latter's work in 1930. And it launched him, from 1933 onwards, into demographic investigations, one fruit of which was the *Morphologie sociale* of 1938—a rather precious but undeservedly neglected work.[26] Incidentally, Halbwachs founded demography as a genuine field of sociology.

But if, in Halbwachs' work, there seems to be an ambivalence of method—an inability or unwillingness to choose between Bergsonian inspiration and Simiand statistics—his theory is integral: that of Durkheim and his group, with which he was, incidentally, a faithful collaborator. From 1903-1904 onward, he contributed reviews to *L'Année Sociologique*. From first to last, Halbwachs did not vary; human data, regardless of the particular science that assembles such data, were explained only in their social contexts.

But Halbwachs' originality lay not only in the methods he thought he employed in advancing a doctrine so widely held that it finally become commonplace. He was capable of providing a new form for this doctrine which was both brilliant and fruitful. We can judge his real significance for social psychology in the future better than at present. Even the title of his most basic work is deceptive: *Les Cadres sociaux de la mémoire*. It would doubtless be better to have called it "Les Contextes sociaux de la mémoire." For even abstract economic laws, such as the well-known law of supply and demand, operate only under specific historical, legal, and cultural conditions. Even psychological phenomena (memory, reasoning, etc.) are related to very specific social conditions. These social conditions constitute frameworks, if you will, but frameworks that, on the one hand, differ from society to society, from group to group, from class to class, and that, on the other hand, are significant for each society, group, and class. They are consequently, frames of reference, contexts, even *content*. In the time realm, these contexts are history, or rather collective memory; indeed there is a great diversity of collective memories—those of different classes, nations, and religions. Each one retains what suits it: "the events that are lessons" (cf. *La Topographie légendaire,* pp. 190, 205). In the economic sphere, these contexts are needs. Halbwachs' works, we can conclude, furnish a concrete reinterpretation (and—it should be stressed—a completely apolitical one) of the sociology of knowledge.

Thus, thanks to Halbwachs, the period is not only a transition, an interim between two active, fertile eras; it possesses a positive character whose value would later appear more and more imposing. Dying at the Buchenwald concentration camp in 1945, Halbwachs, who had latterly left

[26] In addition, we should mention "Recherches statistiques sur la détermination du sexe a la naissance," *Journ. Société de Stat. de Paris* (1933); "La nuptialité en France, pendant et depuis la guerre," *AS* (1935), pp. 1-46; *La population de la terre et des continents* (Paris, 1937); *Sociologie économique et démographie* (Paris, 1940).

the Sorbonne for the Collège de France, bequeathed to French sociology great but unfinished experiments. [See Howard Becker, "Maurice Halbwachs," *ASR*, 11 (April, 1946), pp. 233-235.]

The Period of Empiricism: 1945-1954

We shall not linger long in the occupation period, 1940-1944; production was then very slight. A small number of works, whose publication had been halted by the opening of hostilities in 1939, finally appeared. But research was considerably hampered by the political situation and the enforced isolation of the nation. Teaching was continued under precarious conditions. Certain sociologists had to seek refuge in foreign lands, or in secrecy. Others lived in the greatest anxiety, at their own risk and peril; thus Maurice Halbwachs was finally arrested in July, 1944, and deported. From 1942 the *Annales Sociologiques* had ceased publication. The French Institute of Sociology became dormant. The Centre de documentation sociale was suppressed, and its library was removed from the École normale supérieure.

The end of hostilities did not bring complete recovery. Le Cœur had been killed on the battlefields of Italy. Henri Mougin was deported by the Germans and died in liberated France just after his repatriation. Other sociologists, returning to France, turned to various activities, notably to political and administrative ones on the national and international scene. All told, it is possible that the ordeals of this war were more deranging for French sociology than those of World War I—that the upheavals it experienced were more profound.

We emphasized above the continuity characterizing the revival of 1919. The renewal of 1945 might better be described in terms of discontinuity. Certainly, everything was not new in this third period, neither personnel nor institutions. Thus Georges Davy, who succeeded Halbwachs, had had, as we have seen, a leading influence for more than twenty years. Albert Bayet, emerging from secrecy at the liberation, resumed his teaching at the Sorbonne. Georges Gurvitch, his successor in 1948, had established a reputation in France dating from 1930, besides teaching at the University of Strasbourg before the war. Georges Friedmann, who would be certain of a position of the first rank in industrial sociology, had begun to specialize in the human problems of work at the Centre de documentation sociale. *L'Année Sociologique* reappeared with many of the names that had graced the *Annales Sociologiques*. The French Institute of Sociology resumed its monthly meetings with initially the same members as in 1939. However, we quickly saw the rise of many new faces, new journals, and new institutions. Especially important, whether personnel and institutions were old or young, the framework and the spirit of sociological investigation became considerably altered.

One characteristic of French sociological work since 1945 is, as we have already noted, the empirical bias, a preoccupation with facts. Of course, the great humanistic and philosophical tradition is not dead; quantitatively, it is reflected in numerous works; qualitatively, the best of these works stand comparison with those of preceding periods. But—and a bibliographical analysis shows this—the greatest vitality lies in another direction. The empirical orientation is of course not totally new—far from it. But today it no longer produces only scattered, illustrative, or secondary efforts. Since 1945, analysis of quantitative materials, individual field research, and group investigations have tended to become the rule and virtually the standard of sociological work. This tendency so deeply imbues the spirit of recent French sociology that, rather than being imposed from above, it is even more active among students than teachers. But we should not think, as one might be tempted to do, that this is a matter of foreign importation. It is in fact the culmination of a trend in national sociology, for a long time repressed, or, better still, implicit, which finally burst through and blossomed into full daylight: it represents the monographic influence of LePlay.

A second feature is that sociological work tends more and more to be a group undertaking. In the period of humanistic sociology, groups of investigators, drawn by bonds of friendship, were able to construct a general theory of the nature of social facts and to do this, to a degree, on the basis of related methods: e.g., the group of the *Année Sociologique,* or that of the *Science Sociale*. To designate such groups, the expression "team" has been used. But a possible confusion of ideas should be avoided; these teams never truly practiced "team research." Collaboration, when it occurred, as in the case of the excellent work by Davy and Moret (*Des Clans aux empires*), led to a collaboration of a literary sort. Each coauthor supplied his own original material, which we can easily distinguish from the collective work. At best, therefore—to use Bouglé's term—it is a matter of *convergence* of individual, original works. The situation is quite different in empirical sociology; collective work is both possible and necessary: possible because, if theoretical works are necessarily systematic, being produced by the creative intelligence of dominant personalities, empirical researches are, on the contrary, basically additive and impersonal; necessary, on the other hand, because, quite different from philosophical or even scholarly works, the scope of empirical work—even on a very narrow point—infinitely exceeds the physical possibilities or the special abilities of a single individual.[27] This second trait of

[27] An example of this is supplied by the two volumes published by the Institut national d'études démographiques, *Le Niveau intellectuel des enfants d'âge scolaire* (Paris, 1950, 1954).

French sociology since 1945 is thus a consequence of the first; in pursuing the path of empirical research, French sociologists are henceforth compelled —no longer occasionally, but constantly—to work in teams.

We can likewise conclude that the third feature of the period derives from the second. Team research requires some minimum of organization. In the past ten years of French sociology, we find a clear tendency toward institutionalization. This feature also provides a contrast between the current situation and previous periods. Until very recently, France boasted no institution dedicated to social research. Even the idea of such an institution remained totally foreign to the nation's sociologists. The French Institute of Sociology, as we have seen, was founded in 1924 as an academic institution. The various handbooks published for students of higher education or for the general public only referred in their headings to "centres de documentation" (libraries) or to teaching establishments.[28] Since the war, on the contrary, various institutions of sociological research, public and private, have appeared in France; and that is evidently a very important factor in the development of that science.

The Centre de documentation sociale of the École normale supérieure, cruelly suppressed by the Vichy régime under the German occupation, has not been re-established. To meet the needs it had satisfied, but with new functions, a Centre d'études sociologiques was set up in Paris in 1946 under the auspices of the Centre national de la recherche scientifique. This organization, endowed with an excellent library, has sponsored exploratory conferences and symposia, the most important of which have been published: *Industrialisation et technocratie* (edited by Gurvitch) appeared in 1949; *Villes et campagnes* (edited by Friedmann) in 1953. Besides, the Centre supports and directs a certain amount of research carried on in teams of varying size.[29]

Another new organization for social research is the Institut national d'études démographiques (INED), founded in 1945 as a public entreprise under the authority of the Ministry of Public Health and Population. Directed by a demographer-economist, Alfred Sauvy, very well equipped materially and suitably financed, INED is well organized. It contains seven research sections employing well-known specialists who pursue their careers there—mathematicians and statisticians, biologists, sociologists, psychologists, historians, economists, etc. The operation of the Institut is systematically interdisciplinary, handling all demographic problems (in the broad sense) concerning metropolitan France and the French Union, as well as foreign

[28] See Celestin Bouglé and Marcel Deat, *Le Guide de l'étudiant en sociologie* (3rd ed.; Paris, 1931); Raymond Aron *et al., Les Sciences sociales en France;* and D. Victoroff and B. Gilles, *Nouveau guide de l'étudiant en sociologie et en morale* (Paris, 1949).

[29] See Charles Bettelheim and Suzanne Frère, *Une Ville française moyenne: Auxerre en 1950* (1950); P. H. Chambart de Lauwe (and twenty-two collaborators), *Paris et l'agglomération parisienne* (Paris, 1952), 2 vols.

problems. Emphasis is placed on impelling, concrete problems. The INED publishes a quarterly, *Population,* and several scientific memoranda (twenty-three have appeared between 1945 and 1954).[30]

The founding of the Institut français d'Opinion publique (IFOP) goes back to 1938. Interrupted by the war in 1939, its operation was resumed after the liberation of Paris (August, 1944). The IFOP is directed by Jean Stoetzel, professor of social science at the University of Bordeaux. It specializes in field investigations, but its realm is not limited to political questions or even to opinions and attitudes. It extends to the whole range of social phenomena related to a particular object of empirical investigation (e.g., in 1948 a series of surveys was undertaken on participation in holiday observances). The IFOP publishes a quarterly review, *Sondages: Revue française de l'opinion publique.*

Among those organizations involved in social research, we should mention the operation, long before the war of 1939-1945, of the Musée de l'homme, of the Institut d'ethnologie, and the Musée des arts et traditions populaires. A sixth division was developed in 1950 at the École pratique des hautes études, by two historians, Lucien Febvre and Fernand Braudel, to keep abreast of social research and to promote the integration of various disciplines. In 1952 an Institut des sciences sociales du travail was founded, under the authority of the Minister of Labor. Sociological research in non-continental French territories has been undertaken by the Office de la recherche scientifique d'outre-mer for the whole French Union; by the Institut français d'Afrique noire (IFAN) for French West Africa and the Cameroons; by the Institut d'études centrafricaines for French Equatorial Africa. The scientific interests of these three organizations touch upon all realms of science; they are not limited to sociology but include all departments of ethnographic and sociological research.

Besides these well-organized establishments, from the administrative and material point of view, we might mention other groups quite active and well-versed in team research. Attached to the Fondation nationale des sciences politiques, for example, there is the "electoral sociology" group led by André Siegfried and François Goguel, the Association française de science politique, the "religious sociology" group led by Gabriel LeBras—all of which have conducted many researches, organized symposia, and sponsored several publications. The Catholic group of *Économie et humanisme,* founded in 1942 under the direction of P. L. J. Lebret, likewise produced commendable works of sociological field-research. Many other private organizations might be mentioned: the SAGMA (Société pour l'application généralisée des méthodes d'analyse); the Centre d'informations et d'études d'économie humaine en Lorraine; la Société française d'économie agricole;

[30] See Andre Mayer, "Cinq ans de travail," *Population,* 6 (1951), pp. 5-26.

the ESNA (Études sociales nord-africaines)—all of which, primarily or incidentally, undertake specific sociological investigations. They generally take their methodological cue from LePlay and in fact constitute his modern descendants.[31]

Since 1945, the new tendencies, whose features and institutional aspects have been analyzed and whose fruits should be outlined, have not, however, erased (or even diminished) the philosophical, humanistic, and scholarly orientation that remains the expression of the greatest French sociological tradition.

Thus the current of ideas and theories of the great social thinkers of the past continues to be the object of new editions and critical, exegetical accounts. Hobbes, Rousseau, Marx, and Proudhon, for example, remain of interest to numerous writers.[32] New editions, translations, and selections point to the durability of this theoretical interest.[33] Moreover, a singular revival of interest in utopias has accompanied this trend.[34]

Besides these critical studies, we find many surveys and "systematic" works. Analysis of the relations between sociology and the other social sciences continually produces new observations and reflections.[35] The interpretation of the present in the light of sociological concepts, often more

[31] Paralleling these developments is the creation or revival of many journals: a third series of *Année Sociologique,* in 5 volumes (1949-1953); since 1946, *Cahiers internationaux de sociologie,* as well as *Population; Sondages,* since 1939, though interrupted by the war; *La Revue française de science politique,* since 1951; *Revue de géographie humaine et d'ethnographie* (brief appearance); *Le Bulletin de l'institut français d'Afrique noire; Bulletin de l'institut d'études centrafricains, hommes et techniques,* since 1945; *Arts et traditions populaires; Économie et humanisme; Cahiers d'outre-mer* (University of Bordeaux).

Among series of sociological works, we might mention: *La Bibliothèque de sociologie contemporaine; Recherches en sciences humaines; La Petite bibliothèque sociologique internationale;* and *Cahiers de la fondation nationale des sciences politiques.*

[32] E.g., Georges Davy, *Thomas Hobbes et J. J. Rousseau* (Oxford, 1953); R. Polin, *Politique et philosophie chez Thomas Hobbes* (Paris, 1953); Georges Gurvitch, *Le Concept de classes sociales de Marx à nos jours* (Paris, 1954); J. J. Chevalier, *Les Grandes œuvres politiques de Machiavel à nos jours* (Paris, 1949); Dolleans, *Proudhon* (Paris, 1948).

[33] Among many others, cf. M. Rubel, *Karl Marx: Pages choisies pour une éthique socialiste* (Paris, 1948); Campanella, *La Cité du soleil,* translated by A. Zévaès (Paris, 1950); R. H. Tawney, *La Religion et l'essor du capitalisme,* translated by O. Merlat (Paris, 1951).

[34] R. Ruyer, *L'Utopie et les utopies* (Paris, 1950); G. Duveau, "Introduction à la sociologie de l'utopie," *CIS,* 9 (1950), pp. 17-41; H. Bergues, "La Population vue par les utopistes," *Population,* 6 (1951), pp. 261-286.

[35] M. Merleau-Ponty, "La Philosophie et la sociologie," *CIS,* 10 (1951), pp. 50-69; M. Dufrenne, "Existentialisme et sociologie," *ibid.,* 1 (1946), pp. 161-171; Roger Bastide, *Sociologie et psychanalyse* (Paris, 1950); A. Cuvillier, "Sociologie de la connaissance et idéologie économique," *CIS,* 11 (1951), pp. 80-111; R. Mehl, "Le Dialogue de l'histoire de la sociologie," *ibid.,* 3 (1947), pp. 137-157; A. Cholley, "Géographie et sociologie," *ibid.,* 5 (1948), pp. 3-20.

ambitiously acute than truly scientific, has also attracted a certain number of writers.[36]

But the contemporary philosophical current is specially manifested in the area of general sociology, and in this field no work is more significant than that of Georges Gurvitch.[37] The original orientation of Gurvitch, it will be recalled, was sociologico-juridical.[38] But his *Essais de sociologie* included a study, "Les Formes de la sociabilité," which returned to the subject of a previously published work titled "Essai d'une classification pluraliste des formes de sociabilité," *Annales Sociologiques* (1938). This marked a genuine shift in Gurvitch's sociological work, in the direction of concern for basic concepts and methods, from which he has not substantially deviated.

Gurvitch's conception of sociology is that it is the "culminating point" of the science of man. Its concern is the totality of social reality, taken in its multiplex dimensions, in terms of structure and dynamics. Its method is "hyperempirical dialectic"—a dialectic that works toward the continual upsetting of systems in favor of a constantly renewed deepening of problems; an empiricism made indispensable by (1) the impossibility of knowing facts other than by constantly renewed experience and by (2) the need of choosing between various logical procedures of investigation.[39]

The results of this approach are presented especially in the form of a complicated typology constructed in several dimensions. Social pluralism or diversity manifests itself, horizontally in various forms of sociability, vertically by social layers or levels *(paliers)*. Social reality consists of ten such dimensions: the morphological and ecological exterior; established superstructures; social models or ideals; approved collective behavior; social roles; collective attitudes; social symbols; creative behavior; collective values and ideas; collective circumstances and actions. The forms of sociability are in reality the first of three distinct kinds of social types. The first type is abstract, really microsociological; and since it is based on eight criteria (such as the informal or formal character of sociability, the fact that it derives from partial fusion or partial opposition, etc.), we can therefore construct a very complex table of the forms of sociability—as has been done many times

[36] J. Monnerot, *Sociologie du communisme* (Paris, 1949); Charles Morazé, *Essai sur la civilisation d'occident* (Paris, 1950); Raymond Aron, *Les Guerres en chaîne* (Paris, 1951), and *L'Opium des intellectuels* (Paris, 1955).

[37] However, there are other important works in this field. Cf. J. Monnerot, *Les Faits sociaux ne sont pas des choses* (Paris, 1946), which employs ideas developed by Aron in his thesis of 1938; Roger Caillois, *Quatre essais de sociologie contemporaine* (Paris, 1951).

[38] This interest was not later abandoned. See his *Éléments de sociologie juridique* (Paris, 1940); *Sociology of Law* (New York, 1942); *La Déclaration des droits sociaux;* and "La Magie et le droit," in *Essais de sociologie* (Paris, 1938).

[39] Cf. his "Microsociologie et sociométrie," *CIS,* 3 (1947), pp. 24-67; "L'Hyper-empirisme dialectique: Ses applications en sociologie," *ibid.,* 15 (1953), pp. 3-33; *La Vocation actuelle de la sociologie* (Paris, 1950).

by Gurvitch. But on the other hand, we must recognize two other social types: groupings, which are distinguished with the help of fifteen criteria; and global structures, whose typology results from eight criteria.

Most recently (1955), this great exercise in taxonomy has finally produced some results proclaimed under the title *Déterminisme social et libre arbitre,* dating from 1938, an outline of which appeared in 1951 as "Les Degrés de la liberté humaine" (*Cahiers internationaux de sociologie,* 1951, pp. 3-20). It is a powerfully integrated work, finally entitled *Déterminisme social et liberté humaine* (Paris, 1955). Here Gurvitch for the first time finally attempts the analysis of historical societies by studying the forms and the possibilities of human liberty in a selected number of broad social structures of various types.

Outside general sociology, the philosophical, humanistic, and scholarly orientation is represented in numerous forms, in which there frequently reappear the methods and traditional concerns of prewar French sociology: the sociology of education, sociology of the family, sociology of law, criminology, sociology of language, sociology of art, and sociology of international relations.[40] But we should remark that in these very areas several writers are already turning away from abstract philosophizing and library research for more direct investigation—sometimes even to field research.

Of all the characteristic features of modern French sociology, which is marked as we have said by empiricism, team research, and institutional organization, the most typical is perhaps that which has given rise to a spectacular flourishing of research in urban and rural sociology. In urban sociology, the most important studies are those of the group directed by P. H. Chombatt de Lauwe on Paris (de Lauwe *et al., Paris et l'agglomération parisienne,* 1952, 2 vols.). The first volume undertakes to describe, analyze, and explain the "social space of a great city"—that is, the relation between the land and the location of various social, economic, demographic, and cultural phenomena. The second volume discusses research methods, especially statistical and cartographic types.[41]

For the historian of French sociology, these urban investigations seem especially interesting. As in the parallel studies in rural sociology, and like-

[40] René Hubert, *Histoire de la pédagogie* (Paris, 1949); H. Marrou, *Histoire de l'éducation dans l'antiquité* (Paris, 1948); Jean Bourgeois, "Le mariage, coutume saisonnière," *Population,* 1 (1946), pp 623-642; Jacques Desforges, *Le Divorce en France* (Paris, 1947); J. C. Laurent, *Quelques réflexions sur les causes de divorce* (Paris, 1949); Robert Progent, "Évolution des idées sur la famille," *Population,* 7 (1952), pp. 395-404; R. Savatier, *Les Métamorphoses économiques et sociales du droit civil d'aujourd'hui* (Paris, 1948); Henri Lévy-Bruhl, "Esquisse d'une théorie des sources du droit," *ASo* (1953), pp. 3-33; J. Chazal, *L'Enfance délinquante* (Paris, 1953); Gaston Bouthoul, *Les Guerres: Éléments de polémologie* (Paris, 1951).

[41] Other studies include: Charles Bettelheim and Suzanne Frère, *Une Ville française moyenne: Auxerre en 1950* (Paris, 1950); J. Laurent, *Grenoble d'hier et d'aujourd'hui* (Grenoble, 1948); Jean Gouhier, *Le Mans au milieu du 20e siècle* (1953).

wise in some studies in sociology of religion, they represent a convergence of trends and influences that is specifically national, despite the occasional allusions to foreign schools: the descriptive method of LePlay, the interests of the French geographic school, the borrowing of ethnographic techniques. We should point out that almost none of the cited authors can be referred to a "classical" sociological group (i.e., connected with philosophy). They are sometimes investigators trained by the Musée de l'homme, sometimes geographers, or more or less descendants (disciples) of the "social-science" school.

But these urban monographs do not exhaust the range of recent work on urban sociology in France. A more extensive study would demonstrate that this field is quite diversified. Detailed investigations, for example, on living patterns in cities, on location of professionals, on religious segregation, are numerous.[42] Stanislaus Korzybski, who refers to Simiand and Halbwachs, has made a specialty of statistical-mathematical studies of urban population. The specific delimination of the concept "urban agglomeration" has stimulated various works by statisticians.[43] Geographers and historians, for their part, have made an important contribution to urban sociology, within their own spheres.[44] This whole collection of studies has made modern French urban sociology a complex, energetic field of endeavor.

Rural sociology is no less flourishing since the war's end; we find the same convergence of ethnographic, geographic, and monographic trends (in the style of LePlay) in field research. Some works are strictly geographic or ethnographic; others are historical, or even demographic; some are technological, analyzing the economic and political aspects of rural life and its social problems.[45] The conference organized by Georges Friedmann at the

[42] J. Stoetzel, "Une étude des budgets-temps de la femme dans les agglomérations urbaines," *Population,* 3 (1948), pp. 47-62; J. Daric, "La localisation de quelques professions libérales dans Paris et le departement de la Seine," *ibid.,* 8 (1953), pp. 555-578; Michel Roblin, *Les Juifs de Paris: démographie, économie, culture* (Paris, 1952).

[43] Korzybski, "Le Peuplement des grandes agglomérations urbaines: Londres et Paris aux 19e et 20e siècles," *Population,* 7 (1952), pp. 485-520; Edouard Benard, "Contribution à l'étude des agglomérations françaises," *ibid.* (1952), pp. 95-108; Paul Vincent, "Liste des agglomérations françaises de plus de 5,000 habitants par ordre d'importance décroissante," *ibid.* (1952), pp. 531-536.

[44] G. Chabot, *Les Villes* (Paris, 1948); P. George, *La Ville: Le Fait urbain à travers le monde* (Paris, 1952); Pierre Lavedan, *Histoire de l'urbanisme* (1941); Louis Chevalier, *La Formation de la population parisienne au 19e siècle* (Paris, 1949).

[45] L. Bernot and R. Blancart, *Nouville: Un Village français* (1953); J. Garavel, *Les Paysans de Morette* (Paris, 1948); Daniel Faucher, "Géographie agraire," in A. Cholley (ed.), *Géographie économique et sociale* (Paris, 1949); A. Dauzat, *La Vie rurale en France* (Paris, 1950); I.N.E.D., *Dépeuplement rural et peuplement rational: Six enquêtes locales* (Paris, 1949); André Ramus, *Vie paysanne et technique agricole* (Paris, 1952); Ange-Larribe, *Situation de l'agriculture française: 1930-1939* (2nd ed.; Paris, 1945); Louis Chevalier, *Les Paysans* (Paris, 1947); Henri Lefebvre, "Problèmes de sociologie rurale," *CIS,* 6 (1949), pp. 78-100, and "Les Classes sociales dans les campagnes," *ibid.,* 10 (1951), pp. 70-93.

Centre d'études sociologiques in 1951, which resulted in an important publication—*Villes et campagnes: Civilisation urbaine et civilisation rurale en France* (Paris, 1953)—indicates the extraordinary interest held by various branches of the social sciences in the problems of urban and rural sociology of the past ten years.

But we must emphasize that these areas are not the only ones in which we can observe fruitful collaboration between sociology and other disciplines in France. Indeed, many works officially labeled otherwise could well bear the sociological stamp. This is notably the case in human geography. Bouglé had already noted this in 1935 in his *Bilan* (Chap. 3, p. 61). He argued, it is true, for maintaining the identity of the two sciences; this was also the position tenaciously held by some geographers, who spoke of the "menace" that sociology held for them.[46] If, however, we disregard all doctrinal discussion, we can show that many geographic investigations easily find their place in a sociological bibliography and are accepted by sociologists.[47]

Ethnology is still more closely linked with sociology, if that is possible. A work like Lévi-Strauss' *Les Structures élémentaires de la parenté* (Paris, 1949), for example, constitutes nothing less than a general sociological theory of marriage. *Ethnologie de l'union française,* by A. Leroi-Gourhan and J. Poirier, presents a summary of our knowledge of native societies in French overseas territories. Sociology would particularly claim the later work of the lamented M. Leenhardt, and notably his *Do Kamo: La Personne et le mythe dans le monde mélanésien* (Paris, 1947), as well as the findings of Marcel Graule on the thought and secrets of the Dogons of the French Sudan. These have truly revived in France important conceptions of the cosmogony and metaphysics of the "primitives."[48]

Of course, these do not exhaust the list of recent contributions of ethnology to sociology. In particular, we might briefly mention the numerous works of the staff of the Missions du musée de l'homme in Paris, the Institut des hautes études marocaines in Rabat, the IFAN, the IECA (Institut d'études centrafricaines) in Brazzaville, or of independent researchers. They deal with ethnic groups, demography, rural–urban sociology, and political sociology. In some cases, they contain general descriptions of civilizations with a growing emphasis on the interconnections between cultures.[49] Finally, we

[46] Cf. Maurice LeLannou, *La Géographie humaine* (Paris, 1949), p. 25.

[47] The monumental work of Max Sorre, *Les Fondements de la géographie humaine* (2nd ed.; Paris, 1947, 1948-1952), 3 vols., must certainly be cited; as well as the numerous works in the *Collection de géographie humaine,* edited by P. Deffontaines; and Jean Gottmann, *La Politique des états et leur géographie* (Paris. 1952).

[48] See especially M. Griaule, *Dieu d'eau* (Paris, 1948).

[49] I. Dugast, *Inventaire ethnique du sud-Cameroun, Mémoires de l'IFAN* (Douala, 1949); Marcel Soret, *Démographie et problèmes urbains en A. E. F.* (Brazzaville, 1954); P. Mercier *et al., L'Agglomération dakeroise* (Dakar, 1954); R. Delarozière, *Les Institutions politiques et sociales des populations dites Bamiléké* (Douala, 1950); D. Paulme, *Les Gens du Riz:*

must underscore the reappearance of a research interest in folklore, oriented toward a very general philosophy of civilization and at the same time toward metropolitan ethnography, under the direction of such men as Georges-Henri Rivière, André Varagnac, and M. Maget.[50] It has found a new locus of expression in the quarterly review, *Arts et traditions français* (since 1953).

We cannot end this section without stressing the philosophical as well as the methodological import of this development in rural and urban studies in modern French sociology. They signify that, more or less dimly, sociologists are conscious of the importance of the concept "the situation" in the interpretation and even the description of social phenomena. Consequently, we can see the relevance of these investigations to the increasingly numerous studies that deal with situations involving age and sex factors.[51] Although it might be premature to speak of distinct fields labeled the "sociology of age" and the "sociology of sex," it does not seem foolhardy to foresee the formation of these two new disciplines within French sociology.

Several divisions of sociology have, since the war's end, taken a new turn that insures a genuine rebirth. This is already noticeable in certain aspects of economic sociology. Doubtless, the break with tradition is not complete; the classics of political economy, to begin with, continue to interest sociologists and are reviewed favorably in the sociological journals. Another evidence of continuity with preceding periods is the abiding interest in François Simiand.[52]

However, it is in the realm of production and labor that economic sociology in France has developed most. A cardinal phase of research concerns technology. This is no new interest in France; it goes back to Alfred Espinas, who was among the first to establish sociology as a science and an ideology (cf. *Les Origines de la technologie,* 1897). But recent investigations are

Kissi de Haute-Guinée (Paris, 1954); M. Cardaire, *Contribution à l'étude de l'Islam noir* (Douala, 1949); P. Mercier, "L'Affaiblissement des processus d'intégration dans les sociétés en changement," *Bulletin IFAN,* 16 (1954), pp. 143-166.

[50] Andre Varagnac, *Civilisation traditionnelle et genres de vies* (Paris, 1948); *De la Préhistoire au monde moderne* (Paris, 1954); M. Maget, *Guide d'étude directe des comportements culturels* (Paris, 1953).

[51] Jean Daric, "Vieillissement de la population, besoins et niveau de vie des personnes âgées," *Population,* 7 (1952), pp. 27-48; E. Peritz, "La Jeunesse dans la population active de la France," *ibid.* (1953), pp. 527-554; Jean Stoetzel, "La Sociologie des âges" (lectures at the University of Bordeaux, 1946-1947); Jean Daric, *L'Activité professionnelle des femmes en France* (Paris, 1947); Institut français d'opinion publique, "La Psychologie politique des femmes," *Sondages* (1952); Maurice Duverger, *La Participation des femmes à la vie politique* (Paris, 1955).

[52] Jean Marchal, *Cours d'économie politique* (Paris, 1950); Robert Mosse. *La Monnaie* (Paris, 1950); Robert Marjolin, *Prix, monnaie et production* (Paris, 1941); J. Aubert, *La Courbe d'offre* (Paris, 1949); B. V. Damalas, *L'Œuvre scientifique de François Simiand* (2nd ed.; Paris, 1947); Charles Morazé, "Essai sur la méthode de François Simiand," in *Mélanges d'histoire sociale* (1942), pp. 5-24 and (1943), pp. 22-42.

a great deal more exact and specialized, particularly dealing with agricultural techniques and animal husbandry, and physical and industrial techniques in the West and among preliterates.[53] A complementary aspect of technology is the social organization of the human factors in production. The sociology of work and the professions has stimulated many investigations.[54] We can logically include here works on the sociology of social classes (so closely related to professional differentiation, at least in the West) and the allied problems of social mobility.[55]

One specific branch of the sociology of work has attracted great interest in France: what is commonly called "industrial sociology." This involves on the one hand historical, geographic, and monographic description; on the other, problems of organization and technology.[56] But the most substantial application of research and thinking has been to human relations in industrial enterprises, and to industrial society in general. In this regard, we cannot overestimate the role of Georges Friedmann during the past twenty years. Industrial work, which was traditionally viewed as a technical datum, involves in reality—as we have lately come to discover—psychological aspects that are in turn determined by sociological factors. Modern industry reflects a novel milieu by comparison to that of industrial civilization, which we can call a "natural environment." This environment has its norms, but norms cannot be completely external and objective with respect to the situations in which they are applied.[57] Friedmann's work, therefore, leads in a very concrete and yet philosophical manner into the realm of values.[58]

[53] A. L. Guyot, *Origine des plantes cultivées* (Paris, 1942); René Thevenin, *Origine des animaux domestiques* (Paris, 1947); Pierre Ducassé, *Histoire des techniques* (Paris, 1945); Henri Janne, "Notes critiques relatives à la sociologie de la technique," *Revue de l'institut de sociologie* (1952) [Brussells], pp. 532-652; Andre Leroi-Gourhan, *L'Homme et la matière* (Paris, 1943); and his *Milieu et techniques* (Paris, 1945).

[54] Guy Chaumel, *Histoire des cheminots et de leurs syndicats* (Paris, 1948); Raymond Gaudriault, *L'Organisation des travaux administratifs* (Paris, 1949); Pierre Naville, *La Vie de travail et ses problèmes* (Paris, 1954); Michele Aumont, *Femmes en usine: Les Ouvrières de la métallurgie Parisienne* (Paris, 1953).

[55] A. Touraine, "Classe sociale et statut socio-économique," *CIS,* 11 (1951), pp. 155-176; R. Montagne (ed.), *Naissance du prolétariat marocain* (Paris, 1952); Françoise Bouriez-Cregg, *Les Classes sociales aux États-Unis* (Paris, 1954); M. Bresard, "Mobilité sociale et dimension de la famille," *Population,* 5 (1950), pp. 533-566; Maurice Halbwachs, *Esquisse d'une psychologie des classes sociales* (Paris, 1955).

[56] B. Gilles, *Les Origines de la grande industrie métallurgique en France* (Paris, 1948); Charles Leger, *La Democratie industrielle et les comités d'entreprise en Suède* (Paris, 1950); Georges Brunerie, *Organisation et réorganisation des entreprises* (Paris, 1947); J. P. Palewski, *L'Organisation scientifique du travail* (Paris, 1948); Georges Gurvitch (ed.), *Industrialisation et technocratie* (Paris, 1949).

[57] Cf. Georges Friedmann, *Problèmes humains du machinisme industriel* (Paris, 1946); "De quelques incidences psychologiques, sociales, et morales dans l'évolution contemporaine des métiers industriels," *ASo* (1949), pp. 529-577.

[58] Cf. the article that the philosopher Canguilhem has devoted to Friedmann's

Political sociology is no less developed and changed. We have already noted above the tenacious interest among French writers in ideological problems, treated either historically or in an expository manner. We must, however, make special mention of Raymond Aron, as much for the abundance and vigor of his work in political philosophy[59] as for the recognition that has just been accorded to him by his recent election to the Sorbonne (1955). Constitutional law, on the other hand, remains a field in which writers are quite active and productive; it quite naturally is marked by studies on political institutions and their operation in various historical periods.[60]

If we can, nevertheless, speak of a revival in political sociology in France (formalized, so to speak, in the creation of the Association française de science politique, and the appearance in 1951 of the *Revue française de science politique*—preceded until 1947 by the *Cahiers de la fondation nationale des sciences politiques*), it is due to three circumstances. The first is a conscientious interest on the part of many writers, many of them legal theorists originally, in an independent discipline, whose problems should be more studies in the field than in legal texts or historical documents. This is of course political science. The very title of M. Duverger's work, published in 1948, might be described as a manifesto. The translation in 1951 of Lasswell and Lerner's *The Policy Sciences* was especially significant in sharpening the concepts in this field. Even the idea of "political science" continues to stimulate thinking and criticism (cf. the article by P. Duclos, "Grandeur, faiblesses, aspirations de la 'political science,'" *Revue française de science politique,* 1954, pp. 156-184). This field has nevertheless been bolstered in the past few years —notably by the efforts of Maurice Duverger, his friends and students—by sufficient studies[61] to warrant a secure place in France in the family of social sciences.

The second circumstance that contributed to the expansion of political sociology has been the sudden infatuation with studies in electoral geography, sometimes conceived as studies in electoral sociology. André Siegfried has, virtually through his own efforts, blazed a trail in this area since 1913; he has

work: Georges Canguilhem, "Milieu et normes de l'homme au travail," *CIS,* 3 (1947), pp. 120-136.

[59] Raymond Aron, *L'Homme contre les tyrans* (New York, 1944); *De l'Armistice à l'insurrection nationale* (Paris, 1945); *Le Grand schisme* (Paris, 1948); *Les Guerres en chaîne* (Paris, 1951); *L'Opium des intellectuels* (Paris, 1955).

[60] Maurice Duverger, *Manuel de droit constitutionnel et de science politique* (Paris, 1948); G. Burdeau, *Traité de science politique* (Paris, 1949-1952), 4 vols.; B. Chapman, *L'Administration locale en France* (Paris, 1954); André Mathiot, *Le Régime politique Britannique* (Paris, 1955); Jean Gottmann, *La Politique des états et leur géographie* (Paris, 1952); Pierre Duclos, *L'Évolution des rapports politiques depuis 1750* (Paris, 1950).

[61] Maurice Duverger *et al., L'Influence des systèmes électoraux sur la vie politique* (Paris, 1950); *Les Partis politiques* (Paris, 1951); *Partis politiques et classes sociales* (Paris, 1955); M. Dogan and J. Narbonne, *Le Français face à la politique* (Paris, 1955); Raymond Fusilier, *Le Parti socialiste suèdois* (Paris, 1954).

unceasingly illustrated in his publications and especially in his unpublished lectures at the College de France the possibilities of a meticulous method based entirely on analysis of local voting trends.[62] Writers have not failed to pay homage to the ingenuity and industry of Siegfried, nor to recognize the worth of his conclusions. However, it seemed that this work would not attract followers. Only since 1947 has François Goguel, a writer who had distinguished himself by an important work in political history, turned toward electoral "geography"; and thanks to the aid of a group of collaborators and students, he has produced one of the most original works in political sociology.[63]

It would, however, be unfair to disregard the third favorable factor: the contribution of public opinion surveys in the political field to the current vitality of political sociology. These surveys have helped in understanding that political life is not limited to statics—that, in addition, the problems of political behavior go beyond the mere act of voting.[64] We can add, before ending this brief review of French political sociology, that international relations—until recently approached from the viewpoint of diplomatic history—has begun to appear as a field marked by analytical observation, J. B. Duroselle constituting the leading figure.[65]

The sociology of religion presents a very similar situation. The historical and scholarly works, ethnographic studies, and ambitious overviews connect recent work with previous eras, at the same time contributing to the progress of our knowledge and theory.[66] But the originality of recent French sociology of religion is elsewhere; it is rather in the sociographic viewpoint, in the determination to avoid reference to religious phenomena in the abstract, in favor of describing detailed practices with numerical exactitude. The

[62] André Siegfried, *Tableau politique de la France de l'Ouest sous la IIIe République* (Paris, 1913); *Une Géographie de l'opinion politique est-elle possible?* (Paris, 1937); *Géographie electorale de l'ardèche sous la IIIe République* (Paris, 1949).

[63] François Goguel, *La Politique des partis sous la IIIe République* (Paris, 1946), 2 vols.; Charles Morazé *et al.*, *Études de sociologie electorale* (Paris, 1948); André Siefried, *Colloque de sociologie electorale* (Paris, 1948); Jacques Fauvet, *Les Forces politiques en France: Étude et géographie des divers partis* (Paris, 1951); Jacques Gouault, *Comment la France est devenue républicaine* (Paris, 1954).

[64] J. Pouillon, "Les sondages et la science politique," *Rev. franc. de sc. polit.*, 1 (1951), pp. 83-106; IFOP, "A la recherche de la 'gauche,'" *Les Temps Modernes*, 10 (1955), pp. 1576-1625; Jean Stoetzel, "Voting Behavior in France," *BJS*, 6 (1955), pp. 104-122.

[65] J. B. Duroselle (ed.), *La Politique étrangère et ses fondements* (Paris, 1954); Raymond Aron, "Enquête d'une philosophie de la politique étrangère," *Rev. franc. de sc. polit.*, 3 (1953), pp. 69-91.

[66] Charles Picard, *Les Religions préhelleniques* (Paris, 1948); G. Bardy, *La Conversion au christianisme durant les premiers siècles* (Paris, 1949); Prosper Alfaric, *Les Origines sociales du christianisme* (Paris, 1947); G. Dieterlen, *Essai sur la religion Bambara* (Paris, 1951); Mircea Eliade, *Traité d'histoire des religions* (Paris, 1949).

pioneer has been Gabriel LeBras, whose first explorations we have already noted. The statements and researches of LeBras have finally had their effect, supported by the work of a priest, Canon Boulard.[67] LeBras has formed a genuine school; and the monographs in sociology of religion now are models for monographs in urban and rural sociology, as well as in electoral sociology.[68]

The role of demography, it will be recalled, had been acknowledged by Durkheim and Mauss since the earliest period of French sociology. But if we except Halbwachs' works, its role had remained unfilled for lack of an occupant. With Alfred Sauvy and his team of coworkers over a decade, demographic studies have become an important division of sociology. By combining the techniques and special interests of various specialties, as previously indicated, the Institut national d'études démographiques has broadened and developed the field and the scope of various classical departments of demography and has genuinely integrated them with sociology. Thus, population questions have been approached in their diversity and complexity: the evaluation of population groups that are not well-known and are difficult to enumerate; growth and depopulation; demographic viewpoints and past population features; national, continental, and world populations,[69] natural increase, birth, death, and marriage rates—all have been considered, beyond the simple statistical facts, as sociological phenomena to be described and accurately explained.[70] They are approached as social facts that have causes and that produce effects—migrations and their consequences, i.e., immigration phenomena.[71]

[67] G. LeBras, *Introduction à l'histoire de la pratique religieuse en France* (Paris, 1942, 1945), 2 vols., and *Études de sociologie religieuse* (Paris, 1955) [contains a bibliography of LeBras' works in religious sociology, pp. xi-xix]; F. Boulard, *Problèmes missionaires de la France rurale* (Paris, 1945), 2 vols., and *Essor ou declin du clergé français* (Paris, 1950).

[68] Mgr. Lucien Gros, *La Pratique religieuse dans le diocèse de Marseille* (Paris, 1945); Paul Schmitt-Eglin, *Le Mécanisme de la déchristianisation* (Paris, 1952); Mme. Jean Perrot, *Grenoble: Essai de sociologie religieuse* (Grenoble, 1953); Robert Anchel, *Les Juifs en France* (Paris, 1946); E. G. Leonard, *Le Protestant français* (Paris, 1953).

[69] P. George, *Introduction à l'étude géographique de la population du monde* (Paris, 1951); L. Chevalier, *Le Problème démographique nord-africain* (Paris, 1947); M. Reinhard, *Histoire de la population mondiale de 1700 à 1948* (Paris, 1949).

[70] Jean Bourgeois-Pichat, *Mesure de la fécondité des populations* (Paris, 1950); S. Ledermann, "La Mortalité des adultes en France," *Population,* 1 (1946), pp. 663-680; P. Vincent, "Vieillissement de la population," *Population,* 1 (1946), pp. 213-244; L. Henry, "Mesure de la fréquence des divorces," *ibid.,* 7 (1952), pp. 267-282.

[71] A. Sauvy, "Besoins et possibilités de l'immigration française," *Population,* 5 (1950), pp. 209-228, 417-434; X. Lannes, *L'Immigration en France depuis 1945* (1953); J. Vernant, *Les Réfugiés dans l'après-guerre* (Monaco, 1954); F. Nourrissier and A. Pillepich, *Enracinement des immigrés* (1951); A. Girard and Jean Stoetzel, *Français et immigrés* (Paris, 1953-1954), 2 vols.

A final remark on the state of social psychology. We have here the perpetual question of whether this discipline should be legitimately included in psychology or in sociology. The historical fact is that in France it has developed first under sociological auspices. The source of the most recent works, in which we recognize the same tendency to prefer empirical investigations (although the philosophical approach has not been completely abandoned), certainly does not contradict this trend.[72] Indeed, the teaching of social psychology, recently begun in the Faculté des lettres of Paris, has been entrusted to a sociologist.

SELECTED BIBLIOGRAPHY

Becker, Howard, and H. E. Barnes, *Social Thought from Lore to Science,* 2nd ed. (New York: Dover Publications, 1952), Chap. 22, "Sociology in the French Language," I., "France and French Switzerland," sections by Emile Benoît-Smullyan (see Table of Contents).

Bastide, Roger, *Sociologie et psychoanalyse* (Paris: Presses Universitaires de France, 1950).

Benoît-Smullyan, Émile, "The Sociologism of Émile Durkheim and His School," in H. E. Barnes (ed.), *An Introduction to the History of Sociology* (Chicago: University of Chicago Press, 1948), pp. 499-537.

Bouglé, Celestin, *Bilan de la sociologie française contemporaine* (Paris: Alcan, 1935).

Gurvitch, Georges, *Essais de sociologie* (Paris: Sirey, 1938).

Halbwachs, Maurice, *Les Cadres sociaux de la mémoire* (Paris: Alcan, 1925).

———, *Les Causes du suicide* (Paris: Alcan, 1930).

Lévi-Strauss, Claude, "French Sociology," in Georges Gurvitch and W. E. Moore (eds.), *Twentieth Century Sociology* (New York: Philosophical Library, 1945), pp. 503-537.

[72] Jean Stoetzel, "Une Étude des budgets-temps de la femme dans les agglomérations urbaines," *Population,* 3 (1948), pp. 47-62; G. Vedel, "Le Rôle des croyances économiques dans la vie politique," *Rev. franc. de sc. polit.,* 1 (1951), pp. 40-55; Jean Maisonneuve, *Psychologie sociale* (1951); Mikel Dufrenne, *La Personnalité de base* (Paris, 1953); Jean Stoetzel, *Jeunesse sans chrysanthème ni sabre* (Paris, 1954).

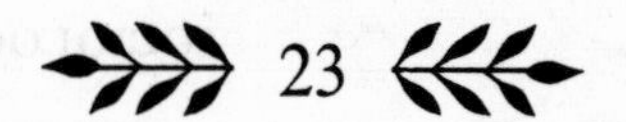

SOCIOLOGY IN GERMANY: SHIFT IN ALIGNMENT*

W. E. MÜHLMANN

A DETAILED HISTORICAL SUMMARY OF GERMAN SOCIOLOGY FROM 1918 to the present has not yet been produced. There are, on the other hand, a number of publications whose goals are either more circumscribed or comprehensive than this, but that can be profitably consulted only with critical reading. Theodore Abel's *Systematic Sociology in Germany* treats only sociological systems (those of Simmel, Vierkandt, Wiese, and Max Weber) and extends only to the middle of the 1920's.[1] Raymond Aron's *Die deutsche Soziologie der Gegenwart* does not fulfill the promise of its title, since it too is concerned only with the sociological systems of the past.[2] The presentation of German sociology that Salomon has written for the collected work *Die Soziologie im 20. Jahrhundert* is also biased. Disregarding the fact that it does not cover present developments, German sociology is too one-sidedly presented as an extension of the argument, pro and con, concerning Hegel and Marx.[3] In all these works, much too much emphasis has been placed upon intellectual-historic and systematic connections, whereas the results of soci-

* Translated by Leon Fannin, University of Wisconsin.

[1] Theodore Abel, *Systematic Sociology in Germany* (New York, 1929). For criticism, cf. Leopold von Wiese, in *KVS*, 8 (1930), pp. 141-164.

[2] Raymond Aron, *Die deutsche Soziologie der Gegenwart,* translated into German by Irving Fetscher (Stuttgart, 1953).

[3] Albert Salomon, "German Sociology," in Georges Gurvitch and W. E. Moore (eds.), *Twentieth Century Sociology* (New York, 1945), pp. 586-614. The same error characterizes the treatment by Franz Oppenheimer, "Tendencies in Recent German Sociology," *Sociological Review* (British), 24 (1932), pp. 1-13, 125-137, 249-260.

ological research receive little or no attention. Sociological bibliographies which take into account the preponderant part of this German literature have been provided by H. Maus and H. Schoeck.[4]

The Culture Area of German Sociology. In attempting to review the contribution of German sociology since the end of World War I, it becomes difficult to decide precisely how this contribution should be delimited. Political borders cannot always be decisive, since they do not coincide with culture areas. Therefore the achievements of Austrian scholars have been mentioned in many cases—not because Austria was annexed in 1938 into the "Great German Reich," but because no cultural and scientific boundary between Germany and Austria has ever existed. German professors often taught in Austria, and Austrians in Germany; and the works of both could as well be printed in Berlin or Leipzig as in Vienna. Many Central European authors preferred to have their works published in the German language, as did, above all, the significant Dutch sociologist, S. R. Steinmetz. In this manner, he contributed for decades to German sociological discussions. Although his influence upon German sociology is not to be overlooked, I have nevertheless largely resisted the temptation to mention his works. The case of Robert Michels (1876-1936), who was German by birth but later became an Italian (he taught in Turin, Perugia, and Rome), is different: his most important works were published in German and they refer so pointedly to German events and figured so prominently in German academic discussions that Michels belongs as much to German academic discussions as to Italian sociology.

The German political emigrants are a special problem. In most cases, they were lost to German sociology after 1933. There are, however, a few individuals to whom the Nazi period caused only an interruption of their participation in German debates. Such was the case of Theodor Geiger (1891-1952), one of the most capable German sociologists in pre-Hitler times. He emigrated to Denmark and became a professor at Aarhus, where he carried out important investigations on social mobility. Soon after the end of World War II, however, he again published works in German (printed partly in Germany), which returned to the problems with which he had been occupied around 1930 in Germany.

The attempt to delimit the contributions to sociology according to countries and national boundaries is, however, generally problematical. It is true, of course, that ethnocentrism, regionalism, and provincialism are evident in scientific endeavor (with the exception of the physical sciences)

[4] Heinz Maus, "Soziologie," *Universitas Litterarum, Handbuch der Wissenschaftskunde* (Berlin, 1955), p. 328; Helmut Schoeck, *Soziologie: Geschichte ihrer Probleme* (Freiburg, 1952), pp. 353-398. In addition there is Hans Proesler (ed.), *Literatur zur Soziologie* (2nd ed.; Nürnberg, 1951), which is very incomplete. The *Jahrbuch für Sozialwissenschaft* has presented, since 1950, bibliographies of the social-science literature.

and that social scientists have trouble in achieving a cosmopolitan perspective even if they wish to do so. Moreover, many sociological problems have a merely practical significance, regionally or nationally delimited; the theoretical interest of a researcher frequently extends no further than the practical significance of the problem with which he is occupied. In this respect it is remarkable that German sociology before 1933 had a comparatively wide horizon. For instance, many American sociologists furnished articles for German periodicals (for example, H. E. Barnes, Howard Becker, R. M. MacIver, W. F. Ogburn, R. E. Park, P. A. Sorokin, and others); one of Sorokin's earliest articles on experiments in altruism was published in 1928 in the *Zeitschrift für Völkerpsychologie und Soziologie* (Vol. IV, pp. 1-10). When Richard Thurnwald in the same periodical arranged a symposium on *Soziologie von heute* (separate publication, Leipzig, 1932), five German sociologists participated (J. Plenge, A. Walther, H. Freyer, F. Tönnies, and Thurnwald himself) and five foreigners (Sorokin, Ogburn, and MacIver of America, Ginsberg of England, and Steinmetz of Holland). But when Thurnwald in 1932 began reorganizing his periodical as a bilingual, German-American organ, and when as editor he included in it articles on the life of the American farmer and on American statistical methods, this was too much "Americanism" for most German sociologists—at that time; it was a premature experiment. There are problems in the social sciences concerning which discussions reach an international level relatively quickly—above all, those that lie more in the area of social history, as for example connections between Calvinism and capitalism, first treated by Max Weber (see the contributions by J. B. Kraus, H. M. Robertson, R. H. Tawney, and others). But there are other problems that are delimited nationally for a long time before it becomes apparent that they are general problems of Western societies at least. There are, for instance, problems of the family, social mobility, social-class structure, industry, mass communications, the assimilation of strangers, and many others.

The Period of the Weimar Republic: 1919-1933

The Construction of Sociological Systems. The era of the Weimar Republic was a "golden age" of sociology in Germany. It can be designated as a period in which theoretical thinking and the inclination toward the construction of comprehensive sociological systems predominated. It was, at the same time, an era of great, imposing personalities who built schools of thought and whose influence continued in effect for a long time. Even today, there are still many sociologists in Germany who designate themselves with a certain pride as students of, for example, Vierkandt or Wiese; and this acknowledgement carries with it a certain charismatic aura.

The Range of Weber's Contributions. The first of these great personalities was undoubtedly Max Weber. Although this extraordinary person died in 1920, his major influence began only in our period, has lasted until today, and will not soon be at an end. His writings on the sociology of religion, social and economic history, general sociology, social policy, and theories of science were first published in collected form after 1920, edited by his widow, Marianne Weber, who also wrote his biography.[5] It has just been announced that there has appeared a new edition of Weber's posthumously published work, *Wirtschaft und Gesellschaft*, edited by Johannes Winckelmann. Having offered evidence that Weber's great work has not hitherto been presented in its authentic arrangement, Winckelmann has attempted to restore this authentic version.

The number of writers who have individually analyzed Max Weber is legion. By far the most valuable works of this kind were those of A. Walther and A. von Schelting.[6] Two articles of Weber's, through which he achieved the most telling results, appeared while he was still alive: "Wissenschaft als Beruf" and "Politik als Beruf" (1919). In the first of these he advocated, as in earlier writings, the thesis of "no value-judgments" *(Wertfreiheit)* in science, which is as pertinent today as it was then, although many scholars seem incapable of maintaining this attitude. The second article can be regarded as the inauguration of political sociology in Germany. Max Weber was a politician himself, but he believed that the teacher should not advocate politics in the lecture hall; this viewpoint is still (or again) prevalent.

Tönnies: Major Concepts in Sociological Analysis. After Max Weber, Ferdinand Tönnies (1856-1936) must be mentioned; he was a professor at Kiel and for a long time president of the *Deutsche Gesellschaft für Soziologie.* Tönnies' main work, *Gemeinschaft und Gesellschaft*, appeared in its first edition as early as 1887, but made a profound impression only in the later editions; the last (the eighth) appeared in 1935.[7] There are few German sociologists who have not been influenced by the dichotomized concepts *Gemeinschaft* and *Gesellschaft*, and even foreign sociologists have been influenced by them, although the terms are *not* translatable in a denotative sense. They reflect *only* a specific German viewpoint of the problems that have been produced since the nineteenth century with the transformation of the old estate society into the modern industrial or class society. *Gemeinschaft* is associated with the family, village life, concord, custom, religion, domestic economy, agriculture, and art; *Gesellschaft* with the large city, the nation,

[5] Marianne Weber, *Max Weber, Ein Lebensbild* (new ed., Heidelberg, 1950).

[6] Andreas Walther, "Max Weber als Soziologe," *JS,* 2 (1926), pp. 1-65; Alexander von Schelting, *Max Weber's Wissenschaftslehre* (Tübingen, 1934).

[7] Cf. also the short and clear exposition by Tönnies: "Gemeinschaft und Gesellschaft," in Vierkandt's *HS* (Stuttgart, 1931), pp. 180-191; also Victor Leemans, *F. Tönnies et la sociologie contemporaine en Allemagne* (Paris, 1933).

convention, politics, public opinion, business, industry, and science. In its social-psychological aspect, "essential will" *(Wesenwille)* corresponds to *Gemeinschaft*, "conscious selective will" *(Kürwille)* to *Gesellschaft*.

There is no doubt that the simplicity of this antithesis, as well as its emotionalized value-connotation, has facilitated its reception in Germany, as with the dichotomized concepts "culture and civilization" and "feeling and intellect." We Germans have a barely concealed inclination for a romantic espousal of the cause of *Gemeinschaft* (culture, feeling) against *Gesellschaft* (civilization, intellect). However, I do not want to imply that Tönnies' distinction is false or worthless; it refers to a structural distinction in the kind of unity among persons; but we should attempt to make the distinction more incisive and to express it in an internationally understandable language.[8] Tönnies himself intrinsically stood on the side of *Gemeinschaft*; he was a Schleswig peasant's son, deeply rooted in a rural environment. In his last work, he attempted to relax the rigid antithesis *Gemeinschaft* and *Gesellschaft* through the introduction of new concepts, but without much success.[9]

The application of these concepts in his great work, *Kritik der öffentlichen Meinung* (Berlin, 1922), was more fruitful. Public opinion, according to Tönnies, is a form of the social will—that form labeled the "conscious selective will." It shares this voluntaristic character with religion, which is also a form of the social will (but of the "essential will"). Common to both is "the inwardly uniting power and the obligatory will, which express themselves often as moral indignation and intolerance against dissenting views." The quasi-religious character of public opinion has not yet been much noticed because it seldom achieves the condensed status of firmer "doctrines"; usually it remains in a much more "fluid" or "airlike" condition. Tönnies analyzes in detail the power factors of public opinion and its role in the civil life of the United States, France, England, and Germany. In this analysis he shows himself not only as a conceptualizer, but also as an incisive thinker. The same is true for his empirical, sociographic works on the problem of social pathology, which have a value quite independent of his theoretical concept-formulations.[10]

[8] Cf. Theodor Geiger, "Die Gruppe und die Kategorien Gemeinschaft und Gesellschaft," *ASS,* 58 (1927). To be sure, Geiger has since disavowed this interpretation of Tönnies; see *Ideologie und Wahrheit* (Stuttgart, 1953), pp. 105-106.

[9] Ferdinand Tönnies, *Einführung in die Soziologie* (Stuttgart, 1931). Cf. the admirable criticism by Georges Gurvitch, *La vocation actuelle de la sociologie* (Paris, 1950), pp. 214-215.

[10] Cf. Ferdinand Tönnies, "Der Selbstmord von Männern in Preussen 1884-1914," *Mensch en Maatschappij,* 9 (1932), pp. 234-254; "Der Selbstmord in Schleswig-Holstein," *Veröffentlichungen der Schleswig-Holsteinischen Universitäts-Gesellschaft,* 9 (Breslau, 1927); Tönnies and E. Jurkat, "Die schwere Kriminalität von Mannern Schleswig-Holstein in den Jahren 1899-1914," *ZVS,* 5 (1929), pp. 26-39. Many of the shorter works by Tönnies have been collected in *Soziologische Studien und Kritiken* (Jena, 1925, 1926, 1929), 3 vols.

Vierkandt and Simmel: Intellectual Heirs of Tönnies. The influence of Tönnies is also perceptible in the theories of Alfred Vierkandt (1867-1953), who was a professor at Berlin. However, Vierkandt relaxed the rigid antithesis of *Gemeinschaft* and *Gesellschaft* by distinguishing between those human relations which are closer to and those which are further from *Gemeinschaft* relations. The second strong influence upon Vierkandt came from Georg Simmel (1858-1918). Although Simmel died before the time with which we concern ourselves here, he has exercised a lasting influence on German sociology.[11] Although purely deductive in his approach, Simmel is unrivaled in the psychological description of the social atmosphere in human relations, in the description of the political "party," of superordination and subordination, of power relations, the relations to strangers, and so on.

Vierkandt profited much from this "atmospheric" social psychology of Simmel, but his thinking underwent profound changes—and here he is different from Tönnies—which were related to his rejection of positivism.[12] This rejection Vierkandt made under the influence of phenomenological philosophy, especially as mediated by Theodor Litt's book, *Individuum und Gemeinschaft* (3rd ed.; Leipzig, 1926), and also, it seems to me, by Max Scheler, although he does not mention the latter so often. The change has been manifested in the second edition of his *Gesellschaftslehre* (1928), in which the essential nature of group life is no longer sought in the "interaction of individuals" but in an "inner unity." Psychologically, Vierkandt joined company with William McDougall, from whom he took over the differentiation of numerous social "instincts." Thus, Vierkandt's sociology is less an original creation than an impressionable syncretism derived from varying contemporary influences. Still, he was a sober, pessimistic, and illusionless thinker, deeply impressed by the preponderant triviality of human motivation. As a teacher he was more liberal than is good for the development of one's own school; however, he at least once succeeded in publishing an organized symposium, the *Handwörterbuch der Soziologie* (Stuttgart, 1931). This work gives a very good cross section of the status of German sociology on the eve of the Nazi era.

Wiese and a Systematic Theory of Sociation. Much more energetic, less changeable, and with more impetus was Leopold von Wiese (born in 1876, professor at Cologne), who held to the basic views of his sociological system of the "theory of social relations" with unchangeable fidelity. He worked

[11] Georg Simmel, *Soziologie: Untersuchungen über die Formen der Vergesellschaftung* (1st ed., 1908; Munich, 1922); and *Grundfragen der Soziologie* (Berlin, 1917). Cf. M. Steinhoff, "Die Form als soziologische Grundkategorie bei Georg Simmel," *KVS,* 4 (1925), pp. 215-259.

[12] Alfred Vierkandt, "Die Überwindung des Positivismus in der deutschen Soziologie der Gegenwart," *JS,* 2 (1926), pp. 66-90.

out his system in the 1920's.[13] His basic concepts are "social relation," "social distance," "attitude," and "situation." All human relations can be reduced to processes of association and dissociation This sounds schematic, and everything therefore depends on whether this schema can be put into operation in sociological research in the empirical world. That this is indeed possible is shown by the discussions on the theory of social relations which took place about 1930 in the *Kölner Zeitschrift für Soziologie* edited by Wiese.[14] We must deal with his work in more detail later.

Freyer and the Historicist Strain. The Leipzig philosopher of culture and sociologist, Hans Freyer (born in 1887), has supplied a very remarkable program rather than a finished system of sociology. He was a student of Wilhelm Dilthey, the epistemologist of the German humanities and social sciences, and his original predilection was (and still is today) less for sociology than for the theory of history.[15] Freyer even today is quite as fond of calling himself a historian as a sociologist. Nevertheless, this involves no detrimental mixture of both fields, but rather an intellectual coexistence on the two levels and a continual dialectical exchange.

In his *Soziologie als Wirklichkeitswissenschaft*, Freyer opened fire on "formal sociology," under which he subsumed not only Simmel but also Wiese. His argument can be best reproduced in his own words: "The fact 'society' with which sociology is concerned is not a multiplicity of relational and structural forms that repeat themselves identically, and that can therefore leave their particular historical situations and be systematized purely as forms. The fact 'society' is much more an *irreversible* succession of total situations, through which the stream of historical life moves."[16] In this argument Freyer overlooks an insight that, to be sure, has only recently been worked out by ethnologists through the comparison of the cultures of different societies: namely, that there are typical forms of temporal processes

[13] Leopold von Wiese, *System der allgemeinen Soziologie als Lehre von den sozialen Prozessen und den sozialen Gebilden der Menschen (Beziehungslehre): I. Teil: Beziehungslehre* (Munich, 1924; 2nd. ed., 1933); *II. Teil: Gebildelehre* (Munich, 1929). An augmented American adaptation was provided by Howard Becker, *Systematic Sociology on the Basis of the* Beziehungslehre *and* Gebildelehre *of Leopold von Wiese* (New York, 1932; 2nd ed.; with a new preface, Gary, Ind., 1950). The number of additional writings in which Wiese has detailed, annotated, and supplemented his system is legion.

[14] I shall mention only the works by Johann Plenge, "Zum Ausbau der Beziehungslehre," *KVS,* 9 (1931), pp. 271-288, 448-493, and "Die Philosophie des 'Wir' als Tiefenbegründung der Soziologie," *KVS,* 11 (1932), pp. 135-138.

[15] Hans Freyer, *Theorie des objektiven Geistes: Eine Einleitung in die Kulturphilosophie* (Leipzig, 1923; 3rd ed., 1934); *Soziologie als Wirtlichkeitswissenschaft: Logische Grundlegung des Systems der Soziologie* (Leipzig, 1930); *Einleitung in die Soziologie* (Leipzig, 1930). Freyer has also published noteworthy contributions to political theory: *Die politische Insel* [*eine Geschichte der Utopien von Platon hin zur Gegenwart*] (Leipzig, 1936); and *Machiavelli* (Leipzig, 1938).

[16] *Soziologie als Wirklichkeitswissenschaft,* p. 67.

which do repeat themselves independently of a distinct place and a distinct time. Thus, temporal sequence is not necessarily unique historical sequence, and irreversibility is not a historical but an evolutionary concept.[17] Freyer's view, therefore, that even the most abstract categories of sociology must be "historicized" to a certain degree cannot yet be convincingly proven.[18] Freyer's historicizing standpoint is also expressed in his conception of sociology itself as a historical phenomenon originating out of bourgeois society's "feeling of the situation." In sociology, "a dialectical event becomes scientific self-consciousness." Real changes and crises each time produce a new phase of social-scientific thought.[19] But if this is so, then it is possible, for instance, that the fascistic "feeling of the situation" of an epoch produces or reflects a fascistic sociology. Freyer himself has not drawn this relativistic conclusion, but others have, successfully intermingling opportunism, ideology, and sociology.

Abortive Sociological Systems: Oppenheimer and Others. The systems or incipient systems of Max Weber, Tönnies, Vierkandt, Wiese, and Freyer are by far the most meaningful in the epoch treated here. Other systems have exercised only a temporary influence, such as that of Franz Oppenheimer (1864-1943), which really presented a particular view of social history,[20] or that of Othmar Spann (born in 1878), a social philosophy influenced by Adam Müller that for some time was not without ideological influence on the romantic program for an organic estate society in Germany.[21] Because of the dozens of sociological "systems" that were produced in Germany at that time, Andreas Walther (professor at Hamburg) raised energetic protests against the "continuing overproduction by system-sketchers who know nothing of their predecessors."[22] Their solipsistic systems also remained without influence in actual research.

The Organization of Sociology. Since sociology in Germany at that time was still not a consolidated body of coordinated activities, its history can be only scantily reproduced in terms of professorial chairs, institutes, periodicals, serial publications, and sc on. It will be sufficient to mention briefly the most important of these.

[17] Cf. in addition, W. E. Mühlmann, "Ethnologie und Geschichte," *Studium Generale,* 7 (1954), pp. 165-177; "Gibt es 'Rück-Entwicklung'?" *Forschungen und Fortschritte,* 26 (1950), pp. 71-74.

[18] Cf. the criticism by Wiese, *System der Soziologie* (1933 ed.), pp. 77-78; and Andreas Walther, "Das Problem einer 'deutschen' Soziologie," *KVS,* 9 (1931), pp. 513-530.

[19] Hans Freyer, *Einleitung in die Soziologie,* p. 32.

[20] Franz Oppenheimer, *System der Soziologie* (Jena, 1922-1929), 4 vols.

[21] Othmar Spann, *Gesellschaftslehre* (3rd ed.; Leipzig, 1930).

[22] Andreas Walther, "Zur neueren Entwicklung der deutschen Soziologie," *ZS,* 91 (1931), p. 348. Still noteworthy "systems" are: Karl Dunkmann (with the collaboration of Gerhard Lehmann and Heinz Sauermann), *Lehrbuch der Soziologie und Sozialphilosophie* (Berlin, 1931); and Max Graf zu Solms, *Bau und Gliederung der Menschengruppen* (Karlsruhe, 1929; Leipzig, 1932).

Sociology was taught at all German universities and at some technical institutes in the 1920's and until 1933, although regularly appointed professorial chairs existed at only a few, and institutes and seminars at fewer still. (Thus, the university of Germany's capital city, Berlin, where Vierkandt occupied a regular chair, had no institute or seminar for sociology.)

German sociologists were organized in the *Deutsche Gesellschaft für Soziologie*, founded in 1910, which held five congresses between 1922 and 1930. Subjects treated at these concerned the nature of revolution (Jena, 1922); sociology and social policy, science and social structure (Heidelberg, 1924); democracy, natural law, the theory of social relations (Vienna, 1926); competition, change, understanding, beginnings of art (Zürich, 1928); press and public opinion, construction of concepts in sociology, sociology of art, and German ethnic subdivisions (Berlin, 1930).[23]

Three periodicals were expressly devoted to sociology:

1. *Kölner Vierteljahrshefte für Sozialwissenschaft,* edited by Christian Eckert, Hugo Lindemann, Max Scheler, and Leopold von Wiese; twelve volumes, 1921-1933. From the third year of publication on, the periodical bore the title *Kölner Vierteljahrshefte für Soziologie* and Wiese was for all practical purposes sole editor.

2. *Zeitschrift für Völkerpsychologie und Soziologie (ZVS)* edited by Richard Thurnwald; nine volumes, 1925-1933. Since the eighth volume the periodical carried the main title *Sociologus* and appeared as a bilingual, German-American organ.

Both periodicals were cosmopolitan in orientation. The Cologne periodical carried a research report on American sociology in the very first number of the first volume, as well as further regular reports on sociology in France, Britain, Belgium, Italy, India, Yugoslavia, and so on. From the beginning, a section on the "theory of social relations" was also included under the leadership of Leopold von Wiese. The *ZVS* had been directed perhaps still more decisively internationally; it had several foreign coeditors (B. Malinowski, W. F. Ogburn, P. A. Sorokin, and S. R. Steinmetz, to whom L. L. Bernard and Edward Sapir were added in 1932). Thurnwald represented an empirical and functional sociology and social psychology. His inclination for American sociology was known and became strengthened through repeated visits in the United States, although his polemic rejection of "speculative" and "philosophizing" German sociology did not always induce comprehension of the American brand.[24] The intermixture of sociology and ethnology and the faulty—if any at all—systematic distinction between the disciplines also worked to the disadvantage of the periodical.

[23] The "transactions" of the first eight German sociologists' sessions have been published in eight volumes (Stuttgart, 1911-1948).

[24] Richard Thurnwald, "Sociology in America: Impressions of a Visitor," *SF*, 11 (1932), pp. 161-175.

In addition, Thurnwald edited the serial publication *Forschungen zur Völkerpsychologie und Soziologie* (fourteen volumes, 1925-1935), which treated such subjects as sociology and psychology of animals, national psychology, social psychology, political sociology, ethnology, and so on.

3. *Archiv für angewandte Soziologie*, edited by Karl Dunkmann; five volumes, Berlin, 1928-1933. Karl Dunkmann (1868-1932) was originally a Protestant theologian and taught sociology at the Technische Hochschule in Berlin.[25] Applied sociology was understood by him primarily as social pedagogy.

The enumeration of these periodicals does not, however, yield a complete picture. Many sociological works appeared in periodicals (economic, social historic, juristic, statistical, and others), of which the most important are the *Archiv für Sozialwissenschaft und Sozialpolitik, Schmollers Jahrbuch,* and the *Zeitschrift für Sozialforschung* (Leipzig, 1932-1933), edited by the Institute of Social Research in Frankfurt/Main, appeared in Germany; the periodical was then moved to Paris, and later still to New York.

The *Jahrbuch für Soziologie: Eine internationale Sammlung,* edited by Gottfried Salomon (three volumes, Karlsruhe, 1925-1927), contained many valuable contributions and should also be mentioned as of great importance.

Empirical Sociology. Empirical sociological research produced most in the fields of social mobility and social stratification—with an emphasis on the problem of social classes—whereas in a few other fields (industrial sociology, ethnological and historical sociology, and others), remarkable individual results were obtained.

Problems of Mobility and Class Stratification. These problems encountered special interest in Germany because a tradition of socialism (of "scientific socialism" also) and a labor movement existed and oriented many sociologists toward Marxism, or at least had influenced them. (It is characteristic that some important research workers began as ardent socialists, only to abandon it more violently later: Sombart, Michels, and Geiger.) Political economists and economic and social historians had begun to analyze the historical foundations that make possible the understanding of our modern industrial capitalistic society.

The greatest influence in this connection was exerted by Werner Sombart (1863-1941), who also produced sociological writings in the narrower sense of the word and played an important role in the *Deutsche Gesellschaft für Soziologie.* His most important works on the history and sociology of capitalism originated in the period before the World War I, but they exercised a powerful effect,[26] undiminished even in a later period. The historical

[25] Cf. Heinz Sauermann (ed.), *Probleme deutscher Soziologie: Gedächtnisgabe für Karl Dunkmann* (Berlin, 1933).

[26] Werner Sombart, *Der moderne Kapitalismus: Historisch-systematische Darstellung des gesamteuropäischen Wirtschaftslebens von seinen Anfängen bis zur Gegenwart* (revised ed.;

and systematic sociological points of view were combined in the presentation and orientation of the material. In any event, the goal sought was not antiquarian and historical, but the understanding of the present and the attainment of directives for social-political activity.

Direct investigations of the social situation of the industrial proletariat had already taken place before World War I. Of these I shall mention only the study of the *Verein für Sozialpolitik*, which treats the selection and adaptation of industrial workers. Max Weber's methodological introduction to these studies and his *Zur Psychophysik der industriellen Arbeit* (1908-1909) must in any case be mentioned in this connection.[27] Thus the ground was well prepared for further studies on the social position and economic environment of the industrial worker.[28]

The New Middle Class. Meanwhile, another problem had advanced into the foreground. Not only did the industrial proletariat, with its rising standard of living, prove more and more open to the attraction and ideology of the "petty bourgeois," by which its revolutionary socialistic impetus was impaired and the Marxist prognoses discredited,[29] but in addition the rise of a new middle class, which consisted chiefly of employees *(Angestellten)*, was also observed. It could be proved that this new "class" expanded faster statistically than the industrial proletariat and that it was about to change decisively the social structure of German society. (It was recognized already at that time, however, that this phenomenon was international.) Since the beginning of the twenties numerous investigations were concerned with this new middle class, which was soon designated the "new middle estate" (after the "old middle estate" had been decimated or de-classed by the inflation).[30]

Munich, 1916-1927; 4th ed., 1921-1927) 3 vols.; *Der Bourgeois Zur Geistesgeschichte des modernen Wirtschaftsmenschen* (Munich, 1913); *Luxus und Kapitalismus* (2nd ed.; Munich, 1922); und *Die Juden und das Wirtschaftsleben* (Munich, 1928). Sombart treated the topics of "Worker," "Vocation," "Basic Forms of Human Group Life," "Capitalism," "City Settlements," and "Economy" in Alfred Vierkandt's *Handwörterbuch der Soziologie* (Stuttgart, 1931).

[27] Reprinted in *Gesammelte Aufsätze zur Soziologie und Sozialpolitik* (Tübingen, 1924).

[28] See especially Goetz Briefs, "Das gewerbliche Proletariat," *GSO,* 9 (Tübingen, 1926), Part 1, pp. 142-240; "Betriebssoziologie," *HS* (Stuttgart, 1931), pp. 31-52. Also L. H. A. Geck, *Die sozialen Arbeitsverhältnisse im Wandel der Zeit* (Berlin, 1930); Walter Jost, *Das Sozialleben des industriellen Betriebs* (Berlin, 1932); H. Lechtape, "Soziale Prozesse im industriellen Betrieb," *KVS,* 8 (1929-1930), pp. 293-301; Richard Woldt, "Die wirtschaftliche Organisationsumwelt des Arbeiters. Sammelbericht," *ZVS,* 2 (1926), pp. 187-194; *Die Lebenswelt des Industriearbeiters* (Leipzig, 1926); and "Die Fabrik als Umwelt des Arbeiters," *ZVS,* 4 (1928), pp. 161-181.

[29] Paul Krische, "Die Krise des Sozialismus," *ZVS,* 7 (1931), pp. 279-305, 420-441.

[30] Emil Lederer and Jakob Marschak, "Der neue Mittelstand," *Grundriss der Sozialökonomik,* 9 (Tübingen, 1926), Part I, pp. 120-141; Paul Krische, "Die soziale Schichtung der Erwerbstätigen im Zeitalter der Dampfmaschine und in dem der Elektrizität," *ZVS,*

A majority of these investigations wrestled with the difficulty of defining this "class" (or "non-class") sociologically, of determining its social position, and of comparing the latter with its prestige attitudes and its very intense ideology of social climbing. At the same time, all these studies perceived the disquieting aspect of a phenomenon that did not fulfill Marxist prognoses and whose future development seemed in no way predictable. Lederer and Marschak speak of a "new middle estate," which at the time (1926) still was labile ("between the classes"), but which in the future, however, would probably amalgamate with the working class. Others, such as Schumpeter, believed they were able to predict that the "white-collar workers" would develop their own class-consciousness. Both alternative prognoses have proved false, but the following statement of Schumpeter's still remains worth noting: "Whatever position this class of the future assumes, it will in any case impress deeper and deeper on the German intellect the stamp of the salaried minion on the one side and the specialized expert on the other: the world of the future will doubtless be a world of bureaucracy."

As soon as the results of the 1925 census of vocations were published, the problems of stratification and social mobility were attacked more sharply.[31] The methodologically most important investigations in this field derived from Theodor Geiger.[32] One of his most important findings was that mentality and ideology do not regularly correspond with social status, but were in many cases "foreign to the system." Through analyses of the Reichstag election results, Geiger demonstrated, moreover, that a probable connection existed between the labile stratum of the "new middle estate," which was demanding prestige and social security, and the Nazi movement. "National Socialism" seemed the answer to the social situation of the new middle class. This was a completely new and unexpected aspect of the middle-class problem. It was at the same time a contribution to the sociology of the Nazi movement—and thus, nearly the only one which was produced at the time.

The Distinction Between "Class" and "Estate." However, the problem of the "new middle estate" could not be completely solved without clar-

4 (1928), pp. 11-18; Siegfried Kracauer, *Die Angestellten* (Frankfurt/Main, 1930); Carl Dreyfuss, *Beruf und Ideologie der Angestellten* (Munich, 1933); Svend Riemer, "Sozialer Aufsteig und Klassenschichtung," *ASS,* 67 (1932), 531-560; Hans Tobis, *Das Mittelstandsproblem der Nachkriegszeit und seine statistische Erfassung. Unter gleichzeitiger Berücksichtigung der französischen Verhaltnisse* (Grimmen, 1930); Emil Grünberg, *Der Mittelstand in der kapitalistischen Gesellschaft: Eine ökonomische und soziologische Untersuchung* (Leipzig, 1932).

[31] J. Nothaas, "Sozialer Auf- und Abstieg im deutschen Volk: Statistische Methoden und Ergebnisse," *Beiträge zur Statistik Bayerns*, No. 117 (Munich, 1930); and "Sozialer Auf- und Abstieg im deutschen Volke," *KVS,* 9 (1930), pp. 61-81.

[32] Theodor Geiger, *Die soziale Schichtung des deutschen Volkes: Soziographischer Versuch auf statistischer Grundlage* (Stuttgart, 1932).

ifying its relation to the "old middle estate" (the bourgeois) and the latter's ideal patterns, which had been transmitted and accepted although not truly assimilated and realized socially. This involved the mutual relation of "class" and "estate." We find around 1930 only fragments of the solution to this problem. Whereas Schumpeter in general strives to avoid a terminological distinction between "class" and "estate," corresponding to the English-American usage, the majority of authors have been convinced of the necessity of this distinction (F. Tönnies, H. Mitgau, T. Geiger, and others).[33] In this they more or less follow Max Weber, who likewise had differentiated "estate situation" and "class situation." As a matter of fact, the peculiarly labile position of the "new middle estate" cannot be understood without recognizing the after-effects of patterns that originated from the old estate-bourgeois traditions. Indeed, it is simply not true that the class society had merely replaced, in a discontinuous manner, the old estate society of the nineteenth century. The estate society, on the contrary, was inserted (with important residues) into the new class structure, and continues to exist by virtue of these survivals. Thus we would say today that the "new middle estate" indeed is in a certain sense still an "estate" (but only ideologically and subjectively), marked by the vain attempt to copy and conserve antiquated estate patterns, although its real situation is that of a "floating" class. Infected with this "false consciousness," the new middle estate is a "spurious social formation." The above items were not formulated *in this manner* at that time, but are the conclusions that we can draw today when we read the works of that time from our modern perspective.

Geiger has in addition stressed the after-effects of estate customs and conceptions of life. He characterizes the interposition of the old (estate) and the new (class) structure as "social-historical faulting," a geological simile appropriate to the situation, thereby indicating that structural traits which on the whole follow one another historically, nevertheless can still be found simultaneously in the present. Hermann Mitgau particularly stressed the fact that estate values and attitudes have been chiefly linked with the family (that is, with *certain* families), through which they will be transmitted as approved styles of life—a trait that the social class proper completely lacks. For the study of vertical mobility (social ascent and descent), Mitgau correctly recommended and applied the genealogical method.[34]

[33] Joseph Schumpeter, "Die sozialen Klassen im ethnischhomogenen Milieu," *ASS,* 57 (1927), pp. 1-57 [reprinted in *Aufsätze zur Soziologie* (Tübingen, 1953), pp. 147-213. Cf. the English edition by the same author, "Social Classes in an Ethnically Homogeneous Environment," *Imperialism Social Classes* (New York, 1951)]; Ferdinand Tönnies, "Stande und Klassen," *HS* (Stuttgart, 1931), pp. 617-638.

[34] Max Weber, *Wirtschaft und Gesellschaft* (3rd ed.; Tübingen, 1947), pp. 177-180; Hermann Mitgau, *Familienschicksal und soziale Rangordnung: Untersuchungen über sozialen Aufstieg und Abstieg* (Leipzig, 1928); and "Grundlagen des sozialen Aufstieges," *Soziologische Studien, Alfred Weber gewidmet* (Potsdam, 1930), pp. 278-298.

Political Sociology. The problems of mobility and social stratification extend into political sociology as soon as the relations between the dominant and dependent strata, their conflicts, and their organizations in regard to the outcome of this conflict ("class conflict") are considered. This field was the domain of Robert Michels. In his *Psychologie der antikapitalistischen Massenbewegungen*, he treated the organizational forms of the proletariat, and in a later work the problem of the circulation of ruling classes (after World War I).[35] It should not be omitted that Michels thereby also treated the problem of the "circulation of the élite" (Pareto)—and, to be sure, in a very striking manner. He, likewise, returns to his earlier thesis that a tendency toward oligarchy also exists in democratic countries and their political parties. Michels was also especially interested in the political role of intellectuals.[36] Tönnies' work on "public opinion" was mentioned earlier (see p. 662).

Psychological Analyses of Political Issues. In political psychology there appeared at that time some works of surprising quality.[37] Walter Sulzbach had already presented in 1923 the quite modern view that antipathies toward other races rest not on "instincts" but on "prejudices."[38] No political sociology is possible without a discussion of the problems of the "masses"; around 1930 an excellent and very instructive discussion was devoted to these problems, in which Geiger, Vleugels, Wiese, and Colm notably participated.[39] Opinions clashed obdurately and not even agreement on the con-

[35] Robert Michels, "Psychologie der antikapitalistischen Massenbewegungen," *GSO*, 9 (Tübingen, 1926), Part 1, pp. 241-359, and *Umschichtungen in den herrschenden Klassen nach dem Kriege* (Stuttgart, 1934).

[36] Robert Michels, "Historisch-kritische Untersuchungen zum politischen Verhalten der Intellecktuellen," *SJ*, 57 (1933). On the nature of the political party, cf. in addition: Herbert Sultan, "Zur Soziologie des modernen Parteisystemes," *ASS*, 55 (1926), pp. 91-140; M. Jaffe, "Demokratie und Partei," *ASS*, 65 (1931), pp. 101-127; Walter Sulzbach, "Politische Parteien," *HS* (Stuttgart, 1931), pp. 425-436. In addition, see the articles in Richard Thurnwald (ed.), *Partei und Klasse im Lebenspsychologie und Soziologie (Forschungen zur Völkerpsychologie und Soziologie)*, vol. 2 (Leipzig, 1926).

[37] Gaston Roffenstein, "Das Problem der Ideologie in der materialistischen Geschichtsauffassung und das moderne Parteiwesen," in *Partei und Klasse, loc. cit.*, and, "Zur Psychologie der politischen Meinung," *ZVS*, 3 (1927), pp. 385-412; Gustav Ichheiser, "Die Antinomie zwischen Politik und Moral nach Machiavelli: Ein Beitrag zu einer 'Soziologie des Erfolges," *ZVS*, 3 (1927), pp. 294-309; Richard Behrendt, *Politischer Aktivismus: Ein Versuch zur Soziologie und Psychologie der Politik* (Leipzig, 1932).

[38] Walter Sulzbach, *Vorteile und Instinkte* (Berlin, 1923).

[39] Wilhelm Vleugels, "Neuere massempsychologische Literatur," *KVS*, 2 (1922), pp. 79-82; "Zur Diskussion über die Massentheorie Le Bons," *ibid.*, 6 (1927), pp. 168-185; and *Die Masse: Ein Beitrag zur Lehre von den sozialen Gebilden* (Munich, 1930); Theodor Geiger, *Die Masse und ihre Aktion: Ein Beitrag zur Soziologie der Revolutionen* (Stuttgart, 1926), and "Revolution," *HS* (Stuttgart, 1931), pp. 511-518; Gerhard Colms, "Masse," *ibid.*, pp. 353-360; Wilhelm Vleugels, "Zur Massentheorie," *KVS*, 10 (1932), pp. 387-399. Wiese's standpoint is set forth in the 1933 edition of his *Allgemeinen Soziologie*, pp. 405-446.

cept of "masses" was obtained. But in 1933 the debate stopped: the "masses" of the "new middle estate" had begun to march and wished to be neither objective nor objectified.

A number of additional works in the twenties and early thirties revolved around the following themes: nation, national feeling and consciousness, nationalism, patriotism, colonialism, and imperialism. After the experiences and disillusionments of World War I, many Central European scholars were willing to undertake sober and dispassionate investigation of these topics whose impact they had directly experienced. Two non-German sociologists, who published many of their works in Germany, led the way: S. R. Steinmetz and Robert Michels. The products of both are characterized by a wealth of knowledge, clarity of presentation, versatility of viewpoint, and a penetration in the analyses of effective factors, including the psychic.[40] Beside these, the works of Scheler, Hertz, Mitscherlich, and Ziegler deserve to be cited.[41] The works of Hans Kohn extended the problematical aspects of nationalism also to the Soviet Union and the Near East.[42] In addition, a number of excellent investigations on imperialism were made.[43] On the eve of the Nazi dictatorship unanimity ruled among German sociologists that "nations" are *historical* structures, not products of "nature."

Cultural Sociology and Related Fields. The term "cultural sociology," as distinct from "pure sociology," had been coined by Max Scheler.[44] Real

[40] S. R. Steinmetz, *De nationaliteiten in Europa, eine sociographische en politische Studie* (Amsterdam, 1920), and "Die Nationalität und ihr Wille," *Gesammelte kleinere Schriften zur Ethnologie und Soziologie,* 3 (Groningen, 1935), pp. 251-285; Robert Michels, "Elemente zu einer Soziologie des Nationalliedes," *ASS,* 55 (1926), pp. 317-361; "Vaterlandsliebe und Heimatgefühl," *KVS,* 6 (1927), pp. 219-231; "Prolegomena zur Analyse des nationalen Elitegedankens," *JS,* 3 (1927), pp. 184-199; "Über den amerikanischen Nationalitätsbegriff," *Weltwirtschaftliches Archiv,* 28 (1928), pp. 257-299; and *Der Patriotismus: Prolegomena zu seiner sociologischen Analyse* (Munich, 1929); K. Stavenhagen, "Soziologie als Wirklichkeitswissenschaft und die nationalsoziologischen Probleme," *Nation und Staat,* 5 (1931), pp. 78-98.

[41] Max Scheler, *Nation und Weltanschauung* (Leipzig, 1923); Friedrich Hertz, "Die allgemeinen Theorien über den Nationalcharakter," *ASS,* 54 (1926), pp. 1-35, 657-715, and "Zur Soziologie der Nation und des Nationalbewusstseins," *ASS,* 65 (1931), pp. 1-60; Waldemar Mitscherlich, *Nationalismus: Die Geschichte einer Idee* (2nd ed.; Leipzig, 1929); Heinz O. Ziegler, *Die moderne Nation: Ein Beitrag zur politischen Soziologie* (Tübingen, 1931).

[42] Hans Kohn, *Der Nationalismus in der Sowjet-Union* (Frankfurt/Main, 1932), and *Nationalismus und Imperialismus im Vorderen Orient* (Frankfurt/Main, 1932).

[43] Joseph Schumpeter, "Zur Soziologie der Imperialismen," *ASS,* 46 (1919), pp. 1-39, 275-310 [reprinted in his *Imperialism and Social Classes* (New York, 1951), pp. 3-130.]; Heinrich Schnee, *Nationalismus und Imperialismus* (Berlin, 1928); Christian Eckert, *Alter und neuer Imperialismus* (Jena, 1932); Albert Lauterbach, "Zur Problemstellung des Imperialismus," *ASS,* 65 (1931), pp. 580-599; Arthur Salz, *Das Wesen des Imperialismus: Umrisse einer Theorie* (Leipzig, 1931); Walther Sulzbach, "Imperialismus," *HS* (Stuttgart, 1931), pp. 253-258; Robert Michels, "Die Theorien des Kolonialismus," *ASS,* 67 (1932), pp. 693-710.

[44] Max Scheler, *Die Wissensformen und die Gesellschaft* (Leipzig, 1926), pp. 1-20.

sociology, according to Scheler, has to do with real factors; it is based upon a theory of human motivation and is a sociology of the substructure of the content of human life. Cultural sociology is concerned with ideal factors, is based upon a theory of the human intellect, and is a sociology of the superstructure of the content of human life. Perhaps one could say more clearly that real sociology has to do with the factual behavior of human beings, cultural sociology with the ideal patterns by which humans orient their actions and which naturally vary from culture to culture. Although the term "cultural sociology" is rather unwieldy, it is perhaps still suitable for designating those studies that refer to the culturally variant orientation or background of human action—to the "typical *probabilities*" of action, to use Max Weber's term.

This implies the *comparative* study of different cultures or epochs and requires, accordingly, the detailed technical knowledge of historians, philologists, jurists, political economists, theologians, ethnographers, and so on. This work as a rule will not be done by professional sociologists, but by representatives of other disciplines who have absorbed the sociological viewpoint; or the sociologist himself must carry out intensive historical and related studies. In practice, they amount to the same thing.

The Comparative Method: Weber and Thurnwald. In this sense, the earliest works of cultural sociology in Germany are the investigations by Max Weber in the sociology of religion, which deal with the careful extraction of the typical probabilities or orientation-patterns that are presented by different religious systems (the Protestant sects, Confucianism, Hinduism, Mohammedanism, and Judaism). Although Max Weber was originally concerned with the probabilities of *economic* action, actually he contributed a great deal regarding social action in general. Toward the end of his life, Weber began to concern himself also with ethnological data; if he had lived longer, he probably would have attempted to utilize this material systematically. It is clear that without a thorough knowledge of the so-called primitive cultures, or of non-Western cultures in general, our knowledge remains extraordinarily limited regarding the probabilities of action and their variations, which, being culturally possible in time and space, have been developed and realized. A sociology that considers only the phenomena of the modern Western world gives a false anthropological perspective.

For that very reason Richard Thurnwald (1869-1954) has for decades energetically and repeatedly advocated the viewpoint that sociology must base its generalizations on all social facts for all mankind in all times and places, not only on the small territorial and historical sector of the "Western world." (This view stands in diametrical opposition to that of Freyer, to whom sociology reflects the concentrated self-consciousness of our contemporary industrial society.) Thurnwald's program therefore implies the integration of a great deal of ethnographic-historical (and even prehistorical) material in sociology. It is the logical continuation of Max Weber's intentions. The result of Thurnwald's program is to be found in his five-volume work, *Die menschliche Gesellschaft in ihren ethno-soziologischen Grundlagen* (Berlin, 1931-1935).[45] This work could be accomplished only by a research worker who had acquired mastery of his trade, as an ethnographical field worker in the South Seas and Australia, and who, moreover, had completely digested the most important ethnographical literature and had captured the social-psychological atmosphere of his own field experience.

Although it is no *literary* masterpiece, it is the work of a master. Thurnwald had an immense knowledge of ethnographic data, but he was not the encyclopedic type of scholar; rather, he clearly disclosed *relationships*. As a person of abundant empirical knowledge, he always remained skeptical toward "theoretical principles," although the fourth volume of the work mentioned above contains penetrating theoretical analyses of the functioning of social, cultural, and civilizational processes. Thurnwald was also one of the first to investigate systematically changes in aboriginal cultures under the influence of Western civilization.[46] The sociology of colonialism is indebted to him for important contributions. Unfortunately, he was not a very good *Dozent* and teacher, and seldom met with congenial understanding. Because he never troubled himself about the systematic demarcations among sociology, ethnology, and psychology (although he drew material predominantly out of his ethnographic experience), most of his students devoted themselves to ethnology, and only a few to sociology.

The tragedy of Thurnwald's career lies in the fact that he conserved the cosmopolitan disposition prevalent in Germany's imperial era, which was less often to be observed after 1918. The cosmopolitan perspective had been coupled with the colonial era in our country. Germany's being deprived of her colonies after World War I not only led to a diminution of interest in ethnology, strange lands, and peoples generally, but also favored in the long run an attitude of introverted provincialism. Only a horde of Thurnwalds would have been able to counteract this. To be sure, there existed here and there a continuing interest in cultural data from strange and distant lands and peoples, but since ethnographic and sociographic experience was lacking among sociologists, attempts to utilize ethnographic data sociologically turned out to be more or less subjective and dilettantish. The facts were selected and interpreted more or less arbitrarily and assimilated into previously well-established "principles."

The Decline of the Comparative Method. This is true also of the sociolog-

[45] For the latest bibliography of Thurnwald's writings see *Beiträge zur Gesellungs- und Völkerwissenschaft, Richard Thurnwald zu seinem 80. Geburtstage gewidmet* (Berlin, 1950), pp. 469-476.

[46] Richard Thurnwald, *Koloniale Gestaltung: Methoden und Probleme überseeischer Ausdehnung* (Hamburg, 1939), and *Black and White in East Africa* (London, 1935).

ical system of Franz Oppenheimer, especially of his views on the origin of the state. Oppenheimer's view that the state originated through violence and exploitation, especially through the "monopoly of land" *(Bodensperre)*, can be related to a one-sided and incomplete interpretation of ethnological facts, which he would have been able to avoid only by a more ample knowledge of the material and by intensive criticism and analysis of the sources. The antithesis between "cooperative" and "hierarchical" organizational forms, which is also found in Vierkandt and still plays a role in modern publications, is also untenable.[47]

The contrast between the "intuitive" interpretation of culture and the analysis of factors based on ethnography becomes especially obvious when one compares, say, Alfred Weber's statements on "culture and civilization" with those of Thurnwald on the same theme.[48] Possibly the two standpoints are now capable of being brought to a synthesis on a new plane. At that time, however, the result was that many ethnologists were repelled by the subjective and insufficient analyses of cultural data by sociologists, which was not conducive to the further development of either field in mastering scientific problems. Unfortunately, the number of writings that, under the mask of "sociology" or "intellectual history," disseminated unrealistic conceptions of non-Western man is not small. The tortuous treatment of non-Occidental data—in spite of the examples of Max Weber and Thurnwald—is also a source of thoroughgoing error in almost all the special sociologies of economics, the state, and of law that were written at the time.

Cultural History of European Social Strata. As soon as cultural sociology moved to the firm ground of *European* history, it produced results of a considerably higher level. Because of their sociological flavor, the works of the social and cultural historian, Eberhard Gothein (1853-1924), must be appreciatively cited here. Gothein belonged for a long time to the Heidelberg circle around Max Weber.[49] This tradition, as in Ernst Troeltsch's work *Die Soziallehren der christlichen Kirchen und Gruppen* (1912), intellectually unites a number of additional cultural–sociological investigations (by Groethuysen and Martin) on certain phases of European history that are of great significance, especially on the origins of bourgeois society. The shortcomings of this concentration on bourgeois society are compensated by the sociological works on folklore by Max Rumpf, who turned his attention to the

[47] Frans Oppenheimer, *The State* (Indianapolis, 1913); Alfred Vierkandt, *Gesellschaftslehre* (2nd ed.; Stuttgart, 1931), pp. 285-286.

[48] Alfred Weber, "Ideen zur Staats- und Kultursoziologie," in Alfred Weber (ed.), *Probleme der Staats- und Kultursoziologie* (Karlsruhe, 1927); Richard Thurnwald, "Contributions towards an Analysis of the Mechanisms of Culture," *ASR,* 1 (1936), pp. 387-395, 604-613, and 2 (1937), pp. 26-42.

[49] Eberhard Gothein, *Schriften zur Kulturgeschichte der Renaissance, Reformation und Gegenformationen* (Munich, 1924), 2 vols. See also his "Über einige soziologische Grundfragen," *Erinnerungsgabe für Max Weber,* 1 (1923), pp. 193-234.

social and cultural life of the "low folk," that is, the lower social strata.[50]

Sociology of Knowledge: Mannheim and the Critics. In a wider sense, the so-called sociology of knowledge can also be regarded as part of cultural sociology; it was instituted originally by Max Scheler, but was first developed as a subject of intensive study by his pupil, Karl Mannheim (1893-1947).[51] This branch of sociology treated, first of all, the simple fact that even the forms of "knowledge" are determined by commitment to a way of life, ideological suppositions, and the more or less conscious and veiled interests of individuals or groups, especially "classes." Mannheim extended this sound proposition by the thesis that all thinking is bound to "being," or existence. The resulting relativity of the concept "truth" he endeavored to overcome by the concept "relationism."

In the ensuing controversy on these topics, Mannheim found supporters as well as opponents.[52] Some authors reproached Mannheim with "sociologism" or even "nihilism" (Julius Kraft, Ernst Robert Curtius, A. von Martin, and A. von Schelting). Vierkandt retreated to a "perspectivism": objectivity would still be possible; "we must transform the concept of truth or knowledge, so that it encompasses the standpoint which the observer incorporates in his decision about ultimate values."[53] (But are not decisions by the observer about ultimate values really in the realm of the subjective?) The controversy over the sociology of knowledge, however, was soon extinguished. The reason for this was not simply that the majority of protagonists, as well as opponents, emigrated. The entire argument mirrored the perplexity of a generation that was not intellectually able to cope with the ferment bequeathed by Marx, Nietzsche, Freud, and Spengler.

Analyses of Success and Genius. A special field of cultural sociology concerns the realm of success norms and success mechanisms that facilitate or hinder the approbation of certain cultural products (by the persons or groups, respectively, that bear them). These mechanisms naturally vary from culture to culture, from epoch to epoch, and they can even be affected by change in

[50] See especially Bernhard Groethuysen, *Die Entstehung der bürgerlichen Welt- und Lebensanschauung in Frankreich* (Halle, 1927, 1930), 2 vols.; A. von Martin, *Soziologie der Renaissance* (2nd ed.; Frankfurt/Main, 1949); Max Rumpf, *Soziale Lebenslehre, ihr System und ihr wissenschaftlicher Ort* (Nurnberg, 1931), and *Religiöse Volkskunde* (Stuttgart, 1933).

[51] Max Scheler, *Die Formen des Wissens und der Bildung* (Bonn, 1925), and *Die Wissensformen und die Gesellschaft* (Leipzig, 1926); Karl Mannheim, "Ideologische und soziologische Betrachtung der geistigen Gebilde," *JS,* 2 (1926), pp. 424-440, and *Ideology and Utopia,* translated by Louis Wirth and Edward Shils (New York, 1936).

[52] See Karl Mannheim, "Wissenssoziologie," *HS* (Stuttgart, 1931), pp. 659-680. The later works that are particularly important are Alexander von Schelting, *Max Webers Wissenschaftslehre* (Tübingen, 1934); Ernst Grünwald, *Das Problem der Soziologie des Wissens* (Vienna, 1934).

[53] Alfred Vierkandt, "Was die Wissenssoziologie uns lehrt," *Pädagogische Warte,* No. 9 (1932).

fashion or style. In Germany, amazingly little has been produced in this field, so that in the area of literary production, for instance, the prominent work by Levin L. Schücking stands completely alone and has as yet found no successor.[54]

On the other hand, the preliminary problems of success in their social-psychological aspects have been worked out very well by the Viennese psychologist Ichheiser.[55] At the very time that the naïve reduction of "success" to criteria of achievement and biologically inherited "excellence" began to become an officially approved dogma of naturalistic social biologists, Ichheiser showed that a discrepancy existed between the ideally esteemed behavior patterns in our society ("honesty is the best policy," "the capable person succeeds," and so on) and the *factual* success mechanisms. Ichheiser even thinks this constitutes an antinomy, an interpretation which can be questioned. The mechanisms used in attaining ends must therefore be investigated independently from verbalized norms and values.

The work of the psychiatrist Wilhelm Lange-Eichbaum, *Genie, Irrsinn und Ruhm,*[56] stems from the same basic methodological viewpoint; he is thus distinguished from his putative predecessors, such as Lombroso. For Lange-Eichbaum "genius" is not the emanation of an especially gifted disposition (as it was for Francis Galton in his *Hereditary Genius*) but the result of an often very long-lasting, ambiguous (in its results as well as in its nature) social-psychic process of value-formation. The origin of a genius-myth can best be understood by means of the psychology of religion, which studies the effect of "numinous" or religiously charismatic qualities. The usual view of the genius, which Lange-Eichbaum opposes, is fixed by value-judgments deriving from the genius-worshiping community. We can surmount these value-judgments only when we sociologically analyze the process of value-formation itself. (See Chap. 6.)

Genius, therefore, is not an inherent quality; it is a "myth." It is not personality, but a nimbus. The values that the genius contributes to the community are projected back on him and are interpreted as "gifted talent." This fundamental methodological standpoint is propounded by Lange-Eichbaum with an overwhelming abundance of psychologically interpreted material. He also investigates the "curves of fame" of a few gifted men and shows how these curves fluctuate from epoch to epoch, from apotheosis to complete obscurity. Not only does the recognition of famous men undergo

[54] Leyin L. Schücking, *Soziologie der literarischen Geschmacksbildung* (2nd ed.; Berlin, 1931).

[55] Gustav Ichheiser, "Kritik des Erfolges: Eine soziologischen Untersuchung," *FVS,* 9 (Leipzig, 1930); "Einige typische Deutungen von Erfolgstatschen," *KVS,* 10 (1931), pp. 51-66; "Erfolgsnormen und Erfolgsgesetze," *ASS,* 68 (1932), pp. 61-74.

[56] See also Wilhelm Lange-Eschbaum, *Das Genie-Problem* (Munich, 1931; 2nd ed. under the title, *Das Genie als Problem,* 1943).

quantitative fluctuations, but they mean something qualitatively different for each cultural period (Schücking had stressed the same thing previously).

The view that there exists a necessary connection between genius and psychosis is not tenable. There are psychological personality traits, however, which facilitate the genesis of a genius-myth. Psychologically and sociologically, Lange-Eichbaum's book summarizes some main tendencies of German thinkers in this epoch. It is influenced psychologically by the studies on the mentality of "primitive" peoples and by the social psychology of Vierkandt, whereas its sociological perspective is related to the "relationism" of Mannheim. It is very strange that this book, replete with practical psychological applications to events of the present, and interpreting "genius" as "nimbus," could reach a third edition in Germany in 1942.

The Period 1933-1945

The Dominance of Ideology. Under the domination of Nazism, sociology no longer played a role in Germany. The leap to ideology as the new "absolute" basis, which was executed quite consciously by many intellectuals, took the place of sociological "relativism," and conscious subjectivity took the place of objectivity. The "folkish" position of the German nation and the "heroic" race were made absolute. It was a rather desperate psychological operation of self-violence, as the basic feeling of nihilism was still preserved by it, though often hidden by a cynicism worn for show.

Political measures liquidated the organizational forms of German sociology. The publication of Wiese's *Kölner Vierteljahrshefte für Soziologie* and Thurnwald's *Sociologus* was stopped in 1933-1934, as well as the *Archiv für Sozialwissenschaft und Sozialpolitik*, and other important periodicals. The *Deutsche Gesellschaft für Soziologie* was dissolved. There was a meeting of German sociologists in Jena from January 5-7, 1934, which was held under the auspices of the political philosopher of the Nazi movement, Ernst Krieck, and the protagonist of Nordic racism, Hans F. K. Günther (who was not the political activist type himself, but an idealist, "escapist" German pedagogue); but this meeting was without consequence. Many German and (after 1938) Austrian sociologists and social scientists emigrated: P. Honigsheim, H. Plessner, A. von Schelting, K. Mannheim, R. Heberle, F. K. Mann, J. Schumpeter, E. Lederer, G. Briefs, E. Voegelin, G. Ichheiser, F. Hertz, M. Horkheimer, T. W. Adorno, T. Geiger, and many others. Many who remained in Germany "emigrated" to neutral fields (ethnology, folklore, human geography, and so on) where political controls were less severe.

Political Eugenics Enthroned. The fate of Theodor Geiger is especially interesting because of his attempt to analyze critically the National Socialist program for the improvement of the human race ("eugenics" or "race hygiene"). The eugenic program in Germany had a long and by no means merely dilettantish tradition, deriving from the Social Darwinism of the late nineteenth century and the social biology of the beginning of the twentieth century. The writings of Ammon, Schallmayer, Ploetz, and others had been widely read. Sociologists such as Thurnwald and Vierkandt had contributed to the *Archiv für Rassen- und Gesellschafts-Biologie*, founded by Alfred Ploetz in 1904, Max Weber had debated with Ploetz (1910), and Tönnies had entered into controversies with Schallmayer.[57] Also Steinmetz, the Dutch sociologist, had concerned himself intensively with social biologic and eugenic problems.

But in the course of time, the relations between sociology and eugenics had become distant. The *Archiv*, cited above, was dedicated more and more on the one hand to problems of the heredity of man, on the other to programs for raising the fertility of the "talented" and for lowering the fertility of the "less worthy," whereas the indispensable *sociological* examination of these problems was neglected. The blame for this lies on both sides: the human geneticists and eugenicists, mostly medical men and physical scientists, considered sociologists unqualified to discuss the problem because of their lack of knowledge of fundamental biological facts; and sociologists scorned the eugenicists as ideologists and utopians. When Geiger in 1933 attempted to tie the threads together again, it was far too late, since political activism was already at the point of appropriating this problem.[58] Geiger's elucidations on the dilettantism of eugenicists with respect to treatment of the problem of social stratification, on the naiveté of identifying genetic quality and social status, and on the constant interchange of biological and social measuring devices, were ignored. They interested no one, since the Nazi state and its functionaries believed they knew more than the professors.

"Race" and "Folk": The Ideology of a Rural Past. In place of *Gesellschaft,* the concept *Gemeinschaft* advanced to the foreground—not altogether in Tönnies' sense, but as a slogan devaluated by inflationary propagandistic methods. In addition, "race" naturally played a role, and some scientific efforts are recognizable under the disciplinary designations of "folk research," "science of folklore," and so on, whereas "Völkerkunde" was not approved, since its explicit plurality contradicted the ideological solipsism. The term

[57] W. E. Mühlmann, *Geschichte der Anthropologie* (Bonn, 1948), pp. 124-128, 198-199; Max Weber, *Gesammelte Aufsätze zur Soziologie und Sozialpolitik* (Tübingen, 1924), pp. 456-472; Ferdinand Tönnies, *Soziologische Studien und Kritiken* (Jena, 1925), vol. 1, Chaps. 9-14, 16.

[58] Theodor Geiger, *Soziologische Kritik der eugenischen Bewegung* (Berlin, 1933), and *Erbpflege: Grundlagen, Planung, Grenzen* (Stuttgart, 1934).

"folk" (also translatable as "people") had a thoroughly mystic connotation, which had been transmitted from German Romanticism of the early nineteenth century. There is, in this connection, no analogy in Western European tradition, because "nation" signifies something else.[59] Precisely for this reason, the adjective "folkish" signifies something different from "national": "folk" signifies being deeply rooted in race and soil *(Blut und Boden)*—precisely what the greater part of the German population had lost through urbanization.

In its association with rural life and the protest against urbanization, this folk concept is somewhat reminiscent of Robert Redfield's polarity, "folk society" and "urban society." However, to German folk propagandists everything is firmly imbedded in romantic schemes. Hans F. K. Günther, who at that time occupied a professor's chair in social anthropology and rural sociology in Berlin, was inspired by the ideal of re-ruralization and a new rural life through which a new "élite" would be cultivated.[60] Mitgau published a very good investigation of urbanization by genealogical methods. Günther Ipsen sketched programs for sociological investigation of the German people and especially the rural population, which, though good, were not carried out. Uninfluenced by ideological considerations, other authors also devoted themselves to investigation of the hated metropolis.[61]

Some Rays of Light Through the Ideological Curtain. Excellent work could often be done under the titles of "population biology," "social anthropology," etc.—that is to say, in fields peripheral to sociology. There were also some noteworthy works on folklore, in which sociological points of view predominated. The discussion of race questions was more difficult, because official doctrine was attached more firmly to the word "race" than to the word "folk." Nevertheless, I prepared a work that stressed the *interrelations* of racial biology, social biology, sociology, and ethnology, and likewise presented an objective discussion of the factors studied by these disciplines. It was cosmopolitan in outlook and emphasized the role of the physical, social, and cultural-historical environment, the processes of mobility and cultural diffusion, and the social-psychological aspects of modern groups and cul-

[59] W. E. Mühlmann, "L'idée nationale allemande et l'idée nationale française," *Revue de Psychologie des Peuples,* 7 (1952), pp. 348-362.

[60] Hans F. K. Günther, *Die Verstädterung* (Leipzig, 1934; 2nd ed., 1936), and *Das Bauertum als Lebens- und Gemeinschaftsform* (Leipzig, 1939). Cf. Peter Quante, *Die Flucht aus der Landwirtschaft* (Berlin, 1933).

[61] Hermann Mitgau, "Verstädterung und Grossstadtschicksal," *Archiv für Bevölkerungswissenschaft* (1941), pp. 339-364; Gunther Ipsen, *Programm einer Soziologie des deutschen Volkstum* (Berlin, 1933), and *Das Landvolk: Ein soziologischer Versuch* (Hamburg, 1933); Willy Hellpach, *Mensch und Volk der Grossstadt* (Stuttgart, 1939; 2nd. ed., 1952), and "Bevölkerungsbiologie der Grossstadt," *Zeitschrift für Rassenkunde and die gesamte Forschung am Menschen,* 12 (1941).

tural contacts. "Race," in the biological sense of the word, was not conceived as a culturally productive factor, but as a set of biological dispositions which could be developed or not, through the powers of the environment.[62]

In the middle thirties some new periodicals were founded that focused on problems of population, ethnic groups (national minorities), ethnic boundaries, etc.[63] They contained works on population and social history, historical geography, cultural geography, folklore, and statistics, many of which possessed sociographic value. Interest concentrated naturally on the cultural importance of German minorities in foreign countries, but much material was also offered on other nationalities in eastern Central Europe, Southeastern, and Eastern Europe. Even an extensive study of minorities in the United States is to be found.[64]

Investigations of Assimilation. Finally, of special sociological significance are the investigations on "ethnic transposition" *(Umvolkung)*—that is, on the exchange of nationality by certain groups: for instance, Germans acquiring the traits of Poles and Czechoslovakians, and vice versa, Germans and Slovaks acquiring those of Magyars, and so on. It had been discovered that such processes play a great role in historical and modern times, and they began to be studied in their social, political, and psychological aspects. But it was hardly perceived that the admission of the possibility of an actual exchange of nationality contradicted the thesis of "racial" determinism of the national character. Robert Beck introduced the concept "suspended nationality" to designate that phase of a situation in which intentions are labile, when persons or groups in the process of ethnic transposition are themselves uncertain about their own ethnic membership. K. V. Müller pointed out, in investigations that could be published only after the war, that assimilation between Germans and Czechs in Bohemia had been reciprocal for generations and that no difference in anthropological type existed between the two nationalities. Stimulated by such investigations, I examined ethnographical material and discovered that ethnic transposition had played a great role also with "primitive" and non-Western peoples, that these processes showed typical regularities, and that they have a fundamental significance also for the understanding of ethnic developments.[65]

[62] W. E. Mühlmann, *Rassen- und Völkerkunde: Lebensprobleme der Rassen, Gesellschaften und Völker* (Braunschweig, 1936). Cf. also Erich Voegelin, *Rasse und Staat* (Tübingen, 1933), and *Die Rassenidee in der Geistesgeschichte* (Berlin, 1933).

[63] E.g., *Auslandsdeutsche Volksforschung,* entitled *Volksforschung* from the third volume on (6 vols., 1937-1943).

[64] See especially Helmut Klocke, "Landvolk und Dorf in madjrischer und rumänischer Sicht," *DALV,* 1 (1937), pp. 990-1023; Hubert Lendl, "Das gesellschaftliche Gefüge des Landvolks im deutsch-madjarischen Grenzraum östlich des Neusiedler Sees," *ibid.,* 2 (1938), pp. 800-835; Heinrich Krieger, *Das Rassenrecht in den Vereinigten Staaten* (Berlin, 1936).

[65] Robert Beck, *Schwebendes Volkstum im Gesinnungswandel* (Stuttgart, 1938); K. V.

The Period of Reconstruction: 1945 to the Present

The Reorganization of Sociology and the "Great Old Men." Restorative and progressive tendencies can be recognized in the development of sociology in Germany after the catastrophe of World War II. That the restorative aspect predominated at first is clear, for in 1945 nothing organizational existed any longer in sociology; and one had to be able to fall back on the experience of the "great old men." In particular, Leopold von Wiese revived the *Deutsche Gesellschaft für Soziologie*, which was relocated in Bad Godesberg, on April 5-6, 1946. Since then it has arranged five congresses (8th, 9th, 10th, 11th, and 12th sessions), whose dates, locations, and main themes were as follows:

8th Session (Frankfurt/Main, 1946). Reports and discussions on "The Contemporary Situation Sociologically Considered" (Wiese), association theory, circulation of social classes, political economy and the problem of monopoly, natural and national law, and German trade unions.

9th Session (Worms, 1948). Reports and discussions on the problems of German youth, making politics a science, terror, and the development of sociological research outside Germany.

10th Session (Detmold, 1950). Reports and discussions on the themes "Home and 'Foreign' Environment" *(Heimat und Fremde)* and "Bureaucratization."

11th Session (Weinheim, 1952). Reports and discussions on the themes "The Contemporary State and Interest-Groups" and "Cells and Cliques."

12th Session (Heidelberg, 1954). Reports and discussions on the themes "The Problem of Ideology" and "The Free Vocations."

In addition, Wiese, in association with other scholars, organized three "anthropological–sociological conferences" with the purpose of illuminating certain complex problems from as many viewpoints as possible. The term "anthropology" was, in this respect, very broadly conceived, and there were included psychologists, educators, biologists, medical men, ethnologists, jurists, philosophers, theologians, etc. The following conferences were held:

1st Conference (Mainz, 1949). Themes: "Individual and Collectivity" and

Müller, "Volksbiologische Beziehungen zwischen Tschechen und Deutschen," in Helmut Preidel (ed.), *Die Deutschen in Böhmen und Mähren* (Gräfelfing, 1950), pp. 291-203. Cf. in addition the periodical *Auslandsdeutsche Volksforschung,* No. 4, 1 (1937) [the entire volume is dedicated to the problem of "Umvolkung"]; W. E. Mühlmann, *Assimilation, Umvolkung, Volkwerdung: Ein globaler Überblick und ein Programm* (Prague, 1944). [These investigations were continued after the war.]

"The Social and Cultural Consequences of the Great Population Increase in the 19th Century."

2nd Conference (Mainz, 1951). Themes: "Growing, Maturing, and Dying" and "The European."

3rd Conference (Heidelberg, 1954). Theme: "The Child."

The *Deutsche Gesellschaft für Soziologie* is the main organization of German sociologists, but it is not the only one. There is in addition a "Society for Empirical Sociology" directed by Karl Valentin Müller (Nürnberg), as well as a number of more informally organized *work-circles* attached to specific institutes or institutions.

Revival of Sociological Journals. There are also the sociological periodicals. Wiese restored his own periodical, which at first was entitled *Kölner Zeitschrift für Soziologie* (six volumes, 1948-1954). From the seventh volume on, it carried the title *Kölner Zeitschrift für Soziologie und Sozialpsychologie* and is now edited by René König (Cologne). Richard Thurnwald resumed his *Sociologus*, which is dedicated chiefly to ethnology, but since his death in 1954 it has not appeared. Since 1950 the periodical *Soziale Welt* has appeared, dedicated to the problems of empirical and applied sociology and edited by the "Social Research Office" in Dortmund. In 1953 a *Zeitschrift für Agrargeschichte und Agrarsoziologie* was founded, edited by Günther Franz. But the periodical in whose titles "sociology" appears are, as before 1933, not completely representative of sociological activity in Germany. Now as before, many important works are published in other social-science organs. The *Jahrbuch für Sozialwissenschaft*, dating from 1950, publishes sociological contributions as well as voluminous bibliographies. And since 1952 there has appeared one of many anticipated volumes of the *Handwörterbuch der Sozialwissenschaften*, edited by H. Jecht and R. Schaeder, and including several sociological articles.

It is to be understood that everything said here about the organization of sociology, as well as the following statements, applies exclusively to the West German Federal Republic (and West Berlin). In the "German Democratic Republic" there is no sociological research and instruction in our sense of the term. At present, there is no longer the same lively communication with Austrian and other Central European scholars as in earlier times. The division of the former German Reich and its reduction to a "truncated Germany" means for West Germany not only a shrinkage in population but also a contraction of the geographic and intellectual horizon.

The Roles of Wiese and Brinkmann. The reintroduction of German sociology after the war is due above all to the "great old men." The activity of Leopold von Wiese was tireless. His extensive organizational activity did not hinder him from continually presenting, annotating, and justifying his personal systematic-sociological views, with an unswerving fidelity to his convictions. If the "theory of social relations" presented in his earlier publications appeared too rigid and formal, then his *Ethik*, published after the war, may give important insights into the personal and human premises of this theory. The symposium *Abhängigkeit und Selbständigkeit im soziale Leben*, edited by Wiese, one would think, should also be based on relational-sociological categories; still, to some extent, the collaborators deviate from the conceptions of Wiese.[66]

Carl Brinkmann (1885-1954), known especially as an economic historian in earlier decades, also edited a collected work, *Soziologie und Leben.* His theoretical standpoint is completely different from that of Wiese. He views sociology less as a *special* science than as a "new view of the worlds of perception generally" that is becoming more and more dominant. Brinkmann in addition wrote a penetrating but barely readable book on "revolution." Shortly before his death he was occupied with a German translation and selection of Pareto's *Trattato di sociologia* (Tübingen, 1955).[67] Indeed, Brinkmann's sociology, which in its last phases unfortunately has not been coherently presented, approaches Pareto's theory of "derivations" and "residues."

The Philosophy of History: Alfred Weber and Hans Freyer. Alfred Weber (born in 1868) in his postwar writings more and more approaches a universal philosophy of history, in which many contemporary sociologists are able to find a *sociological* dimension only with great difficulty.[68] Weber shares a general historical tendency with Hans Freyer (born in 1887), but the similarity is only superficial, since it would never occur to Freyer to pursue history *as* sociology. Moreover, Freyer has completed the shift to history (announced in 1930) in so thorough a fashion that he even designates himself today as a "historian" (to be sure, also always as a sociologist).

Freyer, who was obliged to quit his professorial chair in Leipzig in 1948 and later taught in Münster in Westphalia and Ankara (Turkey), wrote during the war the *Weltgeschichte Europas* (2nd ed.; Stuttgart, 1955), a work that one must consider a philosophy of history, although it is unmistakably the work of a sociologist philosophizing.

Empirical Sociology. Despite the role of these men, the main tendencies of contemporary German sociology lie in a quite different direction. This

[66] Leopold von Wiese, *Ethik in der Schauweise der Wissenschaften vom Menschen und von der Gesellschaft* (Bern, 1947); Leopold von Wiese (ed.), *Abhängigkeit und Selbständigkeit im sozialen Leben* (Cologne, 1951). Another work inspired and edited by Wiese is *Die Entwicklung der Kriegswaffe und ihr Zusammenhang mit der Sozialordnung* [with contributions by W. E. Mühlmann, P. Stotten, and J. Volkmann] (Cologne, 1953).

[67] Carl Brinkmann (ed.), *Soziologie und Leben* (Tübingen, 1952). Cf. Brinkmann's own article in this work: "Die soziologische Dimension in den Fachwissenschaften," pp. 9-27, and *Soziologische Theorie der Revolution* (Gottingen, 1948).

[68] Alfred Weber, *Kulturgeschichte als Kultursoziologie* (2nd ed.; Munich, 1950); *Prinzipien der Geschichts- und Kultursoziologie* (Munich, 1951); and *Der dritte oder der vierte Mensch? Vom Sinn des geschichtlichen Daseins* (Munich, 1953).

direction can be designated as "empirical sociology" or "sociography," with a clear tendency toward "applied sociology." Two principal factors are responsible: (1) the practical necessities of rebuilding devastated cities after the catastrophe of World War II, of reorganizing the economy and social structure, and of adapting and assimilating the millions of refugees who streamed into West Germany; (2) the elaboration of new methods for empirical work, in which the influence of American sociology and "Americanism" is evident in general.[69] Both factors are interrelated.

Sociography and Statistics. In this area, "sociography" is plainly dominant. The concept "sociography," coined by Robert Michels in 1908 and later adopted by S. R. Steinmetz and Tönnies, signifies nothing more than empirical discovery and the most complete description possible of the elementary data of a definite (and usually regionally delimited) problem-complex, and the systematic organization of facts thus determined by means of quantitative methods.[70] When sociography extends beyond this problem, when it *interprets* relationships, for instance, then it becomes *sociology*. Actually many sociographic works do not remain in the narrow realm of description, but already contain sociological elements.

The application of statistical methods has been greatly stimulated by the example of American sociology. It also has a German tradition, however. Georg von Mayr's book, *Statistik und Gesellschaft* (Tübingen, 1914-1922, 3 vols.), was a classic. When one compares the second volume of this work (2nd ed.) with the *Bevölkerungslehre* (1953) by Gerhard Mackenroth (1903-1955), a remarkable progress is obvious. Although the author offers this work as sociography (in this case demography), he actually presents a sociological theory of population. In no other area of sociology since 1945 has the construction of theory been so decisively furthered.

Social Ecology. Since sociography examines the elementary facts of social life, it also has a close relation to problems of the spatial environment in which man and human groups live. *Social ecology* in this connection seems at present to form a special branch of sociology. It has three sources. The first source is to be recognized in some works stemming from around 1930, of which the most prominent example is Adolf Günther's *Alpenländische Gesellschaft* (Jena, 1930). There it was shown that the Central European Alpine environment possesses a commonly grounded significance which extends far beyond political-territorial, religious, and other borders. The second lies in the suggestions that emerged from biological and anthro-

[69] Andreas Walther's book, *Soziologie und Sozialwissenschaften in Amerika,* which had paved the way for an understanding of American sociology years ago, is now long out-dated.

[70] Roberto Michels, *Il proletariato e la borghesia nel movimento socialista italiano: Saggio di scienza sociografico-politica* (Turin, 1908); Rudolf Heberle, "Soziographie," *HS* (Stuttgart, 1931), pp. 564-568.

pological research on the "environment."[71] The third source lies in American community research.

Techniques in Social Psychology. Other methods (or rather techniques) that have been adopted are the questionnaire and interview. The two are often combined and, although they encounter continued criticism, they gain more and more ground and are constantly refined.[72] Social-psychological methods have also been much refined, due in great measure to Peter R. Hofstätter.[73] The application of these methods to problems of German society, however, has not yet been accomplished.

The Refugee Problem. A particularly urgent practical problem in recent years has been that of the refugees. The number of "expellees," or *Heimatvertriebenen* (as the official designation in the Federal Republic reads), who according to the provisions of the Potsdam Agreement had to emigrate from the eastern provinces of Germany, Czechoslovakia, and southern European countries, is estimated at some fourteen millions. The number who died during the flight is estimated at 2,100,000. On December 31, 1953, there were 8,450,000 refugees in the Federal Republic and in addition 2,150,000 "escapees" from the East Zone (German Democratic Republic) and Berlin. Impelling practical problems included the settlement of the refugees in the various provinces of the Federal Republic, their vocational and social assimilation into the indigenous population, the overcoming of the social distance (often at hand and often stressed) between the two population groups, the conquest of the "homesickness complex," and the promotion of intermarriage between the two groups.

Karl Valentin Müller collected much valuable knowledge in this area, and with his collaborators carried out a great many investigations, especially on refugee youth in Lower Saxony, Schleswig-Holstein, and Bavaria. He established, among other things, by very careful investigations that were methodically checked again and again and extended over several years, that the school achievements and social progress of children from refugee families were not lower, but typically a trifle higher, than the children of the old, settled population. On the whole, the pressure of the new citizen population for "achievement" and "social ascent" is very great, even greater than that of the indigenous families. Müller devotes special attention to the correlation between social and intellectual accomplishment on the one hand and social status on the other. With respect to intermarriage between the

[71] Cf. W. E. Mühlmann, "Das Problem der Umwelt beim Menschen," *Zeitschrift für Morphologie und Anthropologie,* 44 (1952), pp. 153-181.

[72] René König *et al., Das Interview: Formen, Technik, Auswertung* (Dortmund, 1953); Ludwig von Friedeburg, "Die Umfrage in der Intimspäre," *Beiträge zur Sexualforschung,* 4 (Stuttgart, 1953).

[73] Peter R. Hofstätter, *Einfuhrung in die quantitativen Methoden der Psychologie* (Munich, 1953); *Die Psychologie der öffentlichen Meinung* (Vienna, 1949); and *Einführung in die Sozialpsychologie* (Stuttgart, 1954).

two groups, the "connubial index" has risen from an average of 70 percent in 1950 to nearly 100 percent in 1955, which is a very good indicator of assimilation by the younger generation.[74]

Sociology of the Large City. A second urgent, practical problem has been the reconstruction of German cities. That this posed not only technical and organizational, but also sociological, problems was first energetically stressed by Elisabeth Pfeil after the war. She could refer in this respect not only to the model of American "urban sociology," but also to a noteworthy *German* tradition (Georg Hansen, Richard Thurnwald, Max Weber, Willy Hellpach, and others). To be sure, the new German sociology of the city has been first engaged in construction. Compared with urban sociology, rural sociology lags behind. A study by Kötter shows that the social and cultural gradient at present is unequivocally from the city to the country.[75]

Industrial Sociology or Sociology of the Factory. It has been known for a long time that the problems of the "industrial work-world" concern a definite aspect of the sociology of the city. Industrial sociology (or sociology of the factory—*Betriebssoziologie*, as it is usually labeled in Germany) perceives new problems before it today in West Germany that are closely connected with the labor situation, the relationship of the social partners (labor and management), and the political influences of the unions. Naturally, interrelations also exist with the problems of refugees and the family. In line with the earlier works by Woldt and others, effort is being made today to study the social and basic milieu of "industrial man."[76]

The position of the employer has changed a great deal since earlier times, so that the older analyses of management by Schumpeter and others are no longer correct for the present state of affairs. In spite of an inspiring book by Sauermann,[77] not very much has been accomplished in this area.

[74] Of K. V. Müller's numerous publications only the following will be cited: *Die Begabung in der sozialen Wirklichkeit* (Gottingen, 1951); *Die Eingliederung der Heimatvertriebenen als soziologischer Vorgang* (Munich, 1953). For a broader social-historical approach, see Wilhelm Brepohl, *Der Aufbau des Ruhrvolkes im Zuge der Ost-West-Wanderung: Beiträge zur deutschen Sozialgeschichte des 19. und 20. Jahrhunderts* (Recklinghausen, 1948).

[75] Elisabeth Pfeil, "Grossstadtforschung," *Raumforschung und Landesplanung*, 19 (Bremen, 1950), and *Die Wohnwünsche der Bergarbeiter: Soziologische Erhebung, Deutung und Kritik der Wohnvorstellungen eines Berufes* (Tübingen, 1954); Martin Rumpf, "Die Grossstadt als Lebensform in ihrer sozialen Prägekraft," *KVS*, 10 (1931), pp. 200-219; Willy Hellpach, *Mensch und Volk der Grossstadt* (2nd ed.; Stuttgart, 1952); Herbert Kotter, *Struktur und Funktion von Landgemeinden im Einflussbereich einer deutschen Mittelstadt* [Darmstadt] (Darmstadt, 1952).

[76] Ernst Michel, *Sozialgeschichte der industriellen Arbeitswelt, ihrer Krisenformen und Gestaltungsversuche* (3rd ed.; Frankfurt/Main, 1953); Walther Hoffmann (ed.), *Beiträge zur Soziologie der industriellen Gesellschaft* (Dortmund, 1952); Theo Pirker *et al.*, *Arbeiter, Management, Mitbestimmung: Industriesoziologische Untersuchung* (Stuttgart, 1955).

[77] Heinz Sauermann, *Die Gestalt des Unternehmers* (Berlin, 1937). See also Wolfgang Kellner, *Die Wirtschaftsführung als menschliche Leistung* (Braunschweig, 1949).

Although some seminars and institutes have promoted studies on the role of leadership and authority in business, this theme still seems to touch upon a peculiar trait in our national psychology—that we can only with great difficulty attain a compromise of responsible and controlled leadership between the extremes of absolute domination and absolute freedom.

Burnham's *Managerial Revolution* has been translated into German. Schelsky has recently stressed the fact that our educational organizations do not provide well enough for the far-sighted and humane type of economic leadership that has become necessary today. Although we have a *de facto* regime of managers, we have no managerial élite; and the general orientation of our society does not even provide for the development of such an élite.[78]

Sociology of the Family. This field had only very modest beginnings before 1933 in Germany.[79] The supposed encouragement of the family by the Nazi régime had demographic-political purposes that transcended the family as a social structure. Consequently there currently exists an inclination in the Federal Republic to identify the "healthy" and "socially intact" family with the "family with many children" and therefore to substitute the demographic-political aspect for the sociological. Nevertheless, there is already in West Germany a scientific sociology of the family.

The impact of the war and postwar events on the family, the disorganization brought about by decimation and the wretchedness of the refugees, and the social de-classing of many families through de-Nazification measures were also in this case the practical starting points for sociographic investigations. René König's studies and publications in Switzerland made German sociologists familiar for the first time after the war with the American sociology of the family. The role of disorganization also came into view in the criminological-sociological studies of Bader. Then came Hilde Thurnwald's great study on Berlin families, followed by the investigations of Schelsky and Wurzbacher.[80]

The conclusion of these studies seems to be that the family as a social unit has held out better than one would have expected in view of the strains to which it had been exposed. Over against the demands made by business, the public, and politics, the modern German family forms a kind of refuge

[78] Helmut Schelsky, "Industrie- und Betriebssoziologie," in Arnold Gehlen and Helmut Schelsky (eds.), *Soziologie* (Düsseldorf, 1955), pp. 157-197.

[79] Cf. the reports in *Soc.,* 8 (1932), pp. 228-229; 471-475; and Ferdinand Tönnies, "Die moderne Familie," *HS,* (Stuttgart, 1931), pp. 122-131.

[80] René König, *Materialien zur Soziologie der Familie* (Bern, 1946); Hilde Thurnwald, *Gegenwartsprobleme Berliner Familien: Eine soziologische Untersuchung an 498 Familien* (Berlin, 1948); Helmut Schelsky, *Wandlungen der deutschen Familie in der Gegenwart* (3rd ed.; Stuttgart, 1955); Gerhard Wurzbacher, *Leitbilder gegenwärtigen deutschen Familienlebens* (2nd ed.; Stuttgart, 1954). Cf. Howard Becker, "German Families Today," Chap. 2 in symposium ed. by H. J. Morgenthau, *Germany and the Future of Europe* (Chicago, 1951).

(perhaps the only one) in which intimacy, feeling, and socialization by primary human relations can still be carried on without reserve. To be sure, the "in-group" feeling bound with it also has its doubtful aspects. Yet when Schelsky summarizes the findings in approximately this manner, this interpretation attracts vehement criticism by other sociologists. Until now such investigations have not extended their scope in the direction of ascertaining whether the "asylum character" of the modern family will suffice to make it again an effective organizing focus in the larger society. The establishment of a Ministry of the Family by the Federal government in Bonn shows how strong are the "patriarchal" residues.

A number of additional problems are related to those problems of marriage and family that touch on sexual psychology, pedagogy, and morals. This area has not yet been well explored, although Michel's *Kritik der Moralstatistik* long since smoothed the way for an unprejudiced treatment of the actual facts.[81]

Stratification and the Structure of the Larger Society. However, nothing can be predicted about the fate of the family without more exact knowledge of the degree and kind of its determination by the larger society. But what do we know about this larger society itself?

If, in the last works of Geiger before 1933 on the social stratification of the German people, the problematical character of the class concept had already been recognized, then the development of the last decade has been characterized by a formal reduction of the concept and even by a certain depreciation of the concept "social stratification." Geiger, who indeed was the leading student of the stratification problem on the Continent, produced, on the basis of his investigation of social stratification in Denmark, a devastating critique of the class concept in its classical Marxist form. Marx's class theory was never correct in the sense of a universally valid empirical law. The temporally delimited phase of the society, for which it proved applicable to a certain extent, has already passed. Quite false, for example, are the "theory of increasing impoverishment" and the assumption of a "true class interest"; likewise false is Marx's prognosis of a disappearance of the middle classes. Stratification based largely on income has broken through the earlier class boundaries and the majority of workers have ascended to the petty bourgeois level. Indeed, it has generally become evident today that the "heroic age" of the workers' movement has passed. This means that the possibilities of a genuine "working-class" style of life are perhaps no longer capable of realization.[82]

On the other hand, Geiger believes he is able to demonstrate (on the basis of his Danish experiences) that vocational strata have become increas-

[81] Robert Michels, *Sittlichkeit in Ziffern? Kritik der Moralstatistik* (Munich, 1928).

[82] Theodor Geiger, *Die Klassengesellschaft im Schmelztiegel* (Cologne, 1949); Gerhard Weisser, *Freiheitlich-sozialistische Stilelemente im Leben der Arbeiterschaft* (Gottingen, 1948).

ingly more rigid in the last seventy years. Consequently, the widespread assertion that the class society is "open" in contrast to "closed estate society" is false—or at least exaggerated. The openness of class lines had been characteristic only of the short period of transition from the highly integrated estate-society in the epoch of early capitalism to the current class-society. I believe, rather, that "estate" elements have never been completely lost, even in the class society, and that they again became powerful after the opposition to estate privileges subsequent to the lapse of these privileges. Mitgau has recently pointed again to the numerous estate "residues" in our secularized culture,[83] by which it is so impressively distinguished from American society, for instance.

It is not at all asserted, however, that these residues will wither away simply because they are perceived as "feudal relics" by liberals. Rather, the prognosis for liberalism is unfavorable. An investigation carried out by Mackenroth shows that the differential social prestige of occupations, combined with the notions of achievement and intellectual qualification, are the most highly esteemed criteria for a ranking of occupations in wide circles of the population, quite independent of "class status."[84]

Geiger has also taken up Michels' old theme: the function of the "intelligentsia," showing that this group is to be defined neither by class situation and class consciousness nor by estate situation.[85]

The Process of De-Stratification. One can today pose the question whether or not the point has been reached in which traditional concepts of "vertical mobility," "social ascent and descent," and "social status" have become catchwords which will no longer exorcise the decisive events in society. On the basis of this rough sketch, contemporary processes must be designated as "leveling" or "de-stratification," although it is doubtful that the essential nature of the processes is revealed by such terms. Sober consideration shows the following: (1) Former class tensions have been more and more replaced in West Germany by tensions that cut across former class lines. The opposition between, on the one hand, the solidarity of interests in the production of goods (employer and worker), and the rest of society, especialy those who only consume, on the other, is perhaps the most important point (Geiger). Furthermore, there are a great number of tensions of the

[83] Theodor Geiger, "Umschichtungen in einer dänischen Mittelstadt," *Acta jutlandica, Aarsskrift for Asrhus Universitet,* 23 (Aarhus and Copenhagen, 1951); Hermann Mitgau, *Ständische Daseinsformen genealogisch gesehen: Untersuchungen über das Generationsschicksal im Gesellschaftsaufbau* (Gottingen, 1953). Cf. Howard Becker, "Changes in the Social Stratification of Contemporary Germany," *ASR,* 15, 3 (June, 1950), pp. 333-342.

[84] Gerhard Mackenroth and K. M. Bolte, "A report on the research plan used in 'Wandlungen der deutschen Sozialstruktur,'" *Transactions of the Second World Congress of Sociology,* 2 (London, 1954), pp. 91-102.

[85] Theodor Geiger, *Aufgaben und Stellung der Intelligenz in der Gesellschaft* (Stuttgart, 1949). Cf. Josef Dobretsberger, "Krise der Intelligens," *ZS,* 107 (1951), pp. 1-35.

second or third order of importance between indigenous and refugee populations, between religious groups, etc. (2) As a consequence of surplus production there exists a widespread pressure for raising the standard of living,[86] which derives less from the image of the "elevated" social strata than from the attraction of the supply itself and the covetous "squinting" at the style of life of one's neighbor who belongs to the same status level. Since this inclination is almost universal, it is therefore not specific to classes and thus must not be confused with the urge for social *ascent*, although the latter can be a subsidiary factor.

Political Sociology. The attempt to establish political science, under American influence, more firmly in academic instruction in the Federal Republic than in the period before 1933 is connected with sociology in several ways, although, naturally, not all political science is political sociology. Of the discussions in which the sociological orientation plays a role, those by Flechtheim and Grabowsky are prominent. The latter has also attempted to formulate a theory of the "masses." Stammer and Gablentz represent a pronounced political sociology.[87] Themes such as international relations, colonialism, imperialism, national ideas, and nationalism are still scarcely treated sociologically. There are, however, a few good studies of European nationalism by historians that the sociologist should not overlook.[88]

From Thurnwald's school, a social-psychological investigation of national prejudices should be cited.[89] A thorough sociological-functional examination of the problems of government and constitutions, and the comparative sociology of democratic and authoritarian ruling systems are still in their early stages. Promising beginnings have been made in the study of external and internal organization and the function of political parties, cells, and interest groups. Flechtheim made a sociological analysis of the German Communist Party during the Weimar Republic. Borkenau's book on Communism and the older works of Gurian are more historical.[90] They lack

[86] Gehlen speaks of a "limitless pleonexia," modifying a term of Scheler's; Arnold Gehlen, *Sozialpsychologische Probleme der industriellen Gesellschaft* (Tübingen, 1949).

[87] Ossip K. Flechtheim, *Politik als Wissenschaft* (Berlin, 1953); Adolf Grabowsky, *Politik im Grundriss* (Freiburg, 1952); Otto Stammer, "Herrschaftordnung und Gesellschaftsstruktur: Erkenntnisobjekt und Aufgaben der politischen Soziologie," *SJ*, 71 (1951), pp. 257-296; O. H. von der Gablenz, *Politische Parteien als Ausdruck gesellschaftlicher Kräfte* (Berlin, 1952).

[88] Eugen Lemberg, *Geschichte des Nationalismus in Europa* (Stuttgart, 1950); Alexander von Schelting, *Russland und Europa im russischen Geschichtsdenken* (Bern, 1948); Reinhard Wittram, *Das Nationale als europäisches Problem* (Gottingen, 1954).

[89] K. S. Sodhi and R. Bergius, *Nationale Vorurteile: Eine sozialpsychologische Untersuchung von 881 Personen* (Berlin, 1953).

[90] See Adolf Grabowsky, *Demokratie und Diktatur* (Zurich, 1949); Ossip K. Flechtheim, *Die KPD in der Weimarer Republik* (Offenbach, 1948); Franz Borkenau, *Der europäische Kommunismus: Seine Geschichte von 1917 bis zur Gegenwart* (Munich, 1952); Waldemar

the brilliant sociological illumination that distinguishes the books of the Frenchman Monnerot on the same themes, yet they offer more plentiful and reliable factual material.

Power, Propaganda, and Political Influence. In the area of political propaganda we now possess much more abundant material than in earlier times, but we lack a person of the caliber of the deceased Roffenstein for a thorough psychological examination of these factual riches.[91]

A problem-complex that attracts historians, sociologists, and ethical philosophers with particular intensity is that of power, domination, and violence; Max Weber had treated this complex earlier with great perception. Mühlmann, for example, dealt with the relation of theory and practice of Gandhi's non-violent resistance in the Indian revolution. On a wider basis, the book by the Chicago political scientist Ludwig Freund, published recently in Germany, treats the relation of politics and ethics and must be mentioned here because it is deeply rooted in the German philosophical tradition and in a sociological sense draws on Simmel and Max Weber.[92] These influences, however, are combined with American realism.

A great deal of thought has also been directed toward the problem of political leadership, political selection, and élite-formation in their historical, sociological, and practical aspects. Here the influence of Italian political sociology (Pareto, Mosca, and Michels) is quite conspicious.[93]

The Current Status of German Sociology: A Break with the Past. The fields of cultural sociology and comparative sociology have in recent years generally receded into the background compared with the activity of sociography and, recently, political sociology.

Gurian, *Der Bolschewismus: Einführung in Geschichte und Lehre* (Freiburg, 1931) R. M. MacIver's *The Web of Government* (New York, 1947) was translated into German under the title, *Macht und Autorität* (Frankfurt/Main, 1953).

[91] Walther Hagemann, *Publizistik im Dritten Reich* (Hamburg, 1949) and *Vom Mythos der Masse: Ein Beitrag zur Psychologie der Öffentlichkeit* (Heidelberg, 1951). Cf. Howard Becker, "The Regimented Man: Interviews with German Officials under the Nazis," *SF,* 28, 1 (Oct., 1949), pp. 19-24; ———, "Intellectuals, Concentration Camps, and Black Propaganda," *American Journal of Economics and Sociology,* hereinafter *AJES,* 10,2 (Jan., 1951), pp. 139-144; ———, "Propaganda and the Impotent German Intellectual," *SF,* 39, 3 (March, 1951), pp. 273-276; ———, "Max Weber, Assassination, and German Guilt," *AJES,* 10,4 (July, 1951), pp. 401-406.

[92] See Gerhard Ritter, *Vom sittlichen Problem der Macht* (Bern, 1948); W. E. Mühlmann, "Aspekte einer Soziologie der Macht," *ARS,* 40 (1952), pp. 84-114; Arnold Gehlen, *Macht, einmal anders gesehen* (Zurich, 1954); W. E. Muhlmann, *Mahatma Gandhi: Der Mann, sein Werk und seine Wirkung* (Tubingen, 1950); Ludwig Freund, *Politik und Ethik;* (Frankfurt/Main, 1955).

[93] See Theodor Geiger, "Führung," *HS* (Stuttgart, 1931), pp. 136-141; Max Graf zu Solms, *Führerbestellung* (Leipzig, 1932); W. E. Mühlmann, "Zur Theorie der sozialen Siebung," *Jahrbuch für Sozialwissenschaft,* 1 (1950), pp. 197-212; Otto Stammer, "Das Elitenproblem in der Demokratie," *SJ* (1951), pp. 1-28.

Ethnographic sociology is pursued only sporadically;[94] the majority of German ethnographers have been little interested in sociology. Unfortunately, the ever-widening breach between sociology and ethnology has developed to the point that the theoretical exploitation of ethnographic data (where this is attempted independently by sociologists) always turns out to be uncritical and dilettantish. Under American influence, many speak readily of "cultural anthropology"; dilettantish efforts, however, are often hidden behind this pretentious label.

It is doubtful whether the sociology of knowledge has a future, in spite of the renewed discussions over it. The high promise with which this special discipline emerged in its time does not seem to be vindicated by the results. It is quite different with the problem of ideology, but little has yet been produced in the investigations of political implications, although a refreshing book by Geiger, published posthumously, has appeared.[95]

There have been a great number of works that claimed to offer a total sociological interpretation of the present situation of mankind, at least of Western man. These efforts at the same time assume the air of being a critique of culture (or of civilization), and contain sociological elements, although they markedly overlap with a philosophy of history. Works of this kind, which can be recognized by their similar titles, already had a tradition in Germany. Nietzsche's and Spengler's works are the model. In 1931 *Die geistige Situation der Zeit* appeared, by the philosopher Karl Jaspers, who had been a pupil of Max Weber. Karl Mannheim wrote his *Diagnosis of Our Time* after emigrating; Max Horkheimer and Theodor W. Adorno likewise planned their deeply pessimistic *Dialektik der Aufklärung* in the emigration period. After the war the works of Alfred Weber, Alfred Müller-Armack, and Alexander Rüstow appeared in Germany.[96] The former sees the main evil in secularization, the latter in the proto-historic subjugation of ethnic groups by conquerors, through which the poison of a dominating arrogance has come into the world.

Although such works are taken today as accumulated wisdom or the condensed philosophy of a "great old man," there hardly exists an inclination to emulate them in the younger generation of sociologists. Theor-

[94] W. E. Mühlmann, "Abhängigkeit und Selbständigkeit bei den Naturvölkern in ihrem Verhältnis zur Zivilisation," in Leopold von Wiese (ed.), *Abhängigkeit und Selbständigkeit im Sozialen Leben* (Cologne, 1951), pp. 82-110; Ilse Schwedetzky, *Das Problem des Völkertodes* (Stuttgart, 1954).

[95] Egon Tuchfeldt, "Zur heutigen Problemstellung der Wissenssoziologie," *ZS*, 107 (1951), pp. 723-731; Hans Joachim Lieber, *Wissen und Gesellschaft: Die Probleme der Wissenssoziologie* (Tübingen, 1952); Theodor Geiger, *Ideologie und Wahrheit: Eine soziologische Kritik des Denkens* (Stuttgart, 1953).

[96] Alfred Weber, *Abschied von der bisherigen Geschichte* (Hamburg, 1946); Alfred Müller-Armack, *Das Jahrhundert ohne Gott: Zur Kultursoziologie unserer Zeit* (Münster, 1945); Alexander Rüstow, *Ortsbestimmung der Gegenwart* (Erlenbach-Zurich, 1950, 1952), 2 vols.

etic and systematic-sociological designs in general have become extremely rare.[97] Where such attempts are made, their proponents usually have neither the tenacity nor the intellectual eminence of the older German sociologists. In earlier times we had in sociology dominant personalities with ideas, and, if luck would have it, they made empirical observations also. Today we have teams of special research workers, united in cohesive working units, that work on definite social problems; and occasionally, they may have ideas also. The advantages of this procedure lie in the freshness, technical knowledge, and methodological security with which social problems are grasped. The disadvantages are the same as those in other countries: provincialism, and sometimes subjectivism and dilettantism. The age of the apparently great, definitive sociological systems and broad theories seems in any event to be ended, at least for the present. Whether it once more will return, no one can predict.[98]

SELECTED BIBLIOGRAPHY

Aron, Raymond, *La Sociologie allemande contemporaine* (Paris: Presses Universitaires de France, 1936).

Barnes, H. E. (ed.), *An Introduction to the History of Sociology* (Chicago: University of Chicago Press, 1948), Chap. 10-20.

Becker, Howard, and H. E. Barnes, *Social Thought from Lore to Science*, 2nd ed. (New York: Dover Publications, 1952). Chap. 23, "Sociology in the Germanic Languages," I., "Germany and Austria," pp. 878-933.

Gehlen, Arnold, and Helmut Schelsky (eds.), *Soziologie* (Düsseldorf: E. Diederich, 1955).

Horkheimer, Max, *Survey of the Social Sciences in Western Germany* (Washington: Library of Congress, 1952).

Salomon, Albert, "German Sociology," in Georges Gurvitch and Wilbert E. Moore (eds.), *Twentieth Century Sociology* (New York: Philosophical Library, 1945), Chap. 20.

Wiese, Leopold von, *Soziologie: Geschichte und Hauptprobleme* (Berlin: Walter de Gruyter, 1950).

Ziegenfuss, Werner, *Handbuch der Soziologie,* Erste Hälfte (Stuttgart: Ferdinand Enke Verlag, 1955), especially Chaps. 1 and 2.

[97] For example, Max Graf zu Solms, "Gesellungslehre," *Verhandlungen des 8. Deutschen Soziologentages 1946* (Tübingen, 1948), pp. 57-91; Gerhard Mackenroth, *Sinn und Ausdruck in der sozialen Formenwelt* (Meisenheim, 1952).

[98] Some examples of team research are: Wilhelm Bernsdorf and Friedrich Bülow (eds.), *Wörterbuch der Soziologie* (Stuttgart, 1955); Arnold Gehlen and Helmut Schelsky (eds.), *Soziologie: Lehr- und Handbuch zur modernen Gesellschaftskunde* (Düsseldorf, 1955); Werner Ziegenfuss (ed.), *Handbuch der Soziologie,* 2 vols. (Stuttgart, 1955-56).

SOCIOLOGY IN ITALY: PROBLEMS AND PERSPECTIVES*

FRANCO FERRAROTTI

THE PURPOSE OF THIS ESSAY IS THE IMPARTING OF A FEW OBSERVATIONS ON THE fortunes and present status of sociological studies in Italy, especially since World War I. This will not, therefore, be a comprehensive study or a critical analysis of the works that have been produced and that, rightly or wrongly, have been considered particularly important on the Italian cultural scene in the field of sociology. This study proposes simply to reopen discussion on several fundamental problems with which, in the Italian cultural situation, sociology must first reckon if it really intends to eliminate from its path certain obstacles that even now seriously hinder its possibilities of development.

THE EPHEMERAL NATURE OF ITALIAN SOCIOLOGY

The position of sociological studies in Italy remains precarious. There are, it is true, signs of an awakening interest that in certain instances reveals some of the enthusiasm of a rediscovery. However, it is a fact that in the modern Italian cultural picture true and independent sociological inquiries are still sporadic enterprises, generally the result of the inspiration and efforts of isolated individuals. Only in exceptional cases do they succeed in giving their investigations an organic foundation and a coherent unity sufficient to save them from unwarranted fragmentary dispersion.[1]

* Translated by Walter G. Langlois, University of Wisconsin.

[1] See Filippo Barbano's bibliographical essay in *Il Politico* (December, 1954). In spite of its disputable viewpoint, this article is particularly imoprtant when considered as a first step toward that organic unity which is sadly lacking in Italian sociological studies.

Understood in its modern sense, sociology is an inductive inquiry not overly preoccupied with fitting itself into a universal metaphysical system. Furthermore, it is a descriptive analysis of human collectivities and of their various interdependent behavior patterns, insofar as these are uniform, recurrent, and therefore—it is well to add—predictable. It is possible to affirm without fear of contradiction that sociology as such is almost non-existent in Italy today. Such an affirmation may seem polemically motivated and unjustified, especially when one considers the abundance of "sociological" titles and phrases in our country, where everyone seems to be interested—in varying degrees—in social problems. But these are really only phrases and not in the majority of cases investigations that are clearly delimited and definite in their working hypotheses and method. They are rather more or less utopian and unjustified projects in which the characteristic note is struck by the constant—and one could say innate—confusion between empirical *apprehension* and guiding *concepts*. Sociological research, strictly speaking, is in reality very rare.

THE BLIGHT OF CROCEAN IDEALISM

According to a rather prevalent point of view, the responsibility for this situation—that is, for the difficulties and in the final analysis for the bankruptcy and almost complete absence of sociology in Italy today, rests principally on the idealistic philosophies of neo-Hegelian origin (Croce and Gentile). In this there is certainly a notable element of truth, although it is easy, viewing the situation exclusively in such terms, to be led to reason mechanically in either-or terms and neglect to consider and evaluate all the variables. As I have had occasion to remark elsewhere, there is no doubt that the prolonged, decisive influence of neo-idealism on the development of our cultural life, in its interests and in its most important directions of study, has contributed and still contributes to a marked degree in making difficult a critical overhauling of the traditions on which sociological studies in Italy must undoubtedly rely. It is a fact that, in the course of the last forty years, neo-idealism has exerted a detrimental influence on sociology, an influence even now not completely dead. The negative position of Croce still makes its effects felt, even in controversies in various areas outside the purely academic world of the specialists, to such an extent that it sometimes becomes the subject of journalistic arguments.[2]

This should not be especially surprising. The influence of neo-idealism,

[2] See for example the bitter polemic exchange of a few years ago between Carlo Antoni, Camillo Pellizzi, and Liberio Lenti about the political science faculties that had seriously compromised themselves during the Fascist period: C. Antonio, "La Facoltà degli spostati," *Il Mondo* (July 23, 1949); C. Pellizzi, "La Facoltà degli spostati," *La Fiera Letteraria* (July 24, 1949); L. Lenti, "La Cultura dei diciottisti," *Il Mondo* (August 6, 1949); C. Antonio, "La Facoltà della seconda laurea," *Il Mondo* (August 13, 1949).

particularly the philosophy of Croce (it seems that Gentile was never anything but an "able exponent"),[3] on Italian cultural life has been so complete and all-pervasive that it is no longer noticed. The thing that is really startling is that the negative position of Croce regarding the possibilities of sociology as a science continues to be blissfully repeated as if it were a hallowed formula. No attempt has been made to go into it more deeply in order to extract all its logical implications. That such a deeper critical examination of his position has not been undertaken, that the urgency of such a re-evaluation has not been realized, testifies in a very evident manner to the enduring presence and acceptance *en bloc* of the fundamental elements of Croce's philosophy in every field of our traditional cultural activity.[4] His veto continues to give evidence of persistent vitality and is still taken up uncritically and regurgitated in various forms as a philosophical *ne plus ultra*.

The success of Croce's philosophy and its extraordinary capacity for *penetration* were, in fact, related to the real exigencies of the situation of the nation, which Croce met by furnishing the philosophical foundation for a first attempt at synthesis and intellectual reorganization. As Gramsci wrote, "While it is true that in Croce the preoccupations of a world *leader* are always present and induce him to assume balanced, Olympian positions without compromising commitments of a temporal or episodic character, it is also true that he himself inculcated the principle that in Italy—if one wanted to de-provincialize culture and custom (and provincialism still remains as a relic of the political and moral particularism of the past)—it was necessary to elevate the level of intellectual life through contact and exchange of ideas with the whole world. . . . Consequently there is immanent in his position and in his function an essentially nationalistic principle. The function of Croce may be compared to that of the Roman Catholic Pope."[5]

Whether the comparison made by Gramsci between Croce and the Pope appears acceptable or whether it sounds irreverent and even offensive, it is certain that Croce as well as Gentile knew how to use the disciplinary rod *(ferula)* very well. Both of them, but especially the indefatigable Croce, may be considered good examples of "organizers" of culture. As early as the first decade of this century, Croce—who from 1903 was publishing *La Critica* and who had already become known both for his critical studies of history and literature and for his reappraisals of Marxism and Hegelianism —was ready to assume the task of being an intellectual guide. He set himself up as the central driving force of a renovation of Italian culture in anti-

[3] See Franco Lombardi, *Nascita del mondo moderno* (Asti, 1953), p. 145.

[4] It is Antonio Gramsci who has probably furnished the most exact scientific explanation of the socio-cultural interpenetration that was to emerge and establish itself as a true "cultural dictatorship" with Croce as a kind of lay Pope. See especially his *Il materialismo storico et la filosofia di Benedetto Croce* (Turin, 1948).

[5] *Ibid.*, pp. 246-247.

positivist terms. This renovation, based on a broad doctrinal clarification having serious consequences, is nevertheless expressed in an unpretentious and almost journalistic discussion. Any fundamental complexities are well concealed by the free-flowing simplicity of the text.

The resulting price paid by Italian culture for this "clarification" was rather high. Although on the one hand it fortunately tempered certain mechanistic excesses of the old positivism, on the other it proposed a new concept of the natural sciences and mathematics that really indicated the impoverishment and dissolution of a whole series of scientific disciplines. As Remo Cantoni has justly observed, "it became necessary to disdain any classification whatever that had a pragmatic, empirical, naturalistic, or social character. The whole of science was put aside as a form of knowledge that was governed by practical—not speculative—exigencies. Everywhere idealism discovered 'pseudo-concepts.'"[6]

In fact, a purely abstractive function was restored to mathematics, whereas all value as knowledge, properly speaking, was denied to the natural sciences and to sociology. They were reduced to little more than convenient classifications. Nor is it accurate to assert, as has often been done by the disciples of Croce and by those who came after them, that Croce did not devaluate science when he transferred it from logic to practice, since in his thought theory and practice constituted a relationship for which it was not logically possible to establish a hierarchy of values. The truth is that by denying science any cognitive value and by reducing it to convenient classification, Croce initiated a divergence between philosophy and science. Not only did philosophy come less often to the aid of scientific research, especially insofar as the fundamental systematic methodology and working hypotheses were concerned, but instead of being enriched with new ideas, it was itself progressively reduced to being a "soloist," to philosophizing with concepts that were "pure"—that is, irrelevant and gratuitous.

Those who hold the widespread opinion that the "dictatorship of idealism" is the fundamental reason for the progressive impoverishment and final extinction of the once vigorous Italian sociological trends are without doubt justified to a certain extent. This position takes into account a series of factors that in the Italian cultural picture of this first half-century have had a very perceptible influence. It is, however, a position that has now become traditional and is everyday more and more in danger of becoming a platitude and a bias. It is really much more interesting to ask why those who carried out empirical social research were not able to resist the idealistic "dictatorship." The limitations of their capacity for resisting the teachings of the followers of Croce and Gentile is truly astonishing.

In other words, it is certainly important to examine the criticisms that

[6] See Remo Cantoni, "La Dittatura dell'Idealismo," *Il Politecnico,* 38 (November, 1947).

the idealists made of sociology and of science in general. In part at least, this has been done.[7] But even more important is the examination of the intrinsic reasons for the weaknesses—from the point of view of methodology and content—of the most notable of the Italian sociologists of the past fifty years, of these "isolates" in the time of Croce, who represent a chapter in the history of Italian culture that is still to be fully written.

THE INFLUENCE OF COMTE

The bibliographical survey by J. M. Robertson notes that "in few countries has there been more sociological activity than in Italy."[8] But to avoid gross misunderstandings, a few clarifications are necessary from the very beginning. Rarely did the promoters of Italian sociology, who at one time were legion, succeed in freeing themselves from the fascination of the philosophy of Comte. They found in the thought of Auguste Comte a combination of emphasis on empirical research and the necessity for an organic, systematic structure, together with a mystical spirit of reform, that appeared remarkably congruent with the tradition of social studies in Italy. In this tradition the *sociological,* as the specific field of descriptive analysis, and the *social,* as the rule of conduct or Utopian plan of reform, were often presented as intimately intermingled. The base given by Comte to sociological research may with a certain justice be defined as "imperialistic" because he considered sociology the crown and summation of all the other sciences, which were consequently to find their justification in it. In reality, sociology—understood according to the conception of Comte—does not appear sufficiently explicit and sure, insofar as its specific object of inquiry is concerned, precisely because of its generalizing tendencies. It is possible to find concrete verification of such an absence of methodology—besides the criticism of Croce, which amply capitalized on this fundamental defect—in Italian sociological production, and particularly in the heterogeneous and erratic character which, save for a few exceptions, distinguishes it.

This inability to fix and guarantee philosophically the specific object of sociological research becomes clearly evident even when one glances through the copious indexes of the *Rivista di Sociologia,* which made its first appearance in 1897. In this review can be found, under the protection of a disconcerting eclecticism, essays on the most varied themes and researches alien to the spirit of a rigorous methodology.[9]

Such methodological chaos, and more precisely the almost complete absence of well-defined, clearly formulated working hypotheses capable of

[7] See Franco Ferrarotti, *Sociologia—saggi e ricerche* (Asti, 1955), pp. 30-33.

[8] J. M. Robertson, *Courses of Study* (3rd ed.; London, 1932), p. 217.

[9] See in this connection the acute criticisms of Constantine Panunzio, "Italian Sociology," in Georges Gurvitch and W. E. Moore (eds.), *Twentieth Century Sociology* (New York, 1945), pp. 650-651.

orienting research and avoiding the pitfalls of false problems and mistaken aims, is characteristic of these works, and it undermines the validity of a whole series of them. The following appear to belong to this class: the *Prime linee di un programma critico di sociologia* (Perugia, 1888) by Icilio Vanno; *Dottrine sociologiche* (Verona, 1901) of Achille Loria; *Saggi di sociologia* (Milan, 1902) and numerous other works of Alessandro Groppali.

Little is worthy of being retained of all this voluminous production, dedicated to questions of a sociological character but in reality profoundly disoriented in its choice of subjects and largely saturated with mechanistic concepts that tend to apply *extrinsic* laws to the world of human beings, conceived as naturalistically valid in accordance with the methodological postulates of Spencerian organismic theory. However, for the clarity of its organization and for the precise sense of the limits that are placed on sociology as a science in relation to the other sciences, the little book of Emilio Morselli, entitled *Elimenti di sociologia generale* (Milan, 1898), is noteworthy. The work is deliberately expository and has explicit intentions of popularization. The thing that stands out as its most positive quality (in an epoch and cultural climate in which sociology as a whole was still conceived essentially as the "science of humanity" using the other sciences as subordinate disciplines to develop to the utmost a monistic, socio-centric system that took the form of a kind of lay "religion" is the clear awareness that "sociology is a science still in process of formation and consequently cannot present dogmatic, established concepts like a treatise in mathematics or physics."[10]

MICHELS: THE CONFLICT OF HISTORICISM AND SOCIOLOGICAL ANALYSIS

It is possible to discern a fundamentally mechanistic and ahistorical orientation in the sociological works of Roberto Michels, who is justly remembered for his studies on the oligarchical tendencies of political parties and particularly for his work on the sociology of the political party in modern democracy.[11] Michels conducted his research along the lines laid down by Vilfredo Pareto, on the one hand; and on the other, according to the concept of "political class" elaborated by Gaetano Mosca.

Michels' observations and the investigations he conducted—in large part the fruit of his direct experience with the internal life of the Italian Socialist Party and of the German Social-Democratic Party to which he often refers in his works[12]—led him to formulate what he defines as the "iron law

[10] Emilio Morselli, *Elementi di sociologia generale* (Milan, 1898), p. xi.

[11] Roberto Michels, *La Sociologia del partito politico nella democrazia moderna* (Turin, 1912).

[12] A bibliography, however summary, of the works of Roberto Michels should probably include the following titles: *Il proletariato e la borghesia nel movimento socialista italiano—saggio di scienza sociografico-politica* (Turin, 1908); *I limiti della morale sessuale* (Turin, 1912); *Saggi economico-statistici sulle classi popolari* (Milan, 1914); *Problemi di sociologia*

of oligarchical tendencies." According to this law, the verification and actual practical operation of democracy as a political régime and therefore as an organizational structure appear severely limited by the "necessity of organization." Organizations, in fact, in order to survive and attain a certain degree of security and stability, are for the most part linked to an "active minority" on whom it is necessary to lean and to which one must unavoidably trust oneself, given the "mechanical and technical impossibility of direct control on the part of the masses." Michels' studies on democracy and authority and his observations on the internal dynamics and organizational structure of the modern political party still constitute rather stimulating reading today —so much so that his volume on the sociology of the political party was first translated in 1915 and reissued in 1951 in the United States.[13]

Yet it is difficult not to perceive in the sociological analyses of Michels the artificial nature of similar typologies and the poverty of certain paradigms, rarely aided by a historical perspective that is organic and critically based—that is, united to a rigorous methodology. The consequence of these deficiencies is that—in spite of copious documentation, of which Michels gives proof in many places—his research sometimes descends to the level of historical anecdote and erudite curiosity, rarely escaping from a diffuseness that undermines its scientific exactitude. This is the case with his critical history of the Italian socialist movement,[14] in which the absence of a clear organic design is amply compensated for by the interest of the abundant citations. Rather useful and worthy of note, among other things, are the attempts to describe on the basis of empirical research what happens in the actual daily routine of social movements (in particular the Italian Socialist Party) generally studied only from the historical and ideological viewpoint.

In the work of Michels these factual descriptions appear as the necessary complement of the purely genetic or historical narration and may rightly be considered as true and appropriate descriptive sociological analyses. In this connection, one can cite the pages dealing with the "veneration of the heads of the Party,"[15] or the interesting inquiry into the reasons for the scant activity and ineffective functioning of the socialist deputies in Parliament.[16] Equally illuminating are the passages regarding the "instituting of leadership *(Führertum)* in democratic organizations." Here Michels points out how

applicata (Turin, 1919); *Corso di sociologia politica* (Milan, 1927); *La teoria di Carlo Marx sulla miseria crescente e le sue origini* (Turin, 1922); *Sunto di storia economica germanica* (Bari, 1930); *Der Patriotismus—Prolegomena zu seiner soziologischen Analyse* (Leipzig, 1929); *Studi sulla democrazia e sull'autorità* (Florence, 1933); *Il boicottagio—saggio su un aspetto delle crisi* (Turin, 1934); *Nuovi studi sulla classe politica—saggio sugli spostamenti sociali e intellettuali nel dopoguerra* (Milan, 1936).

[13] See Michels, *Political Parties* (New York, 1915; Glencoe, Ill., 1951).

[14] See Michels, *Storia critica del movimento socialista italiano* (Florence, 1926).

[15] *Ibid.*, p. 196.

[16] *Ibid.*, p. 279.

"the politically necessary principle of organization, although it avoids that pitfall of disunity of the masses so propitious to its adversaries, conceals within itself other dangers, and thus flees from Scylla only to fall into Charybdis."[17]

In spite of the sometimes violent criticisms leveled against Michels from many sides,[18] such analytical descriptions indubitably contribute to the subject, or rather illuminate the background against which the events take place and which promotes their evaluation. For this reason, even if from a methodological point of view Michels leaves something to be desired and in certain research gathers data indiscriminately, his works still have some degree of validity and interest.

PARETO AND POSITIVISM

The adherents of Croce, together with all those learned men who from the early years of this century accepted his neo-Hegelian premises, in the final analysis had an easy time in attacking the theories of the most noted of the Italian sociologists,. Vilfredo Pareto,[19] from a philosophical and more specifically methodological point of view. The task of the critics was indubitably facilitated by Pareto's obstinate refusal to make any effort to assure the preciseness and autonomy of sociological research on the level of its philosophical base. "Let's forget the names," he writes," and look at the things . . . we have better things to do than to waste time trying to determine whether sociology is or is not an autonomous science—whether it is anything other than the philosophy of history under another name—or arguing at length concerning the methods to be followed in its study."[20] Although he begins his work with this declaration, which might seem to be devoid of pragmatism, Pareto in reality tries—and it is an ambitious effort because of its breadth and vastness of plan—to found sociology as an exact science, particularly in the three large volumes of his treatise on general sociology (four volumes in English translation).

In contrast to the sociological studies inspired by the philosophy of Comte—studies which are inclined to fall into metaphysics in spite of all protestations of "positivism"—Pareto uses the logico-experimental method; that is to say, he declares that his research is based exclusively on experience and observation. The repugnance that dogmatic or *a priori* sociologies arouse

[17] See Michels, *La sociologia del partito politico nella democrazia,* p. 21 *ff*.

[18] See, among others, Antonio Gramsci, *Note sul Machiavelli, sulla politica e sullo stato moderno* (Turin, 1949), pp. 95-100.

[19] Among the works of Vilfredo Pareto, the following are particularly noteworthy: *Les systèmes socialistes* (Paris, 1902) [Italian translation, *I sistemi socialisti* (Turin, 1951)]; *Manuale di economia politica* (Milan, 1906); *Il mito virtuista e la letteratura immorale* (2nd ed.; Rome, 1914); *Trattato di sociologia generale* (Florence, 1916-1923); *Trasformazione della democrazia* (Milan, 1921); *Fatti e teorie* (Florence, 1920).

[20] Pareto, *Trattato di sociologia generale,* vol. I, p. 1.

in him finds vituperative expression: "We have an abundance of 'humanitarian' sociologies, for all those that are being published now are of that sort; we don't lack metaphysical sociologies, and among them are to be classed all those which are 'positivist' and humanitarian; we have a small number of Christian sociologies, Catholic and other; let it be conceded, without wanting to slight all these sociologies, that we are here engaged in the exposition of a kind that is exclusively experimental, like chemistry, physics, and other similar sciences."[21] Guided by this method and with these criteria, Pareto presents an analysis of a huge, heterogeneous collection of evidence, including among other things entire historical periods, the rise and fall of cultures and nations, and the classic description of the "circulation of the élites." The fundamental aim of this long, ponderous work of research, and its ultimate justification, probably consists in the attempt to verify inductively the law of "social equilibrium," which Pareto conceives in accordance with his own methodological premises in mechanistic terms and which he can therefore express in mathematical language through a system of equations.

Aside from the intrinsic limitations of his "social equilibrium," concerning which serious doubts have been raised even recently,[22] and the traditional series of objections that can be leveled against a purely mathematical method when it is applied to the descriptive analysis of the world of human beings and its manifold, multidimensional relationships, the weakness of the monumental sociological work of Pareto seems to lie, from the point of view of recent developments in the social sciences, in its *macrosociological* character. This is particularly true in a period in which sociology is renouncing in ever more decisive manner those ambitions typical of the "imperialism" or encyclopedism of Comte, in favor of the study of well-defined social phenomena, such as the primary group and the community. It appears to be constantly more cognizant of the necessity of going beyond the essentially mechanistic organization from which Spencer's teaching is not immune. We are in fact going from a *macrosociology,* or a general, encyclopedic sociology characteristic of the last century, toward a sociology that is both extremely careful in circumscribing the field of its own specific inquiry and philosophically more sophisticated and defensible. To express it with the suggestive phrase of Gurvitch, we are evolving a sociology *en profondeur*[23] that recognizes its obligation—at a certain stage of its development—to take into account both psychology and history.

All this is certainly not sufficient to justify the critical demolition of Pareto by the neo-idealist followers of Croce and Gentile, particularly Guido de Ruggiero, who writes in so many words: "Without bothering with the

[21] *Ibid.,* p. 4.

[22] See David Easton, "Limits of the Equilibrium Model in Social research," *Profits and Problems of Homeostatic Models in the Behavioral Sciences* (Chicago, 1953), pp. 26-40.

[23] Georges Gurvitch, *La Vocation actuelle de la sociologie* (Paris, 1950), p. 49.

Pleiad of minor authors, I shall restrict myself to calling attention to a very conspicuous and recent example of a man who is generally considered a great master in Italy—I mean Vilfredo Pareto. I have read his treatise on general sociology with a great sense of sadness. The author, a writer of great historical erudition, of acute political sense and of admirable scientific restraint, has succeeded in wasting his outstanding qualities in a work organized abstractly and mechanistically."[24]

The judgment of de Ruggiero, effectively summing up the position of a more mature Crocean philosophy *vis-à-vis* sociology, accused of burying "the laws (of thought) beneath the chaotic mass of facts,"[25] has found followers and has often been amplified in recent works.[26] Pareto is reproached above all for the schematic character of his theoretical analysis, which results in the famous dichotomy of the *residues* (or part that is constant, instinctive, nonlogical) on the one hand, and the *derivations* (or part that is variable and deductive, tending to explain and justify the residues) on the other. Another point of reproach and criticism is found in the unwarranted, confused, and undoubtedly complex subdivisions to which this dichotomy gives rise. Pareto divides the residues into six classes: (1) residues of the instinct of combination; (2) residues of the persistence of aggregates; (3) residues (or needs) of the manifestation of sentiments through overt acts; (4) residues of sociability; (5) residues of the integrity of the individual; (6) sexual residues. Moreover he distinguishes the four classes of *derivations,* masks by means of which facts are rationalized: (1) simple affirmations; (2) affirmations supported by an authority; (3) affirmations in accordance with sentiments or principles; (4) affirmations dependent on exclusively verbal proofs. Each class of residues is formed by many elements and the four classes of derivations include seventeen different forms. The 52 residues (Pareto actually enumerated this many) can enter into various combinations among themselves and with the 17 forms of the derivations. Thus one can easily see that certain reproaches were not completely unjustified and that, in the heat of argument, all sorts of criticisms were leveled against him.

Whatever may be our over-all opinion of the scientific validity of the sociological work of Pareto, there is no doubt that the contributions of this man, who time and time again has been compared with Voltaire and even with Abbot Galiani, and by North American scholars with Thorstein Veblen,[27] have been numerous and of great importance. Among these it is sufficient to note the definition of the logico-experimental method applied

[24] Guido de Ruggiero, *La Filosofia contemporanea* (Bari, 1941), II, pp. 230-231.

[25] *Ibid.,* p. 231.

[26] This is the case with Giuseppe La Ferla, *Vilfredo Pareto, filosofo volteriano* (Florence, 1954).

[27] W. Rex Crawford, "Representative Italian Contributions to Sociology," in H. E. Barnes (ed.), *An Introduction to the History of Sociology* (Chicago, 1948), pp. 555.

to the social sciences, the distinction between the logical and the non-rational elements in human conduct, the recognition that beliefs, myths, and dreams are very real "facts" for the social scientists, the theory of residues and derivations (however artificial and complicated it may appear), the concept of the élite, and, finally, the conception of social causation as a process in which many variables may be functionally interactive.

MOSCA AND METHODOLOGICAL BALANCE

In general, the criticism of the Croceans has been less sharp towards Gaetano Mosca, one of the most noted and astute promotors of the Italian social sciences.[28] It is probable that this results from the fact that Gaetano Mosca, in contrast to other eminent Italian social scientists (such as Roberto Michels, Vilfredo Pareto, and Achille Loria), accepts fully and with all its implications the historical method, rejecting the "single-factor fallacy," which he characterizes as consisting in "simplist formulas that claim to explain very complex phenomenon by means of a single cause."[29] The same Benedetto Croce, reviewing Mosca's work on the elements of political science, wrote:

> The dominating concept of the book is by this time well-known because it is linked to the name of Mosca: it is the idea of the political or ruling class in which the political life of the state is really focused: a class which is quantitatively a minority but qualitatively a majority because it possesses awareness and possibilities for action. This concept is of the greatest importance for the interpretation of political history, an interpretation that is sought in vain in such external causes as climate, ethnic situation, etc., or in any other kind of externals, i.e., political forms considered as values in themselves, that is to say abstract and empty, such as monarchy, republic, and the like.[30]

In spite of this clear recognition of the validity of the methodological base of his research, the historical method to which Mosca claims he conforms is evidently strictly inductive and hence comparable to the empirical method of the natural sciences. As such Croce cannot accept it. However, in order not to be accused of pedantry, Croce abstains from a criticism that might appear purely formalistic. He writes: "While Mosca enunciates and demonstrates truth, it is evident that he is philosophizing and philosophizing well," even

[28] Among Mosca's works, those particularly worthy of mention are: *Teoria dei governi e governo parlamentare* (2nd ed.; Milan, 1925); *Elementi di scienza politica* (2nd ed.; Turin, 1923), 2 vols.; *Il principio aristocratico e il democratico nel passato e nell'avvenire* (Turin, 1903); *Cenni storici e critici sulle dottrine razziste* (Rome, 1933); *Storia delle dottrine politiche* (Rome, 1933; 6th ed.; Bari, 1951).

[29] See Mosca, *Elementi di scienza politica* (5th ed.; Bari, 1953), I, p. 19.

[30] See Benedetto Croce, in *Critica,* XXI (November, 1923), pp. 374-378, reprinted as *Premessa* to Mosca's *Elementi di scienza politica* (5th ed.; Bari, 1953), p. viii.

if it would be easy to demonstrate that Mosca "reaches those truths by means of a method different from the inductive, naturalistic one."[31]

Besides the exact formulation of the concept of the "ruling class," Mosca is particularly apt and effective in those passages where he attacks the banalities and false problems that in his time were still taken as accepted truths. Thus, for example, in pointing out the various biases and prejudices against which Spencer warned scholars of social phenomena to guard themselves (national, religious or political prejudices, etc.), Mosca is able to point out that "the true safeguard against this sort of error is in knowing how to elevate criticism itself above the beliefs and opinions that are general in our epoch or in the particular social or national environment of which we are a part."[32] Further along in his treatment of the question, he takes the opportunity to explode the myth of a presumed antagonism or opposition between the state and society, about which so much has been written.

Starting in fact from his fundamental proposition that "in all societies . . . there exist two classes of people, the governing and the governed,"[33] Mosca affirms that

> antagonism between state and society cannot exist since it is possible to consider the state as that part of the society that fulfills its political function. Thus all questions regarding the interference of the state come to be viewed in a new light. Rather than study what should be the limits of the action of the state, one should seek to ascertain what is the best type of political organization—that is to say, the one that permits all the elements having a given political value in a given society to be best utilized and developed, best subjected to reciprocal control and to the principle of individual responsibility for the acts which they carry out in their respective functions.[34]

The position of Gaetano Mosca appears particularly convincing when he criticizes the concept of "social law" as elaborated by Auguste Comte as being simplist and schematic. Rather judiciously, he notes how the famous Comtean "law of the three stages" cannot logically provide the base for "making a clear and precise chronological distinction between the various human societies by assigning them to one of the three periods Comte names, i.e., theological, metaphysical, and positive."[35] He concludes that "in this, as in so many other cases, simplification does not adapt itself well to the sciences that have to do with the mentality of man, a very complex animal, full of contradictions, who is not always concerned with being logical and coherent."[36]

[31] Croce, *op. cit.*, p. ix.
[32] Mosca, *op. cit.*, p. 73.
[33] *Ibid.*, p. 78.
[34] *Ibid.*, p. 212.
[35] *Ibid.*, p. 218.
[36] *Ibid.*, p. 221.

Equally incisive and appropriate is the criticism advanced by Mosca against the Spencerian distinction between military states, founded on the coercion which the governing class exerts on the governed, and industrial states, based, on the contrary, on a contract—that is, on the free consent of those who make up the state. In opposition to the thesis of Spencer, Mosca demonstrates how "any political organization whatsoever . . . is concurrently spontaneous and coercive; spontaneous since it derives from the nature of man, as has been observed ever since Aristotle, and at the same time coercive because it is a *necessary* condition, man not being able to live otherwise."[37]

Moreover, the ideas of Mosca, like those of Pareto and of Michels, for that matter, were able—in the field of politics—to lend themselves to a justification of Fascism (or at least to a justification of the principle of the "charismatic leader" which was reminiscent of Weber's principle and which at the time was personified by Mussolini) independently of the personal political positions of these writers. Ironically, on the other hand, with the advent of Fascism to power the possibility of conducting free research in the social sciences ended, and in the universities the chairs of sociology and of political science became chairs of "Fascist doctrine."

"THE MARXIST OPPOSITION": IDEOLOGY UNLEASHED

The most interesting characteristic of the present situation of sociological studies in Italy—especially in relation to the critical reappraisal of the traditions of social studies of the pre-Fascist period—seems to be not so much the persistent opposition of those qualified as followers of Croce[38] as the position assumed by the Marxist intellectuals. We have already alluded to the criticisms of the social sciences, and in particular of sociology, put forward by Italian neo-Hegelians. Such criticisms are almost too well known. It should be equally well known that on the level of philosophical and methodological foundations, these criticisms meet only scattered and inadequate resistance.

This is so evident that some Italian sociologists save themselves only by walling themselves up in clearly circumscribed specializations. This seems to be the case with Corrado Gini,[39] internationally known statistician and author of valuable studies on demography, who is responsible for—among other things—an attempt to furnish a biologistic interpretation of history

[37] *Ibid.*, p. 230.

[38] See, for example, the argument between the disciple of Croce, Carlo Antoni, in *Il Mondo* (November 17, 1951), p. 6, and Nicola Abbagnano in *Quaderni di Sociologia* (Winter, 1952), p. 137.

[39] For a bibliography of the numerous contributions of Corrado Gini, see the bibliographical appendix of his *Patologia economica* (5th ed.; Turin, 1954). Particularly noteworthy are: *I fattori demografici dell' evoluzione delle nazioni* (Turin, 1912); *Le rilevazioni statistiche tra le popolazioni primitive* (Rome, 1942); *Il neo-organicismo* (Catania, 1927).

and society[40] which he called "demographic metabolism." It seems to follow the Spencerian tradition with the addition of a vast superstructure derived from the philosophy of Comte.

In relation to sociological research and to its present prospects, far removed from those implicit in the positions of Comte and Spencer, it is the Marxists who in Italy today have assumed the role of foremost opposition. The recent resolution of the cultural section of the central committee of the Italian Communist Party, entitled "Against the Ideologies of the Monopolies,"[41] did not surprise anyone who follows the vicissitudes of the internal ideological debate and the "cultural politics" promulgated by the Communists. This document, of undoubted interest, clearly sums up the position of the Italian Communist intellectuals, as well as those points of view that had found scattered expression in the press organs of the party.

With regard to sociology, the resolution mentioned above is very critical. We read in it, for example, that "the ideological action of the monopolies does not limit itself to business. It tends to spread and diffuse those theories that conceal exploitation and monopolistic surplus-profits. The increase of this ideological action of the monopolies among the intellectuals is without a doubt favored by the accompanying growing penetration into Italian culture of the most recent neo-positivist and sociological theories." This statement, which even in its circumspect language seems to signify the reduction of the sociological disciplines to the defense of parochial interests, or to being no more than simple instruments in the hands of the industrial monopolies, may have justified in the eyes of some commentators the accusation of economic determinism inherent in Italian Marxism of today.

In reality, the Italian exponents of Marxism openly admit that "in truth certain of the technical accomplishments [of American sociological currents] are objectively linked to the amplification of the knowledge of what is real and to the development of productive forces." (Cf. the *Resolution.*) Yet they reproach the representatives of these currents for "the refutation of whatever historical and dialectical vision of the world there is." Here there is probably a fundamental misunderstanding. It is a misunderstanding that seriously impedes the development of empirical social research in Italy and that—insofar as the Italian Marxists of today are concerned—seems to betray in a rather evident manner their origin, not so much in Croce, but rather in Gentilian dialectics—that is, as followers of Giovanni Gentile. In any case they are "Marxists steeped in idealism," as one of them even admitted.[42]

In truth, to reproach modern sociology with the renunciation of an evolutionary, total vision of reality and the study of its internal dynamism

[40] See in particular, Corrado Gini, *Nascita, evoluzione e morte delle nazioni—La teoria ciclica della popolazione e i vari sistemi di politica demografica* (Rome, 1930).

[41] See the Communist newspaper *L'Unità*, August 2nd, 1955, p. 3.

[42] See the Communist weekly *Il Contemporaneo,* II, no. 32, p. 11.

conceived in traditional historical terms simply means to exchange for a methodological confusion the refutation with which the new sociology knowingly confronts the Marxists. Their necessary historical-evolutionary preconceptions seem to exempt them from true and appropriate inductive research from the moment that their dialectical line becomes so rigid that it cannot tolerate exceptions. All the results they obtain are therefore to be disallowed. Moreover, such a situation indicates a lack of understanding that sociology, rather than being "prophecy" or "militant philosophy," is a descriptive analysis, not necessarily static, of all kinds of human groupings in their various interpersonal manifestations. Whereas the dialectical materialist is essentially interested in the problems of change and deploys his particular analyses in such a manner as to put himself in a position to advance historical-evolutionary hypotheses, the sociologist, on the other hand, appears intent on carefully identifying and describing the variable elements of a determinate social cross section (institution or structure) beyond—and even against—the temptations of futuristic visions, the dogmatic absolutism of ideologies, or the formal perfection of juridical formulas.

It is easy to realize how such a circumspect analysis developed by sociologists may sometimes seem tiresome, above all when it is a question of "militant philosophies," and, strictly speaking, there cannot be Marxist philosophies that are not militant. Militant philosophy is nothing but politics on another plane. And politics is, above all, action, not commentary or description; determination, not objective research. But precisely because it refutes the lines of a social development conceived according to a kind of natural law, a true and proper *Naturgesetz* through which it is easy to fall into the old metaphysical positions (and, in fact, the "Philistine" Marxists—the mechanists, economists, Messianists, etc.—relapse into them continually), sociological analysis can be of great practical or political use. After all, it contributes in a very decisive manner by helping to demolish myths and ideological prepossessions and by establishing the life-process of society on the basis of autonomous research.

THE BLEAK FUTURE OF SOCIOLOGICAL RESEARCH

The difficulties that impede the development of empirical social research in Italy seem to be caused by the fact that the Italian situation is dominated by ideological conflicts to a point that makes it impossible—or at least difficult—to carry out research that is really independent, that is, not linked to ideological preconceptions of a purely fideist or doctrinaire character. Let us take, for example, the case of the inquiry into the conditions of the workers in Italy, recently approved by the Parliament. Whereas some naive Marxists present it as the "great case for the prosecution" against the industrial middle class, anticipating the results of a research that has not yet been made, representatives of the Right and the more sophisticated conservatives are attempting by means of the inquiry to offer an unobjectionable "scientific" alibi for their entrepreneurial paternalism. It is now clear that such an inquiry will be useless—or worse, harmful—if it is unable to free itself from the sterile dialectic of rigidly contrasted ideologies, if it is not faithfully carried out according to the principles of rigorously independent scientific research. Naturally this does not mean that the inquiry should resolve itself into a kind of academic *tour de force* of descriptive analysis as an end in itself. It is evident that the results of the investigation, whatever they may be, will furnish material for definite policies tending to ameliorate the condition of workers in the various fields of production. But in the factual situation, and in the systematic gathering of data, the inquiry should be strictly autonomous with respect to any ideological or doctrinal preconceptions whatsoever.

There are few scholars in the present-day Italian cultural situation who realize how much sociological research—if it is to be truly scientific and reliable—has need of the guidance of clearly defined working hypotheses. However, sociology must at the same time affirm its proper independence from closed ideological systems that would be snares and not models for research.[43] The problems with which sociology must reckon in Italy are varied and deeply rooted in the Italian cultural tradition. This tradition is particularly inclined to grandiose philosophical systems and is sadly unaware of the necessity of minute, specific investigations; it is a tradition rich in utopian plans and noble attempts at social reconstruction, but it often wavers between ideological preconceptions and empirical descriptive analysis.

SELECTED BIBLIOGRAPHY

Becker, Howard, and H. E. Barnes, *Social Thought from Lore to Science,* 2nd ed. (New York: Dover Publications, 1952), Chap. 25.

Crawford, W. Rex, "Representative Italian Contributions to Sociology," in H. E. Barnes (ed.), *An Introduction to the History of Sociology* (Chicago: University of Chicago Press, 1948), Chap. 29.

Mosca, Gaetano, *The Ruling Class,* translated by Hannah D. Kahn (New York: McGraw-Hill, 1939).

Panunzio, Constantine, "Italian Sociology," in Georges Gurvitch and W. E. Moore (eds.), *Twentieth Century Sociology* (New York: Philosophical Library, 1945), Chap. 22.

Pareto, Vilfredo, *Mind and Society,* translated by Andrew Bongiorno and Arthur Livingston (New York: Harcourt, Brace, 1935), 4 vols.

[43] We should like to mention here the group that centers around the review *Comunità* (Milan, Via Manzoni, 12) and *Il Politico* (Pavia). The review *Quaderni di Sociologia* (Turin, Via Valeggio, 26) is particularly noteworthy because it is specifically dedicated to sociological problems and encourages research and true "field work." It began publication in 1951 with a bold and precise work program in which are to be examined the problems on whose solution the future of sociological studies in Italy depends.

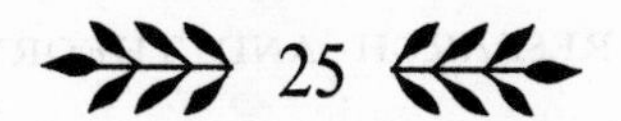

25

SOCIOLOGY IN JAPAN: ACCOMMODATION OF WESTERN ORIENTATIONS

KUNIO ODAKA

MANY OF THE READERS OF THIS VOLUME WOULD PERHAPS IMAGINE THAT sociology in Japan, on the whole, must be only a recent development. Although this is true in the sense that the science began to arouse the interest of the public at large quite recently, this is not true as far as the historical origin is concerned. It was 1893, or about sixty years ago, that the first chair or professorship of sociology was established in the former Tokyo Imperial University, now the University of Tokyo. This date compares favorably with the date of the establishment of sociology in the University of Chicago, the first university to have a separate department of sociology in the United States. Moreover, sociology had already been taught in Japan prior to this time. One can say, therefore, that sociology in Japan has a history comparable in length to that of American sociology.

Furthermore, the Japanese institutions where sociology is taught are quite numerous in comparison to those in most other countries. This has been especially true in the postwar period. According to our estimate, based upon a recent survey, we have now some 140 universities and colleges that have either a separate department or one or more courses of sociology. The number of persons who teach sociology in these institutions is estimated at about 340. It is, therefore, no wonder that the Japanese Sociological Society, a nation-wide association for sociology, has also quite a large membership as compared to similar associations in other countries. At present the Japanese Sociological Society has a membership of about 800. Although this figure includes a good many economists, social workers, journalists, and university students, the figure is by no means a small one, even when compared to the membership of the American Sociological Society, the world's largest sociological association, which has about 4,500 members. In this sense, it is probably safe to say that, next to the United States, Japan has the most flourishing sociological circle in the world, at least quantitatively.

The history of sociology in Japan may be roughly divided into the following four periods:

I: *Early Developments*, beginning in the 1870's and lasting until the time of World War I.

II: *Institutionalization*, covering the period from World War I until the early 1930's.

III: *Cross-currents*, including the period from the early 1930's until the end of World War II.

IV: *Postwar Developments*, covering the period since the end of World War II.

This paper will deal with the last two of these four periods in more detail than the first two, since despite its early origin, it was not until late in the 1930's that Japanese sociology came to be established as an empirical science. Before entering into the discussion of the more recent trends since the third period, however, a brief historical sketch may be necessary as to the origin and earlier developments of Japanese sociology—that is, the developments during the first two periods.[1]

Origin and Early Developments

Early Developments: The Dominance of Social Philosophy. The first period, which lasted some forty years, may also be called the "prehistory" of Japanese sociology. If we use the word "sociology" in the strict sense, works of the leading scholars in this period, such as *Shakaigaku* (Sociology) by Nagao Aruga[2] or *Riron Futsû Shakaigaku* (General Principles of Theoretical

[1] For developments up to the late 1930's, see Teizô Toda, "The Social Sciences as Disciplines: Japan," *ESS,* vol. 1 (New York, 1930), pp. 321-23; Jesse F. Steiner, "The Development and Present Status of Sociology in Japanese Universities," *AJS,* 41 (May, 1936), pp. 707-22; Howard Becker, "Sociology in Japan," *ASR,* 1 (June, 1936), pp. 455-71, or the chapter (29, 3) of the same title in Howard Becker and H. E. Barnes, *Social Thought from Lore to Science,* 2nd ed. New York, 1952); Japanese Sociological Society (ed.), *Sociology, Past and Present, in Japan* (Tokyo, 1937); Earle Eubank, "Sociology, Past and Present, in Japan," *SSR,* 22 (March-April, 1938), pp. 347-56. For more recent developments, see John C. Pelzel, "Japanese Ethnological and Sociological Research," *AA,* 50 (Jan.-March, 1948), pp. 54-72; Kunio Odaka, "Japanese Sociology: Past and Present," *SF,* 28 (May, 1950), pp. 400-409.

[2] Nagao Aruga, *Sociology* (Tokyo, 1883-1884), 3 vols.

Sociology) by Tongo Takebe,[3] may be classified as social philosophy rather than sociology. Although their ultimate goals were different, these scholars were similar insofar as they were endeavoring to rationalize certain social ideals or political viewpoints. Their sociological theories or systems became the vehicles of this rationalization. The nineteenth-century Western thinkers who became their models were also social philosophers, as for example Auguste Comte and Herbert Spencer.

It was in the year 1875 when the word *shakai*, meaning "society" in the Western sense, was first coined, and it was four years later when the word *shakaigaku*, or "sociology," first appeared in print. The first sociology or social philosophy in Japan, as with many other sciences, was an importation from the West. In the earlier part of this period, that is, from the beginning until the early years of the twentieth century, the translation and introduction of Spencer's works was especially influential. Counting those published in book form alone, there appeared thirty translations of his various works. His *Social Statics* was translated into Japanese in 1881, *The Principles of Sociology* in 1882. The reason why Spencer's works were so welcome may be found in the fact that they offered suitable arguments for the so-called *jiyû-minken-ron*, or "liberal democratic thought," which was prevalent in those days. Ernest Fenollosa, an American philosopher and the first person to give lectures on sociology in a Japanese university, also used the works of Spencer as textbooks. He came to Japan in 1878 as professor in the former Tokyo Imperial University, and besides teaching philosophy, political science, and finance, he gave lectures on sociology as a background for political science. As previously mentioned, the first chair of sociology was established in Tokyo Imperial in 1893. The professor in charge of the chair was Shôichi Toyama, then Dean of the Faculty of Letters of that University. He also used Spencer as texts. Moreover, the aforementioned *Shakaigaku* (Sociology) by Aruga, probably the most important work of the first part of this period, was, on the whole, based upon Spencer's ideas.

The latter part of the first period covered about fifteen years, beginning in the early 1900's. During this period, the Japanese nation began to gain prestige abroad as the result of her victories both in the Sino-Japanese and Russo-Japanese Wars. At the same time, with the growth of a consciousness of strength among the Japanese people, a conservative nationalistic current of thought became predominant, offering contrast to the former liberal democratic perspective. One of the leading representatives of this new viewpoint was Tongo Takebe, then head professor of sociology in Tokyo Imperial. The Seminar Room of Sociology was established in that University in 1903, and Takebe, making this his base, led the sociological circle of Japan. He attempted to combine the rather conservative social philosophy

[3] Tongo Takebe, *General Principles of Theoretical Sociology* (Tokyo, 1905-1918), 4 vols.

of Comte with the Confucian political ideal of statecraft. It is said that his conservative orientation resulted in defending sociology against the growing ultra-nationalistic elements. He also established in 1913 the *Nihon Shakaigaku-In*, or the Japanese Institute of Sociology. The Institute held annual conferences and published as its organ the *Nihon Shakaigaku-In Nempô* (Annual of the Japanese Institute of Sociology), ten volumes of which were published by 1922. Although he was very influential as a teacher, very few of his former students advocated or developed his organismic theory of society.

Institutionalization: A Psychological Emphasis

From this time onward, sociology in Japan came to be acknowledged as an independent, well-specialized branch of learning, and in 1919, an independent Department of Sociology was established at Tokyo Imperial. What characterized this period was the introduction and diffusion of psychological sociology in its broader sense, including the formal sociology of Simmel and Wiese; the *verstehende* sociology of Max Weber; the phenomenological sociology of Vierkandt, Litt, and Max Scheler; the psychological sociology of France, especially that of Tarde; and the American psychological sociologies of Small, Giddings, Ross, and Ellwood. In particular, theoretical arguments of German sociologists, such as Simmel's separation of "form" and "content" of social interaction; Max Weber's concepts of "ideal type," *Verstehen*, and "freedom from value-judgments"; Tönnies' concepts of *Gemeinschaft* and *Gesellschaft*, and others had an important influence upon Japanese sociology in this period.

Prior to this period, at about the turn of the century, sociology was introduced at Kyoto Imperial, now the University of Kyoto, by Shôtarô Yoneda. He was primarily a philosopher, but, having a keen interest in various trends of Western social theory, he became the first advocate of psychological sociology in Japan. Yoneda was especially influenced by such Western sociologists as Tarde and Giddings. Although he did not establish his own theory, he had produced a number of able students, among whom Yasuma Takada was the most outstanding figure. Takada, who is known as one of the leading political economists in Japan today, also taught sociology at both Kyushu and Kyoto Imperial. His *Shakaigaku Genri* (Principles of Sociology), a voluminous work of over a thousand pages, and *Shakaigaku Gairon* (General Sociology), his main work in sociology,[4] may be regarded

[4] Yasuma Takada, *Principles of Sociology* (Tokyo, 1919), and *General Sociology* (Tokyo, 1923).

as the turning point in Japanese sociology. From then on, sociology in Japan grew out of the synthetic philosophy of society, in the fashion of Comte or Spencer, and reached the stage of a special science. Takada asserted that sociology was the "commoner" and not the "crowned head" in the domain of the social sciences and constructed a theoretical system of his own, utilizing the viewpoints both of Simmel's formal sociology and Giddings' psychological sociology. He was at the same time the founder of the so-called "Kyoto School," which, in its theoretical, or rather philosophical, character, provided a contrast with the more empirical "Tokyo School." Tendencies similar to Takada's were also seen in Kazuta Kurauchi, now Dean of the Faculty of Letters of the University of Osaka,[5] and Jishô Usui, now Professor of Sociology at the University of Kyoto and President of the Japanese Sociological Society. The position of both of these contemporary representatives of the theoretical group in the Kansai District (area around Kyoto and Osaka) may be called a blend of formal and phenomenological sociology.

In 1923, the *Nihon Shakaigaku-Kai*, or the Japanese Sociological Society, was established, replacing the older *Nihon Shakaigaku-In*. This is a nation-wide association, at present having as many as eight hundred members. It holds annual conventions to report the results of its members' current research. In recent years, the attendance at these annual conventions has increased markedly. For example, on the occasion of its Twenty-Fifth Annual Meeting, held in Tokyo in the fall of 1952, some five hundred people were reported in attendance, and more than eighty papers were presented. Until 1943, the Society published as its organ the *Shakaigaku Zasshi* (Journal of Sociology)[6] and the *Nempô Shakaigaku* (Annual of the Japanese Sociological Society).[7] After the end of World War II, the name of the periodical was changed to *Shakaigaku Hyôron* (Japanese Sociological Review).[8] The Society has at present three district branches—the *Kanto* (area around Tokyo), *Kansai*, and *Seibu* (Kyushu) *Shakaigaku-Kai*, each of which also holds its annual meetings independently.

[5] See Kazuta Kurauchi, *Shakaigaku Gairon* General Sociology] (Tokyo, 1953).

[6] Published monthly, 1924-1930, inclusive.

[7] Published 1933-1943, inclusive. Between these two, the *Kikan Shakaigaku* (Sociological Quarterly) was published from 1931 to 1932.

[8] Published quarterly since 1950. Prior to this, the *Shakaigaku Kenkyû* (Sociological Research) was published from 1947 to 1948.

The Period of Cross-currents

The third period in the history of Japanese sociology, characterized by what we shall call "cross-currents," covers the time from the early thirties until the end of World War II. This period was mainly characterized by a reaction to the preceding period with its psychological and more analytical inclinations. At the same time, the contents of sociological studies became more diversified. Certain influences from German thought that were predominant throughout the preceding period remained active. However, in this period, instead of formal or phenomenological sociology, the cultural sociology of Alfred Weber and the sociology of knowledge of Karl Mannheim and Max Scheler of Germany came to be preferred. On the other hand, the viewpoints of the Durkheimian School of France, as well as of the modern social anthropology of Britain and the United States, gradually came to be absorbed. Influences from Marxist theory also became more conspicuous, at least during the earlier part of this period. In this sense, as John C. Pelzel has pointed out,[9] this period may be characterized by its confusion of theoretical and methodological cross-currents. On the whole, however, a broader, synthetic—"macroscopic"—view of social life seems to have been more characteristic than the previous psychological and more analytical—"microscopic"—viewpoint. Also, because of the more conspicuous presence of Marxist theory within sociology and of the increase in power of the conservative, ultranationalistic ideologies, sociology in Japan came to be looked upon with suspicion by the authorities. Or one might better say that sociology came to be looked upon with greater suspicion, since, even during the preceding periods, sociology was often confused with socialism and thus had often suffered from undue suspicion and oppression by the government as well as by the public. However, from about the mid-thirties, sociological theories such as those of Hans Freyer, whose ideological background was closely related to the totalitarian ideology of the Nazis, were introduced.

The aforementioned broader, synthetic view of social life was, at least from a theoretical standpoint, most clearly represented by Masamichi Shimmei, now Professor of Sociology at Tohoku University. From about 1935, he has cultivated a viewpoint resembling that of Durkheim, Ginsberg, or Sorokin, criticizing the analytical view of formal and psychological sociology as abstract and sterile. In asserting this point of view, he seems to have been most influenced by the synthetic views of the late Karl Mannheim in

[9] Pelzel, *op. cit.*, p. 60.

his *Die Gegenwartsaufgaben der Soziologie*.[10] According to Shimmei, sociology is not a mere special science with a limited scope and a definite subject matter, but rather a synthesizing science whose mission is to study the interrelation of the various fields of social life (for example, the political, economic, religious, moral, or ideological), and, in so doing, to become the mediator for the integration of the other social sciences dealing with these fields separately.[11] A similar reaction to a view of sociology as a special science can also be seen in the works of Uichi Iwasaki, now President of Kansai University at Osaka,[12] and the late Jun'ichirô Matsumoto, former Professor of Sociology at Hôsei University in Tokyo, although their orientation is somewhat different from that of Shimmei. Matsumoto, writing in the mid-thirties, tried to establish a comprehensive system of sociology resembling the so-called "*vollständige Soziologie*" of Andreas Walther of Germany.[13]

Empiricism and Field Studies. However, the more noteworthy trend in this period was the first appearance of sociological research of an empirical or "positivistic" character. The primary objective of such studies was mainly a description of family and rural community structure. The pioneer who introduced this new trend into Japan was Teizô Toda, my teacher and former Professor of Sociology at Tokyo Imperial. He studied sociology at the University of Chicago around 1920 and, after returning to Japan, made strong efforts to transplant the methods of social research then popular in the United States. Since even the word "social research" at that time sounded rather strange to most Japanese scholars, he published in 1933 a manual, *Shakai-Chôsa* (Social Research), which became a standard guide for research methods.[14] He lectured and gave seminars on social research, using American works such as F. Stuart Chapin's *Field Work and Social Research*[15] and Vivien Palmer's *Field Studies in Sociology*.[16] Toda himself, an authority on family studies in Japan, confined most of his research to extensive studies on the

[10] Karl Mannheim, *Die Gegenwartsaufgaben der Soziologie* (Tübingen, 1932).

[11] See Masamichi Shimmei, *Shakaigaku Yôkô* [Essentials of Sociology] (Tokyo, 1935); *Shakaigaku Jiten* [Dictionary of Sociology] (Tokyo, 1943): the articles on "Systems of Sociology" and "Synthetic Sociology"; *Shakaigaku no Tachiba* [The Position of Sociology] (Tokyo, 1948).

[12] See Uichi Iwasaki, *Shakaigaku Gairon* [General Sociology] (Kyoto, 1952).

[13] Cf. Andreas Walther, "Zur Verwirklichung einer vollständigen Soziologie," in Richard Thurnwald (ed.), *Soziologie von Heute* (Leipzig, 1932), pp. 5*ff*. Matsumoto's system is developed in his trilogy, *Shakaigaku Genron* [Foundations of Sociology] (Tokyo, 1935); *Shûdan Shakaigaku Genri* [Principles of Sociology of the Group] (Tokyo, 1937); and *Bunka Shakaigaku Genri* [Principles of Sociology of Culture] (Tokyo, 1938).

[14] Recently a new edition of this manual was published with the title of "Methods of Social Research." In 1952, Eitarô Suzuki and Seiichi Kitano also published a fieldwork manual for rural sociological studies. See Suzuki and Kitano, *Nôson Shakai-Chôsa* [Social Research of Rural Communities] (Tokyo, 1952).

[15] F. Stuart Chapin, *Field Work and Social Research* (Chicago, 1920).

[16] Vivien Palmer, *Field Studies in Sociology* (Chicago, 1928).

formal structure of the family as a social group, using statistical methods. His main theme concerned quantitative determination of such factors as household size and range of kin relationships, and the correlations of these with locality, economic status, or occupation.[17] These tendencies initiated by Toda—that is, the tendency to prefer the family or other kinship groupings as subject matter—and the tendency to attach more importance to the extensive type of statistical research, were for a long time so dominant that social research appeared exclusively as a statistical study of the family or kinship relations. It is, therefore, with good reason that most sociologists who were under the influence of Toda have found their special interest in the field of family studies, and that most of their studies have, to date, devoted little attention to the internal structure of the family and to the psychological relations among members. However, his effort to transplant the empirical viewpoint of American sociology has, on the whole, proved successful. As the head of the Sociology Department in Tokyo Imperial from 1922 to 1947, he trained a number of able sociologists who, in contrast to the "Kyoto School," are often classified as the "Tokyo School." Throughout his term of office, he stressed the significance of empirical studies, and it is not surprising that the "Tokyo School" has tended to ignore the significance of theory and the need for a basic conceptual scheme in research.

Beginning about the end of the thirties, a new type of research similar to the social-anthropological studies of Britain and the United States began appearing in rural sociology. Although the development of rural sociology in Japan had an earlier origin, it was not until about this time that sociologists became aware of the potentialities of the techniques of intensive analysis for their studies of rural communities. In the same period, the methods and viewpoints of contemporary American rural sociology were also introduced to Japan, primarily by Eitarô Suzuki, now Professor of Sociology at Hokkaido University. In addition to the introduction and explanation of the American type of research in this field, he has made a comprehensive analysis of modern rural communities in Japan.[18] Two other representatives of this new type of research in the same field of study are Seiichi Kitano, now Professor of Sociology at Kyushu University, and Kizaemon Ariga, now Professor of Sociology at Tokyo University of Education. Both scholars, building upon intensive field studies of various farming villages in Japan, have constructed theories concerning the structure and function of the family and kinship within rural communities. Ariga, in particular, being both an empiricist and a theoretical thinker, has had an important effect upon younger students through his theory of the *dôzoku-dan*, or

[17] See Teizô Toda, *Kazoku Kôsei* [Family Structure] (Tokyo, 1937).

[18] See Eitarô Suzuki, *Nihon Nôson Shakaigaku Genri* [Principles of Rural Sociology in Japan] (Tokyo, 1940).

extended family group, in Japan.[19] Yet these works, like the products of the "Tokyo School," neglect the internal and psychological structure of the group.

Sociological Specialization until World War II. Another development which characterized this period was the emergence of specialized research. We have already mentioned the interest in the family and rural life.[20] In addition, interest was shown in such fields as the sociology of knowledge, the sociology of language, the sociology of religion, ethno-sociology, political sociology, economic sociology, urban sociology, population studies, class studies, and others.[21] The new field of occupational sociology also

[19] See Kizaemon Ariga, *Nihon Kazoku Seido to Kosaku Seido* [The Family and Tenancy Systems of Japan] (Tokyo, 1943). In 1948 Ariga published a collection of articles, *Sonraku Seikatsu* [Village Life] in which he dealt with the same topic. He also developed his theory of the *dôzoku-dan* in his recent paper, "*Nihon no Ie*" [The Japanese Family], in *Minkan Denshô* [Folklore], Special Issue on the Japanese Nation (April, 1949). The relations between the *dôzoku-dan* system and the so-called "feudalistic" character of Japanese society were discussed by Kitano in his recent article "Dôzoku-dan to Hôken Isei" [Extended Family Group and Feudalistic Remnants], in Nihon Jimbun-Kagaku-Kai [Japanese Cultural Science Society] (ed.), *Hôken Isei* [Feudalistic Remnants] (Tokyo, 1951). A discussion in English of the *dôzoku-dan* system may be found in Michio Nagai and John W. Bennett, *Dôzoku: A Preliminary Study of the Japanese "Extended Family" Group and Its Social and Economic Functions,* Ohio State University Research Foundation Report, No. 7 (September, 1953).

[20] Among family studies and rural sociology, besides works previously mentioned, the following may be considered representative for this period: Morimitsu Shimizu, *Shina Kazoku no Kôzô* [The Structure of the Chinese Family] (Tokyo, 1941); Tatsumi Makino, *Shina Kazoku Kenkyû* [Studies in the Chinese Family] (Tokyo, 1944); Tadashi Fukutake, *Chûgoku Nôson Shakai no Kôzô* [The Structure of Chinese Rural Society] (Kyoto, 1946).

[21] The following may be noted: In the sociology of knowledge are the publications of the *Shakaigaku Kenkyûkai* [Society for Sociological Studies], such as *Ideologie-Ron* [Theories of Ideology] (Tokyo, 1931); *Chishiki Shakaigaku* [Sociology of Knowledge] (Tokyo, 1932); and Masamichi Shimmei, *Chishiki Shakaigaku no Shosô* [Aspects of the Sociology of Knowledge] (Tokyo, 1932). In the sociology of language is Hisatoshi Tanabe, *Gengo Shakaigaku* [Sociology of Language] (Tokyo, 1936). In the sociology of religion, Kiyoto Furuno, *Shûkyô Shakaigaku* [Sociology of Religion] (Tokyo, 1938). In ethno-sociology and the sociology of primitive culture, Takashi Akiba, *Mam-Mô no Minzoku to Shûkyô* [The Race and Religion of Manchuria and Mongolia] (Osaka, 1940); Kentarô Komatsu, *Minzoku no Riron* [Theory of the Nation] (Tokyo, 1941); Eizô Koyama, *Minzoku to Jinkô no Riron* [Theory of the Nation and Population] (Tokyo, 1942); Yuzuru Okada, *Mikai Shakai ni okeru Kazoku* [The Family in Primitive Societies] (Tokyo, 1942); Yuzuru Okada and Kunio Odaka, *Kainantô Reizoku no Shakai Soshiki to Keizai Soshiki* [The Social and Economic Organizations of the Li Tribes of Hainan Island] (Tokyo, 1944) The latter half of this monograph was later translated into English and published in mimeographed form by the Yale University Southeast Asia Studies in 1950. In political sociology, Tomoo Odaka, *Kokka Kôzô-Ron* [The Social Structure of the State] (Tokyo, 1936); Uichi Iwasaki, *Kokka Honshitsu-Ron Kenkyû* [Studies in the Nature of the State] (Kyoto, 1942). In economic sociology, Zenya Takashima, *Keizai Shakaigaku no Kompon Mondai* [The Fundamental Problems of Economic Sociology] (Tokyo, 1942). In urban sociology, Matatarô Okui, *Gendai Daitoshi-Ron* [The Modern Metropolis] (Tokyo, 1940).

began, late in the thirties, to be explored by the present writer.[22] All these, however, were only moderately developed when compared to family and rural research. In particular, urban sociology and class studies were very poorly developed. Moreover, most studies in the fields of the sociology of knowledge, the sociology of religion, political sociology, and economic sociology have been mainly conceptual or methodological, or confined to works of introduction and explanation of Western theories.

The last few years of this period coincided with those of World War II, during which the activities of our sociologists were drastically curtailed. As already noted, studies of sociology during this period suffered oppression from the conservative nationalistic elements and from the government itself, and this tendency became much more conspicuous during the war years. There is no doubt that some segments of the sociological circle were influenced strongly by the National Socialist ideology of Germany, and it is also true that there were some scholars who assumed an ingratiating attitude toward ultranationalistic policies. But on the whole, Japanese sociologists were in hibernation during the war years.

Postwar Developments

The Search for Focus. A considerable change has taken place since the termination of World War II. In fact, one can say at present that, on the whole, sociology in Japan has at last entered a period of full and free growth. Factors that appear to have contributed to this change are, among other things, the collapse of ultranationalistic influences; the reopening of scientific communication between Western countries, particularly the United States, and Japan; and the adoption of a new system of higher education.

However, the third period of the history of Japanese sociology was characterized by what we shall call "a state of prolific confusion and diversity." And this confusion and diversity became even more marked in the present period because scientific communication with Western countries was reopened. In this sense, the flourishing and prosperous growth in the postwar years contained its own dangers. As was seen in the previous sections, Japanese sociology in its second period was a special science with a limited scope and a definite subject matter, independent of the other social

In population studies, Megumi Hayashi, *Nôka Jinkô no Kenkyû* [Studies in the Population of Rural Families] (Tokyo, 1940). In class studies, Yasuma Takada, *Kokka to Kaikyû* [The State and Social Class] (Tokyo, 1934).

[22] See Kunio Odaka, *Shokugyô Shakaigaku* [Occupational Sociology] (Tokyo, 1941; rev. ed., vols. I and II, Tokyo, 1953).

sciences. However, since this view of sociology proved to be abstract and sterile, a reaction appeared in the third period, and, at this time an all-too-inclusive orientation appeared, resulting in considerable confusion and diversity. Sociology at this stage might be called "a sociology of syncretism." Therefore, it is urgent today for Japanese sociology to bring together its many diverse and contrasting viewpoints and to fashion an integrated discipline. This is in harmony with Parsons' corrective advice to American sociologists.[23] Thus in America as in Japan, the science of sociology today faces a crucial task.[24]

We may now discuss some of the new major tendencies in Japanese sociology since the end of World War II. These new tendencies may be summarized under the following six headings: (1) growing importance in higher education; (2) greater emphasis on empirical research; (3) increasing popularity of statistical methods; (4) development of new fields in empirical research; (5) closer association with neighboring sciences; and (6) opening of international collaboration.

Growing Importance of Sociology in Higher Education. Along with the collapse of ultranationalistic influences, the public interest in and demand for sociology has become more active. Moreover, because of the adoption of a new system of higher education, encouraged by the American occupation authorities, there have been established a large number of courses devoted to sociology in universities and colleges all over the country. Before the War, the number of institutions where sociology was taught was less than thirty, of which only Tokyo Imperial had an independent department of sociology. By contrast, as already noted, there are at present 22 universities that have separate departments of sociology, and in addition about 120 universities and colleges that have at least one course in sociology—a total of some 140 institutions. Of these 140 institutions, 58 are national universities, 9 are public, and about 75 are private. Although most of these institutions have the courses only at the undergraduate level, 20 have so far established a

[23] Cf. Talcott Parsons and Bernard Barber, "Sociology, 1941-46," *AJS*, 53 (Jan., 1948), p. 246.

[24] On this point, see Odaka's *Shakaigaku no Honshitsu to Kadai* [Sociology: Its Nature and Themes] (Tokyo, 1949), vol. I. In the writer's view, the present state of sociology can be summarized in the following four principal sets of opposing propositions: (1) the opposite views concerning its scope, that is, the question whether sociology is a synthetic or a special science; (2) the three antagonistic views of its subject matter, that is, the question whether sociology is a science of the group, of action, or of culture; (3) the opposing views on the problem of theory and research, that is, the question whether sociology is a theoretical ("systematic") or an empirical ("positivistic") science, or the question concerning which is more vital to sociology, the construction of a general theory or empirical research; and (4) the conflicting views on the problem of theory and practice, that is, the question whether sociology is theoretical ("pure") or practical ("realistic").

graduate course in sociology under the new system of higher education.[25] The enrollment of students majoring in sociology at those universities where an independent department of sociology is established amounts to some 3,200. In addition, there is an even larger number of students who either major in sociology or at least attend sociology courses at other universities and colleges.[26] The teaching personnel in the 140 institutions is, as previously mentioned, estimated at about 340, including 138 who teach at national and public universities. These figures may be sufficient to show how remarkable the advance of Japanese sociology has been in the postwar years. Except for the United States, there is hardly any other country where so many persons are engaged in sociology as in Japan.

This does not necessarily mean, however, that the public interest in and demand for sociology has become sufficiently active since the war. Sociology in Japan has received far less attention from the government as well as from the public at large than the other social sciences, particularly law or economics. For example, in Japan, most universities have a faculty of law, and most larger universities have also a faculty of economics, whereas there is only one university where an independent faculty of sociology has been established—namely, Hitotsubashi University in Tokyo.[27] In most cases, sociology is given only one or two chairs as a subdivision in the faculty of letters. Since each chair includes as a rule one professor and perhaps one assistant professor, the number of professors who teach sociology is between one and four in most universities. Even the University of Tokyo, probably the largest university in the Orient, has only four chairs of sociology—that is, two in the Faculty of Letters, one in the College of General Education, and another one in the Faculty of Education. Therefore, the present staff consists of four professors, four assistant professors, and three lecturers. On the other hand, in the same university, the Faculty of Law has 38 chairs, and the Faculty of Economics has 23. Moreover, this imbalance between sociology and law or economics in the faculty and departmental organization of universities is reflected in the classification of sciences adopted by the *Nihon Gakujutsu Kaigi*, or the Japanese Science Council, the supreme organ for

[25] In contrast to the large number of courses in sociology, there have been very few courses devoted to social anthropology and social psychology. At present, there are only two universities that have a separate department of social anthropology, and no university where a separate department of social psychology is established.

[26] With the increase in number of students majoring in sociology, many textbooks on sociology have been published since the end of the war. The number of textbooks or works entitled "general sociology" or "introductory sociology" published during the period from 1948 through 1953 is estimated at thirty.

[27] Although it is formally called the "Faculty of Sociology," it contains only two chairs of sociology—the present staff consisting of one professor and one lecturer. On the other hand, the same Faculty includes such chairs as those of literature, linguistics, philosophy, ethics, religion, psychology, education, etc.

promoting the development of scientific studies. According to the present regulations of the Council, sociology has only one-sixteenth the representation of law and one-tenth that of economics.[28] Again, because of this lower esteem, sociology has not received as much financial support from the government as have law or economics.[29] Here one might point to the fact that in Japan, unlike the United States, efficient research cannot be carried on without subsidization by the government. There are no Rockefeller Foundations in Japan. Consequently, even in recent years when empirical research of some importance began to appear, the scope and validity was limited by a slender supply of data. Probably one of the reasons why theoretical studies were predominant in the past in Japanese sociology is that they are less expensive than empirical field studies.

Greater Emphasis on Empirical Research. Since the end of World War II, empirical research on practical problems is coming to occupy a more important position in Japanese sociology. Formerly, even after the transplantation of methods of American social research to Japan around the mid-thirties, the dominance of theory in the German fashion remained active. But in recent years, this tendency seems to be replaced by the empirical viewpoint of American sociology, and even the scholars who formerly were considered to be the leading representatives of theoretical orientation have been converted to the empirical viewpoint. Edward Shils, in his interesting booklet, *The Present State of American Sociology,* pointed out that American sociology is at present showing signs of passing out of its recent "atheoretical prehistory" into a more sophisticated stage.[30] On the contrary, in the case of Japanese sociology, we may say that it is now passing out of its all-too-theoretical prehistory into a more empirical stage.

One of the most serious problems we are now facing in this connection is that of bridging the gap between the existent sociological theories and the increasing tendency toward empirical social research. Although the dominance of theoretical studies has been one of the major characteristics of Japanese sociology, these studies have been lacking in theory in its proper sense—

[28] The Japanese Science Council, established in 1949, divides sciences into seven divisions: the first division includes literature in its broad sense; the second law; the third economics; the fourth through the seventh are devoted to the various natural sciences. The regulations provide that each division has thirty representatives with equal weight given to each of these seven. The first division, literature in its broad sense, is divided into literature proper, history, and philosophy. The province of philosophy is further subdivided into at least eight branches; philosophy in its narrow sense, pedagogy, psychology, sociology, religion, ethics, esthetics, etc.

[29] According to a list of research projects carried out with the Grants-in-Aid for Fundamental Scientific Research in 1954, research funds allotted to twenty-nine items of research belonging to the Branch of Sociology amount to 2,290,000 yen, or about one-third the allotment to 56 items of the Division of Law, and about one-fifth that to 92 items of the Division of Economics. See *Japanese Scientific Monthly,* 7 (July, 1954).

[30] Edward Shils, *The Present State of American Sociology* (Glencoe, Ill., 1948), p. 55.

that is, theory that is based upon empirical research and that simultaneously points the way toward further research. What is meant by the word "theory" in Japanese sociology has hitherto been mainly a methodological reflection on the nature of sociology, or an attempt to make definitions and classifications of some basic concepts, or even a manifestation of a metaphysical doctrine without any empirical basis. Accordingly, sociological research in Japan has, until recently, often been "research for its own sake"—that is, research neither guided by nor aimed at theory in its proper sense. It is, therefore, just as necessary for the future of Japanese sociology to elaborate a general theory of social life as to promote the collection of social facts. Perhaps it is not a mere coincidence that, in recent years, the works of Parsons and his associates are coming to be studied among some theoretically minded young Japanese scholars. The *Riron Shakaigaku-Kai* (Social Theorists' Association), founded in 1953 in Kyoto, may be looked upon as further evidence of the gradually mounting interest in the proper development of sociological theory.[31]

Increasing Popularity of Statistical Methods. A variety of statistical methods that have been developed in recent years are coming to be more widely applied to sociological research. This does not necessarily mean, however, that statistical methods or techniques of measurement in general were neglected by Japanese sociologists in previous periods. Most of the works of Toda, for example, were statistical studies of the structure of the Japanese family. Again, techniques of attitude measurement, such as those of Thurstone, Likert, or Bogardus, were well known at least among the sociologists in the "Tokyo School." There were, however, very few studies, if any, in which such techniques were really used. There had been, in previous periods, not a single case in which a group of sociologists actually conducted a sample survey using a set of techniques—sampling, scaling, testing, etc.—that are now considered in the United States to be standard. The type of research mostly used before World War II was the so-called community-study type, consisting of a more or less impressionistic approach, participant observations, personal interviews with loosely constructed schedules, and so on. Although this type of research is still preferred by some sociologists, particularly among those interested in rural culture, the general trend has been toward the increasing popularity of various measurement techniques that have recently been developed in America as well as in Japan and the wider use of them by sociologists in empirical research. This is especially true of the period since 1950.[32] In fact, the use of recent techniques of measurement

[31] The members of this Association mainly consist of the sociologists who belong to the so-called "Kyoto School." It has been decided, more recently, that the Association should be affiliated with the *Kansai Shakaigaku-Kai,* or the Kansai Branch of the Japanese Sociological Society.

[32] A good example of this trend may be seen in the sample survey on social

is now a fashion among younger sociologists in Japan. As a result, a growing discrepancy may be observed in knowledge of, and attitudes toward, quantitative procedures between senior and junior members of the departments of sociology in several universities.

Development of New Fields in Empirical Research. Interest in empirical research has extended into a number of new fields such as those of industrial sociology, urban sociology, educational sociology, and public opinion research. As already noted, until the end of the third period, the majority of empirical studies had traditionally been undertaken in the field of rural sociology, the main emphasis having been placed on the family or other kinship groupings in the rural community. This tendency remains active in the postwar years[33] and, as can be seen in the table presented later in this paper, rural sociology ranks first numerically among nineteen fields of sociological research. Although research methods traditionally used in this field have been somewhat crude, in recent years a new tendency has been observed among younger researchers to introduce more rigorous techniques that have been developed in the United States.[34]

However, the more noteworthy trend in recent years is the emergence and development of new fields of research. Of these new developments, probably the advance of industrial sociology, which has also been experienced in the United States, is most conspicuous. There were very few Japanese

stratification and social mobility in the six largest cities of Japan conducted by the Research Committee, Japanese Sociological Society, in 1952. Recently a research manual explaining some of the newly developed techniques and instruments for social research was published by a group of young Japanese sociologists. See Tadashi Fukutake (ed.), *Shakai-Chôsa no Hôhô* [Methods of Social Research] (Tokyo, 1954).

[33] In late 1952, the *Sonraku Shakai Kenkyûkai* [Society for Rural Social Studies] was established in order to promote association and collaboration among those interested in the study of rural culture. Although according to the regulations the Society is open to other social scientists, the present membership largely consists of rural sociologists. At present it has a membership of about 180. The Society has held annual conferences since 1953 and published in 1954 its first annual report, *Sonraku Kenkyû no Seika to Kadai* [Rural Social Studies: Their Recent Results and Themes].

[34] To mention a few recent works published by younger researchers in this field: Tetsundo Tsukamoto, "*Dôzoku Soshiki no Ichi Kôsatsu*" [A Study of the Extended Family System], *Shakaigaku Hyôron* [Japanese Sociological Review], 2 (May, 1951); Tadashi Fukutake, *Nihon no Nôson Shakai* [Japanese Rural Society] (Tokyo, 1954); Fukutake and Tsukamoto, *Nihon Nômin no Shakaiteki Seikaku* [The Social Characteristics of Japanese Peasants] (Tokyo, 1954). In the years 1953 through 1954, a series of intensive case studies of social stratification were conducted in three rural villages in the areas of Kyushu, Kansai, and Kanto by a group of rural sociologists, including Seiichi Kitano and Kanji Naitô of Kyushu University, Takashi Koyama and Kazue Kôda of the University of Osaka, and Kizaemon Ariga and Kiyomi Morioka of Tokyo University of Education, using some recent techniques of measurement. The principal objective of these studies was to find some basic criteria upon which to measure social stratification in Japanese rural communities.

sociologists who specialized in this field before World War II. Even after the end of the War, during the few years up to 1950, there were only a handful of sociologists who began to work in this field.[35] A long-range study of human relations and labor-attitudes of foundry workers in Kawaguchi City, near Tokyo, was carried out from 1947 through 1950 by the present writer and several members of the Sociology Department of the University of Tokyo and may be considered as representative of the studies made in this field during the pre-1950 period.[36] In recent years, however, most large universities have had at least one sociologist engaged in the study of such problems as human relations and employee work morale, productivity and supervisory practices, the status and role of foremen, and the leadership structure and decision-making process in local unions.[37] According to our estimate, based upon a recent survey, this field is second only to rural sociology in number of research projects, as is shown in the table below. The present writer, with the collaboration of a few younger sociologists in the University of Tokyo and Tokyo University of Education, conducted an intensive study at a large steel mill near Yokohama and in a coal mine in Yamaguchi Prefecture on the identification of Japanese industrial workers with their unions and

[35] In early 1947, a study of attitudes of industrial workers in a variety of industries (nine manufacturing, five transportation, three mining, etc.) in the Tokyo area was undertaken by several members of the Department of Sociology, University of Tokyo. See Shizuo Matsushima, *Rôdô Shakaigaku Josetsu* [An Introduction to the Sociology of Labor] (Tokyo, 1951); Kunio Odaka (ed.), *Rôdô Shakaigaku* [Sociology of Labor] (Tokyo, 1952). In the same year, an extensive survey of the existing structure and functions of labor unions all over the country was undertaken by several members of the *Shakai-Kagaku Kenkyûjo* (Institute for Social Science) of the University of Tokyo. See University of Tokyo, Institute for Social Science (ed.), *Sengo Rôdô-Kumiai no Jittai* [The Existing Conditions of Labor Unions in the Postwar Years] (Tokyo, 1950); Kazuo Ôkôchi (ed.), *Nihon Rôdô-Kumiai-Ron* [Theory of Japanese Labor Unions] (Tokyo, 1954). The latter study, however, was conducted mainly from the viewpoint of labor economics.

[36] See Kunio Odaka (ed.), *Imono no Machi: Sangyô Shakaigakuteki Kenkyû* [A Foundry Workers' Town: A Study in Industrial Sociology] (Tokyo, 1955).

[37] See *Shakaigaku Hyôron* [Japanese Sociological Review], Special Issue on Human Relations in Industry, 2 (January, 1952). Mikio Saegusa, of the Institute of Industrial Physiology and Psychology, has published several papers on similar problems. See his "*Sangyo ni okeru Ningen Kankei no Shikenteki Sokutei*" [A Pilot Study in the Measurement of Human Relations in Industry], *Japanese Sociological Review,* 3 (October, 1952). Yoshirô Tomita, of the Nageoya Institute of Technology recently published *kôjô no Shakaigaku* [Sociology of Factories] (Tokyo,1953). In 1952, a sample survey on opinions and attitudes of the officers of 550 local unions all over the country was conducted in connection with the Social Tensions Survey by a group of sociologists under the guidance of the present writer. See Akira Takahashi, "*Rôdô-Kumiai o meguru Shakaiteki Kinchô*" [Social Tensions Inside and Outside Labor Unions], *Nichirôken Shiryô* [Japanese Institute of Labor Research Materials], Nos. 248 and 249 (November, 1953). Since late 1954, an intensive study of political orientations of industrial workers in a large steel mill near Yokohama has been carried on by a group of sociologists and social psychologists in the newly established *Shimbun Kenkyûjo* (Institute of Journalism) of the University of Tokyo.

management in 1952. This study may be regarded as an example of the more recent developments in this field.[38]

Although less conspicuous when compared with the advance of industrial sociology, noteworthy developments have been observed also in such fields as urban sociology,[39] social psychology,[40] public opinion research,[41] ethno-sociology,[42] educational sociology,[43] and others.

[38] See Kunio Odaka, *Sangyô ni okeru Ningen Kankei no Kagaku* [Science of Human Relations in Industry] (Tokyo, 1953), pp. 311 *ff.* The report of this study was originally prepared in English for the presentation at the Second World Congress of Sociology held in Liège, Belgium, in the summer of 1953. A German translation of this report appeared in a special issue on "Betriebssoziologie—eine internationale Aufgabe für Forschung und Lehre," in *Sozial Welt,* the official journal of the Arbeitsgemeinschaft sozialwissenschaftlicher Institute, 5 (1954).

[39] For example, Eiichi Isomura of Tokyo Municipal University recently published two introductory works, *Toshi Shakaigaku* [Urban Sociology] (Tokyo, 1953), and *Shakai Byôrigaku* [Social Pathology] (Tokyo, 1954). On the other hand, extended family systems found in urban districts of Japan have been studied by Ariga, Takashi Nakano, and others. See Nakano, "*Toshi ni okeru Dôzoku to Shinzoku*" [Extended Families and Kinship Relations in an Urban District], in *Gendai Shakaigaku no Shomondai* [Current Problems of Sociology], a symposium commemorative of Dr. Teizô Toda's sixty-first anniversary (Tokyo, 1949). Along with the increasing interest in the study of urban culture, the *Nihon Toshigaku-Kai* [Japanese Municipal Research Association] was established in 1953.

[40] Two introductory works on social psychology have been published since the end of World War II. See Hiroshi Minami, *Shakai Shinrigaku* [Social Psychology] (Tokyo, 1947); Ikutarô Shimizu, *Shakai Shinrigaku* [Social Psychology] (Tokyo, 1951). A comparative study of mass communication processes in urban and rural communities of Japan has been carried out by several members of the Institute of Journalism, University of Tokyo, since 1951. See Hajime Ikeuchi, "*Aru Nôson ni okeru Mass Communication no Jittai*" [Mass-Communication Processes in a Rural Community], *Shimbun Kenkyûjo Kiyô* [Institute of Journalism Bulletin], No. 2 (1952); Rokurô Hidaka, Akira Takahashi, Kôtarô Kido, and Jôji Watanuki, "*Mass Communication to Kaikyû Ishiki*" [Mass Communication and Class Consciousness], *ibid.,* No. 4 (1954).

[41] Since the end of the war, there have been established a number of institutes and associations devoted to public opinion research, including the *Kokuritsu Yoron Chôsajo* [National Opinion Research Institute], attached to the Prime Minister's Office, founded in 1948 and recently transferred to a private enterprise. Several sociologists have been working in these institutes.

[42] Before the war, the scope of Japanese ethno-sociological research was limited to the areas of the Orient and Japan; but in recent years, increasing interest has been shown in the study of such areas as Latin America and Africa. See, for example, Seiichi Izumi and Hiroshi Saitô, *Amazon: Sono Fûdo to Nihonjin* [Amazon: Its Natural Environment and Japanese Immigrants] (Tokyo, 1954). On the other hand, an all-round study of the Ainu and their culture has been carried out by a group of ethnologists and sociologists since 1950. See *Minzokugaku Kenkyû* [Japanese Journal of Ethnology], Special Issue on Joint Research on the Saru Ainu, 16 (March, 1952).

[43] Along with the establishment of departments and courses devoted to educational sociology in a majority of universities under the new system of education, the *Nihon Kyôiku Shakaigaku-Kai* [Japanese Educational Sociological Society] was founded in 1949. At present the Society has a membership of some 450. It has held annual conventions

The following table, based upon the Census of Current Research Projects undertaken by the Japanese Sociological Society in October, 1952, as well as the study reports presented at the annual meetings of the Japanese Sociological Society from 1950 through 1952, and the list of subjects of research subsidized by the government from 1950 through 1952, will furnish some guidance for an understanding of how recent sociological studies are distributed in various fields.

DISTRIBUTION OF RESEARCH PROJECTS IN 19 FIELDS, 1950-1952

Field	*Number of Projects*			
	1950	*1951*	*1952*	*Total*
Rural Sociology	16	15	16	47
Industrial Sociology	12	11	17	40
Theory and History	8	12	11	31
Family Studies	11	9	10	30
Methodology	9	11	5	25
Social Stratification Studies	5	3	7	15
Criminal Sociology	6	6	2	14
Urban Sociology	3	5	5	13
Social Psychology	4	3	6	13
Public Opinion Research	4	4	5	13
Sociology of Religion	4	5	2	11
Population Studies	2	4	4	10
Ethno-Sociology	5	3	1	9
Educational Sociology	3	3	2	8
Sociology of Knowledge	3	3	2	8
Sociology of Law	5	2	1	8
Economic Sociology	4	3	0	7
Moral Sociology	2	2	2	6
Social Work	5	1	0	6
Miscellaneous	5	3	3	11
TOTAL	116	108	101	325

Closer Association with Related Sciences. A tendency for Japanese sociologists to enter into partnership with neighboring sciences has now made its appearance. An expression of this tendency can be seen in the cooperative research conferences of the *Kyû Gakukai Rengô,* or the Nine Associations of the Social Sciences, held annually since 1948. On these occasions, a number

since 1950 and has published annually as its organ the *Kyôiku Shakaigaku Kenkyû* (Educational Sociological Research) since 1951. On the other hand, under the auspices of the Japanese National Commission for UNESCO, continuous research on the attitudes of Japanese youth toward international relations has been carried out by a number of sociologists, psychologists, and social anthropologists since 1953.

of researchers in each of the nine disciplines, including archeology, anthropology, human geography, science of religion, psychology, and sociology, met together and reported on the results of their studies.[44] The Social Tensions Surveys that have continually been undertaken by the *Nihon Jimbun-Kagaku-Kai* (Japanese Cultural Science Society) since 1951 also deserve mention here, since it is probably the most outstanding example of a multidisciplinary research venture ever attempted by Japanese social scientists, and since sociologists have taken a leading part throughout its four-year program. The survey was originally undertaken in connection with a UNESCO research project and was designed to study various kinds of tensional relations found in Japanese society. Some eighty social scientists, organized into about ten sections according to the kind of tensions with which they were to deal, participated in the survey each year.[45]

On the other hand, it has become evident that some scholars whose specialties are primarily law or economics are showing keener interest in sociology. Moreover, there also exists a trend toward a mutual approach on research problems among psychologists and sociologists, especially those interested in small group studies. At the same time, closer association and collaboration within the sphere of sociology itself is developing.

Beginnings of International Collaboration. Finally, it is to be noted that Japanese sociologists have now begun to accustom themselves to performing on an international scientific stage. Generally speaking, they have hitherto worked in narrow national boundaries, hence few monographs have been fully meaningful in terms of Western theoretical and methodological trends. But in recent years, there has been an unequivocal tendency for Japanese sociologists to launch into international collaboration. When the International Sociological Association was founded under the auspices of UNESCO in 1950, the Japanese Sociological Society promptly became a regular member of the Association and, at that time, the present writer was elected to membership on its executive committee. Since then, the Japanese Sociological Society has sent its representatives to report on its activities as well as on the results of its members' current research on each occasion of the Association's triennial conventions.

However, a more pertinent example of this tendency can be found in the sample survey of social stratification and social mobility in the six largest

[44] Area studies of Tsushima Island, Nagasaki Prefecture, and the Noto Peninsula, Ishikawa Prefecture, were conducted by members of the Nine Associations in 1950 and 1952. See *Kyû Gakukai Rengô* [Nine Associations of the Social Sciences] (ed.), *Tsushima no Shizen to Bunka* [The Natural Environment and Culture of Tsushima Island] (Tokyo, 1954).

[45] See *Nihon Jimbun-Kagaku-Kai* [Japanese Cultural Science Society] (ed.), *Shakaiteki Kinchô no Kenkyû* [Studies in Social Tensions] (Tokyo, 1953). A condensed report, prepared in English, of the results of the first-year program was published by the Japanese National Commission for UNESCO in 1953.

cities of Japan, conducted in 1952 by the Research Committee of the Japanese Sociological Society. The survey was undertaken in cooperation with a cross-national research program of the International Sociological Association, and the findings were presented at its Second World Congress held at Liège, Belgium, in the summer of 1953. Major objectives of this survey were to determine in the six largest cities: (1) the proportion of the population in each stratum, (2) the self-identification of the members of each stratum concerning stratum affiliation, (3) the relationship between stratum affiliation and class consciousness, and (4) intra-and inter-generation status mobility. Standard procedures of interviewing, coding, IBM machine tabulation, and analysis were applied to a stratified random sample of about 2,000 individuals drawn from the populations of the six cities. Some fifty sociologists, representing eighteen institutions all over the country, took part in the survey.[46] Although the survey had some shortcomings, it was really an epoch-making event in the history of Japanese sociology in at least two outstanding respects. In the first place, it was the largest scale cooperative research ever undertaken in the history of the Japanese Sociological Society; secondly, it was the first venture, not only of Japanese sociologists, but of Japanese social scientists as a whole, in this sort of international cooperative research work. It is the writer's sincere hope that similar international undertakings will become the rule in the future of Japanese sociology.

SELECTED BIBLIOGRAPHY

Becker, Howard, "Sociology in Japan," *ASR,* 1 (June, 1936), pp. 455-471.

Eubank, Earle E., "Sociology, Past and Present, in Japan," *SSR,* 22 (March-April, 1938), pp. 347-356.

Odaka, Kunio, "Japanese Sociology: Past and Present," *SF,* 28 (May, 1950), pp. 400-409.

Pelzel, John C., "Japanese Ethnological and Sociological Research," *AA,* 50 (Jan.-March, 1948), pp. 54-72.

Steiner, Jesse F., "The Development and Present Status of Sociology in Japanese Universities," *AJS,* 41, 6 (May, 1936), pp. 707-722.

[46] See Kunio Odaka and Shigeki Nishihira, "*Waga Kuni Roku Daitoshi no Shakaiteki Seisô to Idô*" [Social Stratification and Social Mobility in the Six Largest Cities of Japan], *Japanese Sociological Review,* 3 (September, 1953), pp. 2-51. A condensed report of this survey, prepared in English by the present writer, is included in *Transactions of the Second World Congress of Sociology,* edited and published in 1955 by the International Sociological Association.

BIBLIOGRAPHIES OF THE EDITORS*

I

HOWARD BECKER

University of Wisconsin

"Future of Man" (trans. of art. by Max Scheler), *The Monthly Criterion* (London) (Feb., 1928), pp. 100–119.

"Sargasso Iceberg: A Study in Cultural Lag and Institutional Disintegration" (study of German [Hunsrück in the Palatinate] peasant village), *American Journal of Sociology*, 34, 3 (Nov., 1928), pp. 492–506.

"Distribution of Space in the *American Journal of Sociology*, 1895-1927," *American Journal of Sociology*, 36, 3 (Nov., 1930), pp. 461–66. (Content analysis; charts and comment.)

"Forms of Population Movement, Part I," *Social Forces*, 9, 2 (Dec., 1930), pp. 147–160; Part II, *ibid.*, 3 (March, 1931), pp. 351–361.

"Some Forms of Sympathy: A Phenomenological Analysis," *Journal of Abnormal and Social Psychology*, 26, 1 (Apr.–June, 1931).

"Pastoral Nomadism and Social Change," *Sociology and Social Research*, 15, 5 (May–June, 1931), pp. 417–427.

"Conquest by Pastoral Nomads," *Sociology and Social Research*, 15, 6 (July–Aug., 1931), pp. 511–526.

Systematic Sociology on the Basis of the Beziehungslehre *and* Gebildelehre *of Leopold von Wiese* (New York: Wiley, 1932), pp. xxi+772. Reissued, with 1950 preface, Norman Paul Press, 1148 St. Joseph St., Gary, Ind., 1950. (*Not* a translation as such; see 1932 preface. Sections on value-judgment, constructed types, migration and personality change, crowd action and structure, sociology of religion, etc., by HB in whole or in part.

"Space Apportioned Forty-eight Topics in the *American Journal of Sociology*," *American Journal of Sociology*, 38, 1 (July, 1932), pp. 71–78. (Content analysis; charts and comment.)

* These include only items relevant for the themes of this volume.

"Processes of Secularisation: An Ideal-typical Analysis with Special Reference to Personality Change as Affected by Population Movement, Part I," *Sociological Review* (British) (Apr.–July, 1932), pp. 135–54. Part II, *ibid.* (Oct., 1932), pp. 266–86.

"Some Aspects of Taboo and Totemism" (with D. K. Bruner), *Journal of Social Psychology,* 3, 3 (Aug., 1932), pp. 337–353. (Critique of Freudian phylogenetic assumptions, and offering of alternatives.)

"Ionia and Athens: Studies in Secularization," abstract of dissertation, *The University of Chicago Abstract Series,* 1933.

"The Sorrow of Bereavement," *Journal of Abnormal and Social Psychology,* 27, 4 (Jan.–March, 1933), pp. 391–410.

"Vicinal Isolation and Mental Immobility," *Social Forces,* 11, 3 (March, 1933), pp. 326–334.

Fields and Problems of Sociology, L. L. Bernard, ed. (New York: Ray Long and R. R. Smith, 1933). Chap. II, "Historical Sociology."

"Mental Mobility and Secularization in Hellenic History: a Study of Some Effects of Migration and Culture Contact," *Revista di Sociologia,* 7, 1 (Jan.–March, 1934), pp. 14–30.

"Culture Case Study and Ideal-Typical Method, with Special Reference to Max Weber," *Social Forces,* 12, 3 (March, 1934), pp. 399–405.

"A New Classification of Culture" (discussion of paper by James W. Woodard), *American Sociological Review,* 1, 1 (Feb., 1936), pp. 102–104.

Social Thought From Lore to Science, 2 vols.: I, "A History and Interpretation of Man's Ideas about Life with His Fellows"; II, "Sociological Trends throughout the World." With Harry Elmer Barnes (Boston: D. C. Heath & Co., 1938), 193 pages preface, notes, etc. plus 1178 text. Second edition, 1952, with new introductory note, 1951 preface, value-system commentary, and 1937–1950 appendix—about 125 pages additional. (New York: Dover Publications, 1956). Portuguese and Spanish translations.

Contemporary Social Theory (New York: Appleton-Century, 1940), symposium edited with Frances Bennett Becker and Harry Elmer Barnes. Chaps. 2 and 25 by HB. Pp. xx+947.

"The Limits of Sociological Positivism," *Journal of Social Philosophy,* 6, 4 (July, 1941), pp. 362–70.

"Max Scheler's Sociology of Knowledge," *Philosophy and Phenomenological Research,* 2, 3 (March, 1942), pp. 309–22. With Helmut Otto Dahlke.

"Sociology in 1941," *Encyclopaedia Britannica Yearbook for 1942.* Thereafter in successive yearbooks until present (1957), for events of 1956—15 articles thus far.

"Peoples of Germany," chap. 16 in symposium, *Problems of the Post-war World,* T. C. McCormick, ed. (New York: McGraw-Hill, 1945), pp. 342–390. ("Personality and culture" description and analysis of 15 pre-World War II German regions.)

German Youth: Bond or Free (London: Routledge Kegan Paul, 1946; New York: Oxford University Press, 1947; Wiesbaden, Germany: Verlag Der Greif 1949 [latter edition in German, with new title, *Vom Barette Schwankt die Feder,* and two chapters added.] Pp. xv+286, 31 illustrations. British edition

reissued by American publishers, 1950, 1954, and 1956 (latter date, The Humanities Press, 55 E. 11th St., New York).
"Sociology and Related Social Sciences, 1937–1946," art. in *Ten Eventful Years,* special volume issued by the *Encyclopaedia Britannica,* 1947.
"In Defense of Morgan's 'Grecian Gens': Ancient Kinship and Stratification," *Southwestern Journal of Anthropology,* 6, 3 (Autumn, 1950), pp. 309–339.
Through Values to Social Interpretation: Essays on Social Contexts, Actions, Types, and Prospects (Durham, N.C.: Duke University Press, 1950), pp. xviii+341. Unabridged and revised versions of six articles, etc., previously published in abridged form. Extensive bibliography by Hopkins and Mills added.
"What the Hitler Youth Inherited," *Phylon,* 12, 1 (March, 1951), pp. 39–54.
"Science, Culture and Society," *Philosophy of Science,* 19, 4 (Oct., 1952), pp. 273–287.
"Anthropology and Sociology," Chap. 5 in John Gillin, ed., *For a Science of Social Man: Convergences in Anthropology, Sociology, and Psychology* (New York: Macmillan, 1954).
"Vitalizing Sociological Theory," *American Sociological Review,* 19, 4 (Aug., 1954), pp. 377–388.
Man in Reciprocity (New York: Frederick A. Praeger, Inc., 1956), pp. xx+459.
"*Systematic Sociology* and Leopold von Wiese" in J. L. Moreno, ed., *Sociometry and the Science of Man* (New York: Beacon House, 1956), pp. 262–268. Also appears in *Sociometry,* 18, 4, pp. 518–524.
"Church and State in the Cosmos of Crete," *International Journal of Social History,* 1, 2 (Autumn, 1956), pp. 253–295.
"Field Work among Scottish Shepherds and German Peasants: 'Wholes' and Their Handicaps," *Social Forces,* 35, 1 (Oct., 1956), pp. 10–15.
"Empathy, Sympathy, and Scheler," *International Journal of Sociometry,* 1, 1 (Sept., 1956), pp. 15–22

II

ALVIN BOSKOFF

College of William and Mary
(Norfolk, Virginia)

"An Ecological Approach to Rural Society," *Rural Sociology,* 14 (December, 1949). Reprinted in A. N. Desai, *Introduction to Rural Sociology in India* (Bombay, 1951).
"Structure, Function, and Folk Society," *American Sociological Review,* 14 (December, 1949).
"The Systematic Sociology of Talcott Parsons," *Social Forces,* 28 (May, 1950).
"Negro Class Structure and the Technicways," *Social Forces,* 29 (December, 1950).
"Postponement of Social Decision in Transitional Society," *Social Forces,* 31 (March, 1953).
"Social Indecision in Two Classical Societies," *Midwest Sociologist,* 15 (Spring, 1953).

[illegible] by American publishers, [illegible] and 1956 (latter date, The Humanities Press, [illegible] St., New York).
"Sociology and Related Social Science, [illegible]," art. in *The Twentieth Year*, special volume issued by the [illegible], 1942.
In Defense of Morgan's [illegible] Ancient Kinship and [illegible] [illegible] *Journal of* [illegible] (Autumn, 1950), pp. 309–336.
[illegible] to [illegible] Interpretation [illegible] (Durham, N.C.: Duke University Press, [illegible]), pp. xviii+[illegible].
[illegible], of revised versions of six articles, [illegible] previously published in abridged form. Extensive bibliography [illegible] and [illegible] added.
"What the [illegible] Learn [illegible]," [illegible] (March, [illegible]), pp. [illegible].
"[illegible] Culture and Society," [illegible] (Oct., 1951), pp. [illegible].
"[illegible] and Sociology," Chap. [illegible] in John Gillin, ed., *[illegible] of [illegible]* (New York: Macmillan, [illegible]).
"[illegible] Theory," *American Sociological Review*, [illegible] (Aug., 1954), pp. [illegible].
[illegible] (New York: [illegible] Praeger, Inc., 1956), pp. xx+[illegible].
"[illegible] Society and Leopold von Wiese," in [illegible] (New York: [illegible] House, 1956), pp. [illegible]. Also [illegible].
"[illegible] and [illegible] of [illegible]," *[illegible] Journal of [illegible]* (Autumn, 1956), pp. [illegible].
"Field Notes [illegible] German Peasants [illegible] and Their [illegible]," [illegible] (Oct., 1928), pp. [illegible].
"[illegible] and Secular," *[illegible] Journal of* [illegible] (Sept., 1959), pp. [illegible].

II

[illegible]

[illegible]

Norfolk, Virginia

"An [illegible] Approach to Rural Society," *[illegible]* (December, 1950). Reprinted in [illegible] (Bombay, 1951).
"[illegible], Function, and [illegible]," *[illegible]* (December, [illegible]).
"[illegible]," [illegible] (May, 1950).
"[illegible] Structure and [illegible]," *Social Forces*, [illegible] (December, 1950).
"[illegible] of Social Decision in Transitional Society," *Social Forces*, [illegible] ([illegible]).
"[illegible]," [illegible] (Spring, 1951).

Index